PEARSON
mydevelopmentlab™

Save Time.

Improve Results.

More than 6 million students have used a Pearson MyLab.

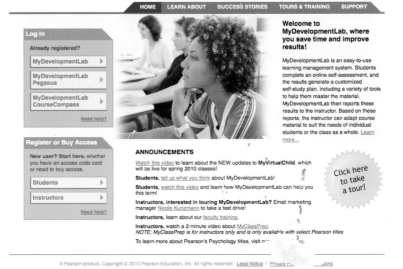

MyDevelopmentLab is an all-in-one learning environment for developmental psychology. This easy-to-navigate site provides students with a variety of resources, including

- An interactive Pearson eText
- Personalized learning opportunities—YOU choose what, where, and when you want to study
- Self-assessment tests that create a personalized study plan to guide you on making the most efficient use of study time

To take advantage of all that MyDevelopmentLab has to offer, you will need an access code. If you do not already have an access code, you can buy one online at

www.mydevelopmentlab.com

PEARSON
mydevelopmentlab™

Improve Your Grade

It's easy to prepare wisely with practice quizzes and tutorials.

MyDevelopmentLab helps you focus your efforts where they are needed. Know your strengths and weaknesses before your first in-class exam.

Go to **www.mydevelopmentlab.com** and follow the simple registration instructions on the Student Access Code Card provided with this text. Your unique access code is hidden there.

Save Time. Improve Results. www.mydevelopmentlab.com

Pearson eText

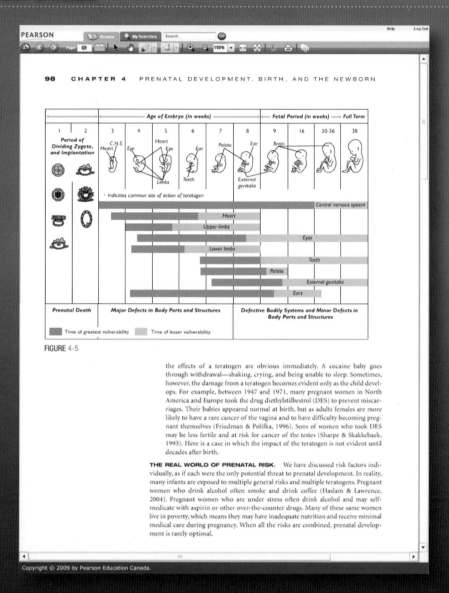

Pearson eText gives students access to the text whenever and wherever they have access to the internet. eText pages look exactly like the printed text, offering powerful new functionality for students and instructors.

Users can create notes, highlight text in different colours, create bookmarks, zoom, click hyperlinked words and phrases to view definitions, and choose single-page or two-page view.

Pearson eText allows for quick navigation using a table of contents and provides full-text search. The eText may also offer links to associated media files, enabling users to access videos, animations, or other activities as they read the text.

Save Time. Improve Results. www.mydevelopmentlab.com

Personalized Learning

In MyDevelopmentLab you are treated as an individual with specific learning needs.

The study and assessment resources that come with your textbook allow you to review content and master what you need to know, on your own time, at your own pace.

MyDevelopmentLab provides

- Access to MyVirtualChild, Pearson's dynamic and interactive web-based simulation that allows you to raise a child from birth to age 18 and monitor the effects of your parenting decisions over time
- Audio and video material that helps bring life to the subject
- Quizzes with immediate grades
- A personalized study plan that tells you where to study based on your results
- A gradebook where you can find your grades to see your progress as the term unfolds
- A full Pearson eText: your textbook, online, in an interactive and dynamic format
- A multimedia library that contains all of the media assets from your Pearson eText in one easy-to-use, searchable format

Lifespan
Development

Denise **BOYD**   Paul **JOHNSON**   Helen **BEE**   Fourth Canadian Edition

Library and Archives Canada Cataloguing in Publication

Boyd, Denise Roberts
    Lifespan development / Denise Boyd, Helen Bee, Paul Johnson.—4th Canadian ed.

Includes bibliographical references and indexes.
ISBN 978-0-205-75428-1

    1. Developmental psychology—Textbooks. I. Bee, Helen L., 1939–
II. Johnson, Paul A III. Title.

BF713.B437 2011   155   C2010-905290-0

ISBN: 978-0-205-75428-1

Vice President, Editorial Director: Gary Bennett
Editor-in-Chief: Ky Pruesse
Acquisitions Editor: Matthew Christian
Sponsoring Editor: Carolin Sweig
Executive Marketing Manager: Judith Allen
Senior Developmental Editor: Patti Altridge
Project Manager: Sarah Lukaweski
Production Editor: Laura Neves
Copy Editor: Deborah Cooper-Bullock
Proofreader: Patricia Jones
Photo and Permissions Research: Dawn du Quesnay
Composition: MPS Limited, a Macmillan Company
Art Director: Julia Hall
Cover and Interior Design: Miriam Blier
Cover Image: Rick Gomez/Corbis

1 2 3 4 5   15 14 13 12 11

Printed and bound in the United States of America.

This book is dedicated to my husband, Jerry Boyd, in appreciation for the help and support he provided to me while I was preparing this edition of *Lifespan Development*.

Denise Boyd

To my best friend, my wife Bonnie Johnson, and our newest psychology graduate, Jessica, and to the newlyweds, Alexandra and Michael.

Paul Johnson

BRIEF CONTENTS

LIST OF FEATURES

DEVELOPMENT IN THE REAL WORLD

RESEARCH REPORTS

POLICY QUESTIONS

CONTENTS

UNIT 2   INFANCY AND EARLY CHILDHOOD

4   PHYSICAL, SENSORY, AND PERCEPTUAL DEVELOPMENT IN INFANCY   93

5   COGNITIVE DEVELOPMENT IN INFANCY   121

6   SOCIAL AND PERSONALITY DEVELOPMENT IN INFANCY   147

PREFACE

Welcome to the fourth Canadian edition of *Lifespan Development*. In preparation for the study of human development across the lifespan from the Canadian perspective, it is important to reflect for a moment on what an incredibly fascinating, complex, and indispensable field of study it is. To convey this richness, *Lifespan Development* covers a great deal of information and, fortunately, this book includes a number of features that will help manage and sort out all this information in a meaningful and rewarding manner.

NEW CONTENT HIGHLIGHTS

The fourth Canadian edition has been thoroughly revised and updated to reflect the latest research in the field of human development. Notably, one of the recognized strengths of this textbook continues to be its breadth of current Canadian content. To provide you with a brief overview, we offer some chapter-by-chapter highlights:

Chapter 1: Basic Concepts and Methods

- Streamlined discussion of the scientific study of human development and descriptive research methods

Chapter 2: Theories of Development

- New coverage of genomics including Canadian researchers' decoding of the DNA of a common type of breast cancer
- Refocused contributions from the humanistic perspective
- New studies connecting scaffolding during the preschool years with higher levels of achievement in elementary school

Chapter 3: Prenatal Development and Birth

- Latest coverage of multiple births and assisted human reproduction in Canada
- Expanded coverage of the fetal stage including new material on the fetal brain
- Updated discussion of teratogens including new material on critical periods and viral infections; psychotropic, prescription, and over-the-counter drugs; diet and weight gain; and maternal age
- New research on the paternal reproductive risks

Chapter 4: Physical, Sensory, and Perceptual Development in Infancy

- Updated Canadian infant nutrition and immunization guidelines
- Revised discussion of pre-term and low-birth-weight infant care in Canada
- Updated infant mortality outcomes including First Nation and Inuit rates
- New Canadian research on intersensory integration in infants

Chapter 5: Cognitive Development in Infancy

- Updated discussion on the impact of babies watching television
- Revised coverage of object permanence and young infants' understanding of objects
- Expanded coverage of what infants learn by observing others
- Updated discussion of infant intelligence
- Streamlined coverage of theoretical perspectives of language including the interactionist view and environmental influences on language development

Chapter 6: Social and Personality Development in Infancy

- Revised coverage of establishing attachment in infancy
- Updated research on infant temperament
- Updated research on the impact of nonparental care in Canada

Chapter 7: Physical and Cognitive Development in Early Childhood

- Updated material on brain development and infantile amnesia
- New research on the impact of obesogenic environments on the unhealthy weight gain in Canadian children
- Revised coverage of unintentional injuries and child maltreatment in Canada
- Revised coverage of information-processing theories
- New section on language and numeracy

Chapter 8: Social and Personality Development in Early Childhood

- New research and discussion of aggression in young Canadian children
- New and updated discussions of temperament, the emotional self, and gender and sex-role development in early childhood

Chapter 9: Physical and Cognitive Development in Middle Childhood

- Updated research on brain development
- New focus on excessive weight gain in Canadian children
- Updated discussion of literacy including second-language learners and the balanced approach to reading
- New commentary on emotional intelligence

Chapter 10: Social and Personality Development in Middle Childhood

- Revised sections on personality traits and Bandura's social-cognitive perspective
- New coverage of self-efficacy, self-esteem, and meaningfulness
- New section on screen time and media influences

Chapter 11: Physical and Cognitive Development in Adolescence

- Updated coverage of puberty including the secular trend and the timing of puberty in social development
- New material on body weights and fitness in Canadian adolescents
- New section on Canadian adolescent sexuality including homosexual, bisexual, and transgendered teens
- Updated material on eating disorders
- New trends in gender and academic achievement and early school-leavers in Canada

Chapter 12: Social and Personality Development in Adolescence

- Updated coverage of friendships and peer groups
- Revised discussion of romantic relationships including heterosexual and homosexual relationships

Chapter 13: Physical and Cognitive Development in Early Adulthood

- Updated discussion of primary and secondary aging including new Canadian demographics

- New discussion of how a sense of control affects health
- New discussion of intimate partner abuse in same-sex relationships and the psychological effects of sexual violence
- Revised section on mental health problems
- Revised coverage of formal operations and the developmental impact of post-secondary education on young Canadian adults

Chapter 14: Social and Personality Development in Early Adulthood

- New section on emerging adulthood
- Updated review of marriage relationship quality
- New section on gay and lesbian couples in Canada
- Revised coverage of life without children
- Updated review of choosing an occupation in Canada
- Updated discussion of career development including Donald Super's stages
- New section on the quality of work life movement

Chapter 15: Physical and Cognitive Development in Middle Adulthood

- Updated research on changes in the adult brain
- Revised section on the secular trend in menopause and women's attitudes towards menopause across ethnic groups
- Updated coverage of cancer and cardiovascular disease in Canada
- New discussion of the Type D personality type
- New material on alcoholism
- New coverage of balancing gains and loses associated with aging
- Updated discussion on the changes in memory and creativity

Chapter 16: Social and Personality Development in Middle Adulthood

- New discussion of Vaillant's revision of Erikson's theory
- New coverage of the life events approach
- Updated discussion of caring for aging parents in Canada
- New coverage of the Big Five personality traits
- Updated research on burnout and sex differences in worker satisfaction

Chapter 17: Physical and Cognitive Development in Late Adulthood

- New material on life expectancy in Canada
- New review of glaucoma and macular degeneration
- New Canadian research on terminal decline and impending death
- Updated research on how Alzheimer's disease and dementia affect Canadians

Chapter 18: Social and Personality Development in Late Adulthood

- New coverage of the process of life review and continuity theory
- Updated coverage of the value of religious coping in elderly Canadians
- Updated coverage of living arrangements of Canadian seniors
- Updated discussion of elder abuse in Canada
- Updated discussion of the protective nature of marriage for older adults, the impact of retirement and the future direction of long-term care for Canadians

Chapter 19: Death, Dying, and Bereavement

- Extensive revision of end-of-life care in Canada including hospital care and hospice palliative care that promotes the value of dignity and well-being
- Revised research on children's and adolescents' understanding of death
- New coverage of the response to impending death
- Revised discussion of the grieving process

In addition, several Canadian research projects, such as the Canadian Perinatal Surveillance System (CPSS), the National Longitudinal Survey of Children and Youth (NLSCY), the Concordia Longitudinal Risk Project (CLRP), the Québec Longitudinal Study of Child Development (QLSCD), and the General Social Survey (GSS), are highlighted throughout the textbook.

NEW TO THE FOURTH CANADIAN EDITION: TAKING AN INTERACTIVE APPROACH TO LEARNING

A textbook isn't like a magazine or a novel. Learners should keep in mind that the goal of working with a textbook is to understand and remember the information in it so that it can be applied effectively in their professional and personal lives. To this end, interacitve *learning tools* have been integrated into the textbook and Pearson eText to help learners to get the most out of each chapter.

MY VIRTUAL CHILD. This interactive simulation allows you to raise a child from birth to age 18 and monitor the effects of your parenting decisions over time. This engaging resource is fully integrated into MyDevelopmentLab and lets you apply the key concepts that you learn in class. And just like in real life, certain unplanned events will be presented to you. See the Connect to MyDevelopmentLab box in Chapter 1 and get started. An Instructor's Manual for My Virtual Child can be downloaded by instructors from a password-protected location on Pearson Canada's online catalogue (http://vig.pearsoned.ca).

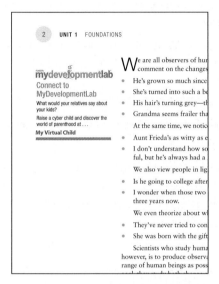

NEW CONNECT TO MYDEVELOPMENTLAB BOXES. Having problems grasping a difficult concept? These boxes help you engage in alternate ways of learning. You can watch a video or interact with a simulation to improve your understanding.

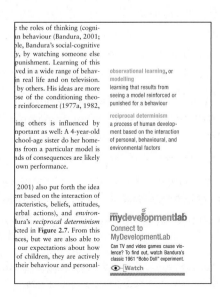

NEW MYDEVELOPMENTLAB ICONS. Throughout the text and Pearson eText, icons connect you to topic-related activities. Look for these symbols associated with MyDevelopmentLab to find engaging content for further learning.

👁-[Watch] See video clips of real researchers at work and observe various behaviours. If you are a visual learner this is for you; real help for your next test.

((•-[Listen] Listen to audio versions of key points and explanations to help you learn concepts, definitions, and proper pronunciations. Repeat as often as you wish to achieve familiarity and mastery.

←●-[Simulate] Engage in animated diagrams, narrated captions, and thought-provoking case studies that put concepts into action and bring the text to life.

✳-[Explore] Head towards a deeper understanding of concepts by exploring a variety of interesting and challenging activities.

RETAINED FEATURES

CHAPTER OUTLINES. Before you read each chapter, read over the outline at its beginning. More information will stick in your mind if you have an idea of what to expect.

PREVIEW QUESTIONS. The introduction to each chapter ends with a list of questions to keep in mind as you read. Like the chapter outline, the questions create a set of mental "hooks" on which to hang the information in the chapter.

BEFORE GOING ON. To help you review, this feature at the end of each major section in a chapter provides questions to assess your understanding of the material.

MARGINAL GLOSSARY. Key terms are defined in the margin near where they are first used in the text.

CRITICAL THINKING QUESTIONS. These questions encourage you to relate material in the book to your own experiences. They can also help you remember the information in the text, because linking new information to things you already know is a highly effective memory strategy.

THEMED ESSAYS. There are two kinds of themed essays throughout the book. Research Report essays recount the findings of important studies, and Development in the Real World essays help you understand the complexities involved in trying to apply developmental

theories and research to real-life problems. They offer practical advice on parenting, teaching, caregiving, and other aspects of daily life to which developmental psychology is relevant.

POLICY QUESTIONS. Discussions of Canadian social policy issues relevant to human development appear at the end of each unit. These discussions will provide you with insight into how the findings of developmental research may be used to influence policy changes in the real world. They may also serve as starting points for group discussions and research projects.

CHAPTER SUMMARIES. Looking over the chapter summary can help you assess how much of the information you remember.

REVIEW QUESTIONS. Here's your opportunity to assess your understanding. You'll find a sampling of questions at the end of every chapter in your textbook. When you finish reading a chapter, take the practice test. If you prefer interactive testing, go to MyDevelopmentLab for the self assessment.

TAKING THE INTERACTIVE APPROACH TO LEARNING

How did you do on your practice test? Were you confused between Bronfenbrenner and Bandura? Did you mix up Piaget and Pavlov? Perhaps a video or simulation would help. For more practice, quizzes, and solutions to review questions, visit your online resource:

PEARSON
mydevelopmentlab

👁-[Watch]   ←●-[Simulate]

((•-[Listen]   ✳-[Explore]

MyDevelopmentLab offers a wealth of resources to help you succeed.

SUPPLEMENTS FOR THE STUDENT

MYDEVELOPMENTLAB. Supplied with every new copy of this textbook, MyDevelopmentLab provides students with videos, simulations, and audio segments, *plus*:

- Diagnostic tests assess your understanding of the text.
- A custom study program that creates a personalized study plan using the eText and based on your diagnostic test results.

- Pearson eText gives students access to the text whenever and wherever they have access to the Internet. eText pages look exactly like the printed text, offering powerful new functionality for students and instructors. Users can create notes, highlight text in different colours, create bookmarks, zoom, click hyperlinked words and phrases to view definitions, and view in single-page or two-page view. Pearson eText allows for quick navigation to key parts of the eText using a table of contents and provides full-text search.

COURSESMART. CourseSmart goes beyond traditional expectations by providing instant, online access to the textbooks and course materials you need at an average savings of 60%. With instant access from any computer and the ability to search your text, you'll find the content you need quickly, no matter where you are. And with online tools like highlighting and note-taking, you can save time and study efficiently. See all the benefits at **www.coursesmart.com/students.**

SUPPLEMENTS FOR THE INSTRUCTOR

MYDEVELOPMENTLAB. Pearson Education Canada's online resource, MyDevelopmentLab, offers instructors and students all of their resources in one place, organized to accompany this text. With MyDevelopmentLab, you will be able to enliven your lectures with a variety of materials. As well, your students will be able to study smarter with an eText and a diagnostic test that creates a customized study plan to help them prepare for, and perform better on, exams. MyDevelopmentLab is available to instructors by going to **www.mydvelopmentlab.com** and following the instructions on that page. Students receive an access code to MyDevelopmentLab at no extra charge with a new textbook.

MYCLASSPREP. This new offering from Pearson makes lecture preparation simpler and less time-consuming. Pearson has collected the very best of instructor resources, including art and figures from our leading texts, videos, lecture activities, classroom activities, demonstrations, and much more. Instructors are able to search through this extensive database by content topic (arranged by standard topics within the introductory psychology curriculum) or by content type (video, audio, simulation, word documents). MyClassPrep allows instructors to select resources appropriate for lectures, many of which can be downloaded directly. Or, instructors may build their own folder of resources and present from within the MyClassPrep program. MyClassPrep can be accessed through MyDevelopmentLab.

IRCD. The Instructor's Resource CD (978-0-205-03179-5) includes the following instructor supplements.

- *Instructor's Manual.* Each chapter includes the following sections:
  - Chapter Preview
  - Learning Goals
  - Extensive Teaching Notes, which include the Learning Objectives
  - Lecture Enhancement notes
  - Instructor Resources, including suggested videos, transparency and handout masters, and references to the full-colour transparency acetates found in the Allyn & Bacon Human Development Transparency Set

- *PowerPoint Presentations.* These slide presentations pair key points covered in the chapters with figures from the textbook to provoke effective classroom discussion.

- *Test Item File.* This test bank in Microsoft Word format includes almost 2000 questions, in multiple-choice, true/false, short answer, and essay formats, each with an answer justification, page references, difficulty rating, and type designation. This test bank is also available in MyTest format (see below).

- *Image Library.* The image library provides you with chapter figures and tables for insertion into PowerPoint presentations.

Most of these instructor supplements are also available for download from a password protected section of Pearson Education Canada's online catalogue (**http://vig.pearsoned.ca**). Navigate to this book's catalogue page to view a list of supplements that are available. See your local sales representative for details and access.

MYTEST. This powerful assessment generation program helps instructors easily create and print quizzes, tests, and exams, as well as homework or practice handouts. Questions and tests can all be authored online, allowing instructors ultimate flexibility and the ability to efficiently manage assessments at any time, from anywhere. MyTest includes almost 2000 questions in multiple-choice, true/false, short answer, and essay format. Go to **www.pearsonmytest.com** to get started. These questions are also available in Microsoft Word format on the Instructor's Resource CD.

VIDEO RESOURCES. The following video resources are available to instructors using this text.

- *Observations Videos: Children and Their Development* (978-0-205-03495-6). This new DVD contains all of the observational videos that are also available online through MyDevelopmentLab and are contextualized within MyVirtualChild.

- *Pearson Teaching Films Lifespan Development Videos* (978-0-205-65602-8). These videos cover all stages of lifespan development, including infancy, preschool, middle childhood, adolescence, early adulthood, middle adulthood, and late adulthood.

COURSESMART FOR INSTRUCTORS. CourseSmart goes beyond traditional expectations by providing instant, online access to the textbooks and course materials you need at a lower cost for students. And even as students save money, you can save time and hassle with a digital eTextbook that allows you to search for the most relevant content at the very moment you need it. Whether it's evaluating textbooks or creating lecture notes to help students with difficult concepts, CourseSmart can make life a little easier. See how when you visit **www.coursesmart.com/instructors**.

TECHNOLOGY SPECIALISTS. Pearson's Technology Specialists work with faculty and campus course designers to ensure that Pearson technology products, assessment tools, and online course materials are tailored to meet your specific needs. This highly qualified team is dedicated to helping schools take full advantage of a wide range of educational resources, by assisting in the integration of a variety of instructional materials and media formats. Your Pearson Education sales representative can provide you with more details on this service program.

ACKNOWLEDGMENTS

Preparing this fourth Canadian edition of *Lifespan Development* was made possible only with the considerable coordinated efforts of many people who each played a vital role in the process.

I am especially grateful to Bonnie Johnson for her feedback on the preliminary drafts; to Jessica Johnson, for her research assistance; and to Annie Enns, for her graphic design updates.

I have also had the good fortune to be able to collaborate with the good-spirited people on the Pearson Education Canada team. As always, they continue to demonstrate the epitome of professionalism. In particular, I wish to express my gratitude to Ky Pruesse, Editor-in-Chief; Carolin Sweig, Sponsoring Editor; Patti Altridge, Senior Developmental Editor; Lila Campbell and Sarah Lukaweski, Project Managers; Laura Neves, Production Editor; Deborah Cooper-Bullock, Copy Editor; and Judith Allen, Executive Marketing Manager. Thank you all—you are a remarkable team to work with.

In closing, I would like to thank the many colleagues who served as reviewers for their valuable comments and suggestions on this fourth Canadian edition:

Noella Comeau, Nova Scotia Community College
Michael Foy, John Abbott
Judith Grad, Concordia University
Laura Loewen, Okanagan College
Cynthia McNairn, George Brown College
Robert W. Milks, Nova Scotia Community College
Cathy Mondloch, Brock University
Verna Pangman, University of Manitoba
Ravi Ramkissoonsingh, Niagara College
Andrew Starzomski, St. Mary's University

Paul Johnson
Confederation College

Wayne R. Bilenduke/Getty Images

CHAPTER 1

Basic Concepts and Methods

We are all observers of human development. For example, at family gatherings, we comment on the changes we notice in our relatives:

- He's grown so much since the last time I saw him.
- She's turned into such a beautiful young lady.
- His hair's turning grey—the hair he has left, that is.
- Grandma seems frailer than last year.

At the same time, we notice the things about people that appear to remain the same:

- Aunt Frieda's as witty as ever.
- I don't understand how someone could go through so much and still be so cheerful, but he's always had a lot of faith.

We also view people in light of the expectations of our culture for their age group:

- Is he going to college after he graduates this year?
- I wonder when those two are going to have children. They've been married for three years now.

We even theorize about why our relatives behave the way they do:

- They've never tried to control that child. No wonder he's such a brat.
- She was born with the gift of the gab.

Scientists who study human development do precisely the same things. Their goal, however, is to produce observations and explanations that can be applied to as wide a range of human beings as possible, in as many contexts as possible. To accomplish this goal, they study both change and stability. In addition, they examine the impact of cultural expectations on individual development. They make predictions about development and use scientific methods to test them. Finally, most hope that their findings can be used to positively influence the development of individual human beings.

When you finish studying the chapter, you will be able to describe how the science of developmental psychology came into being; define lifespan development and how its study has evolved; and identify the research designs and methods used by developmentalists. While you read, keep the following questions in mind:

- If you had been raised by a different set of parents, would you have turned out much differently from the person you are today?
- What biases could you be revealing when you say or think that another person should be "acting their age"?
- What would it take for you to live to be 100 years of age?

THE SCIENTIFIC STUDY OF HUMAN DEVELOPMENT

developmental psychology
the scientific study of age-
related changes in our bodies,
behaviour, thinking, emotions,
social relationships, and
personalities

The field of **developmental psychology** is the scientific study of age-related changes in our bodies, behaviour, thinking, emotions, social relationships, and personalities. Long before the scientific method was used to study development, though, philosophers offered a variety of explanations for differences they observed in individuals of different ages. Their ideas continue to influence the field today, and many Western beliefs about human development are based on them.

TABLE 1.1	Philosophical Approaches to Development	
Historical Philosohical Perspective	Child's Inherent Predisposition	Parental Responsibility
Original Sin	Sinful	Intervene to correct
The Blank Slate	Neutral	Shape behaviours
Innate Goodness	Good	Nurture and protect

PHILOSOPHICAL ROOTS

Early philosophers based their ideas about development on spiritual authorities, deductive logic, and general philosophical orientations. Typically, philosophers' inquiries into the nature of development focused on why babies, who appear to be quite similar, grow up to vary widely (see **Table 1.1**).

ORIGINAL SIN For centuries, the Christian doctrine of *original sin*, often attributed to the 4th-century North African philosopher Augustine of Hippo, taught that all humans are born with a selfish and stubborn nature. To reduce the influence of this inborn tendency toward sinfulness, Augustine taught, humans must seek redemption by leading a disciplined life. Thus, from this perspective, parents facilitate the child's struggle to overcome an inborn tendency to act immorally by restraining and correcting the child's immoral tendencies.

THE BLANK SLATE By contrast, the 17th-century English philosopher John Locke drew on a broad philosophical approach known as *empiricism* when he claimed that the mind of a child is a *blank slate*. Empiricism is the view that humans possess no innate tendencies and that all differences among humans are attributable to experience. As such, the blank slate view suggests that adults can mould children into whatever they want them to be. Therefore, differences among adults can be explained in terms of the differences in their childhood environments rather than as a result of a struggle to overcome their inborn tendencies, as the original sin view proposed.

Critical Thinking

Other cultures and religions have different ways of viewing the process of development. How do the original sin, innate goodness, and blank slate views compare with your own beliefs? How do you think your own culture and religion have contributed to these beliefs?

INNATE GOODNESS Different still was the *innate goodness* view proposed by the 18th-century Swiss philosopher Jean-Jacques Rousseau. He claimed that all human beings are naturally good and seek out experiences that help them grow (Ozman & Craver, 1986). Rousseau believed that children need only nurturing and protection to reach their full potential. Good developmental outcomes happen when a child's environment refrains from interfering in her attempts to nurture her own development. In contrast, poor outcomes occur when a child experiences frustration in her efforts to express the innate goodness with which she was born.

THE STUDY OF HUMAN DEVELOPMENT BECOMES A SCIENCE

Philosophy can provide a framework for ideas about human development. However, in the 19th century, people who wanted to better understand development began to turn to science. By 1930, the foundations of modern developmental psychology had been established and had begun to influence everyday child-rearing practices (see **Development in the Real World**).

Development in the Real World

TOYS: MORE THAN JUST PLAYTHINGS

Today, a vital element of children's development is centred on playing with toys: "If play is the child's work then toys are the child's tools, and appropriate toys can help children do their work well" (Keep Kids Healthy, 2003). Accordingly, it is important to design toys that promote the development of the child (Auerback, 2006). With this in mind, toy designers now create many toys to promote children's

- *physical development*—improving muscle control and eye–hand coordination
- *cognitive development*—understanding about spatial and temporal relationships and fostering reasoning ability through creative expression and problem-solving
- *emotional development*—acting out inner thoughts, feelings, and fantasies in a safe manner and learning persistence and mastery
- *social development*—learning to share with others, practising social and cultural values and rules through make-believe

The Developmental Science Behind Toys

In Canada, the Canadian Toy Testing Council (CTTC) (2010) is a non-profit, volunteer organization that conducts ongoing research to ensure the value and appropriateness of toys. *Age-appropriate* means that a toy not only matches a child's capabilities, but also captures a child's interest. "No matter how promising, if a toy is not fun, it will gather dust" (CTTC, n.d.). While toy-testing research helps to identify what parents and children want in toys, it also considers safety, performance, appeal, usefulness, durability, age-appropriateness, and potential improvements.

At each stage of development a child faces new challenges and different risks (Canadian Child Care Federation [CCCF], 2009). The Canadian and international toy industries have developed age-appropriate recommendations so that toys challenge and stimulate based on a child's chronological age, as well as physical size, skill level, temperament, and maturity. Toys that are beneath or beyond a child's capabilities may discourage the child from developing further interests.

The research that goes into toy design and manufacture is represented by the information contained on toy product labels. The label provides important guidelines for parents when making toy selections (Health Canada, 2009a). For instance, babies tend to put things into their mouths and are therefore at high risk for choking on small toys or toy parts; riding toys for toddlers pose a risk because children at this age do not have well-developed coordination and this can result in a child running into objects or falling down stairs; and projectile toys, although appealing to young children, can cause a variety of injuries, especially eye injuries (CCCF, 2009). As a result, toys are labelled with suitable age ranges—for example, "recommended for children from 18 months to 3 years." In many instances, toy labels may also carry a safety warning—for example, "Choking hazard: This toy contains small parts and is not intended for children under the age of 3." At any age, parental supervision is important, and toys meant for older children should be kept away from smaller children (CCCF, 2009).

LEGO means "play well." The "automatic building brick," invented by a Danish carpenter in 1949, can be considered an ideal toy in that it fosters development in the four key areas of growth: physical, cognitive, emotional, and social (Pisani, 2006; Toy Retailers Association, n.d.).
(*Photo:* Copyright ©Michael Newman/Photo Edit—All rights reserved.)

DARWIN Charles Darwin and other evolutionists believed they could understand the development of the human species by studying child development. Many, including Darwin, kept detailed records of their own children's early development (called *baby biographies*) in the hope of finding evidence to support the theory of evolution (Charlesworth, 1992). These were the first organized studies of human development.

Darwin's theory of evolution is the source of many important ideas in modern developmental psychology. For example, the concept of developmental stages comes from evolutionary theory. However, critics of baby biographies claimed that studying children for the purpose of proving a theory might cause observers to misinterpret or ignore important information.

HALL   G. Stanley Hall of Clark University wanted to find more objective ways to study development. He used questionnaires and interviews to study large numbers of children. His 1891 article titled "The Contents of Children's Minds on Entering School" represented the first scientific study of child development (White, 1992).

Hall agreed with Darwin that the milestones of childhood were similar to those that had taken place in the development of the human species. He thought that developmentalists should identify **norms,** or average ages at which developmental milestones are reached. Norms, Hall said, could be used to learn about the evolution of the species as well as to track the development of individual children.

norms
average ages at which developmental milestones are reached

GESELL   Arnold Gesell's research suggested the existence of a genetically programmed sequential pattern of change (Gesell, 1925; Thelen & Adolph, 1992). Gesell used the term *maturation* to describe such a pattern of change. He thought that maturationally determined development occurred regardless of practice, training, or effort. For example, infants don't have to be taught how to walk—they begin to do so on their own once they reach a certain age. Because of his strong belief that maturation determines many important developmental changes, Gesell spent decades studying children and developing norms. He pioneered the use of movie cameras and one-way observation devices to study children's behaviour. Gesell's findings became the basis for many tests that are used today to determine whether individual children are developing normally.

PIAGET   One of the most influential theories in the history of developmental psychology is that of Swiss developmentalist Jean Piaget (Thomas, 1996). At the age of 10, Piaget published his first scientific article, on sparrows. By the time he was 21, he had published more than 20 scientific articles and had received a Ph.D. in natural science from the University of Geneva. In 1918, he went to Paris to work with Theodore Simon, the co-author of the Binet-Simon IQ test, at the school that Alfred Binet started. Piaget married his colleague and student Valentine Châtenay in 1923, and 2 years later Châtenay gave birth to their first child, Jacqueline. Piaget and Châtenay made detailed notes about Jacqueline's and their two other children's intellectual and language development.

Piaget became a professor at the University of Geneva in 1921 and spent the next 6 decades studying the development of logical thinking in children, until his death in 1980. His studies convinced him that logical thinking develops in four stages between birth and adolescence. At first, infants explore the world by using their senses and motor abilities. Through their actions, they develop basic concepts of time and space. Next, young children develop the ability to use symbols (primarily words) to think and communicate. Once they become proficient in the use of symbols, around age 6 or 7, children are ready to develop the skills needed for logical thinking. They spend the next 5 to 6 years using these skills to solve problems in the everyday world. Finally, in the teenage years, individuals develop the capacity to apply logic to both abstract and hypothetical problems.

The stages Piaget described and the theory he proposed to explain them became the foundation of modern cognitive-developmental psychology. Consequently, you will be reading a great deal more about them in later chapters. Although many developmentalists disagree with Piaget's theoretical explanations, a vast body of research, including numerous cross-cultural studies, supports the existence of the sequence of cognitive development that Piaget observed in his research (Mishra, 1997).

A BRIEF HISTORY OF THE ROOTS OF PSYCHOLOGY IN CANADA

The first psychology course in Canada was taught at Dalhousie University in 1838. Later, in the 1850s, prescientific psychology courses were offered at McGill University in Montreal and the University of Toronto. In these early years, psychology was not considered a distinct discipline but rather a branch of mental and moral philosophy (Wright & Myers, 1982). It wasn't until 1889 that modern scientific psychology came to Canada. James M. Baldwin began lecturing in the fall of that year at the University of Toronto and set up a small psychophysical laboratory (Hoff, 1992).

In the 1920s, funding became available for child-related and family research and, in 1925, William Blatz opened the St. George's School for Child Study in Toronto. Blatz is regarded as "the founder and leader of child study in Canada" (Wright & Myers, 1982). St. George's was later renamed the Institute of Child Study and is now incorporated into the Ontario Institute for Studies in Education (OISE). Blatz is also known for his 3 years of work with the Dionne quintuplets, beginning in 1935.

Prior to World War II, there was no formal organization of practising psychologists in Canada. The impetus for creating a psychological organization came from the threat of war in Europe. In June 1938, psychologists were deliberating how they could provide their services for the war effort. From these discussions, E.A. Bott of the University of Toronto, George Humphrey of Queen's University, and Roy Liddy of the University of Western Ontario founded the Canadian Psychological Association (CPA) in 1939. Also present during these early discussions were Mary Wright and Mary Salter (later Ainsworth). Mary Wright, an assistant to Mary Salter Ainsworth, became the first woman president of the CPA in 1969 (Wright, 1993). Mary Salter Ainsworth, whose work on infant attachment you will encounter in **Chapter 6**, established the theoretical and empirical framework through which developmentalists continue to view infant–caregiver relations.

Canadian psychologists were very active during World War II, especially in Britain, where they focused on personnel selection, recruitment and training methods, morale issues, and all aspects of public opinion. Important strides in early education came about at that time because of the major evacuation of children in Britain away from urban centres. Canadian psychologists were empowered to generate solutions to the ensuing child-care problems. William Blatz was called on to establish a nursery school teachers' training school in Birmingham (Ferguson, 1993). The school was staffed by Canadian child psychologists.

Another early contributor to the CPA was Donald O. Hebb, who was the first editor of the *Bulletin of the Canadian Psychological Association* (which later became the *Canadian Journal of Psychology*). Hebb, an internationally renowned pioneer in the field of

In the early days of psychology, female psychologists seldom received credit for their accomplishments because of societal attitudes toward women. Mary Salter Ainsworth was one of the earliest female psychologists to be recognized in Canada; she was part of a group of psychologists actively involved in the creation of the Canadian Psychological Association. (*Photo:* Courtesy of the Estate of Mary Salter Ainsworth)

experimental psychology at McGill, was president of the CPA in 1953 and the American Psychological Association in 1960. Noel Mailloux, another academic who helped organize the CPA, is credited with establishing the study of modern psychology in French Canada (Ferguson, 1993). He founded the Institut de Psychologie in 1942 at the Université de Montréal (Wright & Myers, 1982).

In 1981, the Developmental Section of the CPA was established. Its goal is to facilitate communication among developmental psychologists in terms of research, teaching, and practice. At present, the Developmental Section provides a forum for collaboration and the sharing of expertise for over 340 members.

Before Going On

- How do the original-sin, blank-slate, and innate-goodness views of human development differ?
- How did the study of human development evolve from its philosophy roots into a science?

CONTEMPORARY DEVELOPMENTAL PSYCHOLOGY

Developmental psychology has changed considerably since the early days. For one thing, the term *development* now encompasses the entire human lifespan rather than just childhood and adolescence. For another, developmentalists have come to understand that inborn characteristics interact with environmental factors in complex ways. Finally, the pioneers thought of change almost exclusively in terms of norms, whereas today's developmentalists view norms as representing only one way to measure change.

THE LIFESPAN PERSPECTIVE

As interest in the lifespan has grown, developmental psychology has become more *interdisciplinary*. Psychologists, who are primarily interested in individuals, have learned that research in other sciences can greatly enhance their understanding of human development. Anthropologists provide information about culture, and sociologists explain the influence of race, socioeconomic status, and other social factors on individual development. Advances in biology are especially critical to an understanding of the physiological foundations of human behaviour.

Until quite recently, psychologists thought of adulthood as a long period of stability followed by a short span of unstable years immediately preceding death. This view has changed because, for one thing, it has become common for adults to go through major life changes, such as divorce and career shifts. There has also been a significant increase in life expectancy that has occurred in the industrialized world. The life expectancy of a Canadian born in 1921 was 59 years for a male and 61 years for a female; a Canadian male born today can expect to live to age 78.4 and a female to 83.0

(Statistics Canada, 2009a). As a result, older adults now constitute a larger proportion of the population than ever before. In fact, adults over the age of 85 are one of the most rapidly growing age groups in Canada, and their numbers are expected to increase five-fold over the next 50 years (Turcotte & Schellenberg, 2007). Thus, the characteristics and needs of older adults are increasingly influencing many disciplines, including developmental psychology.

The changes outlined above have led to the adoption of a **lifespan perspective**. The lifespan perspective maintains that important changes occur during every period of development and that these changes must be interpreted in terms of the cultures and contexts in which they occur (Baltes, Lindenberger, & Staudinger, 2006; Baltes, Reese, & Lipsitt, 1980). Thus, understanding change in adulthood has become just as important as understanding change in childhood, and input from many disciplines is necessary to fully explain human development.

The late Paul Baltes of the Max Planck Institute in Germany was one of the early leaders in the development of a comprehensive theory of lifespan human development (Baltes, Staudinger, & Lindenberger, 1999). Baltes proposed that the capacity for positive change, or *plasticity,* in response to environmental demands is possible throughout the entire lifespan. One such area of positive adult development is the area of personal goals—older adults pursue their goals more intensely than younger adults (Riediger, Freund, & Baltes, 2005). Consequently, one of Baltes's most important contributions to the study of human development was his emphasis on the positive aspects of advanced age. He emphasized that, as human beings age, they adopt strategies that help them maximize gains and compensate for losses. For instance, one of Baltes's most often quoted examples is that of concert pianist Arthur Rubinstein, who was able to outperform much younger musicians well into his 80s (Cavanaugh & Whitbourne, 1999). Rubinstein reported that he maintained his performance capacity by carefully choosing pieces that he knew very well (maximizing gain) and by practising these pieces more frequently than he had at earlier ages (compensating for the physical losses associated with age). You will read more about Baltes's theories and his research later, in the chapters devoted to late adulthood.

THE DOMAINS OF DEVELOPMENT

Scientists who study age-related changes across the lifespan often use three broad categories, called *domains of development*, to classify these changes. The **physical domain** includes changes in the size, shape, and characteristics of the body. For example, developmentalists study the physiological processes associated with puberty. Also included in this domain are changes in how individuals sense and perceive the physical world, such as the gradual development of depth perception over the first year of life.

Changes in thinking, memory, problem-solving, and other intellectual skills are included in the **cognitive domain**. Researchers working in the cognitive domain study topics as diverse as how children learn to read and why some memory functions deteriorate in old age. They also examine the ways in which individual differences among children and adults, such as intelligence test scores, are related to other variables within this domain.

The **social domain** includes changes in variables that are associated with the relationship of an individual to others. For instance, studies of children's social skills fall into the social domain, as does research on individual differences in personality. Individuals' beliefs about themselves are also usually classified within the social domain.

Using domain classifications helps to organize discussions of human development. However, it is always important to remember that the three domains do not function independently of one another. For instance, when a girl goes through puberty, a change

lifespan perspective
the current view of developmentalists that changes happen throughout the entire human lifespan and that changes must be interpreted in light of the culture and context in which they occur; thus, interdisciplinary research is critical to understanding human development

physical domain
changes in the size, shape, and characteristics of the body

cognitive domain
changes in thinking, memory, problem-solving, and other intellectual skills

social domain
changes in variables that are associated with the relationship of an individual to others

in the physical domain, her ability to think abstractly (cognitive domain), and her feelings about potential romantic partners (social domain) change as well. Likewise, older adults who suffer from Alzheimer's disease demonstrate obvious changes in the cognitive domain. But these changes both result from and lead to others in the remaining two domains. Physical changes in the brain are the most likely cause of Alzheimer's disease. The experience of living with the disease may cause a sufferer to be unable to maintain a regular eating and exercise schedule, thus leading to deterioration in physical health. Moreover, individuals who have such severe memory impairments often forget important things about the people with whom they associate, such as their names and relationships. As a result, social relationships are disrupted or may even be impossible.

THE INTERACTIONIST MODEL OF DEVELOPMENT

You may have noticed that some early developmentalists thought of change as resulting from *either* forces outside the person *or* forces inside the person. The debate about the relative contributions of biological processes and experiential factors was known as the *nature–nurture controversy*. In struggling with this important issue, psychologists have moved away from either/or toward more subtle ways of looking at both types of influences. Today, many theorists have adopted an **interactionist model** that considers development to be the result of complex reciprocal interactions between multiple personal and environmental factors.

A good example of research that exemplifies the interactionist model is implicit in the ideas of *vulnerability* and *resilience* (Willms, 2002a). According to this view, each child is born with certain vulnerabilities, such as a tendency toward emotional irritability or alcoholism, a physical abnormality, or an allergy. Each child is also born with some protective factors, such as high intelligence, good physical coordination, an easy temperament, or a lovely smile, that tend to make her more resilient in the face of stress. These vulnerabilities and protective factors then interact with the child's environment so that the same environment can have quite different effects, depending on the qualities the child brings to the interaction.

Studies of Canadian children have shown that a combination of a highly vulnerable child and a poor or unsupportive environment produces by far the most negative outcome (Schonert-Reichl, 2000; Willms, 2002b). Either of these two negative conditions alone—a vulnerable child or a poor environment—can be overcome. A resilient child in a poor environment may do quite well, since she can find and take advantage of all the stimulation and opportunities available; similarly, a vulnerable child may do quite well in a highly supportive environment in which parents help the child overcome or cope with her vulnerabilities.

CONTINUITY AND DISCONTINUITY IN DEVELOPMENT

A key issue in the study of human development is the *continuity–discontinuity* issue. The question is whether age-related change is primarily a matter of amount or degree (the *continuity* side of the debate) or more commonly involves changes in type or kind (the *discontinuity* side). For example, a 2-year-old is likely to have no individual friends among her playmates, while an 8-year-old is likely to have several. We could think of this as a **quantitative change** (a change in amount) from zero friends to some friends. This view implies that the qualitative aspects of friendship are the same at every age—or, as developmentalists would express it, changes in friendship are *continuous* in nature. Alternatively, we could think of the difference in friendships from one age to another as a **qualitative change** (a change in kind or type)—from disinterest in peers to

((•— Listen

✳—Explore

interactionist model
the theory that development
results from complex reciprocal
interactions between multiple
personal and environmental
factors

mydevelopmentlab
Connect to
MyDevelopmentLab
Are you capable of violence? Take
the nature–nurture debate further.
Watch the Zimbardo video about the
Stanford Experiment, and then judge.

◉—Watch

quantitative change
a change in amount

qualitative change
a change in kind or type

interest or from one sort of peer relationship to another. In other words, from this perspective, changes in friendships are *discontinuous,* in that each change represents a change in the quality of a child's relationships with peers. Thus, friendships at 2 are quite different from friendships at 8 and differ in ways that cannot be captured by describing them solely in terms of the number of friends a child has.

Of particular significance is the idea that, if development consists only of additions (quantitative change), then the concept of **stages**, qualitatively distinct periods of development, is not needed to explain it. However, if development involves reorganization or the emergence of wholly new strategies, qualities, or skills (qualitative change), then the concept of stages may be useful. As you'll learn in **Chapter 2**, one of the important differences among theories of development is whether they assume development occurs in stages or is primarily continuous in nature. Nevertheless, most human development theorists and researchers would agree that age-related changes can be classified by using three categories: *universal changes*, *group-specific changes*, and *individual differences*.

stages
qualitatively distinct periods of development

Critical Thinking

How do expectations of 20-year-olds differ from expectations of 70-year-olds in your culture?

UNIVERSAL CHANGES *Universal changes* are common to every individual in a species and are linked to specific ages. Some universal changes happen because we are all biological organisms subject to a genetically programmed maturing process. The infant who shifts from crawling to walking and the older adult whose skin becomes progressively more wrinkled are following a plan that is an intrinsic part of the physical body, most likely something in the genetic code itself.

However, some changes are universal because of shared experiences. A social clock also shapes all (or most) lives into shared patterns of change (Helson, Mitchell, & Moane, 1984). In each culture, the **social clock**, or a set of *age norms*, defines a sequence of normal life experiences, such as the right time to start school, the appropriate timing of marriage and child-bearing, and the expected time of retirement.

Age norms can lead to **ageism**—a set of prejudicial attitudes about older adults, analogous to sexism or racism. In Canadian society, for example, conventional wisdom states that job performance will decline in older adults. As a result, many older adults are denied opportunities to work because employers believe that they are less capable of carrying out required job functions than younger adults. Thus, social expectations about the appropriate age for retirement work together with ageism to shape individual lives, resulting in a pattern in which most people retire or significantly reduce their working hours in later adulthood.

social clock
a set of age norms that defines a sequence of life experiences that is considered normal in a given culture and that all individuals in that culture are expected to follow

ageism
a prejudicial view of older adults that characterizes them in negative ways

GROUP-SPECIFIC CHANGES *Group-specific changes* are shared by all individuals who grow up together in a particular group. One of the most important groups to which we all belong is our culture. The term *culture* has no commonly agreed-on definition, but in essence it describes some system of meanings and customs, including values, attitudes, goals, laws, beliefs, moral guidelines, and physical artifacts of various kinds, such as tools, forms of dwellings, and the like. Culture shapes not only the development of individuals, but also our ideas about what normal development is.

For example, researchers interested in middle and late adulthood often study retirement: why people retire, how retirement affects their health, and so on. But their findings do not apply to older adults in developing nations, where adults gradually shift from one kind of work to another as they get older rather than giving up work altogether and entering a new phase of life called *retirement*. Consequently, developmentalists must be aware that retirement-related phenomena do not constitute universal changes. Instead, they represent developmental experiences that are culturally specific.

The biological clock obviously constrains the social clock to some extent at least. Virtually every culture emphasizes family formation in early adulthood because that is, in fact, the optimal biological time for child-bearing.
(*Photos:* Alan Oddie/PhotoEdit)

Equally important as a source of variation in life experience are historical forces, which affect each generation somewhat differently. Social scientists use the word **cohort** to describe a group of individuals who are born within some fairly narrow span of years and thus share the same historical experiences at the same time in their lives. Within any given culture, successive cohorts may have quite different life experiences.

INDIVIDUAL DIFFERENCES *Individual differences* are changes resulting from unique, unshared events. One clearly unshared event in each person's life is conception; the combination of genes each individual receives at conception is unique. Thus, genetic differences—including physical characteristics, such as body type and hair colour as well as genetic disorders—represent one category of individual differences. Characteristics influenced by both heredity and environment, such as intelligence and personality, constitute another class of individual differences.

Other individual differences are the result of the timing of a developmental event. Child development theorists have adopted the concept of a **critical period**. The idea is that there may be specific periods in development when an organism is especially sensitive to the presence (or absence) of some particular kind of experience.

Most knowledge about critical periods comes from animal research. For baby ducks, for instance, the first 15 hours or so after hatching is a critical period for the development of a following response. Newly hatched ducklings will follow any duck or any other moving object that happens to be around them at that critical time. If nothing is moving at that critical point, they don't develop any following response at all (Hess, 1972).

The broader concept of a sensitive period is more common in the study of human development. A **sensitive period** is a span of months or years during which a child may be particularly responsive to specific forms of experience or particularly influenced by their absence. For example, the period from 6 to 12 months of age may be a sensitive period for the formation of parent–infant attachment. The presence or absence of specific environmental factors during critical and sensitive periods early in life can produce changes, for better or worse, that last a lifetime (Tzschentke & Plagemann, 2006). This important concept will be further examined when we discuss *epigenetics* in later chapters.

In studies of adults, one important concept related to timing has been the idea of *on-time* and *off-time* events (Neugarten, 1979). The idea is that experiences occurring at the expected times for an individual's culture or cohort will pose fewer difficulties for her than will

cohort
a group of individuals who share the same historical experiences at the same times in their lives

critical period
a specific period in development when an organism is especially sensitive to the presence (or absence) of some particular kind of experience

sensitive period
a span of months or years during which a child may be particularly responsive to specific forms of experience or particularly influenced by their absence

Critical Thinking

From birth onward your cohort has and will continue to encounter the same social events and moods and trends at similar ages. What momentous historical events and shifts in society-wide attitudes and trends make your cohort group truly unique? How does your cohort react toward families, sex roles, marriage, careers, religion, social justice, and personal responsibility?

atypical development
development that deviates
from the typical developmental
pathway

off-time experiences. Thus, being widowed at 30 is more likely to produce serious life disruption or forms of pathology, such as depression, than would being widowed at 70.

Atypical development is another kind of individual change. **Atypical development** refers to deviation from a typical, or "normal," developmental pathway. Examples of atypical development include exceptionalities, developmental delay, psychological disorders, and behavioural problems, such as extreme aggressiveness in children and compulsive gambling in adults.

Before Going On

- What is the lifespan perspective?
- What are the three kinds of change contemporary developmentalists study?

RESEARCH DESIGNS AND METHODS

The easiest way to understand research methods is to look at a specific question and the alternative ways we might answer it. For example, older adults frequently complain that they have more trouble remembering people's names than they did when they were younger. Suppose we wanted to find out whether memory really declines with age. How would we go about answering this question?

RELATING GOALS TO METHODS

Developmental psychology uses the scientific method to achieve four goals: to *describe*, *explain*, *predict*, and *influence* human development from conception to death.

DESCRIBE   To describe development is simply to state what happens. A descriptive statement such as "Older adults make more memory errors than young and middle-aged adults" is an example of this first goal of developmental psychology. To meet this goal, all we would have to do is measure memory function in adults of various ages.

EXPLAIN   Explaining development involves telling why a particular event occurs. To generate explanations, developmentalists rely on *theories*—sets of statements that propose general principles of development. Students often say that they hate reading about theories; what they want are the facts. However, theories are important because they help us look at facts from different perspectives. For example, "Older adults make more memory mistakes because of changes in the brain that happen as people get older" is a statement that attempts to explain the fact of age-related memory decline from a biological perspective. Alternatively, we could explain memory decline from an experiential perspective and hypothesize that memory function declines with age because older adults don't get as much memory practice as younger adults do.

PREDICT   Useful theories produce predictions, or *hypotheses*, that researchers can test, such as "If changes in the brain cause declines in memory function, then elderly adults whose brains show the most change should also make the greatest number of memory errors." To test this hypothesis about changes in the brain and memory, we would have to measure some aspects of brain structure or function as well as memory function. Then we would have to find a way to relate one to the other. Alternatively, we could test the experiential explanation by comparing the memories of older adults who presumably get the most memory practice, such as those who are still working, with the memories of those who get less practice. If the working adults do better on tests of memory, the experiential perspective gains support. It is in this way that theories add tremendous depth to psychologists' understanding of the facts of human development and provide them with information they can use to influence development.

INFLUENCE Let's say, for example, that an older adult is diagnosed with a condition that can affect the brain, such as high blood pressure. If we know that brain function and memory are related, we can use tests of memory to make judgments about how much the person's medical condition may have already influenced his brain. At the same time, because we know that experience affects memory as well, we may be able to provide him with training that will help prevent memory problems from developing or worsening.

STUDYING AGE-RELATED CHANGES

✳Explore

When a researcher sets out to study age-related change, she has basically three choices: (1) Study different groups of people of different ages, using what is called a **cross-sectional design**; (2) study the same people over a period of time, using a **longitudinal design**; (3) combine cross-sectional and longitudinal designs in some fashion, in a **sequential design** (see **Table 1.2**).

CROSS-SECTIONAL DESIGNS To study memory cross-sectionally, we might select groups of people of various ages, such as groups of 25-, 35-, 45-, 55-, 65-, 75-, and 85-year-olds. **Figure 1.1** shows the results of just such a study, in which adults 18 to 91 years of age listened to a list of pairs of words being read to them. Once all the word pairs in the list were given, they were supposed to recall the second word of a pair when given the first. You can see that performance was distinctly worse for the 71- to 91-year-olds, a pattern of age-related decline found in a great many memory studies (Salthouse, 1991).

Because these findings fit our hypothesis, it is tempting to conclude that memory ability declines with age, but we cannot say this conclusively based on the cross-sectional data, because these adults differ not only in age, but also in cohort. The differences in

cross-sectional design
a research design in which groups of different ages are compared

longitudinal design
a research design in which people in a single group are studied at different times in their lives

sequential design
a research design that combines cross-sectional and longitudinal examinations of development

TABLE 1.2	Research Designs		
Design	**Description**	**Advantages**	**Limitations**
Cross-sectional	Participants of different ages studied at one time	Quick access to data about age differences	Ignores individual differences; cohort effects
Longitudinal	Participants in one group studied several times	Track developmental changes in individuals and groups	Time-consuming; findings may apply only to the group that is studied
Sequential	Study that combines both longitudinal and cross-sectional components	Cross-sectional and longitudinal data relevant to the same hypothesis	Time-consuming; different attrition rates across groups

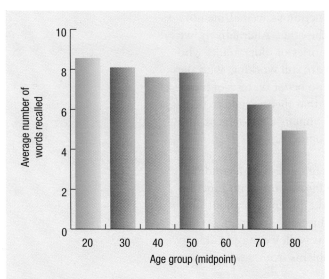

Figure 1.1

In this study, adults of various ages listened to an experimenter reading a series of word pairs. The participant's task was to try to repeat back the second word of a pair when given the first. The scores shown here are the average number of words each age group could repeat back.

(*Source:* Uttl, Graf, & Richter, 2002. Reprinted with permission from Elsevier.)

memory might reflect, for example, differences in education and not changes linked to age or development. Furthermore, cross-sectional studies cannot tell us anything about sequences of change with age or about the consistency of individual behaviour over time, because each participant is tested only once. Still, cross-sectional research is very useful because it can be done relatively quickly and can reveal possible age differences or age changes.

LONGITUDINAL DESIGNS Longitudinal designs seem to solve the problems presented by cross-sectional designs, because they follow the same individuals over a period of time. For example, to examine our hypothesis on memory decline, we could test a group first at age 25, then at 35, again at 45, and so on. Such studies allow psychologists to look at sequences of change and at individual consistency or inconsistency over time. And because longitudinal studies compare performance by the same people at different ages, they get around some aspects of the cohort problem.

Some studies are relatively open-ended. Jane Ledingham and Alex Schwartzman initiated the ongoing Concordia Longitudinal Project in 1976. They studied children living in low-income, inner-city neighbourhoods in Montreal. These children are now in their 30s and 40s and are still part of the study that now includes their offspring. One interesting finding was that at-risk mothers who displayed aggression and withdrawal in childhood had children who were at high risk of serious psychosocial and health problems (see **Figure 1.2**). This suggests significant intergenerational risk, but one mediating factor was the level of education of the mother. A higher level of education predicted better outcomes (Serbin, Cooperman, Peters, Lehoux, Stack, & Schwartzman, 1998; De Genna, Stack, Serbin, Ledingham, & Schwartzman, 2006).

Despite their importance, longitudinal designs have several drawbacks and limitations. They can be time-consuming, and it can be difficult to maintain contact with subjects over a long period of time. Some participants drop out; others die or move away. As a general rule, the healthiest and best educated are most likely to stick it out, and that fact biases the results, particularly if the study covers the final decades of life. Each succeeding set of test results comes from proportionately more and more healthy adults, which may make it look as if there is less change, or less decline, than actually exists.

Some longitudinal studies typically involve giving each participant the same tests over and over again. Over time, people learn how to take the tests. Such *practice effects* may distort the measurement of any underlying developmental changes.

Longitudinal studies don't completely get around the cohort problem either. Longitudinal studies that were conducted decades ago may offer useful information, but they may be contaminated by factors that are unique to that group of subjects at that particular time. Each generation experiences unique cultural, social, economic, and historical conditions that may not apply to subjects living at other times.

SEQUENTIAL DESIGNS One way to avoid the shortcomings of both cross-sectional and longitudinal designs is to use a sequential design. To study our memory hypothesis using a sequential design, we would begin with at least two age groups. One group might

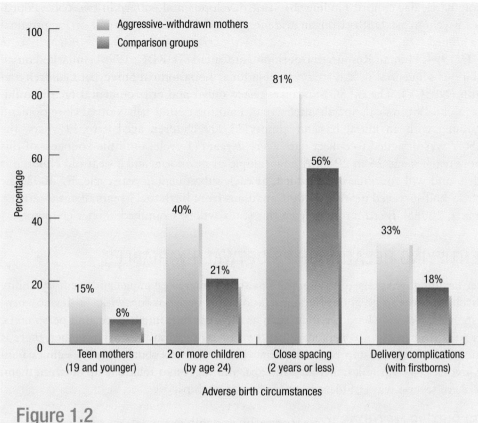

Figure 1.2

These Concordia Longitudinal Risk Project data illustrate the "adverse birth circumstances" associated with mothers who had a history of aggression and withdrawal during their adolescence and early adulthood.

(*Source:* Adapted from Serbin et al., 1998, from Table 1, p. 1251. Copyright © 1998 by the American Psychological Association. Adapted with permission.)

include 25- to 30-year-olds, and the other 30- to 35-year-olds. We would then test each group several times over a number of years, as illustrated in **Figure 1.3**. In a sequential study, each testing point beyond the initial one allows researchers to make two types of comparisons. Age-group comparisons provide them with the same kind of information as a cross-sectional study. Comparison of each group with itself at an earlier testing point allows the researchers to collect longitudinal evidence at the same time.

Sequential designs also allow for comparisons of cohorts. For example, notice in **Figure 1.3** that Group A is 30 to 35 years old at testing point 1, and Group B is 30 to 35 years old at testing point 2. Likewise, Group A is 35 to 40 at point 2, and their counterparts in Group B are this age at point 3. If same-age comparisons of the two groups reveal that their memory performance is different, researchers have evidence that, for some reason, the two cohorts differ. Conversely, if the groups perform similarly, investigators can conclude that their respective performances represent developmental characteristics rather than cohort effects. Moreover, if both groups demonstrate similar age-related patterns of change over time, researchers can conclude that the developmental pattern is not specific

Group	Age at testing point 1	Age at testing point 2	Age at testing point 3
A	30 to 35	35 to 40	40 to 45
B	25 to 30	30 to 35	35 to 40

Figure 1.3

This grid represents a design for a sequential study of memory function.

to any particular cohort. Finding the same developmental pattern in two cohorts provides psychologists with stronger evidence than either cross-sectional or longitudinal data alone.

In 1994, Human Resources Development Canada (HRDC, 1996) embarked on an ambitious sequential design study: the National Longitudinal Survey of Children and Youth (NLSCY). The NLSCY measures how social and environmental factors influence a child's physical, social, intellectual, emotional, and behavioural development. Beginning with an initial base of almost 23 000 children aged 0 to 11 years, the NLSCY was designed to collect data every 2 years (1 cycle) until the youngest of this cohort reaches age 25 in 2018. A new sample of newborns and 1-year-old children is added, and will continue to be added, at each subsequent 2-year cycle. By 2008, the NLSCY had surveyed nearly 38 000 Canadians from birth to 25 years of age (Statistics Canada, 2008a). Interim results from this study will be examined in later chapters.

IDENTIFYING RELATIONSHIPS BETWEEN VARIABLES

After deciding what design to use, the researcher interested in age and memory ability must decide how to go about finding relationships between *variables*. To developmentalists, variables are characteristics, such as physical size, intelligence, and personality, that vary from person to person. When two or more variables vary together, there is some kind of relationship between them. The hypothesis that memory declines with age involves two variables, memory and age, and suggests a relationship between them. There are several ways of identifying such relationships.

case study
an in-depth examination of a
single individual

naturalistic observation
the process of studying people
in their normal environments

Naturalistic observation refers to the research method used by psychologists who observe and study people in their natural, everyday environments.
(*Photo:* ©Michael Doolittle/The Image Works)

DESCRIPTIVE METHODS   **Case studies** are in-depth examinations of single individuals. To test the hypothesis about memory and age, we could use a case study comparing one individual's scores on tests of memory in early and late adulthood. Such a study might tell us a great deal about the stability or instability of memory in the individual studied, but we wouldn't know if our findings applied to others.

Still, case studies are extremely useful in making decisions about individuals. For example, to find out whether a child is mentally retarded, a psychologist would conduct an extensive case study involving tests, interviews of the child's parents, behavioural observations, and so on. Case studies are also frequently the basis of important hypotheses about unusual developmental events, such as head injuries and strokes.

When psychologists use **naturalistic observation** as a research method, they observe people in their normal environments. For instance, to find out more about memory in older adults, a researcher could observe them in their homes or workplaces. Such studies provide developmentalists with information about psychological processes in everyday contexts.

The weakness of naturalistic observation, however, is *observer bias*. For example, if the researcher who is observing teenagers is convinced that most of them have poor table manners, he is likely to ignore any behaviour that goes against this view. Because of observer bias, naturalistic observation studies often use "blind" observers who don't know what the research is about. In most cases, for the sake of accuracy, researchers use two or more observers so that the observations of each observer can be checked against those of the other(s). The measure for this is procedure is known as *inter-rater reliability*.

Like case studies, naturalistic observation studies are limited in the extent to which the results can be generalized.

In addition, naturalistic observation studies are very time-consuming. They must be repeated in a variety of settings so that researchers can be sure people's behaviour reflects development and not the influences of a specific environment.

Have you ever been questioned about health practices, such as sun exposure, alcohol use, or sexual activity, or for whom you plan to vote in the next election? If so, then you have participated in a **survey**, a study in which researchers use interviews and/or questionnaires to collect data about attitudes, interests, values, and various kinds of behaviours. Surveys allow researchers to quickly gather information. They can also be used to track changes over time.

survey
a data collection method in which participants respond to questions

CORRELATIONS   A **correlation** is a relationship between two variables that can be expressed as a number ranging from −1.00 to +1.00. A zero correlation indicates that there is no relationship between those variables. A positive correlation means that high scores on one variable are usually accompanied by high scores on the other. The closer a positive correlation is to +1.00, the stronger the relationship between the variables. Two variables that change in opposite directions result in a negative correlation, and the nearer the correlation to −1.00, the more strongly the two are connected.

 Explore

correlation
a relationship between two variables that can be expressed as a number ranging from −1.00 to +1.00

To understand positive and negative correlations, think about the relationship between temperature and the use of air conditioners and heaters here in Canada. Temperature and air conditioner use are positively correlated. As the temperature climbs, the number of air conditioners in use goes up. Conversely, temperature and heater use are negatively correlated. As the temperature decreases, the number of heaters in use goes up.

If we wanted to know whether age is related to memory, we could use a correlational study. All that would be necessary would be to administer memory tests to adults of varying ages and calculate the numerical correlation between test scores and ages. If there is a positive correlation between age and the number of memory errors people make—if older people make more errors—then we could say that our hypothesis has been supported. Conversely, if there is a negative correlation—if older people make fewer errors—then we would conclude that our hypothesis has not been supported.

Useful as they are, though, correlations have a major limitation: They do not indicate *causal* relationships. For example, even a high positive correlation between memory errors and age would tell us only that memory performance and age are connected in some way. It wouldn't tell us what caused the connection. It might be that younger adults understand the test instructions better. In order to identify a cause, we have to carry out experiments.

experiment
a study that tests a causal hypothesis

EXPERIMENTS   An **experiment** is a study that tests a causal hypothesis. Suppose, for example, that we think age differences in memory are caused by older adults' failure to use memory techniques, such as repeating a list mentally to remember it. We could test this hypothesis by providing memory technique training to one group of older adults and no training to another group. If the trained adults got higher scores on memory tests than they did before training and the no-training group showed no change, then we could claim support for our hypothesis.

A key feature of an experiment is that participants are assigned *randomly* to one of two or more groups. In other words, chance determines which group each participant is placed in. When participants are randomly assigned to groups, the groups have equal amounts of variation with respect to characteristics such as intelligence, personality traits, height, weight, health status, and so on. Consequently, none of these variables can affect the outcome of the experiment.

Participants in the **experimental group** receive the treatment the experimenter thinks will produce a particular effect, while those in the **control group** receive either no special treatment or a neutral treatment. The presumed causal element in the

 mydevelopmentlab
Connect to
MyDevelopmentLab
How's your memory? Be part of this experiment and find out. Challenge your friends to be lab rats.

Simulate

experimental group
the group in an experiment that receives the treatment the experimenter thinks will produce a particular effect

control group
a group in an experiment that receives either no special treatment or a neutral treatment

independent variable
the presumed causal element in an experiment

dependent variable
the characteristic or behaviour that is expected to be affected by the independent variable

experiment is called the **independent variable,** and the characteristic or behaviour that the independent variable is expected to affect is called the **dependent variable.**

In a memory-technique training experiment like the one suggested above, the group that receives the memory training is the experimental group, and the one that receives no instruction is the control group. Memory-technique training is the variable that we, the experimenters, think will cause differences in memory function, so it is the independent variable. Performance on memory tests is the variable we are using to measure the effect of the memory technique training. Therefore, performance on memory tests is the dependent variable.

Experiments are essential for understanding many aspects of development. But two special problems in studying child or adult development limit the use of experiments: First, many of the questions researchers want to answer have to do with the effects of particular unpleasant or stressful experiences on individuals: abuse, prenatal influences of alcohol or tobacco, low birth weight, poverty, unemployment, widowhood. For obvious ethical reasons, researchers cannot manipulate these variables. For example, they cannot ask one set of pregnant women to have two alcoholic drinks a day and others to have none. To study the effects of such experiences, they must rely on nonexperimental methods, such as correlations.

Second, the independent variable that developmentalists are often most interested in is age itself, and researchers cannot assign participants randomly to age groups. They can compare 4-year-olds and 6-year-olds in their approach to some particular task, such as searching for a lost object, but the children differ in a host of ways other than their ages. Older children have had more and different experiences. Thus, unlike psychologists studying other aspects of behaviour, developmental psychologists cannot systematically manipulate many of the variables they are most interested in.

To get around this problem, researchers can use any one of a series of strategies, sometimes called *quasi-experiments*, in which they compare groups without assigning the participants randomly. Cross-sectional studies are a form of quasi-experiment. So are studies in which researchers compare members of naturally occurring groups that differ in some dimension of interest, such as children whose parents choose to place them in daycare programs and children whose parents keep them at home.

Such comparisons have built-in problems, because groups that differ in one way are likely to differ in other ways as well. Parents who send their children to private schools may be wealthier and have different social values compared with parents who keep their children in public schools. If researchers find that the two groups of children differ on a specific academic measure, is it because they have spent their school days in different environments or because of other differences in their families? Researchers can make such comparisons a bit easier if they select comparison groups that are matched on those variables the researchers think might matter, such as income, marital status, or religion. But a quasi-experiment, by its very nature, will always yield more ambiguous results than will a fully controlled experiment.

CROSS-CULTURAL RESEARCH

ethnography
a detailed description of a single culture or context

Increasingly common in developmental psychology are studies comparing cultures or contexts, a task that researchers approach in several ways. One method of study, borrowed from the field of anthropology, is **ethnography.** The ethnographic method creates a detailed description of a single culture or context based on extensive observation. Often the observer lives in the culture or context for a period of time, perhaps as long as several years. Each ethnographic study is intended to stand alone, although it is sometimes possible to combine information from several different studies to see whether similar developmental patterns exist in the various cultures or contexts.

Alternatively, investigators may attempt to compare two or more cultures directly, by testing children or adults in each of the cultures with the same or comparable measures. Sometimes this involves comparing groups from different countries. Sometimes the comparisons are between subcultures within the same country; for example, increasingly common in Canada is research involving comparisons of children or adults living in different ethnic groups or communities, such as First Nations, South Asian, Caribbean, and European Canadians (Statistics Canada, 2009b). This is important in Canada because in 1971 our nation was the first in the world to make multiculturalism an official policy; the *Canadian Multicultural Act* was passed in 1988 (Canadian Heritage, 2001).

Cross-cultural research is important to developmental psychology for two reasons. First, developmentalists want to identify universal changes, that is, predictable events or processes experienced by individuals in all cultures. Developmentalists don't want to make a general statement about development—such as "Memory declines with age"—if the phenomenon in question happens only in certain cultures. Without cross-cultural research, it is impossible to know whether studies involving North Americans and Europeans apply to people in other parts of the world.

Second, one of the goals of developmental psychology is to produce findings that can be used to improve people's lives. Cross-cultural research is critical to this goal as well. For example, developmentalists know that children in cultures that emphasize the community more than the individual are more cooperative than children in more individualistic cultures. However, to use this information to help all children learn to cooperate, they need to know exactly how adults in such cultures teach their children to be cooperative. Cross-cultural research helps developmentalists identify specific variables that explain cultural differences.

RESEARCH ETHICS

Simulate

Research ethics are the guidelines researchers follow to protect the rights of animals used in research and humans who participate in studies. Ethical guidelines are published by professional organizations such as the CPA. Universities, private foundations, and government agencies have review committees that make sure all research sponsored by the institution is ethical. Guidelines for animal research include the requirement that animals be protected from unnecessary pain and suffering. Further, researchers must demonstrate that the potential benefits of their studies to either human or animal populations will be greater than any potential harm to animal subjects.

research ethics
the guidelines researchers follow to protect the rights of animals used in research and humans who participate in studies

The CPA (2000) has published ethical standards for practitioners, researchers, and scientists that include the following principles: respect for the dignity of persons, responsible caring, integrity in relationships, and responsibility to society. These ethical standards address the following major concerns.

PROTECTION FROM HARM It is unethical to do research that may cause participants permanent physical or psychological harm. Moreover, if the possibility of temporary harm exists, then researchers must provide participants with some way of repairing the damage. For example, if the study will remind subjects of unpleasant experiences, such as rape, then researchers must provide them with counselling.

INFORMED CONSENT Researchers must inform participants of any possible harm and have them sign a consent form stating that they are aware of the risks of participating. In order for children to participate in studies, their parents must give permission after the researcher has informed them of possible risks. Children older than 7 must also give their own consent. If the research takes place in a school or daycare centre, then an administrator representing the institution must consent. In addition, both children and adults have the right to discontinue participation in a study at any time. Researchers are obligated to explain this right to children in language they can understand.

CONFIDENTIALITY Participants have the right to confidentiality. Researchers must keep the identities of participants confidential and must report their data in such a way that no particular piece of information can be associated with any specific participant. The exception to confidentiality is when children reveal to researchers that they have been abused in any way by an adult. In Canada, citizens are required to report suspected cases of child abuse.

KNOWLEDGE OF RESULTS Participants, their parents, and the administrators of institutions in which research takes place have a right to a written summary of a study's results.

DECEPTION If deception has been a necessary part of a study, participants have the right to be informed about the deception as soon as the study is over.

Before Going On

- What are the pros and cons of cross-sectional, longitudinal, and sequential research designs?
- How do developmentalists use case studies, naturalistic observation, surveys, correlations, and experiments to identify relationships between variables?

Summary

The Scientific Study of Human Development

- The philosophical concepts of original sin, the blank slate, and innate goodness have influenced Western ideas about human development.

- Darwin studied child development to gain insight into evolution. Hall published the first scientific study of children and introduced the concept of norms. Gesell studied the maturational milestones of development. Piaget identified stages of cognitive development.

Contemporary Developmental Psychology

- Today's developmentalists recognize that change happens throughout the lifespan. They believe that every developmental change is a product of both nature and nurture.

- Development is a matter of changes both in degree (continuity) and kind (discontinuity).

- Contemporary developmental psychologists study three kinds of changes: universal, group-specific, and individual.

Research Designs and Methods

- In cross-sectional studies, separate age groups are each tested once. In longitudinal designs, the same individuals are tested repeatedly over time. Sequential designs combine cross-sectional and longitudinal comparisons.

- Case studies and naturalistic observation provide a great deal of important information about individuals, but it usually isn't generalizable to other individuals or groups. Correlational studies measure relationships between variables and can be done quickly. The information they yield is more generalizable than that from case studies or naturalistic observation. To test causal hypotheses, it is necessary to use experimental designs in which participants are assigned randomly to experimental or control groups.

- Ethical principles governing psychological research include protection from harm, informed consent, confidentiality, knowledge of results, and protection from deception.

Visit **www.mydevelopmentlab.com** to help you get the best grade! Test your knowledge and grasp difficult concepts through

- Custom study plans: See where you are strong and where you go wrong
- Interactive simulations

- Video and audio clips
- Raise your own Virtual Child—and much more!

Review Questions

Answers are provided on MyDevelopmentLab in the Course Resources folder.

The Scientific Study of Human Development

1.1 The philosophy that proposes that adults can mould children into whatever the adults want them to be is called
  a. morality.
  b. the blank slate.
  c. original sin.
  d. innate goodness.

Contemporary Developmental Psychology

1.2 Scientists who study age-related changes across the lifespan often use three broad domains of development to classify these changes. Which of the following is an example of the social domain?
  a. the physiological processes associated with puberty
  b. how some memory functions deteriorate as people age
  c. the relationship of an individual to other people
  d. how individuals sense and perceive their environment

1.3 Developmentalists predict that a child who _____ will have the worst outcomes.
  a. is born with vulnerabilities
  b. is raised in a poor or unsupportive environment
  c. has few vulnerabilities and is raised in a poor or unsupportive environment
  d. has many vulnerabilities and is raised in a poor or unsupportive environment

Research Designs and Methods

1.4 Which of the following is the major limitation of the correlational method?
  a. Observer bias is likely.
  b. It studies only single individuals.

  c. It does not tell us about causal relationships.
  d. Research ethics prevent its use in most developmental studies.

1.5 It would be unethical for psychologists to use experiments to answer which of the following research questions?
  a. At what age do children begin to show preferences for gender-typed toys?
  b. What circumstances elicit altruistic or prosocial behaviours from teenagers?
  c. How does a pregnant woman's stressful job affect her fetus?
  d. How quickly can an 85-year-old interpret and understand puzzling instructions for operating an electronic game?

Critical-Thinking Questions

1.6 Suppose a cross-sectional study of sex-role attitudes reveals that adults between ages 20 and 50 have the most egalitarian attitudes, while teenagers and adults over 50 have more traditional attitudes. How might cohort differences influence your interpretation of these results?

1.7 Researchers have found a positive correlation between the socioeconomic status (SES) of a child's family and the child's academic achievement: Higher SES predicts higher academic achievement. Describe as many different explanations for this correlation as you can.

CHAPTER 2

Theories of Development

Features

Every parent knows it's a constant struggle to keep babies from putting everything in their mouths. Whether it's an attractive toy or a dead insect they encounter while crawling across the living room floor, infants seem to be driven to use their mouths to explore. Have you ever wondered why? An inborn drive to explore the environment may be responsible, or babies may find the physical sensation of mouthing an object highly pleasurable. Perhaps babies use their mouths more than toddlers and preschoolers do because they don't yet have the ability to fully control other parts of their bodies. Clearly, there are many possible explanations.

As you learned in **Chapter 1**, developmental psychologists use theories to formulate *hypotheses*, or testable answers, to such "why" questions. For this reason, you'll be reading about theories in every chapter of this book. To help you make sense of all these theories, this chapter will introduce you to five influential families of theories that have quite different ways of answering questions about development. Theories in these families will come up again and again as you make your way through this book.

When you finish studying the chapter, you will be able to explain why biological and evolutionary theories have recently captured the attention of developmental psychologists; compare how the three "families" of psychology theories explain developmental changes; and explain how systems theory integrates multiple theoretical perspectives into a comprehensive theory of human development. While you read, keep the following questions in mind:

- If genes control your bodily functions, then what controls your genes?

- Why do some teens prefer video gaming over dating?

- How might parents' conflict between their work and family life contribute to their child's school problems?

BIOLOGY AND EVOLUTIONARY THEORIES

A knowledge of biological processes is an important foundation for understanding evolutionary theories of development. Both *genetic* and *epigenetic* factors interact with environmental variables to shape our level of health and well-being across the lifespan. We are just beginning to understand how epigenetic processes integrate nature and nurture—*epigenetics* is positioned to profoundly change the way we think of human development in the 21st century.

Evolutionary theories propose that the genetic and physiological processes that underlie human behaviour changed gradually over time through genetic mutation and natural selection. Evolution is used to explain cognitive and, by extension, social and cultural behaviour.

GENETICS

Our body cells' nuclei contain 23 pairs of **chromosomes** that are made up of about, an astounding, 2.0 metres of finely coiled **deoxyribonucleic acid (DNA)** molecules. Each chromosome is divided into segments, called **genes**, each of which influences a particular feature or developmental pattern. A gene controlling a specific characteristic always appears in the same place (the *locus*) on the same chromosome in every individual of the same species. For example, the locus of the gene that determines whether a person's blood is type A, B, or O is on chromosome 9. A **genome** is all the DNA an organism possesses (see **Figure 2.1**). To appreciate the complexity of the genome, consider that, in humans, each of our 46 chromosomes contains anywhere from 231 to 3141 genes

---

mydevelopmentlab

Connect to MyDevelopmentLab

Continue to raise your cyber child and discover the world of parenthood at . . .

My Virtual Child

---

chromosomes
strings of genetic material in the nuclei of cells

deoxyribonucleic acid (DNA)
a chemical material that makes up chromosomes and genes

 Explore

genes
a complex chemical units of a chromosome that control or influence inherited traits

genome
all the DNA that an organism possesses

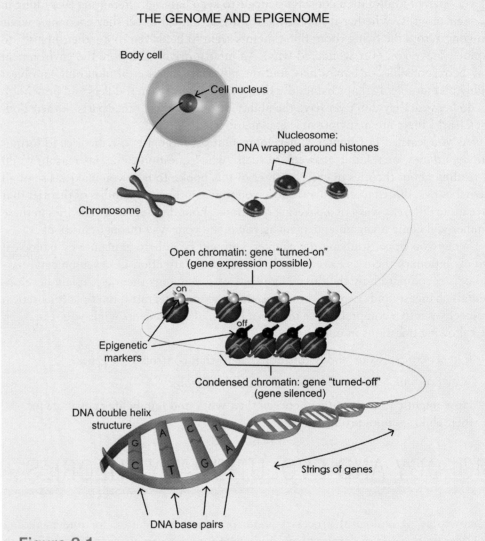

THE GENOME AND EPIGENOME

Body cell

Cell nucleus

Nucleosome:
DNA wrapped around histones

Chromosome

Open chromatin: gene "turned-on"
(gene expression possible)

on

off

Epigenetic
markers

Condensed chromatin: gene "turned-off"
(gene silenced)

DNA double helix
structure

Strings of genes

DNA base pairs

Figure 2.1

The human genome—the DNA contained in the nucleus of our body cells—is comprised of 23 pairs of chromosomes containing loops of genes. The DNA is further wound around histones (a protein material) that resemble beads-on-a-string, called the *nucleosomes*. Deposited along the nucleosomes are epigenetic markers, which, collectively, make up the epigenome. Epigenetic markers control gene expression by either opening up or tightly packing the nucleosomes. When the nucleosome space is open, gene expression is possible, but when nucleosomes are packed tightly together, genes are silenced. Four essential organic compounds, A – adenine, T – thymine, C – cytosine, and G – guanine, are organized into base pairs along the double helix structure of DNA. When the epigenome unpacks the nucleosome, the genetic code (the sequence of base pairs) is ready to be transcribed and translated into proteins.

(*Source:* Nevid et al., 2005, *Essentials of Abnormal Psychology*, Canadian Edition, Figure 2.1. Reprinted with permission from Pearson Education Canada. Artwork copyright © Alexandra Johnson. Printed with permission.)

(read about genetic disorders in **Chapter 3**). In all, each human body cell nucleus possesses an estimated 23 000 genes.

An essential function of genes is to instruct body cells to combine 20 standard amino acids to build the 35 000 or so *proteins* that our bodies need to function properly. **Proteins** are organic compounds that form the structures of the body and regulate its maintenance. Basic structural elements of our bodies—for example, muscle, brain, and bone—are made up of different proteins. Proteins also control all biological processes ranging from metabolic and immune functions to intercellular communications.

proteins
organic compounds, consisting of amino acids, that perform most life functions and make up the majority of cellular structures

GENOTYPES, PHENOTYPES, AND PATTERNS OF INHERITANCE

The **genotype** is the actual DNA material that determines each person's unique genetic blueprint. The **phenotype** is the individual's whole set of observable characteristics. One way to remember the distinction is that the phenotype can be identified by directly observing the individual. For example, you can easily see that a woman has brown eyes, which are part of her phenotype. Her genotype, though, can't be so easily determined. In many cases, you would have to know the eye colour of her parents and offspring to determine whether she carries genes for another eye colour, because complex rules govern the way genotypes influence phenotypes. Three principles of genetic transmission explain such patterns of inheritance.

genotype
an individual's unique genetic blueprint

phenotype
an individual's whole set of observable characteristics

DOMINANT AND RECESSIVE GENES The simplest genetic rule is the **dominant-recessive pattern**, in which a single dominant gene strongly influences phenotype. (**Table 2.1** lists several normal phenotypical traits and indicates whether they arise from dominant or recessive genes.) People whose chromosomes carry either two dominant or two recessive genes are referred to as *homozygous*. Those with one dominant and one recessive gene are said to be *heterozygous*.

dominant-recessive pattern
a pattern of inheritance in which a single dominant gene influences a person's phenotype but two recessive genes are necessary to produce an associated trait

If a child receives a single dominant gene for a trait from one parent, the child's phenotype will include the trait determined by that gene. In contrast, a child's phenotype will include a recessive trait only if she inherits a recessive gene from both parents. For example, geneticists have found that the curliness of hair is controlled by a single pair of genes (see **Figure 2.2**). The gene for curly hair is dominant; therefore, if a man has curly hair, his genotype includes at least one gene for curly hair and at least half of his sperm carry this gene. Conversely, straight hair is recessive, so a straight-haired man's genotype must include two straight-hair genes for his phenotype to include straight hair. Geneticists also know that the only kind of hair type a straight-haired father can pass on to his children is straight hair, because all his sperm carry recessive, straight-hair genes.

Critical Thinking

Think about your hair type and that of your siblings. What does your hair suggest about your parents' genotypes?

In addition, human geneticists have learned that both dominant and recessive genes differ in *expressivity*, meaning that the degree to which any gene influences phenotypes varies from person to person. For example, all individuals who have the gene for curly hair don't have equally curly hair. So, even when a child receives a dominant gene for curly hair from her father, the amount and type of curl in her hair probably won't be exactly the same as his.

TABLE 2.1	Genetic Sources of Normal Traits	
Dominant Genes	**Recessive Genes**	**Polygenic (many genes)**
Broad lips	Thin lips	Height
Nearsightedness	Flat feet	Eye colour
Coarse hair	Fine hair	Body type
Curly hair	Red hair	Skin colour
Dark hair	Blond hair	Personality
Types A and B blood	Type O blood	
Rh-positive blood	Rh-negative blood	
Freckles		
Dimples		

(*Source:* **Tortora & Grabowski, 1993.**)

mydevelopmentlab
Connect to
MyDevelopmentLab
Watch the Junk DNA video to see how we connect to rodents.
Watch

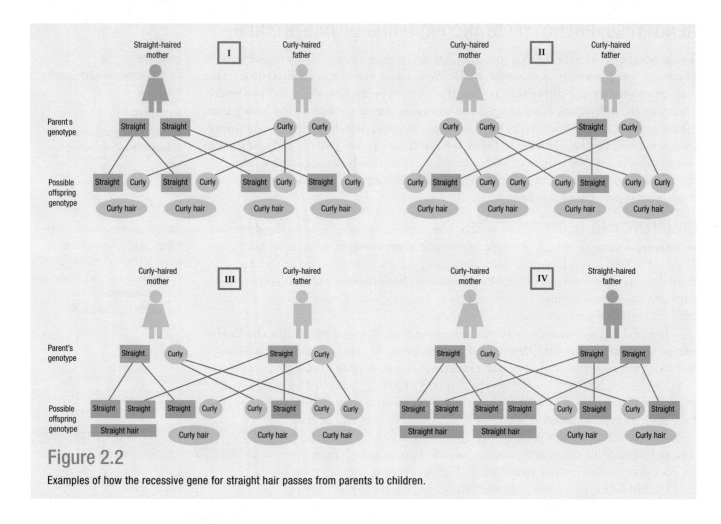

Figure 2.2

Examples of how the recessive gene for straight hair passes from parents to children.

Blood type is also determined by a dominant-recessive pattern of inheritance. Because a person must have two recessive genes to have type O blood, the genotype of every person who has this type is clear. However, the genotype of people with type A or B blood is not obvious because types A and B are dominant. Thus, when a person's phenotype includes either type A or type B blood, one of the person's blood type genes must be for that type, but the other could be for some other type. However, if a type A father and a type B mother produce a child with type O, each of them carries a gene for type O, because the child must receive one such gene from each parent to have the type O phenotype.

polygenic inheritance
a pattern of inheritance in which many genes influence a trait

POLYGENIC AND MULTIFACTORIAL INHERITANCE With **polygenic inheritance,** many genes influence the phenotype. There are many polygenic traits in which the dominant-recessive pattern is also at work. For example, geneticists believe that children get three genes for skin colour from each parent (Tortora & Grabowski, 1993). Dark skin is dominant over light skin, but the skin colours also blend together. Thus, when one parent is dark-skinned and the other is fair-skinned, the child will have skin that is somewhere between the two. The dark-skinned parent's dominant genes will ensure that the child will be darker than the fair parent, but the fair-skinned parent's genes will prevent the child from having skin as dark as that of the dark-skinned parent.

Eye colour is another polygenic trait with a dominant-recessive pattern (Tortora & Grabowski, 1993). Scientists don't know for sure how many genes influence eye colour. They do know, however, that these genes don't cause specific colours. Instead, they cause the coloured part of the eye to be dark or light. Dark colours (black, brown, hazel, and green) are dominant over light colours (blue and grey). However, blended colours are also possible. People whose chromosomes carry a combination of genes for green, blue, and grey eyes can have blue-grey, green-blue, or blue-green eyes. Likewise, genes that cause different shades of brown can combine their effects to make children's eye colour phenotypes different from those of their brown-eyed parents.

Many genes influence height, and they are not subject to a dominant-recessive pattern of inheritance. Most geneticists believe that each height gene has a small influence over a child's size (Tanner, 1990). Thus, a child's height will be the sum of the effects of all these genes.

Height, like most polygenic traits, is also a result of **multifactorial inheritance**—that is, it is affected both by genes and by the environment. For this reason, doctors use a child's height as a measure of his general health (Sulkes, 1998; Tanner, 1990). If a child is ill, poorly nourished, or emotionally neglected, he may be smaller than others his age. Thus, when a child is shorter than 97% of his age-mates, doctors try to determine if he is short because of his genes or because something is causing him to grow poorly (Tanner, 1990).

MITOCHONDRIAL INHERITANCE Scientists have discovered some additional principles of genetic inheritance. In **mitochondrial inheritance**, children inherit genes that are carried in structures called *mitochondria*, which are found in the fluid that surrounds the nucleus of the ovum before it is fertilized. Consequently, mitochondrial genes are passed only from mother to child. Geneticists have learned that several serious disorders, including some types of blindness, are transmitted in this way. In most such cases, the mother herself is unaffected by the harmful genes (Amato, 1998).

EPIGENETICS

Recent genetics research has revealed that our genome accounts for only one aspect of heredity influences. In particular, one question has remained unanswered until now—if each of our cells carries the identical genome, how is it that the cells of our body can be so different? Put another way, how can cells that have the same genotype differentiate into specialized cells (phenotype), such as liver, heart, or brain tissue? The answer comes to us from the discovery of molecular biological compounds that overlay our DNA, known collectively as the **epigenome** (Callinan & Feinberg, 2006) (see **Figure 2.1**).

Possessing the gene for a specific trait does not guarantee that it will be *expressed*. Although each cell in our body contains the same genetic code (the same genotype), our unique set of epigenetic markers regulate *gene expression* (our phenotype). Epigenetic markers work by signalling some genes to "turn on" (**gene expression**) and others to "turn off" (**gene silencing**). For example, soon after conception, epigenetic markers "tell" "brain genes" to be active in brain tissue but inactive in liver tissue. Epigenetic structures also control ongoing cellular functioning in a similar way. They signal a gene or polygene to turn on (e.g., when a cell needs to produce a specific protein) or turn off (e.g., when protein production needs to stop until further notice). In this way, epigenetic mechanisms regulate normal bodily processes, such as regulating blood sugar levels, activating immune functions, or controlling brain cell activity.

Moshe Szyf and Michael Meaney, two pioneers in the emerging field of **epigenetics** and their McGill University colleagues have found that **epigenetic factors** play a pivotal role in development across the lifespan (McDevitt, 2006; Rutter, 2007). Through animal studies, they were the first researchers to demonstrate that maternal care can physically alter molecular epigenetic structures in offspring. For example, a mother rat's increased postnatal levels of feeding and grooming of her pups resulted in calmer rat pups by actually altering the molecular epigenetic structures in the rat pups

multifactorial inheritance
a pattern of inheritance affected by both genes and the environment

mitochondrial inheritance
a pattern of inheritance in which a cell's mitochondrial DNA (mtDNA) is inherited from the mother's egg and not the father's sperm

epigenome
the sum total of inherited and acquired molecular modifications to the genome that leads to changes in gene regulation without changing the DNA sequence of the genome

gene expression
when a gene sequence is activated ("turned on") and ready to be translated into gene products—proteins, for the most part

gene silencing
when a gene sequence is made inactive ("turned off") and is prevented from being translated into gene products—proteins, for the most part

epigenetics
the study of the gene regulation patterns that alter gene function (phenotype) without changing gene structure (genotype)

epigenetic factors
inheritable and acquired gene regulation patterns that alter gene function (phenotype) without changing gene structure (genotype)

(Weaver et al., 2004; Weaver et al., 2007; Weaver, Meaney, & Szyf, 2006). In follow-up studies, they found that although these early-life epigenetic changes persist into adulthood, they could be reversed experimentally (Weaver et al., 2005).

Although epigenetic modifications acquired during a lifetime are typically expunged during the earliest stages of prenatal development of subsequent generations (Kimmins & Sassone-Corsi, 2005), recent studies have shown that some acquired epigenetic modifications can be passed on. For example, animal studies have shown that epigenetic changes to liver, heart, and brain proteins in mice and endocrine, reproductive, and behavioural changes in rats acquired during the lifetime of the parent can be transmitted to the offspring (Anway, Cupp, Uzumca, & Skinner, 2005; Roemer, Reik, Dean, & Klose, 1997). Even epigenetic changes caused by changes to maternal diet have been shown to transfer across generations in mice populations (Cropley, Suter, Beckman, & Martin, 2006). In addition, some preliminary evidence shows that acquired epigenetic traits linked to chromosome structure alterations may be inherited in humans (Amor et al., 2004; Peaston & Whitelaw, 2006; Whitelaw & Whitelaw, 2006).

EVOLUTIONARY THEORIES

Evolutionary theories attempt to explain our differences as individuals and our commonalities as a species. These theories often focus on the genetic and environmental mechanisms that underlie development throughout the lifespan and across generations.

NATIVISM **Nativism** is the view that humans possess unique genetic traits that will be manifested in all members of the species, regardless of differences in their environments. Nativist theory is supported when developmentalists identify behaviours that appear early in life, develop in almost all individuals in every culture, and do not exist in other species. For example, all healthy children learn language early in life without any specific instruction from adults, and, to date, scientists have found no evidence of grammatical language in nonhuman species.

ETHOLOGY **Ethology** emphasizes genetically determined survival behaviours that are assumed to have evolved through natural selection. For example, nests are necessary for the survival of young birds. Therefore, ethologists say, evolution has equipped birds with nest-building genes.

Similarly, ethologists believe that emotional relationships are necessary to the survival of human infants (Bowlby, 1969, 1980). They claim that evolution has produced genes that cause humans to form these relationships. For example, most people feel irritated when they hear a newborn crying. Ethologists say the baby is genetically programmed to cry in a certain way, and adults are genetically programmed to get irritated when they hear it. The caretaker responds to a crying baby's needs to remove the irritating stimulus of the noise. As the caretaker and infant interact, an emotional bond is created between them. Thus, genes for crying in an irritating manner increase infants' chances of survival.

BEHAVIOUR GENETICS A related area of study, **behaviour genetics** focuses on the effect of heredity on individual differences. Traits or behaviours are believed to be influenced by genes when those of related people, such as children and their parents,

nativism
the view that humans possess unique genetic traits that will be manifested in all members of the species, regardless of differences in their environments

ethology
a perspective on development that emphasizes genetically determined survival behaviours presumed to have evolved through natural selection

behaviour genetics
the study of the role of heredity in individual differences

Ethologists assert that the first 2 years of life are a critical period for the establishment of relationships between infants and caregivers. (*Photo:* © Jose Luis Pelaez, Inc./ CORBIS)

are more similar than those of unrelated people. Behaviour geneticists have shown that heredity affects a broad range of traits and behaviours, including intelligence, shyness, and aggressiveness.

SOCIOBIOLOGY **Sociobiology** is the study of society using the methods and concepts of biological science. When applied to human development, sociobiology emphasizes genes that aid group survival. Sociobiologists claim that individual humans have the best chance for survival when they live in groups. Therefore, they claim, evolution has provided humans with genetic programming that helps us cooperate.

To support their views, sociobiologists look for social rules and behaviours that exist in all cultures. For example, every society has laws against murder. Sociobiologists believe that humans are genetically programmed to create rules based on respect for other people's lives. Evolution has selected these genes, they claim, because people need to respect each other's lives and to be able to cooperate.

EVOLUTIONARY PSYCHOLOGY **Evolutionary psychology** is the study of how genetically inherited cognitive and social characteristics have evolved through natural selection. Accordingly, cognitive abilities that underlie social relations and interactions are a major focus. Evolutionary psychology is an interdisciplinary approach to explaining human behaviour that involves biology, anthropology, cognitive science, and neuroscience (Cosmides & Tooby, 2000).

Harvard psychologist Steven Pinker (1997, 2002), a Canadian from Montreal, has been a leading advocate of evolutionary psychology. His basic premise is that, through a process of biological evolution, the mind, like the body, has been shaped by natural selection to serve adaptive functions and promote survival. Moreover, Pinker (2002) contends that we have hard-wired inherited patterns of thinking and feeling shaped over time by the demands made on the species for survival. Today, this "human nature," as he calls it, affects every aspect of our lives, from child-rearing practices to the formation of our political views to our taste in art and music.

Epigenetic theorists suggest that epigenetic variations have evolved alongside genetic ones. They contend that cellular structures, behaviour, culture, and language are all inherited along with, but independent of, genetic variables. They also point out that epigenetic modifications that occur over the course of a lifetime can be transmitted to future generations (Jablonka & Lamb, 1995, 2002, 2005; Mandrioli, 2004). These ideas about epigenetic inheritance are broadening the scope of evolutionary psychology beyond the traditional gene-centred perspective of evolution.

EVOLUTIONARY DEVELOPMENTAL PSYCHOLOGY The proponents of this view say that, contrary to what philosopher John Locke thought about infants (refer to **Chapter 1**), a newborn's mind is not a blank slate. Rather, the mind has been genetically programmed with a predisposition to learn and develop in certain ways—for instance, it has a readiness to learn language and recognize human faces (Bjorklund & Pellegrini, 2002; Pinker, 2002; Tooby, Cosmides & Barrett, 2005).

Evolutionary developmental psychology theorists agree that nature (genes) and nurture (environment) interact in determining individual intelligence, personality, and social behaviour (Bjorklund & Pellegrini, 2002). But they also suggest that we need the ability to display different forms of behaviour at different times over the course of our lives. For example, the cognitive and emotional abilities that help infants and children adapt and survive are qualitatively different from those that adults require to adapt and survive. Specifically, infants need to form attachments while adults must contend with mating and, once children arrive, parenting and, later, grandparenting (Buss, 1999). From this perspective, then, evolutionary forces have contributed to the

sociobiology
the study of society using the methods and concepts of biology; when used by developmentalists, an approach that emphasizes genes that aid group survival

evolutionary psychology
the view that genetically inherited cognitive and social characteristics have evolved through natural selection

evolutionary developmental psychology
the view that genetically inherited cognitive and social characteristics that promote survival and adaptation appear at different times across the lifespan

development of age-dependent traits that promote survival and adaptation across the lifespan.

EVOLUTIONARY PRENATAL PROGRAMMING AND ADULT HEALTH AND DISEASE

Changing one's lifestyle habits later in life to reduce the risk of disease may be a case of "too little, too late." In addition to genetic and lifestyle factors, the risk of developing noncommunicable diseases such as heart disease, diabetes, and obesity may have its roots in very early life influences. This is the case according to evolutionary theorists, Peter Gluckman of the University of Auckland, NZ, and Mark Hanson of the University of Southampton, UK, and their colleagues, who have proposed some intriguing ideas (Gluckman & Hanson, 2006a, 2006b, 2007; Gluckman et al., 2009; Gluckman, Hanson, & Beedle, 2007; Gluckman, Hanson, & Spencer, 2005). They suggest that the *prenate* (i.e., the fetus) picks up cues about existing environmental conditions from its mother and is thereby able to predict what kind of environment it can expect to live in after birth. In response, the fetus undergoes epigenetic changes that ensure the best chance for survival in the anticipated future environment. These so called **predictive-adaptive responses** are adaptive only if the forecast is correct. Where there is a mismatch between the early (prenatal) and later (postnatal) environment, physiological adaptations may be ill-suited to the postnatal environment and thus contribute to lifestyle-related diseases in adulthood—the greater the mismatch, the greater the risk. **Figure 2.3** depicts an example of how these mismatches predict metabolic disease.

predictive-adaptive responses

the prenate's ability to use information about the current environment to adjust its physiology in anticipation that it will match future environmental conditions and optimize the chances to survive and reproduce in adulthood

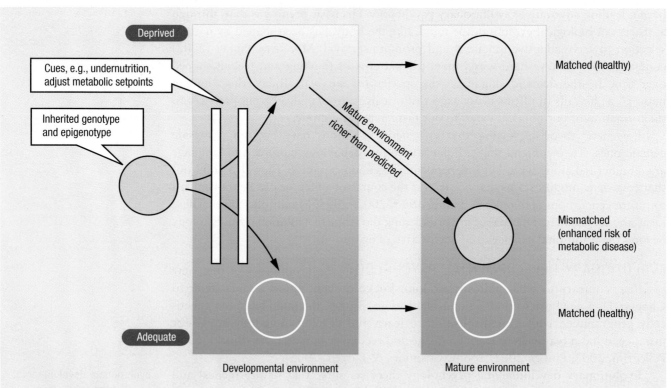

Figure 2.3

The developing organism senses maternally transmitted environmental cues, such as undernutrition, during prenatal and early postnatal life. Developmental flexibility in response to these cues modifies the default trajectory defined by the inherited fetal genome and epigenome according to whether the environment is perceived as adequate (dark background) or deprived (light background), resulting in metabolic adjustments. If the eventual mature environment, whether adequate or deprived, matches the prediction, then the risk of metabolic disease in later life is low. If there is a mismatch between the predicted and actual mature environments, particularly if the mature environment is richer than anticipated, then the risk of metabolic disease is enhanced.

(*Source:* Gluckman, Nansen and Beedle, 2007. Reprinted with permission of Wiley–Liss, Inc., a subsidiary of John Wiley & Sons, Inc.)

Some responses of the embryo or the fetus to its environment may, however, be developmentally disruptive with no adaptive value—for example, a response to an environmental toxic agent that goes beyond the organism's ability to adapt (Gluckman & Hanson, 2004a; Heindel & Lawler, 2006) (you'll read about these *teratogens* later in **Chapter 3**). Epigenetic changes in the DNA made prenatally can persist throughout the lifespan and the response made to the predicted future environmental conditions in one generation may also extend over several generations (Gluckman, Hanson, & Spencer, 2005; Waterman, 2006). The **Research Report** illustrates how a gene variation, which may have aided adaptation for generations, can suddenly give rise to an epidemic when lifestyle behaviours are altered.

EVALUATION OF BIOLOGY AND EVOLUTIONARY THEORIES

Biological principles that underlie genetics and epigenetics are expanding our understanding of disease processes. Scientists are discovering the complex role that inheritance plays in human health and the related importance of early intervention. As well, we use theories of evolution to explain how adaptive behaviours are transmitted across generations, but they are difficult to prove.

DISEASE CONTROL Advances in **human genomics** will likely play a vital role in predicting and preventing diseases in the 21st century (Collins & McKusick, 2001). Some scientists claim that developments in relatively rare single-gene diseases, such as *hemophilia*, *Huntington's disease*, and *sickle-cell disease*, will have a limited impact on overall national health care (Hall, Morley, & Lucke, 2004; Holtzman & Marteau, 2000). In total, these types of genetic diseases account for only about 5% of all human disease in developed countries (Khoury, 2003). Other scientists, predict that the greatest impact of advances in human genomics will likely be seen in the treatment of *multifactoral diseases*, such as heart disease and cancer. In these cases, having a genome-wide perspective will be an advantage (Hall, Morley, & Lucke, 2004). For example, the British Columbia Cancer Agency research team headed by Samuel Aparicio recently decoded the 3 billion letters in the DNA sequence of a type of breast cancer that accounts for 10% of all breast cancers (Shah et al., 2009). Shortly after this discovery, Canadian scientists joined an international partnership that intends to decode the genomes and epigenomes of some 25 000 cancers samples, with the aim of developing new strategies for early detection and prevention (International Cancer Genome Consortium, 2010).

Although the study of the relationship between the epigenome and human health is still in its infancy, early indications suggest that both external and personal factors influence epigenetic mechanisms (Esteller, 2006; Fraga et al., 2005; Hiltunen et al., 2002; Luch, 2005; Mathers & Hesketh, 2007; Rossman, 2003; Weinhold, 2006). In turn, epigenetic changes alter gene expression, which can increase the risk for developing both physical and psychological disorders (Petronis et al., 2000; Petronis, 2003, 2004; Schumacher & Petronis, 2006; Szyf, 2006). Epigenetic markings on DNA are continually modified throughout the lifespan (Bennett-Baker, Wilkowski, & Burke, 2003; Martin, 2005; Richardson, 2003) and any acquired epigenetic traits may be passed onto the next generation (Feil, 2006; Jablonka, 2004; Jablonka & Lamb, 2005). Epigenetic research is rapidly contributing to our understanding of the inheritance factors involved in vulnerability and resilience and may one day lead to new ways of diagnosing and treating diseases and disorders in humans ("Learning Without Learning; Epigenetics," 2006; Jablonka, 2004; Meaney & Szyf, 2005; Wong, Gottesman, & Petronis, 2005). Indeed, newly discovered epigenetic factors may prove to be the proverbial "missing link" that helps us explain how nurture interacts with nature.

human genomics
the study of the human genome including the location of genes, their function and their role in disease processes

Research Report

TYPE 2 DIABETES EPIDEMIC IN A REMOTE COMMUNITY

Prior to the middle of the last century, Type 2 diabetes was rare among Aboriginal populations (Health Canada, 1999a). By the 1970s, however, research suggested that an epidemic might be emerging; two decades later, this was confirmed (Young, Reading, Elias, & O'Neil, 2000). Today, in Canada, Type 2 diabetes is three times as prevalent (and the incidence rate is escalating) in First Nations Peoples as in the general population. An estimated 20% of all First Nations Peoples currently live with the disease (Picard, 2010).

Type 2 diabetes generally occurs later in life and carries with it serious health and social ramifications. It leads to conditions such as heart disease, blindness, kidney failure, and gangrene (Young et al., 2000) and is a leading cause of death and disability among First Nations Peoples (Health Canada, 1999a).

Robert Hegele and his research team at the John P. Robarts Research Institute in London, Ontario, discovered a strong genetic effect related to a single gene variant. This genetic mutation was discovered in the Oji-Cree, who reside on the Sandy Lake Reserve in Northern Ontario. The adults of the community were found to have a high incidence of the G319S mutation, which affects the structure of a specific liver protein. The incidence of Type 2 diabetes was found to be five times higher than it is in the general Canadian population. This rate is the third highest in the world (Hegele, Cao, Harris, Hanley, & Zinman, 1999).

The Type 2 diabetes epidemic demonstrates how we can study the interaction between genes and behaviour and suggests that a genetic susceptibility interacts with multiple environmental factors. The sudden increase in the incidence of the disease may be related to a significant change in lifestyle. For instance, the Oji-Cree's traditional low-carbohydrate diet has been replaced by a "junk food" and high "fatty" content diet and is coupled with a more sedentary level of physical activity. This modern lifestyle encourages obesity of the mid-body area in Oji-Cree who have the G319S mutation, and this is connected to a higher risk of diabetes (Hegele et al., 1999; Young et al., 2000).

This new understanding of the interplay between genetics and environment has led to a complex health care initiative. Community-wide prevention and health education programs that actively involve Oji-Cree residents and demonstrate an appreciation for their language and cultural concerns begin in Grade 3. The focus is on healthy lifestyle practices that include a balanced diet and physical exercise. Moreover, a screening program for detecting diabetes and a lifestyle support program for those who are living with the disease were both established to decrease the severity of its effects (Health Canada, 2010a; John P. Robarts Research Institute, 2000).

EARLY INTERVENTION Evolutionary theory and research are making scientists more aware of the relative importance of early-life events in making accurate predictive-adaptive responses that match expected future environments. This growing awareness has focused attention on the need to promote early interventional strategies during prenatal development (e.g., to support good health and nutrition in females of reproductive age) versus those instituted later in adult life. This important element will prevent chronic disease in future generations across the globe (Gluckman & Hanson, 2004b, 2005, 2006b).

REMAINING QUESTIONS Critics of evolutionary theories claim that they underestimate the impact of the environment and place too much emphasis on heredity. For example, it is true that children learn all languages in the same way; however, environmental factors, including characteristics of different languages, affect the rate at which children learn language. Moreover, when describing social behaviour, critics say that societies have similar rules because, over many generations, people have learned which rules work. When social rules no longer work, say critics, people invent new ones. Both the new rules and the reasons for them are passed on from one generation to the next through language, not genes.

Another major concern is that these theories are difficult to prove. How could a researcher test the idea that infants attach to caregivers because attachment has survival value that has evolved over time? Furthermore, even if there is a strong biological basis for specific cognitive strategies or social behaviours, they can still be modified by experience and learning.

Before Going On

- How do genetic and epigenetic mechanisms interact to determine health and behaviour?
- How can diseases such as diabetes or obesity be programmed prenatally?

PSYCHOANALYTIC THEORIES

One theoretical approach to explaining babies' fascination with mouthing objects might suggest that infants derive more physical pleasure from mouthing objects than from manipulating them with other parts of their bodies. Such an approach would most likely belong to the family of **psychoanalytic theories**, a school of thought that originated with Sigmund Freud (1856–1939). Psychoanalytic theorists believe that developmental change happens because internal drives and emotions influence behaviour.

FREUD'S PSYCHOSEXUAL THEORY

Although much of Freud's formal theory remains contentious, his ideas still influence our understanding of personality development. One of Freud's most distinctive concepts is the idea that behaviour is governed by both conscious and unconscious processes. The most basic of these unconscious processes is an internal drive for physical pleasure that Freud called the **libido**. He believed the libido to be the motivating force behind most behaviour.

PERSONALITY DEVLOPMENT Freud also argued that personality has three parts. The **id** contains the libido and operates at an unconscious level; the id is a person's basic sexual and aggressive impulses, which are present at birth. The **ego**, the conscious, thinking part of personality, develops in the first 2 to 3 years of life. One of the ego's jobs is to keep the needs of the id satisfied. For instance, when a person is hungry, it is the id that demands food immediately, and the ego is supposed to find a way to obtain it. The **superego**, the portion of the personality that acts as a moral judge, contains the rules of society and develops near the end of early childhood, at about age 6. Once the superego develops, the ego's task becomes more complex. It must satisfy the id without violating the superego's rules.

The ego is responsible for keeping the three components of personality in balance. According to Freud, a person experiences tension when any of the three components is in conflict with another. For example, if a person is hungry, the id may motivate her to do anything to find food, but the ego—her conscious self—may be unable to find any. Alternatively, food may be available, but the ego may have to violate one of the superego's moral rules to get it. In such cases, the ego may generate **defence mechanisms**— ways of thinking about a situation that reduce anxiety. Without defence mechanisms,

psychoanalytic theories theories proposing that developmental change happens because of the influence of internal drives and emotions on behaviour

 Explore

libido in Freud's theory, an instinctual drive for physical pleasure present at birth that forms the motivating force behind virtually all human behaviour

id in Freud's theory, the part of the personality that comprises a person's basic sexual and aggressive impulses; it contains the libido and motivates a person to seek pleasure and avoid pain

ego according to Freud, the thinking element of personality

superego Freud's term for the part of personality that is the moral judge

defence mechanisms strategies for reducing anxiety, such as repression, denial, or projection, proposed by Freud

Freud thought, the degree of tension within the personality would become intolerable, leading to mental illness or suicide.

FIVE PSYCHOSEXUAL STAGES Freud proposed a series of **psychosexual stages** through which a child moves in a fixed sequence determined by maturation. In each stage, the libido is centred on a different part of the body. In the infant, the mouth is the focus of the drive for physical pleasure; the stage is therefore called the *oral stage*. As maturation progresses, the libido becomes focused on the anus (hence, the *anal stage*), and later on the genitals (the *phallic stage* and, after a period of dormancy called the *latency stage*, the *genital stage*).

Optimum development, according to Freud, requires an environment that will satisfy the unique needs of each period. For example, the infant needs sufficient opportunity for oral stimulation. An inadequate early environment will result in *fixation*, characterized by behaviours that reflect unresolved problems and unmet needs. Thus, emphasis on the formative role of early experiences is a hallmark of psychoanalytic theories.

ERIKSON'S PSYCHOSOCIAL THEORY

Apart from Freud, Erik Erikson (1902–1994) is the psychoanalytic theorist who has had the greatest influence on the study of development (Erikson, 1950, 1959, 1980b, 1982; Erikson, Erikson, & Kivnick, 1986; Evans, 1969). Erikson, like many of Freud's other early followers, accepted many of Freud's ideas but later went on to expand on them. For instance, Erikson claimed that development results from the interaction between internal drives and cultural demands; thus, his theory refers to **psychosocial stages** rather than to *psychosexual* ones. Furthermore, Erikson thought that development continued through the entire lifespan.

EIGHT PSYCHOSOCIAL STAGES In Erikson's view, to achieve a healthy personality, an individual must successfully resolve a psychosocial crisis at each of the eight stages of development, as summarized in **Table 2.2**. Each crisis is defined by a pair of opposing possibilities, such as trust versus mistrust or integrity versus despair. Successful resolution of a crisis results in the development of the characteristic on the positive side of the dichotomy. A healthy resolution, however, does not mean moving totally to the positive side. For example, an infant needs to have experienced some mistrust to learn to identify people who are not trustworthy. But healthy development requires a favourable ratio of positive to negative. Of the eight stages described in **Table 2.2**, four have been the focus of the greatest amount of theorizing and research: trust in infancy, identity in adolescence, intimacy in early adulthood, and generativity in middle adulthood.

EIGHT CRISES TO RESOLVE Erikson believed that the behaviour of the major caregiver (usually the mother) is critical to the child's resolution of the first life crisis: *trust versus mistrust*. To ensure successful resolution of this crisis, the caregiver must be consistently loving and must respond to the child predictably and reliably. Infants whose early care has been erratic or harsh may develop mistrust. In either case, the child carries this aspect of personality throughout her development, and it affects the resolution of later tasks.

Erikson's description of the central adolescent dilemma, *identity versus role confusion*, has been particularly influential. He argued that, to arrive at a mature sexual and occupational identity, every adolescent must examine his identity

---

psychosexual stages
Freud's five stages of personality development through which children move in a fixed sequence determined by maturation; the libido is centred in a different body part in each stage

psychosocial stages
Erikson's eight stages, or crises, of personality development in which inner instincts interact with outer cultural and social demands to shape personality

Critical Thinking

In which of Erikson's psychosocial stages would you place yourself? Does Erikson's description of this stage correspond to the challenges and concerns you are confronting?

TABLE 2.2	Erikson's Psychosocial Stages	
Approximate Ages	**Stage**	**Positive Characteristics Gained and Typical Activities**
Birth to 1 year	Trust versus mistrust	Hope; trust in primary caregiver and in one's own ability to make things happen (secure attachment to caregiver is key)
1 to 3	Autonomy versus shame and doubt	Will; new physical skills lead to demand for more choices, most often seen as saying "no" to caregivers; child learns self-care skills, such as toileting
3 to 6	Initiative versus guilt	Purpose; ability to organize activities around some goal; more assertiveness and aggressiveness (harsh parental criticism may lead to guilt)
6 to 12	Industry versus inferiority	Competence; cultural skills and norms, including school skills and tool use (failure to master these leads to sense of inferiority)
12 to 18	Identity versus role confusion	Fidelity; a unified and consistent sense of self that integrates pubertal changes into a mature sexual identity, assumes adult social and occupational roles, and establishes personal values and attitudes
18 to 30	Intimacy versus isolation	Love; person develops intimate relationships beyond adolescent love; many become parents
30 to old age	Generativity versus stagnation	Care; people rear children, focus on occupational achievement or creativity, and train the next generation; turn outward from the self toward others
Old age	Integrity versus despair	Wisdom; person conducts a life review, integrates earlier stages and comes to terms with basic identity; develops self-acceptance

and the roles he must occupy. He must achieve an integrated sense of self, of what he wants to do and be, and of his appropriate sexual role. The risk is that the adolescent will suffer from confusion arising from the profusion of roles opening up to him at this age.

In the first of the three adult stages, the young adult builds on the identity established in adolescence to confront the crisis of *intimacy versus isolation*. Erikson defined intimacy as "the ability to fuse your identity with someone else's without fear that you're going to lose something yourself" (Erikson, in Evans, 1969). Many young people, Erikson thought, make the mistake of thinking they will find their identity in a relationship, but in his view only those who have already formed (or are well on the way to forming) a clear identity can successfully enter this fusion of identities that he called *intimacy*. Young adults whose identities are weak or unformed will remain in shallow relationships and will experience a sense of isolation or loneliness.

The middle adulthood crisis is *generativity versus stagnation*, which is "primarily the concern in establishing and guiding the next generation" (Erikson, 1963, p. 267). The rearing of children is the most obvious way to achieve a sense of generativity, but it is not the only way. Doing creative work, giving service to an organization or to society, or serving as a mentor to younger colleagues can help the mid-life adult achieve a sense of generativity. Failing that, the self-absorbed, nongenerative adult may feel a sense of stagnation.

The key idea underlying Erikson's theory is that each new crisis is thrust on the developing person because of changes in social demands that accompany changes in age. The fourth stage of *industry versus inferiority*, for example, begins when the child starts school and must learn to read and write. If the child fails to read and write at grade level, she is often still able to advance with her same-aged peers. As the child enters the higher grade levels lacking the essential reading and writing skills, she may experience an increasing sense of inferiority. This evolving negative self-image may adversely affect the child's transition to the next stage of psychosocial development—the formation of a healthy identity. Thus, childhood crises set the stage for those of adolescence and adulthood.

EVALUATION OF PSYCHOANALYTIC THEORIES

Psychoanalytic theories such as Freud's and Erikson's, summarized in **Table 2.3**, have several attractive aspects. Most centrally, they highlight the importance of the child's earliest relationships with caregivers. Furthermore, they suggest that the child's needs change with age, so that parents and other caregivers must constantly adapt to the changing child. One of the implications of this is that we should not think of "good parenting" as an unchanging quality. Some people may be very good at meeting the needs of an infant but less capable of dealing with teenagers' identity struggles. The child's eventual personality and her overall mental health thus depend on the interaction pattern that develops in a particular family. The idea of changing needs is an extremely attractive element of these theories, because more and more of the research in developmental psychology is moving developmentalists toward just such a conception of the process.

Psychoanalytic theory has also given psychologists a number of helpful concepts, such as the unconscious, the ego, and identity, which have become a part of everyday language as well as theory. Moreover, psychologists are taking a fresh look at Freud's ideas about the importance of defence mechanisms in coping with anxiety (Cramer, 2000). Freud is also usually credited with the invention of psychotherapy, which is still

TABLE 2.3	Psychoanalytic Theories		
		Evaluation	
Theory	**Main Idea**	**Strengths**	**Weaknesses**
Freud's Psychosexual Theory	Personality develops in five stages from birth to adolescence; in each stage, the need for physical pleasure is focused on a different part of the body.	Emphasizes importance of experiences in infancy and early childhood; provides psychological explanations for mental illness.	Sexual feelings are not as important in personality development as Freud claimed.
Erikson's Psychosocial Theory	Personality develops through eight life crises across the entire lifespan; a person finishes each crisis with either a good or a poor resolution.	Helps explain the role of culture in personality development; important in lifespan psychology; useful description of major themes of personality development at different ages.	Describing each period in terms of a single crisis is probably an oversimplification.

practised today. An additional strength of the psychoanalytic perspective is the emphasis on continued development during adulthood found in Erikson's theory. His ideas have provided a framework for a great deal of new research and theorizing about adult development.

The major weakness of psychoanalytic theories is the fuzziness of many of their concepts. For example, how could researchers detect the presence of the id, ego, superego, and so on? Without more precise definitions, it is extremely difficult to test these theories, despite their provocative explanations of development.

THE HUMANISTIC ALTERNATIVE

In addition to criticizing the fuzziness of some psychoanalytic concepts, psychologists have taken issue with the psychoanalytic emphasis on atypical development. Some have proposed alternative theories that focus on the positive aspects of development while accepting the psychoanalytic assumption that behaviour is motivated by internal drives and emotions. These *humanistic theories* share Jean-Jacques Rousseau's basic premise of *innate goodness* (refer back to **Chapter 1**), and they begin with the optimistic assumption that the most important internal drive is each individual's motivation to achieve his or her full potential. A key figure in the humanistic tradition is Abraham Maslow (1908–1970), who used the term **self-actualization** to describe this ultimate goal of human life (Maslow, 1968, 1970).

self-actualization
the process of fulfilling one's unique personal potential

MOTIVES Maslow's greatest interest was in the development of **motives**, or needs, which he divided into two subsets: deficiency motives and being motives. *Deficiency motives* involve drives to maintain physical or emotional homeostasis (inner balance), such as the drive to get enough to eat or drink, the sexual drive, or even the drive to obtain sufficient love or respect from others. *Being motives* involve the desire to understand, to give to others, and to grow—that is, to achieve *self-actualization*. In general, the satisfaction of deficiency motives prevents or cures illness or re-creates homeostasis. In contrast, the satisfaction of being motives produces a general sense of well-being. The distinction is like the "difference between fending off threat or attack and positive triumph and achievement" (Maslow, 1968, p. 32).

motives
internal factors or conditions that tend to initiate, direct, or sustain behaviour

Maslow described these various needs or motives in his famous needs hierarchy, shown in **Figure 2.4**. He argued that the various needs must be met in order from the bottom up. For example, only when physiological needs are met do safety needs come to the fore; only when love and esteem needs are met can the need for self-actualization become dominant. For that reason, Maslow thought that being motives were likely to be significant only in adulthood, and only in those individuals who had found stable ways to satisfy both love and **esteem needs**. In this sense, Maslow's theory sounds very similar to Erikson's stages of intimacy and generativity.

esteem needs
the need for a person to have a sense of value and acceptance based, in part, on their experience of respect and admiration from others and on their perceived self-confidence and self-worth

PERSONAL GROWTH Another prominent humanistic psychologist, Carl Rogers (1902–1987), talked about the capacity of each individual to become a "fully functioning person," without guilt or seriously distorting defences (Rogers, 1961). Early experience with caregivers whose acceptance of the child is conditional on the child behaving in an approved manner can diminish the child's sense of self-worth. The child begins to think of himself as worthwhile only when he behaves in approved ways. In Carl Rogers' view, it is never too late to overcome early conditioning or the residue of unresolved dilemmas. He believed people have the potential and motivation to try to do just that—a concept known as *personal growth*.

The inherent optimism in humanistic theories makes them very appealing. However, as is true of psychoanalytic theories, humanistic models such as Maslow's are

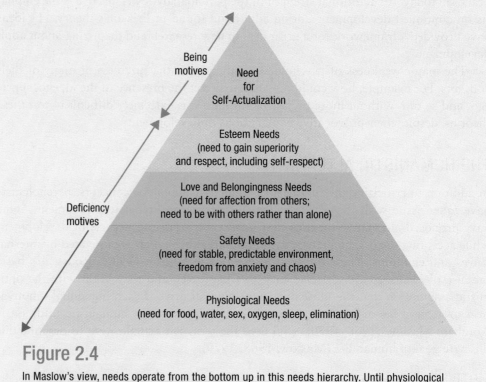

Figure 2.4

In Maslow's view, needs operate from the bottom up in this needs hierarchy. Until physiological needs are met, no other need will be prominent; until love needs are met, esteem needs will not emerge; and so on. Similarly, there is a developmental aspect: A baby is primarily dominated by physiological needs, a toddler by safety needs, and so forth. Only in adulthood may the need for self-actualization become central.

(*Sources:* Maslow, Abraham H., Frager, Robert D., and Fadiman, James. *Motivation and Personality*, 3rd Edition, © 1987. Adapted by permission of Pearson Education, Inc., Upper Saddle, NJ.)

✳–[Explore

stated in broad, rather imprecise terms. They have appealed to a great many people because they seem to resonate with some aspects of everyday experience. But they are difficult to test empirically because the propositions are not stated clearly enough.

Before  Going On

✳–[Explore

- How do Erikson's stages differ from Freud's?
- What are the key assumptions of Maslow's humanistic theory?

LEARNING THEORIES

learning theories
theories that assert that development results from an accumulation of experiences

In general, **learning theories** assert that development results from an accumulation of experiences. Learning theories are aligned with the philosophy of John Locke who, as you recall from **Chapter 1**, said that children are born with neither good nor bad tendencies, but their behaviour is shaped, for better or worse, by their environment. Thus, in contrast to psychoanalysts, learning theorists would say that infants repeat the behaviour of putting objects in their mouths because they find the sensations it produces rewarding. Alternatively, when they put something in their mouths that tastes bad, infants learn not to mouth such an object again.

A central learning theory, know as **behaviourism**, views development in terms of behaviour changes caused by environmental influences—a process called *conditioning*. As you will see, there are two ways that conditioning changes our behaviour.

behaviourism
the view that defines development in terms of behaviour changes caused by environmental influences

classical conditioning
learning that results from the association of stimuli

PAVLOV'S CLASSICAL CONDITIONING

Russian physiologist and Nobel prize winner, Ivan Pavlov (1849–1936), discovered that organisms can acquire new signals for existing responses (behaviours). The term **classical conditioning** refers to this principle. Each incidence of learning begins with a biologically programmed stimulus-response connection, or *reflex*. For example, salivation happens naturally when you put food in your mouth. In classical conditioning terms, the food is the *unconditioned (unlearned, natural) stimulus*; salivating is an *unconditioned (unlearned, natural) response*.

THE CONDITIONING PROCESS
Stimuli presented just before or at the same time as the unconditioned stimulus are those that are likely to be associated with it. For example, most foods have odours, and, to get to your mouth, food has to pass near your nose. Thus, you usually smell food before you taste it. Food odours eventually become *conditioned (learned) stimuli* that elicit salivation. In effect, they act as a signal to your salivary glands that food is coming. Once the connection between food odours and salivation is established, smelling food triggers the salivation response even when you do not actually eat the food. When a response occurs reliably in connection with a conditioned stimulus in this way, it is known as a *conditioned (learned) response*.

EARLY CONDITIONING
Classical conditioning is of interest in the study of development because of the role it plays in the acquisition of emotional responses. For example, things or people that are present when you feel good will become conditioned stimuli for pleasant feelings, while those associated with uncomfortable feelings may become conditioned stimuli for a sense of unease. Classical conditioning is especially important in infancy. Because a child's mother or father is present so often when nice things happen, such as when the child feels warm, comfortable, and cuddled, the mother and father usually serve as conditioned stimuli for pleasant feelings, a fact that makes it possible for the parents' presence to comfort a child.

operant conditioning
learning to repeat or stop behaviours because of their consequences

reinforcement
any immediate consequence that follows a behaviour and increases the likelihood that the behaviour will be repeated

punishment
any immediate consequence that follows a behaviour and decreases the likelihood that the behaviour will be repeated

SKINNER'S OPERANT CONDITIONING

Another type of learning is **operant conditioning**, a term coined by B.F. Skinner (1904–1990), the most famous proponent of this theory (Skinner, 1953, 1980). Operant conditioning involves learning to repeat or stop behaviours because of the consequences they bring about. **Reinforcement** is any immediate consequence that follows a behaviour that increases the likelihood that the behaviour will be repeated. **Punishment** is any immediate consequence that follows a behaviour that decreases the likelihood that the behaviour will be repeated.

REINFORCEMENT
Positive reinforcement entails adding a consequence (usually something pleasant) that follows a behaviour and increases the chances that the behaviour will occur again. Some kinds of pleasant consequences, such as attention, serve as reinforcers for most people most of the time. But strictly speaking, reinforcement is defined by its effect; we don't know something is reinforcing unless we see that its presence increases the probability of some behaviour.

Laboratory research involving animals was important in the development of Skinner's operant conditioning theory. (*Photo:* Ken Hayman/Black Star)

mydevelopmentlab

Connect to MyDevelopmentLab

Could you beat Skinner's pigeons to the pellet? Check how quickly you can learn a new behaviour in the shaping simulation.

Simulate

extinction
the gradual elimination of a behaviour through repeated nonreinforcement

Negative reinforcement entails the taking away of a condition (usually something unpleasant) following a behaviour and increases the chances that the behaviour will occur again. For example, coughing is an unpleasant experience for most of us, and taking a dose of cough medicine usually stops it. As a result, the next time we begin to cough, we reach for the cough syrup because the behaviour of consuming a spoonful of cough syrup is reinforced by the cessation of coughing. In other words, we make the unpleasant experience of coughing go away when we engage in the behaviour of swallowing cough syrup. Thus, the behaviour of taking cough syrup is learned through negative reinforcement.

Definitions and simple examples of positive and negative reinforcement may be misleading when it comes to understanding how the two operate in real-life contexts. For example, most people understand that paying attention to a preschooler's whining is likely to increase it. This case shows positive reinforcement—a child's whining is reinforced whenever a parent shows attention. At the same time, however, a parent learns to attend to a whining preschooler because whining is irritating, and responding to it usually makes it stop. As a result, the parent's behaviour of responding to whining is negatively reinforced by its consequence—namely, that the child *stops* whining. In this case of negative reinforcement, parental attention is reinforced when the child stops whining.

PUNISHMENT There are two general forms of punishment but, in contrast to both kinds of reinforcement, both forms of punishment stop a behaviour. Sometimes punishments involve eliminating nice things, for example, taking away TV privileges. This is referred to as *negative punishment* and entails taking away a condition (usually something pleasant) that follows a behaviour and decreases the chances that the behaviour will occur again. Negative punishment can be considered a type of **extinction**, which is the gradual elimination of a behaviour through repeated nonreinforcement. If a teacher succeeds in eliminating a student's undesirable behaviour by ignoring it, the behaviour is said to have been *extinguished*.

However, punishment may also involve unpleasant things such as scolding. A *positive punishment* entails adding a consequence (usually something unpleasant) that follows a behaviour and decreases the chances that the behaviour will occur again. Like reinforcement, however, punishment is defined by its effect. Consequences that do not stop behaviour can't be properly called punishments.

Critical Thinking

Describe instances in your everyday life when your behaviour is affected by classical or operant conditioning, or when you use these principles to affect others' behaviour.

CHANGING BEHAVIOUR Such examples illustrate the complex manner in which reinforcements and punishments operate in the real world. In laboratory settings, operant conditioning researchers usually work with only one participant or animal subject at a time; they needn't worry about the social consequences of behaviours or consequences. They can also control the situation so that a particular behaviour is reinforced every time it occurs. In the real world, *partial reinforcement*—reinforcement of a behaviour on some occasions but not others—is more common (see **Development in the Real World**). Studies of partial reinforcement show that people take longer to learn a new behaviour under partial

Development in the Real World

LEARNING PRINCIPLES IN REAL LIFE

Let's consider how principles of learning work in some common real-life situations. For example, suppose your 3-year-old daughter repeatedly demands your attention while you are fixing dinner. Because you don't want to reinforce this behaviour, you ignore her the first six or eight times she calls you or tugs at your clothes. But after the ninth or tenth repetition, with her voice getting whinier each time, you can't stand it any longer and finally say something like "All right! What do you want?"

Since you have ignored most of her demands, you might think you have not been reinforcing them. But what you have actually done is create a partial reinforcement schedule. By responding to every ninth or tenth demand, you have in essence, taught her that persistent whining will eventually be rewarded with attention. This intermittent pattern of reinforcement helps create behaviour that is very hard to extinguish. So your daughter may continue to be overly demanding for a very long time.

Another thing we know about reinforcement is that, when two people interact, they mutually shape each other's behaviour—for better or for worse. For example, if a child begins to holler at his mother to fetch his school lunch bag before he goes out the door, and the mother

complies, two things happen. First, the mother has just strengthened the child's hollering behaviour through positive reinforcement by giving him what he wanted when he hollered; in this case, the school lunch bag. Second, the child has just strengthened the mother's obliging behaviour through negative reinforcement by taking away something the mother finds distressing; in this case, hollering.

We would predict that the next time the boy wants something from his mother, he is more likely to holler and, unfortunately, his mother is more likely to comply if the boy stops hollering once his mother gets him what he wants. As you can see, we can easily and inadvertently set up reciprocal patterns of reinforcement and expectations that can benefit one person, but disadvantage the other. Moreover, once such a pattern of reciprocal parent–child interaction is established, it can be very difficult to break, especially if you are not aware of the reinforcing sequence of events.

If such situations are all too familiar to you, then it may pay to keep careful records for a while, noting each incident and your response. Then see whether you can figure out which principles are really at work and how you might change the pattern.

reinforcement conditions; once established, however, such behaviours are very resistant to extinction.

Shaping is the reinforcement of intermediate steps until an individual learns a complex behaviour. For example, you wouldn't start learning to play tennis by challenging a skilled player to a match. Instead, you would first learn to hold the racquet properly. Next, you would learn the basic strokes and practise hitting balls hit or thrown to you by an instructor. Next, you would learn to serve. Finally, you would put all your skills together and play an actual match. All along the way, you would be encouraged by the sense of satisfaction gained from accomplishing each step toward the goal.

shaping
the reinforcement of intermediate steps until an individual learns a complex behaviour

EVALUATION OF LEARNING THEORIES

Several implications of learning theories, summarized in **Table 2.4**, are worth emphasizing. First, learning theories can explain both consistency and changes in behaviour. If a child is friendly and smiling both at home and at school, learning theorists would explain the child's behaviour by saying that the child is being reinforced for that behaviour in both settings. It is equally possible to explain why a child is happy at home but miserable at school. We need only hypothesize that the home environment reinforces cheerful behaviour but the school setting does not.

Learning theorists also tend to be optimistic about the possibility of change. Children's behaviour can change if the reinforcement system, or their beliefs about themselves, change. So, problem behaviour can be modified.

TABLE 2.4   Learning Theories

| Theory | Main Idea | Evaluation | |
		Strengths	Weaknesses
Pavlov's Classical Conditioning	Learning happens when neutral stimuli become so strongly associated with natural stimuli that they elicit the same response.	Useful in explaining how emotional responses, such as phobias, are learned.	Explanation of behaviour change is too limited to serve as comprehensive theory of human development.
Skinner's Operant Conditioning Theory	Development involves behaviour changes that are shaped by reinforcement and punishment.	Basis of many useful strategies for managing and changing human behaviour.	Humans are not as passive as Skinner claimed; the theory ignores hereditary and cognitive, emotional, and social factors in development.

The great strength of learning theories is that they seem to give an accurate picture of the way in which many behaviours are learned. However, the traditional learning theorists' approach is not really developmental; it doesn't tell us much about change over a lifespan, in either childhood or adulthood. Thus, learning theories help developmentalists understand how specific behaviours are acquired.

Before Going On

- Describe instances of everyday situations where behaviour is changed through classical and operant conditioning.
- What are the strengths and weaknesses of learning theories as an explanation of human development?

COGNITIVE THEORIES

cognitive theories theories that emphasize mental processes in development, such as logic and memory

The group of theories known as **cognitive theories** emphasize mental aspects of development, such as logic and memory. A cognitive theorist might propose that babies use their senses, including the sense of taste, to build mental pictures of the world around them. Thus, infants mouth everything in their environment until they have learned all they can from this behaviour, and then they move on to a more mature way of interacting with the world.

PIAGET'S COGNITIVE-DEVELOPMENTAL THEORY

For Jean Piaget (1896–1980), as you should remember from **Chapter 1**, the central question of interest in developmental psychology was "How does thinking develop?"

(Piaget, 1952, 1970, 1977; Piaget & Inhelder, 1969). He was struck by the fact that all children seem to go through the same sequence of discoveries about their world, making the same mistakes and arriving at the same solutions. For example, all 3- and 4-year-olds seem to think that if water is poured from a short, wide glass into a taller, narrower one, there is then more water, because the water level is higher in the narrow glass than it was in the wide glass. In contrast, most 7-year-olds realize that the amount of water has not changed. To explain such age differences, Piaget proposed several concepts that continue to guide developmental research.

Piaget based many of his ideas on naturalistic observations of children of different ages on playgrounds and in schools.
(*Photo:* © Bill Anderson/Photo Researchers, Inc.)

SCHEMES A pivotal idea in Piaget's model is that of a **scheme**, an internal cognitive structure that provides an individual with a procedure to follow in a specific circumstance. For example, when you pick up a ball, you use your picking-up scheme. To throw the ball to someone, you use your looking scheme, your aiming scheme, and your throwing scheme. Piaget proposed that each of us begins life with a small repertoire of sensory and motor schemes, such as looking, tasting, touching, hearing, and reaching. As we use each scheme, it becomes better adapted to the world; in other words, it works better.

We possess mental schemes as well, most of which develop in childhood and adolescence. Mental schemes allow us to use symbols and think logically. Piaget proposed three processes to explain how children get from built-in schemes, such as looking and touching, to the complex mental schemes used in childhood, adolescence, and adulthood.

Assimilation is the process of using schemes to make sense of events or experiences. Piaget would say that a baby who grasps a toy is *assimilating* it to his grasping scheme. The complementary process is **accommodation**, which involves changing the scheme as a result of some new information acquired through assimilation. When the baby grasps a square object for the first time, he will accommodate his grasping scheme; so the next time he reaches for a square object, his hand will be more appropriately bent to grasp it. Thus, the process of accommodation is the key to developmental change. Through accommodation, we improve our skills and reorganize our ways of thinking.

Equilibration is the process of balancing assimilation and accommodation to create schemes that fit the environment. To illustrate, think about infants' tendency to put things in their mouths. In Piaget's terms, they assimilate objects to their mouthing scheme. As they mouth each object, their mouthing scheme changes to include the instructions "*Do* mouth this" or "*Don't* mouth this." The accommodation is based on mouthing experiences. A pacifier feels good in the mouth, but a dead insect has an unpleasant texture. So, eventually, the mouthing scheme says it's okay to put a pacifier in the mouth, but it's not okay to mouth a dead insect. In this way, an infant's mouthing scheme attains a better fit with the real world.

scheme
in Piaget's theory, an internal cognitive structure that provides an individual with a procedure to follow in a specific circumstance

assimilation
the process of using schemes to make sense of events or experiences

accommodation
changing a scheme as a result of some new information

equilibration
the process of balancing assimilation and accommodation to create schemes that fit the environment

STAGES Piaget's research suggested to him that logical thinking evolves in four stages. During the *sensorimotor stage*, from birth to 18 months, infants use their sensory and motor schemes to act on the world around them. In the *preoperational stage*, from 18 months to about age 6, youngsters acquire symbolic schemes, such as language and fantasy, that they use in thinking and communicating. Next comes the *concrete operational stage*, during which 6- to 12-year-olds begin to think logically and become capable of solving problems such as the one illustrated in **Figure 2.5**. The last phase is the *formal operational stage*, in which adolescents learn to think logically about abstract ideas and hypothetical situations.

Explore

Critical Thinking

Describe three or four examples of assimilation and accommodation in your everyday life.

Figure 2.5

In one of the problems Piaget devised, a child is shown two clay balls of equal size and asked if they both contain the same amount of clay. Next, the researcher rolls one ball into a sausage shape and asks the child if the two shapes still contain the same amount of clay. A preoperational child will say that one now contains more clay than the other and will base his answer on their appearance: "The sausage has more because it's longer now." A concrete operational thinker will say that the two still contain the same amount of material because no clay was added or taken away from either.

(*Photo:* © T. Lindfors/Lindfors Photography)

Table 2.5 describes these stages more fully; you will read about each of them in detail later in the book. For now, it is important to understand that in Piaget's view, each stage grows out of the one that precedes it, and each involves a major restructuring of the child's way of thinking. It's also important to know that research has confirmed Piaget's belief that the sequence of the stages is fixed. However, children progress through them at different rates. In addition, some individuals do not attain the formal operational stage in adolescence or even in adulthood. Consequently, the ages associated with the stages are approximations.

INFORMATION-PROCESSING THEORY

The goal of **information-processing theory** is to explain how the mind manages information (Klahr, 1992). Information-processing theorists use the computer as a model of human thinking. Consequently, they focus on what happens to information as it enters the mind (*input*), is transformed by mental programs (*throughput*), and is used to perform actions (*output*).

information-processing theory theoretical perspectives that use the computer as a model to explain how the mind manages information

TABLE 2.5	Piaget's Cognitive-Developmental Stages	
Approximate Ages	**Stage**	**Description**
Birth to 18 months	Sensorimotor	The baby understands the world through her senses and her motor actions; she begins to use simple symbols, such as single words and pretend play, near the end of this period.
18 months to 6 years	Preoperational	By age 2, the child can use symbols both to think and to communicate; he develops the abilities to take others' points of view, classify objects, and use simple logic by the end of this stage.
6 years to 12 years	Concrete operational	The child's logic takes a great leap forward with the development of new internal operations, such as conservation and class inclusion, but is still tied to the known world; by the end of the period, he can reason about simple "what if" questions.
12+ years	Formal operational	The child begins to manipulate ideas as well as objects; she thinks hypothetically and, by adulthood, can easily manage a variety of "what if" questions; she greatly improves her ability to organize ideas and objects mentally.

MEMORY PROCESSES Theorizing about and studying memory processes are central to information-processing theory. This theory breaks memory down into the subprocesses of encoding, storage, and retrieval. *Encoding* is organizing information to be stored in memory. For example, you may be encoding the information in this chapter by relating it to your own childhood. *Storage* is keeping information, and *retrieval* is getting information out of memory. As information flows through these memory processes, we use mental strategies to manipulate information so that we can complete mental operations, solve everyday problems, and learn new tasks.

MEMORY COMPONENTS Most memory research assumes that the human memory is made up of multiple components. The idea is that information moves through these components in an organized way (see **Figure 2.6**). The process of understanding a spoken word serves as a good example.

First, you hear the word when the sounds enter your *sensory memory.* Your experiences with language allow you to recognize the pattern of sounds as a word. Next, the word moves into your *short-term memory,* the component of the memory system where all information is processed. Thus, short-term memory is often called *working memory.* Knowledge of the word's meaning is then called up out of *long-term memory,* the component of the system where information is permanently stored, and placed in short-term memory, where it is linked to the word's sounds to enable you to understand the word.

Each memory component manages information differently. Information flows through the sensory memory in a constant stream. Bits of information that are not attended to drop out quickly. The short-term memory is extremely limited in capacity—it can contain only about seven items at a time. However, information can be retained in short-term memory as long as it is processed in some way—as you do when you repeat your grocery list to yourself on the way to the store.

MEMORY CAPACITY Long-term memory is unlimited in capacity, and information is often organized and stored in terms of meaningful associations. For example, suppose you read a sentence such as "Bill wrote a letter to his brother." When you think about the sentence later, you might mistakenly recall that it contained the word *pen.* This

Using Piaget's terminology, we would say this infant is assimilating the object to her grasping scheme. What scheme is being accommodated at the same time as she adapts her grasping scheme?
(*Photo:* Getty Images)

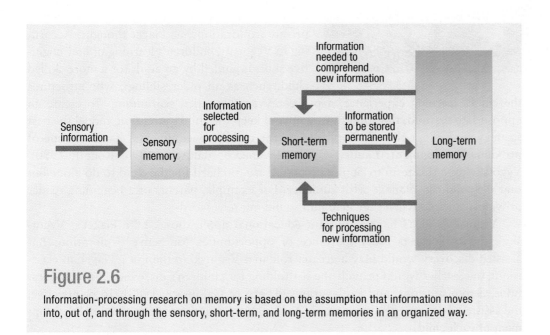

Figure 2.6

Information-processing research on memory is based on the assumption that information moves into, out of, and through the sensory, short-term, and long-term memories in an organized way.

happens because information about the process of writing and the tools used to do it are stored together in long-term memory.

York University psychologist Juan Pascual-Leone established **neo-Piagetian theories** by using information-processing theory to explain Piaget's stages (1987). As fellow Canadian theorist Robbie Case (1944–2000) put it, neo-Piagetian theories expand on Piaget's theory rather than contradict it (Case, 1985; 1997). According to neo-Piagetians, older children and adults can solve complex problems such as those in Piaget's research because they can hold more pieces of information in their short-term memories at the same time than younger children can. To solve the problem described in **Figure 2.5**, for example, a child must be able to think about the appearance of the two balls of clay before one was rolled into a sausage shape and their appearance afterward in her working memory at the same time. She must also think about how the transformation was carried out. Neo-Piagetians maintain that children are incapable of performing all this mental work in short-term memory until after age 6 or 7 (Case, 1985; 1997).

neo-Piagetian theory
an approach that uses information-processing principles to explain the developmental stages identified by Piaget

sociocultural theory
Vygotsky's view that complex forms of thinking have their origins in social interactions rather than in an individual's private explorations

⊙—Watch ## VYGOTSKY'S SOCIOCULTURAL THEORY

Following the Bolshevik revolution of 1917, the new Soviet government hired Russian psychologist Lev Vygotsky (1896–1934), among others, to create a school system that would serve the ends of the new communist regime (Vygotsky, 1978). The historical events that followed his death—World War II and the Cold War—resulted in his work remaining largely unknown outside the former Soviet Union for decades. Since then, however, developmentalists have become interested in his views on the influence of cultural forces on individual development (Thomas, 1996).

Developmental psychologist Lev Vygotsky hypothesized that social interactions among children are critical to both cognitive and social development.
(*Photo:* David Young-Wolff/PhotoEdit)

scaffolding
a process in which the learning of new cognitive skills is guided by someone who is more skilled

zone of proximal development
signifies tasks that are too hard for a child to do alone but that can be managed with guidance

SOCIAL INTERACTIONS BUILD COGNITIVE SKILLS Vygotsky's **sociocultural theory** asserts that complex forms of thinking have their origins in social interactions rather than in the child's private explorations, as Piaget thought. According to Vygotsky, children's learning of new cognitive skills is guided by an adult (or a more skilled child, such as an older sibling), who structures the child's learning experience, a process Vygotsky called **scaffolding**. To create an appropriate scaffold, the adult must gain and keep the child's attention, model the best strategy, and adapt the whole process to the child's developmental level, or **zone of proximal development** (Landry, Garner, Swank, & Baldwin, 1996; Rogoff, 1990). Vygotsky used this term to signify tasks that are too hard for the child to do alone but that the child can manage with guidance. For example, parents of a beginning reader provide a scaffold when they help him sound out new words.

Vygotsky's ideas have important educational applications. Like Piaget's, Vygotsky's theory suggests the importance of opportunities for active exploration. But assisted discovery would play a greater role in a Vygotskian than in a Piagetian classroom; the teacher would provide the scaffolding for children's discovery, through questions, demonstrations, and explanations (Tharp & Gallimore, 1988). To be effective, the assisted discovery processes would have to be within the zone of proximal development of each child.

BANDURA'S SOCIAL-COGNITIVE THEORY

Learning theorist Albert Bandura was born and raised in Alberta and graduated with a bachelor's degree in psychology from the University of British Columbia in 1949 and a Ph.D. from the University of Iowa in 1952. His theory emphasizes the importance of psychological *modelling* in shaping our thoughts, emotions, and behaviour. As well, he describes how we exert influence over the events that affect our lives.

LEARNING BY OBSERVING Bandura's ideas emphasize the roles of thinking (cognition) and of learning by observation (modelling) in human behaviour (Bandura, 2001; Pajares, 2004; Zimmerman & Schunk, 2002). For example, Bandura's social-cognitive theory suggests that phobias may be learned *vicariously*, by watching someone else perform some action and experience reinforcement or punishment. Learning of this type, called **observational learning**, or **modelling**, is involved in a wide range of behaviours. Children learn to hit by watching other people in real life and on television. Adults learn job skills by observing or being shown them by others. His ideas are more influential among developmental psychologists than those of the conditioning theorists, as he contends that learning does not always require reinforcement (1977a, 1982, 1989, 2001).

Furthermore, what a person learns from observing others is influenced by processes such as attention and memory. Maturation is important as well: A 4-year-old probably won't learn geometry from watching his high-school-age sister do her homework. Bandura also suggests that what an observer learns from a particular model is influenced by his own goals, expectations about what kinds of consequences are likely if he adopts the model's behaviour, and judgments of his own performance.

RECIPROCAL DETERMINISM Bandura (1977a, 1986, 2001) also put forth the idea of **reciprocal determinism**, a process of human development based on the interaction of three factors: *personal* (cognitive abilities, physical characteristics, beliefs, attitudes, and expectations), *behavioural* (physical-motor and verbal actions), and *environmental* (other people and physical surroundings). Bandura's *reciprocal determinism* *model* forms a triangle of bidirectional influence as depicted in **Figure 2.7**. From this perspective, we are not only affected by our circumstances, but we are also able to exert influence over our situation, which in turn affects our expectations about how much influence we have over future events. In the case of children, they are actively involved in shaping the very environments that influence their behaviour and personality development.

observational learning, or **modelling**
learning that results from seeing a model reinforced or punished for a behaviour

reciprocal determinism
a process of human development based on the interaction of personal, behavioural, and environmental factors

mydevelopmentlab
Connect to
MyDevelopmentLab
Can TV and video games cause violence? To find out, watch Bandura's classic 1961 "Bobo Doll" experiment.
Watch

Modelling is an important source of learning for both children and adults. What behaviours have you learned by watching and copying others? (*Photos:* left, Kathy Sloane, 1992, Photo Researchers; right, © LWA-Dann Tardif/CORBIS)

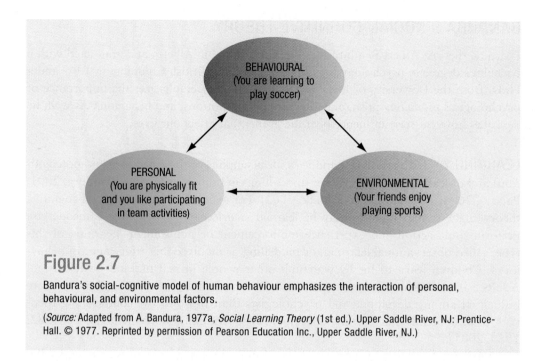

Figure 2.7

Bandura's social-cognitive model of human behaviour emphasizes the interaction of personal, behavioural, and environmental factors.

(*Source:* Adapted from A. Bandura, 1977a, *Social Learning Theory* (1st ed.). Upper Saddle River, NJ: Prentice-Hall. © 1977. Reprinted by permission of Pearson Education Inc., Upper Saddle River, NJ.)

self-efficacy

the belief in one's own capacity to cause an intended event to occur or to perform a task

SELF-EFFICACY   With respect to personal factors, Bandura (1997a, 1997b) has placed particular emphasis on a concept he called **self-efficacy**—the belief in one's own capacity to cause an intended event to occur (a topic we will cover in later chapters). People who have a strong sense of self-efficacy have higher expectations for success and will put forth more effort and persistence when faced with a challenge. Conversely, a person with low self-efficacy has a lower expectation for success, which is associated with acquiescence or avoidance when confronted with a difficult task.

EVALUATION OF COGNITIVE THEORIES

Research based on cognitive theories, especially the work of Piaget, has demonstrated that simplistic views such as those of the conditioning theorists cannot explain the development of the complex phenomenon that is logical thinking. Moreover, Piaget's research findings have been replicated in virtually every culture and in every cohort of children since his work was first published in the 1920s. Thus, not only did he formulate a theory that forced psychologists to think about child development in a new way, but he also provided a set of findings that were impossible to ignore and difficult to explain. In addition, he developed innovative methods of studying children's thinking that continue to be important today.

PIAGET'S INEXACT AGES   Piaget was inexact about some of the ages at which children develop particular skills. As you will see in later chapters, researchers have found that children develop some intellectual skills at earlier ages than Piaget's findings suggested. Furthermore, Piaget was probably incorrect about the generality of the stages themselves. Most 8-year-olds, for example, show concrete operational thinking on some tasks but not on others, and they are more likely to show complex thinking on familiar tasks than on unfamiliar ones. Thus, the whole process seems to be a great deal less stage-like than Piaget proposed. Not surprisingly, most information-processing theorists have abandoned the stage model of cognitive development in favour of a continuous model in which they believe cognitive development takes place continuously and gradually over time. Their focus is on the incremental changes that take place in a specific mental process, such as analytic problem-solving skills, rather than on global cognitive skills.

THE BRAIN IS MORE THAN A COMPUTER
Piagetians claim that information-processing theory emphasizes explanations of single cognitive tasks at the expense of a comprehensive picture of development. Still other critics of information-processing theory point out that human thinking is more complex than that of a computer. For example, University of Waterloo cognitive scientist Paul Thagard (1996, 2002) suggests that information is processed through a complex network of mental rules that simultaneously shape and are shaped by the information. This explains how we do not just passively react to environmental forces, but actively respond to and alter our environment. Critics also point out that much information-processing research involves artificial memory tasks, such as learning lists of words. Therefore, they say, research based on the information-processing approach doesn't always fully describe how memory works in the real world.

SOCIAL FACILITATION IS IMPORTANT
At present, there is insufficient evidence to either support or contradict most of Vygotsky's ideas (Thomas, 2000). However, studies have shown that children in pairs and groups do produce more sophisticated ideas than individual children who work on problems alone (Tan-Niam et al., 1998). Moreover, researchers have found that young children whose parents provide them with more scaffolding during the preschool years exhibit higher levels of achievement in elementary school than peers whose parents provide less support of this kind (Neitzel & Stright, 2003). Thus, future research may support the conclusion that Vygotsky's theory constitutes an important contribution to a full understanding of human development.

BI-DIRECTIONAL INFLUENCES
Bandura's addition of social and environmental elements to cognitive theory adds further to our understanding of human development, since it allows an integration of cognitive models with other approaches. Bandura's variation on cognitive theory tells us how a child's level of cognitive development affects his or her impressions and reactions to the environment. In turn, the child's perception directs her behaviour in particular situations (Bandura, 1991, 1997a; Bandura & Schunk, 1981; Schunk, 1983). Social-cognitive theory also contributes to an understanding of age-related change.

Critics of cognitive theories in general say that these theories ignore the role of other important cognitive functions such as emotions, imagination, and creativity in development (Thagard, 2002). The cognitive theories are summarized in **Table 2.6**.

Before Going On

- What did Piaget discover about the development of logical thinking in children, and how did he explain it?

- How did Vygotsky use the concepts of scaffolding and the zone of proximal development to explain cognitive development?

TABLE 2.6   Cognitive Theories

Theory	Main Idea	Strengths	Weaknesses
		Evaluation	
		Strengths	Weaknesses
Piaget's Theory of Cognitive Development	Reasoning develops in four universal stages from birth through adolescence; in each stage, the child builds a different kind of scheme.	Helps explain how children of different ages think about and act on the world.	Stage concept may cause adults to underestimate children's reasoning abilities; there may be additional stages in adulthood.
Information-Processing Theory	The computer is used as a model for human cognitive functioning; encoding, storage, and retrieval processes change with age, causing changes in memory function; these changes happen because of both brain maturation and practice.	Helps explain how much information people of different ages can manage at one time and how they process it; provides a useful framework for studying individual differences in people of the same age.	Human information-processing is much more complex than that of a computer; the theory doesn't provide an overall picture of development.
Vygotsky's Sociocultural Theory	Cognitive development is strengthened through social interactions that involve speaking during guided problem-solving tasks.	Stresses the importance of sociocultural interaction for cognitive development.	Verbal instructions may not benefit cognitive development in some cultures.
Bandura's Social-Cognitive Theory	People learn from models; what they learn from a model depends on how they interpret the situation cognitively and emotionally.	Helps explain how models influence behaviour; explains more about development than other learning theories because of addition of cognitive and emotional factors.	Does not provide an overall picture of development.

SYSTEMS THEORY

systems approach
the view that personal factors together with external factors form a dynamic integrated system

holism
the view that the whole is greater than the sum of its parts

wellness
a measure of optimal holistic health

The **systems approach** to human development takes into consideration the ever-changing (dynamic) interaction of personal factors with external factors. Personal factors may include biophysical, spiritual, intellectual, emotional, behavioural, and interpersonal aspects of functioning. External factors typically include the physical environment and social and cultural influences. A basic tenet of systems theory is that of holism. **Holism** maintains that the "whole" is primary and is greater than the sum of its parts. By way of example, consider that a loaf of bread is more than the sum of its ingredients: wheat flour, yeast, and water. A person develops in relation to changes in any part of the whole dynamic system. From this perspective, growth is the result of a reorganization of the system as it adjusts to change. When adjustment is adaptive, it promotes a high level of holistic health called **wellness;** when it is maladaptive, it can lead to disorder or dysfunction.

BRONFENBRENNER'S BIOECOLOGICAL SYSTEMS THEORY

One prominent systems approach in developmental psychology is Bronfenbrenner's **bioecological systems theory**. It explains development in terms of the relationships among individuals and their environments, or interconnected *contexts* (as Bronfenbrenner called them) over the passage of time, called the *chronosystem* (Bronfenbrenner, 1979, 2005). Urie Bronfenbrenner (1917–2005) attempted to classify the individual and contextual variables that affect development and to specify how they interact.

bioecological systems theory Bronfenbrenner's theory that explains development in terms of the relationships among individuals and their environments, or interconnected contexts

MACROSYSTEM According to Bronfenbrenner's theory, the contexts of development are like spheres within spheres (see **Figure 2.8**). The outermost sphere, the *macrosystem* (the sociocultural context), is the manifestation of the overarching sociocultural ideologies, values, and beliefs, and organization of the social systems and public policy through macroinstitutions, such as the federal government, in which a child is growing up. For example, Canadians' beliefs about the importance of education exist in the cultural context.

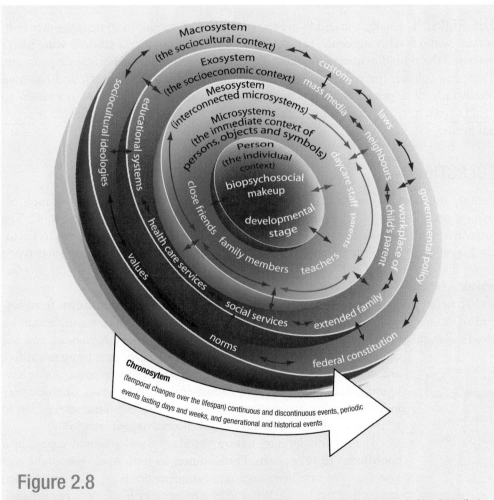

PEARSON
mydevelopmentlab
Connect to MyDevelopmentLab
Does Bronfenbrenner's bioecological systems theory have you going in circles? Explore No Man is an Island to understand what this means.

✳ Explore

Figure 2.8

Bronfenbrenner's bioecological theory proposes that people are exposed to interconnected contexts that interact in complex ways over time to influence development.

(*Source:* Artwork copyright © Alexandra Johnson. Printed with permission.)

EXOSYSTEM The next level, the *exosystem* (the socioeconomic context), includes the institutions of the culture that affect children's development indirectly (e.g., the workplace of a child's parent, the social services, and the health care and educational systems). For example, funding for education exists in the socioeconomic context. The citizens of a specific nation may strongly believe that all children should be educated (sociocultural context), but their ability to provide universal education may be limited by the country's wealth (socioeconomic context).

MICROSYSTEM The *microsystem* (the immediate context) includes those variables to which people are exposed directly, such as their families, schools, religious institutions, and neighbourhoods. The *mesosystem* is made up of the interconnections between these components. For example, the specific school a child attends and her own family are part of the microsystem. Her parents' involvement in her school and the response of the school to their involvement are part of the mesosystem. Thus, the culture a child is born into may strongly value quality education. Moreover, her nation's economy may provide ample funds for schooling. However, her own education will be more strongly affected by the particular school she attends and the connections, or lack thereof, between her school and her family. Thus, the child's immediate context may be either consistent with the cultural and socioeconomic contexts or at odds with them.

THE PERSON Finally, the child's genetic makeup and developmental stage—her *individual context*—also influence her development. For example, a student who hasn't mastered the skill of reading isn't likely to benefit from an enriched literature program. Thus, her culture, the socioeconomic situation, the school she attends, and her own family may all be geared toward providing a quality education; however, her ability to benefit from it will be determined by the degree to which her education fits her individual needs.

ECLECTICISM

Perhaps the most important current trend in the field is **eclecticism**, the use of multiple theoretical perspectives to explain and study human development (Parke, 2004). The interdisciplinary nature of the study of human development you read about in **Chapter 1** is reflected in this new trend as well. Thus, today's developmental scientists try to avoid the kind of rigid adherence to a single theoretical perspective that was characteristic of theorists such as Freud, Piaget, and Skinner.

To better understand the eclectic approach, think about how ideas drawn from several of the major systems and schools of psychology might help us better understand a child's disruptive behaviour in school. Observations of the child's behaviour and her classmates' reactions may suggest that her behaviour is being rewarded, and therefore reinforced, by the other children's responses (a behavioural explanation). Deeper probing of the child's family situation may indicate that her acting-out behaviour may be an emotional reaction to a family event such as divorce (a psychoanalytic explanation).

The interdisciplinary nature of today's developmental science also contributes to eclecticism. For instance, an anthropologist might suggest that the rapid-fire communication media (e.g., television, video games, and the Internet) found in almost every home now require children to develop attention strategies that differ from those that are appropriate for classroom environments. As a result, children today exhibit more disruptive behaviour in school than children in past generations because of the mismatch between the kinds of information delivery to which they are accustomed at home and those found at school.

eclecticism
the use of multiple theoretical perspectives to explain and study human development

Critical Thinking

What personal assumptions about human development do you have? What evidence do you have to support them?

EVALUATION OF SYSTEM THEORIES

Bronfenbrenner's bioecological systems theory provides a way of thinking about development that captures the complexity of individual and contextual variables. To date, its greatest contribution to developmental psychology has been its emphasis on the need for research examining interactions among these variables (Thomas, 2000). For example, this theory has helped developmentalists understand that studies of infant daycare can't just compare infants in daycare with infants in home care. Such studies must also consider family variables, such as parents' educational level, and daycare variables, such as the ratio of caretakers to infants. Bronfenbrenner's theory largely ignored physical environmental influences (ranging from pollutants and toxins to noise levels, crowding, and housing to neighbourhood, daycare, and school quality and type), leaving the role of cumulative exposure to multiple physical environmental conditions on child development for further study (Evans, 2006).

By adopting an eclectic approach, developmentalists can devise more comprehensive theories from which to derive questions and hypotheses for further research. In other words, their theories and studies may more closely match the behaviour of real people in real situations.

Before Going On

- From the systems theory perspective, what causes healthy development?
- What is the main idea of Bronfenbrenner's bioecological systems theory?

Summary

Biology and Evolutionary Theories

- Biological theories focus on the contribution of hereditary genetic mechanisms in development.

- Geneticists distinguish between the genotype (the pattern of inherited genes) and the phenotype (the individual's observable characteristics).

- Inherited and acquired epigenetic mechanisms regulate gene expression.

- Evolutionary psychology is the view that, through a process of biological evolution, the mind, like the body, has been shaped by natural selection to serve adaptive functions and promote survival.

- Evolutionary developmental psychology theorists suggest that heredity and the environment interact in determining the cognitive abilities that promote survival and adaptation at different times across the lifespan.

Psychoanalytic Theories

- Freud emphasized that behaviour is governed by both conscious and unconscious motives and that the personality develops in steps.

- Erikson emphasized social forces more than unconscious drives as motives for development. He proposed that personality develops in eight psychosocial stages over the course of the lifespan.

- Humanistic theorist Abraham Maslow suggested that individuals are motivated to fulfill inner needs in order to ultimately attain self-actualization.

Learning Theories

- Classical conditioning—learning through association of stimuli—helps explain the acquisition of emotional responses.

- Operant conditioning involves learning to repeat or stop behaviours because of their consequences.

Cognitive Theories

- Piaget focused on the development of logical thinking. He discovered that such thinking develops across four childhood and adolescent stages.

- Information-processing theory uses the computer as a model to explain intellectual processes such as memory and problem-solving.

- Information-processing theory has been important in explaining Piaget's findings and memory processes.

- Vygotsky's sociocultural theory has become important to developmentalists' attempts to explain how culture affects development.

- Bandura's social-cognitive theory assumes reciprocal interactions among persons and behavioural factors and the environment.

Systems Theory

- Systems theory considers the reciprocal interactions of personal and external factors in development.

- Bronfenbrenner's bioecological systems theory has helped developmental psychologists categorize environmental factors and think about the ways in which they influence individuals.

- The eclectic approach uses theories derived from all the major systems and schools of psychology, as well as those of many other disciplines, to explain and study human development.

PEARSON
mydevelopmentlab™

Visit **www.mydevelopmentlab.com** to help you get the best grade! Test your knowledge and grasp difficult concepts through

- Custom study plans: See where you are strong and where you go wrong
- Interactive simulations

- Video and audio clips
- Raise your own Virtual Child—and much more!

Review Questions

Answers are provided on MyDevelopmentLab in the Course Resources folder.

Biology and Evolutionary Theories

2.1 Which of the following is not a true statement about the epigenetic influences upon human development?
   a. epigenetic structures are responsible for genotypic expression
   b. epigenetic alterations continue throughout the lifespan
   c. environmental influences can change the epigenome
   d. physical and psychological disorders may be linked to epigenetic errors

Psychoanalytic Theories

2.2 Which of the following represents the most common way individuals achieve generativity?

a. Since her 80th birthday, Mrs. Jabar has seemed increasingly withdrawn, preoccupied, and thoughtful. She seems to wish to be alone with her thoughts.
b. At age 28, Dylan believes he is ready to marry. He feels he is mature, knows what he wants from life, and believes he has many positive qualities to contribute to a relationship.
c. Angelina is in the process of evaluating possible careers and occupations and is beginning to understand how she wants to engage in roles such as worker, wife, mother, and citizen.
d. Mr. and Mrs. Fenwick take pride in parenting a healthy family of four children.

Learning Theories

2.3 Mr. Britton, an elementary school teacher, is planning to change the disruptive behaviour of some of the students in his class by using B.F. Skinner's techniques. We can expect that Mr. Britton's plan would involve

a. extinction and shaping.

b. relaxation and positive imagery.

c. innate conditioning responses.

d. scaffolding within the zone of proximal development.

Cognitive Theories

2.4 According to the principles of Vygotsky's socio-cultural theory of development, when parents help a child learn to ride a bicycle by putting training wheels on the bike and keeping a steadying hand on the seat as the child rides, they are providing a/an _____ for the learning experience.

a. zone of proximal development

b. scaffold

c. intrinsic reinforcement

d. ecology

Systems Theory

2.5 According to Bronfenbrenner's ecological theory of development, the microsystem of a child's development would not include which of the following developmental influences?

a. church, synagogue, or mosque

b. parents and siblings

c. values and beliefs

d. community or neighbourhood

Critical-Thinking Questions

2.6 If physiological processes can be programmed prenatally to match expected environments, do you think personality traits, such as aggression, nurturance, curiosity, or irritability, could be preset in a similar way? What prenatal conditions do you think would contribute to specific personality traits?

2.7 How is scaffolding involved when a parent helps a child with homework?

CHAPTER
3

Prenatal Development and Birth

Like any good story, human development has a beginning, a middle, and an end. Genes and chromosomes passed on to the new individual at the moment of conception and the prenatal environment of the first months set the stage for all that is to follow. From conception to birth, prenatal development follows a truly amazing course that begins with a single cell and ends with a crying, but curious, newborn making his or her debut in the outside world.

Throughout pregnancy, most parents speculate about the baby's inherited characteristics, confident that all will be well. ("Will she be tall like her father?" "Will he be musically talented like his mother?") However, for those few parents-to-be whose babies are affected by a variety of agents that can cause congenital anomalies or whose children are born too soon or too small, pregnancy and birth can bring more anxiety than joy. Nevertheless, it's important to keep in mind that, in many of these cases, there are ways of limiting the damage.

When you finish studying this chapter, you will be able to explain the process of conception and reproduction; trace the milestones of pregnancy and prenatal development from conception to birth; identify the potential negative effects of genetic disorders, chromosomal errors, diseases, drugs, and other factors on prenatal development; and summarize the birth process and the circumstances, choices, and complications that have an impact on childbirth and the neonate. While you read, keep the following questions in mind:

- What role does modern technology play in the process of conception?

- What can prospective parents do to reduce the risk of babies being born with congenital anomalies—abnormalities of structure, function, or body metabolism that are present at birth?

- When it comes to the birthing process, what choices are available for Canadian parents? What are the risks and benefits of each choice?

CONCEPTION

The first step in the development of an individual human being happens at conception, when each of us receives a combination of genes that will shape our experiences throughout the rest of our lives.

THE PROCESS OF CONCEPTION

✳—Explore

Ordinarily, a woman produces one ovum (egg cell) per month from one of her two ovaries, roughly midway between menstrual periods. If the ovum is not fertilized, it travels from the ovary down the fallopian tube toward the uterus, where it gradually disintegrates and is expelled as part of the menstrual fluid. However, if a couple has intercourse during the crucial few days when the ovum is in the fallopian tube, one of the millions of sperm ejaculated as part of each male orgasm may travel the full distance through the woman's vagina, cervix, uterus, and fallopian tube and penetrate the wall of the ovum.

CONCEPTION As you read in **Chapter 2**, every cell in the human body contains 23 pairs of chromosomes, or strings of genetic material. However, sperm and ovum, collectively called **gametes**, contain 23 single (unpaired) chromosomes.

gametes

cells that unite at conception (ova in females; sperm in males)

zygote
a single cell created when
sperm and ovum unite

At conception, chromosomes in the ovum and the sperm combine to form 23 pairs in an entirely new cell called a **zygote**. Twenty-two of these pairs of chromosomes, called *autosomes*, contain most of the genetic information for the new individual. The 23rd pair, the *sex chromosomes*, determines the sex. One of the two sex chromosomes, the X *chromosome*, is one of the largest chromosomes in the body and carries a large number of genes. The other, the Y *chromosome*, is quite small and contains only a few genes. Zygotes containing two X chromosomes develop into females, and those containing one X and one Y chromosome develop into males. Since the cells in a woman's body contain only X chromosomes, all her ova carry X chromosomes. Half of a man's sperm contain X chromosomes; the other half contain Y chromosomes. Consequently, the sex of the new individual is determined by the sex chromosome in the sperm.

MULTIPLE BIRTHS In most cases, human infants are conceived and born one at a time. However, in about 3.2 out of every 100 births in Canada, more than one baby is born, usually twins (Statistics Canada, 2009c). Roughly two-thirds of twins are *fraternal twins,* or twins that come from two sets of ova and sperm. Such twins, also called *dizygotic twins* (meaning that they originate from two zygotes), are no more alike genetically than any other pair of siblings and need not even be of the same sex.

The remaining one-third of twins are *identical twins* (*monozygotic,* or arising from one zygote). Identical twins result when a single zygote, for unknown reasons, separates into two parts, each of which develops into a separate individual. Because identical twins develop from the same zygote, they have identical genes. Research involving identical twins is one of the major investigative strategies in the field of behaviour genetics (see the **Research Report**).

Since the late 1980s, the annual number of multiple births has tripled in Canada (Bushnik & Garner, 2008). Furthermore, births of triplets, quadruplets, and quintuplets have increased even more dramatically—over 230% since the mid-1990s (Public Health Agency of Canada [PHAC], 2008a). One reason for the increase is that the number of women over age 35 giving birth for the first time has grown. Two factors underlie the association between multiple births and maternal age. First, for reasons that researchers don't yet understand, women are far more likely to naturally conceive twins and other multiples after age 35. Second, women over age 35 are more likely than younger women to experience difficulty becoming pregnant and thus are more likely to be treated with *assisted human reproduction* procedures—including ovulation stimulation drugs (Society of Obstetricians and Gynaecologists of Canada [SOGC], 2007b). Women of all ages who use these procedures are more likely to deliver multiples than women who conceive naturally.

**assisted human
reproduction (AHR)**
"any activity undertaken for the
purpose of facilitating human
reproduction" (Health Canada,
2001a)

ASSISTED HUMAN REPRODUCTION In Canada, new legislation now regulates **assisted human reproduction (AHR)** and related research. The Act, introduced as Bill C-6, protects the health and safety of Canadians undergoing AHR treatment and the children born from such procedures (Communication Canada, 2004).

The use of fertility drugs is one of many AHR procedures available to couples who have trouble conceiving. Another is *in vitro fertilization* (IVF), popularly known as the "test-tube baby" method (*in vitro* is Latin for "in glass"). This technique involves uniting an ovum and a sperm in a laboratory dish and implanting the resulting embryo in a woman's uterus. The egg can come from the woman who will carry the child or from a donor. Likewise, sperm can be from the woman's partner or a donor.

cryopreservation
preserving cells or tissues
through a freezing process that
stops all biological activity

Typically, IVF laboratories create numerous embryos, which are then frozen, or *cryopreserved,* prior to being implanted. Until recently, slow-cooling **cryopreservation** has been the most widely used method for freezing and storing embryos, but this technique results in high rates of cellular damage and destruction due to ice-crystal formation and dehydration (Liebermann & Tucker, 2002; 2006). Newer cryopreservation protocols involve immersing embryos in *cryoprotectants* (an antifreeze-like liquid that permeates the embryo) and then plunging them into super-cooled liquid nitrogen (210°c), which freezes the embryos almost instantly (Huang et al., 2005). This **vitrification** protocol significantly improves the survival rate of embryos during the thawing process, implantation success, and pregnancy in comparison with the slow-cooling method (Escribá, Grau, Escrich, & Pellicer, 2010; Kim, Laufer, & Wook Hong, 2010; Loutradi et al. 2008). This newer protocol reduces the need to transfer multiple fertilized embryos to a woman's womb, which lowers the potential risk of multiple gestations.

vitrification
the use of cryoprotectants along with rapid cooling to prevent the fluid in biological tissues (e.g., eggs, semen, embryos) from forming ice crystals (that act like glass shards on cell structures) and from dehydrating. The tissue becomes an intact, non-crystalline, glass-like solid that can be preserved for years.

Research Report

TWINS IN GENETIC AND EPIGENETIC RESEARCH

Researchers interested in the role of heredity in human development have been comparing identical and fraternal twins since the earliest days of developmental psychology. The logic is this: If identical twins (whose genes are exactly the same) who are raised apart are more similar than fraternal twins or non-twin siblings (whose genes are similar, but not identical) who are raised together, heredity must play a role in the trait being studied. For example, the numbers below are correlations based on several studies of twins' intelligence test scores (Eliot, 1999). Recall from **Chapter 1** that the closer to 1.00 a correlation is, the stronger the relationship.

Identical twins reared together	0.86
Identical twins reared apart	0.72
Fraternal twins reared together	0.60
Non-twin siblings reared apart	0.24

As you can see, intelligence test scores are more strongly correlated in identical twins than in fraternal twins or non-twin siblings, even when the identical twins are raised in different families. Such findings are taken to be evidence for the heritability of intelligence.

Canadian researchers from the universities of Western Ontario and British Columbia have also studied the heritability of other human traits, such as attitudes. They surveyed 195 pairs of identical and 141 pairs of fraternal adult twins and found that about 35% of the difference in attitudes could be attributed to genetic factors. Measures of how strongly twins favoured various issues, activities, and social settings revealed that twins' attitudes about, for example, abortion on demand, roller-coaster rides, playing organized sports, and the death penalty for murder yielded a high genetic influence (Olson, Vernon, Aitken Harris, & Jang, 2001).

Taken together, the findings of these studies point to strong genetic components in both intelligence and attitudes. However, what these studies reveal about environment may be even more significant. If psychological characteristics such as intelligence and attitudes were determined solely by heredity, identical twins would be exactly alike, and researchers would find correlations of +1.00. The correlations that twin researchers have found are less than +1.00, even for identical twins who grow up in the same home. Moreover, the correlations for identical twins raised apart are lower than those for identical twins raised together.

To help explain these puzzling facts, scientists are now looking closely at a third component, epigenetic variables, to help explain phenotypic differences (Barros & Offenbacher, 2009; Fraga, 2009; Haque, Gottesman & Wong, 2009; Richards, 2006; Rutter, 2007)—especially in cases of complex non-Mendelian conditions, such as Alzheimer's, breast cancer, or psychotic disorders (Kaminsky et al., 2009; Rutten & Mill, 2009; Wong, Gottesman, & Petronis, 2005). A landmark study of 80 pairs of monozygotic (Mz) twins, conducted by Fraga et al., (2005, 2009), helps to illustrate the point that discordance in behaviour and disease observed in pairs of identical twins is linked to epigenetic variables. Researchers in the study found that younger pairs of Mz twins had indistinguishable epigenetic patterns and physical traits. In comparison, middle-aged pairs of Mz twins showed sizeable differences in their epigenetic patterns and phenotypic characteristics and, in these pairs, twins who lived dissimilar lifestyles and spent less time together during their lifetimes had even greater epigenetic differences. The researchers suggest that, over the course of a lifetime, environmental variables (e.g., differences in diet, smoking, fitness levels) bring about changes in epigenetic markers in genetically identical pairs of twins which, in turn, produce phenotypic changes, including the frequency and onset of disease.

To date, genetic twin studies have proved useful, although not altogether complete. Epigenetic analysis of twins will likely spur on the next wave of heritability research. As Canadian epigeneticist, Arturas Petronis (2006, p. 349), contends, "epigenetics could emerge as a unifying concept for the large variety of non-Mendelian features in complex traits."

Developmentalists have addressed concerns about the possible side effects of cryopreservation on children's development in several studies. Both comparative (IVF infants and children versus non-IVF ones) and longitudinal studies have failed to find any significant side effects of the procedure (Levy-Shiff et al., 1998; van Balen, 1998). However, IVF is not a highly successful procedure. For one thing, the older a woman is, the lower the probability that she will be able to achieve a successful IVF pregnancy. Roughly 32% of Canadian women under age 35 undergoing IVF achieve a live birth, but only about 10% of IVF procedures involving women aged 40 and over are successful (Canadian Fertility and Andrology Society [CFAS], 2006). And even though younger Canadian women can now delay motherhood until a later age and harvest, freeze, and store their "younger" eggs (gametes) for many years, there is no guarantee that using her "youthful" eggs will increase the odds of successful fertilization of those eggs when she is older (Roberts, 2007). Also, the failure of IVF treatment can lead to depression (Weaver, Clifford, Hay, & Robinson, 1997). Even with successful IVF procedures, some women remain emotionally detached from their fetuses for fear of losing them. However, once an IVF baby is born, some studies suggest that parents are more likely to express emotional warmth toward their child than parents who conceive naturally (Eugster & Vingerhoets, 1999).

Multiple births are more frequent among women who become pregnant by using IVF because doctors typically transfer several embryos at once to increase the likelihood of at least one live birth, but multiple births place both mother and babies at risk. This increased risk has contributed to an ongoing debate in Canada and across the globe as to what constitutes a relevant standard of success in reproductive technology. Some argue that successful AHR outcomes should be defined as a single, term-gestation, live baby per fertility cycle (e.g., Min, Breheny, MacLachlan, & Healy, 2004). Others emphasize that once couples who are undergoing AHR are made aware of the maternal and neonatal mortality rates and they accept the risk associated with the possibility of having more than one baby, then having either one or more could be considered an AHR success (e.g., Buckett & Tan, 2004). All the same, *single embryo transfer* (SET) will likely become the international norm in IVF treatment. Nordic countries, for example, have high rates of SET (~70%) and a consistent pregnancy rate of ~30% per embryo transfer (Nygren, 2007). To reduce the chance of multiple births following IVF, Canadian guidelines now recommend that women under the age of 35 years should receive no more than two embryos per fertility cycle and women over 39 years of age should be transferred no more than four, unless there are exceptional circumstances when a woman with a poor conception prognosis has history of multiple failed IVF attempts (Min, Claman, & Hughes, 2006).

Another technique, *artificial insemination*, is more successful and less likely to result in multiple births. In artificial insemination, sperm are injected directly into a woman's uterus, usually during the part of her menstrual cycle when she is most likely to conceive. The procedure can employ the sperm of a woman's partner or that of a donor. This method is most often used by couples in which the male partner has a low sperm count or by fertile women who want to conceive without a male partner. However, as in any invasive medical procedure, artificial insemination carries some risk of infection.

Assisted human reproductive techniques have been somewhat controversial. For example, if donated ova and sperm are provided by anonymous donors, it is impossible to determine the genetic heritage of children conceived through these donations. Canada's *AHR Act* has addressed this concern by legislating the maintenance of a personal health information registry that contains nonidentifying medical information about the sperm and egg donors (Clement, 2006). This registry will allow children of donated sperm and ova to have access to their medical histories.

Before Going On

- Explain the process by which gametes from a woman and a man unite to form a zygote. What are the characteristics of the new cell?
- Describe three common assisted human reproduction techniques used in Canada.

PREGNANCY AND PRENATAL DEVELOPMENT

Pregnancy is a physical condition in which a woman's body is nurturing a developing embryo or fetus. *Prenatal development*, or *gestation*, is the process that transforms a zygote into a newborn. Thus, the process that ends with the birth of a baby involves two sets of experiences: those of the pregnant woman, and those of the developing zygote, embryo, and fetus.

THE MOTHER'S EXPERIENCE

Pregnancy is customarily divided into *trimesters,* three periods of 3 months each (see **Table 3.1**).

FIRST TRIMESTER Pregnancy begins when the zygote implants itself in the lining of the woman's uterus (also called the *womb*). The zygote then sends out chemical messages that cause the woman's menstrual periods to stop. Some of these chemicals are excreted in her urine, making it possible to diagnose pregnancy within a few days after conception. Other chemicals cause physical changes, such as breast enlargement.

The *cervix* (the narrow, lower portion of the uterus, which extends into the vagina) thickens and secretes mucus that serves as a barrier to protect the developing embryo from harmful organisms that might enter the womb through the vagina. The uterus begins to shift position and put pressure on the woman's bladder, causing her to urinate more often. This and other symptoms, such as fatigue and breast tenderness, may interfere with sleep. Another common early symptom of pregnancy is *nausea and vomiting in pregnancy* (NVP), more commonly known as *morning sickness*—feelings of nausea, often accompanied by vomiting, that usually occur in the morning but can occur at any time of the day or the night.

Prenatal care during the first trimester is critical to prevent congenital anomalies, because all the baby's organs form during the first 8 weeks. Early prenatal care can identify maternal conditions, such as sexually transmitted diseases, that may threaten prenatal development. Health professionals can also urge women to abstain from drugs and alcohol early in prenatal development, when such behaviour changes may prevent congenital anomalies.

Early prenatal care can also be important to the pregnant woman's health. For example, in a small

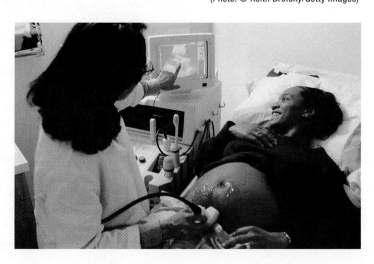

During the second trimester of pregnancy, an ultrasound test allows for the diagnosis of fetal deformities and growth problems, the fetus's position in the uterus, and the position of the placenta. As well, sometimes it is possible to identify the sex of the fetus.
(*Photo:* © Keith Brofsky/Getty Images)

TABLE 3.1 Pregnancy Summary

Trimester	Events	Prenatal Care	Serious Problems
First trimester: From first day of last menstrual period (LMP) to 12 weeks	Missed period Breast enlargement Abdominal thickening	Confirmation of pregnancy Calculation of due date Blood and urine tests (and other tests if needed) Monthly doctor visits to monitor vital functions, uterine growth, weight gain, and sugar and protein in urine	Ectopic pregnancy Abnormal urine or blood tests Increased blood pressure Malnutrition Bleeding Miscarriage
Second trimester: From 12 weeks after LMP to 24 weeks after LMP	Weight gain "Showing" Fetal movements felt Increased appetite	Monthly doctor visits continue Ultrasound to measure fetal growth and locate placenta	Gestational diabetes Excessive weight gain Increased blood pressure Rh incompatibility of mother and fetus Miscarriage 13 to 20 weeks Premature labour 21+ weeks
Third trimester: From 25 weeks after LMP to beginning of labour	Weight gain Breast discharge	Weekly visits beginning at 32nd week Ultrasound to assess position of fetus, if needed Treatment of Rh incompatibility if needed Pelvic exams to check for cervical dilation	Increased blood pressure Bleeding Premature labour Bladder infection

number of cases, a zygote implants in one of the fallopian tubes instead of in the uterus, a condition called *ectopic pregnancy*. Early surgical removal of the zygote is critical to the woman's future ability to have children.

About 15% of pregnancies end in miscarriage, or *spontaneous abortion*. From the woman's point of view, an early-term miscarriage is similar to a menstrual period, although feelings of discomfort and blood loss are usually greater. Medical care is always necessary after a late-term miscarriage because the woman's body may fail to completely expel the embryo.

SECOND TRIMESTER During the second trimester of pregnancy, from the end of week 12 through week 24, morning sickness usually disappears, resulting in increased appetite. The pregnant woman gains weight, and the uterus expands to accommodate a rapidly growing fetus. Consequently, the woman begins to "show" sometime during the second trimester. She also begins to feel the fetus's movements, usually at some point between the 16th and 18th weeks.

At monthly prenatal checkups, the doctor or midwife monitors both the mother's and the baby's vital functions and keeps track of the growth of the baby in the womb. An ultrasound test may be performed to check fetal growth and locate the placenta. Sometimes, if the angle is right, the sex of the baby can also be determined from the ultrasound after about the 13th week. Monthly urine tests check for *gestational diabetes*, a kind of diabetes that happens only during pregnancy. A woman who has any kind of diabetes, including gestational diabetes, has to be carefully monitored during the second trimester because her baby may grow too rapidly, leading to premature labour or a baby that is too large for vaginal delivery.

The risk of miscarriage drops in the second trimester. However, a few fetuses die between the 13th and 20th weeks of pregnancy. In addition, premature labour after the 21st week can result in delivery of a living but extremely small baby. A small percentage of such infants survive, but most have significant health problems.

THIRD TRIMESTER At 25 weeks, the pregnant woman enters her third trimester. Weight gain and abdominal enlargement are the main experiences of this period. In addition, the woman's breasts may begin to secrete a substance called *colostrum* in preparation for nursing.

Supportive partners, friends, and relatives can help third-trimester mothers-to-be maintain positive attitudes and balance negative emotions that often accompany their feelings of physical awkwardness against the anticipated joy of birth. (*Photo:* Michael Newman/PhotoEdit)

Most women begin to feel more emotionally connected to the fetus during the third trimester. Individual differences in fetal behaviour, such as hiccupping or thumb-sucking, sometimes become obvious during the last weeks of pregnancy. In addition, most women notice that the fetus has regular periods of activity and rest.

Monthly prenatal visits continue in the third trimester until week 32, when most women begin visiting their doctor or midwife once a week. Monitoring of blood pressure is especially important, as some women develop a life-threatening condition called *toxemia of pregnancy* during the third trimester. This condition is signalled by a sudden increase in blood pressure and can cause a pregnant woman to have a stroke.

PRENATAL DEVELOPMENT

In contrast to the trimesters of pregnancy, the three stages of prenatal development are defined by specific developmental milestones and are not of equal length. Moreover, the entire process follows two developmental patterns that you can see at work in the photographs in **Table 3.2**. With the **cephalocaudal pattern**, development proceeds from the head downward. For example, the brain is formed before the reproductive organs. With the **proximodistal pattern**, development happens in an orderly way from the centre of the body outward to the extremities. In other words, structures closer to the centre of the body, such as the rib cage, develop before the fingers and toes.

cephalocaudal pattern
growth that proceeds from the head downward

proximodistal pattern
growth that proceeds from the middle of the body outward

THE GERMINAL STAGE The first 2 weeks of gestation, from conception to *implantation*, constitute the **germinal stage**. During this stage, cells specialize into those that will become the fetus's body and those that will become the structures needed to support its development. Cell division happens rapidly, and by the 4th day, the zygote contains dozens of cells.

On day 5, the cells become a hollow, fluid-filled ball called a *blastocyst*. Inside the blastocyst, cells that will eventually become the embryo begin to clump together. On day 6 or 7, the blastocyst comes into contact with the uterine wall, and by the 12th day,

germinal stage
the first stage of prenatal development, beginning at conception and ending at implantation (approximately 2 weeks)

TABLE 3.2   Milestones in Prenatal Development

Stage/Time Frame	Milestones
Germinal Stage Day 1: Conception	Sperm and ovum unite, forming a zygote containing genetic instructions for the development of a new and unique human being. (Photo: P. Motta & J. Van Blerkom, Photo Researchers) 
Days 10 to 14: Implantation	The zygote burrows into the lining of the uterus. Specialized cells that will become the placenta, umbilical cord, and embryo are already formed. (Photo: Lennart Nilsson/Albert Bonniers/Forlag AB) 
Embryonic Stage Weeks 3 to 8: Organogenesis	All the embryo's organ systems form during the 6-week period following implantation. (Photo: Petit Format/Nestlé/Science Source Library, Photo Researchers) 
Fetal Stage Weeks 9 to 38: Growth and Organ Refinement	The fetus grows from 2.5 cm and 7 grams to a length of about 51 cm and a weight of 3.2 kg. By week 12, most fetuses can be identified as male or female. Changes in the brain and lungs make viability possible by week 24; optimum development requires an additional 14 to 16 weeks in the womb. Most neurons form by week 28, and connections among them begin to develop shortly thereafter. In the last 8 weeks, the fetus can hear and smell, is sensitive to touch, and responds to light. Learning is also possible.

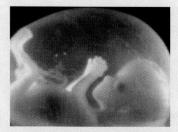

(Photo: Petit Format/Nestlé/Science Source Library, Photo Researchers)

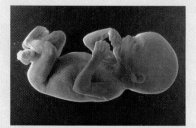

(Photo: James Stevenson/Science Source Library, Photo Researchers)

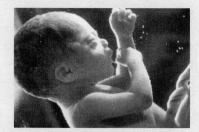

(Photo: Petit Format/Nestlé/Science Source Library, Photo Researchers)

(*Sources:* Kliegman, 1998; Tortora & Grabowski, 1993.)

it is completely buried in the uterine tissue, a process called **implantation**. Some cells from the blastocyst's outer wall combine with cells of the uterine lining to begin creating the **placenta**, an organ that allows oxygen, nutrients, and other substances to be transferred between the mother's and baby's blood. The placenta's specialized structures bring the mother's and baby's blood close to one another without allowing them to mix.

Like the zygote, the placenta secretes chemical messages (hormones) that stop the mother's menstrual periods and keep the placenta connected to the uterus. Other placental hormones allow the bones of the woman's pelvis to become more flexible, induce breast changes, and increase the mother's metabolic rate. At the same time, the blastocyst's inner cells begin to specialize. One group of cells will become the **umbilical cord**, the organ that connects the embryo to the placenta. Vessels in the umbilical cord carry blood from the baby to the mother and back again. Other cells will form the *yolk sac*, a structure that produces blood cells until the embryo's blood-cell-producing organs are formed. Still others will become the **amnion**, a fluid-filled sac in which the baby floats until just before it is born. By the 12th day, the cells that will become the embryo's body are also formed.

THE EMBRYONIC STAGE The **embryonic stage** begins at implantation, approximately 2 weeks after conception, and continues until the end of week 8. By the time many women first suspect a pregnancy, usually 3 weeks after conception, the embryo's cells are starting to specialize and come together to form the foundations of all the body's organs. For example, the cells of the nervous system, the **neurons**, form a structure called the *neural tube*, from which the brain and spinal cord will develop. A primitive heart and the forerunners of the kidneys also develop during week 3, along with three sacs that will become the digestive system.

In week 4, the end of the embryo's neural tube swells to form the brain. Spots that will become the eyes appear on the embryo's head, and its heart begins to beat. The backbone and ribs become visible as bone and muscle cells move into place. The face starts to take shape, and the endocrine system begins to develop.

By week 5, the embryo is about 6.5 millimetres long, 10 000 times larger than the zygote. Its arms and legs are developing rapidly. Five fingers are visible on each hand. Its eyes have corneas and lenses, and its lungs are beginning to develop.

In week 6, the embryo's brain begins to produce patterns of electrical activity. It moves in response to stimuli, and the **gonads**, or sex glands (ovaries in females and testes in males), develop. At first, the gonads of male and female embryos are identical. However, between the 4th and 6th weeks, genes on the Y chromosome cause the male embryo to produce the male hormone *testosterone*. The testosterone causes the gonads to become testes. In the absence of testosterone, the gonads develop into ovaries.

During week 7, a male embryo begins to develop a penis. Also by this time, both male and female embryos begin to move spontaneously (Joseph, 2000). They have visible skeletons and fully developed limbs. The bones are beginning to harden and the muscles are maturing; by this point, the embryo can maintain a semi-upright posture. The eyelids seal shut to protect the developing eyes. The ears are completely formed, and X-rays can detect tooth buds in the jawbones.

During the last week of the embryonic stage, week 8, the liver and spleen begin to function. These organs allow the embryo to make and filter its own blood cells. Its heart is well developed and efficiently pumps blood to every part of the body. The embryo's movements increase as the electrical activity in its brain becomes more organized. Connections between the brain and the rest of the body are also well established. The embryo's digestive and urinary systems are functioning. By the end of week 8, **organogenesis**, the technical term for organ development, is complete.

---

implantation
attachment of the blastocyst to the uterine wall

placenta
specialized organ that allows substances to be transferred from mother to embryo and from embryo to mother without their blood mixing

umbilical cord
organ that connects the embryo to the placenta

amnion
fluid-filled sac in which the fetus floats until just before it is born

embryonic stage
the second stage of prenatal development, from week 2 through week 8, during which the embryo's organ systems form

neurons
specialized cells of the nervous system

gonads
sex glands (ovaries in females; testes in males)

PEARSON
mydevelopmentlab
Connect to
MyDevelopmentLab
Many women don't realize that they are pregnant until they are several weeks into their pregnancy. Does it matter? Find out why weeks 3–7 are critical by exploring the Embryonic Period.

✱ Explore

organogenesis
process of organ growth

TABLE 3.3   Milestones of the Fetal Stage

Period	What Develops
Weeks 9–12	Fingerprints; grasping reflex; facial expressions; swallowing and rhythmic "breathing" of amniotic fluid; urination; genitalia appear; alternating periods of physical activity and rest
Weeks 13–16	Hair follicles; responses to mother's voice and loud noises; 8 to 12 centimetres long, crown to rump; weighs 25 to 100 grams
Weeks 17–20	Fetal movements felt by mother; heartbeat detectable with stethoscope; lanugo (hair) covers body; eyes respond to light introduced into the womb; eyebrows; fingernails; 13 to 17 centimetres long, crown to rump; weighs 140 to 300 grams
Weeks 21–24	Vernix (oily substance) protects skin; lungs produce surfactant (vital to respiratory function); viability becomes possible, although most born now do not survive
Weeks 25–28	Recognition of mother's voice; regular periods of rest and activity; 35 to 38 centimetres long, crown to heel; weighs 660 to 1000 grams; good chance of survival if born now
Weeks 29–32	Very rapid growth; antibodies acquired from mother; fat deposited under skin; 39 to 43 centimetres long, crown to heel; weighs 1.2 to 1.7 kilograms; excellent chance of survival if delivered now
Weeks 33–36	Movement to head-down position for birth; lungs mature; approximately 44 to 48 centimetre-long, crown to heel; weighs about 1.9 to 2.6 kilograms; virtually 100% chance of survival if delivered
Weeks 37+	Full-term status; about 49 centimetres long, crown to heel; weighs about 3 kilograms

fetal stage
the third stage of prenatal development, from week 9 to birth, during which growth and organ refinement take place

viability
ability of the fetus to survive outside the womb

cell bodies
the part of a neuron that contains the cell body and is the site of vital cell functions

mydevelopmentlab

Connect to
MyDevelopmentLab

Watch the amazing growth of the fetus from week 8 until birth.

Watch

THE FETAL STAGE The final phase is the **fetal stage**, beginning at the end of week 8 and continuing until birth. The fetus grows from a weight of about 2 grams and a length of 2.5 centimetres to a baby born around 38 weeks weighing about 3.2 kilograms and having a length of about 50 centimetres. In addition, this stage involves refinements of the organ systems—especially the lungs and brain—that are essential to life outside the womb (see **Table 3.3**).

By the end of week 23, a small number of babies have attained **viability**, the ability to live outside the womb (Moore & Persaud, 1993). However, most babies born this early die, and those who do survive struggle for many months. Remaining in the womb just 1 week longer, until the end of week 24, greatly increases a baby's chances of survival. The extra week probably allows time for lung function to become more efficient. In addition, most brain structures are completely developed by the end of the 24th week. For these reasons, most experts accept 24 weeks as the average age of viability.

THE FETAL BRAIN As you learned earlier, the foundational structures of all the body's organ systems are formed during the embryonic stage. Yet most of the formation and fine-tuning of the brain takes place during the fetal stage. Recall that neurons, the specialized cells of the nervous system, begin developing during the embryonic stage in week 3. But the pace of neural formation picks up dramatically between the 10th and 18th weeks, a process known as *neuronal proliferation*.

Between the 13th and 21st weeks, the newly formed neurons migrate to the parts of the brain where they will reside for the rest of the individual's life (Chong et al., 1996). While migrating, neurons consist only of **cell bodies**, the part of the cell that contains the nucleus and in which all the cell's vital functions are carried out (see **Figure 3.1**). Once they have reached their final destinations in the fetal brain, the neurons begin to develop connections. These connections are called **synapses,** tiny spaces between neurons across which neural impulses travel from one neuron to the next. Several changes in fetal behaviour signal that the process of synapse formation is underway. For instance, the fetus exhibits alternating periods of activity and rest and begins to yawn (Walusinski et al., 2005). When observed, these changes tell physicians that fetal brain development is proceeding normally.

Synapse formation requires the growth of two neuronal structures. **Axons** are tail-like extensions that range in length from 1 to 200 millimetres within the brain, but they can grow to be more than a metre, (e.g., between the spinal cord and the body's extremities). **Dendrites** are tentacle-like branches that extend out from the cell body (see **Figure 3.1**). Dendrite development is thought to be highly sensitive to adverse environmental influences such as maternal malnutrition and defects in placental functioning (Dieni & Rees, 2003).

Simultaneously with neuronal migration, **glial cells** begin to develop. These cells are the "glue" that hold the neurons together to give shape to the brain's major structures. As glial cells develop, the brain begins to assume a more mature appearance, one that can be observed using *magnetic resonance imaging* (MRI) and other modern technologies that you will read more about later in the chapter (see **Figure 3.2**).

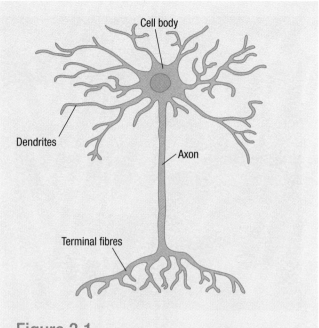

Cell body

Dendrites

Axon

Terminal fibres

Figure 3.1

The structure of a single developed neuron. The cell bodies are the first to be developed, primarily between weeks 12 and 24. Axons and dendrites develop later, especially during the final 12 weeks, and continue to increase in size and complexity for several years after birth.

synapses
tiny spaces across which neural impulses flow from one neuron to the next

axons
tail-like extensions of neurons

dendrites
branch-like protrusions from the cell bodies of neurons

glial cells
specialized cells in the brain that support neurons

SEX DIFFERENCES

Because prenatal development is strongly influenced by maturational codes that are the same for both males and females, there are only a few sex differences in prenatal development. One fairly well-documented difference is that male fetuses, on average, are more physically active (DiPietro, Hodgson, Costigan, & Johnson, 1996; DiPietro, Hodgson, Costigan, Hilton, & Johnson, 1996). Further, activity level is fairly stable from the fetal stage through childhood (Accardo et al., 1997). This means that the sex differences in children's activity level you'll read about in later chapters probably begin in the womb.

Sometime between 4 and 8 weeks after conception, the male embryo begins to secrete the male hormone *testosterone*. If this hormone is not secreted or is secreted in inadequate amounts, the embryo will be "demasculinized," even to the extent of developing female genitalia. Female embryos do not appear to secrete any equivalent hormone. However, the presence of male hormone at the critical time (from a drug the mother takes or from a genetic disease called *congenital adrenal hyperplasia*) acts to "masculinize" the female fetus, sometimes resulting in genitalia that appear to be male.

In addition, male fetuses secrete small amounts of testosterone into the amniotic fluid. If a male shares the womb with a female fraternal twin, she is likely to swallow the secreted testosterone. Although the research is fairly new, studies suggest that these girls have some neurological characteristics that are more similar to the average male than to the average female (McFadden, 1998).

Subtle sex differences in prenatal brain development probably contribute to different patterns of growth hormone secretions in adolescence as well. Researchers have

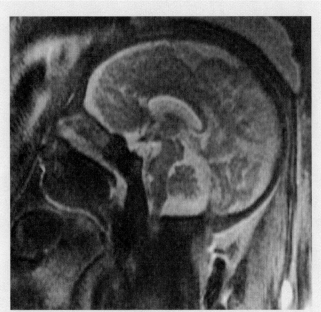

Figure 3.2

This image shows a normal third-trimester fetal brain. Glial cells that develop during the last few months of prenatal development hold neurons together and give form and structure to the fetal brain.

(*Source:* Brown, Estroff, & Barnewolf, 2004. Reprinted with permission of Anderson Publishing Ltd.)

linked prenatal hormones to sex differences in the dominance of the right and left hemispheres of the brain, physical aggression, and connections between brain and motor patterns (Pressman et al., 1998; Todd, Swarzenski, Rossi, & Visconti, 1995).

Developmentalists aren't sure why, but female fetuses appear to be more sensitive to external stimulation and to advance more rapidly in skeletal development (Groome et al., 1999; Tanner, 1990). Female infants are about 1 to 2 weeks ahead in bone development at birth, even though newborn boys are typically longer and heavier. Female superiority in skeletal development persists through childhood and early adolescence, causing girls to acquire many coordinated movements and motor skills, especially those involving the hands and wrists, earlier than boys. The gap between the sexes gets wider every year until the mid-teens, when boys catch up and surpass girls in general physical coordination.

Boys are more vulnerable to all kinds of prenatal problems. Many more boys than girls are conceived—from 120 to 150 male embryos to every 100 female ones—but more of the males are spontaneously aborted. At birth, there are about 105 boys for every 100 girls. Male fetuses also appear to be more sensitive to variables such as marijuana and maternal stress, which may negatively affect prenatal development (Bethus, Lemaire, Lhomme, & Goodall, 2005; Wang, Dow-Edwards, Anderson, Minkoff, & Hurd, 2004).

PRENATAL BEHAVIOUR

Centuries before scientists began to study prenatal development, pregnant women noticed fetal responses to music and other sounds. However, in recent years, developmentalists have learned a great deal about how such stimuli affect the fetus. The use of techniques such as ultrasound imaging, for example, has provided researchers with a great deal of information about fetal behaviour, some of which are shown in **Figure 3.3**.

For one thing, researchers have discovered that the fetus can distinguish between familiar and novel stimuli by the 32nd or 33rd week (Sandman, Wadhwa, Hetrick, Porto, & Peeke, 1997). Evidence for fetal learning comes from studies in which newborns appear to remember stimuli to which they were exposed prenatally: their mother's heartbeats, the odour of the amniotic fluid, and the stories or pieces of music they heard in the womb (Righetti, 1996; Schaal, Marlier, & Soussignan, 1998). For example, in a classic study of prenatal learning, pregnant women read Dr. Seuss's children's story *The Cat in the Hat* out loud each day for the final 6 weeks of their pregnancies. After the infants were born, they were allowed to suck on special pacifiers that turned a variety of sounds off and on. Each kind of sound required a special type of sucking. Researchers found that the babies quickly adapted their sucking patterns in order to listen to the familiar story, but did not increase their sucking in order to listen to an unfamiliar story (DeCasper & Spence, 1986). In other words, babies preferred the sound of the story they had heard *in utero* (in the womb). In another study, researchers from Queen's University and Zhejiang University in China exposed full-term fetuses to either their mother's voice or to the voice of a female stranger via loudspeaker. In both cases the same poem was read to each fetus. The fetuses demonstrated

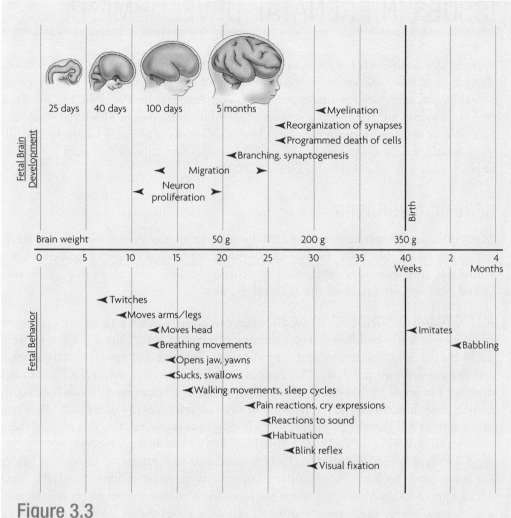

Figure 3.3

Researchers have discovered numerous correlations between fetal brain development and behaviour.

(Source: Walusinski, O., Kurjak, A., Andonotopo, W., & Azumendi, G., 2005. Fetal yawning: A behavior's birth with 4D US revealed. *The Ultrasound Review of Obstetrics & Gynecology, 5,* 210–217.)

a significantly different heart-rate pattern in response to the poem read by their mother (heart rate increase) than to that read by a stranger (heart rate decrease), suggesting that fetuses can remember and recognize their mother's voice (Kisilevsky et al., 2003).

Stable individual differences in behaviour are also identifiable in fetuses. Longitudinal studies have shown that very active fetuses, both males and females, tend to become children who are very active. Moreover, these children are more likely to be labelled "hyperactive" by parents and teachers. In contrast, fetuses who are less active than average are more likely to be intellectually delayed (Accardo et al., 1997).

Before Going On

〔Explore

- Outline the milestones of the germinal, embryonic, and fetal stages of prenatal development.

- What do developmentalists know about prenatal behaviour?

ISSUES IN PRENATAL DEVELOPMENT

Prenatal development is not immune to outside influences, as you'll see in this section. Keep in mind that most of the problems you'll read about are very rare, many are preventable, and many need not have permanent consequences for the child. In Canada, 2 to 3% of babies are born with a serious **congenital anomaly**—an abnormal structure, function, or body metabolism present at birth that results in physical or mental disability or death (see the Canadian Congenital Anomalies Surveillance Network for details at www.phac-aspc.gc.ca) (Health Canada, 2002a).

congenital anomaly
an abnormality present at birth

GENETIC DISORDERS

Many disorders appear to be transmitted through the operation of dominant and recessive genes (see **Table 3.4**). *Autosomal disorders* are caused by genes located on the autosomes (chromosomes other than sex chromosomes). The genes that cause *sex-linked* disorders are found on the X chromosome.

AUTOSOMAL DISORDERS Most disorders caused by recessive genes are diagnosed in infancy or early childhood. For example, a recessive gene causes a baby to have problems digesting the amino acid phenylalanine. Toxins build up in the baby's brain and cause developmental delay. This condition, called *phenylketonuria (PKU)*, is found in about 1 in every 10 000 babies (Nicholson, 1998). If a baby consumes no foods containing phenylalanine, however, he will not become intellectually delayed. Milk is one of the foods PKU babies can't have, so early diagnosis is critical. For this reason, there is universal screening for PKU soon after birth in all Canadian provinces.

Like many recessive disorders, PKU is associated with ethnicity. Caucasian babies are more likely to have the disorder than infants in other groups. Similarly, West African and African American infants are more likely to suffer from *sickle-cell disease*, a recessive disorder that causes red blood cell deformities (Scott, 1998). In sickle-cell disease, the blood can't carry enough oxygen to keep the body's tissues healthy. Few children with sickle-cell disease live past the age of 20, and most who survive to adulthood die before they are 40 (Scott, 1998).

TABLE 3.4   Some Genetic Disorders

Autosomal Dominant Disorders	Autosomal Recessive Disorders	Sex-Linked Recessive Disorders
Huntington's disease	Phenylketonuria	Hemophilia
High blood pressure	Sickle-cell disease	Fragile-X syndrome
Extra fingers	Cystic fibrosis	Red–green colour blindness
Migraine headaches	Tay-Sachs disease	Missing front teeth
Schizophrenia	Kidney cysts in infants	Night blindness
	Albinism	Some types of muscular dystrophy
		Some types of diabetes

(*Sources:* Amato, 1998; Tortora & Grabowski, 1993.)

About 1 in every 3000 babies born to couples of Eastern European Jewish ancestry suffers from another recessive disorder, *Tay-Sachs disease*. Another group that is at risk for the disease is French Canadians in the Gaspé region of Quebec (Triggs-Raine, Richard, Wasel, Prence, & Natowicz, 1995). They carry the gene for a severe form of Tay-Sachs disease at a rate 10 times that of the general population (Myerowitz & Hogikyan, 1987). A baby with Tay-Sachs is likely to be severely intellectually delayed and blind. Very few survive past the age of 3 (Painter & Bergman, 1998).

Disorders caused by dominant genes, such as *Huntington's disease*, are usually not diagnosed until adulthood (Amato, 1998). This disorder causes the brain to deteriorate and affects both psychological and motor functions. The risk of Huntington's in Canada is 1 in 10 000, and the child of a parent with Huntington's has a 50% chance of developing the disease (Huntington Society of Canada, 2001). A blood test can now identify the Huntington's gene. Thus, people who have a parent with this disease can now make better decisions about their own child-bearing, as well as prepare themselves to live with a serious disorder when they get older.

SEX-LINKED DISORDERS Most sex-linked disorders are caused by recessive genes. One fairly common sex-linked recessive disorder is *red–green colour blindness*. People with this disorder have difficulty distinguishing between the colours red and green when these colours are adjacent. About 7 to 8% of men and 0.5% of women have this disorder. Most learn ways of compensating for the disorder and thus live perfectly normal lives.

A more serious sex-linked recessive disorder is *hemophilia*. The blood of people with hemophilia lacks the chemical components that cause blood to clot. Thus, when a person with hemophilia bleeds, the bleeding doesn't stop naturally. Approximately 1 in 5000 baby boys is born with this disorder, which is almost unknown in girls (Scott, 1998).

About 1 in every 1500 males and 1 in every 2500 females has a sex-linked disorder called *fragile-X syndrome* (Amato, 1998). A person with this disorder has an X chromosome with a "fragile," or damaged, spot. Fragile-X syndrome can cause developmental delay that becomes progressively worse as a child gets older (Adesman, 1996). In fact, experts estimate that 5 to 7% of all developmentally delayed males have fragile-X syndrome (Zigler & Hodapp, 1991).

CHROMOSOMAL ERRORS

A variety of problems can be caused by a child having too many or too few chromosomes, a condition referred to as a *chromosomal error*, or *chromosomal anomaly*. Like genetic disorders, these are distinguished by whether they involve autosomes or sex chromosomes.

TRISOMIES A *trisomy* is a condition in which a child has three copies of a specific autosome. The most common is *trisomy 21*, or *Down syndrome*, in which the child has three copies of chromosome 21. The number of infants born with this anomaly has remained fairly constant in Canada, averaging one in 800 births (Mamayson, 2009). These children are intellectually delayed and have distinctive facial features and often other health concerns such as hypothyroidism, hearing loss, or heart anomalies.

This child shows the distinctive facial features of a child with Down syndrome.
(*Photo:* Mark Richards/PhotoEdit)

The risk of bearing a child with trisomy 21 is greatest for mothers over 35. Among Canadian women aged 35 to 39, the rate of Down syndrome is about 1 in 350 births. Among women 40 to 45, it climbs to 1 in 150 births and for women above age 45, Down syndrome is present in almost one-quarter of all births (Health Canada, 2002a). These figures underestimate the true rates by 15 to 24% because they exclude spontaneous abortions and terminated pregnancies (Benn & Egan, 2000).

Scientists have identified children with trisomies in the 13th and 18th pairs of chromosomes as well (Amato, 1998). These disorders have more severe effects than trisomy 21. Few trisomy 13 or trisomy 18 children live past the age of 1 year. As with trisomy 21, the chances of having a child with one of these disorders increase with a woman's age.

SEX-CHROMOSOME ANOMALIES A second class of anomalies is associated with the sex chromosomes. The most common is an XXY pattern, called *Klinefelter's syndrome,* which occurs in 1 or 2 out of every 1000 males (Amato, 1998). Affected boys usually look normal but have underdeveloped testes and, as adults, very low sperm production. Most are not intellectually delayed, but many have language and learning disabilities. At puberty, these boys experience both male and female changes. For example, their penises enlarge and their breasts develop.

A single-X pattern (X0), called *Turner's syndrome*, may also occur. Individuals with Turner's syndrome are anatomically female but show stunted growth and are usually sterile. Without hormone therapy, they do not menstruate or develop breasts at puberty. About one-quarter have serious heart anomalies (Amato, 1998). These girls also show an imbalance in their cognitive skills: They often perform particularly poorly on tests that measure spatial ability but usually perform at or above normal levels on tests of verbal skill (Golombok & Fivush, 1994).

Neither Klinefelter's nor Turner's syndrome is associated with the mother's age. However, older mothers are more likely to produce normal-appearing girls with an extra X chromosome and boys with an extra Y chromosome (Amato, 1998). Females with an XXX pattern, about 1 in every 1000 female births, are usually of normal size but develop more slowly than their peers (Amato, 1998). Many, though not all, have poor verbal abilities, score low on intelligence tests, and do more poorly in school than other groups with sex chromosome anomalies (Bender, Harmon, Linden, & Robinson, 1995).

Approximately 1 in 1000 boys has an extra Y chromosome. Most are taller than average and have large teeth. They usually experience normal puberty, and they have no difficulty fathering children (Amato, 1998). Developmentalists now know that it is only a myth that an extra Y chromosome causes below-average intelligence and high aggression (Tortora & Grabowski, 1993).

TERATOGENS: MATERNAL DISEASES

teratogens
substances such as viruses and drugs that can cause birth defects

Deviations in prenatal development can result from exposure to **teratogens,** agents that cause damage to an embryo or a fetus. The general rule is that each organ system is most vulnerable to harm when it is developing most rapidly (Moore & Persaud, 1993). Because most organ systems develop most rapidly during the first 8 weeks of gestation, this is the period when exposure to teratogens carries the greatest risk (see **Figure 3.4**). Because of space limitations, we will discuss only a few of the most significant teratogens. **Table 3.5** lists several others.

Several viruses pass through the placental filters and attack the embryo or fetus directly. For example, *rubella*, or *German measles*, causes a short-lived mild reaction in adults but may be deadly to a fetus. Most infants exposed to rubella in the first 4 to 5 weeks show some abnormality (Moore & Persaud, 1993). Deafness, cataracts, and heart anomalies are the most common ones.

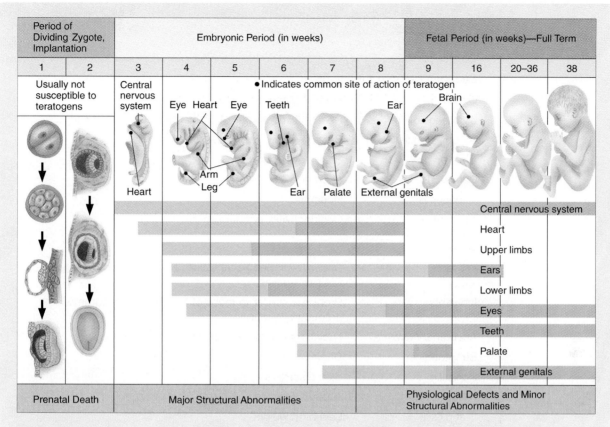

Figure 3.4

Sensitivity to teratogens peaks during the first eight weeks of gestation, although damage can occur throughout the prenatal period.

(*Source:* K.L. Moore & T.V.N. Persaud, 1998, *Before We Are Born* (5th ed.). Philadelphia, PA: Saunders, p. 166. Reprinted with permission from Elsevier.)

A much less well-known viral infection is *cytomegalovirus (CMV)*. CMV is in the herpes group and is transmitted through contact with body fluids, including saliva, breast milk, vaginal fluids, semen, urine, and stool. As many as 60% of all women carry CMV, but most have no recognizable symptoms. A recent Canadian study found that 0.2 to 2.4% of babies whose mothers are infected with CMV become infected prenatally (Vaudry, Lee, Rosychuk, & Pelletier, 2009). The highest risk for the fetus is when the mother is infected or has a reactivation of the infection during preganancy. About 10% of infected newborns display serious symptoms of CMV and have a variety of serious problems, including deafness, central nervous system damage and intellectual delay (Ontario Hospital Association, 2009; Vaudry et al., 2009). Another 5 to 17% of infected newborns who don't initially show symptoms later develop varying degrees of abnormality.

HIV, the virus that causes AIDS, is one of many sexually transmitted organisms that can be passed directly from mother to fetus. The virus can cross the placenta and enter the fetus's bloodstream, the infant may contract the virus in the birth canal during delivery, or the virus can be passed through the breast milk after delivery. Eighty-three percent of Canadian children (aged 0 to 14) with AIDS acquired the virus through these means (PHAC, 2006a). The rate of HIV infection among pregnant women in Canada's provinces is about 3 to 4 per 10 000 (Health Canada, 2004c). Moreover, one Canadian study found that six in 10 women who are infected with HIV intend to become pregnant in the future (Loutfy et al., 2009). Transmission appears to be more likely when the mother has AIDS than when she is HIV-positive but not yet ill (Abrams et al., 1995). In addition, Canadian researchers have demonstrated that

TABLE 3.5	Some Important Teratogens and Their Effects
Teratogens	**Possible Effects on Fetus**
Maternal Diseases/Infections	
Cancer	Fetal or placental tumour
Cytomegalovirus	Deafness, neurological problems, intellectual delay
Toxoplasmosis	Brain swelling, spinal abnormalities
Chicken pox	Scars, eye damage
Parvovirus	Anemia
Hepatitis B	Hepatitis
Chlamydia	Conjunctivitis, pneumonia
Drugs	
Warfarin	Underdeveloped nasal tissue, abnormal long bone growth, CNS anomalies
Inhalants	Problems similar to those of fetal alcohol syndrome, premature labour
Accutane/Vitamin A	Facial, ear, and heart deformities
Streptomycin	Deafness
Penicillin	Skin disorders
Tetracycline	Tooth deformities
Diet pills	Low birth weight

(*Sources:* Amato, 1998; Kliegman, 1998; Martinez, 2002).

HIV-positive pregnant women who take anti-HIV drugs in combination with Caesarean section birth and formula feeding have a markedly lower risk of transmitting the disease to their children (Robinson & Lee, 2000; Walmsley, 2003).

Infants who acquire HIV from their mothers typically become ill within the first 2 years of life (Prince, 1998). The virus weakens children's immune systems, allowing a host of other infectious agents, such as the bacteria that cause pneumonia and meningitis, to attack their bodies. Even children who remain symptom-free must restrict their exposure to viruses and bacteria. For example, HIV-positive children cannot be immunized with vaccines that utilize live viruses, such as the polio vaccine (Prince, 1998).

Other sexually transmitted diseases (STDs), including *syphilis*, *genital herpes*, and *gonorrhea*, cause a variety of congenital anomalies. Unlike most teratogens, the bacterium that causes syphilis is most harmful during the last 26 weeks of prenatal development and causes eye, ear, and brain anomalies. Genital herpes is usually passed from mother to infant during birth. One-third of infected babies die, and another 25 to 30% suffer blindness or brain damage. Thus, doctors usually advise surgical delivery for the babies of women who have herpes. Gonorrhea, which can cause the infant to be blind, is also usually transmitted during birth. For this reason, the eyes of newborns are usually treated with a special ointment that prevents damage from gonorrhea.

TERATOGENS: DRUGS

Any drug, including many whose safety we take for granted (e.g., antibiotics), can be teratogenic. That is why doctors always ask women of child-bearing age whether they might be pregnant before prescribing medication for them. Unless a drug is absolutely necessary to a woman's health, doctors recommend avoiding drugs of any kind during pregnancy. However, sorting out the effects of drugs (prescription and nonprescription, legal and illegal) on prenatal development has proven to be an immensely challenging task because many pregnant women take multiple drugs. Other factors, such as maternal stress, lack of social support, or poverty and poor prenatal care, also often accompany illegal drug use (Johnson, Nusbaum, Bejarano, & Rosen, 1999). Nevertheless, several drugs seem to affect infant development, independent of other variables.

You may have heard about the thalidomide tragedy that occurred in the 1960s. The drug involved was a mild tranquilizer that doctors prescribed to pregnant women who were experiencing severe symptoms of morning sickness. Sadly, the drug caused serious malformations of the limbs in thousands of fetuses that were exposed to it (Vogin, 2005).

Even relatively common prescription drugs used in the treatment of aniety and depression have been found to have teratogic effects (Calderon-Margalit, Qiu, Ornoy, Siscovick, & Williams, 2009). For example, benzodiazepine tranquilizers taken during pregnancy has been associated with an increased risk of preterm delivery, low birthweight, low Apgar score (see page 87), neonatal intensive-care–unit admissions, and respiratory distress syndrome. As well, selective serotonin reuptake inhibitors (SSRIs) were associated with preterm deliveries among women who started treatment after the first trimester.

In general, doctors advise against taking any unnecessary medicines during pregnancy. Nevertheless, some pregnant women must take drugs to treat health conditions that may be threatening to their own and their unborn child's life. For instance, pregnant women with epilepsy must take antiseizure medication because the seizures themselves are potentially harmful to their unborn children. Other drugs that pregnant women may have to risk taking, even though they can be harmful, include medications that treat heart conditions and diabetes, those that control asthma symptoms, and some kinds of psychiatric drugs. In all such cases, physicians weigh the benefits of medication against potential teratogenic effects and look for a combination of drug and dosage that will effectively treat the mother's health condition while placing her unborn child at minimal risk.

In contrast to prescription drugs, most people, pregnant or otherwise, take over-the-counter medicines on a casual, as-needed, basis without consulting a doctor. Many of these drugs, such as acetaminophen, are safe for pregnant women unless taken to excess (Organization of Teratology Information Specialists [OTIS], 2005). However, experts advise pregnant women to discuss the medicines they usually take with physicians at the outset of their pregnancies. These discussions should deal both with drugs and with any vitamins or supplements that the pregnant woman usually takes. Their doctors will advise them as to which of the substances are safe and which are risky. Often, too, physicians can suggest safer alternatives. Typically, most look to older drugs that have been thoroughly tested (Vogin, 2005).

TOBACCO Infants of mothers who smoke are on average about 150 grams lighter at birth than infants of nonsmoking mothers, and lower birth weight has a variety of potential negative consequences (Ghadirian, 2008; Health Canada, 2007a). For instance, pregnant women who smoke have higher rates of miscarriage, stillborn babies, premature birth, neonatal death, and low-birth weight babies (Osadchy, Kazmin, & Koren, 2009). Overall rates of smoking during pregnancy are on the decrease in Canada, but younger women (33%) are more likely to smoke during pregnancy than women over 30 (13%). Even among nonsmoking women, reportedly 36% of younger women and 13% of older women are regularly exposed to second-hand smoke during their pregnancy (Millar & Hill, 2004). Moreover, a recent Canadian study found that roughly twice as many Aboriginal as non-Aboriginal women smoked throughout their pregnancy (Heaman & Chalmers, 2005). In comparison, immigrant mothers had, by far, the lowest rates of smoking during pregnancy—just 2% smoked (Millar & Hill, 2004).

Watch

ALCOHOL Researchers have also documented the effects of alcohol on prenatal development. In fact, recent studies show that alcohol can even adversely affect an ovum prior to ovulation or during its journey down the fallopian tube to the uterus. Likewise, a zygote can be affected by alcohol even before it has been implanted in the uterine lining (Kaufman, 1997).

Children with fetal alcohol syndrome have distinctive features.
(*Photo*: © 2000 George Steinmetz)

Mothers who are heavy drinkers or alcoholics are at significant risk of delivering infants with *fetal alcohol syndrome (FAS)*. Children with FAS are generally smaller than normal, with smaller brains. They frequently have heart anomalies and hearing losses, and their faces are distinctive, with smallish-looking, wide-set eyes, a somewhat flattened nose, a thin upper lip, and often a long, flattened space between the nose and mouth (Bertrand et al., 2004; Sokol, Delaney-Black, & Nordstrom, 2007; Wedding et al., 2007). As children, adolescents, and adults, they are shorter than normal and have smaller heads, and their intelligence test scores indicate mild developmental delay. Children with FAS who are not intellectually delayed often have learning and behaviour difficulties (Bertrand et al., 2004; Chudley, 2006; Mattson & Riley, 1999).

The term *Fetal Alcohol Spectrum Disorders (FASD)* is often used to encompass a continuum of effects caused by the consumption of alcohol while pregnant. At one end, FASD includes FAS; at the other, it includes *Fetal Alcohol Effects (FAE)*, which characterizes the milder or partial adverse effects of ethanol. For example, a child with FAE may not exhibit the physical characteristics of FAS, but the secondary disabilities, such as mental health problems or behavioural and learning difficulties, will become apparent during childhood (Koren, Nulman, Chudley, & Loocke, 2003; Sokol et al., 2007; Wedding et al., 2007).

The overall alcohol consumption rate during pregnancy is coming down in Canada; roughly 14% of women reported consuming alcohol at some point during their pregnancy and 5% admitted to drinking throughout their pregnancy (Dell & Roberts, 2006). Both younger (under 21) and older Canadian women are more likely to consume alcohol during pregnancy than women 21 to 30 years of age (Dell & Roberts, 2006). Unfortunately, even moderate drinking by a pregnant woman may cause her child to have learning and behavioural difficulties in childhood and adolescence (Chudley, 2006). In the face of this evidence, the safest course for pregnant women is to drink no alcohol at all. In addition, women who are trying to become pregnant should abstain while they are trying to conceive, as women who do not discover their pregnancy immediately may inadvertently continue to drink well into their first trimester.

PSYCHOTROPIC DRUGS Both heroin and methadone, a drug often used in treating heroin addiction, can cause miscarriage, premature labour, and early death (Brockington, 1996). Further, 60 to 80% of babies born to heroin-addicted women are addicted to heroin as well. Addicted babies have high-pitched cries and suffer from withdrawal symptoms, such as irritability, uncontrollable tremors, vomiting, convulsions, and sleep problems. These symptoms may last as long as 4 months. Use of cocaine by pregnant women, in either powder or "crack" form, is linked to many kinds of developmental problems in their children (Ornoy, 2002). However, most cocaine-using pregnant women are poor and abuse multiple substances, making it difficult to separate the effects of cocaine from those of poverty and other drugs. Some studies suggest that cocaine alone has no long-term effects on cognitive or social development (Kilbride, Castor & Fuger, 2006; Kilbride, Castor, Hoffman, & Fuger, 2000).

Studies of the effects of marijuana use during pregnancy have yielded mixed results. Some studies have found a small reduction in birth weight (Centre for Addiction and Mental Health [CAMH], 2010a). To date, chemicals found in marijuana (i.e., THC) have not been implicated as a human teratogen. However, exposure to second-hand smoke should be taken into consideration both pre- and postnatally. As well, cannabis is excreted in moderate amounts in breast milk.

Ecstacy, a so-called "club drug", is another drug that is popular among young people. Of the few studies on the effects of club drugs, some have described an increased risk of congenital anomalies and spontaneous abortions, but other studies have found no such risks (CAMH, 2010b). Still, even though the effects of these drugs are not well established, their use should be avoided during pregnancy.

TERATOGENS: OTHER HARMFUL INFLUENCES ON PRENATAL DEVELOPMENT

Other factors that can adversely affect prenatal development include the mother's diet, her age, and her mental and physical health, as well as environmental factors such as pollution and radiation.

DIET Some specific nutrients are vital to prenatal development. One is folic acid, a B vitamin found in beans, spinach, and other foods. Inadequate amounts of this nutrient are linked to neural tube anomalies, such as *spina bifida* (Daly, Kirke, Molloy, Weir, & Scott, 1995). The potential negative effects of insufficient folic acid occur in the very earliest weeks of pregnancy, before a woman may know she is pregnant. To maximize prevention efforts, pre-conception measures are recommended: Women who could become pregnant should be consuming the equivalent of 0.4 milligrams of folic acid per day (Van Allen, McCourt, & Lee, 2002).

It is also important for a pregnant woman to take in sufficient overall calories and protein to prevent malnutrition. A woman who experiences malnutrition during pregnancy, particularly during the final 3 months, has an increased risk of delivering a low-birth-weight infant (under 2500 grams) who will have intellectual difficulties in childhood (Mutch, Leyland, & McGee, 1993). In addition, researchers have recently identified prenatal malnutrition, along with a variety of obstetrical complications, as an important risk factor in the development of mental illnesses in adulthood (Neugebauer, Hoek, & Susser, 1999; Susser & Lin, 1992).

The impact of maternal malnutrition appears to be greatest on the developing nervous system—a pattern found in studies of both humans and other mammals. For example, rats whose caloric intake has been substantially restricted during the fetal and early postnatal periods show a pattern described as *brain stunting*, in which both the weight and the volume of the brain are reduced. They also develop fewer dendrites and show less rich synaptic formation (Pollitt & Gorman, 1994).

Canadian weight-gain guidelines suggest that a woman with a normal weight based on the **body mass index (BMI)** (BMI is a ratio of weight to height) should gain 11.5 to 16.0 kilograms during a *singleton* pregnancy. Women who are underweight

body mass index (BMI)
a ratio of weight to height that estimates healthy and unhealthy body composition

should gain more weight than those who are overweight or obese (Health Canada, 2009b). Generally, if a woman follows the Eating Well with Canada's Food Guide (Health Canada, 2008a) recommendations for pregnant women from early in her pregnancy, she will likely maintain the necessary degree of weight gain.

AGE One intriguing trend in Canada over the past 20 years is that increasingly more women postpone their first pregnancy until their 30s (Bushnik & Garner, 2008). Roughly half of women giving birth in Canada are now aged 30 and older (Statistics Canada, 2009d). The average age of a woman giving birth in Canada has risen to 29.3 years, and 18.0% of women giving birth are aged 35 and older (Statistics Canada, 2009c).

In most cases, older mothers have uncomplicated pregnancies and deliver healthy babies, but the risks associated with pregnancy do increase somewhat as women get older (Bushnik & Garner, 2008; Martin et al., 2009; Vézina & Turcotte, 2009). Their babies are also at greater risk of weighing less than 2.5 kilograms at birth, a finding that is partly explained by the greater incidence of multiple births among older mothers. Still, infants born to women over the age of 35, whether single or multiple birth, are at higher risk of having problems such as heart malformations and chromosomal disorders.

At the other end of the age continuum, higher rates of congenital anomalies are seen in teenage mothers compared with mothers in their 20s (Chen, Wen, Fleming, Yang, & Walker, 2007; Evans & Fortier, 2006; Reefhuis & Honein, 2004). For example, teenage pregnancy is associated with a higher risk for non-chromosomal congenital anomalies such as neural tube and central nervous system anomalies, gastrointestinal system and female genitalia anomalies, and musculoskeletal/integumental (e.g., cleft lip/palate and club foot) anomalies. However, teenage mothers are also less likely to receive adequate prenatal care, have a healthy diet and sufficient multivitamin and folic acid intake, and avoid exposure to smoke, alcohol, and drugs. Canadian researchers emphasize that this makes it hard to sort out the causal factors, but it does point to the need for preventative measures where lifestyle factors contribute to negative outcomes for mother and baby (Chen et al., 2007; Langille, 2007).

CHRONIC ILLNESSES Chronic illnesses, whether emotional or physical, can also affect prenatal development. For example, long-term severe depression and other mood disorders can lead to slow fetal growth and premature labour (Weinstock, 1999). Moreover, developmentalists have learned that depressed mothers are less likely to feel attached to their fetuses. At least one study suggested that infants whose mothers do not develop a prenatal attachment to them are less socially responsive than other infants of the same age (Oates, 1998).

Conditions such as heart disease, diabetes, lupus, hormone imbalances, and epilepsy can also affect prenatal development negatively (Kliegman, 1998; McAllister, Kaplan, Edworthy, Martin, & Crawford, et al., 1997; Sandman, Wadhwa, Chicz-DeMet, Porto, & Garite, 1999). In fact, one of the most important goals of the new specialty of *fetal-maternal medicine* is to manage the pregnancies of women who have such conditions in ways that will support the health of both mother and fetus. For example, pregnancy often makes it impossible for a diabetic woman to keep her blood sugar levels under control. In turn, erratic blood sugar levels may damage the fetus's nervous system or cause it to grow too rapidly (Allen & Kisilevsky, 1999; Kliegman, 1998). To prevent such complications, a fetal-maternal specialist must find a diet, a medication, or a combination of the two that will stabilize the mother's blood sugar but will not harm the fetus. Similarly, fetal-maternal specialists help women who have epilepsy balance their own need for antiepileptic medication against possible harm to the fetus. Interestingly, Canadian researchers have found that recent immigrants experience fewer chronic health problems (the so-called "immigrant effect"), which is related to significantly lower prenatal complications, such as common placental disorders, in comparison to original residents (Ray, Vermeulen, Schull, Singh, Shah, & Redelmeier, 2007).

MATERNAL EMOTIONS Some psychologists have suggested that maternal emotions can affect prenatal development. Their rationale is that stressful psychological states such as anxiety and depression lead to changes in body chemistry. In a pregnant woman, these changes result in both qualitative and quantitative differences in the hormones and other chemicals to which the fetus is exposed.

⊙ Watch

One fairly consistent finding is that the fetuses of severely distressed mothers are more likely to have emotional or cognitive disorders later in childhood (Talge, Neal, & Glover, 2007). Developmentalists do not really know whether this effect results directly from emotion-related hormones or is an indirect effect of the mother's emotional state. A stressed or depressed mother may eat less, or her weakened immune system may limit her ability to fight off viruses and bacteria—either of these situations may retard fetal growth. Recent evidence suggests that providing stressed and at-risk pregnant women with social support and counselling during home visits by nurses can lead to improvements in prenatal and infant health and development, especially within high-risk families (Olds, Sadler, & Kitzman, 2007).

TERATOGENS: MUTAGENIC, ENVIRONMENTAL, AND EPIMUTAGENIC

Current research suggests that teratogens fall within three broad categories: mutagenic, environmental, and unknown (Brent, 2004a). Researchers suspect that much of the unknown category is composed of epigenetic factors and that a single teratogen may fit more than one category.

MUTAGENIC TERATOGENS One group of teratogens is composed of **mutagens**, agents that cause alterations (mutations) to *genomic* DNA. Exposure to mutagens, such as radiation and biological or chemical toxins, can cause *germinal mutations* that interfere with both conception and the normal development of the embryo and the fetus. For example, if gametes are exposed to high levels of X-rays, then infertility can result, but if conception does occur, then the resulting genetic mutation can lead to a failure to implant or a miscarriage (Brent, 2004b; Edwards, n.d.; Finnell, 1999; Kalter, 2003; Mutagens, 1995). In other instances, embryos that are exposed to mutagens may develop *somatic mutations*—chromosomal or genetic errors that can cause congenital anomalies that can be transmitted to future generations (Finnell, 1999; Prasad, Cole, & Hasse, 2004).

mutagens
agents that cause changes (mutations) in genomic DNA

ENVIRONMENTAL TERATOGENS Environmental agents can have direct, non-heritable effects on prenatal development by damaging cells or disrupting normal cell development (Brent, 2004b; Finnell, Waes, Eudy, & Rosenquist, 2002; Kalter, 2003). These agents may interfere with normal **cell proliferation** in the embryo (the formation of specific body tissues, such as neurons, muscles, and bones) or with **cell migration** (the movement of differentiated cells to their genetically predetermined location; for example, when neural cells migrate along the threads of glial cells to their proper location in the brain). They can also cause cellular *structural* and *functional abnormalities* (the destruction or degeneration of cells; for example, when damaged neurons disrupt neural networks in the brain).

cell proliferation
the increase in cell numbers by means of cell growth and cell division

cell migration
the movement of cells to their genetically predetermined destinations in the body

EPIMUTAGENIC TERATOGENS Mutagens account for about 15 to 25% of congenital anomalies, and environmental factors account for another 10% (Brent, 2004a).

epimutagens
agents that cause abnormal
gene silencing or expression
without changing the
genomic DNA

That leaves more than two-thirds unaccounted for, but scientists suspect that a large proportion of these "unknown" factors may turn out to be epigenetic in nature (Holliday, 1998, 2006; Horsthemke, 2006; Jiang, Bressler, & Beaudet, 2004; Martin, Ward, & Suter, 2005; Szyf, 2009). **Epimutagens** are agents that cause alterations (epimutations) to epigenetic structures without changing the genomic DNA. In most cases, any *teratogenic* damage is limited to an individual in only one generation because any acquired epimutations are usually reset following conception. In other instances, however, some acquired epimutations can be passed on to the next generation and sometimes beyond (Calvanese, Lara, Kahn, & Fraga, 2009; Feil, 2006, 2008; Fraga, 2009; Herceg, 2007; Trasler, 2009). Animal studies, for example, have shown that a mother's diet can produce enduring changes on successive generations independent of later changes in diet of the offspring (Cropley, Suter, Beckman, & Martin, 2006). There is now good reason to believe that our current dietary habits may, by means of *epimutagenic* processes, have an impact on "grandchildren who will be born decades from now, independent of the diets that their parents consume" (Cropley et al., 2006, p. 17311).

PATERNAL INFLUENCES: PRECONCEPTUAL AND PRENATAL

Scientists have not researched the father's role in reproductive risk as well as they have researched the mother's; however, researchers suspect that at least a portion of the unknown causes of malformations—which account for 60% of all malformations—are related to paternal factors (Trasler & Doerksen, 1999). Some of the existing research has focused on how the production, abnormalities, or performance of sperm contributes to conditions such as infertility, decreased fertility, miscarriage, and congenital anomalies (OTIS, 2010). Epidemiological studies have shown that there is a higher reproductive risk associated with men working in specific occupations, such as janitors, painters, printers, firefighters, and woodworkers, as well as occupations related to agriculture, such as farmers, gardeners, and butchers, and the art and textile industries (Chia & Shi, 2002; Fear, Hey, Vincent, & Murphy, 2007; Regidor, Ronda, Garcia, & Dominguez, 2004; Trasler & Doerksen, 1999). Paternal exposure to toxic substances, including heavy metals (e.g., lead and mercury), solvents, wood preservatives, pesticides, hydrocarbons, and radiation, is suspected of producing male-mediated teratogenic and mutagenic effects (Chia & Shi, 2002; OTIS, 2010; Trasler & Doerksen, 1999).

Sperm adversely affected up to 3 months before conception can impact the prenate. Genetic effects (gene mutation and chromosomal abnormality) and epigenetic effects (altered gene expression) have the greatest impact during the first two trimesters of pregnancy. The means of contaminating the mother and prenate may involve toxins in seminal fluids that can be transmitted after intercourse or indirect exposure by way of toxic agents transmitted from work clothes, shoes, and equipment that are brought into the home (Trasler & Doerksen, 1999). DNA damage to sperm resulting in genetic and chromosomal changes after fertilization has been shown to contribute to congenital and genetic anomalies in offspring as well as to childhood cancer (Sartorius & Nieschlag, 2010; Schmid et al., 2007). Concerns have also been raised regarding the impact the father's age. For example, evidence links adverse birth outcomes and congenital anomalies with both teenage fathers (Chen et al., 2008; Yang et al., 2007) and, at the other end of the age spectrum, older fathers (Green et al., 2010; Sartorius & Nieschlag, 2010; Schmid et al., 2007; Yang et al., 2007).

Physical abuse of the mother during pregnancy is another serious threat to maternal and child health. It can lead to premature labour, a premature breaking away of the placenta from the uterine wall, and/or low birth weight (Murphy, Schei, Myhr, & Du Mont, 2001). Canadian researchers have reported that the prevalence of physical abuse increases during pregnancy, affecting roughly 6% of pregnant Canadian women

(Cox et al., 2004; Muhajarine & D'Arcy, 1999; Murphy et al., 2001). One Canadian study found that almost two-thirds of the violence was perpetrated by a pregnant woman's husband, boyfriend, or ex-husband (Muhajarine & D'Arcy, 1999). Abuse during pregnancy is preventable, and perhaps the place to start intervening would be to screen newly pregnant women or women planning to conceive for potential abuse along with other preventable lifestyle risk factors such as maternal smoking and unhealthy nutrition during pregnancy (Campbell, 2001; Sarkar, 2008).

FETAL ASSESSMENT AND TREATMENT

Genetic counsellors help women who are at risk of bearing a child with a congenital anomaly to understand potential outcomes and choices. Preconception and first trimester screening procedures assay the potential for developmental complications and determine if prenatal diagnostic testing is warranted or even desired. If diagnostic tests are performed and they detect abnormal results, then a genetics counsellor can help the mother and her family make informed decisions about her options.

Certain diagnostic tests, including *chorionic villus sampling (CVS)* and *amniocentesis*, can be used to identify chromosomal errors and many genetic disorders prior to birth (see **Figure 3.5**). With CVS, cells are extracted from the placenta and used in a variety of laboratory tests during the early weeks of prenatal development. With amniocentesis, which is done between weeks 14 and 16 of a woman's pregnancy, a needle is used to extract amniotic fluid containing fetal cells. Fetal cells filtered out of the fluid are then tested in a variety of ways to diagnose chromosomal and genetic disorders. In addition, ultrasound technology is useful in monitoring fetal growth during high-risk pregnancies.

In addition, many laboratory tests use maternal blood, urine, and/or samples of amniotic fluid to help health care providers monitor fetal development. For example,

PEARSON mydevelopmentlab
Connect to MyDevelopmentLab
See what the chorionic villus sampling procedure looks like on an ultrasound.
👁 Watch

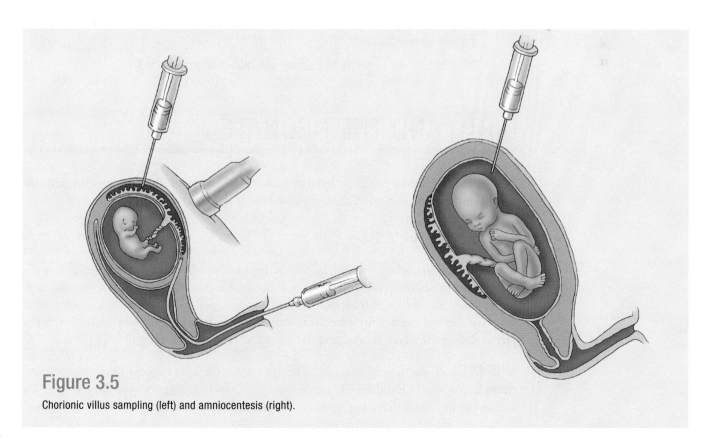

Figure 3.5
Chorionic villus sampling (left) and amniocentesis (right).

the presence of a substance called *alpha-fetoprotein* in a pregnant woman's blood is associated with a number of prenatal anomalies, including abnormalities in the brain and the spinal cord. Doctors can also use a laboratory test to assess the maturity of fetal lungs (Kliegman, 1998). This test is critical when doctors advise early delivery of a baby because of the mother's health.

Fetoscopy involves insertion of a tiny camera into the womb to directly observe fetal development. Fetoscopy makes it possible for doctors to correct some kinds of anomalies surgically (Kliegman, 1998). Likewise, fetoscopy has made techniques such as fetal blood transfusions and bone marrow transplants possible. Specialists also use fetoscopy to take samples of blood from the umbilical cord. Laboratory tests performed on fetal blood samples can assess fetal organ function, diagnose genetic and chromosomal disorders, and detect fetal infections (Curry, 2002). For example, fetal blood tests can help doctors identify a bacterial infection that is causing a fetus to grow too slowly. Once diagnosed, the infection can be treated by injecting antibiotics into the amniotic fluid (so that they will be swallowed by the fetus) or into the umbilical cord (Kliegman, 1998).

Researchers have examined how prenatal diagnosis affects parents-to-be. Compared with parents of 1-year-olds with disabilities who did not know about the problems prior to birth, parents whose infants' difficulties were diagnosed prenatally report greater feelings of stress and depression (Hunfeld et al., 1999). However, specialists in fetal medicine suggest that the negative emotional effects of prenatal diagnosis can be moderated by providing parents-to-be with counselling and specific information about treatment at the time the diagnosis is made, rather than waiting until after the birth.

Before Going On

- Briefly describe the known and suspected causes of congenital anomalies and adverse birth outcomes.
- What options are available to women with high-risk pregnancies?

BIRTH AND THE NEONATE

Once gestation is complete, the fetus must be born—an event that holds some pain for the mother as well as a good deal of joy for most parents.

BIRTH CHOICES

In most places around the world, tradition dictates how babies are delivered. However, in industrialized countries, especially in Canada, hospital deliveries became routine in the second half of the 20th century. Today, though, parents have several choices as to who will attend their baby's birth, whether medication will be used to manage the physical discomforts of labour and delivery, and where the birth will take place.

MIDWIVES Midwifery is a regulated health care profession in most provinces and territories in Canada. Midwife practice involves assessing, supervising, and caring for women prior to and during pregnancy, labour, and the postpartum period. A midwife is

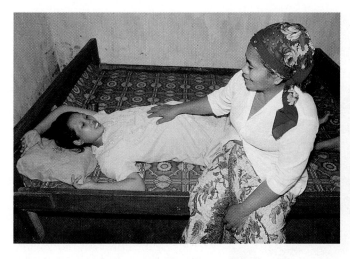
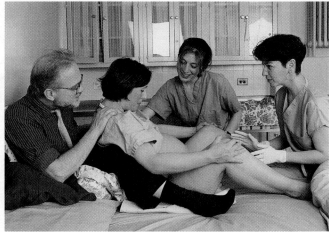

In the developing world, tradition determines where a baby is born and who attends its birth. Hospital deliveries are common in Canada, but many hospitals offer parents the option of delivering their babies in nonsurgical settings such as the birthing room pictured on the right. (*Photos:* left, Sean Sprague/Stock Boston; right, © Margaret Miller, 1992/Photo Researchers)

licensed to conduct deliveries and to care for the newborn infant. To become a midwife in Canada, one must graduate from a midwifery education program at a recognized institution.

DRUGS DURING LABOUR AND DELIVERY   One key decision for expectant mothers concerns whether to use drugs during labour and delivery. *Analgesics* may be given during labour to reduce pain. *Sedatives* or *tranquillizers* can be administered to reduce anxiety. *Anaesthesia*, when used, is usually given later in labour to block pain, either totally (by using general anaesthesia) or in certain portions of the body (by using local anaesthesia).

Studying the causal links between drug use during labour and delivery and the baby's later behaviour or development has proven to be difficult. First, it's clear that nearly all drugs given during labour pass through the placenta, enter the fetal bloodstream, and may remain there for several days. Not surprisingly, then, infants whose mothers have received any type of drug are typically slightly more sluggish, gain a little less weight, and spend more time sleeping in the first few weeks than do infants of non-drugged mothers (Maurer & Maurer, 1988).

Second, there are no consistently observed effects from analgesics and tranquillizers beyond the first few days, and only a few studies hint at the long-term effects of anaesthesia (Rosenblith, 1992). Given such inconclusive findings, only one specific piece of advice seems warranted: If you are a new mother who receives medication during childbirth, bear in mind that your baby is also drugged, and that this will affect her behaviour in the first few days. If you allow for this effect and realize that it will wear off, your long-term relationship with your child is likely to be unaffected.

Nevertheless, many women choose to avoid drugs altogether. The general term *natural childbirth* is commonly used to refer to this particular choice. This approach is also often called the *Lamaze method*, after the physician who popularized the notion of natural childbirth and devised a variety of pain management techniques. In natural childbirth, women rely on psychological and behavioural methods of pain management rather than on pain-relieving drugs.

Natural childbirth involves several components. First, a woman selects someone, typically the baby's father or another supportive person, to serve as a labour coach. *Prepared childbirth classes* psychologically prepare the woman and her labour coach for the experience of labour and delivery. For example, they learn to use the term *contraction* instead of *pain*. Further, believing that her baby will benefit from natural childbirth provides the woman with the motivation she needs to endure labour without

Many fathers take prenatal classes like this one so that they can provide support to their partners during labour.
(*Photo:* © Purestock/Getty Images.)

the aid of pain-relieving medication. Finally, relaxation and breathing techniques provide her with behavioural responses to contractions that serve to replace the negative emotions that typically result from physical discomfort. Aided by her coach, the woman focuses attention on her breathing rather than on the pain.

THE LOCATION OF BIRTH

Another choice parents must make is where the baby is to be born. In most of the industrialized world, women deliver their babies in specialized maternity clinics. However, in Canada there are four alternatives in most communities:

- A traditional hospital maternity unit

- A birth centre or birthing room located within a hospital, which provides a more homelike setting for labour and delivery and often allows family members to be present throughout the birth

- A free-standing birth centre, like a hospital birth centre except that it is located apart from the hospital, with delivery typically attended by a midwife rather than (or in addition to) a physician

- The mother's home

Most babies in Canada are born in hospitals. Home deliveries are appropriate for uncomplicated pregnancies during which the woman has received good prenatal care. When these conditions are met, with a trained birth attendant present at delivery, the rate of home delivery complications or infant problems in Canada is no higher than for hospital deliveries (Janssen et al., 2009).

THE PHYSICAL PROCESS OF BIRTH

Labour is typically divided into three stages (see **Figure 3.6**). Stage 1 covers the period during which two important processes occur: dilation and effacement. The cervix (the opening at the bottom of the uterus) must open up like the lens of a camera (*dilation*) and also flatten out (*effacement*). At the time of actual delivery, the cervix must normally be dilated to about 10 centimetres.

Customarily, stage 1 is itself divided into phases. In the *early* (or *latent*) phase, contractions are relatively far apart and typically not too uncomfortable. In the *active* phase, which begins when the cervix is 3 to 4 centimetres dilated and continues until dilation has reached 8 centimetres, contractions are closer together and more intense. The last 2 centimetres of dilation are achieved during a phase usually called *transition*. It is this phase, when contractions are closely spaced and strong, that women typically find the most painful. Fortunately, transition is also ordinarily the shortest phase.

Figure 3.7 shows the typical length of these various phases of labour for first births and later births. What the figure does not convey is the wide individual variability that exists. Among women delivering a first child, stage 1 may last as few as 3 hours or as many as 20 (Biswas & Craigo, 1994; Kilpatrick & Laros, 1989).

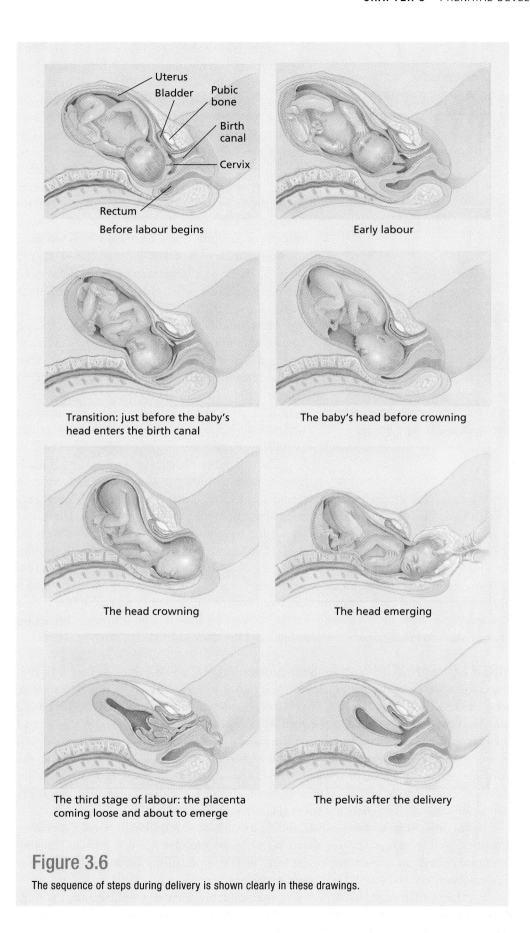

Before labour begins

Early labour

Transition: just before the baby's head enters the birth canal

The baby's head before crowning

The head crowning

The head emerging

The third stage of labour: the placenta coming loose and about to emerge

The pelvis after the delivery

Figure 3.6

The sequence of steps during delivery is shown clearly in these drawings.

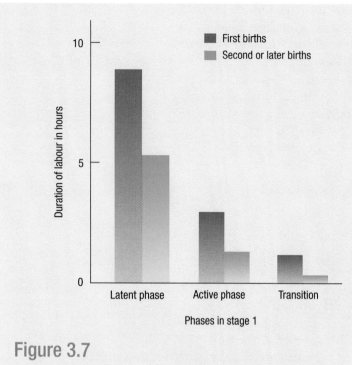

Figure 3.7

Typical pattern of the stages of labour for first births and subsequent births.

(*Source:* Based on Biswas & Craigo, 1994, from Figures 10–16, p. 216 and 10–17, p. 217.)

At the end of the transition phase, the mother will normally have the urge to help the infant emerge by "pushing." When the birth attendant (physician or midwife) is sure the cervix is fully dilated, she or he will encourage this pushing, and stage 2 of labour, the actual delivery, begins. The baby's head moves past the stretched cervix, into the birth canal, and finally out of the mother's body. Most women find this part of labour markedly less distressing than the transition phase because at this point they can assist the delivery process by pushing. Stage 2 typically lasts less than an hour and rarely takes longer than 2 hours. Stage 3, also typically quite brief, is the delivery of the placenta (also called the *afterbirth*) and other material from the uterus.

Most infants are delivered head first, facing toward the mother's spine; 3 to 4%, however, are oriented differently, either feet first or bottom first (called *breech* presentations) (Brown, Karrison, & Cibils, 1994). In Canada today, infants in breech positions are nearly all delivered through an abdominal incision (a *Caesarean section*) rather than vaginally.

Though most physicians agree that a breech presentation requires a Caesarean delivery, the procedure itself is somewhat controversial. Critics argue that the operation is often performed unnecessarily. There are concerns about possible increased risk due to complications and the increased health care cost arising from unnecessary Caesarean sections. In the late 1960s, only about 5% of babies in Canada were delivered by Caesarean section. By 2001, the frequency of surgical delivery had risen above 21% (Health Canada, 2003a), among the highest in the world. The Society of Obstetricians and Gynaecologists of Canada does not promote Caesarean section on demand and recommends that the decision to have an elective Caesarean delivery be based on an informed discussion about risks and benefits between a woman and her doctor (SOGC, 2004).

BIRTH COMPLICATIONS During the process of birth, some babies go into *fetal distress*, signalled by a sudden change in heart rate. In most cases, doctors don't know why a baby experiences fetal distress. However, one cause of distress is pressure on the umbilical cord. For example, if the cord becomes lodged between the baby's head and the cervix, each contraction will push the baby's head against the cord. The collapsed blood vessels can no longer carry blood to and from the baby. When this happens, the baby experiences **anoxia**, or oxygen deprivation. Anoxia can result in death or brain damage, but doctors can prevent long-term effects by acting quickly to surgically deliver infants who experience distress (Handley-Derry et al., 1997).

Infants may also dislocate their shoulders or hips during birth. Some experience fractures, and in others, nerves that control facial muscles are compressed, causing temporary paralysis on one side of the face. Such complications are usually not serious and resolve themselves with little or no treatment.

If a labouring woman's blood pressure suddenly increases or decreases, a Caesarean delivery may be indicated. In addition, some women's labour progresses so

anoxia
oxygen deprivation experienced by a fetus during labour and/or delivery

slowly that they remain in stage 1 for more than 24 hours. This can happen if the infant's head is in a position that prevents it from exerting enough pressure on the cervix to force it open. In such cases, surgery is often indicated, because continuing labour can cause permanent damage to the mother's body.

After giving birth, most women require a period of a month or so to recover. During this time, the mother's body experiences a variety of hormonal changes, including those required for nursing and for returning to the normal menstrual cycle. A few women experience a period of depression after giving birth (a potential problem that you will read more about in the chapters on early adulthood). However, most recover quickly, both physically and emotionally, from the ordeal of pregnancy and birth.

ASSESSING THE NEONATE

A baby is referred to as a **neonate** for the first month of life. The health of babies born in hospitals and birthing centres, as well as most who are delivered at home by professional midwives, is usually assessed with the *Apgar scale* (Apgar, 1953). The baby receives a score of 0, 1, or 2 on each of five criteria, listed in **Table 3.6**. A maximum score of 10 is fairly unusual immediately after birth, because most infants are still somewhat blue in the fingers and toes at that stage. At a second assessment, usually 5 minutes after birth, however, 85 to 90% of infants score 9 or 10. Any score of 7 or better indicates that the baby is in no danger. A score of 4, 5, or 6 usually means that the baby needs help establishing normal breathing patterns; a score of 3 or below indicates a baby in critical condition.

neonate
baby between birth and 1 month of age

Standard screening procedures across Canada have been expanded to include the detection of rare metabolic disorders in newborns (Dyack, 2004). New *tandem mass spectrometry* technology is capable of running multiple tests at the same time in an efficient and cost-effective way. This test means that inborn metabolic anomalies can now be detected presymptomatically, which allows for early treatment measures and better outcomes for infants and their families.

Health professionals often use the *Brazelton Neonatal Behavioral Assessment Scale* to track a newborn's development over the first 2 weeks or so following birth (Brazelton & Nugent, 1995). A health professional examines the neonate's responses to stimuli, reflexes, muscle tone, alertness, cuddliness, and ability to quiet or soothe himself after being upset. Scores on this test can be helpful in identifying children who may have significant neurological problems.

TABLE 3.6 The Apgar Scale

Aspect Observed	Score Assigned		
	0	1	2
Heart rate	Absent	< 100 beats per minute	> 100 beats per minute
Respiratory rate	No breathing	Weak cry and shallow breathing	Good cry and regular breathing
Muscle tone	Flaccid	Some flexion of extremities	Well-flexed extremities
Response to stimulation of feet	None	Some motion	Crying
Colour	Blue, pale	Body pink, extremities blue	Completely pink

(*Source:* **Francis, Self, & Horowitz, 1987, pp. 731–732.**)

A new developmental screening tool developed in Canada, the *Nipissing District Developmental Screen* (NDDS), is a comprehensive screening tool that assists professionals and parents to identify various aspects of a child's development that may require early intervention. The NDDS can be used with children aged 1 month to 6 years to screen for problems in any of these critical areas: vision, hearing, speech, language, communication, gross motor, fine motor, cognitive, social/emotional, and self-help. This culturally sensitive tool is now being used in many jurisdictions across Canada and is available in English, French, Spanish, Chinese, and Vietnamese. (**NDDS** webpage: www.ndds.ca).

LOW BIRTH WEIGHT

low birth weight (LBW)
newborn weight below 2500 grams

Classification of a neonate's weight is another important factor in assessment. All neonates below 2500 grams are classified as having **low birth weight (LBW)**. The proportion of LBW infants is relatively stable in Canada, ranging between 5.4 and 5.7% of newborns, but hospitalization rates are higher for LBW infants and the incidence of illness and mortality is also elevated (Canadian Institute of Child Health, 2000a).

Most LBW infants are *preterm*, or born before the 38th week of gestation. However, it is possible for an infant to have completed 38 weeks or more of gestation and still be an LBW baby. In addition, some preterm babies weigh the right amount for their gestational age, while others are smaller than expected. These *small-for-date* neonates appear to have suffered from retarded fetal growth and, as a group, have poorer prognoses than do infants who weigh an appropriate amount for their gestational age.

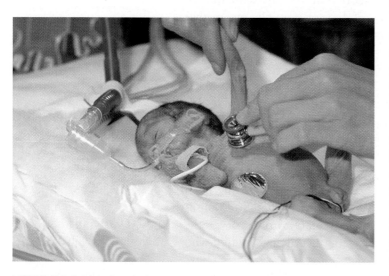

LBW infants' chances of survival are better when they receive care in a neonatal intensive care unit. (*Photo:* Susan Leavines/Photo Researchers)

LBW infants display markedly lower levels of responsiveness at birth and in the early months of life. Those born more than 6 weeks early also often suffer from *respiratory distress syndrome* (also referred to as *hyaline membrane disease*). Their poorly developed lungs cause serious breathing difficulties. In 1990, physicians began treating this problem by administering surfactant (the chemical that makes it possible for the lungs to exchange oxygen and carbon dioxide in the blood) to preterm neonates, a therapy that has reduced the rate of death among very-low-birth-weight infants by about 30% (Corbet, Long, Schumacher, Gerdes, & Cotton, 1995; Schwartz, Anastasia, Scanlon, & Kellogg, 1994).

The majority of LBW babies who weigh more than 1500 grams and who are not small-for-date catch up to their normal peers within the first few years of life. But those below 1500 grams remain smaller than normal and have significantly higher rates of long-term health problems, lower intelligence test scores, and more problems in school (Breslau et al., 1994; Breslau, Johnson, & Lucia, 2001; Weindrich, Jennen-Steinmetz, Laucht, & Schmidt, 2003). In fact, 40 to 50% of such babies show some kind of significant problem later.

An LBW neonate's general health also makes a difference. For example, LBW babies who experience bleeding in the brain immediately after birth are more likely to have later problems (Bendersky & Lewis, 1994). The economic circumstances of an LBW infant's family matter as well. Children in low-income families are more likely to

Critical Thinking

What three pieces of advice would you give a pregnant friend after reading this chapter?

suffer from long-term effects of low birth weight, such as attention problems, than are those who grow up in more affluent homes (Breslau & Chilcoat, 2000).

Boys are more likely than girls to show long-term effects of low birth weight. In fact, one recent study involving more than 700 6-year-olds found a higher rate of learning disabilities and other problems in LBW boys than among their normal-birth-weight (NBW) peers (Johnson & Breslau, 2000). By contrast, LBW girls did not differ at all from their NBW counterparts. The difference between LBW and NBW boys persisted when they were examined again at age 11.

Before Going On

- What happens in each of the three stages of labour?
- Explain how neonates are assessed, and list the risks of low birth weight.

Summary

Conception

- At conception, the 23 chromosomes from the sperm join with the 23 chromosomes from the ovum to make up the set of 46 that will be reproduced in each cell of the new individual.
- Fertility drugs, in vitro fertilization, and artificial insemination are used for assisted human reproduction.

Pregnancy and Prenatal Development

- Prenatal development occurs in three stages of unequal length (germinal, embryonic, fetal) that are marked by specific developmental milestones.
- The fetus is responsive to stimuli and appears to learn in the womb. Prenatal temperamental differences (for example, activity level) persist into infancy and childhood, and some aspects of the prenatal sensory environment may be important to future development.

Issues in Prenatal Development

- Genes for specific diseases can cause a variety of disorders at conception.
- Abnormal numbers of chromosomes or damage to chromosomes causes a number of serious disorders, including Down syndrome.

- Teratogens can change genomic DNA, damage cell structure and function, and alter epigenetic structures.
- Several methods of prenatal diagnosis and treatment of congenital anomalies or fetal abnormalities have become available in recent years.

Birth and the Neonate

- Most babies are delivered by physicians in Canada; however, midwifery care is becoming more available. In uncomplicated low-risk pregnancies, delivery at home or in a birthing centre is as safe as hospital delivery.
- The normal birth process has three parts: dilation and effacement, delivery, and placental delivery. Most drugs given to the mother during delivery pass through to the infant's bloodstream and have short-term effects on infant responsiveness and feeding patterns.
- Neonates weighing less than 2500 grams are designated as having low birth weight. The lower the weight, the greater the risk of significant lasting problems, such as low intelligence test scores or learning disabilities.

Review Questions

Answers are provided on MyDevelopmentLab in the Course Resources folder.

Conception

3.1 A scientist examines a cell under a microscope and finds only 23 chromosomes. Which of the following conclusions would a logical scientist make?
   a. The cell is not a human cell because all human cells have 46 chromosomes.
   b. The cell could be a human cell, but would have chromosomal abnormalities or mutations.
   c. The cell is in a stage of development when it is normal for cells to have only half of their genes.
   d. The cell is a gamete.

Pregnancy and Prenatal Development

3.2 Why is prenatal care during the first trimester important?
   a. It can help identify women with gestational diabetes.
   b. It can ensure that the pregnant woman is gaining enough weight to nourish the growing fetus.
   c. It can identify ectopic pregnancies.
   d. It can identify women at risk for toxemia of pregnancy.

Issues in Prenatal Development

3.3 Which of the following factors would put a couple at risk for having a child with trisomy 21?
   a. the woman being under age 21
   b. the woman being over age 45
   c. the man being over age 45
   d. the couple being in a higher socioeconomic status group

3.4 Which of the following is *not* an accurate statement? Epimutations
   a. may account for a large percentage of congenital anomalies.
   b. can be acquired prenatally.
   c. can be inherited.
   d. cause changes to genomic DNA.

Birth and the Neonate

3.5 Which of the following would be true of an infant who has received a score of 10 on the Apgar scale?
   a. The infant was most likely delivered by Caesarean section.
   b. The infant is in need of immediate resuscitation to establish a normal breathing pattern.
   c. The infant is most likely 5 minutes old.
   d. The infant is in critical condition.

Critical-Thinking Questions

3.6 What are some of the reasons why women become emotionally attached to the fetus during the third trimester?

3.7 New technology developed at Toronto's Hospital for Sick Children can screen a newborn's first bowel movement (meconium) for telltale signs that a mother drank too much alcohol during her pregnancy, thus putting her baby at risk for Fetal Alcohol Spectrum Disorder (FASD). Early detection can aid early intervention, but detractors say universal automatic testing is a violation of a mother's rights and comes too late to prevent harm to the baby. What are some key pros and cons of standard meconium testing for both mother and baby?

Policy Question

What Legal Protection Exists for the Pregnant Mother and Her Fetus?

Society has developed laws to protect a person's rights while prescribing consequences for those who violate those rights. In the case of a pregnant woman and her fetus, society wants to act in the best interests of both. However, because of the integral relationship between mother and fetus, we are sometimes faced with a legal dilemma when their respective needs conflict. The relationship between mother and fetus from a physical point of view seems obvious, but when we try to define the relationship in legal terms we are faced with an imperfect description of that relationship.

We can look to the history of Canadian law for guidance regarding what behaviour constitutes a criminal act. The Canadian *Criminal Code* specifies what acts against a human being are criminal acts, but it does not recognize the fetus as a human being and therefore we do not have laws that recognize the killing of a fetus as homicide or infanticide. This state of affairs has a long tradition that is based in the common law, which did not recognize a fetus as a person until it was born alive. This line of thinking was incorporated into the first Canadian *Criminal Code* of 1892 and persists to this day. There have been laws against procuring a miscarriage (an abortion), and, in 1969, Section 287 of the *Criminal Code* made abortions illegal. However, doctors were exempted from prosecution if a hospital ethical review committee deemed that the mother's health or life was endangered if she carried the fetus to full term. In 1982, the *Canadian Charter of Rights and Freedoms* stated in Section 7 that "everyone has the right to life, liberty and security of the

person and the right not to be deprived thereof . . . ." At about the same time, Henry Morgentaler was testing the "lawfulness" of the abortion law of the day by setting up nonhospital abortion clinics. In 1988, his case went before the Supreme Court of Canada, which ruled that the abortion law violated Section 7 of the *Charter* in that the law interfered with a woman's body and liberty. As a result, the abortion law, Section 287 (Department of Justice Canada, 2001a), was modified. This essentially decriminalized abortions, and by implication a fetus is not protected under the Charter. Henceforth, abortions, at any stage of pregnancy, have not been prohibited in Canada.

At the end of the 20th century, this turn of events led to some challenging legal questions with regard to the rights of a pregnant woman versus the status and well-being of her fetus. Three court challenges in particular exemplify the difficulty we have in deciding what to do when a fetus, and subsequently a child that has been born, are at risk of harm.

What is the legal status of the pregnant mother and her fetus in Canada? The three court cases supply clues.

The first case involved the Winnipeg Child Family Services and a woman who was 5 months pregnant. The agency wanted to detain her in a health centre for treatment of her glue-sniffing addiction until her child was born because glue sniffing can produce permanent nervous-system damage in the developing fetus. Two of the woman's three children had already been made wards of the state at birth because they had been born with brain damage associated with

glue sniffing. The intention of the social agency was to protect the health of the fetus until it was born, but in doing so it was judged to be in violation of the mother's rights and freedom.

The case made its way to the Supreme Court of Canada, which, in 1997, ruled that the mother's rights prevail over those of the fetus. The decision was based on the *Charter of Rights and Freedoms*, which in its present form applies only to human beings (not to fetuses). Therefore, in this instance, protecting the fetus by detaining the mother for treatment violated the liberties of the mother. Moreover, it was noted that if this mother could be detained for sniffing glue, then the ruling could be extended and applied to all pregnant women. It would set a precedent that would allow pregnant

(Photo: Thinkstock)

women to be scrutinized and incarcerated for lifestyle choices that allegedly cause harm to the fetus. This leads to questions about who would set the standard for appropriate maternal behaviour. The judgment in this case reaffirmed that a fetus has no legal rights (although a fetus does retain a moral right to be treated well).

The second case, Dobson v. Dobson, involved a New Brunswick woman who was 27 weeks pregnant. She had been driving on a snow-covered road when she lost control and collided with a pickup truck. The child, a boy, was later delivered by Caesarean section and has permanent mental and physical problems attributable to the accident. The mother's father was suing her for negligence on behalf of the boy. There was already a legal precedent that permits legal action to be taken by a child born alive against a third party for injuries that the child incurred while in the womb. For example, children of mothers who took thalidomide for morning sickness in the 1950s were able to receive compensation from the manufacturer of the drug. The drug caused birth defects such as missing or deformed limbs, which limited the children's ability to have a full life. The courts were asked to decide if the mother in Dobson v. Dobson could be sued as if she were a third party to the case. The New Brunswick Courts ruled that the boy was indeed entitled to compensation. An appeal of this ruling was sent to the Supreme Court in 1999 and was overturned on several grounds. It was noted that the relationship between a mother and her fetus is unlike any other.

Mother and fetus are essentially one until birth. Therefore, no analogy can be made between the role of the mother and that of a third party in terms of any damage committed upon the fetus. Furthermore, there is no practical way to determine what standard of care a pregnant mother should have to live up to in caring for her fetus that wouldn't violate her privacy and autonomy.

The third case concerned Brenda Drummond, an Ontario woman who was charged with attempted murder and failing to provide the necessities of life. The woman apparently kept her pegnancy hidden from co-workers and her husband, and late in her pregnancy she fired a pellet through her vagina into the head of her full-term fetus. The boy was born 2 days later and over the following week his health deteriorated to a critical level. A brain scan was taken and revealed a pellet lodged in his skull. An operation removed the pellet and the boy recovered, but the mother didn't explain what had happened until after the operation.

In an Ontario Provincial Court, the judge ruled that at the time of the shooting the fetus could not be legally considered a victim separate from its mother. Thus, because the fetus has no separate rights in law, no crime was committed and the case was dismissed. However, the mother was then charged with the lesser offence of failing to provide the necessities of life for her newborn child when she failed to inform the doctors that she had shot her son, thereby allowing his health to be dangerously compromised. She pleaded guilty to this charge and was given a suspended sentence.

YOUR TURN

- What do you think the result would be if the outcome of the court decision were different in each case? For instance, what problems do you foresee if pregnant women could be forced into treatment, or what may happen if children could sue their mothers for damages that were sustained prenatally?

- Describe a hypothetical legal standard of conduct for pregnant women.

- If Canadian laws were changed to protect the fetus from a mother's potentially damaging behaviour, then how do you think the laws should address the following concerns? How would the rights of Canadian mothers be affected? What lifestyle behaviours of the mother would be considered harmful to the fetus? Who would decide how much protection is sufficient? How would you enforce such a law?

- In what ways would forcing a woman to seek treatment do more harm than good?

- To what extent do you think society is at least indirectly responsible for harm to fetuses?

© Craig Holmes/Alamy

CHAPTER 4

Physical, Sensory, and Perceptual Development in Infancy

One of the most fascinating features of babies' behaviour is their "busyness." They seem to be constantly on the go, manipulating objects with their hands, looking at them, feeling them, tasting them, and making sounds with them. At times, such activities seem purposeless, but they provide just the kind of skill practice and information infants need for both physical and cognitive development. Considering the energy it takes to keep up with infants' level of activity, it's little wonder their parents seem to be exhausted much of the time.

When you finish studying the chapter, you will be able to trace the processes through which a relatively unskilled newborn becomes a 2-year-old who can move about efficiently; summarize the ways that infants respond to a variety of sensory stimuli; and describe how perception develops in infants and how they come to perceive the world as older children and adults do. While you read, keep the following questions in mind:

- What changes occur in infants' bodies, and how can parents promote healthy physical development?

- What are infants' sensory abilities, and in what ways do babies' sensory skills contribute to the development of parent-infant relationships?

- To the extent that early perceptual learning depends on experience, what kinds of objects and activities would be helpful in promoting an infant's perceptual development?

PHYSICAL CHANGES

What comes to mind when you think about the first two years of life? If you reflect on this period, you will realize that, apart from prenatal development, it is the period during which the greatest degree of physical change occurs. Babies grow 25 to 30 centimetres and triple their body weight in the first year of life. By age 2 for girls and about 2½ for boys, toddlers are half as tall as they will be as adults. This means a 2- to 2½-year-old's adult height can be reliably predicted by doubling his or her current height. But 2-year-olds have proportionately much larger heads than do adults—which they need to hold their nearly full-sized brains.

Explore

THE BRAIN AND THE NERVOUS SYSTEM

The body's systems grow and develop at different rates and at different times. The reproductive system, for instance, is completely formed at birth but doesn't grow or change much until puberty. In contrast, the brain and nervous system develop rapidly during the first 2 years. **Figure 4.1** shows the main structures of the brain. At birth, the midbrain and the medulla are the most fully developed. These two parts, both of which are in the lower part of the skull and connected to the spinal cord, regulate vital functions such as heartbeat and respiration, as well as attention, sleeping, waking, elimination, and movement of the head and the neck—all actions a newborn can perform at least moderately well. The least-developed part of the brain at birth is the cortex, the convoluted grey matter that wraps around the midbrain and is involved in perception, body movement, thinking, and language.

SYNAPTIC DEVELOPMENT You'll recall from **Chapter 3** that all brain structures are composed of two basic types of cells: neurons and glial cells. Millions of these cells are present at birth, and synapses, or connections between neurons, have already begun to form (Monk, Webb, & Nelson, 2001). Synapse development results from growth of both dendrites and axons (look back at **Figure 3.1** on page 67). **Synaptogenesis,** the creation of synapses, occurs rapidly in the cortex during the first few years after birth, resulting in a quadrupling of the overall weight of the brain by age 4 (Spreen, Risser, & Edgell, 1995). However, synaptogenesis is not smooth and continuous. Instead, it happens in spurts.

Typically, each synaptic growth spurt generates many more connections between neurons than the individual actually needs. Thus, each burst of synaptogenesis is followed by a period of **synaptic pruning** in which unnecessary pathways and connections are eliminated (Huttenlocher, 1995). For example, each muscle cell seems to develop synaptic connections with several motor neurons (nerve cells that carry impulses to muscles) in the spinal cord. As the infant works to gain control over his movements, some of these connections are used repeatedly, while others are ignored. Soon, the unused connections die off, or get "pruned" by the system. Once the pruning process is completed, each muscle fibre is connected to only one motor neuron.

This cycle of synaptogenesis followed by synaptic pruning continues through the lifespan. With each cycle, the brain becomes more efficient. Consequently, a 1-year-old actually has denser dendrites and synapses than an adult does, but the 1-year-old's network operates far less efficiently than that of the adult. However, efficiency comes at a price. Because infants have more unused synapses than adults, they can bounce back from a host of insults to the brain (e.g., malnutrition, head injury) much more easily than an adult. Neuroscientists use the term **neuroplasticity** to refer to the brain's ability to change in response to experience. Developmentalists draw several important implications from the cyclical synaptogenesis–pruning feature of neurological development. First, it seems clear that brain development follows the old dictum "Use it or lose it." A child growing up in a rich or intellectually challenging environment will retain a more complex network of synapses than one growing up with fewer forms of stimulation. In addition, as mentioned earlier, the brains of infants possess greater neuroplasticity than those of older children and adults. Paradoxically, though, the period of greatest neuroplasticity is also the period in which the child may be most vulnerable to major deficits—just as a fetus is most vulnerable to teratogens during the time of most rapid growth of any body system (Uylings, 2006). Thus, a young infant needs sufficient stimulation and order in his environment to maximize the early period of rapid growth and neuroplasticity (de Haan, Luciana, Maslone, Matheny, & Richards, 1994). A really inadequate diet or a serious lack of stimulation in the early months may thus have subtle but long-range effects on the child's later cognitive progress. Some have even argued that watching too much television in the early months may impede brain development, as discussed in the **Development in the Real World** feature in **Chapter 5** on page 125.

Finally, new information about the continuation of synaptogenesis and synaptic pruning throughout the lifespan has forced developmental psychologists to change their ideas about the links between brain development and behaviour. If the brain were almost completely organized by age 2, as most developmentalists believed until recently, then it would seem logical to assume that whatever developments occurred

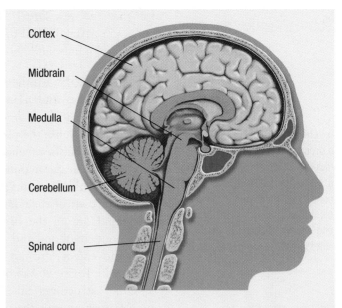

Figure 4.1

The medulla and the midbrain are largely developed at birth. In the first 2 years after birth, it is primarily the cortex that develops, with each neuron going through an enormous growth of dendrites and a vast increase in synapses.

synaptogenesis
the process of synapse development

synaptic pruning
process by which unused or unnecessary neural pathways and connections are eliminated

neuroplasticity
the ability of the brain to reorganize brain structures in response to experience

after that age were largely the product of experience. But researchers now know that changes in psychological functioning are linked to changes in the brain throughout the entire human lifespan.

myelinization

a process in neuronal development in which sheaths made of a substance called myelin gradually cover individual axons and electrically insulate them from one another to improve the conductivity of the nerve

MYELINIZATION   Another crucial process in the development of neurons is the creation of sheaths, or coverings, around individual axons, which insulate them from one another electrically and improve their conductivity. These sheaths are made of a substance called myelin; the process of developing the sheath is called **myelinization**.

The sequence of myelinization follows both cephalocaudal and proximodistal patterns (these were defined in **Chapter 3**). For example, nerves serving muscle cells in the neck and shoulders are myelinized earlier than those serving the abdomen. As a result, babies can control their head movements before they can roll over. Myelinization is most rapid during the first 2 years after birth, but it continues at a slower pace throughout childhood and adolescence. For example, the parts of the brain that govern motor movements are not fully myelinized until a child is about 6 years old (Todd, Swarzenski, Rossi, & Visconti, 1995).

reticular formation

the part of the brain that regulates attention

Other structures take even longer to become myelinized. For example, the **reticular formation** is the part of the brain responsible for keeping your attention on what you're doing and for helping you sort out important and unimportant information. Myelinization of the reticular formation begins in infancy but continues in spurts across childhood and adolescence. In fact, the process isn't complete until a person is in her mid-20s (Spreen, Risser, & Edgell, 1995). Consequently, during the first 2 years, infants improve their ability to focus on a task. Likewise, a 12-year-old is much better at concentrating than an infant but is still fairly inefficient when compared to an adult.

REFLEXES AND BEHAVIOURAL STATES

✳ Explore

Changes in the brain result in predictable changes in babies' reflexes, sensory capacities, and patterns of waking and sleeping. In fact, such changes, or the absense of such changes, can be important indicators of nervous system health.

adaptive reflexes

reflexes, such as sucking, that help newborns survive; some adaptive reflexes persist throughout life

REFLEXES   Humans are born with many **adaptive reflexes** that help them survive. Some, such as automatically sucking any object that enters the mouth, disappear in infancy or childhood. Others protect us against harmful stimuli over the whole lifespan. These adaptive reflexes include withdrawal from a painful stimulus and the opening and closing of the pupil of the eye in response to variations in brightness. Weak or absent adaptive reflexes in neonates suggest that the brain is not functioning properly and that the baby requires additional assessment.

primitive reflexes

reflexes, controlled by "primitive" parts of the brain, that disappear during the first year of life

The purposes of **primitive reflexes**, so called because they are controlled by the less sophisticated parts of the brain (the medulla and the midbrain), are less clear. For example, if you make a loud noise or startle a baby in some other way, you'll see her throw her arms outward and arch her back, a pattern that is part of the *Moro*, or *startle*, *reflex*. Stroke the bottom of her foot and she will splay out her toes and then curl them in, a reaction called the *Babinski reflex*.

Some evidence suggests that stimulation of reflexes may facilitate later motor development. For instance, University of Toronto psychologist Philip Zelazo has found that infants who were encouraged to exercise the stepping reflex were more likely to spontaneously display the stepping movements and began walking at an earlier age (Zelazo, Zelazo, Cohen, & Zelazo, 1993; Zelazo, Zelazo, & Kolb, 1972). By 6 to 8 months of age though, primitive reflexes begin to disappear. If such reflexes persist past this age, the baby may have some kind of neurological problem (DiMario, 2002).

BEHAVIOURAL STATES Researchers have described five different states of sleep and wakefulness in neonates, referred to as **states of consciousness** and summarized in **Table 4.1**. Most infants move through these states in the same sequence: from deep sleep to lighter sleep and then to alert wakefulness and fussing. After they are fed, they become drowsy and drop back into deep sleep. The cycle repeats itself about every 2 hours.

Neonates sleep as much as 80% of the time, as much in the daytime as at night (Sola, Rogido, & Partridge, 2002). By 8 weeks of age, the total amount of sleep per day has dropped somewhat and signs of day/night sleep rhythms (called *circadian rhythms*) become evident. Babies of this age begin to sleep through two or three 2-hour cycles in sequence without coming to full wakefulness and are thus often said to have started to "sleep through the night." By 6 months, babies are still sleeping a bit over 14 hours per day, but sleep is more regular and predictable. Most have clear nighttime sleep patterns and nap during the day at more predictable times.

Of course, babies vary a lot around these averages. Of the 6-week-old babies in one study, one slept 22 hours per day and another slept only 8.8 hours per day (Bamford et al., 1990). (Now, *that* must have been one tired set of parents!) And some babies do not develop a long nighttime sleep period until late in the first year of life. Moreover, cultural beliefs play an important role in parents' responses to infants' sleep patterns. For example, North American parents typically see a newborn's erratic sleep cycle as a behaviour problem that requires "fixing" through parental intervention (Harkness, 1998). As a result, they focus a great deal of attention on trying to force babies to sleep through the night. In contrast, European parents are more likely to regard newborns' patterns of sleeping as manifestations of normal development and tend to expect babies to acquire stable sleeping patterns naturally, without parental intervention, during the first 2 years.

Infants have different cries for pain, anger, or hunger. The basic cry, which often signals hunger, usually has a rhythmical pattern: cry, silence, breath, cry, silence, breath, with a kind of whistling sound often accompanying the in-breath. An anger cry is typically

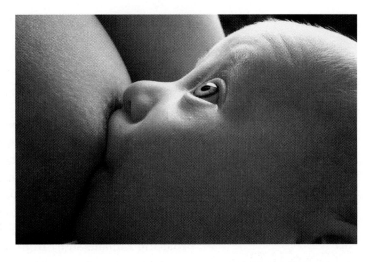

This 4-week-old baby is using the inborn adaptive reflex of sucking. (*Photo:* Richard Meats/Getty Images)

states of consciousness
different states of sleep and wakefulness in infants

TABLE 4.1   The Basic States of Infant Sleep and Wakefulness

State	Characteristics
Deep sleep	Eyes closed, regular breathing, no movement except occasional startles
Active sleep	Eyes closed, irregular breathing, small twitches, no gross body movement
Quiet awake	Eyes open, no major body movement, regular breathing
Active awake	Eyes open, movements of the head, limbs, and trunk, irregular breathing
Crying, fussing	Eyes partly or entirely closed, vigorous diffuse movement with crying or fussing sounds

(*Sources*: Based on the work of Hutt, Lenard, & Prechtl, 1969; Parmelee, Wenner, & Schulz, 1964; Prechtl & Beintema, 1964.)

louder and more intense, and the pain cry normally has a very abrupt onset—unlike the other two kinds of cries, which usually begin with whimpering or moaning.

Cross-cultural studies suggest that crying increases in frequency over the first 6 weeks and then tapers off (St. James-Roberts, Bowyer, Varghese, & Sawdon, 1994). Moreover, parents across a variety of cultures use very similar techniques to soothe crying infants. Most babies stop crying when they are picked up, held, and talked or sung to. Getting a baby to suck on a pacifier also usually helps. Parents sometimes worry that picking up a crying baby will lead to even more crying. But research suggests that prompt attention to a crying baby in the first 3 months actually leads to less crying later in infancy (Sulkes, 1998).

There is one fairly common exception to the typical pattern of crying, however. McGill University Professor of Pediatrics Paul Roumeliotis (2010a, 2010b) estimates that 1 in 5 infants suffer from **colic**, a pattern involving intense bouts of crying totalling 3 or more hours a day for no immediately apparent reason, such as hunger or a wet diaper, that nothing seems to help. Typically, colic appears at about 2 or 3 weeks of age and then disappears on its own at about 3 to 4 months. The crying is generally worst in late afternoon or early evening.

Although neither psychologists nor physicians know why colic begins or why it stops without any intervention, dietary needs have often been blamed as the culprit. To test this common belief, University of Western Ontario medical researchers tracked the feeding patterns of 856 mother–infant pairs of which almost one in four of the infants were rated as colicky (Clifford, Campbell, Speechley, & Gorodzinsky, 2002). They found that there was no significant difference in colic ratings regardless of whether an infant was exclusively breastfed, formula-fed, or fed by a combination of breast milk and nonhuman milk. This study suggests that changing an infant's diet or early weaning is generally uncalled for. It is a difficult pattern to live with, but the good news is that it does go away.

DEVELOPING BODY SYSTEMS AND MOTOR SKILLS

Like behavioural states, the acquisition of motor skills also depends on brain development. Substantial changes in other body systems—bones, muscles, lungs, and heart, for example—are required as well. As you read about them, recall from **Chapter 3** that physical development proceeds from the head downward (cephalocaudal pattern) and from the centre of the body outward (proximodistal pattern).

BONES During infancy, bones change in size, number, and composition. Increases in the lengths of the body's long bones—those in the legs and arms—underlie increases in height (Tanner, 1990). Changes in the number and density of bones in particular parts of the body are responsible for improvements in coordinated movement.

For example, at birth, the wrist contains a single mass of cartilage; by 1 year of age, the cartilage has developed into three separate bones. The progressive separation of the wrist bones is one of the factors behind gains in manipulative skills over the first 2 years. Wrist bones continue to differentiate over the next several years until eventually, in adolescence, the wrist has nine separate bones (Tanner, 1990).

The process of bone hardening, called *ossification*, occurs steadily, beginning in the last weeks of prenatal development and continuing through puberty. Bones in different parts of the body harden in a sequence that follows the typical proximodistal and cephalocaudal patterns. Motor development depends on ossification to a large extent. Standing, for example, is impossible if an infant's leg bones are too soft, no matter how well developed the muscles and nervous system are.

Critical Thinking

What advice would you give to parents who believe that picking up a baby when she cries will "spoil" her?

colic
an infant behaviour pattern involving intense bouts of crying, totalling 3 or more hours a day

MUSCLES The body's full complement of muscle fibres is present at birth, although the fibres are initially small and have a high ratio of water to muscle (Tanner, 1990). In addition, a newborn's muscles contain a fairly high proportion of fat. By 1 year of age, the water content of an infant's muscles is equal to that of an adult, and the ratio of fat to muscle tissue has begun to decline (Tershakovec & Stallings, 1998). Changes in muscle composition lead to increases in strength that enable 1-year-olds to walk, run, jump, climb, and so on.

LUNGS AND HEART The lungs also grow rapidly and become more efficient during the first 2 years (Kercsmar, 1998). Improvements in lung efficiency, together with the increasing strength of heart muscles, give a 2-year-old greater *stamina*, or ability to maintain activity, than a newborn. Consequently, by the end of infancy, children are capable of engaging in fairly long periods of sustained motor activity without rest (often exhausting their parents in the process!).

MOTOR SKILLS Changes in all of the body's systems are responsible for the impressive array of motor skills children acquire in the first 2 years. Developmentalists typically divide these skills into three groups (Malina, 1982). *Locomotor skills*, also often called *gross motor skills*, include abilities such as crawling that enable the infant to get around in the environment. *Nonlocomotor skills*, such as controlling head movements, improve babies' ability to use their senses and motor skills to interact with the objects and the people around them. Many of these skills are used in play as well. *Manipulative skills*, or *fine motor skills*, involve use of the hands, as when a 1-year-old stacks one block on top of another. **Table 4.2** summarizes developments in each of these three areas over the first 24 months.

TABLE 4.2 Milestones of Motor Development in the First 2 Years

Age (in months)	Locomotor Skills	Nonlocomotor Skills	Manipulative Skills
1	Stepping reflex	Lifts head slightly; follows slowly moving objects with eyes	Holds object if placed in hand
2–3		Lifts head up to 90-degree angle when lying on stomach	Begins to swipe at objects in sight
4–6	Rolls over; sits with support; moves on hands and knees ("creeps")	Holds head erect while in sitting position	Reaches for and grasps objects
7–9	Sits without support; crawls		Transfers objects from one hand to the other
10–12	Pulls self up and walks grasping furniture; then walks alone	Squats and stoops; plays patty cake	Shows some signs of hand preference; grasps a spoon across palm but has poor aim when moving food to mouth
13–18	Walks backward, sideways; runs (14–20 mos.)	Rolls ball to adult; claps	Stacks two blocks; puts objects into small container and dumps them out
19–24	Walks up and down stairs, two feet per step	Jumps with both feet off ground	Uses spoon to feed self; stacks 4 to 10 blocks

The typical pattern of motor skill development follows the basic cephalocaudal and proximodistal patterns that are characteristic of much of physical development. However, one important exception to this pattern has been discovered by researchers James Galloway and Esther Thelen (2004). In their research, they found that babies reached for objects with their feet several weeks prior to reaching with their hands. These studies show that, in younger infants, the legs can be more effectively controlled than the arms, exactly the opposite of the cephalocaudal pattern. Additional research is required before we can conclude that the feet-first reaching pattern precedes reaching with the arms in all infants. Furthermore, we need more information about how babies use this skill to explore and learn. However, Galloway and Thelen's groundbreaking research suggests that future human development textbooks may add "reaches for object with feet" to lists such as the one in **Table 4.2.**

Canadian norms are currently being developed as part of University of Manitoba psychologist Warren Eaton's ongoing *Infant Milestone Study*. About 200 babies are being tracked to determine week-to-week changes as they progress toward motor skills milestones. Although the timing of the first time a baby sits, creeps, crawls, and walks is variable, the researchers have so far observed a seasonal trend whereby babies born in the spring reach crawling and walking milestones at a younger age (Eaton, 2003).

EXPLAINING MOTOR SKILL DEVELOPMENT The sequence of motor skill development is virtually the same for all children, even those with serious physical or mental handicaps. Developmentally delayed children, for example, move through the various motor milestones more slowly than normal children do, but they do so in the same sequence. Furthermore, motor skill development follows the cephalocaudal and proximodistal patterns. Whenever developmentalists find such consistencies, maturation of some kind seems an obvious explanation (Thelen, 1995).

However, Wayne Dennis's (1960) classic early study of children raised in Iranian orphanages demonstrated that babies who were routinely placed on their backs in cribs learned to walk eventually, but they did so about a year later than babies in less restrictive settings. Research involving infants living in normal environments supports the notion that experience influences motor development. In one such study, very young babies who were given more practice sitting were able to sit upright longer than those without such practice (Zelazo, Zelazo, Cohen, & Zelazo, 1993). Consequently, developmentalists are fairly certain that severely restricting a baby's movement slows down acquisition of motor skills, and many are beginning to accept the idea that a baby's movement experiences in normal environments may also influence motor skill development.

GENDER DIFFERENCES Just as they were prenatally, girls continue to be ahead of boys in some aspects of physical maturity during infancy. For example, the separate bones of the wrist appear earlier in girls than in boys (Tanner, 1990). This means that female infants may have a slight advantage in the development of manipulative skills such as self-feeding. In addition, boys are more likely to suffer from developmental delays, are less healthy, and have higher mortality rates (Halpern, 1997; MacDorman & Atkinson, 1999).

University of Montreal researchers found that boys are typically more physically active, but some investigators report no difference at all (Cossette, Malcuit, & Pomerleau, 1991). However, both in human and primate studies, male infants display a clear preference for rough-and-tumble play even during the first few months of life (Brown & Dixson, 2000; Humphreys & Smith, 1987). Likewise, differences between boys and girls in physical aggression are already evident near the end of the second year, a finding that has been replicated in studies of many cultures (e.g., Archer, 2004; Hyde, 2005).

The striking improvements in motor development in the early months are easy to illustrate. Between 6 and 12 months of age, babies progress from sitting alone, to creeping and crawling, to walking.
(*Photos:* left and right, © Myrleen Ferguson Cate/PhotoEdit; centre, courtesy of Sylvia M. Scott and Owen K. Sloan)

HEALTH PROMOTION AND WELLNESS

Babies depend on the adults in their environments to help them stay healthy. Specifically, they need the right foods in the right amounts, and they need regular medical care.

NUTRITION   After several decades of extensive research in many countries, experts agree that, for most infants, breastfeeding is substantially superior nutritionally to bottle-feeding. The Canadian Paediatric Society (CPS), the Dieticians of Canada, and Health Canada (Health Canada, 2006a) recommend that breastfeeding should be the sole source of infant nutrition for at least the first 6 months of life (see **Development in the Real World**).

For one thing, breast milk contributes to more rapid weight and size gain (Prentice, 1994). On average, breastfed infants are less likely to suffer from problems such as diarrhea, gastroenteritis, bronchitis, ear infections, and colic, and they are less likely to die in infancy (Barness & Curran, 1996; Beaudry, Dufour, & Marcoux, 1995; Golding,

Eating Well with Canada's Food Guide
guidelines for a balanced and healthy diet based on the four major food groups: vegetables and fruits, grain products, milk and alternatives, and meat and alternatives

Development in the Real World

NUTRITION FROM BIRTH TO ONE YEAR

In Canada, 90% of mothers initiate breastfeeding of their babies (Chalmers et al., 2009), up from just 38% in 1963 (McNally, Hendricks, & Horowitz, 1985). However, there is a wide disparity in breastfeeding trends across the country. Mothers in the western provinces and Yukon have the highest rates, while mothers in Quebec, the Maritime provinces, and eastern territories have had the lowest rates (Chalmers et al., 2009). As well, breastfeeding practices vary greatly between and within Canadian subgoups. For instance, recent immigrant mothers tend to bottle-feed regardless of what the dominant feeding practice was in their home country (Health Canada, 1997). This tendency is believed to be reflective of the newcomers' perception that bottle-feeding is the preferred method of feeding infants in Canada and is considered a sign of adaptation to what they perceive as Canadian culture. Within any given subculture, a mother's breastfeeding pattern has more in common with the health beliefs of women from the same socioeconomic status (SES) than with the beliefs of her subculture

(Masi, 1988). Women who are older, are better educated, have higher incomes, and are not single parents are more likely to initiate and maintain breastfeeding (Chalmers et al., 2009; Girard, 2004).

Health care experts recommend exclusive breastfeeding for 6 or more months (Kramer & Kakuma, 2009; PHAC, 2009a), yet only about half of mothers exclusively breastfeed their infants by 3 months of age, even though breastfeeding can continue, with the introduction of solid foods, to beyond 2 years (Chalmers et al., 2009; PHAC, 2009a).

At 6 months, healthy term infants are ready to try new foods, which helps meet the infant's increasing nutritional needs. The first foods should include iron-fortified infant cereal, followed by puréed vegetables, fruits, and, lastly, meat or meat substitutes. A gradual introduction of new foods allows for better identification of possible allergic reactions. By 1 year of age, the baby should have a wide variety of foods based on **Eating Well with Canada's Food Guide** (Health Canada, 2007b).

Emmett, & Rogers, 1997a, 1997b; López-Alarcón, Villapando, & Fajardo, 1997). Breast milk also appears to stimulate better immune system function (Pickering et al., 1998). For these reasons, physicians strongly recommend breastfeeding, even if the mother can nurse for only a few weeks after birth or if her breast milk must be supplemented with formula feedings (Tershakovec & Stallings, 1998).

Surprisingly, though, there are situations in which breast milk is not sufficient to meet babies' nutritional needs. For instance, preterm babies' intestinal tracts are not as mature as those of full-term infants. As a result, preterm babies require diets supplemented with amino acids and fats that full-term infants' bodies can manufacture on their own (Guesry, 1998; Kliegman, 1998). However, these babies also need the immunological benefits of breast milk. Thus, physicians typically recommend feeding preterm babies a combination of breast milk and a supplemental formula that contains exactly the proteins, fats, vitamins, and minerals their bodies need. Bottles can be used to give the baby the supplemental formula. However, it is also possible to attach a very small tube to the mother's breast through which the baby can be fed the supplement while nursing. When preterm babies are too weak or too ill to be nursed, mothers are urged to use breast pumps to express milk that can then be fed to the babies through tubes inserted directly into the babies' stomachs. This practice allows the mother's breasts to become accustomed to nursing so that breastfeeding can begin as soon as the baby is well enough.

However, Canadian experts caution that breastfeeding is not recommended for all babies (Newman & Pittman, 2003). For example, drugs are often present in the breast milk of mothers who are substance abusers or who depend on medications to maintain their own health. Many of these drugs can negatively affect infant development. Consequently, doctors recommend that these women avoid breastfeeding. In such cases, babies who are fed high-quality infant formula, prepared according to the manufacturer's instructions and properly sterilized, usually thrive on it (Tershakovec & Stallings, 1998). Moreover, a wide variety of formulas are available today to fulfill the requirements of infants who have special needs, such as those who are lactose intolerant. It is also reassuring to know that when bottle-fed babies are held and cuddled in the same ways that breastfed babies are and when their mothers appear to be just as sensitive and responsive to them, mother–infant social interactions appear to be identical to those of nursing mothers and their babies (Field, 1977).

MALNUTRITION Malnutrition in infancy can seriously impair a baby's brain because the nervous system is the most rapidly developing body system during the first 2 years of life. **Macronutrient** malnutrition results from a diet that contains too few calories. Macronutrient malnutrition is the world's leading cause of death of children under the age of 5 (Tershakovec & Stallings, 1998).

When the calorie deficit is severe, a disease called *marasmus* results. Infants with marasmus weigh less than 60% of what they should at their age, and many suffer permanent neurological damage from the disease. Most also suffer from parasitic infections that lead to chronic diarrhea. This condition makes it very difficult to treat marasmus by simply increasing an infant's intake of calories. However, a program of dietary supplementation with formula combined with intravenous feedings and treatment for parasites can reverse marasmus (Tershakovec & Stallings, 1998).

Some infants' diets contain almost enough calories but not enough protein. Diets of this type lead to a disease called *kwashiorkor*, which is common in countries where infants are weaned too early to low-protein foods. Kwashiorkor-like symptoms are also seen in children who are chronically ill because of their bodies' inability to use the protein from the foods they eat. Like marasmus, kwashiorkor can lead to a variety of health problems as well as permanent brain damage (Tershakovec & Stallings, 1998).

macronutrients
large amounts of carbohydrates, fats, and proteins that are needed for energy and for body- and brain-building elements

A small proportion of infants in North America have feeding problems, such as a poorly developed sucking reflex, that place them at risk for macronutrient malnutrition (Wright & Birks, 2000). However, most nutritional problems in industrialized societies involve **micronutrient** malnutrition, a deficiency of certain vitamins and/or minerals. The exception is Canada, which is a world leader in food fortification. Micronutrients have been added to our food supply for about 50 years (Lofti, 2001). Specifically, vitamin D has been added to fluid milk since the 1960s, essentially eliminating childhood rickets; iodine is added to table salt, which has eliminated endemic goitre; and vitamin A is added to low-fat milk and butter substitutes, such as margarine (Health Canada, 1999c). Canada is also a leader in promoting and distributing three essential micronutrients—vitamin A, iodine, and iron—throughout developing countries (CIDA, 2000). As a result, for example, George Beaton, professor emeritus of the University of Toronto and a world-renowned pioneer in the study of human nutrition requirements, found that mortality rates can be reduced by 23% by supplying young children living in at-risk countries with vitamin A (Beaton et al., 1993).

micronutrients
essential vitamins and minerals that are needed in small amounts to regulate physical and mental processes

HEALTH CARE AND IMMUNIZATIONS Infants need frequent medical checkups. Much of *well baby care* may seem routine, but it is extremely important to development. For example, during routine visits to the doctor's office or health clinic, babies' motor skills are usually assessed. An infant whose motor development is less advanced than expected for his age may require additional screening for a developmental or intellectual disability (Sulkes, 1998).

One of the most important elements of well baby care is vaccination against a variety of diseases. Although immunizations later in childhood provide good protection, the *Canadian Immunization Guide* (7th edition) recommends that routine immunization should commence at 2 months of age and continue through childhood and adolescence (Public Health Agency of Canada [PHAC], 2006b). Still, it is important to be informed of the benefits and possible adverse reactions and risks of vaccines when consenting to immunization services (e.g., answers to parent's questions about vaccine effectiveness, safety, and side effects can be found on the Canadian Paediatric Society's "Caring for Kids" website, **www.cps.ca/caringforkids/immunization/VaccinationChild.htm**).

At the beginning of the last century, infectious diseases were a leading cause of childhood death, but they have since been virtually eradicated as the result of mass vaccination programs (Trovato, 1991). At present, Canadian children typically receive vaccinations at 2 months of age for DTaP (diphtheria, tetanus, pertussis [acellular]), IPV (inactivated poliovirus vaccine), Hib (haemophilus influenzae type b), PC (pneumococcal conjugate vaccine), and MC (meningococcal conjugate vaccine). Vaccinations for MMR (measles, mumps, and rubella), Hep B (hepatitis B vaccine), and V (varicella) are administered around an infant's first birthday (PHAC, 2006b).

The public can easily become complacent about immunizations (PHAC, 2006b). For example, declines in whooping cough immunizations during the late 1980s and early 1990s led to outbreaks of this serious illness in Canada (Trovato, 1991). Thus, it is important to remember that diseases such as measles will remain rare only as long as parents are diligent in having their children immunized.

ILLNESSES IN THE FIRST 2 YEARS The average baby has seven respiratory illnesses in the first year of life. Interestingly, research in a number of counties shows that babies in daycare centres have about twice as many infections as those reared entirely at home, with those in small-group daycare falling somewhere in between, presumably because babies cared for in group settings are exposed to a wider range of germs and viruses (Collet et al., 1994; Hurwitz, Gunn, Pinsky, & Schonberger, 1991). In general, the more people a baby is exposed to, the more often she is likely to be sick.

Neuropsychologists have suggested that respiratory illnesses that can lead to ear infections have developmental implications. Many note that infants who have chronic ear infections are more likely than their peers to have learning disabilities, attention disorders, and language deficits during the school years (Asbjornsen et al., 2005). These psychologists hypothesize that, because ear infections temporarily impair hearing, they may compromise the development of brain areas that are essential for language learning during the first 2 years of life (Spreen, Risser, & Edgell, 1995). Thus, most pediatricians emphasize the need for effective hygiene practices in daycare centres, such as periodic disinfection of all toys and prompt treatment of infants' respiratory infections.

PRETERM AND LOW-BIRTH-WEIGHT INFANTS

Infants born live before 37 weeks of gestation are considered preterm. The Canadian preterm rate has steadily increased since the early 1980s, reaching 8.2 per 100 live births by the mid-2000s (PHAC, 2008a). Although preterm rates are significantly higher for multiple birth infants, singleton births still account for about 80% of all preterm births (see **Figure 4.2**) (PHAC, 2008a).

Infants born before 32 weeks of gestation may not have adaptive reflexes that are sufficiently developed to enable them to survive. Sucking and swallowing, for example, are extremely difficult for these tiny infants. Consequently, many preterm infants must be fed intravenously or through a tube inserted into the esophagus or the stomach (Kliegman, 1998). Preterm babies are also at higher risk for neurological impairment, respiratory difficulties, gastrointestinal complications, immunologic deficiencies which cause a susceptibility to infections, and neonatal infant mortality (Berkowitz & Papiernik, 1993; PHAC, 2008a). Over the long haul, preterm babies are also more likely to experience motor, cognitive, visual, hearing, behavioural, and growth problems.

Preterm and low-birth-weight babies (weighing less than 2.5 kilograms at birth) also move more slowly from one developmental milestone to the next because the preterm baby is, in fact, maturationally younger than the full-term baby. If a correction is made for the baby's gestational age, then most (but not all) of the difference in physical development disappears. For example, a 12-month-old who was born 2 months early would have a corrected age of 10 months. Parents of preterms need to keep this in mind when they compare their babies' progress with that of full-term babies. By age 2 or 3, the physically normal preterm can catch up to his peers, but in the early months he is definitely behind.

Although experience influences the developmental progress in preterm infants just as it does full-term infants, it is especially important for parents to know that their responses to the child contribute to how rapidly she develops (White-Traut et al., 2002). For example, a relatively recent innovation in the care of preterm newborns is an intervention called *kangaroo care* in which parents are shown how to increase the amount of skin-to-skin contact infants engage in with them. An important part of the intervention involves allowing parents to hold these tiny newborns for very long periods of time. Researchers from Canada and across the globe have found that preterm babies who receive kangaroo care grow and develop more rapidly than preterm infants given conventional neonatal care (Cooper et al., 2007; Moore, Anderson,

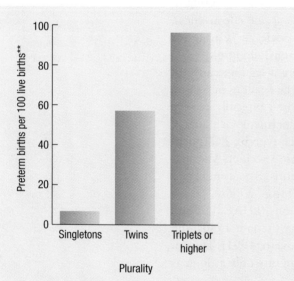

Figure 4.2

Preterm birth rates, by single and multiple births, Canada (excluding Ontario*), 2004.

* Ontario is excluded because of data quality concerns.

** Excludes live births with unknown age and gestational age.

(*Source:* Adapted from PHAC, 2008a, Figure 20.2.)

& Bergman, 2007; Suman, Udani, & Nanavati, 2008; Tessier et al., 2009). McGill University researchers (Johnston et al, 2008) have also found that kangaroo mother care aleviates the pain response in premature neonates.

POST-TERM INFANTS

Infants born after 42 or more weeks of gestation are referred to as *post-term*. Post-term pregnancies are associated with higher risk for maternal medical complications and with fetal and neonatal mortality (PHAC, 2008a). Fortunately, the rate of post-term deliveries in Canada has decreased substantially from 4.4% in 1991 to a low of 0.8% by the mid-2000s (PHAC, 2008a). This decrease can be attributed in part to the effective use of ultrasound dating and the practice of inducing post-term pregnancies. However, the rates of post-term deliveries vary dramatically among Canada's provinces and territories (see **Figure 4.3**) (PHAC, 2008a).

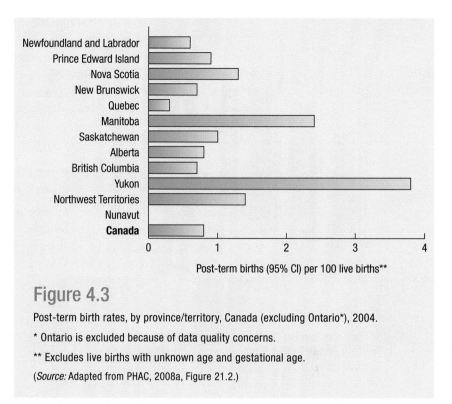

Figure 4.3

Post-term birth rates, by province/territory, Canada (excluding Ontario*), 2004.

* Ontario is excluded because of data quality concerns.

** Excludes live births with unknown age and gestational age.

(*Source:* Adapted from PHAC, 2008a, Figure 21.2.)

INFANT MORTALITY IN CANADA

About half of infant deaths in Canada occur in the neonate and the rest between 4 weeks and 1 year of age. Over the past century, Canada's rate of **infant mortality** has shown a dramatic rate of decline—from 134 per 1000 live births in 1901 to 27 in the 1960s to just 5 in 2006 (Conference Board of Canada [CBofC], 2010; Health Canada, 1998a, 2003b; Wilkens, Houle, Berthelot, & Ross, 2000). Still, despite Canada's high calibre of health care, it has made less progress in reducing infant deaths than many other nations: Of 17 peer countires, Canada is now tied with the United Kingdom for the second highest infant mortality rate—only the United States performs worse (CBofC, 2010).

infant mortality
death within the first year of life

Even though regional disparities in infant mortality rates across Canada have diminished significantly, income disparity stubbornly remains a problem: Lower-income families experience higher infant mortality rates than middle- and upper-income groups (see **Figure 4.4**). Moreover, infant mortality rates for First Nations and Inuit are two and four times higher, respectively, than the general Canadian population (McShane, Smylie, & Adomako, 2009). Although living closer to an urban setting is associated with lower infant mortality rates for non-First Nations, there is no such difference for First Nations (Luo et al., 2010). The rates of infant mortality for First Nations were the same in rural and urban environments, suggesting a need for improved urban First Nations' infant care in light of increasing urban migration.

SUDDEN INFANT DEATH SYNDROME Sudden infant death syndrome (SIDS) is the term associated with the sudden and unexpected death of an apparently healthy infant. The rate of SIDS in Canada has declined quite dramatically from 12 per 1000 in 1980 to 0.3 per 1000 in the 2000s (PHAC, 2008a; Health Canada, 1999d). However, there

sudden infant death syndrome (SIDS)
the term used to describe the sudden and unexpected death of an apparently healthy infant

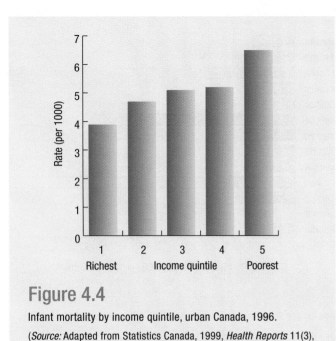

Figure 4.4

Infant mortality by income quintile, urban Canada, 1996.

(*Source:* Adapted from Statistics Canada, 1999, *Health Reports* 11(3), cited in Wilkins, Houle, Berthelot, & Ross, 2000.)

are significant differences in the incidence of SIDS across Canada, with lower rates in British Columbia, Quebec, and Ontario. Rates for First Nations infants are three times the national average.

Researchers have not yet uncovered the underlying cause(s) of SIDS, but some factors have been shown to reduce risk. Parents and caregivers can provide a safe sleep environment that reduces the risk of SIDS by

- placing the baby on his back when he sleeps (CPS, 2009; Carpenter et al., 2004; Trifunov, 2009)

- eliminating quilts, duvets, pillows, soft toys, and crib bumpers that may cover the infant's head: a fitted sheet on a crib mattress that meets current Canadian safety regulations is best (CPS, 2009)

- avoiding laying the baby on soft surfaces or on loose bedding (such as bunched-up blankets or cushions) to sleep or nap, either alone or with someone else (CPS, 2009)

- having the baby sleep in a crib or a cot near to the parent's bed for the first 6 months (CPS, 2009; McIntosh, Tonkin, & Gunn, 2009)

- avoiding bed sharing or otherwise sleeping or napping with the baby on a sofa, especially if the parents smoke, are more tired than usual, or have consumed alcohol or other substances that promote fatigue (CPS, 2009; Carpenter et al., 2004; Trifunov, 2009)

- providing a smoke-free environment during pregnancy and in the home after the infant's birth (CPS, 2009; Trifunov, 2009)

Before Going On

 Explore

- What is the typical pattern of motor skill development during a child's first 2 years, and what important changes in the brain, behaviour, and other body systems take place during infancy?

- What are the nutritional and health care needs and risks of infants and neonates with special needs?

SENSORY SKILLS

When we study sensory skills, we are asking just what information the sensory organs receive. Does the structure of the eye permit infants to see colour? Are the structures of the ear and the cortex such that a very young infant can discriminate among different pitches? The common theme running through all of what you will read in this section is that newborns and young infants have far more sensory capacity than physicians or psychologists thought even as recently as a few decades ago.

VISION

Until half a century ago, many medical texts stated that the newborn infant was blind. Now we know that the newborn has poorer visual skills than older children but is quite definitely not blind.

VISUAL ACUITY The usual standard for **visual acuity** in adults is 20/20 vision, which means that you can see and identify something 20 feet (6 metres) away that the average person can also see at 20 feet (6 metres). A person with 20/100 vision, in contrast, has to be as close as 20 feet (6 metres) to see something that the ordinary person can see at 100 feet (30.5 metres). In other words, the higher the second number, the poorer the person's visual acuity. At birth, acuity is in the range of 20/200 to 20/400, but it improves rapidly during the first year as a result of synaptogenesis, synaptic pruning, and myelination in the neurons that serve the eyes' and the brain's vision processing centres. Stated another way, the visual acuity of a newborn is about 40 times worse than that of a normal sighted adult, but, by 6 months of age, vision improves to the point where it is only eight times worse than that of an adult. Gradually, most children reach adult levels of visual acuity at about 7 years of age (Lewis & Maurer, 2005; Maurer, Mondloch, & Lewis, 2007).

visual acuity
how well one can see details at a distance

The fact that the newborn sees so poorly is not so negative a thing as it might seem at first. Of course, it does mean that a baby doesn't see faraway things clearly; he probably can't see well enough to distinguish two people standing nearby. But he sees quite well close-up, which is all that is necessary for most encounters with the people who care for him or with the objects immediately at hand, such as a breast, a bottle, or a mobile hanging above his crib.

TRACKING OBJECTS IN THE VISUAL FIELD The process of following a moving object with your eyes is called **tracking**, and you do it every day in a variety of situations. You track the movement of other cars when you are driving; you track as you watch a friend walk toward you across the room; a baseball outfielder tracks the flight of the ball so that he can catch it. Because a newborn infant can't yet move independently, many of her experiences are with objects that move toward her or away from her. If she is to have any success in recognizing objects, she has to be able to keep her eyes on them as they move; she must be able to track. Classic research by Richard Aslin (1987) and others shows that tracking is initially fairly inefficient but improves quite rapidly. Infants younger than 2 months show some tracking for brief periods if the target is moving very slowly, but somewhere around 6 to 10 weeks a shift occurs and babies' tracking becomes skilful rather quickly.

tracking
the smooth movements of the eye used to follow the track of a moving object

Newborns are quite nearsighted, so they can focus very well at about 25 to 80 centimetres, just the distance between a parent's face and the baby's eyes when the baby is held for feeding.
(*Photo:* Jonathan Nourok/PhotoEdit)

COLOUR VISION Researchers have established that the types of cells in the eye (cones) necessary for perceiving red and green are clearly present by 1 month (and perhaps present at birth); those required for perceiving blue are probably present by then as well (Bornstein, 1992). Thus, infants can and do see and discriminate among various colours. Indeed, researchers have determined that infants' ability to sense colour, even in the earliest weeks of life, is almost identical to that of adults (Pereverzeva, Hui-Lin Chien, Palmer, & Teller, 2002).

Taken together, these findings certainly do not support the notion that an infant is blind at birth. While it is true that the infant's acuity is initially poor, it improves rapidly, and other visual capacities are remarkably well developed early on. Still, a number of visual skills depend on a specific kind of visual stimulation during sensitive periods of development. For example, the onset of visual deprivation beginning at age 6 months through adolescence can prevent the development of normal *peripheral vision*, whereas sensitivity to the *global direction of motion* (e.g., when an observer sees an identifiable group of dots moving together in a particular direction among dots moving randomly) is affected only by visual deprivation that occurs near birth (Lewis & Maurer, 2005).

✴⃞Explore HEARING AND OTHER SENSES

As you learned in **Chapter 2**, babies can hear long before they are born. However, like vision, hearing improves considerably in the early months of life. The other senses follow a similar course.

auditory acuity
how well one can hear

AUDITORY ACUITY Although children's hearing improves up to adolescence, newborns' **auditory acuity** is actually better than their visual acuity. Research evidence suggests that, within the general range of pitch and loudness of the human voice, newborns hear nearly as well as adults do (Ceponiene et al., 2002). Only with high-pitched sounds is their auditory skill less than that of an adult; such a sound needs to be louder to be heard by a newborn than to be heard by older children or adults (Werner & Gillenwater, 1990).

DETECTING LOCATIONS Another basic auditory skill that exists at birth but improves with age is the ability to determine the location of a sound. Because your two ears are separated from each other, sounds arrive at one ear slightly before the other, which allows you to judge location. Only if a sound comes from a source equidistant from the two ears (the *midline*) does this system fail. In this case, the sound arrives at the same time to both ears and you know only that the sound is somewhere on your midline. We know that newborns can judge at least the general direction from which a sound has come because they will turn their heads in roughly the right direction toward a sound. Finer-grained location of sounds, however, is not well developed at birth. For example, Barbara Morrongiello has observed babies' reactions to sounds played at the midline and then sounds coming from varying degrees away from the midline. Among infants 2 months old, it takes a shift of about 27 degrees off of midline before the baby shows a changed response; among 6-month-olds, only a 12-degree shift is needed; by 18 months, discrimination of a 4-degree shift is possible—nearly the skill level seen in adults (Morrongiello, 1988; Morrongiello, Fenwick, & Chance, 1990).

SMELLING AND TASTING The senses of smell and taste have been studied much less than vision and hearing, but we do have some basic knowledge. The two senses are intricately related in infants, just as they are in adults—that is, if you cannot smell for some reason (e.g., because you have a cold), your taste sensitivity is also significantly reduced. Taste is detected by the taste buds on the tongue, which register four basic flavours: sweet, sour, bitter, and salty. Smell is registered in the mucous membranes of the nose and has nearly unlimited variations.

Newborns appear to respond differentially to all four of the basic flavours (Crook, 1987). Some of the clearest demonstrations of this come from an elegantly simple set of early studies by Jacob Steiner (Ganchrow, Steiner, & Daher, 1983; Steiner, 1979). Newborn infants who had never been fed were photographed before and after flavoured water was put into their mouths. By varying the flavour, Steiner could determine whether the babies reacted differently to different tastes. As you can see in **Figure 4.5**, babies responded quite differently to sweet, sour, and bitter flavours.

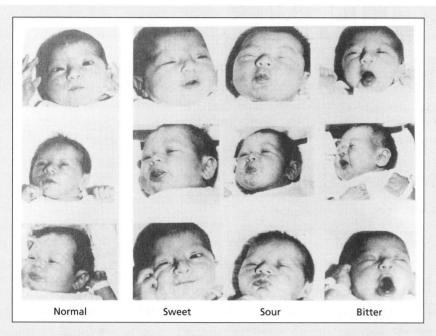

Figure 4.5

Steiner observed these three newborns in his experiments on taste response. The left-hand column shows the babies' normal expressions; the remaining columns show the change in expression when they were given flavoured water with sweet, sour, and bitter tastes. What is striking is how similar the expressions are for each taste.

(*Source:* Steiner, 1979. Reprinted with permission.)

Babies as young as 1 week can differentiate between such complex smells as personal body odours. Specifically, they can identify familiar body odours and can even discriminate their mother's smell from the smell of another woman (Porter, Making, Davis, & Christensen, 1992).

SENSES OF TOUCH AND MOTION The infant's senses of touch and motion may well be the best developed of all. Certainly these senses are sufficiently well developed to get the baby fed. If you think back to the discussion of reflexes earlier in the chapter, then you'll realize that the rooting reflex relies on a touch stimulus to the cheek while the sucking reflex relies on touch in the mouth. Babies appear to be especially sensitive to touches on the mouth, the face, the hands, the soles of the feet, and the abdomen, with less sensitivity in other parts of the body (Reisman, 1987). Likewise, babies display sensitivity to temperature by increasing physical activity in a cold room and to touch by becoming calmer when stroked and crying in protest when pricked with a needle by a nurse drawing blood for a laboratory test.

Everything you have read about these sensory abilities is fairly dry and technical. The important point for you to remember is that, as Reisman puts it, "we think of infants as helpless but they are born with some exquisitely tuned sensory abilities" (1987, p. 265).

Before Going On

- Describe the visual abilities of infants. How do these skills change across the first months?
- How do infants' senses of hearing, smell, taste, touch, and motion compare with those of older children and adults?

PERCEPTUAL SKILLS

When we turn to studies of perceptual skills, we are asking what the individual does with sensory information—how it is interpreted or how different information is combined together. Researchers have found that very young infants are able to make remarkably fine discriminations among sounds, sights, and feelings, and they pay attention to and respond to patterns, not just to individual events.

EXPLAINING PERCEPTUAL DEVELOPMENT

The study of perceptual development was one of the historic battlegrounds for the dispute about the significance of nature versus nurture in development. **Nativists** claimed that most perceptual abilities were inborn, while **empiricists** argued that these skills were learned. Developmentalists are now rethinking the relationship that exists between nature and nurture and how they interact with each other to determine development.

nativists
theorists who claimed that perceptual abilities are inborn

empiricists
theorists who argued that perceptual abilities are learned

INNATE ASPECTS OF PERCEPTUAL DEVELOPMENT It is not hard to find evidence that supports the importance of the nativist aspects of perceptual development. As researchers have become more and more clever in devising ways to test infants' perceptual skills, they have found more and more skills already present in newborns or very young infants: Newborns have good auditory acuity, poor but adequate visual acuity, and excellent tactual and taste perception. They have at least some colour vision and at least rudimentary ability to locate the source of sounds around them. More impressive still, they are capable of making quite sophisticated discriminations from the earliest days of life, including identifying their mother by sight, smell, or sound.

Newborns also appear to be guided by inborn "rules" for determining which stimuli in a stimulus-rich environment are important enough to pay attention to. The fact that these rules seem to change abruptly can also be explained in nativist terms, since changes due to learning typically happen more gradually. For instance, one such change seems to occur at about 2 months, when infants appear to shift away from fixation on contours or edges and toward more detailed analysis of objects or figures. At about the same age, babies become able to track objects smoothly. Another such shift seems to occur at about 4 months.

EXPERIENTIAL ASPECTS OF PERCEPTUAL DEVELOPMENT On the other side of the ledger, we find evidence from research with other species that some minimum level of experience is necessary to support the development of the perceptual systems. For example, animals deprived of light show deterioration of the whole visual system and a consequent decrease in perceptual abilities (Hubel & Weisel, 1963). Likewise, animals deprived of auditory stimuli display delayed or no development of auditory perceptual skills (Dammeijer, Schlundt, Chenault, Manni, & Anteunis, 2002). Similarly, Wayne Dennis's (1960) classic study of babies living in orphanages in Iran found that infants who didn't have a chance to look at things and to explore objects with hands, eyes, and tongue and who were deprived of the opportunity to move around freely were delayed in the development of perceptual skills.

INTEGRATING NATIVISM AND EMPIRICISM We can best understand the development of perceptual skills by thinking of it as the result of an interaction between inborn and experiential factors. The relationship between the built-in process and the role of the environment is a little like the difference between a computer's hardware and its

software. The perceptual hardware (specific neural pathways, rules for examining the world, a bias toward searching for patterns, and the like) may be preprogrammed, while the software (the program that governs the child's response to a particular real environment) depends on specific experience. A child is able to make visual discriminations between people or among objects within the first few days or weeks of life. This ability is built into the hardware. The specific discriminations she learns and the number of separate objects she learns to recognize, however, will depend on her experience. She is initially able to discriminate all the sound contrasts that exist in any spoken language, but the specific sound contrasts she eventually focuses on and the actual language she learns depend on the language she hears. The basic system is thus adapted to the specific environment in which the child finds herself. A perfect example of this, of course, is the newborn's ability to discriminate her mother's face from a very similar woman's face. Such a discrimination must be the result of experience, yet the capacity to make the distinction must be built in. Thus, both nature and nurture are involved in the development of perception.

STUDYING PERCEPTUAL DEVELOPMENT Babies can't talk and can't respond to ordinary questions, so how are we to decipher just what they can see, hear, or discriminate? Researchers use three basic methods that allow them to "ask" a baby about what he experiences. In the **preference technique**, devised by Robert Fantz (1956), the baby is simply shown two pictures or two objects, and the researcher keeps track of how long the baby looks at each one. If many infants shown the same pair of pictures consistently look longer at one picture than the other, then this not only tells us that babies see some difference between the two, but also may reveal something about the kinds of objects or pictures that capture babies' attention.

Another strategy takes advantage of the processes of **habituation**, or getting used to a stimulus, and its opposite, **dishabituation**, responding to a somewhat familiar stimulus as if it were new. Researchers first present the baby with a particular sight, sound, or object over and over until he habituates—that is, until he stops looking at it or showing interest in it. Then the researchers present another sight, sound, or object that is novel or slightly different from the original one and watch to see whether the baby shows renewed interest (dishabituation). If the baby does show renewed interest, you know he perceives the slightly changed sight, sound, or object as "different" in some way from the original. What the changes signify to the infant, however, remain unclear (Schöner & Thelen, 2006).

The third option is to use the principles of *operant conditioning*, described in **Chapter 2**. For example, an infant might be trained to turn her head when she hears a particular sound, with the sight of an interesting moving toy used as a reinforcement. After the learned response is well established, the experimenter can vary the sound in some systematic way to see whether the baby still turns her head.

preference technique
a research method in which a researcher keeps track of how long a baby looks at each of two objects shown

habituation
a decline in attention that occurs because a stimulus has become familiar

dishabituation
responding to a somewhat familiar stimulus as if it were new

LOOKING

One important question to ask about visual perception is whether the infant perceives his environment in the same way as older children and adults do. Can he see fine detail clearly or judge how far away an object is by looking at it? Does he visually scan an object in an orderly way? Developmentalists believe that infants' patterns of looking at objects tell us a great deal about what they are trying to gain from visual information.

EARLY VISUAL STIMULATION Appropriate visual stimulation in infancy is vital to the later development of visual perception. Research supporting this was undertaken by McMaster University psychologists Daphne Maurer, Terri Lewis, and their colleagues who were studying infants born with cataracts on their eyes (infants who have cataracts have clouded vision and can see only light and dark). In a longitudinal study, the researchers examined people aged 9 through 21, who, when they were between 2 and 6 months of age, had had cataracts removed and were then fitted with corrective lenses that gave them normal vision. When these individuals were examined years later, they were found to have subtle visual abnormalities. For example, they did not develop the ability to distinguish the relative position of facial features in the same way that sighted people do (Le Grand, Mondloch, Maurer, & Brent, 2001).

Although early deprivation of visual stimulation does not affect all visual processes, there are critical periods of time in early infancy and beyond when an infant or child needs a specific quality of visual stimulation to develop normal visual perception (Le Grand et al., 2001; Lewis & Maurer, 2005; Maurer et al., 2007). In some instances, early visual input of a type that visually normal newborns cannot yet detect (e.g., mid- to high spatial frequency stimuli such as thin-striped patterns) acts to set up the neural foundations that will enable later visual development to proceed normally (Maurer, Ellemberg, & Lewis, 2006). When early experience is lacking, visual capability fails to develop normally many years later. In particular, this so-called *"sleeper effect"* in the development of visual perception is apparent for sensitivity to mid- and high narrow-striped images, face processing, and facial identity based on the spacing of internal facial features (e.g., the eyes, nose, and mouth) (Maurer et al., 2007).

DEPTH PERCEPTION   One of the perceptual skills that has been most studied is **depth perception**. You need this ability any time you reach for something or decide whether you have room to make a left turn before an oncoming car gets to you. Similarly, an infant needs to judge depth to perform all kinds of simple tasks, including determining how far away an object is so that he can reach for it, how far it is to the floor if he has ideas about crawling off the edge of the couch, or how to aim a spoon toward a bowl of chocolate pudding.

It is possible to judge depth by using any (or all) of three rather different kinds of information: First, *binocular cues* involve both eyes, each of which receives a slightly different visual image of an object; the closer the object is, the more different these two views are. In addition, of course, information from the eye muscles tells you something about how far away an object may be. Second, *pictorial information*, sometimes called *monocular cues*, requires input from only one eye. For example, when one object is partially in front of another one, you know that the partially hidden object is farther away—a cue called *interposition*. The relative sizes of two similar objects, such as two telephone poles or two people you see in the distance, may also indicate that the smaller-appearing one is farther away. *Linear perspective* (e.g., the impression that railroad lines are getting closer together as they get farther away) is another monocular cue. Third, *kinetic cues* come from either your own motion or the motion of some object: If you move your head, objects near you seem to move more than objects farther away (a phenomenon called *motion parallax*). Similarly, if you see objects moving, such as a person walking across a street or a train moving along a track, closer objects appear to move over larger distances in a given period of time.

How early can an infant judge depth, and which of these cues does he use? This is still an active area of research, so the answer is not final. The best conclusion at the moment seems to be that kinetic information is used first, perhaps by about 3 months of age; binocular cues are used beginning at about 4 months; and linear perspective and other pictorial (monocular) cues are used last, perhaps at 5 to 7 months (Bornstein, 1992; Yonas, Elieff, & Arterberry, 2002).

---

depth perception
ability to judge the relative distances of objects

mydevelopmentlab
Connect to
MyDevelopmentLab

What would it be like to be a 9-month-old infant in the visual cliff experiment? Find out in this simulation.

◄●├ Simulate

In a remarkable clever early study, Eleanor Gibson and Richard Walk (1960) devised an apparatus called a *visual cliff*. You can see from the photograph that it consists of a large glass table with a sort of runway in the middle. On one side of the runway is a checkerboard pattern immediately below the glass; on the other side—the "cliff" side—the checkerboard is about a metre below the glass. The baby could judge depth here by several means, but it is primarily kinetic information that is useful, since the baby in motion would see the nearer surface move more than the farther surface. If a baby has no depth perception, then she should be equally willing to crawl on either side of the runway, but if she can judge depth, then she should be reluctant to crawl out on the cliff side.

Since an infant had to be able to crawl to be tested in the Gibson and Walk procedure, the original subjects were all 6 months old or older. Most of these infants did not crawl out on the cliff side but were quite willing to crawl out on the shallow side. In other words, 6-month-old babies have depth perception.

What about younger infants? The traditional visual cliff procedure can't give us the answer, since the baby must be able to crawl in order to "tell" us whether he can judge depth. With younger babies, researchers have studied kinetic cues by watching babies react to apparently looming objects. Most often, the baby observes a film of an object moving toward him, apparently on a collision course. If the infant has some depth perception, then he should flinch, move to one side, or blink as the object appears to come very close. Such flinching has been observed in 3-month-olds (Yonas & Owsley, 1987). Most experts now agree that this is about the lower age limit of depth perception.

In an experiment using a "visual cliff" apparatus, such as the one used by Gibson and Walk, mom tries to entice her baby out onto the "cliff" side. But because the infant can perceive depth, he fears that he will fall if he comes toward her, so he stays put, looking concerned. (*Photo:* © Mark Richards/PhotoEdit)

WHAT BABIES LOOK AT In the first 2 months, a baby's visual attention is focused on where objects are in her world (Bronson, 1994). Babies scan the world around them—not very smoothly or skilfully, to be sure, but nonetheless regularly, even in the dark. This general scanning continues until they come to a sharp light–dark contrast, which typically signals the edge of some object. Once she finds such an edge, the baby stops searching and moves her eyes back and forth across and around the edge. Thus, the initial rule seems to be "Scan till you find an edge and then examine the edge." Motion also captures a baby's attention at this age, so she will look at things that move as well as things with a great amount of light–dark contrast.

These rules seem to change between 2 and 3 months, perhaps because the cortex has developed more fully. Babies at this age begin to scan rapidly across an entire figure rather than getting stuck on edges. As a result, they spend more time looking at the internal features of an object or an array of objects.

What is amazing about this shift is the degree of detail infants now seem to be able to take in and respond to. They notice whether two pictures are placed horizontally or vertically; they can tell the difference between pictures with two things in them and

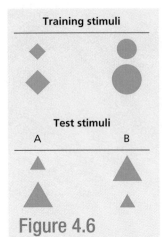

Figure 4.6

In the Carons' study, the researchers first habituated each baby to a set of training stimuli (all "small over large" in this case). Then they showed each baby two test stimuli: one that had the same pattern as the training stimuli (A) and one that had a different pattern (B). Babies aged 3 and 4 months showed renewed interest in stimulus B but not stimulus A, indicating that they were paying attention to the pattern and not just specific stimuli.

(*Source:* Caron & Caron, 1981. By permission.)

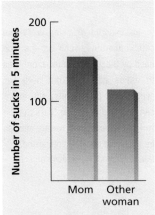

Figure 4.7

The babies in this study were 12 to 36 hours old at the time they were tested. They sucked more to see a picture of Mom than a picture of another woman who looked very much like her, thus showing that they could discriminate between the two faces.

(*Source:* Walton et al., 1992, p. 267.)

pictures with three things in them; and they clearly notice patterns, even such apparently abstract patterns as "big thing over small thing."

One early study that illustrates this point particularly well comes from the work of Albert Caron and Rose Caron (1981), who used stimuli like those in **Figure 4.6** in a habituation procedure. The babies were first shown a series of pictures that shared some particular relationship—for example, a small figure positioned above a larger version of the same figure (small over big). After the baby stopped being interested in these training pictures (i.e., after he habituated), the Carons showed him another figure (the test stimulus) that either followed the same pattern or followed some other pattern. If the baby had really habituated to the pattern of the original pictures (small over big), he should show little interest in stimuli like test stimulus A in **Figure 4.6** ("Ho hum, same old boring small over big thing"), but he should show renewed interest in test stimulus B ("Hey, here's something new!"). Caron and Caron found that 3- and 4-month-old children did precisely that. So even at this early age, babies find and pay attention to patterns, not just specific stimuli.

FACES: AN EXAMPLE OF RESPONDING TO A COMPLEX PATTERN From the beginning of this new era of research on infant perception, researchers have been especially interested in babies' perceptions of faces, not only because of the obvious relevance for parent–infant relationships, but also because of the possibility that there might be a built-in preference for faces or face-like arrangements. After 40 years of research, we do not yet have all the answers. In fact, research brings new surprises all the time. Here is a sample of what we think we know at this point.

First, there is little indication that faces are uniquely interesting to infants; that is, babies do not systematically choose to look at faces rather than other complex pictures. On the other hand, among faces, babies clearly prefer some to others. They prefer attractive faces (an intriguing result, discussed in the **Research Report**), and it now looks as if they prefer their mother's face from the earliest hours of life, a finding that has greatly surprised psychologists, although it may not surprise you.

Several studies have demonstrated that newborns learn to recognize their mother's face in the first few hours after birth (e.g., Pascalis, de Schonen, Morton, Derulle, & Fabre-Grenet, 1995). One of the best examples is a study by Gail Walton and her colleagues (1992). Walton videotaped the faces of 12 mothers of newborns and then matched each of these faces with the face of another woman whose hair colour, eye colour, complexion, and hairstyle were the same as the mother's. Each baby was then tested with one picture at a time in a modification of the preference technique. The babies could keep the picture turned on by sucking on a pacifier. The experimenters counted how often the babies sucked in order to keep Mom's picture available and compared this rate with their sucking rate for the non-Mom photo. These babies, who were only 1 or 2 days old at the time of the testing, clearly preferred to look at their own mother, as you can see in **Figure 4.7**. A newborn's recognition of, and preference for, his mother's face strengthens rapidly with exposure and becomes well established within just 5.5 hours of fixating on his mother's face (Bushnell, 2001).

This result is fascinating. Clearly, the baby can recognize the mother's features in the first hours after birth. How is this possible? Beyond the issue of preference, we also question what babies look at when they scan a face. Before about 2 months of age, babies seem to look mostly at the outer edges of faces (the hairline and the face shape), an observation buttressed by the finding of Pascalis and his colleagues (1995) that newborns could not discriminate Mom's face from a stranger's if the hairline was covered. After 4 months, however, covering the hairline did not affect the baby's ability to recognize Mom. In general, babies appear to begin to focus on the internal features of a face, particularly the eyes, at about 2 to 3 months.

Research Report

BABIES' PREFERENCES FOR ATTRACTIVE FACES

A large number of studies on infant perception seem to point toward the conclusion that many perceptual rules are inborn. One such rule seems to be a preference for attractive faces. In the first study in a classic series of experiments, Langlois and her colleagues (1987) tested 2- to 3-month-olds and 6- to 8-month-olds. Each baby was shown colour slides of adult Caucasian women, half rated by adult judges as attractive and half rated as unattractive. On each trial, the baby was shown two slides simultaneously, with each face approximately life-sized, while the experimenter peeked through a hole in the screen to count the number of seconds the baby looked at each picture. Each baby saw some attractive/attractive pairs, some unattractive/ unattractive pairs, and some mixed pairs. With mixed pairs, even the 2- and 3-month-old babies consistently looked longer at the attractive faces. Several studies, including some in which pictures of individuals of different races were used, produced similar findings in that infants showed a preference for one face in a pair regardless of race (Langlois, Roggman, & Rieser-Danner, 1990; Langlois et al., 1991). Interestingly, studies have shown that infants prefer to look at images of other infants that have been rated as attractive by adults than at images of infants who have been deemed unattractive (Van Duuren, Kendell-Scott, & Stark, 2003).

Just what makes a face attractive? You may be surprised to find out that average faces (as opposed to distinctive featured faces) are rated most attractive (Rhodes et al., 2005). Other aspects of attractiveness include attributes such as facial symmetry and femininity in females and masculinity in males (Rhodes, 2006).

Although experience affects the perception of attractiveness during development and attractiveness is also affected by one's experience with a population of faces (Cooper, Geldart, Mondloch, & Maurer, 2006; Rhodes, 2006; Rhodes et al., 2005), it is hard to imagine what sort of learning experiences could account for such preferences in a 2-month-old. These findings raise the possibility that there is some inborn template for the "correct" or "most desired" shape and configuration for members of our species, and that we simply prefer those who best match this template. From an evolutionary perspective, those very attributes that signal attractiveness may also signal mate quality. As an example, attractiveness is perceived as an indication of good health (Langlois et al., 2000; Rhodes, 2006; Rhodes et al., 2005; Rhodes et al., 2007).

Canadian researchers, for example, Daphne Maurer and Sybil Geldart of McMaster University, Richard Le Grand of Kwantlen University College, Catherine Mondloch of Brock University, and Henry Brent of Toronto's Hospital for Sick Children, have looked at the effects of early visual deprivation caused by congenital cataracts (treated in infancy) on the development of face processing and have reported several key findings. First, early visual input is required for the later development of face-processing expertise in adulthood (Geldart, Mondloch, Maurer, de Schonen, & Brent, 2002). Individuals who were deprived of early visual stimulation did not develop the ability to recognize faces in a holistic manner. That is, they failed to readily process faces as a whole (e.g., automatically recognize faces in terms of the relationship or configuration of features such as the eyes, nose, and mouth). Instead, they tended to process faces as a collection of independent facial features seen in isolation (Le Grand, Mondloch, Maurer, & Brent, 2004). A second characteristic of adults deprived of early visual stimulation is their failure to distinguish the relative spacing of facial features in the same way as normal-sighted people did to sets of faces—as depicted in **Figure 4.8**, for example (Le Grand, Mondloch, Maurer, & Brent, 2001, 2003). Adults who experienced early visual deprivation also had difficulty identifying faces when head orientation or facial expressions changed (Geldart et al., 2002).

Although face recognition increases dramatically between 7 and 11 years of age, adult-like expertise is not achieved before adolescence (Mondloch, Leis, & Maurer, 2006). Distinguishing differences in the spacing among facial features (e.g., the distance between and among the mouth, nose, and eyes) develops much more slowly than distinguishing differences in facial contours (e.g., upright faces have a common external

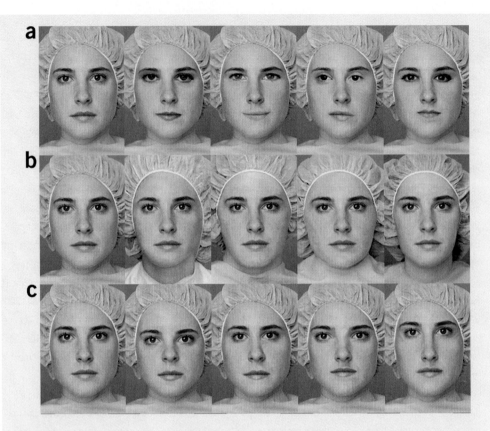

Figure 4.8

In studying sensitivity to facial differences, researchers used three types of facial stimuli: all test samples were presented close to life-size and displayed either variations in eye and mouth shape (set A), variations in facial contours (set B), or variations in the spacing of the eyes and the eyes and mouth (set C). Patients who experienced early visual deprivation caused by congenital cataracts (treated in infancy) had trouble discriminating between faces in the spacing set (C).

(*Source:* Le Grand et al., 2003. Reprinted with permission from Macmillan Publishers Ltd.)

shape along with common internal features—two eyes above a nose and a mouth) (Mondloch, Dobson, Parsons, & Maurer, 2004; Mondloch, Geldart, Maurer, & Le Grand, 2003; Mondloch, Le Grand, & Maurer, 2002; Mondloch, Maurer, & Ahola, 2006). Using fMRI (*functional Magnetic Resonance Imaging*, which will be discussed in greater detail in **Chapter 7**) technology, researchers have confirmed that facial recognition involves distinctively different neural pathways for the processing of facial features than it does for processing the spacing among facial features (Maurer et al., 2007).

LISTENING

When we turn from looking to listening, we find similarly intriguing indications that very young infants not only make remarkably fine discriminations among individual sounds, but also pay attention to patterns.

DISCRIMINATING SPEECH SOUNDS One of the central questions has to do with how early a baby can make discriminations among different speech sounds. This discrimination has obvious relevance for language development, since a baby cannot learn language until he can hear the individual sounds as distinct. Researchers interested in perception have also been investigating this question because the answers may tell us about what may be built into the neurological system.

For starters, early studies established that as early as 1 month old, babies can discriminate between speech sounds such as *pa* and *ba* (Trehub & Rabinovitch, 1972). By 6 months old, they can discriminate between two-syllable "words," such as *bada* and *baga*, and can even respond to a syllable hidden inside a string of other syllables (as in *tibati* or *kobako*) (Fernald & Kuhl, 1987; Goodsitt, Morse, Ver Hoeve, & Cowan, 1984; Morse & Cowan, 1982). Even more remarkable, the quality of the voice making the sound doesn't seem to matter. By 2 or 3 months of age, babies respond to individual sounds, whether they are spoken by a male or a female or by an adult or a child, in the same way (Marean, Werner, & Kuhl, 1992).

That's already pretty impressive evidence that infants listen to quite fine variations in speech sounds, not just at the beginning of words but in other vocal positions as well. Even more striking is the finding that babies are actually better at discriminating some kinds of speech sounds than adults are. Each language uses only a subset of all possible speech sounds. Japanese, for example, does not use the *l* sound that appears in English; Spanish makes a different distinction between *d* and *t* than occurs in English. It turns out that up to about 6 months of age, babies can accurately discriminate all sound contrasts that appear in any language, including sounds they do not hear in the language spoken to them. At about 6 months of age, they begin to lose the ability to distinguish pairs of vowels that do not occur in the language they are hearing; by age 1, the ability to discriminate nonheard consonant contrasts begins to fade (Polka & Werker, 1994) (see how speech perception sets the stage for language in the **Research Report** in **Chapter 5**).

These findings are entirely consistent with what we now know about the pattern of rapid, apparently preprogrammed, growth of synapses in the early months of life, followed by synaptic pruning. Many connections are initially created, permitting discriminations along all possible sound continua, but only those pathways that are actually used in the language the child hears are strengthened or retained.

DISCRIMINATING INDIVIDUAL VOICES Newborns also seem to be able to discriminate between individual voices. DeCasper and Fifer (1980) found that the newborn can tell the mother's voice from another female voice (but not the father's voice from another male voice) and prefers the mother's voice. Moreover, there is a correlation between gestational age and maternal voice recognition: Premature infants are less likely to recognize their mother's voice than are babies born at term (DeRegnier, Wewerka, Georgieff, Mattia, & Nelson, 2002). Thus, in utero learning appears to be responsible for newborns' preference for the maternal voice.

DISCRIMINATING OTHER SOUND PATTERNS As was true with studies of looking, there is also evidence that infants pay attention to patterns or sequences of sounds from the very beginning. For example, University of Toronto psychologist Sandra Trehub and her colleagues (1984, 1985) have found that as early as 6 months of age, babies listen to melodies and recognize the patterns. Trehub trained 6-month-old babies to turn their head toward a loudspeaker for a particular six-tone melody and then tested the babies with melodies that varied in a number of ways. Babies continued to turn their head to new melodies if the melodies had the same contour (notes going up and down in the same sequence) and were in approximately the same pitch range. They responded to the melodies as different if the contour changed or if the notes were much higher or much lower. Thus, as is true with patterns of looking, within the first few months of life, babies appear to pay attention to and respond to patterns and not just the specific sounds.

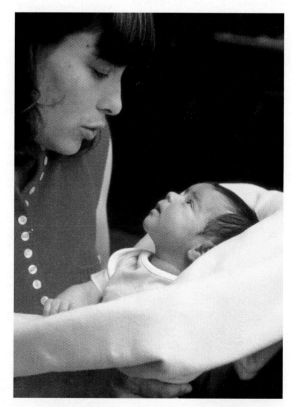

Newborns recognize their mother's voice and by 1 month of age can discriminate between syllables such as *ba* and *pa*.
(*Photo:* © Elizabeth Crews/The Image Works)

COMBINING INFORMATION FROM SEVERAL SENSES

If you think about the way you receive and use perceptual information, then you'll realize that you rarely have information from only one sense at a time. Ordinarily, you have both sound and sight, touch and sight, or still more complex combinations of smell, sight, touch, and sound. Psychologists have been interested in knowing how early an infant can integrate information from several senses (e.g., when does an infant know which mouth movements go with which sounds) and, even more complex, how early a baby can learn something via one sense and transfer that information to another sense (e.g., at what age will a baby recognize solely by feel a toy he has seen but never before felt)? The first of these two skills is usually called **intersensory integration**, while the latter is called **cross-modal transfer**.

Piaget asserted that both these skills were simply not present until quite late in the first year of life, after the infant had accumulated many experiences with specific objects and how they simultaneously looked, sounded, and felt. Other theorists, including James Gibson and Eleanor Gibson, have argued that some intersensory integration or even transfer is built in from birth. The baby then builds on that inborn set of skills through specific experience with objects. Research favours the Gibsonian view: Empirical findings show that cross-modal transfer is possible as early as 1 month and becomes common by 6 months (Rose & Ruff, 1987). Moreover, research comparing these skills in children born prematurely and those born at term suggests that basic maturational processes play an important role in their development (Espy et al., 2002).

Research suggests that intersensory integration is important in infant learning. One group of researchers found that babies who habituated to a combined auditory-visual stimulus were better able to recognize a new stimulus than infants who habituated to either the auditory or the visual stimulus alone (Bahrick & Lickliter, 2000). For example, suppose you played a audiovisual recording of someone singing for one baby, played the same recording without the sound for another, and played an audio recording of the song for a third. Research suggests that the first baby would recognize a change in either the singer (visual stimulus) or the song (auditory stimulus) more quickly than would either of the other two infants.

In older infants, intersensory integration and transfer can be readily demonstrated, not only between touch and sight, but also between other modalities such as sound and sight. For instance, in several delightfully clever early experiments, Elizabeth Spelke (1979) showed that 4-month-old infants can connect sound rhythms with movement. She showed babies two films simultaneously, one depicting a toy kangaroo bouncing up and down and the other a donkey bouncing up and down, with one of the animals bouncing at a faster rate. Out of a loudspeaker located between the two films, the infant heard a tape recording of a rhythmic bouncing sound that matched the bounce pattern of one of the two animals. In this situation, babies showed a preference for looking at the film showing the bounce rate that matched the sound.

An even more striking illustration of the same basic process comes from the work of Sandra Trehub and her fellow University of Toronto researchers (Trehub, Plantinga, & Brcic, 2009). They exposed 6- to 8-month-old babies to audio recordings of speech or singing for 30 seconds. Then the infants watched two silent visual recordings, one of which included the previously heard speaker or singer. The babies in this experiment looked significantly longer at the silent recording of the person heard previously. That is, they appeared to have some understanding of the link between the pattern of sound and the

intersensory integration
coordination of information from two or more senses, as happens when an infant knows which mouth movements go with which sounds

cross-modal transfer
transfer of information from one sense to another, as happens when an infant can recognize by feel a toy he has seen but never before felt

Even though 7-month-old Leslie is not looking at this toy while she chews on it, she is nonetheless learning something about how it ought to look based on how it feels in her mouth and in her hands—an example of cross-modal transfer. (*Photo:* © Laura Dwight Photography)

pattern of movement—knowledge that demonstrates not only intersensory integration, but also a surprisingly sophisticated use of cross-modal cues to match auditory and visual cues to the identify of unfamiliar persons.

Before Going On

 Simulate

- In what ways do babies' perceptual abilities change over the first few months of life, and how does this prepare them to interact with their environment?

- How do infants' abilities to combine information from several senses allow them to make better sense of their world?

Summary

Physical Changes

- In most parts of the brain, development of dendrites and synapses reaches its first peak between 12 and 24 months, after which "pruning" of synapses occurs. Myelinization of nerve fibres also occurs rapidly in the first 2 years.

- Adaptive reflexes disappear within a few months. Neonates move through a series of states of consciousness in a cycle that lasts about 2 hours.

- During infancy, bones increase in number and density; muscle fibres become larger and contain less water. Stamina and motor skills improve rapidly in the first 2 years, as the baby moves from creeping to crawling to walking to running and becomes able to grasp objects.

- The Canadian Paediatric Society recommends breastfeeding, which has been shown to be better for a baby nutritionally. Babies need regular checkups and a variety of immunizations.

- The rates of SIDS in Canada has declined significantly in recent decades. Several factors have been found to reduce the risk for SIDS.

Sensory Skills

- Colour vision is present at birth, but visual acuity and visual tracking skills are relatively poor at birth and then develop rapidly during the first few months after birth.

- Basic auditory skills are more fully developed at birth. The sensory capacities for smelling, tasting, touching, and moving are also well developed at birth.

Perceptual Skills

- The study of perceptual development supports the integration of nativism and empiricism. Many basic perceptual abilities appear to be built into the system at birth or to develop in the first few months after birth as the brain develops.

- Early visual stimulation is required for later visual perception to develop normally. Depth perception is present in at least rudimentary form by 3 months. Facial recognition begins early in life but isn't complete before adolescence. Babies can discriminate the mother's face from other faces, and the mother's voice from other voices, almost immediately after birth.

- Month-old babies appear to attend to and discriminate among speech contrasts present in all possible languages; by 1 year of age, the infant makes fine discriminations only among speech sounds salient in the language he is actually hearing. By 6 months of age, babies also attend to and discriminate among different patterns of sounds, such as melodies or speech.

- Touch/sight and sound/sight cross-modal transfers have been demonstrated in babies as early as 1 month old and are found reliably in 4-month-old babies.

Review Questions

Answers are provided on MyDevelopmentLab in the Course Resources folder.

Physical Changes

4.1   Why can infants bounce back from head injury more easily than adolescents and adults can?
  a.   They have not yet experienced synaptic pruning.
  b.   Their brains have greater neuroplasticity.
  c.   Their brains operate more efficiently.
  d.   They have fewer dendrites and synapses to lose.

4.2   Nathan is a newborn. If his mother usually picks him up promptly when he begins crying,
  a.   she will spoil him.
  b.   his crying will tend to increase.
  c.   he will cry less later in infancy.
  d.   he will probably not stop crying.

4.3   Which of the following factors or influences is not associated with sudden infant death syndrome?
  a.   a history of physical abuse
  b.   sleeping with quilts, duvets, pillows, or soft toys that may cover the baby's head
  c.   sleeping on the stomach
  d.   smoking by the mother during pregnancy or anyone in the home after the child's birth

Sensory Skills

4.4   Which of the following visual abilities appears to be almost identical in newborns and adults?
  a.   tracking
  b.   visual acuity
  c.   colour sensation
  d.   scanning of objects

Perceptual Skills

4.5   Which of the following illustrates the concept of habituation?
  a.   learning habits simply by being exposed to them
  b.   no longer noticing a ticking clock after a few moments of exposure
  c.   hearing someone whisper your name across a loud, crowded room
  d.   learning how to categorize information into schemes through practice

Critical-Thinking Questions

4.6   What are the social implications of newborns' poor visual acuity?

4.7   What would you say to a mother who believed that her preterm infant was unresponsive to her because the baby didn't appear to recognize her voice

© JUPITERIMAGES/Brand X/Alamy

Cognitive Development in Infancy

What do you think of when someone says that an infant is "bright" or "smart"? If you're like most people, then you probably think in terms of both age-related and individual differences: "Lucinda is a little bit ahead of most other 6-month-olds"; "Jamal seems to be typical of most 2-year-olds." Such statements assume both that there is a typical pattern or outline for cognitive development in the early years and that some children deviate from the common pattern.

When you finish studying the chapter, you will be able to characterize Piaget's explanation of the universal changes in thinking that happen in the first 2 years of life, as well as how other theorists explain Piaget's research findings; summarize learning, memory, and individual differences in intelligence among infants; and outline the pattern of language development in infants. While you read, keep the following questions in mind:

- How do psychologists and others measure what babies think, learn, and remember when babies can't use language to express themselves?

- What do babies learn from watching television and other electronic media?

- When is the best time in life to learn a second language? Why?

COGNITIVE CHANGES

The remarkable cognitive advances that happen in infancy are highly consistent across environments. Of course, 2-year-olds are still a long way from cognitive maturity, but some of the most important steps toward that goal are taken in the first 2 years of life (see **Table 5.1**).

 Watch

PIAGET'S VIEW OF THE FIRST 2 YEARS

Recall from **Chapter 2** that Piaget assumed that a baby *assimilates* incoming information to the limited array of schemes she is born with—looking, listening, sucking, grasping—and *accommodates* those schemes based on her experiences. He called this form of thinking *sensorimotor intelligence*. Thus, the **sensorimotor stage** is the period during which infants develop and refine sensorimotor intelligence.

SENSORIMOTOR STAGE In Piaget's view, the newborn who is in substage 1 of the sensorimotor stage is entirely tied to the immediate present, responding to whatever stimuli are available. She forgets events from one encounter to the next and does not appear to plan. This characteristic gradually changes across six substages during the first 24 months (Piaget & Inhelder, 1969).

Each substage represents a definite advance over the one that came before. Substage 2 is marked by the beginning of the coordinations between looking and listening, between reaching and looking, and between reaching and sucking that are such central features of the 2-month-old's means of exploring the world. The technique that distinguishes substage 2, **primary circular reactions**, refers to the many simple repetitive actions seen at this time, each organized around the infant's own body. For example, the baby may accidentally suck his thumb one day, find it pleasurable, and repeat the action.

In substage 3, the baby repeats some action to trigger a reaction outside her own body, a **secondary circular reaction**. The baby coos and Mom smiles, so the baby coos again to get Mom to smile again. These initial connections between body actions and external consequences seem to be simple, almost mechanical, links between stimuli and

sensorimotor stage
Piaget's first stage of development, in which infants use information from their senses and motor actions to learn about the world

primary circular reactions
Piaget's phrase to describe a baby's simple repetitive actions in substage 2 of the sensorimotor stage; the actions are organized around the baby's own body

secondary circular reactions
Piaget's prhase to describe the repetitive actions in substage 3 of the sensorimotor period; the actions are oriented around external objects

	TABLE 5.1	Substages of Piaget's Sensorimotor Stage	

Substage	Age (in months)	Primary Technique	Characteristics
1	0–1	Reflexes	Use of built-in schemes or reflexes such as sucking or looking. Primitive schemes begin to change through very small steps of accommodation. Limited imitation, no ability to integrate information from several senses.
2	1–4	Primary circular reactions	Further accommodation of basic schemes, as the baby practises them endlessly—grasping, listening, looking, sucking. Beginning coordination of schemes from different senses, so that the baby now looks toward a sound and sucks on anything he can reach and bring to his mouth. But the baby does not yet link his body actions to results outside of his body.
3	4–8	Secondary circular reactions	The baby becomes much more aware of events outside his own body and makes them happen again in a kind of trial-and-error learning. Scientists are unsure whether babies this young understand the causal links yet, however. Imitation may occur, but only of schemes already in the baby's repertoire. Beginning understanding of the "object concept" can also be detected in this period.
4	8–12	Coordination of secondary schemes	Clear, intentional means–end behaviour. The baby not only goes after what she wants but also may combine two schemes to do so, such as moving a pillow aside to reach a toy. Imitation of novel behaviour occurs, as does transfer of information from one sense to the other (cross-modal perception).
5	12–18	Tertiary circular reactions	"Experimentation" begins, in which the infant tries out new ways of playing with or manipulating objects. Very active, very purposeful trial-and-error exploration.
6	18–24	Beginning of mental representation	Development of use of symbols to represent object or events. The child understands that the symbol is separate from the object. Deferred imitation can occur only after this point because it requires the ability to represent internally the event to be imitated.

responses. However, in substage 4, the baby shows the beginnings of understanding causal connections, at which point she moves into exploratory high gear. One consequence of this new drive to explore is **means–end behaviour,** or the ability to keep a goal in mind and devise a plan to achieve it. Babies show this kind of behaviour when they move one toy out of the way to gain access to another. The end is the toy they want; the means to the end is moving the other toy.

In substage 5, exploration of the environment becomes more focused, with the emergence of **tertiary circular reactions**. In this pattern, the baby doesn't merely repeat the original behaviour but tries out variations. He may try out many sounds or facial expressions to see if they will trigger Mom's smile, or he may try dropping a toy from several heights to see if it makes different sounds or lands in different places. At this stage, the baby's behaviour has a purposeful, experimental quality. Nonetheless, Piaget thought that the baby still did not have mental symbols to stand for objects in this substage.

The ability to manipulate mental symbols, such as words or images, marks substage 6, which lasts from roughly 18 to 24 months of age. This new capacity allows the infant to generate solutions to problems simply by thinking about them, without the trial-and-error behaviour typical of substage 5. As a result, means–end behaviour

means–end behaviour
purposeful behaviour carried out in pursuit of a specific goal

tertiary circular reactions
deliberate experimentation with variations of previous actions that occurs in substage 5 of the sensorimotor period

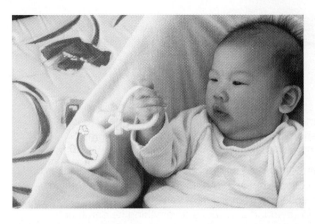

Three-month-old Andrea may be showing a secondary circular reaction here, shaking her hand repeatedly to hear the sound of the rattle. A learning theorist would say that the pleasure she experiences from hearing the sound is reinforcing her hand-shaking behaviour.
(*Photo:* © Laura Dwight/PhotoEdit)

object permanence
the understanding that objects continue to exist when they can't be seen

deferred imitation
imitation that occurs in the absence of the model who first demonstrated it

Critical Thinking

Think about children's television shows that you are familiar with. How would any of them benefit or harm the development of infants and toddlers?

becomes far more sophisticated than in earlier stages. For example, a 24-month-old who knows there are cookies in the cookie jar can figure out how to get one. Furthermore, she can find a way to overcome just about any obstacle placed in her path (Bauer, Schwade, Wewerka, & Delaney, 1999). If her parents respond to her climbing on the kitchen counter in pursuit of a cookie by moving the cookie jar to the top of the refrigerator, then the substage 6 toddler's response will likely be to find a way to climb to the top of the refrigerator. Thus, changes in cognition are behind the common impression of parents and other caregivers that 18- to 24-month-olds cannot be left unsupervised, even for very short periods of time.

OBJECT PERMANENCE   You know that this book continues to exist even when you are unable to see it—an understanding that Piaget called **object permanence**. In a series of studies, many of which involved his own children, Piaget discovered that babies acquire this understanding gradually during the sensorimotor period. According to his observations, replicated frequently by later researchers, the first sign that a baby is developing object permanence comes at about 2 months of age (in substage 2). Suppose you show a toy to a child of this age and then put a screen in front of the toy and remove the toy. When you then remove the screen, the baby will show some indication of surprise, as if he knows that something should still be there. The child thus seems to have a rudimentary expectation about the permanence of an object. But infants of this age show no signs of searching for a toy that has fallen over the side of the crib or that has disappeared beneath a blanket or behind a screen.

In substage 3 (at about 6 to 8 months), however, babies will look over the edge of the crib for dropped toys or on the floor for food that was spilled. (In fact, babies of this age may drive their parents nuts playing "dropsy" from the high chair.) Infants this age will also search for partially hidden objects. If you put a baby's favourite toy under a cloth but leave part of it sticking out, then the infant will reach for the toy, which indicates that in some sense she "recognizes" that the whole object is there even though she can see only part of it. But if you cover the toy completely with the cloth or put it behind a screen, then the infant will stop looking for it and will not reach for it, even if she has seen you put the cloth over it.

This behaviour changes again between 8 and 12 months (in substage 4). Infants of this age will reach for or search for a toy that has been covered completely by a cloth or hidden by a screen. Thus, by 12 months, most infants appear to grasp the basic fact that objects continue to exist even when they are no longer visible. Read about the influence of television viewing on cognitive development in **Development in the Real World** feature.

IMITATION   Piaget also studied infants' ability to imitate the actions of others. He observed that as early as the first few months of life, infants could imitate actions they could see themselves make, such as hand gestures. But he found that they could not imitate other people's facial gestures until substage 4 (8 to 12 months). This second form of imitation seems to require some kind of cross-modal perception, combining the visual cues of seeing the other's face with the kinesthetic cues (perceptions of muscle motion) from one's own facial movements. Piaget argued that imitation of any action that wasn't already in the child's repertoire did not occur until about 1 year, and that **deferred imitation**—a child's imitation of some action at a later time—was possible only in substage 6, since deferred imitation requires some kind of internal representation.

Development in the Real World

WHAT DO BABIES REALLY LEARN FROM WATCHING TELEVISION?

By the age of 24 months, television is a regular part of 9 out of 10 babies' daily routine (Christakis, 2009) although it has been recommended that children under the age of 2 years should be discouraged from watching television (American Academy of Pediatrics [AAP], 2009). In one longitudinal study of American infants, researchers assessed both the amount of time infants spent in front of the television and the trajectory of TV viewing over time (Certain & Kahn, 2002). They found that TV viewing of 3 or more hours a day increased from 7% in infants under 12 months of age to 41% in children between 24 and 35 months. They also found that the amount of time spent watching television at ages 24 to 35 months was associated with how much time 6-year-olds spent watching television. In contrast to children who watched less than 3 hours of television, children who watched 3 or more hours at age 2 were three times as likely to watch more than 3 hours of television at age 6. Thus, greater TV viewing in early childhood predicted greater viewing at school age.

The effects of viewing so much television during childhood remain uncertain. When asked, parents of babies younger than 2 years say they use television for its educational value, entertainment, and babysitting (Zimmerman, Christakis, & Meltzoff, 2007). Moreover, parents often believe that exposing babies to intellectual stimulation via television, especially programs produced specifically for infants, will enhance their cognitive development (Harkness, 1998). A research review by University of Winnipeg's Wendy Josephson (1995), for Child & Family Canada found that 3-month-old infants pay minimal attention to television. But, by 10 months of age, infants could imitate what they saw on television and point at familiar characters on shows that they viewed regularly. Parents should be concerned about what infants watch because later TV-viewing patterns are becoming established at this age. For instance, if left unmonitored, toddlers prefer to watch fast-paced programs, such as cartoons, which often have violent content. And, although many studies have indicated that watching TV shows with prosocial themes can have a positive impact in terms of social interactions and altruistic behaviour, viewing television with antisocial themes has been connected with negative outcomes, such as aggression and the development of stereotypes (Mares & Woodard, 2001, 2005).

It also seems clear that the extraordinary amounts of stimulation that comes from watching television contributes little or nothing to basic cognitive processes, such as the acquisition of object permanence (Bruer, 1999). In fact, studies have shown that TV viewing by children under 3 years of age, may be harmful in terms of a child's cognitive and language development in the areas of reading recognition, reading comprehension, and attentional abilities (Christakis, 2009; Zimmerman & Christakis, 2005), as well as delayed speech development, by the time they enter school (Tanimura, Okuma, & Kyoshima, 2007). Moreover, research suggests that ordinary infant toys, such as rattles and balls, and even common household items such as pots and pans, are just as useful in an infant's attempts to learn about the world as TV programs or videos (Bruer, 1999). Thus, many developmentalists suggest that, at best, the main thing babies learn from watching television is the behaviour of watching television.

CHALLENGES TO PIAGET'S VIEW

Many studies since Piaget's time have suggested that he underestimated the cognitive capacity of infants. For instance, by changing the methods used to measure object permanence, researchers have found that younger infants than Piaget suggested can understand object movements. Additionally, studies have shown that imitation appears at younger ages than Piaget's research implied.

OBJECT PERMANENCE In Piaget's studies of object permanence, infants were judged as having object permanence if they moved a blanket to retrieve a hidden object. You may recall from **Chapter 4** that infants are unable to grasp and move objects in this way until they are 7 to 8 months old. Thus, Piaget's methods made it impossible to tell whether younger infants failed to exhibit object permanence because they were physically unable to perform the task of moving the blanket.

Thanks to the advent of computers, researchers have been able to measure infants' understanding of objects in ways that do not depend on motor skill development.

In many post-Piagetian studies of object permanence, researchers use computer technology to keep track of how infants' eyes respond when researchers move objects from one place to another. These "looking" studies have demonstrated that babies as young as 4 months show clear signs of object permanence if a visual response rather than a reaching response is used to test it (Baillargeon, 1987, 1994; Baillargeon & DeVos, 1991; Baillargeon, Spelke, & Wasserman, 1985). Moreover, many studies have examined how infants respond to a moving object that temporarily disappears behind a screen (e.g., Rosander & von Hofsten, 2004). In these studies, most 5-month-olds immediately looked to the other side of the screen when the moving object disappeared behind it and were delighted when it reappeared. These findings indicate that infants are holding some kind of representation of the hidden object in mind when it is behind the screen: the essence of object permanence. Nevertheless, such studies typically show that younger infants' understanding of object permanence is tied to the specific experimental situation. By contrast, babies who are nearing or past their first birthday understand object permanence sufficiently to use it across all kinds of situations, such as when they playfully hide objects from themselves and delight in "finding" them.

Piaget assumed that a baby came equipped with a repertoire of sensorimotor schemes, but his most fundamental theoretical proposal was that the child constructed an understanding of the world, based on experience. In contrast, recent theorizing suggests that the development of object permanence is more a process of elaboration than one of discovery. Newborns may have considerable awareness of objects as separate entities that follow certain rules (Valenza, Leo, Gava, & Simion, 2006). Certainly, all the research on the perception of patterns suggests that babies pay far more attention to relationships between events than Piaget's model supposed. Still, no one would argue that a baby comes equipped with a full-fledged knowledge of objects or a well-developed ability to experiment with the world.

IMITATION   With respect to imitation, Piaget's proposed sequence has been supported. Imitation of someone else's hand movement or an action with an object seems to improve steadily, starting at 1 or 2 months of age; imitation of two-part actions develops much later, perhaps around 15 to 18 months (Poulson, Nunes, & Warren, 1989).

Yet there are two important exceptions to this general confirmation of Piaget's theory: Infants imitate some facial gestures in the first weeks of life, and deferred imitation seems to occur earlier than Piaget proposed.

Several researchers have found that newborn babies will imitate certain facial gestures—particularly tongue protrusion, as shown in **Figure 5.1** (Anisfeld, 1991). This seems to happen only if the model sits with his tongue out looking at the baby for a fairly long period of time, perhaps as long as a minute. But the fact that newborns imitate

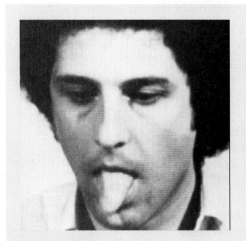
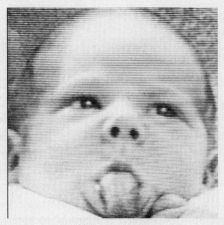

Figure 5.1

Although researchers still disagree on just how much newborns will imitate, everyone agrees that they will imitate the gesture of tongue protrusion, demonstrated here by Andrew Meltzoff from the earliest study of this kind.

(*Source:* Meltzoff & Moore, 1977. Copyright 1997 by the AAAS.)

at all is striking—although it is entirely consistent with the observation that quite young babies are capable of tactile-visual cross-modal transfer, or perception.

Most studies of deferred imitation also support Piaget's model. However, some research indicates that infants as young as 6 weeks of age can defer imitation for at least a few minutes (Bremner, 2002). Moreover, one study showed that babies as young as 6 months can defer their imitation for as long as 24 hours (Collie & Hayne, 1999). By 14 months, toddlers can recall and imitate someone's actions as many as 2 days later (Hanna & Meltzoff, 1993).

These findings are significant for several reasons. First, they make it clear that infants can and do learn specific behaviours through modelling, even when they have no chance to imitate the behaviour immediately. In addition, these results suggest that babies may be more skilful than Piaget thought. Clearly, too, more abilities than he suggested may be built in from the beginning and develop continuously, rather than in stages, throughout infancy (Courage & Howe, 2002).

ALTERNATIVE APPROACHES

The many challenges to Piaget's characterization of infant thinking discussed above have led some developmental researchers to investigate object permanence within the more general context of infants' understanding of what objects are and how they behave. Researchers use the term **object concept** to refer to this understanding. Elizabeth Spelke and her colleagues have done some very thorough and clever work on the development of the object concept (Spelke, 1982, 1985; Spelke, von Hofsten, & Kestenbaum, 1989). Spelke believes that babies are born with certain built-in assumptions that guide their interactions with objects. One of these is the assumption that when two surfaces are connected to each other, they belong to the same object; Spelke calls this the connected surface principle. For instance, you know that all sides of your textbook are connected together in a single, solid object.

In Spelke's early studies of this phenomenon (e.g., Spelke, 1982), a *violation-of-expectancy* type of procedure was used in which she first habituated some 3-month-old babies to a series of displays of two objects; other babies were habituated to the sight of one-object displays. Then the babies were shown two objects touching each other, such as two square blocks placed next to each other so that they created a rectangle. Under these conditions, the babies who had been habituated to two-object displays showed renewed interest, clearly indicating that they "saw" this display as different (e.g., an unexpected outcome), presumably as a single object. Babies who had seen the one-object displays during habituation showed no renewed interest.

In later experiments, Spelke (1991) used a *violation-of-expectancy* procedure shown schematically in the upper part of **Figure 5.2** to demonstrate that babies as young as 2 and 3 months old are remarkably aware of what kinds of movements objects are capable. Two-month-old babies were repeatedly shown a series of events such as that in the "Familiarization" section of **Figure 5.2**: A ball starting on the left-hand side was rolled to the right and disappeared behind a screen. The screen was then taken away, and the baby could see that the ball was stopped against the wall on the right. After the baby got bored looking at this sequence (habituated), he or she was tested with two variations, one "consistent" and one "inconsistent." In the consistent variation (e.g., an expected outcome situation), a second wall was placed behind the screen and the sequence was run as before, except now when the screen was removed, the ball could be seen resting up against the nearer wall. In the inconsistent variation (e.g., an unexpected outcome situation), the ball was surreptitiously placed on the far side of the new wall. When the screen was removed, the ball was visible in this presumably impossible place. Babies in this experiment were quite uninterested in the

object concept
an infant's understanding of the nature of objects and how they behave

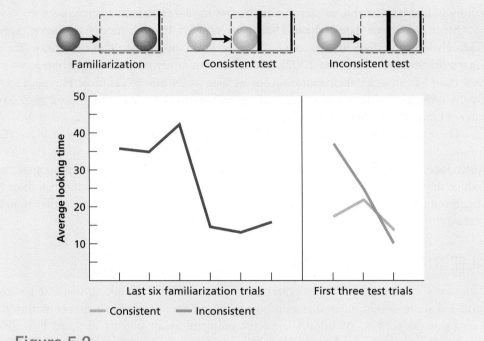

Figure 5.2

The top part of the figure shows a schematic version of the three conditions Spelke used. The graph above shows the actual results. You can see that the babies stopped looking at the ball and the screen after a number of familiarization trials, but they showed renewed interest in the inconsistent version—a sign that the babies saw this as somehow different or surprising. The fact that the babies found the inconsistent trial surprising is evidence that infants as young as 2 months have far more knowledge about objects and their behaviour than most developmentalists had thought.

(*Source:* Spelke, 1991, Figures 5.3 and 5.4. By permission of the publisher and author.)

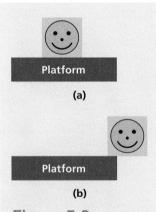

Figure 5.3

Renée Baillargeon's research suggests that 2- and 3-month-old babies think that the smiling-face block will not fall under either of these conditions, but, that by 5 months, they realize that only the condition shown in (a) is stable. The older babies know the block in condition (b) will fall.

(*Source:* Baillargeon, 1994, p. 134, Figure 1. By permission of the publisher.)

consistent condition but showed sharply renewed interest in the inconsistent condition, as you can see in the lower part of **Figure 5.2**, which shows the actual results of this experiment.

Other researchers, such as Renée Baillargeon (1994), argue that knowledge about objects is not built in but that strategies for learning are innate. According to this view, infants initially develop basic hypotheses about the way objects function—how they move and how they connect to one another. Then these early basic hypotheses are quite rapidly modified, based on the baby's experience with objects. For example, Baillargeon finds 2- to 3-month-old infants are already operating with a basic hypothesis that an object will fall if it isn't supported by something, but they have no notion of how much support is required. By about 5 months of age, babies have refined this basic hypothesis, and they understand that the smiling-face block in arrangement (a) at the top of **Figure 5.3** will stay supported, but the block in arrangement (b) on the bottom will not (Baillargeon, 1994).

Other psychologists question Baillargeon's conclusions. For example, developmental psychologist Leslie Cohen and his associates have conducted similar experiments with 8-month-olds and argue that infants respond to the stimuli used in such studies on the basis of novelty, rather than because of an understanding of stable and unstable block arrangements (Cashon & Cohen, 2000). Such varying interpretations demonstrate just how difficult it is to make inferences about infants' thinking from their interactions with physical objects.

An important question remains: When does an infant actually recognize that a particular object seen at one time is actually the *same* object viewed at another time, a process called **object individuation**? University of British Columbia psychologist Fei Xu and her colleagues (Carey & Xu, 2001; Xu, 2003, 2005; Xu & Baker, 2005; Xu & Carey, 1996) have been investigating object individuation by using a *violation-of-expectancy* looking time procedure, as illustrated in **Figure 5.4**. Their research suggests that infants use three broad categories to *individuate* objects; the first relies on *spatiotemporal* information (e.g., information about the location and motion of objects), which is active in infants at 4 months of age. The second category, which is apparent in 10-month-old infants, is based on the use of an object's *property* information (e.g., the perceptual qualities of an object, such as colour texture and size, such that an infant would know that a red ball is a different object from a green ball that is viewed on a separate occasion). The last system to develop involves the awareness of distinct *kinds* of objects (e.g., a duck versus a ball); this adult-like ability first becomes apparent in infants by 9 to 12 months of age.

Recent research has also examined the degree to which infants can make practical use of their understanding of objects and object movements. For example, several

object individuation
the process by which an infant differentiates and recognizes distinct objects based on their mental images of objects in the environment

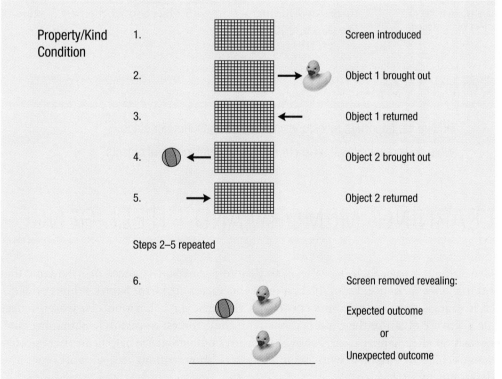

Figure 5.4

In this *violation-of-expectancy* looking time experiment, 10-month-old infants did not spend more time looking at the unexpected outcome of seeing only one object instead of two when the screen was removed. In comparison, 12-month-old infants spent more time looking at the one-object presentation: the unexpected outcome. The researchers concluded that 10-month-old infants failed to grasp that there should be two distinct objects (e.g., a ball and a duck) behind the screen, whereas the 12-month-old infants succeeded in doing so.

(*Source:* Figure 6 in "Categories, Kinds, and Object Individuation in Infancy" by Xu, Fei., 2005. In Lisa Gershkoff-Stowe and David Rakison (Eds.), *Building object categories in developmental time*. New Jersey: Lawrence Erlbaum. This work is protected by copyright and it is being used with the permission of Access Copyright. Any alteration of its content or further copying in any form whatsoever is strictly prohibited.)

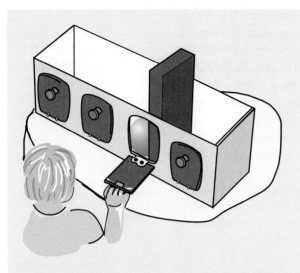

Figure 5.5

Researchers use devices such as the one pictured here to find out whether toddlers can predict that a moving object will be stopped by a barrier that protrudes above the wall of doors. Children younger than 3 years typically fail to identify the door behind which the object will be found.

studies have shown that 2-year-olds experience difficulty when they are required to use this understanding to search for a hidden object (Keen, 2003). In one study, 2-, 2½-, and 3-year-olds were shown a display similar to that in the top portion of **Figure 5.2** on page 128 and responded in exactly the same way as younger infants to the consistent and inconsistent displays (Berthier, DeBlois, Poirier, Novak, & Clifton, 2000). Next, a board containing several doors took the place of the screen, and a larger wall that protruded 8.5 cenimetres above this board was used (see **Figure 5.5**). Across several trials, children were shown the ball rolling behind the board and were asked to open the door behind which they thought the ball would be found. Even though the children could clearly see behind which door the wall was placed in every trial, none of the 2-year-olds and only a few of the 2½-year-olds were able to succeed on this task, in contrast to the large majority of 3-year-olds. Developmentalists interpret such results to mean that young infants' understanding of objects is the foundation on which the object concept is gradually constructed and applied to real-world interaction with objects over the first 3 years of life (Keen, 2003).

Before Going On

- Outline the important milestones of Piaget's sensorimotor stage.
- What does research tell us about infants' understanding of objects?

LEARNING, MEMORY, AND INTELLIGENCE

Generally, the term *learning* is used to denote permanent changes in behaviour that result from experience. From the first moments following birth, babies exhibit evidence of learning—that is, environmental forces change their behaviours. However, babies also actively organize their interactions with these forces, as research examining categorization and memory clearly shows. Measures of intelligence help health care professionals identify infants who require special interventions to support cognitive development.

CONDITIONING AND MODELLING

Critical Thinking

What other classically conditioned emotional responses might develop in early infancy? How may this affect a child's mental health or behaviour later on?

Learning of emotional responses through classical conditioning processes may begin as early as the first week of life. For example, in classic research, pediatrician Mavis Gunther (1955, 1961) found that inexperienced mothers often held nursing newborns in ways that caused the babies' nostrils to be blocked by the breast. Predictably, the babies reflexively turned away from the breast in response to the sensation of smothering. During future nursing sessions, babies who had experienced the smothering sensation while nursing at their mother's right breast refused to nurse on the right side; babies who had associated the smothering sensation with the left breast displayed the opposite pattern of refusal. Gunther hypothesized that classical conditioning was at work in such cases. She developed an intervention based on principles of stimulus-response learning to help babies "unlearn" the response of turning away from the breast they had learned to associate with the sensation of smothering.

Newborns also clearly learn by operant conditioning. Both the sucking response and head turning have been successfully increased by the use of reinforcements such as sweet liquids or the sound of the mother's voice or heartbeat (Moon & Fifer, 1990). At the least, the fact that conditioning of this kind can take place means that whatever neurological wiring is needed for operant learning is present at birth. Such results also tell developmentalists something about the sorts of reinforcements that are effective with very young children; it is surely highly significant for the whole process of mother–infant interaction that the mother's voice is an effective reinforcer for virtually all babies.

Infants can also learn by watching models. In one study, 10- and 12-month-olds were randomly assigned to two learning groups (Provasi, Dubon, & Bloch, 2001). "Observers" first watched an adult demonstrate how to find a toy by lifting the lids of various containers, and then the observers were allowed to play with the containers. "Actors" played with the containers without first watching an adult engage with them. Researchers found that observers were more proficient at finding the toy than actors in both age groups. However, the proficiency was much more pronounced among the older infants.

In an interesting variation on modelling, German researchers conducted experiments in which 9- and 11-month-old infants would play with objects (i.e., a toy car or a ribbon) and then watch a video of adults playing with the same object or a different one (Hauf, Aschersleben, & Prinz, 2007). Researchers found that infants were more interested in watching adults engage with the object the infant had previously played with than with a novel one, which suggests infants' prior experience of playing with an object increases their interest in the actions of other people with the same object. This finding that suggests a relationship between infants' actions and their perception of other peoples' actions.

SCHEMATIC LEARNING

Schematic learning is the organizing of experiences into expectancies, or "known" combinations. These expectancies, often called schemas, are built up over many exposures to particular experiences. Once formed, they help babies distinguish between the familiar and the unfamiliar.

One kind of schematic learning involves categories. Research suggests that by 7 months of age, and perhaps even earlier, infants actively use categories to process information (Pauen, 2000). For example, a 7-month-old is likely to habituate to a sequence of 10 animal pictures, and, if the next picture is of another animal, then the baby will not show surprise or look at it any longer than he looked at any of the first 10 pictures. If, however, researchers show the baby a picture of a human after 10 animal pictures, then he will look surprised and gaze at the picture longer. The same thing is likely to happen if researchers show an infant several pictures of humans and then switch to an animal picture.

Such findings suggest that infants build and use categories as they take in information. However, categorical organization as a cognitive tool is clearly not well developed in 7-month-olds. For one thing, infants of this age clearly do not understand the difference between lower-level and higher-level categories. "Dogs" and "animals," for

schematic learning
organization of experiences into expectancies, called schemas, which enable infants to distinguish between familiar and unfamiliar stimuli

example, can both be thought of as categories, but the higher-level one ("animals") includes the lower-level one. Thus, categories such as "animals" are referred to as *superordinates*. Researchers have found that infants respond to superordinate categories before they display reactions to basic-level categories (Pauen, 2002). In other words, 7- or 8-month-olds view "animals" and "furniture" as different categories, but not "dogs" and "birds." By contrast, 12-month-olds appear to understand both types of categories.

Still, 12-month-olds don't yet know that basic-level categories such as "dogs" and "birds" are nested within the superordinate category "animals." The concept that smaller categories are nested within larger ones, or hierarchical categorization, is demonstrated to some degree by 2-year-olds (Diesendruck & Shatz, 2001). However, full understanding of this kind of categorization is not typical until age 5 or so and is linked to language development and experiences with using words as category labels (Malabonga & Pasnak, 2002; Omiya & Uchida, 2002).

MEMORY

You have probably heard that it is impossible to form memories while you are sleeping, and so playing audio recordings of your textbook while you sleep is not likely to help you perform well on your next exam. However, newborns *do* appear to be able to remember auditory stimuli to which they are exposed while sleeping (Cheour et al., 2002). This interesting characteristics of infant memory is one of several.

An ingenious series of studies by Carolyn Rovee-Collier and her colleagues has shown that babies as young as 3 months of age can remember specific objects and their own actions with those objects over periods as long as a week (Bhatt & Rovee-Collier, 1996; Bhatt, Wilk, Hill, & Rovee-Collier, 2004; Gerhardstein, Liu, & Rovee-Collier, 1998; Hayne & Rovee-Collier, 1995; Rovee-Collier, 1993). A researcher first hangs an attractive mobile over a baby's crib, as shown in **Figure 5.6**, and watches to see how the baby responds, noting how often he kicks his legs while looking at the mobile. After 3 minutes of this "baseline" observation, a string is used to connect the mobile to the baby's leg, so that each time the baby kicks his leg, the mobile moves. Babies quickly learn to kick repeatedly to make this interesting action occur. Within 3 to 6 minutes, 3-month-olds double or triple their kick rates, clearly showing that learning has occurred. The researcher next tests the baby's memory of this learning by coming back some days later and hanging the same mobile over the crib but not attaching the string to the baby's foot. The crucial issue is whether the baby kicks rapidly at the mere sight of the mobile. If the baby remembers the previous occasion, then he should kick at a higher rate than he did when he first saw the mobile, which is precisely what 3-month-old babies do, even after a delay of as long as a week.

Researchers have discovered that infants as young as 3 months make associations between objects that happen to appear together in their physical surroundings (Campanella & Rovee-Collier, 2005). Further research

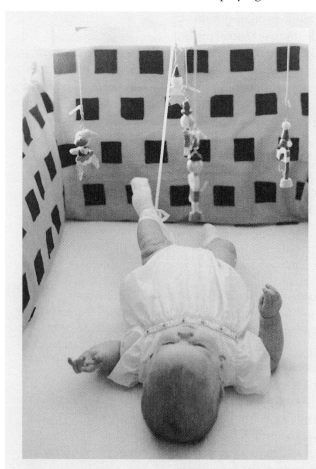

Figure 5.6

This 3-month-old baby in one of Rovee-Collier's memory experiments will quickly learn to kick her foot to make the mobile move. And several days later, she will remember this connection between kicking and the mobile.

(*Source:* Rovee-Collier, 1993, p. 131.)

found that infants as young as 6 months can not only form new associations between objects, but also form new associations with their memories of objects (Cuevas, Rovee-Collier, & Learmouth, 2006). This discovery provides evidence that what infants see when they are just "looking around" can bring to mind things they saw before and combine them in new ways. This highlights the important role of early experiences and rich and varied environments on cognitive development.

Such findings demonstrate that the young infant is more cognitively sophisticated than developmentalists (and Piaget) had supposed. At the same time, these studies support Piaget's view that infants show systematic gains in the ability to remember over the months of infancy. Two-month-olds can remember their kicking action for only 1 day; 3-month-olds can remember it for over a week; and 6-month-olds can remember it longer than 2 weeks. Early infant memories are strongly tied to the specific context in which the original experience occurred, however (Barr, Marrott, & Rovee-Collier, 2003; Bhatt et al., 2004; Houston & Jusczyk, 2003). Even 6-month-olds do not recognize or remember the mobile if the context is changed even slightly—for example, by hanging a different cloth around the crib in which the infant is tested. Thus, babies do remember more than Piaget believed, but their memories are highly specific. With age, their memories become less and less tied to specific cues or contexts.

MEASURING INTELLIGENCE IN INFANCY

As you will learn in **Chapter 7**, psychologists have designed many instruments that measure **intelligence**—an individual's ability to take in information and use it to adapt to the environment—in children and adults. However, it is quite difficult to create a test that can effectively measure intelligence in infants. Tests that measure intelligence in infancy, including the widely used Bayley Scales of Infant Development, measure primarily sensory and motor skills (Bayley, 1969). For example, 3-month-old infants are challenged to reach for a dangling ring; older babies are observed as they attempt to put cubes in a cup (9 months) or build a tower of three cubes (17 months). Some more clearly cognitive items are also included; for example, uncovering a toy hidden by a cloth is a test item used with 8-month-old infants to measure an aspect of object permanence.

Bayley's test and others like it have proven to be helpful in identifying infants and toddlers with serious developmental delays (Dezoete, MacArthur, & Tuck, 2003; Gardner et al., 2006); however, such tests have not been as useful as general predictive tools for forecasting later IQ or school performance. For example, the typical correlation between a Bayley test score at 12 months old and an intelligence test score at 4 years old is only about 0.20 to 0.30 (e.g., Bee et al., 1982)—hardly substantial enough to be used for predicting intellectual performance at later ages. On the whole, it appears that what is being measured on typical infant intelligence tests is not the same as what is tapped by the commonly used childhood or adult intelligence tests (Colombo, 1993). The most recent version of the test, the Bayley-III, includes items that address cognitive and language development in addition to those that assess sensory and motor skills (Bayley, 2006). Future research will determine whether the most recent test better predicts future intellectual performance than previous versions of the test have.

Recent research indicates that habituation tasks have high potential as measures of infant intelligence (Rose & Feldman, 1995; Rose, Feldman, & Jankowski, 2004; Slater, 1995). For example, determining the speed at which a baby habituates to (i.e., loses interest in) an object to which he's been exposed many times may reveal something about the

intelligence
the ability to take in information and use it to adapt to the environment

At 22 months, Katherine would clearly pass the 17-month item on the Bayley Scales of Infant Development that calls for the child to build a tower of three cubes.
(*Photo:* © Laura Dwight Photography)

efficiency of the baby's perceptual/cognitive system and its neurological underpinnings. And if such efficiency lies behind some of the characteristics that psychologists call intelligence, then individual differences in habituation rate during the early months of life may predict later intelligence test scores.

Some developmentalists believe that such tests will be useful indications of infant intelligence. For example, psychologist Joseph Fagan has developed a standardized test of habituation rate known as the Fagan Test of Infant Intelligence (Fagan & Detterman, 1992). Fagan argues that tests of habituation rate—also known as *novelty preference* and *visual recognition*—are particularly appropriate for individuals who are incapable of responding to conventional tests such as the Bayley scales (Fagan, 2000). For example, some infants with cerebral palsy can't perform many of the tasks required by the Bayley scales; however, they are fully capable of viewing visual stimuli and exhibiting habituation to them. Fagan's research and that of others has shown that the Fagan test is a useful measure of cognitive function among such special-case populations (Fagan & Detterman, 1992; Gaultney & Gingras, 2005; Smith, Fagan, & Ulvund, 2002). A recent longitudinal study found that a Fagan test that assessed the information-processing abilty of 6- to 12-month-old infants was moderately predictive of the infants' IQ and academic achievement at 21 years of age (Fagan, Holland, & Wheeler, 2007). This finding tells us that at least one aspect of intelligence is continuous from infancy to adulthood.

Before Going On

- How do infants learn to respond, categorize, and store into memory what they experience?
- How is intelligence measured in infancy?

THE BEGINNINGS OF LANGUAGE

Most of us think of "language" as beginning when a baby uses her first words, at about 12 months of age. But all sorts of important developments precede the first words. Before we look at these developments, though, we'll look at the various theoretical perspectives that try to explain them.

THEORETICAL PERSPECTIVES

The early discussions of language development were steeped in the classic nature–nurture debate (see **Table 5.2**). The child's amazing progress in this domain in the early years of life has been explained from both behaviourist and nativist points of view and as part of the larger process of cognitive development.

INFLUENCES ON LANGUAGE DEVELOPMENT

👁 Watch

Developmentalists better understand how the environment influences language development than they did when Skinner and Chomsky began their historic debate in the 1950s. Moreover, the increasing emphasis on the interactionist approach has led researchers to examine the kinds of environmental influences to which children are

TABLE 5.2	Theoretical Perspectives of Language Development	
Theory and Proponent(s)	**Main Idea**	**Example**
Behaviourist B. F. Skinner (1957)	Behaviourist theories of language development claim that infants learn language through parental reinforcement of word-like sounds and correct grammar.	While babbling, babies accidentally make sounds that somewhat resemble real words as spoken by their parents. Parents hear the word-like sounds and respond to them with praise and encouragement, which serve as reinforcers. Thus, word-like babbling becomes more frequent, while utterances that do not resemble words gradually disappear from babies' vocalizations.
Nativist Noam Chomsky (1959)	Nativist theories of language development state that an innate language processor called the **language acquisition device (LAD)**, which contains the basic grammatical structure of all human language, guides children's comprehension and production of language.	In effect, the LAD tells infants what characteristics of language to look for in the stream of speech to which they are exposed. Simply put, the LAD tells babies that there are two basic types of sounds—consonants and vowels—and enables them to properly divide the speech they hear into the two categories so that they can analyze and learn the sounds specific to the language they are hearing.
Interactionist Lois Bloom (2000) Melissa Bowerman (1985) Michael Tomasello (1999, 2008) Lev Vygotsky (1962)	**Interactionists** assert that infants are biologically prepared to attend to language and that language development is a subprocess of cognitive development. They believe social interactions are critical to language development.	From the beginning of language, the child's intent is to communicate, to share the ideas and concepts in his head. He does this as best he can with the gestures or words he knows, and he learns new words when they help him communicate his thoughts and feelings.

exposed during different phases of language development. For example, adults and older children speak differently to infants than they do to preschoolers, a way of speaking that researchers call **infant-directed speech (IDS)**. This pattern of speech is characterized by a higher pitch than that which is exhibited by adults and children when they are not speaking to an infant. Moreover, adults speaking to infants and young children also repeat a lot, introducing minor variations ("Where is the ball? Can you see the ball? Where is the ball? There is the ball!"). They may also repeat the child's own sentences but in slightly longer, more grammatically correct forms, a pattern referred to as an *expansion* or a *recasting*. For example, if a child said "Mommy sock," the mother might recast the text as "Yes, this is Mommy's sock," or if a child said "Doggie not eating," the parent might say "The doggie is not eating."

We also know that babies as young as a few days old can discriminate between IDS and adult-directed speech and that they prefer to listen to IDS, whether it is spoken by a female or a male voice (Cooper & Aslin, 1994; Pegg, Werker, & McLeod, 1992). This preference exists even when the IDS is being spoken in a language other than the one normally spoken to the child. Janet Werker and her colleagues (1994), for example, have found that both English and Chinese infants prefer to listen to IDS, whether it is spoken in English or Cantonese (one of the major languages of China). Other studies by Werker indicate that IDS helps infants identify the sounds in their mothers' speech that are specific to the language they are learning (e.g., the English schwa, the Spanish rolled *r*) by emphasizing those sounds more than others (Werker et al., 2007).

language acquisition device (LAD) an innate language processor, theorized by Chomsky, that contains the basic grammatical structure of all human language

interactionists theorists who argue that language development is a subprocess of general cognitive development and is influenced by both internal and external factors

infant-directed speech (IDS) the simplified, higher-pitched speech that adults use with infants and young children

IDS may be important to infants' learning of language. Babies appear to find the high-pitched quality of IDS particularly attractive. Once the child's attention is drawn by this special tone, the simplicity and repetitiveness of the adult's speech may help the child to pick out repeating grammatical forms. Children's attention also seems to be drawn to recast sentences. For example, Farrar (1992) found that a 2-year-old was two or three times more likely to imitate a correct grammatical form after he heard his mother recast his own sentences than when the mother used that same correct grammatical form in her normal conversation. Experimental studies confirm this effect of recastings. Children who are deliberately exposed to higher rates of specific types of recast sentences seem to learn the modelled grammatical forms more quickly than do those who hear no recastings (Nelson, 1977). IDS has also been shown to facilitate long-term recognition of words (Singh, Nestor, Parikh, & Yull, 2009).

Developmentalists also know that children whose parents talk to them often, read to them regularly, and use a wide range of words in their speech differ from children whose parents do not. These children begin to talk sooner, develop larger vocabularies, use more complex sentences, and learn to read more readily when they reach school age (Hart & Risley, 1995; Huttenlocher, 1995; Snow, 1997). Thus, the sheer quantity of language a child hears is a significant factor.

Finally, poverty is related to language development. By age 4, the difference in vocabulary between poor and better-off children is already substantial, and the gap only widens over the school years. Similarly, Catherine Snow (1997) found that 4-year-old children reared in poverty use shorter and less complex sentences than do their better-off peers. Many factors no doubt contribute to these differences, but the richness and variety of the language a child hears is obviously highly significant.

((•—[Listen   EARLY MILESTONES OF LANGUAGE DEVELOPMENT

Children across cultures tend to follow a common general pattern of language development, whether they are growing up learning one language or two (Genesee & Nicoladis, 2006; Werker & Byers-Heinlein, 2008; Werker, Byers-Heinlein, & Fennell, 2009). From birth to about 1 month of age, the most common sound an infant makes is a cry, although she also produces other fussing, gurgling, and satisfied sounds. Over the next few months, the number of ways in which a baby can express herself increases tremendously. Although some of these vocalizations may seem to be of little consequence, each of the early milestones of language development makes a unique contribution to the language skills that all healthy children achieve in the first few years of life.

cooing
making repetitive vowel sounds, particularly the *uuu* sound

babbling
the repetitive vocalizing of consonant-vowel combinations by an infant

FIRST SOUNDS AND GESTURES   At about 1 or 2 months, the baby begins to make some laughing and **cooing** vowel sounds. Sounds like this are usually signals of pleasure and may show quite a lot of variation in tone, running up and down in volume or pitch. Consonant sounds appear at about 6 or 7 months, frequently combined with vowel sounds to make a kind of syllable. Babies of this age seem to play with these sounds, often repeating the same sound over and over (such as *babababababa* or *dah-dahdah*). This sound pattern is called **babbling**, and it makes up about half of babies' noncrying sounds from about 6 to 12 months of age (Mitchell & Kent, 1990).

The left side of the brain controls the right side of the body and, in most people, the left brain is also home to our language capacity (see **Chapter 7** for more details on brain specialization). With these facts in mind, McGill University psychologists studied the mouth movements of 5- to 12-month-olds to see if babies display a right mouth bias when babbling similar to the right mouth asymmetry seen in adults when they talk. Indeed the researchers Holowka & Petitto (2002) found that babies differentially used

Research Report

SETTING THE STAGE FOR LANGUAGE ACQUISITION AND WORD LEARNING

Just as there are developmental milestones in motor development, it is intriguing to consider that there may also be developmental stages in speech perception and language development. Janet Werker and her colleagues at the University of British Columbia Infant Studies Centre have been studying the possibility that humans have a predisposition for language acquisition. They contend that language acquisition has two transitional stages: the first is characterized by a "reorganization of communication sounds" (Werker, 1989, p. 58) and the second, by a "reorganization in infants' use of phonetic detail" (Stager & Werker, 1997, p. 381).

To begin with, researchers believe that neonates show a bias for speech that could be innate (Vouloumanos & Werker, 2007a, 2007b). Early in her research, Werker (1995) found that newborns display a special sensitivity to speech sounds and can distinguish between human speech sounds and nonspeech sounds, e.g., dogs barking, traffic bustling, cutlery clanging. By 2½ months of age infants show a strong preference for listening to complex speech sounds compared with equally complex nonspeech sounds (Vouloumanos & Werker, 2004). At 4 to 6 months of age, infants are sensitive to all the essential speech sounds that correspond to the universal body of human language sounds (Werker, 1989); therefore, it seems that infants are perceptually ready to make the necessary sound distinctions required to learn any human language. A perceptual transition occurs, however, by 10 to 12 months of age, whereby infants, like adults, can no longer distinguish between the subtle language sounds that lie beyond the range of the dominant language in which they are being raised. This apparent loss of sensitivity to universal speech sounds is related to perceptual filtering and is not a *sensory-neural* loss, because the sensitivity can be recovered under experimental conditions (Werker & Tees, 1984). Additional evidence for a language acquisition timetable comes from a study comparing bilingual (French and English) with monolingual infants (English only), where it was found that both sets of infants 6 to 8 months of age responded in a similar manner to both French and English words (Burns, Yoshida, Hill, & Werker, 2007). By 10 to 12 months, however, the infants raised from birth in a bilingual environment were able to distinguish phonetic sounds in two language groups (French and English), whereas the monolingual infants could distinguish phonetic sounds corresponding to only one language (English). Collectively, these studies suggest that, from birth to 12 months of age, there is a shift in perceptual sensitivity away from universal speech sounds. This shift in perceptual attention facilitates the processes of language acquisition and word development (J. Werker, personal communication, July 17, 2001).

(*Photo:* Courtesy of Dr. Janet Werker.)

Not only are infants sensitive to auditory sounds, but they have also been shown to visually discriminate languages (e.g., French and English) (Weikum et al., 2007). Infants 4 to 6 months of age can detect when a different language is being spoken when shown silent video clips of bilingual speakers. By 8 months, the monolingual infants lost the ability to detect a switch in language, whereas bilingual infants were still able to visually discriminate the two languages. It seems that both auditory and visual speech information play a vital role in the process of tuning an infant's perceptual sensitivities toward their particular language environment.

Stager and Werker (1997) describe a second developmental stage based on the results of a random word–object association task. They designed an experiment in which infants were tested to see if they could notice a change in either the word, the object, or both the word and object. Stager and Werker discovered that, in the random word–object pairing task, 14-month-old infants could readily link a word with an object but were insensitive to the nuances of fine speech sound distortions. In contrast, 8-month-olds could not associate random words with objects but detected fine differences in speech sounds that the older infants failed to detect. The 8-month-olds were at a stage in which they were still developing familiarity with fundamental speech sounds, but they did not yet have the capacity to make meaningful associations between words and objects. This finding signifies an important change in perception, in which infants at 14 months, having mastered the essential sounds of their dominant language, are capable and ready to learn associations between words and corresponding objects. The ability to identify and remember word–object associations that appears at 14 months of age is an important step in the preparation for the accelerated acquisition of language and vocabulary that occurs at around 18 months of age (Werker, Cohen, Lloyd, Casasola, & Stager, 1998).

Along with the newborn's perceptual sensitivity to subtle speech sound differences, infants come prepared to differentiate words into two categories: *grammatical* and *lexical*. In infancy, a wide assortment of sound cues makes it possible for infants to distinguish between these two word categories. Specifically, **grammatical words** include those words that are primarily structural, such as articles, prepositions, and auxiliaries, which are generally of short vowel duration and have a simple syllable structure, for example, "its, the, in, and you" (Shi, Werker, & Morgan, 1999, pp. B12–B15).

By contrast, **lexical words** have high meaningfulness, such as nouns, verbs, adjectives, and adverbs. These words tend to be longer, have full vowels, and have more complex syllable structure, for example, "mommy, new, bounced, and great" (Shi & Werker, 2001, pp. 70–71).

Shi and Werker (2001) demonstrated that by 6 months infants show a clear preference for lexical words. This finding may help to explain how infants learn and understand lexical words before grammatical words—that is, an inborn preference for lexical words may serve to focus the infant's attention on those words that carry meaning, which prepares the infant for the acquisition of language (Shi, Werker, & Morgan, 1999). This innate perceptual ability to differentiate words into lexical and grammatical categories may be a critical first step in understanding the formal properties of human languages.

grammatical words
words that pertain to the rules of language and proper sentence construction, such as articles, prepositions, and auxiliaries

lexical words
words with a high level of meaning, such as nouns, verbs, adjectives, and adverbs

right mouth openings when babbling, but not when engaging in nonlanguage mouthing activity, such as chewing or crying. This finding suggests that babbling is not just generic oral-motor behaviour but is related to the beginnings of language production.

Any parent can tell you that babbling is a delight to listen to. It also seems to be an important part of the preparation for spoken language. For one thing, infants' babbling gradually acquires some of what linguists call the intonational pattern of the language they are hearing—a process one developmental psychologist refers to as "learning the tune before the words" (Bates, O'Connell, & Shore, 1987). At the very least, infants do seem to develop at least two such "tunes" in their babbling. Babbling with a rising intonation at the end of a string of sounds seems to signal a desire for a response; a falling intonation requires no response.

A second important thing is that when babies first start babbling, they typically babble all kinds of sounds, including some that are not part of the language they are hearing. But at about 9 or 10 months, their sound repertoire gradually begins to narrow to the set of sounds they are listening to, with the nonheard sounds dropping out (Oller, 1981). Such findings do not prove that babbling is necessary for language development, but they certainly make it look as if babbling is part of a connected developmental process that begins at birth.

Another part of that process appears to be a kind of gestural language that develops at around 9 or 10 months. At this age, babies begin "demanding" or "asking" for things by using gestures or combinations of gestures and sound. A 10-month-old baby who apparently wants you to hand her a favourite toy may stretch and reach for it, opening and closing her hand while making whining or whimpering sounds. Interestingly, infants of this age use gestures in this way whether they are exposed to spoken language or sign language. At about the same age, babies enter into those gestural games much loved by parents—"patty cake," "soooo big," and "wave bye-bye" (Bates et al., 1987).

WORD RECOGNITION Research has shown that babies are beginning to store individual words in their memories at around 8 months of age (Jusczyk & Hohne, 1997). By 9 or 10 months, most understand the meanings of 20 to 30 words; this ability to understand words is known as **receptive language**. In the next few months of the babies' lives, the number of words understood increases dramatically. In one

receptive language
comprehension of spoken language

investigation, researchers asked hundreds of mothers about their babies' understanding of various words. Reportedly, 10-month-olds understood an average of about 30 words; for 13-month-olds, the number was nearly 100 words (Fenson et al., 1994).

But how do babies separate a single word from the constant flow of speech to which they are exposed? Many linguists have proposed that children can cope with the monumentally complex task of word learning only because they apply some built-in biases or constraints (Baldwin, 1995; Golinkoff, Mervis, & Hirsh-Pasek, 1994; Jusczyk & Hohne 1997; Markman, 1992; Waxman & Kosowski, 1990). For example, children may have a built-in assumption that words refer to objects or actions but not both.

Learning a language's patterns of word stress may also help babies identify words. Research suggests that infants discriminate between stressed and unstressed syllables fairly early—around 7 months of age—and use syllable stress as a cue to identify single words (Jusczyk, Houston, & Newsome, 1999). For example, first-syllable stress, such as in the word *market*, is far more common in English than second-syllable stress, such as in the word *garage*. Thus, when English-learning infants hear a stressed syllable, they may assume that a new word is beginning. This strategy would help them single out a very large number of individual English words.

All this information—the beginning of meaningful gestures, the drift of babbling toward the heard language sounds, imitative gestural games, and the first comprehension of individual words—reveals a whole series of changes that seem to converge by 9 or 10 months of age. It is as if the child now understands something about the process of communication and is intending to communicate to adults.

THE FIRST WORDS

If you have ever studied another language, then you probably understood the language before you could produce it yourself. Likewise, the 9- to 10-month-old infant understands far more words than she can say. **Expressive language**—the ability to produce, as well as understand and respond to, meaningful words—typically appears at about 12 or 13 months (Fenson et al., 1994). The baby's first word is an event that parents eagerly await, but it's fairly easy to miss. A word, as linguists usually define it, is any sound or set of sounds that is used consistently to refer to some thing, action, or quality. So a child who uses *ba* consistently to refer to her bottle is using a word, even though the sound isn't considered a word in English.

Often, a child's earliest words are used in specific situations and in the presence of many cues. The child may say "bow-wow" or "doggie" only in response to such promptings as "How does the doggie go?" or "What's that?" Typically, this early word learning is very slow, requiring many repetitions for each word. In the first 6 months of word usage, children may learn as few as 30 words. Most linguists have concluded that this earliest word-use phase involves learning each word as something connected to a set of specific contexts. What the child has apparently not yet grasped is that words are symbolic—they refer to objects or events.

Very young children often combine a single word with a gesture to create a "two-word meaning" before they use two words together in their speech. For example, a

Gestures are just one of several skills in infants' repertoire of communication skills.

(*Photo:* © Laura Dwight Photography)

expressive language
the ability to use sounds, signs, or symbols to communicate meaning

These little girls probably haven't yet spoken their first words, but chances are they already understand quite a few. Receptive language usually develops before expressive language.

(*Photo:* © Michael Newman/PhotoEdit)

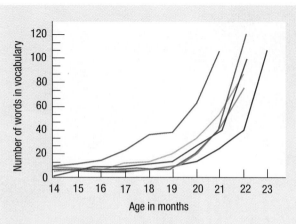

Figure 5.7

Each of the lines in this figure represents the vocabulary growth of one of children studied longitudinally by Goldfield and Reznick. The six children each acquired new words in the most common pattern: slow initial growth followed by a fairly rapid spurt.

(*Source:* Goldfield & Reznick, 1990, Figure 3, p. 177.)

holophrases

combinations of gestures and single words that convey more meaning than just the word alone

naming explosion

the period when toddlers experience rapid vocabulary growth, typically beginning between 16 and 24 months

telegraphic speech

simple two- or three-word sentences that usually include a noun and a verb

inflections

additions to words that change their meaning (e.g., the *s* in toys, the *ed* in waited

child may point to his father's shoe and say "Daddy," as if to convey "Daddy's shoe" (Bates et al., 1987). In such cases, meaning is conveyed by the use of gesture and body language combined with a word. Linguists call these word-and-gesture combinations **holophrases**, and children use them frequently between 12 and 18 months of age.

Between 16 and 24 months, after the early period of very slow word learning, most children begin to add new words rapidly, as if they have figured out that things have names. Developmentalists refer to this period as the **naming explosion**. In this period, children seem to learn new words with very few repetitions, and they generalize these words to many more situations. According to one large cross-sectional study based on mothers' reports, the average 16-month-old has a speaking vocabulary of about 50 words; for a 24-month-old, the total has grown to about 320 words (Fenson et al., 1994).

For most children, the naming explosion is not a steady, gradual process; instead, vocabulary "spurts" begin at about the time the child has acquired 50 words. This pattern, observed by several researchers, is illustrated in **Figure 5.7**, which shows the vocabulary growth curves of six children studied longitudinally (Bloom, 1993; Goldfield & Reznick, 1990). Not all children show precisely this pattern, but a rapid increase over a period of a few months is typical.

Most observers agree that the bulk of new words learned during this early period of rapid vocabulary growth are names for things or people: *ball, car, milk, doggie, he.* Action words tend to appear later (Gleitman & Gleitman, 1992). One study involving a large group of children suggested that as many as two-thirds of the words children knew by age 2 were nouns, and only 8.5% were verbs (Fenson et al., 1994). It appears that infants lack the ability to consistently associate words with actions until about 18 months of age (Casasola & Cohen, 2000). Recent cross-linguistic research also suggests that, compared with Korean-speaking parents, English-speaking parents emphasize nouns more than verbs in speaking and reading to infants (Choi, 2000). Thus, the pattern of learning nouns before verbs may be influenced by the characteristics of the language being learned, as well as by the behaviour of mature speakers as they speak to infants.

THE FIRST SENTENCES

Research suggests that sentences appear when a child has reached a threshold vocabulary of around 100 to 200 words (Fenson et al., 1994). For most children, this threshold is crossed at between 18 and 24 months of age.

The first sentences have several distinguishing features: They are short, generally two or three words, and they are simple. Language development researcher Roger Brown coined the term **telegraphic speech** to refer to this pattern (Brown & Bellugi, 1964). Nouns and verbs are usually included, but virtually all grammatical markers (which linguists call **inflections**) are missing. At the beginning, for example, children learning English do not normally use the *-s* ending for plurals or put the *-ed* ending on verbs to make the past tense.

It is also clear that even at this earliest stage children create sentences following rules—not adult rules, to be sure, but rules nonetheless. They focus on certain types of words and put them together in particular orders. They also manage to convey a variety of different meanings with their simple sentences.

TABLE 5.3	Some Meanings Children Express in Their Earliest Simple Sentences
Meaning	**Examples**
Agent–action	Sarah eat; Daddy jump
Action–object	Eat cookie; read book
Possessor–possessed object	Mommy sock; Timmy lunch
Action–location	Come here; play outside
Object–location	Sweater chair; juice table
Attribute–object	Big book; red house
Nomination	That cookie; it dog
Recurrence	More juice; other book

(*Source*: **Maratsos**, 1983.)

For example, young children frequently use a sentence made up of two nouns, such as "Mommy sock" or "sweater chair" (Bloom, 1973). The child who says "Mommy sock" may mean either "This is Mommy's sock" or "Mommy is putting a sock on my foot" (Bloom, 1973). Thus, to understand what a child means by a two-word sentence, it is necessary to know the context in which it occurred. **Table 5.3** lists typical meanings children convey with their earliest sentences.

INDIVIDUAL DIFFERENCES IN LANGUAGE DEVELOPMENT

The sequences of development of language you've read about are accurate on the average, but the speed with which children acquire language skill varies widely. One factor influencing this rate is the number of languages to which a child has daily exposure (see **Development in the Real World**). There also seem to be important style differences.

DIFFERENCES IN RATE Some children begin using individual words at 8 months, others not until 18 months; some do not use two-word sentences until 3 years or even later. You can see the range of normal variation in sentence construction very clearly in **Figure 5.8**, which shows the average sentence length (referred to by linguists as the **mean length of utterance [MLU]**) of 10 children, each studied longitudinally. Eve, Adam, and Sarah were studied by Roger Brown (1973); Jane, Martin, and Ben by Ira Blake (1994); and Eric, Gia, Kathryn, and Peter by Lois Bloom (1991). The figure includes a line at the MLU level that normally accompanies a switch from simple, uninflected two-word sentences to more complex forms. You can see that Eve was the earliest to make this transition, at about 21 months; Adam and Sarah passed this point about a year later.

More than half of children who talk late eventually catch up. The subset of those who do not catch up is made up primarily of children who also have poor receptive language (Bates, 1993; Thal, Tobias, & Morrison, 1991). This group appears to remain behind in language development and perhaps in cognitive development more generally. In practical terms, these results mean that if your child—or a child you care for—is significantly delayed in understanding as well as speaking language, you

mean length of utterance (MLU)
the average number of meaningful units in a sentence

Development in the Real World

ONE LANGUAGE OR TWO?

Canada's population consists of the world's most diverse cultural, ethnic, and linguistic peoples (Canadian Heritage, 2004). Almost 18% of Canadians are fluent in English and French and, because of recent immigration trends, about one in six Canadians speaks one of 100 other languages (Statistics Canada, 2002a). However, most children of immigrants never acquire native proficiency in their parents' language (Pease-Alvarez, 1993). Many immigrant parents believe that teaching children their language will undermine the children's future educational and economic success—even though knowing two languages is clearly a social and economic benefit for an adult. The research suggests that there are cognitive advantages and disadvantages to growing up bilingual.

On the positive side are the findings of Canadian researchers Elena Nicoladis of the University of Alberta and Fred Genesee of McGill University. They conducted a longitudinal study of infants raised in English/French bilingual homes and found that at about 2 years of age infants would start to speak in the mother's dominant language with the mother and speak the father's dominant language with the father (1996). They also noted that, unlike monolingual children who resist the idea that there can be more than one word for the same object, bilingual children had no difficulty using two translation terms for the same object.

Children are exposed to a variety of circumstances in which they become bilingual—from parents, grandparents, child-care workers, or peer groups who speak different languages—and these different circumstances can influence a bilingual child's proficiency. Consequently, to avoid incomplete acquisition (i.e., vocabulary) and functional competence (i.e., effective social and grammatical usage) in both languages, bilingual children require abundant and regular exposure to both languages.

Pettito and Holowka (2002) found that the earlier a child is exposed to two languages the better: Early exposure promotes higher levels of language competence and mastery. Moreover, bilingual children who are equally fluent in both languages encounter few, if any, learning problems in school (Vuorenkoski, Kuure, Moilanen, & Peninkilampi, 2000). However, most children do not attain equal fluency in both languages. As a result, they tend to think more slowly in the language in which they have less fluency (Chincotta & Underwood, 1997).

Thus, if the language in which they are less fluent is the language they are taught in at school, then they are at risk for learning problems (Anderson, 1998; Thorn & Gathercole, 1999). Therefore, parents who choose bilingualism should probably take into account whether they will be able to help their children become fluent in both languages. In **Chapter 9**, you will discover factors that contribute to bilingual proficiency when considering French immersion programs.

Whatever the cognitive advantages or disadvantages, children who speak their immigrant parents' language appear to develop a stronger sense of attachment to their parents' culture of origin (Buriel, Perez, DeMent, Chavez, & Moran, 1998). Additionally, teaching children about a parent's culture of origin seems to help them acquire the language (Wright, Taylor, & Macarthur, 2000). Finally, the advantages in adulthood of being bilingual are substantial and may outweigh any disadvantages experienced in childhood. Thus, bilingual parents should weigh the various advantages and disadvantages of bilingualism and consider their long-term parenting goals in order to reach an informed decision about the kind of linguistic environment to provide for their babies.

expressive style
a style of word learning characterized by low rates of noun-like terms and high use of personal-social words and phrases

referential style
a style of word learning characterized by emphasis on things and people and their naming and description

should seek professional help to try to diagnose the problem and begin appropriate intervention.

DIFFERENCES IN STYLE Katherine Nelson (1973) was the first developmentalist to point out that some toddlers use an **expressive style** when learning language. Such children's early vocabulary is not made up predominantly of noun-like words. Instead, most of their early words are linked to social relationships rather than objects. They often learn pronouns (*you*, *me*) early and use many more of what Nelson calls "personal-social" words, such as *no*, *yes*, *want*, or *please*. Their early vocabulary may also include some multiword strings, such as *love you*, *do it*, or *go away*. Children who use the expressive style are in sharp contrast to the children who use what Nelson calls a **referential style**, whose early vocabulary is made up predominantly of names for things

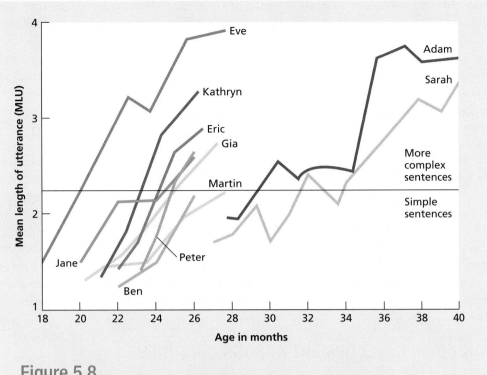

Figure 5.8

The 10 children whose language is charted here, studied by three different linguists, moved at markedly different times from simple one- and two-word sentences to more complex sentences.

(*Source:* Adapted from Brown, 1973, Figure 1, p. 55; Bloom, 1991, Table 3.1, p. 92; Blake, 1994, Table 9.1, p. 169, Figure 9.1, p. 171.)

or people. Later researchers have found further signs of such a difference in both grammar and articulation (see **Table 5.4**).

Elizabeth Bates and her colleagues (Bates, Bretherton, & Snyder, 1988; Thal & Bates, 1990) argue that referential-style children are, in some sense, more cognitively oriented. They are drawn to objects, spend more of their time in solitary play with objects, and interact with other people more often around objects. They are much more likely to show a clear spurt in vocabulary development in the early stages, adding

TABLE 5.4	Some Differences between Expressive and Referential Styles in Early Language	
Aspect of Language	**Expressive**	**Referential**
Early words	Low proportion of nouns and adjectives	High proportion of nouns and adjectives
Vocabulary growth	Slow, gradual; rarely any spurts	Rapid, with clear spurt at one-word stage
Articulation	Less clear speech	Clearer speech
Early sentences	May have inflections at stage 1	Speech is clearly telegraphic at this stage, with no inflections

(*Source:* Shore, 1995; Thal & Bates, 1990.)

many object names in a very short space of time, as if they—more than expressive children—have understood the basic principle that things have names. Such children are also advanced in their ability to understand complex adult language.

Expressive-style toddlers, on the other hand, are oriented more toward people and toward social interactions. Their early words and sentences include a lot of strings of words that are involved in common interactions with adults. Since many such strings include grammatical inflections, expressive children's early language often sounds more advanced than that of referential children, but their vocabularies are typically smaller, with no obvious spurt in vocabulary growth.

Just how these differences come about is still not clear. The most obvious possibility is that a child's early language is a reflection of the type of language she is hearing. There is some evidence, for example, that referential-style children, more than expressive-style children, have mothers who spend time naming objects and describing the child's environment (e.g., Furrow & Nelson, 1984; Goldfield, 1993). Yet it is also likely that the quality of the mother's speech is at least partially a response to the child's own language quality or style rather than—or in addition to—being a cause of it. Thus, referential children appear to elicit much more noun naming and equivalent referential speech from the mother than do expressive-style children (Pine, Lieven, & Rowland, 1997).

LANGUAGE DEVELOPMENT ACROSS CULTURES

Studies in a wide variety of language communities, including Turkish, Serbo-Croatian, Hungarian, Hebrew, Japanese, a New Guinean language called Kaluli, German, and Italian, have revealed important similarities in language development (Maitel, Dromi, Sagi, & Bornstein, 2000). Babies the world over coo before they babble; all babies understand language before they can speak it; babies in all cultures begin to use their first words at about 12 months.

Moreover, holophrases appear to precede telegraphic speech in every language, with the latter beginning at about 18 months. However, the specific word order that a child uses in early sentences is not the same for all children in all languages. In some languages, a noun/verb sequence is fairly common; in others, a verb/noun sequence may be heard. In addition, particular inflections are learned in highly varying orders from one language to another. Japanese children, for example, begin very early to use a special kind of marker, called a *pragmatic marker*, that indicates feeling or context. In Japanese, the word *yo* is used at the end of a sentence when the speaker is experiencing some resistance from the listener; the word *ne* is used when the speaker expects approval or agreement. Japanese children begin to use these markers very early, much earlier than children whose languages contain other types of inflections.

Most strikingly, there are languages in which there seems to be no simple two-word-sentence stage in which the children use no inflections. Children learning Turkish, for example, use essentially the full set of noun and verb inflections by age 2 and never go through a stage of using uninflected words. Their language is simple, but it is rarely ungrammatical from the adult's point of view (Aksu-Koc & Slobin, 1985; Maratsos, 1998).

Before Going On

- Detail what language skills babies develop during their first 2 years.
- What kinds of individual differences are evident in language development?

Summary

Cognitive Changes

- Piaget described the sensorimotor infant as beginning with a small repertoire of basic schemes, from which she moves toward symbolic representation in a series of six substages. The most important cognitive milestone of this stage is object permanence.

- TV-viewing patterns are becoming established at 10 months of age. Parents should be concerned because toddlers prefer to watch fast-paced programs, such as cartoons, which often have violent content.

- Developmentalists, such as Spelke, Baillargeon, and Xu, have studied object permanence within the context of infants' global understanding of objects. Their research shows that Piaget underestimated how much younger infants know about objects and their movements.

Learning, Memory, and Intelligence

- Within the first few weeks of life, babies are able to learn through classical conditioning, operant conditioning, and observing models.

- From an early age, infants use categories to organize information.

- Three- and 4-month-old infants show signs of remembering specific experiences over periods of as long as a few days or a week.

- Infant intelligence tests are not strongly related to later measures of intelligence.

The Beginnings of Language

- Behaviourist theories of language development claim that infants learn language through parental reinforcement of word-like sounds and correct grammar. Nativists say that an innate language processor helps infants learn language rules. Interactionists say that language development is a subprocess of cognitive development.

- Babies' earliest sounds are cries, followed at about 2 months by cooing, and then at about 6 months by babbling. At 9 months, babies typically use meaningful gestures and can understand a small vocabulary of spoken words.

- The first spoken words, usually names for objects or people, typically occur at about 1 year of age, after which toddlers add words slowly for a few months and then rapidly.

- Simple two-word sentences appear in children's expressive language at about 18 months.

- The rate of language development varies from one child to another. In addition, some toddlers display an expressive style in early word learning while others show a referential style.

- Early word learning seems to follow similar patterns in all cultures.

Review Questions

Answers are provided on MyDevelopmentLab in the Course Resources folder.

Cognitive Changes

5.1   An infant sees a toy disappear under a blanket and does not search for it. In fact, the infant acts as though the toy never existed. The infant has not yet developed

    a.   visual tracking.

    b.   intersensory transference.

    c.   primary circular reactions.

    d.   object permanence.

Learning, Memory, and Intelligence

5.2 Schematic learning assumes that
   a. babies attempt to categorize their experiences.
   b. children cannot learn unless the information is organized for them.
   c. babies will learn only if they are reinforced for exploring.
   d. learning is sequential and orderly.

5.3 Which of the following is an accurate statement about infant intelligence tests?
   a. Some studies indicate that babies who habituate quickly when they are 4 or 5 months old are likely to have higher intelligence test scores at later ages.
   b. The Bayley Scales of Infant Development accurately predict a child's intelligence at age 10.
   c. None of the infant intelligence test scores correlate with intelligence test scores at later ages.
   d. Infant intelligence tests are based on individual differences in cognitive abilities.

The Beginnings of Language

5.4 Janet Werker's speech research found that infants 4 to 6 months of age have all the following speech capabilities except
   a. a readiness to link a word with an object.
   b. a sensitivity to all the essential human speech sounds.
   c. the ability to distinguish speech from nonspeech sounds.
   d. a strong preference for lexical words.

5.5 A child's ability to understand a word that is spoken before she can say the word is called
   a. expressive language.
   b. receptive language.
   c. imitation.
   d. innate vocalization.

Critical-Thinking Questions

5.6 How would you explain an infant's habit of throwing things out of her crib to a parent who viewed it as misbehaviour that needed to be corrected?

5.7 Is it reasonable to compare infant intelligence with adult intelligence? Why or why not?

DeVore/Anthro-Photo

Social and Personality Development in Infancy

CHAPTER
6

During infancy, there is more physical closeness, or proximity, between parents and child than in any other period. Proximity is pleasurable for both parents and babies, but it is also practical. For one thing, a mother or father usually has to carry out other duties while simultaneously caring for a baby. Keeping young infants close by helps because they aren't sufficiently mobile to move to the parent when they need care. Once infants become mobile, they can get themselves into all kinds of trouble. Thus, with older babies, one of the goals of maintaining proximity is to protectively restrict their movements.

Practical considerations aside, caregiver–infant proximity contributes to the development of a strong emotional bond. In many parts of the world, mothers carry their babies with them most of the time in some kind of sling or wrap—as the Masai mother is doing in the photo on the previous page. This system is not only practical, but also keeps the caregiver and baby in close physical contact, a factor that seems to promote the development of a secure, affectionate relationship between them. In addition, physical closeness allows parents and babies to interact by exchanging smiles, frowns, or silly faces. Likewise, when parents and babies are close to each other, the parents can easily teach infants the names of objects in the environment.

In industrialized societies, a variety of devices, such as strollers, allow caregivers to easily transport babies just about anywhere an adult can go. You might think that a stroller would restrict contact between caregiver and infant; however, if you observe parents and their stroller-bound infants at a shopping mall or park, then you will see babies taken out of their strollers to be fed and put back in for naps. You will also notice that parents wheel infants to places they think the babies will find interesting—such as a pet-store window where kittens are frolicking—and converse with the babies about what they see: "Look at the kitties. Aren't they cute?" Thus, baby slings such as those used by the Masai may look very different from the industrialized world's strollers, but both help caregivers and infants form relationships.

Developmentalists of diverse theoretical orientations agree that the formation of a strong emotional connection to a primary caregiver early in life is critical to healthy child development and has important implications across the entire human lifespan.

When you finish studying the chapter, you will be able to describe the key points of the psychoanalytic and ethological perspectives of social and personality development; discuss how attachment relationships develop in infancy; explain the inborn biases concerning social interaction that infants bring with them into the world, as well as how their perceptions of themselves develop over the first 2 years; and address the effects of nonparental care on infant development. While you read, keep the following questions in mind:

- Why is it important, and what can a parent do, to help their baby develop a sense of trust?

- What are the signs that a 6- to 8-month-old baby has formed a secure attachment to a parent?

- What can a parent do to build a secure attachment with their child who has a difficult temperament?

THEORIES OF SOCIAL AND PERSONALITY DEVELOPMENT

Psychologists use all the theoretical perspectives you learned about in **Chapter 2** to formulate hypotheses about infant social and personality development. The two most influential perspectives on these issues are the psychoanalytic and the ethological perspectives.

PSYCHOANALYTIC PERSPECTIVES

You may recall from **Chapter 2** that Freud proposed a series of psychosexual stages that extend from birth through adolescence, during which individuals attempt to satisfy certain basic drives in different ways. In the oral stage, from birth to age 2, infants derive satisfaction through the mouth. Freud further believed that the weaning process should be managed in such a way that the infant's need to suck is neither frustrated nor overgratified. The consequences of either, Freud claimed, would be fixation at this stage of development. As a result of fixation, the infant would carry with her into adulthood a need to use her mouth to attain physical gratification of her instinctual drives. Fixation would manifest itself, in Freud's view, in oral behaviours such as nail-biting and swearing.

Freud also emphasized the *symbiotic* relationship between the mother and young infant, in which the two behave as if they were one. He believed that the infant did not understand herself to be separate from her mother. Thus, another result of a gratifying nursing period followed by a balanced weaning process, Freud thought, was the infant's development of a sense of both attachment to and separation from the mother.

Erikson went beyond Freud's view. Nursing and weaning are important, he conceded, but they are only one aspect of the overall social environment. Erikson claimed that responding to the infant's other needs by talking to him, comforting him, and so on, was just as important. He proposed that during the first 2 years of life the infant learns to trust the world around him or becomes cynical about the social environment's ability to meet his needs: the *trust versus mistrust stage*.

One of the best-known studies in developmental psychology demonstrated that Erikson's view of infant development was more accurate than Freud's (Harlow & Zimmerman, 1959). In this study, infant monkeys were separated from their mothers at birth. The experimenters placed two different kinds of surrogate mothers in their cages. The monkeys received all their feedings from a wire mother with a nursing bottle attached. The other mother was covered with soft terrycloth. The researchers found that the monkeys approached the wire mother only when hungry. Most of the time, they cuddled against the cloth mother and ran to it whenever they were frightened or stressed. Subsequent studies with human infants correlating maternal feeding practices with infant adjustment suggested that the infant's social relationships are not based solely on either nursing or weaning practices (Schaffer & Emerson, 1964).

ETHOLOGICAL PERSPECTIVES

 Watch

The strongest theoretical influence in modern-day studies of infant–parent relationships is an ethological approach known as **attachment theory**, based originally on the work of John Bowlby (1969, 1973, 1980, 1988a, 1988b). Bowlby argued that "the propensity to make strong emotional bonds to particular individuals [is] a basic component of human nature, already present in germinal form in the neonate" (1988a, p. 3). Such relationships have survival value, because they ensure that the infant will be nurtured. They are built and maintained by instinctive behaviours that create and sustain proximity between parent and child.

The writings of Ainsworth (described in **Chapter 1** in A Brief History of the Roots of Psychology in Canada) and Bowlby draw a distinction between different types of affectionate human relationships (Ainsworth, Blehar, Waters, & Wall, 1978). An **affectional bond** is defined as "a relatively long-enduring tie in which the partner is important as a unique individual and is interchangeable with none other. In an affectional bond, there is a desire to maintain closeness to the partner" (Bowlby, 1989,

Freud asserted that infant weaning practices were central to the attachment process.
(*Photo:* Thinkstock)

Harlow's ingenious research demonstrated that infant monkeys became attached to a terrycloth covered "mother" and would cling to it rather than to a wire mother that provided them with food.
(*Photo:* © Martin Rogers/Woodfin Camp and Associates)

attachment theory
the view that the ability and need to form an attachment relationship early in life are genetic characteristics of all human beings

affectional bond
the emotional tie to an infant experienced by a parent

Critical Thinking

Think about your own relationships. In Ainsworth's and Bowlby's terms, which are affectional bonds and which are attachments?

attachment
the emotional tie to a parent experienced by an infant, from which the child derives security

reactive attachment disorder
a disorder that appears to prevent a child from forming close social relationships

 Watch

p. 711). An **attachment** is a type of affectional bond in which a person's sense of security is bound up in the relationship. When you are attached, you feel a special sense of security and comfort in the presence of the other, and you can use the other as a "safe base" from which to explore the rest of the world.

Ethologists believe that the first 2 years of life constitute a sensitive period for attachment in human infants. They claim that infants who fail to form a close relationship with a primary caregiver are at risk for future social and personality problems. Studies of infants whose life circumstances do not permit them to engage in extended contact with a single caregiver—such as children who are brought up in orphanages or who are hospitalized for long periods during infancy—seem to confirm ethologists' view (DeAngelis, 1997; Fahrenfort, Jacobs, Miedema, & Schweizer, 1996). For example, children who are adopted after spending more than 2 years in an orphanage are more likely to suffer from a disorder known as **reactive attachment disorder** than those who are adopted in infancy (DeAngelis, 1997). Children with reactive attachment disorder seem to be unable to form close emotional relationships with anyone, including foster and adoptive parents. Long-term institutional care is also associated with cognitive deficits (Castle et al., 1999). Even children whose institutional care does not extend beyond the first 2 years are more likely to display developmental delays and emotional difficulties the later in infancy they are adopted (De Angelis, 1997; see **Research Report**).

Research Report

ADOPTION AND DEVELOPMENT

Most people who adopt a child assume that if they provide enough love and support, then the child will develop both cognitively and emotionally pretty much the way their biological child would. By now, you should know enough about human development to realize that it just isn't that simple. For one thing, many aspects of temperament and personality are inherited. Therefore, an adopted child is more likely than a biological child to be different from his parents in these traits, which may give rise to problems. For example, if two extremely shy parents adopt a very outgoing child, then the parents may view the child's behaviour as difficult or even "disturbed" in some way, rather than just different from theirs.

Adoptive parents also need to take into account the child's circumstances prior to the adoption to form a realistic set of expectations. Children adopted before the age of 6 months who have no history of institutionalization or abuse are generally indistinguishable from nonadopted children in security of attachment, cognitive development, and social adjustment. This is true whether adoptive parents and children are of the same or different races and/or nationalities (Juffer & Rosenboom, 1997).

In special circumstances, however, the outcomes are more equivocal. For instance, researchers from Simon Fraser University have been studying Romanian orphans (RO) who were adopted by Canadian families early in the 1990s. The infants had been raised in Romanian orphanages, where they experienced extreme deprivation, understimulation, malnourishment, and only minimal custodial care. Elinor Ames's (1997) research team found that the infants who had lived in the Romanian orphanages for more than 4 months before being adopted by British Columbian families tended to have more psychological and motor-behaviour problems than nonadopted children. Moreover, the more months an infant had lived in the Romanian orphanage the more serious his or her difficulties were.

Lucy Le Mare has continued the project and last assessed the RO when they were 10 years old (Le Mare, Warford, & Fernyhough, 2001; Le Mare, Fernyhough, & Warford, 2001). Her team found that there was considerable variability between individuals, but as a group the RO continued to show significantly more difficulties than comparable Canadian-born or early-adopted Romanian children. In particular, RO children had lower than average IQs and academic achievement, and more difficulties with attention, learning, and peer relationships.

Despite these challenges, the RO children were just as well liked as any other child and the adoption experience has continued to be mutually rewarding for both the RO children and their adoptive families.

Accordingly, parents who adopt high-risk children should keep the following important facts in mind. Children who are adopted later, who have histories of abuse and/or neglect, or who have lived in institutions for long periods tend to have more problems, both cognitive and emotional, than nonadopted children (Castle et al., 1999; Howe & Fearnley, 2003). All the same, adopted children are better off developmentally than their peers who remain institutionalized or who are returned to biological parents who abused and/or neglected them (Bohman & Sigvardsson, 1990). Further, despite increased risks, the large majority of adopted children are indistinguishable from nonadopted children in social behaviour and emotional functioning by the time they reach late adolescence or adulthood (Brand & Brinich, 1999; Cederblad, Hook, Irhammar, & Mercke, 1999).

Before Going On

- How do Freud's and Erikson's views of personality development in the first 2 years differ?
- What is attachment theory, and what evidence suggests that the first 2 years of life are a critical period for forming an attachment?

ATTACHMENT

Somehow, in the midst of endless diaper changes, food preparation, baths, and the periods of exhaustion that exceed anything they have ever experienced before, the overwhelming majority of parents manage to respond to their infants in ways that foster the development of a close relationship. To understand the early relationship between parent and infant, it is important to look at both sides of the equation—at the development of both the parents' bond to the child and the child's attachment to the parents.

synchrony
a mutual, interlocking pattern of attachment behaviours shared by a parent and a child

THE PARENTS' ATTACHMENT TO THE INFANT

Contact between mother and infant immediately after birth does not appear to be either necessary or sufficient for the formation of a stable long-term bond between them (Wong, 1993). What is essential in the formation of that bond is the opportunity for mother and infant to develop a mutual, interlocking pattern of attachment behaviours, called **synchrony** (Moore, 2007). Synchrony is like a conversation. The baby signals his needs by crying or smiling; he responds to being held by quieting or snuggling; he looks at the parents when they look at him. The mother, in turn, enters into the interaction with her own repertoire of caregiving behaviours.

The father's bond with the infant, like the mother's, seems to depend more on the development of synchrony than on contact immediately after birth. Aiding the development of such mutuality is the fact that fathers seem to have the same repertoire of attachment behaviours as do mothers. In the early weeks of the baby's life, fathers touch, talk to, and cuddle their babies in the same ways that mothers do (Parke & Tinsley, 1981).

After the first weeks of the baby's life, however, signs of a kind of specialization of parental behaviours begin to emerge. Fathers spend more time playing with the baby, with more physical roughhousing; mothers spend more time in routine caregiving and

Fathers engage in physical play with infants more often than mothers do. (*Photo:* © Lynne J. Weinstein/Woodfin Camp and Associates)

also talk to and smile at the baby more (Walker, Messinger, Fogel, & Karns, 1992). This difference does not mean that fathers have a weaker affectional bond with the infant; it simply means that fathers and mothers use different attachment behaviours in interacting with their infants. For instance, Canadian researchers found that fathers can be as sensitive to the needs of their children as mothers. However, fathers are less consistent than mothers in responding to infant cues, sometimes reacting and sometimes not (Harrison, Magill-Evans, & Benzies, 1999). It has also been found that fathers who reported that they felt accepted during their childhood were more responsive to their offspring. Moreover, if the father's current level of marital satisfaction was high he was more responsive to his child's needs, regardless of his perception of his own childhood experiences (Onyskiw, Harrison, & Magill-Evans, 1997).

By 6 months, infants display distinctive patterns of responding to these mother–father differences (Feldman, 2003). Signs of positive emotional states, such as smiling, appear gradually and subtly when babies are interacting with their mothers. In contrast, babies laugh and wriggle with delight in short, intense bursts in interactions with their fathers. Again, it isn't a matter of babies' preference for one parent or the other. Instead, such results mean that infants recognize the same behavioural differences in mothers and fathers that developmental scientists do when they observe parental behaviour. In fact, some researchers have noted that measures of attachment behaviours based on typical mother–infant interactions may cause researchers to inappropriately conclude that fathers are less involved with babies than mothers and, therefore, less important to infants' development (Lewis & Lamb, 2003). To the contrary, research clearly indicates that babies benefit tremendously when both kinds of interaction are available to them.

THE INFANT'S ATTACHMENT TO THE PARENTS

Like the parents' bond to the baby, the baby's attachment emerges gradually and is based on her ability to discriminate between her parents and other people. As you learned in **Chapters 3** and **5**, an infant can recognize her mother's voice prior to birth. By the time the baby is a few days old, she recognizes her mother by sight and smell as well (Cernoch & Porter, 1985; Walton, Bower, & Bower, 1992). Thus, the cognitive foundation for attachment is in place within days after birth.

ESTABLISHING ATTACHMENT   Bowlby suggested four phases in the development of the infant's attachment (Bowlby, 1969). Bowlby and other ethologists claim that these phases appear in a fixed sequence over the first 24 to 36 months of life that is strongly influenced by genes that are present in all healthy human infants. The infant exhibits a distinctive set of attachment-related behaviours and interaction patterns in each phase.

- Phase 1: *Nonfocused orienting and signalling (birth to 3 months)*. Babies exhibit what Ainsworth (1989) described as "proximity promoting" behaviours: actions that signal their needs and draw the attention of others, such as crying, making eye contact, clinging, cuddling, and responding to caregiving efforts by being soothed. Babies direct these signals to everyone with whom they come into contact.

- Phase 2: *Focus on one or more figures (3 to 6 months)*. Babies direct their "come here" signals to fewer people, typically those with whom they spend the most time, and are less responsive to unfamiliar people.

- Phase 3: *Secure base behaviour (6 to 24 months)*. True attachment emerges. Babies show what Ainsworth called "proximity seeking" behaviours, such as following and clinging to caregivers whom they regard as "safe bases," especially when they are anxious, injured, or have physical needs, such as hunger. Most babies direct

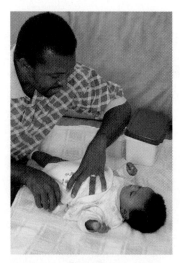

Dads like this one, who get involved with the day-to-day care of their babies, seem to develop stronger attachment relationships with their babies.
(*Photo:* Laura Dwight/PhotoEdit)

these behaviours to a primary caregiver when that person is available and to others only when the primary caregiver, for some reason, cannot or will not respond to them or is absent (Lamb, 1981). Not all infants have a single attachment figure, even at this stage. Some may show strong attachment to both parents or to a parent and another caregiver, such as a babysitter or a grandparent. But even these babies, when under stress, usually show a preference for one of their favoured persons over the others.

- Phase 4: *Internal model (24 months and beyond)*. An internal model of the attachment relationship allows children older than 2 years to imagine how an anticipated action might affect the bonds they share with their caregivers (van IJzendoorn, 2005). The internal model plays a role in later relationships with early caregivers (i.e., adult children and their parents) and in other significant relationships (i.e., romantic partnerships) throughout life.

ATTACHMENT BEHAVIOURS Once the child has developed a clear attachment, at about 6 to 8 months of age, several related behaviours also begin appearing. *Stranger anxiety* and *separation anxiety*, attachment behaviours that are rare before 5 or 6 months, rise in frequency until about 12 to 16 months, and then decline. Infants express **stranger anxiety** with behaviours such as clinging to their mothers when strangers are present. **Separation anxiety** is evident when infants cry or protest being separated from the primary caregiver. The research findings are not altogether consistent, but fear of strangers apparently emerges first. Separation anxiety starts a bit later but continues to be visible for a longer period. Such an increase in fear and anxiety has been observed in children from a number of different cultures, and in both home-reared children and children in daycare.

Another attachment behaviour is **social referencing** (Walden, 1991). By roughly 10 months, infants use cues from the facial expressions of their attachment figures to help them figure out what to do in novel situations, such as when a stranger comes to visit. Babies this age will first look at Mom's or Dad's face to check for the adult's emotional expression. If Mom looks pleased or happy, then the baby is likely, for example,

stranger anxiety
expressions of discomfort, such as clinging to the mother, in the presence of strangers

separation anxiety
expressions of discomfort, such as crying, when separated from an attachment figure

social referencing
infants' use of others' facial expressions as a guide to their own emotions

Whether a child cries when he is separated from his mother is not a helpful indicator of the security of his attachment. Some securely attached infants cry when separated from their mothers; others do not. The same is true of insecurely attached infants.
(*Photo:* Laura Dwight/Photo Edit)

to accept a stranger with less fuss. If Mom looks concerned or frightened, then the baby responds to those cues and reacts to the novel situation with equivalent fear or concern.

Social referencing also helps babies learn to regulate their own emotions. For example, an infant who is angry because an enjoyable activity is no longer available may use his caregiver's pleasant, comforting emotional expressions to transition himself into a more pleasant emotional state. By contrast, a baby whose caregiver responds to his anger with more anger may experience an escalation in the level of his own angry feelings. Researchers use the term **affect dysregulation** to refer to this kind of interaction pattern. The pattern is more common in infant–mother pairs in which the mother displays low levels of sensitivity to the infant's needs and the infant is insecurely attached (National Institute of Child Health and Human Development [NICHD] Early Child Care Research Network, 2004a). Most developmentalists think that the quality of the emotional give-and-take in interactions between an infant and his caregivers is important to the child's ability to control emotions such as anger and frustration in later years (Cole, Martin, & Dennis, 2004).

affect dysregulation
an interaction pattern in which a caregiver's emotional responses to an infant interfere with the baby's ability to learn how to regulate his or her emotions

INTERNAL MODELS In Bowlby's terminology, infants create different internal models of their relationships with parents and other key adults. These models include elements such as the child's confidence (or lack of it) that the attachment figure will be available or reliable, the child's expectation of rebuff or affection, and the child's sense of assurance that the caregiver is really a safe base for exploration. The internal model begins to be formed late in the child's first year of life and becomes increasingly elaborated and better established through the first 4 or 5 years. By age 5, most children have a clear internal model of the mother (or other primary caregiver), a self model, and a model of relationships. Once formed, such models shape and explain experiences and affect memory and attention. Children notice and remember experiences that fit their models and miss or forget experiences that don't match. As Piaget might say, a child more readily assimilates data that fit the model. More importantly, the model affects the child's behaviour: The child tends to re-create in each new relationship the pattern with which he is familiar.

VARIATIONS IN ATTACHMENT QUALITY

Virtually all babies seem to go through the three phases of attachment first identified by Bowlby, but the quality of the attachments they form differs from one infant to the next.

Connect to
MyDevelopmentLab
Be the researcher and assess these children's attachment types in the *Strange Situation*.

Simulate

SECURE AND INSECURE ATTACHMENTS Variations in the quality of the first attachment relationship are now almost universally described using Ainsworth's category system (Ainsworth et al., 1978). The Ainsworth system distinguishes between secure attachment and two types of insecure attachment, which psychologists assess by using a procedure called the *Strange Situation*.

The Strange Situation consists of a series of eight episodes played out in a laboratory setting, typically with children between 12 and 18 months of age. The child is observed in each of the following situations:

- With the mother
- With the mother and a stranger
- Alone with the stranger
- Completely alone for a few minutes
- Reunited with the mother
- Alone again

- With the stranger again
- Reunited with the mother

Ainsworth suggested that children's reactions in these situations—particularly to the reunion episodes—showed attachment of one of three types: **secure attachment, avoidant attachment**, and **ambivalent attachment**. A fourth type, **disorganized/disoriented attachment**, includes attachment reactions that do not readily fit into the other two insecure patterns (Main & Solomon, 1990).

A child's crying upon separation from his mother does not indicate the security of his attachment. The entire pattern of a child's response to the Strange Situation is critical, not any one response. These attachment types have been observed in studies in many different countries, and secure attachment is the most common pattern in every country.

David Pederson and Greg Moran (1996) of the University of Western Ontario have refined the measurement of attachment. Unlike the Strange Situation, which is laboratory-based, they observed mother–infant interactions in the more natural and convenient surroundings of the home environment. The use of either method revealed that in a secure type of relationship, mothers were more sensitive to their infant's needs and their infant tended to be less fussy and enjoyed physical contact with the mother (Pederson & Moran, 1996; Pederson, Gleason, Moran, & Bento, 1998).

STABILITY OF ATTACHMENT CLASSIFICATION Researchers have found that the quality of a child's attachment can be either consistent or changeable. It seems that, when a child's family environment or life circumstances are reasonably consistent, the security or insecurity of her attachment also seems to remain consistent, even over many years (Hamilton, 1995; Weinfield & Egeland, 2004). However, when a child's circumstances change in some major way, such as when the parents divorce or the family moves, the security of the child's attachment may change as well, either from secure to insecure, or the reverse. For example, in one important study, developmentalists followed one group of middle-class white children from 1 to 21 years of age (Waters, Treboux, Crowell, Merrick, & Albersheim, 1995). Those whose attachment classification changed over this long interval had nearly all experienced some major upheaval, such as the death of a parent, physical or sexual abuse, or a serious illness.

The fact that the security of a child's attachment can change over time does not refute the notion of attachment as arising from an internal model. Bowlby suggested that, for the first 2 or 3 years, the particular pattern of attachment a child shows is in some sense a property of each specific relationship. For example, studies of toddlers' attachments to mothers and fathers show that about 30% of the children are securely attached to one parent and insecurely attached to the other, with both possible combinations equally likely (Fox, Kimmerly, & Schafer, 1991). It is the quality of each relationship that determines the security of the child's attachment to that specific adult. If the relationship changes markedly, the security of attachment may change, too. But, Bowlby argued, by age 4 or 5, the internal model becomes more a property of the child and more generalized across relationships, and thus more resistant to change. At that point, the child tends to impose the model on new relationships, including relationships with teachers or peers.

CAREGIVER CHARACTERISTICS AND ATTACHMENT

Researchers have found that several characteristics of caregivers influence the attachment process. These characteristics include the caregivers' emotional responses to the infant, their marital and socioeconomic status, and their mental health.

secure attachment
a pattern of attachment in which an infant readily separates from the parent, seeks proximity when stressed, and uses the parent as a safe base for exploration

avoidant attachment
a pattern of attachment in which an infant avoids contact with the parent and shows no preference for the parent over other people

ambivalent attachment
a pattern of attachment in which the infant shows little exploratory behaviour, is greatly upset when separated from the parent, and is not reassured by his or her return or efforts to comfort him

disorganized/disoriented attachment
a pattern of attachment in which an infant seems confused or apprehensive and shows contradictory behaviour, such as moving toward the parent while looking away from him or her

EMOTIONAL RESPONSIVENESS Studies of parent–child interactions suggest that one crucial ingredient for secure attachment is *emotional availability* on the part of the primary caregiver (Biringen, 2000). An emotionally available caregiver is one who is able and willing to form an emotional attachment to the infant. For example, economically or emotionally distressed parents may be so distracted by their own problems that they can't invest emotion in the parent–infant relationship. Such parents may be able to meet the baby's physical needs but unable to respond emotionally.

Contingent responsiveness is another key ingredient of secure attachment (Isabella, 1995; Pederson & Moran, 1995; Pederson et al., 1990; Seifer, Schiller, Sameroff, Resnick, & Riordan, 1996). Parents who demonstrate **contingent responsiveness** are sensitive to the child's cues and respond appropriately. They smile when the baby smiles, talk to the baby when he vocalizes, pick him up when he cries, and so on (Ainsworth & Marvin, 1995). Infants of parents who display contingent responsiveness in the early months after birth are more likely to be securely attached at 12 months (Heinicke et al., 2000).

A low level of parental responsiveness thus appears to be an ingredient in any type of insecure attachment. However, each of the several subvarieties of insecure attachment is affected by additional distinct factors. For example, if the mother rejects the infant or regularly withdraws from contact with her, the baby is more likely to show an avoidant pattern of attachment, although the pattern also seems to occur when the mother is overly intrusive or overly stimulating toward the infant (Isabella, 1995). An ambivalent pattern is more common when the primary caregiver is inconsistently or unreliably available to the child. A disorganized/disoriented pattern seems especially likely when the child has been abused and in families in which either parent had some unresolved trauma in his or her own childhood, such as abuse or a parent's early death (Cassidy & Berlin, 1994; Main & Hesse, 1990).

MARITAL STATUS AND SES One caregiver variable that predicts attachment quality is marital status. Researchers have found that infants whose parents are married are more likely to be securely attached than babies whose parents are either cohabiting or single (e.g., Rosenkrantz, Aronson, & Huston, 2004). However, the effects of marital status may be due to other characteristics of parents who choose to marry, cohabit, or remain single. One such characteristic is educational background, with married parents typically having the most education of the three. Another is socioeconomic status (SES), with married parents less likely to be poor than parents in the other groups.

Married parents are also, on average, older than parents in the other two groups (Rosenkrantz et al., 2004). Most of the information about the influence of maternal age on the attachment process comes from studies comparing adolescent mothers with older mothers. These studies suggest that, with increasing age, mothers become less likely to describe their babies as "difficult" (Miller, Eisenberg, Fabes, & Shell, 1996). Moreover, older mothers display more sensitive caregiving behaviours than teenagers. Of course, teenaged mothers are likely to have less education and fewer economic resources than older mothers. Thus, it's hard to say whether age or maturity is responsible for the associations between maternal age and parenting characteristics. Finally, marital conflict poses risks for the development of attachment. Researchers have found that 6-month-olds who are exposed to parental arguments, especially those in which parents are verbally aggressive toward each other, are more likely to display signs of emotional withdrawal than babies who are not so exposed (Crockenberg, Leerkes, & Lekka, 2007). Emotional withdrawal on the part of the infant interferes with synchrony, thereby lessening the chances that he will develop a secure attachment to his primary caregiver.

contingent responsiveness being sensitive to the child's verbal and nonverbal cues and responding appropriately

MENTAL HEALTH Psychiatric illness is another caregiver characteristic that appears to be related to attachment quality (Murray et al., 1999; Teti, Gelfand, Messinger, & Isabella, 1995). Developmentalists have found that babies who interact regularly with a depressed mother express more negative and fewer positive emotions. Some even resist their mother's efforts to nurse them; others refuse to eat altogether (Coulthard & Harris, 2003). As a result, compared with infants of nondepressed mothers, a higher proportion of the infants of depressed mothers are undernourished (Rahman, Lovel, Bunn, Igbal, & Harrington, 2004). All these effects interfere with synchrony and can predispose the infant of a depressed mother to develop an insecure attachment. As a result, infants of depressed mothers are at higher risk for later problems. For example, they are more likely than other children to exhibit either heightened aggression or social withdrawal in school (Cummings & Davies, 1994). They are also at higher risk of developing psychiatric illnesses themselves in adulthood (Maki et al., 2004).

It is important to note that maternal depression itself doesn't necessarily doom an infant to an insecure attachment. The critical factors appear to be how and to what extent depression affects mother–infant interactions. There seem to be three problematic behaviour patterns in depressed mothers. In one pattern, mothers are withdrawn and detached; they look at, touch, or talk to their babies less often and are less affectionate toward their infants than are nondepressed mothers (Field, 1995; Hart, Jones, Field, & Lundy, 1999). In the second pattern, mothers are overly involved with their infants, often interrupting and overstimulating them (Hart et al., 1999). The third group of depressed mothers overreact and respond angrily to babies' undesirable behaviours (O'Leary, Smith Slep, & Reid, 1999).

Of course, many depressed mothers are just as sensitive and responsive to their babies' needs as mothers who do not suffer from depression. And, as you might expect, infants whose depressed mothers exhibit sensitive parenting behaviours are less likely to display long-term negative effects than babies of less sensitive depressed mothers (NICHD Early Child Care Research Network, 1999). In other words, when depressed mothers exhibit the same kinds of parenting behaviours as most nondepressed mothers, their emotional status doesn't appear to have negative effects on their babies' development.

Research examining the relationship between infant temperament and responsiveness in depressed mothers lends weight to this conclusion. These studies show that the combination of difficult temperament in an infant and inappropriate responses in a depressed mother carries more risk for the baby's development than either variable alone (Meritesacker, Bade, Haverkock, & Pauli-Pott, 2004). Thus, the infant of a mother with depression whose responses are tailored to the baby's temperament is less likely to display the kinds of problems that are correlated with maternal depression.

Studies involving many mothers with panic disorder have shown that these mothers, like mothers with depression, exhibit behaviours that may interfere with synchrony (Warren et al., 2003). Because it is through behaviour that maternal psychiatric illnesses affect infants, parent training may provide an avenue through which the potential negative effects of this caregiver characteristic can be moderated. Indeed, several studies have shown that training can increase the frequency of sensitive behaviours in depressed mothers and, as a result, lead to changes in infants' attachment status (van den Boom, 1994, 1995). Moreover, appropriate medications may positively affect many aspects of psychiatrically ill mothers' behaviours (e.g., Kaplan, Bachorowski, Smoski, & Zinser, 2001).

LONG-TERM CONSEQUENCES OF ATTACHMENT QUALITY

As we noted earlier, attachment theory proposes that early emotional relationships shape later ones. Thus, researchers have examined the links between Ainsworth's classification system and a wide range of other behaviours in infants, children, adolescents, and adults. Dozens of studies show that children rated as securely attached to their mothers in infancy are later more sociable, more positive in their behaviour toward friends and siblings, less clinging and dependent on teachers, less aggressive and disruptive, more empathetic, and more emotionally mature in their interactions in school and other settings outside the home (e.g., Booth-LaForce et al., 2006; Carlson, Sampson, & Sroufe, 2003; Jacobsen, Husa, Fendrich, Kruesi, & Ziegenhain, 1997; Leve & Fagot, 1995).

Adolescents who were rated as securely attached in infancy or who are classed as secure on the basis of interviews in adolescence are also more socially skilled, have more intimate friendships, are more likely to be rated as leaders, and have higher self-esteem and better grades (Black & McCartney, 1995; Jacobsen & Hofmann, 1997; Lieberman, Doyle, & Markiewicz, 1995; Ostoja, McCrone, Lehn, Reed, & Sroufe, 1995). Those with insecure attachments—particularly those with avoidant attachments—not only have less positive and supportive friendships in adolescence, but also are more likely to become sexually active early and to practise riskier sex (Carlson, Sroufe, Egeland, 2004; O'Beirne & Moore, 1995; Sroufe, Carlson, & Schulman, 1993; Urban, Carlson, Egeland, & Sroufe, 1991).

Quality of attachment in infancy also predicts sociability through early, middle, and late adulthood (Van Lange, DeBruin, Otten, & Joireman, 1997). Moreover, one study found a link between attachment history and sexual dysfunction in adult males (Kinzl, Mangweth, Traweger, & Biebl, 1996). In fact, that investigation found that quality of attachment in infancy predicted sexual dysfunction in adulthood better than a history of sexual abuse did.

Developmentalists have also found that an adult's internal model of attachment affects his or her parenting behaviours (Crittenden, Partridge, & Clausesen, 1991; Steele, Hodges, Kaniuk, Hillman, & Henderson, 2003). For example, mothers who are themselves securely attached are more responsive and sensitive in their behaviour toward their infants or young children (Hammond, Landry, Swank, & Smith, 2000; van IJzendoorn, 1995). Researchers have even found marked consistency across three generations of Canadian grandmothers, young mothers, and infants (Benoit & Parker, 1994). Attachment history affects parental attitudes as well. Some studies have shown that parents with a history of insecure attachment are more likely to view their infants negatively (Pesonen, Raikkonnen, Strandberg, Kelitikangas-Jarvinen, & Jarvenpaa, 2004). Such parents may also lack confidence in their ability to perform effectively in the parenting role (Huth-Bocks, Levendosky, Bogat, & von Eye, 2004).

Examinations of the long-term consequences of quality of attachment suggest that both psychoanalysts and ethologists are correct in their assumption that the attachment relationship becomes the foundation for future social relationships. Certainly, it appears to be critical to the relationship most similar to it—the relationship an individual ultimately develops with her or his own child.

Before Going On

- What are the four phases of attachment and the behaviours that are associated with them?
- Define the four types of attachment and discuss their origins and stability.

PERSONALITY, TEMPERAMENT, AND SELF-CONCEPT

Psychologists typically use the word **personality** to describe patterns in the way children and adults relate to the people and objects in the world around them. Individual differences in personality appear to develop throughout childhood and adolescence, based on a basic set of behavioural and emotional predispositions present at birth (McCrae, Costa, Ostendord, & Angleitner, 2000). These predispositions are usually referred to as **temperament** (Rothbart, Ahadi, & Evans, 2000).

DIMENSIONS OF TEMPERAMENT

Psychologists who study infant temperament have yet to agree on a basic set of temperament dimensions. One influential early theory, proposed by Alexander Thomas and Stella Chess, listed nine dimensions: activity level, rhythmicity, approach/withdrawal, adaptability to new experience, threshold of responsiveness, intensity of reaction, quality of mood (positive or negative), distractibility, and persistence (1977). Thomas and Chess further proposed that variations in these nine qualities tended to cluster into three types, which they called the **easy child** (40% of infants), the **difficult child** (10% of infants), and the **slow-to-warm-up child** (15% of infants).

Other researchers have examined temperament from a trait perspective rather than a categorical perspective. These developmentalists view an individual infant's temperament as a function of how much or how little of various characteristics she possesses. For example, an infant in whom a high level of physical activity was combined with emotional irritability would have a different temperamental profile than an infant in whom high activity was combined with a more easygoing nature. Some developmentalists who have adopted the trait perspective disagree as to what the component characteristics of temperament are, but their research has revealed a few key dimensions (Ahadi & Rothbart, 1994; Belsky, Hsieh, & Crnic, 1996; Kagan, 1994; Martin, Wisenbaker, & Huttunen, 1994.) *Activity level* refers to an infant's tendency either to move often and vigorously or to remain passive or immobile. *Approach/positive emotionality* is a tendency to move toward rather than away from new people, things, or objects, usually accompanied by positive emotion (this dimension is similar to what others call *sociability*). *Inhibition*—a tendency to respond with fear or withdrawal to new people, new situations, or new objects—is the flip side of the approach characteristic. *Negative emotionality* is a tendency to respond to frustrating circumstances with anger, fussing, loudness, or irritability. Finally, *effortful control/task persistence* is an ability to stay focused and to manage attention and effort.

ORIGINS AND STABILITY OF TEMPERAMENT

Because temperamental differences appear so early in life, even during the prenatal period (see **Chapter 3**), it may seem that genes are entirely responsible for them. However, research suggests that both nature and nurture contribute to individual differences in temperament.

HEREDITY   Clear, strong evidence, both from studies of adult personality and from studies of children's temperament, supports the assertion that temperamental differences are inborn (Caspi, 1998; Goldsmith, Lemery, Buss, & Campos, 1999). Studies of twins in many

personality
a pattern of responding to people and objects in the environment

temperament
inborn predispositions, such as activity level, that form the foundations of personality

easy temperament
a predisposition to approaching new events positively, displaying predictable sleeping and eating cycles, being generally happy, and adjusting easily to change

difficult temperament
a predisposition for irregular sleeping and eating cycles, emotional negativity and irritability, and resistance to change

slow-to-warm-up temperament
a predisposition for inactivity and turning away from and adjusting slowly to unfamiliar people and new experiences. They display mild signs of negativity and discomfort.

((•—Listen

Critical Thinking

How would you describe your own temperament as a child? Is your adult personality similar to the temperament you displayed in childhood?

countries show that identical twins are more alike in their temperament than are frater-nal twins (Rose, 1995). For example, one group of researchers studied 100 pairs of identical twins and 100 pairs of fraternal twins at both 14 and 20 months. At each age, mothers rated their children's temperaments by using Buss and Plomin's three basic temperament dimensions: activity level, emotionality, and sociability (Buss, 1989; Buss & Plomin, 1986). In addition, each child's level of behavioural inhibition was meas-ured by observing how the child reacted to strange toys and a strange adult in a special laboratory playroom. Did the child approach the novel toys quickly and eagerly, or hang back and seem fearful? Did the child approach the strange adult or remain close to the mother? The correlations between temperament scores on all four of these dimensions were consistently higher for identical than for fraternal twins, indicating a strong genetic effect (Emde et al., 1992; Plomin et al., 1993).

NEUROLOGICAL PROCESSES Many temperament theorists take the heredity argu-ment a step further and trace the basic differences in behaviour to variations in under-lying physiological patterns (e.g., Gunnar, 1994; Rothbart, Derryberry, & Posner, 1994). For example, Jerome Kagan has suggested that differences in behavioural inhi-bition (or shyness) are based on differing thresholds for arousal in the parts of the brain that control responses to uncertainty—the amygdala and the hypothalamus (Kagan, 1994; Kagan, Reznick, & Snidman, 1990; Kagan, Snidman, & Arcus, 1993). Arousal of these parts of the brain leads to increases in muscle tension and heart rate. Shy or inhibited children are thought to have a low threshold for such a reaction. That is, they more readily become tense and alert in the presence of uncertainty, perhaps even interpreting a wider range of situations as uncertain. What we inherit, then, according to this view, is not "shyness" or some equivalent, but a tendency for the brain to react in particular ways (Davidson, 1994).

Studies examining the genes that control the functions of two important neuro-transmitters, *dopamine* and *serotonin*, support Kagan's hypothesis (Lakatos et al., 2003). These neurotransmitters regulate the brain's responses to new information and unusual situations, precisely the kinds of stimuli that appear to overstimulate shy chil-dren in Kagan's research.

Researchers have also found that another important neurological variable associ-ated with shyness is *frontal lobe asymmetry*. In most people, the left and right hemi-spheres of the frontal lobes respond similarly to new stimuli; in other words, they exhibit *symmetry*. In shy infants, however, the two hemispheres respond differently—that is, *asymmetrically*—to such stimuli. Specifically, these children exhibit higher lev-els of arousal in the right hemisphere than in the left (Fox, Henderson, Rubin, Calkins, & Schmidt, 2001; Henderson, Marshall, Fox, & Rubin, 2004). Such findings make it tempting to conclude that temperamental differences are based in neurological processes. Research, however, suggests that it is difficult to say whether neurological differences are a cause or an effect of temperament. Developmentalists have found that shy infants whose temperaments change over the first 4 years of life—that is, those who become more outgoing—also become less likely to exhibit the asymmetrical pat-tern of arousal (Fox et al., 2001).

ENVIRONMENT Critics of neurological studies point out that it is impossible to know whether such findings are causes or effects (Johnson, 2003). They argue that behaviour shapes the brain. Thus, shy children may exhibit different neurological patterns than outgoing children because their exhibition of shy behaviour contributes to the neural networks that developmental processes in the brain, such as pruning, allow to develop and those that are shut down due to lack of use.

Consistent with these critics' claims, researchers have found that temperament–environment interactions tend to strengthen built-in qualities. For one thing, people of all ages choose their experiences, a process Sandra Scarr refers to as **niche-picking** (Scarr & McCartney, 1983). Our choices reflect our temperaments. For example, highly sociable children seek out contact with others; children low on the activity dimension are more likely to choose sedentary activities, such as puzzles or board games, than baseball.

Parents may also be able to either increase or decrease the effects of an infant's inborn temperamental tendencies. In one longitudinal study, researchers recorded play sessions in which Chinese parents interacted with their 4-year-old children (Hou, Chen, & Chen, 2005). When the children were 7 years old, the researchers found that parent behaviour at age 4 predicted behavioural inhibition (shyness) at age 7. Specifically, the more controlling parents were during the play sessions, the more likely their children were to be rated as more behaviourally inhibited at age 7 than they had been at age 4. Such findings suggest that, perhaps contrary to what you might expect, parents who accept an inhibited child's temperament may contribute more to the child's ability to overcome shyness later in life than parents who try to force a child to be more outgoing. Some experts suggest that parental influences may be greatest for children who are at the extremes of a given temperamental continuum. That is, children who are extremely inhibited may be more subject to parental influence than those who are moderately so (Buss & Plomin, 1984).

Developmentalists argue that the **goodness-of-fit** between children's temperaments and their environments influences how inborn temperamental characteristics are manifested later in life (Thomas & Chess, 1977). For example, if the parents and caregivers of an irritable baby are good at tolerating his irritability and persist in establishing a synchronous relationship with him, then his irritability doesn't lead to the development of an insecure attachment or inhibit social adjustment (Pluess & Belsky, 2010).

LONG-TERM STABILITY Research showing that temperament is stable across infancy and into children's later years supports the view that temperament is strongly influenced by heredity. A growing amount of evidence shows that temperamental ratings are consistent over long periods of infancy and childhood (Kagan & Herschkowitz, 2005). For example, Australian researchers studying a group of 450 children found that mothers' reports of children's irritability, cooperation/manageability, inflexibility, rhythmicity, persistence, and tendency to approach rather than avoid contact were all quite consistent from infancy through age 8 (Pedlow, Sanson, Prior, & Oberklaid, 1993). Similarly, in an American longitudinal study of a group of children from age 1 through 12, psychologists found strong consistency in parents' reports of their children's overall "difficultness" as well as approach versus withdrawal, positive versus negative mood, and activity level (Guerin & Gottfried, 1994a, 1994b). Other research suggests that temperamental differences are stable from the preschool years into adulthood (Caspi, 2000).

Researchers have also found considerable consistency at various ages in Kagan's measure of inhibition, which is based on direct observation of the child's behaviour rather than on the mother's ratings of the child's temperament. In one study, for example, children who had been classified as inhibited at 4 months were less socially responsive to both adults and children at 2 years than uninhibited peers (Young, Fox, & Zahn-Waxler, 1999). In Kagan's own longitudinal study, half of the children who had shown high levels of crying and motor activity in response to a novel situation when they were 4 months old were still classified as highly inhibited at 8 years of age, and three-fourths of those rated as uninhibited at 4 months remained in that category 8 years later (Kagan et al., 1993). Subsequent studies showed that these trends continued into the children's teen and early adulthood years (Kagan & Herschkowitz, 2005).

niche-picking
the process of selecting experiences on the basis of temperament

goodness of fit
the degree to which an infant's temperament is adaptable to his or her environment, and vice versa

SELF-CONCEPT

During the same months when a baby is creating an internal model of attachment and expressing her own unique temperament, she is also developing an internal model of self. Freud suggested that the infant needed to develop a sense of separateness from her mother before she could form a sense of self. Piaget emphasized that the infant's understanding of the basic concept of object permanence was a necessary precursor for the child's attaining self-permanence. Both of these aspects of early self-development reappear in current descriptions of the emergence of the sense of self (Lewis, 1990, 1991).

Canadian researchers have demonstrated that an infant's capacity to differentiate objects emerges well before object permanence is achieved. For instance, an infant can begin to discriminate between objects and people by 2 months of age (Legerstee, Pomerleau, Malcuit, & Feider, 1987). An infant can also differentiate between images of itself, other infants, and dolls between 5 and 8 months of age (Legerstee, Anderson, & Schaffer, 1998).

THE SUBJECTIVE SELF The child's first task is to figure out that he is separate from others and that this separate self endures over time and space. Developmentalists call this aspect of the self-concept the **subjective self**, or sometimes the *existential self*, because the key awareness seems to be "I exist." The roots of this understanding lie in the myriad everyday interactions the baby has with the objects and people in his world that lead him to understand during the first 2 to 3 months of life that he can have effects on things (Thompson & Goodvin, 2005). For example, when the child touches a mobile, it moves; when he cries, someone responds; when he smiles, his mother smiles back. Through this process, the baby separates self from everything else and a sense of "I" begins to emerge.

By the time the infant has constructed a fairly complete understanding of object permanence, at about 8 to 12 months, the subjective self has fully emerged. Just as he is figuring out that Mom and Dad continue to exist when they are out of sight, he is figuring out—at least in some preliminary way—that he exists separately and has some permanence.

subjective self
an infant's awareness that she or he is a separate person who endures through time and space and can act on the environment

objective (categorical) self
the toddler's understanding that she or he is defined by various categories, such as gender, or qualities, such as shyness

Research that has examined babies' ability to recognize themselves suggests that self-awareness develops in the middle of the second year. (*Photo:* Joseph Pobereskin/Getty Images)

THE OBJECTIVE SELF The second major task is for the toddler to come to understand that she is also an object in the world (Thompson & Goodvin, 2005). Just as a ball has properties—roundness, the ability to roll, a certain feel in the hand—so the "self" also has qualities or properties, such as gender, size, a name, or qualities such as shyness or boldness and coordination or clumsiness. This self-awareness is the hallmark of the second aspect of identity, the **objective self**, sometimes called the **categorical self**, because once the child achieves self-awareness, the process of defining the self involves placing oneself in a whole series of categories.

It has not been easy to determine just when a child has developed the initial self-awareness that delineates the formation of the objective self. The most commonly used procedure involves a mirror. First, the baby is placed in front of a mirror, just to see how she behaves. Most infants between about 9 and 12 months old will look at their own images, make faces, or try to interact with the baby in the mirror in some way. After allowing this free exploration for a time, the experimenter, while pretending to wipe the baby's face with a cloth, puts a spot of rouge on the baby's nose, and then lets the baby look in the mirror again. The crucial test of self-recognition, and thus of awareness of the self, is whether the baby reaches for the spot on her own nose, rather than the nose on the face in the mirror.

Figure 6.1 shows the results of a classic study using this procedure. As you can see, few of the 9- to 12-month-old babies in this study touched their own noses, but three-quarters of the babies aged 21 months showed that level of self-recognition, a result confirmed in a variety of other research studies, including studies in Europe (Asendorpf, Warkentin, & Baudonnière, 1996; Lewis & Brooks, 1978). **Figure 6.1** also shows the rate at which children refer to themselves by name when they are shown a picture of themselves, which is another commonly used measure of self-aware-ness. You can see that this development occurs at almost exactly the same time as self-recognition in a mirror. Both are present by about the middle of the second year of life, a finding confirmed by other investigators (Bullock & Lütkenhaus, 1990). At this point, toddlers begin to show a newly proprietary attitude ("Mine!") toward toys or other treasured objects.

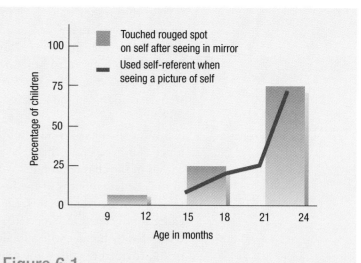

Figure 6.1

Mirror recognition and self-naming develop at almost exactly the same time.
(*Source:* Lewis & Brooks, 1978, pp. 214–215.)

As self-awareness develops, infants begin to refer to themselves by name and, near the end of the second year, to label themselves as "boys" or "girls." In addition, infants recognize that they belong to the "child" category. They also use categorical terms such as "good" and "big" to describe themselves. For example, a girl might say "good girl" when she obeys her parent or "big girl" when she is successful at a task, such as using the toilet (Stipek, Gralinski, & Kopp, 1990).

THE EMOTIONAL SELF Development of the *emotional self* begins when babies learn to identify changes in emotion expressed in others' faces, at 2 to 3 months of age. Ini-tially, they discriminate emotions best when they receive information on many chan-nels simultaneously—such as when they see a particular facial expression and hear the same emotion expressed in the adult's voice (Walker-Andrews, 1997). Moreover, in these early weeks, infants are much better at discerning the emotional expressions of a familiar face than those of an unfamiliar face (Kahana-Kalman & Walker-Andrews, 2001). By 5 to 7 months, babies begin to "read" one channel at a time, responding to facial expression alone or vocal expression alone, even when the emotions are dis-played by a stranger rather than Mom or Dad (Balaban, 1995). They also respond to a much wider variety of emotions than younger infants do and can distinguish among happy, surprised, angry, fearful, interested, and sad faces (Soken & Pick, 1999; Walker-Andrews & Lennon, 1991).

Near the end of the first year, infants' perceptions of others' emotions help them anticipate others' actions and guide their own behaviour (Phillips, Wellman, & Spelke, 2002). For instance, they react to another infant's neutral facial expression by actively trying to elicit an emotional expression from that child (Striano & Rochat, 1999). Just as adults often work at getting a baby to smile at them, babies seem to be following the same sort of script by 8 to 10 months of age.

As the infant's understanding of others' emotions advances, it is matched by paral-lel progression in expression of emotions. At birth, infants have different facial expres-sions for interest, pain, and disgust, and an expression that conveys enjoyment develops very quickly.

This baby's emotional reaction is best described as joy or delight rather than pride; her sense of self is not yet well-enough developed that she can feel pride in learning to walk.
(*Photo:* © Laurance Monneret/Stone/ Getty Images)

By the time a baby is 2 to 3 months old, adult observers can also distinguish expressions of anger and sadness, with expressions of fear appearing by 6 or 7 months (Izard et al., 1995; Izard & Harris, 1995). At about the same time, infants begin to smile more to human faces than to dolls' faces or other inanimate objects, suggesting that at this early stage babies are already responding to the added social signals available in the human face (Ellsworth, Muir, & Hains, 1993; Legerstee et al., 1987).

Over the next several months, the infant's emotional expressions, and the behaviours that arise from them, become more sophisticated. For example, as you learned earlier in the chapter, infants who have formed an attachment to a caregiver (typically in the last few months of the first year) use the caregiver's emotions to guide their own feelings. Moreover, by this age, babies have learned to calm themselves when their caregivers behave in expected ways (Cole et al., 2004). For example, a baby who is frustrated by hunger will calm down when she sees her caregiver preparing to nurse her or to provide her with some other kind of nourishment. Finally, near the middle of the second year, at about the same time that a child shows self-recognition in the mirror, such self-conscious emotional expressions as embarrassment, pride, and shame emerge (Lewis, Allesandri, & Sullivan, 1992; Lewis, Sullivan, Stanger, & Weiss, 1989; Mascolo & Fischer, 1995).

AWARENESS OF THE INTENTIONS OF OTHERS Developmentalists have also begun to examine when an infant becomes aware that other people have separate intentions or "internal mental states" (D'Entremont, Hains, & Muir, 1997). University of New Brunswick psychologist Barbara D'Entremont has been studying this inquiry by observing infants' reactions to an adult's gaze and by studying a child's finger pointing. D'Entremont (2000) contends that, although infants between 3 and 6 months are capable of following the direction of the gaze of another person, following the gaze is more likely a response to an attention-getting cue than true social communication. In another study, finger pointing was used as a measure of an infant's awareness of what another person is paying attention to. It was discovered that 1-year-olds point as a means to heighten "social interaction," whereas 2-year-olds point in an attempt to redirect another person's attention. This research implies an age-related shift in development whereby, at 2 years, a child has developed the capacity to appreciate that other people are not always paying attention to what she is paying attention to and that she can redirect another person's attention by pointing. This capability to pay attention to both another person's intentions and an object at the same time is a form of **joint attention,** and it is related to later language, intellectual, behavioural, and emotional adjustment (D'Entremont & Hartung, 2003; Moore & D'Entremont, 2001).

Other Canadian theorists, such as Jeremy Carpendale of Simon Fraser University, Timothy Racine of the University of Manitoba, and Ulrich Müller of the University of Victoria (Carpendale & Lewis, 2004; Müller, Carpendale, Bibok, & Racine, 2006; Racine & Carpendale, 2007), propose that *joint attention* is a good example of the infant's dawning awareness that other people have separate mental states—an understanding that other people have "minds of their own." Joint attention shows that the infant appreciates the import of paying attention to another person's intentions. According to this perspective, an infant begins to construct an understanding of mental states and the social world primarily within the context of her social interactions with others, seemingly from birth onward (Markova & Legerstee, 2008). (We will revisit this idea later in **Chapter 7.**) Researchers have linked both joint attention and secure emotional attachment to mother–infant social interactions that occur early in life (D'Entremont & Hartung, 2003).

joint attention
when two people are focusing their attention on an object and each is aware that the other is attending to that same object

Before Going On

- Discuss the roles of heredity, neurological processes, and environment in the formation of temperament.

- How do the subjective self, the objective self, and the emotional self develop during the first 2 years of life?

EFFECTS OF NONPARENTAL CARE

In virtually every industrialized country in the world, women have entered the workforce in great numbers over the past several decades. In Canada, the change has been particularly rapid and massive. In 1967, only 17% of Canadian mothers with preschool children were in the labour force; by 2007, roughly 70% of such women were working outside the home (HRDC, 2003; Roy, 2006; Statistics Canada, 2009e). **Figure 6.2** shows how employment rates have doubled over the past 25 years for both dual income and single-parent families with children under the age of 6 years. More recently however, changes in 2000 to the Federal *Employment Insurance Act* that extended the duration of benefit payments for parental leave had an immediate effect in the first year; the length of parental leaves and the number of parents staying home from work to care for their infants rose sharply (Marshall, 2003). The good news for infants is that the trend

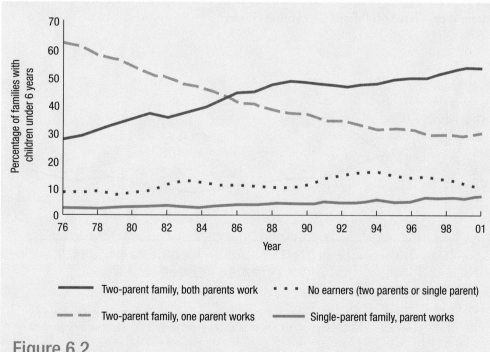

Figure 6.2

Trends in dual earner and single earner families.

(*Source: A New Generation of Canadian Families Raising Young Children* (Cat. No. SP-579-09-03E). Human Resources and Social Development Canada. Reproduced with the permission of Her Majesty the Queen in Right of Canada 2007.)

has had a particularly dramatic effect on fathers: In 2007, 55.2% of fathers took time off from work for the birth or the adoption of a child, up from 37.9% in 2001 (Beaupré & Cloutier, 2007). And when changes were made to Quebec's Parental Insurance Plan in 2006 (which includes higher benefits and no waiting period), the proportion of Quebec fathers' participation in paternal leave jump to the highest levels of anywhere in Canada and North America (Marshall, 2008; Tremblay, 2010).

Even with all the additional support, the duration of fathers' leaves has remained far briefer than that of mothers—only about 33% of men took more than a month off before returning to work. In contrast, roughly 50% of mothers remained with the baby for a period of 1 to 2 years (Beaupré & Cloutier, 2007). The evidence suggests a continued preference for Canadian mothers to spend considerable time with their infants and toddlers (Beaujot & Ravanera, 2009).

In addition to contributing to a better work–family balance for both mothers and fathers, better parental leave plans in Canada and especially in Quebec (Marshall, 2008; Tremblay, 2010) have contributed to one more added benefit. More Canadian mothers have now met the global breastfeeding standard set by public health organizations, including the World Health Organization (Baker & Milligan, 2007). The proportion of mothers who breastfed exclusively for at least 6 months (28%) increased about 40% after the child care reforms took effect—an increased health benefit for both infant and mother.

Still, many children have had some form of nonparent care before their first birthday. Moreover, about 54% of Canadian children under age 5 are cared for by someone other than a parent on a regular basis (Bushnik, 2006). A closer look at the data illustrated in **Figure 6.3** reveals that arrangements for child care differ based on income level: A relative is more likely to care for children from lower income families, but a nonrelative is more likely to care for children from higher income families (HRDC, 2003). The key question for psychologists is as follows: What effect does such nonparental care have on infants and young children?

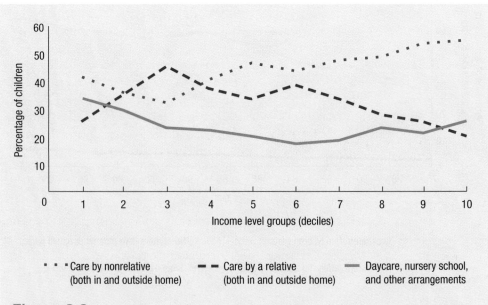

Figure 6.3

Family income level and type of child-care arrangements for children aged 0–5 years (1998/99).

(*Source:* National Longitudinal Survey of Children and Youth, cited in Human Resources Development Canada, 2003. Reproduced with the permission of Her Majesty the Queen in Right of Canada 2007.)

DIFFICULTIES IN STUDYING NONPARENTAL CARE

It might seem that the effect on infant development of this trend toward nonparental care could easily be determined by comparing babies receiving nonparental care with those cared for by their parents. However, both "nonparental care" and "parental care" are really complex interactions among numerous variables rather than single factors whose effects can be studied independently. Thus, interpretation of research on nonparental care has to take into account a variety of issues.

First, an enormous range of different care arrangements in Canada are all lumped under the general title of "nonparental care." Infants who are cared for by grandparents in their own homes as well as those who are enrolled in daycare centres receive nonparental care. In addition, infants enter these care arrangements at different ages, and they remain in them for varying lengths of time. Some have the same nonparental caregiver over many years; others shift often from one care setting to another. Moreover, nonparental care varies widely in quality.

The majority of infants in North America now experience at least some nonparental care.
(*Photo*: © Syracuse Newspapers/Dick Blume/The Image Works)

Furthermore, even distinguishing among the various types of care arrangements does not begin to convey the numerous hybrid solutions Canadian parents use to organize alternative care for their children (Cleveland, Forer, Hyatt, Japel, & Krashinsky, 2008). For example, children may be in some type of combined care, such as family daycare some of the time and care by a relative part of the time (in family daycare, people take care of other parents' children in their own homes). Since the majority of researchers have studied only children in daycare centres, it is not known whether these findings will generalize to children in family daycare or to children who are given at-home care by someone other than a parent. Moreover, it's not clear whether the results of these studies apply to non-Western cultures.

Nonparental care of children is now a part of the Canadian way of life. The most common pattern, especially for infants and toddlers, is for a nonrelative to care for the child in a setting outside the child's home (Bushnik, 2006). Nonparental child care is provided about equally (~30%) either by nonrelatives outside the home or in regulated licensed daycare centres. The remaining 40% of care is either provided outside the home by relatives or within the home by either relatives or nonrelatives. To further complicate matters, families who place their children in nonparental care are different in a whole host of ways from those who care for their children at home. How can researchers be sure that effects attributed to nonparental care are not, instead, the result of these other family differences? Mothers also differ in their attitudes toward the care arrangements they have made. Some mothers with children in nonparental care would far rather be at home taking care of their children; others are happy to be working. Similarly, some mothers who are at home full time would rather be working, and some are delighted to be at home. Some studies suggest that children show more positive reactions to their situations when the mother is satisfied with her situation, whether she is working or at home. For instance, Canadian researchers have found that when a mother's employment preference and her employment decision agree, she is less depressed and provides her children with more stable care (McKim, Cramer, Stuart, & O'Conner, 1999).

Most of the research on nonparental versus parental care has not taken these complexities into account. Researchers have frequently compared children "in daycare" with those "reared at home" and assumed that any differences between the two groups were attributable to the daycare experience. Recent studies are often better, but clear answers to even the most basic questions about the impact of nonparental care on children's development are still not available. Nonetheless, because the issue is so critical, you need to be aware of what is and is not yet known.

EFFECTS ON COGNITIVE DEVELOPMENT, PEER RELATIONS, AND ATTACHMENT

enriched daycare
daycare that provides structured programming to build skills, such as literacy, numeracy, social, art, and physical skills

A good deal of evidence indicates that high-quality, cognitively **enriched daycare** has beneficial effects on many children's overall cognitive and language development. This effect is particularly strong for children from socioeconomically disadvantaged families, who show significant and lasting gains in IQ and later school performance after attending enriched daycare throughout infancy and early childhood (Belsky, 2007; Belsky et al., 2007; Burger, in press; Loeb, Fuller, Kagan, & Carrol, 2004). Moreover, most children, regardless of their social backgrounds, show some cognitive and language benefit when they are in high-quality daycare (for a list of characteristics of "high-quality" daycare, see **Development in the Real World**).

According to researchers, the impact of daycare on children's personalities is not entirely rosy. Recent Canadian and American studies link the number of hours spent in daycare with later behaviour problems at school age (Baker, Gruber, & Milligan, 2008; Belsky, 2007; Belsky et al., 2007). However, the association is not a simple one—subsequent findings suggest that the number of hours spent in daycare is more strongly related to *externalizing behaviour* (e.g., heightened aggression with peers and lower compliance with teachers and parents) when children were in low-quality daycare and

Development in the Real World

CHOOSING A DAYCARE CENTRE

You may be wondering what criteria a parent can use to identify a high-quality daycare setting. Of course, it's important to realize that the "fit" between an infant and her daycare setting is what really matters. Some babies do well no matter where they are cared for or by whom. Others, perhaps those with more difficult temperaments, seem to have problems adjusting to even the best of settings. Consequently, parents can't really judge the quality of a given setting until their babies have spent some time in it. Nevertheless, a few general characteristics are common to high-quality daycare settings.

Canadian child care experts suggest that the following characteristics should be considered for both centre- and home-based daycare:

- low child to staff ratios
- warm, friendly, patient, capable caregivers who are trained in child development, first aid, and CPR
- stable, committed, experienced caregivers (low turnover rate) who respond to the child"s individual needs
- a variety of enjoyable activities that support healthy development (i.e., emotional, physical, motor, social, moral, linguistic, and cognitive development)

- daily routines that are predictable but flexible
- a relaxed, caring, and stimulating environment that is safe, clean, and tidy
- written program policies and plans
- a variety of toys, equipment, and learning materials at the child's level
- space for active and quiet activities, indoor and outdoor play, and rest
- the promotion of good hygiene to prevent the spread of bacteria and adherence to policies for sick children
- nutritious meals and snacks
- cultural sensitivity
- regular communication between parent and caregiver
- compatible child-rearing philosophy and goals (with those of parents)
- mutual respect and trust
- access to community resources and supports

(*Sources*: Centre of Excellence for Early Childhood Development [CEECD], 2009a; CEECD, 2009b; Cleveland et al, 2008; and Co-ordinated Access for Child Care, 2009.)

spent proportionally more time with large groups of peers (McCartney et al, 2010). Of course, a child's level of aggressiveness in elementary school is influenced by a wide variety of things, including temperament and the effectiveness of the parents' disciplinary techniques, but daycare's implication in this equation certainly sounds a cautionary note (Pluess & Belsky, 2010).

Lastly, can an infant or toddler develop secure attachments to her mother and father if she is repeatedly separated from them? This question has been at the centre of a hot debate. Until the mid-1980s, most psychologists believed that infant daycare had no negative effect on attachment. But then developmental psychologist Jay Belsky (1985) sounded an alarm. After decades of research, he concluded that daycare and attachment are connected, although in a complex way. For example, he participated in an American study that revealed that, when coupled with insensitive mothering, insecure attachment was amplified by any one of three conditions: averaging more than 10 hours per week in any type of care, irrespective of quality; multiple child-care arrangements; or exposure to low-quality daycare (NICHD Early Child Care Research Network, 2005). However, this result was found to be at odds with other national studies—that is, one in Israel (Sagi, Koren-Karie, Gini, Ziv, & Joels, 2002) and another in Australia (Harrison & Ungerer, 2002). Belsky (2009) concluded that there are likely no inevitable effects of daycare on attachment and that the quality of attachment seems dependent on the larger familial, community, societal, and cultural context in which child care occurs.

INTERPRETING RESEARCH ON NONPARENTAL CARE

((•— Listen

What is it about nonparental care that may predispose infants to become aggressive, disobedient kindergartners? Studies of infants' psychological responses to nonparental care may hold a clue. Researchers have found that levels of the stress hormone cortisol increase from morning to afternoon in infants who are enrolled in centre-based care (Watamura, Donzella, Alwin, & Gunnar, 2003; Vermeer & van IJzendoorn, 2006). By contrast, cortisol levels decrease over the course of the day in home-reared infants. Interestingly, cortisol levels of home-reared and centre-care infants are identical on weekends and holidays. Thus, some developmentalists argue that the higher levels of cortisol experienced by centre-care infants affect their rapidly developing brains in ways that lead to problem behaviours. However, no direct evidence supports this hypothesis currently.

Some developmentalists argue that nonparental care arrangements probably vary in the degree to which they induce stress in infants and young children. In other words, they say, quality of care may be just as important as quantity of care (Maccoby & Lewis, 2003). For example, some researchers have found that, when infants are cared for in high-quality centres, the amount of time they spend in such care is unrelated to social behaviour (Love et al., 2003). Thus, developmentalists urge parents, especially those who must leave their infants in centre-based care for extended periods of time, to make every effort to ensure that the arrangement they choose has the characteristics discussed in **Development in the Real World**.

Another point to keep in mind is that individual and gender differences have been found to interact with nonparental care. For example, infants who are behaviourally inhibited, in Kagan's terms, may be more sensitive to the stresses associated with centre-based care (Watamura et al., 2003). Moreover, boys in nonparental care are more likely than girls in similar care settings to be insecurely attached to their caregivers (Crockenberg, 2003). For these reasons, more research that takes both temperament and gender into account is needed before we can say for certain that nonparental care has uniformly negative effects on children's social development (Crockenberg, 2003).

Finally, it is important to understand that, on average, the differences between children in nonparental care and their home-reared peers, both positive and negative, are not large (NICHD Early Child Care Research Network, 2006). Moreover, studies that have attempted to examine all the complex variables associated with parental and nonparental care have shown that parenting quality variables (e.g., warmth, affection, acceptance, and sensitivity) are more important than the type of daycare arrangements a family chooses (Adi-Japha & Klein, 2009; Belsky et al, 2007; Lugo-Gil & Tamis-LeMonda, 2008). The confusion inherent in the mixed findings on nonparental care serves to underline the importance of the quality of child care. We can draw the general conclusion that high-quality care is generally linked with positive or neutral outcomes, while inconsistent or poor-quality care can be actively detrimental to children (see **Development in the Real World**). Canadian researchers are now turning their focus on the value of integrating the child care and formal education for young children (McMillan, 2010). For instance, in a new Ontario program called *Full-Day Learning*, both early childhood educators and kindergarten teachers will see to the care and learning of 4- and 5-year-olds (Government of Ontario, 2010).

Before Going On

- Do children who experience nonparental care develop differently from those of children who are cared for at home in infancy?
- What does research suggest about the potential risks of nonparental care?

Summary

Theories of Social and Personality Development

- Freud suggested that individual differences in personality originated in the nursing and weaning practices of infants' mothers. Erikson emphasized the roles of both mothers and fathers, as well as other adults in the infant's environment, in providing for all the infant's needs, thereby instilling a sense of trust concerning the social world.

- Attachment develops in the first 2 years of life and is the foundation of later personality and social development.

Attachment

- Synchrony is crucial to the formation of a strong attachment relationship between parent and infant.

- Bowlby proposed that the child's attachment to a caregiver develops in four phases: nonfocused orienting and signalling, focus on one or more figures, secure base behaviour, and an internal model.

- Caregiver characteristics such as age, emotional state, a history of abuse, and psychiatric health can affect infants' attachment quality.

- The security of the initial attachment is reasonably stable, and, later in childhood, securely attached children appear to be more socially skilful, more curious and persistent in approaching new tasks, and more mature. The internal model of attachment that individuals develop in infancy affects how they parent their own babies.

Personality, Temperament, and Self-Concept

- Temperament theorists generally agree on the following basic temperamental dimensions: activity level, approach/positive emotionality, inhibition, negative emotionality, and effortful control/task persistence.

- There is strong evidence that temperamental differences have a genetic component and are at least somewhat stable over infancy and childhood. A child's built-in temperament shapes the child's interactions with others.

- The goodness-of-fit between an infant's temperament and the ways his environment responds to him affects attachment quality.

- The infant develops a sense of self, including the awareness of a separate self and the understanding of self-permanence (the subjective self); an awareness of self as an object in the world (the objective self); and an emotional self, the ability to make use of information about emotions, such as facial expressions. The infant also develops an awareness that other people have separate thoughts and intentions.

Effects of Nonparental Care

- Comparing parental with nonparental care is difficult because there are so many types of nonparental care arrangements.

- Daycare often has positive effects on the cognitive and language development of socioeconomically disadvantaged children and is also some benefit for middle-class children.

- The impact of daycare on children's social relationships and attachment is unclear, but high-quality care is generally linked with positive or neutral outcomes, while inconsistent or low-quality care can be actively detrimental to the child.

Review Questions

Answers are provided on MyDevelopmentLab in the Course Resources folder.

Theories of Social and Personality Development

6.1 Harlow's research demonstrated that, within a monkey population,
   a. the infant–mother relationship is based on the mother's ability to comfort and cuddle the infant when the infant is frightened or stressed.
   b. the infant–mother relationship is based solely on weaning practices.
   c. the infant–mother relationship is not as important as the infant–father relationship.
   d. the infant–mother relationship is based solely on nursing practices.

Attachment

6.2 The parents of 10-month-old Eduardo have noticed that Eduardo will crawl to follow them as they move from room to room and that he will look at them before he responds to a stranger or before he attempts a new adventure. How would you explain Eduardo's behaviour?
   a. This type of emotional dependency indicates that Eduardo may have developed reactive attachment disorder.
   b. These dependent behaviours represent a form of insecure attachment in which the infant cannot successfully separate from his parents.
   c. Eduardo is in the first stage of development of an attachment relationship in which an infant

uses proximity-promoting behaviours to orient himself toward others and signal his needs.

d. Eduardo is demonstrating proximity seeking and secure base behaviours, which means that he has developed an attachment relationship with his parents.

Personality, Temperament, and Self-Concept

6.3 What is the general conclusion of research that has examined the consistency of temperament over time?

a. Temperament is stable and consistent only through infancy and the preschool years and becomes highly variable once the child is exposed to school and peer influences.

b. Researchers have found consistency and stability of temperament, including qualities of inhibition and difficultness, across infancy and childhood.

c. Inhibition is the only quality of temperament that shows stability across infancy and childhood.

d. Temperament is useful for understanding how infants respond to their environment, but the construct is not valid for understanding reactions or behaviours beyond infancy.

6.4 Goodness-of-fit is

a. the process of selecting experiences on the basis of temperament.

b. when infants realize they can have affect things.

c. selecting a daycare setting staffed with caregivers who understand your infant's special needs.

d. the degree to which an infant's temperament is adaptable to his or her environment, and vice versa.

Effects of Nonparental Care

6.5 Which of the following seems to strongly influence the effects of daycare?

a. the age at which a child begins daycare

b. the gender of the child and the gender of the daycare personnel

c. the number of hours per week that the child spends in care

d. whether the daycare personnel have children of their own

Critical-Thinking Questions

6.6 What could be done to break the cycle of insecure attachment that can be perpetuated from generation to generation? What kind of external interventions would be required?

6.7 An experimental study could answer cause-and-effect questions about the effects of nonparental care, but why would such a study be unethical?

CHAPTER 7

Physical and Cognitive Development in Early Childhood

Watch a 2-year-old playing near her mother or father and you'll notice that she glances at her parent regularly, as if checking to make sure the safe base is still there. Her play is dominated by sensory explorations of objects; she seems motivated to touch and manipulate everything in her environment. In contrast to infants, however, most 2-year-olds have added a new dimension to sensorimotor play—the idea that objects have names. Consequently, almost every object manipulation is accompanied by an important question for nearby adults: "Whazit?" (i.e., What is it?) A few years later, by about age 4, sophisticated forms of pretending, such as "dress-up," become the pre-ferred modes of play.

Profound changes in the physical and cognitive domains underlie these shifts in play behaviour. From 2 to 6 years of age, the period known as *early childhood*, the child changes from a dependent toddler able to communicate only in very primitive ways to a remarkably competent, communicative, social creature, ready to begin school.

When you finish studying the chapter, you will be able to summarize the important physical, motor, neurological, and health and wellness changes and issues associated with early childhood; explain the rapid changes in thinking that happen during the early childhood years, from manipulating symbols to making accurate judgments about others' thoughts, feelings, and behaviours; trace the dramatic advances in vocab-ulary and grammar development and phonological awareness in young children; and gain a better understanding of the issues involved in intelligence testing. While you read, keep the following questions in mind:

- Does a child's knowledge of the home safety rules significantly reduce the inci-dence of childhood injuries? Which strategies work best?

- On a day-to-day basis, what can parents do to encourage language skills in their toddlers? What tips would you give parents to encourage receptive and expressive vocabulary development?

- What are the five indicators that a child is ready to begin school? As a group, who is more developmentally ready, boys or girls? How do you account for this?

PHYSICAL CHANGES

Chapter 4 chronicled the many rapid changes in the infant's body. The physical changes between ages 2 and 6 are less dramatic.

GROWTH AND MOTOR DEVELOPMENT

Changes in height and weight happen far more slowly in the preschool years than in infancy. Each year, the child adds about 5 to 8 centimetres in height and 2.7 kilograms in weight. At the same time, the young child makes steady progress in motor develop-ment. The changes are not as dramatic as the child's first steps, but they enable the child to acquire skills that markedly increase his independence and exploratory ability.

University of Manitoba developmentalists, using stringent motor-behaviour assess-ment techniques, have uncovered some intriguing findings about children's activity lev-els and behavioural self-control. The researchers discovered that children who exhibited higher motor activity levels demonstrated a significantly better ability to con-trol or inhibit their behaviour, allowing for successful task achievement. They suggest that children's extraneous motor activity is an important form of purposeful, exploratory behaviour, especially in children less than 5½ years of age (Campbell,

TABLE 7.1	Milestones of Motor Development	
Age	**Gross Motor Skills**	**Fine Motor Skills**
18–24 months	Runs (20 months); walks well (24 months); climbs stairs with both feet on each step; pushes and pulls boxes or wheeled toys; unscrews lid on a jar	Shows clear hand preference; stacks four to six blocks; turns pages one at a time; picks up things without overbalancing
2–3 years	Runs easily; climbs on furniture unaided; hauls and shoves big toys around obstacles	Picks up small objects; throws small ball while standing
3–4	Walks upstairs one foot per step; skips on two feet; walks on tiptoe; pedals and steers tricycle; walks in any direction pulling large toys	Catches large ball between outstretched arms; cuts paper with scissors; holds pencil between thumb and fingers
4–5	Walks up and down stairs one foot per step; stands, runs, and walks on tiptoe	Strikes ball with bat; kicks and catches ball; threads beads on a string; grasps pencil properly
5–6	Skips on alternate feet; walks on a line; slides, swings	Plays ball games well; threads needle and sews large stitches

(*Sources:* Connolly & Daigleish, 1989; The Diagram Group, 1977; Fagard & Jacquet, 1989; Mathew & Cook, 1990; Thomas, 1990.)

Eaton, & McKeen, 2002). The researchers also found that children's motor activity levels increase linearly with age and tend to peak between 7 and 9 years of age—later than previously thought (Eaton, 1994; Eaton, McKeen, & Campbell, 2001).

Table 7.1 lists the major motor skills that emerge in these preschool years. What is most striking are the impressive gains the child makes in large-muscle skills. By age 5 or 6, children are running, jumping, hopping, galloping, climbing, and skipping. They can ride a tricycle; some can ride a two-wheeled bike. The degree of confidence with which the 5-year-old uses her body for these movements is impressive, particularly in contrast to the somewhat unsteady movements of the 18-month-old.

Fine motor skills also improve in these years, but not to the same level of confidence. Three-year-olds can indeed pick up Cheerios, and 5-year-olds can thread beads on a string. But even at age 5 or 6, children are not highly skilled at such fine motor tasks as cutting accurately with scissors or using a pencil or crayon. When a young child uses a crayon or a pencil, he uses his whole body—his tongue is moving and his whole arm and back are involved in the writing or drawing motion.

These are important facts for teachers of young children to understand. It is the rare kindergartner who is really skilled at such fine motor tasks as writing letters. Younger preschoolers, of course, are even less skilled at these tasks. However, a "wait and see" strategy isn't the best approach for helping children learn to write letters and draw simple forms. Researchers have found that early training, beginning at about age 2½, can accelerate the rate at which young children acquire school-related fine motor skills, such as writing letters (Callaghan & Rankin, 2002).

By age 3, most preschoolers discover the thrill of running at full stride. (*Photo:* Courtesy of Sylvia M. Scott and Owen K. Sloan)

	Drawing Model	
Category	**Cube**	**Cylinder**
1 Scribbles (up to 30 mos.)		
2 Single Units (30 mos. to 46 mos.)		
3 Differentiated Figures (46 mos. to 7 years)		
4 Integrated Whole (7 years +)		

Figure 7.1

Examples of drawings in each category of two object forms.
(*Source:* Toomela, 1999.)

Training effects are evident in studies of children's drawing as well (Callaghan & Rankin, 2002). Nevertheless, drawing appears to follow the developmental sequence shown in **Figure 7.1**, even when accelerated by training (Toomela, 1999). Moreover, the effectiveness of training seems to depend on how well young children understand the figures that experimenters attempt to teach them how to draw. That is, a child who has some grasp of what letters are will be more responsive to training in letter-writing (Callaghan, 1999). Thus, older preschoolers—those beyond age 3—benefit more from training than younger children. Moreover, learning to write letters appears to help children more fully understand them (Callaghan & Rankin, 2002). Thus, research examining young children's writing demonstrates that, in some cases, physical and cognitive development are interactive processes.

THE BRAIN AND NERVOUS SYSTEM

Brain growth, synapse formation, and myelinization continue in early childhood, although at a pace slower than in infancy; however, the slower rate of growth should not be taken to mean that brain development is nearly complete. Indeed, a number of important neurological milestones happen between ages 2 and 6. It is likely that these milestones represent the neurological underpinnings of the remarkable advances in thinking and language that occur during this period.

LATERALIZATION The **corpus callosum**, the brain structure through which the left and right sides of the cerebral cortex communicate, grows and matures more during the

mydevelopmentlab

Connect to
MyDevelopmentLab

Experiment time! Right or left, which side of your brain wins? Link to this simulation and find out.

 Simulate

corpus callosum
the structure that connects the right and left hemispheres of the cerebral cortex

early childhood years than in any other period of life. The growth of this structure accompanies the functional specialization of the left and right hemispheres of the cerebral cortex. This process is called **lateralization**. **Figure 7.2** shows how brain functions are lateralized in most people.

Neuroscientists suspect that our genes dictate which functions will be lateralized and which will not be. However, experience shapes the pace at which lateralization occurs. For example, in 95% of humans, language functions that enable us to understand the meanings of words and the structure of sentences are carried out in the left hemisphere. Studies of fetal responses to different kinds of sounds (i.e., language and music) show that this pattern is evident even before we are born (de Lacoste, Horvath, & Woodward, 1991). The fact that left-side processing of language appears so early in life suggests that lateralization of these functions is dictated by our genes.

Nevertheless, language functions are not as fully lateralized in fetuses as they are in children and adults. Moreover, research indicates that the degree to which these language functions are relegated to the left side of the brain is linked to language production. Preschoolers who display the most advanced language skills in their everyday speech, as well as on standardized tests, show the highest levels of left-side lateralization of these functions (Mills, Coffey-Corina, & Neville, 1994). Of course, we don't know whether children acquire language more rapidly *because* their brains are lateralizing at a faster pace. It seems that the reverse is just as likely to be true—namely, that some children's brains are lateralizing language functions more rapidly because they are learning language faster. But such findings suggest that maturation and experience are both at work in the lateralization process.

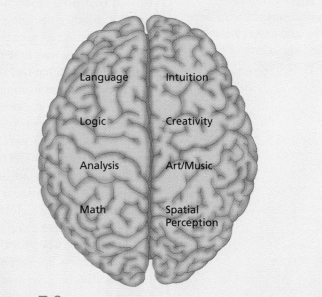

Figure 7.2

Brain functions are lateralized, as shown in the figure. Generally, the left hemisphere specializes in logical sequential processes, such as language and computation, and in the coordination of complex movement. The right hemisphere is associated with holistic simultaneous processes that involve complex perceptual and visual-spatial functions, such as the detection and expression of emotions and nonverbal behaviour. Neurologists think that the basic outline of lateralization is genetically determined, whereas the specific timing of the lateralization of each function is determined by an interaction of genes and experiences.

lateralization
the process through which brain functions are divided between the two hemispheres of the cerebral cortex

THE RETICULAR FORMATION AND THE HIPPOCAMPUS Myelinization of the neurons of the reticular formation, which you will remember from **Chapter 4** is the brain structure that regulates attention and concentration, is another important milestone of early childhood brain development. Neurons in other parts of the brain, such as the *hippocampus*, are also myelinated during this period (Tanner, 1990). The **hippocampus** is involved in the transfer of information to long-term memory. Maturation of this brain structure probably accounts for improvements in memory function across the preschool years (Rolls, 2000). Moreover, maturation of the connections between the hippocampus and the cerebral cortex are probably responsible for our inability to remember much about the first 3 years of life, a phenomenon called *infantile amnesia* (Zola & Squire, 2003). Note that **infantile amnesia** does not involve a complete absence of early memories; thus, some people do have legitimate memories of very early experiences. Typically, though, memories of events that were laid down in the brain prior to age 3 are small in number and fragmentary in character. And, as Piaget's early memory experience suggests, children's early memories are strongly influenced by the verbal recollections of adults that children hear later in their lives, even when those "recollections" turn out to be entirely false.

hippocampus
a brain structure that is essential for the formation of memories

infantile amnesia
the inability of adults and older children to remember more than a few events that took place before they were 3 years of age

handedness
a strong preference for using
one hand or the other that
develops between 3 and
5 years of age

HANDEDNESS

Handedness, the tendency to rely primarily on the right or the left hand, is another neurological milestone of the 2- to 6-year-old period (Tanner, 1990). Scientists used to assume that right-handedness increased among humans along with literacy. The idea was that parents and teachers encouraged children to use their right hands when teaching them how to write. In this way, right-handedness became a custom that was passed on from one generation to the next through instruction.

By examining skeletons that predate the invention of writing, archeologists have determined that the proportions of right- and left-handers were about the same in illiterate ancient populations as among modern humans (83% right-handed, 14% left-handed, and 3% ambidextrous) (Steele & Mayes, 1995). These findings suggest that the prevalence of right-handedness is likely to be the result of genetic inheritance. Moreover, geneticists at the National Cancer Institute (NCI) have identified a dominant gene for right-handedness, which they believe to be so common in the human population that most people receive a copy of it from both parents (Talan, 1998).

Further evidence for the genetic hypothesis can be found in studies demonstrating that handedness appears very early in life—often before the first birthday—although it doesn't become well established until the preschool years (Stroganova, Posikera, Pushina, & Orekhova, 2003). Research comparing children's right-hand and left-hand performance on manual tasks, such as moving pegs from one place to another on a pegboard, also supports the genetic hypothesis. Most of these studies show that older children are better at accomplishing fine motor tasks with the nondominant hand than younger children are (Dellatolas et al., 2003; Roy, Bryden, & Cavill, 2003). Findings from studies comparing nondominant hand use in children and adults follow the same pattern (Annett, 2003; Cavill & Bryden, 2003). Thus, experience in using the hands appears to moderate, rather than strengthen, the advantage of the dominant over the nondominant hand.

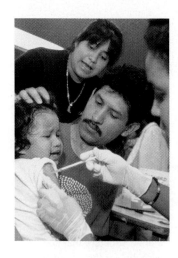

Immunizing young children against a variety of diseases is an important goal of routine health care for this age group.
(*Photo:* Steve Rubin/The Image Works)

HEALTH PROMOTION AND WELLNESS

Young children continue to require periodic medical check-ups as well as a variety of immunizations. Just as they do with infants, doctors monitor preschoolers' growth and motor development. At the same time, doctors and nurses often serve as parents' first source of help with children who have sensory or developmental disabilities that were not diagnosed in infancy (Sulkes, 1998).

EATING PATTERNS Because children grow more slowly during the early childhood years, they may seem to eat less than when they were babies. Moreover, food aversions often develop during the preschool years. For example, a child who loved carrots as an infant may refuse to eat them at age 2 or 3. Consequently, conflicts between young children and their parents often focus on eating behaviour (Wong, 1993).

Parents should also keep in mind that young children eat only about half as much food as adults, and, unlike adults, many don't consume the majority of their daily calories at regular meals (Wong, 1993). Nutritionists suggest that concerned parents keep a daily record of what their children are actually eating for a week. In most cases, parents will find that children are consuming plenty of food.

In Canada, we have seen an uhealthy rise in weight gain over the last quarter century, and roughly 22% of children aged 2 to 5 are now overweight or obese (Shields, 2008). A part of the problem is our increasingly **obesogenic environments**, which foster an overconsumption of high-fat and sugar foods (e.g., fast foods and junk food snacks), inadequate amounts of nutritious foods (e.g., fruits and vegitables), and sedentatry lifestyles—even in youngsters. Recent findings from the Québec Longitudinal Study of Child Development (LSCDQ) found that preschoolers who watched more hours of

obesogenic environments
environments in which social
influences and context contribute to obesity in individuals
or populations

television than their peers also ate more snacks on a daily basis while watching television (Dubois, Farmer, Girard, & Peterson, 2008). And preschoolers who ate more snacks had higher BMIs than children who never or seldom ate snacks in front of the television.

Not only is TV viewing associated with obesity, but also the messages put forth in the content of what is being watched may also be playing a role in TV-watchers weight gain. For example, when University of British Columbia researchers analyzed the messages about food and eating portrayed in preschool TV shows, such as *Barney, Max & Ruby*, and *The Backyardigans*, they found that references to non-nutritious foods are about as equally common as nutritious foods, but the consumption of snacks is more prevalent and is reinforced more than eating proper meals (Anderson & Anderson, 2009). These researchers, using social cognitive theory, suspect that the prevelance of such eating patterns in childrens' TV shows may reinforce eating patterns associated with childhood obesity.

ACCIDENTS   Another concern parents have regarding young children is accidents causing injury and death (Harvey, Towner, Peden, Soori, & Bartolomeos, 2009). Although in any given year fewer than 4 in 1000 children aged 1 to 4 years in Canada have an accident that requires hospitalization (PHAC, 2008b), unintentional injuries account for slightly more than one-quarter of all deaths for children in this age range (PHAC, 2008d). Sadly, an estimated 90% of childhood injuries are preventable (Howard, 2006), and Canadian physicians recommend that caregivers develop ongoing home safety and childproofing measures. These can range, for example, from removing choking hazards from a child's reach, to using child-resistant lids, to lowering household hot water temperature below 50°C, to ensuring that functioning smoke alarms are placed properly in the home (LeBlanc et al., 2006). Urban planners also need to be involved in the design and the construction of safe environments, where, for example, walking and cycling venues can be engineered to reduce injury while promoting healthy activity (Howard, 2010). You can read about other risk factors associated with unintentional injuries in the **Research Report**.

CHILD MALTREATMENT IN CANADA

Certain characteristics of both children and their caregivers can have an impact on risk of maltreatment. Maltreatment has immediate and long-term effects that cross all domains of development. Prevention and protection from harm are important strategies for dealing with abuse.

PATTERNS OF MALTREATMENT   In the Canadian Incidence Study of Reported Child Abuse and Neglect, nationwide statistics were gathered to determine the incidence of child maltreatment in Canada, based on 14 200 cases from 63 sites in all provinces and territories (Trocmé et al., 2005). Overall there were 38.33 investigations of child maltreatment per 1000 children, of which almost half were substantiated. The most common forms of substantiated cases were *neglect* (30%), which involves a failure to supervise, leading to harm or the risk of harm to a child's safety or development; *exposure to domestic violence* (28%), where the child witnessed, overheard, or saw the physical injuries from violence occuring between the caregivers and/or their partners; *physical abuse* (24%), including hitting, shaking, choking, or burning; *emotional maltreatment* (15%), where the child has suffered or is at high risk of suffering from mental, emotional, or developmental problems caused by exposure to family violence, overtly punitive treatment, habitual or extreme verbal abuse or inadequate affection;

Each year, about half of 1% of Canadian children age 1 to 4 have an unintentional injury that requires hospitalization.
(*Photo:* Comstock)

Research Report

UNINTENTIONAL INJURIES IN CANADIAN PRESCHOOLERS

Parents shouldn't assume that children can readily recall safety rules (in one study, 4- to 6-year-olds could recite fewer than half of their home safety rules). Nor should parents assume that a child's knowledge of the rules will protect them. Barbara Morrongiello of the University of Guelph found that a child's knowledge of home safety rules was not significantly related to the incidence of injuries. It is more important that parents see their children demonstrate actions that are consistent with the rules. For instance, researchers have found that the children of parents who practised greater levels of protective supervision and who were more compliant than other children with respect to home safety rules experienced lower rates of injury (Morrongiello, Midgett, & Shields, 2001).

Later studies have shown that being within easy reach of the child was the only technique that lowered risk-taking behaviour and resulted in fewer injuries in young children (Morrongiello & House, 2004; Saluja et al., 2004).

Morrongiello and Rennie (1998) examined cognitive factors that may contribute to a higher risk of injury in boys. They found that boys express greater optimism about their ability to perform activities and believe that they are less susceptible to injury than their peers. This sense of optimism increases with age in both boys and girls. By age 6, boys believe that they will not get hurt and that any injury they may incur will not be severe.

Boys attribute injuries to bad luck rather than a dangerous choice of activity. Parents expect that boys are more likely to be injured than girls, yet they are less likely to intervene in their sons' activities with safety precautions. Conversely, parents see girls as more vulnerable than boys and therefore make their daughters more aware of the potential for harm, although their risk of injury is lower than it is for boys. Parents also assume that boys are natural risk takers, which may foster risk-taking behaviour, as boys are allowed to engage in situations that put them at greater risk for injury.

Another aspect of how cognitive factors affect the rates of injury was found in a study that looked at mothers' differing expectations of risk for different clusters of home injuries. Mothers considered burns, cuts, and falls less severe than injuries caused by such accidents as drowning, poisoning, and suffocation/strangulation/choking (Morrongiello & Kiriakou, 2004). Accordingly, mothers in this study were less motivated to engage in precautionary measures for less severe types of potential injuries. Although most of the earlier research has focused on mothers' supervision beliefs and practices, a subsequent study has determined that there were virtually no differences between the supervisory practices of mothers and fathers (Morrongiello, Walpole, & McArthur, 2009).

Morrongiello and Dawber (1999) investigated socialization factors that contribute to higher rates of injury in boys. They discovered that both mothers and fathers are similar in their interactions with their children, treating boys differently than girls. Both parents put more pressure on their sons, beginning as young as age 3, to play independently with less supervision, and they give them more freedom to roam. By contrast, parents will intervene and support their daughters when they are using play equipment. Furthermore, boys receive more encouragement and direct instructions while girls receive more verbal cautions about safety and possible injury. These differences in parental interaction were evident regardless of the fact that their sons and daughters were all equally physically capable of performing various activities.

As children get a little older, their intended safety practices are influenced by both parental teaching and parental actions (Morrongiello, Corbett, & Bellissimo, 2008). A child's future safety behaviours are best predicted by his parents' actions: If they "walk the talk" by modelling safety practices, their child tends to practise safety behaviours when he is an adult. We might conclude from this that injury-risk behaviours could be passed down from one generation to the next.

and *sexual abuse* (3%), involving a child who has been or is at substantial risk of being sexual molested or sexual exploited. Of all the substantiated cases of child maltreatment, about 19% involved more than one category. The top three combinations included neglect and emotional maltreatment, followed by physical abuse and emotional maltreatment, and then emotional maltreatment coupled with exposure to domestic violence.

Biological parents account for the largest portion of alleged maltreatment. Mothers (54%), followed by fathers (48%), are implicated most often. Stepfathers/common-law partners (12%) or stepmothers/common-law partners (2%) are included in the next largest group of people investigated. About 3% of alleged maltreatment involves nonrelative perpetrators (Trocmé et al., 2005).

CAUSAL FACTORS One useful model for explaining abuse classifies its causes into four broad categories: sociocultural factors, characteristics of the child, characteristics of the abuser, and family stresses (Bittner & Newberger, 1981). The main idea of this model is that episodes of abuse are typically precipitated by everyday interactions between parents and children—for example, when a parent reprimands a young child for spilling a glass of milk. At the time of the episode, several causal factors work together to produce abusive responses in parents. Thus, what differentiates abusive from nonabusive parents, according to this model, is the presence of a number of risk factors that shape how they respond to the ordinary stresses of parenting.

Sociocultural factors include personal or cultural values that regard physical abuse of children as morally acceptable. Parents are more likely to be abusive if they believe that there are few, if any, moral limits on what they can do to their children physically. Sociologists suggest that such beliefs stem from cultural traditions that regard children as property rather than human beings with individual rights (Mooney, Knox, & Schacht, 2010). Moreover, parents who live in communities where others share and act on these beliefs are more likely to be abusive.

Several characteristics of children or parents may set the stage for child abuse. For example, children with physical or mental disabilities or those who have difficult temperaments are more likely to be abused than others (Sulkes, 1998). Indeed, one recent Canadian study found that a child with developmental delay is about 4.4 times as likely as the average Canadian child to be maltreated (Brown & Fudge Schormans, 2004). Parents who are depressed, lack parenting skills and knowledge, have a history of abuse themselves, or are substance abusers are more likely to abuse or neglect their children (Emery & Laumann-Billings, 1998). Family stressors include factors such as poverty, unemployment, and interparental conflict (Sulkes, 1998). Keep in mind that no single factor produces abuse; but the presence of several of these variables in a particular family significantly increases the chances that the children will experience abuse.

OUTCOMES Some children who are frequently or severely abused develop *post-traumatic stress disorder (PTSD)* (Margolin & Gordis, 2000; Morrissette, 1999; Perry, 2001). This disorder involves extreme levels of anxiety, flashback memories of episodes of abuse, nightmares, and other sleep disturbances. Abused children are also more likely than nonabused peers to exhibit poor school performance in middle childhood, to develop substance abuse problems in adolescence, and to exhibit slower rates of brain growth (Glaser, 2000; Malinosky-Rummell & Hansen, 1993; Rogosch, Cicchetti, & Aber, 1995) (see the **Research Report**).

PREVENTIVE MEASURES Preventing abuse begins with education. Informing parents about the potential consequences of some physical acts, such as the link between shaking an infant and brain damage, may help. In addition, parents need to know that injuring children is a crime, even if the intention is to discipline them. Parenting classes, perhaps as a required part of high school curricula, can help inform parents or future parents about principles of child development and appropriate methods of discipline (Mooney et al., 2010).

Another approach to prevention of abuse involves identification of families at risk. Physicians, nurses, and other professionals who routinely interact with parents of infants and young children have a particularly important role to play in this kind of prevention. Parents who seem to have problems attaching to their children can sometimes

Research Report

TRAUMATIC EVENTS AND NEUROBIOLOGICAL AND FUNCTIONAL CHANGES IN THE BRAIN

Bruce Perry, senior consultant to the Alberta Ministry of Children's Services, contends that traumatic experiences from early childhood affect long-term behaviour (Perry, 2002; Perry, Pollard, Blakely, Baker, & Vigilante, 1995). His ideas are supported by neurological studies that have found that severe maltreatment during childhood (physical, sexual, and/or emotional abuse) is related to molecular and neurobiological damage in the emotional and memory areas of the brain that are still growing (Teicher, 2002). In particular, brain imaging studies of adults who were traumatized as children have revealed reductions in the size of the hippocampus, where memory processing takes place, and the **amygdala**, which regulates negative emotions. Atypical left/right cerebral hemisphere functioning was also found.

These findings complement the research of Ruth Lanius, of the University of Western Ontario, who has been using a brain imaging technique called **functional magnetic resonance imaging (fMRI)** to see if people who experience traumatic life events use different regions of the brain when they recall the events. Lanius

and others (Lanius et al., 2003, 2004) compared the brain functioning of people who developed PTSD with those who did not, in the aftermath of comparably traumatic events. When subjects were prompted to recall their traumatic event (e.g., a horrific auto accident or sexual assault), those with PTSD showed arousal in the right brain areas whereas those who did not develop PTSD experienced heightened activation in the left brain. As you recall from **Figure 7.2**, the right brain generally deals with nonverbal information, which may help to explain why people who have PTSD react so strongly to memories that are perceptually vivid and visceral in nature. In comparison, the left brain is better at processing verbal information, which may account for why people who do not develop PTSD recall a less emotionally laden, narrative memory of traumatic events. To what extent traumatic life events either cause these disparities in brain functioning or somehow trigger a predisposition to process emotionally charged information in atypical ways remains unclear.

amygdala
an almond-shaped brain structure that plays a key role in the regulation of defensive emotions like fear and anger

functional magnetic resonance imaging (fMRI)
a form of Magnetic Resonance Imaging (MRI) that records what regions of the brain are active during specific mental activities

be identified during medical office visits. These parents can be referred to parenting classes or to social workers for help. Similarly, parents may ask doctors or nurses how to discipline their children. Such questions provide professionals with opportunities to discuss which practices are appropriate and which are not.

Finally, children who are abused must be protected from further injury. This can be accomplished through vigorous enforcement of existing child abuse laws. Health professionals must report suspected abuse; however, ordinary citizens are also bound by mandatory reporting laws in all provinces and territories except the Yukon, which requests that all concerns be reported. Any person who has reasonable grounds to suspect abuse or neglect of a child or a youth has a duty to report the abuse or neglect to the local child protection agency. Once abuse is reported, steps must be taken to protect injured children from suspected abusers.

Before Going On

- What are the major milestones of physical, motor, and neurological development between ages 2 and 6, and what are the associated changes in nutritional and health care needs?

- What factors can contribute to abuse and neglect, and how does abuse affect children's development?

COGNITIVE CHANGES

The changes in thinking that happen during the early childhood years are staggering. At the beginning of the period, children are just beginning to learn how to accomplish goals. By the time they reach age 5 or 6, they are proficient at manipulating symbols and can make accurate judgments about others' thoughts, feelings, and behaviour.

PIAGET'S PREOPERATIONAL STAGE

According to Piaget, children acquire the **semiotic (symbolic) function** between ages 18 and 24 months. The semiotic function is the understanding that one object or behaviour can represent another—a picture of a chair represents a real chair, a child's pretending to feed a doll stands for a parent's feeding a baby, and so on. Once this understanding has been achieved, children are in Piaget's **preoperational stage**.

During the preoperational stage, children become proficient at using symbols for thinking and communicating but still have difficulty thinking logically. At age 2 or 3, children begin to pretend in their play (Walker-Andrews & Kahana-Kalman, 1999). A broom may become a horse, or a block may become a train. Cross-cultural research suggests that this kind of object use by 2- to 3-year-olds in pretend play is universal (Haight et al., 1999). In fact, observing children at play can provide parents or teachers with a good idea about their levels of cognitive development (see **Table 7.2**). Young children also show signs of increasing proficiency at symbol use in their growing ability to understand models, maps, and graphic symbols, such as letters (Callaghan, 1999; DeLoache, 1995).

*✻⊸[Explore

semiotic (symbolic) function
the understanding that one object or behaviour can represent another

preoperational stage
Piaget's second stage of cognitive development, during which children become proficient in the use of symbols in thinking and communicating but still have difficulty

TABLE 7.2	Children's Play and Cognitive Development
Types of Play	**Description**
Sensorimotor play	A 12-month-old child spends most of her playtime exploring and manipulating objects. She puts things in her mouth, shakes them, and moves them along the floor.
Constructive play	By age 2, children also begin to use objects to build or construct things. Building a tower with blocks, drawing a picture, and digging in sand are typical activities at this stage.
First Pretend play	The first instances of such pretending are usually simple, such as pretending to drink from a toy cup. The toy is used for its actual or typical purpose (a cup is for drinking), and the actions are still oriented to the self, but some pretending is involved. Between 15 and 21 months, the recipient of the pretend action becomes another person or a toy. The child is still using objects for their usual purposes, but now he is using the toy cup with a stuffed bear instead of using it himself.
Substitute Pretend play	Between 2 and 3 years of age, children begin to use objects to stand for something altogether different. Children this age may use a broom as a horse or make "trucks" out of blocks.
Sociodramatic play	Sometime in the preschool years, children also begin to play parts or take roles. For example, in playing house, participants fill roles such as "mommy," "daddy," "sister," "brother," and "baby." At first, children simply take up these roles; later, they name the various roles and may give each other explicit instructions about the right way to pretend a particular role. Interestingly, at about the same age, a great many children seem to create imaginary companions (Taylor, Cartwright, & Carlson, 1993).
Rule-Governed play	By age 5 or 6, children begin to prefer rule-governed pretending and formal games. For example, children of this age use rules such as "Whoever is smallest has to be the baby" when playing "house" and play simple games such as Red Rover and Red Light, Green Light. Younger children play these games as well, but 5- and 6-year-olds better understand their rules and will follow them for longer periods of time.

Figure 7.3

The experimental situation shown here is similar to one Piaget used to study egocentrism in children. The child is asked to pick out a picture that shows how the mountains look to her, and then to pick out a picture that shows how the mountains look to the doll.

egocentrism
the young child's belief that everyone sees and experiences the world the way she does

centration
the young child's tendency to think of the world in terms of one variable at a time

Although young children are remarkably good at using symbols, their reasoning about the world is often flawed. For example, Piaget described the preoperational child's tendency to look at things entirely from her own point of view, a characteristic Piaget called **egocentrism** (Piaget, 1954). This term does not suggest that the young child is a self-centred egomaniac. It simply means that she assumes that everyone sees the world as she does. For example, while riding in the back seat of a car, a 3- or 4-year-old may suddenly call out "Look at that, Dad!"—not realizing that Dad can't see the object she's talking about. Moreover, the child doesn't realize that the car's motion prevents Dad from ever seeing the object in question. As a result, the youngster may become frustrated in her attempts to communicate with her father about what she saw.

Figure 7.3 illustrates a classic experiment in which most young children demonstrate this kind of egocentrism. The child is shown a three-dimensional scene with mountains of different sizes and colours. From a set of drawings, she picks out the one that shows the scene the way she sees it. Most preschoolers can do this without much difficulty. Then the examiner asks the child to pick out the drawing that shows how someone else sees the scene, such as a doll or the examiner. At this point, most preschoolers choose the drawing that shows their own view of the mountains (Flavell, Everett, Croft, & Flavell, 1981; Gzesh & Surber, 1985).

Piaget also pointed out that the preschool-aged child's thinking is guided by the appearance of objects—a theme that still dominates the research on children of this age. Children may believe, for example, that any moving object is an animal of some kind. This kind of thinking reflects the child's tendency to think of the world in terms of one variable at a time, a type of thought Piaget called **centration**. Because of centration, the child reaches the conclusion that all moving objects are animals through a series of false conclusions. The premise on which these conclusions is based is the fact that it is evident in everyday interactions with the world that all animals move—or, as scientists put it, have the capacity for *locomotion* (self-movement). But the preoperational thinker isn't capable of thinking of objects in terms of both their motion and their capacity for self-movement. Thus, movement, without regard to any other relevant characteristic of

At age 2 to 3, children begin to pretend in their play, using one object to stand in for something else, as the child in the photo on the left is doing During the preschool years, children will also begin to play parts or take roles. In playing house, for example (as the children in the photo on the right are doing), participants fill roles such as "mommy," "daddy," "sister," "brother," and "baby." (*Photos:* left, Courtesy of Jerry and Denise Boyd. Used with permission; right, © Stock Connection Blue/Alamy)

objects, becomes the sole criterion for distinguishing between living and nonliving objects. As a result, a child may fear a leaf that blows across the playground because he believes that the leaf is trying to follow him. Piaget used the term *animism* to refer to this particular product of preoperational logic.

Some of Piaget's most famous experiments deal with a cognitive process called **conservation**, the understanding that matter can change in appearance without changing in quantity. Because of centration and irreversibility, children rarely show any kind of conservation before age 5. When they do begin to understand this concept, they demonstrate their understanding with arguments based on three characteristics of appearance-only transformations of matter. The first of these is *identity*, the knowledge that quantities are constant unless matter is added to or subtracted from them. The second is *compensation*, the understanding that all relevant characteristics of the appearance of a given quantity of matter must be taken into account before reaching a conclusion about whether the quantity has changed. The third is *reversibility*, the capacity to mentally compare the transformed appearance of a given quantity of matter to its original appearance. Some of the conservation tasks Piaget used, along with children's typical responses to them, are shown in **Figure 7.4**. As you can see, assessing a child's stage of cognitive development involves finding out how she arrived at her answer to a question, not just evaluating the answer as right or wrong.

conservation
the understanding that matter can change in appearance without changing in quantity

mydevelopmentlab
Connect to
MyDevelopmentLab
Has Piaget confused you? Watch these children as they demonstrate the idea of conservation.

◉─[Watch]

CHALLENGES TO PIAGET'S VIEW

Studies of conservation have generally confirmed Piaget's observations (e.g., Ciancio et al., 1999; Gelman, 1972; Sophian, 1995; Wellman, 1982). Although younger children can demonstrate some understanding of conservation if the task is made very simple, most children cannot consistently solve conservation and other kinds of logical problems until at least age 5. However, evidence suggests that preschoolers are a great deal more cognitively sophisticated than Piaget thought.

EGOCENTRISM AND PERSPECTIVE TAKING Despite their egocentrism, children as young as 14.5 months appear to have at least some ability to understand that another person perceives things or experiences things differently than they do (Song & Baillargeon, 2008). By age 2 or 3, children can adapt their speech or their play to the demands of a companion. They play differently with older and younger playmates and talk differently to a younger or handicapped child (Brownell, 1990; Guralnik & Paul-Brown, 1984).

However, such understanding is clearly not perfect at this young age. Developmental psychologist John Flavell has proposed two levels of perspective-taking ability. At level 1, the child knows that other people experience things differently. At level 2, the child develops a whole series of complex rules for figuring out precisely what the other person sees or experiences (Flavell, Green, & Flavell, 1990). At 2 and 3 years old, children have level 1 knowledge but not level 2; level 2 knowledge begins to be evident in 4- and 5-year-olds.

For example, a child of 4 or 5 understands that another person feels sad if she fails or happy if she succeeds. The preschool child also begins to figure out that unpleasant emotions occur in situations in which there is a gap between desire and reality. Sadness, for example, normally occurs when someone loses something that is valued or fails to acquire some desired object (Harris, 1989).

This young child is able to adapt his speech to the needs of his younger sibling, one of many indications that preschoolers are less egocentric than Piaget thought.
(*Photo:* Copyright ©Spencer Grant/ Photo Edt. All rights reserved.)

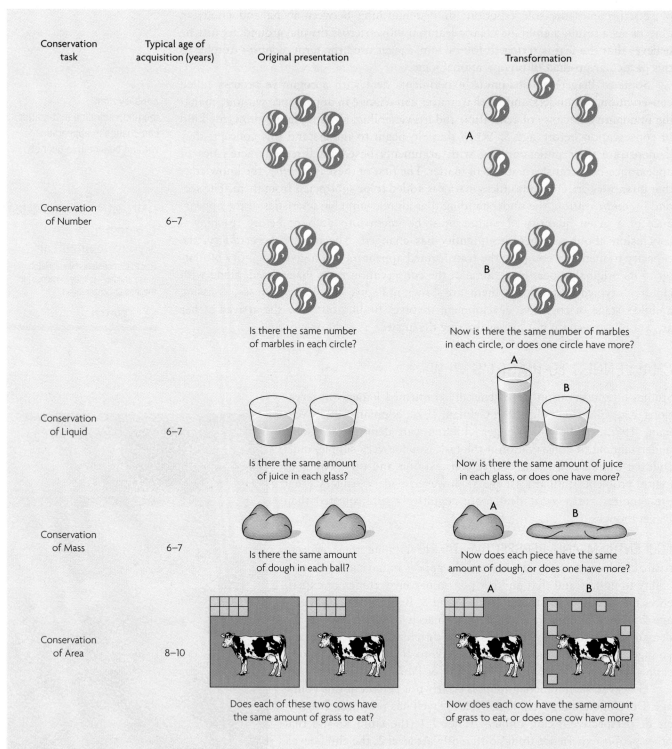

Conservation task	Typical age of acquisition (years)	Original presentation	Transformation
Conservation of Number	6–7	Is there the same number of marbles in each circle?	Now is there the same number of marbles in each circle, or does one circle have more?
Conservation of Liquid	6–7	Is there the same amount of juice in each glass?	Now is there the same amount of juice in each glass, or does one have more?
Conservation of Mass	6–7	Is there the same amount of dough in each ball?	Now does each piece have the same amount of dough, or does one have more?
Conservation of Area	8–10	Does each of these two cows have the same amount of grass to eat?	Now does each cow have the same amount of grass to eat, or does one cow have more?

Figure 7.4

Piaget's research involved several kinds of conservation tasks. He classified children's thinking as concrete operational with respect to a particular task if they could correctly solve the problem and provide a concrete operational reason for their answer. For example, if a child said, "The two circles of marbles are the same because you didn't add any or take any away when you moved them," the response was judged to be concrete operational. Conversely, if a child said, "The two circles are the same, but I don't know why," the response was not classified as concrete operational.

Studies of preschoolers' understanding of emotion have also challenged Piaget's description of the young child's egocentrism. For example, between ages 2 and 6, children learn to regulate or modulate their expressions of emotion to conform to others' expectations (Dunn, 1994). In addition, preschool children use emotional expressions such as crying or smiling to get things they want. These behaviours are obviously based at least in part on a growing awareness that other people judge your feelings by what they see you expressing. These behaviours wouldn't occur if children were completely incapable of looking at their own behaviour from another person's perspective, as Piaget's assertions about egocentrism would suggest.

APPEARANCE AND REALITY The young child's movement away from egocentrism seems to be part of a much broader change in her understanding of appearance and reality. Flavell has studied this understanding in a variety of ways (Flavell, Green, & Flavell, 1989; Flavell, Green, Wahl, & Flavell, 1987). In the most famous Flavell procedure, the experimenter shows the child a sponge that has been painted to look like a rock. Three-year-olds will say either that the object looks like a sponge and is a sponge or that it looks like a rock and is a rock. But 4- and 5-year-olds can distinguish between appearance and reality; they realize that the item looks like a rock but is a sponge (Flavell, 1986). Thus, the older children understand that the same object can be represented differently, depending on one's point of view.

Using similar materials, investigators have also asked when a child can first grasp the **false belief principle**. Individuals who understand this principle can look at a problem or situation from another person's point of view and discern what kind of information would cause that person to believe something that isn't true. For example, after a child has felt the sponge/rock and has answered questions about what it looks like and what it "really" is, a researcher can ask something like this: "John [a playmate of the child] hasn't touched this, he hasn't squeezed it. If John just sees it over here like this, what will he think it is? Will he think it's a rock or will he think it's a sponge?" (Gopnik & Astington, 1988, p. 35). Most 3-year-olds think John will believe the object is a sponge because it is a sponge. By contrast, 4- and 5-year-olds realize that, because John hasn't felt the sponge, he will have a false belief that it is a rock. Some studies show that 3-year-olds can perform more accurately if they are given a hint or clue. For example, if experimenters tell them that a "naughty" person is trying to fool John, more of them will say that he will falsely think the sponge is a rock (Bowler, Briskman, & Grice, 1999). But the child of 4 or 5 more consistently understands that someone else can believe something that isn't true and act on that belief.

A study by Phillip Zelazo and Janet Boseovski (2001) of the University of Toronto helps to clarify the boundaries of the false belief principle. The researchers introduced mnemonic cues that challenged false beliefs in young children. Specifically, they videotaped children during a "representational change task." Children in this situation were shown common objects and asked what they expected would be inside. For example, they were shown a box of Smarties and they guessed that there would be Smarties inside. Then the actual contents of the Smarties box, a piece of string, was revealed to the children. This example illustrates that children had held a false belief about the actual contents. When the children were later asked what they had thought had been in the box originally, most 3-year-olds denied their original (false) belief and said that they thought there had been string in the Smarties box. Even after the videotape was played to them showing that they originally said Smarties would be inside, the 3-year-olds persisted in saying that they had thought string would be inside. By comparison, most 4- and 5-year-olds acknowledged that they had originally been incorrect about the contents.

false belief principle
the ability to look at a problem or situation from another person's point of view and discern what kind of information would cause that person to believe something that isn't true

THEORIES OF MIND

theory of mind
a set of ideas constructed by a
child or an adult to explain other
people's ideas, beliefs, desires,
and behaviour

Evidence like that described in the previous section has led a number of theorists to propose that the 4- or 5-year-old has developed a new and quite sophisticated **theory of mind,** or a set of ideas that explains other people's ideas, beliefs, desires, and behaviour (e.g., Astington & Gopnik, 1991; Gopnik & Wellman, 1994; Harris, 1989).

UNDERSTANDING THOUGHTS, DESIRES, AND BELIEFS The theory of mind does not spring forth full-blown at age 4. Infants as young as 10 months have some beginning understanding of the fact that people (but not inanimate objects) operate with goals and intentions (Legerstee & Markova, 2008). For instance, in a study by Joan Peskin (1992) of the Ontario Institute for Studies in Education, the use of deception by 3- to 5-year-olds was investigated. Unlike previous theory of mind studies that utilized hidden identities or objects, Peskin created a more competitive situation in which children could acquire highly desirable stickers. However, to obtain the stickers a child would have to hide his true feelings about the desired sticker lest a "bad puppet" choose it first. For a child to be able to hide his feelings, he would first need to understand that he had to influence another person's mental state. The results revealed that although 3-year-olds could use physical means to acquire the desirable sticker (including physical blocking and loud protestations), they failed to conceal their true desire for the sticker and thus lost it to the "bad puppet." The 3-year-olds in this study were not able to misinform or withhold information even if it meant that the "bad puppet" would repeatedly end up with the sticker that the child preferred. Therefore, it appears that 3-year-olds lack the capacity to appreciate that someone may misrepresent a situation because they cannot grasp the concept of deceit. In comparison, 4- to 5-year-olds in this situation were able to understand the state of mind of others and could accordingly conceal information that allowed them to succeed in obtaining the desired stickers.

Between ages 3 and 5 years, children understand some aspects of the link between people's thinking or feeling and their behaviour. Still, there is much that the 4- or 5-year-old doesn't yet grasp about other people's thinking. The child of this age understands that other people think but does not yet understand that other people can think about him. The 4-year-old understands "I know that you know." But he does not yet fully understand that this process is reciprocal, namely, "You know that I know."

Furthermore, it is not until about age 6 that most children realize that knowledge can be derived through inference. For example, researchers in one study showed 4- and 6-year-olds two toys of different colours (Pillow, 1999). Next, they placed the toys in separate opaque containers. They then opened one of the containers and showed the toy to a puppet. When asked whether the puppet now knew which colour toy was in each container, only the 6-year-olds said yes.

Understanding of the reciprocal nature of thought seems to develop between ages 5 and 7 for most children. This understanding is likely particularly important because it is probably necessary for the creation of genuinely reciprocal friendships, which begin to emerge in the elementary school years (Sullivan, Zaitchik, & Tager-Flusberg, 1994). In fact, the rate at which an individual preschooler develops a theory of mind is a good predictor of her social skills both later in early childhood and during the school years (Moore, Barresi, & Thompson, 1998; Watson, Nixon, Wilson, & Capage, 1999).

INFLUENCES ON THE DEVELOPMENT OF A THEORY OF MIND Developmentalists have found that a child's theory of mind is correlated with his performance on Piaget's tasks as well as on more recently developed problems designed to assess egocentrism and appearance/reality (Melot & Houde, 1998; Yirmiya & Shulman, 1996). In addition, pretend play seems to contribute to theory of mind development. Shared pretense with other children, in particular, is strongly related to theory of mind (Dockett &

Smith, 1995; Schwebel, Rosen, & Singer, 1999). Furthermore, children whose parents discuss emotion-provoking past events with them develop a theory of mind more rapidly than do their peers who do not have such conversations (Welch-Ross, 1997).

Language skills—such as knowledge of words like *want*, *need*, *think*, or *remember*, which express feelings, desires, and thoughts—are also related to theory of mind development (Astington & Jenkins, 1995). Indeed, some level of language facility may be a necessary condition for the development of a theory of mind. Developmentalists have found that children in this age range simply do not succeed at false-belief tasks until they have reached a certain threshold of general language skill (Astington & Jenkins, 1999; Jenkins & Astington, 1996; Watson et al., 1999).

ALTERNATIVE THEORIES OF EARLY CHILDHOOD THINKING

In recent years, a number of interesting theoretical approaches have attempted to explain both Piaget's original results and the more recent findings that contradict them.

INFORMATION-PROCESSING THEORIES One set of alternative proposals is based on the information-processing model. As you may remember from **Chapter 2**, Robbie Case explained age differences in cognitive development as a function of changes in children's use of their short-term memories (Case, 1985, 1992). Case used the term **short-term storage space** (**STSS**) to refer to the child's working memory. According to Case, how many schemes the STSS can attend to is limited. He referred to the maximum number of schemes that may be put into STSS at one time as **operational efficiency**. Improvements in operational efficiency occur through both practice (doing tasks that require memory use, such as learning the alphabet) and brain maturation as the child gets older. Thus, a 7-year-old is better able to handle the processing demands of conservation tasks than is a 4-year-old because of improvements in operational efficiency of the STSS.

A good example of the function of STSS may be found by examining *matrix classification*, a task Piaget often used with both young and school-aged children (see **Figure 7.5**). Matrix classification requires the child to place a given stimulus in two categories at the same time. Young children fail such tasks because, according to neo-Piagetian theory, they begin by processing the stimulus according to one dimension (either shape or colour) and then either fail to realize that it is necessary to reprocess it along the second dimension or forget to do so.

Nevertheless, researchers have trained young children to perform correctly on such problems by using a two-step strategy. The children are taught to think of a red triangle, for example, in terms of shape first and colour second. Typically, instruction involves a number of training tasks in which researchers remind children repeatedly to remember to reclassify stimuli with respect to the second variable. According to Case, both children's failure prior to instruction and the type of strategy training to which they respond illustrate the constraints imposed on problem-solving by the limited operational efficiency of the younger child's STSS. There is room for only one scheme at a time in the child's STSS, either shape or colour. The training studies show that younger children *can* learn to perform

short-term storage space (STSS)
neo-Piagetian theorist Robbie Case's term for the working memory

operational efficiency
a neo-Piagetian term that refers to the maximum number of schemes that can be processed in working memory at one time

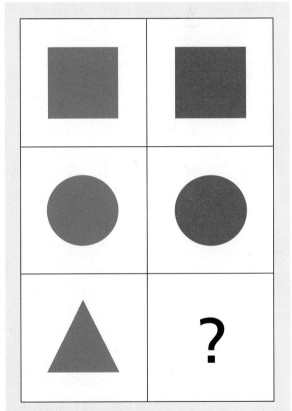

Figure 7.5

Neo-Piagetians have used Piaget's matrix classification task in strategy training studies with young children. Before training, most preschoolers say that a blue triangle or red circle belongs in the box with the question mark. After learning a two-step strategy in which they are taught to classify each object first by shape and then by colour, children understand that a red triangle is the figure that is needed to complete the matrix.

Figure 7.6

On the Flexible Item Selection Task (FIST) children are presented with three cards with pictures of objects that vary on two of four possible dimensions. A child is required to match two cards on one dimension and then to match two cards by using a different dimension. By age 5, children can perform both tasks, which suggests that they are capable of abstraction and cognitive flexibility.

(*Source:* Jacques & Zelazo, 2001, from Figure 2, p. 578.)

correctly, but their approach is qualitatively different from that of older children. The older child's more efficient STSS allows her to think about shape and colour at the same time and, therefore, perform successfully without any training.

Young children can solve simple perceptual matching problems like the ones described above but run into difficulty when they are instructed to solve problems that require higher-level abstract flexible thinking. Sophie Jacques of Dalhousie University and Philip Zelazo of the University of Toronto developed the *Flexible Item Selection Task (FIST)* to measure abstraction and cognitive flexibility (Jacques & Zelazo, 2001). The FIST involves a card-sorting technique to measure if a child can match objects on cards that vary on two of four dimensions (shape, colour, size, and number, as illustrated in **Figure 7.6**). A child is presented with three cards at once and first instructed to pick two cards that match on one of the four dimensions, for example, size (a measure of abstract mental ability), and then to pick two cards that match on a different dimension, for example, shape (a measure of cognitive flexibility—a child has to be able to consider each object on multiple categories). The researchers found that 2-year-olds were unable to grasp the instructions; 3-year-olds could understand the instructions but had difficulty matching cards on even one dimension. The results reflect an underdeveloped abstract reasoning ability in these younger children. By comparison, 4-year-olds could match objects on one dimension but struggled with matching objects on a second dimension, suggesting that although they are capable of abstracting relevant information to solve a problem, they lack the cognitive flexibility to switch between abstract dimensions. However, the 5-year-olds were able to match cards on one or more dimensions. It seems that, even though children as young as 3 years of age can match objects based on concrete perceptual categories, they have a hard time matching objects based on abstract categories required on the FIST. Moreover, it isn't until a child reaches the age of 5 that she demonstrates the ability to show both cognitive abstraction and flexibility.

Jeffrey Bisanz and his colleagues at the University of Alberta have been studying how information-processing capacities affect the development of arithmetic skills in preschoolers. These researchers have been trying to understand what children know about arithmetic prior to formal schooling in terms of the cognitive interplay between arithmetic procedures, concepts, and facts (J. Bisanz, personal communication, July 30, 2001). One problem with testing 4-year-olds' ability to do arithmetic is that they do not have the cognitive ability to use words and symbols to solve number problems. To compensate for their lack of cognitive ability, Klein and Bisanz (2000) developed a novel method of studying arithmetic skills in preschoolers: using poker chips in lieu of numbers for counting. When the researchers studied preschoolers under these new testing procedures, they observed some interesting outcomes. First, in a two-term problem (e.g., a + b) the "representational set size," the maximum number of units of information that must be held in working memory at the same time during problem solution, is a major constraint on the preschooler's success in solving nonverbal addition and subtraction problems. Second, in a three-term problem (e.g., a + b − b), 4-year-olds can spontaneously invent shortcuts to solve this type of problem, thus demonstrating that even at this young age children can apply arithmetic principles to solve nonverbal tasks. Findings such as these may eventually lead to new methods of assessment, early identification, and instruction in the early years.

Information-processing theorists also maintain that children's ability to make efficient use of their memory system is influenced by other cognitive processes. **Metamemory** is knowledge about and control of memory processes. For example, young children know that it takes longer to memorize a list of 10 words than a list of five words (Kail, 1990). However, between ages 2 and 6, children aren't very good at coming up with strategies to apply to more difficult memory tasks. Thus, they can't perform as well as older children on tasks, like those of Piaget, that call for efficient use of the memory system.

metamemory
knowledge about how memory works and the ability to control and reflect on one's own memory function

Metacognition is knowledge about and control of thought processes. For example, a child listening to a story may realize he has forgotten the main character's name and ask the reader what it is. Both knowing that the character's name has been forgotten and knowing that the character's name will make the story easier to understand are forms of metacognition. Moreover, metacognitive processes enable the child to generate a strategy, such as asking the reader, that will solve the problem.

metacognition
knowledge about how the mind thinks and the ability to control and reflect on one's own thought processes

Children's metamemory and metacognition improve during the early childhood period. Between ages 3 and 5, for example, children figure out that to tell whether a sponge painted like a rock is really a sponge or a rock, a person needs to touch or hold it. Just looking at it doesn't give someone enough information (Flavell, 1993; O'Neill, Astington, & Flavell, 1992). Thus, by about age 4 or 5, children seem to have some beginning grasp of these processes, but they still have a long way to go. As a result, their ability to solve complex problems such as those Piaget used is limited compared with that of older children.

VYGOTSKY'S SOCIOCULTURAL THEORY In **Chapter 2** you learned that psychologists' interest in Russian psychologist Lev Vygotsky's views on development has grown recently. Vygotsky's theory differs from both Piagetian and information-processing theory in its emphasis on the role of social factors in cognitive development. For example, two preschoolers working on a puzzle together discuss where the pieces belong. After a number of such dialogues, the participants internalize the discussion. It then becomes a model for an internal conversation the child uses to guide himself through the puzzle-solving process. In this way, Vygotsky suggested, solutions to problems are socially generated and learned. Vygotsky did not deny that individual learning takes place. Rather, he suggested that group learning processes are central to cognitive development. Consequently, from Vygotsky's perspective, social interaction is required for cognitive development (Thomas, 2000).

Chapter 2 described two important general principles of Vygotsky's theory: *the zone of proximal development* and *scaffolding*. Vygotsky also proposed specific stages of cognitive development from birth to age 7. Each stage represents a step toward the child's internalization of the ways of thinking used by the adults around him.

In the first period, called the *primitive stage*, the infant possesses mental processes that are similar to those of lower animals. He learns primarily through conditioning, until language begins to develop in the second year. At that point, he enters the *naive psychology stage*, in which he learns to use language to communicate but still does not understand its symbolic character. For example, he doesn't realize that any collection of sounds could stand for the object "chair" as long as everyone agreed—that is, if all English speakers agreed to substitute the word *blek* for *chair*, we could do so because we would all understand what *blek* meant.

Once the child begins to appreciate the symbolic function of language, near the end of the third year of life, he enters the *egocentric speech stage*. In this stage, he uses language as a guide to solving problems. In effect, he tells himself how to do things. For example, a 3-year-old walking down a flight of stairs might say "Be careful" to himself. Such a statement would be the result of his internalization of statements made to him by adults and older children.

Piaget recognized the existence and importance of egocentric speech. However, he believed that such speech disappeared as the child approached the end of the preoperational stage. In contrast, Vygotsky claimed that egocentric speech becomes completely internalized at age 6 or 7, when children enter the final period of cognitive development, the *ingrowth stage*. Thus, he suggested that the logical thinking Piaget ascribed to older children resulted from their internalization of speech routines they had acquired from older children and adults in the social world rather than from schemes children constructed for themselves through interaction with the physical world.

At present, there is insufficient evidence to either support or contradict most of Vygotsky's ideas (Thomas, 2000). However, studies have shown that young children whose parents provide them with more cognitive scaffolding during the preschool years exhibit higher levels of achievement in the early elementary grades than peers whose parents provide less support of this kind (Neitzel & Stright, 2003). Some intriguing research on children's construction of theory of mind during social interactions lends weight to Vygotsky's major propositions. It seems that children in pairs and groups do produce more sophisticated ideas than individual children who work on problems alone. However, the sophistication of a group's ideas appears to depend on the presence of at least one fairly advanced individual child in the group (Tan-Niam et al., 1998). Thus, Vygotsky's theory may ignore the important contributions of individual thought to group interaction. However, studies strongly support Vygotsky's hypothesis that private speech helps children solve problems (Montero & De Dios, 2006).

By integrating the individualistic "theory of mind" approach (that stemmed from a Piagetian tradition) with Vygotsky's "social interaction" approach, contemporary theorists are attempting to overcome some serious theoretical dilemmas, such as which set of cognitive abilities develops first and which is foremost. The suggestion is that cognitive abilities develop in unison—the child's emerging understanding of the mind helps him interact better with others and in turn his social interactions reinforce his understanding of thoughts, desires, and beliefs. In essence, "concepts about the mind are not just passed on from the social group, nor are they completely formed by individual child-theorists" (Carpendale & Lewis, 2004, p. 84). It is only through his regular and routine interactions with others that a child develops a personal understanding of mind that is distinct from his understanding of the minds of others and which is separate from his understanding of objects in the real world.

Before Going On

- List the characteristics of children's thought during Piaget's preoperational stage.
- How do the theory of mind, information-processing, and sociocultural theories explain the changes in children's thinking that happen between ages 2 and 6?

CHANGES IN LANGUAGE

To his credit, Piaget recognized that the overriding theme of cognitive development in the early childhood years is language acquisition. Of course, the process begins much earlier, as you learned in **Chapter 5**. Amazingly, though, children enter this period producing only a limited number of words and simple sentences but leave it as accomplished, fluent speakers of at least one language.

FAST-MAPPING

The average 2½-year-old's vocabulary of about 600 words is fairly impressive when we compare it with the dozen or so words most 1-year-olds know (E. Bates et al., 1994). This quantity amounts to the acquisition of one or two new words every day between ages 12 and 24 months. Impressive though this feat is, it pales in comparison to the rate of vocabulary growth among preschoolers. By the time a child goes to school at age 5 or 6, total vocabulary has risen to perhaps 15 000 words—an astonishing increase of 10 words a day (Anglin, 1995; Pinker, 1994). Moreover, word learning appears to be the engine that drives the whole process of language development. That is, the more words a child knows, the more advanced she is with regard to grammar and other aspects of language (McGregor, Sheng, & Smith, 2005). What is the impetus behind this amazing rate of word learning?

Researchers have found that a momentous shift in the way children approach new words happens around age 3. As a result of this shift, children begin to pay attention to words in whole groups, such as words that name objects in a single class (e.g., types of dinosaurs or kinds of fruit) or words with similar meanings. In a sense, understanding of the categorical nature of words helps children develop what we might think of as mental "slots" for new words. Once the slots are in place, they seem to automatically organize the linguistic input children receive from parents, teachers, peers, books, TV programs, advertisements, and every other source of language to extract new words and fill the slots as quickly as possible.

Psychologists use the term **fast-mapping** to refer to this ability to categorically link new words to real-world referents (Carey & Bartlett, 1978). (*Referents* are the real objects and events to which words refer.) At the core of fast-mapping, say researchers, is a rapidly formed hypothesis about a new word's meaning (Behrend, Scofield, & Kleinknecht, 2001). The hypothesis is based on information derived from children's prior knowledge of words and word categories and from the context in which the word is used. Once formed, the hypothesis is tested through use of the word in the child's own speech, often immediately after learning it. The feedback children receive in response to use of the word helps them judge the accuracy of the hypothesis and the appropriateness of the category to which they have assumed that the word belongs. Perhaps this helps explain why preschoolers do so much talking and why they are so persistent at getting their listeners to actively respond to them.

fast-mapping
the ability to categorically link new words to real-world referents

inflections
grammatical markers attached to words to indicate tense, gender, number, and the like, such as the use of the ending *ed* to mark the past tense of a verb in English

THE GRAMMAR EXPLOSION

Just as the vocabulary explosion you read about in **Chapter 5** begins slowly, so the grammar explosion of the 2- to 6-year-old period starts with several months of simple sentences, such as "here bottle " or "what that?"

INFLECTIONS The first spoken sentences typically consist of simple two-word utterances that lack **inflections**. If a child was to say "Mommy sock," for example, the addition of *'s* that would tell a child's listeners that she is trying to say that the sock belongs to Mommy. Within each language community, children seem to add inflections and more complex word orders in fairly predictable sequences (Legendre, 2006). In a classic early study, Roger Brown found that the earliest inflection used among children learning English is typically *-ing* added to a verb, as in "I playing" or "Doggie running," expressions that are common in the speech of 2½- to 3-year-olds (Brown, 1973). Over the next year or so come (in

These 2- to 3-year-olds probably speak to each other in short sentences that include uninflected nouns and verbs.
(*Photo:* © Will Faller)

order) prepositions (such as *on* and *in*), the plural *-s* on nouns, irregular past tenses (such as *broke* or *ran*), possessives, articles (*a* and *the* in English), the *-s* added to third-person verbs (as in "He wants,"), regular past tenses (such as *played* and *wanted*), and various forms of auxiliary verbs (as in "I am going").

QUESTIONS AND NEGATIVES There are also predictable sequences in the child's developing use of questions and negatives. In each case, the child seems to go through periods when he creates types of sentences that he has not heard adults use but that are consistent with the particular set of rules he is using. For example, in the development of questions there is a point at which the child can put a *Wh-* word (*who, what, when, where, why*) at the front end of a sentence, but he doesn't yet put the auxiliary verb in the right place, as in "Where you are going now?" Similarly, in the development of negatives, children go through a stage in which they put in *not* or *n't* or *no* but omit the auxiliary verb, as in "I not crying."

overregularization
attachment of regular inflections to irregular words, such as the substitution of *goed* for *went*

OVERREGULARIZATION Another intriguing phenomenon is **overregularization**, or overgeneralization. No language is perfectly regular; every language includes some irregularly conjugated verbs or unusual forms of plurals. What 3- to 4-year-olds do is apply the basic rule to all these irregular instances, thus making the language more regular than it really is (Maratsos, 2000). In English, this is especially clear in children's creation of past tenses, such as "wented," "blowed," and "sitted," or plurals, such as "teeths" and "blockses" (Fenson et al., 1994).

Such overregularizations illustrate yet again that language development is a rule-governed process that cannot be explained by imitation theories. Children show that they are using rules when they create word forms (such as "wented") that they have not heard. Clearly, children cannot have learned these words by imitation. Instead, their presence in children's speech suggests that children actively infer and use language rules.

COMPLEX SENTENCES After children have figured out inflections and the basic sentence forms by using negatives and questions, they soon begin to create remarkably complex sentences, using a conjunction such as *and* or *but* to combine two ideas or using embedded clauses. Here are some examples from children aged 30 to 48 months (de Villiers & de Villiers, 1992, p. 379):

- I didn't catch it but Teddy did!
- I'm gonna sit on the one you're sitting on.
- Where did you say you put my doll?
- Those are punk rockers, aren't they?

When you remember that only about 18 months earlier these children were using sentences little more complex than "See doggie," you can appreciate how far they have come in a short time.

((•—[Listen

PHONOLOGICAL AWARENESS

phonological awareness
children's understanding of the sound patterns of the language they are acquiring

Certain aspects of early childhood language development, such as rate of vocabulary growth, predict how easily a child will learn to read and write when she enters school (Wood & Terrell, 1998). However, one specific component of early childhood language development, *phonological awareness*, seems to be especially important. **Phonological awareness** is a child's sensitivity to the sound patterns that are specific to the language being acquired. It also includes the child's knowledge of that particular language's system for representing sounds with letters. Researchers measure English-speaking children's phonological awareness with questions such as the following: "What would *bat* be if you took away the *b*? What would *bat* be if you took away the *b* and put *r* there instead?"

A child doesn't have to acquire phonological awareness in early childhood. It can be learned in elementary school through formal instruction (Ball, 1997; Bus & van IJzendoorn, 1999). However, numerous studies have shown that the greater a child's phonological awareness *before* he enters school, the faster he learns to read (Christensen, 1997; Gilbertson & Bramlett, 1998; Schatschneider, Francis, Foorman, Fletcher, & Mehta, 1999; Wood & Terrell, 1998). In addition, phonological awareness in the early childhood years is related to rate of literacy learning in languages as varied as English, Punjabi, and Chinese (Chiappe, Glaeser, & Ferko, 2007; Chiappe & Siegel, 1999; Ho & Bryant, 1997; Huang & Hanley, 1997; McBride-Chang & Ho, 2000).

Phonological awareness appears to develop primarily through word play. For example, among English-speaking children, learning and reciting nursery rhymes contributes to phonological awareness (Bryant, MacLean, & Bradley, 1990; Bryant, MacLean, Bradley, & Crossland, 1990; Layton, Deeny, Tall, & Upton, 1996). For Japanese children, a game called *shiritori*, in which one person says a word and another comes up with a word that begins with its ending sound, helps children develop these skills (Norboru, 1997; Serpell & Hatano, 1997). Educators have also found that using such games to teach phonological awareness skills to preschoolers is just as effective as more formal methods, such as flash cards and worksheets (Brennan & Ireson, 1997). *Shared*, or *dialogic*, *reading* has also been found to contribute to growth in phonological awareness (Burgess, 1997) (see **Development in the Real World**).

Preschoolers with good phonological awareness skills—those who have learned a few basic sound–letter connections informally, from their parents or caregivers—often use a strategy called **invented spelling** when they attempt to write (see **Figure 7.7**). In spite of the many errors they make, children who use invented spelling strategies before

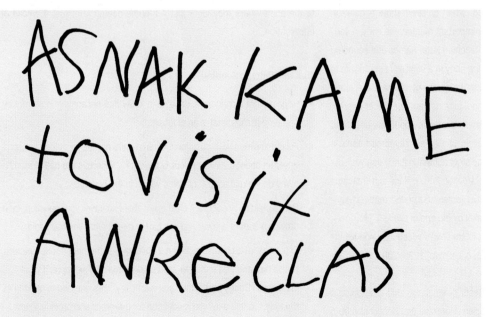

Figure 7.7

Translation: A snake came to visit our class. A 5-year-old used a strategy called "invented spelling" to write this sentence about a snake's visit (accompanied by an animal handler we hope!) to her kindergarten class. Invented spelling requires a high level of phonological awareness. Research suggests that children who have well-developed phonological awareness skills by the time they reach kindergarten learn to read more quickly.

(Courtesy of Jerry and Denise Boyd. Used with permission.)

Development in the Real World

STRENGTHENING LANGUAGE SKILLS IN PRESCHOOLERS

Both the quantity and quality of reading experiences that young children have with their parents influences the children's language and reading development (Evans & Shaw, 2008). Researchers at Monique Sénéchal's language lab at Carleton University have been investigating how young children develop language skills, especially in relation to natural experiences such as storybook reading. A study found that parents who change their communication style when reading to infants between 9 and 18 months of age help the infants' language development. Nine-month-old infants vocalized more when parents talked about a picture book they were reading than when parents simply read a story to their infant (Sénéchal, Cornell, & Broda, 1995). Researched showed that, although reading a storybook just once to a child improves her **receptive vocabulary** (Sénéchal & Cornell, 1993), children who were read the same book three times did much better in later development of both receptive and **expressive vocabulary** (Sénéchal, 1997). Moreover, when children were asked questions about what was being read, their expressive vocabulary increased even more than their receptive vocabulary. It appears that children who actively participate in story-reading by answering questions comprehend and produce more words than do children who passively listen (Sénéchal, Thomas, & Monker, 1995; Sénéchal & Young, 2008).

During the preschool years, it is important to motivate children to begin preparing for independent reading, and, when children show a delay in vocabulary development, it is especially important to intervene early. A variety of formal reading experiences (e.g., teaching letter names and sounding out words) and informal storybook reading early in a child's life contribute to reading performance later on. Even during the course of routine social interactions, such as dinner table conversation, parents and, to a lesser degree, young children have opportunities to share concepts about language and how it's used (e.g., the concepts of telling stories are reinforced when a mother asks her son, "Did you tell dad the story about the funny dog you saw today?") (Ely, Gleason, MacGibbon, & Zaretsky, 2001). Research indicates that both formal and informal parental involvement in a child's reading experiences contribute to improved reading skill by the end of Grade 1. Moreover, a child's reading fluency in Grade 1 predicts a child's vocabulary and listening comprehension in Grade 3 (Sénéchal & LeFevre, 1998, 2002; Sénéchal, LeFevre, Thomas, and Daley, 1998).

As a means of assessing the effects of language skill-development intervention for disadvantaged preschoolers, Hargrave and Sénéchal (2000) studied techniques that could be applied in the preschool daycare settings to improve the acquisition of vocabulary for children with poor vocabularies. They studied preschoolers in a standard daycare reading situation where there was a ratio of eight children to every teacher. Children were divided into two groups. One group experienced the standard story-reading situation

in which the teacher reads the story and the children listen. The other group was exposed to a *dialogic-reading* intervention.

In the dialogic-reading situation, teachers were trained to actively involve the children. The teacher helped the child become the teller of the story, while the teacher became the audience and listened and questioned the child. Dialogic reading included the following techniques: asking *Wh*-questions (i.e., *what, where, when, why, who, which,* and *how*), asking open-ended questions, and expanding on what the child said (Arnold, Lonigan, Whitehurst, & Epstein, 1994). These techniques were designed to teach vocabulary and encourage children to provide more complete descriptions of what they see.

Another part of the procedure involved the parents. Parents of children in the dialogic-reading group received the same training as the teachers. In addition, the parents were encouraged to read to their children at home.

All the children were assessed before and after the dialogic-reading intervention. A comparison of the children's vocabulary scores showed that the children in the dialogic-reading group demonstrated significantly higher expressive vocabulary scores than children in the regular reading group. The children in the dialogic-reading group were on average 13 months behind in their expressive vocabulary before the intervention but advanced to the point where they were just 4 months behind after just 4 weeks of intervention.

Tips for Dialogic Reading

- Repeat what a child says. Let a child know that his answer is correct by restating it: "Yes, that is an elephant."

- Follow answers with questions. When a child names an object, ask a question about it: "What colour is the car?" "Where is the ball hidden?" "Why do we use soap?" or "Who works in the hospital?"

- Help a child as needed. If a child is not able to answer your question, then provide a correct answer and ask him to repeat what you have said.

- Expand what a child says. When a child says something about a picture, praise him and add a little to what's been said. For example, if your child says "Doggy bark," then you might say, "Yes, the dog is barking at the kitty." In this way, you model correct grammar and provide a new piece of information. Later, you might ask a question about this new information: "Who's the dog barking at?"

- Follow a child's interests. If a child shows an interest in a picture either by talking about it or by pointing to it, follow up immediately by asking questions.

- Adapt to a child's growing linguistic abilities. A child who is adept at naming colours should be encouraged to talk about some other aspects of the story.

- Praise and encourage. Tell a child when he is doing well by saying things like "Good answer!" or "That's right. Are you ever brilliant!"

- Have fun. Try to keep reading times fun and like a game. One way to do this is to switch between asking questions and just plain reading.

For example, you could read one page and then have a child tell you about the next page.

- Try to read with a child once a day. Pick a time when a child is interested in sharing a book with you. Before bed is a good time for many children and parents. Even 5 to 10 minutes can make a difference.

(*Source:* Adapted from Arnold, Lonigan, Whitehurst, & Epstein, 1994. Copyright © 1994 by the American Psychological Association. Adapted with permission.)

receiving school-based instruction in reading and writing are more likely to become good spellers and readers later in childhood (McBride-Chang, 1998). Thus, the evidence suggests that one of the best ways parents and preschool teachers can help young children prepare for formal instruction in reading is to engage them in activities that encourage word play and invented spelling.

receptive vocabulary
the words that are understood when heard

expressive vocabulary
the words whose meaning is used correctly when speaking

LANGUAGE AND NUMERACY

In a chapter from his book *Outliers*, Canadian author Malcolm Gladwell put forth the idea that language plays a role in our ability to master numbers. To illustrate his point, he compares number words in Chinese with those in English. He contends that they differ in at least two notable ways. For one, Chinese number words are shorter and take less time to pronounce than their English equivalents, and, thus, they use up less short-term memory capacity. "Most of them can be uttered in less than one-quarter of a second (for instance, 4 is 'si' and 7 'qi'). Their English equivalents—'four,' 'seven'—are longer: pronouncing them takes about one-third of a second" (Dehaene, 1997, quoted in Gladwell, 2008, p. 228). Consequently, the ability to remember a larger quantity of numbers in Chinese is entirely due to this difference in length. Add to this the extra challenge of having to learn more English number words for the same numerals in Chinese. For example, in either language counting from one to 10 means a child needs to learn 10 numeral words (i.e., 1, 2, 3, 4, 5, 6, 7, 8, 9, and 10), but after that, the Chinese numbering system, unlike the English system, doesn't require a child to learn any new words until he reaches the numeral 100 (e.g., 11 is *eleven*, a new word in English, but simply "ten-one" in Chinese; likewise, 12 is *twelve*, another new word in English, but simply "ten-two" in Chinese). Similarly, counting from 20 to 99 requires learning eight more numeral words in English but none in Chinese (30 is *thirty* in English, but simply "three-ten" in Chinese). In sum, to count from 1 to 100 in English, a child must learn 28 words, whereas in Chinese, a child needs only 11—the words for one through 10 and for 100 (Cheng, 2009). This difference gives children who learn numbers in Chinese an early advantage. A 4-year-old Chinese child can usually count to about 40, whereas, their same-age American peers can count only to 15 (Gladwell, 2008).

Although **numeracy**—the ability to use numbers—is a very different skill set from literacy, there are some parallels. For example, the ability to learn both literacy and numeracy can be enhanced through early parental or caregiver influences. In the case of numeracy, Concordia University developmentalists suggest that young children are capable of and interested in number concepts, and parents can encourage children to think about mathematics in everyday situations (Osana & Rayner, 2010). These researchers emphasize that caregivers can take advantage of preschoolers' eagerness to prepare them for the mathematics they will encounter in school. Moreover, the development of numeracy abilities in preschoolers helps to facilitate the learning of more

numeracy
the knowledge and skills required to effectively manage the mathematical demands of diverse situations (Statistics Canada, 2008b)

advanced mathematical concepts in school (Jordan, Kaplan, Locuniak, & Ramineni, 2007; LeFevre et al., 2009). In one Canadian study, researchers found that children who experience more numeracy-related activities at home show greater proficiency at school-based mathematical tasks (LeFevre et al., 2009). Some of these experiences target numeracy skill development directly (e.g., counting objects, sorting objects by category, practising number names, printing numbers). Other experiences involve informal numeracy activities that have quantitative components, such as playing board games with dice, playing card games, measuring quantities while cooking, or setting the table at home. Although both direct and indirect activities in the home are important in promoting numeracy proficiency, these researchers were the first to show a robust relationship between the frequency with which children participate in indirect numeracy activities at home and mathematical proficiency.

Before Going On

- What is happening during the rapid progress in vocabulary and grammar?
- What is phonological awareness, and why is it important?

DIFFERENCES IN INTELLIGENCE

Thanks to advances in language skills, intelligence testing is far more reliable among preschoolers than among infants. Psychologists have constructed standardized tests of intelligence for preschoolers to measure their vocabulary, reasoning skills, and other cognitive processes that depend on language. However, widespread use of these tests has led to an ongoing debate about the origins of score differences and the degree to which scores can be modified.

MEASURING INTELLIGENCE

An important assumption in studying differences in intelligence is that these differences can be measured. Thus, it's important to understand something about the tests psychologists use to measure intelligence as well as the meaning and stability of the scores the tests generate.

THE FIRST TESTS The first modern intelligence test was published in 1905 in France by Alfred Binet and Theodore Simon (Binet & Simon, 1905). From the beginning, the test had a practical purpose—to identify children who might have difficulty in school. For this reason, the tasks Binet and Simon devised for the test were very much like some school tasks, including measures of vocabulary, comprehension of facts and relationships, and mathematical and verbal reasoning. For example, could the child describe the difference between wood and glass? Could the young child identify his nose, his ear, his head? Could he tell which of two weights was heavier?

Lewis Terman and his associates at Stanford University modified and extended many of Binet's original tasks when they translated and revised the test for use in the United States (Terman, 1916; Terman & Merrill, 1937). The Stanford-Binet, the name by which the test is still known, initially described a child's performance in terms of a score called an **intelligence quotient**, later shortened to **IQ**. This score was computed by

intelligence quotient (IQ) the ratio of mental age to chronological age; also, a general term for any kind of score derived from an intelligence test comparing the child's chronological age (in years and months) with his mental age, defined as the level of questions he could answer correctly. For example, a child who could solve the problems for a 6-year-old but not those for a 7-year-old would have a mental age of 6. The formula used to calculate the IQ was

$$\text{mental age/chronological age} \times 100 = \text{IQ}$$

This formula results in an IQ above 100 for children whose mental age is higher than their chronological age and an IQ below 100 for children whose mental age is below their chronological age.

This system for calculating IQ is no longer used. Instead, IQ scores for the Stanford-Binet and all other intelligence tests are now based on a direct comparison of a child's performance with the average performance of a large group of other children of the same age. But the scoring is arranged so that an IQ of 100 is still average.

As you can see in **Figure 7.8**, about two-thirds of all children achieve scores between 85 and 115; roughly 96% of scores fall between 70 and 130. Children who score above 130 are often called gifted; those who score below 70 are referred to by such terms as *intellectually delayed* or as having a *development disability*. A child classified as having a developmental disability will also tend to have problems with "adaptive behaviour," such as an inability to dress or feed himself, a problem getting along with others, or a significant problem adapting to the demands of a regular school classroom.

MODERN INTELLIGENCE TESTS
The test used most frequently by psychologists today is the fourth revision of the Wechsler Intelligence Scales for Children (WISC), the most recent version of a test originally developed by David Wechsler (Wechsler, 2003). In this edition of the WISC, the child is tested with 10 core and five supplemental subtests of different types of problems, each ranging from very easy to very hard. The 15 subtests are categorized into four new sections. The *verbal comprehension index* contains measures for verbal reasoning, comprehension, and the ability to express ideas in words; the *perceptual reasoning index* involves visual nonverbal tasks in the measurement of **fluid reasoning**—the ability to manipulate and use information in a reasoning process; the *working memory index* taps into short-term memory processes, such as the

fluid reasoning
the ability to manipulate and use information in a reasoning process

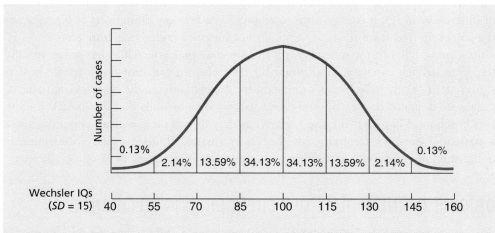

Figure 7.8

IQ scores form what mathematicians call a normal distribution—the famous "bell curve" you may have heard about. The two sides of a normal distribution curve are mirror images of each other. Thus, 34% of children score between 85 and 100, and another 34% score between 100 and 115. Likewise, 13% score between 70 and 85 and another 13% between 115 and 130. A few other human characteristics, such as height, are normally distributed as well.

Critical Thinking

In your opinion, how might having a higher IQ make a child more resilient? For example, in what specific ways might the life of a brighter child be different from the life of a less-bright child in the same environment?

ability to briefly hold onto and pay attention to information in the mind long enough to accurately perform some kind of mental operation or manipulation; and the *processing speed index* is a measure of visual selective attention and speed of mental processing. The four sections are based on recent neurocognitive models of information-processing and can be used to indicate learning disabilities and attentional disorders in children (see **Chapter 9** for details on these conditions). A Full Scale IQ, or measure of overall intellectual ability, is derived from the scores on the subtests of the four sections.

STABILITY AND PREDICTIVE VALUE OF IQ SCORES The correlation between a child's test score and her current or future grades in school is about 0.50 to 0.60 (Brody, 1992; Carver, 1990; Neisser et al., 1996). This correlation is strong but by no means perfect. It indicates that on the whole, children with high IQ scores will be among the high achievers in school, and those who score low will be among the low achievers. But success in school also depends on many factors other than IQ, including motivation, interest, and persistence. Because of this, some children with high IQ scores don't shine in school, while some lower-IQ children do.

IQ scores are also quite stable. If two tests are given a few months or a few years apart, the scores are likely to be very similar. The correlations between IQ scores from adjacent years in middle childhood, for example, are typically in the range of 0.80 (Honzik, 1986). Yet this high level of predictability masks an interesting fact: Many children show quite wide fluctuations in their scores. In fact, about half of all children show noticeable changes from one testing to another and over time (McCall, 1993). Some show steadily rising scores, and some have declining ones; some show a peak in middle childhood and then a decline in adolescence. In rare cases, the shifts may cover a range as large as 40 points.

Such wide fluctuations are more common in young children. The general rule is that the older the child, the more stable the IQ score—although even in older children, scores may still fluctuate in response to major stresses, such as parental divorce, a change of schools, or the birth of a sibling.

LIMITATIONS OF IQ TESTS Before moving on to the question of the possible origins of differences in IQ, it is important to emphasize a few key limitations of IQ tests and the scores derived from them. IQ tests do not measure underlying competence. An IQ score cannot tell you (or a teacher, or anyone else) that your child has some specific, fixed, underlying capacity. Traditional IQ tests also do not measure a whole host of skills that are likely to be highly significant for getting along in the world. Originally, IQ tests were designed to measure only the specific range of skills that are needed for success in school. They do this quite well. What they do *not* do is indicate anything about a particular person's creativity, insight, street smarts, ability to read social cues, or understanding of spatial relationships (Gardner, 1983; Sternberg & Wagner, 1993).

ORIGINS OF INDIVIDUAL DIFFERENCES IN INTELLIGENCE

If a couple whom you perceive to be smart conceive a child, what would you predict about their offspring's IQ scores? Most people know that differences in intelligence run in families. But why do related people seem to be alike in this regard? Is nature or nurture responsible?

EVIDENCE FOR HEREDITY Both twin studies and studies of adopted children show strong hereditary influences on IQ, as you already know from the **Research Report** in

Chapter 3. Identical twins are more like each other in IQ than are fraternal twins, and the IQs of adopted children are better predicted from the IQs of their natural parents than from those of their adoptive parents (Brody, 1992; Loehlin, Horn, & Willerman, 1994; Scarr, Weinberg, & Waldman, 1993). These findings are precisely what researchers would expect if a strong genetic element were at work.

EVIDENCE FOR ENVIRONMENT Adoption studies also provide some strong support for an environmental influence on IQ scores, because the IQ scores of adopted children are clearly affected by the environment in which they have grown up. The clearest evidence for this comes from a study of 38 French children, all adopted in infancy (Capron & Duyme, 1989). Roughly half the children had been born to better-educated parents from a higher social class, while the other half had been born to working-class or poverty-level parents. Some of the children in each group had then been adopted by parents in a higher social class, while the others grew up in poorer families. The effect of rearing conditions was evident in that the children reared in upper-class homes had IQs 15 to 16 points higher than those reared in lower-class families, regardless of the social class level or education of the birth parents. A genetic effect was evident in that the children born to upper-class parents had higher IQs than those from lower-class families, no matter what kind of environment they were reared in.

⊙ Watch

When developmentalists observe how individual families interact with their infants or young children and then follow the children over time to see which ones later have high or low IQs, they begin to get some sense of the kinds of specific family interactions that foster higher scores. For one thing, parents of higher-IQ children provide them with an interesting and complex physical environment, including play materials that are appropriate for the child's age and developmental level (Bradley et al., 1989; Pianta & Egeland, 1994). They also respond warmly and appropriately to the child's behaviour, smiling when the child smiles, answering the child's questions, and in myriad ways reacting to the child's cues (Barnard et al., 1989; Lewis, 1993). These kinds of parental behaviours may even help to limit the effects of poverty and other sources of family stress on children's intellectual development (Robinson, Lanzi, Weinberg, Ramey, & Ramey, 2002).

Parents of higher-IQ children also talk to them often, using language that is descriptively rich and accurate (Hart & Risley, 1995; Sigman et al., 1988). And when they play with or interact with their children, they operate in what Vygotsky referred to as the *zone of proximal development* (described in **Chapter 2**), aiming their conversation, their questions, and their assistance at a level that is just above the level the children could manage on their own, thus helping the children to master new skills (Landry et al., 1996).

In addition, parents who appear to foster intellectual development try to avoid being excessively restrictive, punitive, or controlling, instead giving children room to explore, and even opportunities to make mistakes (Bradley et al., 1989; Olson, Bates, & Kaskie, 1992). In a similar vein, these parents ask questions rather than giving commands (Hart & Risley, 1995). Most also expect their children to do well and to develop rapidly. They emphasize and press for school achievement (Entwisle & Alexander, 1990).

The Concordia Longitudinal Risk Project (see **Chapter 1**), which looked at the intellectual functioning of offspring of mothers who were themselves high-risk children, provides evidence of intergenerational influences on intelligence (Saltaris et al., 2004). In particular, Saltaris and her colleagues found that mothers who had a history of aggression in childhood were less likely to provide effective intellectual stimulation for their own preschool-age children. These mothers displayed less constructive feedback during problem-solving activities and less effective teaching strategies. These characteristics in turn puts the early cognitive development of their offspring at risk.

Children who attend enrichment programs typically do not show lasting gains in IQ, but they are more likely to succeed in school. (*Photo:* Paul Conklin/PhotoEdit)

EVIDENCE FOR PRESCHOOL INFLUENCES Home environments and family interactions are not the only sources of environmental influence. Programs such as Head Start are based squarely on the assumption that it is possible to modify the trajectory of a child's intellectual development, especially if the intervention occurs early enough (Ramey & Ramey, 1998). Children in enriched preschool programs normally show a gain of about 10 IQ points after they are enrolled in them, but this IQ gain typically fades and then disappears within the first few years of school (Zigler & Styfco, 1993).

When the enrichment program is begun in infancy rather than at age 3 or 4, IQ scores remain elevated into adulthood (Campbell, Ramey, Pungello, Sparling, & Miller-Johnson, 2002; Ramey & Ramey, 1998). One very well-designed and meticulously reported infancy intervention was called the Abecedarian project (Campbell & Ramey, 1994; Ramey, 1993; Ramey & Campbell, 1987). Infants from poverty-level families whose mothers had low IQs were randomly assigned either to a special daycare program or to a control group that received nutritional supplements and medical care but no special enriched daycare. The special daycare program began when the infants were 6- to 12-weeks-old and lasted until they began kindergarten.

Figure 7.9 graphs the average IQ scores of the children in each of these two groups from age 2 to 12. You can see that the IQs of the children who had been enrolled in the special program were higher at every age. Fully 44% of the control group children had IQ scores classified as borderline or developmentally delayed (scores below 85), compared with only 12.8% of the children who had been in the special program. In addition, the enriched daycare group had significantly higher scores on both reading and

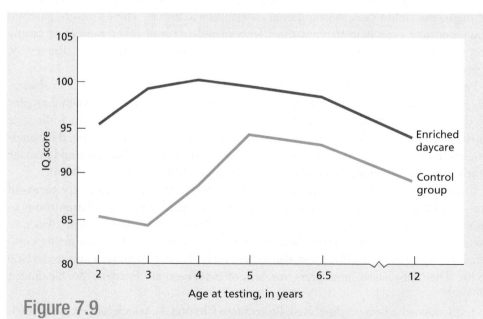

Figure 7.9

In Ramey's study, children from poverty-level families were randomly assigned in infancy to an experimental group that received special daycare or to a control group, with the intervention lasting until age 5. At kindergarten, both groups entered public school. The difference in IQ between the experimental and control groups remained statistically significant even at age 12, seven years after the intervention had ended.

(*Source:* Ramey & Campbell, 1987, Figure 3, p. 135, with additional data from Ramey, 1983, Figure 2, p. 29.)

mathematics tests at age 12 and were only half as likely to have repeated a grade (Ramey, 1992, 1993).

READINESS TO LEARN AT SCHOOL How ready for school is the typical Canadian 3- to 5-year-old? A major Statistics Canada study by Eleanor Thomas (2006) provides an interesting snapshot. Using National Longitudinal Survey of Children and Youth (NLSCY–cycle 5) data, she measured five domains of readiness:

1. Language and communication skill
2. Academic skill
3. Self-regulation of learning
4. Self-control of behaviour
5. Social competence and independence

Girls, she found, enter school with better communication skills, stronger abilities in copying and symbol use, higher scores in attention and in self-control of impulsive behaviour, and higher independence in dressing. Boys were rated above girls on just one measure—curiosity. Although children from lower income households were generally less ready to learn than children from more affluent households, some aspects of the child's home environment were linked with higher levels of readiness regardless of household income. These activities include daily reading, high positive parent–child interaction, participation in organized sports, lessons in physical activities, and lessons in the arts. But the reality is that children from lower income households are less likely to have these experiences.

A recent investigation from the Concordia Longitudinal Risk Project indicates that there can also be inter-generational transfer of risk—that is, mothers with a childhood history of social withdrawl can, in turn, put their childrens' expressive langauge and language-related academic performance at risk (Campisi, Serbin, Stack, Schwartzman, & Ledingham, 2009). Two programs in Canada that target high-risk children are Aboriginal Head Start and HighScope. First, Health Canada (2002b) sponsors several hundred Aboriginal Head Start programs for First Nations, Inuit, Metis, and other Aboriginal children. This early intervention program provides young Aboriginal children with a half-day preschool experience that prepares them for their school years by focusing on education and school readiness, Aboriginal culture and language, parental involvement, health promotion, nutrition, and social support. Second, HighScope, a preschool program that has shown long-term success in high-risk children in the United States, now has three centres across Canada. One HighScope study followed children of poverty into adulthood. The results showed significant differences between those at-risk children who were in the program and those who were not. Children who went through the program had better school readiness skills, spent less time in special education programs, had superior high-school graduation rates, had higher employment income, and had lower rates of criminal arrests (Schweinhart, 2003).

COMBINING THE INFORMATION Virtually all psychologists would agree that heredity is a highly important influence on IQ scores. Studies around the world consistently yield estimates that roughly half the variation in IQ within a given population is due to heredity (Neisser et al., 1996; Plomin & Rende, 1991; Rogers, Rowe, & May, 1994). The remaining half is clearly due to environment or interactions between environment and heredity.

One useful way to think about this interaction is to use the concept of **reaction range**, a range between upper and lower boundaries of functioning that is established by one's genetic heritage; exactly where a child will fall within those boundaries is determined by environment. Some developmental psychologists estimate that the reaction

reaction range
a range between upper and lower boundaries for traits such as intelligence, which is established by one's genes; one's environment determines where, within those limits, one will fall

range for IQ is about 20 to 25 points (Weinberg, 1989). That is, given a specific genetic heritage, a child's actual IQ test performance may vary as much as 20 or 25 points, depending on the richness or poverty of the environment in which he grows up. When the child's environment is changed for the better, the child moves closer to the upper end of his reaction range. When the environment becomes worse, the child's effective intellectual performance falls toward the lower end of his reaction range. Thus, even though intelligence as measured on an IQ test is highly heritable and falls within the reaction range, the absolute IQ score is determined by environment.

Before 🌱 Going On

 Explore

- Briefly describe the history, usefulness, and limitations of IQ tests.
- What kinds of evidence support the nature and nurture explanations for IQ differences?

Summary

Physical Changes

- Physical development is slower from age 2 to 6 than it is in infancy, but it is steady. Large-muscle skills (e.g., running, jumping, galloping) show marked improvement, but small-muscle (fine motor) skills advance more slowly. Higher activity levels have been associated with improved behavioural control that facilitates meaningful exploratory behaviour.
- Significant changes in brain lateralization occur in early childhood. Handedness is weakly related to brain lateralization.
- Slower rates of growth contribute to declines in appetite.
- Unintentional injuries are a major cause of harm and death for preschoolers. Parenting, cognitive, and social factors affect injury rates.
- Long-term consequences of child maltreatment can include a variety of emotional problems and can result in changes in brain structure and function.

Cognitive Changes

- Piaget marked the beginning of the preoperational period as the point when children begin to use mental symbols. In Piaget's view, preschool children are still egocentric, lack understanding of conservation, and are often fooled by appearances.
- Research indicates that young children are less egocentric than Piaget thought. By age 4, they can distinguish between appearance and reality in a variety of tasks.

- By the end of early childhood, children have a well-developed theory of mind.
- Information-processing theory explains early childhood cognitive development in terms of limitations on young children's memory systems. Vygotsky's sociocultural theory asserts that children's thinking is shaped by social interaction through the medium of language.

Changes in Language

- Language and vocabulary develop at a rapid pace between ages 2 and 4, beginning with simple two-word sentences.
- During the grammar explosion (ages 3 to 4), children make large advances in grammatical fluency.
- Development of an awareness of the sound patterns of a particular language during early childhood is important in learning to read during the school years. Children seem to acquire this skill through word play and dialogic reading.

Differences in Intelligence

- Scores on early childhood intelligence tests are predictive of later school performance and are at least moderately consistent over time.
- At least half the variation in IQ scores is due to genetic differences; the remainder is attributable to environment and the interaction of heredity and environment.

Visit **www.mydevelopmentlab.com** to help you get the best grade! Test your knowledge and grasp difficult concepts through

- Custom study plans: See where you are strong and where you go wrong
- Interactive simulations
- Video and audio clips
- Raise your own Virtual Child—and much more!

Review Questions

Answers are provided on MyDevelopmentLab in the Course Resources folder.

Physical Changes

7.1 Melinda is 30 months old. Which of the following activities might she *recently* have begun to do?
   a. stack four blocks to make a tower
   b. climb on a chair to climb to the top of a table
   c. ride a tricycle
   d. hit a ball with a bat

Cognitive Changes

7.2 A child is offered a choice between six pieces of candy laid out in a row and four pieces of candy spread father apart to form a longer row. If the child chooses the longer row with four pieces, we know that the child has not achieved
   a. preoperational thought.
   b. conservation.
   c. a principle of false belief.
   d. a theory of mind.

7.3 A set of ideas that explains other people's ideas, beliefs, desires, and behaviours is called a
   a. false belief principle.
   b. theory of mind.
   c. metamemory.
   d. matrix classification.

Changes in Language

7.4 What explains a child's use of expressions such as "I sitted down," "goed," or "mouses"?
   a. The child is underextending the verb class.
   b. The child has had insufficient practice with inflections.

   c. The child is recasting language heard in the environment.
   d. The child is overregularizing the rules of language.

Differences in Intelligence

7.5 The concept of the reaction range suggests that the upper and lower boundaries of a child's intelligence are established by _____ and the child's actual level of intelligence is determined by _____.
   a. her genes; environment
   b. her parents' IQs; social experiences
   c. a neurological substrate; the quality of formal education
   d. the rate of habituation; hereditary influences

Critical-Thinking Questions

7.6 Overcoming the egocentrism of early childhood is the foundation of many cognitive tasks later in life. For example, students who are writing research papers have to be able to look at their work from their professor's point of view to determine whether what they have written is understandable and in line with the requirements of the assignment. What other situations or tasks can you think of that require taking another person's perspective?

7.7 Consider your own theory of mind. What assumptions do you make about the way other people's behaviour is affected by their beliefs, feelings, or ideas? Although you operate according to such a theory all the time, can you articulate it?

CHAPTER

8

Social and Personality Development in Early Childhood

If you asked a random sample of adults to tell you the most important characteristics of children between ages 2 and 6, the first thing on the list would probably be their rapidly changing social abilities during these years. Nay-saying, oppositional toddlers who spend most of their playtime alone become skilled, cooperative playmates by age 5 or 6. Certainly, the huge improvements in language skills are a crucial ingredient in this transition. But the most obvious thing about 5-year-olds is how socially "grown up" they seem compared with toddlers.

When you finish reading this chapter, you will be able to distinguish the theories of social and personality development; describe the ways that family relationships and structures change during the preschool years and how these changes affect children's development; explain how preschoolers relate to their peers through play and how aggression and prosocial behaviour affect these relationships; identify the important changes in personality and self-concept that happen during early childhood; and summarize children's understanding of gender and how gender roles develop during the preschool years. While you read, keep the following questions in mind:

- Why is parenting style important? What parenting style is associated with the most positive outcomes for children?

- What do you think? Are some children just naturally more aggressive than others, or is aggression a learned behaviour?

- What sex-roles stereotypes influenced you the most when you were growing up? If you were a parent or caregiver of a young child, how would you approach these stereotypes differently?

THEORIES OF SOCIAL AND PERSONALITY DEVELOPMENT

Freud and Erikson's psychoanalytic perspective offered key insights into the emotional components of development in the early childhood years. Modern theorists have focused on the role of cognition. Each point of view contributes something to scientists' understanding of early childhood.

PSYCHOANALYTIC PERSPECTIVES

Freud's theory of stages of personality development emphasized psychosexual stages of maturation (as described in **Chapter 2**), whereas Erikson placed the emphasis for development somewhat differently. Erikson emphasized the importance of internal drives and culture in his psychosocial stages of development. Accordingly, both of the stages Erickson identified in the preschool period (see **Table 2.2**, page 35) are triggered by children's growing physical, cognitive, and social skills. The stage Erikson called *autonomy versus shame and doubt*, for example, centres on the toddler's new mobility and the accompanying desire for autonomy. The stage of *initiative versus guilt* is ushered in by new cognitive skills, particularly the preschooler's ability to plan, which accentuates his wish to take the initiative.

Both Freud and Erikson believed that the key to healthy development during this period is striking a balance between the child's emerging skills and desire for autonomy and the parents' need to protect the child and control the child's behaviour. Thus, the parents' task changes rather dramatically after infancy. In the early months of life, the

mydevelopmentlab

Connect to MyDevelopmentLab

Continue to raise your cyber child and discover the world of parenthood at . . .

My Virtual Child

mydevelopmentlab

Connect to MyDevelopmentLab

For an easy introduction to social and personality development in young children watch this video on self concept. See what Erikson is talking about through the eyes of a child.

Watch

According to Erikson, young children need opportunities to develop autonomy and show initiative within the bounds of parental guidance and direction.
(*Photo:* Thinkstock)

social-cognitive theory
the theoretical perspective that asserts that social and personality development in early childhood is related to improvements in the cognitive domain

person perception
the ability to classify others according to categories such as age, gender, and race

parents' primary task is to provide enough warmth, predictability, and responsiveness to foster a secure attachment and to support basic physiological needs. But once the child becomes physically, linguistically, and cognitively more independent, the need to control becomes a central aspect of the parents' task. Too much control and the child will not have sufficient opportunity to explore; too little control and the child will become unmanageable and fail to learn the social skills he will need to get along with peers as well as adults.

SOCIAL-COGNITIVE PERSPECTIVES

In contrast to the psychoanalytic tradition, **social-cognitive theory** assumes that social and emotional changes in the child are the result of, or at least are facilitated by, the enormous growth in cognitive abilities that happens during the preschool years (Macrae & Bodenhausen, 2000). Over the past few decades, psychologists have devoted a great deal of theoretical and empirical attention to determining just how the two domains are connected.

PERSON PERCEPTION Have you ever heard a child describe a peer as "nice" or "not nice"? Preschoolers' emerging capacity for forming meaningful categories manifests itself in the social domain as a set of ideas and behaviours that psychologists call **person perception**, or the ability to classify others (see **Development in the Real World**). For example, by kindergarten age, children make judgments very similar to those of adults when asked to identify the most intelligent child in their class or play group (Droege & Stipek, 1993). Moreover, they describe their peers in terms of traits such as "grumpy" and "mean" (Yuill, 1997). They also make statements about other people's patterns of behaviour: "Grandma always lets me pick the cereal at the grocery store." They use these observations to classify others into groups such as "people I like" and "people I don't like."

However, young children's observations and categorizations of people are far less consistent than those of older children. A playmate they judge to be "nice" one day may be referred to as "mean" the next. Developmentalists have found that young children's judgments about others are inconsistent because they tend to base them on their most recent interactions with those individuals (Ruble & Dweck, 1995). In other words, a 4-year-old girl describes one of her playmates as "nice" on Monday because she shares a cookie but as "mean" on Tuesday because she refuses to share a chocolate bar. Or, the child declares, "I don't like Grandma any more because she made me go to bed early."

Preschoolers also categorize others on the basis of observable characteristics, such as race, age, and gender. For example, the *cross-race effect*, a phenomenon in which individuals are more likely to remember the faces of people of their own race than those of people of a different race, is established by age 5 (Goodman et al., 2007; Pezdek, Blandon-Gitlin, & Moore, 2003). Similarly, they talk about "big kids" (school-age children) and "little kids" (their age mates), and seem to know that they fit in best with the latter. Self-segregation by gender—a topic you'll read more about later in the chapter—begins as early as age 2.

Development in the Real World

STORYBOOKS AND LEARNING TO CLASSIFY PERSONALITY

You might be familiar with the saying "You are what you read." Carole Peterson at Memorial University of Newfoundland has described how our earliest childhood experiences can be woven into the fabric of our *autobiographical memory* (2002). For example, when you were a youngster, some children's books probably helped you learn about colours, animals, various aspects of your home and neighbourhood, and what other people were like. Have you ever wondered in what way the characters in your childhood storybooks helped to shape your understanding and expectations of others?

The Canadian author of your textbook has at times mused about where his interest in the study of psychology originated. Perhaps it is related to some of his earliest memories of listening to songs and stories. One particular source of early exposure to psychology may have been from the classic recordings of the Winnie-the-Pooh stories. This possibility became evident after he read a whimsical article by Sarah Shea and her colleagues at Dalhousie University titled "Pathology in the Hundred Acre Wood: A Neurodevelopmental Perspective on A.A. Milne" (Shea, Gordon, Hawkins, Kawchuk, & Smith, 2000). The following quotations are from this work. Shea and colleagues contend that "somewhere at the top of the Hundred Acre Wood, a little boy and his bear play. On the surface it is an innocent world, but on closer examination . . . we find a forest where neurodevelopmental and psychosocial

problems go unrecognized and untreated" (p. 1557). It seems that the characters of Milne's stories display a wide range of serious emotional conditions. Pooh, for instance, arguably suffers from both Attention-Deficit/Hyperactivity Disorder (ADHD), Inattentive type, and Obsessive Compulsive Disorder (OCD), related to his "obsessive fixation on honey" and "his repetitive counting behaviours" (p. 1557). Piglet, who is characteristically "anxious, blushing [and] flustered . . . suffers from Generalized Anxiety Disorder" (p. 1558). Eeyore, who displays "chronic negativism, low energy and anhe(haw)donia . . . would benefit greatly from an antidepressant" [and individual therapy] (p. 1558). As for Owl, he is "obviously bright, but dyslexic" (p. 1558). The authors also considered Tigger's character closely and described him as "gregarious and affectionate, but he has a recurrent pattern of risk-taking behaviours . . . in a context of obvious hyperactivity and impulsivity" (p. 1558).

In light of Shea and her colleagues' analysis of Milne's storybook characters, an alternative subtitle for the series of stories could have been "My First Psychology Book." Such insights may lead you to wonder if exposure to these stories could serve to shape an understanding of emotion and personality in early childhood. Research is needed to determine if any significant connection exists between exposure to these stories and later interest in the study of psychology.

UNDERSTANDING RULE CATEGORIES If you attended a formal dinner at which the forks were on the right side of the plates rather than on the left, would you be upset? Probably not, because social conventions, such as customs that govern where to place flatware, are rules that have nothing to do with our fundamental sense of right and wrong. Consequently, most of us are not troubled when the rules are violated and take a dim view of people who are bothered by such trifles. By contrast, we have little tolerance for the breaking of rules that we view as having a basis in morality, such as laws that forbid stealing and unwritten rules such as the one that prohibits you from flirting with your best friend's romantic partner (or with your romantic partner's best friend!). When and how did we learn to make such distinctions?

Researchers have found that children begin to respond differently to violations of social conventions and moral rules between ages 2 and 3 (Smetana, Schlagman, & Adams, 1993). For example, they view taking another child's toy without permission as a more serious violation of rules than forgetting to say "thank you." They also say, just as adults would in response to similar questions, that stealing and physical violence are wrong, even if their particular family or preschool has no explicit rule against them. This kind of understanding seems to develop both as a consequence of preschoolers' increasing capacity for classification and as a result of adults' tendency to emphasize moral transgressions more than social-convention violations when punishing children (Nucci & Smetana, 1996).

UNDERSTANDING OTHERS' INTENTIONS Would you feel differently about a person who deliberately scratched your car paint with a key than you would about someone who accidentally scratched it while washing your car for you? Chances are you would be far more forgiving of the person who unintentionally scratched your car paint because we tend to base our judgments of others' behaviour and our responses to them on what we perceive to be their intentions. Working from his assumptions about young children's egocentrism, Piaget suggested that young children are incapable of such discriminations.

However, later research has demonstrated that young children do understand intentions to some degree (Zhang & Yu, 2002). For one thing, it's quite common for preschoolers to say "It was an accident . . . I didn't mean to do it" when they are punished. Such protests suggest that children understand that intentional wrongdoing is punished more severely than unintentional transgressions of the rules.

Several studies suggest that children can make judgments about actors' intentions both when faced with abstract problems and when personally motivated by a desire to avoid punishment. For example, in a classic study, 3-year-olds listened to stories about children playing ball (Nelson, 1980). Pictures were used to convey information about intentions (see **Figure 8.1**). The children were more likely to label as "bad" or "naughty" the child who intended to harm a playmate than the child who accidentally

Figure 8.1

Pictures like these have been used to assess young children's understanding of an actor's intentions.

hit another child in the head with the ball. However, the children's judgments were also influenced by outcomes. In other words, they were more likely to say a child who wanted to hurt his playmate was "good" if he failed to hit the child with the ball. These results suggest that children know more about intentions than Piaget thought, but that they are still limited in their ability to base judgments entirely on intentions.

Before Going On

- How do the theories of Freud, Erikson, and social-cognitive theorists differ in their emphasis on children's families and peers?
- What are the findings of social-cognitive theorists with respect to preschoolers' skills in person perception, understanding of rules, and understanding of others' intentions?

FAMILY RELATIONSHIPS AND STRUCTURE

Psychologists agree that family relationships constitute one of the most, if not *the* most, influential factors in early childhood development. These relationships reflect both continuity and change. The preschooler is no less attached to her family than the infant but, at the same time, is struggling to establish independence.

ATTACHMENT

You'll remember from **Chapter 6** that by 12 months of age, a baby has normally established a clear attachment to at least one caregiver. By age 2 or 3, the attachment is just as strong, but many attachment behaviours have become less visible. Three-year-olds still want to sit on Mom's or Dad's lap; they are still likely to seek some closeness when Mom returns from an absence. But when she is not afraid or under stress, the 3-year-old is able to wander farther and farther from her safe base without apparent distress. She can also deal with her potential anxiety due to separation by creating shared plans with the parents. For example, a parent might say "I'll be home after your naptime," to which the child may respond "Can we watch a movie then?" (Crittenden, 1992).

Attachment quality also predicts behaviour during the preschool years. Children who are securely attached to parents experience fewer behaviour problems. Those who are insecurely attached display more anger and aggression toward both peers and adults in social settings such as daycare and preschool (DeMulder, Denham, Schmidt, & Mitchell, 2000; Schmidt, DeMulder, & Denham, 2002). For example, in a longitudinal study by University of Montreal researchers, Ellen Moss and colleagues (1999) reported that children between 3 and 5 years of age with mixed-ambivalent attachment are especially prone to displaying outward-focused behavioural problems.

For most children, the attachment relationship, whether secure or not, seems to change at about age 4. Bowlby described this new stage, or level, as a *goal-corrected partnership*. Just as the first attachment probably requires the baby to understand that his mother will continue to exist when she isn't there, so the preschooler grasps that the *relationship* continues to exist even when the partners are apart. Also at about age 4,

Off he goes, into greater independence. A child this age, especially one with secure attachment, is far more confident about being at a distance from his safe base.
(*Photo:* Corbis Digital Stock)

the child's internal model of attachment appears to generalize. Bowlby argued that the child's model becomes less a specific property of an individual relationship and more a general property of all the child's social relationships. Thus, it's not surprising that 4- and 5-year-olds who are securely attached to their parents are more likely than their insecurely attached peers to have positive relationships with their preschool teachers (DeMulder et al., 2000).

At the same time, advances in the internal working model lead to new conflicts. In contrast to infants, 2-year-olds realize that they are independent contributors to the parent–child relationship. This heightened sense of autonomy brings them into more and more situations in which parents want one thing and children another. However, contrary to popular stereotypes, 2-year-olds actually comply with parents' requests more often than not. They are more likely to comply with safety requests ("Don't touch that; it's hot!") or with prohibitions about care of objects ("Don't tear up the book") than they are with requests to delay ("I can't talk to you now, I'm on the phone") or with instructions about self-care ("Please wash your hands now"). On the whole, however, children of this age comply fairly readily (Gralinski & Kopp, 1993). When they resist, it is most likely to be passive resistance—simply not doing what is asked rather than saying "no."

⊙–[Watch]

PARENTING STYLES

Families vary in their responses to preschoolers' increasing demands for independence. Psychologists have struggled over the years to identify the best ways of describing the many dimensions along which families may vary. An early conceptualization was offered by developmentalist Diana Baumrind, who focused on four aspects of family functioning: (1) warmth or nurturance; (2) clarity and consistency of rules; (3) level of expectations, which she describes in terms of "maturity demands"; and (4) communication between parent and child (1972).

Children with nurturant and warm parents are more securely attached in the first 2 years of life than those with more rejecting parents. They also have higher self-esteem and are more empathetic, more altruistic, and more responsive to others' hurts or sufferings. They have higher IQs, are more compliant in preschool and elementary school, do better in school, and are less likely to show delinquent behaviour in adolescence or criminal behaviour in adulthood (Maccoby, 1980; Maughan, Pickles, & Quinton, 1995; Simons, Robertson, & Downs, 1989; Stormshak et al., 2000). Even children from high-risk families (such as low-income, low-parental-education, or dysfunctional families) are less likely to have problems if they are raised in a positive and nurturing environment (Chao & Willms, 1998; Human Resources Development Canada & Statistics Canada, 1996).

A study of Canadian families by Landy and Tam (1996) found that positive and supportive parenting practices reduced the incidence of problems, especially for children in high-risk family situations (such as low income, family dysfunction, or parental depression). In a later study, Landy and Tam (1998) found that, in children 2 to 3 years of age, the likelihood of problems (such as emotional disorder, aggressive behaviour, and hyperactivity) increased significantly with hostile parenting practices. Positive parenting practices tended to have a buffering effect, showing a reduction in these problems by 25 to 52%.

The degree and clarity of the parents' control over the child are also significant. Parents with clear rules, consistently applied, have children who are much less likely to be defiant or noncompliant. Results from the second cycle of the National Longitudinal Survey of Children and Youth (NLSCY) showed that children living in a high-risk family where they are exposed to consistent interactions with parents had fewer behavioural problems (Statistics Canada, 1998). In fact, Landy and Tam (1998) found that the rates of aggressive behaviour and hyperactivity in children of families with consistent parenting styles were less than half the rates found in other families.

Equally important is the form of control the parents use. The most optimal outcomes for the child occur when the parents are not overly restrictive, explain things to the child, and avoid the use of physical punishments. Children whose parents have high expectations (high "maturity demands" in Baumrind's [1971] language) also fare better. Such children have higher self-esteem and show more generosity and altruism toward others.

Finally, open and regular communication between parent and child has been linked to more positive outcomes. Listening to the child is as important as talking to him. Ideally, parents need to convey to the child that what the child has to say is worth listening to, that his ideas are important and should be considered in family decisions. Children of such parents have been found to be more emotionally and socially mature (Baumrind, 1971; Bell & Bell, 1982).

While each of these characteristics of families may be significant individually, they do not occur in isolation but in combinations and patterns. In her early research, Baumrind (1967) identified three patterns, or styles, of parenting. The **permissive parenting style** is high in nurturance but low in maturity demands, control, and communication. The **authoritarian parenting style** is high in control and maturity demands but low in nurturance and communication. The **authoritative parenting style** is high in all four dimensions: nurturance, communication, clarity and consistency, and maturity demands.

Eleanor Maccoby and John Martin have proposed a variation of Baumrind's category system, shown in **Figure 8.2** (Maccoby & Martin, 1983). They categorize families on two dimensions: the degree of demand or control, and the amount of acceptance versus rejection. The intersection of these two dimensions creates four types, three of which correspond quite closely to Baumrind's authoritarian, authoritative, and permissive types. Maccoby and Martin's conceptualization adds a fourth type, the **uninvolved parenting style**.

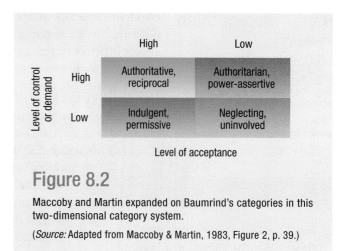

Figure 8.2

Maccoby and Martin expanded on Baumrind's categories in this two-dimensional category system.

(*Source:* Adapted from Maccoby & Martin, 1983, Figure 2, p. 39.)

permissive parenting style a style of parenting that is high in nurturance and low in maturity demands, control, and communication

authoritarian parenting style a style of parenting that is low in nurturance and communication, but high in control and maturity demands

authoritative parenting style a style of parenting that is high in nurturance, maturity demands, control, and communication

uninvolved parenting style a style of parenting that is low in nurturance, maturity demands, control, and communication

THE AUTHORITARIAN TYPE Children growing up in authoritarian families—with high levels of demand and control but relatively low levels of warmth and communication—do less well in school, have lower self-esteem, and are typically less skilled with peers than are children from other types of families. Some of these children appear subdued; others may show high aggressiveness or other indications of being rebellious or "out of control."

THE PERMISSIVE TYPE Children growing up with indulgent or permissive parents also show some negative outcomes. Researchers have found that these children do slightly worse in school during adolescence and are likely to be both more aggressive (particularly if the parents are specifically permissive toward aggressiveness) and somewhat immature in their behaviour with peers and in school. They are less likely to take responsibility and are less independent.

THE AUTHORITATIVE TYPE The most consistently positive outcomes have been associated with an authoritative pattern in which the parents are high in both control and acceptance—setting clear limits but also responding to the child's individual needs.

Connect to MyDevelopmentLab

What do Ozzy Osbourne and Homer Simpson have in common? Try this simulation and find out.

←◉ Simulate

Critical Thinking

Why do you think children of permissive parents are less independent than those from authoritative families?

Children reared in such families typically show higher self-esteem and are more independent, but are also more likely to comply with parental requests and may show more altruistic behaviour as well. They are self-confident and achievement-oriented in school and get better grades than do children whose parents have other parenting styles.

THE UNINVOLVED TYPE The most consistently negative outcomes are associated with the fourth pattern, the uninvolved or neglecting parenting style. You may remember from the discussion of secure and insecure attachments in **Chapter 6** that one of the family characteristics often found in infants rated as insecure/avoidant is the "psychological unavailability" of the mother. The mother may be depressed or may be overwhelmed by other problems in her life and may simply have not made any deep emotional connection with the child. Likewise, a parent may be distracted from parenting by more attractive activities. Whatever the reason, such children continue to show disturbances in their social relationships for many years. In adolescence, for example, youngsters from neglecting families are more impulsive and antisocial, less competent with their peers, and much less achievement oriented in school.

CANADIAN PARENTING STYLES Chao and Willms (1998, 2002) analyzed the key dimensions of Canadian parenting practices from the first cycle of the NLSCY and found that the largest portion of parents (about one-third) were authoritative. The authoritative parents scored above average on all measures of key parenting practices. About one-quarter of the parents were authoritarian and another one-quarter were permissive. A fourth category, similar to uninvolved parenting style, included the remaining 15% of parents who scored low on all key measures of positive parenting. McCain and Mustard (1999) reported that almost half of the children who were raised with this parenting style experienced behavioural problems. In comparison, only one in five children of authoritative parents had behavioural problems.

PARENTING AND CHILD DISCIPLINE The Canadian Paediatric Society (CPS) describes discipline in this way:

> The word discipline means to impart knowledge and skill—to teach. However, it is often equated with punishment and control. There is a great deal of controversy about the appropriate ways to discipline children, and parents are often confused about effective ways to set limits and instil self-control in their child. [The goal of] effective and positive discipline is about teaching and guiding children, not just forcing them to obey. (Canadian Paediatric Society, 2004, p. 37)

Through instruction and practice, parents, teachers and other significant adults help socialize a child in such a way that she has the knowledge, skills, and attitudes required to become a well-functioning person. The purpose of **discipline**, whether physical, mental, or moral, is to develop self-control, moral character, and proper conduct (see how Canadians view discipline in the **Research Report**).

Two key problems make it hard to establish what constitutes effective discipline. First, it is difficult to establish the harmful or beneficial effects of various forms of discipline. For example, do physical punishments, such as spanking or washing a child's mouth out with soap, work any better than nonphysical corrections, such as giving verbal reprimands, reasoning with an explanation of consequences, or enforcing a **time out** away from sources of attention or enjoyment? If nonphysical interventions were found to be at least as effective as physical punishment, then it would be hard to justify the continued use of physical intervention because of its potential to cause pain and harm.

Second, research has not concluded how intense and frequent effective discipline needs to be. The differences among mild, moderate, and severe discipline are not

discipline
training, whether physical, mental, or moral, that develops self-control, moral character, and proper conduct

time-out
removing the child from the situation and from attention and rewards for a short period of time, typically one minute for every year of the child's age, in order to stop unwanted behaviour

Research Report

DISCIPLINING CHILDREN: THE CANADIAN PERSPECTIVE

Although most Canadian parents would agree that disciplining their offspring is an important yet arduous task, many parents disagree about the best ways to discipline. Parents even interpret the term *discipline* in a variety of ways. It can be a means of assuring conformity, a form of punishment, a corrective tool, or a method of shaping desirable behaviour. Proponents of physical discipline generally argue that it serves a useful purpose and does no lasting harm to children; opponents of physical discipline say it does no good and is associated with negative outcomes.

One retrospective health study by McMaster University researchers looked at a large sample of adults in Ontario (MacMillan et al., 1999). Their analysis revealed a significant relationship between the reported frequency of being slapped and/or spanked during childhood and a prevalence of psychiatric disorders later in life: the higher the reported frequency of being slapped or spanked, the greater the lifetime prevalence of anxiety disorders, alcohol abuse or dependence, drug dependence, antisocial behaviours, and, to a lesser extent, major depression. However, in a literature review of 38 studies, Robert Larzelere could find no evidence that nonabusive spanking causes any notable detrimental outcomes in children (Larzelere, 2000). In comparison, an often-cited report by Elizabeth Gershoff that analyzed 88 studies of corporal punishment and behavioural outcomes in children found that physical punishment was associated with aggression and misconduct in children (Gershoff, 2002). Both Larzele and Gershoff agree on one point: punishment does have one desirable effect—it elicits immediate compliance from children. Unfortunately, much of the research to date has methodological problems that preclude any causal inferences about the longer-term outcomes of nonabusive physical punishments, such as mild spanking. As well, the cause-and-effect research needed to provide some decisive answers raises serious ethical concerns and, alternatively, correlational studies need to use more clearly defined variables (Baumrind, 2003; Baumrind, Larzelere, & Cowan, 2002; Lee, 2004).

In January 2004, Canada's highest court ruled that parents, teachers, and caregivers can apply physical force within "reasonable limits" as a form of discipline. The law permits the use of minor corrective force if it "is part of a genuine effort to educate the child, poses no reasonable risk of harm that is more than transitory and trifling, and is reasonable under the circumstances" (Department of Justice Canada, 2004, p. 1). The law disallows hitting a child with objects or delivering blows or slaps to the face or the head. In addition, the use of physical punishment on children under the age of 2 years or over the age of 12 is prohibited. The court has tried to strike a balance between the needs of parents and the rights of children; the judges made it clear that they do not endorse or advocate the use of corporal punishment, such as spanking, but they also don't want to criminalize parents for any and every physical intervention.

University of Manitoba child psychologist Joan Durrant (2004) contends that the Supreme Court's decision affects both parents and child and family professionals alike. She points out that, even though physical discipline is becoming socially unacceptable in Canada, the law still excuses some degree of it, which raises the question: How is a parent to distinguish between physical punishment and physical abuse? How should child welfare professionals advise parents about what is an acceptable degree of and circumstance for physical discipline? For instance, is one spank or two appropriate? Is a tap on the bum or back of the hand permitted? Is it okay to spank with an open hand so long as it leaves no marks or bruising? How calm do parents have to be before they punish? Can you wash a child's mouth out with soap? What about forcing a child to remain motionless in an awkward stance? These are difficult questions to address. In the face of this ambiguity, professionals could tell parents the clear message that physical punishment as a form of discipline is not appropriate (Durrant, 2004) and that alternate forms of effective discipline are available. This approach has been endorsed in policy statements by the Canadian Psychological Association (2004), the Canadian Paediatric Society (2004), and other child-care organizations. Moreover, over 130 Canadian organizations have signed the "Joint Statement on Physical Punishment of Children and Youth," which states that "the physical punishment of children and youth plays no useful role in their upbringing and poses only risks to their development. Parents should be strongly encouraged to develop alternative and positive approaches to discipline" (Children's Hospital of Eastern Ontario, 2003, executive summary).

clearly delineated. In addition, regardless of the type of discipline, *any* corrective measure that is too extreme or too frequent can become child abuse that contributes to detrimental physical and emotional outcomes (Baumrind, Larzelere, & Cowan, 2002; Kazdin & Benjet, 2003; Larzelere, 2003). In fact, punishment is the leading reason given by perpetrators in substantiated cases of child maltreatment in Canada (Trocmé,

Durrant, Ensom, & Marwah, 2004). Although research has yet to provide unequivocal answers to address these issues (Baumrind, 2003; Kazdin & Benjet, 2003), Canadian child-care advocates agree that physical interventions are not appropriate. Instead, they advocate the use of minimal nonphysical interventions in the context of a loving family relationship, and they encourage parents to be proactive by improving parenting skills and anticipating and limiting situations that will require intervention (Canadian Paediatric Society, 2004; Canadian Psychological Association, 2004; Children's Hospital of Eastern Ontario, 2003; Durrant, 2004; Durrant & Ensom, 2004).

inductive discipline
a discipline strategy in which parents explain to children why a punished behaviour is wrong

Another area of complexity is evident in the interaction between parenting style and child temperament. For example, authoritative parents often use **inductive discipline**, a discipline strategy in which parents explain to children why a punished behaviour is wrong (Hoffman, 1970). Inductive discipline helps most preschoolers gain control of their behaviour and learn to look at situations from perspectives other than their own. Research has found that the majority of preschool-aged children whose parents respond to demonstrations of poor self-control, such as temper tantrums, by asserting their social and physical power—as often happens when parents physically punish children— have poorer self-control than preschoolers whose parents use inductive discipline (Kochanska, 1997b; Kochanska, Murray, Jacques, Koenig, & Vandegeest, 1996).

Research suggests that inductive discipline is not equally effective for all children. Children with difficult temperaments or with physically active, risk-taking natures seem to have a greater need for firm discipline and benefit less from inductive discipline than do their peers whose temperamental makeup is different (Kochanska, 1997a). In fact, assumptions about the superiority of inductive discipline, as well as authoritative parenting in general, have been criticized by developmentalists who claim that correlations between discipline strategy and child behaviour may arise simply because parents adapt their techniques to their children's behaviour. Thus, parents of poorly behaved children may be more punitive or authoritarian because they have discovered that this is the kind of parenting their children respond to. In a broader context, corrective intervention for any persistent, severe problem, whether it be for inappropriate behaviour, assistance with homework, a medical condition that requires hospitalization, or a psychological situation, such as suicide risk or delinquency, will demand more intensive intervention, which increases the likelihood of detrimental outcomes (Larzelere, Kuhn, & Johnson, 2004).

Canadian researchers measure four dimensions of parent–child interactions in the NLSCY that complement Baumrind's classification of parenting styles. The four dimensions include the following types of interactions: *hostile/ineffective* (e.g., parents manipulate children through the use of sarcasm or put-downs and/or mix anger with punishment); *punitive/aversive* (e.g., parents intimidate their children by shouting and/ or using physical punishment); *consistent* (e.g., parents ensure compliance with directives and/or follow through with consequences after giving a warning); and *positive* (e.g., parents engage in mutually satisfying activities with their child and/or have fun with them). An analysis of parent–child interactions over the course of two cycles of the NLSCY revealed that the hostile/ineffective parenting style resulted in persistent behavioural problems at a rate nine times higher than what was exhibited in children who were not exposed to that pattern of parenting. Moreover, hostile/ineffective parenting interactions had a stronger negative effect on a child's behaviour than either income level or family structure (Statistics Canada, 1998).

ETHNICITY, SOCIOECONOMIC STATUS, AND PARENTING STYLES

When we consider cultural and social influences in relation to parenting styles, we find that the research reveals some complex patterns. For example, studies in which children provide information about their parents' style as well as those in which researchers conduct direct observation of parents have consistently found that, in general, Asian American parents display an authoritarian style (Chao, 1994; Wang & Phinney, 1998). The finding that Asian American children score higher than their white counterparts on almost all measures of cognitive competence argues against the assumption that authoritative parenting is best. In fact, developmentalists have found a link between Asian American children's achievement and authoritarian parenting—that is, parents who have the most authoritarian parenting style have the highest-scoring children (Wang & Phinney, 1998). Moreover, the authoritarian parenting style was not associated with any negative outcomes in Asian American children, which is not what would be predicted from Baumrind's model. Another example of a parenting style that did not fit Baumrind's prediction of the superiority of the authoritative parenting style for all cultures was reported by Johnson and Cremo (1995). They studied Aboriginal child-rearing practices in Canada and described parenting characteristics that are similar to the permissive style, but they found no association with negative outcomes in Aboriginal children. These studies suggest that parenting style may be dependent on the cultural context in which parents and children live, so that as the cultural context changes the best corresponding type of parenting style changes with it.

Other important aspects of the macrosystem to consider include the effect of socioeconomic status (SES) on child development. First, SES factors such as low family income and low level of parental education are risk factors that are associated with an increase in a child's vulnerability to problems (Landy & Tam, 1998) (see **Figure 8.3**). However, several Canadian studies have shown that parenting style is a better predictor

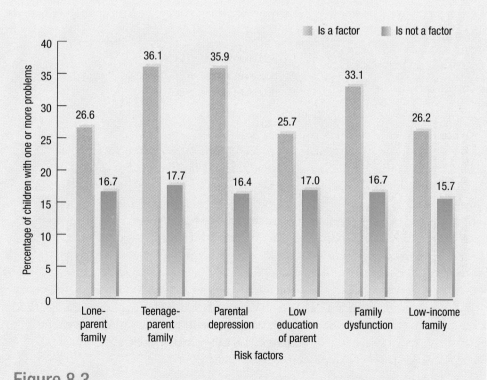

Figure 8.3

Risk factors that are associated with one or more problems for children aged 2 to 3.

(*Source:* Adapted from Landy & Tam, 1998, from Table 1, p.15, Understanding the contribution of multiple risk factors on child development at various ages (Catalogue No. W098_22E). Human Resources and Social Development Canada. Reproduced with the permission of Her Majesty the Queen in Right of Canada 2007.)

of poor outcomes in a child. In particular, the hostile/ineffective parenting style has been shown to be the strongest predictor of behaviour problems in children. At the same time, researchers have found that even when a child was being raised in a high-risk family situation (i.e., low income, parental depression, or family dysfunction), a positive and consistent parenting style acted as a protective factor against these social disadvantages that increase vulnerability for a child (Chao & Willms, 1998, 2002; Landy & Tam, 1998; Miller, Jenkins, & Keating, 2002; Ross, Roberts, & Scott, 1998; Statistics Canada, 1998).

Second, it was found that good parenting practices are common in all SES levels, and that hostile/ineffective parenting practices also cross all income levels (Chao & Willms, 1998, 2002). In a recent study by Brock University psychologist Tanya Martini and others, mothers who held authoritarian beliefs reported that they were less likely to control their hostile emotions in situations where their children were expressing negative emotions. This reaction occurred regardless of whether the mother was from the lower or middle class (Martini, Root, & Jenkins, 2004). All the same, children raised in families in the lower SES are more likely to experience a greater number of risk factors, and this, coupled with hostile or ineffective parenting practices, resulted in proportionally higher levels of vulnerability (see **Figure 8.4**). Overall, however, the majority of children being raised in low-income families are faring well (Ross, Roberts, & Scott, 1998). Therefore, even though low SES is associated with increased vulnerability, effective parenting goes a long way toward compensating for any negative influence associated with the consequences of low SES. The problem remains, however, that a low SES parent may be less capable of providing effective parenting (refer to the **Policy Question** on poverty in Canada at the end of this chapter).

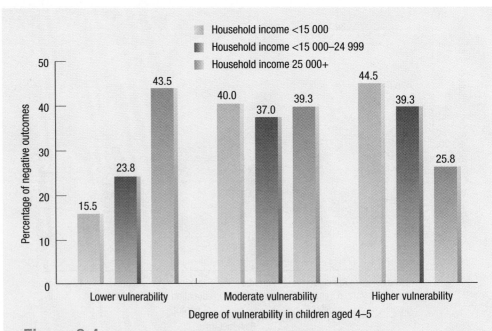

Figure 8.4

Lone-parent household income and the degree of vulnerability (lower, moderate, or high) to negative outcomes in children aged 4 to 5.

(*Source:* Adapted from Ross, Roberts & Scott, 1998, from Table 3.1, p. 20, Mediating factors in child development outcomes: Children in lone-parent families (Catalogue No. W-98-8E). Human Resources and Social Development Canada. Reproduced with the permission of Her Majesty the Queen in Right of Canada 2007.)

FAMILY STRUCTURE

Although in decline, the number of children living with married parents continues to be the dominant structure in Canada (see **Table 8.1**). The percentage of children under the age of 15 years living in two-parent homes fell from 84% in 1981 to 68% in 2001, as the percentage of common-law (3 to 13%) and lone-parent families (13 to 19%) increased over the same time period (Turcotte, 2003). However, there were large inter-provincial/territorial differences. For instance, Nunavut, Northwest Territories, Quebec, and Yukon had the lowest rates of married-couple families and the highest rates of common-law and lone-parent families. At the other extreme, Ontario and Alberta had the highest rates of married-couple families with children (Statistics Canada, 2002b).

DIVERSITY IN TWO-PARENT AND LONE-PARENT FAMILIES The number of two-parent blended families in Canada has risen to 12%. The blended two-parent family consists of stepfamilies that were created when a divorced or never-married single biological parent married another single parent or a nonparent. Half of Canadian stepfamilies comprise children living with the biological mother and a stepfather; 10% consist of the biological father and a stepmother; and 40% are blended—a mix of children that both parents brought into the family (8%) or that combined with children born to the new union (32%) (Statistics Canada, 2002c).

Twenty-seven percent of school-aged children live in a lone-parent family, which represents a 35% increase between 1990 and 1999 (Canadian Council on Social Development, 2001). The largest proportion of lone-parent families consists of separated or

TABLE 8.1   Living Arrangements of Children Under the Age of 15 (by province/territory, Canada, 2001)

	Living with Married Parents (%)	Living with Common-Law Parents (%)	Living with a Lone Parent* (%)
Canada	68.4	12.8	18.8
Newfoundland and Labrador	70.7	10.3	18.9
Prince Edward Island	73.2	8.6	18.2
Nova Scotia	68.0	9.9	22.2
New Brunswick	67.4	12.7	19.9
Quebec	52.1	28.5	19.4
Ontario	75.4	7.3	17.3
Manitoba	70.0	8.8	21.3
Saskatchewan	68.1	9.4	22.5
Alberta	74.0	8.8	17.1
British Columbia	71.5	8.0	20.5
Yukon	52.9	19.8	27.3
Northwest Territories	50.7	25.8	23.5
Nunavut	46.8	30.8	22.3

*Also includes about 1% or less of children with no parents, for example, living with another relative or foster family.

(*Source:* Statistics Canada (2002b). Adapted from Statistics Canada, 2002, *Profile of Canadian families and households: Diversification continues, 2001 Census,* Cat. No. 96F0030, October 22, available at www.12.statcan.ca/english/census01/products/analytic/companion/fam/childfam.cfm)

divorced parents, followed by never-married parents, and a very small proportion of widowed parents. Mothers are five times as likely to be the head of the lone-parent household, and about one-quarter of the mothers are never married (Ambert, 1998). Other lone parents, especially unmarried teenagers, are likely to live with their own parents (Jorgenson, 1993). Consequently, we find that lone-parent households are no more alike than are two-parent households.

FAMILY STRUCTURE EFFECTS Most children being raised in lone-parent families are doing fairly well by all measures, but, there is a subset of these families in which children are more vulnerable to a range of problems (Ross, Roberts, & Scott, 1998). Landy and Tam (1998) found that the impact of lone parenthood had different outcomes depending on the age of the child. For instance, lone parenthood was not related to any specific problem outcome in children aged 2 or 3. However, for children aged 4 to 11, lone parenthood was associated with double the rates of emotional disorder, conduct disorder, hyperactivity, repeating a grade, relationship problems, and having any one or more of these problems. Not surprisingly, lone parents reported experiencing high levels of chronic stress in comparison with two-parent families (see **Figure 8.5**). Moreover, 80% of lone-parent families are headed by women in Canada, and almost half of the female lone-parent families reported experiencing high levels of chronic stress (Health Canada, 1999e; Statistics Canada, 2010a).

OTHER TYPES OF FAMILY STRUCTURES To add to the vast quanitity of research done on two-parent and lone-parent families, recent research has studied the effects of other family structures on children. For example, through studies on custodial grandparenting, researchers have learned that grandparents' responses to children's problems are quite similar to those of parents (Daly & Glenwick, 2000). However, one recent American study found that children raised by custodial grandparents fared less well than children in the general population—children of both genders reportedly had higher levels of behavioural and emotional disturbance (Smith & Palmieri, 2007).

Concerns about children's gender-role identity, personal adjustment, social relationships, and sexual orientation have dominated same-sex parenting research (Patterson, 2009). Parenting by openly same-sex couples is still relatively new in Canada. For the first time, it was measured in Canada's 2006 census, which found that an estimated 4000 same-sex couples were raising children (Sexualityandu.ca, 2009; Statistics Canada, 2009g). More than 25 years' worth of studies have shown no significant differences in sexual orientation, sexual identity, self-esteeem, adjustment, or qualities of social relationships between children raised by gay and lesbian parents and children raised by heterosexual parents (Patterson, 2006, 2009).

Furthermore, most studies suggest that children's development depends more on how parental figures interact with them than on any particular family configuration (Goldberg, 2009). A loving, nurturing home environment provided by parents, whether same-sex or other-sex, is an essential ingredient in raising children who grow up to be healthy, competent, and well-adjusted (Goldberg, 2009; Sexualityandu.ca, 2009). A recent study in the Netherlands

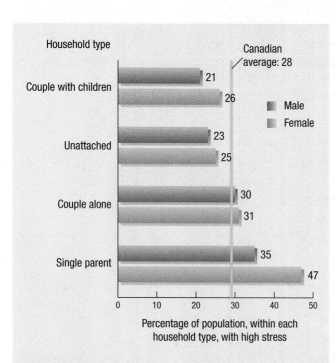

Figure 8.5

High stress, by household type (age-standardized), age 18+, Canada, 1994–1995.

(*Source:* Adapted from Statistics Canada, *National Population Health Survey*, 1994–1995, special tabulations.)

has provided some additional insights into the families of lesbian couples (Bos, van Balen, & van den Boom, 2007). It was found that lesbian biological mothers were much more satisfied with their partners as a co-parent than were heterosexual mothers. Moreover, lesbian mothers were found to be more committed and satisfied with their partner as a co-parent than mothers in heterosexual relationships, and satisfaction with the co-parent was positively associated with child adjustment. It seems that lesbian couples have more egalitarian partnerships than heterosexual couples. For example, in terms of division of family tasks, lesbian partners spend roughly equal amounts of time on household work and child care, as compared with heterosexual couples, where one partner (usually the mother) spends a disproportionate amount of time on such tasks. When considering the above research, take note that roughly 85% of same-sex families are headed by lesbian couples in Canada (Statistics Canada, 2009g).

DIVORCE

The number of divorces in Canada has steadily declined from the all-time peak in 1987; half of all divorces occur within the first 14 years of marriage and one-quarter of all marriages are dissolved by the fourth anniversary (Statistics Canada, 2004a). For many families, divorce happens during the prime child-rearing period, and there can be little doubt that divorce is traumatic for children. It's important to note, however, that some of the negative effects of divorce are due to factors that were present *before* the divorce, such as difficult temperament in the child or excessive marital conflict between the parents (Bailey & Zvonkovic, 2003). It's also important to keep in mind that divorce is not a single variable; children are probably affected by a multitude of divorce-related factors— parental conflict, poverty, disruptions of daily routine, and so on (Hetherington, Bridges, & Insabella, 1998). For this reason, children whose parents separate or who stay in conflict-ridden marriages may experience many of the same effects as children whose parents actually divorce (Ingoldsby, Shaw, Owens, & Winslow, 1999).

Many single parents manage to overcome substantial obstacles to give their children the support and supervision they need.
(*Photos: Top*, Rachael Epstein/ PhotoEdit; *Bottom*, Cindy Charles/ PhotoEdit)

The proportion of children living in post-divorce/separation versus two-parent custody that were found to be experiencing emotional or behavioural problems can be seen in **Figure 8.6**. Most children in either living arrangement are doing well, although children living in post-divorce/separation situations have a higher prevalence of problems in most areas except unsocial behaviour (low prosocial behaviour) (Human Resources Development Canada, 2001a). In the first few years after a divorce, children typically exhibit declines in school performance and show more aggressive, defiant, negative, or depressed behaviour (Greene, Anderson, Doyle, & Ridelbach, 2006). By adolescence, the children of divorced parents are more likely than their peers to engage in criminal behaviour (Price & Kunz, 2003). Children living in step-parent families also have higher rates of delinquency, more behaviour problems in school, and lower grades than do those in intact families (Jeynes, 2006).

The negative effects of divorce seem to persist for many years. For example, about 92% of adult Canadians who had lived in an intact two-parent family from birth to age 15 reported that they had had a very happy childhood. In comparison, only 72% of adult Canadians who had experienced disruption before the age of 15 due to a change in family structure reported that they believe they had been very happy children (Williams, 2001). Moreover, children whose parents divorce have a higher risk of mental health problems in adulthood (Chase-Lansdale, Cherlin, & Kiernan, 1995; Cherlin, Chase-Lansdale, & McRae, 1998; Wallerstein & Lewis, 1998). Many young adults whose parents are divorced lack the financial

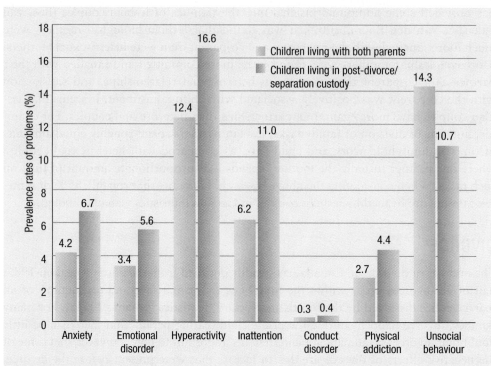

Figure 8.6

The proportion of children with emotional or behavioural problems, comparing those living with both parents with those in post-divorce/separation custody.

(*Source:* Human Resources and Social Development Canada, 1999. The proportion of children with emotional or behavioural problems, published in Bulletin—A special Edition on Child Development. www.hrsdc.gc.ca/eng/cs/sp/sdc/pkrf/publications/bulletins/1999-000002/page02.shtml. Reproduced with the permission of the Minister of Public Works and Government Services Canada, 2010).

resources and emotional support necessary to succeed in post-secondary education; a majority report that they struggle with fears of intimacy in relationships; and they are more likely to rely on social assistance income (Ambert, 1998; Cartwright, 2006). Not surprisingly, adults whose parents divorced are themselves more likely to divorce (Ambert, 1998).

As a general rule, these negative effects are more pronounced for boys than for girls. However, some researchers have found that the effects are delayed in girls, making it more difficult to associate the effects with the divorce. Consequently, longitudinal studies often find that girls show equal or even greater negative effects (Amato, 1993; Hetherington, 1991a, 1991b). Age differences in the severity of the reaction have been found in some studies but not others. For example, one longitudinal study found that the effects of divorce were most severe in a group of 12-year-olds who experienced parental divorce in early childhood rather than during their school years (Pagani, Boulerice, Tremblay, & Vitaro, 1997).

UNDERSTANDING THE EFFECTS OF FAMILY STRUCTURE AND DIVORCE

How are we to understand these various findings? First, lone parenthood or divorce reduces the financial and emotional resources available to support the child. With only one parent, the household typically has only one income and only one adult to respond to the child's emotional needs. Data from Canada indicate that a woman's income drops an average of 50% in the first year after a divorce, while a man's drops by 25%

(Finnie, 2000). Remarriage does indeed add a second adult to the family system, which alleviates these problems to some degree, but it adds others (Hetherington et al., 1999).

Second, any family transition involves upheaval. Both adults and children adapt slowly and with difficulty to the subtraction or addition of new adults to the family system (Hetherington & Stanley-Hagan, 1995). The period of maximum disruption appears to last several years, during which the parents often find it difficult to monitor their children and maintain control over them.

Perhaps most importantly, lone parenthood, divorce, and step-parenthood all increase the likelihood that the family climate or style will shift away from authoritative parenting. This shift is not uncommon in the first few years after a divorce, when the custodial parent (usually the mother) is distracted or depressed and less able to manage warm control; it occurs in stepfamilies as well, where rates of authoritative parenting are lower than in intact families.

Remember, authoritarian or neglectful parenting is linked to poor outcomes whether it is triggered by a divorce, a stressful remarriage, a parent's loss of a job, or any other stress (Goldberg, 1990). Ultimately, the parenting style, rather than any particular type of disruption, is significant for the child. After all, three-quarters of children reared in lone-parent or step-parent families finish high school, and roughly half of those high school graduates go on to attend college (McLanahan & Sandefur, 1994).

Many families construct a social network called an **extended family**, a family structure that includes parents, grandparents, aunts, uncles, cousins, and so on. Extended families seem to serve a protective function for children who are growing up in lone-parent homes (Wilson, 1995). Grandmothers, for example, appear to be important sources of emotional warmth for the children of teenaged mothers (Coley & Chase-Lansdale, 1998). Further, extended family members often help single and divorced mothers with financial and emotional support as well as with child care.

> ## Critical Thinking
>
> How important was your own extended family to you and your parent(s) during your early childhood years?

extended family
a social network of grandparents, aunts, uncles, cousins, and so on

Before Going On

- How do parents differ in their approaches to parenting, and how do these differences affect children's development?
- What are some possible reasons for the relationship between family structure and early childhood development?

PEER RELATIONSHIPS

The child's family experience is undeniably a central influence on emerging personality and social relationships, particularly in early childhood when a good portion of the time is still spent with parents and siblings. But over the years from 2 to 6, relationships with non-sibling peers become increasingly important—this is the critical period when brain development and function is most sensitive to social skills development (McCain & Mustard, 1999).

((•—Listen

RELATING TO PEERS THROUGH PLAY

In **Chapter 7**, you learned about the cognitive aspects of play. But what about the social features of children's play activities? The social dimensions of play were outlined in a classic observational study conducted by Mildred Parten (1932). If you observe young children who are engaged in free play, you will see that Parten's stages of play continue to be useful today.

At every age, children are likely to spend at least some of their time playing alone—a pattern known as *solitary play*. However, children first begin to show some positive interest in playing with others as early as 6 months of age. If you place two babies that age on the floor facing each other, they will look at each other, touch, pull each other's hair, imitate each other's actions, and smile at each other.

By 14 to 18 months, two or more children play together with toys—sometimes cooperating, but more often simply playing side by side with different toys. Developmentalists refer to this as *parallel play*. Toddlers this age express interest in each other and gaze at or make noises at each other. However, it isn't until around 18 months that children engage in *associative play*. In associative play, toddlers pursue their own activities but also engage in spontaneous, though short-lived, social interactions. For example, one toddler may put down a toy to spend a few minutes chasing another toddler or one may imitate another's action with a toy.

By age 3 or 4, children begin to engage in *cooperative play*, a pattern in which several children work together to accomplish a goal. Cooperative play can be either constructive or symbolic. A group of children may cooperate to build a city out of blocks, or they may assign roles such as "mommy," "daddy," and "baby" to one another to play house.

As you learned in **Chapter 7**, play is related to cognitive development. Play is also related to the development of **social skills**, a set of behaviours that usually leads to being accepted as a play partner or friend by others. For example, many researchers have focused on the social skill of *group entry*. Children who are skilled in group entry spend time observing others to find out what they're doing and then try to become a part of it. Children who have poor group-entry skills try to gain acceptance through aggressive behaviour or by interrupting the group. Developmentalists have found that children with poor group-entry skills are often rejected by peers (Fantuzzo, Coolahan, & Mendez, 1998). Peer rejection, in turn, is an important factor in future social development.

According to some studies, sex differences may account for the reasons for and consequences of poor group-entry skills. For example, one study found that 3-year-old girls with poorly developed group-entry skills spent more time in parallel play than in cooperative play (Sims, Hutchins, & Taylor, 1997). In contrast, girls with better group-entry skills engaged in more cooperative than parallel play. Thus, the unskilled 3-year-old girls' patterns of play placed them at risk for future developmental problems, because age-appropriate play experience in the preschool years is related to social development later in childhood (Howes & Matheson, 1992; Maguire & Dunn, 1997).

The same study found that 3-year-old boys with poor group-entry skills tended to be aggressive and were often actively rejected by peers. They typically responded to rejection by becoming even more aggressive and disruptive (Sims, Hutchins, & Taylor, 1997). Thus, the boys in this study seemed to be caught in a cycle: Aggressive behaviour led to peer rejection, which, in turn, led to more aggression. This pattern may place boys at risk for developing an internal working model of relationships that includes aggressive behaviour and, as a result, leads them to routinely respond aggressively to others in social situations.

Because of the risks associated with poor social skills, developmentalists have turned their attention to social-skills training as a preventive measure. For example, in

social skills
a set of behaviours that usually leads to being accepted as a play partner or friend by peers

one study, socially withdrawn 4- and 5-year-olds were taught specific verbal phrases to use when trying to gain acceptance by a group of peers (Doctoroff, 1997). In addition, their socially accepted peers were taught to remind the trained children to use their new skills. For the most part, social-skills interventions like this one lead to immediate gains in social acceptance. However, the degree to which early childhood social-skills training can prevent later social difficulties is unknown at present.

AGGRESSION

Just what is aggression and how common is it in children during their early years? The most common definition of **aggression** is behaviour intended to injure another person or damage an object. The emphasis on intentionality helps separate true aggression from rough-and-tumble play in which children sometimes accidentally hurt one another. Almost every young child shows at least some aggressive behaviour toward siblings, peers, and adults, but the form and frequency of aggression changes over the preschool years and beyond (Tremblay, 2000, 2008a; Tremblay et al., 2004).

aggression
behaviour intended to injure another person or damage an object

PATTERNS IN AGGRESSION A number of psychologists at the University of Montreal and their collaborators used Statistics Canada NLSCY data to track patterns in Canadian children's aggressive behaviour over time. As you can see from **Figure 8.7**, Richard Tremblay (2000) found that *physical aggression* (PA) (e.g., direct confrontation such as reacting with anger, fighting, kicking, hitting, or biting) peaks with toddlers at about age two and begins to decline during the preschool years. However, *indirect aggression* (IA) (e.g., indirect harm such as gossiping, saying bad things about another person behind their back, exposing a person's secrets to others, or telling others to exclude someone) begins to increase throughout the preschool years to the age of 11. In one of two later longitudinal studies, Sylvana Côté and her colleagues found that just over half of the children showed occasional PA (52.2%) and about

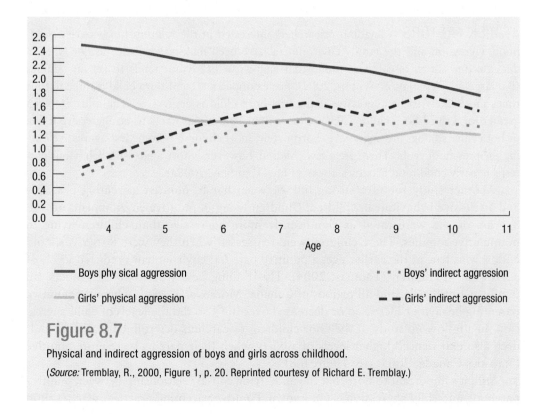

Figure 8.7

Physical and indirect aggression of boys and girls across childhood.

(*Source:* Tremblay, R., 2000, Figure 1, p. 20. Reprinted courtesy of Richard E. Tremblay.)

one-third showed infrequent PA (31.1%) in toddlerhood, which declined to an infrequent level of PA and virtually no expression of PA, respectively, by the time they reached pre-adolescence. A small group (~17%), however, frequently displayed PA during toddlerhood and maintained a high-level of PA throughout childhood (of this group, two-thirds were boys) (Côté, Vaillancourt, LeBlanc, Nagin, & Tremblay, 2006). In the second of these two studies (the first of its kind to track the joint developmental trajectories of both PA and IA), the researchers made some interesting new observations (Côté, Vaillancourt, Barker, Nagin, & Tremblay, 2007). They found, for example, that between 2 and 8 years of age, the majority of children (62.1%) followed a trajectory of declining, occasional, or infrequent use of PA (to the point of virtually no PA) coupled with ongoing low levels of IA. They also found that those preschoolers low on PA to begin with demonstrated a low propensity toward using IA as they entered school (~5.0%). In stark contrast, however, both preschool boys and girls with high levels of PA displayed increasingly higher levels of IA during their transition to elementary school (13.5%). Very few boys or girls displayed a pattern in which PA was experienced separately from the use of IA (1.1%).

In the text below, Richard Tremblay from the University of Montreal summarizes the available data on the development of physical aggression:

- the vast majority of preschool children use physical aggression
- the vast majority also learn with age to use other means of solving problems
- some need more time than others to learn
- girls learn more quickly than boys
- by adolescence, not much more than 5% of males can be considered cases of *chronic physical aggression* (CPA), while female cases are exceptional
- most of the CPA cases during adolescence were CPA cases since early childhood

(Tremblay, 2010, p. 346)

AT-RISK FACTORS Canadian researchers interested in the relationship between childhood aggression and the family environment have been making extensive use of NLSCY data. In one study, researchers found that aggressive behaviour tends to run in families (Baillargeon, Tremblay, & Willms, 2002). For example, a second-born child is three to four times more likely to be aggressive if the first-born child is aggressive. The odds are even greater for a third-born child: They are more than 10 times as likely to be aggressive if one or both elder siblings are aggressive. Fortunately, most children become less aggressive during the preschool years. There are a few children, however, whose aggressive behaviour patterns in early childhood becomes a way of life (Tremblay, 2008a).

Another study found a strong link between harsh, punitive parenting practices and aggressive behaviour in children. Children living in punitive environments at 2 to 3 years of age were rated as significantly more aggressive than children living in nonpunitive families. These children were reassessed when they were 8 to 9 years old and, as was true at the earlier age, a punitive parental environment predicted levels of aggression in children (Thomas, 2004). This finding held true for both genders, all family income levels, and all regions of Canada. Moreover, in cases where the punitive parenting behaviour increased or decreased over time, so did the levels of child aggression. In a follow-up study of the same children, researchers determined that these children also experienced higher levels of anxiety when their parents were more punitive (Statistics Canada, 2005) (see **Figure 8.8**).

Still, it's important to note that the underlying causal relationship between punitive parenting and child aggression is not known. Punitive parenting practices may result in

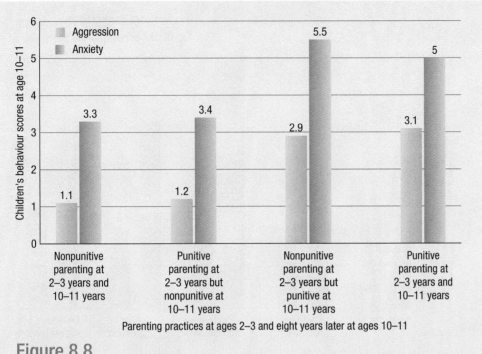

Figure 8.8

A change in parenting practices over time was associated with changes in children's behaviour rating scores on measures of aggression and anxiety.

(*Source:* Adapted from Statistics Canada, 2005, National Longitudinal Survey of Children and Youth: Home environment, income and child behaviour. *The Daily*, Monday, February 21, 2005, at website www.statcan.ca/Daily/English/050221/d050221b.htm)

more aggressive children, but it may be that aggressive behaviour in children results in more punitive approaches to parenting (Thomas, 2004). This contention is supported by an analysis of NLSCY data that showed how parent and child interactions are a two-way street: "Although children presumably respond to their parents' behaviour, it is also true that parents respond to their children's behaviour. That is, more praise may encourage a child to do well, but it is also true that parents may praise more when their children are doing well, censure more severely when the child is misbehaving" (Burton, Phipps, & Curtis, 2005, p. 5).

ORIGINS OF AGGRESSION   Psychologists have suggested several key factors in aggressive behaviour. On the one hand, developmentalists argue that reinforcement and modelling are important. For instance, when a playmate pushes her playmate away and grabs his toy, she is reinforced for her aggression because she gets the toy. In this example, reinforcement clearly plays a vital role in the development of aggressive patterns of behaviour. And when parents give in to their young child's tantrums or aggression, they are reinforcing the very behaviour they deplore, and they thereby unwittingly help to establish a long-lasting pattern of aggression and defiance.

Modelling, too, may play a key role in children's acquisition of aggressive behaviours. In a classic series of studies, psychologist Albert Bandura found that children learn specific forms of aggression, such as hitting, by watching other people perform them (Bandura, Ross, & Ross, 1961, 1963). Although entertainment media offer children many opportunities to observe aggressive behaviour, real-life aggressive models may be more influential. For example, children learn that aggression is a way of

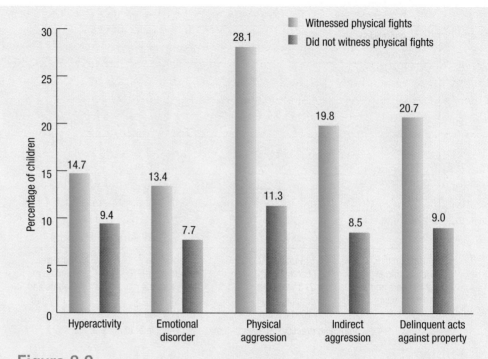

Figure 8.9

Child behaviour in homes where children witnessed and did not witness physical fights. Those children who fell within the bottom 10% of the scales were considered to have behavioural problems.

(*Source:* Statistics Canada, 2001b. Family Violence: Focus on Child Abuse and Children at Risk.)

solving problems by watching their parents, siblings, and others behave aggressively. A NLSCY analysis revealed that children who are exposed to violence in the home are about twice as likely to be physically and indirectly aggressive, commit delinquent acts, and exhibit higher rates of emotional disorders as children not exposed to such violence (Statistics Canada, 2001b) (see **Figure 8.9**).

An alternate view of the development of physical aggression is illustrated in a study which compared gender differences in levels of physical aggression in toddlers in the Québec Longitudinal Study of Child Development (Baillargeon et al., 2007). The researchers found that the ratio of female to male physical aggression was consistent between 17 and 29 months of age; for every girl, five boys displayed physically aggressive behaviour. The essential point is that aggressiveness was likely established by 17 months of age, before socialization of aggression or gender-stereotypic self-regulatory controls could account for this magnitude and consistency of gender difference in physical aggression.

A compelling explanation for children's predisposition toward aggression comes from the emerging field of epigenetics (Tremblay, 2008b). As you read above, theories have long focused on how a child develops aggression (i.e., through reinforcement and modelling), but this new model takes a contrary approach by asking how a child fails to gain control over aggression (Tremblay, 2010). This view is based on the premise that children come into the world with aggressive predispositions rather than starting out as "innocents" who acquire aggressiveness. For example, although gene function likely predisposes a child's aggressive tendencies, environmental factors can modify these tendencies from the moment of conception onward (Meaney, 2010; Shonkoff,

Critical Thinking

Knowing that children's aggressive behaviour or anxiety can change for the better, what does this tell you about the resiliency of children? What does this say about parenting practices over time?

2010) (recall from **Chapter 2** that inherited and acquired epigenetic markers can lead to phenotypal changes—such as aggression—without changing the genotype).

Experiments with long-term follow-ups are now needed to determine if early preventive and corrective interventions can lessen aggression during early childhood (Tremblay, 2010). Preventive measures aimed at modifying epigenetic effects that predispose children to aggressive behaviour need to take place as close to conception as possible and continue through the prenatal and perinatal periods, especially with mothers who are at risk (i.e., mother's who displayed behaviour problems during adolescence, have a low level of education, had their first pregnancy at a young age, and experienced depression). Interventions beginning after a child is 12 to 17 months of age would need to be more corrective in nature and focus more on the families and preschool environment, especially for high-risk families (i.e., families with low income, family dysfunction, lack of stimulation, and the presence of aggressive siblings). Not only may these early interventions lessen the prevalence of aggression in early childhood, but they may also disrupt the intergenerational transmission of aggression. Already, a recent study has shown that early intervention in the parent–child interactions of high-risk families can prevent physical aggression in early childhood (Brotman et al., 2009). Taking this one step further, future prevention strategies could focus on improving the lifestyle of at-risk pregnant women early in their pregnancy (Tremblay, 2008b, 2010).

PROSOCIAL BEHAVIOUR AND FRIENDSHIPS

At the other end of the spectrum of peer relationships is a set of behaviours psychologists call *prosocial behaviour*. Like aggression, **prosocial behaviour** is intentional and voluntary, but its purpose is to help another person in some way (Eisenberg, 1992). In everyday language, such behaviour is called *altruism*, and it changes with age, just as other aspects of peer behaviour change.

prosocial behaviour
behaviour intended to help another person

DEVELOPMENT OF PROSOCIAL BEHAVIOUR
Altruistic behaviours first become evident in children of about 2 or 3 years of age—at about the same time as real interest in playing with other children arises. At this age, a child will offer to help another child who is hurt, will share a toy, or will try to comfort another person (Marcus, 1986; Zahn-Waxler, & Radke-Yarrow, 1982; Zahn-Waxler, Radke-Yarrow, Wagner, & Chapman, 1992). As you read in **Chapter 7**, children this young are only beginning to understand that others feel differently than they do, but they obviously understand enough about the emotions of others to respond in supportive and sympathetic ways when they see other children or adults hurt or sad.

Prosocial behaviours such as sharing are influenced by cognitive development and the deliberate efforts of parents and teachers to teach children to behave in such ways.
(*Photo*: © Danita Delimont/Alamy)

Some other kinds of prosocial behaviour, such as taking turns, also seem to increase with age. If you give children an opportunity to donate some treat to another child who is described as needy, older children donate more than younger children do. Helpfulness, too, seems to increase with age through adolescence. But not all prosocial behaviours show this pattern. Comforting another child, for example, seems to be more common among preschoolers and children in early elementary grades than among older children (Eisenberg, 1992).

Children vary a lot in the amount of altruistic behaviour they show, and young children who show relatively more empathy and altruism are also those who regulate their own emotions well. They show positive emotions readily and negative emotions less often (Eisenberg et al.,

1996). They are also more popular with peers (Mayeux & Cillissen, 2003). These variations among children's levels of empathy or altruism seem to be related to specific kinds of child-rearing. In addition, longitudinal studies indicate that children who display higher levels of prosocial behaviour in the preschool years continue to demonstrate higher levels of such behaviour in adulthood (Eisenberg et al., 1999).

THE ROLE OF EMPATHY ON PROSOCIAL BEHAVIOUR William Roberts of the University College of the Cariboo in Kamloops, British Columbia, and Janet Strayer of Simon Fraser University have been studying prosocial behaviour in children. In one study they found that, in general, girls were more prosocial than boys. In boys, level of empathy predicted cooperative, helpful, and responsible behaviours (Roberts & Strayer, 1996). In a later study, they reported that empathy in specific situations was also an important predictor of interpersonal closeness for both genders. For instance, when a child expressed a high level of empathy with a person portrayed in an emotion-laden video vignette, he or she tended to decrease the personal distance with that character. This relationship between personal distance and empathy was generally stronger in girls but increased with age in both genders (Strayer & Roberts, 1997).

Following up on their earlier research, Strayer and Roberts (2004) conducted a comprehensive analysis of the interactive pathways associated with a child's level of empathy. They looked at how child factors, such as age and several emotional qualities (i.e., ability to take the perspective or role of others, emotional insight, and emotional expressiveness), interact with emotional characteristics and practices of parents (i.e., level of empathy and emotional expressiveness, encouragement of their child's emotional expressiveness, warmth, and control). Taken together, the links between child and parent characteristics predicted two-thirds of children's empathy. The researchers also found that children's anger plays an important role in the development of empathy, a finding that requires further investigation.

PARENTAL INFLUENCES ON PROSOCIAL BEHAVIOUR Research suggests that parental behaviour contributes to the development of prosocial behaviour (Eisenberg, 1992). Specifically, parents of altruistic children create a loving and warm family climate. If such warmth is combined with clear explanations and rules about what to do as well as what not to do, then the children are even more likely to behave altruistically. Such parents also often explain the consequences of the child's action in terms of its effects on others—for example, "If you hit Susan, it will hurt her." Stating rules or guidelines positively rather than negatively also appears to be important; for example, "It's always good to be helpful to other people" is more effective guidance than "Don't be so selfish!"

Providing prosocial *attributions*—positive statements about the underlying cause for helpful behaviour—is also useful. For example, a parent might praise a child by saying "You're such a helpful child!" or "You certainly do a lot of nice things for other people." Having heard such statements often during early childhood helps children incorporate them into their self-concepts later in childhood. In this way, parents may help create a generalized, internalized pattern of altruistic behaviour in the child.

Parents of altruistic children also look for opportunities for them to do helpful things. For example, they allow children to help cook, take care of pets, make toys to give away, teach younger siblings, and so forth. Finally, parental modelling of thoughtful and generous behaviour—that is, parents demonstrating consistency between what they say and what they do—is another contributing factor.

FRIENDSHIPS Beginning at about 18 months, a few toddlers show early hints of playmate preferences or individual friendships (Howes, 1983, 1987); however, by age 3, about 20% of children have a stable playmate. By age 4, more than half spend 30% or more of their time with one other child (Hinde, Titmus, Easton, & Tamplin, 1985). Thus, one important change in social behaviour during early childhood is the formation of stable friendships (Hay, Payne, & Chadwick, 2004).

To be sure, these early peer interactions are still quite primitive. However, it is noteworthy that preschool friend pairs nonetheless show more mutual liking, more reciprocity, more extended interactions, more positive and less negative behaviour, and more supportiveness in a novel situation than do nonfriend pairs at this same age—all signs that these relationships are more than merely passing fancies. Moreover, having had a friend in early childhood is related to social competence during the elementary school years (Sebanc, 2003).

Before Going On

- What are the various kinds of play observed among preschoolers?
- How does aggression and prosocial behaviour change during early childhood?

PERSONALITY AND SELF-CONCEPT

As young children gain more understanding of the social environment, their temperaments ripen into true personalities. At the same time, their self-concepts become more complex, allowing them to exercise greater control over their own behaviour.

FROM TEMPERAMENT TO PERSONALITY

Are you familiar with the children's game "Duck, Duck, Goose"? For the benefit of readers who are unfamiliar with the game, here's how it goes. A child who has been assigned the role of "it" walks around the outside of a circle of children who are seated on the floor. As "it" passes by, he touches the head of each child and calls out "duck" until he comes to the child that he chooses to be the "goose." The "goose" then has to jump up and chase "it" around the circle and try to prevent him from taking the goose's seat. If "goose" fails to beat "it," then she becomes "it" for the next round of the game. The difficult part of the game for many young children is waiting to be chosen to be the "goose."

Activities such as "Duck, Duck, Goose" may seem frivolous, but they contribute to the process through which temperament becomes modified into personality during the early childhood years. A child whose temperament includes a low ranking on the dimension of effortful control, for instance, may not be able to tolerate waiting for his turn in a game of "Duck, Duck, Goose" (Li-Grining, 2007). If he obeys his impulse to chase "it" and jumps up from his seat before he is declared the "goose," he will undoubtedly be scolded by his playmates. If his frustration leads him to withdraw from the game with the protest, "I never get to be the goose!", then he will miss out on the fun of participating. Either way, he will learn that controlling his impulses is more beneficial to him than submitting to them. A few such experiences will teach him to moderate the effects of his lack of effortful control on his social behaviour. As a result, his lack of effortful control will become less prominent in the profile of characteristics that constitute his personality and will change how his peers respond to him. Their approval of his modified profile will encourage him to keep his impulses in check.

Similarly, children with difficult temperaments learn that the behaviours associated with difficultness, such as complaining, often result in peer rejection. As a result, many of them change their behaviour to gain social acceptance. Similarly, some shy toddlers are encouraged by their parents to be more sociable (Rubin, Burgess, & Hastings, 2002). Thus, personality represents the combination of the temperament with which children are probably born and the knowledge they gain about temperament-related behaviour during childhood (McCrae Costa, Ostendord, & Angleitner, 2000; Svrakic, Svrakic, & Cloninger, 1996).

The transition from temperament to personality is also influenced by parental responses to the young child's temperament. If the parents reject the difficult child, then the child is likely to emerge from the preschool years with a personality that puts him at risk for developing serious problems in social relationships, and he may suffer from cognitive deficits as well (Bates, 1989; Fish, Stifter, & Belsky, 1991). However, parents can moderate the risks associated with a difficult temperament by helping these children learn to regulate their emotions and behaviour more effectively (Coplan, Bowker, & Cooper, 2003). Thus, infant temperament doesn't necessarily dictate the kind of personality a child will develop. Instead, it is one factor among many that shape an individual child's personality.

You should also remember from **Chapter 6** that psychologists distinguish between temperament and personality, and most believe that inborn infant temperament constitutes the foundation of personality in later childhood and adulthood (Caspi et al., 2003; Hagekull & Bohlin, 2003). It seems likely that the processes through which temperament becomes modified into personality begin during the early childhood years. For example, some shy toddlers are encouraged by their parents to be more sociable (Rubin, Burgess, & Hastings, 2002). Thus, personality represents the combination of the temperament with which children are probably born and the knowledge they gain about temperament-related behaviour during childhood (McCrae, Costa, Ostendord, & Angleitner, 2000; Svrakic, Svrakic, & Cloninger, 1996). As a result, correlations between infant temperament and later measures of personality, though still strong, tend to decline over childhood and adolescence (Shaw, Ryst, & Steiner, 1996).

The transition from temperament to personality is also influenced by parental responses to the young child's temperament. If the parents reject the difficult or shy child, then the child is likely to emerge from the preschool years with a personality that puts him at risk for developing serious problems in social relationships, and he may suffer from cognitive deficits as well (Bates, 1989; Fish, Stifter, & Belsky, 1991). By contrast, when parents encourage shy children to interact with their peers, the children are likely to become more outgoing. Similarly, parents can moderate the risks associated with a difficult temperament by helping these children learn to regulate their emotions and behaviour more effectively (Coplan, Bowker, & Cooper, 2003). Thus, infant temperament doesn't necessarily dictate the kind of personality a child will develop. Instead, it is one factor among many that shape an individual child's personality.

SELF-CONCEPT

The 18- to 24-month-old is beginning to develop categorical and emotional selves. Between ages 2 and 6, the child continues to develop these two aspects of the self and adds to them a *social self*. Gender differences also begin to appear in self-concept during the preschool years. For instance, Brock University researcher Sandra

Children with difficult temperaments may show heightened aggressiveness or other behavioural problems in school—but when such behaviour results in peer rejection, they may be motivated to change their behaviour in order to gain social acceptance.
(*Photo:* Thinkstock)

Bosacki (2001) conducted a longitudinal study of the self-concept–related dimensions of self-knowledge, emotional understanding, and gender-typed play in children aged 3 to 4. She found that girls scored higher than boys in their cognitive ability to solve false-belief tasks (as described in **Chapter 7**), their ability to understand emotions within themselves and in others, and their perceived level of self-control in social situations. Familiarity with the dimensions of preschoolers' self-concepts helps parents, teachers, and others better understand many aspects of their social behaviour.

THE CATEGORICAL SELF By the end of the preschool period, a child can give you quite a full description of herself on a whole range of dimensions. Still, these early self-concepts remain highly concrete. The self-concept of a preschool child tends to focus on her own visible characteristics—whether she's a boy or girl, what she looks like, what or whom she plays with, where she lives, what she is good at—rather than on more enduring inner qualities.

As you learned earlier in this chapter, categories are also important in young children's perceptions of others—"big kids," "little kids," "boys," "girls," and so on. Preschoolers prefer playmates of their own age and gender. Consequently, the categorical self seems to be as much an internal working model for social relationships as for the self.

THE EMOTIONAL SELF In a Canadian study of children's emotional knowledge, Bosacki and Moore (2004) found that preschool girls scored higher than boys in the ability to correctly label emotions and understand complex emotions. Both girls and boys were found to be better at understanding their own emotions as opposed to the emotions of others. Preschool children also demonstrated the ability to conceptualize complex emotions, such as pride, before they could understand them (e.g., knowing why a specific situation would lead to a sense of pride). In general, preschool children with better vocabularies were better able to label and explain emotions.

In recent years, research examining development of the emotional self during the early childhood years has focused on the acquisition of **emotional regulation**, or the ability to control emotional states and emotion-related behaviour (Hoeksma, Oosterlaan, & Schipper, 2004). For example, children exhibit emotional regulation when they find a way to cheer themselves up when they are feeling sad, or when they divert their attention to a different activity when they get frustrated with something. Recent research has shown that emotional regulation in early childhood is linked to a variety of social variables. One study showed that level of emotional regulation at age 2 predicted level of aggressive behaviour at age 4 in both boys and girls (Rubin, Burgess, Dwyer, & Hastings, 2003). Predictably, preschoolers who display high levels of emotional regulation are more popular with their peers than those who are less able to regulate their emotional behaviour (Denham et al., 2003; Fantuzzo, Sekino, & Cohen, 2004). Emotional regulation skills appear to be particularly important for children whose temperaments include high levels of anger proneness (Diener & Kim, 2004). Further, longitudinal research has demonstrated that emotional regulation in early childhood is related to children's ability to obey moral rules and to think about right and wrong during the school years (Kochanska, Murray, & Coy, 1997).The process of acquiring emotional regulation is one in which control shifts slowly from the parents to the child (Houck & Lecuyer-Maus, 2004). Here again, the child's temperament is a factor. For example, preschoolers who have consistently exhibited difficult behaviour since infancy are more likely to have self-control problems in early childhood (Schmitz et al., 1999). Similarly, preschoolers who were born prematurely or who were delayed in language development in the second year of life experience more difficulties with self-control during early childhood (Carson, Klee, & Perry, 1998; Schothorst & van Engeland, 1996).

emotional regulation
the ability to control emotional states and emotion-related behaviour

While bored toddlers often need to have their attention physically redirected to keep them occupied, by preschool age, most children are able to look for things to do on their own, like looking at a magazine or asking a parent to read to them. (*Photo:* JupiterImages/Thinkstock)

Another aspect of the emotional self involves empathy, the ability to identify with another person's emotional state. Empathy has two aspects: apprehending another person's emotional state or condition and then matching that emotional state oneself. An empathizing person experiences either the same feeling he imagines the other person to feel or a highly similar feeling. Empathy is negatively associated with aggression in the early childhood years; the more advanced preschoolers' capacity for empathy is, the less aggression they display (Findlay, Girardi, & Coplan, 2006; Strayer & Roberts, 2004b). Moreover, the development of empathy in early childhood appears to provide the foundation on which a more sophisticated emotion, sympathy (a general feeling of sorrow or concern for another person), is built in later childhood and adolescence.

In addition to empathy, young children's emotional selves include an awareness of emotional states that are linked to their culture's definitions of right and wrong. These feelings, which are sometimes called the *moral emotions*, include guilt, shame, and pride (Eisenberg, 2000). Guilt is usually thought of as the emotional state that is induced when a child breaks a rule. Consequently, a child who takes a forbidden cookie will experience guilt. Feelings of shame arise when she fails to live up to expectations. For instance, most parents and teachers urge young children to share their toys. Thus, when a child behaves selfishly and is reminded about the sharing rule, he likely feels shame. By contrast, children feel pride when they succeed at meeting such expectations.

Research suggests that the interplay among these three emotions and young children's awareness of them influences the development of behaviour that children's cultures regard as morally acceptable (Eisenberg, 2000). Thus, they form the foundation of later moral development. Studies suggest that these feelings evolve in the context of parent–child relationships. Young children who do not have warm, trusting relationships with their parents are at risk of failing to develop moral emotions or of developing feelings of guilt, shame, and pride that are too weak to influence their behaviour (Koenig, Cicchetti, & Rogosch, 2004).

THE SOCIAL SELF   Another facet of the child's emerging sense of self is an increasing awareness of herself as a player in the social game. By age 2, the toddler has already learned a variety of social "scripts"—routines of play or interaction with others. The toddler now begins to develop some implicit understanding of her own roles in these scripts (Case, 1991). So she may begin to think of herself as a "helper" in some situations or as "the boss" when she is telling some other child what to do.

You can see this clearly in children's sociodramatic play, as they begin to take explicit roles: "I'll be the daddy and you be the mommy" or "I'm the boss." As part of the same process, the young child also gradually understands her place in the network of family roles. She has sisters, brothers, father, mother, and so forth.

The development of social role scripts helps young children become more independent. For example, assuming the "student" role provides a preschooler with a prescription for appropriate behaviour in the school situation. Students listen when the teacher speaks to the class, get out materials and put them away at certain times, help their classmates in various ways, and so on. Once a preschooler is familiar with and adopts the student role, he can follow the role script and is no longer dependent on the teacher to tell him what to do every minute of the day.

Not all children make a social adjustment to school in the same way. Carlton University psychologists Robert Coplan and Kavita Prakash (2003) looked at three patterns of child–teacher interactions and found that children rated as more aggressive initiated more interactions with teachers; shy and anxious children received, but didn't initiate, interactions with teachers; and a third group of children who were rated as more sociable and less solitary spent the least amount of time interacting with teachers as they spent more time interacting with other students and exploring learning opportunities in the classroom. A closer look at shy students found that their quietness may be due to either social disinterest (a nonfearful preference for solitude) or conflicted shyness (an approach-avoidance conflict—their desire to interact with others is accompanied by fear or anxiety) (Coplan, Prakash, O'Neil, & Armer, 2004). Moreover, it seems that children's shyness is related to social anxiety rather than a lack of ability to verbally express themselves (Coplan & Armer, 2005).

Before Going On

- Is temperament stable in early childhood? If not, how does it change?
- What changes take place in the young child's categorical, emotional, and social selves during the preschool years?

GENDER DEVELOPMENT

We noted earlier that preschoolers who are asked to describe themselves are likely to begin by stating whether they are boys or girls. In psychologists' terms, their tendency to do so suggests that "boy-ness" and "girl-ness" are salient, or important, categories for young children. Thus, one of the most fascinating developmental processes of the preschool period is the one that involves children's evolving sense of **gender**—the psychological and social associates and implications of biological sex.

gender
the psychological and social associates and implications of biological sex

EXPLAINING GENDER CONCEPT AND SEX-ROLE DEVELOPMENT

Developmentalists have proposed several explanations of gender development.

SOCIAL-COGNITIVE EXPLANATIONS Social-cognitive theorists have emphasized the role of parents in shaping children's sex-role behaviour and attitudes (Bandura, 1977a; Bandura & Bussey, 2004; Mischel, 1966, 1970). Parents reinforce sex-typed activities in children as young as 18 months, not only by buying different kinds of toys for boys and girls, but also by responding more positively when their sons play with "boy-type" toys, such as tools or trucks, than when their sons play with "girl-type" toys, such as dolls and jewellery, and the opposite is true for daughters (Fagot & Hagan, 1991; Leaper & Friedman, 2007). One study found that an infant's sex affected how mothers interacted with them: The mothers' speech and behaviour varied, even when their infants were as young as 6 months of age. The mothers' speech was more conversational and they engaged in more comforting and hugging with their daughters than with their sons. By comparison, the mothers' speech was more instructional and directive and there was less interaction overall with their sons (Clearfield & Nelson, 2006).

((•— Listen

    A second social-cognitive theory suggests that children's understanding of gender is linked to gender-related behaviour. For example, one such view, based strongly on Piagetian theory, is Lawrence Kohlberg's suggestion that the crucial aspect of the process is the child's understanding of the gender concept (Kohlberg, 1966; Kohlberg & Ullian, 1974). Once the child realizes that he is a boy or she is a girl forever, he or she becomes highly motivated to learn how to behave in the way that is expected or appropriate for that gender. Specifically, Kohlberg's **gender constancy theory** predicts that systematic same-sex imitation will become evident only after the child has shown full gender constancy. **Gender constancy** is the understanding that gender is an innate characteristic that can't be changed. Most studies designed to test this hypothesis have supported Kohlberg. Children do seem to become much more sensitive to same-sex models after they understand gender constancy (Frey & Ruble, 1992). Kohlberg's theory allows developmentalists to make highly reliable predictions about the development of children's knowledge about gender.

However, gender constancy theory is less accurate in predicting behaviour. Specifically, it can't explain the obvious fact that children show clearly different sex-role behaviour, such as toy preferences, long before they have achieved full understanding of the gender concept. A third social-cognitive theory derived from the information-processing approach is usually called *gender schema theory* (Martin, 1991; Martin & Halverson, 1981; Martin, Ruble & Szkrybalo, 2002). This approach includes many of Kohlberg's ideas about how gender constancy develops, but it does a better job of predicting behaviour.

GENDER-SCHEMA THEORY

You'll remember from **Chapter 7** that a great deal of *schematic* learning happens in early childhood. A schema is a mental pattern or model that is used to process information. Just as the self-concept can be thought of as a schema, the child's understanding of gender can be seen in the same way. According to **gender schema theory**, the gender schema begins to develop as soon as the child notices the differences between male and female, knows his own gender, and can label the two groups with some consistency—all of which happens between 18 and 24 months (Zosuls et al, 2009). Perhaps because gender is basically an either/or category, children seem to understand very early that this is a key distinction, so the category serves as a kind of magnet for new information. Once the child has established even a primitive gender schema, a great many experiences can be assimilated to it. Thus, as soon as this schema begins to be formed, children may begin to show preference for same-sex playmates or for gender-stereotyped activities (Martin & Little, 1990; Martin & Ruble, 2004; 2010).

Preschoolers first learn some broad distinctions about what kinds of activities or behaviour "go with" each gender, both by observing other children and through the reinforcements they receive from parents. They also learn a few gender *scripts*—whole sequences of events that are normally associated with a given gender, such as "fixing dinner" or "building with tools"—just as they learn other social scripts at about this age (Levy & Fivush, 1993). Then, between ages 4 and 6, the child learns a more subtle and complex set of associations for his own gender—what children of his own gender like and don't like, how they play, how they talk, what kinds of people they associate with. Only between ages 8 and 10 does the child develop an equivalently complex view of the opposite gender (Martin, Wood, & Little, 1990).

The key difference between this theory and Kohlberg's gender constancy theory is that gender schema theory asserts that the child need not understand that gender is permanent to form an initial gender schema. When they do begin to understand gender constancy, at about age 5 or 6, children develop a more elaborate rule, or schema, of "what people who are like me do" and treat this rule the same way they treat other rules—as an absolute. Later, the child's application of the gender rule becomes more flexible. She knows, for example, that most boys don't play with dolls, but that they can do so if they like.

---

gender constancy theory
Kohlberg's assertion that children must understand that gender is a permanent characteristic before they can adopt appropriate sex roles

gender constancy
the understanding that gender is a component of the self that is not altered by external appearance

gender schema theory
an information-processing approach to gender concept development that asserts that people use a schema for each gender to process information about themselves and others

BIOLOGICAL APPROACHES For a long time, developmentalists dismissed the idea that biological differences between males and females were responsible for psychological differences between them. Today, though, they are taking another look at decades-old experimental studies with animals which show that prenatal exposure to male hormones, such as testosterone, powerfully influences behaviour after birth (Lippa, 2005). Female animals exposed to testosterone behave more like male animals; for instance, they are more aggressive than females who do not experience prenatal exposure to testosterone. Similarly, when experimenters block the release of testosterone during prenatal development of male animal embryos, the animals exhibit behaviour that is more typical of the females of their species.

Hormonal influences have been proposed to explain the outcomes of cases involving boys who carry a genetic defect that causes them to develop deformed genitalia. Decades ago, a few such boys were subjected to plastic surgery to give them female-appearing genitals and were raised as girls. At that time, however, doctors did not realize that the genetic defect in question interferes only with testosterone's effects on the sex organs; the brains of these fetuses were exposed to normal amounts of testosterone throughout prenatal development (Rosenthal & Gitelman, 2002). Follow-up studies found that many of these children, when they learned of their status, sought surgery to masculinize their bodies. Moreover, even those who elected to retain the feminine identities they had been given in infancy possessed many attributes and behaviours that are more typical of males than of females (Reiner & Gearhart, 2004). Such findings support the view that hormones play some role in gender development.

THE GENDER CONCEPT

Children seem to develop gender constancy in three steps. First comes **gender identity**, which is simply a child's ability to label his or her own sex correctly and to identify other people as men or women, boys or girls. By 9 to 12 months, babies already treat male and female faces as if they were different categories (Fagot & Leinbach, 1993). Within the next year, they begin to learn the verbal labels that go with these categories. By age 2, most children correctly label themselves as boys or girls and, within 6 to 12 months, most can correctly label others as well.

Accurate labelling, though, does not signify complete understanding. The second step is **gender stability**, which is the understanding that you stay the same gender throughout life. Researchers have measured this by asking children questions such as "When you were a little baby, were you a little girl or a little boy?" or "When you grow up, will you be a mommy or a daddy?" Most children understand the stability of gender by about age 4 (Slaby & Frey, 1975) (see **Figure 8.10**).

The final step is the development of true gender constancy, the recognition that someone stays the same gender even though he may appear to change by wearing different clothes or changing his hair length. For example, boys don't change into girls by wearing dresses. It may seem odd that a child who understands that he will stay the same gender throughout life (gender stability) can nonetheless be confused about the effect of changes in dress or appearance on gender. But numerous studies, including studies of children growing up in other cultures, such as Kenya, Nepal, Belize, and Samoa, show that children go through this sequence (Munroe, Shimmin, & Munroe, 1984; Munroe & Romney, 2006). Moreover, this stage is related to general cognitive development (Trautner, Gervai, & Nemeth, 2003).

The underlying logic of this sequence may be a bit clearer if you think of a parallel between gender constancy and the concept of conservation. Conservation involves recognition that an object remains the same in some fundamental way even though it changes externally. Gender constancy is thus a kind of "conservation of gender" and is

Watch

gender identity
the ability to correctly label oneself and others as male or female

gender stability
the understanding that gender is a stable, lifelong characteristic

Figure 8.10

In describing this self-portrait, the 5-year-old artist said, "This is how I will look when I get married to a boy. I am under a rainbow, so beautiful with a bride hat, a belt, and a purse." The girl knows she will always be female and associates gender with externals such as clothing (gender stability). She is also already quite knowledgeable about gender-role expectations.

(*Source*: Courtesy of Jerry and Denise Boyd. Used with permission.)

not typically understood until about age 5 or 6, when children understand other conservations (Marcus & Overton, 1978).

SEX-ROLE KNOWLEDGE

Figuring out your gender and understanding that it stays constant are only part of the story. Learning what goes with being a boy or a girl in a given culture is also a vital part of the child's task. Researchers have studied this in two ways: by asking children what boys and girls (or men and women) like to do and what they are like (which is an inquiry about gender stereotypes), and by asking children if it is okay for boys to play with dolls or girls to climb trees or do equivalent cross-sex things (an inquiry about roles).

A large study of Canadian children shows that these stereotyped ideas develop early (Serbin, Powlishta, & Gulko, 1993). It would not be uncommon to hear a 3-year-old say "Mommies use the stove, and daddies use the grill." A 4-year-old might define gender roles in terms of competencies: "Daddies are better at fixing things, but mommies are better at tying bows and decorating." Even 2-year-olds already associate certain activities and possessions with men and women, depending on the adult activities they are most often and consistently exposed to in the home. For example, toddlers of both genders can associate feeding a baby, applying makeup, and dresses with women and, to a lesser extent, cars and hammering with men (Serbin, Poulin-Dubois, & Eichstedt, 2002). By age 3 or 4, children can assign stereotypic occupations, toys, and activities to each gender (Blakemore, 2003; Care, Deans, Brown, 2007). By age 5, children begin to associate certain personality traits, such as assertiveness and nurturance, with males or females (Martin, 1993; Serbin, Powlishta, & Gulko, 1993).

Studies of children's ideas about how men and women (or boys and girls) ought to behave add an interesting further element. For example, in an early study, a psychologist told a story to children aged 4 to 9 about a little boy named George who liked to play with dolls (Damon, 1977). George's parents told him that only little girls play with dolls; little boys shouldn't. The children were then asked questions about the story, such as "Why do people tell George not to play with dolls?" or "Is there a rule that boys shouldn't play with dolls?"

Four-year-olds in this study thought it was okay for George to play with dolls: There was no rule against it, and he should do it if he wanted to. Six-year-olds, in contrast, thought it was wrong for George to play with dolls. By about age 9, children had differentiated between what boys and girls usually do, and what is "wrong." One boy said, for example, that breaking windows was wrong and bad, but that playing with dolls was not bad in the same way: "Breaking windows you're not supposed to do. And if you play with dolls, well you can, but boys usually don't."

As their gender concept develops, children change their views about whether it is acceptable for boys to play with dolls or for girls to play sports, such as baseball.
(*Photos: Left*, SUNSTAR/Photo Researchers, Inc.; *Right*, Mary Kay Denny/PhotoEdit.)

This study appeared to reveal that a 5- to 6-year-old, having figured out that gender is permanent, is searching for a rule about how boys and girls behave (Martin & Halverson, 1981). The child picks up information from watching adults, from watching television, and from listening to the labels that are attached to different activities (e.g., "Boys don't cry" or "Girls act nicely"). Initially, children treat these as absolute, moral rules. Later, they understand that these are social conventions; at this point, sex-role concepts become more flexible and stereotyping declines between ages 5 and 11, although stereotype knowledge and spontaneous stereotyping remain at high levels (Banse, Gawronski, Rebetez, Gutt, & Morton, 2010).

SEX-TYPED BEHAVIOUR

The final element in the development of sex roles is the actual behaviour children show with those of the same and the opposite sex. An unexpected finding is that **sex-typed behaviour**, or different patterns of behaviour among girls and boys, develops earlier than ideas about sex roles (Campbell, Shirley, & Candy, 2004). By 18 to 24 months of age, children begin to show some preference for sex-stereotyped toys, such as dolls for girls or trucks or building blocks for boys, which is some months before they can consistently identify their own gender (Campbell, Shirley, & Caygill, 2002; Serbin, Poulin-Dubois, Colbourne, Sen, & Eichstedt, 2001). By age 3, children begin to show a preference for same-sex friends and are much more sociable with playmates of the same sex—at a time when they do not yet have a concept of gender stability (Corsaro, Molinari, Hadley, & Sugioka, 2003) (see **Figure 8.11**).

sex-typed behaviour
different patterns of behaviour exhibited by boys and girls

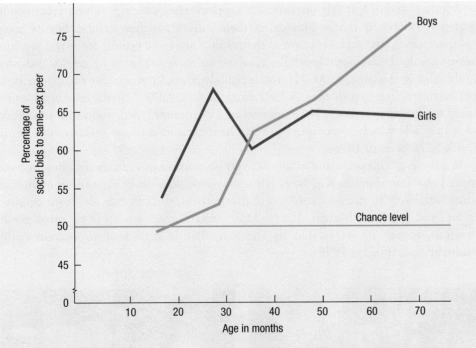

Figure 8.11

In one study of playmate preferences, researchers counted how often preschool children played with same-sex or opposite-sex playmates. Children as young as 2 years old already showed at least some preference for same-sex playmates.

(*Source:* La Freniere, Strayer, & Gautier, 1984, Figure 1, p. 1961. Copyright by the Society for Research in Child Development, Inc.)

Not only are preschoolers' friendships and peer interactions increasingly sex segregated, but it is also clear that boy–boy interactions and girl–girl interactions differ in quality, even in these early years. One important part of same-sex interactions seems to involve instruction and modelling of sex-appropriate behaviour. In other words, older boys teach younger boys how to be "masculine," and older girls teach younger girls how to be "feminine" (Danby & Baker, 1998).

These "lessons" in sex-typed behaviour are subtle. Eleanor Maccoby, one of the leading theorists in this area, describes the girls' pattern as an *enabling style* (Maccoby, 1990). Enabling includes behaviours such as supporting the friend, expressing agreement, and making suggestions. All these behaviours tend to foster a greater equality and intimacy in the relationship and keep the interaction going. In contrast, boys are more likely to show what Maccoby calls a *constricting, or restrictive, style*. "A restrictive style is one that tends to derail the interaction—to inhibit the partner or cause the partner to withdraw, thus shortening the interaction or bringing it to an end" (1990, p. 517). Contradicting, interrupting, boasting, and other forms of self-display are all aspects of this style.

These two patterns begin to be visible in the preschool years. For example, beginning as early as age 3, boys and girls use quite different strategies in their attempts to influence each other's behaviour (Maccoby, 1990). Girls generally ask questions or make requests; boys are much more likely to make demands or phrase things using imperatives (e.g., "Give me that!"). The really intriguing finding is that even at this early age, boys simply don't respond to the girls' enabling style. Thus, playing with boys yields little positive reinforcement for girls, and they begin to avoid such interactions and band together.

Another kind of learning opportunity happens when children exhibit **cross-gender behaviour**, behaviour that is atypical in their culture for their gender. For example, *tomboyishness*, girls' preference for activities that are more typical for boys, is a kind of cross-gender behaviour. Generally, tomboyishness is tolerated by adults and peers (Sandnabba & Ahlberg, 1999). Not surprisingly, then, cross-gender behaviour is far more common among girls than boys (Etaugh & Liss, 1992). Tomboyishness does not appear to interfere with the development of a "feminine" personality in adulthood, and it may allow girls to acquire positive characteristics such as assertiveness (Burn, O'Neil, & Nederend, 1996).

In contrast, both peers and adults actively discourage boys from engaging in cross-gender behaviour. Specifically, boys who play with dolls or behave in an effeminate manner are likely to elicit expressions of disapproval, or even ridicule, from children, parents, and teachers (Martin, 1991). Many adults' reactions to boys' cross-gender behaviour appear to be related to the fear that it may lead to homosexuality (Sandnabba & Ahlberg, 1999).

Critical Thinking

What do you think happens when opposite-sex adults interact in some nonromantic encounter? Is the interaction style some combination of enabling and constricting, or does one style dominate?

cross-gender behaviour
behaviour that is atypical for one's own sex but typical for the opposite sex

Play may provide children with opportunities to learn about gender-role expectations.
(*Photos: Left*, © AGB Photo/Alamy; *Right*, Sue Ann Miller/Getty Images)

It cannot be assumed that the prevalence of sex-typed play among boys is strictly the result of adult and peer influence. For one thing, sex-typed play preferences appear earlier and are more consistent in male infants, which suggests that they begin to develop before environmental forces have had much chance to influence them (Blakemore, LaRue, & Olejnik, 1979). Further, by age 3, boys are likely to show an actual aversion to girls' activities, for example, by saying "yuck" when experimenters offer them toys such as dolls (Bussey & Bandura, 1992). In addition, boys may prefer the company of a girl who is a tomboy to a boy who engages in cross-gender activity (Alexander & Hines, 1994). Finally, researchers have found that it is very difficult to change boys' play preferences with modelling and reinforcement (Paley, 1986; Weisner & Wilson-Mitchell, 1990). These findings suggest that, at least for boys, sex-typed behaviour is part of a complex process of identity development and not just the result of cultural modelling and reinforcement.

Before Going On

- Describe the development of gender identity, gender stability, and gender constancy.
- What are the characteristics of young children's sex-role knowledge, and how is the behaviour of young children sex-typed?

Summary

Theories of Social and Personality Development

- Both Freud's and Erikson's theories of personality development place primary importance on balancing parental control with a child's emerging needs and skills. Erikson described two stages in which autonomy and initiative are developed.

- Three topics of interest to social-cognitive theorists are person perception, understanding rule categories, and understanding others' intentions.

Family Relationships and Structure

- Except in stressful situations, attachment behaviours become less visible as the child gets older. Preschoolers refuse or defy parental influence attempts more than infants do. Outright defiance, however, declines from age 2 to 6.

- Authoritative parenting, which combines warmth, clear rules, and communication with high maturity demands, is associated with the most positive outcomes for children. Most child development experts recommend minimal nonphysical forms of child discipline.

- Good parenting practices are common in all SES levels, but when children of lower SES are exposed to inadequate parenting practices, they become more vulnerable to a wide range of problems.

- Canadian studies found that many lone-parent families experience high levels of stress, yet only a portion of these children have an elevated risk of a range of problems.

- Following a divorce, children typically show disrupted behaviour for several years. Parenting styles also change, becoming less authoritative.

- To understand the influence of family structure on development, a number of variables, such as poverty, associated with differences in family structure must be taken into account.

Peer Relationships

- Play with peers becomes increasingly important through the preschool years.

- Physical aggression toward peers increases and then declines in most children during these early years, while indirect aggression increases among some children more than others.

- Empathy and prosocial behaviour toward others seems to become more common as the child's ability to take another's perspective increases. Stable friendships develop between children in this age range.

Personality and Self-Concept

- Young children's temperaments are modified by social experiences both within and outside of the family to form their personalities.

- The preschooler continues to define himself along a series of objective dimensions but does not yet have a global sense of self. Children make major strides in self-control and in their understanding of their own social roles in the preschool years.

Gender Development

- Social-cognitive, gender-schema, and biological theories each help to explain and predict gender-related understanding and behaviour.

- Between ages 2 and 6, most children move through a series of steps in their understanding of gender constancy: first, labelling their own and others' gender; then, understanding the stability of gender; and, finally, comprehending the constancy of gender.

- Beginning at about age 2, children begin to learn what is appropriate behaviour for their gender. By age 5 or 6, most children have developed fairly rigid rules about what boys or girls are supposed to do and be.

- Children display sex-typed behaviour as early as 18 to 24 months of age.

PEARSON
mydevelopmentlab™

Visit **www.mydevelopmentlab.com** to help you get the best grade! Test your knowledge and grasp difficult concepts through

- Custom study plans: See where you are strong and where you go wrong
- Interactive simulations

- Video and audio clips
- Raise your own Virtual Child—and much more!

Review Questions

Answers are provided on MyDevelopmentLab in the Course Resources folder.

Theories of Social and Personality Development

8.1 The text suggests that both Freud and Erikson believed that the key to the social development of 2- to 6-year-olds is
   a. striking a balance between the child's emerging skills and parents' need for control.
   b. the successful development of peer relationships.
   c. whether potty training goes smoothly.
   d. the ability of the parents to give the child freedom to grow.

Family Relationships and Structure

8.2 A 4- or 5-year old child may have an internal model of attachment that

   a. gradually fades as the child becomes more independent from her parents.
   b. comes to be applied to new relationships, such as that with a preschool teacher.
   c. develops into an external model of attachment as social relationships are developed.
   d. is applied only to relationships with family members.

Peer Relationships

8.3 What is the most dominant trajectory of aggression among Canadian 2- to 8-year-old children?
   a. Preschoolers with high levels of physical aggression display increasingly higher levels of indirect aggression.
   b. Preschoolers with low levels of physical aggression display increasingly higher levels of indirect aggression.

c. Preschoolers low on physical aggression have a low propensity toward using indirect aggression.

d. Preschool children show declining use of physical aggression coupled with ongoing low levels of indirect aggression.

Personality and Self-Concept

8.4   Which of the following is an example of emotional self-regulation?

a. Judy is sad, so she turns on the television to watch a favourite cartoon.

b. Ray gives up on a puzzle that is too difficult for him.

c. Carol gets angry at her mother and storms out of the room.

d. When Dorothy pushes her off a swing, Kathy kicks Dorothy.

Gender Development

8.5   A little boy chooses a toy that he believes is for boys and rejects a shirt based on its colour, saying "That's for girls!" He is using _____ to process information about gender.

a. gender identity

b. a gender schema

c. cross-gender comparison

d. a gender concept

Critical-Thinking Questions

8.6   Think of as many explanations as you can for the fact that children begin to prefer to play with same-sex peers as early as age 3 or 4.

8.7   Why might some children continue to act aggressively when most children's aggressive behaviour changes for the better by the time they start school?

Policy Question

What Are the Effects of Childhood Poverty in Canada?

The proportion of children living in low-income families was hovering around 11% prior to the reccession of 2009 (Statistics Canada, 2009f). However, poverty in Canada is unequally distributed across various family structures and ethnic groups. Just under half of all children in low-income families live in female lone-parent families (40%). Similarly, the low-income rates for Aboriginal (36%) and immigrant children in Canada (41%) are also much higher than the national rate of 18% (Campaign 2000, 2009).

THE EFFECTS OF POVERTY ON FAMILIES AND CHILDREN

For Canadian children, low family income is strongly associated with poorer health and social, emotional, and behavioural problems, as well as lower educational achievement (Phipps & Lethbridge, 2006). The children of low-income families have higher rates of birth defects and early disabilities; they suffer poorer overall health during the first 5 months of life and have higher rates of hospital admission; they recover less readily from early problems; and they are more often ill and undernourished throughout their childhood years (Klerman, 1991; Séguin, Xu, Potvin, Zunzunegui, & Frohlich, 2003). In addition, research shows that as children of low-income families enter school they have higher levels of truancy, lower grades, and 40% higher levels of indirect aggression (Ross, 1998b). In addition, they are more likely to experience hyperactivity, show delayed literacy and math development, have friends who are in trouble, and have lower rates of participation in sports (Ross, 1998a).

Children living in low-income families are also more likely to experience hunger. Although children constitute only 25% of the population, 39% of those using food banks are under age 18 (CCSD, 2001). Specifically, children of the working poor, children of lone-parent families, children of Aboriginal heritage, and children whose families are on social assistance are two to eight times more likely to go hungry than other Canadian children (McIntyre, Walsh, & Conner, 2001). As a result these groups of Canadian children are at risk for malnourishment, which is associated with higher rates of both illness and mortality (Health Canada, 1999f).

It's not poverty per se but the negative consequences it creates that put children at greater risk. Among many other things, poverty reduces options for parents. Children of low-income families have less access to health benefits, child care, safe environments, and recreational and physical activities (CCSD, 2001). Low-income families have little access to services not covered by government health plans, for example, dental care, mental health counselling, and prescription drugs (Health Canada, 1999f). When a low-income mother works, she is likely to have fewer choices of affordable child care. Her children spend more time in poor-quality care and shift more frequently from one care arrangement to another. Low-income families also live in smaller and less-than-adequate housing,

often in decaying neighbourhoods with high rates of violence, and many such families move frequently, which means their children change schools often. The parents are less likely to feel that they have adequate social support, and the children often lack a stable group of playmates (Dodge, Pettit, & Bates, 1994). Parents in these circumstances also tend to be less involved in their children's schools (Griffith, 1998). Overall, the poor live in more chaotic environments, are more highly stressed, and have fewer psychological and social resources than those who are more economically secure (Brooks-Gunn, 1995; Shonkoff, 2010).

Parents living in poverty also tend to treat their children differently than do working-class or middle-class parents. They talk to them less, provide fewer age-appropriate toys, spend less time with them in intellectually stimulating activities, explain things less often and less fully, are less nurturing, and are stricter and more physical in their discipline (Dodge et al., 1994; Sampson & Laub, 1994). A portion of this pattern of parental behaviour is undoubtedly a response to the extraordinary stresses and

(*Photo:* Bruce Ayres/Getty Images)

special demands of living in poverty—a point buttressed by the repeated observation that parents who are poor but who nonetheless feel that they have enough social support are much less likely to be harshly punitive or unsupportive of their children (Hashima & Amato, 1994; Taylor & Roberts, 1995).

Some of the differences in child-rearing patterns between low-income and high-income parents may also result from straightforward modelling of the way the parents themselves were reared, and some may be a product of ignorance of children's needs. Lower-income parents with relatively more education, for example, typically talk to their children more, are more responsive, and provide more intellectual stimulation than do equally poor parents with lower levels of education (Kelley, Sanches-Hucles, & Walker, 1993). But whatever the cause, nearly all children reared in poverty experience physical conditions and interactions with their parents that differ from the experiences of children from high-income families.

THE ROLE OF STRESS

Most children from low-income families develop along the same lines as their more economically secure peers. To help sort out differences between poor children who do well and those who do not, developmentalists think of poverty in terms of accumulated stresses (McLoyd, 1998).

For example, for a child growing up in poverty, perhaps urban poverty especially, the chances of experiencing such multiple stressors are very high indeed. A growing body of evidence shows that the effect of living in a concentrated pocket of poverty is an intensification of all the ill effects of family poverty (Klebanov, Brooks-Gunn, Hofferth, & Duncan, 1995; Kupersmidt, Griesler, DeRosier, Patterson, & Davis,

1995). When the whole neighbourhood is poor, parents have fewer other resources to rely on and children have more violent adult models and fewer supportive ones; rates of child abuse rise, along with rates of aggression and delinquency in children (Coulton, Korbin, Su, & Chow, 1995). When the whole neighbourhood also lacks what sociologists call connectedness and stability—when the adults do not collaborate to monitor the children and do not provide practical or emotional support to one another—the effects are still worse (Wilson, 1995).

IMPETUS FOR CHANGE

In recent years, there has been an upsurge in interest in the importance of early childhood development and how social policy plays a role (Comley & Mousmanis, 2004). In 1999, Fraser Mustard, who received the F.N.G. Starr Award, the Canadian Medical Association's highest honour (CMA, 2001, August 3), and the Honourable Margaret McCain, former new Brunswick Lieutenant-

Governor, co-authored a report for the Ontario government titled "Early Years Study—Reversing the Real Brain Drain." The report emphasizes the impact of nutrition and stimulation on the rapidly developing neural connections within the brain during the first years of life and how these effects persist throughout life. Moreover, the pattern for growth and development later in life is mostly set within the first 3 years of life and thus has an effect on a child's readiness to learn. By age 6, most of the neurological changes that are precursors to lifelong learning, behaviour, and health are complete. Therefore, conditions that contribute to poor neurological development early in life lead to a lifelong disadvantage that is very difficult to reverse and ultimately affects both the individual and Canadian society. The authors of the report call for radical changes in how society supports its young children in all walks of life (McCain & Mustard, 1999, 2002).

(*Photo:* The Canadian Press/Ryan Remiorz)

SOCIAL POLICY ISSUES

There are many different contentious points of view concerning the issues surrounding poverty (CCSD, 2000a; Jackson, 2001; Ross, 1998a). One primary issue is how we should define *low income* itself. Some argue that if you give parents more money they will just squander it on nonessentials, and therefore the poverty line should be drawn at the point where the basic necessities are all that can be provided. This idea, however, fails to address just what constitutes a basic necessity. Some argue that physical needs such as food and shelter are the only needs that require attention. Others suggest that those needs beyond the physical (such as recreation, an intellectually stimulating environment, and health care), if ignored, can lead to long-term outcomes that can carry a major economic cost in the future. They question the wisdom of cutting back on social support to save money today only to create even more difficult and expensive problems in the next generation of adults. Still others argue that Canada is a developed, industrialized nation that values safety, health, civility, and economic and cultural prosperity, and that we who live in such a fair and just society should embrace the ideal that all children should have an equal chance at becoming successful adults.

Generally, as family incomes increase, the children's chances for success increase, but there is no income level below which a child is destined to fail or above which a child is guaranteed to succeed. In addition, it is not just a matter of improving incomes to increase the likelihood of a child's successful transition to adulthood; what is also required is the creation of pathways of opportunity, for example, fair access to public services, education, health care, and recreation. The question of what level of income combined with what level of public support is needed to adequately prepare all Canadian children to meet tomorrow's challenges remains to be answered.

At present a patchwork of social programs exists to deal with the negative consequences of poverty in general and inadequate early childhood support in particular. Some current initiatives include (1) the National Child Benefit (NCB) program, which aims to prevent and reduce the depth of child poverty by providing equalized levels of income support, benefits, and services for children across Canada; (2) the Child Tax Benefit (CTB), which provides relief in the form of tax rebates for the lowest-income families; (3) the Canadian Prenatal Nutrition Program (CPNP) and Community Action Program for Children (CAPC), both of which target the needs of children under 6 years of age; and (4) the on-reserve Aboriginal Head Start (AHS) program.

YOUR TURN

- What are some common perceptions that people have about low-income Canadians and their children?

- In what ways do misconceptions about the poor impede their chances of getting out of poverty?

- Discuss who is responsible for defining the limits of poverty, and justify who should pay for the cost of reducing poverty.

- Explain in what ways it is more than just low family income that creates unfair opportunities for children living in poverty.

- Why should we care about disadvantaged children? Describe how helping all Canadian children to thrive and have the readiness and opportunity to reach their potential can benefit all of society.

CHAPTER 9

Physical and Cognitive Development in Middle Childhood

Throughout the industrialized world, as well as in most developing areas, the years of middle childhood are devoted to formal education. Indeed, the first day of school is considered to be one of the most important transition points in a child's life. In Canada, parents mark the occasion in a variety of ways—with new clothes, fresh school supplies, and carefully selected backpacks and lunch boxes. Some families take pictures of their children's first ride on the school bus or first classroom. All these ways of recognizing this important milestone say to children that this day is unique, and they begin to think of themselves as "big kids" who are engaged in the serious business of going to school, rather than "little kids" who spend most of their time playing.

As important as middle childhood is, however, researchers often pay little attention to these years, as if they were somehow insignificant. Far less research has been done on children in this age group than on either preschoolers or adolescents. Yet it is clear that major cognitive advances occur between ages 6 and 12 and that patterns and habits established during this time will affect not only adolescent experience but also adulthood.

When you finish studying the chapter, you will be able to identify the many physical changes, including those in the brain, that happen between ages 6 and 12; explain how children's linguistic abilities expand significantly during these years, and how children acquire the developmental foundation of adult logic and memory; describe the influence of formal education on a variety of developmental processes; and discuss some factors that shape academic achievement. As you read the chapter, keep the following questions in mind:

- Do you think there is any gain in spatial cognition skills worth the cost of exposing children to the violence found in many video games?
- Why do most societies begin to formally educate children by age 6? What may happen when a child doesn't have a formal education?
- What are some of the advantages of learning to read, write, and speak a second language?

PHYSICAL CHANGES

Although they are more difficult to observe directly, the physical changes of middle childhood are just as impressive as those of early childhood. Standard growth charts that contain height, weight, and body mass indices-for-age percentiles are commonly used for routine monitoring of ideal or optimal physical development and the detection of growth disorders. A collaboration of Canadian health experts (Dietitians of Canada, Canadian Paediatric Society, The College of Family Physicians of Canada, and Community Health Nurses Association of Canada) now recommend using the World Health Organization (WHO) growth charts for monitoring the physical development of Canadian infants, children, and adolescents (Canadian Paediatric Society, 2010).

GROWTH AND MOTOR DEVELOPMENT

Between ages 6 and 12, children grow 5 to 8 centimetres and add about 2.75 kilograms each year. Large-muscle coordination continues to improve, and children become increasingly adept at skills such as bike riding; both strength and speed also increase. Hand–eye coordination improves as well (Woolfolk, Winne, & Perry, 2009). As a result, school-aged children perform more skilfully in activities requiring coordination of vision with body movements, such as shooting a basketball or playing a musical instrument.

Perhaps even more significant is the school-aged child's improving fine motor coordination. Improvements in fine motor coordination make writing possible, as well as the playing of most musical instruments, drawing, cutting, and many other tasks and activities. Such accomplished uses of the hands are made possible by maturation of the wrist, which, as you may recall from earlier chapters, occurs more rapidly in girls than in boys (Woolfolk et al., 2009).

Girls in this age range are ahead of boys in their overall rate of growth as well. By age 12, girls have attained about 93% of their adult height, while boys have reached only 84% of theirs (WHO, 2010). Girls also have slightly more body fat and slightly less muscle tissue than boys. Gender differences in skeletal and muscular maturation cause girls to be better coordinated but slower and somewhat weaker than boys. Thus, girls outperform boys in activities requiring coordinated movement, and boys do better when strength and speed are advantages. Still, the overall gender differences in joint maturation, strength, and speed are small at this age.

When school-aged boys and girls participate in co-ed sports, boys' superior speed and strength is balanced by girls' advantage in coordination. (*Photo:* Cindy Charles/PhotoEdit)

THE BRAIN AND NERVOUS SYSTEM

The overall pattern of brain development during middle childhood shows a steady increase in the myelinization of neural axons across the cerebral cortex (Hua et al., 2009). You'll recall from **Chapter 7** that myelinization is linked to the formation of an increasingly complex network of neural connections. At the beginning of middle childhood, myelinization occurs rapidly in the sensory and motor areas of the brain (Lenroot et al., 2007; Shaw et al., 2008) (see **Chapter 11** for an illustrated description). Development in these areas may be linked to the striking improvements in fine motor skills and hand–eye coordination that usually occur between 6 and 8 years of age.

Brain growth in the frontal lobes of the cerebral cortex becomes the focus of developmental processes later on in middle childhood (Shaw et al., 2008). Of particular importance is the continued myelinization of the reticular formation and of the nerves that link the reticular formation to the frontal lobes (Sowell et al., 2003). Predictably, the areas of the brain that govern logic and planning, two cognitive functions that improve dramatically during this period, are located primarily in the frontal lobes. These connections are essential if the child is to be able to take full advantage of improvements in frontal lobe functions because, as you may recall, the reticular formation controls attention. It is well documented that the ability to control attention increases significantly during middle childhood (Lin, Hsiao, & Chen, 1999; Shaw et al., 2008).

One specific kind of attention, called **selective attention**, is the ability to focus cognitive activity on the important elements of a problem or a situation. For example, suppose your psychology instructor, who usually copies tests on white paper, gives you a test printed on blue paper. You won't spend a lot of time thinking about why the test is blue instead of white; this is an irrelevant detail. Instead, your selective attention skills will prompt you to ignore the colour of the paper and focus on the test questions. In contrast, some younger elementary school children might be so distracted by the unusual colour of the test paper that their test performance is affected. As the nerves connecting the reticular formation and the frontal lobes become more fully myelinated between ages 6 and 12, children begin to function more like adults in the presence of such distractions.

PEARSON
mydevelopmentlab

Connect to MyDevelopmentLab
Participate in this selective attention experiment. See how you compare with other participants in the study.

◄●─ Simulate

selective attention
the ability to focus cognitive activity on the important elements of a problem or a situation

Critical Thinking

Think about how you're using selective attention skills as you read this book. What distractions are you screening out?

association areas
parts of the brain where sensory, motor, and intellectual functions are linked

spatial perception
the ability to identify and act on relationships between objects in space

relative right-left orientation
the ability to identify right and left from multiple perspectives

spatial cognition
the ability to infer rules from and make predictions about the movement of objects in space

The neurons of the **association areas**—parts of the brain where sensory, motor, and intellectual functions are linked—are myelinized to some degree by the time children enter middle childhood. However, from age 6 to 12, the nerve cells in these areas achieve nearly complete myelinization (Shaw et al., 2008). Neuroscientists believe that this advance in the myelinization process contributes to increases in information-processing speed. For example, suppose you were to ask a 6-year-old and a 12-year-old to identify pictures of common items—a bicycle, an apple, a desk, a dog—as rapidly as possible. Both children would know the items' names, but the 12-year-old would be able to produce the names of the items much more rapidly than the 6-year-old. Such increases in processing speed probably contribute to improvements in memory function, which you'll read about later in the chapter (Kail, 1990; Li, Lindenberger, Aschersleben, Prinz, & Baltes, 2004).

Another important advance in middle childhood occurs in the right cerebral hemisphere, with the lateralization of spatial perception, the ability to identify and act on relationships between objects in space. For example, when you imagine how a room would look with a different arrangement of furniture, you are using **spatial perception**. Perception of objects such as faces actually lateralizes before age 6; however, complex spatial perception, such as map-reading, isn't strongly lateralized until about age 8.

A behavioural test of the lateralization of spatial perception neuroscientists often use involves **relative right-left orientation**, the ability to identify right and left from multiple perspectives. Such a test usually shows that most children younger than 8 years old know the difference between their own right and left. Typically, though, only children older than 8 understand the difference between statements like "It's on *your* right" and "It's on *my* right." Lateralization of spatial perception may also be related to the increased efficiency with which older children learn math concepts and problem-solving strategies. In addition, it is somewhat correlated to performance on Piaget's conservation tasks (van der Molen & Molenaar, 1994).

However, the development of spatial perception is more than just a physiological process. Developmentalists know this because this function lateralizes much more slowly in blind children than in those who have sight. Thus, it appears that visual experience plays an important role in this aspect of brain development.

Furthermore, some researchers propose that differences in visual experiences explain gender differences in spatial perception and the related function of **spatial cognition**, the ability to infer rules from and make predictions about the movement of objects in space. For example, when you are driving on a two-lane road and you make a judgment about whether you have enough room to pass a car ahead of you, you are using spatial cognition. From an early age, boys score much higher than girls, on average, on such spatial tasks (Voyer, Voyer, & Bryden, 1995). Some researchers suggest that boys' play preferences, such as their greater interest in constructive activities such as building with blocks, help them develop more acute spatial perception and cognition.

HEALTH PROMOTION AND WELLNESS

Generally speaking, most school-aged children are very healthy as they continue to benefit from regular medical care. However, some school-aged children have undiagnosed health problems, such as vision or hearing problems. Another common childhood problem is sleep disturbance. About one-quarter of children from Grades 6 to 10 have difficulty falling asleep more than once a week, and by Grade 9 about one-third report that they are tired most mornings (Health Canada, 2001b).

IMMUNIZATION Children's immunization history should be reviewed to ensure that optimal vaccination coverage has been achieved. It is also recommended that children age 5 to 13 be vaccinated for Hepatitis B if it was missed during infancy (PHAC, 2006b).

UNINTENTIONAL INJURIES Although the rate of unintentional injury-related deaths has decreased by more than 40% since 1990, unintentional injury remains the most common cause of death (30%) in Canadian children 14 years old and younger (PHAC, 2009b; Statistics Canada, 2009h). The injury-related mortality rate increases with age and is higher for males than females in all age categories. More than half of the fatal injuries in children between ages 5 and 14 are due to motor vehicle crashes, followed by drowning (PHAC, 2009b). By far, the majority of nonfatal unintentional injuries are caused by falls, followed by those caused by being struck by or against an object or another person (e.g., being hit by a puck, colliding with a person).

HEALTHY BODIES AND WEIGHTS Although there has been a reduction across Canada in deaths and hospitalizations due to unintentional injuries, it's not because childrens' environments are necessarily any safer now than in earlier decades. Rather, it's because children are less active: If they don't play outside, walk to school, or ride a bike in their neighbourhood, they are less likely to get injured. Unfortunately, although a convenient and sedentary lifestyle may be safer, it contributes to other health risks (Howard, 2010). Thus, along with unintentional injuries, another significant health risk of the middle childhood period is unhealthy body weights.

Over the past 25 years, we have witnessed an alarming rise in the proportion of Canadian children who have unhealthy body weights. The rates have nearly tripled during this period, and the rates among First Nations children are 2 to 3 times higher than the Canadian average (PHAC, 2010). Nearly 18% of Canadian children between ages 6 and 11 are considered *overweight*, and 8% are *obese* (Shields, 2008).

The primary measure of a child's weight category is the *body mass index* (BMI), which is used to estimate the proportion of body fat to lean body mass. Using the BMI allows health care providers to more accurately identify children who are *underweight*, *overweight*, or *obese* (Canadian Paediatric Society, 2010). A child whose BMI is below the 5th percentile compared to the optimal BMI for his age is considered **underweight**; a BMI above the 85th percentile is generally considered **overweight**, and a child who is above the 95th percentile is classified as **obese**. For optimal growth and health, a child's BMI should fall between the under- and overweight cut-offs.

The longer a child remains overweight, the more likely the child will remain so into the adult years (PHAC, 2010). Only one-fifth of overweight babies become overweight adults, but half of the overweight children in elementary school continue to be overweight in adulthood (Serdula et al., 1993). In addition, overweight and obese children are predisposed to developing a wide range of chronic diseases, such as Type 2 diabetes, cancer, and cardiovascular disease, later in life (PHAC, 2010).

As you might suspect, overeating or eating too much of the wrong foods contributes to obesity in children, just as it does in adults. However, both twin and adoption studies suggest that obesity probably results from a combination of factors: a genetic predisposition, epigenetic modifications set early in life for obesity, and environments that promote overeating and/or low levels of activity (Gluckman & Hanson, 2004a, 2004b; PHAC, 2010). One such environmental factor is the socioeconomic status (SES) of the child's neighbourhood. For example, a NLSCY study found that, for Canadian children between ages 5 and 17, the prevalence of overweight (including obese) children increases from 24% in high SES neighbourhoods to 35% in low SES neighbourhoods and, similarly, the prevalence of obesity alone increases from 7 to 16% respectively (Oliver & Hayes, 2005). An anecdotal finding noted that children's participation in organized sports decreased in less affluent neighbourhoods. Regardless

underweight
a body weight with a low percentage of body fat, which is associated with an increased risk for health problems (i.e., BMI < 18.5)

overweight
a body weight with a high percentage of body fat, which is associated with an increased risk for health problems (i.e., BMI > 25)

obese
a body weight with a high percentage of body fat, which is associated with an increased risk for serious diseases and health problems (i.e., BMI > 30)

An overweight child not only has different kinds of encounters with his peers, but also is more likely to be fat as an adult, with accompanying increased health risks.

(*Photo:* Michael Newman/PhotoEdit)

of the genetic contribution, the decrease in physical activity and increase in the consumption of high-calorie convenience foods has led to the current epidemic of obesity in today's Canadian children (Andersen, 2000).

It's important to keep in mind, though, that weight-loss diets for children can be risky. Since children are still growing, the nutritional needs of obese children differ from those of obese adults (Tershakovec & Stallings, 1998). Consequently, obese children require special diets developed and supervised by nutritional experts. Furthermore, increasing the amount of exercise children get is just as important as changing their eating habits (PHAC, 2010).

The cutbacks in education funding for physical education and after-school sports programs across Canada has helped to decrease children's interest in being physically active as they get older. For instance, both the Canadian Association for Health, Physical Education, Recreation and Dance (CAHPERD) and the Canadian Medical Association (CMA) recommend that children from kindergarten through Grade 12 should have 30 minutes a day of compulsory physical activity, but studies have shown that schools average only 60 minutes a week (Andersen, 2000). An analysis of the NLSCY found that physical activity was especially important for overweight/obese children—an inactive overweight/obese student was more likely to become active and remain active later in childhood if she averaged at least 18 minutes of physical education a day (Pérez, 2003). Not only does a lack of physical exercise contribute to being overweight and poorer health in general, it has also been linked to delayed vocabulary development, lower levels of prosocial behaviour, and lower levels of self-esteem in children (Statistics Canada, 2001c).

One serious consequence of poor nutrition choices and low activity levels is evident in the results from the first major study in 30 years of Canadian childrens' fitness levels. This study highlights a disturbing trend. It compared several measures of fitness (aerobic, flexibility, muscular endurance, and strength), as well as body composition (BMI, waist size, and skinfold measurements) over time. The researchers found significant deterioration in all measures of fitness, coupled with an unhealthy increase in weight due to body fat in both boys and girls across all ages. In short, children are now fatter and weaker than in 1981 (see **Figure 9.1**) (Tremblay et al., 2010).

At the other extreme, fear of developing an unattractive body may become a significant problem for some children. Serious eating disorders (which you'll read about in detail in **Chapter 11**) don't become common until well into adolescence; however, most 6- to 12-year-olds are quite knowledgeable about weight-loss diets and products (Kostanski & Gullone, 1999). Moreover, research suggests that children as young as 7 sometimes express dissatisfaction with their weight or physical appearance, and some begin dieting as early as age 9 (Kostanski & Gullone, 1999; NCHS, 1996; Nutter, 1997). This kind of dissatisfaction can lead to *binge eating and purging*, a pattern that increases the risk of obesity (Tanofsky-Kraff et al., 2004).

It is important to help children develop good eating habits without overemphasizing physical appearance to the extent that children develop patterns of eating that can threaten their later mental and physical health. One way parents can definitely make a difference for all children, regardless of their weight, is to encourage them to be physically active. Simply limiting the time children may spend on television, on computers, and with video games may lead to increases in physical activity (see the **Research Report** below).

But first, more parents need to recognize if their child has a weight problem—a recent Canadian study found that well over one-third of parents were not able to

Research Report

THE EFFECTS OF VIDEO GAMES

Anthropologists propose that video games are one of the many tools industrialized societies can use to teach children the technological and intellectual skills they need as adults (Greenfield, 1994). But like any device we invent, it can have beneficial or damaging effects depending on its use.

Several studies suggest that playing video games has a plus side—video gaming can help boys and, more importantly, girls feel more comfortable with technology; promote teamwork and interpersonal skills when played with others; enhance self-efficacy, self-esteem, and self-confidence through game mastery; foster visual-spatial skills, hand–eye coordination, and fine motor skills; facilitate reading, math, and problem-solving skills; and, in the case of educationally based video games, increase knowledge in various subjects, such as health, history, or science (Atwood, 2004; Chaptman, 2004; Greenfield, Brannon, & Lohr, 1994; Kline, 1998; Lieberman, 1997; Media Awareness Network, 2004a). Despite the positive effects that video gaming can have on learning and development, a strong case has been made that playing video games has a darker side. For one thing, there is some cause for alarm over the amount of time children spend playing video games at the expense of other activities. Communications psychologist Stephen Kline of Simon Fraser University has been investigating the patterns and risks of video gaming. To begin with, he found that almost three-quarters of school-aged children have access to a video game console in the home, and video gaming takes time away from other activities, such as homework, physical activity, and family and peer interactions. Even in the morning, before school, 15.5% of boys, but no girls, reported that they played video games. Kline also found that the majority of parents had rules about video game usage time, but only about one-third of the parents actually monitored or restricted the length of playing time. Of even greater concern, 9 out of 10 children did not have rules about the content of their video games (Kline, 2003). Experts warn us about the adverse effects that video game content can have on personality development and behaviour—especially games with themes of violence, and gender and racial stereotyping (Funk, Buchman, Jenks, & Bechtoldt, 2002; Kline, 1998, 2003; Media Awareness Network, 2004b).

Violent video games appear to be part of a larger set of influences linking preferences for violent stimuli to aggressive behaviour. The more violent TV programs children watch, the more violent the video games they prefer, and the more aggressively they behave toward peers (Mediascope, Inc., 1999). This finding holds for both boys and girls; most girls aren't interested in violent games, but those who are tend to be more physically aggressive than average. In particular, researchers have demonstrated that playing violent video games leads to increased physiological arousal; increased anger, hostility, aggression, and violent behaviour; decreased prosocial behaviours; and is associated with long-term increases in such behaviours (Anderson, 2004; Anderson et al., 2004; Gentile & Anderson, 2003; Anderson, Gentile, & Buckley, 2007; Gentile, Lynch, Linder, & Walsh, 2004). The negative outcomes are even more pronounced for those youth who are "addicted" to playing video games (e.g., those who averaged about 3 hours of video play time a day) (Hauge & Gentile, 2003).

Consequently, parents who observe that aggressive and violent themes characterize most of their children's leisure-time interests as well as their interactions with peers should worry about their children playing video games with violent content (Funk, Buchman, Myers, & Jenks, 2000; Gentile, Walsh, Ellison, Fox, & Cameron, 2004).

Alas, themes of aggression and power dominate the genre, and more than 75% of video games involve violence (Funk & Buchman, 1999). Unfortunately, the very qualities that make video games beneficial teaching tools also make them prime for the building up of aggressive thoughts, feelings, and behaviour. What's more, the engaging, interactive, and reinforcing nature of video games has the potential to be more detrimental than the violence that is transmitted via the relatively more passive medium of television (Anderson et al., 2007; Gentile & Anderson, 2003). Ironically, in Canada, where television and movie content is highly regulated by the Canadian Radio-television and Telecommunications Commission (CRTC), the video gaming industry remains relatively unchecked (Kline, 2002).

Excessive video gaming cuts into the amount of time that is available for other developmentally important activities, such as homework, physical activity, and family and peer interactions.
(*Photo:* Jupiterimages/Creatas Images)

Boy

1981	BODY COMPOSITION	2007–2009
150.9 cm	Height	155.8 cm*
41.6 kg	Weight	48.0 kg*
18.1 kg/m^2	Body mass index	19.2 kg/m^2*
64.9 cm	Waist circumference	66.2 cm
78.0 cm	Hip circumference	84.0 cm*
0.83	Waist-to-hip ratio	0.82*
	FITNESS TEST	
49 kg	Grip strength	44 kg*
26.5 cm	Sit and reach	21.4 cm$_2$*

Girl

1981	BODY COMPOSITION	2007–2009
153.1 cm	Height	155.0 cm
42.7 kg	Weight	47.6 kg
18.4 kg/m^2	Body mass index	19.5 kg/m^2*
62.4 cm	Waist circumference	68.0 cm*
81.2 cm	Hip circumference	86.0 cm*
0.76	Waist-to-hip ratio	0.79*
	FITNESS TEST	
43 kg	Grip strength	40 kg*
32.0 cm	Sit and reach	28.2 cm$_2$*

Figure 9.1

Portrait of Typical 12-year-old Boy and Girl, 1981 and 2007–2009.

Source: Tremblay, M.S., Shields, M., Laviolette, M., Craig, C.L., Janssen, I., & Connor Gorber, S., 2010. Fitness of Canadian children and youth: Results from the 2007–2009 Canadian Health Measures Survey (Catalogue no. 82-003-X). *Health Reports, 21*(1), 7–20. Figure 3, p. 9.

identify their children's weight categories accurately (He & Evans, 2007). Specifically, 22% of parents considered their normal weight children to be underweight; 63% saw their overweight children as normal weight, and the same percentage saw their obese children as merely overweight. Because parents have influence and control over their school-aged children's health behaviour, parents should be encouraged to recognize and acknowledge their children's weight problems. In addition, public health officials suggest that school-based nutrition education and exercise programs can help prevent both obesity and eating disorders (PHAC, 2010).

Before Going On

- Describe the changes in physical development and brain growth, myelinization, and lateralization that happen between ages 6 and 12.
- What are the most important health hazards for 6- to 12-year-olds?

COGNITIVE CHANGES

Along with impressive gains in physical development, children acquire some of the important hallmarks of mature thinking between ages 6 and 12.

LANGUAGE

By age 5 or 6, virtually all children have mastered the basic grammar and pronunciation of their first language, but children of this age still have a fair distance to go before reaching adult levels of fluency. During middle childhood, children become skilled at managing the finer points of grammar (Prat-Sala, Shillcock, & Sorace, 2000; Ragnarsdottir, Simonsen, & Plunkett, 1999). For example, by the end of middle childhood, most children understand various ways of saying something about the past, such as "I went," "I was going," "I have gone," "I had gone," "I had been going," and so on. Moreover, they correctly use such tenses in their own speech. Across the middle childhood years, children also learn how to maintain the topic of conversation, how to create unambiguous sentences, and how to speak politely or persuasively (Anglin, 1993). All these improvements contribute to the school-aged child's emerging mastery of conversation. By age 9, most children are fully capable of engaging in fluent conversation with speakers of any age, and their speech rates approach those of adults (Sturm & Seery, 2007).

Between ages 6 and 12, children also continue to add new vocabulary at a fairly astonishing rate of from 5000 to 10 000 words per year. This estimate comes from several careful studies by developmental psychologist Jeremy Anglin of the University of Waterloo, who estimates children's total vocabularies by testing them on a sample of words drawn at random from a large dictionary (Anglin, 1993, 1995). **Figure 9.2** shows Anglin's estimates for Grades 1, 3, and 5. Anglin found that the largest gain between Grades 3 and 5 occurs in knowledge of the type of words he calls *derived words*—words that have a basic root to which some prefix or suffix is added, such as *happily* or *unwanted*.

Anglin argues that at age 8 or 9 the child shifts to a new level of understanding of the structure of language, figuring out relationships between whole categories of words, such as between adjectives and adverbs (*happy* and *happily*, *sad* and *sadly*), between adjectives and nouns (*happy* and *happiness*), and the like. Once he grasps these relationships, the child can understand and create a whole class of new words, and his vocabulary thereafter increases rapidly.

PIAGET'S CONCRETE OPERATIONAL STAGE

Have you watched a group of children being entertained by a magician? If so, then you may have noticed that younger children, preoperational thinkers in Piaget's terms, don't find magic tricks to be all that interesting. Why? Because, as you'll recall from **Chapter 7**, preoperational thinkers don't really understand the rules that govern physical reality. In middle childhood, children overcome this limitation and, as a result, they know that

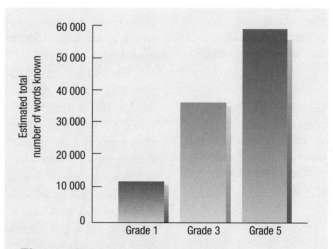

Figure 9.2

Anglin's estimates of the total vocabulary of children in Grades 1, 3, and 5.

(*Source:* Anglin, 1995, from Figure 6, p. 7.)

rabbits cannot be hidden in hats, and birds don't hide in the sleeves of a magician's jacket and fly out on cue. Knowing that the magician is appearing to do something that is physically impossible is what makes his performance interesting. Like adults, the school-aged child wonders "What's the trick?"

There is no better device for demonstrating the school-aged child's capacity for distinguishing between appearance and reality than Piaget's classic conservation tasks (see **Figure 7.4** on page 186). By age 6, most children have begun to show some signs of the **concrete operational stage** and can quickly figure out that a lump of clay has the same mass no matter how its appearance is changed. Thus, this stage is devoted to the construction of schemes that enable children to think logically about objects and events in the real world.

concrete operational stage
Piaget's third stage of cognitive development, during which children construct schemes that enable them to think logically about objects and events in the real world

The stage takes its name from a set of immensely powerful schemes Piaget called *concrete operations*. These operations include mental processes such as *decentration*. You learned about its opposite, centration (thinking in terms of single variables), in the discussion of preoperational thinking in **Chapter 7**. **Decentration** is thinking that takes multiple variables into account. As a result, the school-aged child can see that a clay ball rolled into a sausage shape is not only wider than it was before, but also shorter. Decentration leads him to conclude that the reduced height of the sausage shape compensates for its increased width and that it still has the same amount of clay.

decentration
thinking that takes multiple variables into account

As was mentioned in **Chapter 7**, preoperational children exhibit *irreversibility*, which is the inability to think of some transformed object as it was prior to the transformation. In contrast, concrete operational thinkers display its opposite, **reversibility**—the ability to mentally undo some kind of physical or mental transformation. Piaget thought that reversibility was the most critical of all the concrete operations. The clay sausage in a conservation experiment can be made back into a ball; the water can be poured back into the shorter, wider glass. Understanding of the basic reversibility of actions lies behind many of the gains made during the middle childhood period. For example, if a child has mastered reversibility, then knowing that A is larger than B also tells him that B is smaller than A. The ability to understand hierarchies of classes (such as Fido, spaniel, dog, and animal) also rests on this ability to move both ways in thinking about relationships.

reversibility
the understanding that both physical actions and mental operations can be reversed

Piaget also proposed that during this stage the child develops the ability to use **inductive logic**. She can go from a specific experience to a general principle. For example, she can make assumptions based on specific facts, such as that her friend's parents live in a mansion and have servants working for them; therefore her friend's parents are wealthy.

inductive logic
a type of reasoning in which general principles are inferred from specific experiences

Elementary school children are fairly good observational scientists, and they enjoy activities such as cataloguing rock samples, counting species of trees or birds, and figuring out the nesting habits of guinea pigs. But they are not yet good at **deductive logic** based on hypothetical premises, which requires starting with a general principle and then predicting some outcome or observation—like going from a theory to a hypothesis. For example, children have a general idea of what a fish is from its shape and habitat; a fish is long and sleek and lives underwater. If you ask a child to determine whether a whale is classified as a fish or a mammal, then he may incorrectly classify a whale as a fish because children at this age struggle with the concept that a whale is not a fish even though it has some outward characteristics of a fish. This kind of task is difficult for 6- to 12-year-olds because they must imagine things they have not experienced. The concrete-operations child is good at dealing with things she can see and manipulate or can imagine seeing or manipulating—that is, she is good with *concrete* things; she does not do well with manipulating ideas, abstract concepts, or possibilities. Thus, as the example above illustrates, children respond to deductive problems by generating ideas that are essentially copies of the things they already know about in the concrete world.

deductive logic
a type of reasoning, based on hypothetical premises, that requires predicting a specific outcome from a general principle

DIRECT TESTS OF PIAGET'S VIEW

Piaget understood that it took children some years to apply their new cognitive skills to all kinds of problems, a phenomenon he called *horizontal decalage* (Feldman, 2004). (The French word *decalage* means "a shift.")

HORIZONTAL DECALAGE Researchers have generally found that Piaget was right in his assertion that concrete operational schemes are acquired gradually across the 6- to 12-year-old period. Studies of conservation, for example, consistently show that children grasp conservation of mass or substance by about age 7. That is, they understand that the amount of clay is the same whether it is in a pancake or a ball or some other shape. They generally understand conservation of weight at about age 8, but they don't understand conservation of volume until age 11 (Tomlinson-Keasey, Eisert, Kahle, Hardy-Brown, & Keasey, 1979).

Studies of classification skills show that at about age 7 or 8 the child first grasps the principle of **class inclusion**, the understanding that subordinate classes are included in larger, superordinate classes. Bananas are included in the class of fruit, and fruit is included in the class of food, and so forth. Preschool children understand that bananas are also fruit, but they do not yet fully understand the relationship between the classes.

class inclusion
the understanding that subordinate classes are included in larger, superordinate classes

A good illustration of all these changes comes from an early longitudinal study of concrete operations tasks conducted by Carol Tomlinson-Keasey and her colleagues (Tomlinson-Keasey et al., 1979). They followed a group of 38 children from kindergarten through Grade 3, testing them with five traditional concrete operations tasks each year: conservation of mass, conservation of weight, conservation of volume, class inclusion, and hierarchical classification. (As you recall from **Chapter 7, conservation** is the understanding that matter can change in appearance without changing in quantity.) You can see from **Figure 9.3** that the children got better at all five tasks over the 3-year period, with a spurt between the end of kindergarten and the beginning of Grade 1 (at about the age Piaget thought that concrete operations really arose) and another spurt during Grade 2.

conservation
the understanding that matter can change in appearance without changing in quantity

CONCRETE OPERATIONS AS RULES FOR PROBLEM-SOLVING Other psychologists have conceptualized performance on concrete operational tasks in terms of rules for problem-solving. For example, Robert Siegler's approach is a kind of cross between Piagetian theory and information-processing theory. He argues that cognitive development consists of acquiring a set of basic rules that are then applied to a broader and broader range of problems on the basis of experience. There are no stages, only sequences. Siegler proposes that problem-solving rules emerge from experience—from repeated trial and error and experimentation (Siegler, 1994).

Some of Siegler's own early work on the development of rules illustrates how they may be acquired (Siegler & Chen, 2002). In one test, Siegler used a balance scale with a series of pegs on either side of the centre, like the one in **Figure 9.4**. The child is asked to predict which way the balance will fall, depending on the location and number of disk-shaped weights placed on the pegs. A complete solution requires the child to take into account both the number of disks on each side and the specific location of the disks.

Children do not develop such a complete solution immediately. Instead, Siegler suggests that they develop four rules, in this order: Rule I is basically a preoperational rule, taking into account only one dimension, the number of weights. Children using this rule will predict that the side with more disks will go down, no matter which peg they are placed on. Rule II is a transitional rule. The child still judges on the basis of number, except when the same number of weights appears on each side; in that case the child takes distance from the fulcrum (point of balance) into account. Rule III is basically

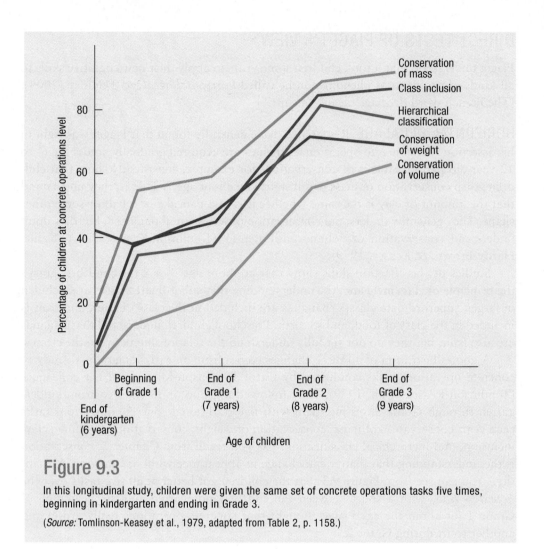

Figure 9.3

In this longitudinal study, children were given the same set of concrete operations tasks five times, beginning in kindergarten and ending in Grade 3.

(*Source:* Tomlinson-Keasey et al., 1979, adapted from Table 2, p. 1158.)

a concrete operational rule; the child tries to take both distance and weight into account simultaneously, except that when the information is conflicting (such as when the side with weights closer to the fulcrum has more weights), the child simply guesses. Rule IV involves the understanding of the actual formula for calculating the combined effect of weight and distance for each side of the balance.

Siegler has found that virtually all children perform on this and similar tasks as if they were following one or another of these rules, and that the rules seem to develop in the given order. Very young children behave as if they don't have a rule (they guess or behave randomly); when they do seem to begin using a rule, Rule I always comes first. But progression from one rule to the next depends heavily on experience. If children are given practice with the balance scale so that they can make predictions and then check which way the balance actually falls, many rapidly develop the next rules in the sequence.

Thus, Siegler is attempting to describe a logical sequence children follow, not unlike the basic sequence of stages that Piaget describes—but Siegler's research shows that a particular child's position in the sequence depends not so much on age as on the child's specific experience with

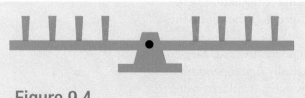

Figure 9.4

This balance scale is similar to what Siegler used in his experiments.

a given set of material. In Piaget's terminology, this is rather like saying that when accommodation of some scheme occurs, it always occurs in a particular sequence, but the rate at which the child moves through that sequence depends on experience.

ADVANCES IN INFORMATION-PROCESSING SKILLS

As they progress through the middle childhood years, children are able to remember longer and longer lists of numbers, letters, or words, as illustrated in **Figure 9.5**. In fact, children's memories function so well that their testimony about events they have witnessed is usually accurate enough to be regarded as reliable in judicial proceedings.

PROCESSING EFFICIENCY Processing **efficiency**, the ability to make efficient use of short-term memory capacity, increases steadily with age, a change that most developmentalists now see as the basis for cognitive development (Case, 1985; Li et al., 2004; Swanson & Kim, 2007). The best evidence that cognitive processing becomes more efficient is that it gets steadily faster with age. Robert Kail has found virtually the same exponential increase in processing speed with age for a wide variety of tasks, including perceptual-motor tasks, such as tapping in response to a stimulus (e.g., pressing a button when you hear a buzzer), and cognitive tasks, such as mental addition (Kail, 1991; Kail & Hall, 1994). He has found virtually identical patterns of speed increases in studies in cross-cultural studies.

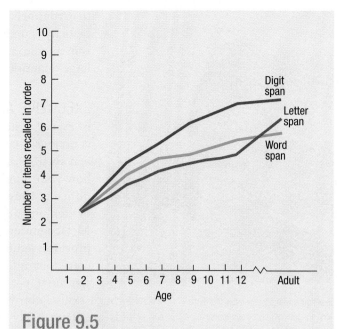

Figure 9.5

Psychologists measure basic memory capacity by asking participants to listen to a list of numbers, letters, or words, and then to repeat back the list in order. This figure shows the number of such items children of various ages are able to remember and report accurately.

(*Source:* Dempster, 1981, from Figures 1, 2, and 3, pp. 66, 67, 68.)

processing efficiency
the ability to make efficient use of short-term memory capacity

AUTOMATICITY One of the most important ways in which processing efficiency grows in middle childhood is through the acquisition of **automaticity**, or the ability to recall information from long-term memory without using short-term memory capacity. For example, when children can respond "49" to the question "How much is 7 times 7?" without thinking about it, they have achieved automaticity with respect to that particular piece of information.

Automaticity is critical to efficient information processing because it frees up short-term memory space for more complex processing. Thus, the child who knows "7 times 7" automatically can use that fact in a complex multiplication or division problem without giving up any of the short-term memory space he is using to solve the problem. As a result, he is better able to concentrate on the "big picture" instead of expending effort trying to recall a simple multiplication fact. Not surprisingly, researchers have found that elementary school children who have *automatized* basic math facts in this way learn complex computational skills more rapidly (Jensen & Whang, 1994).

Automaticity is achieved primarily through practice. For example, when babies first learn to walk, they must focus all their mental effort on the act of walking. After a few weeks of practice, walking becomes automatic, and they can think about chasing the family cat or retrieving a ball that has rolled away. Likewise, adults can think about the grocery list while driving to the supermarket, because driving skills and the routes

automaticity
the ability to recall information from long-term memory without using short-term memory capacity

Experience with a teeter-totter, like these girls are getting, may be one source of knowledge about how balance scales work. (*Photo:* Goodshoot/Thinkstock)

executive processes
information-processing skills that involve devising and carrying out strategies for remembering and problem-solving

memory strategies
learned methods for remembering information

Unless they are rank novices, these school-aged chess players will remember a series of chess moves or an arrangement of chess pieces far better than adults who don't play chess. (*Photo:* © Alistair Berg/Digital Vision/ Getty Images)

they routinely use to get from place to place are automatized. Thus, automaticity is important to information processing throughout the lifespan. It is in middle childhood, however, that children seem to begin automatizing large quantities of information and skills at a fairly rapid rate.

EXECUTIVE AND STRATEGIC PROCESSES If you tried to recall a list of everyday items (e.g., chair, pencil, spaghetti, tree . . .), then you might consciously consider the various alternative strategies for remembering and then select the best one. You could also explain some things about how your mind works, such as which kinds of mental tasks you find most difficult. These are examples of *metacognition*—knowing about knowing or thinking about thinking—a set of skills first mentioned in **Chapter** 7. Metacognition is part of a large group of skills known as **executive processes**—information-processing skills that allow a person to devise and carry out alternative strategies for remembering and problem-solving. Executive processes are based on a basic understanding of how the mind works. Such skills improve a great deal during middle childhood. For example, 10-year-olds are more likely than 8-year-olds to understand that attending to a story requires effort (Parault & Schwanenflugel, 2000).

One of the advantages of having good metacognitive and executive processing skills is that they help the individual devise methods for remembering information, or **memory strategies**. Although many people possess their own unique methods for remembering, **Table 9.1** lists a few common memory strategies. For the most part, these memory techniques first appear between ages 6 and 12.

EXPERTISE A great deal of research shows that the amount of knowledge a person possesses makes a huge difference in how efficiently her information-processing system works. Children and adults who know a lot about a topic (dinosaurs, baseball cards, mathematics, or whatever it may be) categorize information about that topic in highly complex and hierarchical ways. They are also better at remembering and logically analyzing new information on that topic (Ni, 1998).

Even typical age differences in strategy use or memory ability disappear when the younger group has more expertise than the older. For example, psychologist Michelene Chi, in her now-classic early study, showed that expert chess players could remember the placement of chess pieces on a board much more quickly and accurately than novice chess players, even when the expert chess players were children and the novices were adults (Chi, 1978). In addition, children's capacity for creativity appears to greatly depend on how much knowledge they have about a topic (Sak & Maker, 2006).

However, using advanced information-processing skills in their areas of expertise doesn't seem to help children's general memory and reasoning abilities (Ericsson & Crutcher, 1990). For this reason, many information-processing psychologists, such as the Canadian researcher Corinne Zimmerman, now believe that an individual's information-processing skills may depend entirely on the quantity and quality of relevant information stored in long-term memory. Thus, they say, to be able to learn scientific reasoning skills, for example, children must first acquire a body of knowledge about scientific topics (Zimmerman, 2000). To paraphrase developmental psychologist John Flavell, expertise makes any of us, including children, look very smart; lack of expertise makes us look very stupid (Flavell, 1986).

TABLE 9.1	Some Common Information-Processing Strategies Used in Remembering
Strategy	**Description**
Rehearsal	Either mental or vocal repetition; may occur in children as young as 2 years under some conditions, and is common in older children and adults.
Organization	Grouping ideas, objects, or words into clusters to help in remembering them, such as "all animals," or "the ingredients in the lasagna recipe," or "the chess pieces involved in the move called *castling*." This strategy is more easily applied to something a person has experience with or particular knowledge about. Two-year-olds use primitive clustering strategies.
Elaboration	Finding shared meaning or a common referent for two or more things that need to be remembered.
Mnemonic	A device to assist memory; the phrase for the notes of the lines on the musical staff ("Every Good Boy Does Fine") is a mnemonic.
Systematic Searching	"Scanning" one's memory for the whole domain in which a piece of information might be found. Three- and 4-year-old children can begin to do this when they search for actual objects in the real world, but they are not good at doing this in memory. So search strategies may first be learned in the external world and then applied to inner searches.

(*Source:* Flavell, 1985.)

Before Going On

- Describe vocabulary growth during middle childhood and the cognitive advantages children gain as they move through Piaget's concrete operational stage.

- Explain the contributions of processing efficiency, automaticity, metacognition and strategic processes, and expertise to the development of information-processing skills.

SCHOOLING

As you learned at the beginning of this chapter, children all over the world begin school by age 6 or 7. Thus, an examination of the influence of this near-universal experience is important to understanding middle childhood. And, because of its academic focus and the amount of time that children spend in school, formal education is one of the most important influences on the cognitive development of 6- to 12-year-olds.

LITERACY

In the industrialized world, *literacy*, the ability to read and write, is the focus of education in the 6- to 12-year-old period. As you learned in **Chapter 7**, the skills children bring to school from their early childhood experiences may influence early reading as much as formal instruction does (Crone & Whitehurst, 1999). Especially significant among these skills is the set known as *phonological awareness* (Anthony & Lonigan, 2004; Parrila, Kirby, & McQuarrie, 2004; Schatschneider, Fletcher, Francis, Carlson, & Foorman, 2004). Across the early elementary years, phonological awareness skills continue to increase (Shu, Anderson, & Wu, 2000). Thus, children who lack such expertise at the start of school are likely to fall behind unless some systematic effort is made by teachers to provide them with a base of phonological knowledge (Torgesen et al., 1999). However, all beginning readers, both those who have high levels of phonological awareness and those who know less about sounds and symbols, seem to benefit from specific instruction in sound–letter correspondences (Adams & Henry, 1997). Moreover, beginning readers gain a significant advantage when they develop automaticity with respect to sound–letter correspondences and can effectively sound out words, or have "cracked the code," as some researchers put it.

balanced approach
reading instruction that combines explicit phonics instruction with other strategies for helping children acquire literacy

Nevertheless, advocates of the **balanced approach** to reading instruction point out that teachers must move beyond basic phonics. In guided reading sessions, for instance, teachers work with small groups of children on reading books that are somewhat challenging for them (recall Vygotsky's zone of proximal development) (Iaquinta, 2006). When a child makes an error, the teacher uses the opportunity to explain a reading strategy or one of the many idiosyncrasies of written English to all the children in the group. Proponents of the balanced approach also point to studies showing that, in the later elementary grades, attainment of reading fluency requires that children learn about meaningful word parts, such as prefixes and suffixes (Adams & Henry, 1997; McBride-Chang, Shu, Zhou, & Wagner, 2004; Nagy, Berninger, Abbott, Vaughan, & Vermeulen, 2004). At the same time, instruction in comprehension strategies, such as identifying the purpose of a particular text, also helps (Van den Broek, Lynch, Naslund, Ievers-Landis, & Verduin, 2004). Of course, throughout learning to read, children need to be exposed to good literature, both in their own reading and in what teachers and parents read to them.

Some of the strategies used to teach reading also help children learn writing, the other component of literacy; for example, instruction in sound–letter connections helps children learn to spell as well as to read. Of course, good writing is far more than just spelling; it requires instruction and practice, just as reading does. Specifically, children need to learn about writing techniques such as outlining and paragraph development to become good writers. They also need to learn about language mechanics, such as grammar and appropriate uses of words, as well as how to edit their own and others' written work (Graham & Harris, 1997).

Despite educators' best efforts, many children fall behind their classmates in literacy during the early school years. In general, reading researchers have found that poor readers have problems with sound–letter combinations (Agnew, Dorn, & Eden, 2004; Gonzalez & Valle, 2000; Mayringer & Wimmer, 2000). Thus, many children who have reading difficulties benefit from highly specific phonics approaches that provide a great deal of practice in translating letters into sounds and vice versa (Berninger et al., 1999; Koppenhaver, Hendrix, & Williams, 2007).

Curriculum flexibility is also important in programs for poor readers (Johnston, Barnes, & Desrochers, 2008). Some children do not improve when exposed to phonics approaches. In fact, programs that combine sound–letter and comprehension training, such as the Reading Recovery program, have proven to be highly successful in helping poor readers catch up, especially when the programs are implemented in the early elementary years (Klein & Swartz, 1996). Consequently, teachers need to be able to assess the effectiveness of whatever approach they are using and change it to fit the needs of individual students.

SCHOOLING AND COGNITIVE DEVELOPMENT

Studies across a variety of cultures—in Mexico, Peru, Colombia, Liberia, Kenya, Zambia, Nigeria, Uganda, Hong Kong, and many other countries—have led to the conclusion that school experiences are indeed linked to the emergence of some advanced cognitive skills over and above that of normal maturation (Alcock, Holding, Mung'ala-Odera & Newton, 2008; Mishra, 1997). For example, children who do not attend school proceed through Piaget's concrete operational stage at a much slower rate. It's important to note, too, that most of these studies compared children who differed only in schooling; the children were of the same ethnicity and were similar in socioeconomic status.

You might think that rate of cognitive development doesn't matter, so long as everyone gets to the same place developmentally; however, longitudinal studies show that the rate of progression through the concrete operational stage predicts how well children will reason in adolescence and adulthood (Bradmetz, 1999). Thus, the cognitive-developmental advantage that a 6- to 12-year-old gains by attending school is one that probably lasts a lifetime.

Unschooled children are also less proficient at generalizing a learned concept or principle to some new setting. A good illustration comes from studies of South American street vendors, most of whom are of elementary school age. These children can carry out monetary calculations with lightning speed and impressive accuracy, yet they have trouble translating their mental calculations into written mathematical problems (Schliemann, Carraher, & Ceci, 1997). It seems that the "language" of mathematics that children learn in school helps them acquire number knowledge in a far more abstract way than children whose calculation skills originate exclusively from a practical context. Thus, attending school helps children learn to think—precisely what it is intended to do.

MEASURING AND PREDICTING ACHIEVEMENT

Canada lacks a single education system, since each province and territory is entitled to establish its own formal curriculum and school organization. Nonetheless, there has been some harmonization across the nation. For instance, Grades 6 and 10 have a common educational structure and content from province to province. Another initiative to harmonize education has been the creation of the Council of Ministers of Education, Canada (CMEC, 2006). The CMEC has been working on the development of a common Canadian curriculum and national testing standards with measurable outcomes for English, math, and science at Grades 3, 6, and 9.

TYPES OF TESTS Standardized **achievement tests** are designed to assess specific information learned in school, using items such as those in **Table 9.2**. Scores are based on the comparison of an individual child's performance with those of other children in the same grade across Canada. Critics of achievement tests point out that, although these tests are intended to measure what children learn in school, they are actually very similar to IQ tests. For example, suppose an achievement test contains the math problem "4 × 4." Bright children who have not yet learned multiplication may reason their way to the correct answer of 16. Others may answer correctly because they have learned it in school. Still others may know the answer because they learned to multiply from their parents. Thus, critics suggest that comprehensive portfolios of children's school work may be better indicators of actual school learning than standardized achievement tests (Neill, 1998). In comparison to achievement measures, educators conducting a student **assessment** will use a variety of formal and informal assessment

achievement test
a test designed to assess specific information learned in school

assessment
formal and informal methods of gathering information that can be used for programming to improve student learning. No grades or marks are associated with assessment.

Children's experiences in school are similar the world over. The similarities help to explain why cognitive-developmental research involving 6- to 12-year-olds yields pretty much the same results in all cultures where children attend school. (*Photos,* left to right: A. Ramey/Woodfin Camp and Associates; © Joseph Sohm/Visions of America/Corbis; S. Noorani/Woodfin Camp and Associates)

evaluation

the process of assigning a grade or mark to a student's performance, representing the student's highest, most consistent level of achievement over time

Explore

tools to gather information that can be used to improve student learning at a developmentally appropriate level. Assessment is an ongoing process, and students are encouraged to be involved in the assessment process and in finding ways to improve.

In Canada, the trend is toward evaluating a student in terms of age-appropriate provincial or territorial standards. Accordingly, educators make an **evaluation** by calculating each student's highest, most consistent level of performance for each subject to assign a grade or level at any given point. This approach can offer a student a more valid measure of his achievement in terms of his own performance against the provincial standard rather than comparing his performance with that of his peers in the classroom (R. Windsor, personal communication, October 4, 2001). In contrast, the old model of evaluation served primarily to differentiate students based solely on their grade averages and to "ultimately determine who [would] be eligible to attend post-secondary education and reap the status and economic rewards that typically result" (Health Canada, 2001b, p. 14).

THEORIES OF INTELLIGENCE Unlike in previous decades, intellectual assessment in Canadian schools is no longer routinely used to assess students. Intelligence testing (using tools such as the WISC described in **Chapter 7**) is now primarily used to identify a student as exceptional in preparation for special educational programming support (R. Windsor, personal communication, October 4, 2001). In fact, some developmentalists say that the problem with relying on IQ tests to predict achievement is that they fail to provide a complete picture of mental abilities. For example, psychologist Howard

TABLE 9.2	Some Sample Items from a Junior-Grade-Level Achievement Test	
Vocabulary	**Reference Skills**	**Mathematics**
jolly old man 1. angry 2. fat 3. merry 4. sorry	Which of these words would be first in ABC order? 1. pair 2. point 3. paint 4. polish	What does the 3 in 13 stand for? 1. 3 ones 2. 13 ones 3. 3 tens 4. 13 tens
Language Expression	**Spelling**	**Mathematics Computation**
Who wants ____ books? 1. that 2. these 3. them 4. this	Jason took the *cleanest* glass. right ____ wrong ____	79 149 62 +14 −87 ×3

(*Source:* From *Comprehensive Tests of Basic Skills,* Form S. Reprinted by permission of the publisher, CTB/McGraw-Hill, Del Monte Research Park, Monterey, CA 93940. Copyright © 1973 by McGraw-Hill, Inc. All rights reserved. Printed in the USA.)

Gardner proposed a theory of *multiple intelligences* (Gardner, 1983, 1999). This theory claims there are eight types of intelligence:

- *Linguistic*—the ability to use language effectively. People who are good writers or speakers, who learn languages easily, or who possess a lot of knowledge about language possess greater than average linguistic intelligence.

- *Logical/mathematical*—facility with numbers and logical problem-solving. Logical/mathematical intelligence enables individuals to learn math and to generate logical solutions to various kinds of problems.

- *Musical*—the ability to appreciate and produce music. Musicians, singers, composers, and conductors possess musical intelligence.

- *Spatial*—the ability to appreciate spatial relationships. Spatial intelligence is involved in the production and appreciation of works of art, such as paintings and sculptures.

- *Bodily kinesthetic*—the ability to move in a coordinated way, combined with a sense of one's body in space. Professional athletes and top-notch amateur ones must possess high levels of this kind of intelligence.

- *Naturalist*—the ability to make fine discriminations among the flora and fauna of the natural world or the patterns and designs of human artifacts.

- *Interpersonal*—sensitivity to the behaviour, moods, and needs of others. "Helping" professionals—counsellors, social workers, clergy, and the like—usually need to have relatively high levels of interpersonal intelligence.

- *Intrapersonal*—the ability to understand oneself. People who are good at identifying their own strengths and choosing goals accordingly have high levels of intrapersonal intelligence.

Gardner's theory is based on observations of people with brain damage, mental retardation, and other severe mental handicaps. He points out that brain damage usually causes disruption of functioning in very specific mental abilities rather than a general decline in intelligence. He also notes that many individuals with mental deficits have remarkable talents. For example, some are gifted in music, while others can perform complex mathematical computations without using a calculator or pencil and paper.

Robert Sternberg's *triarchic theory of intelligence* proposes three components of human intelligence (Sternberg, 1988). *Contextual intelligence* has to do with knowing the right behaviour for a specific situation. For example, the South American street children you read about earlier (who are good at doing practical calculations but perform poorly on more abstract math problems) are highly "intelligent" in their daily context. However, in the school context, they appear to lack intellectual ability.

Experiential intelligence, according to Sternberg, is measured by IQ tests. It involves learning to give specific responses without thinking about them. For example, you can probably respond without thinking to the question "How much is 7 times 7?" IQ tests contain many such questions.

Componential intelligence is a person's ability to come up with effective strategies. To Sternberg, this component of intelligence is the most important. He claims that intelligence tests put more emphasis on "correctness" of answers than on the quality of the strategies people use to arrive at them.

In general, Sternberg says, IQ tests measure how familiar a child is with "school" culture. Thus, children whose cultural background does not include formal schooling perform poorly because they are unfamiliar with the context of the test. Unfortunately,

PEARSON
mydevelopmentlab
Connect to
MyDevelopmentLab
Challenge yourself. Can you match Gardner's theory to each of these scenarios?

⬅⊙ Simulate

their poor performance is often mistakenly interpreted to mean that they lack intelligence (Sternberg & Grigorenko, 2006). Sternberg believes that intelligence tests should measure all three components of intelligence, and he has produced some research evidence suggesting that testing procedures based on his theory yield better predictions of performance than do conventional IQ tests (Sternberg, Wagner, Williams, & Horvath, 1995).

EMOTIONAL INTELLIGENCE Both Gardner's and Sternberg's theories have become important in helping educators understand the weaknesses of IQ tests. Moreover, psychologist Daniel Goleman's theory of *emotional intelligence* has also added to scientists' understanding of intelligence and achievement (Goleman, 1995). Emotional intelligence has three components: awareness of one's own emotions, the ability to express one's emotions appropriately, and the capacity to channel emotions into the pursuit of worthwhile goals. Without emotional intelligence, Goleman claims, it is impossible to achieve one's intellectual potential. However, research has yet to provide support for Goleman's hypothesis (Humphrey, Curran, Morris, Farrell, & Woods, 2007). Still, research on the relationship between self-control (the third component of emotional intelligence) in early childhood and achievement in adolescence suggests that Goleman's view is correct. Children's ability to exercise control over their emotions in early childhood is strongly related to measures of academic achievement in high school (Denham, 2006).

Before Going On

- List the components of good literacy instruction, and describe how schooled and unschooled children differ in cognitive development.
- Describe the purpose and content of standardized achievement tests.

INDIVIDUAL AND GROUP DIFFERENCES

A number of individual and group variables are associated with school performance (see **Table 9.3**). Various disabilities and attention problems are correlated with achievement in some way, as are language proficiency, gender, and culture. Canadian educators are now moving away from the use of labels for learning problems and instead place emphasis on a child's academic strengths and style of processing information in order to increase the likelihood of her school success (see **Development in the Real World**).

LEARNING DISABILITIES

learning disability
a disorder in which a child has difficulty mastering a specific academic skill, even though she possesses average to above-average intelligence and has no physical or sensory handicaps

Some children are born with or develop differences that may significantly interfere with their education unless they receive some kind of special instruction. For instance, 10 to 15% of the Canadian population may experience learning problems that are a continuation of learning disabilities from early childhood (Learning Disabilities Association of Canada [LDAC], 2000). The **learning disability** concept itself is still controversial, but it is generally associated with a difficulty in attaining a specific academic skill, despite possessing average to above-average intelligence, that is not due primarily to

TABLE 9.3	Categories of Exceptionalities in Canadian Schools
Exceptionality Category	**Description of Exceptionality**
Behaviour Disorders	Conduct disorders, social maladjustment, ADHD, and emotional disorders
Communication Disorders	Language impairment, speech impairment, and learning disability
Sensory Impairments	Deafness and hearing impairment, blindness and low vision
Intellectual Differences	Giftedness, mild intellectual disability, and developmental disability
Pervasive Developmental Disorders	Childhood psychosis, childhood schizophrenia, and infantile autism
Physical Disorders and Impaired Health	Neurological defects, physical disability, and conditions that result from infection and disease
Multiple	Multiple exceptionalities from any of the above categories

(*Sources:* Weber, 1993; Winzer, 1993.)

exceptional child
a child who has special learning needs; the term refers to students with disabilities as well as gifted students

program accommodation
the adjustment of teaching methods to help a child with special needs achieve the outcomes of the standard curriculum

modified program
changes in the curriculum so that the modified outcomes differ from those of the standard curriculum

Development in the Real World

CANADIAN SPECIAL EDUCATION PRACTICES

Educators are following a general trend away from the use of labels for learning problems and toward a focus on a child's academic strengths and style of processing information. Across Canada an **exceptional child** who has special learning needs typically remains integrated in the same class as his same-aged peers. The teacher can introduce a program accommodation or a program modification and adjust her teaching methods to the child's special needs. The exceptional child may also have access to and receive assistance from special education teachers and educational assistants.

In **program accommodations**, an exceptional child is exposed to the same curriculum as his peers and his performance is compared with the same standard outcomes for his grade level, but the classroom teacher makes accommodations for him so that he is allowed to demonstrate his learning in a nonstandard way. Less emphasis is placed on what the student cannot do and more on how he can develop alternative methods of achieving the same outcomes. For example, if a student is required to demonstrate that she understands a specific math concept but she is not good with number functions, then she would be allowed to use a calculator as long as she could explain how she got the answer. In this way, she is measured for her ability to understand math concepts as opposed to being (inadvertently) measured for her ability to use number facts. Other examples include a student who is offered an oral exam because he has difficulty with writing answers down, and a student who is allowed to sit at the front of the classroom because she is easily distracted.

Sometimes a **modified program** is required, whereby the standard curriculum itself is changed so that the modified outcomes are different from the standard outcomes. For example, a student in Grade 5 may be working on a Grade 2 reading program but a Grade 5 program in all other subject areas. Exceptional students are legally designated as such, and require an **Individual Education Plan (IEP)**. The Special Education teacher, in consultation with the child, the parents, the teacher, and any relevant community partners (e.g., social worker or pediatrician), develops the IEP and reviews it annually.

School can be a discouraging and frustrating place for a child with a learning disability.
(*Photo:* Michael Newman/PhotoEdit)

Individual Education Plan (IEP) a written document containing learning and behavioural objectives for the exceptional student, a description of how the objectives will be achieved, and how the objectives will be evaluated

physical or sensory handicaps. It includes a range of conditions that selectively interfere with learning, academic progress, and social competence. To clarify the meaning of learning disability, the LDAC has developed a national definition that educators, parents, and individuals with a learning disability can agree on (see **Figure 9.6**).

Explanations of the problem are subject to disagreement, which makes for inconsistent special education policies across Canada's provinces and territories (Kozey & Siegel, 2008). Some experts argue that children with learning disabilities (especially reading disabilities) may simply have a more general problem with understanding the sound and structure of language (Torgesen et al., 1999). Others, in particular some Canadian neuropsychologists, contend that a learning disability results from a neurobiological problem (Fiedorowicz, 1999; Fiedorowicz et al., 1999, 2002). For example, a large number of small abnormalities, such as irregularity of neuron arrangement,

---

"Learning disabilities" refer to a number of disorders which may affect the acquisition, organization, retention, understanding or use of verbal or nonverbal information. These disorders affect learning in individuals who otherwise demonstrate at least average abilities essential for thinking and/or reasoning. As such, learning disabilities are distinct from global intellectual deficiency.

Learning disabilities result from impairments in one or more processes related to perceiving, thinking, remembering or learning. These include, but are not limited to: language processing; phonological processing; visual spatial processing; processing speed; memory and attention; and executive functions (e.g. planning and decision-making).

Learning disabilities range in severity and may interfere with the acquisition and use of one or more of the following:

- oral language (e.g. listening, speaking, understanding);

- reading (e.g. decoding, phonetic knowledge, word recognition, comprehension);

- written language (e.g. spelling and written expression); and

- mathematics (e.g. computation, problem solving).

Learning disabilities may also involve difficulties with organizational skills, social perception, social interaction and perspective taking.

Learning disabilities are lifelong. The way in which they are expressed may vary over an individual's lifetime, depending on the interaction between the demands of the environment and the individual's strengths and needs. Learning disabilities are suggested by unexpected academic underachievement or achievement which is maintained only by unusually high levels of effort and support.

Learning disabilities are due to genetic and/or neurobiological factors or injury that alters brain functioning in a manner which affects one or more processes related to learning. These disorders are not due primarily to hearing and/or vision problems, socioeconomic factors, cultural or linguistic differences, lack of motivation or ineffective teaching, although these factors may further complicate the challenges faced by individuals with learning disabilities. Learning disabilities may coexist with various conditions including attentional, behavioural, and emotional disorders, sensory impairments, or other medical conditions.

For success, individuals with learning disabilities require early identification and timely specialized assessments and interventions involving home, school, community, and workplace settings. The interventions need to be appropriate for each individual's learning disability subtype and, at a minimum, include the provision of:

- specific skill instruction;

- accommodations;

- compensatory strategies; and

- self-advocacy skills

Figure 9.6

Canadian Definition of Learning Disability

(*Source:* Learning Disabilities Association of Canada (2002). Adopted by the Learning Disabilities Association of Canada on January 30, 2003; reprinted with permission.)

clumps of immature brain cells, scars, or congenital tumours, may develop in the brain during prenatal life. The growing brain compensates for these problems by "rewiring" around the problem areas. These rewirings, in turn, may scramble normal information-processing pathways just enough to make reading or calculation or some other specific task very difficult (Farnham-Diggory, 1992). Some evidence also suggests that learning disabilities, especially dyslexia, may have a genetic basis (Bates et al., 2007; Fiedorowicz et al., 1999, 2002; Gallagher, Frith, & Snowling, 2000).

When reading is the problem skill, the term **dyslexia** is often used (even though, technically speaking, *dyslexia* refers to a total absence of reading). Most children with reading disabilities can read but not as well as others their age. Moreover, it appears that their skill deficits are specific to reading, such as an inability to automatize sound–letter correspondences or weak *morphological awareness* (the ability to understand and correctly use small words, letters, and letter combinations, i.e., prefixes, suffixes, and roots, to create new meanings), rather than the result of a general cognitive dysfunction (Siegel, 2008; Wimmer, Mayringer, & Landerl, 1998).

dyslexia
problems in reading or the inability to read

ATTENTION-DEFICIT/HYPERACTIVITY DISORDER

Some children experience learning difficulties that don't seem to fit the typical special education categories. For example, an estimated 5 to 10% of Canadian school children have a mental disorder called **Attention-Deficit/Hyperactivity Disorder** (ADHD) (Romano, Baillargeon, & Tremblay, 2002). Children with ADHD are more physically active and/or less attentive than their peers. These characteristics often lead to both academic and behavioural problems in school. Therefore, ADHD is considered to be a mental disorder that may cause a child to develop school problems.

Attention-Deficit/Hyperactivity Disorder (ADHD)
a mental disorder that causes children to have difficulty attending to and completing tasks

CAUSES OF ADHD The cause of ADHD is unknown. However, some developmentalists suggest that children with ADHD are neurologically different from their peers. Specifically, some have asserted that children with ADHD have functional deficits in the right hemisphere of the brain (Sandson, Bachna, & Morin, 2000). Indeed, some type of biological factor does seem to be involved, as children who were born at 24 to 31 weeks of gestation are four to six times as likely to suffer from the symptoms of ADHD than their peers who were full-term infants (Barlow & Lewandowski, 2000). Other developmentalists hypothesize that children with ADHD require more sensory stimulation than their peers; thus, they move around more to get the stimulation they need (Antrop, Roeyers, Van Oost, & Buysse, 2000).

Psychologists are fairly sure that diet, environmental toxins, or brain damage is not the cause of ADHD, despite what some promoters of "cures" claim (Spreen et al., 1995). At present, most experts believe that each individual case of ADHD is caused by a complex interaction of factors that are unique to the specific child. These factors may include genetics, temperament, parenting styles, peer relations, the type and quality of school a child attends, and stressors in the child's life, such as poverty, family instability, and parental mental illness.

Researchers at the Ontario Institute for Studies in Education (OISE) have been investigating the association between sleep problems and ADHD. They determined that one of the challenges of studying the relationship between ADHD and sleep problems is that both conditions are intertwined with multiple other conditions. Common to anxiety disorders, depressive disorders, and ADHD is a difficulty in falling asleep and/or staying asleep (Corkum, Moldofsky, Hogg-Johnson, Humphries, & Tannock, 1999). Despite the difficulties of studying ADHD and sleep problems, there are some consistent findings. For example, ADHD children display more movements in their sleep than children without the disorder (Corkum, Tannock, & Moldofsky, 1998).

true sleep
the number of minutes of sleep time excluding all periods of wakefulness, which can be distinguished by electroencephalograph (EEG) activity

ADHD children also display instability in sleep onset, sleep duration, and **true sleep** (the number of minutes of sleep time excluding all periods of wakefulness, which can be distinguished by electroencephalograph [EEG] activity), and therefore it may be important to determine the impact that a disturbed sleep has on daytime behaviour (Gruber, Sadeh, & Raviv, 2000). For instance, sleep-deprived children may display hyperactivity, lack of coordination, and learning difficulty, all signs that could be mistaken for ADHD (Divgi, 2000). Low levels of true sleep time have been accurately predicted from teacher-reported behavioural symptoms such as attention and social problems (Aronen, Paavonen, Fjällberg, Soininen, & Törrönen, 2000).

👁 Watch

CHARACTERISTICS OF ADHD On many kinds of attention tasks, ADHD children do not differ at all from normal children. They seem to vary from their normal peers in activity level, the ability to sustain attention (especially with boring and repetitive tasks), and the ability to control impulses. However, the degree of hyperactivity that ADHD children exhibit is unrelated to their performance on attention tasks. That is, a child can be very physically active and still be good at controlling his attention. Likewise, a child can be very calm yet have little ability to sustain attention. For this reason, there are now two types of ADHD: (1) the hyperactive/impulsive type, in which a high activity level is the main problem; and (2) the inattentive type, in which an inability to sustain attention is the major difficulty (American Psychiatric Association, 2000).

Most children with ADHD are successful in learning academic skills (Chadwick et al., 1999). However, their hyperactivity and/or inattentiveness often cause other kinds of problems. For one thing, children with both types of ADHD usually produce messy school work that is filled with errors, causing them to get poor grades (Cahn et al., 1996). They may be disruptive in class and are often rejected by other children.

TREATING AND MANAGING ADHD By the time their children are diagnosed with ADHD, usually upon entering school, many parents have lost confidence in their ability to control their children (Barkley, 1990). Some cope with their difficult children by being extremely permissive. Others use commands and threats: "Go clean your room right now or I'll whip you with a belt." Thus, parent training can be useful in helping parents cope with children who have ADHD.

The goal of such parenting programs is to help parents regain a sense of control (Barkley, 1990). For example, experts recommend that teachers provide parents with daily reports of their children's work in the various school subjects. Parents can then use the information to enforce a standing rule that the child must have completed all school work before watching television or doing other desired activities. Such approaches, when applied consistently, can help parents of children with ADHD manage their children's difficulties, as well as their own emotional reactions, more effectively.

Many children with ADHD take stimulant medications, such as methylphenidate (Ritalin). In fact, an estimated 82 in 1000 Canadian children are using these types of drugs to treat ADHD (Romano, 2005). The rate of usage for boys climbs from 0.58% in 4- to 5-year-olds to a peak of 6.31% in 10- to 11-year-olds. Girls are much less likely to use these drugs—the highest usage is at age 8 to 9 (1.09%). Seventy percent of the children who use these drugs are found to be calmer and better able to concentrate. However, some studies show that many children's response to the medication may actually be due to changes in expectations on the part of their teachers and parents—sort of a self-fulfilling prophecy (Spreen, Risser, & Edgell, 1995). In addition, studies suggest that the concentration skills of children with ADHD can be improved with training. For example, one study found that the attention skills of a group of children with ADHD were similar to those of a control group of children without attention difficulties following an intensive 18-week training program (Semrud-Clikeman et al., 1999).

It's also important to note that medication doesn't always improve the grades of children with ADHD. Rather, for the most part, it seems that stimulant medications reduce such children's activity levels, help them control their impulses, and somewhat improve their social behaviour. These effects usually result in improvements in classroom behaviour and peer acceptance. Medications such as methylphenidate have the greatest effect on school grades among children whose ADHD symptoms are so severe that they interfere with actual learning (Spreen, Risser, & Edgell, 1995). For this reason, the use of stimulant medications for children who have mild or moderate ADHD symptoms is controversial. Furthermore, Canadian pediatricians caution that there is a lack of evidence about the long-term effectiveness of stimulant medications beyond four weeks of treatment (Schachter, Pham, King, Langford, & Moher, 2001).

SECOND-LANGUAGE LEARNERS

Worldwide patterns of population growth and movement have led to tremendous increases in the number of children attending school in Canada, the United States, Great Britain, and Australia. Educators in English-speaking countries use the term *Limited English Proficient* (LEP) to refer to non-English-speaking children—either immigrant children or native-born children. There are analogous language challenges for educators in those parts of Canada where French is the dominant language but children are not proficient in French.

Historically, Canada has been host to waves of immigrants from all parts of the world. More recently, immigrant children under age 15 have arrived from Asia and the Pacific Region (44%) and Africa and the Middle East (22%). Of these children, 5 in 10 landed in Ontario, 2 in 10 in British Columbia, and slightly more than 1 in 10 in Quebec. More than two-thirds of the children were unable to speak either official language when they arrived (BC Stats, 1998; Canadian Council on Social Development [CCSD], 1999). This immigration has resulted in abnormally high levels of official language deficiency in children in our school system, especially in these three provinces. In the Lower Mainland school districts of British Columbia, for instance, ESL enrolment has more than tripled since 1990, and a large majority of these new students are unfamiliar with both the Roman alphabet and Western cultural practices (British Columbia Ministry of Education, 2001). In the Toronto District School Board (the largest school board in Canada and one of the largest in North America), 41% of the students in elementary schools have a language other than English as their first language. This problem is compounded by the fact that more than 80 languages from all over the world are represented in the Board's schools (Toronto District School Board, 2001).

Bilingual education is a logistical challenge for most school districts that include LEP children. For one thing, if a school system has only a handful of students who speak a particular language, it is not financially feasible to establish a separate curriculum for them. In addition, it may be impossible to find bilingual teachers for children whose language is spoken by very few people outside their country of origin. For these reasons, most LEP students are enrolled in **English-as-a-second-language (ESL) programs,** or if they intend to learn the French language, they are enrolled in French-as-a-second-language (FSL) programs (Canadian Parents for French [CPF], 2001). In ESL programs, children spend part of the day in classes to learn English and part in academic classes that are conducted entirely in English.

Research has shown that no particular approach to second-language learners is more successful than any other (Mohanty & Perregaux, 1997). There is some indication that programs that include a home-based component, such as those that encourage parents to learn the new language along with their children, may be especially effective (Koskinen et al., 2000). But it seems that any structured program, whether

bilingual education
an approach to second-language education in which children receive instruction in two different languages

English-as-a-second-language (ESL) program
an approach to second-language education in which children attend English classes for part of the day and receive most of their academic instruction in English

bilingual education or ESL, fosters higher achievement among non-English-speaking children than simply integrating them into English-only classes, an approach called *submersion*. Although most children in submersion programs eventually catch up to their English-speaking peers, many educators believe that instruction that supports children's home language and culture as well as their English-language skills enhances their overall development (Cushner, McClelland, & Safford, 1992).

With respect to achievement, LEP students' performance in school is very similar to that of English-speaking children (NCES, 1997). In fact, in American schools, native-born English-speaking children are more likely to fail one or more grades than children whose home language is either Asian or European. An exception is Spanish-speaking children, who fail in American schools at about the same rate as English speakers. Thus, there is no evidence that a child who enters school with limited English skills has any greater risk of failure than native-born students.

A cautionary note is necessary, however: An LEP student does not have an increased risk of failure as long as the school provides some kind of transition to English-only instruction and school officials take care to administer all standardized tests in the language with which the child is most familiar (Cushner et al., 1992). Providing a transition to English-only instruction is necessary to optimize the LEP child's potential for achievement. Testing children in their native language ensures that non-English-speaking children will not be misclassified as developmentally delayed or learning disabled because of their limited English skills.

BILINGUAL EDUCATION

Most Canadians have one of Canada's official languages, either English (59.2%) or French (23.3%), as their first language (Statistics Canada, 2000a). Since its experimental roots at St. Lambert in Quebec in 1965, French Immersion programs have become a successful fixture of our Canadian education system and a model for teaching a second language throughout the world (Lambert & Tucker; 1972; Safty, 1995). Children enrolled in early French Immersion programs are taught exclusively in French from kindergarten through to Grade 2 within the classroom. Starting in Grade 3, subjects taught in English are incrementally introduced every year until they receive instruction in both languages approximately equally in the senior grades.

Although initially there is some delay in English language development, by the later grades French Immersion students' English skills are indistinguishable from those of students taught in English (Holobow, Genesee, & Lambert, 1991). By age 15, French Immersion students of both genders have significantly higher reading achievement scores than their nonimmersion counterparts (Allen, 2004). In addition, French Immersion students achieve high proficiency in the French language (Harley & Jean, 1999). Ellen Bialystok (1999) of York University found that early immersion education not only facilitated both spoken and written language skills, but also aspects of thinking, such as improved selective attention on nonlanguage tasks. Even more remarkable, Bialystok and her colleauges have discovered a very important long-term benefit of speaking two languages on a regular basis: In comparison to people who are monolingual, it has the protective effect of delaying the onset of dementia, such as Alzheimer's disease, by four years (Bialystok, Craik, & Freedman, 2007).

The process of learning to read, write, and speak a second language instils an appreciation for another culture, provides an alternative way to think about and value the world, and encourages children to become more objective and open-minded (Canadian Heritage, 1999). With more than 60 nonofficial languages spoken in Canada, heritage language programs are available to help families pass on their language and culture of origin (Settlement.org, 2001). Inherent in federal, provincial, and territorial legislation and policy is the recognition that heritage languages are fundamental to the preservation of the multicultural nature of our country. There is a particular need to preserve the languages of Canadian Aboriginal peoples, since their culture is based on oral tradition and is expressed most fully through their primary heritage language. Historically, more than 60 Aboriginal languages were spoken in Canada, but most are either lost or endangered because so few people who can speak these languages are left (Kirkness, 1999). Heritage language education needs to consist of formal, structured programs designed to increase students' knowledge of these languages.

GENDER DIFFERENCES IN ACHIEVEMENT

Comparisons of IQ test scores for boys and girls do not reveal consistent differences. Only when the total scores are broken down into several separate skills do some serious and perplexing patterns of gender differences emerge. Studies from across Canada show that girls outperform boys in reading and writing (HRDC, 2001b) and in math (although it has been commonly thought that boys were superior in math) on provincial standards tests. Additionally, while girls surpass the provincial standards, boys mostly fail to even meet them (Fine, 2000a, 2000b). The question of where such differences come from remains unanswered. So far, environmental explanations have proven to be more useful than biological theories, particularly in relation to language skills. Some argue that in the early grades boys lack role models with whom they can identify, since most teachers at that level are females. Others suggest that the reading material for boys does not match their interests.

Before Going On

- Describe the controversy surrounding the term *learning disability* and how Attention-Deficit/Hyperactivity Disorder affects a child's development.

- What is the difference between a bilingual and an ESL program? Is one approach more effective than the other?

Summary

Physical Changes

- Physical development from age 6 to 12 is steady and slow.

- Neurological development leads to improvements in selective attention, information-processing speed, and spatial perception.

- Unintentional injuries and unhealthy weights are the most prevalent health problems of this age group.

Cognitive Changes

- Language development continues in vocabulary growth, improvements in grammar, and understanding of the social uses of language.

- Piaget proposed that the 6-year-old child begins to perform powerful operations such as decentration and reversibility. The child also learns to use inductive logic.

- Research on this period confirms many of Piaget's descriptions of sequences of development. The "operations" he observed may actually be rules for solving specific types of problems.

- Most information-processing theorists conclude that there are age-related improvements in children's information-processing speed and efficiency.

Schooling

- To become literate, children need specific instruction in sound–letter correspondences, word parts, and other aspects of written language. They also need to be exposed to good literature and to have lots of opportunities to practise their reading and writing skills.

- School has a significant effect in fostering the 6- to 12-year-old's shift to a more abstract or strategic

form of thinking. Children who lack school experience show less skill of this type.

- School progress in children with exceptionalities is sometimes assessed with both IQ tests and achievement tests. Both types of tests may ignore important aspects of intellectual functioning.

Individual and Group Differences

- Canadian school children with exceptionalities receive special education services while remaining integrated within the classroom.

- Children with limited English perform as well as English-speaking peers when they receive specific kinds of support in school.

- There are no gender differences in overall IQ scores, but girls do somewhat better on reading, writing, and math tasks.

Review Questions

Answers are provided on MyDevelopmentLab in the Course Resources folder.

Physical Changes

9.1   Which of the following is not a significant health risk of middle childhood?
   a.   motor vehicle accidents
   b.   sports injuries
   c.   infectious diseases
   d.   obesity

Cognitive Changes

9.2   Which of the following correctly illustrates inductive logic?
   a.   understanding that adding to a set always makes the set have more

   b.   thinking up examples that illustrate the concept of equality
   c.   knowing how to take a general principle and predict a specific outcome
   d.   demonstrating an ability to process abstract ideals

Schooling

9.3   Which of the following skills is most significant for developing the ability to read well during middle childhood?
   a.   spatial cognition
   b.   class inclusion
   c.   mnemonics
   d.   phonological awareness

Individual and Group Differences

9.4 The term used to describe difficulty mastering a specific academic skill despite possessing average or higher intelligence and no physical or sensory handicaps is called
  a. exceptional mastery.
  b. dyslexia.
  c. communication disorder.
  d. learning disability.

9.5 Behaviour disorders, communication disorders, sensory impairments, and physical disorders are examples of _____ in Canada.

  a. learning disabilities
  b. exceptionalities
  c. dyslexia
  d. horizontal decalage

Critical-Thinking Questions

9.6 How could socioeconomic status affect the eating and physical activity patterns of children from different neighbourhoods? What are some of the social and environmental differences?

9.7 What effect do you think children's elementary school experiences have on the rest of their lives?

Jupiterimages/Thinkstock

CHAPTER
10

Social and Personality Development in Middle Childhood

One mother, who also happened to be a student in a developmental psychology graduate program, had gotten into the habit of trying out research tasks on her 7-year-old daughter, Allison, before using them in actual research. One morning, she asked the girl what she wanted to wear to school. Allison answered, "Do you really want to know, or is this just another one of your studies?" Like most 6- to 12-year-olds, Allison wanted her mother to think of her as an individual, not just another 7-year-old. Children of this age are beginning to realize that they are unique, and they want their uniqueness to be recognized by parents and others.

At the same time, children of this age want to fit into the social world in a meaningful way. Every culture in the world has a *society of childhood*, in which children make up their own social rules that differ from those of adult society. For example, in most Canadian school lunchrooms, food trading is common. A child who refuses to trade may be seen as "stuck-up." But adults who try to talk co-workers into trading lunches are likely to be thought of as pushy or somewhat odd. Such comparisons show that children practise social competence by making up their own social rules rather than simply copying those that exist in the adult world. Creating and enforcing such rules helps children learn to look at things from other people's points of view and to cooperate.

When you finish reading this chapter, you will be able to distinguish among the psychoanalytic, trait, and social-cognitive approaches to social and personality development; summarize the development of self-concept in school-aged children; describe how the advances in social cognition contribute to a more abstract sense of self, others, and moral behaviour; describe the changes in the social relationships of children age 6 to 12; and discuss how influences such as after-school care and television affect the 6- to 12-year-old's development. While you read, keep the following questions in mind:

- What can parents and peers do to help shape a child's level of self-esteem?

- Boys' friendship groups are larger and more accepting of newcomers than are girls'. Girls are more likely to play in pairs or in small, more exclusive groups. Can you think of other differences?

- What advice would you give a parent about controlling what their 6-year-old watches on television?

THEORIES OF SOCIAL AND PERSONALITY DEVELOPMENT

The development of self-perceived competence is the overarching theme of social and personality development in the middle childhood years. How do children develop this critical attribute? Developmentalists representing different theoretical perspectives emphasize different sets of factors in their explanations of the development of self-perceived competence in these years.

PSYCHOANALYTIC PERSPECTIVES

Freud believed that children between age 6 and puberty repress *libidinal* desires to concentrate on developing friendships and social skills. When you think back to your middle childhood years, what kinds of experiences stand out? Most likely, you remember interacting with your peers and siblings. If Freud were called on to explain how your feelings about your own competence developed, then he would appeal to the emotional qualities of these interactions. Freud thought that the challenge of the middle childhood years was to form emotional bonds with peers and to move beyond those that were developed with parents in earlier years. Thus, much of the modern-day research on peer rejection and other emotional features of middle childhood find their roots in Freud's psychoanalytic approach.

Erikson accepted Freud's view of the central role of peer relationships and the emotions that accompany them in middle childhood. He went beyond Freud's perspective, though, when he further characterized middle childhood as the period during which children experience the crisis of **industry versus inferiority**. During this stage, Erikson said, children develop a sense of their own competence through the achievement of culturally defined learning goals (see **Table 2.2** on page 35). The psychosocial task of the 6- to 12-year-old is development of industry, or the willingness to work to accomplish goals. To develop industry, the child must be able to achieve the goals her culture sets for all children her age. In most countries, 6- to 12-year-olds must learn to read and write. If they fail to do so, Erikson's view claims, then they will enter adolescence and adulthood with feelings of inferiority. These feelings of inferiority constitute an emotional mindset that can hamper an individual's ability to achieve for the rest of her life.

Contemporary studies that stress the child's need to feel competent are in tune with Erikson's views. Many of them suggest that he was right about the link between school experiences and an emerging sense of competence. It seems that most 6- to 12-year-olds gradually develop a view of their own competence as they succeed or fail at academic tasks such as reading and arithmetic (Chapman & Tunmer, 1997; Skaalvik & Valas, 1999). Thus, their self-assessments and actual achievements are strongly correlated; that is, those who are most successful judge themselves to be competent, while those who have difficulty perceive themselves as less competent. Individual differences in children's responses to success and failure moderate the effects of the experiences themselves. Some of these differences are found in the emotional realm, as suggested earlier.

Erikson also argued that children who lack success in school can develop it by participating in culturally valued pursuits outside of academic settings. A child who is a mediocre student, for instance, may channel his need to develop self-perceived competence into athletics. Another child who gets poor grades may do so because she spends most of her time reading books that she finds to be more interesting than her school work. Outsiders may worry about her sense of competence, but, internally, she has no doubts about her abilities.

 Explore

THE BIG FIVE PERSONALITY TRAITS

You'll recall from **Chapters 6** and **8** that many developmentalists today think of personality as being built on the foundation of the child's inborn temperament (Caspi et al., 2003; Rothbart, Ahadi, & Evans, 2000). But just how can researchers describe personality? What are the key dimensions on which personalities differ? Over the past few decades most personality researchers have accepted that adult personality can be accurately described as a set of variations along five major dimensions or *traits*: extraversion, agreeableness, conscientiousness, neuroticism, and openness/intellect (Digman, 1990; McCrae & John, 1992). A **trait** is a stable pattern of responding to situations. Trait theorists contend that, by middle childhood, the various dimensions of temperament have evolved into five dimensions of personality (**The Big Five**) that are shown in **Table 10.1**. Personality can be accurately assessed along these five dimensions in youth from ages 9 to 19 to effectively inform decisions concerning children at risk for adjustment problems in school and the community (Klingbeil, 2009).

---

industry versus inferiority stage
the fourth of Erikson's psychosocial stages, during which children develop a sense of their own competence through mastery of culturally defined learning tasks

trait
a stable pattern of responding to situations

The Big Five
a set of five major dimensions of personality, including extraversion, agreeableness, conscientiousness, neuroticism, and openness/intellect

TABLE 10.1	The Big Five Personality Traits	
Trait	**Qualities of Individuals Who Show the Trait**	**Possible Temperament Components**
Extraversion	Active, assertive, enthusiastic, outgoing	High activity level, sociability, positive emotionality, talkativeness
Agreeableness	Affectionate, forgiving, generous, kind, sympathetic, trusting	Perhaps high approach/positive emotionality, perhaps effortful control
Conscientiousness	Efficient, organized, prudent, reliable, responsible	Effortful control/task persistence
Neuroticism (also called emotional instability)	Anxious, self-pitying, tense, touchy, unstable, worrying	Negative emotionality, irritability
Openness/Intellect	Artistic, curious, imaginative, insightful, original, wide interests	Approach, low inhibition

(*Sources:* Ahadi & Rothbart, 1994; John, Caspi, Robins, Moffitt, & Stouthamer-Loeber, 1994, Table 1, p. 161, McCrae & Costa, 1990.)

In longitudinal studies, school-aged children's scores on these five dimensions of personality have been found to strongly predict academic achievement and social skills in adolescence and early adulthood (Shiner, 2000). Researchers have also found strong correlations between parents' ratings of their children's personalities on scales representing the Big Five and objective observations of the children's social behaviour (Markey, Markey, & Tinsley, 2004). In addition, children who receive high ratings on agreeableness are less likely to display aggression than are their less agreeable peers (Sanson, Hemphill, & Smart, 2004). This association may be explained by other research showing that children who are high in agreeableness use more effective conflict resolution strategies than do those who are lower in this trait (Jensen-Campbell, Gleason, Adams, & Malcolm, 2003). Measures of personality in middle childhood also predict antisocial behaviour, such as stealing, in adolescence and later (John et al., 1994; Shiner, 2000). Such longitudinal studies suggest that the Big Five are not only identifiable and stable in middle childhood, but also are extremely important.

The emergence of stable traits in middle childhood are also known to contribute to the development of feelings of competence. For instance, a child who is reasonably extraverted, or outgoing, responds to peer rejection by becoming more determined to be accepted by the group. One who is introverted, or shy, would likely be so emotionally distraught by the taunts of her playmates that she would actively avoid social situations in the future. Still, children are not simply driven by personality-generated impulses in a mechanistic way, and trait theory leaves us wondering why extraversion doesn't always lead to social competence and why some people overcome their tendency toward introversion to become competent in the social arena.

SOCIAL-COGNITIVE PERSPECTIVES

From the social-cognitive perspective, both the psychoanalytic and the trait theorists focus on only one set of factors that shape the development of self-perceived competence in middle childhood. Albert Bandura, for instance, proposed that the emotions described by psychoanalytic theorists and the stable patterns of responding that have been identified by trait theorists, together with cognitive factors, constitute one of three interactive components that influence social and personality development (see **Figure 2.7** on p. 48). Recall that Bandura refers to this emotional/cognitive component as the *personal* factor. The other two factors of his model were the person's *behavioural* responses and the *environmental* influences and pressures.

Bandura proposed that the personal, behavioural, and environmental factors interact in a pattern he termed *reciprocal determinism*. Each of the three components influences, and is influenced by, the other two. By organizing the various interactive influences in the way that it does, Bandura's model provides a more comprehensive explanation of how school-aged children develop ideas about the degrees of competence they possess than either the psychoanalytic or the trait theorists do. Thus, Bandura's social-cognitive approach provides us with a way of taking into account the valuable insights of the psychoanalytic theorists relative to children's emotions with those of the trait theorists. And by integrating both into the three-part model that Bandura proposed, we gain a more comprehensive understanding of the mechanisms that drive the development of self-perceived competence (what Bandura referred to as *self-efficacy*) in the middle childhood years.

 Explore

Before Going On

- How do Freud and Erikson characterize social and personality development in 6- to 12-year-olds?
- What are the main ideas of the psychoanalytic, trait, and social-cognitve theorists?

SELF-CONCEPT

How much insight does a school-aged child really have into her own personality? The answer to this question depends on whether we look at the child at the beginning of this period or near the end of it. Across the years from age 6 to 12, children's understanding of themselves improves quite a bit and, by the end of the middle childhood period, children's self-concepts include two new components: a *psychological self* and a *valued self*.

THE PSYCHOLOGICAL SELF

psychological self
a person's understanding of his or her enduring psychological characteristics

The **psychological self** is a person's understanding of his or her enduring psychological characteristics. It first appears during the transition from early to middle childhood and becomes increasingly complex as the child approaches adolescence. It includes both basic information about the child's unique characteristics and self-judgments of competency.

PERSONALITY TRAITS Children don't use the same terminology as the trait theories that you read about earlier in the chapter, but they do describe their own personalities with increasing degrees of precision across the middle childhood years. For example a

6-year-old might use simple psychological self-descriptors, such as "smart" or "dumb." By 10, a child is more likely to use comparisons in self-descriptions: "I'm smarter than most other kids" or "I'm not as talented in art as my friend" (Rosenberg, 1986; Ruble, 1987).

This developmental trend was illustrated in the results of an older study of the self-concepts of 9- to 18-year-olds (Montemayor & Eisen, 1977). Children who participated were asked to give 20 answers to the question "Who am I?" The researchers found that the younger children were still using mostly surface qualities to describe themselves, as in this description by a 9-year-old:

> My name is Bruce C. I have brown eyes. I have brown hair. I have brown eyebrows. I am nine years old. I LOVE! Sports. I have seven people in my family. I have great! eye site. I have lots! of friends. I live on 1923 Pinecrest Dr. I am going on 10 in September. I'm a boy. I have a uncle that is almost 7 feet tall. My school is Pinecrest. My teacher is Mrs. V. I play Hockey! I'm almost the smartest boy in the class. I LOVE! food. I love fresh air. I LOVE school. (Montemayor & Eisen, 1977, p. 317)

In contrast, consider the self-description of this 11-year-old girl in Grade 6:

> My name is A. I'm a human being. I'm a girl. I'm a truthful person. I'm not very pretty. I do so-so in my studies. I'm a very good cellist. I'm a very good pianist. I'm a little bit tall for my age. I like several boys. I like several girls. I'm old-fashioned. I play tennis. I am a very good swimmer. I try to be helpful. I'm always ready to be friends with anybody. Mostly I'm good, but I lose my temper. I'm not well-liked by some girls and boys. I don't know if I'm liked by boys or not. (Montemayor & Eisen, 1977, pp. 317–318)

This girl, like the other 11-year-olds in the study, describes her external qualities, but she also emphasizes psychological factors such as personality traits.

Thus, as a child moves through the concrete operational period, her psychological self becomes more complex, more comparative, less tied to external features, and more centred on feelings and ideas.

SELF-EFFICACY   As we noted earlier in the chapter, middle childhood is the time when children develop perceptions about their degree of competence. Bandura has greatly advanced developmentalists' understanding of this crucial aspect of the psychological self. He defines *self-efficacy* as an individual's belief in her capacity to cause an intended event to occur (Bandura, 1997a). How does self-efficacy develop?

Bandura proposed that peer models play a primary role in the development of self-efficacy beliefs (Bandura, 1997a). As an example, consider what it's like for a novice bike rider who is prompted by her friends to try some challenging trail riding. Bandura would predict that, when the girl observes her friends riding up a dirt hill, she probably concludes that she can do likewise. Bandura further argued that, to believe that she could follow her peers' example, the girl had to see herself as similar to them. Thus, social comparison, or the process of drawing conclusions about the self based on comparisons to others, plays an integral role in the degree to which children gain insight into their own self-efficacy from observing peers. Thus, simply watching other children model success at a task is insufficient for the development of self-efficacy in a child whom outsiders might see as similar to the models. The child herself must perceive that similarity to be influenced by the models.

Encouragement from knowledgeable people that children value and respect also contributes to self-efficacy. For example, the school cycling coach's willingness to let the girl start training for her school's mountain bike club can play a role in her development of self-efficacy. However, nothing influences self-efficacy more than an individual's real life experiences (Britner & Pajares, 2006). In other words, believing that you can do something is less powerful, emotionally and cognitively, than actually doing it. Consequently, the final hurdle in this girl's development of self-efficacy for bike-racing was surmounted when she succesfully competed in her first cycling race.

THE VALUED SELF

A child can have an accurate view of her personality traits, and even have a solid sense of self-efficacy, but still fail to value herself as an individual. To find out why, developmentalists have studied another aspect of self-concept development in middle childhood: the emergence of the valued self.

self-esteem
a global evaluation of one's own worth

THE NATURE OF SELF-ESTEEM
A child's evaluative judgments have several interesting features. First of all, over the years of elementary school and high school, children's evaluations of their own abilities become increasingly differentiated, with quite separate judgments about academic or athletic skills, physical appearance, social acceptance, friendships, romantic appeal, and relationships with parents (Harter, 1990; Marsh, Craven, & Debus, 1999). Paradoxically, however, it is when they reach school age—around age 7—that children first develop a global self-evaluation. Seven- and eight-year-olds (but not younger children) readily answer questions about how well they like themselves as people, how happy they are, or how well they like the way they are leading their lives. This global evaluation of one's own worth is usually referred to as **self-esteem**, and it is not merely the sum of all the separate assessments a child makes about his skills in different areas. How stable are self-esteem judgments? A number of longitudinal studies of elementary school–aged children and teenagers show that self-esteem is quite stable in the short term but somewhat less so over periods of several years. The correlation between two self-esteem scores obtained a few months apart is generally about 0.60. Over several years, this correlation drops to about 0.40 (Alsaker & Olweus, 1992; Block & Robins, 1993). So, a child with high self-esteem at age 8 or 9 is likely to have high self-esteem at age 10 or 11. But it is also true that self-esteem is subject to a good deal of variation. To some degree, self-esteem is more stable in girls than in boys (Heinonen, Raikkonen, & Keltikangas-Jarvinen, 2003).

Hitting a home run will raise this girl's self-esteem only if she places a high value on being good at sports or at baseball specifically. (*Photo:* © David Young-Wolff/ PhotoEdit)

HOW SELF-ESTEEM DEVELOPS
Developmental psychologist Susan Harter (1987, 1990) has studied the development of self-esteem extensively. She has found that self-esteem is strongly influenced by mental comparisons of children's ideal selves and their actual experiences. For example, social self-esteem, the assessment of one's own social skills, is higher in popular children than in those who are rejected by their peers (Jackson & Bracken, 1998). However, each component of self-esteem is valued differently by different children. Thus, a child who perceives herself to have poor social skills because she is unpopular may not necessarily have low self-esteem. The degree to which her social self-assessment affects her self-esteem is influenced by how much she values social skills and popularity. In addition, she may see herself as very competent in another area—such as academic skills—that balances her lack of social skills.

The key to self-esteem, then, is the amount of discrepancy between what the child desires and what the child thinks he has achieved. Thus, a child who values sports prowess but who isn't big enough or coordinated enough to be good at sports will have lower self-esteem than will an equally small or uncoordinated child who does not value sports skill so highly. Similarly, being good at something, such as singing or playing chess, won't raise a child's self-esteem unless the child values that particular skill.

The second major influence on a child's self-esteem is the overall support the child feels she is receiving from the important people around her, particularly parents and peers (Franco & Levitt, 1998). Apparently, to develop high self-esteem, children must first acquire the sense that they are liked and accepted in their families, by both parents and siblings. Next, they need to be able to find friends with whom they can develop stable relationships. Since childhood friendships begin with shared interests and activities, children need to be in an environment in which they can find others who like the same things they do and are similarly skilled. Athletic children need other athletic children to associate with; those who are musically inclined need to meet peers who are also musical, and so on.

The separate influences of the perceived discrepancy between the ideal and actual self and the amount of social support are clear in the results of Harter's research on self-esteem. She asked children in Grades 3, 4, 5, and 6 how important it was to them to do well in each of five domains, and how well they thought they actually did in each. The total discrepancy between these sets of judgments constituted the discrepancy score. A high discrepancy score indicates that children didn't feel they were doing well in areas that mattered to them. The social support score was based on children's replies to a set of questions about whether they thought others (parents and peers) liked them as they were, treated them as people, or felt that they were important. **Figure 10.1** shows the results for children in Grades 3 and 4; the findings for the children in Grades 5 and 6 are virtually identical to these. Both sets of data support Harter's hypothesis. Note that a low discrepancy score alone does not protect children completely from low self-esteem if they lack sufficient social support. Similarly, loving and accepting familys and peer groups do not guarantee high self-esteem if youngsters do not feel that they are living up to their own standards.

The criteria by which children learn to evaluate themselves vary considerably from one society to another (Miller, Wang, Sandel, & Cho, 2002; Wang & Ollendick, 2001). In individualistic cultures, like that of Canada, parents focus on helping children develop a sense of self-esteem based in the children's own interests and abilities. In collectivist cultures, such as China's, children are taught to value themselves based on cultural ideals about what a "good" person is.

From all these sources, the child fashions her ideas (her internal model) about what she should be and what she is. Like the internal model of attachment, self-esteem is not fixed in stone. It is responsive to changes in others' judgments as well as to changes in the child's own experience of success or failure. But once created, the model does tend to persist, both because the child tends to choose experiences that will confirm and support it and because the social environment—including the parents' evaluations of the child—tends to be at least moderately consistent.

MEANINGFULNESS   One challenging and understudied aspect of self-concept is the spiritual self. Most studies on

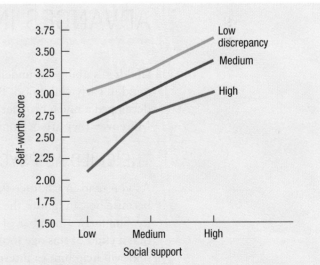

Figure 10.1

For these Grade 3 and 4 children in Harter's studies, self-esteem was about equally influenced by the amount of support the children saw themselves receiving from parents and peers and the degree of discrepancy between the value the children placed on various domains and the skill they thought they had in each of those domains.

(*Source:* Harter, 1987, Figure 9.2, p. 227.)

the topic focus on the cognitive aspects of spirituality without considering the subjective and experiential elements (Bosacki, 2001a, 2001b). The little amount of spiritual education that preadolescents are exposed to commonly focuses more on truisms and facts than on learning to trust one's intuition and emotions in the quest for a meaningful existence—attributes that are important in the formation of a complete and genuine preadolescent self-concept (Bosacki, 2001b). Educational strategies that may strengthen the development of the spiritual aspects of preadolescent self-concept include the use of experiential exercises, such as meditation and visualization, art therapy, and storytelling (Bosacki, 2002, 2005).

For example, one study found that, for spiritual growth to take place, it was helpful to create an environment in which children needed to be more than just passive learners (Sewell, 2009). In such a setting, teachers and children learned together, shared decisions, and respected and trusted one another. In this environment, the focus was more relational than instructional, which may seem counter to our traditional view of teaching. Still, when children were encouraged to be part of this *community of learning*, the children, and their teachers, developed a stronger sense of who they were as humans in the world—another important aspect in the development of the child's self-concept.

Critical Thinking

Take a moment and write down your own 20 answers to the "Who am I?" question. Then compare your answers to the examples given in the text of children's answers. What types of descriptions did you include?

Before Going On

- Characterize the features of the psychological self of 6- to 12-year-olds.
- What is the valued self, and how does it develop?

ADVANCES IN SOCIAL COGNITION

Children's ability to understand others is enhanced by the development of a theory of mind in early childhood. But by the end of the middle childhood period, children have developed a much broader understanding of others than they possessed at its beginning. Moreover, they are beginning to understand the moral aspects of social relationships.

THE CHILD AS PSYCHOLOGIST

As you read in **Chapter 9**, the school-aged child can understand conservation in part because he can ignore the appearance of change and focus on the underlying continuity. Similarly, a number of early groundbreaking social-cognitive studies demonstrated that a child of this age looks beyond appearances and searches for deeper consistencies that will help him to interpret both his own and other people's behaviour.

Like their understanding of the physical world, 6- to 12-year-olds' descriptions of other people move from the concrete to the abstract. If you ask a 6- or 7-year-old to describe others, then he will focus almost exclusively on external features (e.g., what the person looks like, where he lives, what he does). This description by a 7-year-old boy, taken from a classic study of social-cognitive development, is typical:

> He is very tall. He has dark brown hair, he goes to our school. I don't think he has any brothers or sisters. He is in our class. Today he has a dark orange [sweater] and gray trousers and brown shoes. (Livesley & Bromley, 1973, p. 213)

When young children do use internal or evaluative terms to describe people, they are likely to use quite global ones, such as "nice" or "mean," "good" or "bad." Further, young children do not seem to see these qualities as lasting or general traits of the individual, applicable in all situations or over time (Rholes & Ruble, 1984). In other words, the 6- or 7-year-old has not yet developed a concept that might be called "conservation of personality."

Beginning at about age 7 or 8, a rather dramatic shift occurs in children's descriptions of others. The child begins to focus more on the inner traits or qualities of another person and to assume that those traits will be visible in many situations (Gnepp & Chilamkurti, 1988). Children this age still describe others' physical features, but their descriptions are now used as examples of more general points about internal qualities. You can see the change when you compare the 7-year-old's description given above with this description by a child nearly 10 years old:

> He smells very much and is very nasty. He has no sense of humor and is very dull. He is always fighting and he is cruel. He does silly things and is very stupid. He has brown hair and cruel eyes. He is sulky and 11 years old and has lots of sisters. I think he is the most horrible boy in the class. He has a croaky voice and always chews his pencil and picks his teeth and I think he is disgusting. (Livesley & Bromley, 1973, p. 217)

This description still includes many external physical features but goes beyond such concrete surface qualities to the level of personality traits, such as cruelty and lack of humour.

The movement from externals to internals in descriptions of others is well documented by research. For example, in one important early study, researchers asked 6-, 8-, and 10-year-olds to describe three other children; a year later, they asked them to do the same thing again (Barenboim, 1981). **Figure 10.2** shows the results for two of the categories used in the study's data analysis. A *behavioural comparison* was any description that involved comparing a child's behaviours or physical features with those of another child or a norm, such as, "Billy runs a lot faster than Jason," or "She draws the best in our whole class." Any statement that involved some internal personality trait was referred to as a *psychological construct*, such as "Sarah is so kind," or "He's a real stubborn idiot!" You can see that behavioural comparisons peaked at around age 8 but psychological constructs increased steadily throughout middle childhood.

MORAL REASONING

Children's growing understanding of the internal experiences of other people helps them develop a better understanding of how they and others think about actions that have moral implications. *Moral reasoning* is the process of making judgments about the rightness or wrongness of specific acts. As you learned in **Chapter 8**, children learn to discriminate between intentional and unintentional acts between age 2 and 6. However, using this understanding to make moral judgments is another matter. Piaget claimed that the ability to use reasoning about

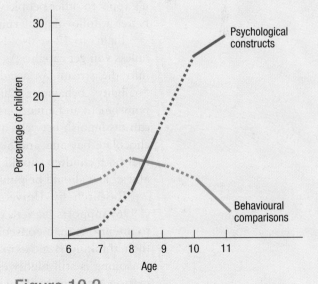

Figure 10.2

These data from Barenboim's study show the change in children's descriptions of their peers during the years of middle childhood. The solid lines represent longitudinal data, the dashed lines cross-sectional comparisons.

(*Source:* Barenboim, 1981, Figure 1, p. 134.)

intentions to make judgments about the moral dimensions of behaviour appears to emerge along with concrete operational reasoning.

PIAGET'S MORAL REALISM AND MORAL RELATIVISM Piaget explained moral conduct by studying how cognitive and social factors act on each other with reciprocal influence. For instance, he studied moral development by observing children playing games. As he watched them play, Piaget noticed that younger children seemed to have less understanding of the rules. Following up on these observations, Piaget questioned children of different ages about rules. Their answers led him to propose a two-stage theory of moral development (Piaget, 1932).

At the beginning of the middle childhood period, children are in what Piaget termed the **moral realism stage**. They believe that the rules of games can't be changed because they come from authorities, such as parents, government officials, or religious figures. For example, one 6-year-old told Piaget that the game of marbles was invented on Noah's ark. He went on to explain that the rules can't be changed because the "big ones," meaning adults and older children, wouldn't like it (Piaget, 1965, p. 60).

Moral realists also believe that all rule violations eventually result in punishment. For example, Piaget told children a story about a child who fell into a stream when he tried to use a rotten piece of wood as a bridge. Children younger than 8 years old told him that the child was being punished for something "naughty" he had done in the past.

After age 8, Piaget proposed, children move into the **moral relativism stage**, in which they learn that people can agree to change rules if they want to. They realize that the important thing about a game is that all the players follow the same rules, regardless of what those are. For example, 8- to 12-year-olds know that a group of children playing baseball can decide to give each batter four strikes rather than three. They understand that their agreement doesn't change the game of baseball and that it doesn't apply to other people who play the game. At the same time, children of this age get better at following the rules of games.

Eight- to 12-year-olds also know that you don't get punished for rule violations unless you get caught. As a result, they view events like the one in which the child fell into the stream as accidents. They understand that accidents are not caused by "naughty" behaviour. Children older than 8 also understand the relationship between punishment and intentions. For example, Piaget's research suggests that children over 8 can distinguish between a child who unintentionally left a store without paying for a chocolate bar and another who deliberately took it. Older children are likely to say that both children should return or pay for the candy, but only the one who intentionally stole it should be punished.

Research by University of Toronto psychologists Zelazo, Helwig, and Lau (1996) supports Piaget's claim that children more than 8 years old give more weight to intentions than consequences when making moral judgments. However, although their thinking is more mature than that of preschoolers, 6- to 12-year-olds' moral reasoning is still highly egocentric. For example, every parent has heard the exclamation "It's not fair!" when a child fails to receive the same treat or privilege as a sibling. It is rare, if not completely unknown, for a 6- to 12-year-old to protest the fairness of receiving something that a sibling didn't. Thus, school-aged children still have a long way to go with respect to mature moral reasoning, and we will return to this topic in the chapters on adolescent development (see **Development in the Real World**).

moral realism stage
the first of Piaget's stages of moral development, in which children believe rules are inflexible

moral relativism stage
the second of Piaget's stages of moral development, in which children understand that many rules can be changed through social agreement

Development in the Real World

ENCOURAGING MORAL REASONING

In his book *Raising Good Children*, developmental psychologist Thomas Lickona reminds readers that the development of mature moral reasoning takes many years (Lickona, 1983). At the same time, he offers parents and teachers several suggestions that will help them assist their 6- to 12-year-olds to prepare for movement to more mature levels. Following are some of his suggestions:

- Require kids to give reasons for what they want.

- Play developmentally appropriate games with them.

- Praise them for observing social conventions, such as saying "please" and "thank you."

- When punishment is necessary, provide them with an explanation, advice on how to avoid punishment in the future, and a way of repairing any damage their misbehaviour has caused.

- Teach them about reciprocity: "We do nice things for you, so you should be willing to help us."

- Give them meaningful chores so that they will think of themselves as important family and community members.

- Help and encourage them to base obedience on love and respect rather than fear.

- Teach them religious and philosophical values, including the idea that some actions are right and others are wrong, regardless of circumstances.

- Challenge their egocentrism by asking questions such as "How would you feel if someone did that to you?" when they violate others' rights.

- Include them in charitable projects, such as food drives, to extend the idea of love and caring beyond their own families.

Before Going On

- What changes occur in children's understanding of others in middle childhood?
- How do children in Piaget's moral realism and moral relativism stages reason about right and wrong?

SOCIAL RELATIONSHIPS

School-aged children's growing ability to understand others changes their social relationships in important ways. Children continue to be attached to parents, but they are becoming more independent. Relationships with peers become more stable and many ripen into long-term friendships. In fact, the quality of 6- to 12-year-olds' peer relationships shapes their futures in many important ways.

FAMILY RELATIONSHIPS

Middle childhood is a period of increasing independence of child from family. Yet attachments to parents and relationships with siblings continue to be important. University of Waterloo researcher Jiri Zuzanek (2000) reports that, after their children are 6 years old, parents spend less time looking after children's physical needs. He also found that the level of social and emotional support lessens considerably once children reach adolescence, to the point where, on average, parents spend 11 minutes a day caring for their teens and only 2 minutes socializing with them. Yet attachments to parents and relationships with siblings continue to be important.

One way that parents can remain connected with their children is by having family meals together. For example, some studies have found that the single best predictor of better childhood outcomes, regardless of family structure, socioeconomic factors, or time spent in school, church, playing sports, or involved in the arts, was having family meals together (five or more meals per week with a parent) (Council of Economic Advisers to the President, 2000; Hofferth, 2001). Children who had regular meals with a parent had significantly better academic success and fewer behavioural problems. Similarly, teens who ate dinner regularly with a parent had significantly better academic success and psychological adjustment, and lowered rates of smoking, drinking, drug use, early sexual activity, violence, and suicide attempts. As an added health bonus, children and teens who regularly ate dinners with their family had nutritionally superior diets (Gillman et al., 2000).

THE CHILD'S UNDERSTANDING OF FAMILY ROLES AND PROCESSES As social-cognitive theory would predict, school-aged children understand family roles and relationships much better than younger children do. For example, psychologist Jenny Jenkins of the University of Toronto found that, by about age 9, children who live in two-parent homes understand that their parents' roles as parents are distinct from their roles as partners or spouses (Jenkins & Buccioni, 2000). Thus, a 9-year-old is better able than a 5-year-old to understand when divorcing parents say that their love for the child hasn't changed, even though their relationship with each other has ended. Emotionally, the divorce experience may be just as difficult, but school-aged children are more capable of understanding it cognitively.

School-aged children also know that marital conflict often arises when spouses have different goals (Jenkins & Buccioni, 2000). Moreover, while younger children seem to believe that the only solution for marital conflict is for one spouse to give in to the other, school-aged children appear to understand that spouses can compromise.

ATTACHMENT It would be a great mistake to assume that, because school-aged children are more independent than they were when younger, the parent–child attachment relationship has weakened. School-aged children continue to use their parents as a safe base; they continue to rely on their presence, support, and affection (Clark & Symons, 2009; Wilson, 2009). Moreover, like infants, school-aged children who experience long-term separations from their parents are at greater risk for a variety of social and emotional problems than are peers who do not experience such separations (Smith, Lalonde, & Johnson, 2004). The quality of attachment matters in middle childhood as well. School-aged children who are securely attached to their parents have more harmonious peer relationships than children who are insecurely attached do (Wilson, 2009).

What does change, though, is the agenda of issues between parent and child. When the child reaches elementary school, disciplinary interactions with parents decline. Key issues now include children's household responsibilities, whether they will receive allowances or be paid for chores, standards for school performance, and the like (Furnham, 1999).

PARENTAL EXPECTATIONS The parent–child agenda changes because parents of 6- to 12-year-olds recognize their children's growing capacity for **self-regulation**, the ability to conform to parental standards of behaviour without direct supervision. As a result, as children get older, parents are more likely to allow them to engage in activities such as bicycle riding and skateboarding without supervision (Soori & Bhopal,

self-regulation
children's ability to conform to parental standards of behaviour without direct supervision

2002). Although, cultures vary to some degree in the specific age at which they expect this to occur, most expect 6- to 12-year-olds to be able to supervise their own behaviour at least part of the time.

Some studies suggest that there are sex differences in parents' expectations with respect to self-regulatory behaviour. For example, mothers make different kinds of demands on boys and girls. They appear to provide both with the same types of guidance but are more likely to give boys more autonomy over their own behaviour than girls. Nevertheless, they are also more likely to hold daughters to a higher standard of accountability for failure than boys (Pomerantz & Ruble, 1998). Developmentalists speculate that this difference may lead to stronger standards of behaviour for girls in later developmental periods.

PARENTING FOR SELF-REGULATION Researchers have learned that several parenting variables contribute to the development of self-regulation. First, the parents' own ability to self-regulate is important, perhaps because they are providing the child with models of good or poor self-regulation (Prinstein & La Greca, 1999). Also, the degree of self-regulation expected by parents influences the child's self-regulatory behaviour. Higher expectations, together with parental monitoring to make certain the expectations are met, are associated with greater self-regulatory competence (Rodrigo, Janssens, & Ceballos, 1999).

Research suggests that only children are just as well adjusted as those who have siblings.
(*Photo:* Michael Newman/PhotoEdit)

You should recall that such parental behaviours are associated with the authoritative style of parenting. Longitudinal research has demonstrated that school-aged children whose parents have been consistently authoritative since they were toddlers are the most socially competent (Baumrind, 1991). Children rated "competent" were seen as both assertive and responsible in their relationships; those rated "partially competent" typically lacked one of these skills; those rated "incompetent" showed neither. In Baumrind's (1991) study, the majority of children from authoritative families were rated as fully competent, while most of those from neglecting families were rated as incompetent.

A study of Canadian mothers and their children was conducted by Rosemary Mills of the University of Manitoba and Kenneth Rubin of the University of Maryland to see if maternal methods of control were related to childhood aggression and social withdrawal. They studied children in kindergarten and Grades 2 and 4 and found that mothers who were behaviourally overcontrolling (e.g., gave more compliance commands, punishment, or criticism, or demonstrated greater devaluation of the child than other parents) had children who were socially withdrawn. In comparison, mothers of aggressive children were generally undercontrolling (e.g., were overly permissive and made fewer requests and were less responsive to a child's behaviour) (Mills & Rubin, 1998).

FRIENDSHIPS

The biggest shift in relationships during middle childhood is the increasing importance of peers, particularly close friends. One frequent manifestation of this trend is the appearance of "best-friend" relationships. Cross-cultural studies show that best-friend relationships, and the belief that having a best friend is important, are universal features of school-aged children's social development (Schraf & Hertz-Lazarowitz, 2003). Younger children, often as early as 3 years of age, express playmate preferences (Hay, Payne, & Chadwick, 2004). Among older school-aged children, however, a best friend is much more than a playmate, reflecting these children's better understanding of the characteristics that distinguish friendships from other kinds of relationships.

Social-cognitive researcher Robert Selman was one of the first to study children's understanding of friendships. He found that if you ask preschoolers and young school-aged children how people make friends, the answer is usually that they "play together" or spend time physically near each other (Damon, 1977, 1983; Selman, 1980).

In the later years of middle childhood, at around age 10, this view of friendship gives way to one in which the key concept seems to be reciprocal trust (Chen, 1997; Hartup & Abecassis, 2004). Older children see friends as special people who possess desired qualities other than mere proximity, who are generous with each other, who help and trust each other, and so on. **Figure 10.3** is a 10-year-old boy's definition of a friend. His characterization of a friend as someone "you can trust," who "will always be there for you when you are feeling down in the dumps" and "always sits by you at lunch," illustrates the older child's understanding of dimensions of friendships such as trust, emotional support, and loyalty.

Researchers have examined the relationship between children's understanding of friendship and the quantity and quality of their friendships. In one such study, researchers Amanda Rose and Steven Asher (2004) presented Grade 5 students with hypothetical situations in which one friend might have an opportunity to help another. For instance, in one scenario, the researchers described a child who was teased by her classmates. Rose and Asher found that children who expressed the view that children should not help others in such situations to avoid putting themselves at risk of being treated similarly by peers had fewer friends than did children who expressed the view that friends should place their relationships above concerns about how their helping behaviour would affect their own social status.

Evidence of the centrality of friends to social development in middle childhood also comes from studies of children's behaviour within friendships. Children are more open and more supportive when with their chums, smiling at, looking at, laughing with, and touching one another more than when they are with nonfriends; they talk more with friends and cooperate and help one another more. Pairs of friends are also more successful than nonfriends are in solving problems or performing some task

My definition of a good friend is someone who you can trust, They will never turn their back on you, They will always be there for you. when you are feeling down in the dumps, They'll try to cheer you up, They will never forget about you. They'll always sit next to you at lunch,

Figure 10.3

This essay on friendship written by a 10-year-old illustrates the way older school-aged children think about friends.

(Courtesy of Denise Boyd. Used with permission.)

together. Yet school-aged children are also more critical of friends and have more conflicts with them; they are more polite with strangers (Hartup, 1996). At the same time, when conflicts with friends occur, children are more concerned about resolving them than they are about settling disagreements with nonfriends. Thus, friendship seems to represent an arena in which children can learn how to manage conflicts (Newcomb & Bagwell, 1995).

Canadian researchers have found that social competence is closely related to a reduction in both internalizing and externalizing behaviour problems in children (Craig, Peters, & Willms, 2002). Unfortunately, as peers begin to play a larger role in social development during late childhood, parents and educators have fewer opportunities to teach social skills to children who need them. Just as children are put into supervised activities in and out of school to develop their athletic and artistic skills, they also need opportunities to get involved with other children in enjoyable activities that support "skills in forming and maintaining positive relationships, dealing with conflict, and understanding their own feelings and behaviour" (Craig, Peters, & Willms, 2002, p. 326). In this way, as children develop their social skills, they become better equipped to build meaningful friendships, which would reduce their likelihood of having behaviour problems.

Critical Thinking

Do you still have any friends from your elementary school years? If not, why do you think those early friendships did not survive? If you do, what do you think differentiates an early friendship that survives from one that does not?

GENDER SEGREGATION

Possibly the most striking thing about peer group interactions in the elementary school years is how gender-segregated they are. This pattern seems to occur in every culture in the world and is frequently visible in children as young as age 3 or 4. Boys play with boys and girls play with girls, each in their own areas and at their own kinds of games (Cairns & Cairns, 1994). In fact, gender seems to be more important than age, race, or any other categorical variable in 6- to 12-year-olds' selection of friends; in addition, the strength of children's preference for same-sex associates increases substantially across middle childhood (Graham, Cohen, Zbikowski, & Secrist, 1998). Moreover, gender segregation is unrelated to sex differences in parenting, suggesting that it is a feature of 6- to 12-year-olds' social relationships that they construct for reasons of their own (McHale, Crouter, & Tucker, 1999).

Shared interests and activities are a critical part of friendship in the early years of middle childhood. For example, rough-and-tumble play is common in boy–boy interactions but is typically avoided by girls. In so doing, the boys learn how to socialize with other boys but acquire few of the skills girls use in their interactions, skills such as self-disclosure (Phillipsen, 1999). Thus, boys establish stable peer groups with dominance hierarchies based on rough-and-tumble play skills (Pelligrini & Smith, 1998). A similar pattern exists for girls: Gender segregation begins with shared activity preferences but leads to the development of social skills that are more useful in interactions with other girls than in interactions with boys.

There are some ritualized "boundary violations" between boys' and girls' groups, such as chasing games. For example, in one universal series of interactions, a girl taunts a boy with a statement like "You can't catch me, nyah nyah." Next, a boy chases and catches her, to the delight of both of their fully supportive same-sex peer groups (Thorne, 1986). As soon as the brief cross-gender encounter ends, both girl and boy return to their respective groups. On the

In middle childhood, boys play with boys and girls play with girls. In fact, children's play groups are more sex-segregated at this age than at any other.
(*Photos: top*, Rolf Bruderer/CORBIS *bottom*, Mary Kate Denny/PhotoEdit)

whole, however, girls and boys between ages 6 and 12 actively avoid interacting with one another and show strong favouritism toward their own gender and negative stereotyping of the opposite gender (Powlishta, 1995).

Gender segregation patterns are even more pronounced in friendships during middle childhood. For example, when researchers ask children to describe the kind of playmate a fictional child would prefer, school-aged children's predictions are largely gender-based (Halle, 1999). Girls' and boys' friendships also differ in quality in intriguing ways. Boys' friendship groups are larger and more accepting of newcomers than are girls'. Boys play more outdoors and roam over a larger area in their play. Girls are more likely to play in pairs or in small, fairly exclusive groups, and they spend more playtime indoors or near home or school (Benenson, 1994; Gottman, 1986).

Sex differences also characterize the interaction between a pair of friends, as you learned in **Chapter 8.** Boys' friendships appear to be focused more on competition and dominance than are girls' friendships (Maccoby, 1995). In fact, among school-aged boys, researchers see higher levels of competition between pairs of friends than between strangers—the opposite of what is observed among girls. Friendships between girls include more agreement, more compliance, and more self-disclosure than is true between boys. For example, "controlling" speech—a category that includes rejecting comments, ordering, manipulating, challenging, defiance, refutation, or resistance of another's attempts to control—is twice as common among pairs of 7- and 8-year-old male friends as among pairs of female friends of that age (Leaper, 1991). Among the 4- and 5-year-olds in Leaper's study, there were no sex differences in controlling speech, suggesting that these differences in interaction pattern arise during middle childhood.

None of this information should obscure the fact that the interactions of male and female friendship pairs have much in common. For example, collaborative and cooperative exchanges are the most common forms of communication in both boys' and girls' friendships in middle childhood. And it is not necessarily the case that boys' friendships are less important to them than girls' are to them. Nevertheless, it seems clear that gender differences, in both form and style, may well have enduring implications for patterns of friendship over the lifespan.

Furthermore, school-aged children appear to evaluate the role of gender in peer relationships in light of other variables. For example, when asked whether a fictitious boy would prefer to play with a boy who is a stranger or with a girl who has been his friend for a while, most school-aged children say the boy would prefer to play with the friend (Halle, 1999). Such results suggest that, even though gender is clearly important in school-aged children's peer relationships, other factors may be more important. This result is yet another example of how children's growing cognitive abilities—specifically, their ability to think about more than one variable at a time—influence their ideas about the social world.

A study of Canadian children shows that about three-quarters of children between Grades 6 and 10 say they have two or more close friends. The percentage of close friendships dips in Grade 9, probably because this is typically a transition year to secondary school and is associated with difficulty in establishing relationships with new fellow students. By age 13, about half of both boys and girls find it easier to talk to opposite-sex friends about more intimate topics (Health Canada, 2001b).

◉⟨Watch   PATTERNS OF AGGRESSION

You may remember from **Chapter 8** that physical aggression declines over the preschool years, while indirect aggression increases. Research on Canadian children shows that, in middle childhood, physical aggression becomes even less common, as children learn the cultural rules about when displaying anger or aggression is acceptable and how much of a display is acceptable (Craig, 2004; Pepler et al., 2006; Tremblay, 2000). Boys at every age show more physical aggression and more assertiveness than do girls, both within friendship pairs and in general (Craig, 2004; Tremblay, 2000). Furthermore, school-aged boys often express approval for the aggressive behaviour of peers (Rodkin, Farmer, Pearl, & Van Acker, 2000). **Table 10.2** gives representative data from a very large, carefully conducted Canadian survey, in which teachers completed checklists describing each child's behaviour (Offord, Boyle, & Racine, 1991). Clearly, boys are described as far more aggressive on all this study's measures of physical aggressiveness.

Results like these have been so clear and so consistent that most psychologists have concluded that boys are simply "more aggressive." But that conclusion may turn out to be wrong. Instead, it begins to look as if girls simply express their aggressiveness in a different way, using what has been termed *relational aggression*, instead of physical aggression. Physical aggression hurts others physically or poses a threat of such damage; **relational aggression** is aimed at damaging the other person's self-esteem or peer relationships, such as by ostracism or threats of ostracism (e.g., "I won't invite you to my birthday party if you do that"), cruel gossip, or facial expressions of disdain. Children are genuinely hurt by such indirect aggression, and they are likely to shun others who often use this form of aggression (Casas & Mosher, 1995; Crick & Grotpeter, 1995; Rys & Bear, 1997).

Girls are much more likely than boys to use relational aggression, especially toward other girls, a difference that begins as early as the preschool years and becomes very marked by Grade 4 or 5. For example, in one study of nearly 500 children in Grades 3 through 6, researchers found that 17.4% of the girls but only 2% of the boys were rated high in relational aggression—almost precisely the reverse of what is observed for physical aggression (Crick & Grotpeter, 1995). Researchers do not yet know whether this difference in form of aggression has some hormonal/biological basis or is learned at an early age, or both. They do know that higher rates of physical aggression in males have been observed in every human society and in all varieties of primates.

Retaliatory aggression—aggression to get back at someone who has hurt you—increases among both boys and girls during the 6- to 12-year-old period (Astor, 1994). Its development is related to children's growing understanding of the difference between intentional and accidental actions. For example, if a child drops his pencil in

relational aggression
aggression aimed at damaging another person's self-esteem or peer relationships, such as by ostracism or threats of ostracism, cruel gossiping, or facial expressions of disdain

retaliatory aggression
aggression to get back at someone who has hurt you

TABLE 10.2	Aggressive Behaviour in Boys and Girls Aged 4 to 11	

Percentages as Rated by Teachers

Behaviour	Boys	Girls
Mean to others	21.8	9.6
Physically attacks people	18.1	4.4
Gets in many fights	30.9	9.8
Destroys own things	10.7	2.1
Destroys others' things	10.6	4.4
Threatens to hurt people	13.1	4.0

(*Source:* **Offord, Boyle, Racine, 1991, from Table 2.3, p. 39.**)

Why do you think competition is such a strong feature of friendship interactions among boys? Do you think this is true in every culture? (*Photo:* Eastcott/Momatiuk/The Image Works)

bullying
the unjust use of power to wilfully, deliberately, and repeatedly upset or hurt another person, their property, reputation, or social acceptance

victimization
repeated, intentional acts that single someone out for hostile, exploitive, unfair, or vindictive treatment

mydevelopmentlab
Connect to
MyDevelopmentLab
Experiment time again. Become the researcher and try to classify these children based on this popularity simulation.

◄●┤Simulate

social status
an individual child's classification as popular, rejected, or neglected

the path of another child who is walking by and that child happens to kick the pencil across the floor, most 8-year-olds can identify this action as an accident. Consequently, the child whose pencil was kicked feels no need to get back at the child who did the kicking. However, children older than age 8 view intentional harm differently. For example, let's say that one child intentionally takes another's pencil off of her desk and throws it across the room. Most children older than age 8 will try to find a way to get back at a child who does something like this. In fact, children who don't try to retaliate in such situations are also more likely to be seen as socially incompetent and to be bullied by their peers in the future (Astor, 1994), as discussed in the **Research Report**.

Peers may approve of retaliatory aggression, but most parents and teachers strive to teach children that, like other forms of intentional harm, such behaviour is unacceptable. Research suggests that children can learn nonaggressive techniques for managing the kinds of situations that lead to retaliatory aggression. In one program, called PeaceBuilders, psychologists have attempted to change individual behaviour by changing a school's overall emotional climate. In this approach, both children and teachers learn to use positive social strategies (Flannery et al., 2000). For example, both are urged to try to praise others more often than they criticize them. Research suggests that when such programs are integrated into students' classes every day for an entire school year or longer, aggression decreases and prosocial behaviour increases. Thus, aggressive interactions between elementary school children may be common, but they do not appear to be an inevitable aspect of development.

SOCIOECONOMIC STATUS (SES) AND FAMILIAL FACTORS OF AGGRESSION

Tremblay et al. (1996) found that there were social class and family differences in rates of aggression in children. In lower SES boys, for instance, the incidence of both physical and indirect forms of aggression was higher, appeared at an earlier age (preschool), and persisted throughout childhood. The corresponding rates of aggression were proportionally less in boys who came from families with higher SES. Similarly, it was found that girls in lower SES families displayed both more physical and indirect aggression than girls from higher SES families.

Another strong predictor of aggression was family influence. Specifically, 38% of the variance in physical aggression and 43% of indirect aggression was found to be attributed to familial factors. The levels of aggressiveness among siblings were especially comparable in lower SES families. Moreover, physically aggressive boys were also more likely to have siblings who displayed both emotional disorders and hyperactivity. Aggressive girls were also more likely to have siblings who were more aggressive and had behavioural problems.

SOCIAL STATUS

Developmentalists measure popularity and rejection by asking children to list peers they would not like to play with or by observing which children are sought out or avoided on the playground. These techniques allow researchers to group children according to the degree to which they are accepted by peers—a variable often called **social status**. Typically, researchers find three groups: *popular*, *rejected*, and *neglected*.

Research Report

BULLIES AND VICTIMS

At first glance, aggressive interactions between children might appear to be fairly simple: one child hurts another child. However, Canadian psychologists Wendy Craig of Queen's University and Debra Pepler of York University and their colleagues have found that, in the middle childhood years, aggressive interactions become increasingly complex (Craig, 2004; Pepler et al., 2006). **Bullying** and **victimization** involving physical aggression decline with age in both boys and girls but are replaced with indirect forms of aggression. For example, *sexual harassment*, such as unwanted sexual comments, brushing up against someone in a sexual way, spreading sexual rumours about someone, or calling someone a *faggot* or a *sleaze*" as well as *dating aggression*, such as slapping or kicking a romantic partner, spreading rumours about him, or ignoring or excluding him from the group in anger, emerge in Grades 6 to 8 and peak by Grade 10—in accord with the physical and psychosocial sexual development associated with puberty (Pepler et al., 2006). Nonphysical bullying also becomes more ethnocultural as children age, taking the forms of racial and religious harassment (Craig, 2004).

Internet communication has provided a new means of attacking others: cyber-bullying. A recent Canadian study suggests that the popularity of instant messaging and social networking websites such as MySpace and Facebook have given rise to this new form of aggression (Lines, 2007). The study by Kids Help Phone, based on 2474 responses to an online survey, indicated that over 70% of the respondents had been bullied online and 44% admitted to having bullied someone online at least once.

Children are also using cellphones to bully others; for example, they send abusive text messages and embarrassing photos. Electronic bullying is rising in popularity because of its seeming anonymity—it allows kids to "act mean and get away with it" (Media Awareness Network, 2005).

As children get older, they tend to take on consistent roles across aggressive interactions—perpetrator, victim, assistant to the perpetrator, reinforcing onlooker, nonparticipant onlooker, defender of the victim, and so on (Andreou & Metallidou, 2004). Children's personality traits to some degree determine the roles they assume. For example, shy children usually take the nonparticipant onlooker role, while children who are emotionally unstable are more likely to serve as assistants to the perpetrator or as reinforcing onlookers (Tani, Greenman, Schneider, & Fregoso, 2003). The occupant of each of these roles plays a part in maintaining a particular aggressive incident and in determining whether another aggressive interaction involving the same perpetrator and victim will occur in the future. Sometimes, however, there is an exception to this pattern: in some cases, children who are victimized by others, or who are onlookers, may in turn be drawn into bullying others (Craig, 2004).

Until fairly recently, both research on and interventions aimed at reducing aggression focused on the habitual perpetrators, or bullies. However, most developmentalists now believe that changing the behaviour of children who occupy the other roles in aggressive interactions, especially those who are habitual victims, may be just as important as intervening with the aggressive children (Green, 2001). Victims have certain characteristics in common, including anxiety, passivity, sensitivity, low self-esteem or self-confidence, lack of humour, and a lack of high quality relationships with friends (Egan & Perry, 1998; Goldbaum, Craig, Pepler, & Connolly, 2003; Hodges, Malone, & Perry, 1997; Olweus, 1995). Cross-cultural studies show that these characteristics are common to habitual victims across a wide variety of cultural settings (Eslea et al., 2004). And in the case of boys, victims are also often physically smaller or weaker than their peers.

Whether boys or girls, victims seldom assert themselves with their peers, neither making suggestions for play activities nor displaying prosocial actions. Instead, they submit to whatever suggestions others make. Other children do not like this behaviour and thus do not like the victims (Crick & Grotpeter, 1995; Schwartz, Dodge, & Coie, 1993). The consequences of such victimization can include loneliness, school avoidance, low self-esteem, and significant depression at later ages (Kochenderfer & Ladd, 1996; Olweus, 1995).

Still, not all children faced with a passive and unresponsive playmate turn into bullies. Bullies are distinctive because they are typically aggressive in a variety of situations, not just in relationships with selected victims.

Bullies also tend to be more aggressive toward adults than do nonbullies, cannot empathize with their victims' pain or unhappiness, feel little or no guilt or shame about their actions, and are often impulsive (Menesini et al., 2003). Contrary to the common assumption that bullies are basically insecure children who have developed a tough exterior to cover up their insecurity, it appears the opposite is true (Olweus, 1995). Bullies most often have low levels of anxiety and insecurity.

Bullying and victimization are complex phenomena that take many forms at different stages in a child's development. Youths cannot solve these behaviours themselves. Early intervention and prevention methods involving peers, adults, and schools may be the best, first course of action to take (Pepler et al., 2006).

Some of the characteristics that differentiate popular children from those in the other two groups are things outside a child's control. In particular, attractive children and physically larger children are more likely to be popular. Conversely, being very different from her peers may cause a child to be neglected or rejected. For example, shy children usually have few friends (Fordham & Stevenson-Hinde, 1999). Similarly, highly creative children are often rejected, as are those who have difficulty controlling their emotions (Aranha, 1997; Maszk, Eisenberg, & Guthrie, 1999).

However, children's social behaviour seems to be more important than looks or temperament. Most studies show that popular children behave in positive, supporting, nonpunitive, and nonaggressive ways toward most other children. They explain things, take their playmates' wishes into consideration, take turns in conversation, and are able to regulate the expression of their strong emotions. In addition, popular children are usually good at regulating their own emotions and accurately assessing others' feelings (Underwood, 1997). Most are good at looking at situations from others' perspectives as well (Fitzgerald & White, 2003).

There are two types of rejected children. *Withdrawn/rejected* children realize that they are disliked by peers (Harrist, Zaia, Bates, Dodge, & Pettit, 1997). After repeated attempts to gain peer acceptance, these children eventually give up and become socially withdrawn. As a result, they often experience feelings of loneliness. *Aggressive/rejected* children are often disruptive and uncooperative and usually believe that their peers like them (Zakriski & Coie, 1996). Many appear to be unable to control the expression of strong feelings (Eisenberg et al., 1995; Pettit, Clawson, Dodge, & Bates, 1996). They interrupt their play partners more often and fail to take turns in a systematic way.

As you learned in **Chapter 8,** aggressive behaviour persists into adulthood in some individuals, and it is most likely to become a stable characteristic among children who are *both* aggressive and rejected by peers. Of course, not all aggressive children are rejected. Among girls, aggression, whether physical or relational, seems to lead to peer rejection consistently. Among boys, however, aggression may result in either popularity or rejection (Rodkin et al., 2000; Xie, Cairns, & Cairns, 1999). For instance, Université Laval psychologists François Poulin and Michel Boivin have been studying the role of aggression in the formation and development of boys' friendships in Grades 4 through 6. They found that, irrespective of aggressive boys' general popularity, their close friends tend to be aggressive as well. Furthermore, aggressiveness seems to precede these relationships. In other words, boys who are aggressive seek out boys like themselves as friends, and being friends doesn't seem to make either member of the pair more aggressive (Poulin & Boivin, 2000). Research also suggests that children have more positive attitudes toward aggressive peers whose aggressive acts are seen as mostly retaliatory and toward those who engage in both prosocial and aggressive behaviour (Coie & Cillessen, 1993; Newcomb, Bukowski, & Pattee, 1993; Poulin & Boivin, 1999). Social approval may not increase aggressiveness, but it does seem to help maintain it; interventions to reduce aggressive behaviour typically have little effect on aggressive boys who are popular (Phillips, Schwean, & Saklofske, 1997).

Neglect seems to be much less stable over time than rejection; neglected children sometimes move to the popular category when they become part of a new peer group. However, children who experience prolonged neglect are more prone to depression and loneliness than are popular children (Cillessen, van IJzendoorn, van Lieshout, & Hartup, 1992; Rubin, Hymel, Mills, & Rose-Krasnor, 1991; Wentzel & Asher, 1995). The association between peer neglect and depression may be explained by recent brain-imaging studies showing that, among school-aged children, social exclusion stimulates the same area of the brain as physical pain does (Eisenberger, 2003). In addition, this tendency toward depression among neglected children may be fostered by unrealistic expectations about adults' ability to "fix" the social situation—for example, "Why doesn't the teacher make them be my friends?" (Galanaki, 2004).

Before Going On

- Describe school-aged children's changing relationships with their parents and peers.
- Describe the changing patterns of aggression and social status in middle childhood.

INFLUENCES BEYOND FAMILY AND PEERS

 Watch

The daily life of the school-aged child is shaped by more than the hours she spends in school. The circumstances in which a child lives also affect her. For example, some parents are at home when children come home from school; others are still at work. A child is also affected by her family's economic circumstances, by the neighbourhood she lives in, and by the TV programs she watches.

AFTER-SCHOOL CARE

In Canada, many children are at home by themselves after school for an hour or more each weekday. They are often referred to as **self-care children**. Self-care arrangements differ so much from child to child that it is impossible to say whether, as a group, self-care children differ from others. For example, some self-care children are home alone but are closely monitored by neighbours or relatives, while others are completely without supervision of any kind (Brandon, 1999). Developmentalists have learned that the effects of self-care on a child's development depend on behavioural history, age, gender, the kind of neighbourhood the child lives in, and how well parents monitor the child during self-care periods (Casper & Smith, 2002; NICHD, 2004b; Posner & Vandell, 1994).

self-care children
children who are at home by themselves after school for an hour or more each day

Research consistently demonstrates that self-care children are more poorly adjusted in terms of both peer relationships and school performance. They tend to be less socially skilled and to have a greater number of behaviour problems. However, some of these differences between self-care children and others arise from the effect of self-care on children who already have social and behavioural difficulties before self-care begins. Investigators have found that children who have such problems in the preschool years, before they experience any self-care, are the most negatively affected by the self-care experience (Pettit, Laird, Bates, & Dodge, 1997).

With respect to age, most developmentalists agree that children less than age 9 or 10 should not care for themselves. The age at which children may be legally left to care for themselves and/or other children varies by province or territory from 10 to 12 years (Canada Safety Council, 2007). Before allowing their child to look after himself or other children, parents can find out what to consider by contacting the Canadian Red Cross, St. John Ambulance, or other community agencies that offer babysitting courses for youth.

From a developmental perspective, children younger than age 9 do not have the cognitive abilities necessary to evaluate risks and deal with emergencies. Children who

Many Canadian children are at home by themselves after school for an hour or more each weekday. (*Photo:* Thinkstock)

start self-care in the early elementary years are vulnerable to older self-care children in their neighbourhoods who may hurt or even sexually abuse them and are more likely to have adjustment difficulties in school (Pettit et al., 1997). High-quality after-school programs can help these younger children attain a higher level of achievement (Peterson, Ewigman, & Kivlahan, 1993; Zigler & Finn-Stevenson, 1993).

Children older than age 9 may be cognitively able to manage self-care, but they, too, benefit from participation in well-supervised after-school programs. Even part-time participation in supervised activities after school seems to make a difference in the adjustment of self-care children (Pettit et al., 1997). Good programs provide children with opportunities to play, do homework, and get help from adults (Posner & Vandell, 1994).

Self-care has the most negative effects for children in low-income neighbourhoods with high crime rates (Marshall et al., 1997). Self-care children in such areas may use after-school time to "hang out" with socially deviant peers who are involved in criminal activity or who have negative attitudes about school. Predictably, then, the positive effects of organized after-school programs on academic achievement are greater for children in low-income neighbourhoods (Mason & Chuang, 2001; Posner & Vandell, 1994).

When everything is taken into consideration, the most important factor in self-care seems to be parental monitoring. Many parents, particularly single mothers, enlist the help of neighbours and relatives to keep an eye on their self-care children (Brandon & Hofferth, 2003). Most require children to call them at work when they get home from school to talk about their school day and get instructions about homework and chores. For example, a working mother might tell a fifth-grader, "By the time I get home at 5:00, you should be finished with your math and spelling. Don't work on your history project until I get home and can help you with it. As soon as you finish your math and spelling, start the dishwasher." Research suggests that children whose periods of self-care are monitored in this way are less likely to experience the potential negative effects of self-care (Galambos & Maggs, 1991).

MEDIA INFLUENCES

Another important feature of children's environment is the wide array of today's informational and entertainment media. Televisions, computers, and video games are found in the majority of homes in the industrialized world. Only 10% of Canadian children meet the Canadian Paediatric Society (2003) recommended guideline of only 2 hours or less of screen time per day. On the contrary, most Canadian children average more than 6 hours daily in front of a screen (Active Healthy Kids Canada, 2010). How do these media affect children's development?

TELEVISION Nearly every Canadian home has at least one TV set and nine out of ten households have access to hundreds of cable or satellite channels, providing children with exposure to a wide variety and quality of TV programming (CRTC, 2006; Natural

Resources Canada, 2010). Canadian children between ages 2 and 11 spend an average of 14 hours a week watching television, down from a peak of 19.2 hours a week in 1990 (Statistics Canada, 2001d, 2006). Although this decline in TV viewing is related to an increase in recreational computer use and video gaming, television still has a major impact on Canadian children (Mark, Boyce, & Janssen, 2006).

In North America, children between ages 6 and 12 spend more time watching television than they do playing.
(*Photo:* Thinkstock)

POSITIVE EDUCATIONAL EFFECTS Programs specifically designed to be educational and/or teach children social values do indeed have demonstrable positive effects (Linebarger & Wainwright, 2006). For example, children who regularly watched quality educational programs, such as *Sesame Street*, *Dora the Explorer*, or *Blue's Clues*, developed better early literacy and math skills than did children who did not watch or who watched less often (Anderson, Huston, Schmitt, Linebarger, & Wright, 2001; Ennemoser & Schneider, 2007; Linebarger & Walker, 2005). In fact, one follow-up study of adolescents whose TV-viewing patterns had been tracked when they were preschoolers, found that those who watched more quality educational programs than entertainment-types of TV programming were less aggressive, had higher grades, read more books, and were more achievement oriented and creative (Anderson et al., 2001). These studies suggest that the TV content viewed is more important than the raw amount watched. In addition, children can have learning experiences through TV viewing—such as witnessing the migration of whales—that they would not likely have otherwise. As you learned in **Chapter 9**, the advances in information-processing skills that children undergo between ages 6 and 12 enable them to remember more from such viewing experiences. Moreover, previously acquired knowledge is important to each new learning experience; Television can be an important means by which school-aged children acquire experiences that can make them more efficient learners at school; for example, a child who has seen a TV program about whale migration is likely to get more out of a school science lesson about whales than a student who has no relevant knowledge.

NEGATIVE EFFECTS OF TELEVISION ON COGNITIVE SKILLS Despite the potential positive effects of watching quality educational television on cognitive development, research has demonstrated that heavy TV viewing is associated with lower scores on achievement tests, including measures of such basic skills as reading, arithmetic, and writing. For example, one study of Grade 3 students found a significant relationship between the type and placement of household media and academic achievement; those students who had no computer in the home but had a television in their bedroom watched more hours of television per week and had the worst test scores on mathematics, reading, and language arts. In contrast, children who had home computer access and use but no bedroom television watched fewer hours of television per week and had the highest achievement test scores (Borzekowski & Robinson, 2005). In a New Zealand longitudinal study, the researchers found that the more hours of television students watched during childhood and adolescence, the lower their academic qualifications achieved by age 26 (Hancox, Milne, & Poulton, 2005). Thus, television can help teach children things they do not already know, but overall, TV-viewing time appears to have a negative effect on school performance, especially television of low educational quality.

TELEVISION AND AGGRESSION Bandura demonstrated the effects of televised violence on children's behaviour in his classic "Bobo doll" studies (Bandura, Ross, & Ross, 1961, 1963). In these experiments, children were found to imitate adults' violent treatment of an inflatable clown that was depicted on film. Recent research suggests that such effects persist into the adult years. For example, in one important 15-year longitudinal study, researchers found that the more TV violence children were exposed to when they were aged 6 to 9 years, the higher the amount of direct physical aggression in adults of both genders and indirect aggression in adult females, regardless of how aggressive they were as children (Huesmann, Moise-Titus, Podolski, & Eron, 2003). Brain-imaging studies suggest that these long-term effects may be the result of patterns of neural activation that underlie emotionally laden behavioural scripts that children learn while watching violent programming (Murray et al., 2006). These patterns of neural activation may also explain the finding that repeated viewing of TV violence leads to long-term aggressive biases, such as emotional desensitization regarding violence, a belief that aggression is a good way to solve problems, and a greater readiness to act aggressively, and to a reduction in prosocial behaviour (Funk, Baldacci, Pasold, & Baumgardner, 2004; Ostrov, Gentile, & Crick, 2006; Van Mierlo & Van den Bulck, 2004).

Sociocultural research has examined the conditions surrounding the emergence of a pattern of aggressive behaviour in several different countries to see whether researchers could identify common antecedents. For example, one researcher looked at changes in homicide rates in the whole population in Canada, and among whites in the United States and South Africa, as a function of the time since television was introduced into each country (Centerwall, 1989, 1992). Television was introduced in both the United States and Canada in about 1950; in South Africa, television became widely available about 25 years later. In each of these three countries, the homicide rate began to rise rapidly 10 to 15 years after TV viewing became widespread. That is, as soon as the first generation of children who had grown up watching television became adults, homicide rates soared. Moreover, statistical analyses showed that the rise in homicides could not be attributed to urbanization, civil unrest, alcohol use, availability of firearms, or any other social condition that had changed over the same period of time.

For parents, the clear message from all the research on television is that television is an educational medium. Children learn from what they watch—vocabulary words, helpful behaviours, dietary preferences, as well as aggressive behaviours and attitudes. The overall content of television—violence and all—may indeed reflect general cultural values. But families can pick and choose among the various cultural messages by controlling what their children watch on television.

Before Going On

- How does self-care affect girls' and boys' development?
- How are televised violence and violent behaviour related?

Summary

Theories of Social and Personality Development

- Freud claimed that the libido is dormant between ages 6 and 12, a period he called the *latency stage*. Erikson theorized that 6- to 12-year-olds acquire a sense of industry by achieving educational goals determined by their cultures.

- The Big Five personality traits are evident in 6- to 12-year-olds. Variations appear to be related to temperament in infancy and early childhood.

- Social-cognitive theories, such as Bandura's reciprocal determinism, indicate that personality is shaped from personal, environmental, and behavioural factors.

Self-Concept

- Between ages 6 and 12, children construct a psychological self. As a result, their self-descriptions begin to include personality traits, such as intelligence and friendliness, along with physical characteristics.

- Self-esteem appears to be shaped by two factors: the degree of discrepancy a child experiences between goals and achievements, and the degree of perceived social support from peers and parents.

Advances in Social Cognition

- Between ages 6 and 12, children's understanding of others' stable, internal traits improves.

- Piaget claimed that moral reasoning develops in sequential stages that are correlated with his cognitive-developmental stages.

Social Relationships

- Relationships with parents become less overtly affectionate, with fewer attachment behaviours, in middle childhood. The strength of the attachment, however, appears to persist.

- Friendships become stable in middle childhood. Children's selection of friends depends on variables such as trustworthiness as well as overt characteristics such as play preferences and gender.

- Gender segregation of peer groups is at its peak in middle childhood and appears in every culture. Individual friendships also become more common and more enduring.

- Physical aggression declines during middle childhood, although verbal aggression increases. Boys show markedly higher levels of physical and direct verbal aggression, and higher rates of conduct disorders, than girls. Girls show higher rates of relational aggression.

- Rejected children are most strongly characterized by high levels of aggression or bullying and low levels of agreeableness and helpfulness, but some aggressive children are very popular. Neglected children may suffer depression.

Influences Beyond Family and Peers

- Self-care is associated with several negative effects. Girls, children who live in safe neighbourhoods, and children whose parents closely monitor their activities after school are the least likely to be negatively affected by self-care.

- Preschoolers can learn vocabulary, prosocial behaviour, and other social skills from moderated viewing of quality educational television. The more television school children watch, the lower their grades are. Experts agree that watching violence on television increases the level of personal aggression or violence shown by a child.

Review Questions

Answers are provided on MyDevelopmentLab in the Course Resources folder.

Theories of Social and Personality Development

10.1 According to Erikson's view of children's psychosocial development in middle childhood, what factor is instrumental in children's development of a sense of industry or inferiority?

a. their developing relationships with cross-gender friends and peers
b. their growing independence from their parents
c. their success or failure at academic tasks
d. their developing motor skills and athletic accomplishments

Self-Concept

10.2 What are the key influences on a child's self-esteem in middle childhood?
   a. her skills and abilities in key developmental areas such as academics, sports, and hobbies
   b. the amount of support she receives from important people around her and the discrepancy between what she has achieved and what she desires to achieve
   c. her perceptions about what children of her age should be able to accomplish or achieve
   d. her popularity with other children and her popularity with the adults she knows

Advances in Social Cognition

10.3 According to Piaget, children who are at the beginning of middle childhood are in which stage of moral development?
   a. moral realism
   b. moral emotional
   c. moral judgmental
   d. moral relativism

Social Relationships

10.4 In middle childhood,
   a. boys and girls play well together.
   b. boys play with boys and girls play with girls.
   c. rough-and-tumble is common in girl–boy interactions.
   d. children prefer to associate with one intimate friend than with groups.

Influences Beyond Family and Peers

10.5 Self-care children who are monitored closely are
   a. more likely to be involved in criminal behaviour.
   b. more likely to make poor grades.
   c. less likely to experience the negative effects of self-care.
   d. less likely to complete their homework.

Critical-Thinking Questions

10.6 Think back to your own elementary school experiences. Do you think you gained a sense of industry or inferiority from them? How did they affect your subsequent development?

10.7 Given all that you have read about television and children's development, how could you as a parent maximize the benefits and limit the negative effects of television? Would you be willing to give up having television altogether if you thought that was necessary for your child's optimum development?

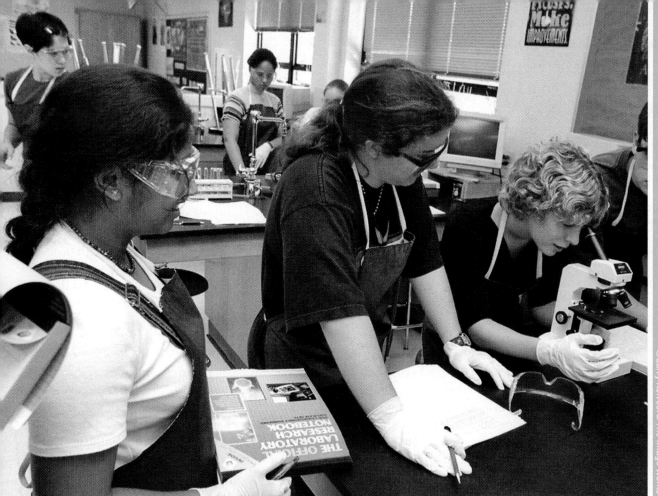

©Larry Kolvoord/The Image Works

When people think about adolescence, puberty is usually the first developmental milestone that comes to mind. However, the physical changes of puberty, as dramatic as they are, are only one component of this important period of transition from childhood to adulthood. For example, if you ask an 8-year-old what she wants to be when she grows up, she is likely to give you an answer like "a firefighter" or "a veterinarian." Ask a 15-year-old the same question, and you are likely to hear something like this: "Well, I'm thinking about several things. I know I want to go to college, but I don't know where, and I'm not sure what I want to study." Such differences reflect age-related changes in the overall quality of thought.

The second idea most people have about adolescence is that it is filled with problems. Mention teenagers and many people automatically think of shouting matches between parents and their teenaged children or of high-risk behaviours such as drug use and unprotected sex. Such stereotypical images stem from people's tendency to focus on the negative aspects of this period rather than on the enormous strides adolescents take toward maturity.

When you finish studying the chapter, you will be able to describe how the reproductive system, the brain, and other body systems change during adolescence; identify the key patterns, issues, and challenges of adolescent sexual development; discuss the risks associated with substance abuse and describe potential mental health problems during adolescence; summarize the cognitive changes in formal operational thinking and information-processing skills during adolescence; and describe the influences of schooling and employment on adolescent development. As you read, keep the following questions in mind:

- How is sexuality influenced by the interaction of biopsychosocial and environmental factors?

- Why do you suppose teens are more likely to engage in risky behaviours than other age groups?

- What sociocultural factors in Canada influence adolescents' perception of desirable body types?

PHYSICAL CHANGES

When we think of the physical changes of adolescence, we usually give the greatest amount of attention to the reproductive system. Reproductive changes are important, as the text will point out. But momentous changes occur in other systems, and we will discuss those as well.

 Watch

MILESTONES OF PUBERTY

The growth and development of teenagers' brains and bodies is remarkable. The physical change that most people associate with adolescence is the attainment of sexual maturity. **Puberty** is a collective term that encompasses all the changes, both seen and unseen, that are needed for reproductive maturity. It begins when the **pituitary gland,** the gland that controls all the body's other glands, signals a child's adrenal gland to step up its production of androgen (see **Table 11.1**). This milestone is called *adrenarche* and occurs around age 7 or 8. Next, the pituitary begins secreting hormones that stimulate the growth of the ovaries in girls and the testes in boys. As they grow, these glands secrete hormones—testosterone in boys and a form of estrogen called *estradiol* in girls—that cause the sex organs to develop.

puberty
collective term for the physical changes that culminate in sexual maturity

pituitary gland
gland that triggers other glands to release hormones

TABLE 11.1	Major Hormones That Contribute to Physical Growth and Development	
Gland	**Hormone(s)**	**Aspects of Growth Influenced**
Thyroid gland	Thyroxine	Normal brain development and overall rate of growth
Adrenal gland	Adrenal androgen	Some changes at puberty, particularly the development of secondary sex characteristics in girls
Testes (boys)	Testosterone	Crucial in the formation of male genitals prenatally; also triggers the sequence of changes in primary and secondary sex characteristics in the male
Ovaries (girls)	Estrogen (estradiol)	Development of the menstrual cycle and breasts in girls; has less to do with other secondary sex characteristics than testosterone does for boys
Pituitary gland	General growth hormone, thyroid stimulating hormone, and other activating hormones	Rate of physical maturation; signals other glands to secrete

The pituitary also secretes two other hormones: *thyroid stimulating hormone* and *general growth hormone*. These, along with adrenal androgen, interact with the specific sex hormones and affect growth. Adrenal androgen, which is chemically very similar to testosterone, plays a particularly important role for girls, triggering the growth spurt and affecting development of pubic hair. For boys, adrenal androgen is less significant, presumably because boys already have so much male hormone in the form of testosterone in their bloodstreams. These hormonal changes trigger two sets of body changes: development of the sex organs and a much broader set of changes in the brain, bones, muscles, and other body organs.

The most obvious changes of puberty are those associated with sexual maturity. Changes in **primary sex characteristics** include growth of the testes and penis in the male and of the ovaries, uterus, and vagina in the female. Changes in **secondary sex characteristics** include breast development in girls, voice pitch changes and beard growth in boys, and body hair growth in both sexes. These physical developments occur in a defined sequence that is customarily divided into five stages, following a system originally suggested by J.M. Tanner (Tanner, 1990), examples from which are shown in **Table 11.2**.

primary sex characteristics
the sex organs: ovaries, uterus, and vagina in the female; testes and penis in the male

secondary sex charactersitics
body parts such as breasts in females and pubic hair in both sexes

SEXUAL DEVELOPMENT IN GIRLS
Studies of preteens and teens in both Europe and North America show that the various sequential changes are interlocked in a particular pattern in girls. The first steps are the early changes in breasts and pubic hair, closely followed by the peak of the growth spurt and by the beginnings of stages 4 and 5, the development of breasts and pubic hair. First menstruation, an event called **menarche** (pronounced men-AR-kee), typically occurs 2 years after the beginning of other visible changes and is succeeded only by the final stages of breast and pubic hair development. Among girls in industrialized countries today, menarche occurs, on average, between ages 12 and 13; 99% of all girls experience this event between ages 9 and 12 (Adelman & Ellen, 2002).

menarche
the beginning of the menstrual cycle

It is possible to become pregnant shortly after menarche, but irregular menstrual cycles are the norm for some time. In as many as three-quarters of the cycles in the first year and in one-half of the cycles in the second and third years after menarche, the girl's body produces no ovum (Adelman & Ellen, 2002). Full adult fertility thus develops over a period of years. Such irregularity no doubt contributes to the widespread (but false) assumption among younger teenaged girls that they cannot get pregnant.

TABLE 11.2	Examples of Tanner's Stages of Pubertal Development	
Stage	Female Breast Development	Male Genital Development
1	No change except for some elevation of the nipple.	Testes, scrotum, and penis are all about the same size and shape as in early childhood.
2	Breast bud stage: elevation of breast and the nipple as a small mound. Areolar diameter increases compared with stage 1.	Scrotum and testes are slightly enlarged. Skin of the scrotum reddens and changes texture, but little or no enlargement of the penis.
3	Breast and areola both enlarge and elevate more than in stage 2, but no separation of their contours.	Penis slightly enlarged, at first mainly in length. Testes and scrotum are further enlarged. First ejaculation.
4	Areola and nipple form a secondary mound projecting above the contour of the breast.	Penis further enlarged, with growth in breadth and development of glans. Testes and scrotum further enlarged, and scrotum skin still darker.
5	Mature stage. Only the nipple projects, with the areola recessed to the general contour of the breast.	Genitalia achieve adult size and shape.

(*Source:* Petersen & Taylor, 1980, p. 127.)

secular trend
the decline in the average age of menarche, along with changes such as an increase in average height for both children and adults, that happened between the mid-19th and mid-20th centuries in Western countries and occurs in developing nations when nutrition and health improve

SECULAR TREND Interestingly, the timing of menarche changed rather dramatically between the mid-19th and the mid-20th centuries. In 1840, the average age of menarche in Western industrialized countries was roughly 17; the average dropped steadily at a rate of about 3 to 4 months per decade until the 1950s. This steady drop among European populations is an example of what psychologists call a **secular trend**. The decline has levelled off in most industrialized countries but is still happening in developing nations where women's diets and general health have been improving (Bagga & Kulkarni, 2000; Roche, 1979; Tanner, 1990). The change is most likely caused by significant changes in lifestyle and diet, particularly increases in protein and fat intake, along with reductions in physical exercise that resulted in an increase in the proportion of body fat in females.

Data collected over much shorter periods of time in developing countries support the nutritional explanation of the secular trend. In one study, researchers found that the average age of menarche was 16 among North Korean girls who lived in squalid refugee camps (Ku et al., 2006). By contrast, studies involving impoverished groups in which food supplies suddenly increase reveal that the age of menarche can plummet from 16 to 13 within just a few years after improvements in nutrition are experienced (Khanna & Kapoor, 2004). Consequently, any change in eating patterns that affects girls' body fat, which must reach a critical value of 17% before menarche can occur, is likely to lead to a change in the age of menarche (Adelman & Ellen, 2002). But is there a lower limit on how early menarche can occur?

The average ages at which girls show secondary sex characteristics, such as the appearance of breast buds and pubic hair, have dropped significantly in recent decades (Anderson, Dallal, & Must, 2003). On average, girls now show these signs 1 to 2 years earlier than their mothers and grandmothers did, resulting in a lengthening of the average time between the appearance of secondary sex characteristics and menarche (Parent et al., 2003). Researchers have found that this trend is attributable to the increased prevalence of overweight children that you read about in **Chapter 9** (Wang, 2002).

Being overweight is both a cause and a consequence of early secondary sex characteristic development, because the hormonal changes that trigger the appearance of these characteristics also signal the body's weight regulation mechanisms to increase fat stores (Pierce & Leon, 2005; Remsberg et al., 2004). Little is known about how these early hormonal shifts affect girls' later health. Several studies are underway to determine whether overweight girls who exhibit early secondary sex characteristic development are at increased risk for breast cancer, adult obesity, and heart disease (National Cancer Institute, 2006; Pierce & Leon, 2005). Interestingly, too, researchers are also investigating why being overweight delays pubertal development in boys and whether such delays affect boys' health later in life (Wang, 2002).

SEXUAL DEVELOPMENT IN BOYS In boys, as in girls, the peak of the growth spurt typically comes fairly late in the sequence of physical development. Studies suggest that, on average, a boy completes stages 2, 3, and 4 of genital development and stages 2 and 3 of pubic hair development before reaching the peak of the growth spurt (Adelman & Ellen, 2002). His first ejaculation, or *spermarche*, occurs between age 13 and 14, but the production of viable sperm does not happen until a few months after the first ejaculation. Most boys do not attain adult levels of sperm production until stage 5 of genital development. The development of a beard and the lowering of the voice occur near the end of the sequence. Precisely when in this sequence the boy begins to produce viable sperm is very difficult to determine, although current evidence places this event some time between ages 12 and 14, usually before the boy has reached the peak of the growth spurt (Adelman & Ellen, 2002).

TIMING OF PUBERTY Although the order of physical developments in adolescence seems to be highly consistent, there is quite a lot of individual variability. In any random sample of 12- and 13-year-olds, you will find some who are already at stage 5 and others still at stage 1 in the steps of sexual maturation. We have already discussed the contribution of diet, exercise, and body fat to the timing of puberty. Researchers think that hereditary and behavioural factors also contribute to hormonal secretions in the bodies of individual teenagers, thereby controlling the timing of puberty (Dorn, Susman, & Ponirakis, 2003). Discrepancies between an adolescent's expectation and what actually happens determine the psychological effect of puberty. Those whose development occurs outside the desired or expected range are likely to think less well of themselves, to be less happy with their bodies and with the process of puberty. They may also display other signs of psychological distress.

A Canadian study based on NLSCY data determined that girls who are early developers (experience major body changes before age 10 or 11) showed no problems with self-esteem or academics, and they had fewer behavioural problems than other girls their age (Japal, Tremblay, McDuff, & Willms, 2002). Although early maturing girls didn't smoke, drink alcohol, or do drugs any more or less than other girls their age, they did tend to belong to groups of older peers who displayed antisocial behaviours and who smoked, drank alcohol, and did drugs. Associating with older youths who get into trouble may set these early maturing girls up for sexual and school problems later

Adolescent girls reach adult height sooner than boys because their bones grow and their joints develop more rapidly.
(*Photo:* Copyright © David Young Wolff/Photo Edit—All rights reserved)

on. Among boys, those who are slightly ahead of their peers in pubertal development often occupy leadership roles and are more academically and economically successful in adulthood (Taga, Markey, & Friedman, 2006). In addition, substance use is associated with early puberty in both girls and boys, because, based on their appearance, early maturers are often invited to join groups of older teens among whom substance use is an important social activity (Costello, Sung, Worthman, & Angold, 2007).

OTHER BODY SYSTEMS

For most individuals, adolescence is one of the healthiest periods of life and the changes in other body systems allow adolescents to acquire new cognitive and motor skills.

THE BRAIN Although a 6-year-old's brain is approximately 95% of its adult size, many significant anatomical changes continue to unfold in the brain up to adulthood (Lenroot & Giedd, 2006). As you may recall from earlier chapters, postnatal brain development occurs in two basic ways: There are growth spurts that entail *synaptogenesis* (the overproduction of neural branches and connection) followed by synaptic *pruning* (which follows the "use it or lose it" principle whereby neural connections that are not used will wither and die). Evidence to support this comes from brain imaging studies of Mz and Dz twins, which indicate an increasing environmental influence on *grey matter* (GM) volumes in response to *plastic* synapses changing in response to activity (Wallace et al., 2006). The changes in GM are thought to reflect changes in the size and complexity of neurons, not a change in actual number. During adolescence though, we observe some dramatic changes in grey matter volume. **Figure 11.1** illustrates how the brain's volume of GM follows an inverted U-shaped trajectory from early childhood to early adulthood with peak volumes being reached in different brain regions at different times in boys and girls (Giedd, 2004; Lenroot & Giedd, 2006; Lenroot et al., 2007). A decreasing amount of GM may reflect the process of pruning. Among the last brain regions to reach adult levels are areas within the frontal cortex that are linked to the control of impulses, judgment, and decision making, which raises concerns about adolescents' degree of responsibility for their actions (Lenroot & Giedd, 2006).

In comparison, the trajectory of volume of *white matter* (WM; myelinated axons that speed-up neural processing) steadily increases in the four major lobes of the brain (frontal, temporal, parietal, and occipital)—a developmental pattern that is associated with the cognitive, behavioural, and emotional differences between children and adults (Giedd, 2004; Lenroot & Giedd, 2006). Two other important increases in WM volume take place in areas which are associated with developmental changes during the adolescent years—the corpus callosum (which integrates the activities of the left and right sides of the brain) and the pathways connecting speech reception (Wernicke's area) with speech production (Broca's area). You will find out more about how the brain develops into adulthood in the **Research Report** in **Chapter 13**.

THE SKELETAL SYSTEM An adolescent may grow 5 to 13 centimetres a year for several years. After the growth spurt, teenagers add height and weight slowly until they reach their adult size. Girls attain most of their height by age 16, while boys continue to grow until they are 18 to 20 years old (Tanner, 1990).

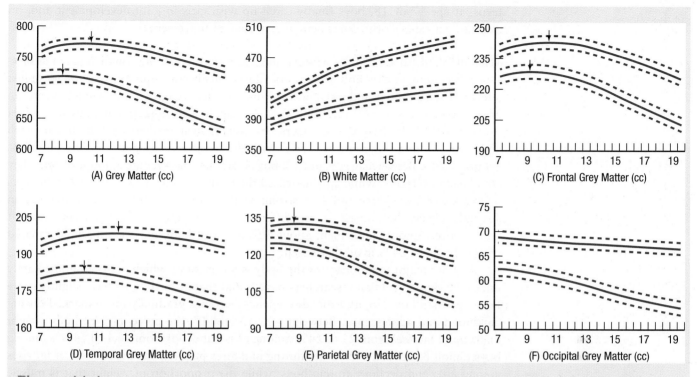

Figure 11.1

Developmental trajectory of brain volume by age in years for males (blue lines) and females (red lines). The middle line in each set of three lines represents the mean value, and the upper and lower lines represent the upper and lower 95% confidence intervals. The arrow indicates the age at which peak volume was attained.

(*Source:* Adapted from Lenroot et al., 2007, Figure 2 and Figure 3, pp. 4–5. Reproduced with the permission of the authors.)

The shape and proportions of the adolescent's body also go through a series of changes. During the growth spurt, the normal *cephalocaudal* and *proximodistal* patterns are reversed. Thus, a teenager's hands and feet are the first body parts to grow to full adult size, followed by the arms and the legs; the trunk is usually the slowest part to grow. In fact, a good signal for a parent that a child is entering puberty is a rapid increase in the child's shoe size. Because of this asymmetry in the body parts, adolescents are often stereotyped as awkward or uncoordinated. Adolescents may look awkward, but they are better coordinated than school-aged children (Malina, 1990).

The skeletal system goes through other changes as it increases in size. For example, during the elementary-school years, the size and shape of a child's jaw change when the permanent teeth come in. In adolescence, both jaws grow forward and the forehead becomes more prominent. This set of changes often gives teenagers' faces (especially boys') an angular, bony appearance.

Joint development enables adolescents to achieve levels of coordination that are close to those of adults. As they do at younger ages, boys continue to lag behind girls. You may remember from earlier chapters that boys' fine motor skills are poorer than girls' because their wrists develop more slowly. In early adolescence, this sex difference is very large; girls achieve complete development of the wrist by their mid-teens (Tanner, 1990). A similar pattern of sex differences is evident in other joints as well, enabling early-adolescent girls to outperform boys of the same age on a variety of athletic skills that require coordination, such as pitching a softball. However, by the late teens, at age 17 or 18, boys finally catch up with girls in joint development and, on average, gain superiority over them in coordinated movement.

THE MUSCULAR SYSTEM Muscle fibres also go through a growth spurt at adolescence, becoming thicker and denser, and adolescents become quite a lot stronger in just a few years. Both boys and girls show this increase in strength, but it is much greater in boys (Buchanan & Vardaxis, 2003). For example, in a cross-sectional study in Canada involving 2673 children and teenagers, researchers measured strength by having each child hang from a bar, with eyes level with the bar, for as long as possible (Smoll & Schutz, 1990). Between ages 9 and 17, boys increased the average amount of time they could hang by 160%, while girls increased their time by only 37%. By age 17, the boys in this study were three times as strong as the girls. This substantial difference in strength reflects the underlying sex difference in muscle tissue that is accentuated at adolescence: Among adult men, about 40% of total body mass is muscle, compared with only about 24% in adult women.

Another major component of the body is fat, most of which is stored immediately under the skin. Canadian researchers have found that at birth, girls have slightly more fat tissue than boys do, and this discrepancy becomes gradually more marked during childhood and adolescence. Between ages 13 and 17, the percentage of body weight made up of fat rises from 21 to 24% among girls but drops from 16.1 to 14.0% among boys (Smoll & Schutz, 1990). So, during and after puberty, the proportion of fat rises among girls and declines among boys, while the proportion of weight that is muscle rises in boys and declines in girls of healthy weight. However, over the past few decades we have seen dramatic changes in the eating and physical activity patterns in youth, which has resulted in a doubling of the number of overweight young teens and a tripling in the rates of obesity. Now Canadian teen boys are about twice as likely as teen girls to be overweight (6%) or obese (17%) (Carrière, 2003; Dietitians of Canada, 2003).

THE HEART AND LUNGS During the teenaged years, the heart and lungs increase considerably in size, and the heart rate drops. Both of these changes are more marked in boys than in girls—another of the factors that make boys' capacity for sustained physical effort greater than that of girls. Before about age 12, boys and girls have similar endurance limits, although even at these earlier ages, when there is a difference, it is usually boys who have greater endurance because of their lower levels of body fat. After puberty, boys have a clear advantage in endurance, as well as in size, strength, and speed (Klomsten, Skaalvik, & Espnes, 2004).

BODY WEIGHT AND FITNESS Becoming overweight/obese and under fit is an increasing, two-pronged problem in Canadian adolescents (see **Figure 11.2**). Since the early 1980s, the rate of the overweight and obese in 12- to 19-year-olds has risen substantially: The rate of overweight adolescents increased from 12 to 19.8%, and the obesity rate tripled, going from 3 to 9.4% (Shields, 2008; Tremblay, Shields et al., 2010). During the same period, fitness levels have declined significantly (e.g., aerobic fitness, flexibility, muscular strength, and endurance) (Tremblay et al., 2010).

It may not be surprising to learn that measures of leisure time and physical activity have shown that obese teens are less active and have a higher screen time (i.e., time spent watching television, playing video games, or using a computer) than non-obese teens. For instance, sedentary boys were significantly more likely than active boys to be obese (16% versus 9%), although the difference in girls was less pronounced—9% of sedentary girls were obese compared to 6% of active girls. When overweight and obese teens were considered as one group, significant differences were found between those

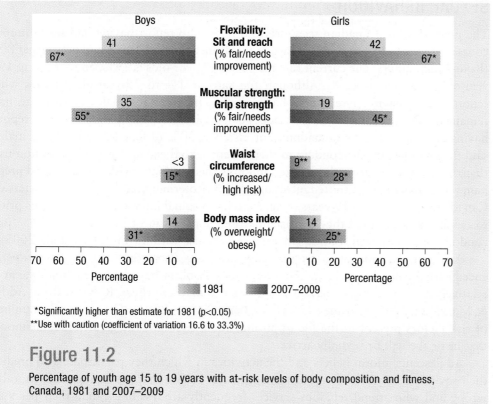

Figure 11.2

Percentage of youth age 15 to 19 years with at-risk levels of body composition and fitness, Canada, 1981 and 2007–2009

(*Source:* Tremblay, M.S., Shields, M., Laviolette, M., Craig, C.L., Janssen, I., & Connor Gorber, S. (2010). Fitness of Canadian children and youth: Results from the 2007–2009. Canadian *Health Measures Survey* (Cat. No. 82-003-X). *Health Reports, 21*(1), 7–20.)

with high and low weekly hours of screen time. Sixty-six percent of youth who clocked more than 20 hours of screen time per week were overweight/obese. In comparison, only 23% of those who logged less than 10 hours per week were overweight/obese (Shields, 2008).

Before Going On

- How do patterns of hormone function change at adolescence, and what are the pubertal milestones for girls and boys?

- How are the brain and other body systems of adolescents different from those of younger children?

ADOLESCENT SEXUALITY

Puberty brings with it the hormonal changes that underlie both sexual attraction and sexual behaviour. Still, these important domains of experience are not entirely controlled by hormones. Each has psychological and social components, as you will see.

mydevelopmentlab

**Connect to
MyDevelopmentLab**

Check out this teenage mini soap
opera, *Choices: The Good, the Bad,
the Ugly—A Look at Issues Facing
Teenage Males.* Have you seen these
behaviours before?

◉─|Watch

SEXUAL BEHAVIOUR

The proportion of Canadian teen girls and boys who report having had sexual intercourse before age 15 has declined by one-third since the mid-1990s and now sits at 8% (Rotermann, 2008). The current rate for 15- to 17-year-olds is 29%, and for 18- to 19-year-olds, the rate is 65%. Although the rate of 15- to 19-year-old females who reported ever having intercourse has declined, the rate for males at this age has remained constant over the past decade. Females are more likely than males to report having sex without using a condom. For instance, 30% of females and 20% of males said they had not used a condom in their recent sexual encounters—a rate of non-use that increases with age for both sexes and puts them at higher risk for unwanted pregnancy and sexually transmitted infections (STIs) (Rotermann, 2008). Three-quarters of Canadian females 15 to 19 years of age who had vaginal intercourse in 6 months prior to being asked reported they consistently used some form of birth control: 74% use condoms, 67% use oral contraceptives, and 17% use withdrawal (Black et al., 2009).

Among girls, those who are sexually active are also more likely to have experienced early menarche, to have low interest in school, to have had their first date at a relatively early age, and to have a history of sexual abuse (Buzi, Roberts, Ross, Addy, & Markham, 2003; Schvaneveldt, Miller, Berry, & Lee, 2001). The greater the number of risk factors present in the life of an individual teenager, the greater the likelihood that he or she will be sexually active.

Adolescents' moral beliefs and the activities in which they participate also predict their sexual activity. For example, teenagers who believe that premarital sex is morally wrong and who attend religious services frequently are less likely than their peers to become sexually active before reaching adulthood (Miller et al., 1998). Rates of sexual activity are also lower among teens who are involved in sports or other after-school pursuits than they are among their peers who do not participate in such activities (Savage & Holcomb, 1999). Moreover, alcohol use is associated with 25 to 30% of adolescent sexual encounters; thus, teens who do not use alcohol are less likely to be sexually active than are their peers who drink (CDC, 2000).

SEXUALLY TRANSMITTED INFECTIONS Even when they are knowledgeable about STIs, many teens may lack the assertiveness necessary to resist sexual pressure from a romantic partner or to discuss condom use—a health risk factor that has become increasingly important for young Canadians. For example, although infection rates declined dramatically since the early 1980s in Canada, since 1997 the rates of new HIV, chlamydia, gonorrhea, and syphilis infections have been on the upswing in youth aged 15 to 19 (PHAC, 2006c; Rotermann, 2008). Chlamydia, a disease that is preventable through condom use, continues to be the most commonly reported STI in Canada. Infection rates are among the highest in 15- to 19-year-old females, who have an infection rate of ~14.4 cases per 1000, five times higher than the incidence found in males of the same age (PHAC, 2006c).

Public health experts estimate that 70% of women and 50% of men who suffer from chlamydia are symptomless (Health Canada, 2006b). Thus, routine chlamydia screening of asymptomatic, sexually active teens and young adults is critical to reducing the prevalence of this disease. Left untreated, chlamydia can lead to **pelvic inflammatory disease (PID)**, ectopic pregnancy, and infertility in women and a number of genital and urinary tract disorders in men.

A more serious viral STI is genital warts caused by the human papillomavirus (HPV). The primary symptom of the disease, the presence of growths on the genitals, is not its most serious effect. The virus is strongly associated with cervical cancer, accounting for more than 70% of all cases (Canadian Cancer Society, 2007). Studies

**pelvic inflammatory
disease (PID)**
an infection of the female
reproductive tract that may
result from a sexually transmitted disease and can lead to
infertility

indicate that, in Canada, the peak prevalence of HPV of any type tends to occur in adolescent girls and young women (25 years of age or younger) and then decreases with age. Canadian public health experts recommend nationwide HPV vaccination of females between ages 9 and 26, as well as continued Pap tests for cervical cancer (Canadian Cancer Society, 2007; National Advisory Committee on Immunization [NACI], 2007; SOGC, 2007).

SEX EDUCATION In addition to routine screening, many developmentalists and public health advocates say that more effective sex education programs are needed. Most suggest that programs that include training in social and decision-making skills, as well as information about STIs and pregnancy, are more likely than information-only approaches to reduce the prevalence of sexual activity and to increase the number of teens who protect themselves against disease and pregnancy when they do have sex. However, no clear consensus about the effectiveness of various approaches to sex education has emerged (Hovell et al., 1998).

Some adults object to sex education because they believe it will cause teenagers who are not sexually active to become so. Research suggests that such fears are unfounded (Berne & Huberman, 1996). There are also debates over the degree to which sex education programs should emphasize abstaining from sex or using contraceptives. No scientific research shows that abstinence-only sex-education programs significantly increase the delay of first intercourse or reduce the prevalence of sexual behaviour in teens (Kirby, 2000; Thomas, 2000). Moreover, making condoms more readily available to teenagers does not increase their rate of sexual activity but does increase the use of condoms by teenagers who are already sexually active (Schuster, Bell, Berry, & Kanouse, 1998).

The PHAC (2008c) *Canadian Guidelines for Sexual Health Education* emphasizes the importance of equipping youth with the information, motivation, and skills they need to make informed and responsible sexual decisions. It focuses on reducing specific risk-taking behaviour, which includes teaching teenagers about proper use of contraceptives. Despite hot debates about what should and should not be taught in sexual education programs, the large majority of Canadian parents and teens believe that sex education that provides explicit information on topics such as reproduction, birth control, STI/AIDS prevention, relationships, sexual orientation, sexual abuse, and societal beliefs about sexual morals is vitally important and is best provided in our schools (McKay, 2005).

Teens who date in early adolescence, as these two may be doing, are more likely to become sexually active while still in school than peers who begin dating later. (*Photo:* © Maria Taglienti-Molinari/ Brand X/Corbis)

TEENAGED PREGNANCY

In Canada, the rate of teenage pregnancy for females aged 15 to 19 has declined from 54 per 1000 in 1974 to 29.2 per 1000 in 2005 (Statistics Canada, 2000b; 2008c). In comparison, the birth rate for teens aged 15 to 19 is 13.3 per 1000, which is less than half the pregnancy rate. Among the developed nations of the world, the teenage birth rate is highest in the United States, where it is about three times as high as in Canada, and lowest in Sweden, which is about seven times lower than in Canada (Luong, 2008).

Teenaged pregnancy statistics can be confusing because they usually refer to all pregnancies among women under age 20. To clarify the extent of the

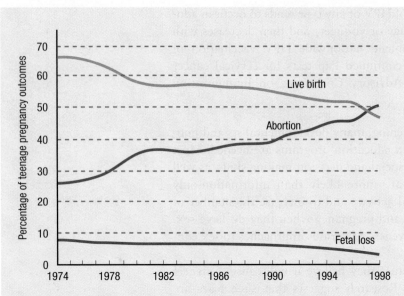

Figure 11.3

Percentage distribution of outcomes of teenaged pregnancy, women aged 15 to 19, Canada, 1974 to 1997.

(*Source:* Adapted from Statistics Canada, *Health Reports*, Cat. No. 82-003, Vol. 12, No.1, Chart 3, available at www.statcan.ca/english/kits/preg/preg3.htm)

teen pregnancy problem, it is useful to break down the statistics by adolescent subgroups. For example, in Canada, the annual pregnancy rate was 15.8 per 1000 in girls aged 15 to 17 and 49.0 per 1000 in girls aged 18 and 19 (Statistics Canada, 2008c). Looking at the numbers this way shows that teen pregnancy is far more frequent among older adolescents and, in fact, is most likely to happen after a girl leaves secondary school.

The age at which an adolescent becomes a parent is only one aspect of the teen pregnancy issue. As noted above, the live birth rate for teenagers has actually dropped in Canada since 1974, when pregnancy statistics were first compiled (Health Canada, 1999h; Statistics Canada, 2008c). During the same time, the abortion rate for teens aged 15 to 19 continued to rise from 14 per 1000 in 1974 to a peak of about 22 per 1000 in the mid-1990s and declined considerably since then, down to 15.3 per 1000 by the mid-2000s. The abortion rate among 18- and 19-year-old teens was higher at ~25 per 1000, which reflects the higher pregnancy rate among older teenagers. In 1997, the percentage of pregnant teens aged 15 to 19 ending their pregnancy in abortion (50.3%) surpassed the percentage of live births (46.8%) and miscarriage or stillbirths (2.9%) for the first time (see **Figure 11.3**) (Statistics Canada, 2000b), and this appears to be a continuing trend.

Whether a girl becomes pregnant during her teenaged years depends on many of the same factors that predict sexual activity in general. The younger a girl is when she becomes sexually active, the more likely she is to become pregnant. Among teenaged girls from poor families, from single-parent families, or from families with relatively uneducated parents, pregnancy rates are higher. Likewise, girls whose mothers became sexually active at an early age and who bore their first child early are likely to follow a similar path. Peer rejection also increases the likelihood that a girl will become pregnant, especially among girls who are high in aggressiveness (Underwood, Kupersmidt, & Coie, 1996).

In contrast, the likelihood of pregnancy is lower among teenaged girls who do well in school and have strong educational aspirations. Such girls are both less likely to be sexually active at an early age and more likely to use contraception if they are sexually active. Girls who have good communication about sex and contraception with their mothers are also less likely to get pregnant.

When teenaged girls become pregnant, in most cases they face the most momentous set of decisions they have encountered in their young lives. The children of teenaged mothers are more likely to grow up in poverty than children born to older mothers, with all the accompanying negative consequences for the child's optimum development (Osofsky, Hann, & Peebles, 1993). However, the children of teenaged mothers whose own parents help with child care, finances, and parenting skills are less likely to suffer such negative effects (Birch, 1998; Uno, Florsheim, & Uchino, 1998). Moreover, social programs that provide teenaged mothers with child care and the support they need to remain in school positively affect both these mothers and their babies. Such programs also improve outcomes for teenaged fathers (Kost, 1997).

SEXUAL MINORITY YOUTH

The emergence of a physical attraction to members of the opposite sex, or heterosexuality, is one of the defining features of adolescence for the great majority of teenagers. For some, though, adolescence is the time when they discover, or confirm a long-standing suspicion, that they are attracted to people of the same sex (homosexuality) or to both sexes (bisexuality). Still others become increasingly convinced that their psychological gender is inconsistent with their biological sex (transgenderism).

GAY, LESBIAN, AND BISEXUAL ADOLESCENTS Surveys involving thousands of teens have found that about 92% identify themselves as exclusively heterosexual in sexual orientation, a person's preference for same- or opposite-sex partners (Austin et al., 2004; Remafedi, Resnick, Blum, & Harris, 1998). About 7% of teens report that they are still unsure of their sexual orientation, and 1% say that they classify themselves as exclusively gay, exclusively lesbian, or bisexual. By adulthood, 94% of teens report being exclusively heterosexual, and just over 5% describe themselves as gay, lesbian, or bisexual, leaving only a very small proportion who are still undecided as to their sexual orientation (Langer, Arnett, & Sussman, 2004).

Lay people and researchers alike have wondered what causes some people to develop a gay, lesbian, or bisexual orientation. Several twin studies show that when one identical twin is homosexual, the probability that the other twin will also be homosexual is 50 to 60%, whereas the concordance rate is only about 20% for fraternal twins and only about 11% for pairs of biologically unrelated boys adopted into the same family (Dawood, Pillard, Horvath, Revelle, & Bailey, 2000; Kendler, Thornton, Gilman, & Kessler, 2000). Family studies also suggest that male homosexuality runs in families—that is, the families of most gay men have a higher proportion of homosexual males than do the families of heterosexual men (Bailey et al., 1999). Such findings strengthen the hypothesis that homosexuality has a biological basis (Dawood et al., 2000). Such evidence does not mean that environment plays no role in homosexuality. For example, when one of a pair of identical twins is homosexual, the other twin does not share that sexual orientation 40 to 50% of the time. Something beyond biology must be at work, although developmentalists do not yet know what environmental factors may be involved.

Prenatal hormone patterns may be one factor in homosexuality (Rahman & Wilson, 2003). For example, women whose mothers took the drug diethylstilbestrol (DES, a synthetic estrogen) during pregnancy are more likely to be homosexual as adults than are women who were not exposed to DES in the womb (Meyer-Bahlburg et al., 1995). These studies are consistent with the hypothesis that homosexuality is programmed in at birth.

Whatever the cause of variations in sexual orientation, the process through which an individual comes to realize that he or she is homosexual appears to be a gradual one. Some researchers think that the process begins in middle childhood as a feeling of doubt about one's heterosexuality (Carver, Egan, & Perry, 2004). Retrospective studies have found that many gay men and lesbians recall having had homosexual fantasies during their teen years, but few fully accepted their homosexuality while still in adolescence (Wong & Tang, 2004). Instead, the final steps toward full self-awareness and acceptance of one's homosexuality appear to take place in early adulthood.

TRANSGENDERED TEENS **Transgendered** teens and adults are those whose psychological gender is the opposite of their biological sex. Some studies suggest that transgendered individuals may have been exposed to atypical amounts of androgens in the womb (Lippa, 2005). However, most do not have such histories, so the cause

transgendered
a person whose psychological gender is the opposite of his or her biological sex

of transgenderism remains a mystery. Transgendered adolescents usually report that, since early childhood, they have been more interested in activities that are associated with the opposite sex than in those that are typical for their own (Lippa, 2005). However, most children who are attracted to cross-gender activities, and even those who express a desire to be the opposite gender, do not exhibit transgenderism after puberty (Cohen-Kettenis & van Goozen, 1997). Thus, such behaviours on the part of children are not considered to be predictive of the development of transgenderism in adolescence.

Out of fear of being stigmatized, most teens who suspect that they are transgendered keep their feelings to themselves. The denial and anger that is often expressed by family members when transgendered adolescents do venture to "come out" amplifies these teens' distress (Zamboni, 2006). As a result, like gay, lesbian, and bisexual teens, transgendered teens are more likely to suffer from depression and are at higher risk of suicide than heterosexual adolescents are (Rosenberg, 2003).

Once individuals accept their transgendered status, some choose to live as the opposite gender on a full-time basis, a pattern called *transsexualism*. Most transsexuals are content with their lives, but others are so anguished by the conflict between their sex and their psychological gender that they seek sex reassignment—a process involving hormonal treatment, reconstructive surgery, and psychological counselling—to achieve a match between the two. Typically, sex reassignment is reserved for adults, but some sex reassignment specialists accept teenaged patients (Smith, van Goozen, Kuiper, & Cohen-Kettenis, 2005). Regardless of the age at which sex reassignment is sought, at least half of those who explore this option, with the help of skilled counsellors, ultimately reject it in favour of less drastic ways of coping with their dilemma. Among those who do actually go through the procedure, most are happy with the results and experience relief from their preoperative emotional distress.

Before Going On

- What are the patterns and consequences of adolescent sexual behaviour in Canada?
- Describe the development of sexual preferences and gender identity during adolescence.

SUBSTANCE ABUSE AND MENTAL HEALTH PROBLEMS

Despite the stereotype of adolescence as a period of "storm and stress," most teenagers are well adjusted. For a few, however, serious substance abuse or mental health problems arise during this period.

⊙ Watch

SENSATION-SEEKING

Teenagers also appear to have what many developmentalists describe as a heightened level of *sensation-seeking*, or a desire to experience increased levels of arousal, such as those that accompany fast driving or the "highs" that are associated with drugs.

Sensation-seeking leads to recklessness, which, in combination with lifestyle factors and inexperience, leads to increased rates of accidents and injuries in this age range. For example, adolescents drive faster, follow too closely, switch traffic lanes and pass other cars more often, and use seat belts less often than adults do (Chamberlain & Solomon, 2006). To reduce the number of accidents among teenaged drivers, six provinces have enacted laws establishing "graduated" driver's licences, and two more have provisional or probationary licence systems (Safety Canada Online, 2000; Traffic Injury Research Foundation, 2001). Sixteen-year-olds can drive in most provinces (except Alberta, where 14-year-olds are eligible for a learner's permit), but they must remain alcohol-, accident-, and ticket-free for a certain period of time before they can have privileges such as driving at night. Other countermeasures include driver education programs and advertising campaigns to discourage risk-taking behaviour. Although car accidents remain the leading cause of death among teens aged 15 to 19, impressive progress has been achieved in reducing road crash death and injury in Canadian adolescents since 1980. After adjusting for population, the fatality rates have dropped by 55% and injuries have fallen by 38%. Alcohol-related deaths have also declined. In 1980, nearly 70% of teen drivers killed in motor vehicle accidents had been drinking. This figure has dropped to around 40% (Chamberlain & Solomon, 2006).

Sensation-seeking and risky behaviours may help teens achieve peer acceptance. Consequently, these behaviours are more likely to happen when adolescents are with peers than when they are alone or with family.
(*Photo:* Eyewire)

Risky behaviours may be more common in adolescence than other periods because they help teenagers gain peer acceptance and establish autonomy with respect to parents and other authority figures (Jessor, 1992). In fact, researchers have found that teens who show high rates of reckless behaviours are likely to have been unsuccessful in school or to have experienced early rejection by peers, neglect at home, or some combination of these problems (Robins & McEvoy, 1990). In addition, adolescents who are not involved in extracurricular activities at school or to whom popularity is important are more likely than their peers who value popularity less to engage in risky behaviour (Carpenter, 2001; Stein, Roeser, & Markus, 1998). (Refer to the Policy Question on gambling among Canadian Youth at the end of **Chapter 12**.)

The messages conveyed in the popular media about sex, violence, and drug and alcohol use may influence teens' risky behaviour. In North America, 12- to 17-year-olds spend more time watching television, listening to music, and playing video games than they do in school (Vanier Institute of the Family, 2001). Surprisingly, though, most teenagers report that their parents have few, if any, rules regarding media use (Mediascope Press, 2000).

Prime-time TV programs contain about five sexual incidents per hour, and only 4% of these impart information about the potential consequences of sex (Henry J. Kaiser Family Foundation, 1999). Drugs and alcohol are even more prevalent than sex in the popular media. One survey found that 98% of 200 movies surveyed portrayed characters using some kind of substance, and, in most cases, characters used more than one substance (Mediascope Press, 1999). Another group of researchers found that 51% of films they surveyed depicted teenagers smoking (Mediascope Press, 1999). In another 46%, teenagers were shown consuming alcohol, and 3% contained images of teens using illegal drugs. Again, references to the consequences of drug or alcohol use were rare; they occurred in only 13% of films surveyed.

DRUGS, ALCOHOL, AND TOBACCO

Teenagers who express the most interest in sensation-seeking are those who are most likely to use drugs and consume alcohol (Donohew et al., 1999). Indeed, researchers have found that individual levels of sensation-seeking predict peer associations—that is, teens who are high sensation-seekers choose friends who are similar. Once such groups are formed, sensation-seeking becomes a central feature of their activities. So, for example, if one member tries marijuana or alcohol, others do so as well. However, teens who spend a lot of time alone may also be vulnerable to substance abuse. Researchers have found that shy adolescents, particularly those who are high in neuroticism, are more likely to use alcohol and drugs than are peers who are more outgoing (Kirkcaldy, Siefen, Surall, & Bischoff, 2004).

Sensation-seeking also interacts with parenting style to increase the likelihood of drug use. Authoritative parenting seems to provide high sensation-seeking teenagers with protection against their reckless tendencies (Pilgrim, Luo, Urberg, & Fang, 1999). Parents who have realistic perceptions of the prevalence of teenaged drinking are also less likely to have teenaged children who are drinkers. These parents who are aware of the prevalence of alcohol use among adolescents try to prevent their children from getting into situations, such as unsupervised social events, where drinking is likely to happen (Bogenschneider, Wu, Raffaelli, & Tsay, 1998).

DRUG USE Drug use among Canadian youth had been steadily declining since the late 1970s. After a slight rebound in the late 1990s, the use of cigarettes, hallucinogens, amphetamines, ecstasy, and barbiturates has been dropping. But indications suggest that the use of some drugs is on the rise again—marijuana, in particular (Adlaf & Paglia, 2003a; Health Canada, 1999g, 2001b). For example, the use of cannabis (i.e., marijuana and hashish) has been on the rise from 1990 onward and, after alcohol, is the substance most commonly used by students. The average age of first-time drug use (including alcohol intoxication) is age 13 to 14 (Hotton & Haans, 2004). The use of substances generally increases with age, with alcohol being the top choice of Canadian students followed, in order, by marijuana, cigarettes, hallucinogens (including LSD, PCP, and mescaline), cocaine/crack, and ecstasy (Adlaf & Paglia, 2003b; Health Canada, 2001b). **Figure 11.4** shows the results of an annual survey of Ontario students (average rate of drug use, Grades 7 through 12).

ALCOHOL As you can see, alcohol use is also very common among Canadian youth. For example, about two-thirds of children in Grade 6 have tried alcohol and by Grade 10 about 90% of students have consumed it (Health Canada, 2001b). Moreover, about one-third of young Canadian drinkers aged 15 to 19 are reportedly heavy drinkers (defined as consuming 5 or more drinks on a single occasion at least 12 times in the past year)—up from 18% in 1995 (Statistics Canada, 2001e). One serious consequence is that 15- to 19-year-old youth have had higher rates of drinking and driving than any other age group except 20- to 24-year-olds (CICH, 2000). On the positive side, even though the rate of drivers under the age of 21 with illegal levels of blood alcohol is still high, it has fallen by about 20% since 1977 (Health Canada, 1999g).

TOBACCO Although cigarette smoking by Canadian youth had generally declined since the 1970s, it saw a

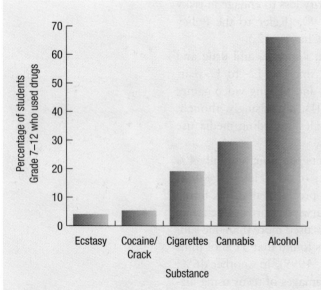

Figure 11.4

The percentage of Canadian students in Grades 7 through 12 who used drugs in the past year.

(*Source:* Adlaf & Paglia, 2003b, from Table 4.3, p. 216. Reprinted by permission of Edward Adlaf.)

resurgence during the mid-1990s (Bondy, Cohen, & Rehm, 2000). Fortunately, the rate has begun to fall again and has hit its lowest point in decades; for the first time, the youth smoking rate is lower than it is for the general population (Health Canada, 2004a). Slightly more teen boys were daily smokers (~17%) than teen girls (~15%); as well, boys smoked more cigarettes per day (~13) than teen girls, whose smoking averaged almost 11 cigarettes per day. The youth rates of smoking varied considerably across the provinces, however, from a low in Ontario of 13% to a high of 27% in Quebec (Health Canada, 2004a) (see **Figure 11.5**).

In addition to the increased risk for a number of diseases, tobacco use in Canadian youth is correlated with use of a variety of other illicit or harmful substances (Davis, 2006). Cigarette smoking has sometimes been referred to as a "gateway" drug to other drugs. Although it's not clear that tobacco use leads to the consumption of other drugs, tobacco is an effective marker of other substance use. For instance, in youth younger than age 20, smokers, in comparison to nonsmokers, are more than 14 times as likely to have used alcohol, 25 times as likely to have used cannabis, and 12.5 times as likely to have used other drugs (i.e., cocaine, heroin, amphetamine, ecstacy, or halluncinogens) in the past year.

Peer influence plays an important role in teen smoking. A nonsmoking teenager who begins associating with a cohesive group of adolescents among whom smoking is a prominent behaviour and a sign of group membership is likely to take up the habit. In fact, some developmentalists advise parents that if their teenaged child's friends smoke, especially close friends with whom the child spends a lot of time, parents should probably assume that their child smokes as well (Urberg, Degirmencioglu, & Pilgrim, 1997). The period between ages 15 and 17 seems to be the time during which a teenager is most susceptible to peer influences with regard to smoking (West, Sweeting, & Ecob, 1999). Clearly, then, monitoring the friends of 15- to 17-year-olds and

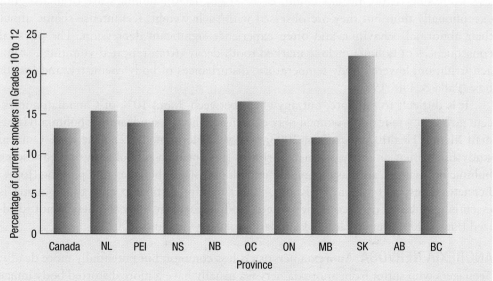

Figure 11.5

The estimated percentage of current smokers* in Grades 10 to 12, by province, in 2008–09.

*Current smoker is daily smokers and nondaily smokers

(*Source:* Adapted from Health Canada, 2010b, Controlled Substances and Tobacco Directorate, Health Canada Supplementary Tables, Youth Smoking Survey 2008–09, Table 4b. Reproduced with the permission of the Minister of Public Works and Government Services Canada, 2010.)

discouraging these teens from associating with smokers may help parents prevent their teen from smoking (Mott, Crowe, Richardson, & Flay, 1999).

Parental influence is important, too—a pattern that is especially clear for mothers and daughters (Kandel & Wu, 1995). When an adult stops smoking, the likelihood that her children will smoke decreases. Moreover, the daily smoking rate was half for those living in smoke-free homes (4%) compared with those were smoking was permitted (8%) (Shields, 2005). Thus, another way to prevent teenaged smoking is to encourage parents to give up the habit. In addition, having a family rule against substance use—including drugs, alcohol, and tobacco—has a lot more influence on teenagers' decisions about using such substances than most parents think (Abdelrahman, Rodriguez, Ryan, French, & Weinbaum, 1998; Mott et al., 1999).

👁 Watch

EATING DISORDERS

Eating disorders, once considered rare in Canada, are now among the most significant mental health problems during adolescence (Health Canada, 2002c). Canadian sources indicate that these disorders, which can be fatal, typically develop during adolescence or early adulthood when the pressures to be thin are the strongest (Jilek, 2001; Government of Canada, 2006a). As these social pressures have increased, so too have the rates of eating disorders. About 9 out of 10 cases occur in women, especially young women (Bitomsky, 2002; HealthyOntario.com, 2003). Although more common among girls than boys, gay and lesbian youth as well as teens who are unsure about their sexual orientation are at higher risk than their heterosexual peers (Austin et al., 2004).

bulimia
an eating disorder characterized by binge eating and purging

BULIMIA **Bulimia** (sometimes called *bulimia nervosa*) involves an intense concern about weight combined with twice-weekly or more frequent cycles of binge eating followed by purging through self-induced vomiting, excessive use of laxatives, or excessive exercising (Attie, Brooks-Gunn, & Petersen, 1990). Bulimics are ordinarily not exceptionally thin, but they are obsessed with their weight, feel intense shame about their abnormal behaviour, and often experience significant depression. The physical consequences of bulimia include marked tooth decay (from repeated vomiting), stomach irritation, lowered body temperature, disturbances of body chemistry, and loss of hair (Palla & Litt, 1988).

It is difficult to estimate, but anywhere between 3 and 10% of Canadian adolescent girls and young adult women may experience the full syndrome of bulimia (Canadian Mental Health Association, 2003; Polivy & Herman, 2002). One large Ontario study found that as many as one-quarter of girls in high school show at least some bulimic behaviours, such as dieting along with occasional bingeing and purging (Jones, Bennett, Olmsted, Lawson, & Rodin, 2001). It's interesting to note that bulimia is essentially unheard of in countries where food is scarce or body thinness is not idealized (Pies, 2003; Mental Health Foundation of New Zealand, 2002).

👁 Watch

anorexia nervosa
an eating disorder characterized by self-starvation

ANOREXIA NERVOSA **Anorexia nervosa** is less common but potentially more deadly. Teenagers who suffer from anorexia nervosa usually have a more distorted body image than those who have bulimia. It is characterized by extreme dieting, intense fear of gaining weight, and obsessive exercising. In girls or women, the weight loss eventually produces a variety of physical symptoms associated with starvation: sleep disturbance, cessation of menstruation, insensitivity to pain, loss of hair on the head, low blood pressure, a variety of cardiovascular problems, and reduced body temperature. Estimates are that between 1 and 2% of female adolescents and young adults in Canada develop anorexia (Canadian Mental Health Association, 2003). Tragically, anywhere from 10 to 15% of anorexics literally starve themselves to death; others die as a result of some type of cardiovascular dysfunction (Deter & Herzog, 1994).

Although anorexia in women is far more common than in men, an increasing number of young men are suffering from anorexia. Many are involved in sporting activities, such as wrestling and gymnastics, in which they have experienced pressure to maintain a lower weight classification. Similarly, pressure to be thin also comes from the men's fashion industry, where tall, ultra-thin male models have become the norm (Trebay, 2008). In this regard, it seems both young men and women experience similar pressures to achieve weight loss and be lean (Ricciardelli & McCabe, 2004).

RISK FACTORS Some theorists have proposed biological causes for eating disorders—for example, some kind of brain dysfunction in the case of bulimics, who often show abnormal brain waves. Others argue for a psychoanalytic explanation, such as a fear of growing up. The most promising explanation, however, may lie in the discrepancy between the young person's internal image of a desirable body and her (or his) perception of her (or his) own body.

When this anorexic 15-year-old looks at herself in the mirror, chances are she sees herself as "too fat," despite being obviously emaciated. (*Photo:* Tony Freeman/PhotoEdit)

This explanation is supported by cross-cultural research demonstrating that adolescents in Western societies, who have the highest rates of eating disorders, are more likely to have negative body images than are adolescents in non-Western societies (Akiba, 1998). In addition, girls who participate in activities such as ballet and gymnastics, in which thinness is highly valued, are at greater risk of developing eating disorders (Picard, 1999; Stoutjesdyk & Jevne, 1993). However, a recent survey suggests that a fairly large proportion of the general population of teenaged girls may be at risk. When the eating habits of 1739 Ontario girls between ages 12 and 18 were examined, 27% were found to have what the authors described as "disordered eating attitudes and behaviours." Twenty-three percent were dieting to lose weight, and 7% of girls 12 to 14 years of age reported that they had used self-induced vomiting as a weight-loss method (Jones et al., 2001).

Some developmentalists suggest that an emphasis on thinness as a characteristic of attractive women, which is common in Western cultures, contributes to the prevalence of eating disorders (Pelletier, Dion, & Levesque, 2004). In one approach to testing this hypothesis, 6- to 12-year-old girls' responses to images of thin, "sexy" women were compared to boys' reactions to images of muscular, hyper-"masculine" men to find out how early children become aware of cultural stereotypes about ideal male and female body types (Murnen, Smolak, Mills, & Good, 2003). Researchers found that even the youngest children in this age group express admiration for the appearance of the models depicted in such images and that children are most interested in idealized images of adults of their own gender. However, girls are more likely than boys to compare their own appearance to that of the models. Moreover, among girls, those who are happiest with their own physical appearance are the least likely to compare their own bodies to media images of "attractive" women (Murnen et al., 2003; Rabasca, 1999).

Critical Thinking

If you had the power to change Canadian society to greatly reduce the rates of bulimia and anorexia, what changes would you want to make? Why and how?

These findings support the assertion of many developmentalists that girls internalize images representing what might be called the "thin ideal" during the middle childhood years and use them as standards against which to compare the changes in their bodies that happen during puberty (Hermes & Keel, 2003). In fact, research shows that, by age 11, girls are significantly more dissatisfied with their bodies than boys are with theirs, and the gender gap in body satisfaction increases across the teen years (Sweeting & West, 2002). As you might expect, given these results, researchers have also found that the tendency of girls to compare themselves to the thin ideal increases as they advance through puberty (Hermes & Keel, 2003).

Recent thinking, however, has placed more emphasis on the pre-existing psychological health of people who develop eating disorders than on cultural influences. Some researchers assert that the body images of individuals who suffer from eating disorders are the result of a general tendency toward distorted thinking (Dyl et al., 2006). In other words, these researchers say that people who have eating disorders tend to think in distorted ways about many things, not just their bodies. From this perspective, internalized images of the "perfect" body fuel the sales of diet products among psychologically healthy people, but they trigger a far more serious outcome, a true eating disorder, in individuals who have a mentally unhealthy tendency toward thought distortion. Longitudinal evidence seems to support this view. In one such study, young women who had been anorexic in adolescence (94% of whom had recovered from their eating disorders) were found to be far more likely than the general population to suffer from a variety of mental disorders (Nilsson, Gillberg, Gillberg, & Rastam, 1999). *Obsessive-compulsive personality disorder*, a condition characterized by an excessive need for control of the environment, seemed to be especially prevalent in this group. The study's authors further stated that the young women's mental difficulties did not appear to be the result of having previously suffered from an eating disorder. Instead, both the adolescent eating disorders and the women's problems in adulthood seem to have been produced by a consistent tendency toward distorted perceptions.

DEPRESSION AND SUICIDE

Studies reveal that more woman than men experience depression in their late teens, but more male teens commit suicide compared with their female peers. Suicide rates among Canada's Aboriginal youth are among the highest in the world.

DEPRESSION A revealing study by Nancy Galambos and her colleagues at the University of Alberta found that 25% of young women and half as many young men aged 16 to 19 had experienced at least one major depressive episode (MDE) (Galambos, Leadbeater, & Barker, 2004). This sex difference persists throughout adolescence and into adulthood and has been found in a number of industrialized countries (Nolen-Hoeksema & Girgus, 1994; Petersen et al., 1993; Roberts & Sobhan, 1992).

Neuroimaging studies show that adolescent depression is associated with some kind of dysfunction in the pituitary gland (MacMaster & Kusumakar, 2004). But what causes the pituitary to function inappropriately in the first place? Genetic factors may be involved, as children growing up with depressed parents are much more likely to develop depression than are those growing up with nondepressed parents (Eley et al., 2004; Merikangas & Angst, 1995). The genetic hypothesis has also received support from at least a few studies of twins and adopted children (Petersen et al., 1993). However, the link between parental and child depression may also be explained in terms of the parenting behaviours of depressed parents, which you read about in earlier chapters. Furthermore, the contributions of a variety of family stressors to adolescent depression are just as clear among children whose parents are not depressed. Any combination of stresses—such as the parents' divorce, the death of a parent or another loved person, the primary caregiver's loss of job, a move, or a change of schools—increases the likelihood of depression or other kinds of emotional distress in the adolescent (Compas, Ey, & Grant, 1993; D'Imperio, Dubow, & Ippolito, 2000). Even smoking has been linked to depression—teen smokers were 1.4 times more likely to develop an MDE (Galambos et al., 2004).

You'll remember from **Chapter 10** that low self-esteem is also part of the equation. Harter's studies reveal that a young person who feels she (or he) does not measure up to her (or his) own standards is much more likely to show symptoms of depression. A great many teenagers are convinced that they do not live up to culturally defined standards of physical appearance. Self-esteem thus drops in early adolescence, and depression rises.

Depression isn't simply an emotional "low" period. It can also hinder academic achievement, because it interferes with memory. For example, depressed adolescents are more likely to remember negative information than positive information (Neshat-Doost, Taghavi, Moradi, Yule, & Dalgleish, 1998). If a teacher says to a depressed adolescent, "You're going to fail algebra unless you start handing in your homework on time," the teenager is likely to remember the part about failing algebra and forget that the teacher also provided a remedy: getting homework done on time. Further, depressed adolescents seem to be less able than their nondepressed peers to store and retrieve verbal information (Horan, Pogge, Borgaro, & Stokes, 1997).

SUICIDE In some teenagers, sadly, the suicidal thoughts that often accompany depression lead to action. Although depression is more common among girls than boys, the likelihood of actually completing a suicide attempt is about 3 times higher for adolescent boys. Suicide is the second leading cause of death for Canadian young people aged 15 to 19, and the 2003 suicide rate was 5.3 per 100 000 for females and 14.8 per 100 000 for males (Government of Canada, 2006a). In contrast, suicide attempts are estimated to be three times more common among girls than among boys based on hospital admissions for nonfatal self-inflicted injuries. Girls use methods that are less likely to succeed, such as self-poisoning. The major exception to this national trend is the disproportionately high rate of suicide among First Nations youth, girls in particular (Health Canada, 1999k) (see **Development in the Real World**).

Although at least three neurobiological systems have been found to be involved in the neurobiology of suicidal behaviour (van Heeringen, 2003), most medical treatment has focused on the treatment of depression associated with suicidal behaviour. The most controversial of these treatments is the use of the newer antidepressant drugs known as *selective serotonin (and noradrenalin) reuptake inhibitors* (SSRIs/SNRIs). Recent disclosures about the outcomes of these drugs on children and adolescents have not only cast doubt on their effectiveness for treating depression, but also revealed evidence that SSRIs/SNRIs can contribute to increased suicidal ideation, attempts and risk of suicide, and hostile aggression in these young populations (Garland, 2004; Herxheimer & Mintzes, 2004; Meek, 2004; Sibbald, 2004). In 2003, the United Kingdom banned the use of SSRIs/SNRIs, with the exception of fluoxetine (Prozac), for children and adolescents. In response, Health Canada issued a rare public warning that advised parents to consult with the primary care physician about the risks and benefits of prescribing these drugs for patients under the age of 18 (Health Canada, 2004b; Kondro, 2004).

It is obviously very difficult to uncover the contributing factors in completed suicides. Although we know that suicide is related to depression, other factors also play a role. Canadian teens diagnosed with personality disorders, such as antisocial, borderline, and narcissistic in particular, have been found to be at increased risk for suicide and suicidal behaviour (Links, Gould, & Ratnayake, 2003). Behaviour problems such as aggression are also common in the histories of those who complete suicides, as is a family history of psychiatric disorder or suicide or a pattern of drug or alcohol abuse (Garland & Zigler, 1993). In addition, psychologists suggest at least three other contributing factors (Shaffer, Garland, Gould, Fisher, & Trautman, 1988; Swedo et al., 1991):

- *Some triggering stressful event.* Studies of suicides suggest that this triggering event is often a disciplinary crisis with the parents or some rejection or humiliation, such as breaking up with a girlfriend or boyfriend or failing in a valued activity.

Development in the Real World

FIRST NATIONS YOUTH SUICIDE CRISIS

The suicide rate for First Nation and Inuit peoples in Canada is two and eleven times higher, respectively, than for non-Aboriginal people (Government of Canada, 2006a). Even more alarming is the high rate of suicides among First Nation youth: Suicide and self-inflicted injury is the leading cause of death (38%) for Aboriginal children 10 to 19 years of age (Health Canada, 2003a). The suicide rate for young Aboriginal females is eight times higher than the national rate for same-aged female peers (Health Canada, 2001c; 2003a). In addition, there are some communities in which the incidence of suicide is unmatched in the rest of the world (Canadian Aboriginal, 1999). For example, the community of Pikangikum in Northwestern Ontario, with a population of about 1700, experienced 12 suicides in the 18 months prior to June 2001 (Kent, 2001). Of these, in the year 2000 alone, eight were young girls and five of them were just 13 years old (Barnsley, 2001; Elliott, 2000). This represents a suicide rate of 470 per 100 000 compared with the Canadian average of 13 per 100 000 (Barnsley, 2001). Another small community, the Siksika Nation near Calgary, reported eight suicides and 247 attempted suicides in 2000 (Barnsley, 2001).

Crisis support can be supplied in the short term, but a long-term prevention plan that involves significant change is the prime goal. British Columbia psychologists, led by Michael Chandler of University of British Columbia, have shown that factors that promote cultural continuity in Aboriginal communities are related to significant suicide reduction in Aboriginal youth (Chandler & Lalonde, 1998; Chandler, Lalonde, Sokol, & Hallet, 2003). The six factors associated with cultural continuity are

- local self-government (the single strongest factor)
- security over traditional lands
- band-controlled school systems
- band-controlled health services
- communal-use cultural facilities
- band-controlled police and fire services

The researchers found that suicide rates varied inversely with the number of indicators of cultural continuity that Aboriginal communities embraced to strengthen and preserve their cultural heritage. For example, British Columbia First Nation bands that had established all the factors had no youth suicides. In comparison, bands that had none of the six factors had close to 140 youth suicides per 100 000—a rate about 100 times the provincial average. Sadly, in the face of nearly two generations of high suicide rates, the challenge of implementing a nationwide strategy to assist Aboriginal communities reduce the risk of suicide is daunting.

- *An altered mental state.* Such a state might be a sense of hopelessness, reduced inhibitions from alcohol consumption, or rage.
- *An opportunity.* A loaded gun in the house or a bottle of sleeping pills in the parents' medicine cabinet creates an opportunity for a teenager to carry out suicidal plans.

A comprehensive suicide prevention strategy is essential for decreasing suicide and suicide attempts (Government of Canada, 2006). Efforts have focused on education—for example, providing training for teachers and teenagers on how to identify students who are at risk for suicide, in the hope that vulnerable individuals might be reached before they attempt suicide. Special training in coping abilities has also been offered to teenaged students so that they might be able to find a nonlethal solution to their problems. Nationwide initiatives, such as community-based suicide prevention programs, respecting diversity and culture, and reducing the availability and lethality of suicide methods are also required.

Before Going On

- Describe how sensation-seeking is related to adolescents' drug, alcohol, and tobacco use in Canada.
- What are the characteristics of eating disorders, depression, and suicide?

CHANGES IN THINKING AND MEMORY

At some point in adolescence, most people become capable of several types of thought that appear to be impossible at earlier ages. Piaget was the first psychologist to offer an explanation of this important developmental milestone.

PIAGET'S FORMAL OPERATIONAL STAGE

Piaget carried out a number of studies suggesting that an entirely new form of thought emerges between about age 12 and 16. He called the stage associated with this kind of thought the **formal operational stage**. Typically, this stage is defined as the period during which adolescents learn to reason logically about abstract concepts. Formal operational thinking has a number of key elements.

SYSTEMATIC PROBLEM-SOLVING One important feature of formal operations is **systematic problem-solving**, the ability to search methodically for the answer to a problem. To study this, Piaget and his colleague Barbel Inhelder (Inhelder & Piaget, 1958) presented adolescents with complex tasks, mostly drawn from the physical sciences. In one of these tasks, subjects were given varying lengths of string and a set of objects of various weights that could be tied to the strings to make a swinging pendulum. The teens were shown how to start the pendulum different ways: by pushing the weight with differing amounts of force and by holding the weight at different heights. The subject's task was to figure out which factor or combination of factors—length of string, weight of object, force of push, or height of push—determines the "period" of the pendulum (i.e., the amount of time for one swing). (In case you have forgotten your high school physics, the answer is that only the length of the string affects the period of the pendulum.)

If you give this task to a concrete operational child, then she will usually try out many different combinations of length, weight, force, and height in an inefficient way. She might try a heavy weight on a long string and then a light weight on a short string. Because she has changed both string length and weight in these two trials, there is no way she can draw a clear conclusion about either factor. In contrast, an adolescent using formal operations is likely to be more organized, attempting to vary just one of the four factors at a time. She may try a heavy object with a short string, then with a medium string, and then with a long one. After that, she might try a light object with the three lengths of string. Of course not all adolescents (or all adults, for that matter) are quite this methodical in their approach. Still, there is a very dramatic difference in the overall strategies used by 10-year-olds and 15-year-olds that marks the shift from concrete to formal operations.

LOGIC Another facet of this shift is the appearance in the adolescent's repertoire of skills of what Piaget called **hypothetico-deductive reasoning**, or the ability to derive conclusions from hypothetical premises. You may remember from **Chapter 9** that Piaget suggested that the concrete operational child can use inductive reasoning, which involves arriving at a conclusion or a rule based on many individual experiences, but performs poorly when asked to reason deductively. Recall that deductive reasoning involves considering hypotheses or hypothetical premises and then deriving logical outcomes. For example, the statement "If all people are equal, then you and I must be equal" involves logic of this type. Although children as young as

formal operational stage
the fourth of Piaget's stages, during which adolescents learn to reason logically about abstract concepts

systematic problem-solving
the process of finding a solution to a problem by testing single factors

hypothetico-deductive reasoning
the ability to derive conclusions from hypothetical premises

High school science classes may be one of the first places where adolescents are required to use deductive logic—a skill Piaget did not think was developed until the period of formal operations.
(*Photo:* © James Shaffer/Photo Edit—All rights reserved)

Research Report

ELKIND'S ADOLESCENT EGOCENTRISM

Psychologist David Elkind hypothesized that another common manifestation of hypothetico-deductive reasoning is a type of thought he called *adolescent egocentrism*, the belief that one's thoughts, beliefs, and feelings are unique. One component of adolescent egocentrism, Elkind said, is the **personal fable**, the belief that the events of one's life are controlled by a mentally constructed autobiography (Elkind, 1967). For example, a sexually active teenage girl might be drawing on such a personal fable when she says "I just don't see myself getting pregnant" in response to suggestions that she use contraception. In contrast to this inappropriately rosy view of the future, a teen who is involved in a violent street gang may say "I'll probably get shot before I make 18" when advised to leave the gang and focus on acquiring the academic skills needed to graduate from high school.

Elkind also proposed that adolescent egocentrism drives teenagers to try out various attitudes, behaviours, and even clothing choices in front of an **imaginary audience**, an internalized set of behavioural standards usually derived from a teenager's peer group. Think about the example of a teenaged girl who is habitually late for school because she changes clothes two or three times every day before leaving home. Each time the girl puts on a different outfit, she imagines how her peers at school will respond to it. If the imaginary audience criticizes the outfit, the girl feels she must change clothes to elicit a more favourable response. Similarly, a boy may spend hours in front of the mirror trimming his sideburns in an effort to achieve a look he thinks his peers will approve of.

Many developmentalists have found Elkind's personal fable and imaginary audience to be helpful in explaining a variety of adolescents' everyday behaviours. However, research examining these constructs has produced mixed results (Bell & Bromnick, 2003; Vartanian, 2000). While it is true that adolescents use idealized mental models to make all kinds of decisions about their own and others' behaviour, researchers have found that school-aged children exhibit similar forms of thought (Vartanian, 2001). Nevertheless, developmentalists agree that the tendency to exaggerate others' reactions to one's own behaviour and to base decisions on unrealistic ideas about the future are two characteristics that distinguish adolescents from younger children.

personal fable
the belief that the events of one's life are controlled by a mentally constructed autobiography

imaginary audience
an internalized set of behavioural standards usually derived from a teenager's peer group

age 4 or 5 can understand some deductive relationships when the premises given are factually true, both cross-sectional and longitudinal studies support Piaget's assertion that only at adolescence are young people able to understand and use the basic logical relationships (Ward & Overton, 1990; Mueller, Overton, & Reene, 2001).

Piaget suggested that hypothetico-deductive thinking underlies many ideas and behaviours that are common to adolescents (see the **Research Report**). For instance, hypothetico-deductive thinking leads to an outlook he called *naive idealism* in many adolescents (Piaget & Inhelder, 1969). Naive idealism is manifested when adolescents use formal operational thinking to mentally construct an ideal world and then compare the real world with it. Not surprisingly, the real world often falls short. As a result, some teenagers become so dissatisfied with the world that they resolve to change it. For many, the changes they propose are personal. So a teen whose parents have been divorced for years may suddenly decide she wants to live with the noncustodial parent because she expects that her life will be better. Another may express naive idealism by becoming involved in a political or religious organization.

DIRECT TESTS OF PIAGET'S VIEW

In an early cross-sectional study, researchers tested 20 girls in each of four grades (Grades 6, 8, 10, and 12) on 10 different tasks that required one or more of what Piaget called formal operational skills (Martorano, 1977). Indeed, many of the tasks the researchers used were those Piaget himself had devised. Results of performance on two of these tasks are graphed in **Figure 11.6**. The pendulum problem is the one described earlier in this section; the balance problem requires a youngster to predict whether two different weights, hung at varying distances on each side of a

Critical Thinking

Think of a few real-life examples of tasks that demand systematic problem-solving.

scale, will balance, a task similar to the balance scale problem Siegler used (recall **Figure 9.4** on page 258). To solve this problem by using formal operations, the teenager must consider both weight and distance simultaneously. You can see from **Figure 11.6** that older students generally did better, with the biggest improvement in scores between children in Grades 8 and 10 (i.e., between ages 13 and 15).

Formal operational reasoning also seems to enable adolescents to understand figurative language, such as metaphors, to a greater degree. For example, one early study found that teenagers were much better than younger children at interpreting proverbs (Saltz, 1979). Statements such as "People who live in glass houses shouldn't throw stones" are usually interpreted literally by 6- to 11-year-olds. By age 12 or 13, most adolescents can easily understand them, even though it isn't until much later that teenagers actually use such expressions in their everyday speech (Gibbs & Beitel, 1995).

Take another look at **Figure 11.6**: Only about 50 to 60% of twelfth-graders solved the two formal operations problems, and only two of the 20 Grade 12 participants used formal operational logic on all 10 problems. Further, recent studies have found rates of formal operational thinking in high school students that are very similar to those found in studies conducted in the 1960s, 1970s, and 1980s (Bradmetz, 1999). The consistency of such findings over several cohorts of adolescents suggests that Piaget's predictions about adolescents' thinking abilities were overly optimistic—in contrast to his overly pessimistic estimates of young children's abilities, which you read about in earlier chapters.

In adulthood, rates of formal operational thinking increase with education. Generally, the better educated the adult participants in a study of formal operational thinking, the greater the percentage who display this kind of reasoning (Mwamwenda, 1999). Piaget's belief in the universality of formal operations may have resulted from his failure to appreciate the role of education in the development of advanced forms of thought. The current consensus among developmentalists is that all teenagers and adults without mental retardation have the capacity for formal operational thinking, but they actually acquire it in response to specific demands, such as those imposed by higher levels of education. Thus, people whose life situations or cultures do not require formal operational thinking do not develop it.

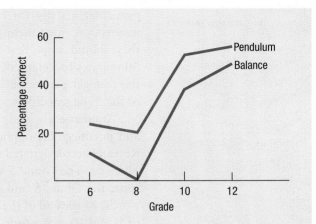

Figure 11.6

These are the results from two of the 10 different formal operational tasks used in Martorano's cross-sectional study.

(*Source:* Martorano, 1977, p. 670. Copyright by the American Psychological Association.)

ADVANCES IN INFORMATION PROCESSING

Adolescents process information faster, use processing resources more efficiently, understand their own memory processes better, and have more knowledge than do elementary school children (Kail, 1990, 1997). As a result, their working memories function more efficiently and they outperform school-aged children even on such simple memory tasks as recognizing faces (Gathercole, Pickering, Ambridge, & Wearing, 2004; Itier & Taylor, 2004). Moreover, they are much better at using strategies to help themselves remember things and can more easily understand and remember complex information, such as that presented in a textbook.

METACOGNITION, METAMEMORY, AND STRATEGY USE By age 14 or 15, the metacognitive and metamemory skills of adolescents far exceed those of younger children. For example, in one classic study, 10- and 14-year-olds were instructed to do a particular activity for exactly 30 minutes (Ceci & Bronfenbrenner, 1985). Experimenters provided them with a clock and instructed them to use it to determine when they should stop. Few of the 10-year-olds periodically checked the time to see if 30 minutes had elapsed, but most of the 14-year-olds did. As a result, less than half of the younger participants succeeded in stopping on time, but more than three-quarters of the teenagers did so.

Another early study of metamemory involved offering students in Grades 5 and 8 and in college the opportunity to earn money for remembering words (Cuvo, 1974). Researchers designated the words to be recalled as being worth either 1 cent or 10 cents. The Grade 5 students rehearsed 1-cent and 10-cent words equally. In contrast, the Grade 8 and college students put more effort into rehearsing the 10-cent words. At the end of the rehearsal period, the Grade 5 students recalled equal numbers of 1- and 10-cent words, while the older participants remembered more 10-cent words. Further, the college students outperformed those in Grade 8 in both rehearsal and recall. This finding suggests that the capacity to apply memory strategies selectively, based on the characteristics of a memory task, appears early in the teenaged years and continues to improve throughout adolescence.

Training studies, in which children and adolescents are taught to use a particular memory strategy, also suggest that metacognitive abilities enable teenagers to benefit more from training than younger children do. For example, researchers taught elementary school students and secondary school students a strategy for memorizing the manufacturing products associated with different cities (e.g., Detroit—automobiles) (Pressley & Dennis-Rounds, 1980). Once participants had learned the strategy and were convinced of its effectiveness, researchers presented them with a similar task, memorizing Latin words and their English translations. Experimenters found that only the secondary school students made an effort to use the strategy they had just learned to accomplish the new memory task. The elementary school children used the new strategy only when researchers told them to and demonstrated how it could be applied to the new task. Secondary school students' success seemed to be due to their superior ability to recognize the similarity between the two tasks: an aspect of metamemory.

TEXT LEARNING Differences between younger children's and adolescents' processing of and memory for text are even more dramatic. In a classic study of text processing, experimenters asked 10-, 13-, 15-, and 18-year-olds to read and summarize a 500-word passage. The researchers hypothesized that participants would use four rules in writing summaries (Brown & Day, 1983). First, they would delete trivial information. Second, their summaries would show categorical organization (i.e., they would use terms such as *animals* rather than use the specific names of animals mentioned in the text). Third, the summaries would use topic sentences from the text. Finally, the participants would invent topic sentences for paragraphs that didn't have them.

The results of the study suggested that participants of all ages used the first rule, because all the summaries included more general than detailed or trivial information about the passage. However, the 10-year-olds and 13-year-olds used the other rules far less frequently than did the 15- and 18-year-olds. There were also interesting differences between the two older groups. Fifteen-year-olds used categories about as frequently as 18-year-olds did, but the oldest group used topic sentences far more effectively. This pattern of age differences suggests that the ability to summarize a text improves gradually during the second half of adolescence.

Studies of text outlining reveal a similar pattern (Drum, 1985). Both elementary and secondary school students know that an outline should include the main ideas of a passage along with supporting details. However, research suggests that 17-year-olds generate much more complete outlines than 14-year-olds do. Moreover, 11-year-olds' outlines usually include only a few of the main ideas of a passage and provide little or no supporting details for those main ideas.

Before Going On

- What are the characteristics and major reseach findings regarding Piaget's formal operational stage?
- List the advances in information-processing capabilities that occur during adolescence.

SCHOOLING

School experiences are clearly formative in middle childhood, as you'll recall from **Chapter 9**, but school is no less central a force in the lives of adolescents.

TRANSITION TO SECONDARY SCHOOL

In many places in the world, including Canada, children attend elementary school for 8 years before moving on to a secondary school for 4 years. In Canada, the exceptions are British Columbia and Quebec, where students switch from elementary to secondary school after Grade 7 and Grade 6 respectively. Because students typically show achievement declines after entering secondary school, educators have developed a model that includes a transitional school—a junior high school or middle school—between elementary and secondary school. The junior high system typically includes 6 or 7 years of elementary school followed by 2 or 3 years of junior high and 3 or 4 years of secondary school. As a consequence, the organization and structure of instruction is most likely to vary for Grade 8 across Canada, whereas Grades 6 and 10 are relatively stable.

However, the junior high/middle school approach does not seem to have solved the transition problem. Students show losses in achievement and in self-esteem across both transition points in these systems. Further, students in both of these systems show greater losses during the transition to secondary school than those in standard elementary–secondary track systems (Alspaugh, 1998; Anderman, 1998). Consequently, educators and developmentalists are currently searching for explanations and practical remedies.

MIDDLE SCHOOL One potential explanation for transition-related achievement declines is that students' academic goals change once they enter junior high/middle school. Researchers classify such goals into two very broad categories: *task goals* and *ability goals*. **Task goals** are goals based on personal standards and a desire to become more competent at something. For example, a runner who wants to improve her time in the 100-metre dash has a task goal. An **ability goal** is one that defines success in competitive terms, being better than another person at something. For example, a runner

Some developmentalists argue that the transition to middle school or junior high school is difficult for many young adolescents because they are not developmentally ready for the secondary-school model. Children who attend middle and junior high schools where close relationships between teachers and students are encouraged, as they are in elementary school, show smaller declines in achievement and self-esteem.
(*Photo:* AP/Wide World Press)

task goals
goals based on a desire for self-improvement

ability goals
goals based on a desire to be superior to others

who wants to be the fastest person on her team has an ability goal. Longitudinal research shows that most Grade 5 students have task goals, but by the time they have been in Grade 6 a few months, most children have shifted to ability goals (Anderman & Anderman, 1999; Anderman & Midgley, 1997).

A student's goal influences his behaviour in important ways. Task goals are associated with a greater sense of personal control and more positive attitudes about school (Anderman, 1999; Gutman, 2006). A student who takes a task-goal approach to school work tends to set increasingly higher standards for his performance and attributes success and failure to his own efforts. For example, a task-goal-oriented student is likely to say he received an A in a class because he worked hard or because he wanted to improve his performance.

In contrast, students with ability goals adopt relative standards—that is, they view performance on a given academic task as good as long as it is better than someone else's. Consequently, such students are more strongly influenced by the group with which they identify than by internal standards that define good and bad academic performance. Ability goal-oriented students are also more likely than others to attribute success and failure to forces outside themselves. For example, such a student might say he got an A in a class because it was easy or because the teacher liked him. Moreover, such students are likely to have a negative view of school (Anderman, 1999).

Because junior high/middle schools emphasize ability grouping more than elementary schools, it is likely that many middle school students change their beliefs about their own abilities during these years (Anderman, Maehr, & Midgley, 1999; Roeser & Eccles, 1998). Thus, high-achieving elementary students who maintain their levels of achievement across the Grade 6 transition gain confidence in their abilities (Pajares & Graham, 1999). In contrast, the changes in self-concept experienced by high achievers who fail to meet expectations in middle school as well as average and low-achieving students do probably lead to self-esteem losses for many of them. Once an ability goal-oriented student adopts the belief that her academic ability is less than adequate, she is likely to stop putting effort into school work. In addition, such students are likely to use ineffective cognitive strategies when attempting to learn academic material (Young, 1997). Consequently, achievement suffers along with self-esteem.

Critical Thinking

What was your first year of high school like? Did your grades and self-esteem decline? What do you think teachers and administrators could do differently to make the transition easier for students?

SECONDARY SCHOOL Regardless of the type of school teenagers attended previously, the early days of secondary school set a general pattern of success or failure for teenagers that continues into their adult years. For example, teenagers who fail one or more courses in the first year of secondary school are far less likely than their peers to graduate (Neild & Balfanz, 2006; Roderick & Camburn, 1999). It appears that minority students have a particularly difficult time recovering from early failure.

Some psychologists emphasize the positive aspects of transition to secondary school, however, claiming that participation in activities that are usually offered only in secondary school allows students opportunities to develop psychological attributes that can't be acquired elsewhere. To demonstrate the point, a number of research studies had secondary school students use pagers to signal researchers whenever they were experiencing high levels of intrinsic motivation along with intense mental effort (Larson, 2000). The results showed that students experienced both states in elective classes and during extracurricular activities far more often than in academic classes (Larson, 2000). In other words, a student engaged in an art project or sports practice is more likely to experience this particular combination of states than one who is in a history class. Consequently, educators may be able to ease the transition to secondary school for many students by offering a wide variety of elective and extracurricular activities and encouraging students to participate.

GENDER AND ACADEMIC ACHIEVEMENT

Canadian 15-year-olds' academic performance continues to be among the highest of 57 nations on the **Programme for International Student Assessment (PISA)**. The PISA is a measure of the essential knowledge and skills, such as mathematics, reading, and science, that students will need to successfully compete in a global, knowledge-based economy (Bussière, Knighton, & Pennock, 2007). Although top-performing Canadian girls and boys (i.e., those who scored at the highest levels on the PISA) scored equally well on the combined science scale, there were slight gender differences in some aspects of science skill: Girls are better at identifying scientific issues, and boys could better explain phenomena scientifically. Additionally, top-performing girls perform better than boys in reading skills, while top-performing boys outperform girls in math skills (Canadian Education Statistics Council [CESC], 2009).

Programme for International Student Asessment (PISA) a worldwide assessment of how well 15-year-olds can apply their academic ability to solve real-life problems

In addition, consistent relationships have been found between a variety of factors and school achievement. Students who correctly perceived themselves as being higher achievers were more satisfied with school and had better relationships with both school and parents. In contrast, students who correctly perceived themselves as being lower achievers were moderately associated with high-risk behaviours such as smoking, drinking, and using marijuana. Another factor associated with lower achievement levels was skipping classes. Boys were only slightly more likely to skip classes than girls. In Grade 6 almost one-quarter of students skipped classes, but by Grade 10 over 40% of students were skipping classes. When students skip classes, they are more likely to become involved with high-risk behaviours both during school hours and in the evenings. Consequently, skipping classes is associated with lower levels of academic achievement and strained relationship with parents (Health Canada, 2001b).

EARLY SCHOOL LEAVERS

The cumulative effect of academic success over many years of schooling fosters a sense of academic confidence in secondary school students. Those who achieve, especially those who achieve despite backgrounds that include poverty and/or other daunting obstacles, are likely to have parents who have high aspirations for them or an authoritative parenting style (Brooks-Gunn, Guo, & Furstenberg, 1993). To be in a position to contribute to today's society and economy, a person without a high school diploma has very limited opportunities (CESC, 2010). For Canadians, "completing high school is now widely considered as a minimal educational requirement for access to the labour market and lifelong learning" (Bushnik, Bar-Telford, & Bussière, 2004, p. 5).

Family interactive style predicts academic achievement in high school. Adolescents whose parents display authoritative parenting are more likely than those with authoritarian or permissive parents to achieve academic success in high school.
(*Photo:* Will and Deni McIntyre/Photo Researchers)

The percentage of Canadian youth who do not have a secondary school diploma and are not currently enrolled in school has been falling steadily over the last two decades (Bowlby, 2008). In 1990, 17.1% of Canadian young adults aged 20 to 24 had not completed their secondary school. In comparison, by 2006, roughly 9% had not completed their secondary school education—about 11% of men and 7% of women 20- to 24-years-old—and these rates were some of the lowest in the world (HRSDC, 2010).

Early leavers from secondary school, like those who achieve academic success, are shaped by a complex interaction of academic and social variables (Statistics Canada, 2008d). Children growing up in poor

families, especially poor families with a lone parent, are considerably more likely to leave secondary school before graduating than are those from more economically advantaged and/or intact families. Teenagers who are living alone, who come from families that do not provide psychological support for academic achievement, or who have caregivers who have negative attitudes toward education or low levels of education are also more likely to become early school leavers (HRDC, 2000). Plus, when a teenager's peer group puts a low value on achievement, the risk of leaving school early is even higher (Statistics Canada, 2008d).

Longitudinal studies have found three strong predictors of early school leaving: a history of academic failure, a pattern of aggressive behaviour, and poor decisions about risky behaviour (Bushnik, Bar-Telford, & Bussière, 2004; Jimerson, 1999). With respect to risky behaviour, decisions about sexual intercourse seem to be especially critical. For girls, giving birth and getting married are strongly linked to dropping out.

Peer influence may also be a factor in early school leaving. Teens who quit school are likely to have friends who have already left school or who are contemplating leaving school early (Bushnik et al., 2004; Statistics Canada, 2008d). Family variables are also linked to early school leaving. For example, children whose families move a lot when they are in elementary or middle school are at increased risk for leaving secondary school before graduating (Worrell, 1997).

One group of University of Montreal researchers has compiled a general profile of students who are at risk. Their research has identified the type of secondary school student who is likely to become an early school leaver as one who is quiet, disengaged, low-achieving, and poorly adjusted (Janosz, Le Blanc, Boulerice, & Tremblay, 2000). This concurs with the outcomes of another Canadian study that reported that early school leaving was linked with being less involved in social, extracurricular, and academic activities (Bushnik et al., 2004).

Whatever its cause, leaving secondary school before graduating is associated with a number of long-term consequences. For instance, unemployment is higher among adults who don't complete school than among those who graduated, and nongraduates who do manage to find jobs earn lower wages than peers who graduate (Bowlby, 2008). Adults who don't complete school are also more likely to experience depression (Hagan, 1997). Furthermore, research suggests that staying in school may be an important protective factor for boys who have poor self-regulation skills. When boys who are poor self-regulators stay in school, they appear to be less likely than poor self-regulators who left school early to become involved in criminal activity in early adulthood (Henry et al., 1999).

Most teenagers with jobs have low-level, low-responsibility, low-paying ones. Some psychologists believe that the negative effects of employment in adolescence may be caused by the type of work teens do. (*Photo:* Thinkstock)

WORKING TEENS

There is a trend toward staying in school longer because youth employment opportunities are relatively poor and most students are motivated to stay in school and get a better education to improve their chances of finding a better job. In fact, from age 16, it now takes students about 8 years to complete the transition from high school to regular employment (Franke, 2003). Canadian researchers have found that students increase their hours of employment from ages 15 to 19 and are employed in mostly "entry-level" part-time and summer jobs. About one-third of full-time students were employed during the school term. Students who have some paid employment have better school performance, but employment beyond 15 to 20 hours

TABLE 11.3	High School Students with Paid Jobs Don't Cut Back on Study Time					
	Women			Men		
	No job	Job	Difference	No job	Job	Difference
	Average hours per day					
High School						
Time spent on:						
Personal care*	11.2	10.3	−0.9	10.9	10.5	−0.4
Leisure	6.8	6.5	−0.3	7.7	6.2	−1.5
Paid Work	0.2	0.7	0.5	0.1	1.9	1.8
Education	4.4	4.8	0.4	4.4	4.4	0.0
Unpaid work	1.4	1.7	0.3	0.9	1.1	0.2

*Includes sleeping, eating, and hygiene

(*Source:* Adapted from the Statistics Canada, General Social Survey, 1998.)

per week can be detrimental to academic achievement and contributes to higher levels of personal stress (CCSD, 2001; Jackson & Schetagne, 2001; Marshall, 2007). Almost half of all Canadian women ages 18 to 19 feel constant pressure to accomplish more than they can handle, a rate that is higher than that reported by women, or men, at any age (Marshall, 2007).

Some studies that consider the quality of the job as well as the number of hours worked find little or no correlation between the number of hours students work and their school grades or risk of problem behaviour (Mael, Morath, & McLellan, 1997; McNeal, 1997). It seems that students who have positive work experiences develop increased feelings of competence and efficacy.

Studies based on this more complex view of teenagers' employment have also shown that students who seem to benefit from work allocate their time differently from those who experience negative effects (Schoenhals, Tienda, & Schneider, 1998). For example, Canadian teens reduce the amount of time they devote to other activities in order to work—male students start to cut back on leisure activities, such as television and video games, whereas female students reduce their time sleeping (Franke, 2003). In addition, **Table 11.3** shows that male students continue to spend just as much time, and female students actually spend slightly more time, studying as they did before they were employed (when they work 15 hours or fewer per week).

Critical Thinking

Think about females you know who are in their late teens. How stressful do their lives seem to be? How would you account for those high stress levels?

Before Going On

- How do changes in students' goals contribute to the transition to secondary school?
- What are the characteristics of gender differences in academic achievement, early school leavers, and working teens?

Summary

Physical Changes

- Puberty is triggered by a complex set of hormonal changes, beginning at about age 7 or 8. In girls, sexual maturity is achieved as early as age 12 or 13. Sexual maturity is achieved later in boys.

- Myelination progresses steadily throughout the brain during this period and there is an inverted U-shaped developmental pattern in grey matter volumes from early childhood to adolescence as synaptogenesis is followed by synaptic pruning. Puberty is accompanied by a rapid growth spurt in height and an increase in muscle mass and fat. Boys add more muscle, and girls add more fat.

Adolescent Health

- Roughly two-thirds of all Canadian teens have had sexual intercourse by the time they reach 19 years of age.

- Roughly 3 out of every 100 Canadian teenage girls become pregnant. The long-term consequences for the teens that give birth are generally negative, although a minority of such women are able to overcome the disadvantages. Less than half of pregnant teenagers give birth.

- Hormonal, genetic, and environmental factors have been proposed to explain homosexuality. The process of realizing one's sexual orientation is a gradual one that often isn't completed until early adulthood. Transgendered teens are those whose psychological gender differs from their biological sex. Gay, lesbian, bisexual, and transgendered adolescents often must cope with peer rejection and parental anger.

Substance Abuse and Mental Health Problems

- Teens engage in high rates of various kinds of risky behaviour, including unprotected sex, drug use, and fast driving.

- The use of alcohol and marijuana remains high among Canadian teenagers. Those most likely to use or abuse drugs are those who also show other forms of deviant or problem behaviour, including poor school achievement.

- Eating disorders, such as bulimia and anorexia, are more common among teenaged girls than teenaged boys.

- Depression and suicide are other mental health problems that are common during adolescence.

Changes in Thinking and Memory

- For Piaget, the formal operational stage is characterized by the ability to apply basic cognitive operations to ideas and possibilities, in addition to actual objects.

- Although some adolescents exhibit advanced forms of thinking, formal operational thinking is not universal, nor is it consistently used by those who are able to do it.

- Memory function improves in adolescence as teens become more proficient in metacognition, metamemory, and strategy use.

Schooling

- The transition to middle school may be accompanied by changes in children's task and ability goal orientation. Secondary school offers many teens more opportunities to pursue special interests and extracurricular activities.

- When comparing top performing 15-year-old Canadians, females surpass males in literacy, males outperform females in math, and both genders are roughly equivalent in science.

- Those who succeed academically in secondary school are typically from authoritative families. Those who drop out are less likely to find value in school life.

- Teens working more than 10 to 15 hours per week experience more chronic stress and risk of getting lower grades or engaging in more risky behaviour than those who work less. Work can be beneficial for students who have positive work experiences.

Visit **www.mydevelopmentlab.com** to help you get the best grade! Test your knowledge and grasp difficult concepts through

- Custom study plans: See where you are strong and where you go wrong
- Interactive simulations
- Video and audio clips
- Raise your own Virtual Child—and much more!

Review Questions

Answers are provided on MyDevelopmentLab in the Course Resources folder.

Physical Changes

11.1 Which of the following events could be attributed to the secular trend?
   a. Girls begin to date earlier than they did at the beginning of the 20th century.
   b. More sexualized images are available in programming for television, films, and video games.
   c. Cultural values lead people to prefer a thin, angular body type.
   d. The age of menarche has declined.

Adolescent Sexuality

11.2 Which statement best describes the process through which most people identify with a homosexual orientation?
   a. They know it as soon as the hormones of puberty begin to flow.
   b. Most people realize it gradually across the adolescent and early adulthood years.
   c. Peers inform them that they are probably gay or lesbian.
   d. There is no consistent pattern.

Substance Abuse and Mental Health Problems

11.3 Which of the following is not an accurate statement about depression among Canadian adolescents?
   a. At any given time, 5 to 8% of adolescents are experiencing an enduring depression.
   b. Teenaged boys are twice as likely as girls to report having experienced depression.
   c. Adolescent boys are more than three times as likely as girls to commit suicide.
   d. Suicide is the second leading cause of teen death.

Changes in Thinking and Memory

11.4 A teenager who can derive conclusions from hypothetical premises, such as what his mother might say if she finds out that he failed a French test, is engaged in
   a. hypothetico-deductive reasoning.
   b. information processing.
   c. metacognition.
   d. logico-conditional thinking.

Schooling

11.5 Which of the following factors has not been found to be related to early school leavers?
   a. low socioeconomic status
   b. a connection with a peer group that does not value academic achievement
   c. drug use
   d. authoritarian parenting

Critical-Thinking Questions

11.6 What might be some of the psychological issues involved with the awkwardness of the pubertal growth spurt? Give examples.

11.7 In what way do teenagers' ability to engage in formal operational thinking influence the decisions that will inform and impact the rest of their lives?

CHAPTER 12

Social and Personality Development in Adolescence

The change in status from child to adult is considered to be so important that many societies mark it with a *rite of passage*, a formal ritual representing an adolescent's initiation into adult culture. In some nonindustrialized societies, young adolescents begin working or sleeping separately from their families for the first time since birth, emphasizing the child's membership in the larger social group. In other cultures, alterations of a teen's physical appearance or trials of endurance play a part in the rite of passage.

Adolescents in industrialized societies like Canada have no universally shared initiation rites. Social scientists speculate that this is one reason why adolescents in these cultures often emphasize their own separation and distinctness by such means as wearing unusual or even outlandish clothing or hairstyles, getting tattoos and/or body piercings, and using special mannerisms and language.

Nevertheless, all teens in industrialized countries share many changes in status. Graduation from secondary school is one such change. In Canada, young people can have a driver's licence at 16 (14 in Alberta) and can see R-rated movies at 18. At ages 14 to 17, depending on the crime, adolescents can be given adult sentences. At 18, teenagers can vote and now have full adult privileges and legal responsibilities for their behaviour.

When you finish reading this chapter, you will be able to explain the theories of social and personality development in the teenage years; summarize the changes in adolescents' self-concepts and personality; describe Kohlberg's theory of moral development and explain its impact on antisocial behaviour; and identify the changes in social relationships during the teenage years. While you read, keep the following questions in mind:

- What are some reasons for the changes in a teenager's self-esteem across adolescence?

- What are the characteristics of the authoritative parenting style that makes it associated with such positive outcomes for adolescents?

- At what age do adolescents begin to form an awareness of their sexual attraction to others?

THEORIES OF SOCIAL AND PERSONALITY DEVELOPMENT

As you have learned in earlier chapters, psychoanalytic approaches to social and personality development emphasize conflicts between individual needs and societal demands. Psychoanalytic theories identify and clarify the major themes of social and personality development during adolescence, such as the teenager's acquiring a sense of who she is as an individual. Likewise, cultural perspectives derived from other disciplines can reveal the important role culture plays in the adolescent's transition from child to adult.

PSYCHOANALYTIC PERSPECTIVES

According to Freud, the postpubertal years constitute the last stage of personality development; both adolescents and adults are in what Freud called the **genital stage**, the period during which psychosexual maturity is reached. Freud believed that puberty awakens the sexual drive that has lain dormant during the latency stage. Thus, for Freud, the primary developmental task of the genital stage is to channel the libido into a healthy sexual relationship.

genital stage
in Freud's theory, the period during which people reach psychosexual maturity

identity
an understanding of one's unique characteristics and how they have been, are, and will be manifested across ages, situations, and social roles

identity versus role confusion
in Erikson's theory, the stage during which adolescents attain a sense of who they are

identity crisis
Erikson's term for the psychological state of emotional turmoil that arises when an adolescent's sense of self becomes "unglued" so that a new, more mature sense of self can be achieved

Erikson, though not denying the importance of achieving sexual maturity, proposed that achievement of a sense of personal identity is a far more important developmental task faced by adolescents. He described identity as a sense of self-continuity (Erikson, 1969). More recent theorists, elaborating on his idea, define **identity** as an understanding of one's unique characteristics and how they are manifested across ages, situations, and social roles. Thus, in Erikson's model, the central crisis of adolescence is **identity versus role confusion**.

Confusion about all these role choices is inevitable and leads to a pivotal transition Erikson called the *identity crisis*. The **identity crisis** is a period during which an adolescent is troubled by his lack of an identity. Erikson believed that adolescents' tendency to identify with peer groups is a defence against the emotional turmoil engendered by the identity crisis. In a sense, he claimed, teens protect themselves against the unpleasant emotions of the identity crisis by merging their individual identities with that of a group (Erikson, 1980a). The teenaged group thus forms a base of security from which the young person can move toward a unique solution of the identity crisis. Ultimately, however, each teenager must achieve an integrated view of himself, including his own pattern of beliefs, occupational goals, and relationships.

MARCIA'S THEORY OF IDENTITY ACHIEVEMENT

identity achievement
in Marcia's theory, the identity status achieved by a person who has been through a crisis and reached a commitment to ideological or occupational goals

Much of the research on the formation of adolescent identity is based on Simon Fraser University professor emeritus James Marcia's descriptions of *identity statuses*. Marcia's early studies confirmed Erikson's general conceptions of the adolescent identity process (Marcia, 1966, 1980, 2001; Schwartz, 2001). Expanding one of Erikson's ideas, Marcia argued that adolescent identity formation has two key parts: a crisis and a commitment. A *crisis*, according to Marcia, meant a period of decision-making when old values and old choices are re-examined. This may occur as an upheaval—the classic notion of a crisis—or it may occur gradually. The outcome of the re-evaluation is a *commitment* to some specific role, value, goal, or ideology. In sum, the achievement of an "ego identity refers to a sense of who one is, based on who one has been and who one can realistically imagine oneself to be in the future" (Marcia, 2002, p. 202).

If you put these two elements together, as shown in **Figure 12.1**, you can see that four different *identity statuses* are possible:

• **Identity achievement:** The person has been through a crisis and has reached a commitment to ideological, occupational, or other goals.

In the Jewish ceremony called *bar mitzvah* (for boys) or *bat mitzvah* (for girls), 12- or 13-year-olds read from the Torah in Hebrew and are admitted to full adult status in the congregation. The Tanzanian boy has had his face painted with white clay as part of an adolescent rite of passage.
(*Photos:* left, Bill Aron/PhotoEdit, right, The Purcell Team/CORBIS)

- **Moratorium:** A crisis is in progress, but no commitment has yet been made.

- **Foreclosure:** The person has made a commitment without having gone through a crisis. No reassessment of old positions has been made. Instead, the young person has simply accepted a parentally or culturally defined commitment.

- **Identity diffusion:** The young person is not in the midst of a crisis (although there may have been one in the past) and has not made a commitment. Diffusion may thus represent either an early stage in the process (before a crisis) or a failure to reach a commitment after a crisis.

The whole process of identity formation may occur later than Erikson and Marcia thought, perhaps because cognitive development is more strongly related to identity formation than either believed. Research suggests that teens who are most advanced in the development of logical thinking and other information-processing skills are also the most likely to have attained Marcia's status of identity achievement (Klaczynski, Fauth, & Swanger, 1998).

There is also evidence that the quest for personal identity continues throughout the lifespan, with alternating periods of instability and stability (Marcia, 2002). For example, a person's sense of being "young" or "old" and the integration of that idea into a sense of belonging to a particular generation appears to change several times over the course of the adolescent and adult years (Sato, Shimonska, Nakazato, & Kawaai, 1997). Consequently, adolescence may be only one period of identity formation among several. What makes the formation of an identity during adolescence special is that all the essential elements for the formation of identity are present for the first time in a person's life. The person now possesses a sufficient level of physical, sexual, cognitive, and moral maturity. In conjunction with this, society encourages the individual to take on adult roles, such as worker, parent, and citizen (Marcia, 2002).

Finally, Marcia has suggested that there are two key reasons why adolescence is so important in the life cycle. For one, "it is the time during which a fourth personality structure, an *identity*, is added to the previous structures of ego, self, and superego" (Marcia, 2002, p. 201). For another, adolescence defines the period of transition from childhood to adulthood when "the consolidation of *identity* marks the end of childhood" (Marcia, 1993, p. 3).

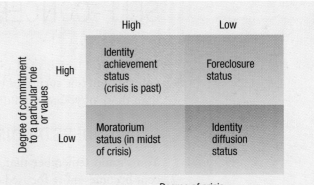

Figure 12.1

The four identity statuses proposed by Marcia, based on Erikson's theory. For a fully achieved identity, the young person must have both examined her values or goals and reached a firm commitment.

(*Source:* Marcia, 1980.)

Critical Thinking

The implication in Marcia's formulation is that foreclosure is a less developmentally mature status—that one must go through a crisis to achieve a mature identity. Does this make sense to you? What is your current identity status? Has it changed much over the past few years?

moratorium
in Marcia's theory, the identity status of a person who is in a crisis but who has made no commitment

foreclosure
in Marcia's theory, the identity status of a person who has made a commitment without having gone through a crisis. The person has simply accepted a parentally or culturally defined commitment

identity diffusion
in Marcia's theory, the identity status of a person who is not in the midst of a crisis and who has made no commitment

Before Going On

- Describe Freud's genital stage and Erikson's stage of identity versus role confusion.

- How does Marcia explain identity development and what makes identity formation during adolescence distinct from subsequent identity development later in adulthood?

SELF-CONCEPT AND PERSONALITY

In **Chapter 11**, you read that thinking becomes more abstract in adolescence. Thus, you shouldn't be surprised to find that teenagers' self-concepts are a lot more complex than those of younger children.

SELF-UNDERSTANDING

You should remember that, through the elementary school years, the child's self-concept becomes more focused on enduring internal characteristics: the psychological self. This trend continues in adolescence, with self-definition becoming more abstract. You may remember the replies of a 9-year-old and an 11-year-old to the question "Who am I?" in Montemayor and Eisen's study, cited in **Chapter 10**. Here's a 17-year-old's answer to the same question:

> I am a human being. I am a girl. I am an individual. I don't know who I am. I am a Pisces. I am a moody person. I am an indecisive person. I am an ambitious person. I am a very curious person. I am not an individual. I am a loner. I am an American (God help me). I am a Democrat. I am a liberal person. I am a radical. I am a conservative. I am a pseudoliberal. I am an atheist. I am not a classifiable person (i.e., I don't want to be). (Montemayor & Eisen, 1977, p. 318)

Clearly, this girl's self-concept is even less tied to her physical characteristics or even her abilities than are those of younger children. She is describing abstract traits or ideology.

You can see the change graphically in **Figure 12.2**, which is based on the answers of all 262 participants in Montemayor and Eisen's study. Each of the answers to the "Who am I?" question was categorized as a reference either to physical properties ("I am tall," "I have blue eyes") or to ideology ("I am an environmentalist," "I believe in God"). As you can see, appearance was a highly prominent dimension in the preteen and early teen years but became less dominant in late adolescence, a time when ideology and belief became more important. By late adolescence, most teenagers think of themselves in terms of enduring traits, beliefs, personal philosophy, and moral standards (Damon & Hart, 1988).

At the same time, adolescents' self-concept becomes more differentiated, as they come to see themselves somewhat differently in each of several roles: as a student, with friends, with parents, and in romantic relationships (Harter & Monsour, 1992). Once these self-concepts are formed, they begin to influence adolescents' behaviour. For example, a longitudinal study of Canadian teens found that a strong self-concept is important to the development of good mental and physical health (Park, 2003). Conversely, a weak self-concept during adolescence puts girls at risk for depression and poor self-perceived health and obesity, and boys at risk for obesity and inactivity in young adulthood.

Adolescents' academic self-concepts seem to come both from internal comparisons of their performance to a self-generated ideal and from external comparisons to peer

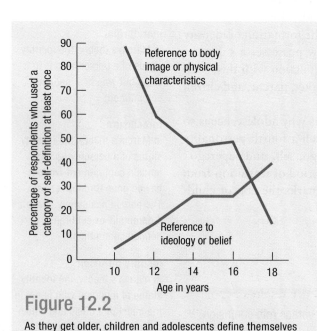

Figure 12.2

As they get older, children and adolescents define themselves less and less by what they look like and more and more by what they believe or feel.

(*Source:* Montemayor & Eisen, 1977, from Table 1, p. 316.)

performance (Bong, 1998). It also appears that perceived competency in one domain affects how a teenager feels about his ability in other areas. For example, if a high school student fails a math course, it is likely to affect his self-concept in other disciplines as well as in math. This suggests that teens' self-concepts are hierarchical in nature: Perceived competencies in various domains serve as building blocks for creating a global academic self-concept (Cheng, Xiaoyan, Dajun, 2006; Yeung, Chui, & Lau, 1999).

Social self-concepts also predict behaviour. For example, a teenager's family self-concept reflects his beliefs about the likelihood of attaining and/or maintaining satisfactory relationships with family members. Developmentalists have found that adolescents who are estranged from their families, such as runaways, perceive themselves to be less competent in the give-and-take of family relations than teens who are close to parents and siblings (Swaim & Bracken, 1997). Indeed, the perceived lack of competency in family relations appears to be distinct from other components of self-concept.

Girls and boys also appear to construct the various components of self-concept somewhat differently. For example, a recent study of teens' evaluations of their own writing abilities found that boys and girls rated themselves as equally capable writers (Pajares & Valiante, 1999). However, the girls scored higher on objective tests of writing ability. In addition, the girls were more likely to describe themselves as being better writers than their peers of both genders. The boys, by contrast, seemed to perceive few ability differences in their peers. In other words, the boys believed they were good writers, but they also thought that their classmates were as good as they were.

Such findings are predictable, given the information in the previous section about girls being influenced by both internal and external comparisons while boys attend more to internal, self-defined standards. The findings also raise interesting questions about the degree to which self-concept development is influenced by cultural ideas about gender roles. Perhaps girls pay more attention to their own and others' writing skills because they know that girls are supposed to be better at language skills than boys.

GENDER ROLES

Developmentalists use the term **gender-role identity** to refer to gender-related aspects of the psychological self. In contrast to younger children, adolescents understand that gender roles are social conventions, so their attitudes toward them are more flexible (Katz & Ksansnak, 1994). Parental attitudes and parental behaviour become increasingly important in shaping teens' ideas about gender and sex roles (Ex & Janssens, 1998; Jackson & Tein, 1998; Raffaelli & Ontai, 2004). In addition, concepts that were largely separate earlier in development, such as beliefs about gender roles and sexuality, seem to become integrated into a conceptual framework that teens use to formulate ideas about the significance of gender in personal identity and social relationships (Mallet, Apostolidis, & Paty, 1997).

In the early days of research on gender-role identity, psychologists conceived of masculinity and femininity as polar opposites. A person could be masculine or feminine, but couldn't be both. However, theories first advanced in the 1970s have resulted in a large body of research in support of the notion that masculinity and femininity are dimensions along a continuum and each may be found in varying quantities in the personalities of both men and women (Bem, 1974; Spence & Helmreich, 1978). A male or a female can be high or low on masculinity or femininity, or both. Indeed, if people are categorized as high or low on each of these two dimensions, based on their self-descriptions, four basic

gender-role identity
gender-related aspects of the psychological self

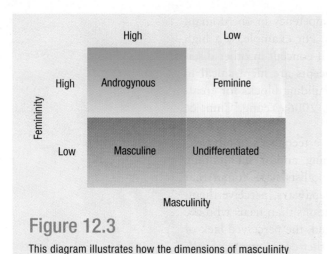

Figure 12.3

This diagram illustrates how the dimensions of masculinity and femininity interact to produce four types of gender-role orientation.

gender-role types emerge: *masculine, feminine, androgynous,* and *undifferentiated* (see **Figure 12.3**).

The masculine and feminine types are the traditional categories; a person in either of these categories sees himself or herself as high in one and low in the other. A "masculine" teenager or adult, according to this view, is thus one who perceives himself (or herself) as having many traditional masculine qualities and few traditional feminine qualities. A feminine teenager or adult shows the reverse pattern. In contrast, androgynous individuals see themselves as having both masculine and feminine traits; undifferentiated individuals describe themselves as lacking both.

SELF-ESTEEM

Interestingly, research suggests that either an androgynous or a masculine gender-role identity is associated with higher self-esteem among both boys and girls (Gurnáková & Kusá, 2004; Woo & Oei, 2006). This finding makes sense in light of the existence of a "masculine bias" in North American and other Western societies, which causes both men and women to value traditionally masculine qualities such as independence and competitiveness more than many traditionally female qualities.

If such a bias exists—and there is good reason to think that it does—then the teenaged boy's task is simpler than the teenaged girl's. He can achieve high self-esteem and success with his peers by adopting a traditional masculine gender role. But a girl who adopts a traditional feminine gender role is adopting a less-valued role, with attendant risks of lower self-esteem and a reduced sense of competence (Rose & Montemayor, 1994). Findings like these suggest the possibility that although the creation of rigid rules, or schemas, for gender roles is a normal—even essential—process in young children, a blurring of those rules may be an important process in adolescence, particularly for girls, for whom a more masculine or androgynous self-concept is associated with more positive outcomes.

Cross-cultural research suggests that adoption of an androgynous or masculine orientation by a girl can lead to lower self-esteem. For example, one study of Israeli girls found that preteens who were tomboys and who rated themselves high on masculine personality traits were less popular and had lower self-esteem than their more feminine peers (Lobel, Slone, & Winch, 1997). Consequently, when considering gender roles and gender-role identity, it is important to remember that both are very strongly tied to culture. A particular society may value the masculine role more highly but also actively discourage girls from adopting it. Thus, it may not be universally true that teens who adopt the more highly valued gender-role identity gain self-esteem.

Self-esteem shows other interesting shifts during the teenage years. The overall trend is a rise in self-esteem through the years of adolescence. The average 19- or 20-year-old has a considerably more positive sense of her global self-worth than she did at age 8 or 11 (Diehl, Vicary, & Deike, 1997; Harter, 1990; Wigfield, Eccles, MacIver, Reuman, & Midgley, 1991). However, the rise to higher self-esteem during adolescence is not steady (see **Figure 12.4**). The 1994–1995 National Population Survey found that psychological well-being in general, and self-esteem in particular, were lowest in adolescent Canadians. For instance, Canadian adolescents not only reported the lowest rates of high self-esteem, but also expressed the

Teenaged boys like these may have an easier time achieving high self-esteem than girls of the same age because both boys and girls seem to place a higher value on certain traditionally "masculine" qualities than on traditionally "feminine" ones. (*Photo:* Myrleen Ferguson Cate/PhotoEdit)

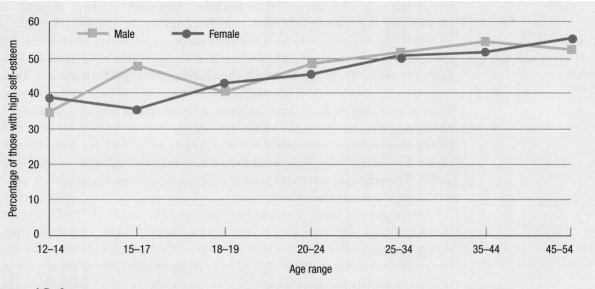

Figure 12.4

The percentage of those with high self-esteem is lowest in adolescence and increases in adulthood.

(*Source:* Adapted from Health Canada, 1999e, from Table 54, p. 222. Reproduced with the permission of the Minister of Public Works and Government Services Canada, 2007.)

highest percentages of low-self esteem. Specifically, almost 20% of 12- to 19-year-olds had low self-esteem, which was the highest rate of all the age groups. The largest gender gap in levels of self-esteem was in 15- to 19-year-olds: 22% of females expressed low self-esteem compared with 13% of males (Health Canada, 1999e; Statistics Canada, 2001f).

To study the relationship of self-esteem to important developmental outcomes, such as school achievement, researchers often divide teens into four groups based on the stability of their self-esteem ratings across adolescence (Diehl et al., 1997; Zimmerman, Copeland, Shope, & Dielman, 1997). The largest group, about half in most studies, display consistently high self-esteem throughout adolescence. The self-esteem of those in the second group steadily increases, and the self-esteem ratings of those in the third group are consistently low. Teens in the fourth group enjoy moderate to high self-esteem at the beginning of the period, but it declines steadily as adolescence progresses. One finding of concern is that girls outnumber boys in the third and fourth groups (Zimmerman et al., 1997). In addition, several studies have found that high self-esteem is correlated with positive developmental outcomes. For example, teens with high self-esteem are better able to resist peer pressure, get higher grades in school and are less likely to be depressed (Repetto, Caldwell, & Zimmerman, 2004). You may also remember from **Chapter 11** that such teens are less likely to become involved in substance abuse or early sexual intercourse.

ETHNIC IDENTITY

There are more than 70 distinct ethnic identities in Canada, and Canadian identities vary along linguistic, national, regional, racial, and religious groupings (Rummens, 2001). Minority teenagers, especially recent immigrant youth, face the task of creating

ethnic identity
a sense of belonging to an ethnic group

two identities in adolescence. Like other teens, they must develop a sense of individual identity that they believe sets them apart from others. In addition, they must develop an **ethnic identity** that includes self-identification as a member of their specific group, commitment to that group and its values and attitudes, and some attitudes (positive or negative) about the group to which they belong (Phinney, Ferguson, & Tate, 1997). Moreover, the process of developing an ethnic identity can be at variance with a social environment that is dominated by the concerns of the majority (Phinney, Ong, & Madden, 2000). For example, immigrant parents' expectations about helping out with family obligations, obeying parents, and dating or socializing can differ from the views of the adolescents who have been exposed to majority cultural values (Sodhi Kalsi, 2003). Furthermore, intergenerational differences tend to become more pronounced the longer the term of residency.

Ethnic identity tends to strengthen with age (Phinney et al., 1997) and progresses through phases. The first phase is typical of younger children who haven't paid attention to or haven't shown much interest in their ethnic identity. Next, as the young person is exposed to the media or experiences racism or inequality in society, she may start to become acutely aware of the gulf that lies between the values and attitudes that exist within the larger culture and her own culture. Following a period of exploration of what it means to be a part of an ethnic group, adolescents may internalize their ethnic identity by developing a secure sense of membership and pride in and commitment to their own ethnic group (Phinney, 1990, 1993; Phinney & Alipuria, 1996; Phinney & Kohastu, 1997). Of course, ethnic identity development does not always progress smoothly or completely, and people may cycle through the phases at different times throughout their lives (Parham, 1989).

Adolescents who form strong and favourable ethnic identities have higher levels of self-esteem and optimism than their peers with weak ethnic identities (Phinney et al., 1997). Moreover, adolescents who form a combined identity based on strong identification and participation in both their own ethnic culture and the larger culture have the highest self-esteem and the best outcomes. Teens who possess a **bicultural identity** not only feel more positive about their own ethnic group, but they have more favourable relationships with people from other ethnic groups as well (Phinney et al., 1997; Phinney & Kohastu, 1997).

bicultural identity
personal identification and satisfaction with more than one culture

Recent-immigrant youth experience mixed feelings toward Canadian society. Although they enjoy the freedom associated with Canadian youth culture, they feel "somewhat overwhelmed and alienated by what they perceive to be its rampant consumerism and superficiality" (**www.ccsd.ca/subsites/cd/docs/iy/hl.htm**). Those who speak neither English nor French face the extra challenge of learning a new language as well as overcoming social isolation when they arrive in Canada (CCSD, 2000b). A Canadian Council on Social Development report on cultural diversity (CCSD, 2000c)

Young recent immigrants often develop two identities: a psychological sense of self and an ethnic identity. Those who succeed at both tasks often think of themselves as "bicultural" and have an easier time relating to peers of the same and other ethnicities.
(*Photos:* left, Jim West/MaXx Images; right, courtesy of Vicky Kasala Pictures)

Development in the Real World

THE STUDENTS COMMISSION

The Students Commission, a diverse, global-minded organization that is run by youth for youth across Canada, was established in 1991 to bring students together to discuss issues and direct public policy both nationally and internationally. Delegates of The Students Commission have had a voice at the tables of the Prime Minister, the Governor General, cabinet ministers, provincial premiers, and business, education, community, and labour leaders across Canada, as well as at many prominent international organizations, such as the United Nations, APEC, and UNESCO (Students Commission, 1995, 2004).

One of the early discussion topics it posed to fellow Canadian youth revolved around the question "What does being Canadian mean?" The following excerpts are some of their responses, which illustrate how Canadian life looked from their point of view:

- We cannot define Canada as only one culture. Canadian society is multicultural, multiracial, multifaith, and multilingual. Your identity is made up of what you value from various cultures that make up your ethnic background.

- Being of the first generation means that one has to keep [one's] cultural heritage and try to combine it with the Canadian lifestyle and values. At one extreme there is the uniqueness of the individual and at the other extreme [we are] all citizens of the earth; somewhere in the middle lies a Canadian identity.

- All Canadian cultures were at one point faced with conflict between their own cultural heritage/ethnic background and the culture of their new surroundings. Differences and adjustments are the things which make the transition to the new culture difficult. These include a change in language, food, value systems, and traditions. These may seem like easy things to change, but to an immigrant, a difficulty with these things could translate to a resentment of their new land. Someone who has lived in Canada for a long time might ask why there is such a big deal about blending two different cultures. Immigrants are faced with this difficult juggling act—a dilemma in which they feel they might have to compromise their traditions [in order] to fit in with the surrounding culture.

- Two [difficulties] facing immigrants have always been adjusting to the new culture and maintaining their own cultural heritage. Often the values and traditions of one ethnic culture get swallowed up by the surrounding environment.

- For many people, the feeling of being Canadian has somewhat erased the feeling of being an immigrant. This may be true for a large number of people in our society. However, we must never lose sight of the fact that we are all immigrants to this country and that our ancestors suffered and sacrificed to reach Canada. Some of our ancestors were escaping from famine, war, [or] religious, social, or political persecution. To escape these things they migrated to Canada just as people migrate today.

(*Source:* http://collections.ic.gc.ca/sharing/B_C_e.html. Students Commission, 1992.)

found that new arrivals have to contend with developing new relationships with friends in whom they can confide. More than one-quarter of immigrant youth aged 12 to 14 who have been in Canada less than 10 years reported that they do not have someone on whom they can rely during a crisis or when making important decisions. Consequently, immigrant youth often seek social support through formal social groups such as volunteer and religious organizations, and actively participate in religious organizations in part as a way to establish a social network (see **Development in the Real World**).

Once they have lived in Canada for at least a decade, immigrant youth adopt patterns of lifestyle behaviours similar to those of Canadian-born youth, especially in terms of changes in participation in religious activities, smoking, and alcohol consumption (CCSD, 2000c). Specifically, immigrant youth who have lived in Canada for more than 10 years have about as many friends in whom they can confide as Canadian-born youth; are about as likely to never attend a religious service; have more friends who drink and smoke than do recent immigrants; and have somewhat increased their own rates of smoking and alcohol consumption.

LOCUS OF CONTROL AND OTHER TRAITS

locus of control
a set of beliefs about the
causes of events

One particularly important component of self- and other-understanding that appears to work in combination with personality traits to shape adolescents' development is **locus of control**. Psychologists use this term to signify a teenager's or an adult's beliefs about the causes of events. Someone with an *external* locus of control attributes the causes of experiences, such as school failure, to factors outside himself. For example, an adolescent with an external locus of control might claim that he failed a class because the teacher didn't like him or because the class was too difficult. Someone with an *internal* locus of control views personal variables, such as ability and effort, as responsible for outcomes. A teen who believes either that she failed a class because she lacks ability or because she didn't try hard enough has an internal locus of control.

There are important correlations between locus of control and behaviour (Janssen & Carton, 1999). An external locus of control is associated with procrastination and poor academic performance. In contrast, both teens and adults with an internal locus of control are more likely to complete tasks and succeed in school. They are also more optimistic (Phinney, Baumann, & Blanton, 2001).

For most teens who have an external locus of control, the trait is balanced by other more positive aspects of personality; however, researchers have found that an external locus of control is sometimes part of a cluster of personality variables that includes low self-esteem, along with the and neuroticism dimensions of the Big Five (Beautrais, Joyce, & Mulder, 1999). (You'll recall that introversion is a preference for solitary rather than social activities; individuals who score high on tests of neuroticism are pessimistic, irritable, and worry a lot.) Developmentalists have found that teens across a variety of cultures who possess this particular combination of characteristics have a very negative outlook on life, resist efforts by parents and friends to help them, and are at greater risk for all kinds of adjustment problems than their peers.

For instance, these adolescents are more likely to use avoidant coping when they face problems (Gomez, Bounds, Holmberg, Fullarton, & Gomez, 1999; Medvedova, 1998). This means that they ignore problems or put off dealing with them. For example, a high school student with these traits who finds out he is failing a class may wait until it is too late to try to do anything about it. However, because he tends to blame others for his problems, he is unlikely to be able to learn from the experience.

Before Going On

- In what ways does self-understanding in adolescence differ from that in childhood?
- How do gender-role, self-esteem, ethnic identity, and locus of control influence an adolescent's development?

MORAL DEVELOPMENT

As you read in **Chapter 10**, theorists representing various orientations think differently about moral development. However, the work of theorist and psychologist Lawrence Kohlberg has had the most powerful impact (Bergman, 2002; Colby, Kohlberg, Gibbs, & Lieberman 1983; Kohlberg, 1976, 1981). Moreover, theories of moral reasoning have been important in explanations of adolescent antisocial behaviour.

KOHLBERG'S THEORY OF MORAL REASONING

You may recall from **Chapter 10** that Piaget proposed two stages in the development of moral reasoning. Working from Piaget's basic assumptions, Kohlberg devised a way of measuring moral reasoning based on research participants' responses to moral dilemmas such as the following:

> In Europe, a woman was near death from a special kind of cancer. There was one drug that the doctors thought might save her. It was a form of radium that a druggist in the same town had recently discovered. The drug was expensive to make, but the druggist was charging ten times what the drug cost him to make. He paid $200 for the radium and charged $2000 for a small dose of the drug. The sick woman's husband, Heinz, went to everyone he knew to borrow the money, but he could only get together about $1000. . . . He told the druggist that his wife was dying, and asked him to sell it cheaper or let him pay later. But the druggist said, "No, I discovered the drug and I'm going to make money from it." So Heinz got desperate and broke into the man's store to steal the drug for his wife. (Kohlberg & Elfenbein, 1975, p. 621)

Kohlberg analyzed participants' answers to questions about such dilemmas (e.g., "Should Heinz have stolen the drug? Why?") and concluded that there were three levels of moral development, each made up of two substages, as summarized in **Table 12.1**. It is important to understand that what determines the stage or level of a person's moral judgment is not any specific moral choice but the form of reasoning used to

Critical Thinking

How would you respond to the Heinz dilemma? What does your response suggest about your level of moral reasoning?

TABLE 12.1   Kohlberg's Stages of Moral Development

Level	Stage	Description
Level I: Preconventional	Stage 1: Punishment and Obedience Orientation	The child or teenager decides what is wrong on the basis of what is punished. Obedience is valued for its own sake, but the child obeys because the adults have superior power.
	Stage 2: Individualism, Instrumental Purpose, and Exchange	Children and teens follow rules when it is in their immediate interest. What is good is what brings pleasant results.
Level II: Conventional	Stage 3: Mutual Interpersonal Expectations, Relationships, and Interpersonal Conformity	Moral actions are those that live up to the expectations of the family or other significant group. "Being good" becomes important for its own sake.
	Stage 4: Social System and Conscience (Law and Order)	Moral actions are those so defined by larger social groups or the society as a whole. One should fulfill duties one has agreed to and uphold laws, except in extreme cases.
Level III: Postconventional	Stage 5: Social Contract or Utility and Individual Rights	This stage involves acting so as to achieve the "greatest good for the greatest number." The teenager or adult is aware that most values are relative and laws are changeable, although rules should be upheld to preserve the social order. Still, there are some basic absolute values, such as the importance of each person's life and liberty.
	Stage 6: Universal Ethical Principles	The small number of adults who reason at Stage 6 develop and follow self-chosen ethical principles in determining what is right. These ethical principles are part of an articulated, integrated, carefully thought-out, and consistently followed system of values and principles.

(*Sources:* Kohlberg, 1976; Lickona, 1978.)

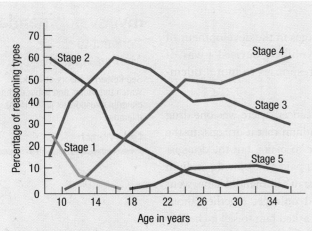

Figure 12.5

These findings are from Colby and Kohlberg's long-term longitudinal study of a group of boys who were asked about Kohlberg's moral dilemmas every few years from age 10 through early adulthood. As they got older, the stage or level of their answers changed, with conventional reasoning appearing fairly widely at high school age. Postconventional, or principled, reasoning was not very common at any age.

(*Source:* Colby et al. 1983, Figure 1, p. 46. © The Society for Research in Child Development.)

justify that choice. For example, either response to Kohlberg's dilemma—that Heinz should steal the drug or that he should not—could be justified with logic at any given stage.

AGE AND MORAL REASONING The stages are correlated somewhat loosely with age. Very few children reason beyond stage 1 or 2, and stage 2 and stage 3 reasoning are the types most commonly found among adolescents (Walker, de Vries, & Trevethan, 1987). Among adults, stages 3 and 4 are the most common (Gibson, 1990). Two research examples illustrate these overall age trends. The first, shown in **Figure 12.5**, comes from Kohlberg's own longitudinal study of 58 boys, first interviewed when they were age 10 and then followed for more than 20 years (Colby et al., 1983). **Table 12.2** shows cross-sectional data from a study by Lawrence Walker and his colleagues (1987). They studied 10 boys and 10 girls at each of four ages, interviewing the parents of each child as well. The results of these two studies, although not identical, point to remarkably similar conclusions about the order of emergence of the various stages and about the approximate ages at which they predominate. In both studies, stage 2 reasoning dominates at around age 10, and stage 3 reasoning is most common at about age 16.

preconventional morality
in Kohlberg's theory, the level of moral reasoning in which judgments are based on authorities outside the self

PRECONVENTIONAL REASONING At level I, **preconventional morality**, the child's judgments are based on sources of authority who are close by and physically superior—usually the parents. Just as descriptions of others are largely external at this level, so the standards the child uses to judge rightness or wrongness are external rather than internal. In particular, the outcome or consequence of an action determines the rightness or wrongness of the action.

In stage 1 of this level—*the punishment and obedience orientation*—the child relies on the physical consequences of some action to decide whether it is right or wrong.

TABLE 12.2	Percentages of Children and Parents Who Show Moral Reasoning at Each of Kohlberg's Stages							
	Stage							
Age	1	1–2	2	2–3	3	3–4	4	4–5	5
6 (grade 1)	10%	70%	15%	5%	—	—	—	—	—
9 (grade 4)	—	25%	40%	35%	—	—	—	—	—
12 (grade 7)	—	—	15%	60%	25%	—	—	—	—
15 (grade 10)	—	—	—	40%	55%	5%	—	—	—
Parents	—	—	—	1%	15%	70%	11%	3%	—

(*Source:* Walker et al., 1987, from Table 1, p. 849, "Moral stages and moral orientations in real-life and hypothetical dilemmas," *Child Development*, 60, 842–858. By permission of the Society for Research in Child Development.)

If he is punished, then the behaviour was wrong; if he is not punished, then it was right. He is obedient to adults because they are bigger and stronger.

In stage 2—*individualism, instrumental purpose, and exchange*—the child or adolescent operates on the principle that you should do things that are rewarded and avoid things that are punished. For this reason, the stage is sometimes called *naive hedonism*. If it feels good, or brings pleasant results, then it is good. Some beginning of concern for other people is apparent during this stage, but only if that concern can be expressed as something that benefits the child or teenager himself as well. So he can enter into agreements such as "If you help me, I'll help you."

To illustrate, here are some responses to variations of the Heinz dilemma, drawn from studies of children and teenagers in a number of different cultures, all of whom were at stage 2:

> He should steal the drug for his wife because if she dies he'll have to pay for the funeral, and that costs a lot. [Taiwan] [He should steal the drug because] he should protect the life of his wife so he doesn't have to stay alone in life. [Puerto Rico] (Snarey, 1985, p. 221)

CONVENTIONAL REASONING At the next major level, the level of **conventional morality**, rules or norms of a group to which the individual belongs become the basis of moral judgments, whether that group is the family, the peer group, a church, or the nation. What the chosen reference group defines as right or good is right or good in the individual's view. Again, very few children exhibit conventional thinking, but many adolescents are capable of this kind of moral reasoning.

Stage 3 (the first stage of level II) is the stage of *mutual interpersonal expectations, relationships, and interpersonal conformity* (sometimes also called the *good boy/nice girl stage*). Regardless of age, individuals who reason at this stage believe that good behaviour is what pleases other people. They value trust, loyalty, respect, gratitude, and maintenance of mutual relationships. Andy, a boy Kohlberg interviewed who was at stage 3, said:

> I try to do things for my parents, they've always done things for you. I try to do everything my mother says, I try to please her. Like she wants me to be a doctor and I want to, too, and she's helping me get up there. (Kohlberg, 1964, p. 401)

Another mark of this third stage is that the individual makes judgments based on intentions as well as on outward behaviour. If someone "didn't mean to do it," then the wrongdoing is seen as less serious than if the person did it "on purpose."

Stage 4, the second stage of the conventional morality level, incorporates the norms of a larger reference group into moral judgments. Kohlberg labelled this the stage of *social system and conscience*. It is also sometimes called the *law-and-order orientation*. People reasoning at this stage focus on doing their duty, respecting authority, and following rules and laws. The emphasis is less on what is pleasing to particular people (as in stage 3) and more on adhering to a complex set of regulations. However, the regulations themselves are not questioned, and morality and legality are assumed to be equivalent. Therefore, for a person at stage 4, something that is legal is right, whereas something that is illegal is wrong. Consequently, changes in law can effect changes in the moral views of individuals who reason at stage 4.

POSTCONVENTIONAL REASONING The transition to level III, **postconventional morality**, is marked by several changes, the most important of which is a shift in the source of authority. Individuals who reason at level I see authority as totally outside of themselves; at level II, the judgments or rules of external authorities are internalized, but they are not questioned or analyzed; at level III, a new kind of personal authority emerges, in which an individual makes choices and judgments based on self-chosen

conventional morality
in Kohlberg's theory, the level of moral reasoning in which judgments are based on rules or norms of a group to which the person belongs

postconventional morality
in Kohlberg's theory, the level of moral reasoning in which judgments are based on an integration of individual rights and the needs of society

Civil disobedience involves intentionally breaking laws one believes to be immoral. For example, in the early years of the U.S. civil rights movement, African Americans broke laws that excluded them from certain sections of restaurants by "sitting in" at whites-only lunch counters. Practitioners of civil disobedience do not try to evade the consequences of their actions, because they believe in upholding the law as a general principle even though they may view some specific laws as immoral. Thus, the thinking that underlies acts of civil disobedience represents Kohlberg's postconventional level of moral reasoning. (*Photo:* Bettman/CORBIS)

principles or on principles that are assumed to transcend the needs and concerns of any individual or group. Postconventional thinkers represent only a minority of adults and an even smaller minority of adolescents.

In stage 5 at this level, which Kohlberg called the *social contract orientation*, such self-chosen principles begin to be evident. Rules, laws, and regulations are not seen as irrelevant; they are important ways of ensuring fairness. But people operating at this level also acknowledge that there are times when the rules, laws, and regulations need to be ignored or changed.

The American civil rights movement of the 1950s and 1960s is a good example of stage 5 reasoning in action. *Civil disobedience*—deliberately breaking laws that were believed to be immoral—arose as a way of protesting racial segregation. For example, African Americans intentionally took seats in restaurants that were reserved for whites. It is important to note that the practice of civil disobedience does not usually involve avoiding the penalties that accompany criminal behaviour. Indeed, some of the most effective and poignant images from that period of U.S. history are photographs of individuals who surrendered and were jailed for breaking segregation laws. This behaviour illustrates the stage 5 view that, as a general principle, upholding the law is important, even though a specific law that is deemed to be immoral can, or even should, be broken when breaking it will serve to promote the common good.

In his original writing about moral development, Kohlberg also included a sixth stage, *the universal ethical principles orientation*. For example, in arguing against capital punishment, some people say that an individual's right to life is more important than society's right to exact retribution on those who are convicted of heinous crimes. Such a claim might or might not be an example of stage 6 reasoning. The same could be said of the assertion that a fetus's right to life should supersede a woman's right to choose whether to bear a child. Remember, the key to assessing an individual's stage of moral development is to fully probe the reasoning behind her answer to a question about a moral dilemma. Sometimes this kind of probing reveals that arguments which, on first glance, appear to represent stage 6 thinking are actually based on the authority of a religious tradition or a highly respected individual, in which case the reasoning is conventional rather than postconventional. Occasionally, though, the individual making such an argument is able to explain it in terms of a universal ethical principle that must always be adhered to regardless of any other considerations. In the case of these two arguments, the universal ethical principle would be the idea that the maintenance of human life is the highest of all moral principles. Note, however, that a person reasoning at stage 6 would not argue that society has no right to punish criminals or that women have no right to decide whether to bear children. Instead, he or she would say that, in situations where upholding such rights involves termination of a human life, the right to life of the person whose life would be ended takes precedence. Moreover, a person reasoning at stage 6 might decide that the right to life is more important than other considerations with regard to the capital punishment question but less important with regard to the abortion question. He or she might also come to an entirely different conclusion when thinking about whether terminally ill people have the right to take their own lives. Thus, stage 6 reasoning involves balancing equally valid, but conflicting, moral principles against one another to determine which should be given precedence with respect to a specific moral issue.

Kohlberg argued that this sequence of reasoning is both universal and hierarchically organized. That is, each stage grows out of the preceding one. Kohlberg did not suggest that all individuals eventually progress through all six stages, or even that each stage is tied to specific ages. But he insisted that the order is invariant and universal. He also believed that the social environment determines how slowly or rapidly individuals move through the stages.

The evidence seems fairly strong that the stages follow one another in the sequence Kohlberg proposed. Long-term longitudinal studies of teenagers and young adults in the United States, Israel, and Turkey show that changes in participants' reasoning nearly always occur in the hypothesized order (Colby et al., 1983; Nisan & Kohlberg, 1982; Snarey, Reimer, & Kohlberg, 1985; Walker, 1989). People do not skip stages, and movement down the sequence rather than up occurs only about 5 to 7% of the time.

Variations of Kohlberg's dilemmas have been used with children in a wide range of countries, including both Western and non-Western, industrialized and nonindustrialized (Snarey, 1985). In every culture, researchers find higher stages of reasoning among older children, but cultures differ in the highest level of reasoning observed. In urban cultures (both Western and non-Western), stage 5 is typically the highest stage observed; in agricultural societies and those in which there is little opportunity for formal education, stage 4 is typically the highest. Collectively, this evidence seems to provide quite strong support for the universality of Kohlberg's stage sequence.

CAUSES AND CONSEQUENCES OF MORAL DEVELOPMENT

The most obvious reason for the general correlations between Kohlberg's stages and chronological age is cognitive development. Specifically, it appears that children must have a firm grasp of concrete operational thinking before they can develop or use conventional moral reasoning. Likewise, formal operations appears to be necessary for advancement to the postconventional level.

To be more specific, Kohlberg and many other theorists suggest that the decline of egocentrism that occurs as an individual moves through Piaget's concrete and formal operational stages is the cognitive-developmental variable that matters most in moral reasoning. The idea is that the greater a child's or adolescent's ability to look at a situation from another person's perspective, the more advanced she is likely to be in moral reasoning. Psychologists use the term **role-taking** to refer to this ability (Selman, 1980). Research has provided strong support for the hypothesized link between role-taking and moral development (Kuhn, Kohlberg, Languer, & Haan, 1977; Walker, 1980).

role-taking
the ability to look at a situation from another person's perspective

Nevertheless, cognitive development isn't enough. Kohlberg thought that the development of moral reasoning also required support from the social environment. Specifically, he claimed that to foster mature moral reasoning, a child's or teenager's social environment must provide him with opportunities for meaningful, reciprocal dialogue about moral issues.

Longitudinal research relating parenting styles and family climate to levels of moral reasoning suggest that Kohlberg was right (Pratt, Arnold, & Pratt, 1999). Parents' ability to identify, understand, and respond to children's and adolescents' less mature forms of moral reasoning seems to be particularly important to the development of moral reasoning. This ability on the part of parents is important because people of all ages have difficulty understanding and remembering moral arguments that are more advanced than their own level (Narvaez, 1998). Thus, a parent who can express her own moral views in words that reflect her child's level of understanding is more likely to be able to influence the child's moral development.

As an individual's capacity for moral reasoning grows, so does her ability to think logically about issues in other domains. For example, the complexity of an individual's political reasoning is very similar to the complexity of her moral reasoning (Raaijmakers, Verbogt, & Vollebergh, 1998). Further, attitudes toward the acceptability of violence also vary with levels of moral reasoning. Individuals at lower levels are more tolerant of violence (Sotelo & Sangrador, 1999).

Perhaps most importantly, teenagers' level of moral reasoning appears to be positively correlated with prosocial behaviour and negatively related to antisocial behaviour (Schonert-Reichl, 1999). In other words, the highest levels of prosocial behaviour are found among teens at the highest levels of moral reasoning (compared with their peers). Alternatively, the highest levels of antisocial behaviour are found among adolescents at the lowest levels of moral reasoning.

CRITICISMS OF KOHLBERG'S THEORY

Criticisms of Kohlberg's theory have come from theorists representing different perspectives.

CULTURE AND MORAL REASONING Cross-cultural research provides strong support for the universality of Kohlberg's stage sequence (Snarey, 1985, 1995). Nevertheless, cross-cultural researchers have argued that his approach is too narrow to be considered truly universal. These critics point out that many aspects of moral reasoning found in non-Western cultures do not fit in well with Kohlberg's approach (Eckensberger & Zimba, 1997). The root of the problem, they say, is that Kohlberg's theory is strongly tied to the idea that justice is an overriding moral principle. To be sure, say critics, justice is an important moral concept throughout the world, and thus it isn't surprising that Kohlberg's stage sequence has been so strongly supported in cross-cultural research. However, these critics argue that the notion that justice supersedes all other moral considerations is what distinguishes Western from non-Western cultures. As these criticisms would predict, research has shown that the responses of individuals in non-Western cultures to Kohlberg's classic dilemmas often include ideas that are not found in his scoring system (Baek, 2002).

For example, in many cultures, respect for one's elders is an important moral principle that often overrides other concerns (Eckensberger & Zimba, 1997). Thus, if researchers alter the Heinz dilemma such that the sick woman is Heinz's mother rather than his wife, Western and non-Western research participants are likely to respond quite differently. Such differences are difficult to explain from the justice-based, stage-oriented perspective of Kohlberg's theory. Advocates for the theory have argued that respect for elders as the basis of moral reasoning represents Kohlberg's conventional level. Critics, by contrast, say that this classification underestimates the true moral reasoning level of individuals from non-Western cultures.

MORAL REASONING AND EMOTIONS Some theorists criticize Kohlberg's failure to connect moral reasoning to moral emotions. Psychologist Nancy Eisenberg (2000), for example, suggests that empathy, the ability to identify with others' emotions, is both a cause and a consequence of moral development. Similarly, Eisenberg suggests that a complete explanation of moral development should include age-related and individual variations in the ability to regulate emotions (such as anger) that can motivate antisocial behaviour.

Likewise, Carol Gilligan claims that an ethic based on caring for others and maintaining social relationships may be as important to moral reasoning as ideas about justice. Gilligan's theory argues that there are at least two distinct "moral orientations":

justice and care (Gilligan, 1982; Gilligan & Wiggins, 1987). Each has its own central injunction—not to treat others unfairly (justice) and not to turn away from someone in need (caring). Research suggests that adolescents do exhibit a moral orientation based on care and that care-based reasoning about hypothetical moral dilemmas is related to reasoning about real-life dilemmas (Skoe et al., 1999). In response, Kohlberg acknowledged in his later writings that his theory deals specifically with development of reasoning about justice and does not claim to be a comprehensive account of moral development (Kohlberg, Levine, & Hewer, 1983). Thus, some developmentalists view Gilligan's ideas about moral development as an expansion of Kohlberg's theory rather than a rejection of it (Jorgensen, 2006).

Possible sex differences in moral reasoning are another focus of Gilligan's theory. According to Gilligan, boys and girls learn both the justice and care orientations, but girls are more likely to operate from the care orientation, whereas boys are more likely to operate from a justice orientation. Because of these differences, girls and boys tend to perceive moral dilemmas quite differently.

Given the emerging evidence on sex differences in styles of interaction and in friendship patterns, Gilligan's hypothesis makes some sense. Perhaps girls, focused more on intimacy in their relationships, judge moral dilemmas by different criteria. But, in fact, research on moral dilemmas has not consistently shown that boys are more likely to use justice reasoning or that girls more often use care reasoning. Several studies of adults do show such a pattern (e.g., Lyons, 1983; Wark & Krebs, 1996); however, studies of children and teenagers generally have not (Jadack, Hyde, Moore, & Keller, 1995; Smetana, Killen, & Turiel, 1991; Walker et al., 1987). Further, recent evidence suggests that such sex differences, if they exist, may be restricted to North American culture (Skoe et al., 1999).

MORAL REASONING AND BEHAVIOUR Finally, critics have questioned the degree to which moral reasoning predicts moral behaviour (Krebs & Denton, 2006). Researchers have found that moral reasoning and moral behaviour are correlated, but the relationship is far from perfect. To explain inconsistencies between reasoning and behaviour, learning theorists suggest that moral reasoning is situational rather than developmental. They point to a variety of studies to support this assertion.

First, neither adolescents nor adults reason at the same level in response to every hypothetical dilemma (Rique & Camino, 1997). An individual research participant might reason at the conventional level in response to one dilemma and at the postconventional level with respect to another. Second, the types of characters in moral dilemmas strongly influence research participants' responses to them, especially when the participants are adolescents. For example, hypothetical dilemmas involving celebrities as characters elicit much lower levels of moral reasoning from teenagers than those involving fictional characters, such as Heinz (Einerson, 1998).

In addition, research participants show disparities in levels of moral reasoning in response to hypothetical dilemmas compared with real-life moral issues. For example, Israeli Jewish, Israeli Bedouin, and Palestinian youths living in Israel demonstrate different levels of moral reasoning when responding to hypothetical stories, such as the Heinz dilemma, than they exhibit in discussing the moral dimensions of the long-standing conflicts among their ethnic groups (Elbedour, Baker, & Charlesworth, 1997). Thus, as learning theorists predict, it appears that situational factors may be more important variables for decisions about actual moral behaviour than the level of moral reasoning exhibited in response to hypothetical dilemmas.

MORAL DEVELOPMENT AND ANTISOCIAL BEHAVIOUR

The consistent finding of low levels of moral reasoning among adolescents who engage in serious forms of antisocial behaviour has been of particular interest to developmentalists (Aleixo & Norris, 2000; Ashkar & Kenny, 2007; Cheung, Chan, Lee, Liu, & Leung, 2001; Ma, 2003). A young person who commits an offence (previously known as a *delinquent* or a *young offender*) is distinguished from other youth who engage in other forms of antisocial behaviour, such as bullying, on the basis of actual lawbreaking (**criminality**). To address youth criminality, Canada's new *Youth Criminal Justice Act* (*YCJA*) focuses in part on rehabilitation and reintegration of a young person into society. Thus, the *YCJA* avoids the practice of labelling a youth as a criminal and instead focuses on the young person's offensive actions, which are malleable to change (see **Development in the Real World**).

criminality
antisocial behaviour that includes lawbreaking

Youth who commit offences appear to be behind their peers in moral reasoning because of deficits in role-taking skills. For example, researchers have found that teenagers who can look at actions they are contemplating from their parents' perspective

Development in the Real World

YOUTH CRIMINAL JUSTICE

In Canada, there are some uneven trends in the incidence of youth crime. From 1991 to 2000, the overall youth crime rate fell steadily, especially for property offences, theft, and break and enter. The rate levelled off in 2000 and rebounded slightly in 2003. Rates of violent youth crime, including homicide, assault, sexual assault, and robbery, increased until 1997, at which time the rates continued to rise, but more gradually (Statistics Canada, 2001f; Sudworth & deSouza, 2000; Wallace, 2003, 2004). Forty-one youth were charged with homicide in 2000, which is 11 fewer than the average since 1990 (Statistics Canada, 2001g).

Youth crime rates vary with location, age, and sex. Demographic data shows that in 2002, Saskatchewan and Manitoba experienced the highest rates of youth crime, while Quebec, Prince Edward Island, and British Columbia experienced the lowest rates (Wallace, 2003). Canadian youth crime rates increase with age and peak at age 15 in females and age 17 in males. Further, males have higher crime rates at every age and account for about 8 out of 10 court cases; males 16 and 17 years of age account for slightly more than half of all youth court cases (Robinson, 2004). At all age groups, youth are more likely to be victims of crimes committed by other youth than by adults. A disproportionately high number of youth are crime victims compared with adults, and girls are more likely to be victims of violent crime than boys (Statistics Canada, 2001f).

Two socializing factors that predict youth crime rates are peer influences and parenting style. The percentage of children engaging in high-risk behaviours such as smoking, fighting, and stealing was four to nine times higher than when children were not part of a group "doing bad things." Children who witnessed violence at home or who were raised by a parent who had either an ineffective or aversive parenting style were very often likely to exhibit conduct disorder behaviours (Statistics Canada, 2001f). Moreover, the rate of violent delinquency was almost five times higher in families where parents failed to consistently monitor where their children were and whom they were with (Fitzgerald, 2010).

It is difficult to understand the motivations that underlie criminal activity, especially violent offences, but a new approach to youth crime has resulted in a major restructuring of our youth justice system. *Canada's Youth Criminal Justice Act* is based on "the values, rights and responsibilities of both society and young people in relation to crime [and has three main objectives:] to prevent crime, rehabilitate and reintegrate offenders into society, and ensure meaningful consequences for offences committed by young people" (Department of Justice Canada, 2001b, p. 1). All the same, it is not easy to balance what should be done to satisfy our need for justice for the suffering of victims of violence against the personal consequences of violent behaviour for the young perpetrators of these crimes, while at the same time reducing future violent offences. Intervention that would reduce future violence would require a considerable commitment of time and resources. Developmentalists play an important role by providing research-based guidance in the mental development factors of individuals as well as a broader perspective of the social factors associated with criminality.

are less likely to engage in criminal behaviour than adolescents who cannot do so (Wyatt & Carlo, 2002). Youth offenders also seem to be unable to look at their crimes from their victims' perspectives or to assess hypothetical crimes from the victims' perspectives. Thus, programs aimed at helping youth who commit offences develop more mature levels of moral reasoning usually focus on heightening their awareness of the victim's point of view. However, few such programs have been successful (Moody, 1997; Putnins, 1997). Consequently, psychologists believe that there is far more to youth criminality than just a lack of role-taking and moral reasoning skills.

First, it appears that there are at least two important subvarieties of youth who commit offences, distinguished by the age at which the criminal behaviour begins. Childhood-onset problems are more serious and more likely to persist into adulthood. Adolescent-onset problems are typically milder and more transitory, apparently more a reflection of peer-group processes or a testing of the limits of authority than a deeply ingrained behaviour problem.

The developmental pathway for early-onset youth criminality seems to be directed by factors inside the child, such as temperament and personality. In early life, these children throw tantrums and defy parents; they may also develop insecure attachments (Greenberg, Speltz, & DeKlyen, 1993). Once the defiance appears, if the parents are not up to the task of controlling the child, the child's behaviour worsens. He may begin to display overt aggression toward others, who then reject him, which aggravates the problem. The seriously aggressive child is pushed in the direction of other children with similar problems, who then become the child's only supportive peer group (Shaw, Kennan, & Vondra, 1994).

By adolescence, these youngsters may exhibit serious disturbances in thinking (Aleixo & Norris, 2000). Canadian researchers have found that most have friends who are almost exclusively other young people who commit crimes (Tremblay, Masse, Vitaro, & Dobkin, 1995). Of course, this situation is reinforced by frequent rejection by noncriminal peers (Brendgen, Vitaro, & Bukowski, 1998). Many of these adolescents have parents with histories of antisocial behaviour as well (Gainey, Catalano, Haggerty, & Hoppe, 1997). Youth who commit crimes at an early age are also highly likely to display a whole cluster of other problem behaviours, including drug and alcohol use, truancy or dropping out of school, and early and risky sexual behaviour, including having multiple sexual partners (Dishion, French, & Patterson, 1995).

For young people whose criminality appears first in adolescence, the pathway is different. They, too, have friends who commit crimes. However, associating with peers who commit crimes worsens their behaviour, while the behaviour of youth who commit crimes at an early age remains essentially the same, whether they have antisocial friends or are "loners" (Vitaro, Tremblay, Kerr, Pagani, & Bukowski, 1997). Moreover, the antisocial behaviour patterns of adolescent-onset youth who commit offences often change as their relationships change (Laird, Pettit, Dodge, & Bates, 1999). Consequently, peer influence seems to be the most important factor in the development of adolescent-onset youth criminality.

Parenting style and other relationship variables seem to be additional factors in this type of antisocial behaviour. Most of these teens have parents who do not monitor them sufficiently; their individual friendships are not very supportive or intimate; and they are drawn to a clique or a crowd that includes some teens who are experimenting with drugs or mild lawbreaking. After a period of months of hanging out with such a group of peers, previously noncriminal adolescents show some increase in risky or antisocial behaviours, such as increased drug-taking (Berndt & Keefe, 1995a; Dishion et al., 1995; Steinberg, Fletcher, & Darling, 1994). However, when parents do provide good monitoring and emotional support, their adolescent child is unlikely to get involved in criminal acts or drug use, even if she hangs around with a tougher crowd or has a close friend who engages in such behaviour (Brown & Huang, 1995; Mounts & Steinberg, 1995).

Before Going On

- What are the features of moral reasoning at each of Kohlberg's stages, and what are some important causes and effects in the development of moral reasoning?

- Describe the moral reasoning abilities and other characteristics of young people who commit criminal offences.

SOCIAL RELATIONSHIPS

As you can see from the solutions for peer conflicts listed in **Table 12.3**, adolescents' ideas about other people and their understanding of social situations are more complex than those of children. These advances in interpersonal understanding lead to changes in family and peer relationships.

RELATIONSHIPS WITH PARENTS

Teenagers have two apparently contradictory tasks in their relationships with their parents: to establish autonomy from them and to maintain a sense of relatedness with them.

TABLE 12.3	Children's and Adolescents' Comments About How to Solve Disagreements Between Friends
Age	**Comments**
5-year-olds	Go away from her and come back later when you're not fighting.
	Punch her out.
8-year-olds	Around our way the guy who started it just says he's sorry.
	Well, if you say something and don't really mean it, then you have to mean it when you take it back.
14-year-olds	Sometimes you got to get away for a while. Calm down a bit so you won't be so angry. Then get back and try to talk it out.
	If you just settle up after a fight that is no good. You gotta really feel that you'd be happy the way things went if you were in your friend's shoes. You can just settle up with someone who is not a friend, but that's not what friendship is really about.
16-year-old	Well, you could talk it out, but it usually fades itself out. It usually takes care of itself. You don't have to explain everything. You do certain things and each of you knows what it means. But if not, then talk it out.

(*Source:* **Selman**, 1980, pp. 107–113.)

CONFLICTS WITH PARENTS The rise in conflict between parents and teenagers has been documented by a number of researchers (e.g., Flannery, Montemayor, & Eberly, 1994; Laursen, 1995; Steinberg, 1988). University of Lethbridge sociologist Reginald Bibby found that Canadian teens disagree with their parents most when it comes to issues such as chores around the house, school, their parents' reaction to the way they talk to them, and their parent's concern about their safety. These issues account for roughly half of the conflicts. It's interesting that there was less parent-teen conflict over issues such as who they are dating, drugs, their appearance (clothing and hairstyle), and sex (about one-fifth of the conflicts) (Bibby, 2001).

Although this increase in discord is widely observed, you should not assume that it signifies a major disruption of the quality of the parent–child relationships. For most Canadian teens, their families are still important to them, especially as a source of enjoyment and support (Bibby, 2001). Furthermore, parent–teen conflicts appear to cause more distress for parents than for adolescents (Dekovic, 1999).

Individual traits of teenagers themselves may contribute to conflicts with parents. The adolescent's temperament, for example, contributes to the amount of conflict. Those who have been difficult from early childhood are the most likely to experience high degrees of conflict with parents in adolescence (Dekovic, 1999). Teens' pubertal status may be a factor as well. Among girls, conflict seems to rise after menarche (Holmbeck & Hill, 1991). Moreover, as noted earlier, cultural factors affect both the degree of parent–teen conflict and perceptions of its meaning.

While it is true that the physical changes of puberty are often followed by an increase in the number of conflicts, it is a myth that conflict is the main feature of the parent–adolescent relationship.
(*Photo:* Penny Tweedie/Getty Images)

ATTACHMENT Teenagers' underlying emotional attachment to their parents remains strong on average. For example, a large study in the Netherlands suggests that the teenager's bond with her parents may weaken somewhat in the middle of adolescence (ages 15 and 16) and then return to former levels (van Wel, 1994). But virtually all the researchers who have explored this question find that a teenager's sense of well-being or happiness is more strongly correlated with the quality of her attachment to her parents than with the quality of her relationships with peers (e.g., Greenberg, Siegel, & Leitch, 1983; Raja, McGee, & Stanton, 1992). Moreover, research findings regarding the centrality of parent–teen relationships have been consistent across a variety of cultures (Claes, 1998; Okamoto & Uechi, 1999).

Research in several countries has also found that teens who remain closely attached to their parents are the most likely to be academically successful and to enjoy good peer relations (Mayseless & Scharf, 2007; Turnage, 2004; Weimer, Kerns, & Oldenburg, 2004; Zimmermann, 2004). They are also less likely than less securely attached teens to engage in antisocial behaviour (Ma, Shek, Cheung, & Oi Bun Lam, 2000). Further, the quality of attachment in early adolescence predicts drug use in later adolescence and early adulthood (Brook, Whiteman, Finch, & Cohen, 2000). Teens who are close to their parents are less likely to use drugs than peers whose bonds with parents are weaker. Thus, even while teenagers are becoming more autonomous, they need their parents to provide a psychological safe base.

PARENTING STYLES For adolescents, as for younger children, authoritative parenting is consistently associated with more positive outcomes. Research suggests that parenting style influences a teen's self-concept and other intrapersonal variables (Dekovic & Meeus, 1997). Internal locus of control, for example, is more common in teens who

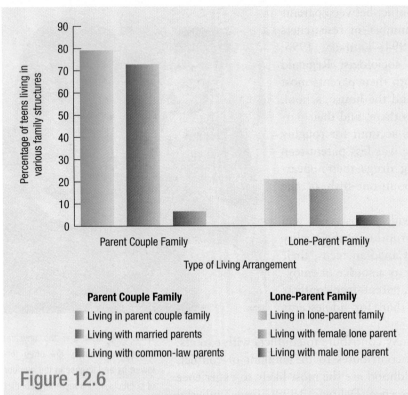

Figure 12.6

The majority of Canadian teens 15 to 19 years of age live within one of two family structures: parent couple and lone parent.

(*Source:* Adapted from Statistics Canada, 2000d; the Statistics Canada table "Age Groups [12B], Family Structure [7] and Sex [3] for Children in Census Families in Private Households, for Canada, Provinces, Territories, Census Metropolitan Areas and Census Agglomerations, 2001 Census—20% Sample Data," Cat. No. 95F0313, October 22, 2002.)

perceive their parents to be authoritative (McClun & Merrell, 1998). Parental acceptance also appears to be important in teens' development of realistic assessments of their academic abilities (Bornholt & Goodnow, 1999).

Parental involvement in education and extracurricular activities seems to be just as important for teenagers as it is for younger children. For example, lack of parental involvement in school and extracurricular activities is strongly related to conduct problems such as disruptive classroom behaviour (Frick, Christian, & Wooton, 1999). In addition, parental involvement in school-based organizations is related to secondary school students' postgraduation plans (Trusty, 1999). Those whose parents are most involved are the most likely to attend a post-secondary institution.

FAMILY STRUCTURE Family structure, too, continues to be an important factor in a teenager's life. Although the vast majority of Canadian youth aged 15 to 19 live with their families (93%) (see **Figure 12.6**), some live with spouses of their own, live common-law, or are lone parents (4%). Still others live on their own, or with relatives or nonrelatives (3%) (Statistics Canada, 2002d).

Adolescents in households including a step-parent are, on average, somewhat less well-adjusted than those who live with two biological parents. These differences are evident even when teens have been living with a step-parent for several years (Hetherington et al., 1999). Among adolescents, girls show more distress when parents divorce, both when the girl lives with her single mother after the divorce and when there is a stepfather in the household (Amato, 1993; Hetherington & Clingempeel, 1992). Adolescent girls have more trouble interacting with a new stepfather than do their brothers, and they treat him more as an intruder. Girls in this situation are also likely to become depressed and are more likely than boys in the same situation to begin using drugs.

Why this pattern occurs is not so obvious. The adolescent girl may feel displaced from a special position in the family system that she held after her parents' divorce and before the mother's remarriage. In contrast, the teenaged boy may benefit from the addition of the stepfather, because he acquires a male role model. Whatever the explanation, findings such as these are reminders that family systems are astonishingly complex.

RELATIONSHIPS WITH PEERS

Despite the importance of family relationships to adolescents, it is an undeniable fact that peer relationships become far more significant in adolescence than they have been at any earlier period, and perhaps than they will be at any time later in life.

FRIENDSHIPS Shared activities and interests continue to be important elements in the selection of friends in adolescence. However, similarity of psychological characteristics and attitudes takes on new significance during the teenaged years. For example, adolescents tend to choose friends who share their beliefs about smoking, drug use, sex, and the importance of academic achievement (Urdan, 1997). And, for many, electronic communication devices that are available today serve as hubs around which their social networks revolve (see the **Research Report**). Many teenagers have one group of friends with whom they communicate by phone, another with whom they exchange online instant messages and email, and yet another with which they associate through online communities, such as myspace.com (Foehr, 2006). As a result, teenagers have a wider range of acquaintances than their parents did in adolescence. However, they do not necessarily have more close friends.

Teens' friendships are increasingly intimate, in the sense that adolescent friends share more and more of their inner feelings and secrets and are more knowledgeable about each other's feelings. Loyalty and faithfulness become more valued characteristics of friendship. However, the ability to display intimacy, loyalty, and faithfulness in the context of a friendship doesn't come automatically with age. In fact, teens vary considerably in these interpersonal skills. The variation may be the result of individual differences in temperament and personality or of teens' experiences with family relationships (Updegraff & Obeidallah, 1999).

Adolescent friendships are also more stable than those of younger children (Degirmencioglu, Urberg, & Tolson, 1998). In one longitudinal study, researchers found that only about 20% of friendships among children in Grade 4 lasted as long as a year, whereas about 40% of friendships formed by these same youngsters when they were in Grade 10 were long-lasting (Cairns & Cairns, 1994). Friendship stability probably increases in adolescence because older teens work harder than younger teens and elementary school children at maintaining positive relationships with friends through negotiation of conflicts (Nagamine, 1999).

In addition, teens often choose friends who are committed to the same activities they are. For example, many teens, especially boys, report that peer companionship is their primary motive for playing computer and video games (Chou & Tsai, 2007; Colwell & Kato, 2005). Some studies suggest that shared video game-playing experiences promote the development of a masculine gender role among male teens (Sanford & Madill, 2006). Some developmentalists also argue that playing these games in group settings helps male adolescents learn to channel aggressive and competitive impulses into socially acceptable ways of expressing them (Jansz & Martens, 2005).

Finally, adolescents' reasons for ending friendships reflect the influence of individual differences in rate of development of social skills. For example, a change in identity status from a less mature to a more mature level often leads to acquisition of new friends (Akers, Jones, & Coyl, 1998). Likewise, girls seem to prefer friendships with other girls whose romantic status is the same as their own—that is, girls who have boyfriends prefer female friends who also have boyfriends. In fact, a girl who gets a boyfriend is likely to spend less time with female peers and to end long-standing friendships with girls who haven't yet acquired a romantic partner (Benenson & Benarroch, 1998; Zimmer-Gembeck, 1999). For boys, differences in athletic achievements can lead to the end of previously important friendships.

PEER GROUPS Like friendships, peer groups become relatively stable in adolescence (Degirmencioglu et al., 1998). Adolescents typically choose to associate with a group that shares their values, attitudes, behaviours, and identity status (Akers et al., 1998; Mackey & La Greca,

As adolescents age, the structures of their peer groups change. (*Photo:* David Young-Wolff/Getty Images)

Research Report

THE SOCIAL ASPECTS OF ELECTRONIC COMMUNICATION

Canada's youth are among the most "wired" of all adolescents in the world (Bell Canada, 2001a; Media Awareness Network [MNet], 2005; Ellison & Clark, 2001). They are the first generation to be raised on cable and satellite television, cellphones with video, and mobile Internet communication, which means that the youth of today have instantaneous access to more information and more people than any other previous generation had. The full impact this will have on this cohort of teenagers' patterns of communication is yet to be realized, in part because the technology is continually becoming more sophisticated, user friendly and pervasive.

Cellphones have helped strengthen the relationship between parents and teenagers. For example, the cellphone allows parents to keep informed about their teen's activities when they are away from home. Cellphones therefore afford teens more independence while providing increased reassurance to parents about their child's safety and whereabouts. Having been raised with cellphone technology, adolescents tend to be savvy yet practical users. A study of Ontario and Quebec 16- to 24-year-olds by Bell Canada (2001b) found that half of the youth surveyed use their cellphones to keep up to date with their friends, but they also use their cellsphones to communicate with relatives, family members, and girlfriends or boyfriends and to deal with emergency situations.

In addition to providing cellphones, most parents stated that they bought a home computer specifically to help their children keep up with their peers. Results from a recent Canada-wide survey found that 94% of students now have Internet in the home, and most of these (61%) have high-speed Internet service (MNet, 2005). Not surprisingly, today's generation of youth, many of whom have had access to a computer since age 3 or 4, perceive computers and the Internet as being a natural and integral part of their daily routines. Even in the classroom, 62% of Grade 4 students prefer using the Internet over books in a

library to gather information, and this figure climbs to above 90% by Grade 9 (MNet, 2005).

MNet (2004b, 2005) surveys indicate that in addition to downloading music, playing games, and researching for personal interest, youth show significant use of the Internet for social purposes, such as instant messaging (IM), email messaging, and visiting chat rooms. **Figure 12.7** shows the proportion of youth in Grades 4 to 11 who engage in online activities on school days. The amount of time children spend on various Internet activities varies considerably from Grades 4 to 11. Most notably, significantly more youth spend more time engaged

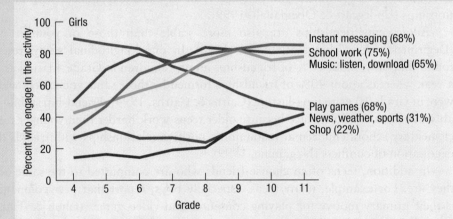

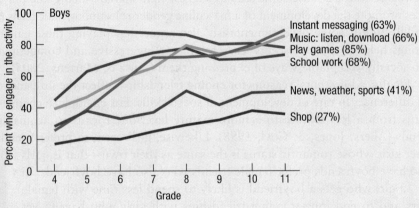

Figure 12.7

The proportion of youth who engage in online activities on an average school day increases with age, except for gaming, which decreases especially in girls. (Note: The overall percent who engage in each activity appears in brackets after the label.)

(*Source:* Media Awareness Network, 2005, p. 19. © 2007 Media Awareness Network, www.media-awareness.ca, reproduced with permission.)

in instant messaging and downloading and listening to music as they get older. In contrast, playing games is the one activity that declines with age, more so in girls than boys, although those boys who continue playing games spend more time doing so. Three-quarters of Canadian students are using the Internet to do their homework by the time they reach Grade 6 and then the usage rates level off.

As is true with most technology, benefits as well as risks are associated with the Internet's use (Clark, 2001). The MNet (2001a, 2005) surveys found that parents provide more instruction and supervision of younger children, but for children aged 13 to 17 parents allow increasing independence. This corresponds with the age when youth, particularly boys, are more likely to engage in risky Internet use (MNet, 2001b, 2005).

Some of the primary risks include the following:

- Sharing personal information—one in five youth said that they would provide both their name and address over the Internet in order to win a prize

- Exploring private and adult-only chat rooms—58% of 11- to 12-year-olds and 70% of 13- to 14-year-olds went into restricted chat rooms

- Meeting Internet acquaintances in person—21% of students in Grades 7 to 11 met someone in person with whom they had first met on the Internet

- Being bullied—of those students in Grades 7 to 11 who reported being bullied, 27% say that it occurred over the Internet

- Being sexually harassed—of those students in Grades 7 to 11 who reported being sexually harassed, 70% say that it occurred over the Internet

As for many high-risk behaviours to which young people are vulnerable, parents should be concerned about equipping their children with the knowledge and skills necessary to prevent harm while at the same time not stifling the creative and beneficial use of electronic media. These are the tools of communication for this generation, and they will likely increase in importance in the future. In fact, youth accept that exposure to violent and sexual content is unavoidable, and at the same time, they have learned to fend off offensive material. Accordingly, teens argue that it is a waste of time and resources trying to keep unsuitable material away from children. Rather, they suggest, children need to develop the critical-thinking skills that will prepare them to make informed choices and decisions about what material to censor (MNet, 2004b).

2007; Urberg, Degirmencioglu, & Tolson, 1998). If the discrepancy between their own ideas and those of their friends becomes too great, teens are more likely to switch to a more compatible group of friends than to be persuaded to adopt the first group's values or behaviours (Verkooijen, de Vries, & Nielsen, 2007). Furthermore, teenagers report that when explicit peer pressure is exerted, it is likely to be pressure toward positive activities, such as school involvement, and away from misconduct.

Only in so-called druggie-tough crowds does there seem to be explicit pressure toward misconduct or lawbreaking, and teens who appear to respond to such pressure may be motivated as much by a desire to prove "I'm as tough as you are" as by explicit pressure from peers (Berndt & Keefe, 1995b; Brown, Dolcini, & Leventhal, 1995). Thus, while Erikson appears to have been quite correct in saying that peers are a major force in shaping a child's identity development in adolescence, peer influence is neither all-powerful, nor uniformly negative.

CHANGES IN PEER GROUP STRUCTURE The structure of the peer group also changes over the years of adolescence. The classic, widely quoted early study is that of Dunphy (1963) on the formation, dissolution, and interaction of teenaged groups in a high school in Sydney, Australia, between 1958 and 1960. Dunphy identified two important subvarieties of groups. The first type, which he called a **clique**, is made up of four to six young people who appear to be strongly attached to one another. Cliques have strong cohesiveness and high levels of intimate sharing.

In the early years of adolescence, cliques are almost entirely same-sex groups—a holdover from the preadolescent pattern. Gradually, however, the cliques combine into larger sets that Dunphy called **crowds**, which include both males and females. Finally, the crowd breaks down again into heterosexual cliques and then into loose associations of couples. In Dunphy's study, the period during which adolescents socialized in

clique
four to six young people who appear to be strongly attached to one another

crowd
a combination of cliques, which includes both males and females

Critical Thinking

Think back to your own high school years and draw a diagram or map to describe the organization of crowds and cliques. Were those crowds or cliques more or less important in the last few years of high school than they had been earlier?

crowds was roughly between ages 13 and 15—the very years when they display the greatest conformity to peer pressure.

Contemporary researchers on adolescence have changed Dunphy's labels somewhat (Brown, 1990; Brown, Mory, & Kinney, 1994). They use the word *crowd* to refer to the *reputation-based group* with which a young person is identified, either by choice or by peer designation. In Canadian schools, these groups have labels such as "all stars," "jocks," "nerds," "skaters," "thugs," "goths," "stoners," "normals," "techies," "preppies," and "loners." Studies in junior high and high schools make it clear that teenagers can readily identify each of the major crowds in their school and have quite stereotypical descriptions of them (e.g., "The partiers goof off a lot more than the jocks do, but they don't come to school stoned like the burnouts do") (Brown et al., 1994, p. 133). Each of these descriptions serves as what Brown calls an *identity prototype*: Labelling others and oneself as belonging to one or more of these groups helps to create or reinforce the adolescent's own identity (Brown et al., 1994). Such labelling also helps the adolescent identify potential friends or foes.

Within any given school, the various crowds are organized into a fairly clear, widely understood pecking order. In North American schools, the groups labelled as some variant of "populars," "jocks," or "normals" are typically at the top of the heap, with "brains" somewhere in the middle and "druggies," "loners," and "nerds" at the bottom (Brown et al., 1994).

Throughout the years of junior high and high school, the social system of crowds becomes increasingly differentiated, with more and more distinct groups (Kinney, 1993). Within (and sometimes between) these crowds, Kinney found, adolescents created smaller cliques. As Dunphy observed, social groups were almost entirely same-sex in early adolescence but, by late adolescence, they had become mixed in gender, often composed of groups of dating couples. Mutual friendships and dating pairs become more central to social interactions in later adolescence than are cliques or crowds (Urberg, Degirmencioglu, Tolson, & Halliday-Scher, 1995).

ROMANTIC RELATIONSHIPS

Heterosexual and homosexual teens follow somewhat different pathways. For both, the ups and downs that are associated with early romances are an important theme of development during adolescence.

HETEROSEXUAL TEENS Most teens display a gradual progression from same-sex friendships to heterosexual relationships. The change happens gradually, but it seems to proceed at a somewhat more rapid pace in girls than in boys. At the beginning of adolescence, teens are still fairly rigid about their preferences for same-sex friends (Bukowski, Sippola, & Hoza, 1999). Over the next year or two, they become more open to opposite-sex friendships (Harton & Latane, 1997; Kuttler, LaGreca, & Prinstein, 1999). The skills they gain in relating to opposite-sex peers in such friendships and in mixed-gender groups prepare them for romantic relationships (Feiring, 1999). Thus, although adults often assume that sexual desires are the basis of emergent romantic relationships, it appears that social factors are just as important. In fact, research suggests that social competence in a variety of relationships—with parents, peers, and friends—predicts the ease with which teens move from exclusive same-sex relationships to opposite-sex friendships and romantic relationships (Theriault, 1998).

By age 12 or 13, most adolescents have a basic conception of what it means to be "in love," and the sense of being in love is an important factor in adolescent dating patterns (Montgomery & Sorel, 1998). In other words, teenagers prefer to date those with whom they believe they are in love, and they view falling out of love as a reason for ending a dating relationship. In addition, for girls (but not for boys), romantic relationships are seen as a context for self-disclosure. Put another way, girls seem to want more psychological intimacy from these early relationships than their partners do (Feiring, 1999).

Early dating and early sexual activity are more common among the poor of every ethnic group and among those who experience relatively early puberty. Religious teachings and individual attitudes about the appropriate age for dating and sexual behaviour also make a difference, as does family structure. Girls with parents who are divorced or remarried, for example, report earlier dating and higher levels of sexual experience than do girls from intact families, and those with a strong religious identity report later dating and lower levels of sexuality (Bingham, Miller, & Adams, 1990; Miller & Moore, 1990). But for every group, these are years of experimentation with romantic relationships.

HOMOSEXUAL TEENS Romantic relationships emerge somewhat differently in the lives of homosexual teens. Researchers have found that homosexual teenagers are more comfortable about revealing their sexual orientation to their parents and to their peers than was true in past cohorts (Floyd & Bakeman, 2006). Consequently, developmentalists have learned a great deal more about the development of a homosexual orientation in the past couple of decades.

One thing that researchers have learned is that homosexual teenagers become aware of same-sex attraction at around age 11 or 12, roughly the same age when their heterosexual peers begin to notice their attraction to the opposite sex (Rosario, Scrimshaw, & Hunter, 2004). In contrast to heterosexual teens, boys notice and act on same-sex attraction at somewhat earlier ages than girls do (Grov, Bimbi, Nanin, & Parsons, 2006). However, girls who ultimately commit to a homosexual orientation express more certainty about their sexual identity than boys do (Rosario, Scrimshaw, Hunter, & Braun, 2006).

Many boys and girls, however, experience some degree of attraction to both sexes prior to self-identifying as gay or lesbian. Thus, many homosexual teens go through a period of sexual discovery that begins with experimentation with heterosexual relationships. Shortly thereafter, these teenagers begin to experiment with same-sex relationships. By age 15 or so, most have classified themselves as primarily heterosexual or committed to a gay, lesbian, or bisexual orientation (Rosario et al., 2004). Many of those who are gay, lesbian, or bisexual participate in clubs and extracurricular activities that are designed to help sexual minority youth form social connections. In the company of these like-minded peers, gay, lesbian, and bisexual teens meet potential romantic partners and find important sources of social support (Rosario et al., 2004).

Before Going On

- Describe adolescents' family relationships in terms of conflict, attachment, parenting styles, and family structure.
- What are the characteristics of adolescents' friendships, peer groups, and romantic relationships?

Summary

Theories of Social and Personality Development

- For Freud, sexual maturity is reached in adolescents in the genital stage. For Erikson, adolescence is a period when a person faces a crisis of identity versus role confusion, out of which the teenager must develop a sense of who he is and where he belongs in his culture.

- Building on Erikson's notion of an adolescent identity crisis, Marcia identified four identity statuses.

Self-Concept and Personality

- Self-definitions become increasingly abstract at adolescence, with more emphasis on enduring, internal qualities and ideology.

- Teenagers also increasingly define themselves in terms that include gender-related traits. When both masculinity and femininity are present, the individual is described as androgynous.

- Self-esteem drops somewhat at the beginning of adolescence and then rises steadily throughout the teenaged years.

- Young people in clearly identifiable minority groups have the additional task in adolescence of forming an ethnic identity.

- Teens who are pessimistic and blame their problems on forces outside themselves encounter more difficulties than peers who have a more positive outlook.

Moral Development

- Kohlberg proposed six stages of moral reasoning, organized into three levels: preconventional, conventional and postconventional morality. These levels and stages are loosely correlated with age, develop in a specified order, and appear in this same sequence in all cultures studied so far.

- The acquisition of cognitive role-taking skills and the social environment are both important to moral development. To foster moral reasoning, adults must provide children with opportunities for discussion of moral issues.

- Other theorists say moral reasoning is based on learning moral behaviour and on emotional factors.

- Youth who commit criminal offences are usually found to be far behind their peers in both role-taking and moral reasoning. Other factors, such as parenting style, may be equally important in criminality.

Social Relationships

- Adolescent–parent interactions typically become somewhat more conflicted in early adolescence.

- Strong attachments to parents remain so and are predictive of good peer relations. Authoritative parenting continues to be the optimal style to use with adolescents.

- Susceptibility to peer-group pressure appears to be at its peak at about age 13 or 14. Reputation-based groups, or crowds, as well as smaller groups, called *cliques*, are important parts of adolescent social relationships.

- Heterosexual teens gradually move from same-sex peer groups to heterosexual couples. The feeling of being "in love" is important to the formation of couple relationships. Many homosexual teens experiment with heterosexual and homosexual relationships before committing to a gay, lesbian, or bisexual orientation in mid-adolescence.

Review Questions

Answers are provided on MyDevelopmentLab in the Course Resources folder.

Theories of Social and Personality Development

12.1 According to Marcia, a *moratorium identity status* is characterized by a person who
    a. has been through a crisis and has become committed to adult goals.
    b. is not in a crisis and who is committed to a childhood identity.
    c. is not in a crisis and who has not made any commitments.
    d. is in a crisis but who has made no commitment.

Self-Concept and Personality

12.2 Which of the following is an accurate statement about self-esteem during adolescence?
    a. Across the teenaged years, girls consistently have higher self-esteem than boys.
    b. Most teens have high self-esteem at the beginning of adolescence but experience a steady decline in self-esteem during the teenaged years.
    c. Self-esteem is typically lower for girls than it is for boys during the mid-teenaged years.
    d. Cross-cultural research shows that in all societies, girls who adopt masculine or androgynous characteristics are more popular and have higher self-esteem.

Moral Development

12.3 According to Kohlberg's theory of moral reasoning, a teen who is in *Stage 4—social system and conscience* of moral reasoning would most likely agree with which of the following statements?
    a. I do the dishes at home because it pleases my mom.
    b. Stealing is wrong because it is against the law.
    c. Might is right.
    d. If it feels good, just do it!

Social Relationships

12.4 Among adolescents, membership in a/an _____ means identification with a *reputation-based group* of peers that carry labels such as "jocks," "geeks," or "skaters."
    a. clique
    b. crowd
    c. prototypical identity
    d. achievement identity

12.5 Jeri is a 12-year-old girl who is sexually attracted to both males and females. Which of the following statements best corresponds to what research would predict about the development of romantic relationships in Jeri's life?
    a. Her romantic relationships will be influenced by the fact that attraction to others of the same sex and self-identification as a homosexual occur simultaneously.
    b. Jeri will probably experiment with both heterosexual and homosexual relationships before committing to a sexual orientation.
    c. She is more likely to hide her attraction to same-sex peers than teenagers in earlier cohorts did.
    d. Jerry will avoid associating with gay and lesbian teens, because they might try to persuade her to commit to a homosexual orientation.

Critical-Thinking Questions

12.6 What are examples of traditional masculine and feminine personality traits? Differentiate between gender-role concepts and a person's sexual orientation or sexuality.

12.7 What are the characteristics of the authoritative parenting style that makes it associated with positive outcomes in adolescents?

Policy Question

What Can Be Done About Gambling Among Canadian Youth?

Today's youth are the first generation of Canadians to live within a culture that views gambling as an everyday and acceptable form of entertainment. Canadian researchers have discovered some startling facts about gambling among Canadian youth and why it is a problem. One factor is that gambling often begins at an earlier age than other high-risk behaviours such as alcohol or drug use. University of Windsor researchers Govoni, Rupcich, and Frisch (1996) found that gambling behaviour can be established by age 14. In addition, McGill University researchers Gupta and Derevensky (1998, 2000) found that "pathological gamblers" started serious gambling by age 10. Although most adult problem gamblers reported that their problem with gambling began in their youth, it is not clear whether adolescent gambling leads to adult gambling problems or whether gambling is related to an underlying propensity for thrill-seeking, risk-taking behaviour that persists into adulthood. The latter contention is supported by research that found adolescent problem gamblers to be more excitable, greater risk-takers, more extraverted, anxious, nonconforming, and lower in self-discipline and self-esteem than non–problem gambling youth (Derevensky & Gupta, 1998; Gupta & Derevensky, 2000). There is also some evidence that a pattern of behaviour showing high impulsivity (such as inattentiveness, distractibility, and hyperactivity) beginning in kindergarten is a significant predictor of self-reported gambling behaviour in students by Grade 6 (Pagani, Derevensky & Japel, 2009).

Gambling and wagering are popular and on the rise among children and adolescents alike (Shaffer & Hall, 1996). The vast majority of adolescents surveyed by researchers from Laval University (Ladouceur, Boudreault, Jacques, & Vitaro, 1999) and Brock University (Lawrence, Yardley, Root, Canham, & McPhee, 2002) acknowledged that they have participated in gaming activities. For instance, studies show that roughly three-quarters or more of teenagers report that they have wagered money in the previous year and anywhere between 9 and 35% did so at least once a week (Derevensky & Gupta, 1998; Gupta & Derevensky, 1998; Lawrence et al., 2002). Of these youths, 55% are considered casual gamblers, 13% have some gambling problems, and 4 to 6% have serious problems with gambling.

Gambling, like many high-risk behaviours, is more prevalent in males than females, and boys are two to four times as likely as girls to have a serious gambling problem (Gupta & Derevensky, 2000; Ladouceur et al., 1999; Lawrence et al., 2002). Adolescents display a higher incidence of gambling problems than adults, and youth are two to four times more likely than adults to have a serious gambling problem (Derevensky, Gupta, & Winters, 2003; Gupta & Derevensky, 2000; Noonan, Turner, & Macdonald, 1999).

Older adolescents and adults prefer to wager money, and a significant number of underage youth engage in age-restricted gambling activities such as lotteries (72%), instant-win tickets (70%), pull-tabs (35%), and PRO-LINE (28%) (Lawrence et al., 2002). In comparison, children wager valued possessions, for example, Pogs (a picture-disk collector's game), marbles, and collector cards (Ladouceur, Dubé, & Bujold, 1995). Some youth activities such as Pogs and marbles may act as a bridge to gambling when played for "keepsies." This gambling could be an ideal opportunity for parental intervention but, like many forms of gambling that are not seen as harmful, these activities are not usually checked by adult caregivers (Noonan et al., 1999). Consequently, children are not informed about the inherent dangers of gambling as they are with smoking, drugs, and alcohol use (Derevensky & Gupta, 1998). On the contrary, children and adolescents often gamble with their parents or other family members, for example, they go together to buy and play lottery tickets, play cards, or play bingo (Gupta & Derevensky, 1997).

Adolescents with gambling problems are twice as likely to have parents who gamble excessively as adolescents whose parents do not gamble excessively (Govoni et al., 1996). Bandura's social learning theory (1977a, 1989) can explain some of the effects that social role models have on gambling behaviour in youth. When children are exposed to family members, peers,

(*Photo:* Paul A. Souders/CORBIS/MAGMA)

neighbours, or celebrities who relish gambling, youth may acquire favourable expectations about gambling (Gupta & Derevensky. 1997). Well-intentioned social groups such as schools and religious groups may inadvertently endorse gambling by sponsoring fundraising events such as bingo or casino nights that are supported by parents and the community (Derevensky & Gupta, 2004).

Cognitively, children and young adolescents are at a disadvantage because they lack an appreciation of what the odds of winning are and have an overly optimistic view of the probability of winning (Turner, Toneatto, & Stanovich, 1999). Moreover, for most teens and adults (including parents and community leaders) gambling is perceived as a relatively benign activity. Even teens who are in treatment for gambling do not see themselves as having a gambling problem (Gupta & Derevensky, 1999, as reported in Derevensky & Gupta, 2000).

Like other addictive behaviours, gambling offers a way to temporarily escape problems, boredom, and stress. At the same time, these benefits are mixed with the excitement of winning. In fact, most adolescents do not gamble primarily for money but for the excitement and sensations of dissociation and escape (Derevensky & Gupta, 1998; Gupta & Derevensky, 1998b). Young problem gamblers have been found to dissociate more frequently when gambling compared with peers who do not have a gambling problem (Gupta & Derevensky, 2000). It has also been shown that when young problem gamblers are away from the gambling situation (a Video Lottery Terminal [VLT], for instance), they can experience withdrawal-like symptoms that make them more likely to want to play again in order to escape these undesirable sensations (Noonan et al., 1999). Not surprisingly, adolescents with serious gambling problems have an increased risk for the development of multiple addictions. They also have

higher rates of depression, which puts them at a heightened risk for suicidal thoughts and suicide attempts. Furthermore, within a social context, adolescents with gambling problems report having a support group, but old friends are often replaced by gambling associates (Gupta & Derevensky, 2000).

Derevensky and Gupta (1998, 2004, 2004) have reported that youth gambling treatment program research remains wanting. Although research into gambling prevention programs is in the formative stages of development, some practical measures can help to inoculate children against the risk of developing a gambling dependence. Parents and caregivers need to first become aware of the seriousness of the problem and then advise and instruct their children accordingly, just as they would with the dangers of other risk-taking behaviours such as smoking and alcohol use or unsafe sexual activity. In terms of social learning theory, "actions speak louder than words." Therefore, if parents believe that they are important role models against gambling, they need to act in ways that are consistent with what they say. Another preventive measure is teaching children about the nature of random events and statistical probability at a level that they can understand. Other cognitive preventive measures include giving a child facts that counter unrealistic expectations and changing inappropriate ideas a child may have concerning the roles of skill, luck, and the illusion of control in gambling activities. It should also be emphasized that gambling is not a method of making money; rather it is another way of spending money. The aim of discussion should be to help modify and change the attitude that gambling is a harmless behaviour.

The school system can provide another important venue for implementing prevention activities that increase knowledge about youth gambling problems.

Indeed, recent studies show that instructional videos can increase the level of accurate knowledge and reduce misconceived attitudes about gambling in students from Grades 6 to 8 (Ferland, Ladouceur, & Vitaro, 2002; Lavoie & Ladouceur, 2004). There is also a need to develop a protocol for the identification, assessment, and referral of students who are at risk of developing a serious gambling problem. Students need to be introduced to both alternative and effective ways of coping with problems and need to improve the skills that would prevent the development of problematic gambling. It would be appropriate for these school-based programs to be integrated into both the elementary and secondary school levels.

YOUR TURN

- Explain whether there is a relationship between the proliferation of gambling opportunities for adults, such as casinos and lottery ticket sales, and adolescent gambling.

- Describe the ways that problem gambling can be harmful to more than just the gambler.

- Explain why youth are more vulnerable to problem gambling than adults.

- Explain how gambling on a computer (no stakes) could help inoculate children against false beliefs they may have about the odds of winning.

- Some young problem gamblers are driven by the excitement and sensations of dissociation they experience when they gamble. What kinds of intervention would help them overcome their dependence on gambling?

- Where do youth get the money to gamble?

JupiterImages/Thinkstock

You probably know someone like one of the people in the following list. What do all of them have in common?

Devon, a 20-year-old second-year university student who is trying to choose between psychology and social work as his major

Cassie, a 22-year-old single mother of a 4-year-old who lives with her parents, works full-time, and attends community college classes part-time

Joe, a 25-year-old married computer programmer who attended a community college after 4 years of working in a computer store

Marta, a 30-year-old remarried mother of a preschooler who works as a registered nurse

Renée, a married 33-year-old mother of two school-aged children who has just started university

Marshall, a 35-year-old single man who has been a public school teacher for 12 years

Each member of this diverse group is a young adult. If you think about the people you know who are between ages 20 and 40, they probably make up just as varied a group.

Clearly, young adulthood is the period of life when individuals' developmental pathways begin to diverge significantly. For example, in contrast to younger individuals, the educational experiences of young adults are highly diverse. Some go on to college or university as soon as they graduate from high school. Others work and attend school part-time. Still others work for a while and then further their education.

Despite these variations, most social science researchers believe that it is still useful to divide the adult years into three roughly equal parts: early adulthood, from 20 to 40; middle adulthood, from 40 to about 65; and late adulthood, from 65 until death. This way of dividing adulthood reflects the fact that optimum physical and cognitive functioning, achieved in the 20s and 30s, begins to wane in some noticeable and measurable ways in the 40s and 50s. Moreover, several important role changes often occur when adults are in their 40s. Children begin to leave home, careers near their peak, and so on.

We will follow the common usage and define "young" or "early" adulthood as the period from age 20 to age 40. When you finish studying the chapter, you will be able to describe how physical functioning changes in the years from 20 to 40; identify the major health issues during early adulthood; summarize how thinking and problem-solving improve in early adulthood; and discuss how post-secondary education helps shape young adults' development. As you read this chapter, keep the following questions in mind:

Critical Thinking

Before you read the rest of the chapter, think about how you might answer the following question for yourself: In what ways have your body and mind changed since you were younger? How do you expect them to change as you get older? How has attending post-secondary school affected your life, and what difference will it make in your future?

- What are some examples of cultural and economic factors that might affect your health?

- What are the major health issues during early adulthood, and how could you change them to slow or even reverse the effects of aging?

- In what ways does post-secondary education help shape your development?

PHYSICAL FUNCTIONING

When developmentalists study children's development, they look at increases or improvements. When developmentalists study adults, especially adults' physical functioning, they ask questions about loss of function, or decline.

PRIMARY AND SECONDARY AGING

Researchers distinguish between two types of aging. The basic, underlying, inevitable aging process is called **primary aging**, sometimes called **senescence**, by most developmentalists. Gray hair, wrinkles, and changes in visual acuity, for example, are attributable to primary aging.

primary aging (senescence)
age-related physical changes that have a biological basis and are universally shared and inevitable

secondary aging
age-related changes that are due to social and environmental influences, poor health habits, or disease

Secondary aging, in contrast, is the product of social and environmental influences, health habits, or disease and is neither inevitable nor experienced by all adults. Research on age differences in health and death rates reveals the expected pattern. For example, a minority of 20- to 34-year-olds die from disease; the majority of deaths are caused by unintentional injuries or suicide (PHAC, 2008d). In addition, researchers have found that socioeconomic status (SES) factors are implicated in health and well-being, a pattern suggesting the influence of secondary aging.

The relationship between an individual's income and measures of health, illness, and longevity is well established in nations worldwide (Hertzman, 1999) especially for young adults (Dorling, Mitchell & Pearce, 2007). Most developmentalists believe that the income-status differences in health, where the rich are generally healthier and live longer than the poor, are caused by secondary aging. (i.e., cultural and economic factors such as diet, stress levels, and access to health care that are associated with social class as well as with disease) (Hertzman & Frank, 2006).

Disability-Adjusted Life Years (DALY)
a measure of the gap between a population's ideal and actual levels of health. It is derived from the number of life-years lost to premature death, illness, or injury and the number of years living with a disability. It assumes a potential life limit of 82½ years for women and 80 for men.

A closer look at the differences in levels of health among developed nations reveals that it is not just a simple case that the wealthy members of a population are healthier than those who are less well off. Rather, as described in the **Research Report** on page 372, the degree of socioeconomic inequality of a country is related to the overall health of its citizens (Kawachi & Kennedy, 2002; United Nations Development Programme [UNDP], 2009). Prosperous nations with high levels of social inequality, most notably the United States, experience poorer overall health than less wealthy but more egalitarian societies, such as Costa Rica. By comparison, Canada distributes its social and economic resources fairly equitably among its citizens (e.g., public funding of and relatively universal access to health care and education) and as a consequence Canadians enjoy relatively good health (Ross et al., 2000; UNDP, 2009).

Health-Adjusted Life Expectancy (HALE)
an estimate of life expectancy at birth. It is the number of years that a newborn can expect to live in full health given current rates of morbidity and mortality.

The study of the factors associated with secondary aging can be viewed in relation to an individual, which we look at later in this chapter, and with respect to a population, an approach that looks at the health indicators that influence populations as a whole. Common indicators of the *population health approach* include mortality statistics and rates of hospitalization, although measures of morbidity are also important because morbidity measures tap into "a key health policy challenge facing Western industrialized nations: that some health interventions may be adding years of sickness to life, rather than years of health" (Chomik, 2001, p. 9). From this perspective it becomes important to measure the health status of populations by looking at *aggregate health indicators* that measure quality of life, such as **Disability-Adjusted Life Years (DALY)**, **Health-Adjusted Life Expectancy (HALE)**, and **Quality-Adjusted Life Years (QALY)**. For example, a recent Canadian study has shown that there are considerable HALE disparities among socio-economic groups (McIntosh, Finès, Wilkins, & Wolfson,

Quality-Adjusted Life Years (QALY)
a measure of how much benefit is gained, and at what cost, for any particular physical or mental intervention. It provides an estimate of the time a person will live at different levels of health over his or her remaining years of life.

2009). At age 25, the average difference in HALE between the highest and lowest income group was 11.4 years for men and 9.7 years for women and, for both sexes, life expectancy tended to rise in step with income (see **Figure 13.1**).

THE BRAIN AND NERVOUS SYSTEM

No matter what age an individual is, new synapses are forming, myelinization is occurring, and old connections are dying off. Further, there is now evidence that, contrary to what neurologists have believed for a long time, some parts of the brain produce new neurons to replace those that die, even in the brains of older adults (Gould, Reeves, Graziano, & Gross, 1999). Interestingly, too, animal research suggests that production of these new neurons is stimulated by an enriched environment, as well as by physical exercise (Cao et al., 2004; Rhodes et al., 2003). Thus, just as is true in childhood and adolescence, a challenging environment probably supports brain development. At some point in development, though, usually in the late teens, developmental processes reach a balance and the brain attains a stable size and weight. Similarly, by early adulthood, most functions have become localized in specific areas of the brain (Gaillard et al., 2000).

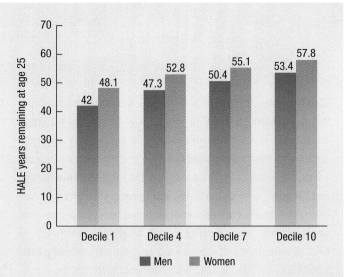

Figure 13.1

Remaining health-adjusted life expectancy (years) at age 25, by income decile and sex, Canada, 1991–2001.

(*Source:* Adapted from Table 4 in "Income disparities in health-adjusted life expectancy for Canadian adults, 1991 to 2001' by McIntosh, Finès, Wilkins, & Wolfson, 2009.)

Neurologists have found that the pattern of peaks and valleys in the development of brain functions that begins during the fetal period continues into adulthood (see the **Research Report** on page 373). In fact, neuroscientists have now found evidence, based on MRI studies, that the human brain continues to mature throughout early adulthood (Giedd et al., 1999; Gogtay et al., 2004; Sowell, Thompson, Holmes, Jernigan, & Toga, 1999; Sowell, Thompson, Tessner, & Toga, 2001). As you may remember from **Chapter 11**, a second major growth spurt of the grey matter of frontal lobes—the area of the brain devoted to logic, planning, and emotional control—begins during preadolescence. The overproduction of neural tissue is followed by a maturing of the frontal lobes that is characterized by the synaptic pruning and myelination that continues through to young adulthood. Many neuropsychologists believe that this pattern of neural development is strongly connected to the increases in the capacity for formal operational thinking and other kinds of abstract reasoning that occur in late adolescence.

Response inhibition is another cognitive skill that emerges in early adulthood that seems to be linked to changes in the brain. For example, when you take a multiple-choice test, you need to be able to keep yourself from responding too quickly to the options in order to carefully weigh all of them. Response inhibition also helps you "bite-your-tongue" to keep from putting your "foot in your mouth" as often as you did at a younger age. Neuropsychologists suggest that response inhibition may depend on the ability of the frontal lobes of the brain to regulate the **limbic system**, or the emotional part of the brain. Many scientists believe that the capacity to integrate various brain functions in this way does not become fully developed until early adulthood (Spreen, Risser, & Edgell, 1995).

mydevelopmentlab

Connect to
MyDevelopmentLab

Why does your brain need exercise? Watch the video and find out.

Watch

Critical Thinking

If teenagers lack the neurological capacity to fully control their emotions, then should they be held to the same level of culpability as adults for committing impulsive criminal acts, such as knifing someone during a brawl?

limbic system

the part of the brain that regulates emotional responses

Research Report

THE DISTRIBUTION OF WEALTH AND HEALTH

Canadian researchers have published the first valid comparison of income to health and mortality rates between Canada and the United States (Ross et al., 2000). The results were surprising. In the United States, as in other industrialized nations, a relationship exists between health and degree of income distribution (the spread between the rich and the poor). In those U.S. states and urban centres where income inequality was the greatest, health outcomes were the poorest, and where relative income equality existed, health outcomes were the best. By contrast, most Canadian cities and provinces showed greater income equality, along with the associated good health and lower mortality rates, than their U.S. counterparts (see **Figure 13.2**).

University of British Columbia health researcher Clyde Hertzman reports that, regardless of the average income level, Americans who live in states that have greater income equality also have longer life expectancy. According to Hertzman, this pattern of income equality and greater longevity holds true in communities in developed nations worldwide. Even more notable is the finding that in jurisdictions where income disparity is greatest (e.g., the United Kingdom), the health status of the wealthy is lower than it is for the wealthy in communities and nations where income distribution is more equitable (e.g., Sweden) (Hertzman, 1999).

In another first-of-its-kind study, the Joint Canada/United States Survey of Health, 2002–03, comparable precise data from both Canada and the United States was analyzed. Although the study found many similarities between our two countries, it also found some significant differences in our health statuses (Sanmartin & Ng, 2004). The greatest disparity in health is related to differences in income: Americans in the lowest income bracket experience significantly lower levels of health, higher obesity, and more severe mobility impairment than their Canadian counterparts.

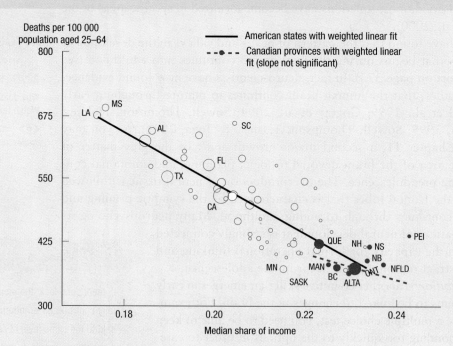

Figure 13.2

Mortality rates of the population aged 25 to 64 in Canadian provinces and American states, by percentage of total household income in province or state received by households with income below the median, 1991 (Canada) and 1990 (United States).

(*Sources:* Health Reports, 1999a, Chart 1, p. 80, 1991 Census of Canada; Canadian Vital Statistics Data Base; Centers for Disease Control, standardized to 1991 Canadian population.)

Research Report

THE BRAIN MATURES INTO ADULTHOOD

The brain contains two types of tissue: grey matter and white matter. Grey matter is made up of neuron cell bodies and axon and dendrite terminals that "connect" neurons to one another (look back at **Figure 3.1** on page 67); white matter is the myelinated axons. Normal brain development seems to follow a cyclical pattern of development. It starts with the rapid proliferation of grey matter and is followed by the simultaneous processes of synaptic pruning, and myelination. Synaptic pruning is a process that results in a decline in grey matter density as unused synapses—neural circuits—are discarded. Any unused neural cells and synaptic connections wither away while those that are used become stronger and more efficient with the help of myelination. During myelination, white matter density increases as a cholesterol-rich fatty substance coats the axons to improve neural transmission. A

period of relative stability follows once this stage of brain maturation is reached, usually around age 30 (Sowell et al., 2003).

Maturation of the brain does not happen all at once—the human brain matures in uneven patterns whereby specific regions of the brain develop at different times and rates than others (Gogtay et al., 2004). For example, the first stage of grey matter proliferation occurs during the first 18 months of life in the parts of the brain that control basic somatosensory functions. The next major cycle of brain development begins just prior to puberty, when there is a surge in grey matter production in areas of the brain associated with higher mental processes, namely the frontal lobes (Giedd et al., 1999; Gogtay et al., 2004). In both instances, the surge in grey matter production is followed by synaptic pruning and myelination. The time-lapse MRI scans in **Figure 13.3** illustrate a part of this

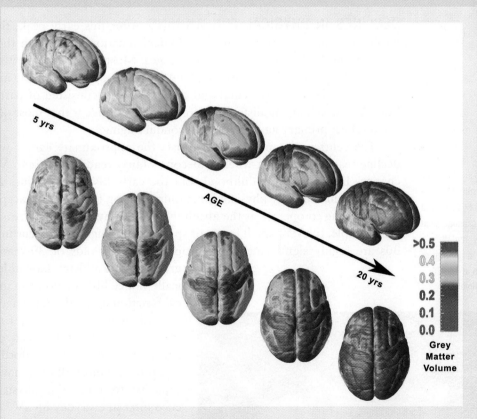

Figure 13.3

Selected slides from MRI scans that tracked brain maturation from ages 5 to 20 (a time-lapse movie can be viewed at **www.loni.ucla.edu/~thompson/DEVEL/dynamic.html**). Grey matter (red) diminishes as the brain matures because of synaptic pruning and myelination (blue). Notice that the region at the front of the brain (the prefrontal cortex that is associated with higher mental functioning) matures last.

(*Source:* Gogtay et al., 2004, Figure 3, p. 8178. Copyright 2004 National Academy of Sciences, U.S.A.)

process—you can see that over time, grey matter recedes at the same time that white matter advances across the surface of the brain (Sowell et al., 2001).

The human brain seems to mature in the primitive areas first and in the newer parts of the brain last (Gogtay et al., 2004). One exception to this pattern is the development of the areas of the brain that are associated with language and vocabulary. Although grey matter formation develops early in life in these brain regions, growth continues until a person reaches middle adulthood. This fits the research that shows that language skills improve continuously through to middle age (Sowell et al., 2003).

A final cycle of brain development is associated with the overall natural degenerative process that occurs in later adulthood (Sowell et al., 2003). This phase is characterized by a decline in grey matter density coupled with an end to white matter growth, resulting in an overall decline in brain volume. In this last stage of development, brain function begins to slow and becomes gradually less efficient, as you'll read later in **Chapters 15** and **17**.

OTHER BODY SYSTEMS

Young adults perform better than do the middle-aged or old on virtually every physical measure. Compared with older adults, adults in their 20s and 30s have more muscle tissue, maximum bone calcium, more brain mass, better eyesight, hearing, and sense of smell, greater oxygen capacity, and a more efficient immune system. The young adult is stronger, faster, and better able to recover from exercise or to adapt to changing conditions, such as alterations in temperature or light levels.

DECLINES IN PHYSICAL FUNCTIONING After this early peak, there is a gradual decline in almost every measure of physical functioning through the years of adulthood. **Table 13.1** summarizes these changes. Most of the summary statements in the table are based on both longitudinal and cross-sectional data; many are based on studies in which both experimental and control groups consisted of participants in good health. So developmentalists can be reasonably confident that most of the age changes listed reflect primary aging and not secondary aging.

The centre column of the table lists the approximate age at which the loss or decline reaches the point where it becomes fairly readily apparent. Virtually all these changes begin in early adulthood. But the early losses or declines are not typically noticeable in everyday physical functioning during these years, except when a person is attempting to operate at the absolute edge of physical ability. Among top athletes, for example, the very small losses of speed and strength that occur in the late 20s and 30s are highly significant, often dropping 25-year-olds or 30-year-olds out of the group of elite athletes. Nonathletes, though, typically notice little or no drop in everyday physical functioning until middle age.

Another way to think of this change is in terms of a balance between physical demand and physical capacity (Welford, 1993). In early adulthood, almost all of us have ample physical capacity to meet the physical demands we encounter in everyday life. We can read the fine print without bifocals, we can carry heavy boxes or furniture when we move, our immune systems are strong enough to fight off most illnesses, and we recover quickly from sickness. As we move into middle adulthood, the balance sheet changes. We find more and more areas in which our physical capacities no longer quite meet the demands.

It's hard to draw a clear line between "early adulthood" and "middle adulthood" because the physical and mental changes are so gradual; even at age 30, adults may find that it takes a bit more work to get into or stay in shape than it did at age 20. (*Photo:* Mark Richards/PhotoEdit)

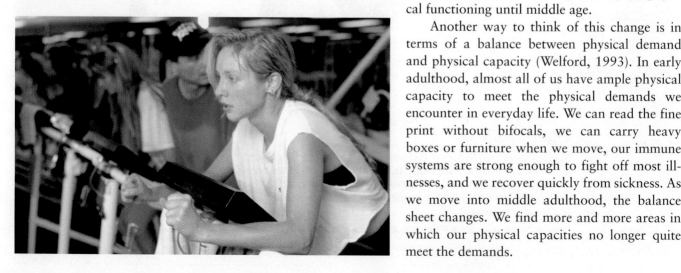

TABLE 13.1 A Summary of Age Changes in Physical Functioning

Body Function	Age at Which Change Begins to Be Clear or Measurable	Nature of Change
Vision	Mid-40s	Lens of eye thickens and loses accommodative power, resulting in poorer near vision and more sensitivity to glare
Hearing	50 or 60	Loss of ability to hear very high and very low tones
Smell	About 40	Decline in ability to detect and discriminate among different smells
Taste	None	No apparent loss in taste discrimination ability
Muscles	About 50	Loss of muscle tissue, particularly in "fast twitch" fibres used for bursts of strength or speed
Bones	Mid-30s (women)	Loss of calcium in the bones, called *osteoporosis*; also wear and tear on bone in joints, called *osteoarthritis*, more marked after about 60
Heart and lungs	35 or 40	Most functions (such as aerobic capacity or cardiac output) do not show age changes at rest but do show age changes during work or exercise
Nervous system	Probably gradual throughout adulthood	Some loss (but not clear how much) of neurons in the brain; gradual reduction in density of dendrites; gradual decline in total brain volume and weight
Immune system	Adolescence	Loss in size of thymus; reduction in number and maturity of T cells; not clear how much of this change is due to stress and how much is primary aging
Reproductive system	Mid-30s (women)	Increased reproductive risk and lowered fertility
	Early 40s (men)	Gradual decline in viable sperm beginning at about age 40; very gradual decline in testosterone from early adulthood
Cellular elasticity	Gradual	Gradual loss of elasticity in most cells, including skin, muscle, tendon, and blood vessel cells; faster deterioration in cells exposed to sunlight
Height	40	Compression of disks in the spine, with resulting loss of height of 2.5 to 5.0cm by age 80
Weight	Nonlinear	In American studies, weight reaches a maximum in middle adulthood and then gradually declines in old age
Skin	40	Increase in wrinkles, as a result of loss of elasticity; oil-secreting glands become less efficient
Hair	About 50	Becomes thinner and may grey

(*Source:* Bartoshuk & Weiffenbach, 1990; Blatter et al., 1995; Braveman, 1987; Briggs, 1990; Brock, Guralnik, & Brody, 1990; Doty et al., 1984; Fiatarone & Evans, 1993; Fozard, 1990; Fozard, Metter, & Brant, 1990; Gray, Berlin, McKinlay, & Longcope, 1991; Hallfrisch, Muller, Drinkwater, Tobin, & Adres, 1990; Hayflick, 1994; Ivy, MacLeod, Petit, & Marcus, 1992; Kallman, Plato, & Tobi, 1990; Kline & Scialfa, 1996; Kozma, Stones, & Hannah, 1991; Lakatta, 1990; Lim, Zipursky, Watts, & Pfefferbaum, 1992; McFalls, 1990; Miller, 1996; Mundy, 1994; Scheibel, 1992, 1996; Shock et al., 1984; Weisse, 1992.)

HEART AND LUNGS The most common measure of overall aerobic fitness is **maximum oxygen uptake (VO$_2$ max)**, which reflects the ability of the body to take in and transport oxygen to various body organs. When VO$_2$ max is measured in a person at rest, scientists find only minimal decrements associated with age. But when they measure VO$_2$ max during exercise (such as during a treadmill test), it shows a systematic decline with age of about 1% per year, beginning between ages 35 and 40 (Goldberg, Dengel, & Hagberg, 1996).

maximum oxygen uptake (VO$_2$ max)
a measure of the body's ability to take in and transport oxygen to various body organs

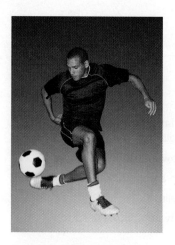

Research on peak performance in various sports suggests that elite athletes reach peak performance levels in their early 20s.
(*Photo:* Polka Dot Images/Thinkstock)

VO_2 max during exercise declines more with age than does VO_2 max at rest for a variety of reasons. Primary aging effects have been demonstrated in studies showing that, even in healthy individuals who exercise regularly, age is associated with a loss of arterial elasticity and with calcification of the valves that regulate the flow of blood to and from the heart (Cheitlin, 2003). As a result, the older adult's heart responds less efficiently to the demands of exercise than the younger adult's. Research has also revealed, however, that aerobic exercise can improve VO_2 max in both younger and older adults (Wilmore et al., 2001). Thus, age-related declines in this variable may reflect the cumulative effects of a sedentary lifestyle.

STRENGTH AND SPEED   The collective effect of changes in muscles and cardiovascular fitness is a general loss of strength and speed with age—not just in top athletes, but in all of us. **Figure 13.4** shows both cross-sectional and 9-year longitudinal changes in grip strength in a group of men who participated in the Baltimore Longitudinal Studies of Aging (Kallman et al., 1990). Clearly, strength was at its peak in the men's 20s and early 30s and then declined steadily. Once again, though, such a difference might be the result of the fact that younger adults are more physically active or more likely to be engaged in activities or jobs that demand strength. Arguing against this conclusion, however, are studies of physically active older adults, who also show loss of muscle strength (e.g., Phillips, Bruce, Newton, & Woledge, 1992).

REPRODUCTIVE CAPACITY   In **Chapter 3**, you read that the risk of miscarriage and other complications of pregnancy is higher in a woman's 30s than in her 20s. An equivalent change occurs in fertility—the ability to conceive—which is at its highest in the late teens and early 20s and drops steadily thereafter (McFalls, 1990; Mosher, 1987; Mosher & Pratt, 1987). Men's reproductive capacity declines as well, but far more slowly than is common among women. Moreover, older men have a diminished sperm count, but, as long as their reproductive organs remain disease free, men retain the ability to father children throughout their lives. Why does this pattern of reproductive aging exist?

Genetic studies in mice suggest that a single protein is responsible for the regulation of reproductive aging in both sexes (Baker et al., 2004). However, the end point of the reproductive aging process is different for men and women. Men's capacity diminishes, as stated earlier, but remains intact. By contrast, the end point of reproductive aging for women involves a total loss of the capacity for reproduction. Because of this difference, fertility problems in men (e.g., low sperm count) are almost always the result of some kind of disease or abnormal developmental process. By contrast, fertility problems in women are more often a by-product of the normal aging process.

As you will learn in **Chapter 15**, in preparation for menopause, ovulation becomes sporadic and unpredictable in many women, sometimes as soon as the early 30s. Consequently, the natural process of reproductive aging leads many women to experience periods of time during which conception is impossible. However, because menstrual cycles continue to occur, many women who are ovulating intermittently are unaware of this. Thus, to achieve conception, many women in their 30s turn to specialists in reproductive medicine who can help them identify the times when they are fertile or can prescribe drugs that stimulate the ovaries to produce more eggs, as discussed in **Chapter 3**.

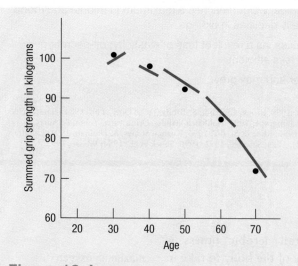

Figure 13.4

These data, from the Baltimore Longitudinal Study of Aging, show both cross-sectional data (the dots) and longitudinal data (the lines) for grip strength among men.

(*Source:* Kallman et al., 1990, Figure 2, p. M84.)

IMMUNE SYSTEM FUNCTIONING The two key organs in the immune system are the thymus gland and the bone marrow. Between them, they create two types of cells, B cells and T cells, each of which plays a distinct role. B cells fight against external threats by producing antibodies against such disease organisms as viruses or bacteria; T cells defend against essentially internal threats, such as transplanted tissue, cancer cells, and viruses that live within the body's cells (Kiecolt-Glaser & Glaser, 1995). It is T cells that decline most in number and efficiency with age (Garcia & Miller, 2001).

Changes in the thymus gland appear to be central to the aging process (Cohen, 2006). This gland is largest in adolescence and declines dramatically thereafter in both size and mass. By age 45 or 50, the thymus has only about 5 to 10% of the cellular mass it had at puberty (Braveman, 1987; Hausman & Weksler, 1985). This smaller, less functional thymus is less able to turn the immature T cells produced by the bone marrow into fully "adult" cells. As a result, both of the basic protective mechanisms work less efficiently. Adults produce fewer antibodies than do children or teenagers. And T cells partially lose the ability to "recognize" a foreign cell, so that the body may fail to fight off some disease cells (cancer cells, for example). Thus, one of the key physical changes over the years of adulthood is an increasing susceptibility to disease.

It is not entirely clear whether this susceptibility is due to primary or secondary aging. These changes in the immune system are found in healthy adults, which makes them look like part of primary aging. But there is also growing evidence that the functioning of the immune system is highly responsive to psychological stress and depression (Hawkley & Cacioppo, 2004). College and university students, for example, show lower levels of one variety of T cells ("natural killer" T cells) during exam periods than at other times (Glaser et al., 1992). And adults who have recently been widowed show a sharp drop in immune system functioning (Irwin & Pike, 1993). Chronic stress, too, has an effect on the immune system, initially stimulating an increase in immune efficiency, followed by a drop (Hawkley & Cacioppo, 2004).

Collectively, this research points to the possibility that life experiences that demand high levels of change or adaptation will affect immune system functioning. Over a period of years and many stresses, the immune system may become less and less efficient. It may well be that the immune system changes with age in basic ways regardless of the level of stress. But it is also possible that what is thought of as normal aging of the immune system is a response to cumulative stress.

Before Going On

- Define primary and secondary aging, and describe how socioeconomic factors affect a nation's health.

- Describe the patterns of brain maturation leading up to early adulthood and the various changes in other body systems that happen in early adulthood.

HEALTH PROMOTION AND WELLNESS

Early adulthood is a relatively healthy period of life, but risky behaviours—having multiple sex partners or engaging in substance use, for example—along with generally poor health habits can be problematic.

SEXUALLY TRANSMITTED INFECTIONS

In contrast to other types of disease, most sexually transmitted infections (STIs), including chlamydia (by far the most widespread) and gonorrhea are more common among young adults (aged 20 to 24) than in any other age group (Public Health Agency of Canada [PHAC], 2006c). Rates of syphilis are relatively low throughout adolescence but climb steadily beginning in early adulthood until about age 60. After declining for two decades, the number of reported new cases of these infections has been increasing, especially for chlamydia (PHAC, 2006c; Sarwal, Wong, Sevigny, & Ng, 2003). The other disease that is more common in young adults than in other age groups is HIV/AIDS.

The precise measurement of HIV infection in the Canadian population is difficult because it relies on individuals to come forward and be tested. This means that HIV infection may be present but remain undiagnosed. Another challenge in determining the levels of current and new HIV infections is that estimates are based on data from major Canadian cities and therefore do not reflect local trends. Even so, we see some disturbing trends appearing from the data that is available.

Early in the Canadian HIV epidemic, those most affected were men who had sex with men (MSM) and to a lesser extent unsuspecting victims who received HIV-contaminated blood products in the 1980s. The rate of new infections for the MSM population has been increasing since the mid-1990s, following more than a decade of decline. In contrast, the rate of new HIV infection for another high-risk group, injection drug users (IDU), has declined after peaking in the mid-1990s (see **Figure 13.5**). The HIV epidemic has recently invaded other segments of the population, with new infections on the rise in heterosexuals, women, and, to a disproportionately high level, in Aboriginal peoples (~7.5%), a rate that is ~2.8 times higher than among non-Aboriginal persons (PHAC, 2006a).

It is estimated that 58 000 Canadians now live with HIV and/or AIDS, of which about 11 800 are women. Three-quarters of the new HIV infections in women are due

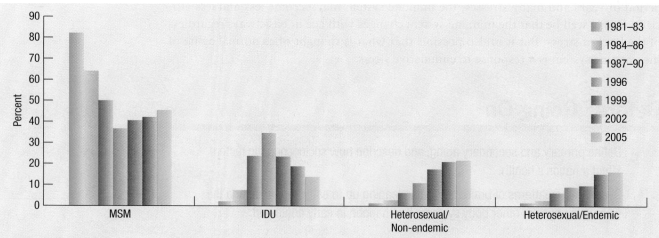

Figure 13.5

Estimated exposure category distributions (%) of new HIV infections in Canada, by time period. Estimates were subclassified according to the following exposure categories: men who have had sex with men (MSM); injecting drug users (IDU); MSM-IDU; heterosexual/endemic (non-IDU heterosexual with origin in a country where heterosexual sex is the predominant mode of HIV transmission and HIV prevalence is high, primarily countries in sub-Saharan Africa and the Caribbean); and heterosexual/non-endemic (heterosexual contact with a person who is either HIV infected or at risk of HIV, or heterosexual as the only identified risk).

(*Source:* HIV/AIDS Epi Updates, August 2006, Surveillance and Risk Assessment Division, Centre for Infectious Disease Prevention and Control, Public Health Agency of Canada. Reproduced with the permission of the Minister of Public Works and Government Services Canada, 2007.)

to heterosexual contact (76%), while the remainder is attributable to IDU (PHAC, 2006a). Women are most likely to test positive for HIV between ages 20 and 39. In comparison, men are more than twice as likely to be diagnosed at ages 30 to 39 than at ages 20 to 29 (Health Canada, 2000b). The highest percentage of newly diagnosed AIDS cases in Canada occurs between ages 30 and 39 (Health Canada, 2000c). Age determinants are difficult to measure because of the lengthy delay between exposure and diagnosis. In many cases, the onset of AIDS occurs in individuals who were exposed to HIV infection in their early 20s.

PREVENTION   Like adolescents, many young adults engage in high-risk behaviours that are specifically linked to STIs: having multiple sexual partners, having sex without adequate protection, and frequently using drugs or alcohol. However, for most young adults, STIs remain one of the taboo topics. Many young adults are unwilling to insist on the use of condoms; many do not seek medical attention when they develop symptoms and do not inform their partners of potential problems (Lewis, Malow, & Ireland, 1997; Schuster, 1997). The risks of these behaviours are considerable, especially with the increase in drug-resistant strains of gonorrhea and syphilis. So take note: Safe sex practices—including knowledge of your partner's sexual history—are worth the effort.

HEALTH HABITS AND PERSONAL FACTORS

As you might expect, individual health habits, such as exercise, influence health in the early adult years and beyond. Social support networks and attitudes also affect health.

HEALTH HABITS   The best evidence for the long-term effects of various health habits comes from the Alameda County Study, a major longitudinal epidemiological study conducted in one county in California (Berkman & Breslow, 1983; Breslow & Breslow, 1993; Kaplan, 1992; Stallworth & Lennon, 2003). The study began in 1965, when a random sample of all residents of the county, a total of 6928 people, completed an extensive questionnaire about many aspects of their lives, including their health habits and their health and disability. These participants were contacted again in 1974 and in 1983, when they again described their health and disability. The researchers identified five good health habits: getting physical exercise; not smoking, drinking, over- or undereating; and getting regular sleep. They found that, in every age group, those with poorer health habits had a higher risk of mortality. Not surprisingly, poor health habits were also related to disease and disability rates over the 18 years of the study. Those who described poorer health habits in 1965 were more likely to report disability or disease symptoms in 1974 and in 1983 (Breslow & Breslow, 1993; Guralnik & Kaplan, 1989; Strawbridge, Camacho, Cohen, & Kaplan, 1993). Moreover, the study showed that a sedentary lifestyle in early adulthood predisposes people to develop life-threatening illnesses such as diabetes in later years (Hu, Li, Colditz, Willet, & Manson, 2003).

The Alameda study is not the only one to show these connections between health habits and mortality. For example, a 20-year longitudinal study in Sweden confirms the link between physical exercise and lower risk of death (Lissner, Bengtsson, Bjorkelund, & Wedel, 1996). In addition, the Nurses' Health Study, a longitudinal investigation that examined the health behaviours of more than 115 000 nurses in the United States for almost two decades, found that the lower a woman's initial body mass index (BMI—the ratio of weight to height), the lower her likelihood of death (Manson et al., 1995).

These longitudinal studies suggest that the lifestyle choices of early adulthood have cumulative effects. For example, the effect of a high-fat diet coupled with a sedentary lifestyle appears to add up over time. However, a radical lowering of fat levels in the

Sexually transmitted diseases are one of the most significant health risks of young adulthood. Casual sexual encounters with multiple partners carry with them a higher risk of contracting such diseases than do more careful relationship choices.
(*Photo:* Timothy Shonnard/Getty Images)

diet along with regular exercise can reduce the risk of heart disease and diabetes (Health Canada, 1999b). Thus, the long-term effects of lifestyle choice made in early adulthood may be either negative or positive. So there is likely to be a payoff for changing your health habits.

SOCIAL SUPPORT Abundant research shows that adults with adequate *social support* have lower risk of disease, death, and depression than do adults with weaker social networks or less supportive relationships (e.g., Berkman, 1985; Berkman & Breslow, 1983; Cohen, 1991). The link between social support and health was revealed in some of the findings from the Alameda study. In this study, the *social network index* reflected an objective measurement—number of contacts with friends and relatives, marital status, and church and group membership. Even using this less-than-perfect measure of support, the relationship was vividly clear: Among both men and women in three different age groups (30 to 49, 50 to 59, and 60 to 69), those with the fewest social connections had higher death rates than those with more social connections. Since similar patterns have been found in other countries, including Sweden and Japan, this link between social contact and physical hardiness is not restricted to Western cultures (Orth-Gomér, Rosengren, & Wilhelmsen, 1993; Sugisawa, Liang, & Liu, 1994).

How does social support contribute to health? One reason may be that the size and perceived adequacy of a person's social network is correlated with the functioning of her immune system (Bouhuys, Flentge, Oldehinkel, & van den Berg, 2004). Likewise, adults who have adequate social support are less likely than their peers to be depressed, a factor that indirectly affects the immune system (Symister & Friend, 2003).

A SENSE OF CONTROL Another personal characteristic that affects health is an individual's level of *self-efficacy*, the belief in one's ability to perform some action or to control one's behaviour or environment, to reach some goal or to make something happen (Bandura, 1977b, 1986; 1997a, b). As you learned in **Chapter 10**, this aspect of the psychological self first appears in middle childhood. In adulthood, it is linked to many health outcomes. For instance, individuals who are high in self-efficacy are more likely than those who are low in self-efficacy to follow medical advice with regard to health problems such as chronic headaches (Nicholson, Houle, Rhudy, & Norton, 2007).

A similar variable, locus of control, which is an individual's set of beliefs about the causes of events, also contributes to health. Recall from **Chapter 12** that a person who has an internal locus of control sees herself as capable of exerting some control over what happens to her (Rotter, 1990). One who has an external locus of control believes that other people or uncontrollable forces, such as luck, determine the future.

To understand how locus of control influences health, think about what would happen if you had an ear infection for which a doctor prescribed an antibiotic that you took for only half as long as directed. How would you explain your ear infection if it failed to go away? If you have an internal locus of control, then you would have no difficulty acknowledging the fact that your failure to take the medicine as directed was responsible for your still-aching ear. However, if you have an external locus of control, then you might respond to the pain in your ear with a remark such as "Just my luck! Nothing ever goes my way."

Research suggests that the tendency to make realistic attributions is what counts when it comes to health (Frick, Fegg, Tyroller, Fischer, & Bumeder, 2007). The best outcomes for patients happen when they are able to accurately determine which aspects of their conditions are controllable and which are not. For instance, with regard to our ear infection example, a person who is able to balance attributions in this way would realize that taking medicine is under her control and would take responsibility for that aspect of her treatment. However, she would understand that the physician is responsible for

◉—Watch

determining which antibiotic to prescribe. Balancing her thinking about the reasons for her recovery or her failure to recover helps her cope with the stress of being ill.

Both self-efficacy and locus of control are related to yet another control-related psychological characteristic, the continuum that ranges from optimism to pessimism (Seligman, 1991). The pessimist, who feels helpless, believes that misfortune will last a long time, will undermine everything, and is his own fault. The optimist believes that setbacks are temporary and usually caused by circumstances. He is convinced that there is always some solution and that he will be able to work things out. Confronted by defeat, the optimist sees it as a challenge and tries harder, whereas the pessimist gives up. Not surprisingly, optimism affects health in many ways, including enhancing the effects of medication (Geers, Kosbab, Helfer, Weiland, & Wellman, 2007). That is, optimists show larger benefits from medication than pessimists do. These results are in line with other studies showing that optimism has positive effects on the immune system (Segerstrom, Taylor, Kemeny, & Fahey, 1998). In addition, it fits with the results of a classic longitudinal study which found that pessimism at age 25 was correlated with poor health in middle and late adulthood (Peterson, Seligman, & Vaillant, 1988).

INTIMATE PARTNER ABUSE

Researchers define **intimate partner abuse** as physical acts or other behaviour intended to cause physical, psychological, or sexual harm to an intimate partner. Intimate partners are couples who are dating, cohabiting, engaged, or married, or who were formerly partners. The more common term, *domestic abuse*, refers only to incidents involving individuals who live in the same household.

intimate partner abuse
physical acts or other behaviour intended to intimidate or harm an intimate partner

PREVALENCE When intimate partners get into a physical altercation, men and women are about equally likely to push, slap, or kick their partners. However, analyses of medical records show that, throughout the world, women are more likely than men to be injured during physical confrontations between intimate partners (McHugh, 2005). And as **Figure 13.6** reveals, the rates of abuse of women vary significantly around the world (World Health Organization [WHO], 2000). In Canada, a 1999 survey suggested that, over a 5-year period, about 8% of women had been physically abused by a spouse, compared with 7% of men. Spousal violence within the Aboriginal population is higher than average, with 25% of Aboriginal women and 13% of Aboriginal men being assaulted by their spouse (Statistics Canada, 2001h). In both Aboriginal and non-Aboriginal populations, persons living in common-law relationships are more likely to be victims of lethal and nonlethal spousal violence than those who are legally married (Hotton, 2001). Both women (28%) and men (22%) who had contact with an ex-marital or common-law partner reported violence committed by an ex-partner (Statistics Canada, 2001h). Moreover, violence by former partners is reportedly more severe and lethal than assault by a current partner (Statistics Canada, 2000c).

Researchers estimate that gay men and lesbians are about as likely to be abused by a partner as are women in heterosexual relationships (Freedberg, 2006); however, the exact prevalence rate of abuse in same-sex relationships is difficult to ascertain because homosexuals are less likely than heterosexuals to seek medical attention for their injuries because of fear of discrimination. When gays and lesbians do seek help, researchers have found that health care professionals tend to overlook intimate partner abuse as a possible source of their injuries. As a result, emergency medical personnel may fail to question gays and lesbians about intimate partner abuse as they would heterosexuals.

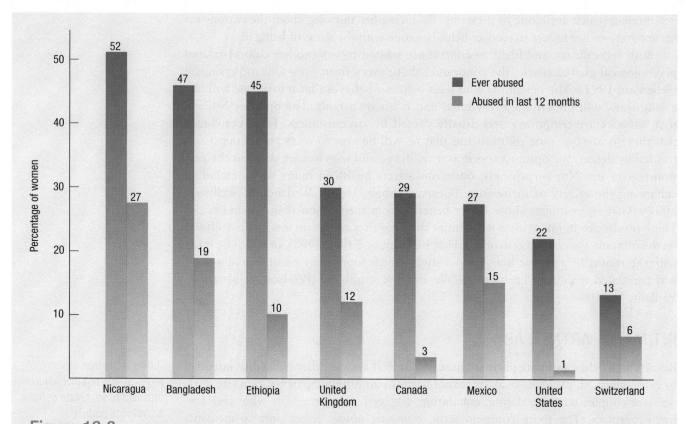

Figure 13.6

These data on physical abuse are based on a World Health Organization international survey of medical records.
(*Source:* WHO, 2000.)

Criminologists point out that intimate partner abuse happens most often in the context of arguments over long-standing disagreements that take place when partners are home from work in the evening, on holidays or weekends, and/or have been drinking or using drugs.
(*Photo:* Jonathan Nourok/PhotoEdit)

CAUSES OF PARTNER ABUSE Cultural attitudes contribute to rates of abuse (McHugh, 2005). Specifically, in many societies, women were regarded as property, and a man's "right" to beat his partner was at times protected by law. In fact, there was a time when, based on English common-law traditions, this was true in British-governed parts of North America.

Gender-role prescriptions may also contribute to abuse. For example, rates of abuse are particularly high among Japanese women, over 50% of whom claim to have been victimized (Kozu, 1999). Researchers attribute the prevalence of abuse to the cultural belief that Japanese husbands are absolute authorities over their wives and their children. Further, to avoid bringing dishonour on her husband, the Japanese wife is obligated to conceal abusive incidents from those outside the family.

In addition to cultural beliefs, a number of characteristics of abusers and their victims are associated with intimate partner abuse. For example, the same cluster of personality traits contributes to abuse in both heterosexual and homosexual couples (Burke & Follingstad, 1999). The cluster includes a tendency toward irrational jealousy, a need for dependency in the partner and control in a relationship, sudden mood swings, and a quick temper (Landolt & Dutton, 1997). Men who are generally more aggressive than others are also more likely than less aggressive men to abuse their partners (Kane, Staiger, & Ricciardelli, 2000). In addition, men who are high school dropouts or who are frequently unemployed abuse their partners more often than other men (Kyriacou et al., 1999).

Abuse victims are more likely to have been abused as children than are their peers who are not involved in abusive relationships (Smith, White, & Holland, 2003; Wyatt et al., 2000). Age is also a factor. Young women between ages 16 and 24 are more likely to be abused than those who are older (National Center for Injury Prevention and Control [NCIPC], 2006). This pattern of age differences may result from younger women's lesser ability to function independently from abusive partners. They may lack the education or work experience necessary to gain employment. Finally, younger women are more likely to be caring for infants and young children for whom they cannot obtain daycare. As a result, many such women remain in abusive relationships, believing they have no other choice (Kaplan & Sadock, 1991).

Alcohol and drug problems are more common among both abusers and victims than among nonabusive partners (NCIPC, 2006). One extensive study of more than 8000 intrafamily killings found that, in about half of spousal homicides, the perpetrator had been drinking alcohol or using drugs (Dawson & Langan, 1994). Similarly, in 50% of cases, the victim had been using alcohol or drugs.

EFFECTS OF ABUSE ON INDIVIDUALS Women who are abused are at heightened risk for physical injury, sexual and reproductive disorders, and homicide (Heise & Garcia-Moreno, 2002). They may develop feelings of anxiety, depression, and low self-esteem (Buchbinder & Eisikovits, 2003; Kaplan & Sadock, 1991). Such feelings are intensified when victims believe they cannot escape from the abusive relationship. Some become so despondent that they consider or attempt suicide as an escape (NCIPC, 2000).

Witnessing abuse also influences children's development. One study involving 420 adults who had witnessed physical violence between their parents as children suggested that there are strong relationships between parental violence and a variety of negative developmental outcomes (McNeal & Amato, 1998). For one thing, many of these adults were found to have poor relationships with their own partners and children. Moreover, many had become perpetrators or victims of partner abuse themselves.

PREVENTION Vigorous law enforcement is one approach to prevention (Dugan, Nagin, & Rosenfeld, 2003). Advocates of this approach suggest that a stigma of arrest may force abusers to face the reality that they have a serious problem. Training programs for law enforcement officials and hospital emergency room personnel that teach them to recognize signs of abuse are also essential (Hamberger & Minsky, 2000). Many experts also recommend training physicians and nurses to recognize and question patients about signs of abuse during routine medical exams (Scholle et al., 2003). As a result of such training, advocates claim, perpetrators may be identified and prosecuted even when victims do not voluntarily report abusive incidents.

A different approach is to provide victims with problem-solving skills and temporary shelters that may prevent their revictimization (NCIPC, 2000). Further, community-wide and school-based approaches to prevention seek to educate the public about intimate partner abuse and to change attitudes about the acceptability of violence in intimate relationships, so that abuse will not happen in the first place.

SEXUAL ASSAULT

Sexual assault is any form of sexual activity with another person without his or her consent. Engaging in sex with a person who is incapable of consenting or of understanding what is happening to him or her because of a mental disability or a temporary altered state of consciousness is also defined as sexual assault.

sexual assault
any form of sexual activity with another person without his or her consent

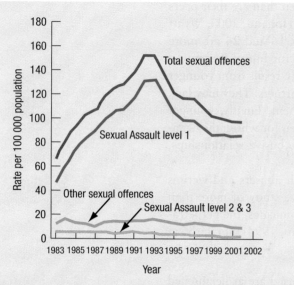

Figure 13.7

The rates of police-reported sexual offences peaked during the 1990s and then declined in Canada.

(*Source:* Adapted from Statistics Canada, 2003, available at: http://www.statcan.ca/Daily/English/030725/d030725.pdf)

Canadian law prescribes three levels of sexual assault: level 1—sexual assault (e.g., kissing, touching, oral or anal sex, intercourse or other forms of penetration); level 2—sexual assault with a weapon or resulting in bodily harm; and level 3—aggravated sexual assault (e.g., wounding, maiming, disfiguring, or endangering the life of the victim).

PREVALENCE The rate of reported sexual assault incidents was 86 per 100 000 in 2002 (see **Figure 13.7**), and of these, 88% were level 1 sexual assaults (Kong, Johnson, Beattie, & Cardillo, 2003). Six of 10 reported sexual assault victims were young—the majority were girls aged 11 to 19 and boys aged 3 to 14. Women are far more likely than men to be sexually victimized, accounting for 85% of all reported cases in 2002.

Most sexual violence occurs within the context of social or romantic relationships; fewer than half of all sexual assaults are committed by strangers. Eighty percent of the victims of reported cases in 2002 knew their assailants: 10% were assaulted by a friend, 41% by an acquaintance, and 28% by a family member (Kong et al., 2003). Like sexual assault by men against women, male rape against males usually involves men who are acquaintances or who are intimate partners (Hodge & Canter, 1998).

Sexual assault rates are quite similar across cultures, with a few rather dramatic exceptions. For example, in an international survey of medical records, 48% of women in Peru were found to have reported being forced into a sexual act during the previous 12 months (WHO, 2000).

EFFECTS The psychological effects of being a victim of sexual violence include the development of sexual dysfunctions and post-traumatic stress disorder, as well as the possibility of physical trauma and pregnancy (Elliott et al., 2004). Men who are raped by other men also sometimes experience doubts about their sexual orientation (Kaplan & Sadock, 1991). Moreover, the psychological effects of sexual violence have been found to persist more than a decade in many victims (Elliott et al., 2004). Thus, being victimized by sexual violence can, overall, be one of the most traumatic episodes in a young adult's life.

One particularly troubling type of sexual violence among young adults is date rape, or rape that occurs in the context of a date. Men's belief that women say no when they mean yes is believed to contribute to such incidents. However, many cases of date rape are premeditated and involve the use of alcohol and drugs to loosen the inhibitions of the victim. Research indicates that such episodes may be more traumatic than rapes perpetrated by strangers because victims of date rape believe they should have been able to prevent the assault. Victims who were coerced with drugs and/or alcohol also frequently have incomplete memories of the event, a factor that increases their vulnerability to long-term negative emotional consequences (Gauntlett-Gilbert, Keegan, & Petrak, 2004).

Prevention of sexual violence often involves training potential victims to avoid situations in which such episodes are likely to occur (Kalmuss, 2004). Training in self-defense techniques, both verbal and physical, can also help women learn how to deal effectively with the initial phases of a threatened sexual assault (Hollander, 2004).

MENTAL HEALTH PROBLEMS

Studies in a number of developed countries show that the risk of virtually every kind of emotional disturbance is higher in early adulthood than in middle age (Kessler et al., 2005). In fact, survey research suggests that as many as 10% of younger adults, those aged 18 to 24, have seriously considered committing suicide (Brener, Hassan, & Barrios, 1999).

CAUSES OF MENTAL DISORDERS

The most plausible explanation for the differing rates of mental disorder between young adults and middle-aged adults is that early adulthood is the period in which adults have both the highest expectations and the highest levels of role conflict and role strain. These are the years when each of us must learn a series of major new roles (e.g., spouse, parent, worker). If we fall short of our expectations, then emotional difficulties such as anxiety and depression become more likely.

Some people respond very effectively to the challenges of young adulthood, while others do not. For example, the personal factors you read about in an earlier section are important to mental health as well as physical health. However, with respect to mental disorder, researchers' attention is becoming more focused on biological causes.

First, mental disorders tend to run in families, suggesting a hereditary factor. In fact, the number of close relatives a person has who suffer from depression or other mood disorders is the best predictor of the likelihood that the individual will develop a mood disorder (Kendler et al., 1995). In addition, an increasing number of studies demonstrate links between mental disorder and disturbances in specific brain functions (Drevets et al., 1997; Monarch, Saykin, & Flashman, 2004). Consequently, the current view of most psychologists is that mental disorders result from an interaction of biological, psychological, and sociocultural factors.

When a young adult develops a mental health problem, the long-term impact of the problem depends on the degree to which it diverts her from an adaptive developmental pathway. For instance, if a college student develops one of these problems, then she may have to leave school. Thus, many mental health professionals believe that once an effective treatment has been identified, educational and vocational rehabilitation services are critical to the young adult's full recovery. Longitudinal studies involving young adults with mental illnesses who have participated in educational/vocational rehabilitation programs support this view (Ellison, Danley, Bromberg, & Palmer-Erbs, 1999; Gralinski-Bakker et al., 2005).

ANXIETY AND MOOD DISORDERS

The most common mental disorders that affect Canadians are those that are associated with intense or prolonged fear and anxiety (Health Canada, 2002c). For example, anxiety disorders, such as *phobias*, *generalized anxiety disorder*, *obsessive-compulsive disorder*, and *panic disorder*, affect a reported 12% of the Canadian adult population in any given year. Anxiety disorders are of such severity as to interfere with normal daily functioning, and because they are so common they also contribute to lost productivity from both absenteeism and unemployment.

After anxiety disorders, problems associated with moods are the most common type of mental difficulty. Depression is the most frequent of these disorders, with the most debilitating type, called *major depression*, affecting between 4 and 5% of Canadians annually (Health Canada, 2002c). Rates of depression are higher in early adulthood than in either adolescence or middle age. Thus, paradoxically, the time of life in which people experience their peak of physical and intellectual functioning is also the time when they may be most prone to feelings of sadness. Depression rates may be higher in early adulthood because these are the years when people must create new attachment relationships while at the same time separating from parents (Erikson's task of *intimacy*). Consequently, brief periods during which a person is alone may result in feelings of loneliness and social failure that may lead to depression (Comninos & Grenyer, 2007).

ALCOHOL AND SUBSTANCE USE DISORDERS Rates of alcoholism and significant drug addiction also peak between ages 18 and 40, after which they decline gradually. The rates of addiction are higher for men than for women, but the age pattern is very similar in both genders (Thompson & Lande, 2007). One Canadian study found the rate of regular heavy drinking to be about 38% for young drinkers aged 20 to 24, compared with 23% among 25- to 34-year-olds, and 6% for those over age 65. The greatest disparity between gender drinking rates was found for the age group 20 to 24, with 53% of male drinkers and 23% of female drinkers considered to be regular heavy drinkers (Statistics Canada, 2001e).

Binge drinking (usually defined as consuming five or more drinks on one occasion) is also particularly common among college and university students in Canada. Although most binge drinkers do not think of themselves as having a problem with alcohol, they clearly display a variety of problem behaviours, including substantially higher rates of unprotected sex, physical injury, driving while intoxicated, and trouble with the police (Wechsler, Davenport, Dowdall, Moeykens, & Castillo, 1994; Wechsler, Dowdall, Maenner, Gledhill-Hoyt, & Lee, 1998). Thus, alarmed by surveys showing that as many as 50% of post-secondary students engage in binge drinking, a growing number of colleges and universities are strictly enforcing rules against on-campus substance use (Wechsler et al., 1998). Many also provide students with treatment for alcohol and substance abuse problems.

PERSONALITY DISORDERS In a few cases, the stresses of young adulthood, presumably in combination with some type of biological factor, lead to serious disturbances in cognitive, emotional, and social functioning that are not easily treated. For example, a **personality disorder** is an inflexible pattern of behaviour that leads to difficulties in social, educational, and occupational functioning. In many cases, the problems that are associated with these disorders appear early in life. However, the behaviour pattern is usually not diagnosed as a mental disorder until late adolescence or early adulthood (American Psychiatric Association [APA], 2000). The five most common types of personality disorders are listed in **Table 13.2**.

personality disorder
an inflexible pattern of behaviour that leads to difficulty in educational, occupational, and social functioning

TABLE 13.2	Personality Disorders
Type	**Characteristics**
Antisocial	Difficulty forming emotional attachments; lack of empathy; little regard for the rights of others; self-centred; willingness to violate the law or social rules to achieve a desired objective
Paranoid	Suspicious of others' behaviour and motives; emotionally guarded and highly sensitive to minor violations of personal space or perceived rights
Histrionic	Irrational, attention-seeking behaviour; inappropriate emotional responses; sexually seductive behaviour and clothing
Narcissistic	Exaggerated sense of self-importance; craves attention and approval; exploits others; lack of empathy
Borderline	Unstable moods and relationships; fear of abandonment; tendency to self-injury; highly dependent on others; impulsive and reckless behaviour

(*Source:* APA, 2000.)

Generally, to be diagnosed with any of the disorders in **Table 13.2**, a young adult has to have been exhibiting the associated behaviour since mid- or late adolescence. In addition, the person should demonstrate the behaviour consistently, across all kinds of situations. For example, a person who steals from an employer but generally respects the property rights of others outside the work environment would probably not be diagnosed with antisocial personality disorder. The individual's functioning at work, at school, or in social relationships also must be impaired to some degree. Psychological tests can be helpful in distinguishing whether an individual simply has a troublesome personality trait, such as suspiciousness, or a genuine mental disorder, such as paranoid personality disorder.

Some personality disorders, such as antisocial and borderline disorders, become less severe in their manifestations with age (APA, 2000). However, most of these disorders remain problematic throughout adult life. In addition, they are not easily treated. They often do not respond to psychotherapy, because those who suffer from them seem to believe their problems result from others' behaviour rather than their own.

SCHIZOPHRENIA One of the most serious mental disorders that is often first diagnosed in early adulthood is **schizophrenia**. This mental disorder affects an estimated 1% of Canadians and is characterized by confused thinking, false beliefs known as *delusions*, and false sensory experiences called *hallucinations* (Health Canada, 2002c). For example, a first-year biology student who breaks into a laboratory on his university campus to work on a cure for cancer he has just thought of may suffer from a *delusion of grandeur*. Likewise, a young woman who hears voices that guide her behaviour is likely to be experiencing hallucinations.

For most people with schizophrenia, these disturbances of thought become so severe that they can no longer function at work, at school, or in social relationships. In fact, many engage in behaviour that endangers themselves or others. For example, a person with schizophrenia may believe that he can fly and jump out of an upper-story window. Consequently, people with schizophrenia are frequently hospitalized. Fortunately, powerful antipsychotic medications can help most people with schizophrenia regain some degree of normal functioning (Lauriello, McEvoy, Rodriguez, Bossie, & Lasser, 2005). Yet many continue to experience recurring episodes of disturbed thinking, even when medication helps them gain control over their behaviour.

schizophrenia
a serious mental disorder characterized by disturbances of thought such as delusions and hallucinations

Before Going On

- How are risky behaviours, health habits, and stress, as well as social support networks and attitudes, related to health and illness?

- What factors are involved in the social problems of intimate partner abuse and sexual assault, and in the emotional disturbances found in early adulthood?

COGNITIVE CHANGES

Like most aspects of physical functioning, intellectual processes are at their peak in early adulthood. Indeed, it now seems clear that the intellectual peak lasts longer than many early researchers had thought and that the rate of decline is quite slow. Current research also makes it clear that the rate and pattern of cognitive decline varies widely—differences that appear to be caused by a variety of environmental and lifestyle factors, as well as by heredity.

FORMAL OPERATIONS AND BEYOND

As you should recall from **Chapter 11**, Piaget's formal operational stage emerges in mid- to late adolescence, but some theorists dispute Piaget's hypothesis that the formal operations stage is the last stage of cognitive development (Labouvie-Vief, 2006). These theorists hypothesize that a fifth stage emerges in early adulthood, typically in the early 20s, in response to the kinds of problems that are unique to adult life. The term **postformal thought** is collectively applied to the types of thinking that these theorists propose to be characteristic of the fifth stage of cognitive development.

The work of postformal theorists owes its origins to the ideas of Lawrence Kohlberg, whose theory of moral development you read about in **Chapter 12**, and William Perry (Labouvie-Vief, 2006). Kohlberg and Perry emphasized the shift toward **relativism**, the idea that some propositions cannot be adequately described as either true or false, that occurs in early adulthood (Kohlberg, 1969; Perry, 1968). Perry studied undergraduates at Harvard University in the 1960s and concluded that they began their studies with the view that knowledge comprises truthful statements and that the purpose of education is to accumulate an increasing number of such propositions. As young adults progress through higher education, Perry's work suggested, conflicts among the many ideas to which they are exposed push them toward a relativistic approach that enables them to evaluate propositions in terms of their underlying assumptions and the contexts in which they occur. For example, in the United States, most high school history students learn that slavery was the main cause of the Civil War (1861–1865). According to Perry's view, a student who is presented with a different idea about the main cause of the war is likely to dismiss it as "false" rather than to analyze it with regard to the supporting evidence that is cited by the person who advocates it. Perry argued that higher education classes reframe the "facts" that students acquired in earlier years in just this way and, in the process, help students develop a postformal approach to such complex issues.

Other theorists place more emphasis on everyday thought processes than they do on thinking that occurs in academic contexts. One such theorist, Gisela Labouvie-Vief argues that adults learn how to solve the problems associated with the particular social roles they occupy or the particular jobs they hold (Labouvie-Vief, 1980, 1990). In the process, they trade the deductive thoroughness of formal operations for what Labouvie-Vief calls *contextual validity*. In her view, this trade-off does not reflect a regression or a loss, but rather a necessary structural change.

Another theorist, Michael Basseches, points out that many young adults turn away from a purely logical, analytic approach, toward a more open, perhaps deeper, mode of understanding that accepts paradox and uncertainty. He calls this new adult type of thinking **dialectical thought** (Basseches, 1984, 1989). According to this view, adults do not give up their ability to use formal reasoning. Instead, they acquire a new ability to deal with the fuzzier problems that make up the majority of the problems of adulthood—problems that do not have a single solution or in which some critical pieces of information may be missing. Choosing what type of refrigerator to buy might be a decision aided by formal operational thought. But such forms of logical thought may not be helpful in making a decision about whether to adopt a child or whether to place an aging parent in a nursing home. Basseches argues that such problems demand a different kind of thinking—not a "higher" kind of thinking, but a different one.

Psychologists Patricia King and Karen Kitchener (2004) have proposed that **reflective judgment**, the capacity to identify the underlying assumptions of differing

postformal thought
types of thinking that are associated with a hypothesized fifth stage of cognitive development

relativism
the idea that some propositions cannot be adequately described as either true or false

dialectical thought
a form of thought involving recognition and acceptance of paradox and uncertainty

reflective judgement
the ability to identify the underlying assumptions of differing perspective on controversial issues

perspectives on controversial issues, is an important feature of postformal thought. For example, reflective thinkers are capable of ascertaining that a person who argues that the key to reducing drug use is to educate people about the adverse effects of drugs is assuming that those who use drugs do so because they lack such knowledge. According to the studies that King and Kitchener have carried out, the capacity to analyze arguments in this way develops in a series of seven stages across childhood, adolescence, and adulthood (King & Kitchener, 2004). Like Kohlberg's stages of moral judgment, these stages are loosely tied to age and are influenced by an individual's level of education.

Many of these new theories of adult cognition are intriguing, but they remain highly speculative, with little empirical evidence to back them up. More generally, psychologists do not yet agree on whether these new types of thinking represent "higher" forms of thought, built on the stages Piaget described, or whether it is more appropriate simply to describe them as different forms of thinking that may or may not emerge in adulthood. What may be most important about such theories is the emphasis on the fact that the normal problems of adult life, with their inconsistencies and complexities, cannot always be addressed fruitfully by using formal operational logic. It seems entirely plausible that adults are pushed toward more pragmatic, relativistic forms of thinking and use formal operational thinking only occasionally, if at all. Postformal theorists agree that this change should not be thought of as a loss or a deterioration, but rather as a reasonable adaptation to a different set of cognitive tasks.

Critical Thinking

List two personal problems you have had to solve in the past 6 months. What kind of logic or thought process did you use to solve each one? Did your mode of thinking change in response to the nature of the problem?

INTELLIGENCE AND MEMORY

Examination of intelligence and memory in early adulthood suggests that both continuity and change characterize these components of cognitive functioning (Schroeder & Salthouse, 2004). Verbal abilities, such as the number of words in one's vocabulary, grow during early adulthood. By contrast, spatial skills decline a bit. Thus, you may be wondering—does an individual become more intelligent or less so over the years from 20 to 40? The answer to this question depends on how intellectual functioning is measured.

IQ SCORES   IQ scores remain quite stable across middle childhood, adolescence, and early adulthood. For example, a study of Canadian army veterans, first tested when they were in their early 20s and then again in their early 60s, yielded similar results; there was a correlation of 0.78 between verbal IQ scores achieved at the two ages (Gold et al., 1995). Over shorter intervals, the correlations were even higher.

The best single source of evidence on the stability of IQ in adulthood is a remarkable 35-year study by Werner Schaie, referred to as the Seattle Longitudinal Study (Schaie & Willis, 2005). Schaie's study has provided developmentalists with a number of important insights into how intellectual functioning changes across adulthood. One is the finding that longitudinal and cross-sectional data yield somewhat different pictures of these changes, a phenomenon first reported by Schaie in 1983 (Schaie & Hertzog, 1983). He began in 1956 with a set of cross-sectional samples; the participants in different samples were 7 years apart in age and ranged in age from 25 to 67. All participants took an IQ test at the outset of the study; a subset of the participants in each age group was then followed over 35 years and retested every 7 years. In 1963, another set of cross-sectional samples, covering the same age ranges, was tested, and a subset of these was retested 7, 14, 21, and 28 years later. Further samples were added in 1970, 1977, 1984, and 1991. This remarkable data-collection process enabled Schaie to look at IQ changes over 7-, 14-, 21-, and 28-year intervals for several sets of participants, each from a slightly different cohort. **Figure 13.8** graphs one set of cross-sectional

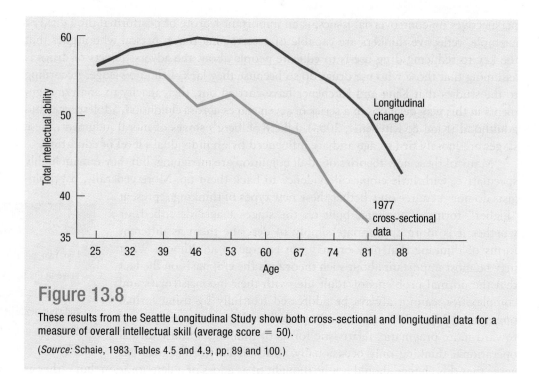

Figure 13.8

These results from the Seattle Longitudinal Study show both cross-sectional and longitudinal data for a measure of overall intellectual skill (average score = 50).

(*Source:* Schaie, 1983, Tables 4.5 and 4.9, pp. 89 and 100.)

comparisons made in 1977 as well as 14-year longitudinal results smoothed over the whole age range. The test involved in this case is a measure of global intelligence on which the average score is set at 50 points (equivalent to an IQ of 100 on most other tests).

You can see that the cross-sectional comparisons show a steady drop in IQ. But the longitudinal evidence suggests that overall intelligence test scores actually rise in early adulthood and then remain quite constant until perhaps age 60, when they begin to decline. Since this pattern has also been found by other researchers (e.g., Sands, Terry, & Meredith, 1989; Siegler, 1983), there is good support for the temptingly optimistic view that intellectual ability remains essentially stable through most of adulthood.

CRYSTALLIZED AND FLUID INTELLIGENCE

Looking at different components of intellectual ability gives a clearer picture of change and stability across the adult years. Theorists have suggested several ways to subdivide intellectual tasks. However, the most influential of these theories has been Raymond Cattell and John Horn's distinction between crystallized intelligence and fluid intelligence (Cattell, 1963; Horn, 1982; Horn & Donaldson, 1980).

crystallized intelligence
knowledge and judgment acquired through education and experience

Crystallized intelligence depends heavily on education and experiences. It consists of the set of skills and bits of knowledge that every adult learns as part of growing up in any given culture, such as vocabulary, the ability to read and understand the newspaper, and the ability to evaluate experience. Technical skills you may learn for your job or your life—balancing a chequebook, using a computer, making change, finding the mayonnaise in the grocery store—also represent crystallized intelligence.

fluid intelligence
the aspect of intelligence that reflects fundamental biological processes and does not depend on specific experiences

Fluid intelligence, in contrast, involves more "basic" abilities—it is the aspect of intelligence that depends more on the efficient functioning of the central nervous system and less on specific experience. A common measure of fluid intelligence is a "letter series test," in which a participant is given a series of letters (e.g., *A C F J O*) and must figure out what letter should go next. This problem demands abstract reasoning rather than reasoning about known or everyday events. Most tests of memory also measure fluid intelligence, as do many tests measuring response speed and those measuring higher-level or abstract mathematical skills. Schaie's results, and the results of many other investigators, suggest that adults maintain crystallized intelligence throughout early and middle adulthood, but that fluid intelligence declines fairly steadily over adulthood, beginning at perhaps age 35 or 40 (Li et al., 2004; Schaie & Willis, 2005).

So where does this leave us in answering the question about intellectual maintenance or decline over adulthood? It seems safe to conclude, at least tentatively, that intellectual abilities show essentially no decline in early adulthood except at the very top levels of intellectual demand. In middle adulthood, though, declines on fluid intelligence abilities—those tasks that are thought to represent the efficiency of the basic physiological process—become evident (Salthouse, 1991).

Before Going On

- What are some theoretical proposals regarding a stage of cognitive development beyond Piaget's formal operational stage?

- How do the concepts of crystallized and fluid intelligence help to explain age-related changes in IQ scores?

POST-SECONDARY EDUCATION

In today's high-tech, global economy, **post-secondary education**, any formal educational experience that follows high school, has become a necessity for virtually everyone. This requirement helps to explain why the number of students enrolled in some level of post-secondary education in Canada has been on the rise. Moreover, a higher proportion of highly educated immigrants and recessionary labour markets have also encouraged young adults to further their studies (Clark, 2003a).

post-secondary education
any formal educational experience that follows high school

DEVELOPMENTAL IMPACT

Canada has the world's highest proportion of 25- to 64-year-old college (24%) and university (25%) graduates combined (49%)—higher than Japan, New Zealand, or the United States (CESC, 2009; Statistics Canada, 2009i). Notably, for the first time, more Canadian women than men 25 to 34 years of age now possess a bachelor's degree (62%) or a master's degree (54%), although slightly fewer women than men have doctoral degrees (45%) (Statistics Canada, 2009j). Additionally, a recent study found that 17% of students left high school before graduating, but by age 28, only 6% of those early school leavers still hadn't graduated from high school or entered post-secondary education (CESC, 2010).

There is no longer any doubt about the economic value of post-secondary education, as **Figure 13.9** suggests. Further, although some post-secondary education is better than none, people who succeed in completing a degree have a clear income advantage. Of those Canadians 24 to 64 years of age who have not completed high school, roughly 57% are employed compared with an employment rate of 77% for high school or trade/vocational graduates and 83% for college and university graduates (Statistics Canada, 2009k). Moreover, a review of the HRDC School Leavers Follow-up Survey, which tracked Canadian employment and income trends, found that workers with post-secondary qualifications rated themselves as "very satisfied" with their primary job more

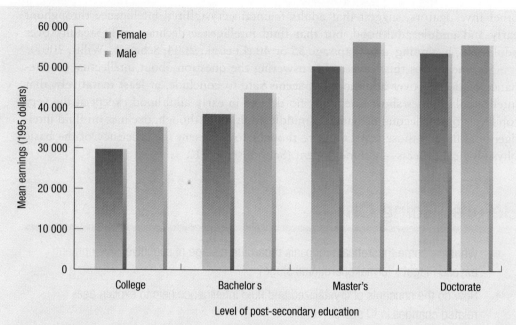

Figure 13.9

Mean earnings of post-secondary graduates in Canada (1990 cohort) 5 years after graduation (1995 dollars). Note: The calculations of the mean earnings omit individuals with reported earnings below $5000. Earnings have been truncated to $143 035.

(*Source:* Human Resources and Social Development Canada. Reproduced with the permission of Her Majesty the Queen in Right of Canada, 2007.)

College and university attendance is associated with developmental advances in both the cognitive and social domains.
(*Photo:* Royalty Free/CORBIS)

often than non-post-secondary graduates (Marquardt, 1998). Interestingly, although there are sex differences in the earnings of men and women at all educational levels, the advantage of post-secondary education seems to be as great for women as for men. (We will return to the issue of sex differences in earnings in **Chapter 14**.)

College and university graduates earn more than nongraduates for a variety of reasons (CESC, 2009; Pascarella & Terenzi, 1991). First, graduates get more promotions and are far less likely than nongraduates to be unemployed for prolonged periods of time. In addition, college and university graduates have higher status. This means that they are more likely than nongraduates to get high-status managerial, technical, and professional positions, and they are viewed by those who make hiring decisions as more desirable employees than are nongraduates. This finding raises the question of whether graduates of post-secondary schools are really different from nongraduates or are simply perceived to be. Longitudinal evidence suggests that the longer a person remains in a post-secondary school, the better her performance on Piaget's formal operational tasks and other measures of abstract reasoning (Lehman & Nisbett, 1990; Pascarella, 1999).

There is also evidence that, during their years of post-secondary school enrolment, students' academic and vocational aspirations change (Sax & Bryant, 2006). For example, a woman may enter university with the goal of becoming a biology teacher but graduate with the intention of going on to medical school. What seems critical about post-secondary education for making such decisions is that college- and university-level classes enable students to make realistic assessments of their academic abilities. Thus, another student who may have intended to be a doctor when he began his first year may soon conclude that becoming a biology teacher is a more realistic, attainable goal, given his performance in university-level classes.

In addition to cognitive and motivational benefits, going to college or university provides students with new socialization opportunities. Many students encounter people from racial or ethnic groups other than their own for the first time in a post-secondary school setting. Advances in moral and social reasoning, as well as increases in the capacity to empathize with others' feelings, are also linked to college or university attendance (Chickering & Reisser, 1993; Pascarella & Terenzi, 1991). However, the relationships among authoritative parenting, academic performance, and social adjustment you have read about so often in earlier chapters hold true for college and university students as well (Wintre & Yaffe, 2000). Thus, students' social experiences prior to entering post-secondary education seem to be critical to their ability to benefit fully from the college or university experience.

Before Going On

- Describe how post-secondary education influences employment.
- List some of the ways in which a post-secondary education affects individual development.

Summary

Physical Functioning

- It is important to distinguish between the unavoidable effects of primary aging and the preventable consequences of secondary aging.

- There is strong evidence that the frontal lobes of the brain do not fully mature until young adulthood. This mirrors the development of cognitive abilities, such as abstract reasoning, logic, planning, and emotional control.

- Adults are at their peak physically between ages 20 and 40; that is, a person has more muscle tissue, more calcium in the bones, better sensory acuity, greater aerobic capacity, and a more efficient immune system.

Health Promotion and Wellness

- Sexually transmitted infections are more common among young adults than among older adults.

- The rate of loss of physical and cognitive abilities varies widely across individuals, in part because of varying health habits. Adults with good health habits have lower risk of death and disease at any age.

- Social support and a sense of personal control also affect rates of disease and death.

- Intimate partner abuse involves cultural beliefs about gender roles, as well as personal variables such as alcohol and drug use.

- Sexual assault usually involves individuals who are acquaintances or intimate partners.

- Rates of mental disorder are higher in early adulthood than in middle adulthood; young adults are more likely to be depressed, anxious, or lonely than are the middle-aged. Early adulthood is the period during which personality disorders and schizophrenia are usually diagnosed.

Cognitive Changes

- Some theorists sugggest that cognitive development goes beyond Piaget's formal operational stage.

- Intellectual decline occurs quite late for well-exercised abilities (crystallized abilities), such as recall of vocabulary, everyday memory use, and normal problem-solving. A measurable decline occurs earlier for so-called fluid abilities.

Post-secondary Education

- Post-secondary education has beneficial effects on both cognitive and social development and career opportunities.

Review Questions

Answers are provided on MyDevelopmentLab in the Course Resources folder.

Physical Functioning

13.1 Which of the following is not an example of primary aging?
   a. decline in ability to detect and discriminate among various smells
   b. reduction in the density of dendrites
   c. lowered fertility of women
   d. obesity

Health Promotion and Wellness

13.2 Which of the following terms represents the belief in one's capacity to master tasks or control one's behaviour or environment?
   a. dialectical thought
   b. external locus of control
   c. postformal thinking
   d. self-efficacy

13.3 Which of the following is not a level of sexual assault under Canadian law?
   a. sexual harassment (e.g., sexual innuendo)
   b. any form of sexual activity with another person without his or her consent
   c. sexual assault with a weapon
   d. aggravated sexual assault (e.g., wounding)

Cognitive Changes

13.4 Which form of intelligence depends heavily on education and experience, such as the skills and knowledge learned while growing up as part of a culture?
   a. contextual
   b. crystallized
   c. dialectical
   d. fluid

Post-secondary Education

13.5 Which statement about post-secondary education in Canada is not true?
   a. Graduates are less likely to be unemployed for long periods of time.
   b. On average, graduates earn higher incomes.
   c. Female graduates are more satisfied with their careers than male graduates.
   d. Graduates perform better on Piagetian formal operational type tasks.

Critical-Thinking Questions

13.6 What reasons could explain why a society's distribution of income makes such a difference to health and mortality?

13.7 Given that only so much money can be spent on health care, what priorities would you recommend for Canadian society? How important is it for you to have a "good quality life" rather than just a "long life"? Do you think it would be wise for the government to reallocate some hospital funds for illness prevention and health promotion programs?

CHAPTER 14

Social and Personality Development in Early Adulthood

In early adulthood, individuals turn away from the preoccupation with self-definition that is characteristic of adolescence and take on a series of roles that involve new relationships with other people. For example, from their wedding day forward, newlyweds will be known both as individuals and as spouses. The bride is also now a daughter-in-law as well as a daughter; the groom has become a son-in-law in addition to continuing to be his parents' son. It is also likely that the two young adults have already taken on occupational roles, and they may also become parents within a few years.

The timing and content of the various adult roles obviously differ from one culture to another, from one cohort to another, and even from one individual to another. For example, the median age for first marriage among women in Canada rose from about 21 in the 1960s and 1970s to 28.5 by 2003. The median age of first marriage for men similarly rose from about 23 to 30.6 during the same time period (Beaujot & Kerr, 2004; HRSDC, 2010a; Statistics Canada, 2007). Marriage remains an important milestone of the young adult years, as evidenced by the fact that only 12% of Canadians aged 25 to 29 do not expect to marry and, in fact, nine in ten do get legally married by age 50 (Crompton, 2005). In addition, most people become parents for the first time in early adulthood. Thus, regardless of variations in timing, adults' social connections become far more complex between ages 20 and 40—through marriage, divorce, parenthood, and career development.

When you finish studying this chapter you will be able to explain the theories of social and personality development in the early adulthood years; summarize the issues involved in establishing intimate relationships as a young adult; discuss the effects of parenthood and other relationships on development in early adulthood; and identify the issues involved in assuming the role of a worker as a young adult. While you read, keep the following questions in mind:

* What are the possible consequences of not establishing an identity before reaching early adulthood?

* What impact does cohabiting before marriage have on later marital satisfaction?

* How much influence does family have on a person's choice of career or job?

THEORIES OF SOCIAL AND PERSONALITY DEVELOPMENT

Psychoanalytic theories view adult development, like development at younger ages, as a result of a struggle between a person's inner thoughts, feelings, and motives and society's demands. Other perspectives provide different views of this period. Integrating ideas from all of them allows us to better understand early adult development.

ERIKSON'S STAGE OF INTIMACY VERSUS ISOLATION

intimacy versus isolation
Erikson's early adulthood stage, in which an individual must find a life partner or supportive friends to avoid social isolation

intimacy
the capacity to engage in a supportive, affectionate relationship without losing one's own sense of self

For Erikson, the central crisis of early adulthood is **intimacy versus isolation**. The young adult must find a life partner, someone outside her own family with whom she can share her life, or face the prospect of being isolated from society. More specifically, **intimacy** is the capacity to engage in a supportive, affectionate relationship without losing one's own sense of self. Intimate partners can share their views and feelings with each other without fearing that the relationship will end. They can also allow each other some degree of independence without feeling threatened.

Social scientists have not done very well at devising theories to explain lovely romantic moments like these. (*Photos:* left, Simon Marcus/Corbis; right, Gallo Images—Hayley Baxter/ Getty Images)

As you might suspect, successful resolution of the intimacy versus isolation stage depends on a good resolution of the identity versus role confusion crisis you read about in **Chapter 12.** Erikson predicted that individuals who reached early adulthood without having established a sense of identity would be incapable of intimacy—that is, such young adults would be, in a sense, predestined to social isolation.

Still, a poor sense of identity is only one barrier to intimacy. Misunderstandings stemming from sex differences in styles of interaction can also get in the way. To women, intimacy is bound up with self-disclosure. Thus, a woman who is involved with a partner who does not reveal much that is personal perceives the relationship as lacking in intimacy. However, most men don't see self-disclosure as essential to intimacy. Consequently, many men are satisfied with relationships that their female partners see as inadequate.

Though many people involved in intimate relationships wish their relationships were better, most adults succeed in establishing some kind of close relationship. Not everyone marries, of course, but many adults develop affectionate, long-lasting friendships that are significant sources of support for them and may, in some cases, serve the same functions as an intimate life partner.

Critical Thinking

Have you experienced periods of loneliness? If so, how do you think the state of your love life at the time contributed to your feelings?

LEVINSON'S LIFE STRUCTURES

Daniel Levinson's concept of *life structure* represents a different approach to adult development (Levinson, 1978, 1990). A **life structure** includes all the roles an individual occupies, all his or her relationships, and the conflicts and balance that exist among them. **Figure 14.1** illustrates how life structures change over the course of adulthood.

Like Erikson, Levinson theorized that each of these periods presents adults with new developmental tasks and conflicts. He believed that individuals respond psychologically to these tasks and conflicts by creating new life structures. Consequently, adults cycle through periods of stability and instability.

As adults enter a period in which a new life structure is required, there is a period of adjustment, which Levinson called the *novice* phase. In the *mid-era* phase, adults become more competent at meeting the new challenges through reassessment and reorganization of the life structure they created during the novice phase. Stability returns in the *culmination* phase, when adults have succeeded in creating a life structure that allows them to manage the demands of the new developmental challenges with more confidence and less distress.

For example, marriage requires a new life structure. Even if the newlyweds have known each other for a very long time or have been living together, they have not known each other in the roles of husband and wife. Moreover, they have never had in-laws. So,

life structure
a key concept in Levinson's theory: the underlying pattern or design of a person's life at a given time, which includes roles, relationships, and behaviour patterns

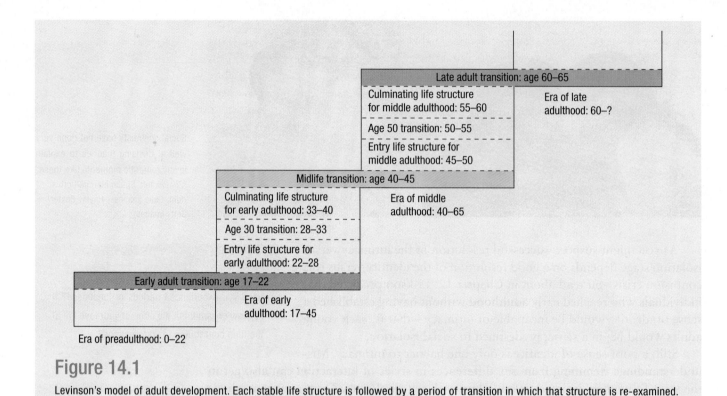

Figure 14.1

Levinson's model of adult development. Each stable life structure is followed by a period of transition in which that structure is re-examined.
(*Source:* Levinson, 1986, adapted from Levinson, 1978. Copyright © 1978 by Daniel J. Levinson. Reprinted by permission of Alfred A. Knopf, Inc.)

young adults who marry acquire a whole new set of relationships. At the same time, they face many new day-to-day, practical issues, such as how finances will be managed, how housekeeping chores will be done, and whose family they will visit on which holidays. As Levinson's theory predicts, newlyweds usually go through a period of adjustment, during which they experience more conflict than before the wedding and after which things are much calmer. The calm comes, as Levinson would put it, when each spouse has achieved a new life structure that is adapted to the demands of marriage.

EMERGING ADULTHOOD

emerging adulthood
the period from the late teens to early 20s when individuals explore options prior to committing to adult roles

Like Levinson, a growing number of developmentalists view the period between ages 17 and 22 as a transitional one. Psychologist Jeffrey Arnett has proposed that the educational, social, and economic demands that modern cultures make in individuals in this age range have given rise to a new developmental period he calls **emerging adulthood**. Arnett defines this phase as the period from the late teens to the early twenties when individuals experiment with options prior to taking on adult roles (Arnett, 2000, 2004). Research examining the self-concepts of men and women in this age group support Arnett's view. His studies and those of other researchers indicate that, at least in Canada and the United States, young people do not tend to think of themselves as having fully attained adulthood until age 25 or so (Galambos, Turner, & Tilton-Weaver, 2005).

Neuroimaging studies have provided some support for the notion that emerging adulthood is a unique period of life. These studies suggest that the parts of the brain that underlie rational decision making, impulse control, and self-regulation mature during these years (Crone, Wendelken, Donohue, van Leijenhorst, & Bunge, 2006; Gotay et al., 2004). As a result, early on in this phase of life, individuals make poorer decisions about matters such as risky behaviours (e.g., unprotected sex) than they do when these brain areas reach full maturity in the early to mid-20s.

The neurological changes of the emerging adult period combine with cultural demands to shape the psychosocial features of this period of development. Researcher Glenn Roisman and his colleagues have hypothesized that emerging adults must address developmental tasks in five domains: academic, friendship, conduct, work, and romantic (Roisman, Masten, Coatsworth, & Tellegen, 2004). Roisman's research suggests that skills within the first three of these domains transfer easily from adolescence to adulthood. Useful study skills (academic) acquired in high school, for instance, are just as helpful in college. Likewise, the skills needed to make and keep friends (friendship) are the same in both periods, and the process of adapting to rules (conduct) is highly similar as well.

By contrast, emerging adults must approach the work and romantic domains differently than they did as adolescents, according to Roisman. Certainly, many teenagers have jobs and are involved in romances. However, the cultural expectations associated with emerging adulthood require them to commit to a career path that will enable them to achieve full economic independence from their families. Likewise, emerging adults must make decisions about the place of long-term romantic relationships in their present and future lives, as well as participate in such relationships. As predicted by his hypothesis, Roisman's findings and those of other researchers suggest that emerging adults experience more adjustment difficulties related to these two domains than they do in the academic, friendship, and conduct domains (Korobov & Thorne, 2006).

Finally, psychologists speculate that the tendency that most emerging adults acquire in their late teens of pushing the limits of their independence from their families contributes to the remarkable neurological changes that occur during this phase. Thus, the road that leads to fulfillment of the developmental tasks outlined by Roisman is often a bumpy one.

Before Going On

- What did Erikson mean when he described early adulthood as a crisis of intimacy versus isolation?

- What is a life structure and how does it change? What are the characteristics of emerging adulthood?

INTIMATE RELATIONSHIPS

Theories help to explain what everyday observations of adults reveal—an intimate relationship forms the secure base from which most young adults move out into the adult world. In many cases, marriage is the context in which such a relationship is established. Marriages in Canada are quickly starting to mirror our sociodemographic diveristy. In addition to the legalization of same-sex marriages, we've seen a dramatic increase in mixed unions among those with differing sociodemographic and cultural characteristics, such as age, education, religion, or ethnic origin (Milan, Maheux & Chui, 2010). The largest shift is in the number of intermarriages of visible minorites, which has increased more than threefold over the past 25 years (see **Figure 14.2**). Also, as society has become more accepting of nonmarital relationships—gay and lesbian partners and cohabiting heterosexual couples—behavioural scientists have had to expand research on intimacy to include these relationships as well. Further, Internet relationships have added a new dimension to courtship and dating (see **Development in the Real World**).

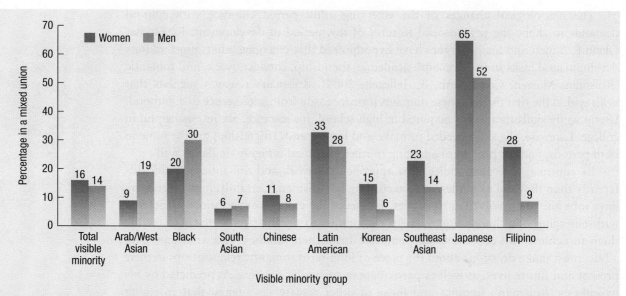

Figure 14.2

This figure shows the proportion of all the married or partnered couples within a visible minority group who are in mixed unions*. Overall, men and women who belong to visible minority groups and are in couples are equally likely to be in mixed union relationships, although there are some differences within specific minority groups.

* Common-law or marital relationships made up of one spouse or partner who is a member of a visible minority group and the other who is not, as well as couples composed of two different visible minority group members

(*Source:* Milan, Maheux, & Chui, 2010. *A portrait of couples in mixed unions* (Statistics Canada—11-008-X.)

 Watch

THEORIES OF MATE SELECTION

What are the characteristics that men and women look for in an intimate partner? Some theorists claim that males and females answer this question differently because of evolutionary pressures. Others argue that the roles that men and women occupy in the cultures in which they live shape their ideas about what kind of person would be an ideal mate.

EVOLUTIONARY THEORIES As you should remember from **Chapter 2**, evolutionary explanations of behaviour focus on survival value. Heterosexual relationships ensure the survival of the species, of course, because they are the context in which conception takes place. However, when choosing a mate, heterosexuals don't simply look for someone of the opposite sex. Instead, mating is a selective process, and evolutionary theorists often cite research on sex differences in mate preferences and mating behaviour in support of their views. Cross-cultural studies conducted over a period of several decades suggest that men prefer physically attractive, younger women, while women look for men whose socioeconomic status is higher than their own, who offer earning potential and stability (Buss, 1999; Crompton, 2005; Schmitt, Shackelford, & Buss, 2001).

The reasons behind men's and women's divergent mating goals are explained by **parental investment theory** (Trivers, 1972). This theory proposes that men value health and availability in their mates and are less selective because their minimum investment in parenting offspring—a single act of sexual intercourse—requires only a few minutes. In contrast, women's minimum investment in childbearing involves nurturing an unborn child in their own bodies for 9 months as well as enduring the potentially physically traumatic experience of giving birth. Given their minimum investments, men seek

PEARSON
mydevelopmentlab
Connect to
MyDevelopmentLab
Play the dating game and try to match the personal ad to its author.
✳ Explore

parental investment theory
the theory that sex differences in mate preferences and mating behaviour are based on the different amounts of time and effort men and women must invest in child-rearing

Development in the Real World

INTERNET RELATIONSHIPS ⊙–Watch

Do you have friends you associate with exclusively online? If so, you have something in common with millions of other North Americans, especially those in younger age groups, 70 to 90% of whom have online-only friends (Parks & Roberts, 1998; Wolak, Mitchell, & Finkelhor, 2002). Many of these friendships blossom into in-person dating relationships. Internet dating has become so popular that many websites are now devoted to matching cyber-daters with others who have similar interests. An *Online Dating for Dummies* book is even available for individuals who want to learn how to start cyber-dating (Silverstein & Lasky, 2003).

The appeal of Internet dating for many seems to be its capacity to allow individuals to bypass conventional relationship "filters": physical attractiveness, socioeconomic status, and age. Through email, bulletin boards, and chat rooms, cyber-daters can get to know each other psychologically, without the distraction of characteristics that are easily discernible in face-to-face relationships. Cross-cultural research also suggests that interpersonal communication on the Internet is viewed as more pleasurable than in-person communication (Chou, Chou, & Tyang, 1998).

Some psychologists speculate that, in contrast to conventional dating, Internet relationships may retard development of social skills in young people, because online relationships don't allow for the kind of immediate behavioural feedback, such as facial expressions, that face-to-face relationships typically provide (Schnarch, 1997). Further, the more time people spend on the Internet, the less time they spend in other kinds of social interactions where such feedback is available (Kraut et al., 1998).

Another major drawback to Internet dating is the possibility of being deceived. A recent poll found that, although three-quarters of

Canadians 25 to 34 years of age believe the Internet makes it easier to meet people, about 80% of Canadians agree that online dating is dangerous because you do not know who you are dealing with (Wyatt, 2004). For some, Internet relationships may be preferable in situations where deception is desirable. For example, married people who want to present themselves to potential partners as single can do so more easily online.

Not surprisingly, extramarital affairs that begin or are carried out exclusively on the Internet are a growing phenomenon.

One Canadian website that caters to customers who want to have extramarital affairs boasts that it has 60 000 client profiles (Durbin, 2003). Historically, an affair has involved sexual contact. But online affairs often lack any face-to-face contact, sexual or otherwise. Still, sexual tension and stimulation are typically a large part of online affairs. While online, partners trade pictures, sometimes sexually provocative ones, and engage in flirtatious sexual banter. Researchers have found that most men and women believe that these kinds of interactions represent sexual infidelity (Whitty, 2003). Consequently, marital counsellors now define an affair as a relationship that involves psychological intimacy, secrecy, and sexual chemistry. This definition helps clients understand that marital fidelity involves something more than just sexual monogamy (Glass, 1998).

No doubt the phenomenon of Internet dating will continue to grow. Thus, there is a need for research that will lead to a better understanding of how online relationships develop and dissolve, as well as how they affect individual development.

to maximize the likelihood of survival of the species by maximizing the number of their offspring; women seek to minimize them because their investment is so much greater.

Further, evolutionary theorists argue that both men and women realize that a truly adaptive approach to child-rearing requires much more than a minimum investment (Buss, 1999). Human offspring cannot raise themselves. Therefore, men value health and youth in their mates not only because these traits suggest fertility, but also because a young, healthy woman is likely to live long enough to raise the children. Similarly, women realize that to be able to nurture children to adulthood, they must have an economic provider so that they will be able to invest the time needed to raise offspring. Consequently, they look for men who seem to be capable of fulfilling these requirements.

As mentioned above, consistent sex differences in mate preferences and mating behaviour have been found across many cultures, and evolutionary theorists suggest that this cross-cultural consistency is strong evidence for a genetic basis for the behaviour. However, these claims take us back to the basic nature-versus-nurture arguments we have examined so many times before. Certainly, these sex differences are consistent, but they could be the result of variations in gender roles that are passed on within cultures.

social role theory
the idea that sex differences in mate preferences and mating behaviour are adaptations to gender roles

SOCIAL ROLE THEORY **Social role theory** provides a different perspective on sex differences in mating (Eagly & Wood, 1999). According to this view, such sex differences are adaptations to gender roles that result from present-day social realities rather than from natural selection pressures that arose in a bygone evolutionary era. To test this hypothesis, social role theorists reanalyzed a very large set of cross-cultural data, a data set produced and interpreted by evolutionary psychologist David Buss in support of parental investment theory (Buss et al., 1990). In their reanalysis, advocates of social role theory found that both men's and women's mate preferences changed as women gained economic power (Eagly & Wood, 1999): Women's emphasis on potential mates' earning power declined, and men's focus on potential mates' domestics skills decreased.

Researchers have also found that higher-educated women with high earning potential prefer to date and marry men whose income potential is higher than their own (Wiederman & Allgeier, 1992). In fact, the more a woman expects to earn herself, the higher are her income requirements in a prospective mate. This study was widely cited by evolutionary theorists as supporting their view that such preferences are genetic and are not influenced by cultural conditions. However, a different perspective on the same study, proposed by social role theorists, led to a different conclusion (Eagly & Wood, 1999). These theorists suggest that many of today's high-income women desire to take time off to have and raise children. To be able to do so without lowering their standard of living substantially, these women require a mate who can earn a lot of money. Thus, social role theorists say, such research findings can be explained by social role theory just as well as by evolutionary theory.

In addition, social role theorists point out that high-income women desire high-income husbands because members of both sexes prefer mates who are like themselves. People are drawn to those who are similar in age, education, social class, ethnic group membership, religion, attitudes, interests, and temperament. Sociologists refer to this tendency as **assortative mating**, or **homogamy**. Further, partnerships based on homogamy are much more likely to endure than are those in which the partners differ markedly (Murstein, 1986).

assortative mating (homogamy)
a sociologist's term for the tendency to mate with someone who has traits similar to one's own

PSYCHOLOGICAL ASPECTS OF MARRIAGE

In predicting who will mate with whom as well as the quality of these relationships, several psychological factors seem to be of importance—attachment, love, and conflict management.

RELATIONSHIP QUALITY While we often discuss differences across sociocultural groups, there is a remarkable amount of agreement across groups about what makes a marriage work (Taylor, Funk, & Clark, 2007). Importantly, a large majority of adults in all groups believe that intimacy issues, that is, faithfulness and a satisfactory sexual relationship, are more important than the material aspects of marriage, such as dividing labour and having an adequate income. Thus, relationship quality appears to be what most people look for to judge whether their marriages are satisfactory.

Many powerful influences on marital success are in place long before a marriage even begins. Each partner brings to the relationship certain skills, resources, and traits that affect the emerging partnership. The personalities of the partners seem to be especially important (Arrindell & Luteijn, 2000; Haring, Hewitt, & Flett, 2003). For example, a high degree of neuroticism in one or both partners usually leads to dissatisfaction and instability in the relationship (Robins, Caspi, & Moffitt, 2000). As well,

Canadian studies show that attitudes toward marriage affect marital stability (Clark & Crompton, 2006). Couples who do not believe that marriage is important for them to be happy are at greater risk of marital breakdown (170% higher risk) than those who believe it is very important.

THE ROLE OF ATTACHMENT Another important factor appears to be the security of each partner's attachment to his or her family of origin. Theorists speculate that the parental attachment relationship contributes to the construction of an internal model of intimate relationships that children bring with them into adulthood and into their marriages (e.g., Crowell & Waters, 1995; Feeney, 1994; Fuller & Fincham, 1995; Hazan & Shaver, 1987; Owens et al., 1995; Rothbard & Shaver, 1994). Research supports this hypothesis. For example, one study found that nearly two-thirds of a sample of about-to-be-married young people showed the same attachment category (secure, dismissing, or preoccupied) when they described their love relationship as when they described their relationship with their parents (Owens et al., 1995). Once the marriage takes place, however, spouses must know when and how to let go of their families of origin in favour of the new family they are in the process of establishing. Research shows that, among newlyweds, the frequency of arguments about in-laws is exceeded only by the frequency of disagreements about financial matters (Oggins, 2003).

THE ROLE OF LOVE Emotional affection contributes to relationship quality as well. The most compelling theory of romantic love comes from Robert Sternberg, who argues that love has three key components: (1) *intimacy*, which includes feelings that promote closeness and connectedness; (2) *passion*, which includes a feeling of intense longing for union with the other person, including sexual union; and (3) *commitment to a particular other*, often over a long period of time (Sternberg, 1987). When these three components are combined in all possible ways, you end up with the seven subvarieties of love listed in **Figure 14.3**. Sternberg's theory suggests that the characteristics of the emotional bond that holds a couple together influence the unique pattern of interaction that develops in each intimate relationship.

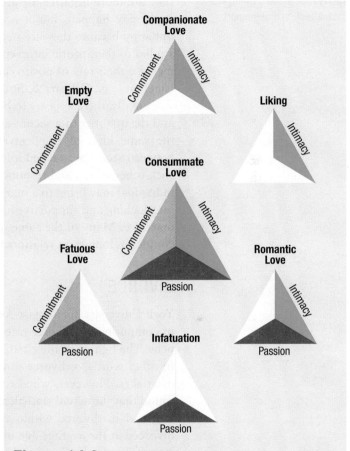

Figure 14.3

Sternberg's theory postulates three components of love: passion, intimacy, and commitment. Relationships can be classified according to which of the three components is present.

CONFLICT MANAGEMENT How a couple manages conflict is also an important predictor of relationship quality. Drawing on a large body of research, psychologists have identified three quite different types of stable, or enduring, marriages (Gottman, 1994). **Validating couples** have disagreements, but the disagreements rarely escalate. Partners express mutual respect, even when they disagree, and listen well to each other. **Volatile couples** squabble a lot, disagree, and don't listen to each other very well when they argue, but they still have more positive than negative encounters, showing high levels

validating couples partners who express mutual respect, even in disagreements, and are good listeners

volatile couples partners who argue a lot and don't listen well, but still have more positive than negative interactions

Connect to MyDevelopmentLab: Check out these 8 cases. Can you match the people to their attachment styles? Can you recognize these styles in people you have dated? Simulate

avoidant couples
partners who agree to disagree
and who minimize conflict by
avoiding each other

hostile/engaged couples
partners who have frequent arguments and lack the balancing
effect of humour and affection

hostile/detached couples
partners who fight regularly,
rarely look at each other, and
lack affection and support

of laughter and affection. **Avoidant couples,** called *conflict minimizers,* don't try to persuade each other; they simply agree to disagree, without apparent rancour, a pattern sometimes described as "devitalized."

Similarly, psychologists find two types of unsuccessful marriages. Like volatile couples, **hostile/engaged couples** have frequent hot arguments, but they lack the balancing effect of humour and affection. **Hostile/detached couples** fight regularly (although the arguments tend to be brief), rarely look at each other, and lack affection and support. In both unsuccessful types, the ratio of negative to positive encounters gets out of balance, and the marriage spirals downward toward dissolution.

What can we conclude about causality here? Do couples become unhappy because they are more negative, or are they more negative because they are already unhappy? Both may happen, but it appears that it is more common for couples to become unhappy because they are negative. The best support for this conclusion comes from studies of therapeutic interventions with unhappy couples: Couples who are trained to increase their rate of positive interactions typically show increases in their marital satisfaction (e.g., O'Leary & Smith, 1991).

Finally, there appears to be a parallel between the qualities of a successful marriage and the qualities of a secure attachment. Adults in good marriages have a high level of the same kind of responsiveness to the other's signals that developmentalists see between securely attached infants and their parents. Satisfied partners take turns, read each other's cues, and respond positively. Whatever internal model of attachment each individual may bring to a marriage, the ability of the partners to create such a mutually interlocking and supportive interactive system seems to be critical to the survival of the marriage. Many of the same qualities characterize both heterosexual and homosexual couples in long-term relationships.

DIVORCE

York University sociologist Anne-Marie Ambert (2002) describes how different ways of computing the divorce rate can distort our ideas about how frequently divorce happens. The figure usually cited, 50%, is the ratio of divorces to marriages in a given year. In other words, a divorce rate of 50% means that there is one divorce for every two marriages. However, when researchers followed married couples longitudinally, they found that the actual statistical likelihood is that roughly 38% of marriages in Canada will end in divorce within 30 years of marriage (Statistics Canada, 2004a). Men divorced at the average age of 43.1 years and women at the age of 40.5. Although the rate of divorce had peaked before the fifth wedding anniversary, the average marriage lasted 14.2 years.

PSYCHOLOGICAL EFFECTS At a psychological level, divorce is clearly a major stressor. It is associated with increases in mental health problems, especially depression. For example, results from a National Population Health Survey of Canadian couples between ages 20 and 64 found that men who experienced marital breakup were six times more likely to exhibit symptoms of depression within 2 years of a breakup than men who remained married (Rotermann, 2007). Women who divorced were three and a half times more likely to experience depression in this time period than those who remained married. Even after controlling for other factors that are associated with depression, such as the effects of changes in income and employment status, social support, presence of children, as well as education, age, and a history of depression, the rates of depression remained significant for both sexes—men were still three times more likely to become depressed following marital breakdown and women were two and a half times more likely.

ECONOMIC EFFECTS The psychological effects of divorce are often significantly worsened by serious economic effects, particularly for women. Because most men have had continuous work histories, they commonly leave a marriage with far greater earning power than do women. Women not only typically lack high earning capacity, but also usually retain custody of any children, with attendant costs. Several longitudinal studies in Canada, the United States, and European countries show that divorced men slightly improve in their economic position, while divorced women are strongly adversely affected (Ambert, 2002). For example, men's incomes were above the average Canadian household income following a breakup, whereas women's incomes declined to below average (Rotermann, 2007). Furthermore, this negative economic effect does not disappear quickly—and for some women, it doesn't disappear at all. Such a long-term economic loss from divorce is especially likely for working-class women or those with relatively low levels of education, especially if they do not remarry. Women who were earning above-average incomes before their divorce are more likely to recover financially, even if they do not remarry (Ambert, 2002).

EFFECTS ON LIFE PATHWAYS For many adults, divorce also affects the sequence and timing of family roles. Even though divorced women with children are less likely to remarry than those who are child-free, remarriage expands the number of years of child-rearing for many divorced women (Lampard & Peggs, 1999; Norton, 1983). The total number of years of child-rearing may also be significantly increased for divorced men, especially for those who remarry younger women with young children. One effect of this change in timing is to reduce the number of years a remarried couple may have between the departure of the last child and the time when their elderly parents may need economic or physical assistance.

COHABITING HETEROSEXUAL COUPLES

Given today's high divorce rate, many young people want to be sure the person they marry is someone they want to be with for the rest of their lives. Thus, today it is relatively common for couples to live together before marriage. In fact, the latest Canadian census shows that almost half of all 20- to 29-year-old couples who lived together were not married (48%) (Turcotte, 2003). It was also found that, given the opportunity, the large majority of young adults would live common-law (Milan, 2003). Many such couples conceive of cohabitation as a final "filter," a sort of "test" before marriage: Can we really get along together? Are we sexually compatible? In Levinson's terms, they believe that cohabitation will lessen the likelihood of divorce because it will provide them with an opportunity to build a life structure they can use in adapting to marriage. Interestingly, the great bulk of the evidence shows exactly the opposite.

Studies in Canada, the United States, and several European countries show that those who cohabit before marriage are less satisfied with their subsequent marriages. Research has also shown that this relationship exists across historical cohorts. That is, couples who cohabited prior to marriage during the 1980s and 1990s display the same rates of marital dissatisfaction and divorce as those who cohabited in the 1960s and 1970s (Dush, Cohan, & Amato, 2003). In Canada, the divorce rate for those who lived together before marriage is double that of those who did not cohabitate prior to marriage (Ambert, 2002, 2005; Clark & Crompton, 2006). The most likely explanation of this surprising set of findings is twofold.

First, cohabiting leads to development of a life structure for cohabiting, not for marriage, because the two relationships are fundamentally different (Ambert, 2003, 2005). For example, moving in together is seldom accompanied by the public announcements and celebratory fanfare that are associated with marriage (Lindsay,

2000). Further, cohabiting couples regard their relationships as ambiguous in nature—they may or may not be permanent. In contrast, marriage involves a public declaration of lifelong commitment to another person. Thus, when a cohabiting couple marries, the social and psychological aspects of the relationship change, because of the deepened sense of commitment and the expectation that the relationship is permanent.

Second, adults who choose to live together before marriage are different, in key ways, from those who marry without cohabiting (Ambert, 2003, 2005). For example, cohabiting couples are less homogamous (less similar) than married couples (Blackwell & Lichter, 2000). Couples in which partners are of different races, religions, educational levels, and socioeconomic statuses, are more likely to cohabit prior to marriage. Moreover, a closer look reveals that cohabiters are more than twice as likely to have sexual affairs (Treas & Geisen, 2000), are more likely to be unhappy or depressed (Brown, 2000), and have an increased risk for domestic violence (Brownridge & Halli, 2001; Salari & Baldwin, 2002; Shackelford, 2001).

Other developmentalists believe that these findings result from the tendency of researchers to lump all kinds of cohabiting couples into a single category. This kind of aggregation, they say, may distort a study's findings because it ignores that there are two rather distinct types of heterosexual cohabitation (Kline, Stanley, Markman, & Olmos-Gallo, 2004). One type involves couples who are fully committed to a future marriage. In most cases, these couples have firm wedding plans and choose to live together for convenience or for economic reasons. In the second type of cohabitation, the relationship between the two partners is more ambiguous. Many such couples regard future marriage as a possibility but also believe that the relationship may be temporary.

Sociologist Jay Teachman points out that one important difference between these two types of couples is previous cohabitation and premarital sexual experience (Teachman, 2003). His findings are derived from the National Survey of Family Growth, a longitudinal study that focuses on women's family transitions. Teachman's analyses of these data show that married women whose premarital cohabitation and sexual experience was limited to their future husband are no more likely to divorce than women who did not cohabit prior to marriage. Thus, says Teachman, the critical variable at work in the cohabitation–divorce relationship is the fact that a large proportion of cohabitants have been in prior cohabiting or sexual relationships.

Researchers have also identified interaction differences between cohabitants with firm intentions to marry and those whose future plans are less clear. For instance, cohabiting men who intend to marry their partners do more housework than men who are not so committed (Ciabittari, 2004). This difference may be the result of communication patterns that distinguish cohabiting women of the two types. In other words, cohabiting women who intend to marry their partners may do a better job of communicating their expectations about a fair division of labour. Another important finding is that cohabiting couples who are clear about their intentions to marry are happier during the period of cohabitation than couples whose future plans are more ambiguous (Brown, 2003). Thus, looking at the kinds of interaction patterns that exist among cohabitants who intend to marry helps us understand why, after marriage, they differ little in satisfaction and stability from those who do not cohabit until after marriage (Brown, 2003; Kline et al., 2004; Teachman, 2003).

GAY AND LESBIAN COUPLES

In 2006, for the first time, Canadian census data included same-sex couples. This census indicated that about one in five couples are married (7 500), while the majority are in common-law relationships (37 885) (Statistics Canada, 2008e). One factor that appears to be just as important in same-sex unions as it is in opposite-sex relationships is attachment security (Elizur & Mintzer, 2003). As is true for heterosexual couples, neuroticism in one or both partners is related to relationship quality and length (Kurdek, 1997, 2000). Moreover, homosexual couples argue about the same things as heterosexual couples, and gay/lesbian relationships are of higher quality if the two partners share similar backgrounds and are equally committed to the relationship (Krueger-Lebus & Rauchfleisch, 1999; Kurdek, 1997; Peplau, 1991; Solomon, Rothblum, & Balsam, 2004).

Despite these similarities, there are important differences between the two kinds of relationships. For one, gay and lesbian partners are often more dependent on each other for social support than men and women in heterosexual partnerships are. This happens because many homosexuals are isolated from their families, primarily because of their families' disapproval of their sexual orientation (Hill, 1999). Thus, many gays and lesbians build families of choice for themselves. These social networks typically consist of a stable partner and a circle of close friends. They provide for gay and lesbian couples the kind of social support that most heterosexual adults receive from their families of origin (Kurdek, 2003; Weeks, 2004).

Another difference is in the nature of the power relation between the partners. Homosexual couples seem to be more egalitarian than heterosexual couples, with less specific role prescriptions. It is quite uncommon in homosexual couples for one partner to occupy a "male" role and the other a "female" role. Instead, power and tasks are more equally divided. However, some research indicates that this is more true of lesbian couples, among whom equality of roles is frequently a strong philosophical ideal, than of gay couples (Kurdek, 1995).

Finally, homosexual and heterosexual partners appear to differ with regard to expectations for monogamy. Both men and women in heterosexual relationships overwhelmingly state that they expect their partners to be sexually faithful to them. Similarly, lesbian partners often insist on sexual exclusivity. However, gay men, even those in long-term partnerships, do not necessarily regard sexual fidelity as essential to their relationships. Couples therapists report that monogamy is important to gay men, but it is an issue that is considered to be negotiable by most (LaSala, 2001).

SINGLEHOOD

Many adults are single by preference. The impact of singlehood on an adult's life often depends on the reason for his or her relationship status. One Canadian study found that mature singles who do not intend to marry have less conventional views about the importance of love, marriage, and family: They don't value being part of a couple or a family as highly as singles who do expect to marry (Crompton, 2005). Continuous singlehood is also associated with greater individual autonomy and capacity for personal growth than is a life path that has included divorce or loss of a spouse (Marks & Lamberg, 1998). Another important point to keep in mind is that many single adults participate in intimate relationships that do not involve either cohabitation or marriage. These people show up in surveys and census reports as "single" but might be better described as "partnered." Even among singles who have an intimate partner, though, close relationships with their families of origin are more likely to be an important source of psychological and emotional intimacy than they are for individuals who are married or cohabiting (Allen & Pickett, 1987; Campbell, Connidis, & Davies, 1999). Further, close friends are likely to play a more prominent role in the social networks of singles than of marrieds or cohabitants.

The number of years an individual has been single appears to be an important factor in the influence of singlehood on his development. Developmentalists have found that there is a transition time during which long-term singles move from thinking of themselves as people who will be married or partnered in the future to viewing themselves as single by choice (Davies, 2003). At this point, singlehood becomes an important, positive component of the individual's identity. This kind of self-affirmation may protect singles from some of the negative health consequences associated with singlehood that you read about earlier.

Before Going On

- How can evolutionary and social role theories contribute to an understandanding of partner selection?
- In what ways do intimate relationships change during early adulthood? How do marriage and divorce, cohabitation, same-sex couples, and singlehood have an impact on early adult life?

PARENTHOOD AND OTHER RELATIONSHIPS

The second major new role typically acquired in early adulthood is that of "parent." The transition into this new role brings with it unique stresses, and, to make matters more complicated, it usually happens at a time when most other social relationships are in transition as well.

 Watch

PARENTHOOD

Most parents would agree that parenthood is a remarkably mixed emotional experience. On one hand, the desire to become a parent is, for many adults, extremely strong; thus, fulfilling that desire is an emotional high point for most. On the other hand, parenthood results in a number of stressful changes.

For most couples in long-term relationships, especially those who are married, having a child is an important goal.
(*Photo:* JUPITERIMAGES/Thinkstock/ Alamy)

THE DESIRE TO BECOME A PARENT In Canada, the vast majority of both young men and young women expect to have at least one child; only about 7 to 8% of 20- to 34-year-olds report that they do not expect to have children (Stobert & Kemeny, 2003). Not surprisingly, a major Canadian survey found that most parents (92%) believe that parenting is the most important thing they could do and most individuals enjoyed the role of being a parent (94%) (Oldershaw, 2002). The percentage of men who strongly feel they want to become parents and view parenting as a life-enriching experience is actually greater than the percentage of women who feel this way (Horowitz, McLaughlin, & White, 1998; Muzi, 2000). Furthermore, most expectant fathers become emotionally attached to their unborn children during the third trimester of pregnancy and eagerly anticipate the birth (White, Wilson, Elander, & Persson, 1999).

THE TRANSITION EXPERIENCE Even when new mothers are emotionally healthy, the transition to parenthood can be very stressful. New parents may argue about child-rearing philosophy as well as how, when, where, and by whom child-care chores should be done (Reichle & Gefke, 1998). Both parents are usually also physically exhausted, perhaps even seriously sleep-deprived, because their newborn keeps them up for much of the night. Predictably, new parents report that they have much less time for each other—less time for conversation, for sex, for simple affection, or even for doing routine chores together (Belsky, Lang, & Rovine, 1985).

Some cultures have developed ritualized rites of passage for this important transition, which can help new parents manage stress. For example, in Hispanic cultures, *la cuarenta* is a period of 40 days following the birth of a child, during which fathers are expected to take on typically feminine tasks such as housework. Extended family members are also expected to help out. Researchers have found that Hispanic couples who observe *la cuarenta* adjust to parenthood more easily than those who do not (Niska, Snyder, & Lia-Hoagberg, 1998).

POSTPARTUM DEPRESSION Between 10 and 25% of new mothers experience a severe mood disturbance called *postpartum depression (PPD)*—a disorder found among mothers in Canada (Pearce, 1997) as well as in many countries around the world, including Australia, China, Sweden, Scotland, and the United States (Guo, 1993; Lundh & Gyllang, 1993; Oates et al., 2004; Webster, Thompson, Mitchell, & Werry, 1994). Women who develop PPD suffer from feelings of sadness for several weeks after the baby's birth. Most cases of PPD persist only a few weeks, but 1 to 2% of women suffer for a year or more. Moreover, more than 80% of women who suffer from PPD after their first pregnancy experience the disorder again following subsequent deliveries (Garfield, Kent, Paykel, Creighton, & Jacobson, 2004).

Women whose bodies produce unusually high levels of steroid hormones toward the end of pregnancy are more likely to develop postpartum depression (Harris et al., 1994). The disorder is also more common in women whose pregnancies were unplanned, who were anxious about the pregnancy, or whose partners were unsupportive (O'Hara, Schlechte, Lewis, & Varner, 1992). The presence of major life stressors during pregnancy or immediately after the baby's birth—such as a move to a new home, the death of someone close, or job loss—also increases the risk of PPD (Swendsen & Mazure, 2000). Fatigue and difficult temperament in the infant can also contribute to PPD (Fisher, Feekery, & Rowe-Murray, 2002).

The best predictor of postpartum depression is depression during pregnancy (Da Costa, Larouche, Dritsa, & Brender, 2000). Thus, many cases of PPD can probably be prevented by training health professionals to recognize depression in pregnant women. Similarly, family members of women with absent or unsupportive partners can help them locate agencies that provide material and social support.

DEVELOPMENTAL IMPACT OF PARENTHOOD Despite its inherent stressfulness, the transition to parenthood is associated with positive behaviour change. Sensation-seeking and risky behaviour decline considerably when young adults become parents (Arnett, 1998). All the same, marital satisfaction tends to decline after the birth of a child. The general pattern is that such satisfaction is at its peak before the birth of the first child, after which it drops and remains at a lower level until the last child leaves home. **Figure 14.4** illustrates the pattern, based on results from an early and widely quoted study (Rollins & Feldman, 1970). The best-documented portion of this curvilinear pattern is the drop in marital satisfaction after the birth of the first child, for which there is both longitudinal and cross-sectional evidence. More recent studies suggest that the decline in marital satisfaction is characteristic of contemporary cohorts of

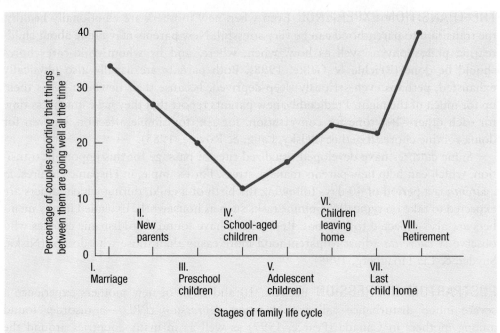

Figure 14.4

This pattern of change in marital satisfaction over the stages of the family life cycle is one of the best-documented findings in family sociology research.

(*Source:* Rollins & Feldman, 1970, Tables 2 and 3, p. 24. Copyright 1970 by the National Council on Family Relations.)

new parents as well, and researchers have found a pattern of marital satisfaction similar to that reported by Rollins and Feldman across a variety of cultures (Ahmad & Najam, 1998; Gloger-Tippelt & Huerkamp, 1998; Twenge, Campbell, & Foster, 2003). Nevertheless, studies that examine the relationship between marital satisfaction and parenthood in a more complex fashion suggest that it is neither universal nor inevitable. Longitudinal studies show that the length of time that a couple has been together before having their first child, the amount of education they have, and the number of children that they have are all positively related to marital satisfaction (Jose & Alfons, 2007).

A number of variables contribute to just how dissatisfied a couple may become. One important factor is achieving a balance between work and family (Marshall, 2006)—a success factor that Canadian workers valued even more than a range of other factors, such as job challenges, levels of responsibility, or salary (Ipsos-Reid/Globe and Mail, 2003). However, achieving balance seems to be an ever-elusive goal. General Social Survey (GSS) data show that Canadians have less time to spend with their families as their number of hours of paid work increases (Turcotte, 2007). In fact, the amount of time paid workers spend with their families has decreased significantly over the past two decades, down from 250 minutes a day on average in 1986 to 209 minutes in 2005 (Marshall, 2006; Turcotte, 2007).

Some developmentalists suggest that the relative effectiveness of the coping strategies couples use to adjust to their new roles determines how their relationship satisfaction will be affected by the birth of a child (Belsky & Hsieh, 1998). For example, couples who have established effective conflict-resolution strategies before the birth of a child experience less loss of satisfaction (Cox, Paley, Burchinal, & Payne, 1999; Lindahl, Clements, & Markman, 1997). The quality of new parents' attachment to their own parents also predicts how much their relationship satisfaction declines after the birth of a child (Gloger-Tippelt & Huerkamp, 1998). In fact, young adults with anxious or avoidant attachments to their own parents expect the transition to parenthood to be a negative experience more often than do those whose attachments are secure (Rholes, Simpson, Blakely, Lanigan, & Allen, 1997).

It's important to keep in mind, though, that new parents who are married or cohabiting experience a much smaller decline in overall life satisfaction than new single parents, whose lives are far more complicated and stressful (Lee, Law, & Tam, 1999). Likewise, single parents are more likely to suffer from health problems and are less likely to advance to management positions at work (Khlat, Sermet, & Le Pape, 2000; Tharenou, 1999). Instead of focusing on declines in relationship satisfaction, some developmentalists suggest that more attention should be paid to the consistent finding that having a parenting partner—especially one to whom one is married—is a significant protective factor in managing the stressful transition to parenthood.

LIFE WITHOUT CHILDREN Like parenthood, having no children affects the shape of an adult's life, both within marriage and in employment patterns. To begin with, those Canadians who place less value on the importance of marriage or being part of a couple are more likely to expect to remain without children than those who do value committed relationships (Stobert & Kemeny, 2003). For couples who marry and remain without children, marital satisfaction fluctuates little over time. However, as is true of all couples, those without children are also likely to experience some drop in satisfaction in the first months and years of marriage. But over the range of adult life, the curve of marital satisfaction for couples without children is much flatter than the one shown in **Figure 14.4** (Houseknecht, 1987; Somers, 1993). Couples in their 20s and 30s without children consistently report higher cohesion in their marriages than do couples with children.

Not having children affects employment patterns, especially for women. Women without children are much more likely to have full-time, continuous careers (Abma & Martinez, 2006; Zhang, 2009). A recent study comparing Canadian women with and without children found some sizable earnings differences (Zhang, 2009). This so-called **motherhood earnings gap** shows how much the earnings of women with children fall below those of women without childen. For example, at any given age, women with children averaged roughly 12% lower hourly earnings than their counterparts without children and this gap increases with the number of children. As well, the earnings gap was larger yet for mothers with higher education than those with no more than a high school education. Thus, raising children affects not only marital satisfaction, but also income.

motherhood earnings gap
a measure showing how much the earnings of women with children are below those of women without childen

SOCIAL NETWORKS

Creating a partnership may be the most central task of the process of achieving intimacy, but it is certainly not the only reflection of that basic process. In early adult life, each of us creates a social network made up of family and friends as well as our life partner.

FAMILY If you ask children and adults "Who is the person you don't like to be away from?" or "Who is the person you know will always be there for you?" children and teenagers most often list their parents, while adults most often name their spouses or partners and almost never mention their parents (Hazan, Hutt, Sturgeon, & Bricker, 1991). However, most adults feel emotionally close to their parents and see or talk to them regularly (Belsky, Jaffee, Caspi, Moffitt, & Silva, 2003; Campbell, Connidis, & Davies, 1999).

> ## Critical Thinking
>
> List all the people in your current social network. What is the relative importance of family and friends for you?

Not surprisingly, the amount and kind of contact an adult has with kin is strongly influenced by proximity. Adults who live within 2 hours of their parents and siblings see them far more often than those who live farther away. But distance does not prevent a parent or sibling from being part of an individual adult's social network. These relationships can provide support in times of need, even if physical contact is infrequent.

There are also important cultural differences in young adults' involvement with their families. For example, one study compared the development of social independence among Australian, Canadian, and Japanese children and adults (Takata, 1999). In all three cultures, the sense of being independent from parents and family increased with age. However, Australian and Canadian participants appeared to develop self-perceptions of independence earlier in life. Consequently, Japanese young adults reported a greater sense of connectedness to their families of origin than either Australian or Canadian young adults.

FRIENDS Friends, too, are important members of a social network, even those with whom young adults interact exclusively online (Sherman, Lansford, & Volling, 2006). We choose our friends as we choose our partners, from among those who are similar to us in education, social class, interests, family background, or family life-cycle stage. Cross-sex friendships are more common among adults than they are among 10-year-olds, but they are still outnumbered by same-sex friendships. Young adults' friends are also overwhelmingly drawn from their own age group. Beyond this basic requirement of similarity, close friendship seems to rest on mutual openness and personal disclosure.

Because of the centrality of the task of intimacy in early adulthood, most researchers and theorists assume that young adults have more friends than do middle-aged or older adults. Research has offered some hints of support for this idea, but it has been a difficult assumption to test properly. Developmentalists lack longitudinal data and do not agree on definitions of friendship, which makes combining data across studies very difficult.

SEX DIFFERENCES IN RELATIONSHIP STYLES As in childhood, there are very striking sex differences in both the number and quality of friendships in the social network of young adults (Radmacher & Azmitia, 2006). Women have more close friends, and their friendships are more intimate, with more self-disclosure and more exchange of emotional support. Young men's friendships, like those of boys and older men, are more competitive. Male friends are less likely to agree with each other or to ask for or provide emotional support to each other (Dindia & Allen, 1992; Maccoby, 1990). Adult women friends talk to each other; adult men friends do things together.

Another facet of this difference is that women most often fill the role of **kin-keeper** (Moen, 1996; Salari & Zhang, 2006). They write the letters, make the phone calls, arrange the gatherings of family and friends. (In later stages of adult life, it is also the women who are likely to take on the role of caring for aging parents—a pattern you'll learn more about in **Chapter 16**.)

Taken together, all this means that women have a much larger "relationship role" than men do. In virtually all cultures, it is part of the female role to be responsible for maintaining the emotional aspects of relationships—with a spouse, with friends, with family, and, of course, with children.

kin-keeper
a family role, usually occupied by a woman, which includes responsibility for maintaining family and friendship relationships

Before Going On

- Describe the transition to parenthood and the developmental effects of becoming a parent and of remaining child-free.
- How are family and friends important to young adults?

THE ROLE OF WORKER

In addition to the roles of "spouse" or "partner" and of "parent," a large percentage of young adults are simultaneously filling yet another major and relatively new role, that of "worker." Most young people need to take on this role to support themselves economically, but that is not the only reason for the centrality of this role. Satisfying work also seems to be an important ingredient in mental health and life satisfaction, for both men and women (Meeus, Dekovic, & Iedema, 1997; Tait, Padgett, & Baldwin, 1989). Before looking at what developmentalists know about career steps and sequences in early adulthood, let's examine how young people choose an occupation.

CHOOSING AN OCCUPATION

As you might imagine, a multitude of factors influence a young person's choice of job or career: family background and values; gender; and personality (in addition to other factors such as intelligence and education, ethnic group, self-concept, and school performance).

FAMILY INFLUENCES Typically, young people tend to choose occupations at the same general social class level as their parents, although this is less true today than it was in decades past (Biblarz, Bengtson, & Bucur, 1996). In part, this effect is perpetuated through the medium of education. Canadian parents who have higher-than-average levels of education typically influence the aspirations and preparedness of their children for post-secondary education over the course of their children's lives (Finnie, Mueller, Sweetman, & Usher, 2010). This ongoing influence engenders motivation, engagement with school, good study habits, and academic success in high school that increases a student's preparedness for, and decision to attend, post-secondary education. Higher education, in turn, makes it more likely that the young person will qualify for middle-class jobs, for which a post-secondary education is frequently required.

Families also influence job choices through their value systems (Jacobs, Chin, & Bleeker, 2006). In particular, parents who value academic and professional achievement are far more likely to have children who attend a post-secondary school and choose professional-level jobs. This effect is not just social-class difference in disguise. Among working-class families, the children of those who place the strongest emphasis on achievement are most likely to move up into middle-class jobs (Finnie et al, 2010; Gustafson & Magnusson, 1991). Further, families whose career aspirations for their children are high tend to produce young adults who are more intrinsically motivated as employees (Cotton, Bynum, & Madhere, 1997).

Similarly, parental moral beliefs influence young adults' willingness to enter various occupations (Bregman & Killen, 1999). For example, young adults whose families believe that drinking alcohol is morally wrong are unlikely to choose alcohol-related occupations such as bartending, waiting tables in a restaurant where liquor is served, or working at a liquor store.

GENDER Canadian researchers Thiessen and Nickerson (2001) contend that "the nature and extent of women's and men's educational and labour market activities evolves continuously" (p. 10). Academically, for instance, more women than men are now enrolled in all the major fields of study except for architecture and engineering; mathematics and computer sciences; and personal, protective and transportation services (Parsons & McMullen, 2009). Nonetheless, specific job selection remains strongly affected by gender. Despite the women's movement and despite the vast increase in the proportion of women working, about 70% of women occupy traditionally female occupations, such as nursing, teaching, and clerical (Cooke-Reynolds & Zukewich, 2004; McMullen et al., 2010; Statistics Canada, 2004b). However, the trend is shifting—Canadian women are increasing their presence in traditionally male-dominated jobs, such as medicine, dentistry, and senior managagement, as well as doubling their ranks in agriculture and manufacturing (see **Figure 14.5**) (Cooke-Reynolds & Zukewich, 2004; McMullen et al., 2010). It is not surprising that, in Canada, the gap between women's income and that of their male counterparts has been decreasing steadily. In 2007, the median earnings of women working full-time was roughly three-quarters of men's wages (Phillips, 2010).

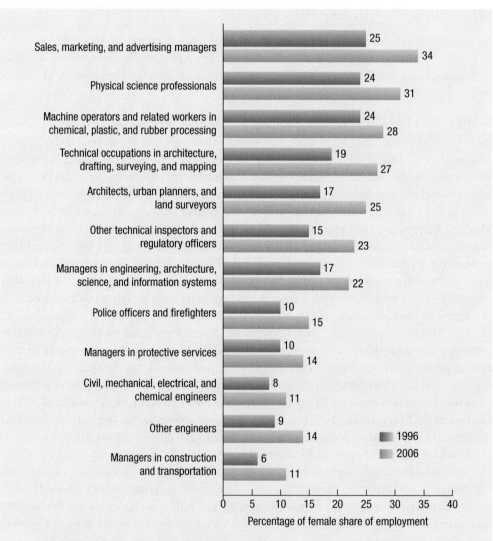

Figure 14.5

In Canada, the proportion of women in most occupational fields has been steadily increasing, although many occupations still reflect historical gender roles.

(*Source:* McMullen, K., Gilmore, J., & Le Petit, C., 2010. Occupations and Fields of Study. (Statistics Canada—81-004-X). Chart 3. *Education Matters: Insights on Education, Learning and Training in Canada* April 29, 7(1). Retrieved from http://www.statcan.gc.ca/pub/81-004-x/2010001/article/11151-eng.htm)

TABLE 14.1	Holland's Personality Types and Work Preferences
Type	**Personality and Work Preferences**
Realistic	Aggressive, masculine, physically strong, often with low verbal or interpersonal skills; prefer mechanical activities and tool use, choosing jobs such as mechanic, electrician, or surveyor
Investigative	Oriented toward thinking (particularly abstract thinking), organizing, and planning; prefer ambiguous, challenging tasks but are low in social skills; are often scientists or engineers
Artistic	Social; prefer unstructured, highly individual activity; are often artists
Social	Extraverts; people-oriented, sociable, and attention-seeking; avoid intellectual activity and dislike highly ordered activity; prefer to work with people, choosing service jobs such as nursing and education
Enterprising	Highly verbal and dominating; enjoy organizing and directing others; are persuasive and strong leaders, often choosing careers in sales
Conventional	Prefer structured activities and subordinate roles; like clear guidelines and see themselves as accurate and precise; may choose occupations such as bookkeeping or filing

(*Source:* Holland, 1973, 1992.)

Children learn the cultural definitions of "appropriate" jobs for men and women in their early years, just as they learn all the other aspects of sex roles. So it is not surprising that most young women and men choose jobs that fit these sex-role designations. Nonstereotypical job choices are much more common among young people who see themselves as androgynous or whose parents have less conventional occupations. For instance, young women who choose traditionally masculine careers are more likely to have a mother who has had a long-term career and are more likely to define themselves either as androgynous or as masculine (Betz & Fitzgerald, 1987; Fitzpatrick & Silverman, 1989).

PERSONALITY   Another important influence on job choice is the young adult's personality. John Holland, whose work has been the most influential in this area, proposes six basic personality types, summarized in **Table 14.1** (Holland, 1973, 1992). Holland's basic hypothesis is that each of us tends to choose and be most successful at an occupation that matches our personality.

Research in non-Western as well as Western cultures has generally supported Holland's proposal (Spokane & Cruza-Guet, 2005). Ministers, for example, generally score highest on Holland's social scale, engineers highest on the investigative scale, car salespeople on the enterprising scale, and career army officers on the realistic scale.

People whose personalities match their jobs are also more likely to be satisfied with their work. Moreover, obtaining a personality assessment prior to making an occupational choice is associated with greater feelings of confidence about the decision (Francis-Smythe & Smith, 1997).

CAREER DEVELOPMENT

Once the job or career has been chosen, what kinds of experiences do young adults have in their work life? **Career development** is the process of adapting to the workplace,

Parents who have higher-than-average levels of education themselves are more likely to encourage their children to pursue post-secondary studies.
(*Photo:* Fotosearch/PhotoDisc)

career development
the process of adapting to the workplace, managing career transitions, and pursuing goals through employment

managing career transitions, and pursuing personal goals through employment. Psychologists who study career development focus on issues such as the phases of workplace adaptation and job satisfaction.

SUPER'S STAGE OF CAREER DEVELOPMENT Psychologist Donald Super claims that the roots of the career development process are found in infancy. Between birth and age 14, Super says, we are in the *growth stage*, a period during which we learn about our abilities and interests. Next comes the *exploratory stage*, roughly from age 15 to 24. In this stage, the young person must decide on a job or a career, and he searches for a fit between his interests and personality and the jobs available. The whole process involves a good deal of trial and error as well as luck or chance. Perhaps because many of the jobs available to those in this age range are not terribly challenging and because many young adults have not yet found the right fit, job changes are at their peak during this period.

Next comes the *establishment stage* (also called the *stabilization stage*), roughly from age 25 to 45. Having chosen an occupation, the young person must learn the ropes and begin to move through the early steps in some career ladder as he masters the needed skills, perhaps with a mentor's help. In this period, the worker also focuses on fulfilling whatever aspirations or goals he may have set for himself. In Levinson's terms, he tries to fulfill his dream. The young scientist pushes himself to make an important discovery; the young attorney strives to become a partner; the young business executive tries to move as far up the ladder as he can; the young blue-collar worker may aim for job stability or promotion to foreman. Most promotions occur in these years.

The final phase of career development in Super's model is the *maintenance stage*. It begins around age 45 and ends at retirement. The primary goals of the maintenance stage are to protect and maintain the gains that were made during the establishment stage. To accomplish these goals, older workers must keep up with new developments in their fields. They must also acquire new skills to avoid becoming obsolete. Moreover, individuals in the maintenance phase must make preparations for retirement.

Super's model is useful for describing the challenges that individuals face in the various phases of their careers. However, to be validly applied in today's rapidly changing economy, Super's stages must be thought of independently from the ages to which he originally linked them (Super, 1990). This is necessary because of the frequency with which adults now change careers or move from one workplace to another. Thus, regardless of age, a person who makes a major career change probably exhibits the characteristics of Super's exploratory stage prior to doing so and experiences some of the features of his establishment and maintenance phases in the years following the change.

JOB SATISFACTION Early studies of job satisfaction found that job satisfaction was at its lowest in early adulthood and rose steadily until retirement (Glenn & Weaver, 1985). More recently, however, researchers have found that satisfaction is lowest at mid-career, usually toward the end of the early adulthood period (Fullerton & Wallace, 2007). This trend is attributable to changes in workers' perceptions of job security. In the past, security increased with time on the job. Nowadays, job security is elusive because of the speed with which job requirements and employers' priorities shift. Thus, workers who have been on the job for some time are no longer assured of having greater security, higher incomes, or higher status positions than beginning workers do.

Research also suggests that a number of important variables contribute to job satisfaction in young adults. As with almost every life situation, individual personality traits, such as neuroticism, affect job satisfaction (Judge, Bono, & Locke, 2000; Wright

& Bonett, 2007). In addition, young adults engaged in careers for which they prepared in high school or college have higher levels of satisfaction (Blustein, Phillips, Jobin-Davis, & Finkelberg, 1997).

GENDER DIFFERENCES IN WORK PATTERNS

It is estimated that it now takes the average Canadian youth about 7 years to make the transition from school to full-time work. The transition begins at the point at which most young people are attending only school, continues through a period of schooling mixed with part-time work, and reaches the point at which more than half are working full-time (Beaujot, 2004). This transitional delay has meant that young men today are economically worse off than young men of previous generations. Young women, however, especially if they have continued to advance their education, are better off than young women of earlier generations. From a heterosexual couple's standpoint, the woman's greater financial contribution compensates for the man's lower contribution, as most couples form a two-worker family. In the long-term, most studies show that it is advantageous to delay the transition to full-time work, provided that you pursue an advanced education and delay starting a family.

Some of what you have read so far about work patterns is as true for women as it is for men. For example, women's work satisfaction goes up with age (and with job tenure), just as men's does. But women's work experience in early adulthood differs from men's in one strikingly important respect: The great majority of women move in and out of the workforce at least once, often many times (Moen, 2005). This pattern has numerous repercussions for working women. For example, Canadian women who work continuously or delay motherhood to keep working have higher salaries and achieve higher levels in their jobs than do those who have moved in and out of employment (Drolet, 2003). Of women who have not worked continuously, those who worked for several short bursts during their in-and-out stage do better economically than those who were unemployed for a single long stretch, even when the total months or years of employment are the same in the two groups (Gwartney-Gibbs, 1988). Very likely these short bursts of work allow the woman to keep up her work skills, especially if she works at the same type of job each time she re-enters the workforce. Continuous part-time work also seems to serve the same function. It seems that some strategies can help a woman maximize her work success while still allowing her to spend time with her family, but accomplishing both takes a good deal of thought and planning.

Canadian women have one of the highest labour force participation rates in the world.
(*Photos:* left, JupiterImages/Thinkstock; right, Thomas Northcut/Thinkstock)

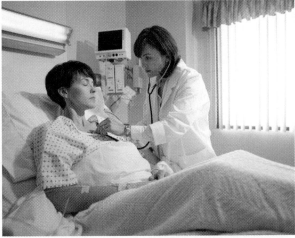

Women's work patterns and attitudes are changing rapidly. For example, one Canadian study found that most of the high school girls the researchers interviewed in the early 1990s expected both to be continuously employed and to have a family in adulthood (Davey, 1998). However, when they were re-interviewed 4 years later, these young women had begun to think about potential conflicts between career and family goals. Most still expected to be continuously employed, but many indicated that they preferred to take time out from their careers to achieve family goals, such as raising children. So although the cultural climate has changed considerably with regard to women's work patterns, the essential conflict women feel with regard to work and family, which is an ongoing factor behind discontinuous patterns of employment, continues to be evident in current cohorts.

The evidence on women's patterns of discontinuous employment raises the more general question of how individuals and couples balance the roles of worker, parent, and spouse. In Canada at least, the division of labour in the home is steadily diminishing. (Marshall, 2006). **Figure 14.6** shows that women between ages 25 and 54 now spend more time in paid work than their coequals in 1986. In comparison, men in the same age category, whether single or married with or without children, have increased their time spent on housework. To be sure, married women, especially those with children, still continue to do more of the housework than married men, but the overall difference is narrowing.

Kerry Daly (2000) of the University of Guelph found that Canadian adults aged 25 to 44 experience the most time pressure of all age groups. Both single mothers and married parents who were employed full-time reported the highest levels of time-related stress. In addition, Daly determined that there was a curvilinear relationship between age and leisure time, whereby youth and late middle-aged adults had the high-

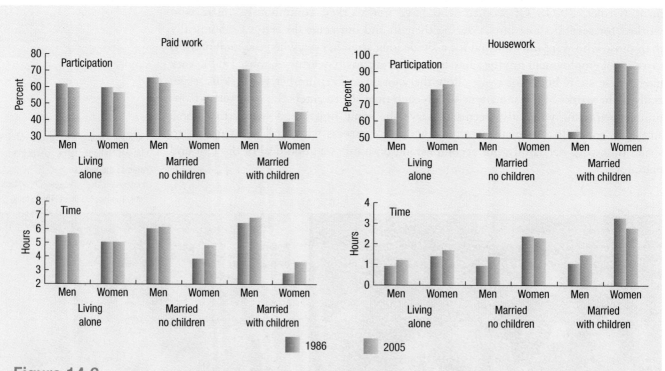

Figure 14.6

Daily participation in, and time spent on, paid work and housework, by living arrangements of Canadian men and women ages 25 to 54. (Note: Except paid work for those living alone, all other differences between men and women are statistically significant.)

(*Source:* Marshall, 2006. Converging gender roles. *Perspectives on Labour and Income, 18*[2], p. 10. Cat. No. 75-001-XPE.)

est proportion of leisure time per day and 35- to 44-year-olds reported the least amount. Men in this latter age bracket averaged 4.8 hours and women averaged only 4.5 hours of leisure per day over a week. Of course, parents with children had even less leisure time than average.

Not all the effects of combining family and work roles are problematic for women. For example, working women have more power in their marriages or partnerships than do nonworking women (Blumstein & Schwartz, 1983; Spitze, 1988). The more equal the earnings of the partners, the more equality there is in decision-making and in household work. But it remains true that the most striking single fact about combining work and family roles in this age of high female employment is that women struggle more than men do to resolve the conflict between the two. It is also clear that this conflict is vastly greater during early adulthood, when children are young and need constant care, than it is in middle or later adult life. In many respects, this complex intersection of spousal, parental, and work roles is the defining feature of early adult life in industrialized societies (see **Development in the Real World**).

Critical Thinking

What plans do you have to combine work and family? Might your planning or your thinking change as a result of what you have read so far?

Before Going On

- What factors influence a person's choice of occupation, and what kinds of experiences do young adults have in their work life?

- Describe women's patterns of work and how they relate to on-the-job performance and income. What are the potential conflicts between work and family roles, and how do they differ for men and women?

Development in the Real World

STRATEGIES FOR COPING WITH CONFLICT BETWEEN WORK AND FAMILY LIFE

If you are like many of today's college or university students, then you view your future as including marriage, parenthood, and a successful career (Hoffnung, 2004; Turcotte, 2007). But can a person really successfully balance the demands of all three of these roles? While there is no magic formula for creating such a balance and eliminating conflict and distress, some strategies can help. These suggestions are phrased as advice to women, because it is women who experience the greatest role conflict. But men can certainly profit from the same information.

The most helpful strategy overall is something psychologists call *cognitive restructuring*—recasting or reframing the situation for yourself in a way that identifies the positive elements. Cognitive restructuring might include reminding yourself that you had good reasons for choosing to have both a job and a family and recalling other times when you have coped successfully with similar problems (Paden & Buehler, 1995).

Another related kind of restructuring, involves redefining family roles. In several older studies, psychologists found that women who found ways to redistribute basic household tasks to other family members (husband and children) or who simply gave up doing some tasks experienced less stress and conflict (Hall, 1972, 1975). You might make a list of all the household chores you and your partner do and go over the list together, eliminating whatever items you can and reassigning the others. Men can clean toilets; clutter can be dealt with less frequently (or not at all!); meals can be simpler. If economic resources are sufficient, it's all right to delegate—reassure yourself that help can be hired. In fact, as Canadians work longer hours, they see their household incomes rise, which provides the means to get some relief from housework by hiring someone to do it as you can see in **Figure 14.7**.

If you feel you do the most amount of the work in the home, it may be helpful to try to determine whether the current division of labour in your household exists because others in the household don't do their share or because of your own inner resistance to changing your view of yourself and your basic contribution to the family unit.

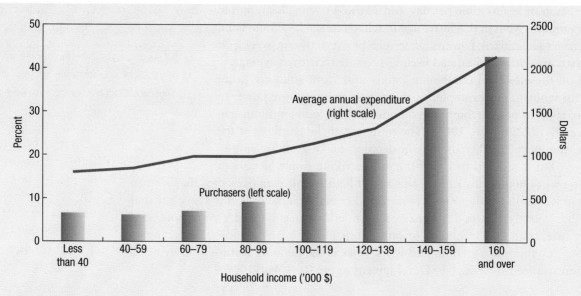

Figure 14.7

A greater percentage of higher income Canadian households are more likely to hire and spend more money annually on domestic help than lower income households.

(*Source:* Marshall, 2006. Converging gender roles. *Perspectives on Labour and Income, 18* [2], p. 10. Cat. No. 75-001-XPE.)

Finally, you may find it helpful to take a class in time management. Research reveals that good planning can, in fact, reduce the sense of strain you feel (Paden & Buehler, 1995). You have probably already heard lots of advice about how to organize things better. Easier said than done! But there are techniques that can help, and many of these are available online and in self-help books and are taught in workshops and classes in most cities.

What does not help is simply trying harder to do it all yourself. Women who continue to try to fulfill several roles perfectly report maximum strain and stress. Something has to give, whether it is your standards for housework or your sense of your female role. Combining a number of roles is inherently full of opportunities for conflict. At best, you may manage a delicate balance. At worst, you will find yourself overwhelmed.

Summary

Theories of Social and Personality Development

- Erikson proposed that young adults face the crisis of intimacy versus isolation. Those who fail to establish a stable relationship with an intimate partner or a network of friends become socially isolated.Levinson said adults cycle through periods of stability and instability as they build and refine life structures.

- The parts of the brain involved in decision-making and self-control mature between the late teens and early 20s. Once emerging adults accomplish developmental tasks in the academic, conduct, and friendship domains, new skills are required for tasks in the work and romantic domains.

Intimate Relationships

- Evolutionary theories of mate selection suggest that sex differences in mate preferences and mating behaviour are the result of natural selection. Social role theory emphasizes gender roles, similarity, and economic exchange in explaining sex differences in mating.

- Personality characteristics, as well as attachment and love, contribute to marital success. Marriage is associated with a number of health benefits, while divorce tends to increase young adults' risk of depression.

- People who cohabit prior to marriage are more likely to divorce. However, research has shown that among cohabiting couples in which the intention to marry is firm and the woman has had no prior cohabitation experience, divorce or dissatisfaction with the relationship is no more likely than among couples who do not live together before marriage.

- The factors that contribute to relationship satisfaction are similar across homosexual and heterosexual couples. However, the two types of couples often differ in the power relation within the partnership. Further, monogamy is not as important to gay male couples as it is to lesbian or heterosexual partners.

- Singles who do not have intimate partners rely on family and friends for intimacy. After many years of singlehood, unpartnered adults tend to incorporate "singleness" into their sense of personal identity.

Parenthood and Other Relationships

- Most men and women want to become parents because they view raising children as a life-enriching experience. The transition to parenthood is stressful and leads to a decline in relationship satisfaction. Factors such as the division of labour between mother and father, individual personality traits, and the availability of help from extended family members contribute to relationship satisfaction.

- Young adults' relationships with their parents tend to be steady and supportive, even if they are less central to the young adults' lives than they were at earlier ages. The quality of attachment to parents

continues to predict a number of important variables in early adulthood. Each young adult creates a network of relationships with friends as well as with a partner and family members.

The Role of Worker

- The specific job or career a young adult chooses is affected by her family background and values, personality, and gender. The majority of adults choose jobs that fit the cultural norms for their social class and gender. More intelligent young people and those with more education are more upwardly mobile. Super's stage theory proposes that career development involves the growth, exploratory, establishment, and maintenance stages.

- Job satisfaction rises steadily throughout early adulthood, in part because the jobs typically available to young adults are less well paid, are more repetitive, are less creative, and allow the worker very little power or influence.

- For many women, the work role also includes an "in-and-out" stage in which periods of focusing on family responsibilities alternate with periods of employment. The more continuous a woman's work history, the more successful she is likely to be at her job.

- When both partners work, the family responsibilities are not equally divided. In Canada, the division of labour is steadily diminishing.

PEARSON
mydevelopmentlab™

Visit **www.mydevelopmentlab.com** to help you get the best grade! Test your knowledge and grasp difficult concepts through

- Custom study plans: See where you are strong and where you go wrong
- Interactive simulations

- Video and audio clips
- Raise your own Virtual Child—and much more!

Review Questions

Answers are provided on MyDevelopmentLab in the Course Resources folder.

Theories of Social and Personality Development

14.1 According to Levinson, the first phase of a period of adjustment is called the
a. culmination phase.
b. beginning phase.

c. mid-era phase.
d. novice phase.

Intimate Relationships

14.2 Which of the following factors does *not* contribute to marital satisfaction?
a. personality characteristics of the partners
b. sexual compatibility

c. negative attitudes toward divorce

d. emotional affection

Parenthood and Other Relationships

14.3 Of the following couples, which would most likely report the lowest level of marital satisfaction?

a. a recently married couple who do not have children

b. a couple who have three children in elementary school

c. a couple whose children are in college or employed

d. a retired couple who frequently take care of their grandchildren

The Role of Worker

14.4 As a scientist with a national research institute, Maria has conceived, planned, and organized a number of national research initiatives that have examined influences on the physical and mental health of adolescents. According to Holland's personality and work typology, Maria is most likely of which personality type?

a. conventional

b. enterprising

c. investigative

d. social

14.5 Donald Super proposes that the work sequence of young adulthood has two stages, the _____ stage and the _____ stage.

a. familial; external

b. investigative; realistic

c. interrupted; continuous

d. trial; establishment

Critical-Thinking Questions

14.6 What are the similarities and differences among Erikson's, Levinson's, and Arnett's approach to early adulthood?

14.7 Having children often means that a couple's social networks change such that the parents of their children's playmates take the place of other adults with whom they have associated in the past. What are the long-term advantages and disadvantages of this trend for parents' future post-child-rearing lives?

Comstock Images/Thinkstock

CHAPTER 15

Physical and Cognitive Development in Middle Adulthood

The great baseball player Satchel Paige, who was still pitching in the major leagues at age 62, once said, "Age is mind over matter. If you don't mind, it doesn't matter."

It's a nice summary of the physical changes of the middle years. Yes, there are changes. Memory does get less efficient in some situations in mid-life; vision and hearing get worse; people slow down slightly and become somewhat weaker. But among adults who are otherwise healthy, the amount of loss is far less than folklore would have us believe. Further, along with obvious losses come important gains. Indeed, although early adulthood may be the physical high point of adulthood, there is a great deal of evidence that middle adulthood is the intellectual and creative peak.

In this chapter you will learn that, with advancing age, the story of human development seems to become more an account of differences than a description of universals. This happens because so many factors—behavioural choices, poor health, and so on—determine the specific developmental pathway an adult follows. Most middle-aged adults are healthy, energetic, and intellectually productive, but others are in decline. Moreover, because developmental psychology has focused more on younger individuals, there simply isn't as much knowledge about universal changes in adulthood.

When you finish studying the chapter, you will be able to trace the physical changes that occur during middle age; summarize the issues relevant to health promotion and wellness during middle adulthood, and describe the changes in cognitive functioning during middle adulthood. While you study this chapter, keep the following questions in mind:

- In addition to a drop in sex hormone levels, what other explanations might there be for the gradual decline in frequency of sexual activity during the middle adult years?

- How would you convince adolescents and young adults of the importance of getting enough calcium and exercise? What arguments do you think would work?

- Give examples of how practice and expertise in a particular field can help compensate for age-related deficits in cognitive functioning.

PHYSICAL CHANGES

For a quick overview of the common physical changes of middle age, take another look at **Table 13.1** on page 375, which summarizes most of the evidence. Changes or declines in many physical functions occur very gradually through the 40s and 50s. For a few physical functions, however, change or decline is already substantial in the middle adult years.

THE BRAIN AND NERVOUS SYSTEM

Our knowledge of what happens to the normal, undamaged brain during middle adulthood has increased dramatically over the past few years because of the findings of recent MRI studies. One of the first studies of its kind, based at the UCLA Department of Neurology, compared brain development in a cross-sectional study of people ranging from their first to their ninth decade of life (Sowell et al., 2003). For example, **Figure 15.1** shows significant changes in two main components of the brain. Broadly speaking, it shows that white matter volume crests during middle adulthood and that grey matter volume continues the decline that it began in childhood and does not level off until about age 60. The volume of *cerebrospinal fluid* (CSF) also increases steadily

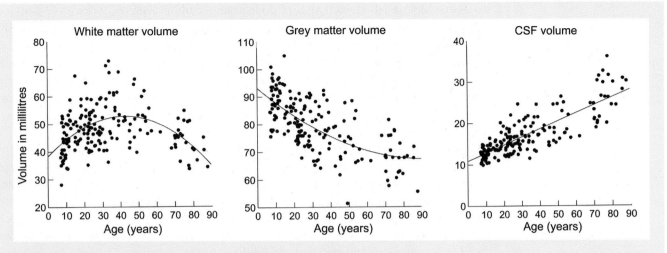

Figure 15.1

These graphs illustrate the changes that take place in the brain across the lifespan. White matter volume increases until middle adulthood and then declines. Grey matter volume declines from childhood and then levels off at the end of middle adulthood. Cerebrospinal fluid increases at a regular rate across the lifespan.

(*Source:* Image courtesy of Elizabeth R. Sowell, Ph.D., UCLA Laboratory of Neuro Imaging. From Sowell et al, 2003, Figure 6, p. 314.)

across the lifespan. It is important to note that new synapses are continuing to form in middle age. Earlier in life, though, new synapses form more rapidly or at the same rate as old connections are lost. In middle age, it appears, more synapses are lost than are formed; this net loss is associated with the cognitive declines seen in older adults.

As noted in **Chapter 13**, hidden within the global changes depicted in **Figure 15.1** are localized changes that occur in various parts of the brain at different times and rates. It is suspected that the decline in grey matter density that occurs after age 40 is associated with subtle degenerative processes—this is the time when white matter growth peaks and total brain weight begins to decline (Sowell et al., 2003; Sowell, Thompson, & Toga, 2004). With the exception of specific regions in the left temporal lobe that are associated with language comprehension skills, the general rule of brain maturation is that the areas of the brain that develop last are the ones that begin to decline first, namely areas located within the frontal and parietal lobes. You can read more about the associated changes in cognitive function later in the chapter.

In addition, developmentalists know that behavioural choices and mental health affect the adult brain. For example, alcoholics and nonalcoholics differ in the distribution of electrical activity in the brain (Duffy, 1994). The brains of depressed and non-depressed adults differ as well. Further, a number of serious mental illnesses, such as schizophrenia, are associated with structural variations in the brain. What researchers don't know yet is whether the brains of alcoholics, depressed persons, or schizophrenics were different from others before the onset of their difficulties. The longitudinal research necessary to answer such questions hasn't yet been done.

Besides studying the effects of trauma and disease, neuropsychologists are also involved in investigating a very important issue in the study of aging—whether declines in cognitive functions are caused by a loss of neurological processing resources. To find out, researchers examine how the brains of young and middle-aged people respond to cognitive tasks. Such studies have produced a rather complex set of findings.

One fairly consistent finding is that middle-aged adults' brains respond more slowly to cognitive tasks than those of younger adults (Zysset, Schroeter, Neumann, & von Cramon, 2007). Another finding is that such tasks activate a larger area of brain tissue in middle-aged adults than they do in younger adults (Gunter, Jackson, & Mulder, 1998). Of course, neuropsychologists don't know why, but they speculate that cognitive processing in middle-aged adults is less selective than it is in younger adults. It's as if the middle-aged brain has a more difficult time finding just the right neurological tool to carry out a particular function, and so it activates more tools than are necessary. This lack of selectivity could account for differences between age groups in the speed at which cognitive tasks are carried out.

The brains of middle-aged and younger adults also respond differently to sensory stimuli. For example, patterns of brain waves in different areas vary across age groups when participants are presented with a simple auditory stimulus such as a musical tone (Yordanova, Kolev, & Basar, 1998). Research along this line has suggested that middle-aged adults may have less ability to control attention processes by inhibiting brain responses to irrelevant stimuli (Amenedo & Diaz, 1998, 1999). Their difficulty with attentional control could be another reason for the average difference in processing speed between young and middle-aged adults.

Such findings might lead you to conclude that, in everyday situations requiring intense concentration and rapid judgments, middle-aged adults would perform more poorly than their younger counterparts. Interestingly, though, some research on lapses of concentration and poor decision-making among drivers shows just the opposite (Dobson, Brown, Ball, Powers, & McFadden, 1999). Younger drivers exhibit more lapses in attention and driving errors than middle-aged drivers. These lapses and errors, combined with younger drivers' greater likelihood of driving after drinking alcohol, help account for the different accident rates of young and middle-aged adults. Such findings, when considered with those on age differences in brain function, illustrate the difficulty researchers face in finding direct relationships between age-related brain differences and cross-age variations in behaviour.

Another point to keep in mind about studies of the middle-aged brain is that the results of these studies are likely due to both primary and secondary aging. That is, part of the difference in brain function between young and middle-aged adults is due to natural aging processes. The remainder is attributable to the effects of health. Studies show, for example, that health-related changes in the circulatory system cause damage in the parts of the brain that are critical to processing speed, planning, and memory in middle age (Raz & Rodrigue, 2006; Raz, Rodrigue, Kennedy, & Acker, 2007). Consequently, healthy middle-aged adults exhibit both neurological and cognitive functioning that is more similar to that of young adults than their peers who suffer from health conditions that affect the circulatory system.

THE REPRODUCTIVE SYSTEM

If you were asked to name a single significant physical change occurring in the years of middle adulthood, chances are you'd say *menopause*—especially if you're a woman. The term **climacteric** refers to the years of middle or late adulthood in both men and women during which reproductive capacity declines or is lost.

climacteric
the years of middle or late adulthood in both men and women during which reproductive capacity declines or is lost

MALE CLIMACTERIC In men, the climacteric is extremely gradual, with a slow loss of reproductive capacity, although the rate of change varies widely from one man to the next, and there are documented cases of men in their 90s fathering children. On average, the quantity of viable sperm produced declines slightly, beginning perhaps at about age 40. The testes also shrink very gradually, and the volume of seminal fluid declines after about age 60.

The causal factor is most likely a very slow drop in testosterone levels, beginning in early adulthood and continuing well into old age. This decline in testosterone is implicated in the gradual loss of muscle tissue (and hence strength) that becomes evident in the middle and later years, as well as in the increased risk of heart disease in middle and old age. It also appears to affect sexual function. In particular, in the middle years, the incidence of erectile dysfunction begins to increase—although many things other than the slight decline in testosterone contribute to this change, including an increased incidence of poor health (especially heart disease), obesity, use of blood pressure medication (and other medications), alcohol abuse, and smoking. *Erectile dysfunction*, sometimes called *impotence*, is the inability to achieve or maintain an erection.

During middle age, supportive partners help each other cope with the changes in sexual function that are brought about by the natural aging of the reproductive system. (*Photo:* Rhoda Sidney/The Image Works)

Lifestyle changes can sometimes restore sexual function. In one study, researchers enrolled 35- to 55-year-old obese men with erectile dysfunction in a 2-year weight loss program that required participants to make changes in their diets and exercise habits (Esposito et al., 2004). About one-third of the men experienced improvements in erectile dysfunction along with reductions in body fat.

Among healthy middle-aged men, performance anxiety is a frequent cause of erectile dysfunction. The drug *sildenafil* (Viagra) has been found to be effective in treating this problem (Chen, Paik, & Ishii, 2007; Skoumal et al., 2004). However, physicians warn that men with erectile dysfunction should avoid so-called natural treatments such as food supplements because most of them have not been studied in placebo-controlled experiments (Rowland & Tai, 2003). Moreover, men who turn to supplements for symptom relief may delay seeking medical attention and, as a result, may continue to suffer from a serious underlying condition without realizing it.

MENOPAUSE Declines in key sex hormones are also clearly implicated in the set of changes in women called **menopause**, which means literally the cessation of the menses. You'll remember from **Chapter 11** that secretion of several forms of estrogen by the ovaries increases rapidly during puberty, triggering the onset of menstruation as well as stimulating the development of breasts and secondary sex characteristics. In the adult woman, estrogen levels are high during the first 14 days of the menstrual cycle, stimulating the release of an ovum and the preparation of the uterus for possible implantation. *Progesterone*, which is secreted by the ruptured ovarian follicle from which the ovum emerges, rises during the second half of the menstrual cycle and stimulates the sloughing off of accumulated material in the uterus each month if conception has not occurred.

menopause
the cessation of monthly menstrual cycles in middle-aged women

The Society of Obstetricians and Gynaecologists of Canada (SOGC; 2001) regularly sponsors the annual National Menopause Awareness Month (October 15–November 15) to provide accurate information and tips for coping with symptoms of both perimenopause and menopause. About 4 million Canadian women are currently experiencing menopause. The transition phase of menopause, called *perimenopause*, can be expected to begin after age 40. Menopause usually occurs when a woman is between her late 40s and early 50s, and can last beyond age 55 (SOGC, 2001). About one woman in 12 experiences menopause before age 40, referred to by physicians as *premature menopause* (Wich & Carnes, 1995).

MENOPAUSAL PHASES Menopause, like puberty, is often thought of as a single event. However, it actually occurs over several years, and researchers generally agree that it consists of three phases. First, during the **premenopausal phase**, estrogen levels

premenopausal phase
the stage of menopause during which estrogen levels fall somewhat, menstrual periods are less regular, and anovulatory cycles begin to occur

begin to fluctuate and decline, typically in the late 30s or early 40s, producing irregular menstrual periods in many women. The ovaries are less sensitive to cyclical hormonal signals, and many women experience *anovulatory cycles*, or cycles in which no ovum is released. Even though no ovum is produced, estrogen levels are high enough in pre-menopausal women to produce periodic bleeding. However, the lack of ovulation results in a dramatic drop in progesterone. Thus, many experts believe that the menstrual irregularity associated with the premenopausal period is due to progesterone loss rather than estrogen loss (Lee, 1996).

perimenopausal phase
the stage of menopause during which estrogen and progesterone levels are erratic, menstrual cycles may be very irregular, and women begin to experience symptoms such as hot flashes

During the **perimenopausal phase**, estrogen levels decrease and women experience more extreme variations in the timing of their menstrual cycles. In addition, about 75% of perimenopausal women experience *hot flashes*, sudden sensations of feeling hot. Of those who have hot flashes, 85% will have them for more than a year; one-third or more will have them for 5 years or more (Kletzky & Borenstein, 1987). It is hypothesized that fluctuating levels of estrogen and other hormones cause a woman's blood vessels to expand and contract erratically, thus producing hot flashes.

During a hot flash, the temperature of the skin can rise as much as 4°C in some parts of the body, although the core body temperature actually drops (Kronenberg, 1994). Hot flashes last, on average, about 3 minutes and may recur as seldom as daily or as often as three times per hour (Bellantoni & Blackman, 1996). Most women learn to manage these brief periods of discomfort if they occur during the day. However, hot flashes frequently disrupt women's sleep. When this happens, it sets in motion a series of changes that are actually due to sleep deprivation rather than menopause. For example, lack of sleep can lead to mental confusion, difficulty with everyday memory tasks, and emotional instability. Thus, perimenopausal women may have the subjective feeling that they are "going crazy" when the real problem is that hot flashes are preventing them from getting enough sleep. The general light-headedness and shakiness that accompany some women's hot flashes can add to this sensation.

postmenopausal phase
the last stage of menopause; a woman is postmenopausal when she has had no menstrual periods for at least a year

Eventually, estrogen and progesterone drop to consistently low levels and menstruation ceases altogether. Once a women has ceased to menstruate for a year, she is in the **postmenopausal phase**. In postmenopausal women, estradiol and estrone, both types of estrogen, drop to about one-quarter or less of their premenopausal levels. Progesterone decreases even more, as a result of the cessation of ovulation, although the adrenal glands continue to provide postmenopausal women with some progesterone.

The reduction in estrogen during the perimenopausal and postmenopausal phases also has effects on genital and other tissue. The breasts become less firm, the genitals and the uterus shrink somewhat, and the vagina becomes both shorter and smaller in diameter. The walls of the vagina also become somewhat thinner and less elastic and produce less lubrication during intercourse (McCoy, 1998; Wich & Carnes, 1995).

Research Report

THE PROS AND CONS OF HORMONE REPLACEMENT THERAPY

Most of the physical symptoms and effects of menopause—including hot flashes, thinning of the vaginal wall, and loss of vaginal lubrication—can be dramatically reduced by taking estrogen and progesterone. Moreover, hormone replacement is associated with a reduction in mood swings in menopausal women (Klaiber, Broverman, Vogel, Peterson, & Snyder, 1997). However, researchers have found that women are very poorly informed about both menopause itself and the potential risks and benefits of hormone replacement therapy. Apparently, unlike women in nonindustrialized societies, who rely on older women for information, women in the industrialized world rely on drug manufacturers' advertisements on television and in women's magazines for information about menopause (Berg & Lipson, 1999; Clinkingbeard, Minton, Davis, &

McDermott, 1999; Whittaker, 1998). Analyses of these sources of information have shown that they contain more misleading than helpful information (Gannon & Stevens, 1998). Thus, a woman who wants to make an informed decision about alternatives for dealing with the effects of menopause has to look beyond these information sources.

Hormone replacement therapy has had a somewhat checkered history. In the 1950s and 1960s, estrogen therapy became extremely common. In some surveys, as many as half of all postmenopausal women in the United States reported using replacement estrogen, many of them over periods of 10 years or more (Stadel & Weiss, 1975). In the 1970s, however, new evidence showed that the risk of endometrial cancer (cancer of the lining of the uterus) increased threefold to tenfold in women taking replacement estrogen (Nathanson & Lorenz, 1982). Not surprisingly, when this information became public, the use of estrogen therapy dropped dramatically.

The third act in this drama was the discovery that a combination of estrogen and progesterone, at quite low dosages, had the same benefits as estrogen alone and eliminated the increased risk of endometrial cancer. Furthermore, studies also made clear that the use of replacement estrogen significantly retards the bone loss of osteoporosis (Barrett-Connor & Bush, 1991; Ross, Paganini-Hill, Mack, & Henderson, 1987). Research reveals that this benefit occurs with the newer estrogen–progesterone combinations as well as with estrogen alone (e.g., Cauley et al., 1995; Stampfer et al., 1991; Working Group for the PEPI Trial, 1995).

This sounds almost too good to be true, doesn't it? Why shouldn't every postmenopausal woman be on a program of hormone replacement? There are serious counter-arguments: First, many women consider the process of aging, including the changes of menopause, to be natural physical processes with which they do not want to tinker. Second, although scientists have evidence that hormone replacement therapy is linked to slightly lower overall cancer risks, some studies have found that it is associated with somewhat higher rates of breast cancer and very slightly higher rates of ovarian cancer (Posthuma, Westendorp, & Vandenbroucke, 1994). In the Nurses' Health Study (which you read about in **Chapter 13**), researchers found that for every woman diagnosed with breast cancer who did not take replacement hormones, there were roughly 1.4 cases of breast cancer diagnosed among women who did use hormone therapy (Colditz et al., 1995). The equivalent comparison for ovarian cancers, drawn from another study (Rodriguez et al., 1995), was 1.0 case of ovarian cancer in women who did not take hormones and 1.15 cases in women who did. Third, the latest milestone in this story is the NIH's Women's Health Initiative (WHI) study of HRT. Findings included increased risk of heart attack, stroke, blood clots, dementia, and breast cancer. There was so much concern that certain parts of the study were stopped. Since the release of these findings, prescriptions of estrogen–progesterone for HRT have dropped off the charts (Heiss et al., 2008; NIH, 2005; Toh et al., 2010; WHI Steering Committee, 2004).

How can an individual woman add up these various benefits and risks? Among other things, a woman should consider not only her present discomfort, but also her overall risk of heart disease and cancer (heart disease is actually the larger overall risk in the years of middle and late adulthood), which includes her family history of these diseases. Above all, a woman entering menopause should commit herself to seeking information beyond what can be learned from television and women's magazines. For example, Canadian experts (Blake, Collins, Reid, Fedorkow, & Lalonde, 2002) advise that women should discuss their concerns with health care professionals in order to make an informed choice based on their unique medical history. Moreover, it is recommended that hormone replacement therapy should be used primarily for the treatment of menopausal symptoms rather than solely for the prevention of disease, especially among postmenopausal women in whom alternative lifestyle changes should be encouraged, including exercising, eating a healthy diet, smoking cessation, and the like (SOGC, 2002).

PSYCHOLOGICAL EFFECTS OF MENOPAUSE One other aspect of the climacteric in women deserves some mention. It has been part of folklore for a very long time that menopause involves major emotional upheaval as well as clear physical changes. However, research findings are mixed. Longitudinal studies show that depressive symptoms increase during menopause (Freeman et al., 2004). Nevertheless, experts note that serious depression, as defined by the DSM-IV-TR criteria for major depressive disorder, is no more frequent among menopausal women than among those who are nonmenopausal (Bromberger et al., 2007).

A woman's overall negativity and number of life stressors before entering menopause contributes to her emotional state (Dennerstein, Lehert, & Guthrie, 2002). In other words, a woman's negativity may be attributed to menopause when, in reality, it may be a longstanding component of her personality. Alternatively, she may have a particularly stressful life, and menopausal symptoms are just one more source of difficulty.

In addition, the actual level of symptoms women experience makes a difference. It isn't surprising that women who are most uncomfortable because of hot flashes and other physical changes, and whose symptoms last the longest, experience the most depression and negative mood. Researchers have also found that menopausal women who suffer from sleep deprivation because of hot flashes at night, or *night sweats*, may be misdiagnosed with generalized anxiety disorder. Not only are the symptoms of the two conditions similar, but electroencephalographic studies reveal that the patterns of brain activity across the two conditions are quite similar, too (Terashima et al., 2004).

Women's attitudes toward menopause vary somewhat across ethnic groups. Interestingly, one study suggested that these views are linked to women's general feelings about getting older (Sommer et al., 1999). For example, researchers in the United States have found that women who agreed with the statement "The older a woman is, the more valued she is" were likely to disagree with the statement "A woman is less attractive after menopause." Compared with Hispanic, Japanese American, white, and Chinese American women, African American women expressed a more positive view of aging and a less negative view of menopause than did women in the other groups. Interestingly, however, African American women, on average, experience more menopause symptoms, such as hot flashes, than women in other groups do (Gold et al., 2006). Thus, having a positive outlook on aging and menopause does not appear to protect women against its symptoms. Moreover, across all groups, menopausal status is only one of many aspects of mid-life that women consider when they are asked to evaluate the quality of their lives (Beyene, Gillis, & Lee, 2007). Thus, some researchers argue that menopause should be studied within the whole context of a middle-aged woman's life rather than as the universal defining feature of this period of life.

SEXUAL ACTIVITY Despite changes in the reproductive system, the great majority of middle-aged adults remain sexually active, although the frequency of sex declines somewhat during these years (Association of Reproductive Health Professionals [ARHP], 2000; Laumann, Gagnon, Michael, & Michaels, 1994; Michael, Gagnon, Laumann, & Kolata, 1994). It is unlikely that this decline during mid-life is due wholly or even largely to drops in sex hormone levels; women do not experience major estrogen declines until their late 40s, but the decline in sexual activity begins much sooner. And the drop in testosterone among men is so gradual and slight during these years that it cannot be the full explanation. An alternative explanation is that the demands of other roles are simply so pressing that middle-aged adults find it hard to find time for sex. Increasing rates of chronic diseases such as diabetes and arthritis may also explain the declines in the frequency of sexual activity among people in their 50s (ARHP, 2000).

THE SKELETAL SYSTEM

osteoporosis
loss of bone mass with age, resulting in more brittle and porous bones

Another change that begins to be quite significant in middle adulthood is a loss of calcium from the bones, resulting in reduced bone mass and more brittle and porous bones. This process is called **osteoporosis**. Bone loss begins at about age 30 for both men and women, but in women the process is accelerated by menopause. The major consequence of this loss of bone density is a significantly increased risk of fractures, beginning as early as age 50 for women, and much later for men. Among older women (and men), such fractures can be a major cause of disability and reduced activity, so osteoporosis is not a trivial change. In fact, University of Toronto researchers found that, with advancing age, there was an exponential increase in hip fractures, in accompanying lengths of stay in the hospital, and in death rates following the fracture for both men and women (Papadimitropoulos, Coyte, Josse, & Greenwood, 1997).

In women, it is clear that bone loss is linked quite directly to estrogen and progesterone levels. Researchers know that these hormones fall dramatically after menopause, and it is the timing of menopause rather than age that signals the increase in rate of bone loss (Recker, Lappe, Davies, & Heaney, 2000). Researchers also know that the rate of bone loss drops to premenopausal levels among women who take replacement hormones, all of which makes the link quite clear (Rossouw et al., 2002). While the overall pattern of bone loss seems to be a part of primary aging, the amount of such loss nonetheless varies quite a lot from one individual to another. **Table 15.1** lists the known risk factors for osteoporosis.

Aside from taking replacement hormones, women can help prevent osteoporosis by using one or all of the following strategies. First, they can get enough calcium during early adulthood, so that peak levels of bone mass are as robust as possible. Second, throughout adult life women can get regular exercise, particularly weight-bearing exercise such as walking or strength training. In one study, a group of middle-aged or older women were randomly assigned to a strength-training program consisting of twice-weekly sessions for a year. They showed a gain in bone density over the year, whereas women in a control group without such weight training showed a loss (Nelson et al., 1994). Third, bone mineral density (BMD) tests can identify osteoporosis long before it causes serious damage to bones. Once it is diagnosed, women can take bone-building medications such as alendronate sodium (Fosamax). Studies show that the combination of BMD testing and medication dramatically reduces the risk of fractures among women over the age of 50 (Jaglal et al., 2005).

Any weight-bearing exercise—including walking—will help prevent osteoporosis.
(*Photo:* David Madison/Getty Images)

TABLE 15.1	Risk Factors for Osteoporosis
Risk Factor	**Explanation**
Race	Whites are at higher risk than other races.
Gender	Women have considerably higher risk than men.
Weight	Those who are underweight are at higher risk.
Timing of climacteric	Women who experience early menopause and those who have had their ovaries removed are at higher risk, presumably because their estrogen levels decline at earlier ages.
Family history	Those with a family history of osteoporosis are at higher risk.
Diet	A diet low in calcium during adolescence and early adulthood results in lower peak levels of bone mass, and hence greater risk of falling below critical levels later. Whether there is any benefit in increasing intake of calcium postmenopausally remains in debate. Diets high in either caffeine (especially black coffee) or alcohol are also linked to higher risk.
Exercise	Those with a sedentary lifestyle are at higher risk. Prolonged immobility, such as bedrest, also increases the rate of bone loss. Exercise reduces the rate of bone loss.

(*Sources:* Dalsky et al., 1988; Duursma, Raymakers, Boereboom, & Scheven, 1991; Gambert, Schultz, & Hamdy, 1995; Goldberg & Hagberg, 1990; Gordon & Vaughan, 1986; Lindsay, 1985; Morrison et al., 1994; Smith, 1982.)

VISION AND HEARING

One of the most noticeable physical changes occurring in the middle years is a loss of visual acuity. Most people find that they need reading glasses or bifocals by the time they are 45 or 50 years old. Two changes in the eyes, collectively called **presbyopia**, are involved. First, the lens of the eye thickens. In a process that begins in childhood but produces noticeable effects only in middle adulthood, layer after layer of slightly pigmented material accumulates on the lens. Because light coming into the eye must pass through this thickened, slightly yellowed material, the total light reaching the retina decreases, which reduces a person's overall sensitivity to light waves, particularly to short wavelengths that are perceived as blue, blue-green, and violet (Fozard, 1990).

By age 45 or 50, nearly everyone needs glasses, especially for reading. (*Photo*: Myrleen Ferguson Cate/ PhotoEdit)

presbyopia
normal loss of visual acuity with aging, especially the ability to focus the eyes on near objects

Because of this thickening of the lens, it is also harder and harder for the muscles surrounding the eye to change the shape of the lens to adjust the focus. In a young eye, the shape of the lens readily adjusts for distance, so no matter how near or far away some object may be, the light rays passing through the eye converge where they should, on the retina in the back of the eye, giving a sharp image. But as the thickening increases, the elasticity of the lens declines and it can no longer make these fine adjustments. Many images become blurry. In particular, the ability to focus clearly on near objects deteriorates rapidly in the 40s and early 50s. As a result, middle-aged adults often hold books and other items farther and farther away, because only in that way can they get a clear image. Finally, of course, they cannot read print at the distance at which they can focus, and they are forced to wear reading glasses or bifocals. These same changes also affect the ability to adapt quickly to variations in levels of light or glare, such as from passing headlights when driving at night or in the rain. So driving may become more stressful. All in all, these changes in the eyes, which appear to be a genuine part of primary aging, require both physical and psychological adjustment.

presbycusis
normal loss of hearing with aging, especially of high-frequency tones

The equivalent process in hearing is called **presbycusis**. The auditory nerves and the structures of the inner ear gradually degenerate as a result of basic wear and tear, resulting primarily in losses in the ability to hear sounds of high and very low frequencies. But these changes do not accumulate to the level of significant hearing loss until somewhat later in life than is typical for presbyopia. Hearing loss is quite slow until about age 50, and only a small percentage of middle-aged adults require hearing aids (Fozard, 1990). After age 50 or 55, however, the rate of hearing loss accelerates. Such a pattern of loss also appears to be an aspect of primary aging, but some secondary aging processes are involved as well. In particular, the amount of hearing loss is considerably greater in adults who work or live in very noisy environments—or who listen regularly to very loud music (Baltes, Reese, & Nesselrode, 1977).

Before Going On

- What do researchers know about brain function in middle age?
- How does the reproductive system, the skeletal system, and vision and hearing change in men and women in middle age?

HEALTH PROMOTION AND WELLNESS

No single variable affects the quality of life in middle and late adulthood as much as health. A middle-aged person in good health often functions as well and has as much energy as much younger adults. However, mid-life is the era during which the poor health habits and risky behaviours of earlier years begin to catch up with us.

HEALTH TRENDS AT MID-LIFE

👁 Watch

In general, middle-aged adults report that they experience annoying aches and pains with greater frequency than when they were younger (Helme, 1998). Moreover, many middle-aged adults, especially women, are unhappy with their bodies; most would prefer to be thinner (Allaz, Bernstein, Rouget, Archinard, & Morabia, 1998). In addition, the number of truly healthy adults declines in mid-life. Perhaps half of adults between ages 40 and 65 have either some diagnosed disease or disability or a significant but undiagnosed problem, such as the early stages of heart disease. Still, a 40-year-old's life expectancy is remarkably high, as you can see from **Figure 15.2**, and has been rising over the past few decades (Statistics Canada, 2000a). In addition, even though middle-aged adults have more chronic diseases and disabilities, such as diabetes and arthritis, than those who are younger, the risk of having chronic health problems is significantly lower now than it was in the 1970s (Crompton, 2000; Statistics Canada, 2000d). Similarly, disease-related death rates increase significantly in middle adulthood, as you can see in **Figure 15.3**. The two leading causes of death in middle age are cancer and heart disease (Statistics Canada, 2009l).

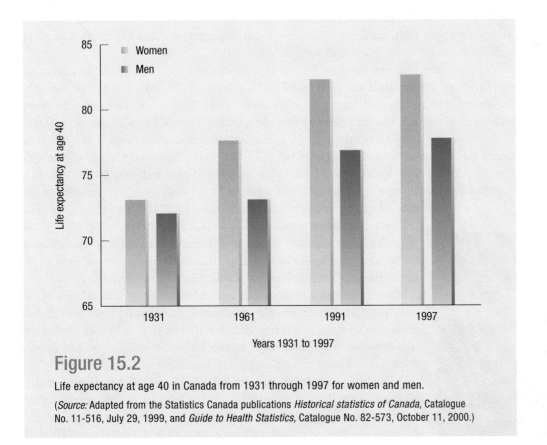

Figure 15.2

Life expectancy at age 40 in Canada from 1931 through 1997 for women and men.

(*Source:* Adapted from the Statistics Canada publications *Historical statistics of Canada*, Catalogue No. 11-516, July 29, 1999, and *Guide to Health Statistics*, Catalogue No. 82-573, October 11, 2000.)

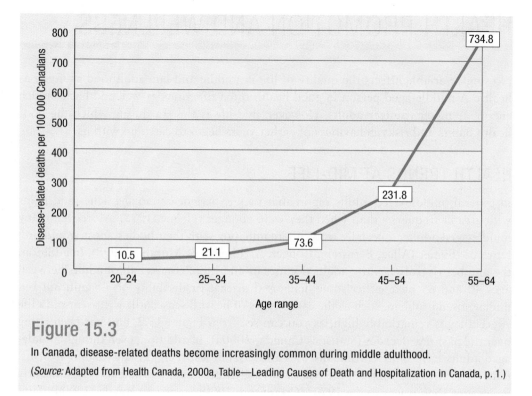

Figure 15.3

In Canada, disease-related deaths become increasingly common during middle adulthood.

(*Source:* Adapted from Health Canada, 2000a, Table—Leading Causes of Death and Hospitalization in Canada, p. 1.)

CANCER

The leading cause of death of Canadians in middle and old age is cancer (Statistics Canada, 2009l). The lifetime probability of developing cancer is 45% for men and 40% for women. In addition, men have a 29% and women have a 24% lifetime probability of dying from cancer (National Cancer Institute of Canada, 2000; Canadian Cancer Society's Steering Committee [CCSSC], 2010).

Lung cancer remains the number one type of cancer death in Canada and accounts for 28.1% of cancer deaths in men and 25.8% in women (CCSSC, 2010). For men, the incidence of new cases of lung cancer peaked in the 1980s and has been dropping steadily; for women, the bad news is that the number of new cases of lung cancer has jumped nearly fivefold over the past 40 years, although the good news is that the incidence rate has recently begun to level off (CCSSC, 2010; National Cancer Institute of Canada, 2000). After lung cancer, the next leading type of cancer deaths for Canadians is colorectal cancer in men (12.5%) and breast cancer in women (14.8%). The third major type of cancer death in Canadian men (10.8%) is prostate cancer and colorectal cancer in women (11.4%) (CCSSC, 2010).

Like heart disease, which you'll read about later in the chapter, cancer does not strike in a totally random fashion. Indeed, as you can see in the left-hand column of **Table 15.2**, some of the same risk factors are implicated in both diseases. Most of these risk factors are at least partially under your own control. It helps to have established good health habits in early adulthood, but it is also clear from the research that improving your health habits in middle age can reduce your risks of both cancer and heart disease.

The most controversial item listed in **Table 15.2** is diet; in particular, scientists debate the role of dietary fat as a potential risk factor. Some evidence suggests that reducing consumption of red meat may decrease the risk of colorectal cancer (Kushi & Giovannucci, 2002).

The Japanese, whose diet is very low in fat, have lower rates of some kinds of cancer than North Americans and Europeans.

(*Photo:* Ryan McVay/Thinkstock)

TABLE 15.2	Risk Factors for Cancer and Heart Disease	
Risk	**Cancer**	**Heart Disease**
Smoking	Substantially increases the risk of lung cancer; also implicated in other cancers.	Major risk; the more you smoke, the greater the risk. Quitting smoking reduces risk.
Blood pressure	No known risk.	Systolic pressure above 140 or diastolic pressure above 90 linked to higher risk.
Weight	Being overweight is linked to increased risk of several cancers, including breast cancer, but the risk is smaller than for heart disease.	Some increased risk with any weight above the normal range; risk is greater for those with weight 20% or more above recommended amount.
Cholesterol	No known risk.	Clear risk with elevated levels of low-density lipoproteins.
Inactivity	Inactivity is associated in some studies with higher rates of colon cancer.	Inactive adults have about twice the risk as those who exercise.
Diet	Results are still unclear; a high-fat diet is linked to risks of some cancers; high-fibre diets appear to be protective for some cancers.	High-fat, low-fibre diet increases risk; antioxidants, such as vitamin E, vitamin C, or beta carotene, may decrease risk.
Alcohol	Heavy drinking is associated with cancers of the digestive system.	Moderate intake of alcohol, especially wine, is linked to decreased CVD risk. Heavy drinking can weaken the heart muscle.
Heredity	Some genetic component with nearly every cancer.	Those with first-degree relatives with CVD have seven to ten times the risk; those who inherit a gene for a particular protein are up to twice as likely to have CVD.

(*Sources:* Centers for Disease Control, 1994; Gaziano & Hennekens, 1995; Hunter et al., 1996; Lee, Manson, Hennekens, & Paffenbarger, 1993; Manson et al., 1995; Morris, Kritchevsky, & Davis, 1994; Rich-Edwards, Manson, Hennekens, & Buring, 1995; Risch, Jain, Marrett, & Howe, 1994; Rose, 1993; Stampfer et al., 1993; Woodward & Tunstall-Pedoe, 1995.)

While the debate over the role of diet continues, there is now little doubt that several types of cancers are caused by infectious agents (Ewald, 2000). For example, in **Chapter 11** you learned about the link between the human papillomavirus (HPV) and cervical cancer (Canadian Cancer Society, 2007; Castellsagué et al., 2002). This sexually transmitted disease is apparently also responsible for many cancers of the mouth, nose, and throat, presumably because of oral sex, and for some cases of anal cancer in gay men (Frisch et al., 1997; Mork et al., 2001).

Studies have shown that Epstein-Barr virus is also associated with cancers of the nose and throat, as well as one type of non-Hodgkin's lymphoma (Chien et al., 2001). Another virus, hepatitis B, is linked to liver cancer (Yang et al., 2002). Thus, screening people who do not yet have symptoms of these viral infections may help to identify cancers at very early stages of development, when they are most curable.

Correlations between bacterial infections and cancer have also been identified. For example, *Helicobacter pylori* has been implicated in many studies of stomach cancer and one type of non-Hodgkin's lymphoma (Uemura et al., 2001). This micro-organism also causes stomach ulcers. Typically, antibiotic treatment clears up both the infection and the ulcers and, coincidentally, reduces the risk of stomach cancer. However, most people who carry *H. pylori* do not have ulcers or any other symptoms. Moreover, a fairly high proportion of people, especially those in developing nations with poor water purification systems, carry the infection (Brown, 2000). Consequently, researchers are currently trying to determine whether treating carriers who are asymptomatic will reduce rates of stomach cancer. Others are examining whether improvements in sanitary conditions in developing nations will lead to lower rates of *H. pylori* infection and stomach cancer.

Studies of the role of infection in the development of cancer provide yet another example of the importance of health-related choices. Specifically, safe sex practices can limit an individual's risk of contracting sexually transmitted diseases and the cancers in which they have been implicated. Moreover, vaccines against many viruses, including hepatitis B, are widely available.

CARDIOVASCULAR DISEASE

cardiovascular disease (CVD)
a set of disease processes in the heart and circulatory system

atherosclerosis
narrowing of the arteries caused by deposits of plaque, a fatty substance

The term **cardiovascular disease (CVD)** covers a variety of physical problems, but the key problem is in the arteries. In individuals suffering from CVD, the arteries become clogged with *plaque* (a fibrous or fatty substance), in a process called **atherosclerosis**. Eventually, vital arteries may become completely blocked, producing what laypeople call a *heart attack* (if the blockage is in the coronary arteries) or a *stroke* (if the blockage is in the brain). Atherosclerosis is not a normal part of aging. It is a disease, increasingly common with age, but not inevitable.

The rate of CVD has been dropping steadily in Canada over the past half century. Between 1956 and 2002, for example, it decreased by 70%, a fairly startling decline that has contributed greatly to the increased life expectancy among today's adults (Health Canada, 2002d; Heart & Stroke Foundation, 2010). Although the CVD mortality rate has been declining at roughly 3% annually since the mid-1990s (Tu et al., 2009), CVD remains a leading cause of death among middle-aged adults in Canada, accounting for 20% of deaths among those ages 45 to 54 and 24% among those ages 55 to 64 (PHAC, 2009c).

**Connect to
MyDevelopmentLab**

Can stress contribute to cardiovascular disease and other health issues? See how there are good and bad stresses and test your stress level with this simulation

◄●┤Simulate

GENERAL RISK FACTORS The best information about who is at risk for CVD comes from a number of long-term epidemiological studies, such as the Framingham Heart Study and the Nurses' Health Study, in which the health and habits of large numbers of individuals have been tracked over time. In the Framingham study, 5209 adults were first studied in 1948, when they were 30 to 59 years old. Their health (and mortality) has since been assessed repeatedly, which makes it possible to identify characteristics that predict CVD (Anderson, Castelli, & Levy, 1987; Dawber, Kannel, & Lyell, 1963; Garrison, Gold, Wilson, & Kannel, 1993; Kannel & Gordon, 1980). More recent studies continue to suggest the same risk factors (Heart and Stroke Foundation of Canada, 2010; PHAC, 2009c). The right side of **Table 15.2** lists the well-established risk factors that emerged from the Framingham study and similar studies, along with a few other risk factors that are more speculative.

Because lists like the one in **Table 15.2** have appeared in numerous popular magazines and newspapers, the list does not likely contain information that will be new to you, but a couple of critical points must still be made. First, many Canadians have the risk factors listed in **Table 15.2**. In fact, one-third of Canadians older than age 20 have three or more risk factors for CVD, and the risks increase as we age (Canadian Heart Health Strategy and Action Plan, 2009). Canadian researchers have found that the prevalence of most of the major CVD risk factors (high blood pressure, diabetes mellitus, and obesity) has increased dramatically over the last decade (Lee et al., 2009). So, although mortality rates have declined, national trends indicate a rise in the risk factors, particularly among younger Canadians. Such trends have significant implications; the presence of the risk factors in young and middle-aged adults predisposes them to earlier onset of CVD and increases the potential that they will lose quality life-years. This trend has the potential of reducing life expectancy in the 21st century, something that has not occurred in two centuries (Bibbins-Domingo, Coxson, Pletcher, Lightwood, & Goldman, 2007; Lee et al., 2009; Olshansky et al., 2005). Thus, it is important to do a much better job of reducing heart disease risks in younger age groups (Heart and Stroke Foundation of Canada, 2010).

Second, it is important to understand that these risks are cumulative in the same way that the health habits investigated in the Alameda County Study (which you learned about in **Chapter 13**) seem to be cumulative: The more high-risk behaviours or characteristics you have, the higher your risk of heart disease; the effect is not just additive. For example, high cholesterol is more serious for a person who has diabetes and high blood pressure than it is for adults who do not suffer from these conditions (Cohen, Hailpern, & Alderman, 2004).

PERSONALITY AND HEALTH Personality may also contribute to heart disease. The **type A personality pattern** was first described by two cardiologists, Meyer Friedman and Ray Rosenman (1974; Rosenman & Friedman, 1983). They were struck by the apparently consistent presence among patients who suffered from heart disease of several other characteristics, including competitive striving for achievement, a sense of time urgency, and hostility or aggressiveness. These people, whom Friedman and Rosenman named type A personalities, were perpetually comparing themselves with others, always wanting to win. They scheduled their lives tightly, timed themselves in routine activities, and often tried to do such tasks faster each time. They had frequent conflicts with their co-workers and family. Type B people, in contrast, were thought to be less hurried, more laid back, less competitive, and less hostile.

Early research by Friedman and Rosenman suggested that type A behaviour was linked to higher levels of cholesterol, and hence to increased risk of CVD, even among people who did not suffer from observable heart disease. Contradictory results from more extensive studies since then, however, have forced some modifications in the original hypothesis (e.g., Miller, Turner, Tindale, Posavac, & Dugoni, 1991; O'Connor, Manson, O'Connor, & Buring, 1995). However, not all facets of the type A personality, as originally described, seem to be equally significant for CVD. The most consistent link has been found between CVD and hostility (Mohan, 2006; Olson et al., 2005). Moreover, careful studies have shown that anger and hostility may be part of a larger complex of variables that includes anger, anxiety, cynicism, and other negative emotions (Kubzansky, Cole, Kawachi, Vokonas, & Sparrow, 2006; Olson et al., 2005). The finding that negative emotions are correlated with CVD has led some researchers to propose a new classification, *type D personality* (*D* for distress) (Denollet, 1997). People with this profile exhibit a chronic pattern of emotional distress combined with a tendency to suppress negative emotions. In one study of men who were enrolled in a rehabilitative therapy program after having had a heart attack, those with the type D profile were found to have four times the risk of death as other patients in the program (Sher, 2004).

Critical Thinking

In addition to the personal costs, what are the societal costs attributable to the higher prevalence of health risk factors among Canadians?

type A personality pattern
a personality type associated with greater risk of coronary heart disease. It includes competitive achievement striving, a sense of time urgency, and, sometimes, hostility or aggressiveness.

Chances are this man will die before his wife does, but she will be more troubled by chronic illnesses in her middle and later years.
(*Photo:* Pixland/Thinkstock)

Most people who have analyzed this research would now agree that there is some kind of connection between personality and CVD. What is less clear is just which aspect(s) of personality are most strongly predictive. Some research suggests that measures of neuroticism or depression may be even better risk predictors than hostility (e.g., Cramer, 1991).

◉─⌐Watch

GENDER AND HEALTH

Figure 15.2 makes it clear that women's life expectancy is greater than men's. But what is not evident is an interesting paradox: Women live longer, but they have more diseases and disabilities. Women are more likely to describe their health as poor, to have more chronic conditions such as arthritis, and to be more limited in their daily activities. Such differences have been found in every country in which the pattern has been studied, including nonindustrialized countries (Rahman, Strauss, Gertler, Ashley, & Fox, 1994).

This difference is already present in early adulthood and grows larger with age. By old age, women are substantially more likely than men to be chronically ill (Guralnik, Land, Blazer, Fillenbaum, & Branch, 1993; Kunkel & Applebaum, 1992). In early adulthood, this gender difference in disease rate can be largely attributed to health problems associated with child-bearing. At later ages, the difference cannot be explained in this same way.

How is it possible that men die younger but are healthier while they are alive? Researchers suggest that the apparent paradox can be resolved by considering sex differences in potentially fatal conditions such as CVD (Verbrugge, 1989). In Canada, 101 of every 100 000 men between ages 45 and 54 die of heart disease annually, compared with only 35 of every 100 000 women (Health Canada, 2002d). This difference in rates of heart disease diminishes once women are past menopause, although it does not disappear totally even in late old age.

It isn't just that men have higher rates of CVD; they are also more likely to die from the disease once they have it. One reason for this may be that the heart muscles of women who have CVD seem to be better able to adapt to stresses such as physical exertion (van Doornen, Snieder, & Boomsma, 1998). In addition, once they suffer a heart attack, women recover to a higher level of physical functioning than men do (Bosworth et al., 2000). Sex differences in health habits also seem to contribute to women's greater ability to recover from CVD. For example, women are more likely to get regular checkups and seek help earlier in an illness than men are (Addis & Mahalik, 2003; Verbrugge & Wingard, 1987).

By contrast, women are more likely than men to suffer from nonfatal chronic ailments, such as arthritis. Because chronic pain is characteristic of arthritis, the activities of women who suffer from it are often limited. Understandably, too, living with chronic pain affects their general sense of well-being.

MENTAL HEALTH

As you learned in **Chapter 13**, most types of mental health problems are considerably more common in early adulthood than in the middle years of adult life. In fact, both Canadian men and women report improved mental health with increasing age. One measure of mental health in particular, self-esteem, reportedly peaks between ages 35 and 54 (Health Canada, 1999e). However, about two-thirds of adults diagnosed with serious mental disorders in early adulthood continue to have difficulties in middle age (Meeks, 1997). Further, though most addictive disorders begin in adolescence or early adulthood, they frequently go undiagnosed until the middle adulthood years, when they begin to have dramatic effects on health and other areas of functioning that sufferers or their families can no longer deny.

ALCOHOL USE DISORDERS The Statistical Report on the Health of Canadians (Health Canada, 1999e) found that Canadian men are more likely to be regular heavy drinkers than women, which means that men consumed five or more drinks at least once a month on average. For instance, 9% of men versus 3% of women reported drinking heavily on more than 52 occasions in the previous year. The rate of heavy regular drinking peaks during the young adult years, with more than half of young adults drinking heavily at least some of the time. The rates begin to decline between ages 34 and 44 and continue to decline thereafter.

Alcoholism, defined as physical and psychological dependence on alcohol, takes a particularly heavy toll during middle age. For example, some parts of the brains of middle-aged alcoholics are smaller and less responsive to stimuli than the brains of nonalcoholics (Laakso et al., 2000; Polo, Escera, Gual, & Grau, 1999). Functional deficits among alcoholics include problems with memory and language. CVD is more prevalent among alcoholics as well, because long-term exposure to alcohol weakens the muscles of the heart along with the valves and walls of the body's blood vessels. Further, long-term heavy drinking damages the digestive system, impairs the immune system, and contributes to losses in muscle strength (Laso et al., 1999; Tarter et al., 1997). In women, alcoholism is associated with a delay in the course of the phases of menopause (Torgerson, Thomas, Campbell, & Reid, 1997).

The result of this interaction between aging and alcohol abuse is that alcoholics face an increased risk of health problems and death (Dawson, 2000). A longitudinal study involving more than 40 000 males in Norway found that the rate of death prior to age 60 was significantly higher among alcoholics than among nonalcoholics (Rossow & Amundsen, 1997). Studies further indicate that the death rates of men with alcoholism who are in their 50s and early 60s are five to six times higher than those of nonalcoholics in the same age group (Kristenson, Österling, Nilsson, & Lindgärde, 2002).

Thankfully, the effects of alcohol on the brain may be reversible if an alcoholic quits drinking (Kensinger, Clarke, & Corkin, 2003). Likewise, giving up alcohol is essential to stopping the progression of alcohol-induced liver damage. A drug called acamprosate can be prescribed to help recovering alcoholics deal with withdrawal symptoms and maintain abstinence from alcohol (Mason, Goodman, Chabac, & Lehert, 2006).

alcoholism
physical and psychological dependence on alcohol

Critical Thinking

Considering all the risk factors for the various health problems that were described in this section, what can you predict about your own health in middle age? Which factors can you change?

Before Going On

- What are the major trends in health during middle adulthood?
- What are some important differences in the physical and mental health of middle-aged men and women?

COGNITIVE FUNCTIONING

In the middle adult years, some cognitive abilities improve, while others slow down a bit. Still, many adults have acquired large bodies of knowledge and skill that help them compensate for losses and solve problems within their areas of expertise more efficiently than younger adults do.

◉—[Watch

A MODEL OF PHYSICAL AND COGNITIVE AGING

Many of the various bits and pieces of information you've encountered so far about physical and cognitive changes in adulthood can be combined in a single model, suggested by Nancy Denney and illustrated in **Figure 15.4** (Denney 1982, 1984). Denney proposed that, on nearly any measure of physical or cognitive functioning, age-related changes follow a typical curve, like those shown in the figure. But she also argued that the height of this curve varies depending on the amount an individual exercises some ability or skill. Denney used the word *exercise* very broadly, to refer not only to physical exercise, but also to mental exercise and to the extent some specific task may have been performed before. Unexercised abilities generally have a lower peak level of performance; exercised abilities generally have a higher peak.

Many laboratory tests of memory, for example, such as memorizing lists of names, tap unexercised abilities. Everyday memory tasks, such as recalling details from a newspaper column, tap much more exercised abilities. The distinction is somewhat similar to the distinction between crystallized and fluid intelligence (see **Chapter 13**). Most crystallized abilities are at least moderately exercised, whereas many fluid abilities are relatively unexercised. But Denney was making a more general point: Whether abilities are crystallized or fluid, those that are more fully exercised will have a higher peak.

The gap between the curve for unexercised abilities and the curve for maximally exercised abilities represents the degree of improvement that would be possible for any given skill. Any skill that is not fully exercised can be improved if the individual begins to exercise that ability. There is clear evidence, for example, that aerobic capacity (VO_2 max) can be increased at any age if a person begins a program of physical exercise (e.g., Buchner, Beresford, Larson, LaCroix, & Wagner, 1992; Cheitlin, 2003).). Nonetheless, in Denney's model, the maximum level an adult will be able to achieve, even with optimum exercise, will decline with age, just as performance of top athletes declines, even with optimum training regimens. One implication of this is that young adults are more likely to be able to get away with laziness or poor study habits and still perform well; as adults age, this becomes less and less true, because they are fighting against the basic decay curve of aging.

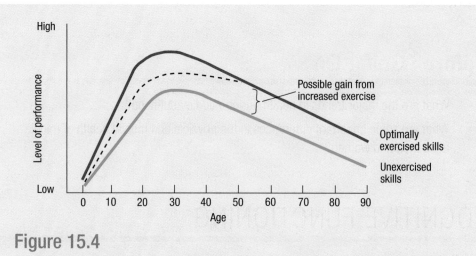

Figure 15.4

Denney's model suggests both a basic decay curve and a fairly large gap between actual level of performance on exercised and unexercised abilities.

(*Source:* Denney, 1982, 1984.)

A somewhat different approach was taken by researchers Paul Baltes (1939–2006) and Margaret Baltes (1939–2000). In their view, the physical declines of middle age give rise to a strategy they call **selective optimization with compensation**, the process of balancing the gains and losses associated with aging (Baltes & Baltes, 1990). The idea is that since a body's resources, such as physical agility and working memory capacity, decrease as the body ages, aging adults, to manage the demands of competing tasks, select one task to which they devote most or all of their resources. Moreover, adults optimize the skills that they believe can be improved by exercising them as much as possible. At the same time, they use compensatory strategies to offset the effects of aging.

selective optimization with compensation
the process of balancing the gains and losses associated with aging

Selection occurs when a middle-aged adult reduces distractions to more efficiently carry out a cognitive task. For example, a middle-aged college student might be more likely than a younger student to turn off the television when she studies. Optimization is involved when middle-aged adults work to improve their physical fitness or expand their knowledge. Compensation takes many forms, including the use of reading glasses to correct for presbyopia and the development of organizational strategies, such as being diligent about recording important events on a calendar, to offset declines in memory.

HEALTH AND COGNITIVE FUNCTIONING

 Watch

You should remember from **Chapter 13** that it is often difficult to separate the effects of primary and secondary aging because they happen at the same time. Denney's model helps illuminate the links between primary aging and cognitive functioning in middle age. Research examining correlations between health and cognition helps developmentalists understand the effects of secondary aging. Specifically, many of the same characteristics that are linked to increased or decreased risk of heart disease and cancer are also linked to the rate of change or the maintenance of intellectual skill in the middle years.

One illustration of this relationship comes from Walter Schaie's analysis of data from the Seattle Longitudinal Study (Schaie & Willis, 2005). He found that those research participants who had some kind of CVD (either coronary heart disease or high blood pressure) showed earlier and larger declines on intellectual tests than did those who were disease-free. Other researchers have found similar linkages. Even adults whose blood pressure is controlled by medication seem to show earlier declines (Sands & Meredith, 1992; Schultz, Elias, Robbins, Streeten, & Blakeman, 1986). Schaie cautions against taking these findings too far. The size of the effect is quite small, and it may operate indirectly rather than directly. For example, adults with CVD may become physically less active as a response to their disease. The lower level of activity, in turn, may affect the rate of intellectual decline. This raises the possibility that exercise may be one of the critical factors in determining an individual person's overall physical health and cognitive performance during middle adulthood. A growing amount of information confirms such an effect.

One particularly large and well-designed study of the effects of exercise on physical health involved 17 321 Harvard alumni who had been students between 1916 and 1950. In 1962 or 1966, when the men were in their 30s, 40s, or 50s, each man provided information about his daily levels of physical activity (Lee, Hsieh, & Paffenbarger, 1995). (The measures of physical activity were quite detailed. Each man reported how many blocks he normally walked each day, how often he climbed stairs, the amount of time per week he normally engaged in various sports, and so on. All the answers were then converted into estimates of calories expended per week. For example, walking 1 mile [1.6 kilometres] on level ground uses roughly 100 calories;

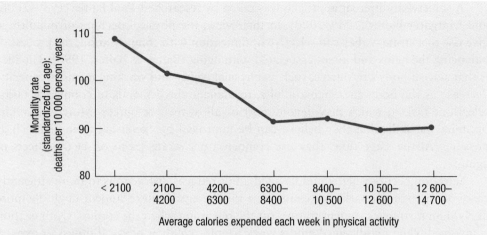

Figure 15.5

Results from the Harvard Alumni Study show clearly that those who are more physically active in middle adulthood have lower risk of mortality over the next decades.

(*Source:* Lee et al., 1995, adapted from data from Table 2, p. 1181.)

climbing one flight of stairs uses about 17.) The researchers tracked all these men until 1988 to identify who had died and of what cause. The link between the level of physical activity and death rates over the succeeding 25 years is shown clearly in **Figure 15.5**: The more exercise a man reported, the lower his mortality risk.

Researchers were careful to exclude from the study any man who was known to suffer from heart disease or other disease at the outset of the study, in the 1960s. Furthermore, the groups differed *only* in level of energy expenditure; they did not differ in age, or whether they smoked, had high blood pressure, were overweight, or had a family history of early death—which makes the effect of exercise even clearer. To be sure, because the level of exercise was each man's own choice, there may have been other differences that separated the various exercise groups that could account for the different death rates. But the pattern, which has been replicated in other groups of both men and women, is so substantial and striking that alternative explanations are hard to come by (e.g., Blair et al., 1995; Lissner et al, 1996). By far, the most likely explanation is that there is a causal connection between longevity and level of physical activity.

Physical exercise also seems to help maintain cognitive abilities in the middle adult years, very likely because it helps to maintain cardiovascular fitness (Rogers, Meyer, & Mortel, 1990). Among physically healthy middle-aged and older adults, those who are more physically active—doing gardening, heavy housework, or aerobic exercise such as walking, running, or swimming—score higher on tests of reasoning, reaction time, and short-term memory (Van Boxtel et al., 1997).

A different approach to studying exercise and cognitive functioning would involve randomly assigning some people to an exercise program and some to a nonexercise control group and then seeing whether the two groups differed in their cognitive functioning after a period of exercise. The results of the small number of studies of this type have been quite mixed. Every study finds that exercise increases measures of physical functioning, such as VO_2 max, even in very elderly adults. Some—but not all—such studies also show that exercise improves thinking (Hawkins, Kramer, & Capaldi, 1992; Hill, Storandt, & Malley, 1993). Other studies do not come to that conclusion (e.g., Buchner et al., 1992; Emery & Gatz, 1990). In most cases, the experimental exercise program lasts only a few months, and that may not be sufficient to make any difference in mental functioning. Still, because researchers already know that exercise is linked to lower levels of disease and greater longevity, prudence alone would argue for including it in your life.

CHANGES IN MEMORY AND COGNITION

◉─Watch

When developmentalists study changes in cognitive functioning in middle age, they find almost precisely what Denney's model and Schaie's longitudinal study suggest. That is, lack of mental exercise tends to be correlated with declines in memory and cognitive skills, but major deficits are not found until between ages 60 and 65.

MEMORY FUNCTION Drawing conclusions about memory function in middle age is difficult, because studies of age differences in adult memory rarely include middle-aged people. Typically, researchers compare very young adults, such as college students, to adults in their 60s and 70s. When the two groups are found to differ, psychologists often infer that middle-aged adults' performance falls somewhere between the two. In other words, they assume that memory function declines steadily, in linear fashion, across the adult years—an assumption that may not be true.

One thing developmentalists do know about memory is that the subjective experience of forgetfulness clearly increases with age. The older we get, the more forgetful we think we are (Commissaris, Ponds, & Jolles, 1998). However, it may be that the memory demands of middle-aged adults' everyday lives are greater than those of young adults. Remember, working memory is limited, and the more you try to remember at one time, the more you will forget.

Nevertheless, there seem to be some real differences in the memory performance of young and middle-aged adults. For example, visual memory, the ability to remember an object you have seen for just a few seconds, declines in middle age (Fahle & Daum, 1997; Giambra, Arenberg, Zonderman, Kawas, & Costa, 1995). Further, the more complex the visual stimulus and the longer the interval between presentation and recall, the greater the difference. By contrast, memory for auditory stimuli seems to remain stable throughout adulthood.

Performance on more complex memory tasks, such as remembering lists of words and passages of text, also declines with age, but usually not until after about age 55. In contrast, recognition of words and texts appears to remain stable throughout adulthood (Zelinski & Burnight, 1997). Such findings suggest that there are age differences in working memory. Research examining short-term memory capacity at various ages shows that it remains very stable throughout early, middle, and late adulthood. What changes, apparently, is the ability to make efficient use of available capacity (Lincourt, Rybash, & Hoyer, 1998).

SEMANTIC AND EPISODIC MEMORIES Researchers can gain additional insight into age-related memory changes by studying how well young and middle-aged adults encode different kinds of memories. In the 1960s at the University of Toronto, Endel Tulving (1972, 2004) was the first to distinguish between two important types of memory. **Episodic memories** have to do with the ability to re-experience personal events or episodes (Tulving, 1999); **semantic memories** represent our general knowledge of the world, facts, and the meaning of words. For example, a person's memories of a vacation in Newfoundland and Labrador are episodic, and her knowledge that Newfoundland became the last Canadian province in 1949 is semantic.

Researchers find that young and middle-aged adults differ more with respect to new episodic memories than they do with respect to semantic memories (Maylor, 1998; Nilsson, Baeckman, Erngrund, & Nyberg, 1997). For example, a middle-aged person

episodic memories
recollections of personal events

semantic memories
recollections of general knowledge, facts, and word meanings

attending a hockey game may forget where he parked his car (episodic memory). How-ever, he is unlikely to forget the basic rules of the game (semantic memory).

Middle-aged adults are very proficient at overcoming episodic memory limitations by using reminders, or cues, to help themselves remember information. Thus, the mid-dle-aged person who knows that she may forget where her car is parked makes a point of noting nearby landmarks that will help her remember its location. The tendency to use cues may exist because middle-aged adults, in contrast to those who are older, continue to have a high sense of self-efficacy with respect to memory (Lineweaver & Hertzog, 1998). In other words, they believe their efforts will make a difference, so they actively work to improve their memories. This effect is strengthened when the person perceives themselves as belonging to a positive aging stereotype category, such as those who are self-accepting, fun-loving, sociable, and independent (Lineweaver, Berger, & Hertzog, 2009).

USE IT OR LOSE IT? In general, most adults maintain or even gain in skill on any task that they practise often or that is based on specific learning. For example, verbal abilities increase in middle age (Giambra et al., 1995; Salthouse, 2004). It appears that vocabulary—or, more precisely, performance on vocabulary tests—doesn't begin to decline until about age 65. And the "use it or lose it" dictum seems to hold true for cognitive abilities. That is, adults who engage in intellectually challenging activities show fewer losses in cognitive skills than those who do not (Salthouse, 2004; Schaie, Nguyen, Willis, Dutta, & Yue, 2001).

Similarly, expertise in a particular field helps to compensate for age-related deficits in cognitive functioning (Colonia-Willner, 1999; Morrow et al., 2003; Tsang, 1998). For example, in one study, researchers examined 17- to 79-year-old participants' abil-ity to recognize melodies performed at varying tempos (Andrews, Dowling, Bartlett, & Halpern, 1998). Some tunes were played very rapidly and then slowed until partici-pants could recognize them. Both age and years of musical training predicted partici-pants' ability to recognize melodies presented in this way, but the relationship between age and recognition was much weaker than the relationship between recognition and musical training. Other melodies were played too slowly to be recognized at the begin-ning and then speeded up. Interestingly, only musical training correlated with recogni-tion of tunes played this way; there was no association with age whatsoever.

NEW LEARNING Because of the accumulated effects of many years of using some cog-nitive skills and the development of a large body of relevant information in long-term memory, middle-aged adults outperform those who are younger on tasks that involve comprehending and remembering reading material. For instance, researchers have found that middle-aged and younger adults take different approaches to learning from expository text (the kind of text you're reading right now!) (Noh et al., 2007). Younger adults focus on creating a word-for-word representation of the text in their memories. By contrast, middle-aged adults pay more attention to overarching themes than to details. In memory, this difference might be reflected in a decline in memory for surface detail, accompanied by an increase in memory for themes and meanings.

A study in which researchers asked adults of various ages to read a story and then to recall it immediately afterward, in writing, yielded support for this hypothesis (Adams, 1991). Younger adults were more likely to report specific events or actions in the story, while middle-aged adults recalled more of the psychological motivations of the characters and offered more interpretations of the story in their recall. What this may mean is that, along with a shift in schematic processing, the encoding process changes as we get older. We may not attempt to encode as much detail but may store more summarizing information.

CREATIVITY

A somewhat different question about cognitive functioning in the middle years of adulthood has to do with **creativity**, the ability to produce original, appropriate, and valuable ideas and/or solutions to problems. One psychologist looked at the lifetime creativity and productivity of thousands of notable scientists from the 19th century and earlier (Simonton, 1991, 2000). Dean Simonton identified the age at which these individuals (nearly all men) published their first significant work, their best work, and their last work. In every scientific discipline represented, the thinkers produced their best work at about age 40, on average. But most of them were publishing significant, even outstanding, research through their 40s and into their 50s.

Lifetime creative output of modern-day scientists follows a similar pattern. Mathematicians, psychologists, physicists, and other scientists born in the 20th century have consistently shown their maximum productivity (usually measured by the number of papers published in a single year) when they were about 40 years old. But research quality (as measured by the number of times each research paper is cited by peers) remains high through age 50 or even age 60 (Horner, Rushton, & Vernon, 1986; Simonton, 1988).

Among musicians or other artists, peak creativity may occur later or be maintained far longer. For example, in one study, researchers asked judges to rate the aesthetic qualities of musical compositions by the 172 composers whose works are most often performed (Simonton, 1988). Works created late in life ("swan songs") were most likely to be evaluated as masterpieces by the judges.

You might be wondering how the creative process actually works (see **Development in the Real World**). Psychologists have been studying it for some time and still

creativity
the ability to produce original, appropriate, and valuable ideas and/or solutions to problems

Development in the Real World

MAINTAINING THE CREATIVE "EDGE" IN MID-LIFE AND BEYOND

The songwriting career of music legend Willie Nelson began when he started writing poetry at age 5. When his grandparents gave him a guitar, he figured out how to set his poems to music. Nearly 3000 songs later, Nelson continues to be inspired more by lyrics than he is by melodies. And even though Nelson is in his late 70s, he doesn't seem to have lost his creative edge. What is the secret to maintaining one's creativity and productivity through middle age and into the later years?

In a fascinating set of interviews, a number of highly successful and creative people described how they viewed creativity ("The creators," 2000). Interestingly, all reported that they viewed themselves as more creative than they had been when they were younger. Their comments suggested that the creative process is a highly individualized intellectual activity. However, what was remarkable was that, by middle age, all had arrived at firm conclusions about what did and did not work for them. So, some part of the maintenance of creativity included acceptance of their own creative idiosyncrasies. Some, for example, expressed the need for external motivation, such as a deadline. Guitarist B.B. King, age 74, said, "If you want me to be creative, give me the line to cross and when I have to cross it" (p. 44). Others were more motivated by self-imposed standards than by external

influences. For example, writer Isabel Allende, age 57, reported that she always begins a new work on January 8, because the date is a personally meaningful anniversary for her. Advertising writer Stan Freberg, age 73, claimed that when he needs an idea, he takes a shower, because he often gets inspiration while in the shower.

A second theme pervaded these reports. Each creative person, in one way or another, recognized the value of accumulated knowledge and experience. They also tended to acknowledge important sources of this knowledge, such as parents, spouses, and friends.

Consequently, these people saw their creative work not only as the product of their own abilities, but also as the result of a complex network of influential individuals, life experiences, and their own capacity to reflect on their lives.

From these extraordinary individuals, we can learn two important things about maintaining creativity and productivity in the middle and late adult years: First, being consciously aware of one's own creative process—and accepting its boundaries—seems to be critical. Second, some degree of humility, a sense of indebtedness to those who have contributed to and supported one's creative development, appears to be associated with continuing productivity in the middle and late adult years.

have much to learn. However, one useful approach describes creativity as a type of thought process called *divergent thinking* (Guilford, 1967). A person who uses divergent thinking can provide multiple solutions to problems that have no clear answer. Thus, divergent thinking is as vital to science as it is to art. For instance, when scientists were faced with the problem of identifying the cause of AIDS, they proposed and tested many hypotheses before it became clear that the disease was caused by a virus. Likewise, a novelist who wants to provide readers with insight into a character's motivations tries out several ways of communicating the information before she settles on the one that works best.

Creative solutions sometimes pop into the mind of a creative person fully formed, but most of the time they arise from bits and pieces of several solutions that she has been mulling over for a while. Psychologist Daniel Goleman describes this mulling over process as involving four stages when it is used to solve problems (Goleman et al., 1992). During *preparation*, relevant information is gathered. The next phase, *incubation*, involves digesting the information without actually trying to work on the problem. *Illumination* occurs when this digestive process produces an "aha!" moment in which the solution to the problem becomes clear. Finally, during *translation*, the solution is applied to the problem and adjustments are made as needed. As you probably know from experience, the last step is the most difficult and time-consuming because, in the real world, things don't often go as we imagine they will. As Thomas Edison put it, "Genius is 1% inspiration and 99% perspiration." Edison should know; after working out how to design a commercially viable electric light bulb theoretically, he spent over a year making prototypes before he finally found the design that worked. Thus, Edison believed that failure was essential to the creative process.

Before Going On

- What does research reveal about the link between health and cognitive functioning?
- Describe differences between young and middle-aged adults in cognition, memory function, and creativity.

Summary

Physical Changes

- Brain volume peaks during the middle adult years. Middle-aged adults often outperform younger adults on everyday tasks that require concentration and rapid judgments, such as driving.

- The loss of reproductive capacity, *climacteric*, occurs very gradually in men, but more rapidly in women. Menopause is a three-phase process that results from a series of hormonal changes.

- Bone mass declines significantly after age 30; accelerated declines in women at menopause are linked to decreased levels of estrogen and progesterone.

- Thickening of the lens of the eye, with accompanying loss of elasticity, reduces visual acuity noticeably in the 40s or 50s. Hearing loss is more gradual.

Health Promotion and Wellness

- Chronic illness and death rates rise noticeably toward the end of middle adulthood. The two major causes of death in middle adulthood are heart disease and cancer.

- Risk factors for cancer include smoking, obesity, an inactive lifestyle, and likely a high-fat diet.

- Risk factors for cardiovascular disease include smoking, high blood pressure, high blood cholesterol, obesity, and a high-fat diet.

- Women tend to live longer than men but are more likely to suffer from chronic illnesses.

- Middle-aged adults have lower rates of mental health problems of virtually every kind than young adults. Alcoholism usually starts at younger ages but often remains undiagnosed until middle age.

Cognitive Functioning

- Denney's model of aging suggests that exercising either physical or cognitive abilities can improve performance at any age, but the upper limit on improvement declines with increasing age. Paul and

Margaret Baltes assert that middle-aged adults balance the gains and losses associated with aging by selecting tasks on which to focus limited resources, optimizing some skills through practice, and compensating for declines.

- Exercise clearly affects the physical health of middle-aged adults, but research is less conclusive with regard to its effects on cognitive functioning.

- Verbal abilities continue to grow in middle age. Some loss of memory speed and skill occurs. Expertise helps middle-aged adults compensate for losses in processing speed.

- Creative productivity also appears to remain high during middle adulthood. Goleman descibes four stages in the creative process: preparation, incubation, illumination, and translation.

Review Questions

Answers are provided on MyDevelopmentLab in the Course Resources folder.

Physical Changes

15.1 Which of the following statements is true about the brain at mid-life?
  a. The distribution of electrical activity is the same in the brains of alcoholics and those of nonalcoholics.
  b. Cognitive tasks activate a larger area of brain tissue in middle-aged adults than in younger adults.
  c. In middle age, more new synapses are formed than are lost.
  d. Synaptic density continues to increase across adulthood.

15.2 Which of the following is the best summary of the current research on hormone replacement therapy?

  a. Hormone replacement therapy has no positive effects.
  b. Hormone replacement therapy reduces the incidence of heart disease and Alzheimer's disease, but also has some negative effects.
  c. Hormone replacement therapy has some positive effects, but there are ways of achieving these results without the risks associated with hormone replacement therapy.
  d. Hormone replacement therapy has many benefits and no known risks.

Health Promotion and Wellness

15.3 Middle aged Canadian men are more likely to _____, while women _____.
  a. have higher rates of cancer; higher rates of heart disease

b. live longer and healthier lives; have more dis-
    abilities
c. be chronically ill; have good health
d. die from disease; suffer from nonfatal chronic
    ailments

Cognitive Functioning

15.4 A review of the research findings on cognitive
      change in middle adulthood reveals that
      a. vocabularies decline.
      b. problem-solving ability is significantly impaired.
      c. mental processes get slower, but actual losses are
          small.
      d. performance is maintained or even slightly
          improved on tasks of fluid intelligence.

15.5 According to Simonton's review of the lifetime cre-
      ativity and productivity of thousands of notable sci-
      entists, people are most creative
      a. in their adolescent years.
      b. in their 20s.

c. at about age 40.
d. in their 60s.

Critical-Thinking Questions

15.6 Given the changes in the brain, reproductive system,
      bones, and sensory abilities that you have learned
      about in the section on physical changes, how would
      you evaluate a statement such as "age is just a state
      of mind"?

15.7 Given what you have learned in the section on cog-
      nitive functioning, where would you place cognitive
      functioning in middle age on a 10-point scale rang-
      ing from "age and health have no effect on cognitive
      functioning" at the low end to "age and health cause
      inevitable declines in cognitive functioning" at the
      high end? What reasons would you give if you were
      asked to explain your assessment?

Polka Dot Images/Thinkstock

Social and Personality Development in Middle Adulthood

What is the best age for a woman to initiate a new business venture? When is the best time for a man to be at the peak of his career? When is the best time to complete an advanced university degree? What is the best age to retire? People within any given society carry general social expectations about how a person's life should progress and unfold, and these expectations are closely associated with a person's age. Most often, expectations reflect cultural beliefs about the social clock. Middle adulthood is commonly seen as the time when people are best able, developmentally, to manage the weighty demands associated with positions of authority and responsibility.

Such beliefs and expectations are not entirely unfounded. When middle-aged adults get together with acquaintances, friends, or relatives at events such as high school or family reunions, they find most of their age-mates to be in the most powerful positions of their lives. Most have higher incomes than they ever had before or ever will again, and a greater proportion of them hold positions of authority in business, education, and government than was true when they were younger.

The social clock is evident in family relationships as well. The middle-aged cohort of any family tends to have the most responsibility. They are "sandwiched" between adolescent or young adult children and aging parents. When a younger or older family member requires help, the middle-aged members are expected to respond.

What seems most striking about everyday life in middle age, however, is how much less constricting social roles feel. Most middle-aged adults are married, parents, and workers, but by age 40 or 50, these roles have changed in important ways. Children begin to leave home, which dramatically alters and reduces the intensity of the parental role; job promotions have usually reached their limit, so workers have less need to learn new work skills. And when both parenting and work are less demanding, partners can find more time for themselves and for each other.

When you finish studying the chapter, you will be able to explain the theories of social and personality development in the middle adulthood years; trace the changes in relationships across middle adulthood; and identify the changes in the importance of work in middle adulthood. While you read this chapter, keep the following questions in mind:

- What are some reasons why marital stability and satisfaction may increase in middle adulthood?

- Speculate as to how the role of caregiver of an aging parent may change in the next few decades.

- Why do you suppose those who dread retirement do the least planning?

THEORIES OF SOCIAL AND PERSONALITY DEVELOPMENT

generativity versus stagnation stage
the seventh of Erikson's stages, in which middle-aged adults find meaning in contributing to the development of younger individuals

generativity
a sense that one is making a valuable contribution to society by bringing up children or mentoring younger people in some way

You should remember from **Chapter 2** that Erik Erikson viewed middle age as a period when attention turns to creation of a legacy that nutures and guides the next generation. Adults do this by influencing the lives of those in younger generations. Yet many have characterized middle age less positively, suggesting that it is a period of intense crisis.

ERIKSON'S GENERATIVITY VERSUS STAGNATION STAGE

Middle-aged adults are in Erikson's **generativity versus stagnation stage**. Their developmental task is to acquire a sense of **generativity**, which involves an interest in establishing and guiding the next generation. Generativity is expressed not only in bearing or rearing one's own children, but also through teaching, serving as mentor, or taking on leadership roles in various civic, religious, or charitable organizations. Merely having children is not enough for developing generativity in Erikson's terms. The optimum expression of generativity requires turning outward from a preoccupation with self, a kind of psychological expansion toward caring for others. Those who fail to develop generativity often suffer from a "pervading sense of stagnation and personal impoverishment [and indulge themselves] as if they were their own one and only child" (Erikson, 1963, p. 267).

RESEARCH ON GENERATIVITY   Research has produced hints of such a developmental stage, but the findings are much less clear than data on changes in earlier years. One cross-sectional study of young, mid-life, and older women found that generativity increased in middle age, as Erikson's theory suggests (Zucker, Ostrove, & Stewart, 2002). Contrary to what his theory would predict, however, the oldest group of participants, whose average age was 66, cited generative concerns as being important to them just as frequently as the middle-aged group did. These findings support Erikson's claim that generativity is more common in middle age than in early adulthood, but they also indicate that generativity continues to be important in old age. Other research suggests that generativity is a more prominent theme in the lives of middle-aged women than in the lives of middle-aged men (Morfei, Hooker, Carpenter, Mix, & Blakeley, 2004).

Despite these inconsistencies, studies support Erikson's belief that generativity is related to mental health among middle-aged adults. For instance, researchers have found that generativity is positively related to satisfaction in life and work and to emotional well-being (Ackerman, Zuroff, & Moskowitz, 2000). Further, in a study that measured middle-aged women's sense of being burdened by caring for elderly parents, those who exhibited the highest levels of generativity felt the least burdened by elder care (Peterson, 2002).

Erikson's theory also raises questions about the impact of childlessness on adult development. One very interesting analysis comes from a 40-year longitudinal study of a group of inner-city, nondelinquent boys who had originally served as a comparison group in a study of delinquent boys (Snarey, Son, Kuehne, Hauser, & Vaillant, 1987). Of the 343 married men who were still part of this sample in their late 40s, 29 had fathered no children. Researchers found that the way a man had responded earlier to his childlessness was predictive of his psychological health at age 47. At that age, each man was rated on his degree of generativity. A man was considered to be "generative" if he had participated in some kind of mentoring or other teaching or supervising of children or younger adults. Among those with no children, those who were rated as most generative were likely to have responded to their childlessness by finding another child to nurture. They adopted a child, became Big Brothers, or helped with the rearing of someone else's child, such as a niece or a nephew. Those childless men rated as nongenerative were more likely to have chosen a pet as a child substitute.

VAILLANT'S REVISION OF ERIKSON'S THEORY   Psychiatrist George Vaillant has spent the past three decades chronicling the development of several hundred adults through early, middle, and late adulthood. His research has included measures of change in the physical, cognitive, personality, and social domains. His findings for the middle adulthood period prompted him to propose a modification of Erikson's theory of lifespan development (Vaillant, 2002).

Vaillant argued that there is a stage between intimacy and generativity called *career consolidation*. Like Erikson, Vaillant tended to define the domains of life fairly

PEARSON
mydevelopmentlab
Connect to
MyDevelopmentLab
What does generativity versus stagnation mean? Follow along with this pictorial dialogue to understand Erikson's concept.

❋─[**Explore**

Critical Thinking

Make a list of ways to express generativity other than by bringing up your own children and helping them get a start in life.

broadly, so *career* may mean a paid vocation or it could involve a decision to be a stay-at-home mother or father. The outcome of this phase is the creation of a new social network for which the middle-aged adult's primary work serves as a hub. Involvement with this social network helps the individual meet the psychosocial needs of this substage. Such needs include contentment, compensation, competence, and commitment (Vaillant, 2002). Individuals need to be happy with the work-related choices they have made, to feel that they are adequately compensated, to view themselves as competent in their chosen field, and to be able to maintain a sense of commitment to their work.

Following generativity versus stagnation, Vaillant argued, is another stage called *keeper of the meaning*. In this phase, middle-aged adults focus on preserving the institutions and values of their culture that they believe will benefit future generations. For some, religious organizations become paramount. Others focus on the arts, educational institutions, historical preservation societies, or political organizations. The key is that participation in these institutions is motivated by the desire to ensure their survival rather than by a concern for how the institution can benefit the individual middle-aged adult. In other words, the well adjusted adult in the keeper of meaning stage wants to give something to the institution rather than to get something from it. Moreover, the social networks that are created through middle-aged adults' associations with institutions support their need to feel that the work they are doing will make a difference for future generations.

⊙─[Watch]

MID-LIFE CRISIS: FACT OR FICTION?

Canadian psychoanalyst Elliot Jacques (1965) popularized the term *mid-life crisis* in the 1960s, an era when the occurrence of major events along the timeline of life was relatively lockstep and predictable, especially for men. The landmarks of life (particularly in industrialized countries such as Canada) included finishing school, going to work, retiring, and ultimately, dying. Midway between completing school and death there was a change in a person's time perspective that shifted from "time since birth" to "time left till death." At this point, any perceived gap between what one had accomplished thus far in life and where one had expected to be, coupled with the realization that only so much time was left to close the gap, was therefore thought to be responsible for creating a sense of urgency, a sense of having just one last chance at a fulfilled life. The realization of the inevitability of death, along with other tangible indicators of time passing, such as noticeable body aging, children leaving home, or elderly or deceased parents, seemed to be a universal phenomenon that hit people during their 40s.

Decades later, of course, the timing and nature of major life events have changed dramatically. The progression from formal secondary schooling to late adulthood is much less predictable than it was in the 1960s, and it is certainly not a universal, worldwide experience as thought previously. In Canada, for instance, both women and men engage in lifelong learning, have different family living arrangements at various times in their lives, and generally hit the major milestones later in life. By the 1980s, the concept of a mid-life crisis was being challenged. For example, by using a mid-life crisis scale, including items about inner turmoil, marital or job dissatisfaction, and a sense of declining power, researchers compared the responses of over 500 participants in a cross-sectional study of men ranging in age from 35 to 70 (Costa & McCrae, 1980; McCrae & Costa, 1984). The researchers could find no distinct ages at which measures of "mid-life crisis" occurred.

A LIFE EVENTS APPROACH When developmentalists look at the relevant research evidence, however, they often question NIH's Robert McCrae and Paul Costa's conclusion. Just over one-quarter of middle-aged and older adults report having had a crisis such as the one that Levinson's theory predicts (Lachman, 2004). However, these crises appear to have been triggered by specific events, such as the loss of a job or the death of a close friend or relative. Thus, some developmentalists argue that a **life events approach** to explaining the unique stresses of the middle adulthood period is preferable to a theoretical perspective that proposes a universal crisis. The life events approach focuses on normative and non-normative events and middle-aged adults' responses to them.

The physical changes of middle age that you learned about in **Chapter 15** are the backdrop against which the major life events of this period are played out. Consequently, all middle-aged adults are dealing with new stressors for which they must develop new ways of coping, and research shows that concerns about the limitations imposed by these physical changes increases across the middle adulthood years (Cate & John, 2007). In addition, most middle-aged adults experience the loss of a parent or must cope with major declines in their parents' ability to care for themselves. Most are also dealing with work-related issues. At the same time, for those who have children, major shifts are occurring in the nature of parent–child relationships. Another important factor, one that adds another layer of complexity, is that many of these stressors last for some time. A middle-aged person can spend years, for example, caring for an incapacitated parent. With all these changes going on at the same time, it isn't surprising that middle-aged adults often feel stressed.

Some developmentalists argue that the best way to understand middle adulthood is to study how people in this age group manage to integrate all these changes and their interpretations of them into the coherent stories of their own middle adulthood experiences (Glück, Bluck, Baron, & McAdams, 2005; Ville & Khlat, 2007). It is particularly important to understand how each middle-aged person's understanding of her experiences is influenced by characteristics that she brings to the developmental tasks of middle age. For example, men and women with histories of depression are likely to integrate the life events of middle age differently from those who do not have such histories (Kikhavani & Kunar, 2005). Variations in general optimism and in personality are likely to contribute to the integration process (Clarke & Singh, 2005; McAdams & Pals, 2006). Likewise, adults who face a major health crisis, such as breast cancer, along with the more normative events of middle age are likely to think differently about this period than their peers who are blessed with good health during these years do (Low, Stanton, Thompson, Kwan, & Ganz, 2006).

Finally, the stresses associated with the events of middle age are often complicated by **role conflict**, any situation in which two or more roles are at least partially incompatible, either because they call for different behaviours or because their separate demands add up to more hours than there are in the day. Role conflict happens, for example, when a middle-aged father must choose between helping his aging parents with financial or health problems and attending his teenaged son's hockey games. A person experiences **role strain** when her own qualities or skills do not measure up to the demands of some role. For example, a 40-year-old worker who is forced to return to school to acquire new skills after a job layoff and who feels anxious about her ability to succeed is experiencing role strain.

life events approach a theoretical perspective on middle adulthood that focuses on normative and non-normative events and how adults in this age group respond to them

role conflict any situation in which two or more roles are at least partially incompatible, either because they call for different behaviours or because their separate demands add up to more hours than there are in the day

role strain the strain experienced by an individual whose own qualities or skills do not measure up to the demands of some role

Before Going On

- Briefly describe Erikson's generativity versus stagnation stage and the evidence that supports his theory.
- What does research suggest about the existence of a universal mid-life crisis?

CHANGES IN RELATIONSHIPS AND PERSONALITY

As suggested previously, family roles are still an important part of Canadian life in middle age (Beaujot & Ravanera, 2008). However, these roles change significantly during this period of life.

PARTNERSHIPS

Several lines of evidence suggest that, on average, marital stability and satisfaction increase in mid-life as conflicts over child-rearing and other matters decline (Swensen, Eskew, & Kohlhepp, 1981; Veroff, Douvan, & Kulka, 1981; Wu & Penning, 1997). In addition, as couples get older, the number of shared friends they have increases and the number of non-shared friends decreases (Kalmijn, 2003). As a result, the social network tends to get a bit tighter—and probably more supportive—in middle age, which may be one reason for age-related improvements in relationship satisfaction. So, despite considerable diversity among mid-life marriages or partnerships, overall, they are less conflicted than those of young adults.

Improvements in marital satisfaction may derive from middle-aged adults' increased sense of control—a kind of marital self-efficacy (Lachman & Weaver, 1998). It is likely that middle-aged partners' identification of successful problem-solving strategies contributes to the sense that they have control over their relationship. Research has provided useful illustrations of this point. For example, researchers typically find that marital problem themes among middle-aged couples are remarkably similar to those of younger adults. Wives complain of an unjust division of labour; husbands express dissatisfaction with limits on their freedom. Yet, relationship stability among middle-aged couples is maintained through the practice of what one researcher called *skilled diplomacy*, an approach to solving problems that involves confrontation of the spouse about an issue, followed by a period during which the confronting spouse works to restore harmony (Perho & Korhonen, 1999). Skilled diplomacy is practised more often by wives than by husbands, but it appears to be an effective technique for marital problem solving no matter which spouse uses it.

As age-related increases in marital satisfaction would predict, middle-aged couples are far less likely to divorce than those who are younger (Uhlenberg, Cooney, & Boyd, 1990). Moreover, research suggests that middle-aged women are better able to cope with divorce then younger women (Marks & Lambert, 1998). Perhaps a "mellowing" of personality (which you will read about later in this chapter) renders the middle-aged woman more resilient in the face of such traumatic events. Moreover, some women remain in unsatisfactory marriages through their 20s and 30s because they think that divorce will be harmful to their children. Once the children are grown, such women feel free to move out of these relationships and report that the stress associated with divorce was less problematic than the emotional turmoil they experienced in the years prior to splitting from their husbands (Enright, 2004).

CHILDREN AND PARENTS

The discussion of the relationship between young adults and their families in **Chapter 14** focused almost entirely on connections *up* the chain of family generations—that is, relationships between the young adults and their own middle-aged parents. When looking at family relationships from the perspective of middle age, we have to look in both directions: down the generational chain to relationships with grown children, and up the chain to relationships with aging parents.

One of the striking effects of increased life expectancy in developed countries is that adults are likely to spend many more years focusing on both older and younger generations in their families. For example, in 1800, a woman in North America could expect both of her parents to be dead by the time she was 37 years old (Watkins, Menken, & Bongaarts, 1987). Early in the 21st century, the average woman can expect to have at least one parent still living until she is in her late 50s, and this pattern will become only more prevalent as projected life expectancy increases still further (Health Reports, 2001).

SANDWICH GENERATION Each of the positions in a family's generational chain has certain role prescriptions (Hagestad, 1986, 1990). In middle adulthood, for current age cohorts at least, the family role involves not only giving assistance in both directions in the generational chain, but also shouldering the primary responsibility for maintaining affectional bonds. These responsibilities produce what is sometimes called the mid-life *squeeze*, and those being squeezed form the "sandwich generation."

Such a squeeze was illustrated in the results of interviews with over 13 000 American adults in one frequently cited survey. Among many other things, respondents were asked about the amount of help of various kinds—financial, child care, household, and so forth—they gave to and received from both adult children and aging parents (Bumpass & Aquilino, 1995). The results, graphed in **Figure 16.1**, make it clear that those between ages 40 and 65 give help more than they receive help in both directions within the family—to adult children and to aging parents. This pattern was confirmed in a variety of other studies in the United States (e.g., Gallagher, 1994), as well as within the Canadian population by gerontology researchers John Hirdes of the University of Waterloo and Laurel Strain of the University of Manitoba (Hirdes & Strain, 1995).

Whether most middle-aged adults experience this combination of responsibilities as a burden is not answered simply (Williams, 2005). A General Social Survey of

Once the children are grown and gone, many couples find it easier to spend time together—perhaps one of the reasons that marital satisfaction generally rises in middle age. (*Photo:* Ryan McVay/Thinkstock)

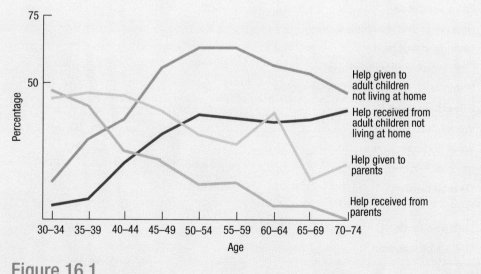

Figure 16.1

The midlife "squeeze," or "sandwich generation," is illustrated in this graph of data from a national survey of adults. Middle-aged adults give more help to both their adult children and their own parents than they receive.

(*Source:* Bumpass & Aquilino, 1995, data from Tables 11, 12, 25, and 26.)

Canadian sandwich generation caregivers who were working full-time reported being somewhat/very stressed (70%), but the survey also found that a significant number of these caregivers were satisfied (34%) or very satisfied (61%) with their lives (Williams, 2005). The degree of infirmity of the aging parents, the nature of the relationship the middle-aged adult has with those aging parents, and the degree of help required by the young adult children make a difference in the level of intensity of care. A 50-year-old whose divorced daughter has returned with young grandchildren to live at home or one who has a parent living nearby and suffering from the early stages of Alzheimer's is far more likely to experience major role strain than is someone of the same age who babysits the grandchildren from time to time and helps her aging parents by doing occasional shopping, snow shovelling, or housecleaning. In addition to the added strain, high-intensity sandwich generation caregivers who spend more time on elder care than those low-intensity caregivers, also incur extra expenses, as **Table 16.1** reveals. But, on

TABLE 16.1	Impact of High-Intensity Elder Care on Sandwich Generation Caregivers	
	Intensity of Elder Care	
	Low (8 hours or less per month)	**High (more than 8 hours per month)**
	%	%
Proportion feeling stressed		
Very/somewhat	67	76*
Not very	23	19
Not at all	9^E	5^E
Don't know/no opinion	F	F
Caregiving has resulted in		
Health repercussions	7^E	23*
Changed sleep patterns	9^E	22*
Extra expenses	32	55*
Change in social activities	28	50*
Change in holidays	17	43*
Care receiver moving closer	7^E	10^E
Caregiver moving in with care receiver	F	6^E
Effects on work		
Work hours shifted	11	35*
Work hours reduced	10	26*
Income reduced	6^E	17*
Overall burden		
None	60	37*
Little/moderate	34	56*
Quite a bit/extreme	3^E	6^E

Note: Percentages may not add to 100 because of some nonresponse.
*Indicates statistically significant difference from the low-intensity sandwiched group.
^{E}Use with caution
^{F}Too unreliable to publish

(*Source:* Statistics Canada, General Social Survey, 2002, in Williams, 2005, p. 18.)

average, it is clear that middle adulthood is likely to be a time when more help is given than is received.

EMPTYING THE NEST

The timing of the "empty nest" stage in the family life cycle obviously depends on a person's (or couple's) age when the last child is born. In conjunction with women delaying child-bearing, men are delaying parenting, which pushes the empty nest stage to a later age in a pattern typical of today's Canadian adults. This pattern is quite different from the historical parenting trends in Canada. For example, McMaster University researchers Carolyn Rosenthal and James Gladstone have been studying trends in contemporary families. They reported that women born in the mid-1800s had their last child, on average, when they were about 40 (Rosenthal & Gladstone, 2000). If we assume that this last child left home when he or she was between 20 and 25, then women in this cohort were roughly 60 years old when their last child left. Since the life expectancy for women during the first decades of the 1900s was less than 60 years (Health Reports, 2001), there was little possibility for women to experience what we now call the *empty nest stage*. By comparison, women born during the 1930s and later were only about 30 when they bore their last child and were in their 50s when the last child left home (Beaujot & Ravanera, 2001). Their life expectancy was somewhat beyond 60 years. Thus, there was greater likelihood that they would experience the empty nest stage. This stage will likely be prolonged even more in the near future because of a number of other factors associated with women born in the late 1940s and 1950s: These women started having fewer, more closely spaced babies at an earlier age (Rosenthal & Gladstone, 2000). This cohort also enjoys a much longer projected lifespan, which increases the likelihood of living well beyond the time when the youngest child leaves home.

A study by University of Western Ontario researchers Ravanera and Rajulton (1998) found that male parenting in Canada parallels the female pattern, whereby male parenting patterns in the later half of the 20th century have been more variable than prior to that time. Both men and women experience nontraditional family patterns, including sole-parenting and step-parenting. Moreover, on average, Canadian men end parenting at just over age 56, and since they are living longer, they too experience the empty nest. Ravanera and Rajulton also reported two other interesting trends in male parenting. First, men of lower status start parenting younger but end parenting at an older age. Second, men in the Atlantic provinces have the longest parenting duration, whereas men from Ontario have the shortest.

The role of parent does not cease when the child leaves home. Support and advice continue to be expected and offered. But the content of the parental role in this "postparental" phase is clearly quite different from what it was when the children were still living at home. The child does not need daily care or supervision. As a result, adults have much more time for their spousal roles, a change that undoubtedly contributes to the higher reported marital satisfaction in this stage of family life.

Folklore in Western cultures predicts that some or even most women become depressed or upset once the "nest" is empty, because they are losing their central role of "mother." Of course, it is possible that such a pattern exists in some cultures, but it

Contrary to popular belief, when this woman's daughter leaves the nest in a few years, it will be a joyful experience.
(*Photo:* Sean Justice/Corbis)

seems not to be true of Canadian society, at least not for the great majority of middle-aged women. Suicide rates do go up for women in mid-life, but the rise begins between ages 35 and 54, when children are still at home, and then drops for women past their mid-50s, which is when the empty nest typically occurs. Similarly, high rates of depression among mid-life women are apparent until after the mid-40s, also before the children have left home. Furthermore, high levels of chronic stress also peak after age 44 and decline thereafter (Statistics Canada, 2010b).

More to the point, when women are asked specifically about positive and negative transitions in their lives, those who list the departure of the last child are more likely to describe this event as positive rather than negative. In one study of 60 women between ages 45 and 60, researchers found that only one-third of the participants described any significant transition point when the last child left home (Harris, Ellicott, & Holmes, 1986). Of these, 25% reported that the transition involved a distinct "mellowing," increased marital satisfaction, or increased inner stability; 17% reported that the transition involved an adjustment to the departure of the children. Those few women who do experience some distress in this role transition appear to be those whose sense of self-identity has been heavily focused on the role of "mother." In contrast, women in this age range who are in the labour force are much more likely to experience the empty nest as positive.

THE REVOLVING DOOR

Because research findings regarding the positive aspects of emptying the nest are so strong, researchers have turned their attention to the *revolving door*, the pattern in which adult children return to their parents' home (Dennerstein, Dudley, & Guthrie, 2002). Studies show that conflicts between parents and resident adult children are common (Muzi, 2000). Both parents and children feel that they have inadequate privacy. Middle-aged parents' sense of obligation to their children may cause them to feel that they can't pursue their own goals until they have helped their late-blooming children become self-sufficient. As a child's departure is further and further delayed, frustrations can accumulate.

The percentage of adult children living with their middle-aged parents is increasing. Gerontologist Barbara Mitchell (2000) of Simon Fraser University reported that 20- to 34-year-olds are staying at home longer (about half are still living with their parents). Many others leave home and then return (about 24% of Canadian parents are living with an adult child who is part of this so-called *boomerang generation*) (Turcotte, 2006). Financial difficulties associated with unemployment and/or extended post-secondary schooling, delayed marriage, and a rise in the divorce rate probably explain this increase (Muzi, 2000; Turcotte, 2006).

Research suggests that, even though conflict occurs, more than half of parents with adult resident children manage to work out good systems for handling the potential stresses and say that they are satisfied with their arrangement (Aquilino & Supple, 1991). In fact, some parents enjoy greater social support from their resident children than from their children who live away from home (Umberson, 1992). But there is little doubt that such an arrangement brings a new set of tasks and roles, and that it is linked to somewhat higher stress levels in many families.

GRANDPARENTING

Middle-aged adults typically move into several new roles, such as becoming "in-laws" as their children marry. In addition, more than half of Canadian adults become "grandparents" by the end of middle adulthood (Milan & Hamm, 2003) (see **Figure 16.2**).

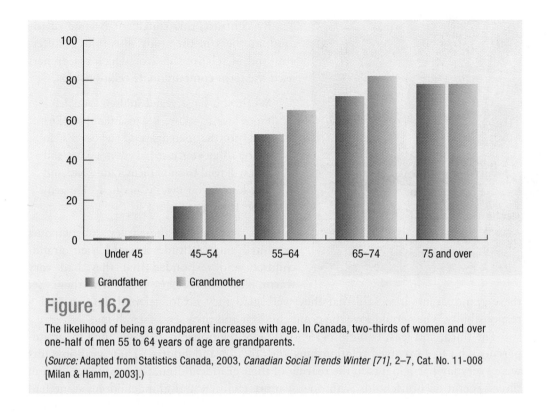

Figure 16.2

The likelihood of being a grandparent increases with age. In Canada, two-thirds of women and over one-half of men 55 to 64 years of age are grandparents.

(*Source:* Adapted from Statistics Canada, 2003, *Canadian Social Trends Winter [71],* 2–7, Cat. No. 11-008 [Milan & Hamm, 2003].)

In Canada, there are about 5.7 million grandparents and almost five grandchildren for each grandparent. Nearly half a million grandchildren share the same household with their grandparents, although a relatively small number (25 200) live with only their grandparents.

Most grandparents—92% in one study—express high levels of satisfaction with this role (Kaufman & Elder, 2003; Segatto & Di Filippo, 2003). A majority see or talk to their grandchildren regularly. They may write, call, or visit as often as every couple of weeks, and most describe their relationships as warm and loving. Likewise, many studies have demonstrated the positive impact of warm relationships with grandparents on children's development (Adkins, 1999).

Grandparents seem to be an especially important source of stability in the lives of children of divorced parents. However, in most cases, grandparents in Canada have privileges, as does any interested third party, but not rights of access to their grandchildren. With the exceptions of Quebec, Alberta, and British Columbia, there is a lack of provincial legislation that provides grandparents with a legal basis for matters such as visitation or access to their grandchildren (Kruk, 1995; Spencer, 2008).

Fortunately, most parents welcome the involvement of their own parents in their children's lives, and surveys suggest that grandparents and grandchildren engage in many of the same activities—watching television, shopping, attending religious services—that parents and children share (Waggoner, 2000). However, while parenthood clearly involves full-time responsibility, there are many degrees of being a grandparent.

Most behavioural scientists place grandparents in one of several categories derived from a study in which researchers interviewed a nationally representative sample of over 500 grandparents (Cherlin & Furstenberg, 1986). Twenty-nine percent of grandparents in the study had **remote relationships**; they saw their grandchildren relatively infrequently and had little direct influence over their grandchildren's lives. The most common reason for this remoteness was physical distance.

remote relationships relationships in which grandparents do not see their grandchildren often

This girl seems delighted with her grandmother, with whom she seems to have what Cherlin and Furstenberg would call a companionate relationship.
(*Photo:* Jack Monnier/Getty Images)

companionate relationships relationships in which grandparents have frequent contact and warm interactions with grandchildren

involved relationships relationships in which grandparents are directly involved in the everyday care of grandchildren or have close emotional ties with them

By contrast, this statement by one of the grandmothers in the study illustrates a different kind of relationship, for which researchers used the term **companionate relationship**:

> When you have grandchildren, you have more love to spare. Because the discipline goes to the parents and whoever's in charge. But you just have extra love and you will tend to spoil them a little bit. And you know, you give. (Cherlin & Furstenberg, 1986, p. 55)

Just over half of the survey's participants exhibited such attitudes toward their grandchildren and responded that they had very warm, pleasurable relationships with them. Yet these grandparents also said that they were glad they no longer had the day-to-day responsibility. They could love the grandchildren and then send them home.

The third, and least common (16%), type of relationship was exhibited by grandparents who had **involved relationships** with their grandchildren. These grandparents were everyday participants in the rearing of their grandchildren. Some of them lived in three-generation households with one or more children and grandchildren; some had nearly full-time care of the grandchildren. But involved relationships also occurred in some cases in which the grandparent had no daily responsibility for the grandchildren's care but created an unusually close link.

Gerontologists Joan Norris and Joseph Tindale (1994) of the University of Guelph determined that grandparents commonly help their children and grandchildren with child care, although most grandparents prefer to avoid full-time child-care arrangements. Full-time grandparent care is especially likely when the grandchild's mother is unmarried. In such cases, the grandmother frequently takes on child-care responsibilities so that her daughter can continue in school or hold down a job. That such assistance is indeed helpful is indicated by the fact that teenaged mothers who have such help from their own mothers complete more years of education and have more successful work careers in adulthood (Taylor, Chatters, Tucker, & Lewis, 1990).

Gender is related to grandparenting as well. Among all ethnic groups, the role of grandmother is likely to be both broader and more intimate than that of grandfather (Hagestad, 1985). In addition, young grandparents, those in their 40s, have less day-to-day contact with grandchildren than those who are older, perhaps because most are still working (Watson, 1997). As a result, they know less about and are less involved in their grandchildren's everyday lives than older grandparents are.

The role of grandparent obviously brings many middle-aged and older adults a good deal of pleasure and satisfaction. However, grandparents who see their grandchildren more often do not describe themselves as happier than those who see theirs less often (Palmore, 1981). Thus, for most adults in middle age, grandparenthood is not central to their lives, to their sense of self, or to their overall morale.

CARING FOR AGING PARENTS

Another role that may be added at mid-life and that *does* have a powerful effect on overall life satisfaction is that of "major caregiver for aging parents" (see **Development in the Real World**). The great majority of adults, in virtually every culture, feel a strong

Development in the Real World

WHO CARES FOR AGING PARENTS IN CANADA?

One of the most difficult dilemmas of mid-life arises when elderly parents become incapable of caring for themselves. Inevitably, the issue of who will care for them creates conflict. Following some form of needs assessment, the caregiver must choose between several care options, each of which carries its own unique blend of quality, convenience, and cost. Options in Canada include in-home care (private and publicly funded); independent-supportive living, for example, full-service residences or apartments, retirement homes; nursing homes and homes for the aged; and palliative care and hospice care facilities. Some caregivers feel a sense of moral obligation or have a desire to care for their parents directly. In fact, Canada's 2001 census data shows that 13% of men and 12% of women aged 65 and over who had adult children now live with one of those children (Statistics Canada, 2002d). Ultimately, even if elders move to long-term care facilities, someone has to take primary responsibility for overseeing their care.

Families typically negotiate the caregiving task along a number of dimensions, including each family member's competing demands and availability of resources. Within a group of siblings, the one most likely to take on the task of caregiving is the one who has no children still at home, is not working, is not married, and lives closest to the aging parent (Brody, Litvin, Albert, & Hoffman, 1994; Stoller, Forster, & Duniho, 1992).

Anne Martin-Matthews (2001), a University of British Columbia gerontologist, points out that Canadian women are the ones most likely to be actively involved in the caregiving of their elderly parents and, in their later years, an elderly spouse. Moreover, women have traditionally married older men, and since men have a shorter life expectancy, proportionally more women than men will outlive their spouse. This

means that, if they require care, these women will be dependent on alternative (rather than spousal) sources of care in their senior years.

Some studies have found that as many as 90% of the primary caregivers for elders with Alzheimer's disease are either daughters or daughters-in-law (Daire, 2004). One factor that increases daughters' involvement in parental care is simple proximity. Perhaps because of greater emotional closeness to their parents or their socialization for the role of kin-keeping, daughters are more likely to live near their parents. And parents, when they approach their later years, are more likely to move to be close to a daughter than to a son.

Even when sons are involved in the care of an elder, research indicates that they experience far less caregiver burden than daughters do (Pinquart & Sorensen, 2006a). This difference results from the tendency of daughters to provide more hours of care, more personal types of care such as bathing, and to view the recipient of care as more difficult to deal with than sons do. The psychological and physical aspects of the types of care that daughters give and their attitudes toward their role of caregiver result in increases in depressive symptoms and decreases in health.

Researchers have found that multidimensional interventions can ease the strain of the caregiver burden (Pinquart & Sorensen, 2006b). These interventions should include education for the caregiver about the care recipient's condition or illness. The educational component should include information on the availability of resources such as daycare and home health aides, both of which can provide the caregiver with a much needed respite from the physical aspects of caring for an elderly parent. Similarly, counselling sessions and support groups can help with the emotional aspects of caregiving.

sense of filial responsibility. When their parents need assistance, they endeavour to provide it (Lachman, 2004).

Just what impact does caregiving have on the middle-aged adult? First off, we know that about one in five Canadians provides care to a senior family member or friend (Cranswick, 2003). We also know that about one-quarter of Canadians aged 45 to 54 provided the greatest proportion of unpaid care for elderly parents (Canadian Council on Social Development, 1999b; Cranswick, 2003). As you can see from **Figure 16.3**, informal caregiving can take time away from other social and recreational activities. Caregivers can incur additional costs as well, such as extra expenses or poor health (Cranswick, 2003).

Not surprisingly, this demanding caregiver role takes its toll. The cumulative evidence indicates that caregivers are more depressed and have lower marital satisfaction than those in comparison groups of similar age and social class (Hoyert & Seltzer, 1992; Jutras & Lavoie, 1995; Li & Seltzer, 2003; Schulz, Visintainer, & Williamson, 1990). Some research also suggests that those who

Daughters, far more than sons, are likely to take on the role of significant caregiver for a disabled or demented parent as this daughter has done, now that her mother is suffering from Alzheimer's disease. (*Photo:* Michael Newman/PhotoEdit)

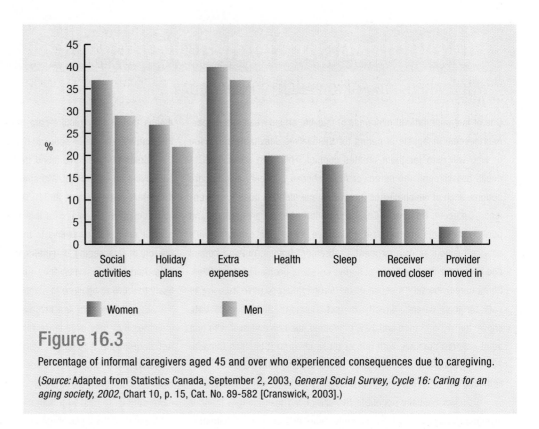

Figure 16.3

Percentage of informal caregivers aged 45 and over who experienced consequences due to caregiving.

(*Source:* Adapted from Statistics Canada, September 2, 2003, *General Social Survey, Cycle 16: Caring for an aging society, 2002*, Chart 10, p. 15, Cat. No. 89-582 [Cranswick, 2003].)

caregiver burden
a term for the cumulative negative effects of caring for an elderly or disabled person

care for frail elders are more often ill themselves or have some reduced efficiency of immune system function (Dura & Kiecolt-Glaser, 1991; Hoyert & Seltzer, 1992; Kiecolt-Glaser et al., 1987). Collectively, these effects are often termed **caregiver burden**.

Still, for the majority of mid-life adults, the relationship with aging parents is far more positive. Most give more assistance to their parents than they did before, but they also continue to see them regularly for ceremonial and celebratory occasions and to feel affection as well as filial responsibility (Stein et al., 1998). Parents are also symbolically important to middle-aged adults, because as long as they are alive, they occupy the role of elder in the family lineage. When they are gone, each generation moves up a notch in the sequence: Those in the middle generation must come to terms with the fact that they have now become the elders and are confronted directly with their own mortality.

FRIENDS

The scant research on friendships in middle adulthood suggests that the total number of friendships is lower in these years than in young adulthood (Kalmijn, 2003). For example, in one small American study, researchers interviewed three generations of women in each of 53 families (Levitt, Weber, & Guacci, 1993). Each woman was asked to describe her close relationships. Among both groups, the young adult women had more friends in their social networks than did their middle-aged mothers.

At the same time, other bits of research suggest that mid-life friendships are as intimate and close as those at earlier ages. For example, researchers have analyzed information from the files of 50 participants in the now-familiar Berkeley/Oakland Longitudinal Study, who had been interviewed or tested repeatedly from adolescence through age 50 (Carstensen, 1992). These analyses revealed that the frequency of interaction with best friends dropped between ages 17 and 50, but that the best-friend relationships remained very close.

These studies suggest that the social network of middle-aged adults is relatively small, although relationships are just as intimate as they were at earlier ages. It may be that the social network shrinks as adults age because there is less need for it. Role conflict and role strain decline significantly in middle age, and the need for emotional support from a social network outside the family seems to decrease accordingly (Due, Holstein, Lund, Modvig, & Avlund, 1999). Yet, because the relationships that do endure are close, the social network is available when needed. Friendship depends less on frequent contact than on a sense that friends are there to provide support as needed. Thus, the nature of friendship itself may be different in middle age.

CONTINUITY AND CHANGE IN PERSONALITY

Can developmentalists tell what kind of person someone will be in middle adulthood, based on what is known about his childhood, adolescence, or early adult life? As you learned in **Chapter 10**, a stable set of personality traits that psychologists call the *Big Five* emerge during middle childhood. Notice in this brief review of the traits that they can be easily remembered by using the acronym *CANOE*:

- *Conscientiousness*: need for order in the environment
- *Agreeableness*: ease with which a person gets along with others
- *Neuroticism*: emotional negativity, pessimism, and irritability
- *Openness*: willingness to try new things
- *Extraversion*: sociability

Many studies show that the Big Five are relatively stable from childhood to old age (Hampson & Goldberg, 2006). Such findings are consistent with the proposition that the five factors are determined very early in life and are stable throughout the lifespan (Caspi, 2000; McCrae & Costa, 1990). However, there are subtle age-related changes in the five factors across the years of adulthood (Terracciano et al., 2005). Longitudinal research indicates that openness, extraversion, and neuroticism decline as adults age. Agreeableness increases, as does conscientiousness, up until around age 70 when it begins to show declines. Thus, the best statement that we can make about the stability of the Big Five is that these traits follow a general pattern of stability in most people but that they are also subject to some degree of modification (Branje, Van Lieshout, & Gerris, 2007).

Studies of negative and positive emotionality suggest a similar pattern. Even though negative emotionality in early adulthood is moderately to strongly correlated with negative emotionality in middle adulthood, longitudinal studies show that many individuals, particularly women, become less negative over time (Helson & Klohnen, 1998; Srivastava, John, Gosling, & Potter, 2003). Similarly, agreeableness appears to increase with age (Srivastava et al., 2003). At the same time, tolerance for risk-taking and impulsivity decline with age (Deakin, Aitken, Robbins, & Sahakian, 2004). Apparently, then, when researchers consider large groups—which they must do to correlate variables such as personality factors—they find that personality is fairly stable over time. However, the correlations can mask a number of individual cases in which there is a great deal of change. Consequently, the best conclusion to draw is that stability is the general pattern, but the increased individual variability in personality that is typically found among middle-aged and older adults suggests that change is clearly possible and may even be common (Nelson & Dannefer, 1992).

Personality is an important contributor to middle-aged adults' capacity for managing stress. For example, in one study researchers found that adults who were higher in extraversion and conscientiousness were less likely to feel strained by work-related stressors (Grant & Langan-Fox, 2007). By contrast, those who were high in neuroticism were less able to cope with on-the-job problems. Likewise, personality moderates the effects of caregiver burden on the subjective sense of well-being among middle-aged adults who are caring for elderly parents (Koerner & Kenyon, 2007).

Before Going On

- What is the quality of marital relationships in middle age and what is the family role of middle-aged adults with respect to older and younger generations?

- What changes are apparent in social networks and personality through middle adulthood?

MID-LIFE CAREER ISSUES

Work in mid-life is characterized by two paradoxes: First, work satisfaction is at its peak in these years, despite the fact that most adults receive few work promotions in middle age. Second, the quality of work performance remains high, despite declines in some cognitive or physical skills.

WORK SATISFACTION

burnout
lack of energy, exhaustion, and pessimism that results from chronic stress

As we have noted before, many aspects of life improve with age. Interestingly, middle-aged workers are less likely than younger workers to experience work-related **burnout** (Freudenberger & Richelson, 1980). People with burnout lack energy and feel emotionally drained and are pessimistic about the possibility of changing their situations. People who feel that their work is unappreciated are more subject to burnout than others. For example, one survey suggested that nearly half of the social workers in the United Kingdom suffer from burnout, and the sense of being unappreciated was the best predictor of the condition (Evans et al., 2006). Developmentalists suggest that middle-aged workers who have avoided burnout in high-stress professions are those who have learned to pace themselves and to rely less on external sources of job satisfaction (Randall, 2007).

In addition, despite the plateau in promotions that occurs for most adults in the middle years, job satisfaction is typically at its peak, as is a sense of power, or job clout. One reason for these increases may be that careers become more stable in middle age, with fewer interruptions caused by either voluntary or involuntary job changes (Boxall, Macky, & Rasmussen, 2003). Still, patterns of work and work satisfaction do vary between men and women in middle adulthood.

Some studies suggest that women and men use the same criteria to assess whether they are satisfied with their jobs. In one study, for example, researchers found that male and female workers across four different countries (China, Japan, Germany, and the

Studies show that men are more likely than women to use problem-focused strategies to cope with job stress. By contrast, women use emotion-focused coping more often than men. These differences help explain why middle-aged men and women differ in work satisfaction. (*Source:* © Ronnie Kaufman/Corbis)

United States) had similar preferences with regard to performance awards and management styles (Gunkel, Lusk, Wolff, & Li, 2007). However, research also suggests that men and women think differently about their work. For instance, one consistent finding is that women worry much more about the effects of having children on their career advancement (Hagan & Kay, 2007; Stewart & Ostrove, 1998).

Similarly, the different paths men and women take to achieve job satisfaction are accompanied by sex differences in coping style at work (Perho & Korhonen, 1999). Men and women cite the same sources of work dissatisfaction in middle age: time pressure, difficult co-workers, boring tasks, and fear of losing one's job. However, they cope with these challenges differently. Men are more likely to negotiate with supervisors and co-workers directly to effect change. In contrast, women tend to withdraw and engage in collective complaining with female co-workers. Still, women are better able than men to balance their dissatisfactions with areas of contentment. Consequently, a statement such as "I don't like the boss, but the hours fit my needs" is more likely to come from a woman than a man. Because of their different coping styles, men are more likely to improve their level of satisfaction in situations where change is possible. By contrast, women are probably better able to cope with work settings where they must adjust to dissatisfaction because the situation can't be changed.

Despite their differences, both men and women in mid-life have a greater sense of control over their work lives than younger adults do (Lachman & Weaver, 1998). One reason for the increased feeling of control may be that social-cognitive skills improve from early to middle adulthood (Blanchard-Fields, Chen, Schocke, & Hertzog, 1998; Hess, Bolstad, Woodburn, & Auman, 1999). Middle-aged adults are better than they were when younger at "sizing up" people, relationships, and situations. At the same time, by middle age, they have become proficient at directing their own behaviour in ways that allow them to maintain levels of personal satisfaction even in unpleasant circumstances.

JOB PERFORMANCE

Early studies suggested that job performance remained high throughout middle adulthood except in professions in which speed is a critical element (Sparrow & Davies, 1988). More recent cohorts of middle-aged adults in such professions, such as air traffic controllers, have been found to perform equally as well as their younger peers (Broach & Schroeder, 2006). Improvements in health that have led to increases in general life expectancy are also credited with producing this historical change. As a result, many governments around the world are examining regulations that force employees in these professions to retire at a certain age. Instead, research-based reform proposals argue that older occupants of these jobs be tested individually to determine whether they can continue.

You should recall from **Chapter 15** that researchers Paul and Margaret Baltes argue that maintaining high job productivity or performance is possible because adults, faced with small but noticeable erosions of cognitive or physical skill, engage in a process the Balteses call *selective optimization with compensation* (Baltes & Baltes, 1990). Three subprocesses are involved:

- *Selection.* Workers narrow their range of activities—for example, by focusing on only the most central tasks, delegating more responsibilities to others, or giving up or reducing peripheral job activities.

- *Optimization.* Workers deliberately "exercise" crucial abilities—such as by taking added training or polishing rusty skills—so as to remain as close to maximum skill levels as possible.

Involuntary career changers must confront a series of stressful situations, such as retraining and relocating to find work.
(*Photo:* Thinkstock)

• *Compensation.* Workers adopt pragmatic strategies for overcoming specific obstacles—for example, getting stronger glasses or hearing aids, making lists to reduce memory loads, or even carefully emphasizing strengths and minimizing weaknesses when talking to co-workers or bosses.

A growing body of evidence supports the Baltes' view (Baltes & Heydens-Gahir, 2003). Researchers tested this model in a study of 224 working adults aged 40 to 69 (Abraham & Hansson, 1995). Measuring each of the three aspects of the proposed compensatory process as well as job competence, they found that the link between the use of selection, optimization, and compensation on the one hand and the quality of work performance on the other got stronger with increasing age. That is, the older the worker, the more it mattered whether she used helpful compensatory practices. In the older groups (primarily those in their 50s and early 60s), those who used the most selection, optimization, and compensation had the highest work performance. But among the younger workers in this sample (those in their early 40s), the same relationship did not hold. These results obviously come from only one study, but the findings provide some support for the idea that job performance remains high during middle age at least in part because adults take deliberate compensatory actions.

UNEMPLOYMENT AND CAREER TRANSITIONS

In today's rapidly changing job market, it is not unusual for men and women to change occupations. However, career transitions can be more difficult in middle age than earlier in adulthood. For one thing, potential employers tend to believe that young adults are more capable of learning a new job than middle-aged applicants, even though research suggests that this generalization is untrue (Forte & Hansvick, 1999). Employers give middle-aged applicants higher ratings on variables such as dependability, but they tend to think that younger applicants will be able to acquire new skills (especially computer skills) more rapidly. Thus, mid-life career changers must often overcome ageism in obtaining new employment.

Career counsellors also point out that to understand mid-life career changes, it is useful to categorize workers on the basis of their reasons for changing occupations (Zunker, 1994). They suggest that people change careers for either external or internal reasons and can thus be classified as either *involuntary* or *voluntary* career changers.

INVOLUNTARY CAREER CHANGERS Involuntary career changers are people who are in transition because of external reasons: Their skills have become obsolete, their jobs have been eliminated through organizational restructuring, or they have been laid off because of shifting economic conditions. They experience heightened levels of mental health disorders, such as anxiety, depression, and substance abuse, and are at higher risk of physical illness in the months after the job loss (Crowley, Hayslip, & Hobdy, 2003; Avison, 1997; He, Colantonio, & Marshall, 2003; Isaksson, Johansson, Bellaagh, & Sjöberg, 2004). William Avison (1997), a University of Western Ontario sociologist, also reported higher levels of mortality associated with unemployment, whereby the longer the period of unemployment, the higher the mortality rate. Avison also noted that negative health effects are heightened during economic recessions. Such effects are not unique to workers in Canada. Similar results have been found in studies in Australia, Denmark, England, the United States, and other Western countries (e.g., Broom et al., 2007; Iversen & Sabroe, 1988; Warr, Jackson, & Banks, 1988). Interestingly, just as remarriage alleviates many of the stresses associated with divorce, re-employment seems to restore health, emotional stability, and a sense of well-being quite rapidly.

The effects of job loss include changes in family relationships and loss of self-esteem. Most strikingly, marital relationships deteriorate rapidly after one or the other spouse has been laid off. The number of hostile or negative interactions increases, and the number of warm and supportive interactions declines—which means that the crucial ratio of positive to negative interactions spirals downward. Separation and divorce become much more common as a result (Ahituv & Lehman, 2004).

Predictably, the Big Five personality dimensions, especially neuroticism and openness to experience, contribute to mental health during involuntary career transitions across all racial and ethnic groups (Heppner, Fuller, & Multon, 1998). Nevertheless, mental health professionals suggest that the impact of an involuntary career change on an individual's life may be more directly affected by his coping skills (Zunker, 1994). For example, the person must be able to assess the situation realistically. If new work skills are needed, then the person must be able to formulate and carry out a plan for obtaining such skills. Researchers have found that mid-life career changers who have good coping skills and use them to manage involuntary transitions are less likely to become depressed (Cook & Heppner, 1997).

As with all types of stress, the effects of unemployment can be partially buffered by having adequate social support (Vinokur & van Ryn, 1993). Further, involuntary career changers benefit from career counselling that addresses both their occupational needs and their psychosocial development (Schadt, 1997). Counsellors can help people who are forced to change jobs learn to think of the transition as an opportunity to re-examine goals and priorities—to treat the crisis as an opportunity (Zunker, 1994).

VOLUNTARY CAREER CHANGERS Voluntary career changers leave one career to pursue another for a variety of internal reasons (Allen, Dreves, & Ruhe, 1999). For example, they may believe that the new job will be more fulfilling. One pattern occurs when workers look at the next step on the career ladder and decide they don't want to pursue further advancement in their current occupation. For example, both male and female certified public accountants are more likely to leave their profession for this reason than for any other (Greenhaus, Collins, Singh, & Parasuraman, 1997). Others change careers to be able to express aspects of their personalities that they believe aren't utilized in their present jobs (Young & Rodgers, 1997).

Twin studies suggest that the tendency to change careers voluntarily in adulthood may have a genetic basis (McCall, Cavanaugh, Arvey, & Taubman, 1997). These findings further suggest that such transitions are a by-product of personality. Specifically, voluntary job changers appear to have a higher tolerance for risk-taking than do people who generally do not actively seek to change jobs (Roth, 2003). Most also appear to be people who do not regard either working or job-seeking as particularly stressful (Mao, 2003). Although voluntary career changers have a better sense of control over their situation than do people whose job changes are forced on them, the transition may still be stressful. Spouses and family members may not understand why the person wants to change careers. Moreover, changing careers can involve periods of unemployment and, often, a reduction in income. Thus, voluntary career changers manifest many of the same symptoms of anxiety and depression seen in involuntary career changers (Ahituv & Lehman, 2004). Consequently, they, too, benefit from social support and career counselling.

PREPARING FOR RETIREMENT

Many middle-aged adults begin to prepare for retirement as early as 15 years before their anticipated retirement date (Herzog, House, & Morgan, 1991). One aspect of such preparation is a gradual reduction in workload. For example, the peak participation rate in the Canadian

Critical Thinking

How do the retirement plans of Baby Boomers fit in with the stage and life events approaches to middle age that you learned about at the beginning of the chapter?

One difference between Baby Boomers and earlier cohorts is that more women are involved in retirement planning.
(*Photo:* Thinkstock/Corbis)

labour force is between ages 25 and 54 for both men and women. However, the participation rates for Canadians aged 55 to 65 drops by about one-third for men and about half for women. This pattern of reduced participation after age 55 is common to many industrialized nations, such as the United States, Japan, Sweden, and the United Kingdom (Statistics Canada, 2001i).

The notion of retirement is relatively new and tends to be exclusive to industrialized cultures, and the retirement preparations of the Baby Boom cohort, who are all now middle-aged, are quite different from those of their parents (Monroy, 2000). For one thing, among their parents, retirement planning was primarily a male responsibility. In contrast, Baby Boom women are also doing retirement planning, sometimes together with their husbands, but sometimes independently (Dietz, Carrozza, & Ritchey, 2003; Glass & Kilpatrick, 1998). Further, retirement-minded Boomers are largely responsible for the growth of electronic financial services because of their enthusiastic response to the availability of such services on the Internet.

Most Baby Boomers expect to die in their mid-80s or later but expect to retire fairly early, in their early 60s (Monroy, 2000). This means that their expected length of retirement is 20 years or more longer than that of earlier generations. Moreover, Baby Boomers believe that they need higher retirement incomes than their parents. Most have enjoyed a comfortable standard of living compared with earlier generations, in part because of the proliferation of the two-income family. They expect some decline in income after their retirement but generally expect much less change in their standard of living. Further, most do not expect that Old Age Security and Canada Pension Plan benefits will be adequate to meet their desired lifestyle needs.

In a survey involving more than 3000 Baby Boomers, gerontologist Ken Dychtwald found that virtually all the respondents intended to continue working into retirement, but most intended to combine paid work with other pursuits (Mauldin, 2005). Dychtwald identified five distinct approaches to what those non-work pursuits should be (Mauldin, 2005). *Wealth Builders* (31%) intend to spend their spare time finding new ways to make money and building on the wealth that they have already accumulated. Predictably, this group plans to devote more hours to paid work than their peers in other groups do. *Anxious Idealists* (20%) would like to do volunteer work and give money to charity after they retire, but they recognize that their tendency toward impracticality has left them with insufficient economic resources to do either. *Empowered Trailblazers* (18%) expect to spend time travelling, taking classes, and doing volunteer work, and they believe that they are financially secure enough to meet these goals. *Stretched and Stressed Boomers* (18%) are in deep trouble financially, and they are well aware of it. Most are worried about how they will be able to pay for basic necessities such as food and health care. *Leisure Lifers* (13%) intend to spend most of their time engaging in recreational pursuits and are geared toward very early retirement in their early to mid-50s.

Clearly, Baby Boomers have devoted a great deal of thought to what they would like to do during their retirement years. However, few have devoted as much energy to preparing for the financial aspects of retirement. Dychtwald's survey found that only 2% had actually saved enough money to be able to do what they said they wanted to do in retirement. Consequently, many Baby Boomers appear to be headed on a path toward disappointment when financial realities set in just a few years from now.

Nevertheless, economic analysts predict that as a group Baby Boomers are likely to enjoy levels of affluence in retirement that far exceed those of their parents. Further, they are projected to be the healthiest, best-educated, and longest-living retirees in history. Thus, they are likely to substantially change ideas about both preparing for retirement and retirement itself.

Before Going On

- What happens to levels of job satisfaction and job performance among middle-aged workers?

- What are the factors that contribute to career transitions in mid-life, and how do Baby Boomers differ from previous cohorts with respect to preparation for retirement?

Summary

Theories of Social and Personality Development

- Erikson proposed that the primary developmental task of middle adulthood is to acquire a sense of generativity through mentoring younger individuals. Vaillant proposed that the stage of career consolidation precedes Erikson's generativity stage, and that of keeper of the meaning follows it.

- Many different models of the "mid-life crisis" in middle adulthood have been proposed but none have been strongly supported by research.

Changes in Relationships and Personality

- Marital satisfaction is typically higher at mid-life than it is earlier. This higher level of satisfaction appears to be due primarily to a decline in problems and conflicts.

- Middle-aged adults have significant family interactions both up and down the generational chain. The two-way responsibilities can create a mid-life "squeeze" or a "sandwich generation." Middle adults provide more assistance in both directions and attempt to influence both preceding and succeeding generations.

- There is little sign that middle-aged parents experience negative reactions to the "empty nest" when the last child leaves home. On the contrary, the reduction in role demands may contribute to the rise in life satisfaction at this age.

- The "revolving door" is the pattern in which adult children who have been living independently return to live in their parents' home. Generally, this pattern is associated with declines in life satisfaction among middle-aged adults. However, some enjoy the companionship provided by adult children.

- Most adults become grandparents in middle age. The majority have warm, affectionate relationships with

their grandchildren, although there are also many remote relationships. A minority of grandparents are involved in day-to-day care of grandchildren.

- Almost one-quarter of middle-aged adults take on the role of caregiver for an aging parent. They report feeling a considerable burden and suffer increased depression, particularly if the parent being cared for suffers from some form of dementia. Women are two to four times as likely as men to fill the role of caregiver to a frail elder.

- Friendships appear to be somewhat less numerous in middle adulthood, although they appear to be as intimate and central to the individual.

- The Big Five personality traits and other aspects of personality are correlated across early and middle adulthood. There is evidence for personality change in middle age as well.

Mid-Life Career Issues

- Job satisfaction is at its peak in middle adulthood, and productivity remains high. But the centrality of the work role appears to wane somewhat, and job satisfaction is less clearly linked to overall life satisfaction than at earlier ages. Research suggests that patterns of work and satisfaction are different for men and women in middle age.

- Levels of job performance in middle adulthood are consistent with those at earlier ages, with the exception of work that involves physical strength or reaction time.

- Involuntary career changes are associated with anxiety and depression. Even many middle-aged adults who make voluntary career transitions experience negative emotions.

- Middle-aged adults prepare for retirement in several ways, not only by specific planning, but also by reducing the number of hours they work.

PEARSON mydevelopmentlab

Visit **www.mydevelopmentlab.com** to help you get the best grade! Test your knowledge and grasp difficult concepts through

- Custom study plans: See where you are strong and where you go wrong
- Interactive simulations
- Video and audio clips
- Raise your own Virtual Child—and much more!

Review Questions

Answers are provided on MyDevelopmentLab in the Course Resources folder.

Theories of Social and Personality Development

16.1 How does generativity affect later mental health?
   a. Generative people are more likely to be satisfied with their lives.
   b. Generative people are less likely to have dementia.
   c. Generative people are more likely to have attachment disorders.
   d. Generative people are less likely to commit suicide.

Changes in Relationships and Personality

16.2 Professionals label the middle adulthood cohort the _____ generation, because their family role involves giving assistance and maintaining affectional bonds in both directions in the generational chain.
   a. enabling
   b. co-dependent
   c. sandwich
   d. pipeline

16.3 Which of the following does *not* characterize social networks in middle age, according to research?
   a. more friends
   b. less frequent interaction among friends
   c. relationships as intimate as they were at earlier ages
   d. less need for emotional support from individuals outside the family

Mid-Life Career Issues

16.4 Which of the following is the best example of optimization in the selective optimization with compensation model of compensatory strategies for job performance?

   a. Eric believes that one of his most effective managerial skills is to delegate important tasks and responsibilities to the junior executives in his department.
   b. To remain up-to-date in her clinical knowledge and therapeutic techniques, Dr. Smith completes approximately 50 hours of continuing education seminars and workshops each year.
   c. When Mrs. Wilson anticipates that her busy day will trouble her arthritic knee, she wears her knee brace and takes anti-inflammatory pain medication.
   d. Carmen has managed to lose 22 kilograms by eating a low-fat, vegetarian diet and following an exercise program recommended by her physician.

16.5 Which of the following does *not* influence mental health status and ability to adjust during involuntary career transitions?
   a. maintaining relationships with former co-workers
   b. personality characteristics, such as neuroticism and openness to experience
   c. coping skills
   d. social support system

Critical-Thinking Questions

16.6 How could the stage models of Erikson and Vaillant be integrated with the life events approach to provide a more comprehensive description of middle adulthood than any of them can provide alone?

16.7 How do the changes in social relationships contribute to maintaining some personality traits while modifying others in middle age?

Policy Question

What Is Canada's Position on Stem Cell Research?

Stem cells are partially developed, unspecialized cells. In response to biochemical signals that scientists don't yet fully understand, they develop into mature, specialized cells (Campbell, Perez-Iratxeta, Andrade-Navarro, & Rudnicki, 2007). The potential of stem cells for curing many diseases associated with aging, such as Parkinson's and Alzheimer's, has received a great deal of attention in recent years (e.g., Goldman & Windrem, 2006; Lindvall, 2003). Some experts believe stem cell research may lead to treatments that reverse the effects of aging. For instance, stem cells may be used to stop the loss of muscle mass that normally accompanies aging, and stem cells in hair follicles have been touted as a potential cure for baldness (Blanpain, Lowry, Geoghegan, Polak, & Fuchs, 2004; Stewart, 2004). Such claims have resulted in widespread public interest in stem cell research. Policymakers are interested in age-related applications of stem cell research because of the anticipated health care costs associated with the demographic crisis you will read about in **Chapter 17**.

CANADIAN STEM CELL RESEARCH REGULATIONS

The Canadian Institutes of Health Research (CIHR) has led the development and implementation of the policy and guidelines that govern human stem cell research. Accordingly, the Stem Cell Oversight Committee (SCOC) ensures that no research with human stem cells is funded without prior approval. Research undertaken must have

- potential health benefits for Canadians;

- free and informed consent;

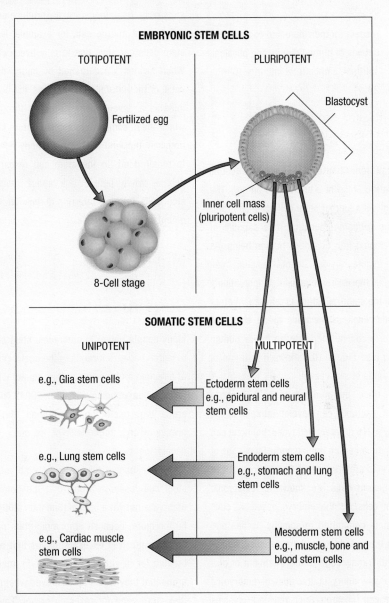

Figure 16.4

Totipotent stem cells will develop into any human cell. *Pluripotent* stem cells will grow into three very broad categories of cells: endoderm (e.g., gastrointestinal and respiratory); ectoderm (e.g., nerves and skin); and mesoderm (e.g., bones, muscle and blood). *Multipotent* stem cells descend from pluripotent stem cells but have a more limited range of development. For example, multipotent nerve stem cells can form into only neural and glial cells. *Unipotent* stem cells can produce only one type of cell. Embryonic stems cells are of particular interest to researchers because of their potential to treat a wide range of human diseases and disorders. Scientists have also found that it is possible to manipulate somatic stem cells into forming other cell types.

(*Source:* Artwork copyright © Alexandra Johnson. Printed with permission.)

- respect for privacy and confidentiality;

- no direct or indirect payment for tissues collected and no financial incentives;

- no creation of embryos for research purposes;

- respect for individual and community notions of human dignity and physical, spiritual, and cultural integrity. (CIHR, 2007)

TYPES OF STEM CELLS

Recall from **Chapter 3** that a zygote results from the union of a sperm and an egg. The zygote is a kind of stem cell scientists refer to as *totipotent* because it is capable of developing into an entire human being. As the zygote divides, each resulting cell retains the characteristic of totipotentiality until the eight-cell stage is reached. In other words, each of the cells in an eight-cell embryo can develop into an entire human body (see **Figure 16.4** for an illustration of the kinds of stem cells).

Once the number of cells exceeds eight, each cell can develop into one of the body's 216 different cell types, but none can become an entire human body. Stem cells of this kind are *pluripotent*. Both totipotent and pluripotent cells are known as **embryonic stem cells**. As the embryo develops, cells become committed to specific tissues and lose their pluripotent characteristics. Applying this knowledge to the treatment of disease and injury is the goal of embryonic stem cell research. Such research involves extracting undifferentiated stem cells from embryos and experimenting with them.

Some cells that are committed to a particular kind of tissue retain a degree of plasticity, even though they are not pluripotent. Such cells represent a second kind of stem cell called **somatic or adult stem cells**. One subtype of somatic cells, *multipotent*,

are present in the body at all stages of development, including adulthood. For example, multipotent stem cells in bone marrow can become any kind of blood cell the body needs. The least plastic somatic stem cells, *unipotent*, normally produce only one type of mature cell, for example, liver stem cells can give rise to only liver cells. When tissues are damaged by injury, disease, or the natural aging process, the body initiates a developmental process through which these somatic stem cells mature into precisely the kind of tissue the body needs to repair itself. In the stem cell research debate, when people talk about "adult" stem cells, they are referring to these multipotent or unipotent cells.

WHY IS STEM CELL RESEARCH CONTROVERSIAL?

Many people object to embryonic stem cell research because it requires the destruction of a human embryo, which they equate with killing a human being (Shannon, 2004). They argue that destruction of human life is always wrong, regardless of its stage of development.

In response, advocates of embryonic stem cell research argue that the human embryo is not yet a person (Shannon, 2004). Furthermore, because embryonic stem cell research involves excess embryos that are created for in vitro fertilization (IVF), many argue that they would be destroyed whether they were used for research or not. Thus, advocates ask, why not use them to benefit others?

The debate takes a turn when the issue of creating embryos strictly for research is raised. Many who would endorse using excess IVF embryos for research balk at the idea that sperm and ova might be joined in a test tube for the

sole purpose of experimentation. They argue that leftover embryos from IVF were conceived with the intention of allowing them to develop into human beings. For this reason, they say, using leftover tissue to help others is morally acceptable, much like organ donation and transplant. By contrast, research involving somatic stem cells extracted from the tissues of children and/ or adults is unhampered by such ethical dilemmas (Stewart, 2004).

CAN STEM CELLS CURE DISEASES?

Experiments have shown that it is possible to extract pluripotent cells from developing embryos and grow them in the laboratory. In fact, a few such cells can turn into millions in a matter of weeks (National Institutes of Health, 2004). Moreover, scientists have learned how to keep them from differentiating into specialized cells. In other words, they know how to maintain the cells' pluripotent characteristics indefinitely. What isn't known, though, is exactly how to initiate and control specialization.

Recently, however, scientists succeeded in developing neurons from embryonic stem cells. These neurons were then implanted in the spinal cords of paralyzed laboratory animals. Remarkably, both mice and rats can recover from paralysis and regain movement (Bernreuther et al., 2006; Cao et al., 2005;

embryonic stem cells
undifferentiated cells found in the zygote and blastocyst that are capable of indefinite self-replication and differentiation into specialized cells

somatic or adult stem cells
non-embryonic stem cells found in differentiated tissue that are capable of self-replicating and differentiating into the kind of tissue from which they originated

Deshpande et al., 2006; Kerr et al., 2001). These types of findings have been widely cited by advocates for embryonic stem cell research.

Even the most ardent advocates of stem cell research warn that much remains to be learned before similar experiments can be carried out with human beings. For one thing, they caution that stem cell transplants, like organ transplants, can be rejected by the body (rejection isn't an issue, of course, when an individual receives new tissue grown from her own stem cells). Moreover, studies suggest that laboratory-grown cells can develop into malignant tumours (e.g., Balch et al., 2005; Egger et al., 2004; Laird, 2005; Maitra et al., 2005; Tai et al., 2005). Consequently, stem cells cannot be used to treat diseases in humans until more is known about controlling the tissue rejection and tumour development.

There is no doubt that stem cells can be used to treat diseases. In fact, bone marrow stem cells have been used in the treatment of blood diseases for decades (Stewart, 2004). And in recent years, scientists have identified many new somatic stem cell "populations"—in muscle tissue, the liver, the brain, skin, hair follicles, and many other tissues, including menstrual blood, which contains some 30 times more stem cells than bone marrow (Kerr, 2006; National Institutes of Health, 2004). Thus, most experts agree that the potential for using stem cells to treat disease—or even to moderate the effects of aging—is tremendous.

Moreover, Canadian scientists affiliated with the Ottawa Health Research Institute, have recently identified a single gene, *Oct4*, that regulates the formation, self-renewal, and differentiation of embryonic stem cells (Campbell et al., 2007). The gene, *Oct4*, is not normally active in mature stem cells but has been found to be active in cancerous cells. In many ways, cancer cells act like stem cells, which supports the theory that cancer is a disease of stem cells. Thus, the discovery that *Oct4* is a master regulator, has implications for finding new approaches to fighting cancer.

STEM CELL RESEARCH POLICIES

Stem cell research policy in Canada can be summarized as follows: (1) emphasis on public rather than private funding for stem cell research, (2) strict regulation of stem cell research, and (3) prioritization of embryonic over somatic stem cell research.

YOUR TURN

- Think about some of the risks associated with stem cell therapy, such as immune rejection and tumour formation. If you had a debilitating medical condition, such as a spinal cord injury, liver disease, multiple sclerosis, or Parkinson's disease, explain why you would or wouldn't be willing to participate in clinical trials.

- Of what benefit is it to society to develop and implement stem cell cures?

- As a Canadian taxpayer, you help fund stem cell research: (1) What benefits, assurances, and protection would you expect to receive from any treatment or cures that result from publicly funded research? (2) What would be a fair price to pay for any needed stem cell therapy? (3) Should stem cell therapy be available to all Canadians regardless of their ability to pay? (4) Should non-Canadians pay the same cost for treatment as we would pay?

- Other than the treatment of diseases, what applications might there be for stem cell research?

CHAPTER 17

Physical and Cognitive Development in Late Adulthood

© Digital Vision/Alamy

In an earlier edition of this book, Helen Bee wrote about her 81-year-old father's tendency to use the term *my brains* to refer to a notebook in which he kept information such as frequently used phone numbers, appointments, and birthdays. He developed this behaviour in response to his self-observed increasing forgetfulness, and the substitute "brains" enabled him to get through each day without having to rely on his own brain. As this anecdote illustrates, for many older adults, the experience of aging is a process of learning to offset weaknesses, such as increasing forgetfulness, with strengths, such as practicality and inventiveness.

As the example of Helen Bee's father illustrates, older adults often find ingenious ways of managing age-related changes. Thus, one of the most striking characteristics of old age is the degree to which the experience of growing old varies from one individual to another. In this chapter, we will examine this variability, along with changes that appear to affect almost everyone.

When you finish studying the chapter, you will be able to describe the variability of characteristics of seniors; identify the physical changes in specific body systems in late adulthood; summarize the impact of mental health in seniors and assess the cognitive changes in late adulthood. While you read, keep the following questions in mind:

- What can we do before we reach late adulthood to help prevent, or at least postpone, the onset of disabilities?

- How might a nap in the middle of the day have a different effect for a 20- to 30-year-old post-secondary student than for a senior?

- What difference does it make if a senior is in an institution voluntarily or involuntarily?

VARIABILITY IN LATE ADULTHOOD

The scientific study of aging is known as **gerontology**. For many years, gerontologists thought about old age almost exclusively in terms of decline and loss. However, perspectives on the later years are rapidly changing, and late adulthood is now thought of as a period of tremendous individual variability rather than one of universal decline (Weaver, 1999).

gerontology
the scientific study of aging

LIFE EXPECTANCY AND LONGEVITY

Animal species vary widely in their expected lifespans. Fruit flies, for instance, live for only a few weeks, while giant Galapagos turtles often live to be more than 100 years old. Among humans, cases such as that of Jeanne Calmet, a French woman who lived to be 122 years old, suggest that the maximum lifespan is about 120 years, but this estimate may change as more individuals pass the centenarian mark. Yet there is no denying that death rates increase dramatically when humans reach their 60s, and scientists are learning more about the variables that distinguish individuals who die in their 60s from those who live for 100 years or more.

LIFE EXPECTANCY You might be surprised to learn that life expectancy increases as adults get older. For example, in Canada, the average 65-year-old man lives to just over age 83, but once a man reaches his early 80s, he is likely to live to be 90 (Statistics Canada, 2004c, 2010c). Life expectancy among women is even longer. The average 65-year-old woman is likely to live slightly over age 86, and the women who make it to their mid-80s can expect to live to over age 92. Because of this sex difference in life expectancy, there are more elderly women than men. However, the gender gap has been narrowing in Canada since 1981, at which time women outlived men by 7.1 years (Statistics Canada, 2001j). The latest estimates indicate that a male baby born in 2007 can expect to live to be 78.3 years old and a female baby 83.0 years old, a difference of only 4.7 years (Statistics Canada, 2010c).

SUBGROUPS Gerontologists point out that there are important differences among the *young old* (aged 60 to 75), the *old old* (aged 75 to 85), and the *oldest old* (aged 85 and over). The oldest old are the fastest-growing segment of the population in Canada, which means that terms such as *octogenarian* (a person in his or her 80s) and *centenarian* (a person over 100 years of age) will be used far more often than in the past. From 1981 to 2000, the over-65 population in Canada increased by about two-thirds, from about 10 to 13% of the total population (Health Canada, 2003c). The over-85 population almost tripled during the same time frame, and it is estimated that by 2051 the over-85 population will grow to almost five times the current figure of 400 000-plus (Health Canada, 2003d).

Another interesting trend is that throughout the industrialized world, including Canada, the subgroup of the elderly who are 100 years old or older is growing at a more rapid rate than any other segment of the population. In 2009, there were an estimated 6000 Canadian centenarians, and demographers project that by 2030 the centenarian population will reach 15 000 (Statistics Canada, 2009l). As in all periods of older adulthood, the overwhelming majority of these 100-year-olds will be women.

HEALTH   👁—[Watch]

Stereotypes may lead you to think that most seniors are in poor health. However, the majority of older adults do not suffer from ailments that seriously impair their day-to-day functioning (FIFARS, 2006). Moreover, the inevitable physical declines that are associated with aging do not seem to decrease older adults' satisfaction with their lives.

SELF-RATED HEALTH As **Figure 17.1** indicates, a majority of older adults across all three age subgroups regard their health as good to excellent (Statistics Canada, 2004d). These data contradict stereotypes of old age as a period of illness. However, the proportion of elderly with fair or poor health is a great deal higher than the equivalent proportions for young and middle-aged adults. For instance, the proportion of fair or poor self-rated health scores jumped from 5% in Canadians aged 25 to 34 up to 32% in seniors aged 75 and older. Thus, as you might suspect, health is the single largest factor determining the trajectory of an adult's physical or mental status over the years beyond age 65. As you read more about the prevalence of disability and disease among older adults, keep **Figure 17.1** in mind. You will see that these data are a testimony to the emotional resilience of older adults, a majority of whom are able to maintain an optimistic view of themselves and their lives in the face of growing physical challenges.

Further, their optimistic view seems to help protect older adults against the long-term effects of serious health threats, such

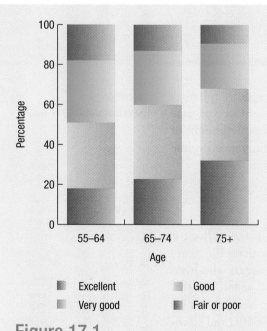

Figure 17.1

Most Canadian seniors rated their health as good to excellent.

(*Source:* Adapted from Statistics Canada, June 2004, *Health Indicators*, 2004[1], Chart—Self-rated health, by age group and sex, household population aged 12 and over, Canada, 2003, Cat. No. 82-221 [Statistics Canada 2004f].)

as strokes. Researchers have found that seniors who rate their health as good, regardless of how an objective observer might rate it, recover more physical and cognitive functions after a stroke than their peers who rate their health more poorly (Hillen, Davies, Rudd, Kieselbach, & Wolfe, 2003). Older adults who are already suffering from one or more chronic diseases at 65 show far more rapid declines than do those who begin late adulthood with no disease symptoms. In part, of course, this is an effect of the disease processes themselves. Cardiovascular disease results, among other things, in restricted blood flow to many organs, including the brain, with predictable effects on an adult's ability to learn or remember. Longitudinal studies show that adults with this disease show earlier declines in all mental abilities (Schaie & Willis, 2005). And of course, those suffering from the early stages of Alzheimer's disease or another disease that causes dementia will experience far more rapid declines in mental abilities than will those who do not have such diseases.

LIMITATIONS ON ACTIVITIES University of Manitoba health care researchers Betty Havens and Marcia Finlayson (1999) define **functional status** as a measure of an individual's ability to perform certain roles and tasks, particularly self-help tasks and other chores of daily living. Daily living tasks are grouped into two categories: **Activities of daily living (ADLs)** include bathing, dressing, using the toilet, and so forth. **Instrumental activities of daily living (IADLs)** include doing housework, cooking, and managing money.

As you can see from **Figure 17.2,** the physical problems or diseases that are most likely to contribute to some functional disability in late adulthood are arthritis and hypertension Turcotte & Schellenberg, 2007). Arthritis is very common in both

functional status
a measure of an individual's ability to perform certain roles and tasks, particularly self-help tasks and other chores of daily living (Havens & Finlayson, 1999)

activities of daily living (ADLs)
self-help tasks such as bathing, dressing, and using the toilet

instrumental activities of daily living (IADLs)
more complex daily living tasks such as doing housework, cooking, and managing money

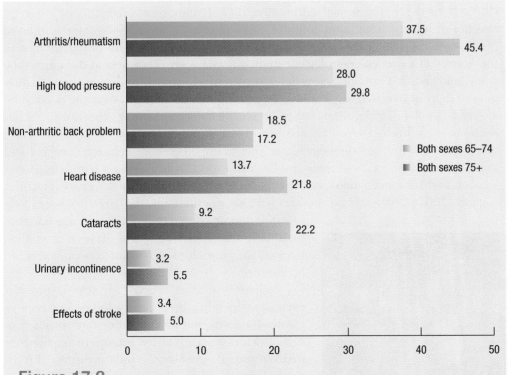

Figure 17.2

This graph shows the proportions of Canadian seniors who suffer from chronic conditions that limit their activity and may necessitate help for activities of daily living.

(*Source:* Adapted from Statistics Canada, March 13, 1996, *Health Reports* 8(3), pp. 7–15, Table 5, Cat. No. 82-003 [Wilkins & Park, 1996].)

genders. However, women aged 65 or higher are considerably more likely than men to suffer from arthritis, so they are also more often limited in their ability to carry out the various movements and tasks necessary for independent life (Brock, Guralnik, & Brody, 1990; Wilkins & Park, 1996). Since women are more likely to be widowed and thus to lack a partner who can assist with these daily living tasks, it is not surprising that more women than men live with their children or in nursing homes.

As you would probably predict, disability rates increase dramatically as seniors get older. Haven and Finlayson (1999) reported that roughly one-third of Canadians over age 65 and 44% of those over age 85 experienced at least some level of difficulty performing some basic daily life activities. The oldest old are more likely to suffer from significant physical and mental impairments than are the young old or old old. Consequently, the increase in their numbers means that the population of **frail elderly**, older adults who cannot care for themselves, is also likely to grow significantly. Consequently, demographers and economists have become concerned about the ability of young and middle-aged adults to support the growing number of elderly.

frail elderly
seniors whose physical and/or mental impairments are so extensive that they cannot care for themselves

HEREDITY
Some general tendency to live a long life is clearly inherited (Heun & Bonsignore, 2004). Identical twins are more similar in length of life than are fraternal twins, and adults whose parents and grandparents were long-lived are also likely to live longer (Plomin & McClearn, 1990). Twin studies in Sweden showed that identical twins have more similar illness rates than do fraternal twins (Pedersen & Harris, 1990). Only about one-quarter of those whose oldest grandparent had lived past age 90 had any kind of chronic illness at age 65, compared with nearly 70% of those whose oldest grandparent had died at age 78 or younger (Vaillant, 1991).

HEALTH HABITS
The same health habits that are important predictors of longevity and health in early adulthood continue to be significant predictors in late adulthood (Turcotte & Schellenberg, 2007). For example, a 17-year follow-up of participants in the Alameda County epidemiological study, who were age 60 or over at the start of the study, showed that smoking, low levels of physical activity, and being significantly underweight or overweight were linked to increased risk of death over the succeeding 17 years (Kaplan, 1992). Many other large epidemiological studies confirm such connections (e.g., Brody, 1996; Paffenbarger, Hyde, Wing, & Hsieh, 1987). For instance, one Canadian study of smokers found significant differences between smokers and nonsmokers—a 65-year-old male smoker can expect to live 6 years less than a nonsmoker, and for female smokers the difference is even greater at 8.5 years (Statistics Canada, 2001a). Not only do smokers have shorter lifespans, they are also more likely to suffer disease-related disabilities—by age 65 more than half of all smokers will have a disability, whereas only one-third of nonsmokers can expect to be disabled.

Perhaps the most crucial variable is physical exercise, which has been clearly linked not only to greater longevity, but also to lower rates of diseases such as heart disease, cancer, osteoporosis, diabetes, gastrointestinal problems, and arthritis (Brody, 1995; Deeg, Kardaun, & Fozard, 1996). Good evidence on this point comes from studies in which older adults were assigned randomly to exercise and nonexercise groups (e.g., Blumenthal et al., 1991; Tsang & Hui-Chan, 2003). In these studies, too, those who exercised had better scores on various

There are many ways to maintain physical fitness in old age. In China, elderly people can often be found practising Tai Chi in the early morning.
(*Photo:* © Visions of America/ Joe Sohm/Getty Images)

measures of physical functioning. One such experiment, with a group of adults who were all over age 80, found that muscular strength increased and motor skills improved after only 12 weeks of exercise (Carmeli, Reznick, Coleman, & Carmeli, 2000).

If anything, physical exercise seems to be even more important in the later years than at earlier ages. For example, one investigation used medical records and self-reports of exercise to examine the degree to which physical activity influenced height loss in the elderly (Sagiv, Vogelaere, Soudry, & Shrsam, 2000). They found that study participants who had exercised regularly lost significantly less height over a 30-year period than those who had not exercised. Further, exercise after age 40 seemed to be especially important in preventing height loss.

Some authors have suggested that as much as half of the decline in various aspects of physical (and perhaps cognitive) functioning in late adulthood could be prevented through an improved lifestyle, particularly exercise. For instance, Statistics Canada (2000e), reporting on the 1998/99 National Population Health Survey, found that just over 52% of Canadians older than age 65 engaged in a minimum of 15 minutes of vigorous activity three or more times a week. Yet only 27% of older adults in Canada are active enough to achieve the desired health benefits associated with exercise, so it would seem that this amount of exercise is not enough (Canadian Fitness and Lifestyle Research Institute [CFLRI], 2001).

One of the reasons for the discrepancy may be a lack of understanding of how much physical activity older adults should engage in. Although more than one-third of adults over age 65 are generally aware of the guidelines for physical activity, roughly half lack a clear understanding of the requirements (CFLRI, 2001). It is worth mentioning that physical activity should be done 30 to 60 minutes per day, but this can be *accumulated* in segments throughout the day.

Of those Canadians over age 65, only 34% of males and 22% of females engage in vigorous exercise (CFLRI, 2001). People give many reasons for not exercising, including poor health, arthritic pain, time demands of caring for an ailing spouse, culturally based assumptions about appropriate behaviour for older persons, embarrassment about exposing an aging body to others in an exercise program, lack of fitness facilities or lack of transportation to such facilities, fears of various kinds, and plain lethargy.

One important part of a strategy to increase the fitness levels of inactive seniors was the development of *Canada's Physical Activity Guide to Healthy Active Living for Older Adults* (see **Figure 17.3**). This guide is a readily available, practical handbook for overcoming misconceptions and excuses regarding inactivity. It promotes the belief that physical activity for health can easily be built into a person's daily routine, regardless of current level of activity. A complement to this guide is the newly revised *Eating Well with Canada's Food Guide*, which provides advice about eating healthy portions based on the four basic food groups (Health Canada, 2007). Eating well and being physically active are important factors in controlling the rising levels of obesity in elderly Canadians (Turcotte & Schellenberg, 2007). The percentage of obesity for Canadians aged 75 and over has reached 19% for men and 27% for women.

Critical Thinking

How would you characterize your own chances for a long life based on the genes you have inherited and on your health habits?

Before Going On

- In what ways do older adults vary across age groups and individually?
- What are the factors that contribute to longevity?

Figure 17.3

Canada's *Physical Activity Guide to Healthy Active Living for Older Adults* and the companion handbook are available free of charge. For a copy or more information, call 1-888-334-9769 or visit **www.paguide.com**.

(*Source:* Public Health Agency of Canada, 2007. This is a reproduction of an official work published by the Government of Canada and has not been produced in affiliation with, or with the endorsement of the Government of Canada.)

PHYSICAL CHANGES

Despite variability in health and functioning among the elderly, several changes in physical functioning characterize the late adult years for almost everyone.

THE BRAIN AND NERVOUS SYSTEM

Four main changes occur in the brain during the adult years: a reduction of brain weight, a loss of grey matter, a decline in the density of dendrites, and slower synaptic transmission speed (i.e., the rate at which information flows among neurons). The most central of these changes is the loss of dendritic density. You'll remember from **Chapter 4** that dendrites are "pruned" during the first few years after birth, so that redundant or unused pathways are eliminated. The loss of dendrites in middle and late adulthood does not seem to be the same type of pruning. Rather, it appears to be a decrease in useful dendritic connections (Sowell et al., 2003).

Research suggests that experience as well as aging is involved in the loss of dendritic density. Neurologists have found that, between ages 60 and 90, adults with higher levels of education show significantly less atrophy of the cerebral cortex than those who have fewer years of schooling (Coffey, Saxton, Ratcliff, Bryan, & Lucke, 1999). Moreover, the brains of well- and poorly educated elderly adults do not differ in areas that are less involved in academic learning than the cerebral cortex is. This finding suggests that education itself is the cause of the reduced atrophying of the cerebral cortex rather than some general factor, such as socioeconomic status, which is coincidentally related to education.

Dendritic loss also results in a gradual slowing of synaptic speed, with a consequent increase in reaction time for many everyday tasks. Neural pathways are redundant enough that it is nearly always possible for a nerve impulse to move from neuron A to neuron B, or from neuron A to some muscle cell. Neurologists usually refer to this redundancy as **synaptic plasticity**. But with the increasing loss of dendrites, the shortest route may be lost, so plasticity decreases and reaction time increases.

One final change in the nervous system (about which physiologists disagree) is the loss of neurons themselves. For many years, it was believed that an adult lost 100 000 neurons every day. It now appears that this conclusion, like many such conclusions about primary aging, was based on cross-sectional comparisons that included many older adults who had diseases known to affect brain composition and functioning. Researchers have not yet reached a consensus on just how much loss occurs among healthy aging adults, but most agree that 100 000 neurons per day is a considerable overestimation (e.g., Ivy et al., 1992; Scheibel, 1996).

Current estimates are that the brain has perhaps 1 trillion neurons (Morgan, 1992). A loss of 100 000 per day, even if it began at birth and lasted for a lifespan of 100 years, would be only about 4 billion neurons, leaving the vast majority (over 99%) still intact. It is only when the brain loses a significant amount of interconnectivity, which occurs as dendrites decrease in number, that "computational power" declines and symptoms of old age appear (Scheibel, 1992, p. 168). In addition, as you learned in **Chapter 13**, scientists have only fairly recently discovered that new neurons are produced in some parts of the brain even in adulthood, although the effect of this neuron regeneration is not yet known (Gould et al., 1999).

synaptic plasticity
the redundancy in the nervous system that ensures that it is nearly always possible for a nerve impulse to move from one neuron to another or from a neuron to another type of cell (e.g., a muscle cell)

THE SENSES

 Explore

In **Chapter 15**, you read about declines in sensory and other physical functions that occur in middle age. Such deficits become larger in late adulthood, and several more serious threats to the health of these systems arise.

VISION In addition to presbyopia (farsightedness), late adulthood can bring other vision defects due to body changes. For example, blood flow to the eye decreases (perhaps as a side effect of atherosclerosis), which results in an enlarged "blind spot" on the retina and thus a reduced field of vision. The pupil does not widen or narrow as much or as quickly as it previously did, which means that the older adult has more difficulty seeing at night and responding to rapid changes in brightness (Kline & Scialfa, 1996).

In addition, a significant minority of older adults suffer from diseases of the eye that further diminish visual acuity and adaptability. For example, among Canadians aged 65 to 74, 9% have *cataracts* (a condition in which the lens inside the eye becomes clouded and obscures vision), 3% have *glaucoma* (a progressive loss of vision caused by optic nerve damage that is often associated with increased fluid pressure buildup in the eye). For those age 75 and older, the rates increase to 22% and 7% respectively (Wilkins & Park, 1996). The leading cause of field restriction for older Canadians is *macular degeneration*, a type of age-related deterioration of the retina that results in loss of central vision. An estimated 20% of those aged 65 to 75, and 37% of those over age 75, have the condition (Somani et al., 2009). Thus, many older adults must often adapt to significant impairments of vision, and the process of adaptation doesn't always go smoothly. Researchers have found that middle-aged adults adjust more easily than older adults to the difficulties associated with living with a serious vision impairment (Lindo & Nordholm, 1999). Moreover, vision loss has a greater negative effect on an elderly adult's sense of well-being. Fortunately, many age-related diseases of the eye can be effectively treated with medications and/or surgery.

◉—Watch

tinnitus
a persistent ringing in the ears

Hearing aids improve many adults' quality of life.
(*Photo:* © Steve Mason/Getty Images)

HEARING You'll recall from **Chapter 15** that wear and tear on the auditory system results in some hearing loss (*presbycusis*) beginning in middle adulthood, but these gradual losses don't typically add up to functionally significant loss until late adulthood. Auditory problems, unlike many other disabilities of old age, are more likely to be experienced by men than by women. This sex difference is normally attributed to differential exposure to noise: More men have worked in environments with high levels of noise (at least in current cohorts of older adults in developed countries).

Hearing difficulties in late adulthood have several components: First, there is the loss of ability to hear high-frequency sounds. Both cross-sectional and longitudinal studies suggest that, for the range of sounds used in normal human speech, the loss after age 60 is such that a given sound has to be about 1 to 2 decibels louder each year for the individual to report that he hears it (Fozard, 1990; Kline & Scialfa, 1996).

Second, most older adults develop difficulties with word discrimination. Even when the sound is loud enough, older adults have more difficulty identifying individual words they have just heard (Schieber, 1992). In addition, many adults over age 60 have problems hearing under noisy conditions. The loss of ability to discriminate individual words is even greater in such situations, so large gatherings become increasingly difficult for older adults.

Tinnitus, a persistent ringing in the ears, also increases in incidence with age, although this problem appears to be independent of the other changes just described. The Tinnitus Association of Canada (2001) reports that 360 000 Canadians experience tinnitus and that 150 000 have an impaired quality of life because of it. It is believed that tinnitus may be caused by exposure to noise, although this cause is not well established.

Even mild hearing loss can pose communication problems in some situations. Those with such problems may also be perceived by others as disoriented or suffering from poor memory, especially if the person with the hearing loss is unwilling to admit the problem and ask for a comment or an instruction to be repeated. Nonetheless, the older adult with a hearing impairment is *not* necessarily socially isolated or unhappy. Mild and moderate hearing losses, even if uncorrected with a hearing aid, are simply not correlated with measures of general social, emotional, or psychological health among elderly adults. Only severe hearing loss is associated with an increase in social or psychological problems, including heightened rates of depression (Corso, 1987; Schieber, 1992).

Presbycusis and the other changes in hearing seem to result from gradual degeneration of virtually every part of the auditory system. Older adults secrete more ear wax, which may block the ear canal; the bones of the middle ear become calcified and less elastic; the cochlear membranes of the inner ear become less flexible and less responsive; and the nerve pathways to the brain show some degeneration (Schieber, 1992).

> ## Critical Thinking
>
> How do you think a hearing impairment is likely to affect the life of an older adult? Aside from wearing a hearing aid, how could a person with a moderate hearing impairment adapt his life so as to reduce the impact of the disability?

TASTE, SMELL, AND TOUCH   The ability to taste the four basic flavours (salty, bitter, sweet, and sour) does not seem to decline over the years of adulthood. Taste receptor cells (taste buds) have short lives and are constantly replaced (Bornstein, 1992). But other changes in the taste system affect older adults, such as the secretion of somewhat less saliva, producing a sensation of "woolly mouth" for some. Many elders also report that flavours seem blander than in earlier years, leading them to prefer more intense concentrations of flavours, particularly sweetness (de Graaf, Polet, & van Staveren, 1994). But it may well be that this perception of flavour blandness is largely due to a loss of the sense of smell.

The sense of smell clearly deteriorates in old age. The best information comes from a cross-sectional study in which researchers tested nearly 2000 children and adults on their ability to identify 40 different smells—everything from pizza to gasoline (Doty et al., 1984). As **Figure 17.4** reveals, young and middle-aged adults had equally good scores on this smell identification test, but scores declined rapidly after age 60. However, the loss of sensitivity to odours is far greater among elderly men than women (Morgan, Covington, Geisler, Polich, & Murphy, 1997).

Interestingly, like hearing loss, the loss of the sense of smell seems to have an environmental component. Specifically, both men and women who worked in factories (where, presumably, they were exposed to more pollutants) show much greater losses of sense of smell in old age than do those who worked in offices (Corwin, Loury, & Gilbert, 1995).

These changes in taste and smell can reduce many pleasures in life. But they can also have practical health consequences. Smells enhance the pleasure of food, so as the sense of smell becomes less acute, elders are less motivated to prepare tasty food. In some cases, this can result in inadequate nutrition or significant dietary imbalances.

Similarly, loss of sensitivity to touch can lead to significant declines in the quality of life. For example, the skin of elderly adults is less responsive to cold and heat (Stevens & Choo, 1998). Research suggests that the loss of sensitivity occurs in a pattern that is a reversal of the proximodistal principle of growth you learned about in **Chapter 3**. In other words, the extremities, usually the feet, are the first body parts that decline in sensitivity. Consequently, elderly people are less able to benefit from the potential comforts associated with physical stimuli. For example, for an elderly person to be able to feel a warm bath, the water temperature may have to be so high that it will burn the skin.

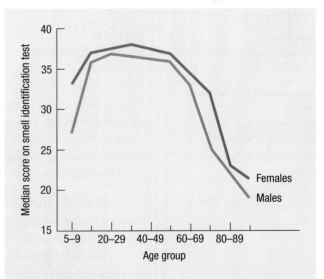

Figure 17.4

Doty's data show a very rapid drop in late adulthood in the ability to identify smells.

(*Source:* Doty et al., 1984.)

THEORIES OF BIOLOGICAL AGING

What are the basic causes of aging? Current theorists agree that the most likely explanation lies in basic cellular processes, which appear to change with age in specific ways that reduce the efficiency of cellular functioning. A number of theoretical variations on this theme have been proposed.

THE HAYFLICK LIMIT

As we pointed out earlier, species vary widely in how long, on average, individuals live. For humans, the maximum lifespan seems to be about 120 years. These differences in life length have persuaded some biologists that there may be a universal genetic process that triggers age-related declines and limits the lifespan (e.g., Hayflick, 1977, 1987). For turtles, the lifespan is far longer, and for chickens, far shorter.

Advocates of this view support their argument with research demonstrating that cells taken from the embryos of different species and placed in nutrient solution double only a fixed number of times, after which the cell colony degenerates. Human embryo cells double about 50 times; those from the Galapagos tortoise double roughly 100 times; chicken cells double only about 25 times. Furthermore, cells taken from human adults double only about 20 times, as if they had already "used up" some of their genetic capacity. The theoretical proposal that emerges from such observations is that each species is subject to a time limit, known as the **Hayflick limit** (because it was proposed by biologist Leonard Hayflick), beyond which cells simply lose their capacity to replicate themselves (Norwood, Smith, & Stein, 1990).

The genetic limits argument has been strengthened by the discovery that each chromosome in the human body (and presumably in other species, too) has, at its tip, a string of repetitive DNA called a **telomere** (Angier, 1992; Campisi, Dimri, & Hara, 1996). Among other functions, telomeres appear to serve as a kind of timekeeping mechanism for the organism. Researchers have found that the number of telomeres is reduced slightly each time a cell divides, so that the number remaining in a 70-year-old is much lower than what is found in a child. This raises the possibility that there may be a crucial minimum number of telomeres; when the total falls below that number, then disease or death comes fairly quickly.

GENETICALLY PROGRAMMED SENESCENCE

Senescence is the gradual deterioration of body systems that happen as organisms age. **Programmed senescence theory** suggests that age-related physical declines result from species-specific genes for aging. Evolutionary theorists argue that programmed senescence prevents older, presumably less fit, individuals from becoming parents at an age when they are unlikely to be able to raise offspring to maturity (Buss, 1999). The idea is that these aging genes are equipped with some kind of built-in clock that prevents the genes from having an effect when humans are in their reproductive years but switches them on once the reproductive peak has passed.

REPAIR OF GENETIC MATERIAL AND CROSS-LINKING

Another theory of aging focuses on the cells' ability to repair breaks in DNA. Breaks in DNA strands are common events, resulting from unknown metabolic processes. Because the organism is apparently unable to repair all the damage, the theory proposes, the accumulation of unrepaired breaks results over time in a loss of cellular function, and the organism ages (Tice & Setlow, 1985).

A related theory focuses on another cellular process called cross-linking, which occurs more often in cell proteins of older adults than in those of younger adults. **Cross-linking** occurs when undesirable chemical bonds form between proteins or fats. In skin and connective tissue, for example, two proteins called *collagen* and *elastin* form cross-linkages,

---

Hayflick limit
the theoretical proposal that each species is subject to a genetically programmed time limit after which cells no longer have any capacity to replicate themselves accurately

telomere
string of repetitive DNA at the tip of each chromosome in the body that appears to serve as a kind of timekeeping mechanism

senescence
physical changes and declines associated with aging

programmed senescence theory
the view that age-related declines are the result of species-specific genes for aging

cross-linking
the formation of undesirable bonds between proteins or fats

either between their molecules or within a given molecule. The resulting molecules cannot assume the correct shape for proper function, leading to effects such as wrinkling of the skin and arterial rigidity. (An equivalent process, by the way, occurs in old rubber, which explains why windshield wipers become stiffer over time.)

FREE RADICALS A third type of cellular process that may contribute to aging relates to the body's ability to deal with free radicals. **Free radicals**, which are molecules or atoms that possess an unpaired electron, are a normal by-product of body metabolism and also arise as a result of exposure to certain substances in foods, sunlight, X-rays, or air pollution. They may also occur more frequently in older than in younger people's bodies because of age-related deterioration of the mitochondria, the cell structures that convert food into energy (Nichols & Melov, 2004). These radicals, especially the subgroup called *oxygen free radicals*, enter into many potentially harmful chemical reactions, resulting in irreparable cellular damage that accumulates with age. For example, oxidation reactions caused by free radicals can damage cell membranes, thereby reducing the cell's protection against toxins and carcinogens.

Research on diet variations also points to the possibility that some foods, especially those high in fat and/or food additives such as preservatives, promote the formation of oxygen free radicals, whereas others, referred to as *antioxidants*, inhibit the formation of these radicals or promote chemical processes that help the body defend against them. Foods high in vitamin C, vitamin E, and beta carotene (vitamin A) all belong in the latter group (Ornish, 1993). Several large epidemiological studies show that people who eat diets higher in antioxidants or who take regular supplements of vitamin E or beta carotene live somewhat longer and have lower rates of heart disease (Blumberg, 1996).

Such findings do not mean that age-related problems, such as heart disease and vision loss, are caused by antioxidant deficiencies. Moreover, some studies suggest that free radicals may not contribute as much to physical aging as researchers once believed (Sanz, Pamplona, & Barja, 2006). Nevertheless, studies showing associations between antioxidants and improvements in health support the general notion that many of the effects of aging are modifiable and perhaps even preventable.

TERMINAL DROP Some theorists claim that physical and mental declines in old age are actually part of the dying process. For example, the **terminal drop hypothesis** asserts that all adults retain excellent physical and mental function until just a few years before death, at which time there are significant declines in all functions (Kleemeier, 1962). In terms of mental functioning, changes in IQ scores (Johansson et al., 2004) and other cognitive measures have been found to fit the terminal drop pattern. For example, a Canadian research team has discovered a reliable marker for changes in cognitive performance that foreshadows terminal decline and impending death (MacDonald, Hultsch, & Dixon, 2008). The researchers found that *inconsistency in speed of performance* was a more sensitive predictor of impending death than the traditional cognitive measures, such as uniformly lower levels of cognitive performance and slower speed of performance on cognitive tasks.

BEHAVIOURAL EFFECTS OF PHYSICAL CHANGES

The great majority of older adults cope effectively with most everyday tasks—buying groceries, managing their finances, reading bus schedules, planning their lives, and so on—despite changes in vision, hearing, and other physical functions (Willis, 1996). Thus, in addition to knowing what these changes are and how they might be explained, it's important to know just how they affect older adults' daily lives.

free radicals
molecules or atoms that possess an unpaired electron

mydevelopmentlab
Connect to MyDevelopmentLab
Be in charge of the aging process in four people in this interactive simulation. See how their facial features change over the years.
Simulate

terminal drop hypothesis
the hypothesis that mental and physical functioning decline drastically only in the few years immediately preceding death

This older man has bought himself a very sporty car and doubtless thinks of himself as still a skilful driver. But it is nonetheless true that many of the physical changes associated with aging will make it harder for him to respond quickly, to see clearly in glare, and to adapt rapidly to changing driving conditions. (*Photo:* Tom Prettyman/PhotoEdit)

GENERAL SLOWING The biggest single behavioural effect of age-related physical changes is a general slowing down. Dendritic loss at the neuronal level clearly contributes substantially to this general slowing, but other factors are also involved, including arthritic changes in the joints and loss of elasticity in the muscles. Everything takes longer—writing things down, tying one's shoes, and adapting to changes in temperature or changes in light conditions (Schaie & Willis, 2005). Even tasks that involve word skills, which tend to decline very little in accuracy with age, nonetheless are done more slowly (Spieler & Griffin, 2006).

Further, many developmentalists believe that the decline in the speed of nerve impulses is responsible for age-related difficulties in translating thoughts into action. For example, neurologists sometimes assess nervous system functioning by having patients demonstrate a physical action involving a tool, such as hammering. Demonstrating an appropriate hand posture and moving the arm in an appropriate way are taken as indicators of neurological health. Developmentalists have found that healthy individuals in late adulthood make more initial errors than younger adults in trying to carry out such activities (Peigneux & van der Linden, 1999). However, they correct their errors just as quickly as those who are younger. Consequently, neuropsychologists think that general slowing of brain activity interferes with older adults' retrieval of the knowledge they need to accomplish the task and that they use behavioural feedback to compensate for mistakes.

Age-related physical changes add up to really significant differences in functioning in a complex motor activity, such as driving. Young adults have more auto accidents than any other age group, primarily because they drive too fast. But older adults have more accidents per kilometres driven (Market Wire, 2003). Of course, other physical changes beyond general slowing contribute to driving problems in old age. Changes in the eyes mean that older adults have more trouble reading signs at night and adjusting to the glare of oncoming headlights. In addition, reduced range of motion in the neck, which often accompanies arthritis, may contribute to automobile accidents involving elderly drivers. Older adults also say that they have more trouble judging their own speed and that the instrument panel is too dim to see (Kline et al., 1992). Similarly, they seem to be less able to judge the speed of oncoming traffic when trying to execute turns and carry out other driving manoeuvres (Keskinen, Ota, & Katila, 1998). And the general increase in reaction time affects elders' ability to switch attention from one thing to the next or to react quickly and appropriately when a vehicle or obstacle appears unexpectedly.

Changes in temperature sensitivity, together with general slowing, lead to increases in accidental burns. For example, the elderly are more likely to burn themselves when they mistakenly pick up a hot pan while cooking. The neurological message "Put down this pan because it's going to burn your skin" moves from the hand to the brain almost instantaneously in a young or middle-aged adult. Among older adults, however, a greater amount of heat is required to initiate the message, the message itself travels to the brain more slowly, and the response from the brain that signals the hand to let go of the pan travels more slowly as well. Consequently, burns are far more common in late adulthood than earlier.

SLEEPING AND EATING PATTERNS Another common effect of physical change is a shift in sleep patterns in old age, which occurs among both healthy and less healthy seniors. Adults older than age 65 typically wake up more frequently in the night and show decreases in rapid eye movement (REM) sleep, the lighter sleep state in which dreaming occurs. Older adults are also more likely to wake early in the morning and go to bed early at night. They become "morning people" instead of "night people" (Cataletto & Hertz, 2005). And because their night sleep is more often interrupted, older adults also nap more during the day to accumulate the needed amount of sleep. These changes in sleep and activity patterns are presumed to be related to changes in nervous system functioning.

The ability of the brain to regulate appetite also changes with advancing age. When you eat, your blood sugar rises, resulting in a chemical message to the brain that creates a sensation called **satiety**, the sense of being full. The feeling of satiety continues until your blood sugar drops, at which time another chemical message is sent to the brain that causes you to feel hunger. In older adults, the satiety part of the pattern seems to be impaired (Keene, Hope, Rogers, & Elliman, 1998). As a result, older adults may feel hungry all the time and may overeat. To compensate, they come to rely more on habits such as taking their meals at certain times and eating the same foods every day. Thus, they may seem to be unnecessarily rigid to those who are younger, when, in reality, their adherence to a particular eating regime is simply a (perhaps unconscious) way of coping with a physiological change.

satiety
the feeling of fullness that follows a meal

MOTOR FUNCTIONS The various physical changes associated with aging also combine to produce a reduction in stamina, dexterity, and balance. The loss of stamina clearly arises in large part from the changes in the cardiovascular system, as well as from changes in muscles. Dexterity is lost primarily as a result of arthritic changes in the joints.

Another significant change, one with particularly clear practical ramifications, is a gradual loss of the sense of balance (Guralnik et al., 1994; Simoneau & Liebowitz, 1996; Slobounov, Moss, Slobounova, & Newell, 1998). Older adults, who may be quite mobile in their home environments, are likely to have greater difficulty handling an uneven sidewalk or adapting their bodies to a swaying bus. Such situations require the ability to adjust rapidly to changing body cues and the muscular strength to maintain body position, both of which decline in old age. So older adults fall more often. About one-quarter of the young old and more than one-third of the old old interviewed for one study reported having fallen in the previous year (Hornbrook, Stevens, & Wingfield, 1994). However, the kinds of activities in which older adults participate affect both the sense of balance and the frequency of falls. Those who practice Tai Chi or who play golf regularly are better able to maintain their balance than their peers who do not engage in these activities (Tsang & Hui-Chan, 2004).

Critical Thinking

How might age-related changes in facial muscles contribute to stereotypes about "grumpiness" in the elderly?

Older adults also have more problems with fine motor movements (Smith et al., 1999). Such losses are small and gradual with respect to well-practised skills, such as handwriting. However, research suggests that some fine motor activities, especially those that require learning a new pattern of movement, may be extremely difficult for elderly people. For example, older adults take far longer than young and middle-aged adults do to learn complex computer mouse skills, such as clicking and dragging objects across the screen (Smith, Sharit, & Czaja, 1999).

SEXUAL ACTIVITY Another behaviour that is affected by the cumulative physical changes of aging is sexual behaviour. You read in **Chapter 15** that the frequency of sexual activity declines gradually in middle adulthood. Both cross-sectional and longitudinal data suggest that this trend continues in late adulthood (Marsiglio & Donnelly, 1991; Palmore, 1981).

The decline in the frequency of sexual activity in late adulthood doubtless has many causes (National Institute on Aging, 2000b). The continuing decline in testosterone levels among men clearly plays some role. The state of one's overall health plays an increasingly larger role with advancing age. For example, blood pressure medication sometimes produces impotence as a side effect; chronic pain may also affect sexual desire. Stereotypes that portray old age as an essentially asexual period of life may also have some effect.

Despite declining frequency, though, more than 70% of adults continue to be sexually active in old age (Bartlik & Goldstein, 2000). Moreover, the physiological capacity to respond to sexual stimulation, unlike other aspects of functioning, appears not to diminish with age. Indeed, some studies suggest that older adults, especially women, are more sexually adventurous; that is, they appear to be more willing to engage in sexual experimentation than young and middle-aged adults (Purnine & Carey, 1998).

Before Going On

- What changes happen in the brain, the nervous system, and other body systems of older adults? How do theories explain these changes in biological aging?

- What are the behavioural effects of changes in the various body systems of older adults?

MENTAL HEALTH

dementia
a neurological disorder involving problems with memory and thinking that affect an individual's emotional, social, and physical functioning

The best-known mental health problems of old age are the **dementias**, a group of neurological disorders involving problems with memory and thinking that affect an individual's emotional, social, and physical functioning. Dementia is the leading cause of institutionalization of the elderly in Canada, especially women (Alzheimer Society of Canada, 2010) (see **Development in the Real World**). However, depression is also a concern in the late adult years.

DEMENTIA

Christopher Patterson, professor of geriatric medicine at McMaster University, states that, as the prevalence of dementia increases in Canadian seniors, so does the rate of cognitive impairment. Alzheimer's disease, an irreversible degenerative condition, is the most common cause of dementia. Other sources of mental confusion include "intercurrent illnesses, infections, metabolic disturbances and drug intoxications" (Patterson, 1994, p. 902). Little of the cognitive impairment associated with the later cluster of disorders is reversible. For instance, Patterson (1994) reported that only 11% of dementing disorders were partially (8%) or completely (3%) cleared up.

The prevalence of mild and severe forms of dementia, which both contribute to cognitive deficits, has been found to be relatively consistent in Canada, Europe, and the United States (Patterson, 1994). Researchers found a great deal of variability in a 7-year longitudinal study of the cognitive abilities of 102 older adults, first tested when they were between ages 62 and 86 (Willis, Jay, Diehl, & Marsiske, 1992). Over the ensuing 7 years, when most of the participants shifted from being young old to old old, 62% of the group either remained at their original level of competence or showed improvement in competence on everyday intellectual tasks, while the remaining 38% showed decline

Development in the Real World

INSTITUTIONALIZATION AMONG CANADIAN SENIORS

Research results such as those graphed in **Figure 17.2** suggest that the average older adult will spend at least a few years with some kind of disability or chronic disease. How often do such problems require nursing-home care? There are several answers to that question, depending on what statistics you look at.

In Canada, roughly the same number of women (2.3%) and men (2.1%) aged 65 to 74 were in any kind of institutional care in 2001 (Cranswick, 2003). However, when we look at the oldest old, far more women (35.4%) than men (22.6%) were living in institutions. Still, these numbers may be lower than you would have guessed.

Another important piece of information examines key questions about the likelihood of institutionalization and what factors most strongly predict that a senior in Canada will live in an institution (Health Reports, 1999b). First, and not surprisingly, age was one strong predictor of institutionalization; the odds of living in an institution increase directly with age. Compared with those who were aged 65 to 74, 75- to 84-year-olds were five times as likely and those over age 85 were 10 times as likely to be institutionalized. Second, two health conditions were also found to be predictive: Those seniors with a serious cognitive impairment were 3.2 times and those with uncorrected visual impairment were 3.0 times as likely to be institutionalized. Third, seniors with low or lower-middle household income had more than a twofold chance of being institutionalized compared with the higher income groups. And fourth, the odds of being institutionalized for those seniors who perceived themselves as having only fair or poor health

were 2.6 times higher than for seniors who had good to excellent self-perceived health status.

The actual experiences of those in nursing homes paint both rosy and gloomy pictures. It is true that placement in a nursing home is often followed by death within a relatively short time. But it is not true that nursing-home care necessarily shortens a person's life. Only when an older adult has been placed in an institution (or any other living situation) involuntarily is there evidence that the move itself is a causal factor in rapid decline and death. Involuntarily institutionalized seniors show much higher death rates in the ensuing months and years than do equivalently disabled seniors who remain at home, although even this effect is not inevitable (Lawton, 1985, 1990). When the institution itself offers residents high levels of warmth, individuation, and opportunity for choice and control, even an involuntary move need not accelerate the process of physical or mental decline (Fields, 1992).

In Canada, there is a growing need to create alternatives to institutionalization as the number of seniors increases over the next several decades, many of whom will have some form of dementia in their later years (Alzheimer Society of Canada, 2010). Two suggested preventative measures include increasing the physical activity levels for all Canadians over age 65 and delaying the onset of dementia through healthy diet and lifestyle programs that target dementia-free Canadian adults. Two supportive measures include the development of informal caregiver skill-building and support program, as well as linking newly diagnosed dementia patients and their informal caregivers with case managers to coordinate care.

(Willis et al., 1992). These results are supported by the graph in **Figure 17.5**, which illustrates that a majority of seniors even among those who are over 85, do not suffer from cognitive impairments.

Gerontologists have also learned that variations in sex hormones are related to variations in cognitive performance. In one study, researchers examined cognitive functioning in men who were receiving sex hormone-blocking drugs in connection with treatment for prostate cancer (Almeida, Waterreus, Spry, Flicker, & Martins, 2004). When these men discontinued treatment, their levels of sex hormones returned to normal, and their cognitive functioning improved dramatically.

Similarly, studies show that estrogen levels and cognitive functioning are correlated in women. Some early studies indicated that postmenopausal women who received hormone replacement therapy showed improved memory function (Costa, Reus, Wolkowitz, Manfredi, & Lieberman, 1999; Duka, Tasker, & McGowan, 2000). However, the collective findings of numerous studies examining the effects of hormone replacement therapy on cognitive functioning suggest that giving women hormone supplements does not improve their cognitive functioning. In fact, as you learned in

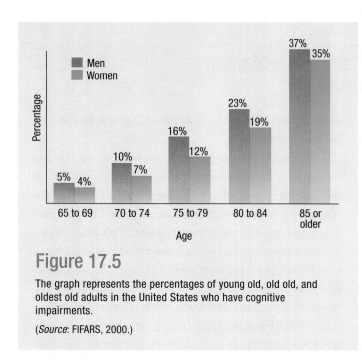

Figure 17.5

The graph represents the percentages of young old, old old, and oldest old adults in the United States who have cognitive impairments.

(*Source*: FIFARS, 2000.)

Alzheimer's disease
a very severe form of dementia, the cause of which is unknown

Chapter 15, hormone replacement therapy may actually increase women's chances of developing serious cognitive dysfunctions (Shumaker et al., 2003). So, the nature of the relationship between sex hormones and cognitive functioning is not yet understood.

ALZHEIMER'S DISEASE

Alzheimer's disease (technically known as *dementia of the Alzheimer's type*) is a severe form of dementia. The early stages of Alzheimer's disease usually become evident very slowly, beginning with subtle memory difficulties, repetitive conversation, and disorientation in unfamiliar settings. Then memory for recent events begins to go. Memory for long-ago events or for well-rehearsed cognitive procedures, such as simple calculations, is often retained until late in the illness, presumably because these memories can be accessed through many alternative neural pathways (Martin et al., 2003).

Eventually, however, an individual with Alzheimer's disease may fail to recognize family members and may be unable to remember the names of common objects or how to perform routine activities such as brushing her teeth or dressing. Those afflicted with Alzheimer's suffer declines in the ability to communicate, as well as the ability to carry out daily self-care routines. The changes in appetite regulation you read about earlier in this chapter are particularly problematic for those with Alzheimer's, because they can't rely on habit to regulate their eating behaviour, as healthy older people do. Left to their own devices, Alzheimer's victims may consume as many as three or four complete meals at one sitting without realizing how much they have eaten. Consequently, their eating behaviour must be closely supervised.

Alzheimer's patients also have difficulty processing information about others' emotions, such as facial expressions (Burnham & Hogervorst, 2004). Some have problems controlling their own emotions and display sudden bursts of anger or even rage. Others exhibit an increased level of dependency and clinginess toward family or friends (Raskind & Peskind, 1992). In addition, research suggests that the incidence of depression among elders with Alzheimer's disease may be as high as 40% (Harwood et al., 2000).

DIAGNOSING AND TREATING ALZHEIMER'S DISEASE
Alzheimer's disease can be definitively diagnosed only after a person has died. At autopsy, the brains of Alzheimer's victims are far more likely to contain extensive *neurofibrillary tangles* than are the brains of individuals with other kinds of dementia (Silver, Newell, Brady, Hedley-White, & Perls, 2002). Neurofibrillary tangles are stringy masses of tissue that appear to "clog" connections between neurons. They are typically surrounded by deposits of proteins and other substances called *plaques*.

The difficulty involved in diagnosing Alzheimer's disease is magnified by the fact that nearly 80% of elderly individuals complain of memory problems (Hanninen et al., 1996). As a result, researchers are currently looking for a set of predictors that may distinguish individuals who are in the process of developing Alzheimer's from those who are suffering from the effects of normal aging. A few indicators, such as the syndrome known as *mild cognitive impairment*, show promise (see **Research Report**). At present, though, a diagnosis of Alzheimer's disease represents a health professional's best educated guess about the source of an individual's cognitive difficulties.

Research Report

MILD COGNITIVE IMPAIRMENT AND ALZHEIMER'S DISEASE

When a senior seeks help for memory problems or difficulties with logical thinking but is clearly not suffering from any kind of dementia, health care professionals usually try to determine whether he should be diagnosed with mild cognitive impairment (MCI) or with age-associated cognitive decline (AACD). Criteria for both diagnoses include a gradual decline in cognitive function, along with low scores on standardized tests (compared with scores of others of the same age). Physicians must also rule out the possibility that the individual is suffering from a specific disorder that might account for his symptoms (e.g., brain tumour, stroke, depression). Of the two disorders, AACD is the more common, afflicting just under one-third of older adults (Hanninen et al., 1996). By contrast, MCI is found in about 9% of elders (Tervo et al., 2004).

The procedures involved in determining which diagnosis is appropriate can take several weeks to complete and must usually be repeated a few months later. Although this process can be frustrating for elderly adults and their caregivers, getting the correct diagnosis is important because MCI is believed to be a precursor to Alzheimer's disease, while AACD is not. Thus, the prognosis for individuals with MCI is quite different from that for elders with AACD. Moreover, many researchers think that the progression to dementia in patients with MCI can be slowed or even prevented through the use of drugs that have shown to be effective against fully developed Alzheimer's (Amieva et al., 2004; Maruyama et al., 2003).

The idea that MCI is an early stage in the development of Alzheimer's disease is somewhat controversial. Some of the strongest evidence in favour of the stage hypothesis has involved brain-imaging and DNA studies. Generally, imaging studies show similar patterns of brain degeneration in individuals with MCI and Alzheimer's disease (Johnson, Vogt, Kim, Cotmam, & Head, 2004), and these patterns appear to be distinguishable from those associated with both normal aging and other kinds of dementia. Similarly, defects in the *apolipoprotein E* gene are strongly associated with both Alzheimer's disease and MCI (Tervo et al., 2004).

Additional support for the stage view comes from other kinds of physiological research. For example, individuals with either MCI or Alzheimer's disease differ from normal older adults in the degree to which free-radical–fighting substances, such as vitamin C, are present in their bloodstreams (Rinaldi et al., 2003). Further, studies examining substances in the cerebrospinal fluid of normal elderly adults, elders with MCI, and Alzheimer's sufferers indicate that both MCI and Alzheimer's are associated with rapid neuronal death (Maruyama et al., 2003).

Despite these compelling lines of evidence, it is abundantly clear that MCI does not inevitably lead to Alzheimer's disease. Longitudinal studies show that only one-third of adults aged 70 and over exhibit full-blown dementia within 2 years of receiving the diagnosis of MCI (Amieva et al., 2004). In addition, the cognitive functioning of many MCI sufferers remains entirely stable for many years.

Scientists on both sides of the debate about the nature of the MCI–Alzheimer's link agree that continued research into the correlation between the two is important to discovering the disease process that underlies the symptoms of Alzheimer's disease. Such research could lead to preventive measures that spare many MCI sufferers from this devastating disease.

A few drugs—such as *galantamine*, a drug that increases the amounts of some neurotransmitters in the brain—appear to slow down progress of Alzheimer's disease (Kurz, Erkinjuntti, Small, Lilienfeld, & Damaraju, 2003). Researchers are also studying the potential uses of anti-inflammatory drugs (e.g., aspirin) and antioxidant supplements (e.g., vitamin E) in the treatment and prevention of the disease (Sano et al., 1997). Experimental studies have shown that training Alzheimer's sufferers to use specific strategies (e.g., making notes in a journal) can to some degree improve their performance of everyday memory tasks, such as associating names with faces and remembering to take medication (Lowenstein, Acevedo, Czaja, & Duara, 2004).

HEREDITY AND ALZHEIMER'S DISEASE Genetic factors seem to be important in some, but not all, cases of Alzheimer's (Heun & Bonsignore, 2004). Researchers have found a gene on chromosome 19 (*apoliprotein E* or *ApoE*) that controls production of a protein that is linked to Alzheimer's disease (Rose, 1995). When errors in the production of this protein occur, the dendrites and axons of neurons in the brain become tangled and, as a result, do not function as efficiently. However, this gene does not act alone. Many other genes combine with *ApoE* in ways that researchers don't yet fully understand to trigger the onset of the disease (Bertram, McQueen, Mullin, Blacker, & Tanzi, 2007; Reiman et al., 2007).

Even in families with very high prevalences of Alzheimer's disease, ages of onset are highly variable. In one family study, age of onset ranged from age 44 to age 67, and in another, onset ranged from the early 60s to the mid-80s (Axelman, Basun, & Lannfelt, 1998; Silverman et al., 2005). Moreover, there were wide variations in the severity of the disease's behavioural effects and in the length of time the victims lived once they developed Alzheimer's.

OTHER TYPES OF DEMENTIA Strictly speaking, dementia is a symptom and not a disease, and neurological research indicates that Alzheimer's and non-Alzheimer's dementias involve very different disease processes (Fokin, Ponomareva, Androsova, & Gavrilova, 1997). For example, signs of dementia frequently appear after a person suffers multiple small strokes; in this case, the condition is called **multi-infarct dementia**. The brain damage caused by such strokes is irreversible. However, in contrast to most cases of Alzheimer's disease, various forms of therapy—occupational, recreational, and physical—can improve victims' functioning.

In addition, dementia can be caused by depression, metabolic disturbances, drug intoxication, Parkinson's disease, hypothyroidism, multiple blows to the head (frequent among boxers), a single head trauma, some kinds of tumours, vitamin B12 deficiency, anemia, or alcohol abuse (Anthony & Aboraya, 1992; Butters et al., 2004; Suryadevara, Storey, Aronow, & Ahn, 2003). Clearly, many of these causes are treatable; indeed, roughly 10% of all patients who are evaluated for dementia turn out to have some reversible problem. So, when an older person shows signs of dementia, it is critical to arrange for a careful diagnosis.

INCIDENCE OF ALZHEIMER'S AND OTHER DEMENTIAS Evidence from research indicates that somewhere between 2 and 8% of all Canadian adults over age 65 show significant symptoms of some kind of dementia, and that almost two-thirds (64%) of those with dementia have Alzheimer's disease (Lindsay, Sykes, McDowell, Verreault, & Laurin, 2004). Experts also agree that the rates of all kinds of dementias, including Alzheimer's disease, rise rapidly among people in their 70s and 80s. For example, large Canadian studies have showed that 11.1% of adults over age 75 and 34.5% of those over age 85 suffered from moderate to severe symptoms of dementia (e.g., Lindsay et al., 2004; Rockwood & Stadnyk, 1994).

multi-infarct dementia
a form of dementia caused by one or more strokes

👁 Watch

DEPRESSION

The earliest studies of age differences in depression suggested that older adults were at higher risk for this disorder than any other age group, which contributed to a widespread cultural stereotype of the inevitably depressed elder. However, several recent Canadian studies have shown that mental health is relatively poor among Canadian youth and improves with age (e.g., Stephens, Dulberg, & Joubert, 2000; Streiner, Cairney, Velhuizen, 2006; Wade & Cairney, 1997). **Figure 17.6** shows the declining prevalence rates for depressive and anxiety disorders in older Canadians. Still, the full story on depression in late adulthood is complex.

DIAGNOSIS, DEFINITIONS, AND PREVALENCE Ageism can influence the diagnosis of depression in the elderly. Signs of depression in older adults may be dismissed as old-age "grumpiness" by family members (NIA, 2000a). And when health care professionals recognize the signs of depression in elderly adults, they often fail to offer them effective treatments (Fischer, Wei, Solberg, Rush, & Heinrich, 2003). Alternatively, as noted earlier, depression may be mistaken for dementia because it can cause confusion and memory loss.

It is also important to distinguish between depressed mood and full-fledged clinical depression. The latter involves problems (e.g., feelings of hopelessness, insomnia, lack of appetite, loss of interest in social activities) that are of long duration and are severe enough to interfere with a person's ability to carry out normal activities (APA, 2000). By contrast, chronic depressed mood among the elderly, known as **geriatric dysthymia**, typically does not progress to clinical depression and has been found to be related to life stresses (Kocsis, 1998).

Although four times as many Canadian men as women commit suicide, about twice as many women are depressed (Health Canada, 2002c). More than 11% of Canadian women aged 20 to 44 have a probable risk of depression, but the rate declines steadily to 3.6% after age 75 (Statistics Canada, 2002e). The trend is reversed for the duration of depressive episodes. Depressive episodes are briefest (about 5 weeks on average) for the youngest age group, whereas the duration of depression lasts an average of 10.3 weeks at age 75 and beyond (Health Canada, 1999e). These findings fit with other evidence that suggests that true clinical depression is, if anything, less common among older adults than among younger adults, while dysthymia increases somewhat in frequency in late old age (Beekman, Copeland, & Prince, 1999; Gatz, Kasl-Godley, & Karel, 1996). In fact, health professor Scott Patten of the University of Calgary reported that the prevalence of major depression in Canadians for both sexes is highest in 12- to 24-year-olds and then drops with every successive age group to 3.1% in females and a nominal level in males aged 65 and older (Patten, 2000).

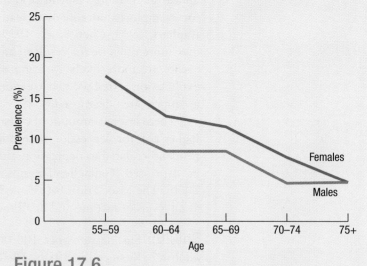

Figure 17.6

Prevalence of lifetime mood disorders for Canadian men and women age 55 years and over.

(*Source:* Streiner, Cairney, & Veldhuizen, 2006, Figure 1, p. 188.)

geriatric dysthymia
chronic depressed mood in older adults

RISK FACTORS The risk factors for depression and dysthymia among the elderly are not difficult to identify: inadequate social support, inadequate income, emotional loss (such as following the deaths of a spouse, family, or friends), and nagging health problems. However, the strongest predictor appears to be health status. Across all ethnic and socioeconomic groups, the more disabling conditions older adults have, the more depressive symptoms they have (Black, Markides, & Miller, 1998; Curyto, Chapleski, & Lichtenberg, 1999; FIFARS, 2000; Lam, Pacala, & Smith, 1997; Okwumabua, Baker, Wong, & Pilgram, 1997). Determining the direction of causation in the association between health status and depression is difficult because depression impairs an older adult's ability to respond to therapeutic interventions that might be helpful (Mast, Azar, MacNeil, & Lichtenberg, 2004). To put it differently, elders who have chronic health conditions, such as arthritis, are more likely to be depressed than their peers who do not, but depression is a risk factor for a poor response to therapy. Thus, for many elderly adults, the link between health and depression becomes circular.

Gender is also a risk factor; in Canada, depressed women outnumber men two to one among the elderly, just as they do at younger ages (Statistics Canada, 2002e). However, sorting out the causes of this difference is difficult. For one thing, women appear to be more resilient in response to many life stressors. The death of a spouse, for example, is more likely to lead to depression in a man than in a woman (Byrne & Raphael, 1999; Chen et al., 1999). Such findings suggest that depression in women may more often be the result of an accumulation of everyday stresses, while traumatic events are more likely to bring on feelings of depression in men. Another possible explanation is that women are more willing to seek help for depression and, as a result, are more often diagnosed.

There is a fair amount of consistency in findings that elders living in poverty are at higher risk for depression than others (Beekman et al., 1999). Education is also independently related to depression; that is, poorly educated older adults are more likely to be depressed (Gallagher-Thompson, Tazeau, & Basilio, 1997; Miech & Shanahan, 2000). The association between education and depression exists among elderly adults at all levels of income and in all racial and ethnic groups.

SUICIDE Suicide rates per 100 000 for all age groups of Canadians have increased almost 75% since the 1950s. Historically, elderly Canadians had higher than average rates of suicide until the late 1980s. Since that time, the suicide rate for the elderly has declined to a level slightly below the national average (Suicide Information & Education Centre, 1998). Despite higher rates of depression among women in Canada, elderly men are more than five times as likely to commit suicide, as illustrated in **Figure 17.7** (Langlois & Morrison, 2002).

The reasons for this dramatic sex difference are not entirely clear. It's important to note, though, that suicide at all ages is predicted by the same factors: a sense of hopelessness, unemployment, psychological disorders, alcoholism, social isolation, and poor physical health (Beck, Brown, Berchick, Stewart, & Steer, 1990; Kaplan & Sadock, 1991). Some theorists believe that elderly men are at higher risk for suicide, even though elderly women are more often depressed, because men are more likely than women to have several of these risk factors in combination (Kaplan & Sadock, 1991).

In addition, loss of economic status through retirement may be more troubling for men than for women in present cohorts of the elderly, because traditional socialization patterns may have led men to equate earnings with self-worth (Mooney et al, 2000b). Similarly, declining health may cause an elderly man to view himself as a burden on others. The death of a spouse may also be a factor in many male suicides because, as you will learn in **Chapter 19**, men do not adjust as well as women do to the death of a spouse (Stroebe & Stroebe, 1993). Finally, as is true of younger people, older women attempt suicide more often than older men do, but the men complete the act more often, mostly because they are more likely than women to choose violent methods, such as firearms.

THERAPY AND MEDICATION Therapies for depression are the same for older adults as for those who are younger. Psychotherapy is often recommended, especially interventions that help sufferers develop optimistic thought

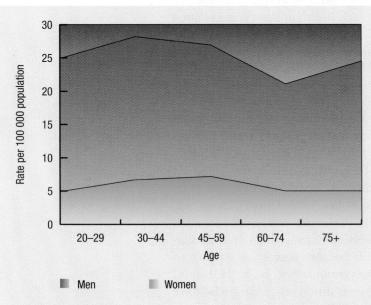

Figure 17.7

Suicide rates in Canada are four times higher for males than for females. The difference is five times higher for males aged 65-plus than for females.

(*Source:* Adapted from Statistics Canada, 2001, *Health Reports 13*(2), Table 2, p. 15, Cat. No. 82-003 [Langlois & Morrison, 2002].)

patterns (NIA, 2000a). However, as with younger adults, therapy appears to be most effective when combined with antidepressant medications ("Depressed elderly," 1999).

Experts point out that appropriate use of antidepressant medications among the elderly is critical. For one thing, antidepressants may reduce the effectiveness of the life-sustaining drugs some older adults take (NIA, 2000a). In addition, antidepressants are linked to an increased incidence of falls among the institutionalized elderly. One study found a remarkable 80% increase in falls within a group of more than 2000 nursing-home residents who began taking antidepressants (Bender, 1999).

PREVENTION Given that poor overall health status predicts depression in the elderly, one important aspect of preventing depression is to help older adults improve their health. For example, arthritis limits the activities of more elderly Canadians than any other chronic condition (Wilkins & Park, 1996). Older adults may be unaware of many new and effective treatments for arthritis. So, one indirect way of preventing depression is to educate older adults and their health care providers about such treatments and to encourage the elderly to get help. One cost-effective strategy that can reduce the risk of depression is a program of regular exercise, as prescribed in *Canada's Physical Activity Guide to Healthy Active Living for Older Adults* (Health Canada, 2000d) (see **Figure 17.3**).

Interacting with children may help prevent depression in late adulthood. (*Photo:* Ellen Senisi/The Image Works)

Social involvement may also be important in preventing depression in the elderly. For example, in one study, researchers in Mexico examined how participation in activities with children, such as attending children's plays or helping plan children's parties, might affect nursing home residents' emotions (Saavedra, Ramirez, & Contreras, 1997). Researchers found that such activities significantly improved participants' emotional states. So periodic involvement with children might be an effective way to prevent depression in institutionalized elders.

In addition, research on the connection between religion and depression suggests that caretakers can help elders avoid depression by supporting their spiritual needs. Many older adults need help getting to religious services; those who live in institutions may need to have services brought to them. Declines in vision may mean that an elderly person can no longer read religious books and may deeply appreciate having someone read to him or provide him with recordings. Helping elders maintain religious faith and practice in these ways may be an important key to reducing depression rates.

Before Going On

- What is Alzheimer's disease, and how does it differ from other dementias?
- What does research suggest about depression among older adults?

COGNITIVE CHANGES

Among the young old (aged 65 to 75), cognitive changes are still fairly small, and these older adults show little or no average decline on a few measures, such as vocabulary knowledge. But the old old and the oldest old show average declines on virtually all measures of intellectual skill, with the largest declines evident on any measures that involve speed or unexercised abilities (Cunningham & Haman, 1992; Giambra et al., 1995).

MEMORY

As you learned in **Chapter 15,** forgetfulness becomes more frequent with age (Ponds, Commissaris, & Jolles, 1997). However, it's important to remember that the same basic rules seem to apply to memory processes among both older and younger adults. For both groups, for example, recognition is easier than recall, and tasks that require speed are more difficult. Further, metamemory and metacognition skills are just as important to memory function in old age as they are earlier in life (Olin & Zelinski, 1997). Further, in many studies, older adults achieve scores very similar to those of younger adults on tests of memory accuracy, although they typically take longer to complete memory tasks and make more errors (Babiloni et al., 2004).

SHORT-TERM MEMORY FUNCTION
One area in which researchers see significant late adulthood changes is in short-term, or working, memory capacity (Hester, Kinsella, & Ong, 2004; Jenkins, Myerson, Hale, & Fry, 1999). You should remember from earlier chapters that there is a limitation on the number of items a person can retain in her memory at once. The more pieces of information she has to handle, the more she forgets, and the poorer her performance on memory and other kinds of cognitive tasks. Thus, the more any given cognitive task makes demands on working memory, the larger the decline with age.

A good illustration comes from a study involving a familiar, everyday task—remembering telephone numbers (West & Crook, 1990). Participants were shown a series of 7-digit or 10-digit telephone numbers on a computer screen, one at a time. The participant said each number as it appeared; then the number disappeared from the screen and the participant had to dial the number she had just seen on a push-button phone attached to the computer. On some trials, the participants got a busy signal when they first dialled and then had to dial the number over again. **Figure 17.8** shows the relationship between age and the correct recall of the phone numbers under these four conditions.

Notice that there is essentially no decline with age in immediate recall of a normal seven-digit telephone number (the equivalent of what you do when you look a number up in the phone book, say it to yourself as you read it, and then dial it immediately). When the length of the number increases to the 10 digits used for long-distance numbers, however, a decline with age becomes evident, beginning at about age 60. And with even a brief delay between saying the number and dialling it, the decline occurs earlier.

Patterns of age differences are not identical for all memory tasks. For example, older adults typically perform more poorly than younger adults on tasks involving *retrospective memory*, or recalling something that has happened recently (Henry, MacLeod, Phillips, & Crawford, 2004). By contrast, older adults outperform younger adults on *prospective* memory tasks in a natural setting, such as their home (Rendell & Thomson, 1999). Prospective tasks

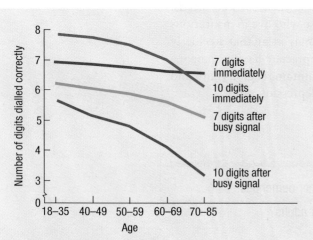

Figure 17.8

The graph shows the results from West and Crook's study of memory for telephone numbers. Notice that there is no loss of memory in middle adulthood for the most common condition: a seven-digit number dialled immediately. But if the number of digits increases, or if you have to remember the number a bit longer, some decline in memory begins around age 50 or 60.

(*Source:* West & Crook, 1990, from Table 3, p. 524.)

require a person to remember an event into the future—for example, remembering to take their medication, show up for a doctor's appointment, or pay a bill. However, University of Victoria memory researchers have found the elderly generally underperform young and middle-aged adults on such tasks when in a controlled laboratory setting where there are no external memory cues, such as a calendar or reminder note (Cohen, Dixon, Lindsay, & Masson, 2003).

STRATEGY LEARNING A study of older adults in Germany provides a good example of research findings on strategy learning and memory in older adults (Baltes & Kliegl, 1992; Kliegl, Smith, & Baltes, 1990). Researchers tested 18 college students and 19 old, but physically healthy, adults between ages 65 and 80, with an average age of 71.7 years. Participants were shown sets of pictures of 30 familiar buildings in Berlin and were asked to use the pictures to create associations that would help them remember a list of 30 words. For example, a castle might be paired with the word *bicycle*. A typical association would be to imagine someone riding a bicycle in front of a castle. The pictures in each set were displayed for different amounts of time, ranging from 20 seconds each to 1 second each. After participants attempted to learn each list of words, the experimenters asked what images they had used and suggested possible improvements. Training sessions were interspersed with test sessions to check on the participants' progress.

Figure 17.9 shows the results for pictures and words presented at 5-second intervals. You can see that the older adults showed improvement after training, but their performance was poorer than that of younger adults. These findings suggest that the learning process simply takes longer for older adults—longer to create the mental image and longer to link that image up with the word in the list. However, when allowed more time to associate each picture and word, older adults' performance was more similar to that of younger participants.

Studies comparing younger and older adults' performance on arithmetic tasks involving the "five rule" show a somewhat different pattern, however. The "five rule" is researchers' term for the common finding that arithmetic problems involving multiples of five are easier to work with than problems that do not involve these multiples. For instance, people more quickly say that 5 × 12 = 50 is false than that 4 × 12 = 50 is false. Researchers have found that the five rule is used far less often by elderly than by younger research participants (Lemaire & Lecacheur, 2004). Such findings suggest that the tendency to apply some cognitive strategies automatically—that is, without giving them much thought—may decline with age.

EVERYDAY MEMORY One common argument from those who take a more optimistic view of the effects of aging on cognitive functioning is that older adults may be able to remember just as well as younger adults, but they are simply less motivated to memorize lists of unrelated words given to them by researchers in a laboratory. However, on virtually all everyday tasks—remembering the main points of a story or a newspaper article; recalling movies, conversations, grocery lists, or recipes; recalling the information from a medicine label; remembering whether they did something ("Did I turn off the stove before I left the house?"); or remembering where they heard something (called *source memory*)—older adults perform less well than younger

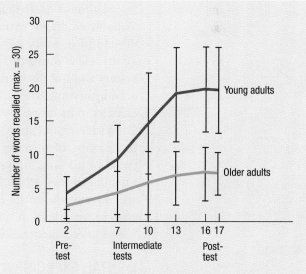

Figure 17.9

These results from Kliegl's study show that older adults can learn complex information-processing skills and improve their performance after training but that they don't gain as much as younger adults do. However, this study also suggested that, given enough time, older adults can learn new strategies.

(*Source:* Kliegl et al., 1990, adapted from figure on p. 899.)

Use it or lose it? These men keep their minds sharp by playing games that require complex memory and strategy skills.
(*Photo:* A. Ramey/PhotoEdit)

adults (Brown, Jones, & Davis, 1995; Salt-house, 1991; Verhaeghen & Marcoen, 1993; Verhaeghen, Marcoen, & Goossens, 1993). These results have been found in longitudinal as well as cross-sectional studies, particularly after age 70 (Hultsch, Hertzog, Small, McDonald-Miszczak, & Dixon, 1992; Zelinski, Gilewski, & Schaie, 1993).

Still, task-specific knowledge seems to make a difference among the elderly. For example, older adults who have larger vocabularies outperform peers who know fewer words on tasks involving rapid recognition of words (Kitzan, Ferraro, Petros, & Ludorf, 1999). Researchers know that prior knowledge is the critical factor in such findings, because elders with large vocabularies perform just as poorly as their less knowledgeable peers on tasks involving nonsense words.

PRELIMINARY EXPLANATIONS How do researchers account for these changes in memory? Neuroimaging studies show that age-related memory decline is associated with changes in the ratio of grey to white matter in the brain (Kramer et al., 2007). In addition, a reduction in the volume of the hippocampus is associated with memory deficits among the elderly.

Functionally speaking, forgetfulness among the elderly may result from the kind of general slowing that you read about earlier in the chapter. Older adults take longer to register some new piece of information, encode it, and retrieve it. Some of the clearest evidence of the important role of speed in memory decline in old age comes from an extensive series of studies by Timothy Salthouse (e.g., Salthouse, 2004).

Salthouse has tested both basic reaction speed and memory or other cognitive skills in adults of various ages. According to him, a very large portion of the age decline in memory can be accounted for simply by slower reaction times in older adults. He is convinced that the loss of speed occurs at the level of the central nervous system and not in the peripheral nerves. So physiological changes in neurons and the accompanying loss of nerve conductance speed may be the root causes of these changes in memory.

Virtually all experts now agree with Salthouse that loss of speed is a key aspect of the process of memory decline, and studies have shown that quantitative losses in speed of information-processing very strongly predict qualitative changes in memory function (Byrne, 1998; Maylor, Vousden, & Brown, 1999). But most also believe that speed is not the entire explanation. There appear to be other factors as well, such as changes in attention strategies that lead to less effective processing of information (Gottlob & Madden, 1999).

MENTAL EXERCISE Can mental exercise improve mental functioning, just as physical exercise improves physical functioning? Studies with rats show that older rats placed in very rich, interesting environments experience growth in brain tissue, whereas rats placed in neutral or boring environments experience a decrease in brain mass (Cotman & Neeper, 1996). Neurophysiologists involved in this animal research are convinced that something analogous occurs among humans—that older adults who continue to challenge themselves with complex mental activities can delay, or even reverse, the normal decline in brain mass that is part of primary aging.

Correlational evidence supports this argument (Salthouse, 2004). For example, in one study, researchers found that older adults who played bridge regularly had higher scores on tests of both memory and reasoning than did non-bridge players. The two groups did not differ in education, health, exercise levels, or life satisfaction or on measures of physical and cognitive functioning that have little relationship to bridge playing, such as reaction time and vocabulary size (Clarkson-Smith & Hartley, 1990).

The difficulties inherent in this research are obvious: Most strikingly, such research suffers from a serious self-selection problem. People who strive to remain mentally active are doubtless different to begin with from those who make less effort (Hultsch, Hertzog, Small, & Dixon, 1999). And teasing out the unique effect of mental activity from the role of education, social class, and health is clearly very difficult. But it seems reasonable that some—perhaps significant—enhancement or better maintenance of intellectual skills results from an "engaged" and intellectually active lifestyle (Gold et al., 1995).

WISDOM AND CREATIVITY

Theorists who study cognition in older adults have also begun to ask whether elders might have some advantages over the young because of their accumulation of knowledge and skills. In other words, older adults might be wiser. Researchers have not yet agreed on a common definition of wisdom, but most authors emphasize that it goes beyond mere accumulations of facts. **Wisdom** reflects understanding of "universal truths" or basic laws or patterns. It is knowledge that is blended with values and meaning systems; it is knowledge based on the understanding that clarity is not always possible, that unpredictability and uncertainty are part of life (Baltes & Kunzmann, 2004).

wisdom
a hypothesized cognitive characteristic of older adults that includes accumulated knowledge and the ability to apply that knowledge to practical problems of living

You may be wondering how researchers measure wisdom. The leading researcher in this field, the late Paul Baltes, devised one useful technique (Baltes & Staudinger, 2000). Baltes presented research participants with stories about fictional characters who were trying to make a major life decision. For example, one dilemma Baltes used involved a 15-year-old girl who wants to get married. Participants' responses to the stories are judged according to five criteria Baltes hypothesizes to be central to wisdom as it relates to solving practical life problems:

- factual knowledge
- procedural knowledge
- understanding of relevance of context
- understanding of relevance of values
- recognition that it is impossible to know in advance how any decision will ultimately affect one's life

A person would be judged to be low in wisdom if her response to the 15-year-old's desire to marry were something like "A 15-year-old getting married? That's stupid. I would tell the girl to forget about it until she's older." The answer of a person judged to be high in wisdom would be more complex. A wise person might point out, "There are circumstances when marriage at such a young age might be a good decision. Is she motivated by a desire to make a home for a child she is expecting? Also, the girl might come from a culture where marriage at 15 is quite common. You have to consider people's motivations and their backgrounds to understand their decisions. You also have to know how the person involved views the situation to be able to give advice."

Critical Thinking

Make a list of the people you think of as wise. How old are they? Is old age necessary for wisdom? If not, how do you think wisdom is acquired?

Seeking advice from an elder who is presumed to be wise is one way young adults act on the belief that those who are older have accumulated knowledge and information that can benefit them.
(*Photo:* David Young-Wolff/ Getty Images)

Virtually all theorists who have written about wisdom assume that it is more likely to be found in the middle-aged and the elderly. However, Baltes has found that younger adults perform as well as older adults in response to the fictional dilemma task. In fact, Baltes has found that, rather than age, intelligence and professional experience are correlated with responses to the dilemma task. So, Baltes's research seems to suggest that the popular idea that age and wisdom are associated is probably not true. Wisdom does not appear to be a characteristic of the elderly that distinguishes them from other subgroups of adults.

Critics have suggested that Baltes is simply measuring general cognitive ability rather than what is usually thought of as wisdom. Nevertheless, Baltes's research has produced an important finding about wisdom and old age: In contrast to performance on information-processing tasks, such as memorizing nonsense words, performance on wisdom tasks does not decline with age (Baltes & Staudinger, 2000). Moreover, the speed of accessing wisdom-related knowledge remains constant across adulthood, unlike speed of information-processing in other domains. In addition, other researchers (e.g., Orwoll & Perlmutter, 1990) have found that those older adults singled out by their peers as wise are more likely to rank high in what Erikson called ego integrity and are more likely to show concern for humanity as a whole.

Enhanced creativity may also be an element of cognition in older adults. As you learned in **Chapter 15**, some highly creative individuals, especially composers and artists, reach their peak in late adulthood. To describe the potential for creative work in the later years, a leading gerontologist, Gene Cohen, has developed a four-stage theory of mid- to late-life creativity (Cohen, 2000). Cohen believes that these phases apply to ordinary people who are more creative than others in their everyday lives as well as to professional creators, such as composers and artists.

Cohen proposes that at around age 50, creative individuals enter a *re-evaluation phase*, during which they reflect on past accomplishments and formulate new goals. The re-evaluation process, along with an increasing sense of time limitations, leads to an intensification of the desire to create and produce. During the next stage, the *liberation phase*, individuals in their 60s become freer to create, because most have retired from everyday work. Most are also more tolerant of their own failures, and thus are willing to take risks that they would not have taken at earlier ages. In the *summing-up phase*, creative people in their 70s have a desire to knit their accomplishments together into a cohesive, meaningful story. They begin to view their early accomplishments in terms of how those accomplishments prefigured later achievements. Finally, in the *encore phase*, during the 80s and beyond, there is a desire to complete unfinished works or to fulfill desires that have been put aside in the past.

Before Going On

- Describe memory differences that distinguish older and younger adults, and suggest some possible explanations for these age differences.

- What do theory and research on wisdom and creativity reveal about cognitive functioning in late adulthood?

Summary

Variability in Late Adulthood

- Developmentalists group the elderly into three sub-groups: the young old (aged 60 to 75), the old old (aged 75 to 85), and the oldest old (aged 85 and older). There are vast individual differences in the timing and pace of all the physical and mental changes associated with aging.

- Heredity, overall health, current and prior health habits (particularly exercise), and availability of adequate social support all influence functioning and longevity.

Physical Changes

- The aging brain experiences a loss of dendritic density of neurons, which has the effect of slowing reaction time for almost all tasks.

- Older adults have more difficulty adapting to darkness and light. Loss of hearing is more common and more noticeable after age 65; many older adults experience loss of hearing for high sounds, some loss of ability to discriminate words, and greater difficulty hearing under noisy conditions. Taste discrimination remains largely unchanged with age, but ability to discriminate smells declines substantially in late adulthood.

- Theories of biological aging emphasize the possible existence of genetic limiting mechanisms and/or the cumulative effects of malfunctions within cells.

- General slowing alters behaviour in old age and makes some tasks, such as driving, more dangerous. Older adults also change their sleeping and eating patterns. Motor abilities decline, causing more accidents because of falls. Sexual activity also decreases in frequency, although most older adults continue to be sexually active.

Mental Health

- Dementia is rare before late adulthood but becomes steadily more common with advancing age. The most common cause of dementia is Alzheimer's disease.

- Mild or moderate depression appears to rise in frequency after age 70 or age 75. Serious clinical depression, however, appears not to become more common in old age.

Cognitive Changes

- The elderly experience difficulties in a variety of mental processes, which appear to reflect both the general slowing of the nervous system and perhaps a loss of working-memory capacity.

- Wisdom and creativity may be important aspects of cognitive functioning in old age.

PEARSON
mydevelopmentlab™

Visit **www.mydevelopmentlab.com** to help you get the best grade! Test your knowledge and grasp difficult concepts through

- Custom study plans: See where you are strong and where you go wrong
- Interactive simulations
- Video and audio clips
- Raise your own Virtual Child—and much more!

Review Questions

Answers are provided on MyDevelopmentLab in the Course Resources folder.

Variability in Late Adulthood

17.1 Which characteristic of elderly Canadians is false?
   a.   Women have a higher life expectancy than men.
   b.   Life expectancy decreases as adults get older.
   c.   The oldest old are the fastest-growing segment of the population
   d.   The gender gap in life expectancy has been narrowing since the 1980s.

17.2 The most important determinant of the trajectory of an adult's mental health after age 65 is
   a.   his parents' health.
   b.   his parents' mental health.
   c.   his family life.
   d.   his health.

Physical Changes

17.3 How do sleep patterns change in old age?
   a.   Older adults go to bed later at night.
   b.   Older adults wake earlier in the morning.
   c.   Older adults enter "deep sleep" more easily.
   d.   Older adults wake up less frequently in the middle of the night.

Mental Health

17.4 What is the leading cause of institutionalization of elderly adults in Canada?
   a.   arthritis
   b.   cardiovascular disease
   c.   dementia
   d.   diabetes

Cognitive Changes

17.5 Which of the following is not one of Paul Baltes' criteria of wisdom?
   a.   understanding of relevance of context
   b.   semantic knowledge
   c.   factual knowledge
   d.   procedural knowledge

Critical-Thinking Questions

17.6 In what ways would better health habits lower the incidence of disabilities in older adults?

17.7 Many of the techniques that mental health professionals use require them to empathize with and develop trusting relationships with the people whom they are trying to help. In what ways do the characteristics of Alzheimer's disease and depression interfere with mental health professionals' efforts to do so with those who suffer from them?

CHAPTER
18

Social and Personality Development in Late Adulthood

In an autobiography written when he was in his late 60s, comedian Groucho Marx, who died at age 87, said, "Age is not a particularly interesting subject. Anyone can get old. All you have to do is live long enough" (1987). Marx's observation implies that there is little value in regarding the attainment of old age as the only thing about oneself that is interesting or remarkable. Indeed, an important part of maintaining a sense of self in late adulthood is recognizing whatever it is about one's life that could not have been done by anyone else. But maintaining a sense of personal uniqueness can be especially challenging for older adults, who are often stereotyped by others as sick, disabled, or incompetent.

As you learned in **Chapter 17**, the biological clock ticks far more loudly in late adulthood than it does earlier in life. But the experiences of these years, as in every period of life, extend far beyond the physical domain. Indeed, as you will learn in this chapter, changes in roles and relationships are perhaps just as significant as physical ones. And for many older adults, these changes are not perceived as losses but as opportunities to create new roles and to make old age a time of personal and social gains.

When you finish studying the chapter, you will be able to explain the theories of social and personality development in late adulthood; examine the individual differences that have an impact on successful aging; describe the social relationships of older adults; and discuss the career issues in late life. While you read this chapter, keep the following questions in mind:

- What can you do to prepare for optimum aging?

- How many different explanations can you think of for the fact that older single men are more likely to remarry than women?

- How might retirement or continued work affect the lives of older adults? What is your internal model for retirement age?

Connect to MyDevelopmentLab

Test yourself on your knowledge of lifespan development and match the milestones to each age. If you make the baby cry, then you have not matched to the right age.

✳ Explore

THEORIES OF SOCIAL AND PERSONALITY DEVELOPMENT

If the social and personality changes of young adulthood can be described as "individuation" and those of middle adulthood can be described (more tentatively) as "mellowing," how might the changes of late adulthood be described? Several theorists have hypothesized specific forms of change, but there is little agreement among them and very little information supporting any of their theories.

ERIKSON'S STAGE OF EGO INTEGRITY VERSUS DESPAIR

ego integrity versus despair stage
the last of Erikson's psychosocial stages, in which older adults must achieve a sense of satisfaction with their lives

ego integrity
the feeling that one's life has been worthwhile

Erikson termed the last of his eight life crises the **ego integrity versus despair stage**. He thought that the task of achieving **ego integrity**, the sense that one has lived a useful life, began in middle adulthood but was most central in late adulthood. To achieve ego integrity, the older adult must come to terms with who she is and has been, how her life has been lived, the choices that she made, the opportunities gained and lost. The process also involves coming to terms with death and accepting its imminence. Erikson hypothesized that failure to achieve ego integrity in late adulthood would result in feelings of hopelessness and despair because there would be too little time to make changes before death.

Developmentalists have essentially no longitudinal or even cross-sectional data to suggest whether older adults are more likely than younger or middle-aged adults to achieve such self-acceptance. What they have instead are a few bits of information suggesting that adults become more reflective and somewhat more philosophical in orientation as they move through the late adulthood years (Prager, 1998). Moreover, those who use their growing capacity for philosophical reflection to achieve a degree of self-satisfaction are less fearful of death. There is also some evidence that older adults are more likely than young and middle-aged adults to respond to thwarted personal goals with feelings of sadness—a hint that the kind of despair Erikson talked about may be more common in old age than earlier in life (Levine & Bluck, 1997).

One aspect of Erikson's theory that has received a great deal of attention from researchers is the notion that the process of **reminiscence**, thinking about the past, is a necessary and healthy part of achieving ego integrity, and thus an important aspect of old age and preparation for death. However, few developmentalists today would say that the only, or even the most important, purpose of these processes is to help an individual prepare for death. Instead, research has examined the link between reminiscence and health.

First, it's important to note that adults of all ages engage in reminiscence. In fact, young adults reminisce more often than middle-aged or older adults (Parker, 1999). However, developmentalists hypothesize that young and older adults feel differently about reminiscence because they use it for different purposes (Webster & McCall, 1999). Young adults often use reminiscence to search for tried and true methods of solving problems ("How did I handle this the last time it happened?"). For older adults, reminiscence is more often seen as a way of communicating their experiences to younger individuals.

Among older adults, reminiscence is also the foundation for the process of **life review**, an evaluative process in which seniors make judgments about their past behavior (Butler, 1963, 2002). Consistent with Erikson's view of the ego integrity/despair crisis, life review results in both positive and negative emotional outcomes, and the overall balance of positive and negative emotions that results from the life review process is correlated with seniors' mental health. Researchers have found that seniors whose life reviews produce more regrets over past mistakes and missed opportunities than satisfaction with how they handled problems earlier in life are more prone to depression than those who have generally positive feelings about their lives.

reminiscence
reflecting on past experience

life review
an evaluative process in which elders make judgments about past behaviour

Some older adults are quite content with solitary lives, but disengagement from social contacts is neither a typical nor optimal choice for most elders.
(*Photo:* Frank Siteman/Getty Images)

OTHER THEORIES OF LATE-LIFE PSYCHOSOCIAL FUNCTIONING

As you learned in **Chapter 16**, the ideas of Paul and Margaret Baltes about selection, optimization, and compensation have been important in the study of middle-aged adults' psychosocial functioning. They are often applied to the study of older adults as well. Recall that the Balteses proposed that, as adults get older, they maintain high levels of performance by focusing on their strengths. In this way, they compensate for weaknesses.

Another theoretical perspective on old age focuses on the question of whether it is normal, necessary, or healthy for older adults to remain

activity theory
the idea that it is normal and healthy for older adults to try to remain as active as possible for as long as possible

active as long as possible, or whether the more typical and healthy pattern is some kind of gradual turning inward. The perspective typically referred to as **activity theory** argues that the psychologically and physically healthiest response to old age is to maintain the greatest possible level of activity and involvement in the greatest possible number of roles.

Activity theorists often cite research demonstrating that the most active older adults report slightly greater satisfaction with themselves or their lives, are healthiest, and have the highest morale (Adelmann, 1994; Bryant & Rakowski, 1992; George, 1990; McIntosh & Danigelis, 1995). The effect is not large, but its direction is consistently positive: More social involvement is linked to better outcomes, even among seniors who suffer from disabilities, such as arthritis, for whom active social participation may be physically painful (Zimmer, Hickey, & Searle, 1995). Yet, it is also true that every in-depth study of lifestyles of older adults identifies at least a few who lead socially isolated lives but remain contented, sometimes because they are engaged in an all-consuming hobby (e.g., Maas & Kuypers, 1974; Rubinstein, 1986).

An alternative theory of social and personality development in old age is disengagement theory, first proposed as a formulation of the central psychological process for older adults (Cumming, 1975; Cumming & Henry, 1961). In its current form, **disengagement theory** proposes that aging has three aspects:

disengagement theory
the theory that it is normal and healthy for older adults to scale down their social lives and to separate themselves from others to a certain degree

- *Shrinkage of life space:* As people age, they interact with fewer and fewer people and fill fewer and fewer roles.

- *Increased individuality:* In the roles and relationships that remain, the older individual is much less governed by strict rules or expectations.

- *Acceptance of these changes:* The healthy older adult actively disengages from roles and relationships, turning increasingly inward and away from interactions with others.

The first two of these aspects seem largely beyond dispute. What has been controversial about disengagement theory is the third aspect. Advocates argue that the normal and healthy response to the shrinkage of roles and relationships is for the older adult to step back still further, to stop seeking new roles, spend more time alone, and turn inward. In essence, they propose a kind of personality change, not just a decline in involvement.

Although it is possible to choose a highly disengaged lifestyle in late adulthood and to find satisfaction in it, such disengagement is neither normal for the majority of older adults nor necessary for overall mental health in the later years. For most seniors, some level of social involvement is a sign—and probably a cause—of higher morale and lower levels of depression and other psychiatric symptoms (Zunzunegui, Alvarado, Del Ser, & Otero, 2003).

Critical Thinking

Think about the oldest person you know. How are the themes of ego integrity, reminiscence, life review, activity, disengagement, and continuity manifested in their lives?

The last theory of social and personality development in old age that we will discuss is *continuity theory*. **Continuity theory** argues that the primary means by which seniors adjust to aging is by engaging in the same kinds of activities that interested and challenged them in their earlier years (Atchley, 1989). For instance, an older woman who was an avid gardener during early and middle adulthood, but whose physical condition renders continuation of this hobby impossible, may adjust to her body's decline by limiting her passion for gardening to a small selection of potted plants. Research supports continuity theorists' assertions that aging adults work to maintain consistency of this kind and that achieving such consistency is essential to older adults' maintenance of a positive outlook on the aging process (Agahi, Ahacic, & Parker, 2006; Greenfield & Marks, 2007). Therefore, they argue, providing ways in which seniors can meet these continuity goals should be integral to their care.

continuity theory
the idea that older adults adapt life-long interests and activities to the limitations imposed on them by physical aging

Before Going On

- Does research support the existence of Erikson's stage of ego integrity versus despair?
- What are the main ideas of activity theory and disengagement theory?

INDIVIDUAL DIFFERENCES

Individual differences continue to make substantial contributions to the experiences of older men and women. In fact, research suggests that differences in a variety of behaviours are related to overall quality of life as well as to longevity. Similarly, individual differences in reliance on religious beliefs and institutions as sources of support are also correlated with well-being in late adulthood.

THE SUCCESSFUL AGING PARADIGM

In recent years, one of the dominant themes in gerontology literature has been the concept of **successful aging**. As defined by authors John Rowe and Robert Kahn, successful aging has three components: good physical health, retention of cognitive abilities, and continuing engagement in social and productive activities (Rowe & Kahn, 1997, 1998). An additional aspect of successful aging is an individual's subjective sense of life satisfaction (**Table 18.1** describes these components). The concept of successful aging is referred to as a *paradigm* because it presents patterns for or examples of such aging. Rather than stating a theory of development, the paradigm of successful aging offers a way of thinking about late adulthood and about how earlier decisions and patterns of behaviour contribute to quality of life at later ages.

STAYING HEALTHY AND ABLE   By now, you should be familiar with the factors that predict health and physical functioning across the lifespan: diet, exercise, avoidance of tobacco, and so on. In a sense, older people reap the consequences of the behavioural choices they made when they were younger. Thus, it isn't surprising that making wise choices in this domain during early and middle adulthood, especially with regard to the

 Watch

successful aging
the term gerontologists use to describe maintaining one's physical health, mental abilities, social competence, and overall satisfaction with one's life as one ages

TABLE 18.1	The Components of Successful Aging
Health	Good health must be maintained through middle and late adulthood.
Mental activity	Engaging in cognitively stimulating activities and hobbies helps older adults retain mental abilities.
Social engagement	Remaining socially active is critical; social contacts that involve helping others are especially important.
Productivity	Volunteer activities can help by engaging retired adults in productive pursuits.
Life satisfaction	Older adults must learn how to adjust expectations such that life satisfaction remains high.

factors that influence cardiovascular health, is essential to successful aging later in life (Hughes & Hayman, 2007). However, there are also aspects to staying healthy and able that most of us never face until old age.

When an older adult suffers a stroke or fractures a bone, for example, his willingness to engage in the sometimes painful process of rehabilitation significantly affects his degree of recovery. Researchers have found that older adults vary considerably in their willingness to comply with physicians and therapists who supervise their rehabilitations after such events. An individual's willingness to adopt recovery goals suggested by rehabilitation professionals is related to recovery prospects (Ushikubo, 1998). Those who believe they can reach the suggested goals appear to be the most willing to do the work required for optimal recovery of functioning. Not surprisingly, these individuals gain the most from rehabilitation. So life-long health habits contribute to successful aging, but individuals' responses to the health crises of old age also matter.

RETAINING COGNITIVE ABILITIES The degree to which seniors maintain cognitive functioning seems to be linked to education. As you learned in **Chapter 17,** those who are the best educated show the least cognitive decline. Moreover, researchers who have examined correlations between cognitive functioning and the other two dimensions of successful aging—physical health and social engagement—have found that verbal intelligence and education are related to both (Jorm et al., 1998). Cross-cultural research has found relationships among cognitive functioning, health, and social involvement in Taiwanese and North American seniors, as well as in Mexican Americans and white Americans (Hazuda, Wood, Lichtenstein, & Espino, 1998; Ofstedal, Zimmer, & Lin, 1999).

In addition to education, the complexity of the cognitive challenges older adults are willing to take on also influences their cognitive functioning. For example, older adults are sometimes reluctant to use new technologies, such as automatic teller machines (Echt, Morrell, & Park, 1998). Psychologists suggest that self-stereotyping contributes to this reluctance; older people may believe that they can't learn as well as younger people can, and so they stick to established routines. However, neuropsychologists suggest that such avoidance of learning may actually contribute to cognitive decline (Volz, 2000). New learning, these scientists hypothesize, helps to establish new connections between neurons, connections that may protect the aging brain against deterioration (Calero & Navarro, 2007). Thus, what might be called *cognitive adventurousness*, a willingness to learn new things, appears to be a key component of successful aging.

● Watch   **SOCIAL ENGAGEMENT** Social connectedness and participation in productive activities are clearly important to successful aging. For example, nursing home residents report greater satisfaction with their lives when they have frequent contact with family and friends (Guse & Masesar, 1999). Similarly, among seniors with disabilities, frequency of contact with family and friends is associated with reduced feelings of loneliness (Bondevik & Skogstad, 1998).

Social engagement contributes to successful aging because it provides opportunities for older adults to give support as well as to receive it. For example, researchers studying Japanese seniors found that a majority of them say that helping others contributes to their own health and personal sense of well-being (Krause, Ingersoll-Dayton, Liang, & Sugisawa, 1999). In addition, researchers who have asked nursing home residents to rate various quality-of-life factors have found that they often give high ratings to "opportunities to help others" (Guse & Masesar, 1999). Thus, even when elderly adults have significant disabilities, many are still oriented toward helping others and feel more satisfied with their lives when they can do so.

PRODUCTIVITY Contributing to a social network may be one important way of remaining productive, especially for older adults who are retired. **Volunteerism,** performing unpaid work for altruistic reasons, has been linked to successful aging. Neena Chappell, past director of the University of Victoria Centre on Aging, conducted an extensive review of the literature on volunteerism in North America and concluded that people who volunteer, especially with helping others, are happier and healthier in their elder years. The social interaction aspect in particular has a beneficial impact on both quality of life and mortality. This finding may not be surprising, since the elderly indicate that their relationships with others are what they value the most in life (Chappell, 1999).

For some elders, remaining productive means venturing into new hobbies, such as painting, sculpting, or other artistic pursuits.
(*Photo:* © Stock Connection Blue/Alamy)

Results from the 2000 National Survey of Giving, Volunteering and Participating show that the percentage of Canadians volunteering has declined in all age groups, including the elderly. However, those aged 65 to 74 clocked the highest number of annual volunteer hours of any age group (272 hours) and those 75 and older came in a close second (265 hours) (Canadian Centre for Philanthropy, 2003). So it seems the volunteer activities of older adults have the potential to benefit society as well as enhance the volunteers' own physical and mental health (Warburton, Le Brocque, & Rosenman, 1998). As you can see from Figure 18.1, older adults in Canada are involved in their communities through a wide range of activities.

volunteerism
performance of unpaid work for altruistic motives

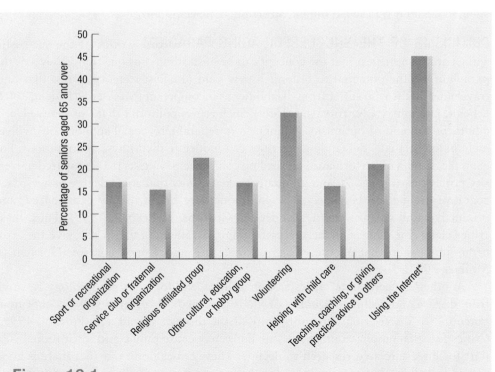

Figure 18.1

This graph shows the participation in social and leisure organizations and activities by Canadians age 65 and older.
*age 65 to 74

(*Source:* Adapted from Turcotte & Schellenberg, 2007, Tables 4.3.2, 4.4.1, and 4.4.2; and Veenhof & Timusk, 2009, Chart 1.)

Some older adults remain productive by venturing into new pursuits, such as taking music lessons, attending college classes, or learning to paint or sculpt. Researchers conducting a study of 36 artists over age 60 asked them to explain how artistic productivity contributed to their successful aging (Fisher & Specht, 1999). Their responses contained several themes: Producing art gave them a purpose in life, opportunities to interact with like-minded peers, and a sense of competence. The older artists also claimed that creating art helped them stay healthy. Thus, creative productivity may help older adults maintain an optimistic outlook, which, as you have learned, contributes to physical and mental health (Flood, 2007).

LIFE SATISFACTION *Life satisfaction*, or a sense of personal well-being, is also an important component of successful aging. What is critical to life satisfaction in almost all cases is an individual's perception of her own situation, which seems to be more important than objective measures (Gana, Alphilippe, & Bailly, 2004). Perceived adequacy of social support and perceived adequacy of income are critical. Moreover, self-ratings of health, rather than objective measures of health, may be the most significant predictors of life satisfaction and morale (Draper, Gething, Fethney, & Winfield, 1999).

Research also suggests that social comparisons—how well an older adult thinks he is doing compared with others his age—are just as important to these perceptions as the older adult's awareness of the changes he has undergone since his younger years (Robinson-Whelen & Kiecolt-Glaser, 1997). A majority of older adults, no matter what their personal circumstances, believe that most others their age are worse off than they are (Heckhausen & Brim, 1997). Developmentalists speculate that the tendency to see others as having more problems is an important self-protective psychological device employed by those who are aging successfully (Frieswijk, Buunk, Steverink, & Slaets, 2004).

CRITICISMS OF THE SUCCESSFUL AGING PARADIGM Critics of the successful aging paradigm suggest that the concept can be misleading. For one thing, they say, the paradigm has the potential to become a new kind of ageist stereotype, one that portrays older adults who suffer from disabilities as incompetent (Minkler & Fadem, 2002; Scheidt, Humpherys, & Yorgason, 1999). Such critics point out that, for many elderly adults, no amount of optimism, willingness to rehabilitate, social support, or involvement in intellectually demanding activities can moderate their physical limitations. For example, studies of performance on reading comprehension tests that compared university professors over age 70 and graduate students show that some degree of age-based cognitive decline can be expected, even among very bright, highly experienced, and productive adults (Christensen, Henderson, Griffiths, & Levings, 1997). Thus, these critics claim, the danger of the successful aging paradigm is that it can give the erroneous impression that all the effects of aging are under one's control (Holstein & Minkler, 2003).

Another danger, some critics say, in shifting the focus of gerontology research from disease and decline to quality of life is that medical research still has enormous potential for discovering cures for many of the diseases of old age (Portnoi, 1999). Critics fear that emphasis on successful aging may cause public and institutional support for disease-related research to decline. These critics point out that there is good reason to believe that many conditions that are now thought to be part of "normal" aging are actually disease processes for which medical science can find effective treatments (Portnoi, 1999).

Nevertheless, critics concede that the successful aging paradigm has broadened gerontologists' approaches to studying old age. Thus, they agree that its influence has been largely positive. Still, keeping their criticisms in mind can help balance the

PEARSON
mydevelopmentlab

Connect to MyDevelopmentLab

Want to age well? George Vaillant offers some key insights from a seven-decade longitudinal study of aging.

👁 Watch

optimism of the successful aging paradigm against the realities of life in late adulthood and the need to continue to encourage researchers to search for treatments for age-related diseases, such as Alzheimer's.

RELIGIOUS COPING

Religion appears to be one factor contributing to individual differences in life satisfaction. Psychologists use the term **religious coping** to refer to the tendency to turn to religious beliefs and institutions in times of stress or trouble. People of all ages use religious coping. However, many developmentalists suggest that religious coping may be particularly important in the later years because of the high number of life stressors, including deaths of loved ones, chronic illnesses, and declining sensory abilities. And seniors themselves often cite religious coping as their primary means of managing stress (Barusch, 1999).

SEX DIFFERENCES Canadian data suggest that women make more use of religious coping than men do (Bibby, 2001; Lindsay, 2008). Most developmentalists attribute this finding to sex differences in social behaviour that are observed across the lifespan. However, it's important to keep in mind that, even though the frequency with which religious coping is used may differ according to ethnicity and gender, its effects seem to be similar in all racial and ethnic groups and for both women and men. These effects are best examined by separating the psychological and social components of religious coping.

RELIGIOUS BELIEFS The psychological component of religious coping involves people's beliefs and attitudes. A number of investigators have examined links between religious beliefs and various measures of well-being among the elderly. For example, seniors who place a great deal of emphasis on religious faith worry much less than those who do not (Tapanya et al., 1997). Moreover, associations between religious faith and physical and mental health have been found among older adults of diverse faiths—Christians, Buddhists, Muslims, Hindus, Taoists, and Sikhs—and from a variety of cultures and ethnic groups (Krause et al., 1999; Meisenhelder & Chandler, 2000; Tapanya et al., 1997; Zhou, Yao, & Xu, 2002). Thus, the positive effects of religious faith may have more to do with a general attitude of *spirituality*, a tendency to focus on the aspects of life that transcend one's physical existence, than on any particular set of doctrines or teachings.

The positive effects of religious coping seem to arise from its influence on how seniors think about their lives. For example, older adults who rate their religious beliefs as highly important to them are more likely than others to think that their lives serve an important purpose (Gerwood, LeBlanc, & Piazza, 1998). In addition, religious faith seems to provide older adults with a theme that integrates the various periods of their lives (Ko, Mehta, & Meng, 2006; Mehta, 1997). As a result, religious seniors are more likely than their nonreligious peers to view old age as a chapter in an ongoing story rather than as primarily a period of loss of capacities. Further, among low-income seniors, divine power is viewed as a resource on which those who have little social power in the material world can rely (Barusch, 1999).

ATTENDANCE AT RELIGIOUS SERVICES The social aspect of religious coping most often examined by researchers is attendance at religious services. Across all ages, adult women attend religious services more regularly

Watch

religious coping
the tendency to turn to religious beliefs and institutions for support in times of difficulty

Strong religious beliefs appear to be positively associated with elders' health and well-being.
(*Photo:* Michael Newman/PhotoEdit)

than men (Clark & Schellenberg, 2006; Statistics Canada, 2010d). Regular religious service attendance dips during early adulthood but rises steadily once Canadians reach their mid-adult years. It is highest for seniors, with roughly four in ten attending at least once a week (Lindsay, 2008). Research suggests that Canadian adults who regularly attend such services are more optimistic, are physically healthier, are longer living, are very satisfied with their lives, and have less stressful lives than their nonattending peers (Clark, 1998). These findings correspond with research on religious people that emphasizes the positive connection between a sense of belonging and a sense of well-being. As well, there appears to be a causal connection wherein feelings of belonging improve a person's level of health. Religious seniors who regularly attend religious services live healthier lives, and this is associated with a strong sense of connectedness to their community and a better personal support network (Clark, 2000). Interestingly, longitudinal studies suggest that patterns of attendance change little even if seniors become ill or disabled (Idler & Kasl, 1997).

Longitudinal studies also suggest that the mortality rate is lower among religious participants. In one study, researchers examined the association between religious attendance and mortality in nearly 2000 older adults over a 5-year period (Oman & Reed, 1998). Researchers compared participants who were associated with other kinds of organizations to those who were involved with religious institutions. They found that the mortality rate during the 5-year period was lower among the religious older adults, even when the amount of organizational involvement and the size of the organizational social networks were the same as for the nonreligious older adults (Oman & Reed, 1998).

Seniors themselves cite a number of reasons for the benefits of religious involvement. For example, many say that religious institutions provide them with opportunities to help others (la Cour, Avlund, & Schultz-Larsen, 2006; Krause et al., 1999). Intergenerational involvement is another aspect of religious participation often mentioned by older adults. For many, religious institutions provide a structure within which they can pass on their knowledge and beliefs to younger individuals (Mehta, 1997).

Critical Thinking

Can you think of any other benefits to the elderly of participating in religious services? What are the benefits to younger members of the religious group?

ALTERNATIVE EXPLANATIONS Researchers must always consider selection effects when examining links between variables such as religious coping and health. There are other possible confounding factors as well. For example, religious and nonreligious seniors may differ in personality traits. It seems likely that those with higher levels of extraversion would be the most comfortable in religious social environments—and scientists know that extraversion is correlated with successful aging. Thus, the connection between religious coping and health in old age may be a manifestation of personality rather than an independent effect of religion.

In addition, research on the association between religious faith and health focuses on the personal relevance of spirituality rather than on intellectual acceptance of a set of doctrines. So it may be the intensity and the personal nature of these beliefs, rather than the fact that they have a religious focus, that are responsible for the correlations. In addition, in most research studies, the participants have had long-standing belief and attendance patterns. Thus, these seniors may persist in religious faith and involvement, even when they are ill or disabled, because it helps them achieve a sense of continuity of identity. That is, religious involvement may allow an older adult to feel that, despite physical losses, she is still the same person. So it may be that the sense of personal integration that religion provides is responsible for the correlations. Whatever the reasons, the research evidence suggests that supporting the spiritual needs of the elderly may be just as important to maintaining their health and functioning as meeting their physical and material needs.

Before Going On

- Describe the successful aging paradigm, noting the ways in which it is manifested in the lives of older adults.

- How does religious coping influence physical and mental health in late adulthood?

SOCIAL RELATIONSHIPS

The social roles older adults occupy are usually different from those they held at younger ages. Nevertheless, most elderly adults cite meaningful social roles as essential to life satisfaction (Bowling et al., 2003). Moreover, there is no doubt that social relationships contribute to older adults' sense of well-being. Both consistency and change characterize social relationships during this period.

SOCIAL ROLES

Clearly, role changes are inevitable in old age, and physical and cognitive changes are responsible for many of them. Some, however, are the result of ageism. Appearance cues—wrinkles and grey hair and the like—are often the basis for judgments about the competence of older people (Hummert, Garstka, & Shaner, 1997). The older people look, the more negatively others stereotype them, and negative stereotypes are more often applied to older women than to older men. Consequently, older adults may be unjustly forced out of roles by younger adults.

In a practical sense, the decline in role content means that the daily routines of many older adults are no longer structured by specific roles. But is this good or bad? Some developmentalists see this loss of role definition as carrying with it a significant risk of isolation or alienation. Further, in one survey, a majority of British seniors cited meaningful social roles as essential to life satisfaction (Bowling et al., 2003). Others see distinct advantages to this "roleless" time in late life. One such advantage is a greater "license for eccentricity" (Bond & Coleman, 1990, p. 78). Because they do not have to fit into the sometimes tight confines of role expectations, older adults feel far freer to express their own individuality—in dress, language, and personal preferences. This change may begin even earlier than late adulthood; the gradual assertion of individuality seems to be characteristic of middle adulthood for many. But certainly older adults benefit from a kind of institutionalized acceptance of eccentricity.

LIVING ARRANGEMENTS

Only about 9% of women and 5% of men over age 65 reside in long-term care institutions, although the percentage increases substantially in seniors who are aged 85 and older (Cranswick, 2003). Most of the seniors who are not institutionalized live alone. The most common living arrangement for middle-aged adults is living with a spouse or partner, but this arrangement becomes much less common in late adulthood.

Figure 18.2 shows the marital status of seniors in Canada. Because men typically marry younger women and because women live longer than men, a man can normally expect to have a spouse or intimate partner until he dies. The normal expectation for a woman is that she will eventually be without such a partner, often for many years. Clearly, gender differences seen in **Figure 18.2** support these expectations, and it is

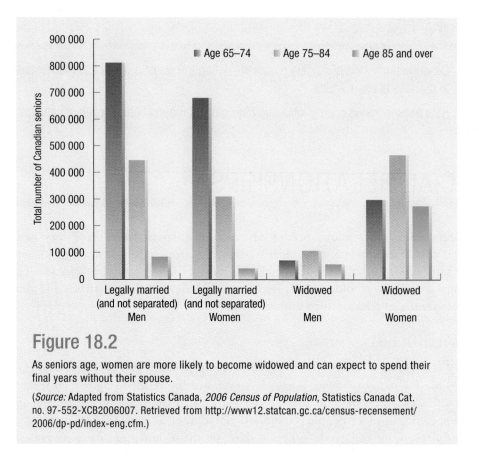

Figure 18.2

As seniors age, women are more likely to become widowed and can expect to spend their final years without their spouse.

(*Source:* Adapted from Statistics Canada, *2006 Census of Population*, Statistics Canada Cat. no. 97-552-XCB2006007. Retrieved from http://www12.statcan.gc.ca/census-recensement/ 2006/dp-pd/index-eng.cfm.)

hard to exaggerate the importance of that difference for the experience of late adulthood for men and women.

The difference is also clearly reflected in **Figure 18.3,** which shows the living arrangements of seniors in Canada. As you can see, older women are more likely to live alone than older men. This pattern is typical in other industrialized countries as well.

Several factors affect the probability that an unattached older adult will live with a child or with other relatives:

- *Health.* Older adults with higher levels of functional health are less likely to move in with family or into institutional living arrangements (Sarma, Hawley, & Basu, 2009). Seniors who need help with activities of daily living (ADLs) are more likely to live in the homes of family members than are those who can manage the physical demands of living independently (Choi, 2003). However, as self-reported health status declines, the probability of institutionalization increases (Sarma et al., 2009).

- *Income.* Older adults with higher household incomes are more likely to live with family members (Sarma et al., 2009).

- *Adult children's characteristics.* Older adults with several daughters are more likely than those with few daughters to live with grown children (Soldo, Wolf, & Agree, 1990). Married adults are more likely than those who are single to take in their aging parents (Choi, 2003).

- *Public home care and social support services.* Older adults who receive home care services are less likely to become institutionalized, and older adults with social support services are less likely to have either family or institutional living arrangements (Sarma et al., 2009).

What do these statistics suggest about the roles and relationships of older adults? First and foremost, of course, they point to a sharp divergence of experience for men and women in the later years. They also indicate that developmentalists need to look beyond the spousal or partnership relationship if they are to understand the patterns of social interactions that are central to the aging individual.

The greatest proportion of their social activities involve contacts with family and friends (Turcotte & Schellenberg, 2007). For widowed or unmarried seniors, relationships with adult children and other family members may become more central in late adulthood than they were in earlier years. But an older adult who is no longer able to live alone may be reluctant to live with an adult child with whom she has long-standing disagreements or whom she does not trust (see the **Research Report**).

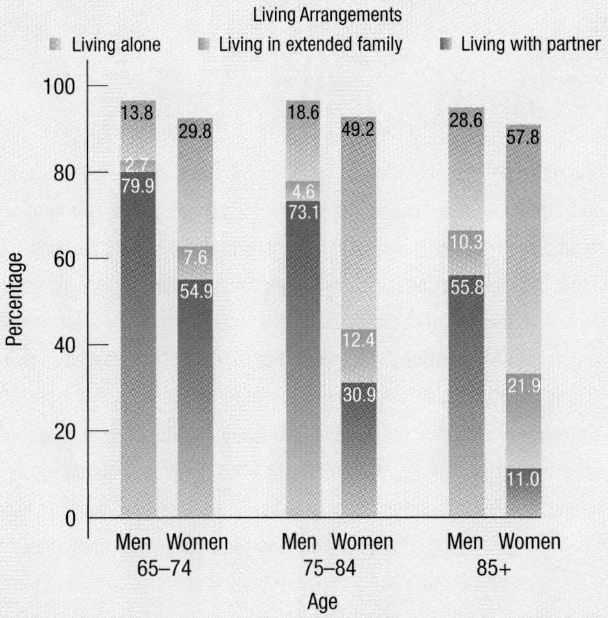

PARTNERSHIPS

Cross-sectional comparisons show that marital satisfaction is higher in the late adult years than when children are still at home. But this high marital satisfaction may have a somewhat different basis than that of the early years of marriage. In late adulthood, marriages tend to be based less on passion and mutual disclosure and more on loyalty, familiarity, and mutual investment in the relationship (Bengtson, Rosenthal, & Burton, 1990; Fouquereau & Baudoin, 2002). In Sternberg's terms (look back at **Figure 14.3,** page 403), late adult marriages are more likely to reflect companionate love than romantic or even consummate love.

Figure 18.3

This graph shows the living arrangements of Canadian seniors. You can see that for those seniors who were not living with a spouse, living alone was the most common alternative, followed by living with extended families.

(*Sources:* Adapted from Health Canada, 2000e, figures from Statistical Snapshots: Most Live at Home, No. 6; Living with Extended Families, No. 7; and Most Living at Home, No. 8. Reproduced with permission of the Minister of Public Works and Government Services Canada, 2005.)

Of course, this does not mean that the marriages of older adults are necessarily devitalized or neutral. That may well be true of some marriages, but there is evidence to the contrary for many. You'll recall from **Chapter 17** that the majority of older adult couples are still sexually active and may be somewhat more sexually adventurous than younger adults. Collectively, older couples also report higher levels of pleasure and lower levels of conflict in their relationships than do middle-aged couples. When older couples do have conflicts, they resolve them in more affectionate and less negative ways (Carstensen, Gottman, & Levenson, 1995; Levenson, Carstensen, & Gottman, 1993). Older couples also spend more time with each other than with family or friends, and although much of this time is spent in passive or basic maintenance activities—watching TV, doing housework, running errands—it is also true that those married seniors who spend more time with their spouses report high levels of happiness (Larson, Mannell, & Zuzanek, 1986).

Further evidence of the deep bond that continues to exist in late-life marriages is the remarkable degree of care and assistance older spouses give each other when one or the other is disabled. For married seniors with some kind of disability, by far the largest source of assistance is the spouse, not children or friends. Many husbands and wives continue to care for spouses who are ill or who suffer from dementia for very long periods of time. And even when both spouses suffer from significant disabilities, they nonetheless continue to care for each other "until death do us part." Marriages may thus be less romantic or less emotionally intense in late adulthood than they were in earlier years, but they are typically satisfying and highly committed.

Research Report

ELDER ABUSE IN CANADA

One extreme manifestation of conflict and strain between older adults and someone in a relationship of trust (such as a family member, a friend, a service provider, or health care providers in institutional settings) is the abuse (physical, psychological, or financial) and neglect of seniors (Government of Canada, 2009). In recent years, the maltreatment of seniors has occasionally received a great deal of media coverage, but it is a largely hidden and growing problem in Canada and worldwide (Dauvergne, 2003; World Health Organization, 2002). Canadian surveys have indicated that 7% of seniors reported emotional abuse, such as yelling, insulting, threatening, or ignoring. In addition, 1% reported financial exploitation and 1% reported being physically or sexually violated. Male abusers are more likely to commit physical abuse, whereas female abusers are more likely to fail to provide needed aid (neglect) (Swanson, 1999). Just less than two-thirds of all the reported instances of senior abuse involve a non-family member, and 6% involve an unknown person (Dauvergne, 2003). The remaining 28% of abuse cases entail family violence and, of these cases, 43% of elderly men reported abuse by their adult children, and elderly women reported being victimized as often by their adult children (37%) as by their spouse (36%).

Researchers have identified several risk factors for elder abuse, including mental illness or alcoholism in the abuser, financial dependency of the abuser on the victim, social isolation, and external stresses (Pillemer & Suitor, 1990, 1992; Swanson, 1999). A likely victim of abuse is an elderly widow sharing her household with a dependent son who has a mental disorder or a drug or alcohol problem; the mother is typically too dependent on her son to kick him out and too ashamed of the abuse to tell others about it (Bengtson et al., 1996). Abuse is also more likely when the senior with dementia is physically violent and when a husband has physically abused his wife throughout their adult lives and simply continues to do so in old age.

The existence of such destructive forms of interaction is a clear reminder that older adults' relationships with their kin are not all sweetness and light. But it is also important to remember that these highly negative patterns are the exception rather than the rule. For most seniors, relationships with children and other kin may be a mixture of positive and negative, but the scale most often tips toward the positive.

Researchers have found similar characteristics and effects in long-term gay and lesbian relationships (Grossman, Daugelli, & Hershberger, 2000). Like heterosexuals, an elderly homosexual who has a long-term partner typically identifies the partner as his most important source of emotional support. In addition, those who live with a partner report less loneliness and better physical and mental health.

The loss of the marriage or partnership relationship through the death of the spouse or partner alters this pattern for so many older adults. The gender difference in marital status among seniors illustrated in **Figure 18.1** is further increased by a higher rate of remarriage for men than for women, a pattern found among both the widowed and the divorced at every age. In Canada, 15% of unattached men over 65 remarry, compared with only 6% of women (Norris, 1994). Older unmarried men are also more likely to date and more likely to live with someone (Bulcroft & Bulcroft, 1991). By contrast, research suggests that widows have little interest in dating or remarriage (Talbott, 1998). Despite older women's reluctance to remarry, studies of the emotional impact of remarriage in late adulthood suggest that both men and women benefit emotionally (Curran, McLanahan, & Knab, 2003; Winter, Lawton, Casten, & Sando, 2000). When researchers examine self-ratings of life satisfaction, elderly newlyweds rate their personal happiness more highly than do either long-married or unattached peers.

Married older adults, like married adults of any age, have certain distinct advantages: They have higher life satisfaction, better health, and lower rates of institutionalization (Iwashyna & Christakis, 2003). Such differential advantages are generally greater for married older men than for married older women (again, this is also true among younger adults). This difference might be interpreted as indicating that marriage affords more benefits to men than to women or that men rely more on their marriage relationship for social support and are thus more affected by its loss. Whatever the explanation, it seems clear that, for older women, marital status is less strongly connected to health or life satisfaction, but still strongly connected to financial security.

The protective nature of marriage for older adults is supported by research showing that single adults over age 65 have higher mortality rates, even when factors such as poverty are controlled (Manzoli, Villari, Pironec, & Boccia, 2007). Moreover, these rates are consistent across gender and culture. Interestingly, though, seniors whose single status is the result of divorce have higher mortality rates than either those who have been widowed or peers who have never married. In addition, divorced older adults have higher rates of alcohol abuse, depression, and suicide (Hahn et al., 2004; Lorant et al., 2005; Onen et al., 2005). This rate may be higher because divorced seniors, especially men, are more likely to be disconnected from their families than their never-married or widowed peers are (Tomassini et al., 2004). However, participation in religious activities and other forms of social engagement appear to moderate the associations among single status, substance abuse, depression, poor health, and mortality risk (Hahn et al., 2004). Thus, the key advantage of intimate partnerships for older adults is that they provide them with readily available sources of support. For single seniors, more effort is required to identify and connect with sources of support, and physical disabilities are more likely to interfere with maintaining them than is the case for partnered seniors who share the same household.

Affection between married partners and pleasure in each other's company clearly do not disappear in old age. (*Photo:* © Paul Barton/CORBIS)

FAMILY RELATIONSHIPS

Folklore and descriptions of late adulthood in the popular press suggest that family, particularly children and grandchildren, form the core of the social life of older adults, perhaps especially those who are widowed. Older adults do describe intergenerational bonds as strong and important; most report a significant sense of family solidarity and support (Bengston et al., 1996). These bonds are reflected, among other things, in regular contact between seniors and family members. Moreover, researchers have found

Most elders enjoy maintaining relationships with younger family members. However, research suggests that such connections are not essential to life satisfaction in old age. (*Photo:* PhotoEdit)

that family relationships become more harmonious as adults get older (Akiyama, Antonucci, Takahashi, & Langfahl, 2003). Thus, they represent an important component of most seniors' overall life satisfaction.

CONTACTS WITH ADULT CHILDREN Canadian studies show that between two-thirds and three-quarters of older parents said their children see them at least once a week (Connidis, 1989; Rosenthal, 1987). The distance between where a senior parent and adult child live has an effect on the frequency of visitation. University of Alberta sociologist Susan McDaniel (1994) reported that of those Canadians who lived within 10 kilometres of one

of their parents, 80% visited daily or at least once a week. Of those who lived between 11 and 50 kilometres away, 52% visited daily or weekly, but the rate of regular visitations dropped to 23% when the parent and child lived 51 to 100 kilometres apart. For those children who do not visit frequently, close family ties are maintained with telephone calls, letters, and email. In addition, it is important to emphasize that the frequency of contact is not the only measure of the closeness of family relationships.

Perhaps more important than the frequency of visitation is the satisfaction seniors experience with family contacts. Havens and Finlayson (1999) reported that seniors do not need to have frequent contact with family members to feel close to them. Regardless of frequency of visitation, 88% of seniors report that they feel close to family members. Moreover, about three-quarters of seniors aged 65 and above are very satisfied with the level of family contact, while fewer than 4% are less than satisfied with the level of contact with family members.

Part of the regular contact between the elderly and their adult children, of course, involves giving aid to or receiving it from the elder person—a pattern you learned

Elderly newlyweds report higher levels of personal happiness than either long-married or single peers.
(*Photo:* David Young-Wolff/PhotoEdit)

about in **Chapter 16.** Havens and Finlayson (1999) found that aging parents in Canada are most likely to need support with activities that involve physical activity (e.g., lifting, bending). Young seniors are most likely to need help with housework, emotional support, grocery shopping, yardwork, and transportation. The oldest old need assistance with, in priority order, transportation, housework, groceries, meals, and yardwork. When older adults need help that cannot be provided by a spouse, the help is most often provided by other family members, principally children. With advancing age, a spouse is less likely to be able to assist, and the rate of spousal help drops from a high of 57% in the young old down to about 23% in the oldest old. Conversely, as parents age, children provide an increasingly larger portion of the care. For parents aged 65 to 74, 29% of sons and more than 35% of daughters provide assistance. The rates of help for parents aged 85 and over increases by about 5% for sons and 7% for daughters.

EFFECTS OF RELATIONSHIPS WITH ADULT CHILDREN Some studies indicate that when relationships between elders and adult children are warm and close, they are more important to elders' sense of well-being than any other kind of social relationship (Pinquart & Soerensen, 2000). By contrast, other researchers have found that seniors who see their children more often or report more positive interactions with their children do not describe themselves as happier or healthier overall than do those who have less frequent or less positive relationships with their children (e.g., Mullins & Mushel, 1992). Moreover, such results have been obtained in very different cultural settings, for example, in India and among Mexican Americans (Lawrence, Bennett, & Markides, 1992; Venkatraman, 1995). In all these studies, the older adults reported regular contact with their children and said that they enjoyed it, but these relationships did not seem to enhance happiness or health. Moreover, research has shown that childless seniors are just as happy and well adjusted as those who have children (Connidis & McMullin, 1993). Many developmentalists have concluded that good relationships and regular contact with adult children can add to an elderly adult's quality of life but are not necessary for it.

One possible explanation for this inconsistency in findings is that the relationship with one's children is still governed by role prescriptions, even in old age. It may be friendly, but it is not chosen in the same way that a relationship with a friend is. With your friend, you feel free to be yourself and feel accepted as who you are. With your children, you may feel the need to live up to their demands and expectations.

GRANDCHILDREN AND SIBLINGS As you learned in **Chapter 16**, interactions between grandchildren and middle-aged grandparents are beneficial to both. However, in late adulthood, contact between grandchildren and grandparents declines as the grandchildren become adults themselves (Barer, 2001; Silverstein & Long, 1998). Thus, grandchildren are rarely part of an elderly adult's close family network.

Interestingly, though, it appears that relationships with siblings may become more important in late adulthood, especially after both parents have died (Taylor et al., 2006). Siblings seldom provide much practical assistance to each other in old age, but they can and often do serve two other important functions. First, siblings can provide a unique kind of emotional support for each other, based on shared reminiscences and companionship. Once parents are gone, no one else knows all the old stories, all the family jokes, the names and history of former friends and neighbours. Second, many seniors see their siblings as a kind of "insurance policy" in old age, a source of support of last resort (Connidis, 1994).

FRIENDSHIPS

Mounting evidence suggests that contact with friends has a significant impact on overall life satisfaction, self-esteem, and the amount of loneliness reported by older adults (Antonucci, Lansford, & Akiyama, 2001; Antonucci, 1990; Hartup & Stevens, 1999). Moreover, for those seniors whose families are unavailable, friendships seem to provide an equally effective support network (Takahashi, Tamura, & Tokoro, 1997). The importance of friendships is particularly true of unmarried seniors but is at least somewhat true for married ones as well.

Friends meet different kinds of needs for older adults than do family members. For one thing, relationships with friends are likely to be more reciprocal or equitable, and developmentalists know that equitable relationships are more valued and less stressful. Friends provide companionship, opportunities for laughter, and shared activities. In one Canadian study, for example, friends were second only to spouses as sources of companionship among those over age 65 (Connidis & Davies, 1992). Friends may also provide assistance with daily tasks, such as shopping or housework, although they typically provide less help of this kind than do family members.

GENDER DIFFERENCES IN SOCIAL NETWORKS

As at earlier ages, women and men in late adulthood appear to form different kinds of social networks, with men's friendships involving less disclosure and less intimacy than women's. In addition, older women's networks tend to be larger and closer than those of older men. Developmentalists attribute these

Critical Thinking

Why do you think most older adults' friends are long-standing ones? What social or psychological barriers might there be to creating new friendships in old age?

Friends seem to play an important role in late adulthood, perhaps because they share the same background and memories—like favourite old tunes and dances. (*Photo:* Michael L. Abramson/Woodfin Camp and Associates)

findings to a continuation of a pattern evident across most of the lifespan (Taylor et al., 2006). Thus, if you think back on what you learned about sex differences in the chapters on childhood, adolescence, early adulthood, and middle adulthood, sex differences in late adulthood social networks should not be surprising.

It would be a mistake to assume, however, that because men have smaller social networks, their relationships are unimportant to them. Some developmentalists suggest that research on social networks may be biased in such a way that women will always be found to have stronger networks. This bias, critics say, originates from the fact that research emphasizes shared activities and frequency of contact more than the quality of the relationships. Indeed, when quality of relationships is considered, research shows that men's social networks are just as important to them and provide them with the same kinds of emotional support as women's networks do, even though men's networks tend to be smaller (Riggs, 1997).

Before Going On

- How do social roles change in late adulthood?
- What is the impact associated with changes in living arrangements, intimate partnerships, family relationships, and friendships experienced in older adulthood?

CAREER ISSUES IN LATE LIFE

A remarkable capacity for adaptation marks the transition from work to retirement.

TIMING OF RETIREMENT

Until a few years ago the normal retirement age was 65 in Canada. With few exceptions (e.g., those in physically demanding jobs, such as firefighting and police work), mandatory retirement has been eliminated across the country (CBC News, 2009). Ironically, survey results of employed Canadians under age 40 found that only 18% were willing to postpone their retirement (Langlois, 2004); this trend was echoed by those nearing retirement age (aged 45 to 59) (Schellenberg & Ostrovsky, 2008). Furthermore, the average age of retirement has been dropping in most industrialized countries; in Canada, the average age of retirement went from age 64.9 in 1982 to a low of 61.0 in 2000 (Statistics Canada, 2001k). Now, however, it seems the trend is reversing and the age of retirement is creeping back up. It rose to 62 years of age in 2007 (Schellenberg & Ostrovsky, 2008). Still, roughly three-quarters of those nearing retirement age expect to retire on or before age 65 (22% before age 60, 25% between 60 and 64, and 25% at age 65).

REASONS FOR RETIREMENT

Research suggests that financial incentives are only one reason for retiring. Studies point to a collection of "pushes" and "pulls" that combine to influence each person's decision to retire (Kohli, 1994; Quadagno & Hardy, 1996).

AGE Age itself is obviously an important ingredient in the retirement equation. Internal models play an important role here. If a person's "expected life history" includes retirement at age 55 or 65, he will be strongly inclined to retire at that age, regardless of other factors.

HEALTH Poor health provides a particularly strong push toward early retirement (Schulz, 1995). Poor health lowers the average age of retirement by 1 to 3 years and is commonly found in industrialized countries (Hayward, Friedman, & Chen, 1996; McDonald & Wanner, 1990; Sammartino, 1987; Stanford, Happersett, Morton, Molgaard, & Peddecord, 1991). However, among those who retire at age 65 or later, health is a less powerful factor, presumably because most of these later retirees are in good health.

FAMILY CONSIDERATIONS Family composition is important in the decision to retire. Those who are still supporting minor children retire later than do those in the postparental stage. Thus, men and women who bear their children very late, those who acquire a second and younger family in a second marriage, and those rearing grand-children are likely to continue to work until these children have left home.

FINANCIAL SUPPORT Equally important in the timing of retirement is the availability of adequate financial support for retirement (Schellenberg & Ostrovsky, 2008). Those who anticipate receiving pension support in addition to Canadian Pension Plan (CPP) or Québec Pension Plan (QPP) benefits, or who have personal savings to draw on, retire earlier than do those who have no such financial backup.

Anticipated pension and health frequently work in opposite directions, because many working-class men and women who have worked in unskilled jobs can expect lit-tle supplementary retirement income and are in poor health. In general, working-class adults retire earlier than do middle-class and upper-class adults, often as a result of ill health and social norms, but many poor and working-class adults continue to work well past the normal retirement age to supplement their incomes.

On the other end of the social class scale, health and the adequacy of pensions work against each other in the opposite way. Adults in higher socioeconomic groups generally have both better health and better pensions; they also tend to have more interesting jobs. The three factors combine to produce somewhat later retirement for this group.

WORK CHARACTERISTICS Median retirement ages across industry categories are different. For example, more non-unionized or self-employed people expect to work beyond age 65 than those who aren't (Schellenberg & Ostrovsky, 2008). People who are highly committed to work they enjoy, including many self-employed adults, retire later—often quite a lot later—than do those who are less gratified by their work. People in challenging and interesting jobs are likely to postpone retirement until they are pushed by ill health or attracted by some extra financial inducement. For them, availability of a pension is less of an influence (Hayward & Hardy, 1985).

The ranks of Canadian seniors who were employed has been on the rise since 1996, and the average age of these generally better educated workers has also increased (Duchesne, 2004). In 2002, 8.4% of seniors were employed. Of these working seniors, the majority were involved with farming and, to a lesser extent, jobs in the retail trade. The largest number of senior professionals included accountants, general practitioners, and religious ministers.

SEX DIFFERENCES In Canada, the median age at which women retire is about 2 years younger than the age at which men retire (Statistics Canada, 2004e). Just when women will retire cannot be predicted by retirement benefits, health, or job character-istics. One factor that tends to keep women in the labour force is the lure of higher earnings that will augment future CPP/QPP benefits—a factor that may be especially important for women who took several years off from full-time work to raise children. However, financial experts point out that even if retirement-aged women have as many years of full-time employment as men do, they are still likely to receive less money from pensions because, on average, their earnings are lower (Powell, 2006).

By contrast, the factors that lead to positive views of retirement are very similar for men and women. For example, one study found that health was the most important predictor of quality of life in retirement for both sexes (Quick & Moen, 1998). However, extensive preretirement planning seemed to be more important for men. Moreover, almost all the study's male participants had worked continuously until retirement. Among the retired women, though, some had worked continuously, but others had spent a significant number of years in the home or in part-time employment. The researchers found that those who had worked continuously expressed more satisfaction with the quality of their retirement.

EFFECTS OF RETIREMENT

A number of shifts, both positive and negative, take place at retirement. But, overall, retirement seems to have positive effects on the lives of older adults.

INCOME One potentially significant change that occurs at retirement is related to the availability of alternative sources of income. Human Resources Development Canada (HRDC) (2001c) suggests that retired adults have several potential sources of income: government pensions, such as Old Age Security (OAS) and CPP/QPP; other pensions, such as those offered through an employer; income from savings, such as registered retirement savings plans (RRSPs), or other assets; and earnings from continued work. For most elderly in Canada, nongovernment sources now provide the largest portion of retirement income (Health Canada, 2003e), which means that young workers need to plan well ahead to ensure that they will have enough retirement income to meet their retirement lifestyle expectations. A common estimation is that you will need about 70% of your current pretax earnings to maintain your standard of living in retirement; for example, if you are earning $50 000 before you retire, you can expect to need $35 000 of annual income once you retire (HRDC, 2001c).

In Canada, as in many developed countries, many retired adults own their own homes and have no mortgage payments, and their children are self-reliant. Additionally, retirees are eligible for provincial health care benefits as well as for many special senior citizen benefits and discounts. When these factors are taken into consideration, on average, retired adults in most developed countries have incomes that are equivalent to 85 to 100% of preretirement levels (Smeeding, 1990). To assist Canadians plan for their future financial security, Service Canada (2010) has created an interactive website as a way to estimate their retirement income needs by using the Canadian Retirement Income Calculator (**www.servicecanada.gc.ca/eng/isp/common/cricinfo.shtml**).

POVERTY It used to be that postretirement income losses resulted in high poverty rates among the elderly. However, over the past several decades, poverty rates among the elderly have declined substantially. Health Canada (2003f) reported that after adjusting for inflation, senior men's income rose 21% and senior women's by 22% between 1981 and 1998. Accordingly, the incidence of seniors who were living below Statistics Canada's Low Income Cut-offs (LICOs) has fallen sharply since the early 1980s, from 34 to 20% in 1998 (Health Canada, 2003g).

A variety of factors are responsible for declining poverty rates among the elderly. For one thing, there have been significant improvements in work-related pensions. As well, there have been moderate improvements in CPP/QPP and regular cost-of-living increases for pension incomes (Health Canada, 2003e). Equivalent progress has been made in reducing the rates of poverty among the elderly in many other countries. These improvements have meant that the relative financial position of the elderly has improved more than that of any other age group in the population. In fact, most elderly adults today had better jobs and earned a great deal more money before retirement than did members of previous generations. As a result, today's seniors have more savings and better retirement benefits.

Unfortunately, the recent trend toward a lower incidence of seniors living below the LICOs (a measure of poverty) obscures much higher rates in two subgroups. **Figure 18.4** shows declines in the elderly poverty rates of senior men and women who either live in families or are unattached. Although rates declined in all groups over the past two decades, large disparities across groups remained. Unattached older adults in particular continue to be more likely to be poor than their peers who live in families, and among the older unattached, women are more likely to be poor than men (48% versus 35%, respectively) (Health Canada, 2003i). Varying poverty rates for elderly unattached men and women arise from a number of differences in adult life experiences. Current cohorts of older women are much less likely than their male peers to have had paid employment, are less likely to

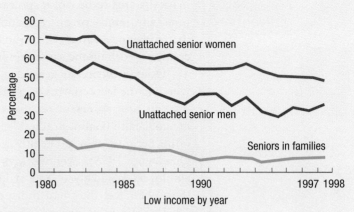

Figure 18.4

This graph illustrates how unattached older adults, in particular, continue to be poorer than their peers who live in families. Among the unattached seniors, women are more likely to be poor than men.

(*Source:* Adapted from Statistics Canada, 2001i, 2001j, figures from Statistical Snapshots: Gender Differences in Low Income, No. 15; and Low Income and Family Status, No. 16. Reproduced with permission of the Minister of Public Works and Government Services Canada, 2005.)

have earned retirement benefits even if they did work, and generally worked for lower wages (Powell, 2006). As a result, many older widows rely entirely on CPP/QPP and OAS income. Younger women are more likely to have been employed and to have participated in a retirement plan, but, as you learned in earlier chapters, gender differences in work patterns still exist. Moreover, many more retirement-age women today are divorced than in past cohorts. The combination of income inequality and the increased prevalence of divorce are likely to lead to a dramatic rise in the number of women who live in poverty after retirement (Powell, 2006).

HEALTH, ATTITUDES, AND EMOTIONS Longitudinal studies indicate quite clearly that health simply does not change, for better or worse, because of retirement (van Solinge, 2007). When ill health accompanies retirement, the causal sequence is nearly always that the individual retired because of poor health. Among those in good health at retirement age, retirement itself has little or no effect on health status over the succeeding years.

In one study of more than 1500 men over a period of years, participants were asked to indicate which of 31 possibly stressful life events they had experienced in the past year and to rate the overall stressfulness of each of these events (Bossé, Aldwin, Levenson, & Workman-Daniels, 1991). Retirement was ranked 30th out of 31 in overall stressfulness, below even such items as "move to a less desirable residence" or "decrease in responsibilities or hours at work or where you volunteer." Of those who had retired in the previous year, seven out of ten said that they found retirement either not stressful at all or only a little stressful. Among the 30% of retired men in this study who did list some problems with retirement, poor health and poor family finances were the most likely causes. Those with marital problems were also likely to report more daily hassles in their retired lives.

In fact, Canadian research suggests that retirement can have a positve impact on overall life satisfaction, especially in situations where dissatisfaction stems from a work–life imbalance (Uriarte-Landa & Hébert, 2009). The most common causes of work–life conflict are caregiving, (i.e., for elderly parents, elderly relatives, and/or grandchildren); disability onset; coping with emotional demands, such as a change in marital status or loss of a spouse or a parent; and changing priorities where spending time with family or on recreational pursuits or volunteering becomes more valuable than pursuing a career. Unfortunately, given a choice, dissatisfied older workers elect to continue working the same number of hours rather than sacrifice pay.

Other evidence suggests that those who respond least well to retirement are those who had the least control over the decision (Smith & Moen, 2004). For example, those who go into retirement because of a late-career job loss show declines in physical and mental health (Gallo, Bradley, Siegel, & Kasl, 2000). Similarly, those who are forced to retire because of poor health typically adjust more poorly to retirement (Hardy & Quadagno, 1995). Even workers who accept special early retirement offers from their employers are likely to report lower satisfaction and higher levels of stress than do those who feel they had more control over the retirement decision (Herzog et al., 1991). Retirement is also likely to be more stressful for those whose economic situation is poor, or for those who must simultaneously cope with both retirement and other major life changes, such as widowhood (Stull & Hatch, 1984). But for those for whom retirement is anticipated and on time, this role loss is not stressful.

It appears that what predicts life satisfaction in late adulthood is not whether a person has retired, but whether he was satisfied with life in earlier adulthood. We take ourselves with us through the years: Grumpy, negative young people tend to be grumpy, negative old people, and satisfied young adults find satisfaction in retirement as well. The consistency of this finding is quite striking and provides very good support for continuity theories of adulthood. Work does shape daily life for 40 years or more of adulthood, but a person's happiness or unhappiness with life, her growth or stagnation, seems less a function of the specifics of the work experience than a function of the attitudes and qualities she brings to the process.

GEOGRAPHIC MOBILITY For many adults, retirement brings an increase in choices about where to live. When your job or your spouse's job no longer ties you to a specific place, you can choose to move to sunnier climes or to live nearer one of your children. Surprisingly, however, most retirees stay fairly close to the place they have called home for many years (Brown, 2004). In fact, Havens and Finlayson (1999) reported that only about 20% of seniors moved within a 5-year period. Moreover, when seniors aged 65 and over did move, most did so because their house was too big or too small; they or a spouse retired; there was a decline in the health of self or a spouse; and/or they wanted access to recreation or leisure. Regardless of whether they moved or remained where they lived before retirement, about seven of every ten seniors lived in Canadian urban centres with a population of 50 000 or more (Turcotte & Schellenberg, 2007). The cities with the highest concentration of seniors were the St. Catharines–Niagara area of Ontario, Victoria, British Columbia, and Trois-Rivières, Quebec.

Elders who have moved to resort communities specifically designed for retired people have made what social scientists call an *amenity move*.
(*Photo:* A. Ramey/PhotoEdit)

Charles Longino, who has been one of the most diligent investigators of residential moves among the elderly, suggests that elderly adults make three types of moves (Jackson, Longino, Zimmerman, & Bradsher, 1991; Litwak & Longino, 1987; Longino, 1990; Longino, Jackson, Zimmerman, & Bradsher, 1991). The first type, which he calls an *amenity move*, is the one most of us probably think of when we think of older adults changing residences. If an older adult makes such a move, it is almost always right around the time of retirement. Most typically, an **amenity move** is in a direction away from the older person's children, frequently to a warmer climate. The Department of Foreign Affairs and International Trade (DFAIT) (2001) suggests that Florida and Arizona are popular destinations for amenity moves to the United States. Other popular international destinations include Mexico, Latin American countries, and islands in the Caribbean, especially where there is a Canadian expatriate community. In Canada, amenity moves are most often westward, particularly to British Columbia. It's not surprising that Victoria, B.C., is among communities with the most seniors per capita (Health Canada, 2003g).

Seniors who make amenity moves are likely to be still married and relatively healthy and to have adequate or good retirement income (De Jong, Wilmoth, Angel, & Cornwell, 1995; Hazelrigg & Hardy, 1995). Often the relocating couple has vacationed in the new location; many have planned the move carefully over a number of years (Cuba & Longino, 1991). Most report higher levels of life satisfaction or morale after such a move, although some move back to where they came from because they find themselves too isolated from family and friends.

Another kind of amenity move is to move seasonally rather than making a permanent move to a new location. Some seniors, often called *snowbirds*, spend the winter months in sunnier areas and the summer months at home, nearer their families. Permanent movers away from Canada and seasonal retirees both have to contend with many essential issues when they leave the country, namely immigration and citizenship, taxation, health care, and real estate matters (DFAIT, 2001).

The second type of move, which Longino calls **compensatory (kinship) migration**, occurs when the older adult—most often, a widow living alone—develops such a level of chronic disability that she has serious difficulty managing an independent household. When a move of this type occurs, it is nearly always a shift to be closer to a daughter, son, or some other relative who can provide regular assistance. In some cases, this means moving in with that daughter or son, but often the move is to an apartment or house nearby or into a retirement community in which the individual can live independently but has supportive services available. The final type of move in late adulthood is what Longino calls **institutional migration**, to nursing-home care (see **Development in the Real World**).

Of course, very few older adults actually move three times. Longino's point is that these are three very different kinds of moves, made by quite different subsets of the population of elderly, and at different times in the late adult years. Amenity moves usually occur early, kinship or compensatory migration is likely to occur in middle to late old age, and institutional migration clearly occurs late in life. Only the first of these types of moves reflects the increase in options that may result from retirement.

amenity move
postretirement move away from kin to a location that has some desirable feature, such as year-round warm weather

compensatory (kinship) migration
a move to a location near family or friends that happens when an elder requires frequent help because of a disability or a disease

institutional migration
a move to an institution, such as a nursing home, that is necessitated by a disability

CHOOSING NOT TO RETIRE

A small number of adults continue working past the typical retirement age. In 1999, 9.8% of men and 3.4% of women over age 65 were employed in Canada (Statistics Canada, 2001i). This subgroup actually includes two types of people: those who have never retired from their long-time occupations and those who retired from their regular occupations and ventured into new lines of work, often part-time.

CONTINUING IN A LIFE-LONG OCCUPATION Research has focused on men who shun retirement. Some are men with very limited education, poor retirement benefits, and thus very low incomes. Many of these men continue working out of economic necessity.

Development in the Real World

DECIDING ON LONG-TERM CARE IN CANADA

In **Chapter 17** you read about the numbers of older adults living in long-term care institutions. A long-term care home in Canada usually denotes either not-for-profit homes for the aged or not-for-profit and for-profit nursing homes. The economics of long-term institutional care can make it unattractive for many older adults, especially seniors in low-income households (Sarma et al., 2009). Such care in Canada now costs anywhere from a minimum of about $1000 up to thousands of dollars per month, costs only partially covered by government or most health insurance plans. A stay of as long as a year is likely to exhaust the disposable assets of the majority of older adults. To be eligible for government subsidization for such care, a person must first use all his own disposable assets, which may leave a surviving spouse in very difficult financial straits. Most Canadian jurisdictions permit ownership of certain assets, such as a home, to be transferred to a surviving spouse, so that this asset need not be disposed of before the partner in the long-term care institution is eligible for government subsidy—an alternative that leaves the surviving spouse in somewhat better financial condition. But the spouse may still suffer significant impoverishment.

The problem for individual families is balancing the older adult's need for independence and control against the needs of younger family members who have lives of their own to lead. What often tips the balance, one way or the other, is whether any family member is able or willing to provide assistance, and whether other community services are available. For some families, Meals on Wheels, visiting nurses, adult day programs, and other help may make it possible to continue to care for a frail or demented senior at home. An intermediate alternative, which is becoming more available, is some kind of "supportive housing," where the older person can have an individual apartment and thus live independently but has nursing and meal services available in the building or complex (Pynoos & Golant, 1996).

Beyond cost considerations, provincial and territorial agencies that serve older adults have suggested several criteria for evaluating a long-term care facility (Government of Canada, 2008). Here are a few:

- Be certain that the facility has the staff and equipment required to meet your elder's physical needs.

- Check with authorities to see whether any complaints have been filed and how they were resolved; avoid facilities with many outstanding complaints.

- Research the results of provincial/territorial inspections and the extent to which any deficiencies were corrected; do not admit your elder to a facility that has any current deficiencies.

- Visit at different times, such as during meals, recreation periods, early morning, and late evening, to note how residents are cared for in different situations.

- Talk to family members of other residents if possible.

- Ask about the facility's policies regarding medical emergencies.

Of course, a facility can receive high marks on these criteria and still not be the best one for an older adult. Thus, once a facility has satisfied these basic criteria, families must determine whether it can meet their older loved one's cognitive, social, and spiritual needs. Moreover, once an elder has been admitted, family members should closely monitor their care and be prepared to make a change if needed.

Only 9.8% of men and 3.4% of women over age 65 are employed in Canada. However, a fairly high proportion of middle-aged people say they plan to work at least part-time after retirement. Consequently, employers are eager to learn how best to train older workers. (*Photos: left*, Don Smetzer/Stone/Getty Images; *right*, Copyright ©Tom Carter/ Photo Edit)

A larger fraction of those who shun retirement are highly educated, healthy, highly work-committed professionals, whose wives often are also still working (Parnes & Sommers, 1994). Many of them have been highly work-committed their entire adult lives. For example, men in the American National Longitudinal Surveys sample, a group that has been studied over a period of 25 years, were asked in their 50s whether they would continue working if they suddenly found themselves with enough money to live comfortably. Those who said they would continue working are much more likely to shun retirement and to be still working in their 70s and 80s (Parnes & Sommers, 1994). For these men, work continues to provide more satisfaction than they expect retirement to offer.

Research suggests that older adults respond to computer training very much the way younger adults do. Most get over any anxieties they have about using computers after receiving training. In addition, they can become as proficient as younger adults, although they may require slower-paced training. (*Photo:* Copyright ©David Young-Wolff/Photo Edit)

LEARNING NEW JOB SKILLS Perhaps the greatest obstacle to employment for older adults is that many potential employers express concerns about older adults' ability to learn new job skills (Forte & Hansvick, 1999). However, studies of age differences in learning demonstrate that the learning process itself does not change with age. The same factors—interest, anxiety, motivation, quality of instruction, self-efficacy, and so on—predict learning success in both older and younger adults (Chasseigne, Grau, Mullet, & Cama, 1999; Gardiner, Luszcz, & Bryan, 1997; Mead & Fisk, 1998; Plaud, Plaud, & von Duvillard, 1999; Truluck & Courtenay, 1999). Thus, it seems reasonable that many aspects of effective training programs designed for younger workers, such as financial incentives for accomplishment of training goals, should also apply to older employees.

Moreover, an extensive body of research shows that, with appropriately paced training, older adults can significantly improve their performance on many cognitive tasks that are relevant to the workplace (Baltes & Kliegl, 1992; Dittmann-Kohli, Lachman, Kliegl, & Baltes, 1991; Kliegl et al., 1989, 1990; Verhaeghen et al, 1992). Pacing is important, because these studies do suggest that learning new skills sometimes takes longer for older adults. However, even training in the use of new technologies usually results in similar or identical skill levels among younger and older adults.

WORKPLACE FUNCTIONING With respect to aspects of job functioning other than learning of new skills, supervisors typically give older adults higher ratings than younger adults (Forte & Hansvick, 1999). For example, they view older employees as more reliable. In addition, managers typically report that, although younger workers produce a greater quantity of work, the quality of older employees' work is better (Rao & Rao, 1997). Consequently, many employers view older adults as desirable employees.

Before Going On

- What are the factors that influence the decision to retire?
- How does retirement affect income, health, attitudes, emotions, and mobility? What does research suggest about the decision not to retire?

Summary

Theories of Social and Personality Development

- Erikson's concept of ego integrity has been influential, but research does not indicate that the development of ego integrity is necessary to adjustment in old age. The notions of reminiscence and life review have been helpful in researchers' attempts to understand development in late adulthood.

- Similarly, disengagement has been found not to be essential in old age; high life satisfaction and good mental health are found most often among seniors who maintain continuity with their earlier interests.

Individual Differences

- Successful aging encompasses maintenance of health, cognitive and social functioning, productivity, and life satisfaction.

- Religious coping has psychological and social components. It is associated with a lower mortality rate as well as with better physical and mental health.

Social Relationships

- Late adulthood is a time when people discard some roles, leaving other roles which may offer greater licence for individuality.

- Among unmarried seniors in Canada, living alone is the most common and preferred living arrangement.

- Marriages in late adulthood are, on average, highly satisfying for both spouses, if the spouses exhibit strong loyalty and mutual affection. Married seniors, as a group, are somewhat healthier and more satisfied with their lives than are single seniors.

- The majority of seniors see their children regularly. There is some indication that relationships with siblings may become more significant in late adulthood than at earlier ages.

- Degree of contact with friends is correlated with overall life satisfaction among older adults.

- Women in this age group continue to have larger social networks than men do.

Career Issues in Late Life

- The typical age of retirement in Canada is roughly age 62.

- Time of retirement is affected by health, family responsibilities, adequacy of anticipated pension income, and satisfaction with one's job.

- Income typically decreases with retirement. Among seniors, women are more likely to live with lower income.

- Retirement appears not to be a stressful life change for most people. The minority of older adults who find retirement stressful are likely to be those who feel they had little control over the decision to retire.

- Those who choose not to retire do so for economic reasons or because of particularly strong commitments to work. Research indicates that older adults can learn new job skills.

Review Questions

Answers are provided on MyDevelopmentLab in the Course Resources folder.

Theories of Social and Personality Development

18.1 The notion that reminiscence is a necessary and healthy aspect of aging and preparation for death is a component of which of the following theories?
   a. Erikson's stage of ego integrity versus despair
   b. disengagement theory
   c. Rowe and Kahn's successful aging paradigm
   d. Loevinger's theory of adult development

Individual Differences

18.2 Which of the following does not accurately describe how religious coping affects older adults?
   a. Seniors who place a great deal of emphasis on religious faith worry less than those who do not.
   b. Seniors who say their religious beliefs are important to them think that their lives serve an important purpose.
   c. Seniors who have strong religious beliefs are more likely to commit suicide to be with God.
   d. Seniors who regularly attend religious services are healthier, both physically and emotionally.

Social Relationships

18.3 In comparison to men's, women's
   a. friendships involve less disclosure.
   b. friendships involve less intimacy.
   c. social networks are smaller.
   d. social networks are larger.

Career Issues in Late Life

18.4 Which of the following is not an accurate statement about the factors that influence the decision to retire?
   a. Poor health lowers the average age of retirement by 1 to 3 years.
   b. Retirement-age adults who have young children at home are likely to retire early in order to rear their children.
   c. Poor health and social norms often cause working-class adults to retire earlier than individuals in the middle or upper socioeconomic groups.
   d. The most reliable predictor of retirement for a woman is whether her spouse has retired.

18.5 According to Charles Longino, those who make *amenity moves* are likely to be
   a. in poor health.
   b. experiencing a health crisis that necessitates nursing care.
   c. married, healthy, and in possession of an adequate income.
   d. women.

Critical-Thinking Questions

18.6 What factors predict successful aging, and how does religious coping affect older adults' physical and mental health?

18.7 Do you suppose the number of seniors living alone is different in non-Western industrialized countries? Explain your answer.

CHAPTER 19

Death, Dying, and Bereavement

We began our study of the human lifespan with an examination of birth and went on to consider the multitude of changes in the physical, cognitive, and social domains from infancy to late adulthood. Now we turn to the end of life. A particularly eloquent expression of the inevitability of death came from Stewart Alsop, a writer who kept a diary of the last years of his life as he was dying of leukemia. In one of the very late entries in this journal, he said, "A dying man needs to die as a sleepy man needs to sleep, and there comes a time when it is wrong, as well as useless, to resist" (1973, p. 299). Alsop's statement calls to mind one of the important individual variables you have read about often in earlier chapters: the timing of a universal developmental event in a particular individual's life.

Like Alsop, many people contract fatal diseases and consciously face the inevitability of impending death for a period of months or years. Sometimes an unexpected event—perhaps an accident or a crime—ends a child's or young adult's life prematurely. For most of us, though, death comes in late adulthood and results from the subtle interplay between primary and secondary aging. Consequently, a good deal of what you will learn about dying and death will concern older adults. But the story must begin earlier, with an examination of people's understanding of and attitudes toward dying and death.

When you finish studying the chapter, you will be able to identify the three definitions of death and care at the end of life; describe how the meaning of death changes over the lifespan; compare Elisabeth Kübler-Ross's stages of dying with the alternative views on the process of dying; and identify some of the ways people respond to death and the issues involved in the grieving process. While you read, keep the following questions in mind:

- What is the value of emphasizing care that seeks to prevent, reduce, or soothe the patients' symptoms rather than care that uses life-prolonging treatments at the end of life?

- Why do you suppose young adults seem to have the need to preserve their belief that bad things, including death, happen to others but not to themselves? What eventually happens to cause them to accept death as final, inevitable, and universal?

- Why do you think widowhood seems to be much harder on men than on women?

THE EXPERIENCE OF DEATH

Most of us use the word *death* as if it described a simple phenomenon. You are either alive or dead. In fact, death is a process as well as a state, and physicians have different labels for different aspects of this process. Moreover, for both the deceased and the bereaved, the experience of death is shaped by the circumstances surrounding the end of life.

DEATH ITSELF

The term **clinical death** refers to the few minutes after the heart has stopped pumping, when breathing has stopped and there is no evident brain function, but during which resuscitation is still possible. Heart attack patients are sometimes brought back from clinical death; presumably, those who report near-death experiences were in a state of clinical death.

clinical death
a period during which vital signs are absent but resuscitation is still possible

brain death
absence of vital signs, including brain activity; resuscitation is no longer possible

Brain death describes a state in which the person no longer has reflexes or any response to vigorous external stimuli and shows no electrical activity in the brain. When the cortex, but not the brain stem, is affected, the person may still be able to breathe without assistance and may survive for long periods in a vegetative state or on life-support systems. When the brain stem is also dead, no body functioning can occur independently, and the individual is said to be legally dead (Detchant, 1995). Brain death most often occurs after a period of 8 to 10 minutes of clinical death, but there are cases in which brain death has occurred because of brain injury, as in an auto accident, and other body functions can still be maintained artificially. In such cases, other body organs, such as the heart and kidneys, can be used for organ donation, as long as they are removed without delay.

social death
the point at which family members and medical personnel treat the deceased person as a corpse

Social death occurs at the point when the deceased person is treated like a corpse by others; for instance, someone may close the eyes or sign a death certificate. Once social death has been acknowledged, family and friends must begin to deal with the loss.

END-OF-LIFE CARE

Until recently, the majority of Canadians died in hospitals. As a result of changing views about the process of dying, more families are turning toward an alternate form of end-of-life care for their terminally ill loved ones: hospice palliative care.

HOSPITAL CARE The majority of Canadians (60%) die in hospitals rather than at home or in long-term care facilities (Statistics Canada, 2009a). Where people die depends on such factors as age, gender, and type of disease or injury (CIHI, 2007a, 2007b). For example, hospital death is more prevalent for older adults, and somewhat more so for women than men, than it is for their younger counterparts. People with a terminal illness, such as cancer, are more likely to die in a hospital than those with organ failure or frailty, or those who die suddenly because of, for example, accidents or trauma. As well, adults with terminal illness or chronic conditions, such as heart disease or organ failure, typically spend more time in the hospital in the year before death than those dying of other causes, such as those who are hospitalized with an acute problem such as a heart attack or an injury and who die soon thereafter, having had no prior hospitalization.

hospice care
a holistic approach to care for the terminally ill that emphasizes individual and family control of the process of dying

HOSPICE PALLIATIVE CARE In recent years, an alternative form of end-of-life care that has become common is **hospice care**, a holistic approach to caring for the dying that embraces individual and family control of the process. The modern-day hospice care movement emerged in England in the late 1960s and in Canada in the mid-1970s (van Bommel, 2002). The hospice care movement was given a boost by the writings of Elisabeth Kübler-Ross, who emphasized the importance of a "good death," or a "death with dignity," in which the patient and the patient's family have an active role in the process (1974). Many health care professionals, particularly in England, Canada, and the United States, believe that death with dignity is more likely if the dying person remains at home, or in a home-like setting in which contact with family and friends is part of the daily experience. The philosophy that underlies this alternative approach to the dying patient has several aspects (van Bommel, 2002):

- Death should be viewed as normal, as something not to be avoided but to be faced and accepted.

- The patient and family should be encouraged to prepare for the death by examining their feelings, planning for after the death, and talking openly about the death.

- The family should be involved in the patient's care as much as is physically possible, not only because this participation gives the patient the emotional support of loved ones, but also because it allows family members to resolve their relationships with the dying person.

- Control over the patient's care should be in the hands of the patient and the family. They decide what types of medical treatment they will ask for or accept; they decide whether the patient will remain at home or be hospitalized.

- Care should be aimed at satisfying the physical, emotional, spiritual, and psychosocial needs of a person with a life-threatening or terminal condition and his family.

- Medical care should be primarily *palliative care* rather than curative. The emphasis is on controlling pain and maximizing comfort, not on invasive or life-prolonging measures.

A related and more bilingual term, **palliative care**, was first coined in 1975 by Canadian oncology specialist Balfour Mount, following his inspiring 1974 visit to Dame Cicely Saunders' St. Christopher's Hospice in England. Founded in 1967, this establishment was the first modern-day hospice. Shortly after his return to Canada, two Canadian palliative care units were opened late in 1974, the first at St. Boniface General Hospital in Winnipeg and weeks later, under the direction of Balfour Mount, the second at the Royal Victoria Hospital in Montreal (McBurney, 2008; Ottawa Citizen, 2005). Although the terms *hospice care* and *palliative care* are still used independently by some organizations in Canada, we have seen the terms converge, and *hospice palliative care* is now widely used across the country (Canadian Hospice Palliative Care Association [CHPCA], 2009a). The philosophy that underlies hospice palliative care focuses on both the relief of suffering and the improvement of the quality of living and dying. Hospice palliative care helps dying patients and their families to

palliative care
a form of care that seeks to prevent, relieve, or soothe the patients' symptoms rather than cure their diseases or disorders

- address physical, psychological, social, spiritual, and practical issues and their associated expectations, needs, hopes, and fears;

- prepare for and manage self-determined life closure and the dying process; and

- cope with loss and grief during illness and bereavement (BC Ministry of Health, 2006)

End-of-life care for terminally ill patients in Canada has shifted away from the purely curative to include hospice palliative care, as illustrated in **Figure 19.1**. While hospice palliative care complements traditional curative biomedical care, it has more of a wellness, whole-person orientation—that is, it encompasses a person's existential/spiritual needs in addition to their physical and psychosocial ones—and is intended to optimize the quality of life for individuals and their families who are living with life-threatening progressive illness or are bereaved. This shift has spawned a new field of research to determine how to best alleviate distress and optimize end-of-life well-being (Chochinov, 2007; Chochinov et al., 2005; Chochinov et al., 2009; Chochinov et al., 2006).

Indeed, research studies are now beginning to demonstrate the tangible value of whole-person end-of-life care (Chochinov, 2006). For example, University of Manitoba research psychiatrist Harvey Chocinov has developed a Model of Dignity that shows that a loss of dignity is associated with increased levels of distress in the terminally ill (Chochinov et al., 2008; Chochinov et al., 2006). In this Model of Dignity, a person's perception of dignity is intertwined with physical, psychological, existential, and spiritual challenges (Chochinov et al., 2009; Chochinov et al., 2006). Subsequently, Chochinov developed the Patient Dignity Inventory (PDI) to

Balfour Mount is considered the founder of the palliative care movement in North America that focuses on improving the quality of life for people with terminal illnesses and their families.
(*Photo:* Courtesy of McGill University)

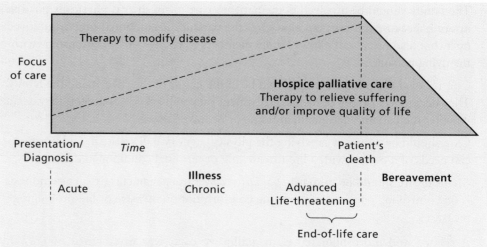

Figure 19.1

This model represents the relative proportions of concurrent therapies at different phases of the dying process. The dashed line distinguishes therapies intended to modify disease (curative care) from therapies intended to relieve suffering and/or improve quality of life (labelled *Hospice palliative care*). The lines are straight for simplicity. In reality, the total quantity of therapy and the mix of concurrent therapies would fluctuate based on the patient's and family's issues, and their goals for care and treatment priorities. At times, there may not be any therapy in use at all.

(*Source:* Ferris et al., 2002. A Model to Guide Hospice Palliative Care: Based on National Principles and Norms of Practice. Ottawa, ON: CHPCA. Adapted from: Expert Working Group on Integrated Palliative Care for Persons with AIDS [1988]. Caring together: summary of a report submitted to Health and Welfare Canada [December, 1987]. *Journal of Palliative Care, 4*(4), 76–86. Figure 8 [The Role of Hospice Palliative Care During Illness].)

objectively measure dignity-related distress in palliative care for the purpose of fostering psychotherapeutic interventions to help patients die with greater dignity (Chochinov et al., 2008). So far, evidence suggests that patients who participate in dignity-based care report a heightened sense of dignity, an increased sense of purpose, a heightened sense of meaning, and an increased will to live (Chochinov et al., 2009; Thompson & Chochinov, 2008; Thompson et al., 2009). In addition, the families of terminally ill patients were better prepared for the future.

Today, most communities in Canada provide some form of hospice palliative care serving thousands of terminally ill patients and their families (CHPCA, 2009b). And yet, no more than 37% of Canadians who are dying have access to quality hospice palliative care (Bacon, 2008).

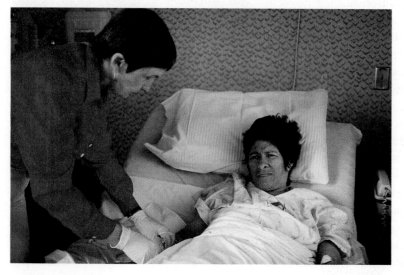

This woman, who is dying of cancer, has chosen to stay at home during her last months, supported by regular visits from hospice nurses. (*Photo:* Bill Aron/PhotoEdit)

CAREGIVER SUPPORT Hospice palliative care providers must recognize that caregivers, as well as patients, have needs (CHPCA, 2007; Kristjanson & Aoun, 2004). In fact, caring for a dying loved one, particularly someone with dementia, induces a grief response (Lindgren, Connelly, & Gaspar, 1999; Rudd, Viney, & Preston, 1999). Consequently, another important element of palliative hospice care is grief support for the primary caregiver, support that includes both psychosocial and educational components (Meredith & Rassa, 1999; Ferris et al., 2005). Similarly, palliative hospice care providers themselves also often require support services because of the emotional strain involved in caring for patients who are terminally ill.

Health Canada (2002g) launched a web-based Canadian Virtual Hospice to help support palliative hospice care providers and their patients, the patient's family, and researchers across Canada. One of the main goals is to provide "Canadians with expert palliative care at home" (Health Canada, 2001e). The Canadian Virtual Hospice enables palliative hospice care experts to interact directly with informal caregivers, provide access to a wide range of palliative hospice care services, and bring medical expertise to the home and to rural and remote areas of Canada.

Before Going On

- Define clinical death, brain death, and social death.
- How do hospice and hospital care differ with respect to their effects on terminally ill patients?

THE MEANING OF DEATH ACROSS THE LIFESPAN

Life teaches us how to survive, while death teaches us how to live. Life is a taskmaster, while death is a master teacher. We cannot learn how to appreciate the preciousness of life without coming to grips with the reality of death. (Wong, 2000, p. 27)

As an adult, you understand that death is irreversible, that it comes to everyone, and that it means a cessation of all function. But do children and teenagers understand these aspects of death? And what does death mean to adults of different ages?

CHILDREN'S AND ADOLESCENTS' UNDERSTANDING OF DEATH

Results from a variety of studies suggest that preschool-aged children typically understand none of these aspects of death. They believe that death can be reversed, for instance, through prayer, magic, or wishful thinking; they believe that dead persons can still feel or breathe. Research shows that young children's ideas about death are rooted in their lack of understanding of life (Slaughter & Lyons, 2003). This link between understanding life and understanding death has been illustrated in a series of studies showing that teaching young children about the nature of biological life helps them understand what causes death and why it is irreversible.

By the time they start school, just about the time Piaget described as the beginning of concrete operations, most children seem to understand both the permanence and the universality of death. Children 6 to 7 years of age comprehend death as a biological event in which the heart ceases to beat, the lungs no longer take in air, and brain activity stops (Barrett & Behne, 2005; Slaughter, 2005). This understanding is clear from children's own comments. In one study, children were told a story about two children who used to go into a candy store kept by an old lady who had recently died (Lansdown & Benjamin, 1985). After they heard the

These children being comforted by an adult at a loved one's grave are likely to have far more mature concepts of death than others their age who have not encountered death first-hand.
(*Photo:* Mark Gibson/MaXx Images Inc.)

story, the participants were asked some questions about the old lady and about what it meant that she was dead.

> A 5-year-old: "Someone came into the shop to kill her. She'll see them again and she'll die again. She can try to get up."
>
> A 7-year-old: "They never come alive again. You can't move because your heart has stopped. People wish you can come alive but you can't. Children can't die because they start at one and go to 100."
>
> A 9-year-old: "Their heart can't take it any longer and they die. Babies can die of cancer, kidney problems. Heaven is much nicer than down here." (Lansdown & Benjamin, 1985, p. 20)

The first of these children did not yet understand the permanence of death; the second did not understand its universality; the third seems to have grasped both ideas.

As is true of so many other milestones of this age range, the child's specific experience seems to make a good deal of difference. Four- and five-year-olds who have had direct experience with the death of a family member are more likely to understand the permanence of death than are those who have had no such personal experience (Stambrook & Parker, 1987). Experiences in which children discover a dead animal, lose a pet, or are exposed to a story in which a character dies (e.g., *Bambi, The Lion King*) can also speed up their understanding of death (Cox, Garrett, & Graham, 2004–2005). Such experiences influence children's understanding of death because they serve as the catalyst for discussions of death with children's parents. Such discussions, when they focus on the concrete, biological aspects of death, provide children with the scaffolding they need to achieve a cognitive understanding of death. Linking death to broader values with which children are familiar helps them grasp the social aspects of death.

Adolescents understand the finality of death better than children do. Moreover, in an abstract sense, they understand that death is inevitable. Unrealistic beliefs about personal death, however, appear to contribute to adolescent suicide. Typically, teens who attempt suicide claim to understand that death is final, but many tell researchers and counsellors that the purpose of their suicidal behaviour was to achieve a temporary escape from a stressful personal problem (Blau, 1996). Further, researchers have found that some teenagers who attempt suicide believe that death is a pleasurable experience for most people who die (Gothelf et al., 1998). Certainly, such distorted beliefs may be the result of the powerful emotions that lead teens to attempt suicide rather than the product of adolescent thinking. However, suicidal adults typically think of death, even when it is desired, as painful and unpleasant. So there may be a developmental difference between suicidal adolescents' and suicidal adults' understanding of death.

Like those of children, adolescents' ideas about death are affected by their personal experiences. Experiencing the death of a family member or a friend, especially someone who is near the teenager's own age, tends to shake an adolescent's confidence in her own immortality. In fact, research suggests that the loss of someone close, such as a sibling, may lead an adolescent to re-examine critically her ideas about death—both as a general concept and as something that is inevitable for herself (Batten & Oltjenbruns, 1999).

THE MEANING OF DEATH FOR ADULTS

Adults' ideas about death vary with age. Death seems remote to most young adults. The notion of personal mortality is a more common focus of thought in middle age, and by the later years, the idea of death becomes very personally relevant for most adults.

EARLY ADULTHOOD In recent years, psychologists examining young adults' views on death have drawn attention to young adults' sense of **unique invulnerability**—a belief that bad things, including death, happen to others but not to themselves. Although young adults are more realistic about personal mortality than adolescents are, researchers find that many believe that they possess unique personal characteristics that somehow protect them against death. For example, researchers often ask participants of various ages to use life-expectancy statistics and risk-factor self-ratings to predict the age at which they will die. Such studies usually find that young adults overestimate their own life expectancy (Snyder, 1997). Moreover, young adults are more likely than those who are middle-aged or older to show increased fear of death following open discussions of the process of dying (Abengozar, Bueno, & Vega, 1999).

Here again, actual experience with death makes a difference. For example, nursing students display less fear of death than college students pursuing other careers, and their anxieties about death lessen with each additional year of training (Sharma, Monsen, & Gary, 1997). Moreover, the sudden loss of a loved one appears to shake a young adult's belief in unique invulnerability and, as a result, is often more traumatic for younger than for older adults (Liu & Aaker, 2007). In fact, such losses frequently lead to suicidal thoughts in young adults. Young adults who have recently lost a loved one in an accident or because of a homicide or a suicide are about five times as likely to formulate a suicide plan as young adults who have not had such a loss, although most never follow through with their plans (Prigerson et al., 1999).

Analyses of public reactions to the deaths of young Canadians, such as 21-year-old Terry Fox or the deaths of our young Canadian soldiers in Afghanistan, provide additional insight into young adults' ideas about death. As you may have noticed, perceptions about young people often change dramatically after their deaths, and they are given heroic status (Bourreille, 1999). Moreover, public interest in the events surrounding their deaths, as evidenced by the frequency of headline stories devoted to them, continues for many years afterward (Brown, Basil, & Bocarnea, 2003). Psychologists hypothesize that such early deaths challenge young people's beliefs in unique invulnerability and, therefore, provoke defensive reactions that cause them to place those who die young in a special category. In other words, to maintain belief in their own unique invulnerability, young adults must come up with reasons why death came early to others but will not happen to them. As a result, they elevate such figures to near-sainthood.

MIDDLE AND LATE ADULTHOOD In middle and late adulthood, an understanding of death goes well beyond the simple acceptance of finality, inevitability, and universality. A death changes the roles and relationships of everyone else in a family. For example, when an elder dies, everyone else in that particular lineage "moves up" in the generational system. The death of a parent can be particularly unsettling for a middle-aged adult if the adult does not yet consider himself ready to assume the elder role.

An individual's death also affects the roles of people beyond the family, such as younger adults in a business organization, who then can take on new and perhaps more significant roles. Retirement serves some of the same function, as an older adult steps aside for a younger one. But death brings many permanent changes in families and social systems.

Images of flag-draped caskets holding the remains of Canadian soldiers killed in Afghanistan promote intense feelings of pride. Here, people line Highway 401 to honour Canada's fallen soldiers as they are repatriated. (*Photo:* The Canadian Press/Frank Gunn)

unique invulnerability
the belief that bad things, including death, happen only to others

At an individual level, the prospect of death may shape one's view of time (Kalish, 1985). In middle age, most people exhibit a shift in their thinking about time, thinking less about "time since birth" and being more aware of "time until death," a transition clearly reflected in the comment of this middle-aged adult:

> Before I was 35, the future just stretched forth. There would be time to do and see and carry out all the plans I had. . . . Now I keep thinking, will I have time enough to finish off some of the things I want to do? (Neugarten, 1970, p. 78)

Critical Thinking

When you think of your own age, do you think of time since birth, or time until death, or both? If you think in terms of time until death, can you remember when you switched to this view?

Such an "awareness of finitude" is not a part of every middle-aged or older adult's view of death (Marshall, 1975). One study of a group of adults aged 72 and older found that only about half thought in terms of "time remaining" (Keith, 1981/1982). Interestingly, those who did think of death in these terms had less fear of death than did those who thought of their lives as "time lived." Other research confirms this: Middle-aged and older adults who continue to be preoccupied with the past are more likely to be fearful and anxious about death (Pollack, 1979/1980).

FEAR OF DEATH

Paul T.P. Wong, an existentialist researcher with Trinity Western University in British Columbia, discusses the nature of death anxiety in the following way:

> Death is the only certainty in life. All living organisms die; there is no exception. However, human beings alone are burdened with the cognitive capacity to be aware of their own inevitable mortality and to fear what may come afterwards. Furthermore, their capacity to reflect on the meaning of life and death creates additional existential anxiety. (Wong, 2003, para. 16)

Wong goes on to suggest that our fear of death stems from six existential uncertainties, as described in **Table 19.1.**

TABLE 19.1   Sources of Fear of Death

Aspects of Death	Implications
The finality of death	There is no reversal, no remedy, no more tomorrow. Therefore, death signifies the cessation of all hope with respect to this world.
The uncertainty of what follows	Socrates has made the case that, since we really don't know what will happen, we should not fear. But uncertainty coupled with finality can create a potential for terror.
Annihilation anxiety or fear of non-existence	The concept of non-being can be very threatening, because it seems to go against a strong and innate conviction that life should not be reduced to non-being.
The ultimate loss	When death occurs, we are forced to lose everything we have ever valued. Those with the strongest attachments toward things of this world are likely to fear death most. Loss of control over affairs in the world and loss of the ability to care for dependents also contribute to death anxiety.
Fear of the pain and loneliness in dying	Many are afraid that they will die alone or die in pain, without any family or friends around them.
Fear of failing to complete life work	According to Goodman's (1981) interviews with eminent artists and scientists, many people are more afraid of a meaningless existence than death itself; their fear of death stems from fear of not being able to complete their mission or calling in life.

(*Source:* Wong, P.T.P. [2003]. From death anxiety to death acceptance: A meaning management model. Langley, BC: International Network on Personal Meaning. Retrieved September 9, 2004, from http://www.meaning.ca/articles/death_acceptance.htm. Courtesy of Paul T.P. Wong, Graduate Program in Counselling Psychology, Trinity Western University.)

Researchers have typically tried to measure fear of death with questionnaires. For example, one strategy is to ask participants to indicate, on a five-point scale, how disturbed or anxious they feel when thinking about various aspects of death or dying, such as "the shortness of life" or "never thinking or experiencing anything again" or "your lack of control over the process of dying" (Lester, 1990). Another approach asks participants to respond to statements such as "I fear dying a painful death" or "Coffins make me anxious" or "I am worried about what happens to us after we die" (Thorson & Powell, 1992).

FEAR OF DEATH ACROSS ADULTHOOD Although you might think that the oldest old, those closest to death, would fear it the most, research suggests that middle-aged adults are most fearful of death (Kumabe, 2006). For young adults, the sense of unique invulnerability probably prevents intense fears of death. In middle age, though, belief in one's own immortality begins to break down, resulting in increasing anxiety about the end of life. However, by late life, the inevitability of death has been accepted, and anxieties are focused on how death will actually come about.

Still, older adults do not become less pre-occupied with death. On the contrary, the elderly think and talk more about death than do those at any other age. Predictably, these discussions lead to less fear and anxiety about death among older adults (Abengozar et al., 1999). Thus, to an older person, death is highly important, but it is apparently not as frightening as it was at mid-life (Cicirelli, 2006). Older adults are more likely to fear the period of uncertainty before death than they are to fear death itself (Sullivan, Ormel, Kempen, & Tymstra, 1998). They are anxious about where they may die, who will care for them until they do, and whether they will be able to cope with the pain and loss of control and independence that may be part of the last months or years of life (Marshall & Levy, 1990).

RELIGIOUS BELIEFS Researchers typically find that adults who are deeply religious or who regularly go to their place of worship for spiritual reasons are less afraid of death than those who describe themselves as less religious or who participate less regularly in religious activities (Ardelt & Koenig, 2006; Neimeyer, Wittkowski, & Moser, 2004; Pyne, 2008). In some instances, however, researchers have found that both those who are deeply religious and those who are totally irreligious report less fear of death. Thus, the most fearful may be those who are uncertain about or uncommitted to any religious or philosophical tradition.

Religious beliefs may moderate fears of death because religious people tend to view death as a transition from one form of life to another, from physical life to a spiritual one. Sociologist Reginald Bibby of the University of Lethbridge has been tracking the attitudes of thousands of Canadians of all ages since 1975. His survey in 2000 revealed some curious intergenerational differences in conventional and less conventional religious beliefs (see **Figure 19.2**). For one, the belief that God exists increases with each age group, from 73% of teens to 85% of grandparents. Yet at the same time, belief in life after death decreases with age, from a high of 78% in teens to a low of 64% in grandparents (Bibby, 2001). This suggests that although youth may be somewhat less eager to participate in an organized set of religious practices, they do have a strong sense of spirituality. Two pioneers of hospice palliative care in Canada, Dorothy Ley and Harry van Bommel, remind us that the spiritual search for meaning in our lives is often intensified by the reality of death. This spiritual struggle is arguably an important philosophical cornerstone of the dying process and thus an important factor behind providing palliative care (Ley & van Bommel, 1994).

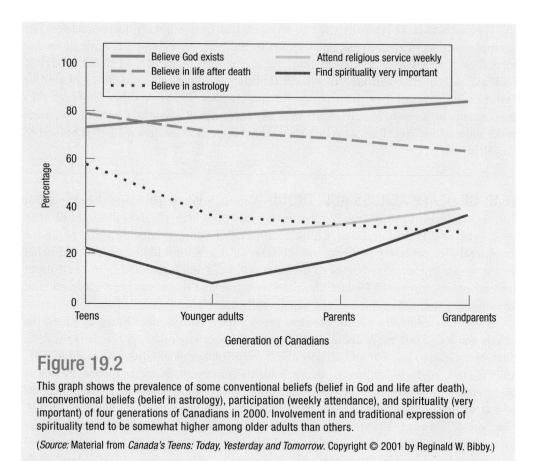

Figure 19.2

This graph shows the prevalence of some conventional beliefs (belief in God and life after death), unconventional beliefs (belief in astrology), participation (weekly attendance), and spirituality (very important) of four generations of Canadians in 2000. Involvement in and traditional expression of spirituality tend to be somewhat higher among older adults than others.

(*Source:* Material from *Canada's Teens: Today, Yesterday and Tomorrow.* Copyright © 2001 by Reginald W. Bibby.)

In addition to framing death as a transition rather than an end, religious beliefs provide adults with death stories that help them cope with both their own deaths and those of loved ones (Winter, 1999). For example, Jewish scriptures, the Christian Bible, and the Muslim Quran all contain many stories that convey the idea that death comes when one's purpose in life has been fulfilled. Many such stories also teach that each individual life is part of a larger, multigenerational story. In this larger context, death is portrayed as a necessary part of the transfer of responsibility from one generation to another. This kind of philosophical approach to death leads believers to focus on the contributions to family and community that they have made during their lives rather than on the losses they will experience at their deaths.

PERSONAL WORTH Feelings about death are also linked to one's sense of personal worth or competence. Adults who feel that they have achieved the goals they set out to achieve, or who believe that they have become the persons they wanted to be, are less anxious about death than are those who are disappointed in themselves (Ardelt & Koenig, 2006). Adults who believe that their lives have had some purpose or meaning also appear to be less fearful of death, as do those who have some sense of personal competence (Neimeyer et al., 2004).

Such findings suggest that adults who have successfully completed the major tasks of adult life, who have adequately fulfilled the demands of the roles they occupied, and who have developed inwardly are able to face death with greater equanimity. Adults who have not been able to resolve the various tasks and dilemmas of adulthood face their late adult years more anxiously, even with what Erikson described as despair. Fear of death may be merely one facet of such despair.

PREPARATION FOR DEATH

Preparation for death occurs on a number of levels. At a practical level, regardless of age, most adults agree that it is important to make preparations for death (Steinhauser et al., 2001). According to most people, in addition to purchasing life insurance and making a will, such preparations should include issuing directives regarding end-of-life care, often called a *living will*. Individuals can use living wills to make clear to health care professionals and to their families that they either do or do not wish to have their lives prolonged with feeding tubes and other devices. Moreover, most people agree that advance funeral planning can help bereaved family members deal with the many decisions they must make in the hours and days following the death of a loved one. However, researchers have found that older adults are far more likely than younger adults to have actually made such preparations (Bravo, Dubois, & Paquet, 2003).

At a somewhat deeper level, adults may prepare for death through some process of reminiscence. Deeper still, there may be unconscious changes that occur in the years just before death, which might be thought of as a type of preparation. You read about the physical and cognitive changes associated with terminal drop in **Chapter 17**. Research has pointed to the possibility that terminal psychological changes may occur as well. For example, in a still-influential study, researchers studied a group of older adults longitudinally, interviewing and testing each participant regularly over a period of 3 years (Lieberman, 1965; Lieberman & Coplan, 1970). After the testing, investigators kept track of the participants and noted when they died. They were able to identify one group of 40 participants who had all died within 1 year of the end of the interviewing and to compare them with another group of 40, matched to the first group by age, sex, and marital status, who had survived at least 3 years after the end of the testing. By comparing the psychological test scores obtained by participants in these two groups during the course of the 3 years of testing, researchers could detect changes that occurred near death.

The study's results revealed that those nearer death not only showed terminal drop on tests of memory and learning, but also became less emotional, introspective, and aggressive or assertive and more conventional, docile, dependent, and warm. In those near death, all these characteristics increased over the 3 years of interviewing, a pattern that did not occur among those of the same age who were further from death. Thus, conventional, docile, dependent, and nonintrospective adults did not die sooner; rather, these qualities became accentuated in those who were close to death.

More recently, in a German longitudinal study spanning 22 years, researchers examined another psychological attribute, life satisfaction, in a representative population sample of 70- to 100-year-olds (Gerstorf et al., 2008). The researchers set out to identify and describe well-being at the end of life. They found sharp declines in life satisfaction, commencing in the 4 years prior to death. They also found that individuals dying at older ages spend more time in the terminal periods of life satisfaction decline than individuals dying at younger ages.

The results of studies such as these are intriguing and suggestive. They paint a picture of a kind of psychological preparation for death—conscious or unconscious—in which an individual "gives up the fight," becoming less active physically and psychologically. Thus, near death, individuals do not necessarily become less involved with other people, but they do seem to show some kind of disengagement.

Before Going On

- How do ideas about death change across the lifespan?
- What factors are related to fear of death in adults?

THE PROCESS OF DYING

Elisabeth Kübler-Ross (1926–2004) was a Swiss-American psychiatrist who studied the experiences of the dying and their loved ones. In the 1960s, she formulated a model that asserted that those who are dying go through a series of psychological stages. These stages of dying, which were formulated on the basis of interviews with approximately 200 adults who were dying of cancer, continue to be highly influential, although Kübler-Ross's model has its critics. For example, research suggests that individual differences affect the process of dying in important ways.

KÜBLER-ROSS'S STAGES OF DYING

In Kübler-Ross's early writings, she proposed that those who know they are dying move through a series of steps, or stages, arriving finally at the stage she called *acceptance*. Kübler-Ross's ideas and her terminology are still widely used. In fact, surveys of death education programs suggest that Kübler-Ross's model is the only systematic approach to the dying process to which health professionals-in-training are exposed (Downe-Wamboldt & Tamlyn, 1997). Thus, you should at least be familiar with the stages she proposed.

Kübler-Ross's model predicts that most people who are confronted with a terminal diagnosis react with some variant of "Not me!" "It must be a mistake," "I'll get another opinion," or "I don't feel sick." All these reactions are forms of *denial*, a psychological defence that may be highly useful in the early hours and days after such a diagnosis. Denial of this kind may be helpful in insulating a person's emotions from the trauma of hearing such news. Keeping emotions in check in this way may help an individual formulate a rational plan of action based on "What if it's true?" Having a plan of action may help moderate the effects of acknowledging the reality of the diagnosis. Kübler-Ross thought that these extreme forms of denial would fade within a few days, to be replaced by *anger*.

The model suggests that anger among the dying expresses itself in thoughts such as "It's not fair!" but a dying person may also express anger toward God, the doctor who made the diagnosis, nurses, or family members. The anger seems to be a response not only to the diagnosis itself, but also to the sense of loss of control and helplessness that many patients feel in impersonal medical settings.

Bargaining follows anger in the Kübler-Ross model. In this form of defence, the patient tries to make "deals" with doctors, nurses, family, or God: "If I do everything you tell me, then I'll live till spring." Kübler-Ross gave a particularly compelling example of this defence reaction: A patient with terminal cancer wanted to live long enough to attend the wedding of her eldest son. The hospital staff, to help her try to reach this goal, taught her self-hypnosis to deal with her pain and she was able to attend the wedding. Kübler-Ross reported, "I will never forget the moment when she returned to the hospital. She looked tired and somewhat exhausted and—before I could say hello—said, 'Now don't forget; I have another son!'" (1969, p. 83).

Bargaining may be successful as a defence for a while, but the model predicts that, eventually, bargaining breaks down in the face of signs of declining health. At this point, Kübler-Ross's theory predicts, the patient enters the stage of *depression*. According to Kübler-Ross, depression, or despair, is a necessary preparation for the final stage of *acceptance*. To reach acceptance, the dying person must grieve for all that will be lost with death.

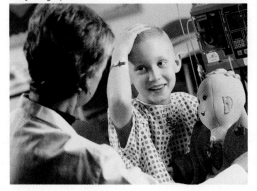

Children use some of the same defences to deal with impending death as adults. Young cancer patients may deny or bargain—for instance, "If I take my medicine, then I'll be able to go back to school in the fall."
(*Photo:* Zigy Kaluzny/Stone/ Getty Images)

CRITICISMS AND ALTERNATIVE VIEWS

Kübler-Ross's model has provided a common language for those who work with dying patients, and her highly compassionate descriptions have, without doubt, sensitized health care workers and families to the complexities of the process of dying. At some moments, what the patient needs is cheering up; at other moments, he simply needs someone to listen to him. There are times to hold his hand quietly and times to provide encouragement or hope. Many new programs for terminally ill patients are clearly outgrowths of this greater sensitivity to the dying process.

These are all worthwhile changes. But Kübler-Ross's basic thesis—that the dying process is universal and necessarily involves these specific five stages—has drawn criticism, in part, because Kübler-Ross bases her hypothesised sequence on a somewhat narrow sample of individuals (i.e., 200 mostly adult cancer patients with Westernized, individualistic cultural values). This small sample raises questions about the generalizability and cross-cultural relevance of her findings.

The most potent criticism of Kübler-Ross's model, however, centres on the issue of stages. Many clinicians and researchers who have attempted to study the process systematically have found that not all dying patients exhibit these five emotions, let alone in a specific order. Of the five, only depression seems to be common among Western patients. Further, neither Kübler-Ross's acceptance nor Cumming and Henry's disengagement (discussed in **Chapter 18**) appears to be a common end point of the dying process (Baugher, Burger, Smith, & Wallston, 1989/1990). Some patients display acceptance, others remain as active and engaged as possible right up to the end. Edwin Shneidman (1980, 1983), a major theorist and clinician in the field of **thanatology** (the scientific study of death and dying), puts it this way:

> I reject the notion that human beings, as they die, are somehow marched in lock step through a series of stages of the dying process. On the contrary, in working with dying persons, I see a wide [array] of human feelings and emotions, of various human needs, and a broad selection of psychological defences and manoeuvres—a few of these in some people, dozens in others—experienced in an impressive variety of ways. (1980, p. 110)

thanatology
the scientific study of death and dying

Instead of stages, Shneidman suggests that the dying process has many "themes" that can appear, disappear, and reappear in any one patient in the process of dealing with death. These themes include terror, pervasive uncertainty, fantasies of being rescued, incredulity, feelings of unfairness, a concern with reputation after death, fear of pain, and so forth.

Another alternative to Kübler-Ross's model is the "task-based" approach suggested by Charles Corr (1991/1992). In Corr's view, coping with dying is like coping with any other problem or dilemma: You need to take care of certain specific tasks. He suggests four such tasks for the dying person:

- Satisfying bodily needs and minimizing physical stress
- Maximizing psychological security, autonomy, and richness of life
- Sustaining and enhancing significant interpersonal attachments
- Identifying, developing, or reaffirming sources of spiritual energy, and thereby fostering hope

Corr does not deny the importance of the various emotional themes described by Shneidman. Rather, he argues that, for health professionals who deal with dying individuals, it is more helpful to think in terms of the patient's tasks, because the dying person may need help in performing some or all of them.

Whichever model one uses, what is clear is that no common patterns typify most or all reactions to impending death. Common themes exist, but they are blended together in quite different patterns by each person who faces this last task.

RESPONSES TO IMPENDING DEATH

Individual variations in responding to imminent death have themselves been the subject of a good deal of research interest in the past few decades. In one study involving 26 terminally ill men, researchers found that many of the men believed that they could avoid entering into the process of actively dying by continuing to engage in their favorite hobbies (Vig & Pearlman, 2003). Such findings raise questions about whether attitudes and behavioural choices can influence the course of a terminal disease.

Some of the early influential research on responses to impending death has been the work of British psychiatrist Steven Greer and his colleagues (Greer, 1991; Greer, Morris, & Pettingale, 1979; Pettingale, Morris, Greer, & Haybittle, 1985). They followed 62 women diagnosed with early stages of breast cancer in the 1970s. Three months after her original diagnosis, each woman was interviewed at some length and her reaction to the diagnosis and her treatment was classed in one of five groups:

- *Denial (positive avoidance).* The person rejects evidence about diagnosis; she insists that surgery was just precautionary.

- *Fighting spirit.* The person maintains an optimistic attitude and searches for more information about the disease. These patients often see their disease as a challenge and plan to fight it with every method available.

- *Stoic acceptance (fatalism).* The person acknowledges the diagnosis but makes no effort to seek any further information; or, the person ignores the diagnosis and carries on normal life as much as possible.

- *Helplessness/hopelessness.* The person acts overwhelmed by diagnosis; she sees herself as dying or gravely ill and as devoid of hope.

- *Anxious preoccupation.* Women in this category had originally been included in the helplessness group, but they were separated out later. The category includes those whose response to the diagnosis is strong and persistent anxiety. If they seek information, they interpret it pessimistically. They monitor their body sensations carefully, interpreting each ache or pain as a possible recurrence.

Greer then checked on the survival rates of these five groups after 5, 10, and 15 years. Only 33% of those whose initial reaction had been a fighting spirit had died of cancer 15 years later, compared with 76% of those whose initial reaction had been denial, stoic acceptance, anxious preoccupation, or helplessness/hopelessness. Because those in the five groups did not differ initially in the stage of their disease or in their treatment, these results support the hypothesis that psychological responses contribute to disease progress—just as coping strategies more generally affect the likelihood of disease in the first place. Moreover, numerous later studies have shown that the helplessness/hopelessness response, in particular, is associated with a significantly increased risk of reoccurrence and death (Greer, 2002).

More recently, Canadian cancer psychologist Alistair Cunningham and his colleagues have been involved in longitudinal studies that have provided a very clear indication of how a patient's involvement in psychological self-help can prolong life (Cunningham, Phillips, Stephen, & Edmonds, 2002; Cunningham & Watson, 2004). In the latest longitudinal analysis, 22 patients with medically incurable metastatic cancers were tracked as they went through group therapy (Cunningham & Watson, 2004).

At the start of the study, expert oncologists examined data on patients' medical charts and predicted each patient's probability of length of survival. The patients' attitudes and behaviours were tracked by using their written homework and therapists' notes. From this, the researchers developed a measure of how engaged the patients became in their self-help work (e.g., their levels of motivation, confidence, and openness to change). In essence, the researchers wanted to look at how much better each person did than expected, and how this correlated with their engagement in the self-help work.

What they found was that the third who became most engaged in self-help lived much longer (about three times on average) than the third who were least engaged, despite the expectation of similar survival length (see **Figure 19.3**). Ten of the patients with medically incurable cancers outlived their prognosis from 2.2 to 12.5 years and two of the patients had complete remission of their disease—the difference being that those with the higher survival rates displayed a much higher degree of early involvement in their psychological self-help than did most of their nonsurviving peers. The survivors' mental state following the self-help routine was characterized by "equanimity and social harmony" and increased "meaning and spiritual connection" (see **Table 19.2**). Long-term survivors also saw their lives as having changed profoundly: They came to understand what was important and meaningful to them (authenticity); to exercise freedom of

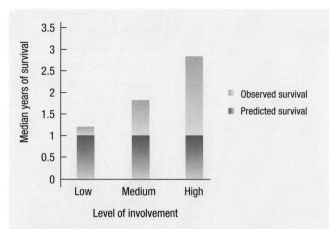

Figure 19.3

Predicted and observed survival for sub-groups rated low, medium, and high for level of involvement in self-help.

(*Source:* Cunningham, A.J., Phillips, C., Lockwood, G.A., Hedley, D.W., & Edmonds, C.V. [2000]. Association of involvement in psychological self-regulation with longer survival in patients with metastatic cancer: an exploratory study. *Advances in Mind-Body Medicine.* Fall; 16(4):276–87. (Table 1 Relationship of subjects' characteristics to survival). Used with the permission of InnoVision Health Media.)

TABLE 19.2	Themes Expressed by Long-Term Survivors		
Theme	**Long-Term Survivors**	**New Registrants[a]**	**Poor Outcome[b]**
Doing what is desired and valued			
Feeling authenticity	95[c]	17	17
Feeling autonomy	95	42	33
Perceiving profound change	75	25	0
Using and valuing self-help	80	25	58
View of cancer and medical treatment, cancer less salient	65	0	0
Achieving mental state			
Feeling equanimity and social harmony[d]	70	13	21
Experiencing meaning and spiritual connection[e]	80	9	13

[a]patients who entered the therapy program but had not yet begun it
[b]patients who went through the therapy program but had the lowest survival rates
[c]numbers are expressed as a percentage of the total possible rating score
[d]includes four subthemes: peace/joy, self-understanding and reflection, more tolerance and love (less conflict), and more expression and sharing of feelings
[e]includes two subthemes: more meaning in life and spiritual connection

(*Source:* Adapted by Cunningham, A.J. & Watson, K. (2004). How psychological therapy may prolong survival in cancer patients: New evidence and a simple theory. *Integrative Cancer Therapies* (September 2004), *3*(3), pp. 214–229. Table 5. Degree to which the main themes were expressed.)

choice in determining how to live their lives (autonomy); and they exhibited greater "acceptance," evidenced by enhanced self-esteem, greater tolerance for and emotional closeness to others, and an affective experience described as more peaceful and joyous. These were common themes among long survivors but were largely absent from the interviews with the comparison groups, who seemed preoccupied with their disease to the relative exclusion of other aspects of their lives.

Studies such as these highlight the growing body of evidence suggesting that suffering can be lessened while survival can be prolonged by psychological interventions. A word of caution: There is no conclusive evidence that the mind can cure cancer or other diseases. All the same, research shows that along with the bodies' own healing mechanisms and medical treatment, mental states and attitudes are associated with healing and can cause people to live longer in some cases (Cunningham, 2004, 2005; Greer, 2000, 2002). When Canadian researchers recently reviewed the last 30 years of research on mind–body connections in cancer outcomes, they concluded that the mind–cancer survival question must be seen as a legitimate and important area worthy of further exploration (Stephen, Rahn, Verhoef, & Leis, 2007).

Before Going On

- Describe Kübler-Ross's stages of dying and some alternate views of the dying process.
- How do people vary in the ways they adapt to impending death?

THE EXPERIENCE OF GRIEVING

In virtually every culture, the immediate response to a death is some kind of funeral ritual. However, a death ritual is only the first step in the process of **grieving**—the emotional response to a death—which may take months or years to complete.

grieving
the emotional response to a death

PSYCHOSOCIAL FUNCTIONS OF DEATH RITUALS

Funerals, wakes, and other death rituals help family members and friends manage their grief by giving them a specific set of roles to play. Like all roles, these include both expected behaviours and prohibited or discouraged behaviours. The content of these roles differs markedly from one culture to the next, but their clarity in most cases provides a shape to the days or weeks immediately following the death of a loved person. In Canadian society, the rituals prescribe what one should wear, who should be called, who should be fed, what demeanour one should show, and far more. Depending on one's ethnic or religious background, one may gather family and friends for a wake or to "sit shiva," a traditional Jewish 7-day period of mourning during which family members stay in the same home and formally mourn a deceased loved one. One may be expected to respond stoically or to wail and tear one's hair. Friends and acquaintances, too, have guiding rules, at least for those first few days. They may bring food, write letters of condolence, offer help, and attend wakes and funerals.

Death rituals also bring family members together as no other occasion does (with the possible exception of weddings). Frequently, cousins and other distant relatives see one another for the first time in many years at funerals. Such occasions typically inspire shared reminiscences and renew family relationships that have been inactive for a long time. In this way, death rituals can strengthen family ties, clarify the new lines of influence or authority within a family, and "pass the torch" in some way to the next generation. Likewise, funerals help to establish deaths as shared milestones for family members— "that was before Grandpa died"

Each culture has its own death rituals. The customarily quiet graveside service in Canada would seem strange to people in many other societies.
(*Photos:* left, Thinkstock; right, A. Ramey/Stock Boston)

or "the last time I saw her was at Grandpa's funeral." A death can become an important organizer of experience that separates the past from the present. Dividing time in this way seems to help survivors cope with grief (Katz & Bartone, 1998).

Death rituals are also designed to help the survivors understand the meaning of death itself, in part by emphasizing the meaning of the life of the person who has died. It is not accidental that most death rituals include testimonials, biographies, and witnessing. By telling the story of a person's life and describing that life's value and meaning, others can more readily accept the person's death.

Finally, death rituals may give some transcendent meaning to death itself by placing it in a philosophical or religious context (Pang & Lam, 2002). In this way, they provide comfort to the bereaved by offering answers to that inevitable question "Why?"

Critical Thinking

Do the various funerals or death rituals you have participated in seem to have served the purposes described in the text?

THE PROCESS OF GRIEVING

The ritual of a funeral, in whatever form it occurs, can provide structure and comfort in the days immediately following a death. But what happens when that structure is gone? How do people handle the sense of loss? Answering that question requires a look at a number of factors associated with grief.

AGE OF THE BEREAVED Children express feelings of grief very much the way teens and adults do (Auman, 2007). Like adults, children demonstrate grief through sad facial expressions, crying, loss of appetite, and age-appropriate displays of anger, such as temper tantrums (Oatley & Jenkins, 1996). Funerals seem to serve the same adaptive function for children as for adults, and most children resolve their feelings of grief within the first year after the loss. In addition, knowing that a loved one or even a pet is ill and in danger of death helps children cope with the loss in advance, just as it does for those who are older (Jarolmen, 1998).

Although the behavioural aspects of adolescents' grief responses vary little from those of adults, teens may be more likely to experience prolonged grief than children or adults. One study found that more than 20% of a group of high school students who had a friend killed in an accident continued to experience intense feelings of grief 9 months after the death (Dyregrov, Gjestad, Bie Wikander, & Vigerust, 1999). Adolescents may also grieve longer than children or adults for lost siblings; in some cases, teens continue to have problems with grief-related behaviours, such as intrusive thoughts about the deceased, for as long as 2 years after the death of a sibling (Lohan & Murphy, 2001/2002). Other research suggests that adolescent girls whose mothers have died run a particularly high risk of developing long-term, grief-related problems (Lenhardt & McCourt, 2000). Teenagers may also be more likely than adults to experience grief responses to the deaths of celebrities or to idealize peers' suicides.

Adolescents' grief responses are probably related to their general cognitive characteristics. You should remember from **Chapters 11** and **12** that adolescents often judge the real world by idealized images. Consequently, a teenager may become caught up in fantasizing about how the world would be different if a friend or loved one had not died. In addition, prolonged grieving among adolescents may be rooted in their tendency to engage in "what if" thinking. This kind of thinking may lead teens to believe that they could have prevented the death and, thus, cause them to develop irrational guilt feelings (Cunningham, 1996).

Connect to MyDevelopmentLab

What do you expect will happen when a loved one dies? What needs to be done to prepare for the funeral and for the grief that follows?

 Watch

MODE OF DEATH How an individual dies also contributes to the grief process of those who are in mourning. For example, widows who have cared for spouses during a period of illness prior to death are less likely to become depressed after the death than those whose spouses die suddenly (Carnelley, Wortman, & Kessler, 1999). Grief-related depression seems to emerge during the spouse's illness rather than after the death. The spouse's death is thought of as an escape from suffering for the one who dies and a release from grieving for the caregiver. Similarly, a death that has intrinsic meaning, such as that of a young soldier who dies defending his country, is not necessarily easier to cope with but does provide the bereaved with a sense that the death has not been without purpose (Malkinson & Bar-Tur, 1999). Consequently, mourners have a built-in cognitive coping device—a rational explanation for the death—that allows them to grieve but also protects them from long-term depression.

Sudden and violent deaths evoke more intense grief responses (Murphy, Johnson, & Lohan, 2003). One study found that 36% of widows and widowers whose spouses had died in accidents or by suicide were suffering from post-traumatic stress disorder (PTSD) symptoms (e.g., nightmares) 2 months after the death, compared with only 10% of widows and widowers whose spouses had died of natural causes (Zisook, Chentsova-Dutton, & Shuchter, 1998). Moreover, almost all those whose spouses had died unnaturally and who had PTSD symptoms were also depressed.

Death in the context of a natural disaster is also associated with prolonged grieving and development of symptoms of PTSD (Kilic & Ulusoy, 2003). Such events bring to mind the inescapable reality of the fragility of human life. Public memorial services in which the common experiences of survivors are recognized and the differences between controllable and noncontrollable aspects of life are emphasized can help survivors cope with this kind of grief.

Public memorials can also be helpful to survivors whose loved ones have died as a result of what might be called "politically motivated" mass murders, such as the terrorist attacks of September 11, 2001 (Shapiro, 2002). Moreover, political activism on the part of survivors aimed at preventing future events of this kind may be helpful to policy-makers and also may serve as a coping mechanism for those who engage in it (Shapiro, 2002).

By contrast, the most frustrating aspect of the grieving process for people who have lost a loved one through a violent crime is the inability to find meaning in the event (Currier, Holland, & Neimeyer, 2006). In the initial phases of the grief process, survivors protect themselves against such frustration through cognitive defenses, such as denial, and by focusing on tasks that are immediately necessary (Goodrum, 2005). Next, survivors often channel their grief and anger into the criminal justice process through which they hope that the perpetrator of the crime will be justly punished. Oftentimes, survivors eventually become involved in organizations that support crime victims and survivors of murdered loved ones or those that seek to prevent violence (Stetson, 2002).

Finally, suicide is associated with a unique pattern of responses among survivors (Bailley, Kral, & Dunham, 1999). In general, family and close friends of someone who commits suicide experience feelings of rejection and anger. Moreover, their grief over the loss of the loved one is complicated by the feeling that they could or should have done something to prevent the suicide. They are also less likely to discuss the loss with other family members or with friends because of their sense that a suicide in the family is a source of shame. For these reasons, suicide survivors may be more likely than others who have lost loved ones to experience long-term negative effects.

WIDOWHOOD

The relationship between the deceased and those who are in mourning affects the grieving process. For example, bereaved parents often report that their health is poorer after a child's death than it was before the death, and many parents continue to experience intense feelings of sadness for several years (Arbuckle & De Vries, 1995; Malkinson & Bar-Tur, 1999) (see **Development in the Real World**). Similarly, children who lose a sibling sometimes worry that thoughts produced by sibling rivalry, such as wishing a brother or sister would die, caused the death (Crehan, 2004). As a general rule, though, the most difficult death to recover from is that of a spouse (Kaslow, 2004).

WIDOWHOOD AND PHYSICAL HEALTH The experience of widowhood appears to have both immediate and longer-term effects on the immune system (Beem et al., 1999; Gallagher-Thompson, Futterman, Farberow, Thompson, & Peterson, 1993; Irwin & Pike, 1993). (The term *widowhood* applies to both men and women; *widow* refers to women and *widower* to men.) In one Norwegian study, researchers measured immune functioning in widows twice, shortly after their husbands' deaths and a year later (Lindstrom, 1997). Investigators found that the widows' immune systems were suppressed somewhat immediately after the death but in most cases had returned to normal a year later.

Similarly, a study comparing widows with married women in the Netherlands found that widows' immune responses continued to differ from those of married participants 7 months after the spouses' deaths (Beem et al., 1999). Interestingly, 7 months after the spouses' deaths, psychological differences (such as feelings of sadness) between the two groups had disappeared, though the immune function differences persisted. Thus, the bereaved may continue to suffer at a biochemical level even after obvious signs of grieving have subsided. Moreover, the association between death of a spouse and ensuing illness in a surviving partner may be the result of the effects of grief on the body's defences against disease agents, such as viruses and bacteria.

WIDOWHOOD AND MENTAL HEALTH In the year following bereavement, the incidence of depression among widows and widowers rises substantially, though rates of death and disease rise only slightly (Onrust & Cuijpers, 2006; Stroebe & Stroebe, 1993). In one important longitudinal study, researchers repeatedly interviewed a sample of 3000 adults, all age 55 or older at the beginning of the study (Norris & Murrell, 1990). Of these adults, 48 were widowed during the 2.5 years of the study, which allowed investigators to look at depression and health status before and immediately after bereavement. They found no differences in physical health between widowed and nonwidowed participants, but they did note a rise in depression among the widowed immediately following the loss and then a decline within a year after bereavement.

Development in the Real World

WHEN AN INFANT DIES

Morgan recently lost her 2-month-old son to SIDS. After the baby's death, she was determined to continue living as normal a life as possible, despite the overwhelming grief she felt. To that end, she went back to work immediately after the funeral and kept up all her social activities. She also forced herself to attend family gatherings, even though she feared having to talk about the experience. To her dismay, her co-workers and relatives kept their distance from her, almost as if they didn't know what to say to her about her child's death. Morgan was torn between the relief she felt over not having to talk too much about what had happened and a desperate need for others to somehow acknowledge her loss.

Many parents grieving for a lost infant do not receive adequate support from either their social networks or health professionals (Vaeisaenen, 1998). It is important for those who are in a position to support grieving parents to understand that the grief that follows the death of an infant is no less intense than any other kind of bereavement. In fact, it may be more complex.

When an older child dies, parents have a relationship history and an intimate knowledge of the child's personality on which to build reminiscences. Such cognitive devices help them reorganize their attachment to the lost child so that they are able to release the child psychologically.

But with an infant, there is little or no relationship history to draw on. The parents, of course, feel deep emotions of attachment, but the cognitive elements that help parents cope with the loss of a child are absent. For these reasons, bereaved parents of a dead infant often have a greater need for support from family, friends, and health professionals than even they themselves realize (Vaeisaenen, 1998).

Well-intentioned friends or family may pressure the couple to cope with their loss by simply replacing the infant with another one.

However, research suggests that starting another pregnancy soon after the loss of an infant doesn't necessarily end either a mother's or a father's grief, although it does tend to protect both against long-term negative effects such as depression (Franche & Bulow, 1999). Moreover, parents may fear that a subsequent child will also die in infancy and may try to avoid becoming emotionally attached to a newborn (Wong, 1993). This reaction could have adverse effects on the whole family.

Health professionals have compiled a few guidelines that can be useful to family members or friends in supporting parents who have lost an infant (Wong, 1993):

- Don't try to force bereaved parents to talk about their grief or the infant if they don't want to.
- Always refer to the deceased infant by name.
- Express your own feelings of loss for the infant, if they are sincere.
- Follow the parents' lead in engaging in reminiscences about the baby's looks or personality.
- Discourage the parents from resorting to drugs or alcohol to manage grief.
- Assure grieving parents that their responses are normal and it will take time to resolve the emotions associated with losing an infant.
- Don't pressure the parents to "replace" the baby with another one.
- Don't offer rationalizations (e.g., "Your baby's an angel now") that may offend the parents.
- Do offer support for the parents' own rationalizations.
- Be aware that the infant's siblings, even those who are very young, are likely to experience some degree of grief.

Other researchers have found that the metal health of older adults whose spouses have died differs for several years following the death from the mental health of peers whose spouses are still alive (Bennett, 1997). So, it appears that declines in physical and mental health follow bereavement fairly consistently, but how long such effects last may be highly variable. Several factors contribute to this variability.

One such factor is mental health history. Older adults who enter widowhood with a history of depression are more likely to experience depression after the death of their spouse (Zisook, Paulus, Shuchter, & Judd 1997). However, regardless of prior mental health, several variables have been associated with mental health problems following widowhood (Onrust, Cuijpers, Smit, & Bohlmeijer, 2007). In particular, depressive symptomology, anxiety, and somatic complaints related to psychological problems or stress were predicted by a combination of risk factors, including lower age, shorter duration of widowhood, the lack of social support (both actual and perceived), more physical illness/disabilites, and a lower sense of mastery (e.g., their perceived sense of influence over outcomes).

Economic changes that accompany the loss of a spouse also add to the overall stress involved in the transition to widowhood. Women typically suffer greater economic losses after the death of a spouse than men do, usually because they lose their husbands' income or pension (Zick & Holden, 2000). However, the household incomes of both widows and widowers are lower than those of married elders (Federal Interagency Forum on Aging-Related Statistics [FIFARS], 2006). Thus, the degree to which an individual's economic status changes as a result of a spouse's death is probably another factor that contributes to individual differences in the long-term effects of bereavement.

PATHOLOGICAL GRIEF Some psychologists argue that **pathological grief**, depression-like symptoms following the death of a loved one, should be thought of as a separate disorder from depression (Stroebe et al., 2000). They suggest that individuals who continue to experience grief symptoms, such as loss of appetite, more than 2 months following the loss of a loved one may be developing pathological grief.

Diagnosis and treatment of pathological grief may be important for preventing problems in both mental and physical health among widows and widowers. Researchers have found that widows and widowers whose grief symptoms continue for 6 months or longer are more likely to suffer long-term depression as well as physical ailments, such as cancer and heart disease (Prigerson et al., 1997). Moreover, they continue to show important differences in physical and mental functioning for up to 2 years after their spouse's death.

It's important to keep in mind, however, that many aspects of grief are culturally determined. Beliefs about how long mourning should last and how the bereaved should behave vary widely from one culture to another (Braun & Nichols, 1997; Rubin & Schechter, 1997). Thus, mental health professionals are advised to learn about an individual's cultural beliefs before forming conclusions about grief-related behaviour. Likewise, friends, neighbours, and co-workers of someone who is mourning the death of a spouse or other close family member should also be careful to interpret any grief-related behaviours within the context of the person's cultural background. Moreover, it is not unusual for nondepressed widows and widowers to express feelings of grief even decades after their spouses have died (Carnelley, Wortman, Bolger, & Burke, 2006).

pathological grief
symptoms of depression brought on by the death of a loved one

SEX DIFFERENCES The death of a spouse appears to be a more negative experience for men than for women, despite the fact that there seem to be no sex differences in the actual grieving process following such a loss (Lee & DeMaris, 2007). The risk of death from either natural causes or suicide in the months immediately after widowhood is significantly greater among men than among women (Stroebe & Stroebe, 1993). Depression and suicidal thoughts are also more common in widowers than in widows (Byrne & Raphael, 1999; Chen et al., 1999). Further, men seem to have a more difficult time than women do in returning to the levels of emotional functioning they exhibited before the spouse's death (van Grootheest, Beekman, van Groenou, & Deeg, 1999).

These differences are most often interpreted as yet another sign of the importance of social support. Social activities are very important in the lives of widows. In contrast, researchers have found that widowers withdraw from social activities to a far greater degree than widows do in the months immediately following bereavement (Bennett, 1998).

Some developmentalists have suggested that activities-oriented studies have led to a stereotype that characterizes widowers as lonely and isolated. In fact, research involving in-depth examinations of widowers' friendships, rather than of just their social activities, suggests that social relationships are very important in the lives of men who have lost a spouse (Riggs, 1997). Thus, differences in social involvement may be part of the explanation for sex differences in health and depression following the death of a spouse, but they do not appear to tell the whole story.

The results of a carefully designed longitudinal study of Australian widowers and married men over age 65 suggest that alcohol use may play a role in the greater prevalence of depression among widowers (Byrne, Raphael, & Arnold, 1999). Researchers found that more than twice as many widowers as married men (19% versus 8%) consumed five or more alcoholic drinks per day. Although alcohol may temporarily relieve unpleasant feelings of grief, it is a central nervous system depressant, and prolonged heavy drinking can lead to depression.

PREVENTING LONG-TERM PROBLEMS Some research suggests that the "talk-it-out" approach to managing grief can be helpful in preventing grief-related depression, especially when feelings are shared with others who have had similar experiences in the context of a support group (Francis, 1997). Research also indicates that developing a coherent personal narrative of the events surrounding the spouse's death helps widows and widowers manage grief (Neimeyer, Prigerson, & Davies, 2002). Participating in support groups, or even jointly recalling relevant events with close family members, can facilitate the formation of such stories. These interventions reinforce what researchers are now suggesting: The most important preventions of depression are those actions that promote a sense of mastery, or an internal locus-of-control, as well as actual and perceived social support (Onrust et al., 2007).

Clearly, this kind of psychosocial management of grief requires time. Mental health professionals advise employers that providing bereaved employees (especially those whose spouses have died) with sufficient time off to grieve may be critical to their physical and mental health. In the long run, illness and depression among bereaved workers who return to their jobs too soon may be more costly to employers than providing additional time off (Eyetsemitan, 1998).

Before Going On

- How do funerals and ceremonies help survivors cope with grief?
- How does grief affect the physical and mental health of widows and widowers?

Summary

The Experience of Death

- *Death* is a somewhat nonspecific term. Medical personnel refer to *clinical death* and *brain death*; *social death* occurs when the deceased person is treated like a corpse by those around the him.

- The great majority of adults in industrialized countries die in hospitals. Hospice care emphasizes

patient and family control of the dying process and palliative care rather than curative treatment.

The Meaning of Death Across the Lifespan

- Until about age 6 or 7, children do not understand that death is permanent and inevitable and involves loss of function. Teens understand the physical aspects of death much better than children do, but they sometimes have distorted ideas about it, especially in regard to their own mortality.

- Many young adults believe they possess unique characteristics that protect them from death. For middle-aged and older adults, death has many possible meanings: a signal of changes in family roles, a transition to another state (such as a life after death), and a loss of opportunity and relationships. Awareness of death may help a person organize her remaining time.

- Many adults prepare for death in practical ways, such as by buying life insurance, writing wills, and making living wills. Reminiscence may also serve as mental preparation. Closer to death, a person can seem less physically active and more psychologically disengaged.

The Process of Dying

- Kübler-Ross suggested five stages of dying: denial, anger, bargaining, depression, and acceptance.

Research fails to support the hypothesis that all dying adults go through all five stages or that the stages necessarily occur in this order. The emotion most commonly observed is depression.

- Research with terminally ill patients suggests that those who are most pessimistic and docile in response to diagnosis and treatment have shorter life expectancies. Those who fight hardest, and even display anger, live longer. Dying adults who have better social support, either from family and friends or through specially created support groups, also live longer than those who lack such support.

The Experience of Grieving

- Funerals and other rituals after death serve important functions, including defining roles for the bereaved, bringing family together, and giving meaning to the deceased's life and death.

- Grief responses depend on a number of variables. The age of the bereaved and the mode of death shape the grief process.

Review Questions

Answers are provided on MyDevelopmentLab in the Course Resources folder.

The Experience of Death

19.1 Which of the following is not an element of the philosophy of hospice care?
   a. Death is normal and should be faced and accepted.
   b. Medical care should be palliative not curative.
   c. The patient and the family should control decisions about the patient's care.
   d. Treatment should be provided by professionals trained in hospice procedures for palliative care.

The Meaning of Death Across the Lifespan

19.2 Which group of adults is most afraid of death?
   a. young adults
   b. middle-aged adults
   c. older adults
   d. men

The Process of Dying

19.3 An individual who says to her physician "You have made a mistake. I am not sick!" is most likely in the _____ stage of Kübler-Ross's model of psychological preparation for death.

   a. denial
   b. defence
   c. rejection
   d. stoicism

19.4 Research into the relationship between an individual's emotional response to impending or probable death and the actual outcome suggests, in general, that

   a. emotional response to a condition does not affect outcome or survival rate.
   b. difficult patients who express their anger and hostility openly die sooner.
   c. individuals who question, challenge, and have a fighting spirit experience a more difficult recovery experience.
   d. emotional responses contribute to disease progress.

The Experience of Grieving

19.5 Which of the following is not a suggestion for friends and family members supporting parents who have lost an infant?

   a. Don't refer to the deceased infant by name.
   b. Don't offer rationalizations that may offend the parents.
   c. Assure the grieving parents that their responses are normal.
   d. Express your own feelings of loss for the infant, if they are sincere.

Critical-Thinking Questions

19.6 What role do age and fear of death play in people's decisions about death preparations, such as living wills and prepaid funeral arrangements?

19.7 In what ways is Kübler-Ross's model helpful to health care professionals who work with terminal patients, and in what ways might the model interfere with their responses to the needs of patients?

Policy Question

Do People Have a Right to Die?

One element of having greater control over the process of dying might be the ability to choose the timing of death—a highly controversial topic. Today, most medical ethicists distinguish between two forms of euthanasia (also known as *mercy killing*). *Passive euthanasia* occurs when a person (typically, a physician) hastens a death by not using life support systems or medication that would prolong the life or by withdrawing life support or other treatment that may be keeping a patient alive. *Active euthanasia* occurs when a physician or other individual (at a patient's request) hastens the patient's death by active means, such as by administering a fatal dose of a drug. Alternatively, when a patient intentionally ends his life with the help of a physician or other individual, the action is referred to as *assisted suicide*.

LIVING WILLS

There is little controversy about passive euthanasia. Most people agree that individuals should be able to determine the degree to which life-support technology will be used to delay their own deaths. Thus, an increasing number of adults have made living wills, specifying that life-support systems or resuscitation should not be used in case of their clinical death or near death. Such living wills essentially ask physicians to participate in passive euthanasia.

All Canadian provinces, except for New Brunswick, have legislation that recognizes the directives expressed in living wills. In Canada, living wills have several formats, depending on which province or territory you live in. These living wills are, and may be known variously as, an *advanced directive*, a *health care directive*, or *powers of attorney for personal care*. A living will generally contains two essential elements: a proxy directive, which specifies who you deem to be responsible to make health care decisions on your behalf if you are no longer able to make your wishes known to others; and an instruction directive, which specifies the health care or other personal care choices that can be fulfilled by you or someone else (your designated proxy) on your behalf. The living will can include any combination of consent or refusal to consent to a diagnostic, therapeutic, preventative, or palliative treatment.

THE ASSISTED SUICIDE DEBATE

By contrast, assisted suicide is far less common and much more controversial. The debate over physician-assisted suicide has been brought to public attention in North America by the actions of Dr. Jack Kevorkian, a physician who has helped several terminally ill or severely handicapped individuals end their own lives. A 2007 Ipsos-Reid poll found that three-quarters (76%) of Canadians surveyed support the notion of the patient's "right to die" and 71% belive that doctor-assisted suicide for terminally ill patients should be legal. Although widespread support of assisted suicide for the terminally ill exists, support is highest among those with a university degree (79%) and somewhat less among those without a high school diploma (38%). Nonetheless, assisted suicides are still illegal in Canada. Doctors also have a legal obligation to prevent patients from harming themselves in a case where there is a risk of suicide.

Assisted suicide is fully and explicitly legal in only a few places in the world: the

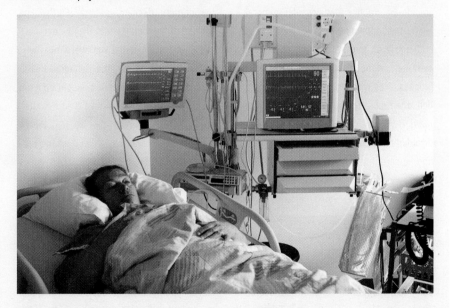

Many hospitals now specifically ask terminal patients during the admission process how they want to be treated in the event that they become mentally incapacitated.
(*Photo:* © Ariadna de Raadt/Shutterstock)

Netherlands, Belgium, Switzerland, and the State of Oregon (CBC News, 2009). The Netherlands passed the first active euthanasia law in 2001. This law essentially legalized the long-standing Dutch custom of providing terminally ill patients with lethal doses of pain-killing drugs ("Dutch Senate OKs Doctor-Assisted Suicide," 2001). Individuals who wish to die must be terminally ill and have no hope of recovery, and must obtain the approval of two physicians. Children under 12 are prohibited from requesting to die, and those between 12 and 15 must have parental consent. The parents of a 16- or 17-year-old must be notified of the child's request but do not have the right to prevent the assisted suicide from being carried out. Since 2001, the only other country that has managed to legalize active euthanasia is Belgium.

Many of those who oppose active euthanasia believe that each individual life is sacred. They believe that decisions about when to end life should be subject only to divine authority. These critics also view assisted suicide as just another form of suicide—a practice they consider immoral.

Other opponents argue against active euthanasia on the grounds that it might be extremely difficult to set limits on the process, even with strict guidelines—a position often labelled *the slippery slope argument* (Twycross, 1996). Advocates for the disabled have been particularly vocal in putting forward this point of view (Smith, 2004), especially in the aftermath of controversial cases, such as the Saskatchewan farmer, Robert Latimer, who was sentenced to life imprisonment for the death (by means of truck engine exhaust) of his daughter, Tracy, who suffered from a severe form of cerebral palsy that resulted in constant and excruciating pain. They claim that once assisted suicide becomes widely viewed as morally acceptable, society may come to the point

where those who are infirm or severely disabled will be subtly (or not so subtly) encouraged to end their own lives to relieve others of the burden of their care. Such critics even fear that things might reach a point where physicians would administer fatal drugs without the patient's consent.

A third argument against any form of active euthanasia is that modern pain management techniques allow even those with extremely painful terminal illnesses to be comfortable in the last days or weeks of their lives. Thus, it is not necessary to hasten death to prevent pain. Over a decade ago, long-time Canadian hospice care advocate Harry van Bommel reasoned that it's not only the fear of death, but also the fear of dying alone or in pain or of creating hardship for others that had helped to feed the pro-euthanasia movement. He suggested that the real fears about the quality of life that a dying person holds could be assuaged with an alternate form of care; namely, a Canadian style of hospice palliative care that meets the full range of human needs in which the patient and family are the primary decision-makers. Further, he warned of the danger that if palliative care and home care initiatives were not supported formally within the Canadian health care policy, then euthanasia would be seen as the only viable alternative (van Bommel, 1992, 2002).

For these reasons, as well as the personal religious beliefs of some, about three-quarters of a sample of 3000 oncologists (physicians who specialize in treating cancer) in a survey carried out by the National Institutes of Health were found to oppose active euthanasia of any kind (Emanuel et al., 2000). Instead, they advocate palliative-care education for all physicians to make them aware of the benefits of hospice care as well as the most effective ways of relieving patients' pain. They also suggest that physicians treating

terminal patients engage their patients in frank discussions about pain relief as early in the course of their illness as possible. Through such discussions, doctors and patients can decide together what pain relief measures will be taken.

Studies involving patients who refuse treatments, such as chemotherapy, suggest that such individuals often want to live as long as possible; however, they do not want to go through the difficulties associated with the treatments (Abrams, 1998). Such findings suggest that observers should be cautious about jumping to the conclusion that a person who doesn't want medical treatment is also interested in hastening death.

Opponents of assisted suicide also question terminally ill patients' psychological fitness for making the decision to end their lives.

Some fear that such patients may be depressed and that a request to hasten death is really no different from any other kind of suicide attempt. In other words, it is an act born of emotional despair, not rationality. The distinction is important, they say, because the philosophical rationale of assisted suicide laws is that choosing to die involves a rational decision-making process.

To address this concern, assisted suicide legislation would have to include a mandatory waiting period between a request for death and the fulfilment of the request. During the waiting period, a psychologist or psychiatrist would be responsible for assessing the mental state of the patient to determine whether she is competent to make the life-ending decision. University of Calgary psychologists Kim Galbraith and Keith Dobson (2000) suggest that in the event that assisted suicide or euthanasia were legalized in Canada, psychologists would play a vital and prominent role in helping patients with end-of-life decisions and with determining the competency of the terminally ill patient to make an informed rational decision.

Those who favour assisted suicide legislation note that modern medical technology has increasingly made it possible to prolong life well past the point at which death, in earlier decades, would naturally have occurred. Further, proponents of assisted suicide argue that many terminal patients are unable to carry out their own suicides, and therefore require the help of a physician. However, opponents counter that asking another person to help with a suicide is a far cry from giving a person "death with dignity." As Jörg-Dietrich Hoppe, a leading voice for German physicians who oppose assisted suicide expressed it, "Everyone has the right to a dignified death, but nobody has the right to be killed" (as cited in Cohen, 2001, April 12).

YOUR TURN

- Find out from a local medical association or health unit whether hospitals and physicians in your area generally honour living wills. Does your province or territory require medical personnel to ask all hospitalized people whether they have a living will?

- The medical association or health unit should also be able to tell you whether your province or territory allows family members to authorize health professionals to terminate aspects of care, such as tube feeding, in cases where a terminally ill or seriously injured individual can't speak for himself.

- Has anyone in your province or territory ever been prosecuted for helping a dying person hasten death? If so, what were the circumstances and outcome of the case(s)?

- Are there efforts underway in your province or territory to legalize assisted suicide? If so, what do opinion polls suggest about public support for such laws?

GLOSSARY

ability goals goals based on a desire to be superior to others *329*

accommodation changing a scheme as a result of some new information *43*

achievement test a test designed to assess specific information learned in school *263*

activities of daily living (ADLs) self-help tasks such as bathing, dressing, and using the toilet *477*

activity theory the idea that it is normal and healthy for older adults to try to remain as active as possible for as long as possible *506*

adaptive reflexes reflexes, such as sucking, that help newborns survive; some adaptive reflexes persist throughout life *96*

affect dysregulation an interaction pattern in which a caregiver's emotional responses to an infant interfere with the baby's ability to learn how to regulate his or her emotions *154*

affectional bond the emotional tie to an infant experienced by a parent *149*

ageism a prejudicial view of older adults that characterizes them in negative ways *10*

aggression behaviour intended to injure another person or damage an object *225*

alcoholism physical and psychological dependence on alcohol *439*

Alzheimer's disease a very severe form of dementia, the cause of which is unknown *490*

ambivalent attachment a pattern of attachment in which the infant shows little exploratory behaviour, is greatly upset when separated from the parent, and is not reassured by his or her return or efforts to comfort him *155*

amenity move postretirement move away from kin to a location that has some desirable feature, such as year-round warm weather *525*

amnion fluid-filled sac in which the fetus floats until just before it is born *65*

amygdala an almond-shaped brain structure that plays a key role in the regulation of defensive emotions like fear and anger *182*

anorexia nervosa an eating disorder characterized by self-starvation *320*

anoxia oxygen deprivation experienced by a fetus during labour and/or delivery *86*

assessment formal and informal methods of gathering information that can be used for programming to improve student learning. No grades or marks are associated with assessment. *263*

assimilation the process of using schemes to make sense of events or experiences *43*

assisted human reproduction (AHR) "any activity undertaken for the purpose of facilitating human reproduction" (Health Canada, 2001a) *58*

association areas parts of the brain where sensory, motor, and intellectual functions are linked *250*

assortative mating (homogamy) a sociologist's term for the tendency to mate with someone who has traits similar to one's own *402*

atherosclerosis narrowing of the arteries caused by deposits of plaque, a fatty substance *436*

attachment the emotional tie to a parent experienced by an infant, from which the child derives security *150*

attachment theory the view that the ability and need to form an attachment relationship early in life are genetic characteristics of all human beings *149*

Attention-Deficit/Hyperactivity Disorder (ADHD) a mental disorder that causes children to have difficulty attending to and completing tasks *269*

atypical development development that deviates from the typical developmental pathway *12*

auditory acuity how well one can hear *108*

authoritarian parenting style a style of parenting that is low in nurturance and communication, but high in control and maturity demands *213*

authoritative parenting style a style of parenting that is high in nurturance, maturity demands, control, and communication *213*

automaticity the ability to recall information from long-term memory without using short-term memory capacity *259*

avoidant attachment a pattern of attachment in which an infant avoids contact with the parent and shows no preference for the parent over other people *155*

avoidant couples partners who agree to disagree and who minimize conflict by avoiding each other *404*

axons tail-like extensions of neurons *67*

babbling the repetitive vocalizing of consonant-vowel combinations by an infant *136*

balanced approach reading instruction that combines explicit phonics instruction with other strategies for helping children acquire literacy *262*

behaviour genetics the study of the role of heredity in individual differences 28

behaviourism the view that defines development in terms of behaviour changes caused by environmental influences 39

bicultural identity personal identification and satisfaction with more than one culture 344

bilingual education an approach to second-language education in which children receive instruction in two different languages 271

bioecological systems theory Bronfenbrenner's theory that explains development in terms of the relationships among individuals and their environments, or interconnected contexts 51

body mass index (BMI) a ratio of weight to height that estimates healthy and unhealthy body composition 77

brain death absence of vital signs, including brain activity; resuscitation is no longer possible 532

bulimia an eating disorder characterized by binge eating and purging 320

bullying the unjust use of power to wilfully, deliberately, and repeatedly upset or hurt another person, their property, reputation, or social acceptance 294

burnout lack of energy, exhaustion, and pessimism that results from chronic stress 464

career development the process of adapting to the workplace, managing career transitions, and pursuing goals through employment 415

caregiver burden a term for the cumulative negative effects of caring for an elderly or disabled person 462

case study an in-depth examination of a single individual 16

cell bodies the part of a neuron that contains the cell body and is the site of vital cell functions 66

cell migration the movement of cells to their genetically predetermined destinations in the body 79

cell proliferation the increase in cell numbers by means of cell growth and cell division 79

centration the young child's tendency to think of the world in terms of one variable at a time 184

cephalocaudal pattern growth that proceeds from the head downward 63

chromosomes strings of genetic material in the nuclei of cells 23

class inclusion the understanding that subordinate classes are included in larger, superordinate classes 257

classical conditioning learning that results from the association of stimuli 39

climacteric the years of middle or late adulthood in both men and women during which reproductive capacity declines or is lost 426

clinical death a period during which vital signs are absent but resuscitation is still possible 531

clique four to six young people who appear to be strongly attached to one another 361

cognitive domain changes in thinking, memory, problem-solving, and other intellectual skills 8

cognitive theories theories that emphasize mental processes in development, such as logic and memory 42

cohort a group of individuals who share the same historical experiences at the same times in their lives 11

colic an infant behaviour pattern involving intense bouts of crying, totalling 3 or more hours a day 98

companionate relationships relationships in which grandparents have frequent contact and warm interactions with grandchildren 460

compensatory (kinship) migration a move to a location near family or friends that happens when an elder requires frequent help because of a disability or a disease 525

concrete operational stage Piaget's third stage of cognitive development, during which children construct schemes that enable them to think logically about objects and events in the real world 256

congenital anomaly an abnormality present at birth 70

conservation the understanding that matter can change in appearance without changing in quantity 185

conservation the understanding that matter can change in appearance without changing in quantity 257

contingent responsiveness being sensitive to the child's verbal and nonverbal cues and responding appropriately 156

continuity theory the idea that older adults adapt life-long interests and activities to the limitations imposed on them by physical aging 506

control group a group in an experiment that receives either no special treatment or a neutral treatment 17

conventional morality in Kohlberg's theory, the level of moral reasoning in which judgments are based on rules or norms of a group to which the person belongs 349

cooing making repetitive vowel sounds, particularly the *uuu* sound 136

corpus callosum the structure that connects the right and left hemispheres of the cerebral cortex 176

correlation a relationship between two variables that can be expressed as a number ranging from -1.00 to $+1.00$ 17

creativity the ability to produce original, appropriate, and valuable ideas and/or solutions to problems 445

criminality antisocial behaviour that includes lawbreaking 354 critical period a specific period in development when an organism is especially sensitive to the presence (or absence) of some particular kind of experience *11*

cross-gender behaviour behaviour that is atypical for one's own sex but typical for the opposite sex *240*

cross-linking the formation of undesirable bonds between proteins or fats *484*

cross-modal transfer transfer of information from one sense to another, as happens when an infant can recognize by feel a toy he has seen but never before felt *118*

cross-sectional design a research design in which groups of different ages are compared *13*

crowd a combination of cliques, which includes both males and females *361*

cryopreservation preserving cells or tissues through a freezing process that stops all biological activity *58*

crystallized intelligence knowledge and judgment acquired through education and experience *390*

decentration thinking that takes multiple variables into account *256*

deductive logic a type of reasoning, based on hypothetical premises, that requires predicting a specific outcome from a general principle *256*

defence mechanisms strategies for reducing anxiety, such as repression, denial, or projection, proposed by Freud *33*

deferred imitation imitation that occurs in the absence of the model who first demonstrated it *124*

dementia a neurological disorder involving problems with memory and thinking that affect an individual's emotional, social, and physical functioning *488*

dendrites branch-like protrusions from the cell bodies of neurons *67*

deoxyribonucleic acid (DNA) a chemical material that makes up chromosomes and genes *23*

dependent variable the characteristic or behaviour that is expected to be affected by the independent variable *18*

depth perception ability to judge the relative distances of objects *112*

developmental psychology the scientific study of age-related changes in our bodies, behaviour, thinking, emotions, social relationships, and personalities *2*

dialectical thought a form of thought involving recognition and acceptance of paradox and uncertainty *388*

difficult temperament a predisposition for irregular sleeping and eating cycles, emotional negativity and irritability, and resistance to change *159*

Disability-Adjusted Life Years (DALY) a measure of the gap between a population's ideal and actual levels of health. It is derived from the number of life-years lost to premature death, illness, or injury and the number of years living with a disability. It assumes a potential life limit of 82½ years for women and 80 for men. *370*

discipline training, whether physical, mental, or moral, that develops self-control, moral character, and proper conduct *214*

disengagement theory the theory that it is normal and healthy for older adults to scale down their social lives and to separate themselves from others to a certain degree *506*

dishabituation responding to a somewhat familiar stimulus as if it were new *111*

disorganized/disoriented attachment a pattern of attachment in which an infant seems confused or apprehensive and shows contradictory behaviour, such as moving toward the parent while looking away from him or her *155*

dominant-recessive pattern a pattern of inheritance in which a single dominant gene influences a person's phenotype but two recessive genes are necessary to produce an associated trait *25*

dyslexia problems in reading or the inability to read *269*

easy temperament a predisposition to approaching new events positively, displaying predictable sleeping and eating cycles, being generally happy, and adjusting easily to change *159*

Eating Well with Canada's Food Guide guidelines for a balanced and healthy diet based on the four major food groups: vegetables and fruits, grain products, milk and alternatives, and meat and alternatives *101*

eclecticism the use of multiple theoretical perspectives to explain and study human development *52*

ego according to Freud, the thinking element of personality *33*

ego integrity the feeling that one's life has been worthwhile *504*

ego integrity versus despair stage the last of Erikson's psychosocial stages, in which older adults must achieve a sense of satisfaction with their lives *504*

egocentrism the young child's belief that everyone sees and experiences the world the way she does *184*

embryonic stage the second stage of prenatal development, from week 2 through week 8, during which the embryo's organ systems form *65*

embryonic stem cells undifferentiated cells found in the zygote and blastocyst that are capable of indefinite self-replication and differentiation into specialized cells *472*

emerging adulthood the period from the late teens to early 20s when individuals explore options prior to committing to adult roles *398*

emotional regulation the ability to control emotional states and emotion-related behaviour *233*

empiricists theorists who argued that perceptual abilities are learned *110*

English-as-a-second-language (ESL) program an approach to second-language education in which children attend English classes for part of the day and receive most of their academic instruction in English *271*

enriched daycare daycare that provides structured programming to build skills, such as literacy, numeracy, social, art, and physical skills *168*

epigenetic factors inheritable and acquired gene regulation patterns that alter gene function (phenotype) without changing gene structure (genotype) *27*

epigenetics the study of the gene regulation patterns that alter gene function (phenotype) without changing gene structure (genotype) *27*

epigenome the sum total of inherited and acquired molecular modifications to the genome that leads to changes in gene regulation without changing the DNA sequence of the genome *27*

epimutagens agents that cause abnormal gene silencing or expression without changing the genomic DNA *80*

episodic memories recollections of personal events *443*

equilibration the process of balancing assimilation and accommodation to create schemes that fit the environment *43*

esteem needs the need for a person to have a sense of value and acceptance based, in part, on their experience of respect and admiration from others and on their perceived self-confidence and self-worth *37*

ethnic identity a sense of belonging to an ethnic group *344*

ethnography a detailed description of a single culture or context *18*

ethology a perspective on development that emphasizes genetically determined survival behaviours presumed to have evolved through natural selection *28*

evaluation the process of assigning a grade or mark to a student's performance, representing the student's highest, most consistent level of achievement over time *264*

evolutionary developmental psychology the view that genetically inherited cognitive and social characteristics that promote survival and adaptation appear at different times across the lifespan *29*

evolutionary psychology the view that genetically inherited cognitive and social characteristics have evolved through natural selection *29*

exceptional child a child who has special learning needs; the term refers to students with disabilities as well as gifted students *267*

executive processes information-processing skills that involve devising and carrying out strategies for remembering and problem-solving *260*

experiment a study that tests a causal hypothesis *17*

experimental group the group in an experiment that receives the treatment the experimenter thinks will produce a particular effect *17*

expressive language the ability to use sounds, signs, or symbols to communicate meaning *139*

expressive style a style of word learning characterized by low rates of noun-like terms and high use of personal-social words and phrases *142*

expressive vocabulary the words whose meaning is used correctly when speaking *197*

extended family a social network of grandparents, aunts, uncles, cousins, and so on *223*

extinction the gradual elimination of a behaviour through repeated nonreinforcement *40*

false belief principle the ability to look at a problem or situation from another person's point of view and discern what kind of information would cause that person to believe something that isn't true *187*

fast-mapping the ability to categorically link new words to real-world referents *193*

fetal stage the third stage of prenatal development, from week 9 to birth, during which growth and organ refinement take place *66*

fluid intelligence the aspect of intelligence that reflects fundamental biological processes and does not depend on specific experiences *390*

fluid reasoning the ability to manipulate and use information in a reasoning process *199*

foreclosure in Marcia's theory, the identity status of a person who has made a commitment without having gone through a crisis. The person has simply accepted a parentally or culturally defined commitment *339*

formal operational stage the fourth of Piaget's stages, during which adolescents learn to reason logically about abstract concepts *325*

frail elderly seniors whose physical and/or mental impairments are so extensive that they cannot care for themselves *478*

free radicals molecules or atoms that possess an unpaired electron *485*

functional magnetic resonance imaging (fMRI) a form of Magnetic Resonance Imaging (MRI) that records what regions of the brain are active during specific mental activities *182*

functional status a measure of an individual's ability to perform certain roles and tasks, particularly self-help tasks and other chores of daily living (Havens & Finlayson, 1999) 477

gametes cells that unite at conception (ova in females; sperm in males) 57

gender constancy the understanding that gender is a component of the self that is not altered by external appearance 236

gender constancy theory Kohlberg's assertion that children must understand that gender is a permanent characteristic before they can adopt appropriate sex roles 236

gender identity the ability to correctly label oneself and others as male or female 237

gender schema theory an information-processing approach to gender concept development that asserts that people use a schema for each gender to process information about themselves and others 236

gender stability the understanding that gender is a stable, lifelong characteristic 237

gender the psychological and social associates and implications of biological sex 235

gender-role identity gender-related aspects of the psychological self 341

gene expression when a gene sequence is activated ("turned on") and ready to be translated into gene products—proteins, for the most part 27

gene silencing when a gene sequence is made inactive ("turned off") and is prevented from being translated into gene products—proteins, for the most part 27

generativity a sense that one is making a valuable contribution to society by bringing up children or mentoring younger people in some way 450

generativity versus stagnation stage the seventh of Erikson's stages, in which middle-aged adults find meaning in contributing to the development of younger individuals 450

genes complex chemical units of a chromosome that control or influence inherited traits 23

genital stage in Freud's theory, the period during which people reach psychosexual maturity 337

genome all the DNA that an organism possesses 23

genotype an individual's unique genetic blueprint 25

geriatric dysthymia chronic depressed mood in older adults 493

germinal stage the first stage of prenatal development, beginning at conception and ending at implantation (approximately 2 weeks) 63

gerontology the scientific study of aging 475

glial cells specialized cells in the brain that support neurons 67

gonads sex glands (ovaries in females; testes in males) 65

goodness of fit the degree to which an infant's temperament is adaptable to his or her environment, and vice versa 161

grammatical words words that pertain to the rules of language and proper sentence construction, such as articles, prepositions, and auxiliaries 138

grieving the emotional response to a death 546

habituation a decline in attention that occurs because a stimulus has become familiar 111

handedness a strong preference for using one hand or the other that develops between 3 and 5 years of age 178

Hayflick limit the theoretical proposal that each species is subject to a genetically programmed time limit after which cells no longer have any capacity to replicate themselves accurately 484

Health-Adjusted Life Expectancy (HALE) an estimate of life expectancy at birth. It is the number of years that a newborn can expect to live in full health given current rates of morbidity and mortality. 370

hippocampus a brain structure that is essential for the formation of memories 177

holism the view that the whole is greater than the sum of its parts 50

holophrases combinations of gestures and single words that convey more meaning than just the word alone 140

hospice care a holistic approach to care for the terminally ill that emphasizes individual and family control of the process of dying 532

hostile/detached couples partners who fight regularly, rarely look at each other, and lack affection and support 404

hostile/engaged couples partners who have frequent arguments and lack the balancing effect of humour and affection 404

human genomics the study of the human genome including the location of genes, their function and their role in disease processes 31

hypothetico-deductive reasoning the ability to derive conclusions from hypothetical premises 325

id in Freud's theory, the part of the personality that comprises a person's basic sexual and aggressive impulses; it contains the libido and motivates a person to seek pleasure and avoid pain 33

identity achievement in Marcia's theory, the identity status achieved by a person who has been through a crisis and reached a commitment to ideological or occupational goals 338

identity an understanding of one's unique characteristics and how they have been, are, and will be manifested across ages, situations, and social roles 338

identity crisis Erikson's term for the psychological state of emotional turmoil that arises when an adolescent's sense of self becomes "unglued" so that a new, more mature sense of self can be achieved 338

identity diffusion in Marcia's theory, the identity status of a person who is not in the midst of a crisis and who has made no commitment 339

identity versus role confusion in Erikson's theory, the stage during which adolescents attain a sense of who they are 338

imaginary audience an internalized set of behavioural standards usually derived from a teenager's peer group 326

implantation attachment of the blastocyst to the uterine wall 65

independent variable the presumed causal element in an experiment 18

Individual Education Plan (IEP) a written document containing learning and behavioural objectives for the exceptional student, a description of how the objectives will be achieved, and how the objectives will be evaluated 268

inductive discipline a discipline strategy in which parents explain to children why a punished behaviour is wrong 216

inductive logic a type of reasoning in which general principles are inferred from specific experiences 256

industry versus inferiority stage the fourth of Erikson's psychosocial stages, during which children develop a sense of their own competence through mastery of culturally defined learning tasks 278

infant mortality death within the first year of life 105

infant-directed speech (IDS) the simplified, higher-pitched speech that adults use with infants and young children 135

infantile amnesia the inability of adults and older children to remember more than a few events that took place before they were 3 years of age 177

inflections additions to words that change their meaning (e.g., the *s* in toys, the *ed* in waited) 140

inflections grammatical markers attached to words to indicate tense, gender, number, and the like, such as the use of the ending *ed* to mark the past tense of a verb in English 193

information-processing theory theoretical perspectives that use the computer as a model to explain how the mind manages information 44

institutional migration a move to an institution, such as a nursing home, that is necessitated by a disability 525

instrumental activities of daily living (IADLs) more complex daily living tasks such as doing housework, cooking, and managing money 477

intelligence quotient (IQ) the ratio of mental age to chronological age; also, a general term for any kind of score derived from an intelligence test 198

intelligence the ability to take in information and use it to adapt to the environment 133

interactionist model the theory that development results from complex reciprocal interactions between multiple personal and environmental factors 9

interactionists theorists who argue that language development is a subprocess of general cognitive development and is influenced by both internal and external factors 135

intersensory integration coordination of information from two or more senses, as happens when an infant knows which mouth movements go with which sounds 118

intimacy the capacity to engage in a supportive, affectionate relationship without losing one's own sense of self 396

intimacy versus isolation Erikson's early adulthood stage, in which an individual must find a life partner or supportive friends to avoid social isolation 396

intimate partner abuse physical acts or other behaviour intended to intimidate or harm an intimate partner 381

involved relationships relationships in which grandparents are directly involved in the everyday care of grandchildren or have close emotional ties with them 460

joint attention when two people are focusing their attention on an object and each is aware that the other is attending to that same object 164

kin-keeper a family role, usually occupied by a woman, which includes responsibility for maintaining family and friendship relationships 412

language acquisition device (LAD) an innate language processor, theorized by Chomsky, that contains the basic grammatical structure of all human language 135

lateralization the process through which brain functions are divided between the two hemispheres of the cerebral cortex 177

learning disability a disorder in which a child has difficulty mastering a specific academic skill, even though she possesses average to above-average intelligence and has no physical or sensory handicaps 266

learning theories theories that assert that development results from an accumulation of experiences 38

lexical words words with a high level of meaning, such as nouns, verbs, adjectives, and adverbs 138

libido in Freud's theory, an instinctual drive for physical pleasure present at birth that forms the motivating force behind virtually all human behaviour 33

life events approach a theoretical perspective on middle adulthood that focuses on normative and non-normative events and how adults in this age group respond to them *453*

life review an evaluative process in which elders make judgments about past behaviour *505*

life structure a key concept in Levinson's theory: the underlying pattern or design of a person's life at a given time, which includes roles, relationships, and behaviour patterns *397*

lifespan perspective the current view of developmentalists that changes happen throughout the entire human lifespan and that changes must be interpreted in light of the culture and context in which they occur; thus, interdisciplinary research is critical to understanding human development *8*

limbic system the part of the brain that regulates emotional responses *371*

locus of control a set of beliefs about the causes of events *346*

longitudinal design a research design in which people in a single group are studied at different times in their lives *13*

low birth weight (LBW) newborn weight below 2500 grams *88*

macronutrients large amounts of carbohydrates, fats, and proteins that are needed for energy and for body- and brain-building elements *102*

maximum oxygen uptake (VO₂ max) a measure of the body's ability to take in and transport oxygen to various body organs *375*

mean length of utterance (MLU) the average number of meaningful units in a sentence *141*

means–end behaviour purposeful behaviour carried out in pursuit of a specific goal *123*

memory strategies learned methods for remembering information *260*

menarche the beginning of the menstrual cycle *305*

menopause the cessation of monthly menstrual cycles in middle-aged women *427*

metacognition knowledge about how the mind thinks and the ability to control and reflect on one's own thought processes *191*

metamemory knowledge about how memory works and the ability to control and reflect on one's own memory function *191*

micronutrients essential vitamins and minerals that are needed in small amounts to regulate physical and mental processes *103*

mitochondrial inheritance a pattern of inheritance in which a cell's mitochondrial DNA (mtDNA) is inherited from the mother's egg and not the father's sperm *27*

modified program changes in the curriculum so that the modified outcomes differ from those of the standard curriculum *267*

moral realism stage the first of Piaget's stages of moral development, in which children believe rules are inflexible *286*

moral relativism stage the second of Piaget's stages of moral development, in which children understand that many rules can be changed through social agreement *286*

moratorium in Marcia's theory, the identity status of a person who is in a crisis but who has made no commitment *339*

motherhood earnings gap a measure showing how much the earnings of women with children are below those of women without children *411*

motives internal factors or conditions that tend to initiate, direct, or sustain behaviour *37*

multifactorial inheritance a pattern of inheritance affected by both genes and the environment *27*

multi-infarct dementia a form of dementia caused by one or more strokes *492*

mutagens agents that cause changes (mutations) in genomic DNA *79*

myelinization a process in neuronal development in which sheaths made of a substance called myelin gradually cover individual axons and electrically insulate them from one another to improve the conductivity of the nerve *96*

naming explosion the period when toddlers experience rapid vocabulary growth, typically beginning between 16 and 24 months *140*

nativism the view that humans possess unique genetic traits that will be manifested in all members of the species, regardless of differences in their environments *28*

nativists theorists who claimed that perceptual abilities are inborn *110*

naturalistic observation the process of studying people in their normal environments *16*

neonate baby between birth and 1 month of age *87*

neo-Piagetian theory an approach that uses information-processing principles to explain the developmental stages identified by Piaget *46*

neurons specialized cells of the nervous system *65*

neuroplasticity the ability of the brain to reorganize brain structures in response to experience *95*

niche-picking the process of selecting experiences on the basis of temperament *161*

norms average ages at which developmental milestones are reached *5* numeracy the knowledge and skills required to effectively manage the mathematical demands of diverse situations (Statistics Canada, 2008b) 197

obese a body weight with a high percentage of body fat, which is associated with an increased risk for serious diseases and health problems (i.e., BMI > 30) 251

obesogenic environments environments in which social influences and context contribute to obesity in individuals or populations 178

object concept an infant's understanding of the nature of objects and how they behave 127

object individuation the process by which an infant differentiates and recognizes distinct objects based on their mental images of objects in the environment 129

object permanence the understanding that objects continue to exist when they can't be seen 124

objective (categorical) self the toddler's understanding that she or he is defined by various categories, such as gender, or qualities, such as shyness 162

observational learning, or modelling learning that results from seeing a model reinforced or punished for a behaviour 47

operant conditioning learning to repeat or stop behaviours because of their consequences 39

operational efficiency a neo-Piagetian term that refers to the maximum number of schemes that can be processed in working memory at one time 189

organogenesis process of organ growth 65

osteoporosis loss of bone mass with age, resulting in more brittle and porous bones 430

overregularization attachment of regular inflections to irregular words, such as the substitution of goed for went 194

overweight a body weight with a high percentage of body fat, which is associated with an increased risk for health problems (i.e., BMI > 25) 251

palliative care a form of care that seeks to prevent, relieve, or soothe the patients' symptoms rather than cure their diseases or disorders 533

parental investment theory the theory that sex differences in mate preferences and mating behaviour are based on the different amounts of time and effort men and women must invest in child-rearing 400

pathological grief symptoms of depression brought on by the death of a loved one 551

pelvic inflammatory disease (PID) an infection of the female reproductive tract that may result from a sexually transmitted disease and can lead to infertility 312

perimenopausal phase the stage of menopause during which estrogen and progesterone levels are erratic, menstrual cycles may be very irregular, and women begin to experience symptoms such as hot flashes 428

permissive parenting style a style of parenting that is high in nurturance and low in maturity demands, control, and communication 213

person perception the ability to classify others according to categories such as age, gender, and race 208

personal fable the belief that the events of one's life are controlled by a mentally constructed autobiography 326

personality a pattern of responding to people and objects in the environment 159

personality disorder an inflexible pattern of behaviour that leads to difficulty in educational, occupational, and social functioning 386

phenotype an individual's whole set of observable characteristics 25

phonological awareness children's understanding of the sound patterns of the language they are acquiring 194

physical domain changes in the size, shape, and characteristics of the body 8

pituitary gland gland that triggers other glands to release hormones 304

placenta specialized organ that allows substances to be transferred from mother to embryo and from embryo to mother without their blood mixing 65

polygenic inheritance a pattern of inheritance in which many genes influence a trait 26

postconventional morality in Kohlberg's theory, the level of moral reasoning in which judgments are based on an integration of individual rights and the needs of society 349

postformal thought types of thinking that are associated with a hypothesized fifth stage of cognitive development 388

postmenopausal phase the last stage of menopause; a woman is postmenopausal when she has had no menstrual periods for at least a year 428

post-secondary education any formal educational experience that follows high school 391

preconventional morality in Kohlberg's theory, the level of moral reasoning in which judgments are based on authorities outside the self 348

predictive-adaptive responses the prenate's ability to use information about the current environment to adjust its physiology in anticipation that it will match future environmental conditions and optimize the chances to survive and reproduce in adulthood 30

preference technique a research method in which a researcher keeps track of how long a baby looks at each of two objects shown 111

premenopausal phase the stage of menopause during which estrogen levels fall somewhat, menstrual periods are less regular, and anovulatory cycles begin to occur 427 preoperational stage Piaget's second stage of cognitive development, during which children become proficient in the use of symbols in thinking and communicating but still have difficulty thinking logically *183*

presbycusis cardiovascular disease (CVD) a set of disease processes in the heart and circulatory system *436*

presbyopia normal loss of visual acuity with aging, especially the ability to focus the eyes on near objects *432*

primary aging (senescence) age-related physical changes that have a biological basis and are universally shared and inevitable *370*

primary circular reactions Piaget's phrase to describe a baby's simple repetitive actions in substage 2 of the sensorimotor stage; the actions are organized around the baby's own body *122*

primary sex characteristics the sex organs: ovaries, uterus, and vagina in the female; testes and penis in the male *305*

primitive reflexes reflexes, controlled by "primitive" parts of the brain, that disappear during the first year of life *96*

processing efficiency the ability to make efficient use of short-term memory capacity *259*

program accommodation the adjustment of teaching methods to help a child with special needs achieve the outcomes of the standard curriculum *267*

Programme for International Student Assessment (PISA) a worldwide assessment of how well 15-year-olds can apply their academic ability to solve real-life problems *331*

programmed senescence theory the view that age-related declines are the result of species-specific genes for aging *484*

prosocial behaviour behaviour intended to help another person *229*

proteins organic compounds, consisting of amino acids, that perform most life functions and make up the majority of cellular structures *24*

proximodistal pattern growth that proceeds from the middle of the body outward *63*

psychoanalytic theories theories proposing that developmental change happens because of the influence of internal drives and emotions on behaviour *33*

psychological self a person's understanding of his or her enduring psychological characteristics *280*

psychosexual stages Freud's five stages of personality development through which children move in a fixed sequence determined by maturation; the libido is centred in a different body part in each stage *34*

psychosocial stages Erikson's eight stages, or crises, of personality development in which inner instincts interact with outer cultural and social demands to shape personality *34*

puberty collective term for the physical changes that culminate in sexual maturity *304*

punishment any immediate consequence that follows a behaviour and decreases the likelihood that the behaviour will be repeated *39*

qualitative change a change in kind or type *9*

Quality-Adjusted Life Years (QALY) a measure of how much benefit is gained, and at what cost, for any particular physical or mental intervention. It provides an estimate of the time a person will live at different levels of health over his or her remaining years of life. *370*

quantitative change a change in amount *9*

reaction range a range between upper and lower boundaries for traits such as intelligence, which is established by one's genes; one's environment determines where, within those limits, one will fall *203*

reactive attachment disorder a disorder that appears to prevent a child from forming close social relationships *150*

receptive language comprehension of spoken language *138*

receptive vocabulary the words that are understood when heard *197*

reciprocal determinism a process of human development based on the interaction of personal, behavioural, and environmental factors *47*

referential style a style of word learning characterized by emphasis on things and people and their naming and description *142*

reflective judgment the ability to identify the underlying assumptions of differing perspective on controversial issues *388*

reinforcement any immediate consequence that follows a behaviour and increases the likelihood that the behaviour will be repeated *39*

relational aggression aggression aimed at damaging another person's self-esteem or peer relationships, such as by ostracism or threats of ostracism, cruel gossiping, or facial expressions of disdain *293*

relative right-left orientation the ability to identify right and left from multiple perspectives *250*

relativism the idea that some propositions cannot be adequately described as either true or false *388*

religious coping the tendency to turn to religious beliefs and institutions for support in times of difficulty *511*

reminiscence reflecting on past experience *505*

remote relationships relationships in which grandparents do not see their grandchildren often *459* research ethics the guidelines researchers follow to protect the rights of animals used in research and humans who participate in studies *19*

retaliatory aggression aggression to get back at someone who has hurt you *293*

reticular formation the part of the brain that regulates attention *96*

reversibility the understanding that both physical actions and mental operations can be reversed *256*

role conflict any situation in which two or more roles are at least partially incompatible, either because they call for different behaviours or because their separate demands add up to more hours than there are in the day *453*

role strain the strain experienced by an individual whose own qualities or skills do not measure up to the demands of some role *453*

role-taking the ability to look at a situation from another person's perspective *351*

satiety the feeling of fullness that follows a meal *487*

scaffolding a process in which the learning of new cognitive skills is guided by someone who is more skilled *46*

schematic learning organization of experiences into expectancies, called schemas, which enable infants to distinguish between familiar and unfamiliar stimuli *131*

scheme in Piaget's theory, an internal cognitive structure that provides an individual with a procedure to follow in a specific circumstance *43*

schizophrenia a serious mental disorder characterized by disturbances of thought such as delusions and hallucinations *387*

secondary aging age-related changes that are due to social and environmental influences, poor health habits, or disease *370*

secondary circular reactions Piaget's phrase to describe the repetitive actions in substage 3 of the sensorimotor period; the actions are oriented around external objects *122*

secondary sex characteristics body parts such as breasts in females and pubic hair in both sexes *305*

secular trend the decline in the average age of menarche, along with changes such as an increase in average height for both children and adults, that happened between the mid-19th and mid-20th centuries in Western countries and occurs in developing nations when nutrition and health improve *306*

secure attachment a pattern of attachment in which an infant readily separates from the parent, seeks proximity when stressed, and uses the parent as a safe base for exploration *155*

selective attention the ability to focus cognitive activity on the important elements of a problem or a situation *249*

selective optimization with compensation the process of balancing the gains and losses associated with aging *441*

self-actualization the process of fulfilling one's unique personal potential *37*

self-care children children who are at home by themselves after school for an hour or more each day *297*

self-efficacy the belief in one's own capacity to cause an intended event to occur or to perform a task *48*

self-esteem a global evaluation of one's own worth *282*

self-regulation children's ability to conform to parental standards of behaviour without direct supervision *288*

semantic memories recollections of general knowledge, facts, and word meanings *443*

semiotic (symbolic) function the understanding that one object or behaviour can represent another *183*

senescence physical changes and declines associated with aging *484*

sensitive period a span of months or years during which a child may be particularly responsive to specific forms of experience or particularly influenced by their absence *11*

sensorimotor stage Piaget's first stage of development, in which infants use information from their senses and motor actions to learn about the world *122*

separation anxiety expressions of discomfort, such as crying, when separated from an attachment figure *153*

sequential design a research design that combines cross-sectional and longitudinal examinations of development *13*

sex-typed behaviour different patterns of behaviour exhibited by boys and girls *239*

sexual assault any form of sexual activity with another person without his or her consent *383*

shaping the reinforcement of intermediate steps until an individual learns a complex behaviour *41*

short-term storage space (STSS) neo-Piagetian theorist Robbie Case's term for the working memory *189*

slow-to-warm-up temperament a predisposition for inactivity and turning away from and adjusting slowly to unfamiliar people and new experiences. They display mild signs of negativity and discomfort. *159*

social clock a set of age norms that defines a sequence of life experiences that is considered normal in a given culture and that all individuals in that culture are expected to follow *10*

social death the point at which family members and medical personnel treat the deceased person as a corpse *532* social domain changes in variables that are associated with the relationship of an individual to others *8*

social referencing infants' use of others' facial expressions as a guide to their own emotions *153*

social role theory the idea that sex differences in mate preferences and mating behaviour are adaptations to gender roles *402*

social skills a set of behaviours that usually leads to being accepted as a play partner or friend by peers *224*

social status an individual child's classification as popular, rejected, or neglected *294*

social-cognitive theory the theoretical perspective that asserts that social and personality development in early childhood is related to improvements in the cognitive domain *208*

sociobiology the study of society using the methods and concepts of biology; when used by developmentalists, an approach that emphasizes genes that aid group survival *29*

sociocultural theory Vygotsky's view that complex forms of thinking have their origins in social interactions rather than in an individual's private explorations *46*

somatic or adult stem cells non-embryonic stem cells found in differentiated tissue that are capable of self-replicating and differentiating into the kind of tissue from which they originated *472*

spatial cognition the ability to infer rules from and make predictions about the movement of objects in space *250*

spatial perception the ability to identify and act on relationships between objects in space *250*

stages qualitatively distinct periods of development *10*

states of consciousness different states of sleep and wakefulness in infants *97*

stranger anxiety expressions of discomfort, such as clinging to the mother, in the presence of strangers *153*

subjective self an infant's awareness that she or he is a separate person who endures through time and space and can act on the environment *162*

successful aging the term gerontologists use to describe maintaining one's physical health, mental abilities, social competence, and overall satisfaction with one's life as one ages *507*

sudden infant death syndrome (SIDS) the term used to describe the sudden and unexpected death of an apparently healthy infant *105*

superego Freud's term for the part of personality that is the moral judge *33*

survey a data collection method in which participants respond to questions *17*

synapses tiny spaces across which neural impulses flow from one neuron to the next *67*

synaptic plasticity the redundancy in the nervous system that ensures that it is nearly always possible for a nerve impulse to move from one neuron to another or from a neuron to another type of cell (e.g., a muscle cell) *481*

synaptic pruning process by which unused or unnecessary neural pathways and connections are eliminated *95*

synaptogenesis the process of synapse development *95*

synchrony a mutual, interlocking pattern of attachment behaviours shared by a parent and a child *151*

systematic problem-solving the process of finding a solution to a problem by testing single factors *325*

systems approach the view that personal factors together with external factors form a dynamic integrated system *50*

task goals goals based on a desire for self-improvement *329*

telegraphic speech simple two- or three-word sentences that usually include a noun and a verb *140*

telomere string of repetitive DNA at the tip of each chromosome in the body that appears to serve as a kind of timekeeping mechanism *484*

temperament inborn predispositions, such as activity level, that form the foundations of personality *159*

teratogens substances such as viruses and drugs that can cause birth defects *72*

terminal drop hypothesis the hypothesis that mental and physical functioning decline drastically only in the few years immediately preceding death *485*

tertiary circular reactions deliberate experimentation with variations of previous actions that occurs in substage 5 of the sensorimotor period *123*

thanatology the scientific study of death and dying *543*

The Big Five a set of five major dimensions of personality, including extraversion, agreeableness, conscientiousness, neuroticism, and openness/intellect *278*

theory of mind a set of ideas constructed by a child or an adult to explain other people's ideas, beliefs, desires, and behaviour *188*

time-out removing the child from the situation and from attention and rewards for a short period of time, typically one minute for every year of the child's age, in order to stop unwanted behaviour *214*

tinnitus a persistent ringing in the ears *482*

tracking the smooth movements of the eye used to follow the track of a moving object *107*

trait a stable pattern of responding to situations *278*

transgendered a person whose psychological gender is the opposite of his or her biological sex *315*

true sleep the number of minutes of sleep time excluding all periods of wakefulness, which can be distinguished by electroencephalograph (EEG) activity *270*

type A personality pattern a personality type associated with greater risk of coronary heart disease. It includes competitive achievement striving, a sense of time urgency, and, sometimes, hostility or aggressiveness. *437*

umbilical cord organ that connects the embryo to the placenta *65*

underweight a body weight with a low percentage of body fat, which is associated with an increased risk for health problems (i.e., BMI < 18.5) *251*

uninvolved parenting style a style of parenting that is low in nurturance, maturity demands, control, and communication *213*

unique invulnerability the belief that bad things, including death, happen only to others *537*

validating couples partners who express mutual respect, even in disagreements, and are good listeners *403*

viability ability of the fetus to survive outside the womb *66*

victimization repeated, intentional acts that single someone out for hostile, exploitive, unfair, or vindictive treatment *294*

visual acuity how well one can see details at a distance *107*

vitrification the use of cryoprotectants along with rapid cooling to prevent the fluid in biological tissues (e.g., eggs, semen, embryos) from forming ice crystals (that act like glass shards on cell structures) and from dehydrating. The tissue becomes an intact, non-crystalline, glass-like solid that can be preserved for years. *59*

volatile couples partners who argue a lot and don't listen well, but still have more positive than negative interactions *403*

volunteerism performance of unpaid work for altruistic motives *509*

wellness a measure of optimal holistic health *50*

wisdom a hypothesized cognitive characteristic of older adults that includes accumulated knowledge and the ability to apply that knowledge to practical problems of living *499*

zone of proximal development signifies tasks that are too hard for a child to do alone but that can be managed with guidance *46*

zygote a single cell created when sperm and ovum unite *58*

REFERENCES

Abdelrahman, A., Rodriguez, G., Ryan, J., French, J., & Weinbaum, D. (1998). The epidemiology of substance use among middle school students: The impact of school, familial, community and individual risk factors. *Journal of Child & Adolescent Substance Abuse, 8,* 55–75.

Abengozar, C., Bueno, B., & Vega, J. (1999). Intervention on attitudes toward death along the life span. *Educational Gerontology, 25,* 435–447.

Abma, J., & Martinez, G. (2006). Childlessness among older women in the United States: Trends and profiles. *Journal of Marriage and Family, 68,* 1045–1056.

Abraham, J.D., & Hansson, R.O. (1995). Successful aging at work: An applied study of selection, optimization, and compensation through impression management. *Journals of Gerontology: Psychological Sciences, 50B,* P94–P103.

Abrams, E.J., Matheson, P.B., Thomas, P.A., Thea, D.M., Krasinski, K., Lambert, G., . . . New York City Perinatal HIV Transmission Collaborative Study Group (1995). Neonatal predictors of infection status and early death among 332 infants at risk of HIV-1 infection monitored prospectively from birth. *Pediatrics, 96,* 451–458.

Abrams, R. (1998). Physician-assisted suicide and euthanasia's impact on the frail elderly: Something to think about. *Journal of Long Term Home Health Care: The Pride Institute Journal, 17,* 19–27.

Accardo, P., Tomazic, T., Fete, T., Heaney, M., Lindsay, R., & Whitman, B. (1997). Maternally reported fetal activity levels and developmental diagnoses. *Clinical Pediatrics, 36,* 279–283.

Ackerman, S., Zuroff, D., & Moskowitz, D. (2000). Generativity in midlife and young adults: Links to agency, communion and subjective well-being. *Aging and Human Development, 50,* 17–41.

Active Healthy Kids Canada (2010). *Healthy habits start earlier than you think: The Active Healthy Kids Canada Report Card on physical activity for children and youth.* Toronto, ON: Author. Retrieved from www.activehealthykids.ca/ecms.ashx/2010ActiveHealthyKidsCanadaReportCard-longform.pdf

Adams, C. (1991). Qualitative age differences in memory for text: A life-span developmental perspective. *Psychology and Aging, 6,* 323–336.

Adams, M., & Henry, M. (1997). Myths and realities about words and literacy. *School Psychology Review, 26,* 425–436.

Addis, M., & Mahalik, J. (2003). Men, masculinity, and the contexts of help seeking. *American Psychologist, 58,* 5–14.

Adelman, W., & Ellen, J. (2002). Adolescence. In A. Rudolph, R. Kamei, & K. Overby (Eds.), *Rudolph's fundamentals of pediatrics* (3rd ed.; pp. 70–109). New York, NY: McGraw-Hill.

Adelmann, P.K. (1994). Multiple roles and physical health among older adults: Gender and ethnic comparisons. *Research on Aging, 16,* 142–166.

Adesman, A.R. (1996). Fragile X syndrome. In A.J. Capute & P.J. Accardo (Eds.), *Developmental disabilities in infancy and childhood: Vol. II. The spectrum of developmental disabilities* (2nd ed., pp. 255–269). Baltimore, MD: Paul H. Brookes.

Adi-Japha, E., & Klein, P.S. (2009). Relations between parenting quality and cognitive performance of children experiencing varying amounts of childcare. *Child Development, 80*(3), 893–906.

Adkins, V. (1999). Grandparents as a national asset: A brief note. *Activities, Adaptation, & Aging, 24,* 13–18.

Adlaf, E.M., & Paglia, A. (2003a). *Drug use among Ontario students 1977–2003: OSDUS highlights* (CAMH Research Document Series, No. 14). Retrieved from Centre for Addiction and Mental Health website: www.camh.net/pdf/OSDUS03_Drug_Report_highlights.pdf

Adlaf, E.M., & Paglia, A. (2003b). *Drug use among Ontario students 1977–2003: Detailed OSDUS findings* (CAMH Research Document Series, No. 13). Retrieved from Centre for Addiction and Mental Health website: www.camh.net/pdf/OSDUS03-drugdetail-final.pdf

Agahi, N., Ahacic, K., & Parker, M. (2006). Continuity of leisure participation from middle age to old age. *The Journals of Gerontology Series B: Psychological Sciences and Social Sciences, 61,* S340–S346.

Agnew, J., Dorn, C., & Eden, G. (2004). Effect of intensive training on auditory processing and reading skills. *Brain & Language, 88,* 21–25.

Ahadi, S.A., & Rothbart, M.K. (1994). Temperament, development, and the Big Five. In C.F. Halverson, Jr., G.A. Kohnstamm, & R.P. Martin (Eds.), *The developing structure of temperament and personality from infancy to adulthood* (pp. 189–207). Hillsdale, NJ: Erlbaum.

Ahituv, A., & Lehman, R. (2004). *Job turnover, wage rates, and marital stability.* Retrieved from Urban Institute website: www.urban.org

Ahmad, G., & Najam, N. (1998). A study of marital adjustment during first transition to parenthood. *Journal of Behavioural Sciences, 9,* 67–86.

Ainsworth, M.D.S. (1989). Attachments beyond infancy. American Psychologist, 44, 709–716.

Ainsworth, M.D.S., Blehar, M., Waters, E., & Wall, S. (1978). Patterns of attachment. Hillsdale, NJ: Erlbaum.

Ainsworth, M.D.S., & Marvin, R.S. (1995). On the shaping of attachment theory and research: An interview with Mary D.S. Ainsworth (Fall 1994). *Monographs of the Society for Research in Child Development, 60* (244, Nos. 2–3), 3–21.

Akers, J., Jones, R., & Coyl, D. (1998). Adolescent friendship pairs: Similarities in identity status development, behaviors, attitudes, and interests. *Journal of Adolescent Research, 13,* 178–201.

Akiba, D. (1998). Cultural variations in body esteem: How young adults in Iran and the United States view their own appearances. *The Journal of Social Psychology, 138,* 539–540.

Akiyama, H., Antonucci, T., Takahashi, K., & Langfahl, E. (2003). Negative interactions in close relationships across the life span. *Journals of Gerontology, Series B: Psychological Sciences & Social Sciences, 58B,* P70–P79.

Aksu-Koc, A.A., & Slobin, D.I. (1985). The acquisition of Turkish. In D.I. Slobin (Ed.), *The crosslinguistic study of language acquisition: Vol. 1: The data* (pp. 839–878). Hillsdale, NJ: Erlbaum.

Alcock, K.J., Holding, P.A., Mung'ala-Odera, V., & Newton, C.R.J.C. (2008). Constructing tests of cognitive abilities for schooled and unschooled children. *Journal of Cross-Cultural Psychology, 39,* 529–551.

Aleixo, P., & Norris, C. (2000). Personality and moral reasoning in young offenders. *Personality & Individual Differences, 28,* 609–623.

Alexander, G., & Hines, M. (1994). Gender labels and play styles: Their relative contribution to children's selection of playmates. *Child Development, 65,* 869–879.

Allaz, A., Bernstein, M., Rouget, P., Archinard, M., & Morabia, A. (1998). Body weight preoccupation in middle-aged and ageing women: A general population survey. *International Journal of Eating Disorders, 23,* 287–294.

Allen, C., & Kisilevsky, B. (1999). Fetal behavior in diabetic and non-diabetic pregnant women: An exploratory study. *Developmental Psychobiology, 35,* 69–80.

Allen, K.R., & Pickett, R.S. (1987). Forgotten streams in the family life course: Utilization of qualitative retrospective interviews in the analysis of lifelong single women's family careers. *Journal of Marriage and the Family, 49,* 517–526.

Allen, M. (2004). Minority language school systems: A profile of students, schools and communities. *Education Quarterly Review, 9*(4), 9–29.

Allen, W., Dreves, R., & Ruhe, J. (1999). Reasons why college-educated women change employment. *Journal of Business & Psychology, 14,* 77–93.

Almeida, O., Waterreus, A., Spry, N., Flicker, L., & Martins, R. (2004). One year follow-up study of the association between chemical castration, sex hormones, beta–amyloid, memory and depression in men. *Psychoneuroendocrinology, 29,* 1071–1081.

Alsaker, F.D., & Olweus, D. (1992). Stability of global self-evaluations in early adolescence: A cohort longitudinal study. *Journal of Research on Adolescence, 2,* 123–145.

Alsop, S. (1973). *Stay of execution.* New York, NY: Lippincott.

Alspaugh, J. (1998). Achievement loss associated with the transition to middle school and high school. *Journal of Educational Research, 92,* 20–25.

Alzheimer Society of Canada (2010). *Rising tide: The impact of dementia on Canadian society.* Toronto, ON: Author. Retrieved from www.alzheimer.ca/docs/RisingTide/Rising%20Tide_Full%20Report_Eng_FINAL_Secured%20version.pdf

Amato, P.R. (1993). Children's adjustment to divorce: Theories, hypotheses, and empirical support. *Journal of Marriage and the Family, 55,* 23–38.

Amato, S. (1998). Human genetics and dysmorphy. In R. Behrman & R. Kliegman (Eds.), *Nelson essentials of pediatrics* (3rd ed., pp. 129–146). Philadelphia, PA: W.B. Saunders.

Ambert, A. (1998). Divorce: Facts, figures and consequences. Ottawa, ON: The Vanier Institute of the Family. Retrieved from www.vifamily.ca/pubs/divorce.htm

Ambert, A. (2002). *Divorce: Facts, causes, and consequences.* Ottawa, ON: The Vanier Institute of the Family. Retrieved from www.vifamily.ca/library/cft/divorce.pdf

Ambert, A. (2003). *Cohabitation and marriage: Are they equivalent?* Ottawa, ON: The Vanier Institute of the Family. Retrieved from the York University Facutly of Arts website: www.arts.yorku.ca/soci/ambert/writings/cohabitation.html

Ambert, A. (2005). Cohabitation and marriage: How are they related? Ottawa, ON: The Vanier Institute of the Family. Retrieved from www.vifamily.ca/library/cft/cohabitation.pdf

Amenedo, E., & Diaz, F. (1998). Aging-related changes in processing of non-target and target stimuli during an auditory oddball task. *Biological Psychology, 48,* 235–267.

Amenedo, E., & Diaz, F. (1999). Aging-related changes in the processing of attended and unattended standard stimuli. *Neuroreport: For Rapid Communication of Neuroscience Research, 10,* 2383–2388.

American Academy of Pediatrics. (2009). Where we stand: TV viewing time. Retrieved from www.healthychildren.org/English/Pages/default.aspx

American Psychiatric Association. (2000). *Diagnostic and statistical manual of mental disorders* (4th ed., text revision). Washington, DC: Author.

Ames, E.W. (1997). *The development of Romanian orphanage children adopted to Canada: Final report.* Ottawa, ON: National Welfare Grants Program, Human Resources Development Canada.

Amieva, H., Lentenneur, L., Dartigues, J., Rouch-Leroyer, I., Sourgen, C., D'Alchée-Birée, F., . . . Fabrigoule C. (2004). Annual rate and predictors of conversion to dementia in subjects presenting mild cognitive impairment criteria defined according to a population-based study. *Dementia & Geriatric Cognitive Disorders, 18,* 87–93.

Amor, D.J., Bentley, K., Ryan, J., Perry, J., Wong, L., Slater, H., et al. (2004). Human centromere repositioning 'in progress'. Proceedings of the National Academy of Sciences of the United States of America, 101(17), 6542–6547.

Anderman, E. (1998). The middle school experience: Effects on the math and science achievement of adolescents with LD. *Journal of Learning Disabilities, 31,* 128–138.

Anderman, E., & Midgley, C. (1997). Changes in achievement goal orientations, perceived academic competence, and grades across the transition to middle-level schools. *Contemporary Educational Psychology, 22,* 269–298.

Anderman, E., Maehr, M., & Midgley, C. (1999). Declining motivation after the transition to middle school: Schools can make a difference. *Journal of Research & Development in Education, 32,* 131–147.

Anderman, L. (1999). Classroom goal orientation, school belonging and social goals as predictors of students' positive and negative affect following the transition to middle school. *Journal of Research & Development in Education, 32,* 89–103.

Anderman, L., & Anderman, E. (1999). Social predictors of changes in students' achievement goal orientations. *Contemporary Educational Psychology, 24,* 21–37.

Andersen, R.E. (2000). The spread of the childhood obesity epidemic. *Canadian Medical Association Journal, 163*(11), 1461–1462.

Anderson, C.A. (2004). An update on the effects of violent video games. *Journal of Adolescence, 27*(1), 113–122.

Anderson, C.A., Carnagey, N.L., Flanagan, M., Benjamin, A.J., Eubanks, J., & Valentine, J.C. (2004). Violent video games: Specific effects of violent content on aggressive thoughts and behavior. In M. Zane (Ed.), *Advances in experimental social psychology, Vol. 36.* New York, NY: Elsevier.

Anderson, C.A., Gentile, D.A., & Buckley, K.E. (2007). *Violent video game effects on children and adolescents: Theory, research, and public policy.* New York, NY: Oxford University Press.

Anderson, D.R., Huston, A.C., Schmitt, K.L., Linebarger, D.L., & Wright, J.C. (2001). Early childhood television viewing and adolescent behavior: The recontact study. *Monographs of the Society for Research in Child Development, 66*(1):I–VIII, 1–147.

Anderson, K.M., Castelli, W.P., & Levy, D. (1987). Cholesterol and mortality: 30 years of follow-up from the Framingham study. *Journal of the American Medical Association, 257,* 2176–2180.

Anderson, L.M., & Anderson, J. (2009). Barney and breakfast: messages about food and eating in preschool television shows and how they may impact the development of eating behaviours in children. *Early Child Development and Care.* doi: 10.1080/03004430903040516

Anderson, R. (1998). Examining language loss in bilingual children. *Electronic Multicultural Journal of Communication Disorders, 1.*

Anderson, S., Dallal, G., & Must, A. (2003). Relative weight and race influence average age at menarche: Results from two nationally representative surveys of U.S. girls studied 25 years apart. *Pediatrics, 111,* 844–850.

Andreou, E., & Metallidou, P. (2004). The relationship of academic and social cognition to behaviour in bullying situations among Greek primary school children. *Educational Psychology, 24*(1), 27–41.

Andrews, M., Dowling, W., Bartlett, J., & Halpern, A. (1998). Identification of speeded and slowed familiar melodies by younger, middle-aged, and older musicians and nonmusicians. *Psychology & Aging, 13,* 462–471.

Angier, N. (1992, June 9). Clue to longevity found at chromosome tip. *New York Times,* pp. B5, B9.

Anglin, J.M. (1993). Vocabulary development: A morphological analysis. *Monographs of the Society for Research in Child Development, 58* (Serial No. 238).

Anglin, J.M. (1995, March). *Word learning and the growth of potentially knowable vocabulary.* Paper presented at the biennial meetings of the Society for Research in Child Development, Indianapolis, IN.

Anisfeld, M. (1991). Neonatal imitation. *Developmental Review, 11,* 60–97.

Annett, M. (2003). Do the French and the English differ for hand skill asymmetry? Handedness subgroups in the sample of Doyen and Carlier (2002) and in English schools and universities. *Laterality: Asymmetries of Body, Brain & Cognition, 8,* 233–245.

Anthony, J., & Lonigan, C. (2004). The nature of phonological awareness: Converging evidence from four studies of preschool and early grade school children. *Journal of Educational Psychology, 96,* 43–55.

Anthony, J.C., & Aboraya, A. (1992). The epidemiology of selected mental disorders in later life. In J.E. Birren, R.B. Sloane, & G.D. Cohen (Eds.), *Handbook of mental health and aging* (2nd ed., pp. 28–73). San Diego, CA: Academic Press.

Antonucci, T., Lansford, J., & Akiyama, H. (2001). Impact of positive and negative aspects of marital relationships and friendships on well-being of older adults. *Applied Developmental Science, 5,* 68–75.

Antonucci, T.C. (1990). Social supports and social relationships. In R.H. Binstock & L.K. George (Eds.), *Handbook of aging and the social sciences* (3rd ed., pp. 205–226). San Diego, CA: Academic Press.

Antrop, I., Roeyers, H., Van Oost, P., & Buysse, A. (2000). Stimulation seeking and hyperactivity in children with ADHD. *Journal of Child Psychology, Psychiatry & Allied Disciplines, 41,* 225–231.

Anway, M.D., Cupp, A.S., Uzumcu, M., & Skinner, M.K. (2005). Epigenetic transgenerational actions of endocrine disruptors and male fertility. *Science, 308*(5727), 1466–1469.

Apgar, V.A. (1953). A proposal for a new method of evaluation of the newborn infant. *Current Research in Anesthesia and Analgesia, 32,* 260–267.

Aquilino, W.S., & Supple, K.R. (1991). Parent-child relations and parent's satisfaction with living arrangements when adult children live at home. *Journal of Marriage and the Family, 53,* 13–27.

Aranha, M. (1997). Creativity in students and its relation to intelligence and peer perception. *Revista Interamericana de Psicologia, 31,* 309–313.

Arbuckle, N.W., & De Vries, B. (1995). The long-term effects of later life spousal and parental bereavement on personal functioning. *The Gerontologist, 35,* 637–647.

Archer, J. (2004). Sex differences in aggression in real-world settings: A meta-analytic review. *Review of General Psychology, 8*(4), 291–322. doi: 10.1037/1089-2680.8.4.291

Ardelt, M., & Koenig, C.S. (2006). The role of religion for hospice patients and relatively healthy older adults. *Research on Aging, 28*(2), 184–215.

Arnett, J. (1998). Risk behavior and family role transitions during the twenties. Journal of Youth & Adolescence, 27, 301–320.

Arnett, J.J. (2000). Emerging adulthood. A theory of development from the late teens through the twenties. *American Psychologist, 55*(5), 469–480.

Arnett, J.J. (2004). *Emerging adulthood: The winding road from the late teens through the twenties.* Toronto, ON: Oxford University Press.

Arnold, D.H., Lonigan, C.J., Whitehurst, G.J., & Epstein, J.N. (1994). Accelerating language development through picture book reading: Replication and extension to a videotape training format. *Journal of Educational Psychology, 86*(2), 235–243.

Aronen, E.T., Paavonen, E., Fjällberg, J., Soininen, M., & Törrönen, J. (2000). Sleep and psychiatric symptoms in school-age children. *Journal of the American Academy of Child & Adolescent Psychiatry, 39*(4), 502–508.

Arrindell, W., & Luteijn, F. (2000). Similarity between intimate partners for personality traits as related to individual levels of satisfaction with life. Personality & Individual Differences, 28, 629–637.

Asbjornsen, A., Obrzut, J., Boliek, C., Myking, E., Holmefjord, A., Reisaeter, S., . . . & Moller, P. (2005). Impaired auditory attention skills following middle-ear infections. *Child Neuropsychology, 11,* 121–133.

Asendorpf, J.B., Warkentin, V., & Baudonnière, P. (1996). Self-awareness and other-awareness. II: Mirror self-recognition, social contingency awareness, and synchronic imitation. *Developmental Psychology, 32,* 313–321.

Ashkar, P., & Kenny, D. (2007). Moral reasoning of adolescent male offender: Comparison of sexual and nonsexual offenders. *Criminal Justice and Behavior, 34,* 108–118.

Aslin, R. (1987). Motor aspects of visual development in infancy. In N. P. Salapatek & L. Cohen (Eds.), *Handbook of infant perception: Vol. 1. From sensation to perception* (pp. 43–113). Orlando, FL: Academic Press.

Association of Reproductive Health Professionals. (2000). *Mature sex.* Retrieved from www.ahrp.org/maturesex

Astington, J., & Jenkins, J. (1999). A longitudinal study of the relation between language and theory-of-mind development. *Developmental Psychology, 35,* 1311–1320.

Astington, J.W., & Gopnik, A. (1991). Theoretical explanations of children's understanding of the mind. In G.E. Butterworth, P.L. Harris, A.M. Leslie, & H.M. Wellman (Eds.), *Perspectives on the child's theory of mind* (pp. 7–31). New York, NY: Oxford University Press.

Astington, J.W., & Jenkins, J.M. (1995, March). *Language and theory of mind: A theoretical review and a longitudinal study.* Paper presented at the biennial meetings of the Society for Research in Child Development, Indianapolis, IN.

Astor, R. (1994). Children's moral reasoning about family and peer violence: The role of provocation and retribution. *Child Development, 65,* 1054–1067.

Atchley, R. (1989). A continuity theory of normal aging. *The Gerontologist, 29,* 183–190.

Attie, I., Brooks-Gunn, J., & Petersen, A. (1990). A developmental perspective on eating disorders and eating problems. In M. Lewis & S.M. Miller (Eds.), *Handbook of developmental psychopathology* (pp. 409–420). New York, NY: Plenum.

Atwood, S. (2004, June). Education Arcade: MIT researchers are creating academically driven computer games that rival commercial products and make learning fun. *Technology Review.* Cambridge, MA. Retrieved from Technology Review website: www.technologyreview.com/articles/atwood0604.asp

Auerbach, S. (2006). *Smart play smart toys: How to raise a child with a high PQ.* San Francisco, CA: Institute for Childhood Resources.

Auman, M. (2007). Bereavement support for children. *The Journal of School Nursing, 23*(1), 34–39.

Austin, S., Ziyadeh, N., Kahn, J., Camargo, C., Colditz, G., & Field, A. (2004). Sexual orientation, weight concerns, and eating-disordered behaviors in adolescent girls and boys. *Journal of the American Academy of Child & Adolescent Psychiatry, 43,* 1115–1123.

Avison, W.R. (1997). National Forum on Health: Summary of the health consequences of unemployment. Ottawa, ON: Health Canada. Retrieved December 21, 2001 from www.nfh.hc-sc.gc.ca/publicat/execsumm/avison.htm

Axelman, K., Basun, H., & Lannfelt, L. (1998). Wide range of disease onset in a family with Alzheimer disease and a His163Tyr mutation in the presenilin-l gene. *Archives of Neurology, 55,* 698–702.

Babiloni, C., Babiloni, F., Carducci, F., Cappa, S., Cincotti, F., Del Percio, C., . . . Rossini, P.M. (2004). Human cortical rhythms during visual delayed choice reaction time tasks: A high–resolution EEG study on normal aging. *Behavioural Brain Research, 153,* 261–271.

Bacon, J. (2008). *Hospice palliative home care in Canada: A progress report.* Ottawa, ON: Quality End-of-Life Care Coalition of Canada.

Baek, H. (2002). A comparative study of moral development of Korean and British children. *Journal of Moral Education, 31,* 373–391.

Bagga, A., & Kulkarni, S. (2000). Age at menarche and secular trend in Maharashtrian (Indian) girls. *Acta Biologica Szegediensis, 44*(1–4), 53–57.

Bahrick, L., & Lickliter, R. (2000). Intersensory redundancy guides attentional selectivity and perceptual learning in infancy. *Developmental Psychology, 36,* 190–201.

Bailey, J., Pillard, R., Dawood, K., Miller, M., Farrer, L., Trivedi, S., & Murphy, R. (1999). A family history study of male sexual orientation using three independent samples. *Behavior Genetics, 29,* 7986.

Bailey, S., & Zvonkovic, A. (2003). Parenting after divorce: Nonresidential parents' perceptions of social and institutional support. Journal of *Divorce & Remarriage, 39,* 59–80.

Baillargeon, R. (1987). Object permanence in very young infants. *Developmental Psychology, 23,* 655–664.

Baillargeon, R. (1994). How do infants learn about the physical world? *Current Directions in Psychological Science, 3,* 133–140.

Baillargeon, R., & DeVos, J. (1991). Object permanence in young infants: Further evidence. *Child Development, 62,* 1227–1246.

Baillargeon, R., Spelke, E.S., & Wasserman, S. (1985). Object permanence in five-month-old infants. *Cognition, 20,* 191–208.

Baillargeon, R., Tremblay, R., & Willms, J.D. (2002). Physical aggression among toddlers: Does it run in families? In J. D. Willms (Ed.), *Vulnerable Children: Findings from Canada's National Longitudinal Survey of Children and Youth* (pp. 71–102). Edmonton, AB: The University of Alberta Press.

Baillargeon, R.H., Zoccolillo, M., Keenan, K., Côté, S., Pérusse, D., Wu, H.X., . . . Tremblay, R.E. (2007). Gender differences in the prevalence of physical aggression: A prospective population-based survey of children before and after two years of age. *Developmental Psychology, 43,* 13–26.

Bailley, S., Kral, M., & Dunham, K. (1999). Survivors of suicide do grieve differently: Empirical support for a common sense proposition. *Suicide and Life-Threatening Behavior, 29,* 256–271.

Baker, D., Jeganathan, K., Cameron, D., Thompson, M., Juneja, S., Kopecka, A., . . . van Deursen, J.M. (2004). BubR1 insufficiency causes early onset of aging-associated phenotypes and infertility in mice. *Nature Genetics, 36,* 744–749.

Baker, M., & Milligan, K. (2007, April). *Maternal employment, breastfeeding and health: Evidence from maternity leave mandates* (Working Paper). Toronto, ON: National Bureau of Economic Research. Retrieved from www.chass.utoronto.ca/cepa/breastfeeding2.9.pdf

Baker, M., Gruber, J., & Milligan, K. (2008). Universal child care, maternal labor supply and family well-being. *Journal of Political Economy, 116*(4), 709–745.

Balaban, M.T. (1995). Affective influences on startle in five-month-old infants: Reactions to facial expressions of emotion. *Child Development, 66,* 28–36.

Balch, C., Montgomery, J.S., Paik, H.I., Kim, S., Huang, T.H., & Nephew, K.P. (2005). New anti-cancer strategies: Epigenetic therapies and biomarkers. *Frontiers in Bioscience, 10*(2), 1897–1931.

Baldwin, D.A. (1995, March). *Understanding relations between constraints and a socio-pragmatic account of meaning acquisition.* Paper presented at the biennial meetings of the Society for Research in Child Development, Indianapolis, IN.

Ball, E. (1997). Phonological awareness: Implications for whole language and emergent literacy programs. *Topics in Language Disorders, 17,* 14–26.

Baltes, P., & Kunzmann, U. (2004). The two faces of wisdom: Wisdom as a general theory of knowledge and judgment about excellence in mind and virtue vs. wisdom as everyday realization in people and products. *Human Development, 47,* 290–299.

Baltes, P., & Staudinger, U. (2000). Wisdom: A metaheuristic (pragmatic) to orchestrate mind and virtue toward excellence. *American Psychologist, 55,* 122–136.

Baltes, P.B., & Baltes, M.M. (1990). Psychological perspectives on successful aging: The model of selective optimization with compensation. In P.B. Baltes & M.M. Baltes (Eds.), *Successful aging* (pp. 1–34). Cambridge, England: Cambridge University Press.

Baltes, B., & Heydens-Gahir, H. (2003). Reduction of work-family conflict through the use of selection, optimization, and compensation behaviors. Journal of Applied Psychology, *88,* 1005–1018.

Baltes, P.B., & Kliegl, R. (1992). Further testing of limits of cognitive plasticity: Negative age differences in a mnemonic skill are robust. *Developmental Psychology, 28,* 121–125.

Baltes, P.B., Lindenberger, U., & Staudinger, U. (2006). Lifespan theory in developmental psychology. In W. Damon & R.M. Lerner (Eds.), *Handbook of child psychology: Vol. 1. Theoretical models of human development* (6th ed., pp. 569–664). New York, NY: Wiley.

Baltes, P.B., Reese, H.W., & Lipsitt, L.P. (1980). Life-span developmental psychology. *Annual Review of Psychology, 31,* 65–70.

Baltes, P.B., Reese, H.W., & Nesselroade, J.R. (1977). *Life-span developmental psychology: Introduction to research methods.* Monterey, CA: Books/Cole.

Baltes, P.B., Staudinger, U.M., & Lindenberger, U. (1999). Lifespan Psychology: Theory and application to intellectual functioning. *Annual Review of Psychology, 50,* 471–507.

Bamford, F.N., Bannister, R.P., Benjamin, C.M., Hillier, V.F., Ward, B.S., & Moore, W.M.O. (1990). Sleep in the first year of life. *Developmental Medicine and Child Neurology, 32,* 718–724.

Bandura, A. (1977a). *Social learning theory.* Englewood Cliffs, NJ: Prentice-Hall.

Bandura, A. (1977b). Self-efficacy: Toward a unifying theory of behavioral change. *Psychological Review, 84,* 91–125.

Bandura, A. (1982). The psychology of chance encounters and life paths. *American Psychologist, 37,* 747–755.

Bandura, A. (1986). *Social foundations of thought and action: A social cognitive theory.* Englewood Cliffs, NJ: Prentice-Hall.

Bandura, A. (1989). Social cognitive theory. *Annals of Child Development, 6,* 1–60.

Bandura, A. (1991). Self-regulation of motivation through anticipatory and self-regulatory mechanisms. In R.A. Dienstbier (Ed.), *Perspectives on motivation: Nebraska symposium on motivation* (Vol. 38, pp. 69–164). Lincoln: University of Nebraska Press.

Bandura, A. (1997a). *Self-efficacy: The exercise of control.* New York, NY: W.H. Freeman.

Bandura, A. (1997b). Self-efficacy. *Harvard Mental Health Letter, 13*(9), 4–6.

Bandura, A. (2001). Social cognitive theory: An agentic perspective. *Annual Review of Psychology, 52*(2), 1–26.

Bandura, A. & Bussey, K. (2004). On broadening the cognitive, motivational, and sociocultural scope of theorizing about gender development and functioning: Comment on Martin, Ruble, and Szkrybalo (2002). *Psychological Bulletin, 130,* 691–701.

Bandura, A., & Schunk, D.H. (1981). Cultivating competence, self-efficacy, and intrinsic interest through proximal self-motivation. *Journal of Personality and Social Psychology, 41,* 586–598.

Bandura, A., Ross, D., & Ross, S.A. (1961). Transmission of aggression through imitation of aggressive models. *Journal of Abnormal and Social Psychology, 63,* 575–582.

Bandura, A., Ross, D., & Ross, S.A. (1963). Imitation of film-mediated aggressive models. *Journal of Abnormal and Social Psychology, 66,* 3–11.

Banse, R., Gawronski, B., Rebetez, C., Gutt, H., & Morton, J.B. (2010). The development of spontaneous gender stereotyping in childhood: Relations to stereotype knowledge and stereotype flexibility. *Developmental Science, 13*(2), 298–306.

Barenboim, C. (1981). The development of person perception in childhood and adolescence: From behavioral comparisons to psychological constructs to psychological comparisons. *Child Development, 52,* 129–144.

Barer, B. (2001). The "grands and greats" of very old black grandmothers. *Journal of Aging Studies, 15,* 1–11.

Barkley, R. (1990). *Attention-deficit hyperactivity disorder.* New York, NY: Guilford Press.

Barlow, J., & Lewandowski, L. (2000, August). *Ten-year longitudinal study of preterm infants: Outcomes and predictors.* Paper presented at the annual meeting of the American Psychological Association, Washington, DC.

Barnard, K.E., Hammond, M.A., Booth, C.L., Bee, H.L., Mitchell, S.K., & Spieker, S.J. (1989). Measurement and meaning of parent-child interaction. In J.J. Morrison, C. Lord, & D.P. Keating (Eds.), *Applied developmental psychology*: Vol. 3 (pp. 40–81). San Diego, CA: Academic Press.

Barness, L., & Curran, J. (1996). Nutrition. In R.E. Behrman, R.M. Kliegman, & A.M. Arvin (Eds.), *Nelson's textbook of pediatrics* (15th ed., pp. 141–184). Philadelphia, PA: Saunders.

Barnsley, P. (2001). Native youth remain in distress. *Windspeaker News.* Retrieved from The Aboriginal Multi-Media Society website: www.ammsa.com/windspeaker/children/JAN2001-youthindistress.html

Barr, R., Marrott, H., & Rovee-Collier, C. (2003). The role of sensory preconditioning in memory retrieval by preverbal infants. *Learning & Behavior, 31,* 111–123.

Barrett, H., & Behne, T. (2005). Children's understanding of death as the cessation of agency: A test using sleep versus death. *Cognition, 96*(2), 93–108.

Barrett-Connor, E., & Bush, T.L. (1991). Estrogen and coronary heart disease in women. *Journal of the American Medical Association, 265,* 1861–1867.

Barros, S.P., & Offenbacher, S. (2009). Epigenetics: Connecting environment and genotype to phenotype and disease. *Journal of Dental Research, 88,* 400–408.

Bartlik, B., & Goldstein, M. (2000, June). Maintaining sexual health after menopause. *Psychiatric Services Journal, 51,* 751–753.

Bartoshuk, L.M., & Weiffenbach, J.M. (1990). Chemical senses and aging. In E.L. Schneider & J.W. Rowe (Eds.), *Handbook of the biology of aging* (3rd ed., pp. 429–444). San Diego, CA: Academic Press.

Barusch, A. (1999). Religion, adversity and age: Religious experiences of low-income elderly women. *Journal of Sociology & Social Welfare, 26,* 125–142.

Basseches, M. (1984). *Dialectical thinking and adult development.* Norwood, NJ: Ablex.

Basseches, M. (1989). Dialectical thinking as an organized whole: Comments on Irwin and Kramer. In M.L. Commons, J.D. Sinnott, F.A. Richards, & C. Armon (Eds.), *Adult development: Vol. 1. Comparisons and applications of developmental models* (pp. 161–178). New York, NY: Praeger.

Bates, E. (1993). Commentary: Comprehension and production in early language development. *Monographs of the Society for Research in Child Development, 58* (3–4, Serial No. 233), 222–242.

Bates, E., Bretherton, I., & Snyder, L. (1988). *From first words to grammar: Individual differences and dissociable mechanisms.* Cambridge, England: Cambridge University Press.

Bates, E., Marchman, V., Thal, D., Fenson, L., Dale, P., Reznick, J.S., . . . Hartung, J. (1994). Developmental and stylistic variation in the composition of early vocabulary. *Journal of Child Language, 21,* 85–123.

Bates, E., O'Connell, B., & Shore, C. (1987). Language and communication in infancy. In J.D. Osofsky (Ed.), *Handbook of infant development* (2nd ed., pp. 149–203). New York, NY: Wiley.

Bates, J.E. (1989). Applications of temperament concepts. In G.A. Kohnstamm, J.E. Bates, & M.K. Rothbart (Eds.), *Temperament in childhood* (pp. 321–356). Chichester, England: Wiley.

Bates, T.C., Lucian, M., Castles, A., Coltheart, M., Wright, M.J., & Martin, NAG. (2007). Replication of reported linkages for dyslexia and spelling and suggestive evidence for novel regions on chromosomes 4 and 17. *European Journal of Human Genetics, 15*(2), 194–203.

Batten, M., & Oltjenbruns, K. (1999). Adolescent sibling bereavement as a catalyst for spiritual development: A model for understanding. *Death Studies, 23,* 529–546.

Bauer, P., Schwade, J., Wewerka, S., & Delaney, K. (1999). Planning ahead: Goal-directed problem solving by 2-year-olds. *Developmental Psychology, 35,* 1321–1337.

Baugher, R.J., Burger, C., Smith, R., & Wallston, K. (1989/1990). A comparison of terminally ill persons at various time periods to death. *Omega, 20,* 103–115.

Baumrind, D. (1967). Child care practices anteceding three patterns of preschool behavior. *Genetic Psychology Monographs, 75,* 43–88.

Baumrind, D. (1971). Current patterns of parental authority. *Developmental Psychology Monograph, 4* (1, Part 2).

Baumrind, D. (1972). Socialization and instrumental competence in young children. In W.W. Hartup (Ed.), *The young child: Reviews of research* (Vol. 2, pp. 202–224). Washington, DC: National Association for the Education of Young Children.

Baumrind, D. (1991). Effective parenting during the early adolescent transition. In P.A. Cowan & M. Hetherington (Eds.), *Family transitions* (pp. 111–163). Hillsdale, NJ: Erlbaum.

Baumrind, D. (2003, March). *When are causal inferences justified in the debate about physical discipline "effects"?* Paper presented at the Institute of Human Development University of California, Berkeley, CA.

Baumrind, D., Larzelere, R.E., & Cowan, P.A. (2002). Ordinary physical punishment: Is it harmful? Comment on Gershoff (2002). *Psychological Bulletin, 128*(4), 580–589.

Bayley, N. (1969). *Bayley scales of infant development.* New York, NY: Psychological Corporation.

Bayley, N. (1993). *Bayley scales of infant development: Birth to two years.* New York, NY: Psychological Corporation.

Bayley, N. (2006). *Bayley scales of infant and toddler development* (3rd ed). San Antonio, TX: Harcourt Assessment, Inc.

BC Stats. (1998). Special feature: A tale of three immigrant cities. Victoria, BC: Author. Retrieved from www.bcstats.gov.bc.ca/pubs/immig/imm973sf.pdf

Beaton, G.H., Martorell, R., L'Abbe, K.A., Edmonston, B., McCabe, G., . . . Harvey, B. (1993). Effectiveness of Vitamin A supplementation in the control of young child morbidity and mortality in developing countries. *Final report to the Canadian International Development Agency (CIDA).* Toronto, ON: University of Toronto.

Beaudry, M., Dufour, R., & Marcoux, S. (1995). Relation between infant feeding and infections during the first six months of life. *Journal of Pediatrics, 126,* 191–197.

Beaujot, R. (2004). *Delayed life transitions: Trends and implications.* Ottawa, ON: The Vanier Institute of the Family. Retrieved from www.vifamily.ca/library/cft/delayed_life.pdf

Beaujot, R., & Kerr, D. (2004). *Population change in Canada.* Toronto, ON: Oxford University Press.

Beaujot, R., & Ravanera, Z. (2008). Family change and implications for family solidarity and social cohesion. *Canadian Studies in Population, 35*(1), 73–101.

Beaujot, R., & Ravanera, Z.R. (2001, January). *An interpretation of family change, with implications for social cohesion.* Paper presented at a conference "Have the Factors of Social Inclusiveness Changed?" organized by the Centre de recherche interuniversitaire sur les transformations et les régulations économiques et sociales (CRITERES) and the Policy Research Secretariat, Montreal, PQ.

Beaujot, R., & Ravanera, Z.R. (2009). Family models for earning and caring: Implications for child care and for family policy. *Canadian Studies in Population, 36*(1-2), 145–166.

Beaupré, P., & Cloutier, E. (2007). Navigating family transitions: Evidence from the General Social Survey, Cycle 20: Family Transitions Survey (89–625–XIE, no. 2). Ottawa, ON: Statistics Canada. Retrieved from www.statcan.ca/english/research/89-625-XIE/89-625-XIE2007002.pdf

Beautrais, A., Joyce, P., & Mulder, R. (1999). Personality traits and cognitive styles as risk factors for serious suicide attempts among young people. *Suicide & Life-Threatening Behavior, 29,* 37–47.

Beck, A., Brown, G., Berchick, R., Stewart, B., & Steer, R. (1990). Relationship between hopelessness and ultimate suicide: A replication with psychiatric outpatients. *American Journal of Psychiatry, 147,* 190–195.

Bee, H.L., Barnard, K.E., Eyres, S.J., Gray, C.A., Hammond, M.A., Spietz, A.L., . . . Clark, B. (1982). Prediction of IQ and language skill from perinatal status, child performance, family characteristics, and mother-infant interaction. *Child Development, 53,* 1135–1156.

Beekman, A., Copeland, J., & Prince, M. (1999). Review of community prevalence of depression in later life. *British Journal of Psychiatry, 174,* 307–311.

Beem, E., Hooijkaas, H., Cleriren, M., Schut, H., Garssen, B., Croon, M., . . . de Vries, M. (1999). The immunological and psychological effects of bereavement: Does grief counseling really make a difference? A pilot study. *Psychiatry Research, 85,* 81–93.

Behrend, D., Scofield, J., & Kleinknecht, E. (2001) Beyond fast mapping: Young children's extensions of novel words and novel facts. *Developmental Psychology, 37,* 690–705.

Bell Canada (2001, 11a). Students move their mouse before they move house. Bell Canada Press Releases (August 22). Retrieved from www.bell.ca/en/about/press/release/2001/pr_20010822.asp

Bell Canada (2001, 11b). Young people show mature attitude toward cell phone use. Bell Canada Press Releases (August 16). Retrieved from www.bell.ca/en/about/press/release/2001/pr_20010816.asp

Bell, J., & Bromnick, R. (2003). The social reality of the imaginary audience: A ground theory approach. *Adolescence, 38,* 205–219.

Bell, L.G., & Bell, D.C. (1982). Family climate and the role of the female adolescent: Determinants of adolescent functioning. *Family Relations, 31,* 519–527.

Bellantoni, M.F., & Blackman, M.R. (1996). Menopause and its consequences. In E.L. Schneider & J.W. Rowe (Eds.), *Handbook of the biology of aging* (4th ed., pp. 415–430). San Diego, CA: Academic Press.

Belsky, J. (1985). Prepared statement on the effects of day care. In Select Committee on Children, Youth, and Families, House of Representatives, 98th Congress, Second Session, *Improving child care services: What can be done?* Washington, DC: U.S. Government Printing Office.

Belsky, J. (2007). Recent child care findings. *Pediatrics for Parents, 9,* 2–3.

Belsky, J. (2009). Early day care and infant-mother attachment security. In R.E. Tremblay, R.G. Barr, R.D. Peters, & M. Boivin (Eds.), *Encyclopedia on early childhood development.* Montreal, QC: Centre of Excellence for Early Childhood Development. Retrieved from www.child-encyclopedia.com/documents/BelskyANGxp-Child_care2.pdf.

Belsky, J., & Hsieh, K. (1998). Patterns of marital change during the early childhood years: Parent personality, coparenting, and division-of-labor correlates. *Journal of Family Psychology, 12,* 511–528.

Belsky, J., Hsieh, K., & Crnic, K. (1996). Infant positive and negative emotionality: One dimension or two? *Developmental Psychology, 32,* 289–298.

Belsky, J., Jaffee, S., Caspi, A., Moffitt, T., & Silva, P. (2003). Intergenerational relationships in young adulthood and their life course, mental health, and personality correlates. *Journal of Family Psychology, 17,* 460–471.

Belsky, J., Lang, M.E., & Rovine, M. (1985). Stability and change in marriage across the transition to parenthood: A second study. *Journal of Marriage and the Family, 47,* 855–865.

Belsky. J., Vandell. D.L., Burchinal. M., Clarke-Stewart. K.A., McCartney. K., & Owen, M.T. (2007). Are there long-term effects of early child care? *Child Development, 78*(2), 681–701.

Bem, S.L. (1974). The measurement of psychological androgyny. *Journal of Consulting and Clinical Psychology, 42,* 155–162.

Bender, B.G., Harmon, R.J., Linden, M.G., & Robinson, A. (1995). Psychosocial adaptation of 39 adolescents with sex chromosome abnormalities. *Pediatrics, 96,* 302–308.

Bender, K. (1999). Assessing antidepressant safety in the elderly. *Psychiatric Times, 16* [Online archives]. Retrieved from www.mhsource.com/pt/p990151.html

Bendersky, M., & Lewis, M. (1994). Environmental risk, biological risk, and developmental outcome. *Developmental Psychology, 30,* 484–494.

Benenson, J., & Benarroch, D. (1998). Gender differences in responses to friends' hypothetical greater success. *Journal of Early Adolescence, 18,* 192–208.

Benenson, J.F. (1994). Ages four to six years: Changes in the structures of play networks of girls and boys. *Merrill-Palmer Quarterly, 40,* 478–487.

Bengtson, V., Rosenthal, C., & Burton, L. (1990). Families and aging: Diversity and heterogeneity. In R.H. Binstock & L.K. George (Eds.), *Handbook of aging and the social sciences* (3rd ed., pp. 263–287). San Diego, CA: Academic Press.

Bengtson, V., Rosenthal, C., & Burton, L. (1996). Paradoxes of families and aging. In R. H. Binstock & L. K. George (Eds.), *Handbook of aging and the social sciences* (4th ed., pp. 253–282). San Diego, CA: Academic Press.

Benn, P.A., & Egan, J.F.X. (2000). Letters to the Editor: Survival of Down syndrome in utero. *Prenatal Diagnosis, 20*(5), 432–433.

Bennett, M. (1997). A longitudinal study of wellbeing in widowed women. *International Journal of Geriatric Psychiatry, 12,* 61–66.

Bennett, M. (1998). Longitudinal changes in mental and physical health among elderly, recently widowed men. *Mortality, 3,* 265–273.

Bennett-Baker, P.E., Wilkowski, J., & Burke, D.T. (2003). Age-associated activation of epigenetically repressed genes in the mouse. *Genetics, 165*(4), 2055–2062.

Benoit, D., & Parker, K.C.H. (1994). Stability and transmission of attachment across three generations. *Child Development, 65,* 1444–1456.

Berg, J., & Lipson, J. (1999). Information sources, menopause beliefs, and health complaints of midlife Filipinas. *Health, 20,* 81–92.

Bergman, R. (2002). Why be moral? A conceptual model from developmental psychology. *Human Development, 45,* 104–124.

Berkman, L.F. (1985). The relationship of social networks and social support to morbidity and mortality. In S. Coen & S.L. Syme (Eds.), *Social support and health* (pp. 241–262). Orlando, FL: Academic Press.

Berkman, L.F., & Breslow, L. (1983). *Health and ways of living: The Alameda County Study.* New York, NY: Oxford University Press.

Berkowitz, G.S., & Papiernik, E. (1993). Epidemiology of preterm birth. *Epidemiological Review, 15,* 414–443.

Berndt, T.J., & Keefe, K. (1995a). Friends' influence on adolescents' adjustment to school. *Child Development, 66,* 1312–1329.

Berndt, T.J., & Keefe, K. (1995b, March). *Friends' influence on school adjustment: A motivational analysis.* Paper presented at the biennial meetings of the Society for Research in Child Development, Indianapolis, IN.

Berne, L., & Huberman, B. (1996, February). Sexuality education works: Here's proof. *Education Digest,* 25–29.

Berninger, V., Abbott, R., Zook, D., Ogier, S., Lemos-Britton, Z., & Brooksher, R. (1999). Early intervention for reading disabilities: Teaching the alphabet principle in a connectionist framework. *Journal of Learning Disabilities, 32,* 491–503.

Bernreuther, C., Dihne, M., Johann, V., Schiefer, J., Cui, Y., Hargus, G., . . . Schachner. (2006). Neural cell adhesion molecule L1-transfected embryonic stem cells promote functional recovery after excitotoxic lesion of the mouse striatum. *The Journal of Neuroscience, 26*(45), 11532–11539.

Berthier, N., DeBlois, S., Poirier, C., Novak, M., & Clifton, R. (2000). Where's the ball? Two- and three-year-olds reason about unseen events. Developmental Psychology, 36, 394–401.

Bertram, L., McQueen, M., Mullin, K., Blacker, D., & Tanzi, R. (2007). Systematic meta-analyses of Alzheimer disease genetic association studies: The AlzGene database. *Nature Genetics, 39,* 17–23.

Bertrand, J., Floyd, R.L., Weber, M.K., O'Connor, M., Riley, E.P, Johnson, K.A., et al.; National Task Force on FAS/FAE. (2004). *Fetal Alcohol Syndrome: Guidelines for Referral and Diagnosis.* Atlanta, GA: Centers for Disease Control and Prevention.

Bethus, I., Lemaire, V., Lhomme, M., & Goodall, G. (2005). Does prenatal stress affect latent inhibition? It depends on the gender. *Behavioural Brain Research, 158*(2), 331–338.

Betz, N.E., & Fitzgerald, L.F. (1987). *The career psychology of women.* Orlando, FL: Academic Press.

Beyene, Y., Gilliss, C., & Lee, K. (2007). "I take the good with the bad, and I moisturize": Defying middle age in the new millennium. *Menopause, 14,* 734–741.

Bhatt, R., Wilk, A., Hill, D., & Rovee-Collier, C. (2004). Correlated attributes and categorization in the first half-year of life. *Developmental Psychobiology, 44,* 103–115.

Bhatt, R.S., & Rovee-Collier, C. (1996). Infants' forgetting of correlated attributes and object recognition. *Child Development, 67,* 172–187.

Bialystok, E. (1997). Effects of bilingualism and biliteracy on children's emerging concepts of print. *Developmental Psychology, 33.*

Bialystok, E. (1999). Cognitive complexity and attentional control in the bilingual mind. *Child Development, 70,* 636–644.

Bialystok, E., & Majumder, S. (1998). The relationship between bilingualism and the development of cognitive processes in problem solving. *Applied Psycholinguistics, 19,* 69–85.

Bialystok, E., Craik, F.I.M. & Freedman, M. 2007. Bilingualism as a protection against the onset of symptoms of dementia. *Neuropsychologia, 45*(2), 459–464.

Bialystok, E., Shenfield, T., & Codd, J. (2000). Languages, scripts, and the environment: Factors in developing concepts of print. *Developmental Psychology, 36,* 66–76.

Bibbins-Domingo, K., Coxson, P., Pletcher, M.J., Lightwood, J., & Goldman, L. (2007). Adolescent overweight and future adult coronary heart disease. *New England Journal of Medicine, 357,* 2371–2379.

Bibby, R.W. (2001). *Canada's teens: Today, yesterday and tomorrow.* Toronto, ON: Stoddart Publishing Co. Limited.

Biblarz, T.J., Bengtson, V.L., & Bucur, A. (1996). Social mobility across three generations. *Journal of Marriage and the Family, 58,* 188–200.

Binet, A., & Simon, T. (1905). Méthodes nouvelles pour le diagnostic du niveau intellectuel des anormaux [New methods for diagnosing the intellectual level of the abnormal]. *L'Anée Psychologique, 11,* 191–244.

Bingham, C.R., Miller, B.C., & Adams, G.R. (1990). Correlates of age at first sexual intercourse in a national sample of young women. *Journal of Adolescent Research, 5,* 18–33.

Birch, D. (1998). The adolescent parent: A fifteen-year longitudinal study of school-age mothers and their children. *International Journal of Adolescent Medicine & Health, 19,* 141–153.

Biringen, Z. (2000). Emotional availability: Conceptualization and research findings. *American Journal of Orthopsychiatry, 70,* 104–114.

Biswas, M.K., & Craigo, S.D. (1994). The course and conduct of 576 normal labor and delivery. In A.H. DeCherney & M.L. Pernoll (Eds.), *Current obstetric and gynecologic diagnosis & treatment* (pp. 202–227). Norwalk, CT: Appleton & Lange.

Bitomsky, M. (2002). Men often untreated for eating disorders. *The Medical Post, 38*(37), 53.

Bittner, S., & Newberger, E. (1981). Pediatric understanding of child abuse and neglect. *Pediatric Review, 2,* 198.

Bjorklund, D.F., & Pellegrini, A.D. (2002). *The origins of human nature: Evolutionary developmental psychology.* Washington, DC: American Psychological Association.

Black, A., Yang, Q., Wen, S.W., Lalonde, A.B., Guilbert, E., & Fisher, W. (2009). Contraceptive use among Canadian women of reproductive age: Results of a national survey. *Journal of Obstetrics and Gynaecology Canada, 31*(7), 627–640.

Black, K.A., & McCartney, K. (1995, March). *Associations between adolescent attachment to parents and peer interactions.* Paper presented at the biennial meetings of the Society for Research in Child Development, Indianapolis, IN.

Black, S., Markides, K., & Miller, T. (1998). Correlates of depressive symptomatology among older community-dwelling Mexican Americans: The hispanic EPESE. *Journals of Gerontology: Series B: Psychological Sciences & Social Sciences, 53B,* S198–S208.

Blackwell, D., & Lichter, D. (2000). Mate selection among married and cohabiting couples. *Journal of Family Issues, 21,* 275–302.

Blair, S.N., Kohl, H.W., III, Barlow, C.E., Paffenbarger, R.S., Gibbons, L.W., & Macera, C.A. (1995). Changes in physical fitness and all-cause mortality. *Journal of the American Medical Association, 273,* 1093–1098.

Blake, I.K. (1994). Language development and socialization in young African-American children. In P.M. Greenfield & R.R. Cocking (Eds.), *Cross-cultural roots of minority child development* (pp. 167–195). Hillsdale, NJ: Erlbaum.

Blake, J.M., Collins, J.A., Reid, R.L., Fedorkow, D.M., & Lalonde, A.B. (2002). The SOGC statement on the WHI report on estrogen and progestin use in postmenopausal women. *The Journal of Obstetrics and Gynaecology Canada, 24*(10), 783–787.

Blakemore, J., LaRue, A., & Olejnik, A. (1979). Sex-appropriate toy preference and the ability to conceptualize toys as sex-role related. *Developmental Psychology, 15,* 339–340.

Blakemore, J.E.O. (2003). Children's beliefs about violating gender norms: Boys shouldn't look like girls and girls shouldn't act like boys. *Sex Roles, 48*(9/10), 411–415.

Blanchard-Fields, F., Chen, Y., Schocke, M., & Hertzog, C. (1998). Evidence for content-specificity of causal attributions across the adult life span. *Aging, Neuropsychology, & Cognition, 5,* 241–263.

Blanpain, C., Lowry, W., Geoghegan, A., Polak, L., & Fuchs, E. (2004). Self-renewal, multipotency, and the existence of two cell populations within an epithelial stem cell niche. *Cell, 118,* 635–648.

Blau, G. (1996). Adolescent depression and suicide. In G. Blau & T. Gullotta (Eds.), *Adolescent dysfunctional behavior: Causes, interventions, and prevention* (pp. 187–205). Newbury Park, CA: Sage.

Block, J., & Robins, R.W. (1993). A longitudinal study of consistency and change in self-esteem from early adolescence to early adulthood. *Child Development, 64,* 909–923.

Bloom, L. (1973). *One word at a time.* The Hague: Mouton.

Bloom, L. (1991). *Language development from two to three.* Cambridge, England: Cambridge University Press.

Bloom, L. (1993). The transition from infancy to language: Acquiring the power of expression. Cambridge, England: Cambridge University Press.

Bloom, L. (2000). The intentionality model of word learning: How to learn a word, any word. In Golinkoff, R., Hirsh-Pasek, K., Bloom. L., Smith, L., Woodward, A., Akhtar, N., Tomasello, M., & Hollich, G. (2000), *Becoming a word learner: A debate on lexical acquisition* (pp. 19–50). New York, NY: Oxford University Press.

Blumberg, J.B. (1996). Status and functional impact of nutrition in older adults. In E.L. Schneider & J.W. Rowe (Eds.), *Handbook of the biology of aging* (4th ed., pp. 393–414). San Diego, CA: Academic Press.

Blumenthal, J.A., Emery, C.F., Madden, D.J., Schniebolk, S., Walsh-Riddle, M., George, L.K., . . . Coleman, R.E. (1991). Long-term effects of exercise on physiological functioning in older men and women. *Journals of Gerontology: Psychological Sciences, 46,* P352–361.

Blumstein, P., & Schwartz, P. (1983). *American couples.* New York: Morrow.

Blumstein, P., & Schwartz, P. (1990). Intimate relationships and the creation of sexuality. In D. McWhirter, S. Sanders, and J. Reinisch (Eds.), *Homosexuality/heterosexuality: Concepts of sexual orientation* (pp. 96–109). New York, NY: Oxford University Press.

Blustein, D., Phillips, S., Jobin-Davis, K., & Finkelberg, S. (1997). A theory-building investigation of the school-to-work transition. *Counseling Psychology, 25,* 364–402.

Bogenschneider, K., Wu, M., Raffaelli, M., & Tsay, J. (1998). "Other teens drink, but not my kid": Does parental awareness of adolescent alcohol use protect adolescents from risky consequences? *Journal of Marriage & the Family, 60,* 356–373.

Bohman, M., & Sigvardsson, S. (1990). Outcome in adoption: Lessons from longitudinal studies. In D.M. Brodzinsky (Ed.), *The psychology of adoption* (pp. 93–106). New York, NY: Oxford University Press.

Bond, J., & Coleman, P. (Eds.). (1990). *Aging in society.* London, England: Sage.

Bondevik, M., & Skogstad, A. (1998). The oldest old, ADL, social network, and loneliness. *Western Journal of Nursing Research, 20,* 325–343.

Bondy, S.J., Cohen, J.E. & Rehm, J.T. (2000). Past trends in tobacco use and some thoughts on future trends. In R. Ferrence, J. Slade, R. Room & M. Pope (Eds.), *Nicotine and public health* (pp. 311–342). Washington: Public Health Association.

Bong, M. (1998). Tests of the internal/external frames of reference model with subject-specific academic self-efficacy and frame-specific academic self-concepts. *Journal of Educational Psychology, 90,* 102–110.

Booth-LaForce, C., Oh, W., Kim, A., Rubin, K., Rose-Krasnor, L., & Burgess, K. (2006). Attachment, self-worth, and peer-group functioning in middle childhood. *Attachment & Human Development, 8,* 309–325.

Bornholt, L., & Goodnow, J. (1999). Cross-generation perceptions of academic competence: Parental expectations and adolescent self-disclosure. *Journal of Adolescent Research, 14,* 427–447.

Bornstein, M.H. (1992). Perception across the life span. In M.H. Bornstein & M.E. Lamb (Eds.), *Developmental psychology: An advanced textbook* (3rd ed., pp. 155–210). Hillsdale, NJ: Erlbaum.

Borzekowski, D.G.L., & Robinson, T.N. (2005). The remote, the mouse and the No. 2 pencil: The household media environment and academic achievement among third grade students. *Archives of Pediatrics and Adolescent Medicine, 159*(7), 607–613.

Bos, H.M.W, van Balen, F., & van den Boom, D.C. (2007). Child adjustment and parenting in planned lesbian-parent families. *American Journal of Orthopsychiatry, 7*(1), 38-48. doi: 10.1037/0002-9432.77.1.38

Bosacki, S. (2001a). "Theory of mind" or "theory of the soul"? The role of spirituality in children's understanding of minds and emotions. In J. Erricker, C. Ota, & C. Erricker (Eds.), *Spritual Education: Cultural, Religious and Social Differences* (pp. 156–169). Portland, OR: Sussex Academic Press.

Bosacki, S. (2005). Religiosity in Children and Youth: Psychoeducational Approaches. In C. Frisby & C.R. Reynolds (Eds.), *Comprehensive Handbook of Multicultural School Psychology* (pp. 611–650). New York, NY: Wiley & Sons.

Bosacki, S., & Moore, C. (2004). Preschoolers' understanding of simple and complex emotions: Links with gender and language. *Sex Roles, 50*(9–10), 659–675.

Bosacki, S.L. (2001). Spirituality, gendered subjectivities, and education in preadolescents: Canadian preadolescents' reflections on gender-roles and their sense of self. *International Journal of Children's Spirituality, 6*(20), 207–221.

Bosacki, S.L. (2002). Spirituality and self in preadolescents: Implications for a connected curriculum. *Journal of Beliefs & Values, 23*(1), 55–67.

Bossé, R., Aldwin, C.M., Levenson, M.R., & Workman-Daniels, K. (1991). How stressful is retirement? Findings from the normative aging study. *Journals of Gerontology: Psychological Sciences, 46*, P9–14.

Bosworth, H., Siegler, I., Brummett, B., Barefoot, J., Williams, R., Clapp-Channing, N., & Mark, D. (2000, August). *Health-related quality of life in a coronary artery sample.* Paper presented at the annual meeting of the American Psychological Association. Washington, DC.

Bouhuys, A., Flentge, F., Oldehinkel, A., & van den Berg, M. (2004). Potential psychosocial mechanisms linking depression to immune function in elderly subjects. *Psychiatry Research, 127*, 237–245.

Bourreille, C. (1999). Diana/Diana. *Cahiers Jungiens de Psychanalyse, 96*, 75–76.

Bowerman, M. (1985). Beyond communicative adequacy: From piecemeal knowledge to an integrated system in the child's acquisition of language. In K.E. Nelson (Ed.), *Children's language: Vol. 5* (pp. 369–398). Hillsdale, NJ: Erlbaum.

Bowerman, M. (2004). From universal to language-specific in early language development. In K. Trott, S. Dobbinson, & P. Griffiths (Eds.), *The child language reader* (pp. 131–146). London, England: Routledge.

Bowlby, G. (2008). Provincial drop-out rates—trends and consequences (81-004-XIE). In *Education Matters*, Ottawa, ON: Statistics Canada. Retrieved from www.statcan.gc.ca/pub/81-004-x/2005004/8984-eng.htm

Bowlby, J. (1969). *Attachment and loss: Vol. 1. Attachment.* New York, NY: Basic Books.

Bowlby, J. (1973). *Attachment and loss: Vol. 2. Separation, anxiety, and anger.* New York, NY: Basic Books.

Bowlby, J. (1980). *Attachment and loss: Vol. 3. Loss, sadness, and depression.* New York, NY: Basic Books.

Bowlby, J. (1988a). Developmental psychiatry comes of age. *American Journal of Psychiatry, 145*, 1–10.

Bowlby, J. (1988b). *A secure base.* New York, NY: Basic Books.

Bowlby, J. (1989). The role of attachment in personality development and psychopathology. In: S.I. Greenspan and G.H. Pollock, (Eds.), *The Course of Life: Vol. II, Early Childhood.* Madison, CT: International Universities Press, Inc.

Bowler, D., Briskman, J., & Grice, S. (1999). Experimenter effects on children's understanding of false drawings and false beliefs. *Journal of Genetic Psychology, 160*, 443–460.

Bowling, A., Fleissig, A., Gabriel, Z., Banister, D., Dyjes, J., Dowding, L., . . . Sutton, S. (2003). Let's ask them: A national survey of definitions of quality of life and its enhancement among people aged 65 and over. *International Journal of Aging & Human Development, 56*, 269–306.

Boxall, P., Macky, K., & Rasmussen, E. (2003). Labour turnover and retention in New Zealand: The causes and consequences of leaving and staying with employers. *Asia Pacific Journal of Human Resources, 41*, 195–214.

Bradley, R.H., Caldwell, B.M., Rock, S.L., Barnard, K.E., Gray, C., Hammond, M.A., . . . Johnson, D.L. (1989). Home environment and cognitive development in the first 3 years of life: A collaborative study involving six sites and three ethnic groups in North America. *Developmental Psychology, 25*, 217–235.

Bradmetz, J. (1999). Precursors of formal thought: A longitudinal study. *British Journal of Developmental Psychology, 17*, 61–81.

Brand, A., & Brinich, P. (1999). Behavior problems and mental health contacts in adopted, foster, and nonadopted children. *Journal of Child Psychology & Psychiatry & Allied Disciplines, 40*, 1221–1229.

Brandon, P. (1999). Determinants of self-care arrangements among school-age children. *Children & Youth Services Review, 21*, 497–520.

Brandon, P., & Hofferth, S. (2003). Determinants of out-of-school childcare arrangements among children in single-mother and two-parent families. *Social Science Research, 32*, 129–147.

Branje, S., Van Lieshout, C., & Gerris, J. (2007). Big Five personality development in adolescence and adulthood. *European Journal of Personality, 21*, 45–62.

Braun, K., & Nichols, R. (1997). Death and dying in four Asian American cultures: A descriptive study. *Death Studies, 21*, 327–359.

Braveman, N.S. (1987). Immunity and aging immunologic and behavioral perspectives. In M.W. Riley, J.D. Matarazzo, & A. Baum (Eds.), *Perspectives in behavioral medicine: The aging dimension* (pp. 94–124). Hillsdale, NJ: Erlbaum.

Bravo, G., Dubois, M., & Pâquet, M. (2003). Advance directives for health care and research prevalence and correlates. *Alzheimer Disease & Associate Disorders, 17*, 215–222.

Brazelton, T.B., & Nugent, J.K. (1995). *Neonatal Behavioral Assessment Scale.* London, England: MacKeith Press.

Bregman, G., & Killen, M. (1999). Adolescents' and young adults' reasoning about career choice and the role of parental influence. *Journal of Research on Adolescence, 9*, 253–275.

Bremner, J. (2002). The nature of imitation by infants. *Infant Behavior & Development, 25*, 65–67.

Brendgen, M., Vitaro, F., & Bukowski, W. (1998). Affiliation with delinquent friends: Contributions of parents, self-esteem, delinquent behavior, and rejection by peers. *Journal of Early Adolescence, 18*, 244–265.

Brener, N., Hassan, S., & Barrios, L. (1999). Suicidal ideation among college students in the United States. *Journal of Consulting & Clinical Psychology, 67*, 1004–1008.

Brennan, F., & Ireson, J. (1997). Training phonological awareness: A study to evaluate the effects of a program of metalinguistic games in kindergarten. *Reading & Writing, 9*, 241–263.

Brent, R.L. (2004a). Environmental causes of human congenital malformations: The pediatrician's role in dealing with these complex clinical problems caused by a multiplicity of environmental and genetic factors. *Pediatrics, 113*(4 S), 957–968.

Brent, R.L. (2004b). Teratology in the 20th century environmental causes of congenital malformations in humans and how they were established by Harold Kalter. *Neurotoxicology and Teratology, 26*(1), 1–12.

Breslau, N., & Chilcoat, H. (2000). Psychiatric sequelae of low birth weight at 11 years of age. *Biological Psychiatry, 47*, 1005–1011.

Breslau, N., DelDotto, J.E., Brown, G.G., Kumar, S., Ezhuthachan, S., Hufnagle, K.G., & Peterson, E.L. (1994). A gradient relationship between low birth weight and IQ at age 6 years. *Archives of Pediatric and Adolescent Medicine, 2148*, 377–383.

Breslau, N., Johnson, E., & Lucia, V. (2001). Academic achievement of low birthweight children at age 11: The role of cognitive abilities at school entry. *Journal of Abnormal Child Psychology, 29*(4), 273–279.

Breslow, L., & Breslow, N. (1993). Health practices and disability: Some evidence from Alameda County. *Preventive Medicine, 22*, 86–95.

Briggs, R. (1990). Biological aging. In J. Bond & P. Coleman (Eds.), *Aging in society* (pp. 48–61). London, England: Sage.

British Columbia Ministry of Education. (2001). English as a second language. Victoria, BC: Author. Retrieved from www.bced.gov.bc.ca/esl/policy/introduction.htm

British Columbia Ministry of Health (2006). *A provincial framework for end-of-life care*. Victoria, BC: Author. Retrieved from www.health.gov.bc.ca/library/publications/year/2006/framework.pdf

Britner, S., & Pajares, F. (2006). Sources of science self-efficacy beliefs in middle school students. *Journal of Research in Science Teaching, 43*(5), 485–499.

Broach, D., & Schroeder, D. (2006). Air traffic control specialist age and en route operational errors. *International Journal of Aviation Psychology, 16*, 363–373.

Brock, D.B., Guralnik, J.M., & Brody, J.A. (1990). Demography and the epidemiology of aging in the United States. In E.L. Schneider & J.W. Rowe (Eds.), *Handbook of the biology of aging* (3rd ed., pp. 3–23). San Diego, CA: Academic Press.

Brockington, I. (1996). *Motherhood and mental health*. Oxford, England: Oxford University Press.

Brody, E.M., Litvin, S.J., Albert, S.M., & Hoffman, C.J. (1994). Marital status of daughters and patterns of parent care. Journals of Gerontology: Social Sciences, 49, S95–103.

Brody, J.E. (1995, October 4). Personal health. *New York Times*, p. B7.

Brody, J.E. (1996, February 28). Good habits outweigh genes as key to a healthy old age. *New York Times*, p. B9.

Brody, N. (1992). *Intelligence* (2nd ed.). San Diego, CA: Academic Press.

Bromberger, J., Matthews, K., Schott, L., Brockwell, S., Avis, N., Kravitz, H., . . . Randolph, J. (2007). Depressive symptoms during the menopausal transition: The Study of Women's Health Across the Nation (SWAN). *Journal of Affective Disorders*. 267–272.

Bronfenbrenner, U. (1979). *The ecology of human development*. Cambridge, MA: Harvard University Press.

Bronfenbrenner, U. (2005). The bioecological theory of human development (2001). In U. Bronfenbrenner (Ed.), *Making human beings human: Bioecological perspectives on human development* (pp. 3–15). Thousand Oaks, CA: Sage Publications, Inc.

Bronson, G.W. (1994). Infants' transitions toward adult-like scanning. *Child development, 65*, 1253–1261.

Brook, J., Whiteman, M., Finch, S., & Cohen, P. (2000). Longitudinally foretelling drug use in the late twenties: Adolescent personality and social-environmental antecedents. *Journal of Genetic Psychology, 161*, 37–51.

Brooks-Gunn, J. (1995). Children in families in communities: Risk and intervention in the Bronfenbrenner tradition. In P. Moen, G.H. Elder, Jr., & K. Lüscher (Eds.), *Examining lives in context: Perspectives on the ecology of human development* (pp. 467–519). Washington, DC: American Psychological Association.

Brooks-Gunn, J., Guo, G., & Furstenberg, F.F., Jr. (1993). Who drops out of and who continues beyond high school? A 20-year follow-up of black urban youth. *Journal of Research on Adolescence, 3*, 271–294.

Broom, D., D'Souza, R., Rennie, M., Strazdins, L., Butterworth, P., Parslow, R., & Rogers, B. (2007). The lesser evil: Bad jobs or unemployment? A survey of mid-aged Australians. *Social Science & Medicine, 63*, 575–586.

Brotman, L.M., O'Neal, C.R., Huang, K-Y., Gouley, K.K., Rosenfelt, A., & Shrout, P.E. (2009). An experimental test of parenting practices as mediator of early childhood physical aggression. *Journal of Child Psychology and Psychiatry, 50*(3), 235–245.

Brown, A., & Day, J. (1983). Macrorules for summarizing text: The development of expertise. *Journal of Verbal Learning and Verbal Behavior, 22*, 1–14.

Brown, A.S., Jones, E.M., & Davis, T.L. (1995). Age differences in conversational source monitoring. *Psychology and Aging, 10*, 111–122.

Brown, B. (2004). Homes for a booming market. Retrieved from www.aarp.org/bulletin/yourlife/a2004-08-11-boomingmarket.html.

Brown, B.B. (1990). Peer groups and peer cultures. In S.S. Feldman & G.R. Elliott (Eds.), *At the threshold: The developing adolescent* (pp. 171–196). Cambridge, MA: Harvard University Press.

Brown, B.B., & Huang, B. (1995). Examining parenting practices in different peer contexts: Implications for adolescent trajectories. In L.J. Crockett & A.C. Crouter (Eds.), *Pathways through adolescence* (pp. 151–174). Mahwah, NJ: Erlbaum.

Brown, B.B., Dolcini, M.M., & Leventhal, A. (1995, March). *The emergence of peer crowds: Friend or foe to adolescent health?* Paper presented at the biennial meetings of the Society for Research in Child Development, Indianapolis, IN.

Brown, B.B., Mory, M.S., & Kinney, D. (1994). Casting adolescent crowds in a relational perspective: Caricature, channel, and context. In R. Montemayor, G.R. Adams, & T.P. Gullotta (Eds.), *Personal relationships during adolescence* (pp. 123–167). Thousand Oaks, CA: Sage.

Brown, G., & Dixson, A. (2000). The development of behavioral sex differences in infant rhesus macaques. *Primates, 41*, 63–77.

Brown, I., & Fudge Schormans, A. (2004). *Maltreatment rates in children with developmental delay*. CECW Information Sheet #9E. Toronto, ON: Faculty of Social Work, University of Toronto. Retrieved from Canadian Child Welfare Portal website: www.cecwcepb.ca/DocsEng/DDMaltreatmentRates9E.pdf

Brown, L., Karrison, T., & Cibils, L. (1994). Mode of delivery and perinatal results in breech presentation. *American Journal of Obstetrics & Gynecology, 171*(1), 28–34.

Brown, R. (1973). *A first language: The early stages*. Cambridge, MA: Harvard University Press.

Brown, R., & Bellugi, U. (1964). Three processes in the acquisition of syntax. *Harvard Educational Review, 334*, 133–151.

Brown, S. (2003). Relationship quality dynamics of cohabiting unions. *Journal of Family Issues, 24*(5), 583–601.

Brown, S., Estroff, J.,& Barnewolf, C. (2004). Fetal MRI. *Applied Radiology, 33*, 9–25.

Brown, S.L. (2000). The effect of union type on psychological well-being: Depression among cohabitors versus marrieds. *Journal of Health and Social Behavior, 41*(3), 241–255.

Brown, W., Basil, M., & Bocarnea, M. (2003). Social influence of an international celebrity: Responses to the death of Princess Diana. *Journal of Communication, 53*, 587–605.

Brownell, C.A. (1990). Peer social skills in toddlers: Competencies and constraints illustrated by same-age and mixed-age interaction. *Child Development, 61*, 836–848.

Brownridge, D.A., & Halli, S.S. (2001). Marital status as differentiating factor in Canadian women's coping with partner violence. *Journal of Comparative Family Studies, 32*(1), 117–125.

Bruer, J. (1999). *The myth of the first three years*. New York, NY: Free Press.

Bryant, P., MacLean, M., & Bradley, L. (1990). Rhyme, language, and children's reading. *Applied Psycholinguistics, 11*, 237–252.

Bryant, P.E., MacLean, M., Bradley, L.L., & Crossland, J. (1990). Rhyme and alliteration, phoneme detection, and learning to read. *Developmental Psychology, 26*, 429–438.

Bryant, S., & Rakowski, W. (1992). Predictors of mortality among elderly African-Americans. *Research on Aging, 14*, 50–67.

Buchanan, P., & Vardaxis, V. (2003). Sex-related and age-related differences in knee strength of basketball players ages 11–17 years. *Journal of Athletic Training, 38*, 231–237.

Buchbinder, E., & Eisikovits, Z. (2003). Battered women's entrapment in shame: A phenomenological study. *American Journal of Orthopsychiatry, 73*, 355–366.

Buchner, D.M., Beresford, S.A.A., Larson, E.B., LaCroix, A.Z., & Wagner, E.H. (1992). Effects of physical activity on health status in older adults II: Intervention studies. *Annual Review of Public Health, 13*, 469–488.

Buckett, W., & Tan, S.L. (2004). What is the most relevant standard of success in assisted reproduction? The importance of informed choice. *Human Reproduction, 19*(5), 1043–1045.

Bukowski, W., Sippola, L., & Hoza, B. (1999). Same and other: Interdependency between participation in same- and other-sex friendships. *Journal of Youth & Adolescence, 28*, 439–459.

Bulcroft, R.A., & Bulcroft, K.A. (1991). The nature and functions of dating in later life. *Research on Aging, 13*, 244–260.

Bullock, M., & Lütkenhaus, P. (1990). Who am I? Self-understanding in toddlers. *Merrill-Palmer Quarterly, 36,* 217–238.

Bumpass, L.L., & Aquilino, W.S. (1995). *A social map of midlife: Family and work over the middle life course.* (Report of the MacArthur Foundation research network on successful midlife development). Vero Beach, FL: Author.

Burger, K. (in press). How does early childhood care and education affect cognitive development? An international review of the effects of early interventions for children from different social backgrounds. *Early Childhood Research Quarterly.*

Burgess, S. (1997). The role of shared reading in the development of phonological awareness: A longitudinal study of middle to upper class children. *Early Child Development & Care, 127/128,* 191–199.

Buriel, R., Perez, W., DeMent, T., Chavez, D., & Moran, V. (1998). The relationship of language brokering to academic performance, biculturalism, and self-efficacy among Latino adolescents. *Hispanic Journal of Behavioral Sciences, 20,* 283–297.

Burke, L., & Follingstad, D. (1999). Violence in lesbian and gay relationships: Theory, prevalence, and correlational factors. *Clinical Psychology Review, 19,* 487–512.

Burn, S., O'Neil, A., & Nederend, S. (1996). Childhood tomboyishness and adult androgeny. *Sex Roles, 34,* 419–448.

Burnham, H., & Hogervorst, E. (2004). Recognition of facial expressions of emotion by patients with dementia of the Alzheimer type. *Dementia & Geriatric Cognitive Disorders, 18,* 75–79.

Burns, T.C., Yoshida, K.A., Hill, K., & Werker, J.F. (2007). The development of phonetic representation in bilingual and monolingual infants. *Applied Psycholinguistics, 28*(3), 455–474.

Burton, P., Phipps, S., & Curtis, L. (2005). All in the family: A simultaneous model of parenting style and child conduct (11F0019MIE). Ottawa, ON: Statistics Canada. Retrieved from www.statcan.gc.ca/pub/11f0019m/11f0019m2005261-eng.pdf

Bus, A., & van IJzendoorn, M. (1999). Phonological awareness and early reading: A meta-analysis of experimental training studies. *Journal of Educational Psychology, 91,* 403–414.

Bushnell, L.W.R. (2001). Mother's face recognition in newborn infants: Learning and memory. *Infant and Child Development, 10,* 67–74. doi: 10.1002/icd.248

Bushnik, T. (2006). Child Care in Canada (89–599–MIE2006003). Ottawa, ON: Minister of Industry. Retrieved from Statistics Canada website: www.statcan.ca/english/research/89-599-MIE/89-599-MIE2006003.pdf

Bushnik, T., Bar-Telford, L., & Bussière, P. (2004). *In and out of school: First results from the second cycle of Youth in Transition Survey, 2002* (Cat. No. 81-595). Ottawa, ON: Statistics Canada.

Bushnik, T., & Garner, R (2008). The children of older first-time mothers in Canada: their health and development. (89-599-M). Ottawa, ON: Statistics Canada. Retrieved from Women's Health Resources website: http://thesurvey.womenshealthdata.ca/pdf_files/89-599-MIE2008005.pdf

Buss, A. (1989). Temperaments as personality traits. In G.A. Kohnstamm, J.E. Bates, & M.K. Rothbart (Eds.), *Temperament in childhood* (pp. 49–58). Chichester, England: Wiley.

Buss, A.H., & Plomin, R. (1984). *Temperament: Early developing personality traits.* Hillsdale, NJ: Erlbaum.

Buss, D., Abbott, M., Algleitner, A., Ahserian, A., Biaggio, A., Blanco-Villasenor, A. . . . Yang, K. (1990). International preferences in selecting mates: A study of 37 cultures. *Journal of Cross-Cultural Psychology, 21,* 5–47.

Buss, D.M. (1999). *Evolutionary psychology: The new science of the mind.* Boston, MA: Allyn & Bacon.

Bussey, K., & Bandura, A. (1992). Self-regulation mechanisms governing gender development. *Child Development, 63,* 1236–1250.

Bussière, P., Knighton, T. & Pennock, D. (2007). Measuring up : Canadian results of the OECD PISA Study; no. 3 (CS81-590-XPE). Ottawa, ON: Minister of Industry. Retrieved from the Programme for International Student Assessment website: www.pisa.gc.ca/81-590-E.pdf

Butler, R. (1963). The life review: An interpretation of reminiscence in the aged. *Psychiatry: Interpersonal & Biological Processes, 26,* 65–76.

Butler, R. (2002). The life review. *Journal of Geriatric Psychiatry, 35,* 7–10.

Butters, M., Whyte, E., Nebes, R., Begley, A., Dew, M., Mulsant, B., . . . Becker, J. (2004). Nature and determinants of neuropsychological functioning in late-life depression. *Archives of General Psychiatry, 61,* 587–595.

Buzi, R., Roberts, R., Ross, M., Addy, R., & Markham, C. (2003). The impact of a history of sexual abuse on high-risk sexual behaviors among females attending alternative schools. *Adolescence, 38,* 595–605.

Byrne, G., & Raphael, B. (1999). Depressive symptoms and depressive episodes in recently widowed older men. *International Psychogeriatrics, 11,* 67–74.

Byrne, G., Raphael, B., & Arnold, E. (1999). Alcohol consumption and psychological distress in recently widowed older men. *Australian & New Zealand Journal of Psychiatry, 33,* 740–747.

Byrne, M. (1998). Taking a computational approach to aging: The SPAN theory of working memory. *Psychology & Aging, 13,* 309–322.

Cahn, D., Marcotte, A., Stern, R., Arruda, J., Akshoomoff, N., & Leshko, I. (1966). The Boston Qualitative Scoring System for the Rey-Osterrieth Complex Figure: A study of children with attention deficit hyperactivity disorder. *Clinical Neuropsychologist, 10,* 397–406.

Cairns, R.B., & Cairns, B.D. (1994). *Lifelines and risks: Pathways of youth in our time.* Cambridge, England: Cambridge University Press.

Calderon-Margalit, R., Qiu, C., Ornoy, A., Siscovick, D.S., & Williams, M.A. (2009). Risk of preterm delivery and other adverse perinatal outcomes in relation to maternal use of psychotropic medications during pregnancy. *American Journal of Obstetrics & Gynecology, 201*(6), 579.

Calero, M., & Navarro, E. (2007). Cognitive plasticity as a modulating variable on the effects of memory training in elderly persons. *Archives of Clinical Neuropsychology, 22,* 63–72.

Callaghan, T. (1999). Early understanding and production of graphic symbols. *Child Development, 70,* 1314–1324.

Callaghan, T., & Rankin, M. (2002). Emergence of graphic symbol functioning and the question of domain specificity: A longitudinal training study. *Child Development, 73,* 359–376.

Callinan, P.A., & Feinberg, A.P. (2006). The emerging science of epigenomics. *Human Molecular Genetics, 15*(Review Issue No. 1), 95–101.

Calvanese. V., Lara. E., Kahn. A., & Fraga. M.F. (2009). The role of epigenetics in aging and age-related diseases. *Ageing Research Reviews, 8*(4), 268–76.

Campaign 2000 (2009). 2009 report card on child and family poverty in Canada: 1989–2009. Toronto, ON: Author. Retrieved from www.campaign2000.ca/reportCards/national/2009EnglishC2000NationalReportCard.pdf

Campanella, J.L., & Rovee-Collier, C. (2005). Latent learning and deferred imitation at 3 months. *Infancy, 7,* 243–262.

Campbell, A., Shirley, L., & Candy, J. (2004). A longitudinal study of gender-related cognition and behaviour. *Developmental Science, 7,* 1–9.

Campbell, A., Shirley, L., & Caygill, L. (2002). Sex-typed preferences in three domains: Do two-year-olds need cognitive variables? *British Journal of Psychology, 93,* 203–217.

Campbell, D.W., Eaton, W.O., & McKeen, N.A. (2002). Motor activity level and behavioural control in young children. *International Journal of Behavioral Development, 26*(4), 289–296.

Campbell, F., Ramey, C., Pungello, E., Sparling, J., & Miller-Johnson, S. (2002). Early childhood education: Young adult outcomes from the Abecedarian Project. *Applied Developmental Science, 6,* 42–57.

Campbell, F.A., & Ramey, C.T. (1994). Effects of early intervention on intellectual and academic achievement: A follow-up study of children from low-income families. *Child Development, 65,* 684–698.

Campbell, J.C. (2001). Abuse during pregnancy: a quintessential threat to maternal and child health—so when do we start to act? *Canadian Medical Association Journal, 164*(5), 1578–1579.

Campbell, L., Connidis, I., & Davies, L. (1999). Sibling ties in later life: A social network analysis. *Journal of Family Issues, 20,* 114–148.

Campbell, P.A., Perez-Iratxeta, C., Andrade-Navarro, M.A., & Rudnicki, M.A. (2007, June 20). Oct4 targets regulatory nodes to modulate stem cell function. *PLoS ONE, 2*(6), e553-e553. Retrieved from www.plosone.org/article/fetchArticle. action?articleURI=info:doi/10.1371/journal.pone.0000553

Campisi, J., Dimri, G., & Hara, E. (1996). Control of replicative senescence. In E.L. Schneider & J.W. Rowe (Eds.), Handbook of the biology of aging (4th ed., pp. 121–149). San Diego, CA: Academic Press.

Campisi, L., Serbin, L.A., Stack, D.M., Schwartzman, A.E., & Ledingham, J.E. (2009). Precursors of language ability and academic performance: An intergenerational, longitudinal study of at-risk children. *Infant and Child Development, 18*(5), 377–403.

Canada Safety Council (2007). *Preparation and Communication the Key for Children Home Alone.* Ottawa, ON: Author. Retrieved from http://archive.safety-council.org/info/child/alone.html

Canadian Aboriginal. (1999). Federal paternalism angers Pikangikum. *Canadian Aboriginal News.* Retrieved from www.canadianaboriginal.com/news/news131a.htm

Canadian Cancer Society. (2007). *The human papillomavirus (HPV) and the HPV vaccine.* Toronto, ON: Author. Retrieved from www.cancer.ca/ccs/internet/standardpf/ 0,3182,3172_1242735771_1242735798_langId-en,00.html

Canadian Cancer Society's Steering Committee. (2010). Canadian cancer statistics 2010. Toronto, ON: Canadian Cancer Society. Retrieved from www.ncic.cancer.ca

Canadian Centre for Philanthropy. (2003). *The giving and volunteering of seniors.* Toronto, ON: Author. Retrieved from Giving and Volunteering website: www.givingandvolunteering.ca/pdf/ factsheets/2000_CA_Giving_and_volunteering_in_Seniors.pdf

Canadian Child Care Federation. (2009). Toy safety. Retrieved from www.cccf-fcsge.ca/docs/cccf/RS_26-e.pdf

Canadian Council on Social Development. (1999). *Immigrant youth in Canada: Arriving in Canada.* Ottawa, ON: Author. Retrieved from www.ccsd.ca/subsites/cd/docs/iy/arriving.htm

Canadian Council on Social Development. (1999b). Work, family and community: Key issues and directions for future research (3.2 Social trends). Ottawa, ON: Author. Retrieved December 23, 2001 from http://labour.hrdc-drhc.gc.ca/worklife/CCSD-CCDS/ c32-en.html

Canadian Council on Social Development. (2000a). *Time to debate social Canada.* Ottawa, ON: Author. Retrieved from www.ccsd. ca/pr/oped00ml.htm

Canadian Council on Social Development. (2000b). Immigrant youth in Canada: Highlights. In *Cultural diversity: A CCSD research program.* Ottawa, ON: Author. Retrieved from www.ccsd.ca/ subsites/cd/docs/iy/hl.htm

Canadian Council on Social Development. (2000c). Immigrant youth in Canada: Lifestyle patterns of immigrant youth. In *Cultural diversity: A CCSD research program.* Ottawa, ON: Author. Retrieved from www.ccsd.ca/subsites/cd/docs/iy/lifestyl.htm

Canadian Council on Social Development. (2001). *Highlights: The progress of Canada's children 2001.* Ottawa, ON: Author. Retrieved from www.ccsd.ca/pubs/2001/pcc2001/hl.htm

Canadian Education Statistics Council (2009). Education indicators in Canada: An international perspective (81-604-X). Ottawa, ON: Statistics Canada. Retrieved from www.statcan.gc.ca/bsolc/olc-cel/ olc-cel?catno=81-604-X&lang=eng

Canadian Education Statistics Council (2010). Interrupting high school and returning to education (81-599-X). Ottawa, ON: Statistics Canada. Retrieved from www.cmec.ca/Publications/Lists/ Publications/Attachments/224/81-599-x2010005-eng.pdf

Canadian Fertility and Andrology Society, The. (2006). *Human assisted reproduction live birth rates for Canada.* Retrieved from www.cfas.ca/2006_Press_Release.pdf

Canadian Fitness and Lifestyle Research Institute. (2001). *2000 physical activity monitor.* Ottawa, ON: Author. Retrieved from www.cflri.ca/pdf/e/2000pamrep.pdf

Canadian Heart Health Strategy and Action Plan. (2009). Building a heart healthy Canada. Retrieved from www.chhs.ca/en/reports

Canadian Heritage. (1999). *Second Language Education*, 2. Second Language Learning: A chance to become bilingual. Ottawa, ON: Author [Online information kit]. Retrieved from www.pch.gc.ca/ offlangoff/publications/kit/EF02b.htm

Canadian Heritage. (2001). *Multiculturalism: Strength through diversity.* Ottawa, ON: Author. Retrieved from www.pch.gc.ca/multi/ reports/ann98-99/multic_e.shtml

Canadian Heritage. (2004). *Canadian diversity: Respecting our differences.* Ottawa, ON: Author. Retrieved from www.pch.gc.ca/progs/ multi/respect_e.cfm

Canadian Hospice Palliative Care Association. (2007). Influencing change: A patient and caregiver advocacy guide. Ottawa, ON: Author. Retrieved from www.living-lessons.org/resources/secured/ eng_advocacy_092107.pdf

Canadian Hospice Palliative Care Association. (2009a). The Canadian Hospice Palliative Care Association . . . A History. Ottawa, ON: Author. Retrieved from www.chpca.net/about_us/history.html

Canadian Hospice Palliative Care Association. (2009b). National directory of hospice palliative care services. Ottawa, ON: Author. Retrieved from www.chpca.net/canadian_directory_of_hospice_ palliative_care_services.htm

Canadian Institute for Health Information (2007b). Health care use at the end of life in Western Canada. Ottawa, ON: Author. Retrieved from http://secure.cihi.ca/cihiweb/products/ end_of_life_report_aug07_e.pdf

Canadian Institute for Health Information. (2007a). HSMR: A new approach for measuring hospital mortality trends in Canada. Ottawa, ON: Author. Retrieved from http://secure.cihi.ca/cihiweb/ products/HSMR_hospital_mortality_trends_in_canada.pdf

Canadian Institute of Child Health. (2000). *The health of Canada's children: A CICH profile* (3rd ed.). Ottawa, ON: Canadian Institute of Child Health.

Canadian Institutes of Health Research. (2007, June 29). Updated guidelines for human pluripotent stem cell research. Ottawa, ON: Author. Retrieved from www.cihr-irsc.gc.ca/e/34460.html

Canadian International Development Agency. (2000). *Micronutrient malnutrition.* Author. Retrieved from www.acdi-cida.gc.ca/cida_ind. nsf/vLUallDocByIDEn/D1509FA7EF751EDF8525686C006D06B8? OpenDocument

Canadian Medical Association. (2001, August 3). *Dr. James Fraser Mustard to receive the CMA's highest honour.* Ottawa, ON: Author. Retrieved from www.cma.ca/cma/common/displayPage.do?pageId=/ staticContent/HTML/N0/l2/MedPost/JamesFraserMustard.htm

Canadian Mental Health Association. (2003). *Eating disorders.* Toronto, ON: Author. Retrieved from www.cmha.ca/english/ info_centre/mh_pamphlets/mh_pamphlet_ed.pdf

Canadian Paediatric Society (2003). Impact of media on children and youth. *Paediatrics & Child Health, 8*(5), 301–306.

Canadian Paediatric Society. (2004). Effective discipline for children. *Paediatrics & Child Health, 9*(1), 37–41.

Canadian Paediatric Society. (2009). *Recommendation for safe sleeping environments for infants and children.* Retrieved from www.cps.ca/english/statements/cp/cp04-02.htm

Canadian Paediatric Society. (2010). Promoting optimal monitoring of child growth in Canada: Using the new World Health Organization growth charts- executive summary. *Paediatric Child Health, 15*(2), 77–79.

Canadian Parents for French. (2001). *The state of French second language in Canada 2001.* Ottawa, ON: Author. Retrieved from www.cpf.ca/English/resources/FSL%202001%20Report/ stateoffsl2001.htm

Canadian Psychological Association. (2004). Policy statement on *physical punishment of children and youth.* Ottawa, ON: Author. Retrieved from www.cpa.ca/documents/policy.html

Canadian Radio-television and Telecommunications Commission (2006). The future environment facing the Canadian Broadcasting System. Ottawa, ON: Author. Retrieved from www.crtc.gc.ca/eng/ publications/reports/broadcast/rep061214.htm

Canadian Toy Testing Council. (2004). *Welcome to the Canadian Toy Testing Council website!* Retrieved from www.toy-testing.org/ CTTCmm.htm

Canadian Toy Testing Council. (2010). Canadian toy testing council: About us. Retrieved from www.toy-testing.org/aboutus.html

Cao, L., Jiao, X., Zuzga, D., Liu, Y., Fong, D., Young, D., & During, M. (2004). VEGF links hippocampal activity with neurogenesis, learning and memory. *Nature Genetics, 36,* 827–835.

Cao, Q., Xu, X-M., DeVries, W.H., Enzmann, G.U., Ping, P., Tsoulfas, P., et al. (2005). Functional recovery in traumatic spinal cord injury after transplantation of multineurotrophin-expressing glial-restricted precursor cells. *Journal of Neuroscience, 25*(30), 6947–6957.

Capron, C., & Duyme, M. (1989). Assessment of effects of socio-economic status on IQ in a full cross-fostering study. *Nature, 340,* 552–554.

Care, E., Deans, J., & Brown, R. (2007). The realism and sex type of four to five-year-old children's occupational aspirations. *Early Childhood Research, 5*(2), 155–68.

Carey, S., & Bartlett, E. (1978). Acquiring a single new word. *Papers & Reports on Child Language Development, 15,* 17–29.

Carey, S., & Xu, F. (2001). Infants' knowledge of objects: Beyond object files and object tracking. *Cognition, 80*(1–2), 179–213.

Carlson, E., Sampson, M., & Sroufe, A. (2003). Implications of attachment theory and research for developmental-behavioral pediatrics. *Journal of Developmental & Behavioral Pediatrics, 24,* 364–379.

Carlson, E., Sroufe, A., & Egeland, B. (2004). The construction of experience: A longitudinal study of representation and behavior. *Child Development, 75,* 66–83.

Carmeli, E., Reznick, A., Coleman, R., & Carmeli, V. (2000). Muscle strength and mass of lower extremities in relation to functional abilities in elderly adults. *Gerontology, 46,* 249–257.

Carnelley, K., Wortman, C., & Kessler, R. (1999). The impact of widowhood on depression: Findings from a prospective survey. *Psychological Medicine, 29,* 1111–1123.

Carnelley, K., Wortman, C., Bolger, N., & Burke, C. (2006). The time course of grief reactions to spousal loss: Evidence from a national probability sample. *Journal of Personality and Social Psychology, 91*(3), 476–492.

Caron, A.J., & Caron, R.F. (1981). Processing of relational information as an index of infant risk. In S. Friedman & M. Sigman (Eds.), *Preterm birth and psychological development* (pp. 219–240). New York, NY: Academic Press.

Carpendale, J.I.M., & Lewis, C. (2004). Constructing an understanding of mind: The development of children's understanding of mind within social interaction. *Behavioral and Brain Sciences, 27*(1), 79–96.

Carpenter, R.G., Irgens, L.M., Blair, P.S., England, P.D., Fleming, P., Huber, J., . . . Schreuder, P. (2004). Sudden unexplained infant death in 20 regions in Europe: Case control study. *Lancet, 363,* 185–191.

Carpenter, S. (2001). Teens' risky behavior is about more than race and family resources. *APA Monitor, 32,* 22–23.

Carrière, G. (2003). Parent and child factors associated with obesity (Statistics Canada, Cat. No. 82-003). *Health Reports, 14*(Supplement), 29–39.

Carson, D., Klee, T. & Perry, C. (1998). Comparisons of children with delayed and normal language at 24 months of age on measures of behavioral difficulties, social and cognitive development. *Infant Mental Health Journal, 19,* 59–75.

Carstensen, L.L. (1992). Social and emotional patterns in adulthood: Support for socioemotional selectivity theory. Psychology and Aging, 7, 331–338.

Carstensen, L.L., Gottman, J.M., & Levenson, R.W. (1995). Emotional behavior in long-term marriage. *Psychology and Aging, 10,* 140–149.

Cartwright, C. (2006). You want to know how it affected me? Young adults' perceptions of the impact of parental divorce. *Journal of Divorce & Remarriage, 44,* 125–143.

Carver, P., Egan, S., & Perry, D. (2004). Children who question their heterosexuality. *Developmental Psychology, 40,* 43–53.

Carver, R.P. (1990). Intelligence and reading ability in grades 2–12. *Intelligence, 14,* 449–455.

Casas, J.F., & Mosher, M. (1995, March). *Relational and overt aggression in preschool: "You can't come to my birthday party unless . . ."* Paper presented at the biennial meeting of the Society for Research in Child Development, Indianapolis, IN.

Casasola, M., & Cohen, L. (2000). Infants' association of linguistic labels with causal actions. *Developmental Psychology, 36,* 155–168.

Case, R. (1985). *Intellectual development: Birth to adulthood.* New York, NY: Academic Press.

Case, R. (1991). Stages in the development of the young child's first sense of self. *Developmental Review, 11,* 210–230.

Case, R. (1992). *The mind's staircase: Exploring thought and knowledge.* Hillsdale, NJ: Erlbaum.

Case, R. (1997). The development of conceptual structures. In B. Damon (General Ed.) and D. Kuhn & R. S. Siegler (Series Eds.), *Handbook of child psychology, Vol. 2: Cognitive, language, and perceptual development.* New York, NY: Wiley.

Cashon, C., & Cohen, L. (2000). Eight-month-old infants' perceptions of possible and impossible events. *Infancy, 1,* 429–446.

Casper, L., & Smith, K. (2002). Dispelling the myths: Self-care, class, and race. *Journal of Family Issues, 23*(6), 716–727.

Caspi, A. (1998). Personality development across the life course. In N. Eisenberg (Ed.), *Handbook of child psychology: Vol. 3. Social, emotional, and personality development* (5th ed., pp. 311–388). New York, NY: Wiley.

Caspi, A. (2000). The child is father of the man: Personality continuities from childhood to adulthood. *Journal of Personality & Social Psychology, 78,* 158–172.

Caspi, A., Harrington, H., Milne, B., Amell, J., Theodore, R., & Moffitt, T. (2003). Children's behavioral styles at age 3 are linked to their adult personality traits at age 26. *Journal of Personality, 71,* 495–513.

Cassidy, J., & Berlin, L.J. (1994). The insecure/ambivalent pattern of attachment: Theory and research. *Child Development, 65,* 971–991.

Castellsagué, X., Bosch, X., Muñoz, N., Meijer, C., Shah, K., Sanjosé, S., . . . Franceschi, S. (2002). Male circumcision, penile human papillomavirus infection, and cervical cancer in female partners. *New England Journal of Medicine, 346,* 1105–1112.

Castle, J., Groothues, C., Bredenkamp, D., Beckett, C., O'Conner, T.G., & Rutter, M. (1999). Effects of qualities of early institutional care on cognitive attainment. *American Journal of Orthopsychiatry, 69,* 424–437.

Cataletto, M., & Hertz, G. (2005). *Sleeplessness and circadian rhythm disorder.* Retrieved from www.emedicine.com/neuro/topic655.htm

Cate, R., & John, O. (2007). Testing models of the structure and development of future time perspective: Maintaining a focus on opportunities in middle age. *Psychology and Aging, 22,* 186–201.

Cattell, R.B. (1963). Theory of fluid and crystallized intelligence: A critical experiment. *Journal of Educational Psychology, 54,* 1–22.

Cauley, J.A., Seeley, D.G., Ensrud, K., Ettinger, B., Black, D., & Cummings, S.R. (1995). Estrogen replacement therapy and fractures in older women. *Annals of Internal Medicine, 122,* 9–16.

Cavanaugh, J., & Whitbourne, S. (1999). *Gerontology: An interdisciplinary perspective.* New York, NY: Oxford University Press.

Cavill, S., & Bryden, P. (2003). Development of handedness: Comparison of questionnaire and performance-based measures of preference. *Brain & Cognition, 53,* 149–151.

CBC News (2009, Aug 20). *Mandatory retirement fades in Canada.* Author. Retrieved from www.cbc.ca/canada/story/2009/08/20/mandatory-retirement-explainer523.html

CBC News (2009, February 9). *Assisted suicide: The fight for the right to die.* Retrieved from www.cbc.ca/canada/story/2009/02/09/f-assisted-suicide.html

Ceci, S., & Bronfenbrenner, U. (1985). "Don't forget to take the cupcakes out of the oven": Prospective memory, strategic time-monitoring, and context. *Child Development, 56,* 152–164.

Cederblad, M., Hook, B., Irhammar, M., Mercke, A. (1999). Mental health in international adoptees as teenagers and young adults: An epidemiological study. Journal of Child Psychology & Psychiatry & Allied Disciplines, 40, 1239–1248.

Centers for Disease Control. (1994). Prevalence of adults with no known major risk factors for coronary heart disease—behavioral risk factor surveillance system, 1992. *Morbidity and Mortality Weekly Report, 43*, 61–69.

Centers for Disease Control. (2000). Youth risk behavior surveillance—United States, 1999. *Morbidity and Mortality Weekly Report, 49*, 1–96.

Centerwall, B.S. (1989). Exposure to television as a cause of violence. In G. Comstock (Ed.), *Public communication and behavior* (pp. 1–58). San Diego, CA: Academic Press.

Centerwall, B.S. (1992). Television and violence. The scale of the problem and where to go from here. *Journal of the American Medical Association, 267*(22), 3059–3063.

Centre for Addiction and Mental Health. (2010a). *Cannabis.* Retrieved from http://knowledgex.camh.net/primary_care/guidelines_materials/Pregnancy_Lactation/Pages/per_cannabis.aspx

Centre for Addition and Mental Health. (2010b). *Club drugs.* Retrieved from http://knowledgex.camh.net/primary_care/guidelines_materials/Pregnancy_Lactation/Pages/per_club_drugs.aspx

Centre of Excellence for Early Childhood Development (CEECD) (2009a). High quality child care services: A stimulating and caring environment for children. In R.E. Tremblay, R.G. Barr, R.D. Peters, & M. Boivin (Eds.), *Encyclopedia on Early Childhood Development.* Montreal, QC: Centre of Excellence for Early Childhood Development. Retrieved from www.child-encyclopedia.com/pages/PDF/Child_careANGmcP.pdf

Centre of Excellence for Early Childhood Development (CEECD) (2009b). Synthesis on child care (0–5 years). In R.E. Tremblay, R.G. Barr, R.D. Peters, & M. Boivin (Eds.), *Encyclopedia on Early Childhood Development.* Montreal, QC: Centre of Excellence for Early Childhood Development. Retrieved from www.child-encyclopedia.com/pages/PDF/child_care.pdf

Ceponiene, R., Kuchnerenko, E., Fellman, V., Renlund, M., Suominen, K., & Naeaetaenen, R. (2002). Event-related potential features indexing central auditory discrimination by newborns. *Cognitive Brain Research, 13*, 101–113.

Cernoch, J.M., & Porter, R.H. (1985). Recognition of maternal axillary odors by infants. *Child Development, 56*, 1593–1598.

Certain, L.K., & Kahn, R.S. (2002). Prevalence, correlates and trajectory of television viewing among infants and toddlers. *Pediatrics, 109*(4), 634–642.

Chadwick, O., Taylor, E., Taylor, A., Heptinstall, E., & Danckaerts, M. (1999). Hyperactivity and reading disability: A longitudinal study of the nature of the association. *Journal of Child Psychology & Psychiatry, 40*, 1039–1050.

Chalmers, B., Levitt, C., Heaman, M., O'Brien, B., Sauve, R., & Kaczorowski, J. (2009). Breastfeeding rates and hospital breastfeeding practices in Canada: A national survey of women. *Birth, 36*(2), 122–132.

Chamberlain, E., & Solomon, R. (2006). *Youth and impaired driving in Canada: opportunities for progress.* Oakville, ON: MADD Canada. Retrieved from www.madd.ca/english/research/youth_and_impaired_driving_may_2006.pdf

Chandler, M.J., & Lalonde, C. (1998). Cultural continuity as a hedge against suicide in Canada's First Nations. *Transcultural Psychiatry, 35*(2), 193–211.

Chandler, M.J., Lalonde, C.E., Sokol, B., & Hallett, D. (2003). Personal persistence, identity development, and suicide: A study of native and non-native North American adolescents. *Monographs of the Society for Research in Child Development, 68*(2), 1–130.

Chao, R. (1994). Beyond parental control and authoritarian parenting style: Understanding Chinese parenting through the cultural notion of training. *Child Development, 65*, 1111–1119.

Chao, R.K., & Willms, J.D. (1998). Do parenting practices make a difference? (Cat. No. W-98-32Es). Retrieved from Human Resources Development Canada website: www.hrdc-drhc.gc.ca/stratpol/arb/conferences/nlscyconf/chao-e.shtml

Chao, R.K., & Willms, J.D. (2002). The effects of parenting practices on children's outcomes. In J.D. Willms (Ed.), *Vulnerable children* (pp. 71–102). Edmonton, AB: The University of Alberta Press.

Chapman, J., & Tunmer, W. (1997). A longitudinal study of beginning reading achievement and reading self-concept. *British Journal of Educational Psychology, 67*, 279–291.

Chappell, N. (1999). *Volunteering and healthy aging: What we know.* Retrieved from Volunteer Canada website: www.volunteer.ca/volunteer/canada_adults_report_printable.htm

Chaptman, D. (2004, January 24). Education Arcade aims for video-game literacy, markets. *Wisconsin Week.* Madison, WI: University of Wisconsin. Retrieved from www.news.wisc.edu/9333.html

Charlesworth, W.R. (1992). Darwin and developmental psychology: Past and present. *Developmental Psychology, 28*, 5–16.

Chase-Lansdale, P.L., Cherlin, A.J., & Kiernan, K.E. (1995). The long-term effects of parental divorce on the mental health of young adults: A developmental perspective. *Child Development, 66*, 1614–1634.

Chasseigne, G., Grau, S., Mullet, E., & Cama, V. (1999). How well do elderly people cope with uncertainty in a learning task? *Acta Psychologica, 103*, 229–238.

Cheitlin, M. (2003). Cardiovascular physiology: Changes with aging. *American Journal of Geriatric Cardiology, 12*, 9–13.

Cheitlin, M. (2003). Cardiovascular physiology: Changes with aging. *American Journal of Geriatric Cardiology, 12*, 9–13.

Chen, J., Bierhals, A., Prigerson, H., Kasl, S., Mazure, C., & Jacobs, S. (1999). Gender differences in the effects of bereavement-related psychological distress in health outcomes. *Psychological Medicine, 29*, 367–380.

Chen, K., Paick, J., & Ishii, N. (2007). The efficacy and safety of vardenafil in East Asian men with erectile dysfunction. *Journal of Sexual Medicine, 4*, 753–761.

Chen, S. (1997). Child's understanding of secret and friendship development. *Psychological Science (China), 20*, 565–545.

Chen, X., Wen, S.W., Fleming, N., Yang, Q., & Walker, M.C. (2007). Teenage pregnancy and congential anomalies: Which system is vulnerable? *Human Reproduction, 22*(6), 1730–1735.

Chen, X., Wen, S.W., Krewski, D., Fleming, N., Yang, Q., & Walker, M.C. (2008). Paternal age and adverse birth outcomes: teenager or 40+, who is at risk? *Human Reproduction, 23*(6), 1290–1296.

Cheng, Q., Xiaoyan, H., & Dajun, Z. (2006). A review of academic self-concept and its relationship with academic achievement. *Psychological Science (China), 29*, 133–136.

Cheng, L. (2009). Thinking about thinking, how language and math intersect: Chinese v. English. Philosophy, Pop Culture Blog. Retrieved from http://larrycheng.com/2009/10/07/how-language-and-math-intersect-chinese-v-english/

Cheour, M., Martynova, O., Naeaetaenen, R., Erkkola, R., Sillanpaeae, M., Kero, P., . . . Haemaelaeinen, H. (2002). Speech sounds learned by sleeping newborns. *Nature, 415*, 599–600.

Cherlin, A., & Furstenberg, F.F. (1986). *The new American grandparent.* New York, NY: Basic Books.

Cherlin, A., Chase-Lansdale, P., & McRae, C. (1998). Effects of parental divorce on mental health throughout the life course. *American Sociological Review, 63*, 239–249.

Cheung, C.K., Chan, W.T., Lee, T.Y., Liu, S.C., & Leung, K.K. (2001). Structure of moral consciousness and moral intentions among youth in Hong Kong. *International Journal of Adolescence and Youth. 9*, 83–116.

Cheung, C.K., Lee, T.Y., Chan, W.T., Liu, S.C., Leung, K.K. (2004). Developing civic consciousness through social engagement among Hong Kong youths. *The Social Science Journal, 41*(4), 651–660.

Chi, M.T. (1978). Knowledge structure and memory development. In R.S. Siegler (Ed.), *Children's thinking: What develops?* (pp. 73–96). Hillsdale, NJ: Erlbaum.

Chia, S.E., & Shi L.M. (2002). Review of recent epidemiological studies on paternal occupations and birth defects. *Occupational and Environmental Medicine, 59*, 149–155.

Chiappe, P., & Siegel, L. (1999). Phonological awareness and reading acquisition in English- and Punjabi-speaking Canadian children. *Journal of Educational Psychology, 91*, 20–28.

Chiappe, P., Glaeser, B., & Ferko, D. (2007). Speech perception, vocabulary, and the development of reading skills in English among Korean- and English-speaking children. *Journal of Educational Psychology, 99,* 154–166.

Chickering, A., & Reisser, L. (1993). *Education and identity* (2nd ed.). San Francisco, CA: Jossey-Bass.

Chien, Y., Cheng, J., Liu, M., Yang, H., Hsu, M., Chen, C., & Yang, C. (2001). Serologic markers of Epstein-Barr virus infection and nasopharyngeal carcinoma in Taiwanese men. *New England Journal of Medicine, 345,* 1877–1882.

Children's Hospital of Eastern Ontario. (2003). *Joint statement on physical punishment of children and youth.* Ottawa, ON: Author. Retrieved from www.cheo.on.ca/english/pdf/joint_statement_e.pdf

Chincotta, D., & Underwood, G. (1997). Estimates, language of schooling and bilingual digit span. *European Journal of Cognitive Psychology, 9,* 325–348.

Chochinov, H.M. (2006). Dying, dignity, and new horizons in palliative end-of-life care. *A Cancer Journal for Clinicians, 56*(2), 84–103.

Chochinov, H.M. (2007). Dignity and the essence of medicine: The A, B, C and D of Dignity Conserving Care. *British Medical Journal, 335*(7612), 184–187.

Chochinov, H.M., Hack, T., Hassard, T., Kristjanson, L.J., McClement, S., & Harlos, M. (2005). Dignity therapy: A novel psychotherapeutic intervention for patients near the end of life. *Journal of Clinical Oncology, 23*(24), 5520–5525.

Chochinov, H.M., Hassard, T., McClement, S., Hack, T., Kristjanson, L.J., Harlos, M. . . . Murray, A. (2008). The Patient Dignity Inventory: A Novel Way of Measuring Dignity-Related Distress. *Palliative Care Journal of Pain and Symptom Management, 36*(6), 559–571.

Chochinov, H.M., Hassard, T., McClement, S., Hack, T., Kristjanson, L.J., Harlos, M., . . . Murray, A. (2009). The landscape of distress in the terminally ill. *Journal of Pain and Symptom Management, 38*(5), 641–649.

Chochinov, H.M., Kristjanson, L.J., Hack, T., Hassard, T., McClement, S., & Harlos, M. (2006). Dignity in the terminally ill: revisited. *Journal of Palliative Medicine, 9*(3), 666–672.

Choi, N. (2003). Nonmarried aging parents' and their adult children's characteristics associated with transitions into and out of intergenerational coresidence. *Journal of Gerontological Social Work, 40,* 7–29.

Choi, S. (2000). Caregiver input in English and Korean: Use of nouns and verbs in book-reading and toy-play contexts. *Journal of Children's Language, 27,* 69–96.

Chomik, T.A. (2001). *The population health template.* Ottawa, ON. Retrieved from Health Canada website: www.hc-sc.gc.ca/hppb/phdd/pdf/discussion_paper.pdf

Chomsky, N. (1959). A review of B.F. Skinner's *Verbal Behavior. Language, 35,* 26–129.

Chong, B., Babcook, C., Salamat, M., Nemzek, W., Kroeker, D., & Ellis, W. (1996). A magnetic resonance template for normal neuronal migration in the fetus. *Neurosurgery, 39,* 110–116.

Chou, C., & Tsai, M. (2007). Gender differences in Taiwan high school students' computer game playing. *Computers in Human Behavior, 23,* 812–824.

Chou, C., Chou, J., & Tyang, N. (1998, February 18–22). *An exploratory study of Internet addiction, usage, and communication pleasure.* Paper presented at the annual meeting of the Association for Educational Communications and Technology. St. Louis, MO. (ERIC No. ED 416 838).

Christakis, D.A. (2009). The effects of infant media usage: What do we know and what should we learn? *Acta Paediatrica, 98,* 8–16.

Christensen, C. (1997). Onset, rhymes, and phonemes in learning to read. *Scientific Studies of Reading, 1,* 341–358.

Christensen, H., Henderson, A., Griffiths, K., & Levings, C. (1997). Does aging inevitably lead to declines in cognitive performance? A longitudinal study of elite academics. *Personality & Individual Differences, 23,* 67–78.

Chudley, A.E. (2006). *Birth defects and fetal alcohol spectrum disorder.* Winnipeg, MB: Public Health Agency of Canada.

Ciabattari, T. (2004). Cohabitation and housework: The effects of marital intentions. *Journal of Marriage & the Family, 66*(1), 118–125.

Ciancio, D., Sadovsky, A., Malabonga, V., Trueblood, L., & Pasnak, R. (1999). Teaching classification and seriation to preschoolers. *Child Study Journal, 29,* 193–205.

Cicirelli, V. (2006). Fear of death in mid-old age. *Journals of Gerontology: Series B: Psychological Sciences and Social Sciences, 61*(B), 75–81.

Cillessen, A.H.N., van IJzendoorn, H.W., van Lieshout, C.F.M., & Hartup, W.W. (1992). Heterogeneity among peer-rejected boys: Subtypes and stabilities. *Child Development, 63,* 893–905.

Claes, M. (1998). Adolescents' closeness with parents, siblings, and friends in three countries: Canada, Belgium, and Italy. *Journal of Youth & Adolescence, 27,* 165–184.

Clark, S.E., & Symons, D.K. (2009). Representations of attachment relationships, the self, and significant others in middle childhood. *Journal of the Canadian Academy of Child and Adolescent, 18*(4), 316–21.

Clark, W. (1998). Religious observance: Marriage and family (Cat. No. 11-008-XPE). *Canadian Social Trends, Autumn*(50), 2–7.

Clark, W. (2000). Patterns of religious attendance (Cat. No. 11-008-XPE). *Canadian Social Trends, Winter*(59), 23–27.

Clark, W. (2001, 11b). Kids and teens on the net. Canadian Social Trends, 62, 6–10.

Clark, W. (2003). Update on Education. Canadian Social Trends, Winter(71), 19–22.

Clark, W., & Crompton, S. (2006). Till death do us part? The risk of first and second marriage dissolution (Statistics Canada Cat. No. 11-008). *Social Trends, 81,* 24–34.

Clark, W., & Schellenberg, G. (2006). Who's religious? In *Canadian Social Trends* (11-008). Ottawa, ON: Statistics Canada. Retrieved from www.statcan.gc.ca/pub/11-008-x/2006001/pdf/9181-eng.pdf

Clarke, D., & Singh, R. (2005). The influence of pessimistic explanatory style on the relation between stressful life events and hospital doctors' psychological distress. *Social Behavior and Personality, 33,* 259–272.

Clarkson-Smith, L., & Hartley, A.A. (1990). The game of bridge as an exercise in working memory and reasoning. *Journals of Gerontology: Psychological Sciences, 45,* P233–238.

Clearfield, M.W., & Nelson, N.M. (2006). Sex differences in mothers' speech and play behavior with 6-, 9-, and 14-month-old infants. *Sex Roles, 54,*(1/2) doi: 10.1007/s11199-005-8874-1

Clement, T. (2006). *Assisted Human Reproduction Agency of Canada 2006–2007 Report on Plans and Priorities.* Ottawa, ON: Health Canada. Retrieved from Treasury Board of Canada Secretariat website: www.tbs-sct.gc.ca/rpp/0607/ahrac-accpa/ahrac-accpa_e.pdf

Cleveland, G., Forer, B., Hyatt, D., Japel, C., & Krashinsky, M. (2008). New evidence about child care in Canada: Use patterns, affordability and quality. *IRPP Choices, 14*(12), 1–42.

Clifford, T.J., Campbell, M.K., Speechley, K.N., & Gorodzinsky, F. (2002). Empirical evidence of the absence of an association with source of early infant nutrition. *Archives of Pediatrics & Adolescent Medicine, 156*(11), 1123–1128.

Clinkingbeard, C., Minton, B., Davis, J., & McDermott, K. (1999). Women's knowledge about menopause, hormone replacement therapy (HRT), and interactions with healthcare providers: An exploratory study. *Journal of Women's Health & Gender-Based Medicine, 8,* 1097–1102.

Coffey, C., Saxton, J., Ratcliff, G., Bryan, R., & Lucke, J. (1999). Relation of education to brain size in normal aging: Implications for the reserve hypothesis. *Neurology, 53,* 189–196.

Cohen, A.-L., Dixon, R.A., Lindsay, D.S., & Masson, M.E.J. (2003). The effect of perceptual distinctiveness on the prospective and retrospective. *Canadian Journal of Experimental Psychology, 57*(4), 274–289.

Cohen, G. (2000). *The creative age: Awakening human potential in the second half of life.* New York, NY: Avon Books.

Cohen, H., Hailpern, S., & Alderman, M. (2004). Glucose-cholesterol interaction magnifies coronary disease risk for hypertensive patients. *Hypertension, 43,* 983.

Cohen, R. (2001, April 12). Horror expressed in Germany over Dutch euthanasia. *New York Times Online.* Retrieved from www.nytimes.com/2001/04/12/world/horror-expressed-in-germany-over-dutch-euthanasia.html

Cohen, S. (1991). Social supports and physical health: Symptoms, health behaviors, and infectious disease. In E.M. Cummings, A.L. Greene, & K.H. Karraker (Eds.), *Life-span developmental psychology: Perspectives on stress and coping* (pp. 213–234). Hillsdale, NJ: Erlbaum.

Cohen, S. (2006). *Aging changes in immunity. Medline: Medical encyclopedia.* Retrieved www.nlm.nih.gov/medlineplus/ency/article/004008.htm.

Cohen-Kettenis, P., & van Goozen, S. (1997). Sex reassignment of adolescent transsexuals: A follow-up study. *American Academy of Child & Adolescent Psychiatry, 36*, 263–271.

Coie, J.D., & Cillessen, A.H.N. (1993). Peer rejection: Origins and effects on children's development. *Current Directions in Psychological Science, 2*, 89–92.

Colby, A., Kohlberg, L., Gibbs, J., & Lieberman, M. (1983). A longitudinal study of moral judgment. *Monographs of the Society for Research in Child Development, 48*(1–2, Serial No. 200).

Colditz, G.A., Hankinson, S.E., Hunter, D.J., Willett, W.C., Manson, J.E., Stampfer, M.J., . . . Speizer, F.E. (1995). The use of estrogens and progestins and the risk of breast cancer in postmenopausal women. *New England Journal of Medicine, 332*, 1589–1593.

Cole, P., Martin, S., & Dennis, T. (2004). Emotion regulation as a scientific construct: Methodological challenges and directions for child development research. *Child Development, 75*, 317–333.

Coley, R., & Chase-Lansdale, L. (1998). Adolescent pregnancy and parenthood: Recent evidence and future directions. *American Psychologist, 53*, 152–166.

Collet, J.P., Burtin, P., Gillet, J., Bossard, N., Ducruet, T., & Durr, F. (1994). Risk of infectious diseases in children attending different types of day-care setting. Epicreche Research Group. *Respiration, 61*, 16–19.

Collie, R., & Hayne, H. (1999). Deferred imitation by 6- and 9-month-old Infants: More evidence for declarative memory. *Developmental Psychology, 35*(2), 83–90.

Collins, F.S., & McKusick, V.A. (2001). Implications of the Human Genome Project for medical science. *Journal of the American Medical Association, 285*(19), 2447–2448.

Colombo, J. (1993). *Infant cognition: Predicting later intellectual functioning.* Newbury Park, CA: Sage.

Colonia-Willner, R. (1999). Investing in practical intelligence: Ageing and cognitive efficiency among executives. *International Journal of Behavioral Development, 23*, 591–614.

Colwell, J., & Kato, M. (2005). Video game play in British and Japanese adolescents. *Simulation & Gaming, 36*, 518–530.

Comley, L., & Mousmanis, P. (2004). *Improving the odds: Healthy child development.* Toronto, ON: Ontario College of Physicians. Retrieved from Best Start website: www.beststart.org/resources/hlthy_chld_dev/pdf/HCD_complete.pdf

Commissaris, C., Ponds, R., & Jolles, J. (1998). Subjective forgetfulness in a normal Dutch population: Possibilities of health education and other interventions. *Patient Education & Counseling, 34*, 25–32.

Communication Canada (2004). *Statutes of Canada 2004 Chapter 2: An Act respecting assisted human reproduction and related research Bill C-6.* Retrieved from Health Canada website: www.hc-sc.gc.ca/english/pdf/protection/ahr/C-6_4_RA.pdf

Comninos, A., & Grenyer, B. (2007). The influence of interpersonal factors on the speed of recovery from major depression. *Psychotherapy Research, 17*, 230–239.

Compas, B.E., Ey, S., & Grant, K.E. (1993). Taxonomy, assessment, and diagnosis of depression during adolescence. *Psychological Bulletin, 114*, 323–344.

Conference Board of Canada. (2009). *Health: Infant mortality.* Retrieved from www.conferenceboard.ca/hcp/details/health/infant-mortality-rate.aspx

Connidis, I.A. (1989). *Family Ties Later in Life.* Toronto, ON, & Vancouver, BC: Butterworths.

Connidis, I.A. (1994). Sibling support in older age. *Journals of Gerontology: Social Sciences, 49*, S309–317.

Connidis, I.A., & Davies, L. (1992). Confidants and companions: Choices in later life. *Journals of Gerontology: Social Sciences, 47*, S115–122.

Connidis, I.A., & McMullin, J.A. (1993). To have or have not: Parent status and the subjective well-being of older men and women. *The Gerontologist, 33*, 630–636.

Connolly, K., & Dalgleish, M. (1989). The emergence of a tool-using skill in infancy. *Developmental Psychology, 25*, 894–912.

Cook, S., & Heppner, P. (1997). Coping control, problem-solving appraisal, and depressive symptoms during a farm crisis. *Journal of Mental Health Counseling, 19*, 64–77.

Cooke-Reynolds, M., & Zukewich, N. (2004). The feminization of work (Cat. No. 11-008). *Canadian Social Trends, Spring*(72), 24–29.

Cooper, L.G., Gooding, J.S., Gallagher, J., Sternesky, L., Ledsky, R., & Berns, S.D. (2007). Impact of a family-centered care initiative on NICU care, staff and families. *Journal of Perinatology, 27*, s32–s37.

Cooper, P.A., Geldart, S.S., Mondloch, C.J., & Maurer, D. (2006). Developmental changes in perceptions of attractiveness: A role of experience? *Developmental Sciences, 9*(5), 530–543.

Cooper, R.P., & Aslin, R.N. (1994). Developmental differences in infant attention to the spectral properties of infant-directed speech. *Child Development, 65*, 1663–1677.

Co-ordinated Access for Child Care (2009). *Choosing quality child care. The Regional Municipality of Hamilton-Wentworth, ON: Arthur.* Retrieved from www.cafcc.on.ca/quality.php?subs=/choose.php

Coplan, R., Bowker, A., & Cooper, S. (2003). Parenting daily hassles, child temperament and social adjustment in preschool. *Early Childhood Research Quarterly, 18*, 376–395.

Coplan, R.J., & Armer, M. (2005). 'Talking yourself out of being shy': Shyness, expressive vocabulary, and adjustment in preschool. *Merrill-Palmer Quarterly, 51*(1), 20–41.

Coplan, R.J., & Prakash, K. (2003). Spending time with teacher: Characteristics of preschoolers who frequently elicit versus initiate interactions with teachers. *Early Childhood Research Quarterly, 18*(1), 143–158.

Coplan, R.J., Prakash, K., O'Neil, K., & Armer, M. (2004). Do you 'want' to play? Distinguishing between conflicted-shyness and social disinterest in early childhood. *Developmental Psychology, 40*(2), 244–258.

Corbet, A., Long, W., Schumacher, R., Gerdes, J., & Cotton, R. (1995). Double-blind developmental evaluation at 1-year corrected age of 597 premature infants with birth weights from 500 to 1350 grams enrolled in three placebo-controlled trials of prophylactic synthetic surfactant. *Journal of Pediatrics, 126*, S5–12.

Corkum, P., Moldofsky, H., Hogg-Johnson, S., Humphries, T. & Tannock, R. (1999). Sleep problems in children with attention-deficit/hyperactivity disorder: Impact of subtype, comorbidity, and stimulant medication. *Journal of the American Academy of Child and Adolescent Psychiatry, 38*(10), 1285–1293.

Corkum, P., Tannock, R. & Moldofsky, H. (1998). Sleep disturbances in children with attention-deficit/hyperactivity disorder. *Journal of the American Academy of Child and Adolescent Psychiatry, 37*(6), 637–646.

Corr, C.A. (1991/1992). A task-based approach to coping with dying. *Omega, 24*, 81–94.

Corsaro, W., Molinari, L., Hadley, K., & Sugioka, H. (2003). Keeping and making friends: Italian children's transition from preschool to elementary school. *Social Psychology Quarterly, 66*, 272–292.

Corso, J.F. (1987). Sensory-perceptual processes and aging. In K.W. Schaie (Ed.), *Annual review of gerontology and geriatrics: Vol. 7* (pp. 29–56). New York, NY: Springer.

Corwin, J., Loury, M., & Gilbert, A.N. (1995). Workplace, age, and sex as mediators of olfactory function: Data from the National Geographic smell survey. *Journals of Gerontology: Psychological Sciences, 50B*, P179–186.

Cosmides, L., & Tooby, J. (2000). Evolutionary Psychology and the Emotions. In M. Lewis & J. Haviland-Jones (Eds.), *Handbook of emotions* (2nd ed.). New York, NY: Guilford.

Cossette, L., Malcuit, G., & Pomerleau, A. (1991). Sex differences in motor activity during early infancy. *Infant Behavior and Development, 14,* 175–186.

Costa, M., Reus, V., Wolkowitz, O., Manfredi, F., & Lieberman, M. (1999). Estrogen replacement therapy and cognitive decline in memory-impaired post-menopausal women. *Biological Psychiatry, 46,* 182–188.

Costa, P.T., Jr., & McCrae, R.R. (1980). Still stable after all these years: Personality as a key to some issues in adulthood and old age. In P.B. Baltes & O.G. Brim, Jr. (Eds.), *Life-span development and behavior* (pp. 65–102). New York, NY: Academic Press.

Costello, E., Sung, M., Worthman, C., & Angold, A. (2007). Pubertal maturation and the development of alcohol use and abuse. *Drug and Alcohol Dependence, 88,* S50–S59.

Côté, S.M., Vaillancourt, T., LeBlanc, J.C., Nagin, D.S., & Tremblay, R.E. (2006). The development of physical aggression from toddlerhood to pre-adolescence: a nation wide longitudinal study of Canadian children. *Journal of Abnormal Child Psychology, 34*(1), 71–85

Côté, S.M., Vaillancourt, T., Barker, E.D., Nagin, D., & Tremblay, R.E. (2007). The joint development of physical and indirect aggression: Predictors of continuity and change during childhood. *Development and Psychopathology, 19*(1), 37–55.

Cotman, C.W., & Neeper, S. (1996). Activity-dependent plasticity and the aging brain. In E.L. Schneider & J.W. Rowe (Eds.), *Handbook of the biology of aging* (4th ed., pp. 284–299). San Diego, CA: Academic Press.

Cotton, L., Bynum, D., & Madhere, S. (1997). Socialization forces and the stability of work values from late adolescence to early adulthood. *Psychological Reports, 80,* 115–124.

Coulthard, H., & Harris, G. (2003). Early food refusal: The role of maternal mood. *Journal of Reproductive & Infant Psychology, 21,* 335–345.

Coulton, C.J., Korbin, J.E., Su, M., & Chow, J. (1995). Community level factors and child maltreatment rates. *Child Development, 66,* 1262–1276.

Council of Economic Advisers to the President. (2000). Teens and their parents in the 21st century: An examination of trends in teen behavior and the role of parental involvement. Washington, DC: Author. Retrieved from Welcome to the White House website: http://clinton4.nara.gov/media/pdf/CEAreport.pdf

Council of Ministers of Education, Canada (CMEC) (2006). *About the Council of Ministers of Education, Canada (CMEC).* Retrieved from www.cmec.ca/abouteng.stm

Courage, M., & Howe, M. (2002). From infant to child: The dynamics of cognitive change in the second year of life. *Psychological Bulletin, 128,* 250–277.

Cox, J., Bota, G.W., Carter, M., Bretzlaff-Michaud, J.A., Sahai, V., & Rowe, B.H. (2004). Domestic violence. Incidence and prevalence in a northern emergency department. *Canadian Family Physician, 50*(1), 90–97.

Cox, M., Garrett, E., & Graham, J. (2004–2005). Death in Disney films: Implications for children's understanding of death. *Omega: Journal of Death and Dying, 50*(4), 267–280.

Cox, M., Paley, B., Burchinal, M., & Payne, C. (1999). Marital perceptions and interactions across the transition to parenthood. *Journal of Marriage & the Family, 61,* 611–625.

Craig, W.M. (2004). Bullying in Canada. In *The Canadian World Health Organization report on young people in Canada and their health and well being* (pp. 87–96). Ottawa, ON: Health Canada.

Craig, W.M., Peters, R.D., & Willms, J.D. (2002). The role of peer group in pre-adolescent behaviour. In J.D. Willms (Ed.), *Vulnerable children* (pp. 71–102). Edmonton, AB: The University of Alberta Press.

Cramer, D. (1991). Type A behavior pattern, extraversion, neuroticism and psychological distress. *British Journal of Medical Psychology, 64,* 73–83.

Cramer, P. (2000). Defense mechanisms in psychology today. *American Psychologist, 55,* 637–646.

Cranswick, K. (2003). *General Social Survey—Cycle 16: Caring for an aging society, 2002* (Cat. No. 89-582-XIE). Ottawa, ON: Statistics Canada.

Creators, The. (2000, March/April). *Modern Maturity,* 38–44.

Crehan, G. (2004). The surviving sibling: The effects of sibling death in childhood. *Psychoanalytic Psychotherapy, 18,* 202–219.

Crick, N.R., & Grotpeter, J.K. (1995). Relational aggression, gender, and social-psychological adjustment. *Child Development, 66,* 710–722.

Crittenden, P.M. (1992). Quality of attachment in the preschool years. *Development and Psychopathology, 4,* 209–241.

Crittenden, P.M., Partridge, M.F., & Claussen, A.H. (1991). Family patterns of relationship in normative and dysfunctional families. *Development and Psychopathology, 3,* 491–512.

Crockenberg, S. (2003). Rescuing the baby from the bathwater: How gender and temperament (may) influence how child care affects child development. *Child Development, 74,* 1034–1038.

Crockenberg, S., Leerkes, E., & Lekka, S. (2007). Pathways from marital aggression to infant emotion regulation: The development of withdrawal in infancy. *Infant Behavior & Development, 30,* 97–113.

Crompton, S. (2000). Health (Cat. No. 11-008-XPE). *Canadian Social Trends, Winter*(59), 12–17.

Crompton, S. (2005). Always the bridesmaid: People who don't expect to marry (Cat. No. 11-008). *Canadian Social Trends, Summer*(77), 2–8.

Crone, D., & Whitehurst, G. (1999). Age and schooling effects on emergent literacy and early reading skills. *Journal of Educational Psychology, 91,* 594–603.

Crone, E.A., Wendelken, C., Donohue, S., van Leijenhorst, L., & Bunge, S.A. (2006). Neurocognitive development of the ability to manipulate information in working memory. *Proceeding for the National Academy of Sciences, 103,* 9315–9320.

Crook, C. (1987). Taste and olfaction. In P. Salapatek & L. Cohen (Eds.), *Handbook of infant perception, Vol. 1: From sensation to perception* (pp. 237–264). Orlando, FL: Academic Press.

Cropley, J.E., Suter, C.M., Beckman, K.B., & Martin, D.I. (2006). Germ-line epigenetic modification of the murine A^vy allele by nutritional supplementation. *Proceedings of the National Academy of Sciences of the United States of America, 103*(46), 17308–17312.

Crowell, J.A., & Waters, E. (1995, March). *Is the parent–child relationship a prototype of later love relationships? Studies of attachment and working models of attachment.* Paper presented at the biennial meeting of the Society for Research in Child Development, Indianapolis, IN.

Crowley, B., Hayslip, B., & Hobdy, J. (2003). Psychological hardiness and adjustment to life events in adulthood. *Journal of Adult Development, 10,* 237–248.

Cuba, L., & Longino, C.F., Jr. (1991). Regional retirement migration: The case of Cape Cod. *Journals of Gerontology: Social Sciences, 46,* S33–42.

Cuevas, K., Rovee-Collier, C., & Learmonth, A. E. (2006). Infants form associations between memory representations of stimuli that are absent. *Psychological Science, 17,* 543–549.

Cumming, E. (1975). Engagement with an old theory. *International Journal of Aging and Human Development, 6,* 187–191.

Cumming, E., & Henry, W.E. (1961). *Growing old.* New York, NY: Basic Books.

Cummings, E.M., & Davies, P.T. (1994). Maternal depression and child development. *Journal of Child Psychology and Psychiatry, 35,* 73–112.

Cunningham, A.J. & Watson, K. (2004). How psychological therapy may prolong survival in cancer patients: New evidence and a simple theory. *Integrative Cancer Therapies, 3*(3), 214–229.

Cunningham, A.J. (2004). *Healing journey level I workbook.* Toronto, ON: Ontario Cancer Institute/The Princess Margaret Hospital. Retrieved from http://individual.utoronto.ca/hayman/HJPlev1.pdf

Cunningham, A.J. (2005). Can the mind heal cancer? A clinician-scientist examines the evidence. Toronto, ON: Hushion House.

Cunningham, A.J., Phillips, C., Lockwood, G.A., Hedley, D., & Edmonds, C.V.I. (2000). Association of involvement in psychological self-regulation with longer survival in patients with metastatic cancer: An exploratory study. *Advances in Mind-Body Medicine, 16*(4), 276–287.

Cunningham, A.J., Phillips, C., Stephen, J., and Edmonds, C. (2002). Fighting for life: A qualitative analysis of the process of psychotherapy-assisted self-help in patients with metastatic cancer. *Integrative Cancer Therapies 1*(2), 146–161.

Cunningham, L. (1996). *Grief and the adolescent.* Newhall, CA: TeenAge Grief, Inc.

Cunningham, W.R., & Haman, K.L. (1992). Intellectual functioning in relation to mental health. In J.E. Birren, R.B. Sloane, & G.D. Cohen (Eds.), *Handbook of mental health and aging* (2nd ed., pp. 340–355). San Diego, CA: Academic Press.

Curran, S., McLanahan, S., & Knab, J. (2003). Does remarriage expand perceptions of kinship support among the elderly? *Social Science Research, 32,* 171–190.

Currier, J., Holland, J., & Neimeyer, R. (2006). Sense-making, grief, and the experience of violent loss: Toward a mediational model. *Death Studies, 30*(5), 403–428.

Curry, C. (2002). An approach to clinical genetics. In A. Rudolph, R. Kamei, & K. Overby (Eds.), *Rudolph's fundamentals of pediatrics.* (pp. 184–220). New York, NY: McGraw-Hill.

Curyto, K., Chapleski, E., & Lichtenberg, P. (1999). Prediction of the presence and stability of depression in the Great Lakes Native American elderly. *Journal of Mental Health & Aging, 5,* 323–340.

Cushner, K., McClelland, A., & Safford, P. (1992). *Human diversity in education.* New York, NY: McGraw-Hill.

Cuvo, A. (1974). Incentive level influence on overt rehearsal and free recall as a function of age. *Journal of Experimental Child Psychology, 18,* 167–181.

D'Entremont, B. (2000). A perceptual-attentional explanation of gaze following in 3- and 6-month-olds. *Developmental Science, 3,* 302–311.

D'Entremont, B., & Hartung, C. (2003). *A longitudinal investigation of joint attention, emotion regulation and attachment.* Poster presented at the Society for Research in Child Development, Tampa, FL.

D'Entremont, B., Hains, S.M.J., & Muir, D.W. (1997). A demonstration of gaze following in 3- to 6-month-olds. *Infant Behavior and Development, 20,* 560–572.

D'Imperio, R., Dubow, E., & Ippolito, M. (2000). Resilient and stress-affected adolescents in an urban setting. *Journal of Clinical Child Psychology, 29,* 129–142.

Da Costa, D., Larouche, J., Dritsa, M., & Brender, W. (2000). Psychosocial correlates of prepartum and postpartum depressed mood. *Journal of Affective Disorders, 59,* 31–40.

Daire, A. (2004). Investigating caregiver distress with the Parental Bonding Instrument (PBI). *Dementia: The International Journal of Social Research & Practice, 3,* 83–94.

Dalsky, G.P., Stocke, K.S., Ehsani, A.I., Slatopolsky, E., Lee, W., & Birge, S.J. (1988). Weight-bearing exercise training and lumbar bone mineral content in post-menopausal women. *Annals of Internal Medicine, 108,* 824–828.

Daly, K. (2000). *It keeps getting faster: Changing patterns of time in families.* Ottawa, ON: The Vanier Institute of the Family. Retrieved from www.vifamily.ca/cft/daly/dalye.htm

Daly, L.E., Kirke, P.N., Molloy, A., Weir, D.G., & Scott, J.M. (1995). Folate levels and neural tube defects: Implications for prevention. *Journal of the American Medical Association, 274,* 1698–1702.

Daly, S., & Glenwick, D. (2000). Personal adjustment and perceptions of grandchild behavior in custodial grandmothers. *Journal of Clinical Child Psychology, 29,* 108–118.

Dammeijer, P., Schlundt, B., Chenault, M., Manni, J., & Anteunis, L. (2002). Effects of early auditory deprivation and stimulation on auditory brainstem responses in the rat. *Acta Oto-Laryngologica, 122,* 703–708.

Damon, W. (1977). *The social world of the child.* San Francisco, CA: Jossey-Bass.

Damon, W. (1983). The nature of social-cognitive change in the developing child. In W.F. Overton (Ed.), *The relationship between social and cognitive development* (pp. 103–142). Hillsdale, NJ: Erlbaum.

Damon, W., & Hart, D. (1988). *Self understanding in childhood and adolescence.* New York, NY: Cambridge University Press.

Danby, S., & Baker, C. (1998). How to be masculine in the block area. *Childhood: A Global Journal of Child Research, 5,* 151–175.

Dauvergne, M. (2003). Family violence against seniors (Cat. No. 11-008-XPE). *Canadian Social Trends, Spring*(68), 10–14.

Davey, F. (1998). Young women's expected and preferred patterns of employment and child care. *Sex Roles, 38,* 95–102.

Davidson, R. (1994). Temperament, affective style, and frontal lobe asymmetry. In G. Dawson & K. Fischer (Eds.), *Human behavior and the developing brain.* New York, NY: Guilford Press.

Davies, L. (2003). Singlehood: Transitions within a gendered world. *Canadian Journal on Aging, 22,* 343–352.

Davis, C.G. (2006). *Risks associated with tobacco use in youth aged 15–19.* Ottawa, ON: Canadian Centre on Substance Abuse. Retrieved from www.ccsa.ca/2006%20CCSA%20Documents/ccsa-011346-2006.pdf

Dawber, T.R., Kannel, W.B., & Lyell, L.P. (1963). An approach to longitudinal studies in a community: The Framingham study. *Annals of the New York Academy of Science, 107,* 539–556.

Dawood, K., Pillard, R., Horvath, C., Revelle, W., & Bailey, J. (2000). Familial aspects of male homosexuality. *Archives of Sexual Behavior, 29,* 155–163.

Dawson, D. (2000). Alcohol consumption, alcohol dependence, and all-cause mortality. *Alcoholism: Clinical & Experimental Research, 24,* 72–81.

Dawson, J., & Langan, P. (1994). *Murder in families.* Washington, DC: U.S. Department of Justice.

De Genna, N.M., Stack, D.M., Serbin, L.A., Ledingham, J.E., & Schwartzman, A.E. (2006). From risky behavior to health risk: Continuity across two generations. *Journal of Developmental & Behavioral Pediatrics, 27*(4), 297–309.

de Graaf, C., Polet, P., & van Staveren, W.A. (1994). Sensory perception and pleasantness of food flavors in elderly subjects. *Journals of Gerontology: Psychological Sciences, 49,* P93–99.

de Haan, M., Luciana, M., Maslone, S.M., Matheny, L.S., & Richards, M.L.M. (1994). Development, plasticity, and risk: Commentary on Huttenlocher, Pollit and Gorman, and Gottesman and Goldsmith. In C.A. Nelson (Ed.), *The Minnesota Symposia on Child Psychology: Vol. 27* (pp. 161–178). Hillsdale, NJ: Erlbaum.

De Jong, G.F., Wilmoth, J.M., Angel, J.L., & Cornwell, G.T. (1995). Motives and the geographic mobility of very old Americans. *Journals of Gerontology: Social Sciences, 50B,* S395–404.

de Lacoste, M., Horvath, D., & Woodward, J. (1991). Possible sex differences in the developing human fetal brain. *Journal of Clinical and Experimental Neuropsychology, 13,* 831.

de Villiers, P.A., & de Villiers, J.G. (1992). Language development. In M.H. Bornstein & M.E. Lamb (Eds.), *Developmental psychology: An advanced textbook* (3rd ed., pp. 337–418). Hillsdale, NJ: Erlbaum.

Deakin, J., Aitken, M., Robbins, T., & Sahakian, B. (2004). Risk taking during decision-making in normal volunteers changes with age. *Journal of the International Neuropsychological Society, 10,* 590–598.

DeAngelis, T. (1997). When children don't bond with parents. *Monitor of the American Psychological Association, 28*(6), 10–12.

DeCasper, A., & Fifer, W. (1980). Of human bonding: Newborns prefer their mothers' voices. *Science, 208,* 1174–1176.

DeCasper, A.J., & Spence, M.J. (1986). Prenatal maternal speech influences newborns' perception of speech sounds. *Infant Behavior and Development, 9,* 133–150.

Deeg, D.J.H., Kardaun, W.P.F., & Fozard, J.L. (1996). Health, behavior, and aging. In J.E. Birren & K.W. Schaie (Eds.), *Handbook of the psychology of aging* (4th ed., pp. 129–149). San Diego, CA: Academic Press.

Degirmencioglu, S., Urberg, K., & Tolson, J. (1998). Adolescent friendship networks: Continuity and change over the school year. *Merrill-Palmer Quarterly, 44,* 313–337.

Dekovic, M. (1999). Parent-adolescent conflict: Possible determinants and consequences. *International Journal of Behavioral Development, 23,* 977–1000.

Dekovic, M., & Meeus, W. (1997). Peer relations in adolescence: Effects of parenting and adolescents' self-concept. *Journal of Adolescence, 20,* 163–176.

Dell, C.A., & Roberts, G. (2006). *Research update: Alcohol use and pregnancy: an important Canadian public health and social issue.* Ottawa, ON: Public Health Agency of Canada.

Dellatolas, G., de Agostini, M., Curt, F., Kremin, H., Letierce, A., Maccario, J., & Lellouch, J. (2003). Manual skill, hand skill asymmetry, and cognitive performances in young children. *Laterality: Asymmetries of Body, Brain & Cognition, 8,* 317–338.

DeLoache, J.S. (1995). Early understanding and use of symbols: The model model. *Current Directions in Psychological Science, 4,* 109–113.

Dempster, F.N. (1981). Memory span: Sources of individual and developmental differences. *Psychological Bulletin, 89*(1), 63–100.

DeMulder, E., Denham, S., Schmidt, M., & Mitchell, J. (2000). Q-sort assessment of attachment security during the preschool years: Links from home to school. *Developmental Psychology, 36,* 274–282.

Denham, S. (2006). Social-emotional competence as support for school readiness: What is it and how do we assess it? *Early Education and Development, 17,* 57–89.

Denham, S., Blair, K., DeMulder, E., Levitas, J., Sawyer, K., & Queenan, P. (2003). Preschool emotional competence: Pathway to social competence. *Child Development, 74,* 238–256.

Dennerstein, L., Dudley, E., & Guthrie, J. (2002). Empty nest or revolving door? A prospective study of women's quality of life in midlife during the phase of children leaving and re-entering the home. *Psychological Medicine, 32,* 545–550.

Dennerstein, L., Dudley, E., & Guthrie, J. (2002). Empty nest or revolving door? A prospective study of women's quality of life in midlife during the phase of children leaving and re-entering the home. *Psychological Medicine, 32,* 545–550.

Dennerstein, L., Lehert, P., & Guthrie, J. (2002). The effects of the menopausal transition and biopsychosocial factors on well-being. *Archives of Women's Mental Health, 5,* 15–22.

Denney, N.W. (1982). Aging and cognitive changes. In B.B. Wolman (Ed.), *Handbook of developmental psychology* (pp. 807–827). Englewood Cliffs, NJ: Prentice-Hall.

Denney, N.W. (1984). Model of cognitive development across the life span. *Developmental Review, 4,* 171–191.

Dennis, W. (1960). Causes of retardation among institutional children: Iran. *Journal of Genetic Psychology, 96,* 47–59.

Denollet, J. (1997). Personality, emotional distress and coronary heart disease. *European Journal of Personality, 11,* 343–357.

Department of Foreign Affairs and International Trade (2001). *Retirement abroad: Seeing the sunsets.* Ottawa, ON: Author, Consular Affairs. Retrieved from Foreign Affairs and International Trade website: www.voyage.gc.ca/Consular-e/Publications/retirement_abroad-e.htm

Department of Justice Canada. (2001a). *Criminal Code. R.S., c. C-34, s. 1.* Ottawa, ON: Author. Retrieved from http://lois.justice.gc.ca/en/C-46/text.html

Department of Justice Canada. (2001b). *Backgrounder: Youth Criminal Justice Act.* Ottawa, ON: Author. Retrieved from http://canada.justice.gc.ca/en/news/nr/2001/doc_25948.html

Department of Justice Canada. (2004). *Fact sheet—Section 43 of the Criminal Code (Corporal Punishment): The Canadian Foundation for Children, Youth and the Law v. The Attorney General of Canada.* Ottawa, ON: Author. Retrieved from http://canada.justice.gc.ca/en/news/fs/2004/doc_31114.html

Depressed elderly react best to a mix of drugs and psychotherapy. (1999, March). *APA Monitor Online* [Archives]. Retrieved from www.apa.org/monitor/mar99/depress.html

DeRegnier, R., Wewerka, S., Georgieff, M., Mattia, F., & Nelson, C. (2002). Influences of postconceptional age and postnatal experience on the development of auditory recognition memory in the newborn infant. *Developmental Psychobiology, 41,* 215–225.

Derevensky, J.L. & Gupta, R. (1998). Youth gambling: Lack of public awareness is contributing to the increasing number. *Psynopsis,* Fall. Retrieved from Canadian Psychological Association website: www.cpa.ca/Psynopsis/Gambling.html

Derevensky, J.L., & Gupta, R. (2004, February). Adolescents with gambling problems: A synopsis of our current knowledge. *eGambling: The Electronic Journal of Gambling Issues, 10,* 1–22. Retrieved from Centre for Addiction and Mental Health website: www.camh.net/egambling/issue10/ejgi_10_derevensky_gupta.html

Deshpande, D.M., Kim, Y-S., Martinez, T., Carmen, J., Dike, S., Shats, I., . . . Kerr, D.A. (2006). Recovery from paralysis in adult rats using embryonic stem cells. *Annals of Neurology, 60*(1), 22–34.

Derevensky, J.L., Gupta, R., & Winters, K. (2003). Prevalence rates of youth gambling problems: Are the current rates inflated? *Journal of Gambling Studies, 19*(4), 405–425.

Detchant, Lord Walton. (1995). Dilemmas of life and death: Part one. *Journal of the Royal Society of Medicine, 88,* 311–315.

Deter, H., & Herzog, W. (1994). Anorexia nervosa in a long-term perspective: Results of the Heidelberg-Mannheim study. *Psychosomatic Medicine, 56,* 20–27.

Dezoete, J., MacArthur, B., & Tuck, B. (2003). Prediction of Bayley and Stanford-Binet scores with a group of very low birthweight children. *Child: Care, Health, & Development, 29,* 367–372.

Diagram Group, The (1977). *Child's body.* New York, NY: Paddington.

Diehl, L., Vicary, J., & Deike, R. (1997). Longitudinal trajectories of self-esteem from early to middle adolescence and related psycho-social variables among rural adolescents. *Journal of Research on Adolescence, 7,* 393–411.

Diener, M., & Kim, D. (2004). Maternal and child predictors of preschool children's social competence. *Journal of Applied Developmental Psychology, 25,* 3–24.

Dieni, S., & Rees, S. (2003). Dendritic morphology is altered in hippocampal neurons following prenatal compromise, *Journal of Neurobiology, 55,* 41–52.

Dieni, S., & Rees, S. (2003). Dendritic morphology is altered in hippocampal neurons following prenatal compromise. *Journal of Neurobiology, 55,* 41–52.

Diesendruck, G., & Shatz, M. (2001). Two-year-olds' recognition of hierarchies: Evidence from their interpretation of the semantic relation between object labels. *Cognitive Development, 16,* 577–594.

Dietitians of Canada. (2003). *Eating, physical activity and body weight trends in Canadian children and youth.* Toronto, ON: Author. Retrieved from www.dietitians.ca/child/pdf/backgrounder.pdf

Dietz, B., Carrozza, M., & Ritchey, P. (2003). Does financial self-efficacy explain gender differences in retirement saving strategies? *Journal of Women & Aging, 15,* 83–96.

Digman, J.M. (1990). Personality structure: Emergence of the five-factor model. *Annual Review of Psychology, 41,* 417–440.

DiMario, F. (2002). The nervous system. In A. Rudolph, R. Kamei, & K. Overby (Eds.), *Rudolph's fundamentals of pediatrics* (3rd ed., pp. 796–846). New York, NY: McGraw-Hill.

Dindia, K., & Allen, M. (1992). Sex differences in self-disclosure: A meta-analysis. *Psychological Bulletin, 112,* 106–124.

DiPietro, J., Hodgson, D., Costigan, K., & Johnson, T. (1996). Fetal antecedents of infant temperament. *Child Development, 67,* 2568–2583.

DiPietro, J., Hodgson, D., Costigan, K., Hilton, S., & Johnson, T. (1996). Fetal neurobehavioral development. *Child Development, 67,* 2553–2567.

Dishion, T.J., French, D.C., & Patterson, G.R. (1995). The development and ecology of antisocial behavior. In D. Cicchetti & D.J. Cohen (Eds.), *Developmental psychopathology: Vol. 2. Risk, disorder, and adaptation* (pp. 421–471). New York, NY: Wiley.

Dittmann-Kohli, F., Lachman, M.E., Kliegl, R., & Baltes, P.B. (1991). Effects of cognitive training and testing on intellectual efficacy beliefs in elderly adults. *The Journals of Gerontology: Psychological Sciences, 46,* P162–164.

Divgi, V. (2000). What about sleep? *Archives of Pediatrics & Adolescent Medicine, 154*(6), 636.

Dobson, A., Brown, W., Ball, J., Powers, J., & McFadden, M. (1999). Women drivers' behaviour, socio-demographic characteristics and accidents. *Accident Analysis & Prevention, 31,* 525–535.

Dockett, S., & Smith, I. (1995, March). *Children's theories of mind and their involvement in complex shared pretense.* Paper presented at the biennial meetings of the Society for Research in Child Development, Indianapolis, IN.

Doctoroff, S. (1997). Sociodramatic script training and peer role prompting: Two tactics to promote sociodramatic play and peer interaction. *Early Child Development & Care, 136*, 27–43.

Dodge, K.A., Pettit, G.S., & Bates, J.E. (1994). Socialization mediators of the relation between socioeconomic status and child conduct problems. *Child Development, 65*, 649–665.

Donohew, R., Hoyle, R., Clayton, R., Skinner, W., Colon, S., & Rice, R. (1999). Sensation seeking and drug use by adolescents and their friends: Models for marijuana and alcohol. *Journal of Studies on Alcohol, 60*, 622–631.

Dorling, D., Mitchell, R., & Pearce, J. (2007). The global impact of income inequality on health by age: An observational study. *BMJ, 335*(7625): 873.

Dorn, L.D., Susman, E.J., & Ponirakis, A. (2003). Pubertal timing and adolescent adjustment and behavior: Conclusions vary by rater. *Journal of Youth and Adolescence, 32*(3), 157–167. doi 10.1023/A:1022590818839

Doty, R.L., Shaman, P., Appelbaum, S.L., Bigerson, R., Sikorski, L., & Rosenberg, L. (1984). Smell identification ability: Changes with age. *Science, 226*, 1441–1443.

Downe-Wamboldt, B., & Tamlyn, D. (1997). An international survey of death education trends in faculties of nursing and medicine. *Death Studies, 21*, 177–188.

Draper, B., Gething, L., Fethney, J., & Winfield, S. (1999). The Senior Psychiatrist Survey III: Attitudes towards personal ageing, life experiences and psychiatric practice. *Australian & New Zealand Journal of Psychiatry, 33*, 717–722.

Drevets, W., Price, J., Simpson, J., Todd, R., Reich, T., Vannier, M., & Raichle, M. (1997). Subgenual prefrontal cortex abnormalities in mood disorders. Nature, *386*, 824–827.

Droege, K., & Stipek, D. (1993). Children's use of dispositions to predict classmates' behavior. *Developmental Psychology, 29*, 646–654.

Drolet, M. (2003). Motherhood and paycheques (Cat. No. 11-008). *Canadian Social Trends, Spring*(68), 7–10.

Drum, P. (1985). Retention of text information by grade, ability and study. *Discourse Processes, 8*, 21–52.

Dubois, L., Farmer, A., Girard, M., & Peterson, K. (2008). Social factors and television use during meals and snacks is associated with higher BMI among preschool children. *Public Health Nutrition, 11*(12), 1–13. doi: 10.1017/S1368980008002887

Duchesne, D. (2004). More seniors at work (Cat. No. 75-001). *Perspectives on Labour and Income, 5*(2). Retrieved from Statistics Canada website: www.statcan.ca/english/studies/75-001/10204/high-1.htm

Due, P., Holstein, B., Lund, R., Modvig, J., & Avlund, K. (1999). Social relations: Network, support and relational strain. *Social Science & Medicine, 48*, 661–673.

Duffy, F. (1994). The role of quantified electroencephalography in psychological research. In K. Fischer & G. Dawson (Eds.), *Human behavior and the developing brain* (pp. 93–136). New York, NY: Guilford Press.

Dugan, L., Nagin, D., & Rosenfeld, R. (2003). Do domestic violence services save lives? *National Institute of Justice Journal, 250*, 1–6.

Duka, T., Tasker, R., & McGowan, J. (2000). The effects of 3-week estrogen hormone replacement on cognition in elderly healthy females. *Psychopharmacology, 149*, 129–139.

Dunn, J. (1994). Experience and understanding of emotions, relationships, and membership in a particular culture. In P. Ekman & R.J. Davidson (Eds.), *The nature of emotion: Fundamental questions* (pp. 352–355). New York, NY: Oxford University Press.

Dunphy, D.C. (1963). The social structure of urban adolescent peer groups. *Sociometry, 26*, 230–246.

Dura, J.R., & Kiecolt-Glaser, J.K. (1991). Family transitions, stress, and health. In P.A. Cowan & M. Hetherington (Eds.), *Family transitions* (pp. 59–76). Hillsdale, NJ: Erlbaum.

Durbin, J. (2003, October 6). Internet sex unzipped. *Maclean's*, 18–22.

Durrant, J. (2004). Distinguishing physical punishment from physical abuse: Implications for professionals. *Ontario Association of Children's Aid Societies Journal, 48*(2), 15–20.

Durrant, J., & Ensom, R. (2004). *Physical punishment of children* (CECW Information Sheet #7E). Ottawa, ON: Child Welfare League of Canada. Retrieved from www.cecw-cepb.ca/DocsEng/PhysPun7E.pdf

Dush, C., Cohan, C., & Amato, P. (2003). The relationship between cohabitation and marital quality and stability: Change across cohorts? *Journal of Marriage & the Family, 65*, 539–549.

Dutch Senate OKs doctor-assisted suicide. (2001, April 11). *Houston Chronicle*, p. 16A.

Duursma, S.A., Raymakers, J.A., Boereboom, F.T.J., & Scheven, B.A.A. (1991). Estrogen and bone metabolism. *Obstetrical and Gynecological Survey, 47*, 38–44.

Dyack, S. (2004). Expanding newborn screening: Lessons learned from MCAD deficiency. *Paediatrics & Child Health, 9*(4), 241–243.

Dyl, J., Kittler, J., Phillips, K., & Hunt, J. (2006). Body dysmorphic disorder and other clinically significant body image concerns in adolescent psychiatric inpatients: Prevalance and clinical characteristics. *Child Psychiatry and Human Development, 36*, 369–382.

Dyregrov, A., Gjestad, R., Bie Wikander, A., & Vigerust, S. (1999). Reactions following the sudden death of a classmate. *Scandinavian Journal of Psychology, 40*, 167–176.

Eagly, A., & Wood, W. (1999). The origins of sex differences in human behavior: Evolved dispositions versus social roles. American Psychologist, *54*, 408–423.

Eaton, W. (2003, Fall). *Infant milestones newsletter*. Winnipeg, MB: University of Manitoba Milestone Study. Retrieved from www.umanitoba.ca/outreach/milestones/fallnewsletter2003.shtml

Eaton, W.O. (1994). Temperament, development, and the five factor model: Lessons from activity level. In C.F. Halverson, G.A. Kohnstamm, & R.P. Martin (Eds.), *The developing structure of temperament and personality from infancy to adulthood* (pp. 173–187). Hillsdale, NJ: Erlbaum.

Eaton, W.O., McKeen, N.A., & Campbell, D.W. (2001). The waxing and waning of movement: Implications for psychological development. *Developmental Review, 21*(2), 205–223.

Echt, K., Morrell, R., & Park, D. (1998). Effects of age and training formats on basic computer skill acquisition in older adults. *Educational Gerontology, 24*, 3–25.

Eckensberger, E., & Zimba, R. (1997). The development of moral judgment. In J. Berry, P. Dasen, & T. Saraswathi (Eds.), *Handbook of cross-cultural psychology:Vol. 2* (pp. 299–328). Boston, MA: Allyn & Bacon.

Edwards, G. (n.d.). *Health and environmental issues linked to the nuclear fuel chain: Health effects* (Section B). Montreal: Canadian Coalition for Nuclear Responsibility. Retrieved from www.ccnr.org/ceac_B.html#b.14

Egan, S.K., & Perry, D.G. (1998). Does low self-regard invite victimization? *Developmental Psychology, 34*(2), 299–309.

Egger, G., Liang, G., Aparicio, A., & Jones, P.A. (2004). Epigenetics in human disease and prospects for epigenetic therapy. *Nature, 429*(6990), 457–463.

Einerson, M. (1998). Fame, fortune, and failure: Young girls' moral language surrounding popular culture. *Youth & Society, 30*, 241–257.

Eisenberg, N. (1992). *The caring child*. Cambridge, MA: Harvard University Press.

Eisenberg, N. (2000). Emotion, regulation, and moral development. *Annual Review of Psychology, 51*, 665–697.

Eisenberg, N., Fabes, R.A., Murphy, B., Karbon, M., Smith, M., & Maszk, P. (1996). The relations of children's dispositional empathy-related responding to their emotionality, regulation, and social functioning. *Developmental Psychology, 32*, 195–209.

Eisenberg, N., Fabes, R.A., Murphy, B., Maszk, P., Smith, M., & Karbon, M. (1995). The role of emotionality and regulation in children's social functioning: A longitudinal study. *Child Development, 66*, 1360–1384.

Eisenberg, N., Guthrie, I., Murphy, B., Shepard, S., Cumberland, A., & Carlo. G. (1999). Consistency and development of prosocial dispositions: A longitudinal study. *Child Development, 70*, 1360–1372.

Eisenberger, N. (2003). Does rejection hurt? An fMRI study of social exclusion. *Science, 302*(5643), 290–292.

Elbedour, S., Baker, A., & Charlesworth, W. (1997). The impact of political violence on moral reasoning in children. *Child Abuse & Neglect, 21*, 1053–1066.

Eley, T., Liang, H., Plomin, R., Sham, P., Sterne, A., Williamson, R., & Purcell, S. (2004). Parental familial vulnerability, family environment, and their interactions as predictors of depressive symptoms in adolescents. *Journal of the American Academy of Child Psychiatry, 43,* 298–306.

Eliot, L. (1999). *What's going on in there? : How the brain and mind develop in the first five years of life.* New York, NY: Bantom Books.

Elizur, Y., & Mintzer, A. (2003). Gay males' intimate relationship quality: The roles of attachment security, gay identity, social support, and income. *Personal Relationships, 10,* 411–435.

Elkind, D. (1967). Egocentrism in adolescence. *Child Development, 38,* 1025–1033.

Elliott, D., Mok, D., & Briere, J. (2004). Adult sexual assault: Prevalence, symptomatology, and sex differences in the general population. *Journal of Traumatic Stress, 17,* 203–211.

Elliott, L. (2000). Aboriginal girls taking their lives in record numbers across Ontario's north. *Canadian Aboriginal News.* Retrieved from www.canadianaboriginal.com/health/health15b.htm

Ellison, J., & Clark, W. (2001). Net shopping. *Canadian Social Trends, 60,* 6–9.

Ellison, M., Danley, K., Bromberg, C., & Palmer-Erbs, V. (1999). Longitudinal outcome of young adults who participated in a psychiatric vocational rehabilitation program. *Psychiatric Rehabilitation Journal, 22,* 337–341.

Ellsworth, C.P., Muir, D.W., & Hains, S.M.J. (1993). Social competence and person-object differentiation: An analysis of the still-face effect. *Developmental Psychology, 29,* 63–73.

Ely, R., Gleason, J.B., MacGibbon, A., & Zaretsky, E. (2001). Attention to language: Lessons learned at the dinner table. *Social Development, 10*(3), 355–373.

Emanuel, E., Fairclough, D., Clarridge, B., Blum, D., Bruera, E., Penley, W., . . . Mayer, R. (2000). Attitudes and practices of U.S. oncologists regarding euthanasia and physician-assisted suicide. *Annals of Internal Medicine, 133,* 527–532.

Emde, R.N., Plomin, R., Robinson, J., Corley, R., DeFries, J., Fulker, D.W., . . . Zahn-Waxler, C. (1992). Temperament, emotion, and cognition at fourteen months: The MacArthur longitudinal twin study. *Child Development, 63,* 1437–1455.

Emery, C.F., & Gatz, M. (1990). Psychological and cognitive effects of an exercise program for community-residing older adults. *The Gerontologist, 30,* 184–192.

Emery, R., & Laumann-Billings, L. (1998). An overview of the nature, causes, and consequences of abusive family relationships: Toward differentiating maltreatment and violence. *American Psychologist, 53,* 121–135.

Ennemoser, M., & Schneider, W. (2007). Relations of television viewing and reading: Findings from a 4-year longitudinal study. *Journal of Educational Psychology, 99*(2), 349–368.

Enright, E. (2004). A house divided. *AARP Magazine.* Retrieved from www.aarpmagazine.org/family/Articles/a2004-05-26-mag-divorce.html

Entwisle, D.R., & Alexander, K.L. (1990). Beginning school math competence: Minority and majority comparisons. *Child Development, 61,* 454–471.

Ericsson, K.A., & Crutcher, R.J. (1990). The nature of exceptional performance. In P.B. Baltes, D.L. Featherman, & R.M. Lerner (Eds.), *Life-span development and behavior: Vol. 10* (pp. 1188–218). Hillsdale, NJ: Erlbaum.

Erikson, E.H. (1950). *Childhood and society.* New York, NY: Norton.

Erikson, E.H. (1959). *Identity and the life cycle.* New York, NY: Norton. (Reissued, 1980.)

Erikson, E.H. (1963). *Childhood and society* (2nd ed.). New York, NY: Norton.

Erikson, E.H. (1968). *Identity: youth and crisis.* New York, NY: W.W. Norton.

Erikson, E.H. (1980a). *Identity and the life cycle.* New York, NY: Norton. (Originally published 1959.)

Erikson, E.H. (1980b). Themes of adulthood in the Freud-Jung correspondence. In N.J. Smelser & E. Erikson (Eds.), *Themes of work and love in adulthood* (pp. 43–76). Cambridge, MA: Harvard University Press.

Erikson, E.H. (1982). *The life cycle completed.* New York, NY: Norton.

Erikson, E.H., Erikson, J.M., & Kivnick, H.Q. (1986). *Vital involvement in old age.* New York, NY: Norton.

Escribá, M.J., Grau, N., Escrich, L., & Pellicer, A. (2010). Vitrification of isolated human blastomeres. *Fertility and Sterility, 93*(2), 667–671.

Esposito, K., Giugliano, F., Di Palo, C., Giugliano, G., Marfella, R., D'Andrea, F., . . . Giugliano, D. (2004). Effect of lifestyle changes on erectile dysfunction in obese men: A randomized controlled trial. *Journal of the American Medical Association, 291,* 2978–2984.

Espy, K., Stalets, M., McDiarmid, M., Senn, T., Cwik, M., & Hamby, A. (2002). Executive functions in preschool children born preterm: Application of cognitive neuroscience paradigms. *Child Neuropsychology, 8,* 83–92.

Esteller, M. (2006). The necessity of a human epigenome project. *Carcinogenesis, 27*(6), 1121–1125.

Etaugh, C., & Liss, M. (1992). Home, school, and playroom: Training grounds for adult gender roles. *Sex Roles, 26,* 129–147.

Eugster, A., & Vingerhoets, A. (1999). Psychological aspects of in vitro fertilization: A review. *Social Science & Medicine, 48,* 575–589.

Evans, G.W. (2006). Child development and the physical environment. *Annual Review of Psychology, 57,* 423–451.

Evans, J.A., & Fortier, A. (2006). *Congenital malformations in infants born to young mothers.* Winnipeg, MB: Public Health Agency of Canada.

Evans, M.A., & Shaw, D. (2008). Home grown for reading: parental contributions to young children's emergent literacy and word recognition. *Canadian Psychology, 49*(2), 89–95. doi:10.1037/0708-5591.49.2.89

Evans, R.I. (1969). *Dialogue with Erik Erikson.* New York, NY: Dutton.

Evans, S., Huxley, R., Gately, C., Webber, M., Mears, A., Pajak, S., . . . Katona, C. (2006). Mental health, burnout and job satisfaction among mental health social workers in England and Wales. *The British Journal of Psychiatry, 188,* 75–78.

Ewald, P. (2000). *Plague time.* New York, NY: Free Press.

Ex, C., & Janssens, J. (1998). Maternal influences on daughters' gender role attitudes. *Sex Roles, 38,* 171–186.

Expert Working Group on Integrated Palliative Care for Persons with AIDS (1988). Caring together: summary of a report submitted to Health and Welfare Canada (December, 1987). Journal of Palliative Care, 4(4), 76–86.

Eyetsemitan, F. (1998). Stifled grief in the workplace. *Death Studies, 22,* 469–479.

Fagan, J. (2000). A theory of intelligence as processing: Implications for society. *Psychology, Public Policy, & Law, 6,* 168–179.

Fagard, J., & Jacquet, A. (1989). Onset of bimanual coordination and symmetry versus asymmetry of movement. Infant Behavior and Development, 12, 229–235.

Fagan, J.F., & Detterman, D.K. (1992). The Fagan Test of Infant Intelligence: A technical summary. *Journal of Applied Developmental Psychology, 13,* 173–193.

Fagan, J.F., Holland, C.R., & Wheeler, K. (2007). The prediction, from infancy, of adult IQ and achievement. *Intelligence, 35*(3), 225–231.

Fagot, B.I., & Hagan, R. (1991). Observations of parent reactions to sex-stereotyped behaviors: Age and sex effects. *Child Development, 62,* 617–628.

Fagot, B.I., & Leinbach, M.D. (1993). Gender-role development in young children: From discrimination to labeling. *Developmental Review, 13,* 205–224.

Fahle, M., & Daum, I. (1997). Visual learning and memory as functions of age. *Neuropsychologia, 35,* 1583–1589.

Fahrenfort, J., Jacobs, E., Miedema, S., & Schweizer, A. (1996). Signs of emotional disturbance three years after early hospitalization. *Journal of Pediatric Psychology, 21,* 353–366.

Fantuzzo, J., Coolahan, K., & Mendez, J. (1998). Contextually relevant validation of peer play constructs with African American

Head Start children: Penn Interactive Peer Play Scale. *Early Childhood Research Quarterly, 13,* 411–431.

Fantuzzo, J., Sekino, Y., & Cohen, H. (2004). An examination of the contributions of interactive peer play to salient classroom competencies for urban Head Start children. *Psychology in the Schools, 41,* 323–336.

Fantz, R.L. (1956). A method for studying early visual development. *Perceptual & Motor Skills, 6,* 13–15.

Farnham-Diggory, S. (1992). *The learning-disabled child.* Cambridge, MA: Harvard University Press.

Farrar, M.J. (1992). Negative evidence and grammatical morpheme acquisition. *Developmental Psychology, 28,* 90–98.

Fear, N.T., Hey, K., Vincent, T., & Murphy, M. (2007). Paternal occupation and neural tube defects: A case-control study based on the Oxford Record Linkage Study register. *Paediatric and Perinatal Epidemiology, 21*(2), 163–168.

Federal Interagency Forum on Aging-Related Statistics (FIFARS). (2000). *Older Americans 2000: Key indicators of well-being.* Retrieved from Aging Stats website: www.agingstats.gov/chartbook2000

Federal Interagency Forum on Aging-Related Statistics. (FIFARS). (2006). *2006 Older American update: Key indicator of wellness.* Retrieved from http://agingstats.gov/agingstatsdotnet/Main_Site/Data/Data _2006.aspx

Feeney, J.A. (1994). Attachment style, communication patterns, and satisfaction across the life cycle of marriage. *Personal Relationships, 1,* 333–348.

Feil, R. (2006). Environmental and nutritional effects on the epigenetic regulation of genes. *Mutation Research/Fundamental and Molecular Mechanisms of Mutagenesis, 600*(1–2), 46–57.

Feil, R. (2008). Epigenetics, an emerging discipline with broad implications. *Molecular Biology and Genetics, 331*(11), 837–843.

Feiring, C. (1999). Other-sex friendship networks and the development of romantic relationships in adolescence. *Journal of Youth & Adolescence, 28,* 495–512.

Feldman, D. (2004). Piaget's stages: The unfinished symphony of cognitive development. *New Ideas in Psychology, 22,* 175–231.

Feldman, R. (2003). Paternal socio-psychological factors and infant attachment: The mediating role of synchrony in father-infant interactions. *Infant Behavior & Development, 25,* 221–236.

Fenson, L., Dale, P.S., Reznick, J.S., Bates, E., Thal, D.J., & Pethick, S.J. (1994). Variability in early communicative development. *Monographs of the Society for Research in Child Development, 59*(5, Serial No. 242).

Ferguson, G.A. (1993). Psychology in Canada 1939–1945. *Canadian Psychology, 33*(2), Abstract.

Ferland, F., Ladouceur, R., & Vitaro, F. (2002). Prevention of problem gambling: Modifying misconception and increasing knowledge. *Journal of Gambling Studies, 18*(10), 19–29.

Fernald, A., & Kuhl, P. (1987). Acoustic determinants of infant preference for motherese speech. *Infant Behavior and Development, 10,* 279–293.

Ferris, F.D., Balfour, H.M., Bowen, K., Farley, J., Hardwick, M., Lamontagne, C. . . . West, P. (2005). *A Model to Guide Hospice Palliative Care: Based on National Principles and Norms of Practice.* Ottawa, ON: Canadian Hospice Palliative Care Association. Retrieved from www.chpca.net/resource_doc_library/model_to_guide_hpc/A+Model+to+Guide+Hospice+Palliative+Care+2002-URLUpdate-August2005.pdf

Fiatarone, M.A., & Evans, W.J. (1993). The etiology and reversibility of muscle dysfunction in the aged. *The Journals of Gerontology, 48*(Special Issue), 77–83.

Fiedorowicz, C. (1999). *Neurobiological basis of learning disabilities: An overview.* Linking Research to Practice: Second Canadian Forum Proceedings Report, Canadian Child Care Federation Symposium (pp. 64–67). Ottawa, ON: Canadian Child Care Federation.

Fiedorowicz, C., Benezra, E., MacDonald, W., McElgunn, B., & Wilson, A. (1999). *Neurobiological basis of learning disabilities.* Ottawa, ON: Learning Disabilities Association of Canada.

Fiedorowicz, C., Benezra, E., MacDonald, W., McElgunn, B., Wilson, A., & Kaplan, B. (2002). The neurobiological basis of learning disabilities: An update. *Learning Disabilities: A Multidisciplinary Focus, 11*(2), 61–73.

Field, T. (1995). Psychologically depressed parents. In M.H. Bornstein (Ed.), *Handbook of parenting: Vol. 4. Applied and practical parenting* (pp. 85–99). Mahwah, NJ: Erlbaum.

Field, T.M. (1977). Effects of early separation, interactive deficits, and experimental manipulations on infant-mother face-to-face interaction. *Child Development, 48,* 763–771.

Fields, R.B. (1992). Psychosocial response to environment change. In V.B. Van Hasselt & M. Hersen (Eds.), *Handbook of social development: A lifespan perspective* (pp. 503–544). New York, NY: Plenum.

Findlay, L., Girardi, A., & Coplan, R. (2006). Links between empathy, social behavior, and social understanding. *Early Childhood Research Quarterly, 21,* 347–359.

Fine, S. (2000a, September 5). Are the schools failing boys? *The Globe and Mail,* pp. A1, A9.

Fine, S. (2000b, November 3). Ontario students score poorly. *The Globe and Mail,* p. A3.

Finnell, R.H. (1999). Teratology: General considerations and principles. *The Journal of Allergy and Clinical Immunology, 103*(2), S337–S342.

Finnell, R.H., Waes, J.G., Eudy, J.D., & Rosenquist, T.H. (2002). Molecular basis of environmentally induced birth defects. *Annual review of Pharmacology and Toxicology, 42,* 181–208.

Finnie, R. (2000). *Earnings of post-secondary graduates in Canada: Holding their own* (Cat. No. MP 32-29/99-12-1E). Retrieved from Human Resources Development Canada website: www.hrdc-drhc.gc.ca/arb/publications/research/1999docs/r-99-12ea.pdf

Finnie, R., Mueller, R., Sweetman, A., & Usher, A. (2010). *New perspectives on access to postsecondary education* (81-004-X). Ottawa, ON: Statistics Canada. Retrieved from www.statcan.gc.ca/pub/81-004-x/2010001/article/11152-eng.htm

Fischer, L., Wei, F., Solberg, L., Rush, W., & Heinrich, R. (2003). Treatment of elderly and other adult patients for depression in primary care. *Journal of the American Geriatrics Society, 51,* 1554–1562.

Fish, M., Stifter, C. A., & Belsky, J. (1991). Conditions of continuity and discontinuity in infant negative emotionality: Newborn to five months. *Child Development, 62,* 1525–1537.

Fisher, B., & Specht, D. (1999). Successful aging and creativity in later life. *Journal of Aging Studies, 13,* 457–472.

Fisher, J., Feekery, C., & Rowe-Murray, H. (2002). Nature, severity and correlates of psychological distress in women admitted to a private mother-baby unit. *Journal of Paediatrics & Child Health, 38,* 140–145.

Fitzgerald, D., & White, K. (2003). Linking children's social worlds: Perspective taking in parent–child and peer contexts. *Social Behavior and Personality: An International Journal, 31*(5), 509–522.

Fitzgerald, R. (2010). *Parenting, school contexts and violent delinquency* (85-561-M, no. 19). Ottawa, ON: Ministry of Industry. Retrieved from www.statcan.gc.ca/pub/85-561-m/85-561-m2010019-eng.pdf

Fitzpatrick, J.L., & Silverman, T. (1989). Women's selection of careers in engineering: Do traditional-nontraditional differences still exist? *Journal of Vocational Behavior, 34,* 266–278.

Flannery, D., Vazsonyi, A., Embry, D., Powell, K., Atha, H., Vesterdal, W., & Shenyang, G. (2000, August). *Longitudinal effectiveness of the PeaceBuilders' universal school-based violence prevention program.* Paper presented at the annual meeting of the American Psychological Association, Washington, DC.

Flannery, D.J., Montemayor, R., & Eberly, M.B. (1994). The influence of parent negative emotional expression on adolescents' perceptions of their relationships with their parents. *Personal Relationships, 1,* 259–274.

Flavell, J.H. (1985). *Cognitive development* (2nd ed.). Englewood Cliffs, NJ: Prentice-Hall.

Flavell, J.H. (1986). The development of children's knowledge about the appearance-reality distinction. *American Psychologist, 41,* 418–425.

Flavell, J.H. (1993). Young children's understanding of thinking and consciousness. *Current Directions in Psychological Science, 2,* 40–43.

Flavell, J.H., Everett, B.A., Croft, K., & Flavell, E.R. (1981). Young children's knowledge about visual perception: Further evidence for the Level 1–Level 2 distinction. *Developmental Psychology, 17,* 99–103.

Flavell, J.H., Green, F.L., & Flavell, E.R. (1989). Young children's ability to differentiate appearance-reality and level 2 perspectives in the tactile modality. *Child Development, 60,* 201–213.

Flavell, J.H., Green, F.L., Wahl, K.E., & Flavell, E.R. (1987). The effects of question clarification and memory aids on young children's performance on appearance-reality tasks. *Cognitive Development, 2,* 127–144.

Flood, M. (2007). Exploring the relationship between creativity, depression, and successful aging. *Activities, Adaptation, & Aging, 31,* 55–71.

Floyd, F., & Bakeman, R. (2006). Coming-out across the life course: Implications of age and historical context. *Archives of Sexual Behavior, 35,* 287–297.

Foehr, U. (2006). *Media multitasking among American youth: Prevalence, predictors and pairings.* Menlo Park, CA: Henry J. Kaiser Foundation. Retrieved from http://kff.org/entmedia/upload/7592.pdf

Fokin, V., Ponomareva, N., Androsova, L., & Gavrilova, S. (1997). Interhemispheric asymmetry and neuroimmune modulation in normal aging and Alzheimer's dementias. *Human Physiology, 23,* 284–288.

Fordham, K., & Stevenson-Hinde, J. (1999). Shyness, friendship quality, and adjustment during middle childhood. *Journal of Child Psychology & Psychiatry & Allied Disciplines, 40,* 757–768.

Forte, C., & Hansvick, C. (1999). Applicant age as a subjective employability factor: A study of workers over and under age fifty. *Journal of Employment Counseling, 36,* 24–34.

Fouquereau, E., & Baudoin, C. (2002). The marital satisfaction questionnaire for older persons: Factor structure in a French sample. *Social Behavior & Personality, 30,* 95–104.

Fox, N., Henderson, H., Rubin, K., Calkins, S., & Schmidt, L. (2001). Continuity and discontinuity of behavioral inhibition and exuberance: Psychophysiological and behavioral influences across the first four years of life. *Child Development, 72,* 1–21.

Fox, N.A., Kimmerly, N.L., & Schafer, W.D. (1991). Attachment to mother/attachment to father: A meta-analysis. *Child Development, 62,* 210–225.

Fozard, J.L. (1990). Vision and hearing in aging. In J.E. Birren & K.W. Schaie (Eds.), *Handbook of the psychology of aging* (3rd ed., pp. 150–171). San Diego, CA: Academic Press.

Fozard, J.L., Metter, E.J., & Brant, L.J. (1990). Next steps in describing aging and disease in longitudinal studies. *Journals of Gerontology: Psychological Sciences, 45,* P116–127.

Fraga, M.F. (2009). Genetic and epigenetic regulation of aging. *Current Opinion in Immunology, 21*(4), 446–453.

Fraga, M.F., Ballestar, E., Paz, M.F., Ropero, S., Setien, F., Ballestar, M.L., . . . Esteller, M. (2005). Epigenetic differences arise during the lifetime of the monozygotic twins. *Proceedings of the National Academy of Sciences of the United States of America, 102*(30), 10604–10609.

Franche, R., & Bulow, C. (1999). The impact of a subsequent pregnancy on grief and emotional adjustment following a perinatal loss. *Infant Mental Health Journal, 20,* 175–187.

Francis, L. (1997). Ideology and interpersonal emotion management: Redefining identity in two support groups. *Social Psychology Quarterly, 60,* 153–171.

Francis, P.L., Self, P.A., & Horowitz, F.D. (1987). The behavioral assessment of the neonate: An overview. In J.D. Osofsky (Ed.), *Handbook of infant development* (2nd ed., pp. 723–779). New York, NY: Wiley-Interscience.

Francis-Smythe, J., & Smith, P. (1997). The psychological impact of assessment in a development center. *Human Relations, 50,* 149–167.

Franco, N., & Levitt, M. (1998). The social ecology of middle childhood: Family support, friendship quality, and self-esteem. *Family Relations: Interdisciplinary Journal of Applied Family Studies, 47,* 315–321.

Franke, S. (2003). Studying and working: The busy lives of students with paid employment (Cat. No. 11-008). *Canadian Social Trends, Spring*(68), 22–25.

Freedberg, P. (2006). Health care barriers and same-sex intimate partner violence: a review of the literature. *Journal of Forensic Nursing, 2*(1), 15–25.

Freeman, E., Sammel, M., Liu, L., García, C., Nelson, D., & Hollander, L. (2004). Hormones and menopausal status as predictors of depression in women in transition to menopause. *Archives of General Psychiatry, 61,* 62–70.

Freudenberger, H.J., & Richelson, G. (1980). Burn-out: the high cost of high achievement. Garden City, NY: Anchor Press.Fagan, J. (2000). A theory of intelligence as processing: Implications for society. *Psychology, Public Policy, & Law, 6,* 168–179.

Frey, K.S., & Ruble, D.N. (1992). Gender constancy and the "cost" of sex-typed behavior: A test of the conflict hypothesis. *Developmental Psychology, 28,* 714–721.

Frick, E., Fegg, M., Tyroller, M., Fischer, N., & Bumeder, I. (2007). Patients' health beliefs and coping prior to autologous peripheral stem cell transplantation. *European Journal of Cancer Care, 16,* 156–163.

Frick, P., Christian, R., & Wooton, J. (1999). Age trends in association between parenting practices and conduct problems. *Behavior Modification, 23,* 106–128.

Friedman, M., & Rosenman, R.H. (1974). *Type A behavior and your heart.* New York, NY: Knopf.

Frieswijk, N., Buunk, B., Steverink, N., & Slaets, J. (2004). The effect of social comparison information on the life satisfaction of frail older persons. *Psychology & Aging, 19,* 183–190.

Frisch, M., Glimelius, B., van den Brule, A., Wohlfahrt, J., Meijer, C., Walboomers, J., . . . Melbye, M. (1997). Sexually transmitted infection as a cause of anal cancer. *New England Journal of Medicine, 337,* 1350–1358.

Fuller, T.L., & Fincham, F.D. (1995). Attachment style in married couples: Relation to current marital functioning, stability over time, and method of assessment. *Personal Relationships, 2,* 17–34.

Fullerton, A., & Wallace, M. (2007). Traversing the flexible turn: US workers' perceptions of job security, 1977–2002. *Social Science Research, 36,* 201–221.

Funk, J., & Buchman, D. (1999). Playing violent video and computer games and adolescent self-concept. *Journal of Communication, 46,* 19–32.

Funk, J., Buchman, D., Myers, B., & Jenks, J. (2000, August). *Asking the right questions in research on violent electronic games.* Paper presented at the annual meeting of the American Psychological Association, Washington, DC.

Funk, J.B., Baldacci, H.B., Pasold, T., & Baumgardner, J. (2004). Violence exposure in real-life, video games, television, movies, and the internet: Is there desensitization? *Journal of Adolescence, 27*(1), 23–39.

Funk, J.B., Buchman, D.D., Jenks, J., & Bechtoldt, H. (2002). An evidence-based approach to examining the impact of playing violent video and computer games. *Studies in Media & Information Literacy Education, 2*(4). Retrieved from University of Toronto Press website: www.utpjournals.com/jour.ihtml?lp=simile/issue8/funkfulltext.html

Furnham, A. (1999). Economic socialization: A study of adults' perceptions and uses of allowances (pocket money) to educate children. *British Journal of Developmental Psychology, 17,* 585–604.

Furrow, D., & Nelson, K. (1984). Environmental correlates of individual differences in language acquisition. *Journal of Child Language, 11,* 523–534.

Galbraith, K.M., & Dobson, K.S. (2000). The role of the psychologist in determining competence for assisted suicide/euthanasia in the terminally ill. *Canadian Psychology, 41*(3), 174–183.

Gaillard, W., Hertz-Pannier, L., Mott, S., Barnett, A., LeBihan, D., & Theodore, W. (2000). Functional anatomy of cognitive development: fMRI of verbal fluency in children and adults. *Neurology, 54,* 180–185.

Gainey, R., Catalano, R., Haggerty, K., & Hoppe, M. (1997). Deviance among the children of heroin addicts in treatment: Impact of parents and peers. *Deviant Behavior, 18,* 143–159.

Galambos, N., & Maggs, J. (1991). Out-of-school care of young adolescents and self-reported behavior. *Developmental Psychology, 27,* 644–655.

Galambos, N.L., Leadbeater, B.J., & Barker, E.T. (2004). Gender differences in and risk factors for depression in adolescence: A 4-year longitudinal study. *International Journal of Behavioral Development, 28*(1), 16–25.

Galambos, N.L., Turner, P.K., & Tilton-Weaver, L.C. (2005). Chronological and subjective age in emerging adulthood: The crossover effect. *Journal of Adolescent Research, 20,* 538–556.

Galanaki, E. (2004). Teachers and loneliness: The children's perspective. *School Psychology International, 25*(1), 92–105.

Gallagher, A., Frith, U., & Snowling, M. (2000). Precursors of literacy delay among children at genetic risk of dyslexia. *Journal of Child Psychology & Psychiatry & Allied Disciplines, 41,* 202–213.

Gallagher, S.K. (1994). Doing their share: Comparing patterns of help given by older and younger adults. *Journal of Marriage and the Family, 56,* 567–578.

Gallagher-Thompson, D., Futterman, A., Farberow, N., Thompson, L.W., & Peterson, J. (1993). The impact of spousal bereavement on older widows and widowers. In M.S. Stroebe, W. Stroebe, & R.O. Hansson (Eds.), *Handbook of bereavement: Theory, research, and intervention* (pp. 227–239). Cambridge, England: Cambridge University Press.

Gallagher-Thompson, D., Tazeau, Y., & Basilio L. (1997). The relationships of dimensions of acculturation to self-reported depression in older Mexican-American women. *Journal of Clinical Geropsychology, 3,* 123–137.

Gallo, W., Bradley, E., Siegel, M., & Kasl, S. (2000). Health effects of involuntary job loss among older workers: Findings from the health and retirement survey. *Journals of Gerontology: Series B: Psychological Sciences & Social Sciences, 55B,* S131–S140.

Galloway, J.C., & Thelen, E. (2004) Feet first: Object exploration in human infants. *Infant Behavior and Development, 27*(1), 107–112.

Gambert, S.R., Schultz, B.M., & Hamdy, R.C. (1995). Osteoporosis: Clinical features, prevention, and treatment. *Endocrinology and Metabolism Clinics of North America, 24,* 317–371.

Gana, K., Alaphilippe, D., & Bailly, N. (2004). Positive illusions and mental and physical health in later life. *Aging & Mental Health, 8,* 58–64.

Ganchrow, J.R., Steiner, J.E., & Daher, M. (1983). Neonatal facial expressions in response to different qualities and intensities of gustatory stimuli. *Infant Behavior & Development, 6*(2-3), 189–200.

Gannon, L., & Stevens, J. (1998). Portraits of menopause in the mass media. *Women & Health, 27,* 1–15.

Garcia, G., & Miller, R. (2001). Single-cell analyses reveal two defects in peptide-specific activation of naive T cells from aged mice. *Journal of Immunology, 166,* 3151–3157.

Gardiner, M., Luszcz, M., & Bryan, J. (1997). The manipulation and measurement of task-specific memory self-efficacy in younger and older adults. *International Journal of Behavioral Development, 21,* 209–227.

Gardner, H. (1983). *Frames of mind: The theory of multiple intelligence.* New York, NY: Basic Books.

Gardner, H. (1999). *Intelligence reframed.* New York, NY: Basic Books.

Gardner, J., Karmel, B., Freedland, R., Lennon, E., Flory, M., Miroschnichenko, I., . . . Harm, A. (2006). Arousal, attention, and neurobehavioral assessment in the neonatal period: Implications for intervention and policy. *Journal of Policy and Practice in Intellectual Disabilities, 3,* 22–32.

Garfield, P., Kent, A., Paykel, E., Creighton, F., & Jacobson, R. (2004). Outcome of postpartum disorders: A 10 year follow-up of hospital admissions. *Acta Psychiatrica Scandinavica, 109,* 434–439.

Garland, A.F., & Zigler, E. (1993). Adolescent suicide prevention: Current research and social policy implications. *American Psychologist, 48,* 169–182.

Garland, E.J. (2004). Facing the evidence: Antidepressant treatment in children and adolescents. *Canadian Medical Association Journal, 170*(4), 489–491.

Garrison, R.J., Gold, R.S., Wilson, P.W.F., & Kannel, W.B. (1993). Educational attainment and coronary heart disease risk: The Framingham offspring study. *Preventive Medicine, 22,* 54–64.

Gathercole, S., Pickering, S., Ambridge, B., & Wearing, H. (2004). The structure of working memory from 4 to 15 years of age. *Developmental Psychology, 40,* 177–190.

Gatz, M., Kasl-Godley, J.E., & Karel, M.J. (1996). Aging and mental disorders. In J.E. Birren & K.W. Schaie (Eds.), *Handbook of the psychology of aging* (4th ed., pp. 365–381). San Diego, CA: Academic Press.

Gaultney, J., & Gingras, J. (2005). Fetal rate of behavioral inhibition and preference for novelty during infancy. *Early Human Development, 81,* 379–386.

Gauntlett-Gilbert, J., Keegan, A., & Petrak, J. (2004). Drug-facilitated sexual assault: Cognitive approaches to treating the trauma. *Behavioral & Cognitive Psychotherapy, 32,* 211.

Gaziano, J.M., & Hennekens, C.H. (1995). Dietary fat and risk of prostate cancer. *Journal of the National Cancer Institute, 87,* 1427–1428.

Geers, A., Kosbab, K., Helfer, S., Weiland, P., & Wellman, J. (2007). Further evidence for individual differences in placebo responding: An interactionist perspective. *Journal of Psychosomatic Research, 62,* 563–570.

Geldart, S., Mondloch, C.J., Maurer, D., de Schonen, S., & Brent, H.P. (2002). The effect of early visual deprivation on the development of face processing. *Developmental Science, 5*(4), 490–501.

Gelman, R. (1972). Logical capacity of very young children: Number invariance rules. *Child Development, 43,* 75–90.

Genesee, F. (2009). Early childhood bilingualism: Perils and possibilities (Special Issue: Article 2). *Journal of Applied Research on Learning, 2,* 1–21

Genesee, F., & Nicoladis, E. (2006). Bilingual acquisition. In E. Hoff & M. Shatz (Eds.), *Handbook of Language Development.* Oxford, England: Blackwell.

Gentile, D.A. & Anderson, C.A. (2003). Violent video games: The newest media violence hazard. In D.A. Gentile (Ed.), *Media violence and children* (pp. 131–152). Westport, CT: Praeger Publishing.

Gentile, D.A., Lynch, P.J., Linder, J.R., & Walsh, D.A. (2004). The effects of violent video game habits on adolescent aggressive attitudes and behaviors. *Journal of Adolescence, 27*(1), 5–22.

Gentile, D.A., Walsh, D.A., Ellison, P.R., Fox, M., & Cameron, J. (2004, May). *Media violence as a risk factor for children: A longitudinal study.* Paper presented at the American Psychological Society 16th Annual Convention, Chicago, IL.

George, L.K. (1990). Social structure, social processes, and social-psychological states. In R.H. Binstock & L.K. George (Eds.), *Handbook of aging and the social sciences* (3rd ed., pp. 186–204). San Diego, CA: Academic Press.

Gerhardstein, P., Liu, J., & Rovee-Collier, C. (1998). Perceptual constraints on infant memory retrieval. *Journal of Experimental Child Psychology, 69,* 109–131.

Gershoff, E.T. (2002). Corporal punishment by parents and associated child behaviors and experiences: A meta-analytic and theoretical review. *Psychological Bulletin, 128*(4), 539–579.

Gerstorf, D., Ram, N., Estabrook, R., Schupp, J., Wagner, G.G., & Lindenberger, U. (2008). Life satisfaction shows terminal decline in old age: Longitudinal evidence from the German Socio-Economic Panel Study (SOEP). *Developmental Psychology, 44*(4), 1148–1159.

Gerwood, J., LeBlanc, M., & Piazza, N. (1998). The Purpose-in-Life Test and religious denomination: Protestant and Catholic scores in an elderly population. *Journal of Clinical Psychology, 54,* 49–53.

Gesell, A. (1925). *The mental growth of the preschool child.* New York, NY: Macmillan.

Ghadirian, P. (2008). Sleeping with a killer: The effects of smoking on human health. Ottawa, ON: Health Canada. Retrieved from www.hc-sc.gc.ca/hc-ps/alt_formats/pdf/pubs/tobac-tabac/swk-dat/swk-dat-eng.pdf

Giambra, L.M., Arenberg, D., Zonderman, A.B., Kawas, C., & Costa, P.T., Jr. (1995). Adult life span changes in immediate visual memory and verbal intelligence. *Psychology and Aging, 10,* 123–139.

Gibbs, R., & Beitel, D. (1995). What proverb understanding reveals about how people think. *Psychological Bulletin, 118,* 133–154.

Gibson, D.R. (1990). Relation of socioeconomic status to logical and sociomoral judgment of middle-aged men. *Psychology and Aging, 5,* 510–513.

Gibson, E.J., & Walk, R.D. (1960). The "visual cliff." *Scientific American, 202,* 80–92.

Giedd, J.N. (2004). Structural magnetic resonance imaging of the adolescent brain. *Annals of the New York Academy of Sciences, 1021,* 77–85.

Giedd, J.N., Blumenthal, J., Jeffries, N.O., Castellanos, F.X., Liu, H., Zijdenbos, A., . . . Rapoport, J.L. (1999). Brain development during childhood and adolescence: A longitudinal MRI study. *Nature Neuroscience, 2*(10), 861–863.

Gilbertson, M., & Bramlett, R. (1998). Phonological awareness screening to identify at-risk readers: Implications for practitioners. *Language, Speech, & Hearing Services in Schools, 29,* 109–116.

Gilligan, C. (1982). *In a different voice: Psychological theory and women's development.* Cambridge, MA: Harvard University Press.

Gilligan, C., & Wiggins, G. (1987). The origins of morality in early childhood relationships. In J. Kagan & S. Lamb (Eds.), *The emergence of morality in young children* (pp. 277–307). Chicago, IL: University of Chicago Press.

Gillman, M.W., Rifas-Shiman, S.L., Frazier, L.A., Rockett, H.R.H., Camargo, C.A., Field, A.E., . . . Colditz, G.A. (2000). Family dinner and diet quality among older children and adolescents. *Archives of Family Medicine, 9*(3), 235–240.

Girard, D.L. (2004). Social determinants of initiation, duration and exclusivity of breast feeding at the population level: The results of the Longitudinal Study of Child Development in Quebec (ELDEQ 1998–2002). *Canadian Journal of Public Health, 94*(4), 300–305.

Gladwell, M. (2008). Outliers: The story of success. New York, NY: Little, Brown and Company.

Glaser, D. (2000). Child abuse and neglect and the brain—a review. *Journal of Child Psychology & Psychiatry & Allied Disciplines, 41,* 97–116.

Glaser, R., Kiecolt-Glaser, J.K., Bonneau, R.H., Malarkey, W., Kennedy, S., & Hughes, J. (1992). Stress-induced modulation of the immune response to recombinant hepatitis B vaccine. *Psychosomatic Medicine, 54,* 22–29.

Glass, J., & Kilpatrick, B. (1998). Gender comparisons of baby boomers and financial preparation for retirement. *Educational Gerontology, 24,* 719–745.

Glass, S. (1998). Shared vows. *Psychology Today, 31,* 34.

Gleitman, L.R., & Gleitman, H. (1992). A picture is worth a thousand words, but that's the problem: The role of syntax in vocabulary acquisition. *Current Directions in Psychological Science, 1,* 31–35.

Glenn, N.D., & Weaver, C.N. (1985). Age, cohort, and reported job satisfaction in the United States. In A.S. Blau (Ed.), *Current perspectives on aging and the life cycle. A research annual: Vol. 1. Work, retirement and social policy* (pp. 89–110). Greenwich, CT.

Gloger-Tippelt, G., & Huerkamp, M. (1998). Relationship change at the transition to parenthood and security of infant-mother attachment. *International Journal of Behavioral Development, 23,* 633–655.

Gluckman, P.D., & Hanson, M.A. (2004a). Living with the past: Evolution, development, and patterns of disease. *Science, 305,* 1733–1736.

Gluckman, P., & Hanson, M. (2004b). *The fetal matrix: evolution, development and disease.* New York, NY: Cambridge University Press.

Gluckman, P., & Hanson, M. (2006a). *Mismatch: Why our world no longer fits our bodies.* New York, NY: Oxford University Press.

Gluckman, P.D., & Hanson, M.A. (2006b). Adult disease: echoes of the past. *European Journal of Endocrinology, 155*(S1), S47–S50. doi: 10.1530/eje.1.02233

Gluckman, P.D., & Hanson, M.A. (2007). Developmental plasticity and human disease: Research directions. *Journal of Internal Medicine, 261*(5), 461–471.

Gluckman, P.D., Hanson, M.A., & Beedle, A.S. (2007). Early life events and their consequences for later disease: A life history and evolutionary perspective. *American Journal of Human Biology, 19*(1), 1–19.

Gluckman, P.D., Hanson, M.A., & Spencer, H.G. (2005). Predictive adaptive responses and human evolution. *Trends in Ecology and Evolution, 20*(10), 527–33. doi:10.1016/j.tree.2005.08.001

Gluckman, P.D., Hanson, M.A., Bateson, P., Beedle, A.S., Law, C.M., Bhutta, Z.A., . . . West-Eberhard, M.J. (2009). Towards a new developmental synthesis: adaptive developmental plasticity and human disease. *Lancet, 373*(9675), 1654–1657.

Glück, J., Bluck, S., Baron, J., & McAdams, D. (2005). The wisdom of experience: Autobiographical narratives across adulthood. *International Journal of Behavioral Development, 29,* 197–208.

Gnepp, J., & Chilamkurti, C. (1988). Children's use of personality attributions to predict other people's emotional and behavioral reactions. *Child Development, 50,* 743–754.

Gogtay, N., Giedd, J.N., Lusk, L., Hayashi, K.M., Greenstein, D., Vaituzis, A.C., . . . Thompson, P.M. (2004). Dynamic mapping of human cortical development during childhood through early adulthood. *Proceedings of the National Academy of Sciences of the United States of America, 101,* 8174–8179.

Gold, D.P., Andres, D., Etezadi, J., Arbuckle, T., Schwartzman, A., & Chaikelson, J. (1995). Structural equation model of intellectual change and continuity and predictors of intelligence in older men. *Psychology and Aging, 10,* 294–303.

Gold, E., Colvin, A., Avis, N., Bromberger, J., Greendale, G., Powell, L., . . . Matthews, K. (2006). Longitudinal analysis of the association between vasomotor symptoms and race/ethnicity across the menopausal transition: Study of women's health across the nation. *American Journal of Public Health, 96,* 1225–1235.

Goldbaum, S., Craig, W.M., Pepler, D.J., & Connolly, J. (2003). Developmental trajectories of victimization: Identifying risk and protective factors. *Journal of Applied School Psychology, 19,* 139–156.

Goldberg, A.E. (2009). Claiming a place at the family table: Gay and lesbian families in the 21st century. *PsycCritiques, 55*(7), 233–235.

Goldberg, A.P., & Hagberg, J.M. (1990). Physical exercise in the elderly. In E.R. Schneider & J.W. Rowe (Eds.), *Handbook of the biology of aging* (3rd ed., pp. 407–428). San Diego, CA: Academic Press.

Goldberg, A.P., Dengel, D.R., & Hagberg, J.M. (1996). Exercise physiology and aging. In E.L. Schneider & J.W. Rowe (Eds.), *Handbook of the biology of aging* (4th ed., pp. 331–354). San Diego, CA: Academic Press.

Goldberg, W.A. (1990). Marital quality, parental personality, and spousal agreement about perceptions and expectations for children. *Merrill-Palmer Quarterly, 36,* 531–556.

Goldfield, B.A. (1993). Noun bias in maternal speech to one-year-olds. *Journal of Child Language, 20,* 85–99.

Goldfield, B.A., & Reznick, J.S. (1990). Early lexical acquisition: Rate, content, and the vocabulary spurt. *Journal of Child Language, 17,* 171–183.

Golding, J., Emmett, P., & Rogers, I. (1997a). Does breast feeding protect against non-gastric infections? *Early Human Development, 49* (Supp.), S105–S120.

Golding, J., Emmett, P., & Rogers, I. (1997b). Gastroenteritis, diarrhea and breast feeding. *Early Human Development, 49*(Supp.), S83–S103.

Goldman, S., & Windrem, M. (2006). Cell replacement therapy in neurological disease. *Philosophical Transactions of the Royal Society of London. Series B, Biological Sciences, 361*(1473), 1463–1475.

Goldsmith, H.H., Lemery, K.S., Buss, K.A., & Campos, J.J. (1999). Genetic analyses of focal aspects of infant temperament. *Developmental Psychology, 35*(4), 972–985.

Goleman, D. (1995). *Emotional intelligence.* New York, NY: Bantam.

Goleman, D. D., Kaufman, P., & Ray, M. (1992). *The creative spirit.* New York, NY: Dutton.

Golinkoff, R.M., Mervis, C.V., & Hirsh-Pasek, K. (1994). Early object labels: The case for a developmental lexical principles framework. *Journal of Child Language, 21,* 125–155. Also in K. Perera (Ed.), *Growing points in child language.* Cambridge, MA: Cambridge University Press.

Golombok, S., & Fivush, R. (1994). *Gender development.* Cambridge, England: Cambridge University Press.

Gomez, R., Bounds, J., Holmberg, K., Fullarton, C., & Gomez, A. (1999). Effects of neuroticism and avoidant coping style on maladjustment during early adolescence. *Personality & Individual Differences, 26,* 305–319.

Gonzalez, J., & Valle, I. (2000). Word identification and reading disorders in the Spanish language. *Journal of Learning Disabilities, 33,* 44–60.

Goodman, G.S., Sayfan, J.S., Lee, M., Sandhai, A., Walle-Olsen, S., Magnussen, K., & Pezdek, P.A. (2007). The development of memory for own and other-race faces. *The Journal of Experimental Child Psychology, 98*(4), 233–242.

Goodman, L.M. (1981). *Death and the creative life: Conversations with eminent artists and scientists as they reflect on life and death.* New York, NY: Springer Publishing Company.

Goodrum, S. (2005). The interaction between thoughts and emotions following the news of a loved one's murder. *Omega: Journal of Death and Dying, 51*(2), 143–160.

Goodsitt, J.V., Morse, P.A., Ver Hoeve, J.N., & Cowan, N. (1984). Infant speech recognition in multisyllabic contexts. *Child Development, 55,* 903–910.

Gopnik, A., & Astington, J.W. (1988). Children's understanding of representational change and its relation to the understanding of false belief and the appearance-reality distinction. *Child Development, 59,* 26–37.

Gopnik, A., & Wellman, H.M. (1994). The theory theory. In L.A. Hirschfeld & S.A. Gelman (Eds.), *Mapping the mind* (pp. 257–293). Cambridge, England: Cambridge University Press.

Gordon, G.S., & Vaughan, C. (1986). Calcium and osteoporosis. *Journal of Nutrition, 116,* 319–322.

Gotay, N., Giedd, J., Lusk, L., Hayashi, K., Greenstien, D., Vaituzis, A., . . . Thompson, P. (2004). Dyanmic mapping of human cortical development during childhood through early adulthood. *Proceeding for the National Academy of Sciences, 101,* 8174–8179.

Gothelf, D., Apter, A., Brand-Gothelf, A., Offer, N., Ofek, H., Tyano, S., & Pfeffer, C. (1998). Death concepts in suicidal adolescents. *Journal of the American Academy of Child & Adolescent Psychiatry, 37,* 1279–1286.

Gottlob, L., & Madden, D. (1999). Age differences in the strategic allocation of visual attention. *Journals of Gerontology: Series B: Psychological Sciences & Social Sciences, 54B,* P165–P172.

Gottman, J.M. (1986). The world of coordinated play: Same- and cross-sex friendship in young children. In J.M. Gottman & J.G. Parker (Eds.), *Conversations of friends: Speculations on affective development* (pp. 139–191). Cambridge, England: Cambridge University Press.

Gottman, J.M. (1994). *Why marriages succeed or fail.* New York, NY: Simon & Schuster.

Gould, E., Reeves, A., Graziano, M., & Gross, C. (1999). Neurogenesis in the neocortex of adult primates. *Science, 286,* 548–552.

Government of Canada (2006). *The human face of mental health and mental illness in Canada* (HP5-19/2006E). Ottawa, ON: Minister of Public Works and Government Services Canada. Retrieved from www.phac-aspc.gc.ca/publicat/human-humain06/pdf/human_face_e.pdf

Government of Canada (2009). Elder abuse: It's time to face the reality (HS4-61/2009). Ottawa, ON: Author. Retrieved from www.seniors.gc.ca/c.4nt.2nt@.jsp?cid=154

Government of Canada. (2008). *Care facilities.* Ottawa, ON: Author. Retrieved from www.seniors.gc.ca/s.2.1rchcat@.jsp?lang=eng&cat=712

Government of Ontario (2010). Full-day learning for 4- and 5-year-olds: Time to learn, grow and play. Toronto, ON: Ministry of Education, Government of Ontario. Retrieved from www.edu.gov.on.ca/earlylearning/EL_FactSheet_Jan2010.pdf

Govoni, R., Rupcich, N. & Frisch, G.R. (1996). Gambling behavior of adolescent gamblers. *Journal of Gambling Studies, 12,* 305–317.

Graham, J., Cohen, R., Zbikowski, S., & Secrist, M. (1998). A longitudinal investigation of race and sex as factors in children's classroom friendship choices. *Child Study Journal, 28,* 245–266.

Graham, S., & Harris, K. (1997). It can be taught, but it does not develop naturally: Myths and realities in writing instruction. *School Psychology Review, 26,* 414–424.

Gralinski, J.H., & Kopp, C.B. (1993). Everyday rules for behavior: Mothers' requests to young children. *Developmental Psychology, 29,* 573–584.

Gralinski-Bakker, J., Hauser, S., Billings, R., Allen, J., Lyons, P., & Melton, G. (2005). Transitioning to adulthood for young adults with mental health issues. *Network on Transitions to Adulthood Policy Brief, 21,* 1–3.

Grant, S., & Langan-Fox, J. (2007). Personality and the occupational stressor-strain relationship: The role of the Big Five. *Journal of Occupational Health Psychology, 112,* 20–33.

Green, R.F., Devine, O., Crider, K.S., Olney, R.S., Archer, N., Olshan, A.F., & Shapira, S.K. (2010). Association of paternal age and risk for major congenital anomalies from the nation birth defects prevention study, 1997 to 2004. *Annals of Epidemiology, 20*(3), 241–249.

Green, S. (2001). Systemic vs. individualistic approaches to bullying. *Journal of the American Medical Association, 286*(7), 787.

Greenberg, M.T., Siegel, J.M., & Leitch, C.J. (1983). The nature and importance of attachment relationships to parents and peers during adolescence. *Journal of Youth and Adolescence, 12,* 373–386.

Greenberg, M.T., Speltz, M.L., & DeKlyen, M. (1993). The role of attachment in the early development of disruptive behavior problems. *Development and Psychopathology, 5,* 191–213.

Greene, S., Anderson, E., Doyle, E., & Ridelbach, H. (2006). Divorce. In Bear, G., & Minke, K. (Eds.), *Children's needs III: Development, prevention, and intervention.* Washington, DC: National Association of School Psychologists.

Greenfield, E., & Marks, N. (2007). Continuous participation in voluntary groups as a protective factor for the psychological well-being of adults who develop functional limitations: Evidence from the National Survey of Families and Households. *The Journals of Gerontology Series B: Psychological Sciences and Social Sciences, 62,* S60–S68.

Greenfield, P. (1994). Video games as cultural artifacts. *Journal of Applied Developmental Psychology, 15,* 3–12.

Greenfield, P., Brannon, C., & Lohr, D. (1994). Two-dimensional representation of movement through three-dimensional space: The role of video game expertise. *Journal of Applied Developmental Psychology, 15,* 87–104.

Greenhaus, J., Collins, K., Singh, R., & Parasuraman, S. (1997). Work and family influences on departure from public accounting. *Journal of Vocational Behavior, 50,* 249–270.

Greer, S. (1991). Psychological response to cancer and survival. *Psychological Medicine, 21,* 43–49.

Greer, S. (2000). Fighting spirit in patients with cancer. *The Lancet, 355*(9206), 847–848.

Greer, S. (2002). Psychological intervention. The gap between research and practice. *Acta Oncologica, 41*(3), 238–243.

Greer, S., Morris, T., & Pettingale, K.W. (1979). Psychological response to breast cancer: Effect on outcome. *Lancet,* 785–787.

Griffith, J. (1998). The relation of school structure and social environment to parent involvement in elementary schools. *Elementary School Journal, 99,* 53–80.

Groome, L., Mooney, D., Holland, S., Smith, L., Atterbury, J., & Dykman, R. (1999). Behavioral state affects heart rate response to low-intensity sound in human fetuses. *Early Human Development, 54,* 39–54.

Gross, J., Carstensen, L., Pasupathi, M., Tsai, J., Gostestam-Grossman, A., Daugelli, A., & Hershberger, S. (2000). Social support networks of lesbian, gay, and bisexual adults 60 years of age and older. *Journals of Gerontology: Series B: Psychological Sciences & Social Sciences, 55B*, P171–P179.

Grov, C., Bimbi, D., Nanin, J., & Parsons, J. (2006). Race, ethnicity, gender, and generational factors associated with the coming-out process among gay, lesbian, and bisexual individuals. *Journal of Sex Research, 43*, 115–121.

Gruber, R., Sadeh, A., & Raviv, A. (2000). Instability of sleep patterns in children with attention-deficit/hyperactivity disorder. *Journal of the American Academy of Child and Adolescent Psychiatry, 379*(4), 495–501.

Guerin, D.W., & Gottfried, A.W. (1994a). Developmental stability and change in parent reports of temperament: A ten-year longitudinal investigation from infancy through preadolescence. *Merrill-Palmer Quarterly, 40*, 334–355.

Guerin, D.W., & Gottfried, A.W. (1994b). Temperamental consequences of infant difficultness. *Infant Behavior and Development, 17*, 413–421.

Guesry, P. (1998). The role of nutrition in brain development. *Preventive Medicine, 27*, 189–194.

Guilford, J. (1967). *The nature of human intelligence*. New York, NY: McGraw-Hill.

Gunkel, M., Lusk, E., Wolff, B., & Li, F. (2007). Gender-specific effects at work: An empirical study of four countries. *Gender, Work & Organization, 14*, 56–79.

Gunnar, M.R. (1994). Psychoendocrine studies of temperament and stress in early childhood: Expanding current models. In J.E. Bates & T.D. Wachs (Eds.), *Temperament: Individual differences at the interface of biology and behavior* (pp. 175–198). Washington, DC: American Psychological Association.

Gunter, T., Jackson, J., & Mulder, G. (1998). Priming and aging: An electrophysiological investigation of N400 and recall. *Brain & Language, 65*, 333–355.

Gunther, M. (1955). Instinct and the nursing couple. *Lancet, 265*(6864), 575–578.

Gunther, M. (1961). Infant behavior at the breast. In B. Foss (Ed.), *Determinants of infant behavior* (pp. 37–44). London: Methuen.

Guo, S.F. (1993). Postpartum depression. *Chung-Hua Fu Chan Ko Tsa Chi, 28*, 532–533, 569.

Gupta, R., & Derevensky, J.L. (1997). Familial and social influences on juvenile gambling. Journal of Gambling Studies, *13*, 179–192.

Gupta, R., & Derevensky, J.L. (1998a). Adolescent gambling behaviour: A prevalence study and examination of the correlates associated with excessive gambling. *Journal of Gambling Studies, 14*, 227–244.

Gupta, R., & Derevensky, J.L. (1998b). An empirical examination of Jacob's General Theory of Addictions: Do adolescent gamblers fit the theory? Journal of Gambling Studies, *14*, 17–49.

Gupta, R., & Derevensky, J.L. (2000). Adolescents with gambling problems: From research to treatment. *Journal of Gambling Studies, 16*(2–3), 315–342.

Guralnik, J.M., & Kaplan, G.A. (1989). Predictors of healthy aging: Prospective evidence from the Alameda County Study. *American Journal of Public Health, 79*, 703–708.

Guralnik, J.M., & Paul-Brown, D. (1984). Communicative adjustments during behavior-request episodes among children at different developmental levels. *Child Development, 55*, 911–919.

Guralnik, J.M., Land, K.C., Blazer, D., Fillenbaum, G.G., & Branch, L.G. (1993). Educational status and active life expectancy among older blacks and whites. *New England Journal of Medicine, 329*, 110–116.

Guralnik, J.M., Simonsick, E.M., Ferrucci, L., Glynn, R.J., Berkman, L.F., Blazer, D.G., . . . Wallace, R.B. (1994). A short physical performance battery assessing lower extremity function: Association with self-reported disability and prediction of mortality and nursing home admission. *Journals of Gerontology: Medical Sciences, 49*, M85–94.

Gurnáková, J., & Kusá, D. (2004). Gender self-concept in personal theories of reality. *Studia Psychologica, 46*, 49–61.

Guse, L., & Masesar, M. (1999). Quality of life and successful aging in long-term care: Perceptions of residents. *Issues in Mental Health Nursing, 20*, 527–539.

Gustafson, S.B., & Magnusson, D. (1991). *Female life careers: A pattern approach*. Hillsdale, NJ: Erlbaum.

Gutman, L. (2006). How student and parent goal orientations and classroom goal structures influence the math achievement of African Americans during the high school transition. *Contemporary Educational Psychology, 31*, 44–63.

Gwartney-Gibbs, P.A. (1988). Women's work experience and the "rusty skills" hypothesis: A reconceptualization and reevaluation of the evidence. In B.A. Gutek, A.H. Stromberg, & L. Larwood (Eds.), *Women and work: An annual review: Vol. 3* (pp. 169–188). Newbury Park, CA: Sage.

Gzesh, S.M., & Surber, C.F. (1985). Visual perspective-taking skills in children. *Child Development, 56*, 1204–1213.

Hagan, J. (1997). Defiance and despair: Subcultural and structural linkages between delinquency and despair in the life course. *Social Forces, 76*, 119–134.

Hagan, J., & Kay, F. (2007). Even lawyers get the blues: Gender, depression, and job satisfaction in legal practice. *Law & Society Review, 41*, 51–78.

Hagekull, B., & Bohlin, G. (2003). Early temperament and attachment as predictors of the Five Factor Model of personality. *Attachment & Human Development, 5*, 2–18.

Hagestad, G.O. (1985). Continuity and connectedness. In V.L. Bengtson (Ed.), *Grandparenthood* (pp. 31–38). Beverly Hills, CA: Sage.

Hagestad, G.O. (1986). Dimensions of time and the family. *American Behavioral Scientist, 29*, 679–694.

Hagestad, G.O. (1990). Social perspectives on the life course. In R.H. Binstock & L.K. George (Eds.), *Handbook of aging and the social sciences* (3rd ed., pp. 151–168). San Diego, CA: Academic Press.

Hahn, C., Yang, M-S., Yang, M-J., Shih, C., & Lo, H. (2004). Religious attendance and depressive symptoms among community dwelling elderly in Taiwan. *International Journal of Geriatric Psychiatry, 19*, 1148–1154.

Haight, W., Wang, X., Fung, H., Williams, K., & Mintz, J. (1999). Universal, developmental, and variable aspects of young children's play. *Child Development, 70*, 1477–1488.

Hall, D.T. (1972). A model of coping with role conflict: The role behavior of college educated women. *Administrative Science Quarterly, 17*, 471–486.

Hall, D.T. (1975). Pressures from work, self, and home in the life stages of married women. *Journal of Vocational Behavior, 6*, 121–132.

Hall, W.D., Morley, K.I., & Lucke, J.C. (2004). The prediction of disease risk in genomic medicine. *EMBO reports, 5*(S1), S22–S26.

Halle, T. (1999). Implicit theories of social interactions: Children's reasoning about the relative importance of gender and friendship in social partner choices. *Merrill-Palmer Quarterly, 45*, 445–467.

Hallfrisch, J., Muller, D., Drinkwater, D., Tobin, J., & Adres, R. (1990). Continuing diet trends in men: The Baltimore Longitudinal Study of Aging. *Journals of Gerontology: Medical Sciences, 45*(6), M186–191.

Halpern, D. (1997). Sex differences in intelligence: Implications for education. *American Psychologist, 52*, 1091–1102.

Hamberger, K., & Minsky, D. (2000, August). *Evaluation of domestic violence training programs for health care professionals*. Paper presented at the annual meeting of the American Psychological Association, Washington, DC.

Hamilton, C.E. (1995, March). *Continuity and discontinuity of attachment from infancy through adolescence*. Paper presented at the biennial meetings of the Society for Research in Child Development, Indianapolis, IN.

Hammond, M., Landry, S., Swank, P., & Smith, K. (2000). Relation of mothers' affective development history and parenting behavior: Effects on infant medical risk. *American Journal of Orthopsychiatry, 70*, 95–103.

Hampson, S., & Goldberg, L. (2006). A first large cohort study of personality trait stability over the 40 years between elementary school and midlife. *Journal of Personality and Social Psychology, 91*, 763–779.

Hancox, R.J., Milne, B.J., & Poulton, R. (2005). Association of television viewing during childhood with poor educational achievement. *Archives of Pediatrics & Adolescent Medicine, 159*(7), 614–618.

Handley-Derry, M., Low, J., Burke, S., Waurick, M., Killen, H., & Derrick, E. (1997). Intrapartum fetal asphyxia and the occurrence of minor deficits in 4- to 8-year-old children. *Developmental Medicine & Child Neurology, 39,* 508–514.

Hanna, E., & Meltzoff, A.N. (1993). Peer imitation by toddlers in laboratory, home, and day-care contexts: Implications for social learning and memory. *Developmental Psychology, 29,* 701–710.

Hanninen, T., Koivisto, K., Reinikainen, K., Helkala, E., Soininen, H., Mykkanen, L., . . . Riekkinen, P. (1996). Prevalence of ageing-associated cognitive decline in an elderly population. *Age & Aging, 25,* 201–205.

Haque, F.N., Gottesman, I.I., & Wong, A.H.C. (2009). Not really identical: Epigenetic differences in monozygotic twins and implications for twin studies in psychiatry. *American Journal of Medical Genetics Part C: Seminars in Medical Genetics, 151C*(2), 136–141.

Hardy, M.A., & Quadagno, J. (1995). Satisfaction with early retirement: Making choices in the auto industry. Journals of Gerontology: Social Sciences, *50B,* S217–228.

Hargrave, A.C. & Sénéchal, M. (2000). Book reading interventions with language-delayed preschool children: The benefits of regular reading and dialogic reading. *Early Childhood Research Quarterly, 15*(1), 75–90.

Haring, M., Hewitt, P., & Flett, G. (2003). Perfectionism, coping, and quality of intimate relationships. *Journal of Marriage & the Family, 65,* 143–158.

Harkness, S. (1998). Time for families. *Anthropology Newsletter, 39,* 1, 4.

Harley, B., & Jean, G. (1999). Vocabulary skills of French immersion students in their second language. *Zeitschrift für Interkulturellen Fremdsprachenunterricht* [online], 4(2), 19. Retrieved from University of Alberta website: www.ualberta.ca/~german/ejournal/harley2.htm

Harlow, H., & Zimmerman, R. (1959). Affectional responses in the infant monkey. *Science, 130,* 421–432.

Harris, B., Lovett, L., Newcombe, R.G., Read, G.F., Walker, R., & Riad-Fahmy, D. (1994). Maternity blues and major endocrine changes: Cardiff puerperal mood and hormone study II. *British Medical Journal, 308,* 949–953.

Harris, P.L. (1989). *Children and emotion: The development of psychological understanding.* Oxford, England: Blackwell.

Harris, R.L., Ellicott, A.M., & Holmes, D.S. (1986). The timing of psychosocial transitions and changes in women's lives: An examination of women aged 45 to 60. *Journal of Personality and Social Psychology, 51,* 409–416.

Harrison, L.J., & Ungerer, J.A. (2002). Maternal employment and infant-mother attachment security at 12 months postpartum. *Developmental Psychology, 38*(5), 758–773.

Harrison, M.J., Magill-Evans, J., & Benzies, K. (1999). Fathers' scores on the nursing child assessment teaching scale: Are they different from those of mothers? *Journal of Pediatric Nursing, 14,* 1–8.

Harrist, A., Zaia, A., Bates, J., Dodge, K., & Pettit, G. (1997). Subtypes of social withdrawal in early childhood: Sociometric status and social-cognitive differences across four years. *Child Development, 68,* 278–294.

Hart, B., & Risley, T.R. (1995). *Meaningful differences in the everyday experience of young American children.* Baltimore, MD: Paul H. Brookes.

Hart, S., Jones, N., Field, T., & Lundy, B. (1999). One-year-old infants of intrusive and withdrawn depressed mothers. *Child Psychiatry & Human Development, 30,* 111–120.

Harter, S. (1987). The determinations and mediational role of global self-worth in children. In N. Eisenberg (Ed.), *Contemporary topics in developmental psychology* (pp. 219–242). New York, NY: Wiley-Interscience.

Harter, S. (1990). Processes underlying adolescent self-concept formation. In R. Montemayor, G.R. Adams, & T.P. Gullotta (Eds.), *From childhood to adolescence: A transitional period?* (pp. 205–239). Newbury Park, CA: Sage.

Harter, S., & Monsour, A. (1992). Developmental analysis of conflict caused by opposing attributes in the adolescent self-portrait. *Developmental Psychology, 28,* 251–260.

Harton, H., & Latane, B. (1997). Social influence and adolescent lifestyle attitudes. *Journal of Research on Adolescence, 7,* 197–220.

Hartup, W.W. (1996). The company they keep: Friendships and their developmental significance. *Child Development, 67,* 1–13.

Hartup, W.W., & Abecassis, M. (2004). Friends and enemies. In P.K. Smith & C.H. Hart (Eds.), *Blackwell handbook of childhood social development* (pp. 285–306). Maiden, MA: Blackwell.

Hartup, W.W., & Stevens, N. (1999). Friendships and adaptation across the life span. *Current directions in psychological science, 8*(3), pp. 76–79.

Harvey, A., Towner, E., Peden, M., Soori, H., & Bartolomeos, K. (2009). Injury prevention and the attainment of child and adolescent health. *Bulletin of the World Health Organization, 87*(5), 390–394. doi:10.2471/BLT.08.059808

Harwood, D., Barker, W., Ownby, R., Bravo, M., Aguero, H., & Duara, R. (2000). Depressive symptoms in Alzheimer's disease: An examination among community-dwelling Cuban American patients. *American Journal of Geriatric Psychiatry, 8,* 84–91.

Hashima, P.Y., & Amato, P.R. (1994). Poverty, social support, and parental behavior. *Child Development, 65,* 394–403.

Hauf, P., Aschersleben, G. & Prinz, W. (2007). Baby do—baby see! How action production influences action perception in infants. *Cognitive Development, 22,* 16–32.

Hauge, M.R., & Gentile, D.A. (2003, April). *Video game addiction among adolescents: Associations with academic performance and aggression.* Paper presented at the Society for Research in Child Development Conference, Tampa, FL.

Hausman, P.B., & Weksler, M.E. (1985). Changes in the immune response with age. In C.E. Finch & E.L. Schneider (Eds.), *Handbook of the biology of aging* (2nd ed., pp. 414–432). New York, NY: Van Nostrand Reinhold.

Havens, B., & Finlayson, M. (1999). *Analysis of Canada's oldest old: From the survey of ageing and independence.* Ottawa, ON: Health Canada. Retrieved from www.hc-sc.gc.ca/seniors-aines/pubs/havens/index_e.htm

Hawkins, H.L., Kramer, A.F., & Capaldi, D. (1992). Aging, exercise, and attention. *Psychology and Aging, 7,* 643–653.

Hawkley, L., & Cacioppo, J. (2004). Stress and the aging immune system. *Brain, Behavior, and Immunity, 18,* 114–119.

Hay, D., Payne, A., & Chadwick, A. (2004). Peer relations in childhood. *Journal of Child Psychology & Psychiatry & Allied Disciplines, 45,* 84–108.

Hayflick, L. (1977). The cellular basis for biological aging. In C.E. Finch & L. Hayflick (Eds.), *Handbook of the biology of aging* (pp. 159–186). New York, NY: Van Nostrand Reinhold.

Hayflick, L. (1987). Origins of longevity. In H.R. Warner, R.N. Butler, R.L. Sprott, & E.L. Schneider (Eds.), *Aging: Vol. 31. Modern biological theories of aging* (pp. 21–34). New York, NY: Raven Press.

Hayflick, L. (1994). *How and why we age.* New York, NY: Ballantine Books.

Hayne, H., & Rovee-Collier, C. (1995). The organization of reactivated memory in infancy. *Child Development, 66,* 893–906.

Hayward, M.D., & Hardy, M.A. (1985). Early retirement processes among older men: Occupational differences. *Research on Aging, 7,* 491–518.

Hayward, M.D., Friedman, S., & Chen, H. (1996). Race inequities in men's retirement. *Journals of Gerontology: Social Sciences, 51B,* S1–10.

Hazan, C., & Shaver, P. (1987). Romantic love conceptualized as an attachment process. *Journal of Personality and Social Psychology, 52,* 511–524.

Hazan, C., Hutt, M., Sturgeon, J., & Bricker, T. (1991, April). *The process of relinquishing parents as attachment figures.* Paper presented at the biennial meetings of the Society for Research in Child Development, Seattle, WA.

Hazelrigg, L.E., & Hardy, M.A. (1995). Older adult migration to the sunbelt: Assessing income and related characteristics of recent migrants. *Research on Aging, 17,* 109–234.

Hazuda, H., Wood, R., Lichtenstein, M., & Espino, D. (1998). Sociocultural status, psychosocial factors, and cognitive functional limitation in elderly Mexican Americans: Findings from the San Antonio Longitudinal Study of Aging. *Journal of Gerontological Social Work, 30*, 99–121.

He, M., & Evans, A. (2007). Are parents aware that their children are overweight or obese? *Canadian Family Physician, 53*, 1493–1499.

He, Y., Colantonio, A., & Marshall, V. (2003). Later-life career disruption and self-rated health: An analysis of General Social Survey data. *Canadian Journal on Aging, 22*, 45–57.

Health Canada. (1997). *A multicultural perspective of breastfeeding in Canada.* (Cat. No. H39-386/1997E). Ottawa, ON: Author. Retrieved from www.hc-sc.gc.ca/hppb/enfancejeunesse/cyfh/pdf/multicultural.pdf

Health Canada. (1998a). *Canadian Perinatal Health Surveillance System: Infant mortality* Ottawa, ON: Author. Retrieved from www.hc-sc.gc.ca/hpb/lcdc/brch/factshts/mort_e.html

Health Canada. (1998b). *Canadian Perinatal Health Surveillance System: Breastfeeding.* Ottawa, ON: Author. Retrieved from www.hc-sc.gc.ca/hpb/lcdc/brch/factshts/brstfd_e.html

Health Canada. (1999a). *The Aboriginal Diabetes Initiative.* Ottawa, ON: Author. Retrieved from www.hc-sc.gc.ca/english/archives/releases/1999/99135ebk2.htm

Health Canada. (1999b). *Weight control and heart disease: How to control your weight and reduce your risk of heart disease.* Ottawa, ON: Author. Retrieved from www.hc-sc.gc.ca/pphb-dgspsp/ccdpc-cpcmc/hhk-tcs/english/pdf_e/weig_eng.pdf

Health Canada. (1999c). *The addition of vitamins and minerals to foods policy recommendations.* Ottawa, ON: Author. Retrieved from www.hc-sc.gc.ca/food-aliment/english/subjects/dietary_reference_intakes/review_of_hc_policies/ q_a.html

Health Canada. (1999d). *Canadian Perinatal Health Surveillance System: Sudden infant death syndrome.* Ottawa, ON: Author. Retrieved from www.hc-sc.gc.ca/hpb/lcdc/brch/factshts/sids_e.html

Health Canada. (1999e). Positive mental health. In *Statistical report on the health of Canadians* (Cat. No. H39-467/1999E) (pp. 220–222). Ottawa, ON: Author. Retrieved from www.hc-sc.ca/hppb/phdd/report/stat/pdf/english/all_english/pdf

Health Canada. (1999f). *Toward a healthy future: Second report on the health of Canadians* (Cat. No. H39-468/1999E). Ottawa, ON: Minister of Public Works and Government Services Canada. Retrieved from www.hc-sc.gc.ca/hppb/phdd/report/toward/pdf/english/toward_a_healthy_english.PDF

Health Canada. (1999g). For the safety of Canadian children and youth. Ottawa, ON: Author. Retrieved October 2, 2001 from http://www.hc-sc.gc.ca/hpb/lcdc/brch/chirrpbk/ch1_e.html

Health Canada. (1999h). *Healthy development of children and youth: The role of the determinants of health.* (Cat. No. H39-501/1999E). Ottawa, ON: Author. Retrieved from www.hc-sc.gc.ca/hppb/childhood-youth/spsc/pdf/child&yo.pdf

Health Canada. (1999j). *Teen pregnancy.* Ottawa, ON: Author. Retrieved from www.hc-sc.gc.ca/hpb/lcdc/brch/measuring/mu_ee_e.html

Health Canada. (1999k). *Suicide.* Ottawa, ON: Author. Retrieved from www.hc-sc.gc.ca/hpb/lcdc/brch/measuring/mu_y_e.html

Health Canada. (2000a). *Leading causes of death and hospitalization in Canada.* Ottawa, ON: Author. Retrieved from www.hc-sc.ca/pphb-dgspsp/publicat/lcd-pcd97/pdf/hos_mrt_e.pdf

Health Canada. (2000b). *Positive HIV test reports in Canada.* Ottawa, ON: Author. Retrieved from www.hc-sc.gc.ca/hpb/lcdc/bah/epi/poshiv_e.html

Health Canada. (2000c). *AIDS and HIV in Canada.* Ottawa, ON: Author. Retrieved from www.hc-sc.gc.ca/hpb/lcdc/bah/epi/ahcan_e.html

Health Canada. (2001a). *Proposal for legislation governing assisted human reproduction: An overview.* Ottawa, ON: Author. Retrieved from www.hc-sc.gc.ca/english/archives/releases/2001/2001_44ebk1.html

Health Canada. (2001b). Coping with life. *Trends in the health of Canadian youth.* Ottawa, ON: Author. Retrieved from www.hc-sc.gc.ca/hppb/childhood-youth/spsc/e_trends.html

Health Canada. (2001c). *National Report—Canada: Ten-year review of the world summit for children.* Ottawa, ON: Author. Retrieved from www.hc-sc.gc.ca/hppb/childhood-youth/spsc/pdf/WSC10FinalEnglish.pdf

Health Canada. (2001d). *Canada's seniors: No. 15—Gender differences in low income.* Ottawa, ON: Author. Retrieved from www.hc-sc.gc.ca/seniors-aines/pubs/factoids_2001/no15_3.htm

Health Canada. (2001e). *News release: Health Minister Allan Rock and Minister with Special Responsibility for Palliative Care Sharon Carstairs announce funding for Canadian Virtual Hospice.* Ottawa, ON: Health Canada. Retrieved from www.hc-sc.gc.ca/english/media/releases/2001/2001_121e.htm

Health Canada. (2002a). *Congenital anomalies in Canada—A perinatal health report, 2002* (H39-641/2002E). Ottawa, ON: Minister of Public Works and Government Services Canada.

Health Canada. (2002b). *ECD strategy for Aboriginal children: Expansion of Aboriginal Head Start (AHS).* Ottawa, ON: Author. Retrieved from www.hc-sc.gc.ca/fnihb/cp/publications/ecd_ahs.htm

Health Canada. (2002c). *A Report on Mental Illnesses in Canada* (Cat. No. 0-662-32817-5). Ottawa, ON: Health Canada Editorial Board Mental Illnesses in Canada. Retrieved from www.hc-sc.gc.ca/pphb-dgspsp/publicat/miic-mmac/pdf/men_ill_e.pdf

Health Canada. (2002d). *Cardiovascular disease surveillance on-line: Mortality by age group.* Ottawa, ON: Author. Retrieved from http://dsol-smed.hc-sc.gc.ca/dsol-smed/cvd/c_age_e.html

Health Canada. (2002g). Needs assessment for the Canadian virtual hospice: Final report. Ottawa, ON: Author, Applied Research Initiative Program. Retrieved September 8, 2004 from http://www.hc-sc.gc.ca/ohih-bsi/pubs/kdec/on_virt_rpt_e.html

Health Canada. (2003a). *Canadian perinatal health report* (H49-142/2003E). Ottawa, ON: Minister of Public Works and Government Services Canada.

Health Canada. (2003b). *A Statistical Profile on the Health of First Nations in Canada.* Ottawa, ON: Author. Retrieved from www.hc-sc.gc.ca/fnihb-dgspni/fnihb/sppa/hia/publications/statistical_profile.pdf

Health Canada. (2003c). *Canada's seniors: No. 2—Canada's oldest seniors.* Ottawa, ON: Author. Retrieved from www.hc-sc.gc.ca/seniors-aines/pubs/factoids/2001/no02_e.htm

Health Canada. (2003d). *Canada's seniors: No. 1—A growing population.* Ottawa, ON: Author. Retrieved from www.hc-sc.gc.ca/seniors-aines/pubs/factoids/2001/no01_e.htm

Health Canada. (2003e). *Canada's seniors: No. 19—Private retirement pensions largest source of income.* Ottawa, ON: Author, Division of Aging and Seniors. Retrieved from www.hc-sc.gc.ca/seniors-aines/pubs/factoids/2001/no19_e.htm

Health Canada. (2003f). *Canada's seniors: No. 13—Gender differences in income.* Ottawa, ON: Author, Division of Aging and Seniors. Retrieved from www.hc-sc.gc.ca/seniors-aines/pubs/factoids/2001/no13_e.htm

Health Canada. (2003g). *Canada's seniors: No. 14—The incidence of low income falling.* Ottawa, ON: Author, Division of Aging and Seniors. Retrieved from www.hc-sc.gc.ca/seniors-aines/pubs/factoids/2001/no14_e.htm

Health Canada. (2003h). *Canada's seniors: No. 15—Gender differences in low income.* Ottawa, ON: Author, Division of Aging and Seniors. Retrieved from www.hc-sc.gc.ca/seniors-aines/pubs/factoids/2001/no15_e.htm

Health Canada. (2003i). *Canada's seniors: No. 6—In cities, towns and elsewhere.* Ottawa, ON: Author. Retrieved from www.hc-sc.gc.ca/seniors-aines/pubs/factoids/2001/no06_e.htm

Health Canada. (2004a). *Canadian Tobacco Use Monitoring Survey (CTUMS).* Ottawa, ON: Author. Retrieved from www.hc-sc.gc.ca/hecs-sesc/tobacco/research/ctums/index.html#prevalence

Health Canada. (2004b). *Health Canada advises Canadians under the age of 18 to consult physicians if they are being treated with newer anti-depressants.* Ottawa, ON: Author. Retrieved from www.hc-sc.gc.ca/english/protection/warnings/2004/2004_02.htm

Health Canada. (2004c). *HIV/AIDS EPI Updates, May 2004.* Surveillance and Risk Assessment Division, Centre for Infectious Disease Prevention and Control. Ottawa, ON: Author.

Health Canada. (2006a). Nutrition for Healthy Term Infants—Statement of the Joint Working Group: Canadian Paediatric Society, Dietitians of Canada and Health Canada. Ottawa, ON: Minister of Public Works and Government Services. Retrieved from www.hc-sc.gc.ca/fn-an/pubs/infant-nourrisson/nut_infant_nourrisson_term_e.html#table

Health Canada (2006b). *Chlamydia*. Ottawa, ON: Author. Retrieved from www.hc-sc.gc.ca/hl-vs/iyh-vsv/diseases-maladies/chlamyd-eng.php

Health Canada. (2007a). *Smoking and your body: health concerns—pregnancy*. Ottawa, ON: Author. Retrieved from www.hc-sc.gc.ca/hc-ps/tobac-tabac/body-corps/preg-gros-eng.php

Health Canada. (2007b). Eating well with Canada's food guide. Advise for different ages and stages. Ottawa, ON: Author. Retrieved on March 31, 2007 from www.hc-sc.gc.ca/fn-an/food-guide-aliment/choose-choix/advice-conseil/index_e.html

Health Canada. (2008a). Canada's food guide: My food guide. Ottawa, ON: Author. Retrieved from www.hc-sc.gc.ca/fn-an/food-guide-aliment/myguide-monguide/index-eng.php

Health Canada. (2008b). *Canada's food guide: My food guide.* Ottawa, ON: Author. Retrieved from www.hc-sc.gc.ca/fn-an/food-guide-aliment/myguide-monguide/index-eng.php

Health Canada. (2009a). *Toy safety tips*. Retrieved from www.hc-sc.gc.ca/cps-spc/alt_formats/hecs-sesc/pdf/pubs/cons/toy_safe-jouet_secur-eng.pdf

Health Canada. (2009b). *Canadian gestational weight gain recommendations*. Ottawa, ON: Author. Retrieved from www.hc-sc.gc.ca/fn-an/nutrition/prenatal/qa-gest-gros-qr-eng.php

Health Canada. (2010a). First Nations, Inuit and Aboriginal health—diabetes. Ottawa, ON: Author. Retrieved from www.hc-sc.gc.ca/fniah-spnia/diseases-maladies/diabete/index-eng.php#a71

Health Canada (2010b). Controlled Substances and Tobacco Directorate, Health Canada Supplementary Tables, Youth Smoking Survey 2008–09. Ottawa, ON: Author. Retrieved from www.hc-sc.gc.ca/hc-ps/alt_formats/hecs-sesc/pdf/tobac-tabac/research-recherche/stat/_survey-sondage_2008-2009/yss-2008-2009-tab-eng.pdf

Health Reports. (1999a). Income inequality and mortality among working-age people in Canada and the U.S. *Health Reports, 11*(3), 77–82.

Health Reports. (1999b). Health among older adults (Cat. No. 82-003-XPB). *Health Reports, 11*(3), 47–61.

HealthyOntario.com. (2003). *Eating disorders: The facts.* Toronto, ON: Ministry of Health and Long-Term Care. Retrieved from www.healthyontario.com/english/printVersion.asp?which=features&text_id=91&channel_id=0

Heaman, M.I., & Chalmers, K. (2005). Prevalence and correlates of smoking during pregnancy: A comparison of Aboriginal and non–Aboriginal women in Manitoba. *Birth, 32*(4), 299–305.

Heart & Stroke Foundation (2010). *Statistics*. Ottawa, ON: Author. Retrieved from www.heartandstroke.com/site/c.ikIQLcMWJtE/b.3483991/k.34A8/Statistics.htm

Heckhausen, J., & Brim, O. (1997). Perceived problems for self and others: Self-protection by social downgrading throughout adulthood. *Psychology & Aging, 12,* 610–619.

Hegele, R.A., Cao, H., Harris, S.B., Hanley, A.J.G., & Zinman, B. (1999). The hepatic nuclear factor—1% G319S variant is associated with early-onset type 2 diabetes in Canadian Oji-Cree. *The Journal of Clinical Endocrinology and Metabolism, 84*(3), 1007–1082.

Heindel, J.J., & Lawler, C. (2006). Role of exposure to environmental chemicals in developmental origins of health and disease. In P. Gluckman, Hanson, M (Eds.), *Developmental origins of health and disease* (pp. 82–97). New York, NY: Cambridge University Press.

Heinicke, C., Goorsky, M., Moscov, S., Dudley, K., Gordon, J., Schneider, C., & Guthrie, D. (2000). Relationship-based intervention with at-risk mothers: Factors affecting variations in outcome. *Infant Mental Health Journal, 21,* 133–155.

Heinonen, K., Raikkonen, K., & Keltikangas-Jarvinen, L. (2003). Maternal perceptions and adolescent self-esteem: A six-year longitudinal study. *Adolescence, 38,* 669–687.

Heise, L. & Garcia-Moreno, C. (2002). Violence by intimate partners. In E.G. Krug, L.L. Dahlberg, J.A. Mercy, A.B. Zwi, & R. Lozano (Eds.), *World report on violence and health* (pp. 87–121). Geneva: World Health Organization. Retrieved from www.who.int/violence_injury_prevention/violence/world_report/en/full_en.pdf

Heiss, G., Wallace, R., Anderson, G.L., Aragaki, A., Beresford, S.A.A., Brzyski, R., . . . Stefanick, M.L. (2008). Health risks and benefits 3 years after stopping randomized treatment with estrogen and progestin. *Journal of the American Medical Association, 299*(9), 1036–1045.

Helme, R. (1998). Pain in the elderly. *Australasian Journal on Aging, 17,* 33–35.

Helson, R., & Klohnen, D. (1998). Affective coloring of personality from young adulthood to midlife. *Personality & Social Psychology Bulletin, 24,* 241–252.

Helson, R., Mitchell, V., & Moane, G. (1984). Personality and patterns of adherence and nonadherence to the social clock. *Journal of Personality and Social Psychology, 46,* 1079–1096.

Henderson, H., Marshall, P., Fox, N., & Rubin, K. (2004). Psychophysiological and behavioral evidence for varying forms and functions of nonsocial behavior in preschoolers. *Child Development, 75,* 236–250.

Henry J. Kaiser Family Foundation. (1999). *Sex on TV.* Washington, DC: Author.

Henry, B., Caspi, A., Moffitt, T., Harrington, H., & Silva, P. (1999). Staying in school protects boys with poor self-regulation in childhood from later crime: A longitudinal study. *International Journal of Behavioral Development, 23,* 1049–1073.

Henry, J., MacLeod, M., Phillips, L., & Crawford, J. (2004). A meta-analytic review of prospective memory and aging. *Psychology & Aging, 19,* 27–39.

Heppner, M., Fuller, B., & Multon, K. (1998). Adults in involuntary career transition: An analysis of the relationship between the psychological and career domains. *Journal of Career Assessment, 6,* 329–346.

Herceg, Z. (2007). Epigenetics and cancer: Towards an evaluation of the impact of environmental and dietary factors. *Mutagenesis, 22*(2), 91–103.

Hermes, S., & Keel, P. (2003). The influence of puberty and ethnicity on awareness and internalization of the thin ideal. *International Journal of Eating Disorders, 33,* 465–467.

Hertzman, C. (1999). Population health and human development. In D.P. Keating & C. Hertzman (Eds.), *Developmental health and the wealth of nations: Social, Biological, and Educational Dynamics* (pp. 21–40). New York, NY: Guilford Press.

Hertzman, C. & Frank, J. (2006). Biological pathways linking the social environment, development, and health. In J. Heymann, C. Hertzman, M.L. Barer, & R.G. Evans (Eds.), *Healthier Societies: From Analysis to Action* (pp. 35–57). New York, NY: Oxford University Press.

Herxheimer, A., & Mintzes, B. (2004). Antidepressants and adverse effects in young patients: Uncovering the evidence. *Canadian Medical Association Journal, 170*(4), 487–488.

Herzog, A.R., House, J.S., & Morgan, J.N. (1991). Relation of work and retirement to health and well-being in older age. *Psychology and Aging, 6,* 202–211.

Hess, E.H. (1972). "Imprinting" in a natural laboratory. *Scientific American, 227,* 24–31.

Hess, T., Bolstad, C., Woodburn, S., & Auman, C. (1999). Trait diagnosticity versus behavioral consistency as determinants of impression change in adulthood. *Psychology & Aging, 14,* 77–89.

Hester, R., Kinsella, G., & Ong, B. (2004). Effect of age on forward and backward span tasks. *Journal of the International Neuropsychological Society, 10,* 475–481.

Hetherington, E., Bridges, M., & Insabella, G. (1998). What matters? What does not? Five perspectives on the association between marital transitions and children's adjustment. *American Psychologist, 53,* 167–184.

Hetherington, E., Henderson, S., Reiss, D., Anderson, E., Edward, R., Bridges, M. . . . Lorraine, C. (1999). Adolescent siblings in stepfamilies: Family functioning and adolescent adjustment.

Monographs of the Society for Research in Child Development, 64, 222.

Hetherington, E.M. (1991a). Presidential address: Families, lies, and videotapes. *Journal of Research on Adolescence, 1,* 323–348.

Hetherington, E.M. (1991b). The role of individual differences and family relationships in children's coping with divorce and remarriage. In P.A. Cowen & M. Hetherington (Eds.), *Family transitions* (pp. 165–194). Hillsdale, NJ: Erlbaum.

Hetherington, E.M., & Clingempeel, W.G. (1992). Coping with marital transitions: A family systems perspective. *Monographs of the Society for Research in Child Development, 57*(2–3, Serial No. 227).

Hetherington, E.M., & Stanley-Hagan, M.M. (1995). Parenting in divorced and remarried families. In M.H. Bornstein (Ed.), *Handbook of parenting: Vol. 3. Status and social conditions of parenting* (pp. 233–254). Mahwah, NJ: Erlbaum.

Heun, R., & Bonsignore, M. (2004). No evidence for a genetic relationship between Alzheimer's disease and longevity. *Dementia & Geriatric Cognitive Disorders, 18,* 1–5.

Hill, C. (1999). Fusion and conflict in lesbian relationships. *Feminism & Psychology, 9,* 179–185.

Hill, R.D., Storandt, M., & Malley, M. (1993). The impact of long-term exercise training on psychological function in older adults. *Journals of Gerontology: Psychological Sciences, 48,* P12–17.

Hillen, T., Davies, S., Rudd, A., Kieselbach, T., & Wolfe, C. (2003). Self ratings of health predict functional outcome and recurrence free survival after stroke. *Journal of Epidemiology & Community Health, 57,* 960–966.

Hiltunen, M.O., Turunen, M.P., Hakkinen, T.P., Rutanen, J.H., Hedman, M., Makinen, M., . . . Yla-Herttula, S. (2002). DNA hypomethylation and methyltransferase expression in atherosclerotic lesions. *Vascular Medicine, 7*(1), 5–11.

Hinde, R.A., Titmus, G., Easton, D., & Tamplin, A. (1985). Incidence of "friendship" and behavior toward strong associates versus nonassociates in preschoolers. *Child Development, 56,* 234–245.

Hirdes, J.P., & Strain, L.A. (1995). The balance of exchange in instrumental support with network members outside the household. *Journals of Gerontology: Social Sciences, 50B,* S134–142.

Ho, C., & Bryant, P. (1997). Learning to read Chinese beyond the logographic phase. *Reading Research Quarterly, 32,* 276–289.

Hodge, S., & Canter, D. (1998). Victims and perpetrators of male sexual assault. *Journal of Interpersonal Violence, 13,* 222–239.

Hodges, E.V.E., Malone, M.J., & Perry, D.G. (1997). Individual risk and social risk as interacting determinants of victimization in the peer group. *Developmental Psychology, 33*(6), 1032–1039.

Hoeksma, J., Oosterlaan, J., & Schipper, E. (2004). Emotion regulation and the dynamics of feelings: A conceptual and methodological framework. *Child Development, 75,* 354–360.

Hoff, T.L. (1992). Psychology in Canada one hundred years ago: James Mark Baldwin at the University of Toronto. *Canadian Psychology, 33*(2), Abstract.

Hofferth, S.L. (2001). How American children spend their time. *Journal of Marriage and the Family, 63*(2), 295–308.

Hoffman, M. (1970). Moral Development. In P. Mussen (Ed.), *Carmichael's manual of child psychology: Vol. 2.* New York, NY: Wiley.

Hoffnung, M. (2004). Wanting it all: Career, marriage, and motherhood during college-educated women's 20s. *Sex Roles, 50,* 711–723.

Holland, J.L. (1973). *Making vocational choices: A theory of careers.* Englewood Cliffs, NJ: Prentice-Hall.

Holland, J.L. (1992). *Making vocational choices: A theory of vocational personalities and work environments* (2nd ed.). Odessa, FL: Psychological Assessment Resources.

Hollander, J. (2004). "I Can Take Care of Myself": The impact of self-defense training on women's lives. *Violence Against Women, 10,* 205–235.

Holliday, R. (1998). The possibility of epigenetic transmission of defects induced by teratogens. *Mutation Research/Fundamental and Molecular Mechanisms of Mutagenesis, 422*(2, 3), 203–205.

Holliday, R. (2006). Epigenetics: A historical overview. *Epigenetics, 1*(2), 76–80.

Holmbeck, G.N., & Hill, J.P. (1991). Conflictive engagement, positive affect, and menarche in families with seventh-grade girls. *Child Development, 62,* 1030–1048.

Holobow, N., Genesee, F., & Lambert, W. (1991). The effectiveness of a foreign language immersion program for children from different ethnic and social class backgrounds: Report 2. *Applied Psycholinguistics, 12,* 179–198.

Holowka, S., & Petitto, L.A. (2002). Left hemisphere cerebral specialization for babies while babbling. *Science, 297*(5586), 1515.

Holstein, M., & Minkler, M. (2003). Self, society, and the "new gerontology." *Gerontologist, 43,* 787–796.

Holtzman, N.A., & Marteau, T.M. (2000). Will genetics revolutionize medicine? *The New England Journal of Medicine, 343*(2), 141–144.

Honzik, M.P. (1986). The role of the family in the development of mental abilities: A 50-year study. In N. Datan, A.L. Greene, & H.W. Reese (Eds.), *Life-span developmental psychology: Intergenerational relations* (pp. 185–210). Hillsdale, NJ: Erlbaum.

Horan, W., Pogge, D., Borgaro, S., & Stokes, J. (1997). Learning and memory in adolescent psychiatric inpatients with major depression: A normative study of the California Verbal Learning Test. *Archives of Clinical Neuropsychology, 12,* 575–584.

Horn, J.L. (1982). The aging of human abilities. In B.B. Wolman (Ed.), *Handbook of developmental psychology* (pp. 847–870). Englewood Cliffs, NJ: Prentice-Hall.

Horn, J.L., & Donaldson, G. (1980). Cognitive development in adulthood. In O.G. Brim, Jr. & J. Kagan (Eds.), *Constancy and change in human development* (pp. 415–529). Cambridge, MA: Harvard University Press.

Hornbrook, M.C., Stevens, V.J., & Wingfield, D.J. (1994). Preventing falls among community-dwelling older persons: Results from a randomized trial. *The Gerontologist, 34,* 16–23.

Horner, K.W., Rushton, J.P., & Vernon, P.A. (1986). Relation between aging and research productivity of academic psychologists. *Psychology and Aging, 1,* 319–324.

Horowitz, A., McLaughlin, J., & White, H. (1998). How the negative and positive aspects of partner relationships affect the mental health of young married people. *Journal of Health & Social Behavior, 39,* 124–136.

Horsthemke, B. (2006). Epimutations in human disease. *Current Topics in Microbiology and Immunology, 310,* 45–59.

Hotton, T. (2001). Spousal violence after marital separation (Cat. No. 85-002). *Juristat, 21*(7), 2–18.

Hotton, T., & Haans, D. (2004). Alcohol and drug use in early adolescence. *Health Reports, 15*(3), 9–19.

Hou, J., Chen, H., & Chen, X. (2005). The relationship of parent-children interaction in the free play session and copy-modeling session with the development of children's behavioral inhibition in Chinese families. *Psychological Science (China), 28,* 820–825.

Houck, G., & Lecuyer-Maus, E. (2004). Maternal limit setting during toddlerhood, delay of gratification and behavior problems at age five. *Infant Mental Health Journal, 25,* 28–46.

Houseknecht, S.K. (1987). Voluntary childlessness. In M.B. Sussman & S.K. Steinmetz (Eds.), *Handbook of marriage and the family* (pp. 369–395). New York, NY: Plenum.

Houston, D., & Jusczyk, P. (2003). Infants' long-term memory for the sound patterns of words and voices. *Journal of Experimental Psychology: Human Perception & Performance, 29,* 1143–1154.

Hovell, M., Blumberg, E., Sipan, C., Hofstetter, C., Burkham, S., Atkins, C., & Felice, M. (1998). Skills training for pregnancy and AIDS prevention in Anglo and Latino youth. *Journal of Adolescent Health, 23,* 139–149.

Howard, A.W. (2006). Injury in childhood: A vexingly simple problem. *Canadian Medical Association Journal, 175*(8), 899–900.

Howard, A.W. (2010). Keeping children safe: Rethinking how we design our surroundings. *Canadian Medical Association Journal, 182*(6), 573.

Howe, D., & Fearnley, S. (2003). Disorders of attachment in adopted and fostered children: Recognition and treatment. *Clinical Child Psychology & Psychiatry, 8,* 369–387.

Howes, C. (1983). Patterns of friendship. *Child Development, 54,* 1041–1053.

Howes, C. (1987). Social competence with peers in young children: Developmental sequences. *Developmental Review, 7,* 252–272.

Howes, C., & Matheson, C.C. (1992). Sequences in the development of competent play with peers: Social and pretend play. *Developmental Psychology, 28,* 961–974.

Hoyert, D.L., & Seltzer, M.M. (1992). Factors related to the well-being and life activities of family caregivers. *Family Relations, 41,* 74–81.

Hu, F., Li, T., Colditz, G., Willet, W., & Manson, J. (2003). Television watching and other sedentary behavior in relation to risk of obesity and type 2 diabetes mellitus in women. *Journal of the American Medical Association, 289,* 1785–1791.

Hua, X., Leow, A.D., Levitt, J.G., Caplan, R., Thompson, P.M., & Toga, W.A. (2009). Detecting brain growth patterns in normal children using tensor-based morphometry. *Human Brain Mapping, 30,* 209–219.

Huang, C., Lee, T., Chen, S., Chen, H., Cheng, T., Liu, C., . . . Lee, M. (2005). Successful pregnancy following blastocyst cryopreservation using super-cooling ultra-rapid vitrification. *Human Reproduction, 20*(1), 122–128.

Huang, H., & Hanley, J. (1997). A longitudinal study of phonological awareness, visual skills, and Chinese reading acquisition among first-graders in Taiwan. *International Journal of Behavioral Development, 20,* 249–268.

Hubel, D.H., & Wiesel, T.N. (1963). Receptive fields of cells in striate cortex of very young, visually inexperienced kittens. *Journal of Neurophysiology, 26,* 994–1002.

Huesmann, L.R., Moise-Titus, J., Podolski, C.L., & Eron, L.D. (2003). Longitudinal relations between children's exposure to TV violence and their aggressive and violent behaviour in young adulthood: 1977–1992. *Developmental Psychology, 39*(2), 201–221.

Hughes, S., & Hayman, L. (2007). Cardiovascular risk reduction: The fountain of youth. *Journal of Cardiovascular Nursing, 22,* 84–85.

Hultsch, D., Hertzog, C., Small, B., & Dixon, R. (1999). Use it or lose it: Engaged lifestyle as a buffer of cognitive decline in aging? *Psychology & Aging, 14,* 245–263.

Hultsch, D.F., Hertzog, C., Small, B.J., McDonald-Miszczak, L., & Dixon, R.A. (1992). Short-term longitudinal change in cognitive performance in later life. *Psychology and Aging, 7,* 571–584.

Human Resources and Skills Development (2010a). *Family life—marriage.* Ottawa, ON: Author. Retrieved from www4.hrsdc.gc.ca/.3ndic.1t.4r@-eng.jsp?iid=78

Human Resources and Skills Development Canada (2010). *Learning—school drop-outs.* Ottawa, ON: Author. Retrieved from www4.hrsdc.gc.ca/.3ndic.1t.4r@-eng.jsp?iid=32

Human Resources Development Canada and Statistics Canada. (1996). *Growing up in Canada 1994/95* (Cat. No. 89-550-MPE). Ottawa, ON: Author.

Human Resources Development Canada. (1996). *National Longitudinal Survey of Children and Youth (NLSCY).* (Cat. No. SP-AH036E-10-96). Ottawa, ON: Author. Retrieved from www11.hrdc-drhc.gc.ca/edd/NLSCY_172000.htm

Human Resources Development Canada (2000). *Dropping out of high school: definitions and costs* (Cat. No. R-01-1E). Ottawa, ON: Author.

Human Resources Development Canada. (2001a). *Does parental separation affect children's behaviour?* Ottawa, ON: Author. Retrieved from www.hrdc-drhc.gc.ca/stratpol/arb/publications/bulletin/child_dev/chi_dev2.shtml

Human Resources Development Canada. (2001b). *Canadian gender trends in education and work* (Cat. No. MP32-30/00-4E). Ottawa, ON: Author. Retrieved from www.hrdc-drhc.gc.ca/stratpol/arb/publications/research/2000docs/t-00-4e.pdf

Human Resources Development Canada. (2001c). *Canada's retirement income system—simply stated.* Ottawa, ON: Author. Retrieved from www.hrdc-drhc.gc.ca/isp/ris/cris_e.shtml

Human Resources Development Canada. (2003). *A new generation of Canadian families raising young children* (Cat. No. SP-579-09-03E). Retrieved from www11.sdc.gc.ca/en/cs/sp/arb/publications/research/2003-001330/2003-001330.pdf

Hummert, M., Garstka, T., & Shaner, J. (1997). Stereotyping of older adults: The role of target facial cues and perceiver characteristics. *Psychology & Aging, 21,* 107–114.

Humphrey, N., Curran, A., Morris, E., Farrell, P., & Woods, K. (2007). Emotional intelligence and education: A critical review. *Educational Psychology, 27,* 235–254.

Humphreys, A., & Smith, P. (1987). Rough and tumble, friendship, and dominance in school children: Evidence for continuity and change with age. *Child Development, 58,* 201–212.

Hunfeld, J., Tempels, A., Passchier, J., Hazebroek, F., & Tibboel, D. (1999). Parental burden and grief one year after the birth of a child with a congenital anomaly. *Journal of Pediatric Psychology, 24,* 515–520.

Hunter, D.J., Spiegelman, D., Adami, H., Beeson, L., van den Brandt, P.A., Folsom, A.R., . . . Willett, W. (1996). Cohort studies of fat intake and the risk of breast cancer—a pooled analysis. *New England Journal of Medicine, 334,* 356–361.

Huntington Society of Canada. (2001). *Huntington disease (HD) is a hereditary brain disorder with devastating effects on both mind and body.* Kitchener, ON: Author. Retrieved from www.hsc-ca.org/english/about_hd.shtml

Hurwitz, E., Gunn, W.J., Pinsky, P.F., & Schonberger, L.B. (1991). Risk of respiratory illness associated with day-care attendance: A nationwide study. *Pediatrics, 87,* 62–69.

Huth-Bocks, A., Levendosky, A., Bogat, G., & von Eye, A. (2004). The impact of maternal characteristics and contextual variables on infant-mother attachment. *Child Development, 75,* 480–496.

Hutt, S.J., Lenard, H.G., & Prechtl, H.F.R. (1969). Psychophysiological studies in newborn infants. In L.P. Lipsitt & H.W. Reese (Eds.), *Advances in child development and behavior: Vol. 4* (pp. 128–173). New York, NY: Academic Press.

Huttenlocher, J. (1995, April). Children's language in relation to input. Paper presented at the biennial meetings of the Society for Research in Child Development, Indianapolis, IN.

Hyde, J.S. (2005). The gender similarities hypothesis. *American Psychologist, 60*(6), 581–592. DOI: 10.1037/0003-066X.60.6.581

Iaquinta, A. (2006). Guided reading: A research-based response to the challenges of early reading instruction. *Early Childhood Education Journal, 33,* 1573–1707.

Idler, E., & Kasl, S. (1997). Religion among disabled and nondisabled persons II: Attendance at religious services as a predictor of the course of disability. *Journals of Gerontology: Series B: Psychological Sciences & Social Sciences, 52B,* S306–S316.

Ingoldsby, E., Shaw, D., Owens, E., & Winslow, E. (1999). A longitudinal study of interparental conflict, emotional and behavioral reactivity, and preschoolers' adjustment problems among low-income families. *Journal of Abnormal Child Psychology, 27,* 343–356.

Inhelder, B., & Piaget, J. (1958). *The growth of logical thinking from childhood to adolescence.* New York, NY: Basic Books.

International Cancer Genome Consortium (2010). International network of cancer genome projects. *Nature, 464,* 993–998.

Ipsos-Reid (2007). As Dr. Kevorkian released, just one quarter (25%) believe doctor-assisted suicide should be illegal. Toronto, ON: Author. Retrieved from www.ipsos-na.com/news/pressrelease.cfm?id=3526#

Ipsos-Reid/Globe and Mail. (2003). *What are Canadians' Top Indicators of Career Success?* Toronto, ON: Author. Retrieved from www.ipsos-na.com/news/pressrelease.cfm?id=1803#

Irwin, M., & Pike, J. (1993). Bereavement, depressive symptoms, and immune function. In M.S. Stroebe, W. Stroebe, & R.O. Hansson (Eds.), *Handbook of bereavement: Theory, research, and intervention* (pp. 160–171). Cambridge, England: Cambridge University Press.

Isabella, R.A. (1995). The origins of infant-mother attachment: Maternal behavior and infant development. *Annals of Child Development, 10,* 57–81.

Isaksson, K., Johansson, G., Bellaagh, K., & Sjöberg, A. (2004). Work values among the unemployed: Changes over time and some gender differences. *Scandinavian Journal of Psychology, 45,* 207–214.

Itier, R., & Taylor, M. (2004). Face inversion and contrast-reversal effects across development: In contrast to the expertise theory. *Developmental Science, 7,* 246–260.

Iversen, L., & Sabroe, S. (1988). Psychological well-being among unemployed and employed people after a company closedown: A longitudinal study. *Journal of Social Issues, 44,* 141–152.

Ivy, G.O., MacLeod, C.M., Petit, T.L., & Marcus, E.J. (1992). A physiological framework for perceptual and cognitive changes in aging. In F.I.M. Craik & T.A. Salthouse (Eds.), *The handbook of aging and cognition* (pp. 273–314). Hillsdale, NJ: Erlbaum.

Iwashyna, T., & Christakis, N. (2003). Marriage, widowhood, and health-care use. *Social Science & Medicine, 57,* 2137–2147.

Izard, C.E., & Harris, P. (1995). Emotional development and developmental psychopathology. In D. Cicchetti & D.J. Cohen (Eds.), *Developmental psychopathology: Vol. 1. Theory and methods* (pp. 467–503). New York, NY: Wiley.

Izard, C.E., Fantauzzo, C.A., Castle, J.M., Haynes, O.M., Rayias, M.F., & Putnam, P.H. (1995). The ontogeny and significance of infants' facial expressions in the first 9 months of life. *Developmental Psychology, 31,* 997–1013.

Jablonka, E. (2004). Epigenetic epidemiology. *International Journal of Epidemiology, 33*(5), 929–935.

Jablonka, E., & Lamb, M.J. (1995). *Epigenetic Inheritance and Evolution: The Lamarckian Dimension.* Oxford, UK: Oxford University Press.

Jablonka, E., & Lamb, M.J. (2002). The Changing Concept of Epigenetics. *Annals of the New York Academy of Sciences, 981*(1), 82–96.

Jablonka, E., & Lamb, M.J. (2005). *Evolution in Four Dimensions.* Cambridge, MA: MIT Press.

Jackson, A. (2001). *The incidence and depth of child poverty in recession and recovery: Some preliminary lessons on child benefits.* Ottawa, ON: Canadian Council on Social Development. Retrieved from www.ccsd.ca/pubs/2001/ajncb.htm

Jackson, A., & Schetagne, S. (2001). *Still struggling: An update on teenagers at work.* Ottawa, ON: Canadian Council on Social Development. Retrieved from www.ccsd.ca/pubs/2001/pcc2001/employ.htm

Jackson, D., & Tein, J. (1998). Adolescents' conceptualization of adult roles: Relationships with age, gender, work goal, and maternal employment. *Sex Roles, 38,* 987–1008.

Jackson, D.J., Longino, C.F., Jr., Zimmerman, R.S., & Bradsher, J.E. (1991). Environmental adjustments to declining functional ability: Residential mobility and living arrangements. *Research on Aging, 13,* 289–309.

Jackson, L., & Bracken, B. (1998). Relationship between students' social status and global and domain-specific self-concepts. *Journal of School Psychology, 36,* 233–246.

Jacobs, J., Chin, C., & Bleeker, M. (2006). Enduring links: Parents' expectations and their young adult children's gender-typed occupational choices. *Educational Research and Evaluation, 12,* 395–407.

Jacobsen, T., & Hofmann, V. (1997). Children's attachment representations: Longitudinal relations to school behavior, and academic competency in middle childhood and adolescence. *Developmental Psychology, 33,* 703–710.

Jacobsen, T., Husa, M., Fendrich, M., Kruesi, M., & Ziegenhain, U. (1997). Children's ability to delay gratification: Longitudinal relations to mother-child attachment. *Journal of Genetic Psychology, 158,* 411–426.

Jacques, E. (1965). Death and the mid-life crisis. *International Journal of Psychoanalysis, 46*(4), 502–514.

Jacques, S., & Zelazo, P.D. (2001). The Flexible Item Selection Task (FIST): A measure of executive function in preschoolers. *Developmental Neuropsychology, 20*(3), 573–591.

Jadack, R.A., Hyde, J.S., Moore, C.F., & Keller, M.L. (1995). Moral reasoning about sexually transmitted diseases. *Child Development, 66,* 167–177.

Jaglal, S., Weller, I., Mamdani, M., Hawker, G., Kreder, H., Jaakkimainen, L., & Adachi, J. (2005). Population trends in BMD testing, treatment, and hip and wrist fracture rates: Are the hip fracture projections wrong? *Journal of Bone and Mineral Research, 20,* 898–905.

Janosz, M., Le Blanc, M., Boulerice, B., & Tremblay, R. (2000). Predicting different types of school dropouts: A typological approach with two longitudinal samples. *Journal of Educational Psychology, 92,* 171–190.

Janssen, T., & Carton, J. (1999). The effects of locus of control and task difficulty on procrastination. *Journal of Genetic Psychology, 160,* 436–442.

Janssen. P.A., Saxell, L., Page, L.A., Llien, M.C., Liston, R.M., & Lee, S.K. (2009). Outcomes of planned home birth with registered midwife versus planned hospital birth with midwife of physician. *Canadian Medical Association Journal, 181*(6–7), 377–383.

Jansz, J., & Martens, L. (2005). Gaming at a LAN event: The social context of playing video games. *New Media & Society, 7,* 333–355.

Japal, C., Tremblay, R., McDuff, P., & Willms, J.D. (2002). Pre-adolescent girls and the onset of puberty. In J.D. Willms (Ed.), *Vulnerable children* (pp. 305–316). Edmonton, AB: The University of Alberta Press.

Jarolmen, J. (1998). A comparison of the grief reaction of children and adults: Focusing on pet loss and bereavement. *Omega: Journal of Death & Dying, 37,* 133–150.

Jenkins, J., & Buccioni, J. (2000). Children's understanding of marital conflict and the marital relationship. *Journal of Child Psychology & Psychiatry & Allied Disciplines, 41,* 161–168.

Jenkins, J.M., & Astington, J.W. (1996). Cognitive factors and family structure associated with theory of mind development in young children. *Developmental Psychology, 32,* 70–78.

Jenkins, L., Myerson, J., Hale, S., & Fry, A. (1999). Individual and developmental differences in working memory across the life span. *Psychonomic Bulletin & Review, 6,* 28–40.

Jensen, A., & Whang, P. (1994). Speed of accessing arithmetic facts in long-term memory: A comparison of Chinese-American and Anglo-American children. *Contemporary Educational Psychology, 19,* 1–12.

Jensen-Campbell, L., Gleason, K., Adams, R., & Malcolm, K. (2003). Interpersonal conflict, agreeableness, and personality development. *Journal of Personality, 71,* 1059–1085.

Jessor, R. (1992). Risk behavior in adolescence: A psychosocial framework for understanding and action. *Developmental Review, 12,* 374–390.

Jeynes, W. (2006). The impact of parental remarriage on children: A meta-analysis. *Marriage & Family Review, 40*(4), 75–102.

Jiang, Y.H., Bressler, J., & Beaudet, A.L. (2004). Epigenetics and human disease. *Annual Review of Genomics and Human Genetics, 5,* 479–510.

Jilek, W.G. (2001). *Anorexia nervosa: Cultural factors in psychiatric disorders.* Paper presented at the 26th Congress of the World Federation for Mental Health, July, 2001. Retrieved from Internet Mental Health website: www.mentalhealth.com/mag1/wolfgangex.html

Jimerson, S. (1999). On the failure of failure: Examining the association between early grade retention and educational and employment outcomes during late adolescence. *Journal of School Psychology, 37,* 243–272.

Johansson, B., Hofer, S., Allaire, J., Maldonado-Molina, M., Piccinin, A., . . . McClearn, G. (2004). Change in cognitive capabilities in the oldest old: The effects of proximity to death in genetically related individuals over a 6-year period. *Psychology & Aging, 19,* 145–156.

John P. Robarts Research Institute. (2000). *New gene helps fight diabetes in Canada's Aboriginal population.* London, ON: Diabetes Research Centre.

John, O.P., Caspi, A., Robins, R.W., Moffitt, T.E., & Stouthamer-Loeber, M. (1994). The "little five": Exploring the nomological network of the five-factor model of personality in adolescent boys. *Child Development, 65,* 160–178.

Johnson, E., & Breslau, N. (2000). Increased risk of learning disabilities in low birth weight boys at age 11 years. *Biological Psychiatry, 47,* 490–500.

Johnson, H., Nusbaum, B., Bejarano, A., & Rosen, T. (1999). An ecological approach to development in children with prenatal drug exposure. *American Journal of Orthopsychiatry, 69*, 448–456.

Johnson, J.K., Vogt, B.A., Kim, R., Cotman, C.W., & Head, E. (2004). Isolated executive impairment and associated frontal neuropathology. *Dementia and Geriatric Cognitive Disorders, 17*(4), 360–367.

Johnson, M. (2003). Development of human brain functions. *Biological Psychiatry, 54*, 1312–1316.

Johnson, N., & Cremo, E. (1995). Socialization and the native family. In K. Covell (Ed.), *Readings in child development*. Toronto, ON: Nelson.

Johnston, A.M., Barnes, M.A., & Desrochers, A. (2008). Reading comprehension: Developmental processes, individual differences, and interventions. *Canadian Psychology, 49*(2), 125–133.

Johnston, C.C., Filion, F., Campbell-Yeo, M., Goulet, C., Bell, L., McNaughton, K., . . . Walker, C.D. (2008). Kangaroo mothercare diminishes pain from heel lance in very preterm neonates: a crossover trial. *BMC Pediatrics, 8*(13), 1–9.

Jones, J.M., Bennett, S., Olmsted, M.P., Lawson, M.L., & Rodin, G. (2001). Disordered eating attitudes and behaviours in teenaged girls: A school-based study. *Canadian Medical Association Journal, 165*(5), 547–552.

Jordan, N. C., Kaplan, D., Locuniak, M. N., & Ramineni, C. (2007). Predicting first-grade math achievement from developmental number sense trajectories. *Disabilities Research and Practice, 22*, 36–46.

Jorgensen, G. (2006). Kohlberg and Gilligan: Duet or duel? *Journal of Moral Education, 35*, 179–196.

Jorgenson, S. (1993). Adolescent pregnancy and parenting. In T. Gullotta, G. Adams, & R. Montemayor (Eds.), *Adolescent sexuality* (pp. 103–140). Thousand Oaks, CA: Sage Publications.

Jorm, A., Christensen, H., Henderson, A., Jacomb, P., Korten, A., & Mackinnon, A. (1998). Factors associated with successful aging. *Journal of Ageing, 17*, 33–37.

Jose, O., & Alfons, V. (2007). Do demographics affect marital satisfaction? *Journal of Sex & Marital Therapy, 33*, 73–85.

Joseph, R. (2000). Fetal brain behavior and cognitive development. *Developmental Review, 20*, 81–98.

Josephson, W.L. (1995). *Television violence: A review of the effects on children of different ages.* (CH4-1/8-1995E). Retrieved from The Department of Canadian Heritage website: http://dsp-psd.communication.gc.ca/Collection/CH4-1-8-1995E.pdf

Judge, T., Bono, J., & Locke, E. (2000). Personality and job satisfaction: The mediating role of job characteristics. *Journal of Applied Psychology, 85*, 237–249.

Juffer, F., & Rosenboom, L., (1997). Infant mother attachment of internationally adopted children in the Netherlands. *International Journal of Behavioral Development, 20*, 93–107.

Jusczyk, P., & Hohne, E. (1997). Infants' memory for spoken words. *Science, 277*.

Jusczyk, P., Houston, D., & Newsome, M. (1999). The beginnings of word segmentation in English-learning infants. *Cognitive Psychology, 39*, 159–207.

Jutras, S., & Lavoie, J. (1995). Living with an impaired elderly person: The informal caregiver's physical and mental health. *Journal of Aging and Health, 7*, 46–73.

Kagan, J. (1994). *Galen's prophecy.* New York, NY: Basic Books.

Kagan, J., & Herschkowitz, N. (2005). *A young mind in a growing brain.* Hillsdale, NJ: Lawrence Erlbaum.

Kagan, J., Reznick, J.S., & Snidman, N. (1990). The temperamental qualities of inhibition and lack of inhibition. In M. Lewis & S.M. Miller (Eds.), *Handbook of developmental psychopathology* (pp. 219–226). New York, NY: Plenum.

Kagan, J., Snidman, N., & Arcus, D. (1993). On the temperamental categories of inhibited and uninhibited children. In K.H. Rubin & J.B. Asendorpf (Eds.), *Social withdrawal, inhibition, and shyness in childhood* (pp. 19–28). Hillsdale, NJ: Erlbaum.

Kahana-Kalman, R., & Walker-Andrews, A. (2001). The role of person familiarity in young infants' perception of emotional expressions. *Child Development, 72*, 352–369.

Kail, R. (1990). *The development of memory in children* (3rd ed.). New York, NY: Freeman.

Kail, R. (1991). Processing time declines exponentially during childhood and adolescence. *Developmental Psychology, 27*, 259–266.

Kail, R. (1997). Processing time, imagery, and spatial memory. *Journal of Experimental Child Psychology, 64*, 67–78.

Kail, R., & Hall, L.K. (1994). Processing speed, naming speed, and reading. *Developmental Psychology, 30*, 949–954.

Kalish, R.A. (1985). The social context of death and dying. In R.H. Binstock & E. Shanas (Eds.), *Handbook of aging and the social sciences* (2nd ed., pp. 149–170). New York, NY: Van Nostrand Reinhold.

Kallman, D.A., Plato, C.C., & Tobin, J.D. (1990). The role of muscle loss in the age-related decline of grip strength: Cross-sectional and longitudinal perspectives. *Journals of Gerontology: Medical Sciences, 45*, M82–88.

Kalmijn, M. (2003). Shared friendship networks and the life course: An analysis of survey data on married and cohabiting couples. *Social Networks, 25*, 231–249.

Kalmuss, D. (2004). Nonviolational sex and sexual health. *Archives of Sexual Behavior, 33*, 197–209.

Kalter, H. (2003). Teratology in the 20th century: Environmental causes of congenital malformations in humans and how they were established. *Neurotoxicology and Teratology, 25*(2), 131–282.

Kaminsky, Z.A., Tang, T., Wang, S., Ptak, C., Oh, G.H.T., Wong, A. H.C., . . . Petronis, A. (2009). DNA methylation profiles in monozygotic and dizygotic twins. *Nature Genetics, 41*, 240–245.

Kandel, D.B., & Wu, P. (1995). The contributions of mothers and fathers to the intergenerational transmission of cigarette smoking in adolescence. *Journal of Research on Adolescence, 5*, 225–252.

Kane, T., Staiger, P., & Ricciardelli, L. (2000). Male domestic violence: Attitudes, aggression and interpersonal dependency. *Journal of Interpersonal Violence, 15*, 16–29.

Kannel, W.B., & Gordon, T. (1980). Cardiovascular risk factors in the aged: The Framingham study. In S.G. Haynes & M. Feinleib (Eds.), *Second conference on the epidemiology of aging.* NIH Publication No. 80–969 (pp. 65–89). U.S. Department of Health and Human Services. Washington, DC: U.S. Government Printing Office.

Kaplan, G.A. (1992). Health and aging in the Alameda County study. In K.W. Schaie, D. Blazer, & J.M. House (Eds.), *Aging, health behaviors, and health outcomes* (pp. 69–88). Hillsdale, NJ: Erlbaum.

Kaplan, H., & Sadock, B. (1991). *Synopsis of psychiatry* (6th ed.). Baltimore, MD: Williams & Wilkins.

Kaplan, P., Bachorowski, J., Smoski, M., & Zinser, M. (2001). Role of clinical diagnosis and medication use in effects of maternal depression on infant-directed speech. *Infancy, 2*, 537–548.

Kaslow, F. (2004). Death of one's partner: The anticipation and the reality. *Professional Psychology: Research & Practice, 35*, 227–233.

Katz, P., & Bartone, P. (1998). Mourning, ritual and recovery after an airline tragedy. *Omega: Journal of Death & Dying, 36*, 193–200.

Katz, P.A., & Ksansnak, K.R. (1994). Developmental aspects of gender role flexibility and traditionality in middle childhood and adolescence. *Developmental Psychology, 30*, 272–282.

Kaufman, G., & Elder, G. (2003). Grandparenting and age identity. *Journal of Aging Studies, 17*, 269–282.

Kaufman, M. (1997). The teratogenic effects of alcohol following exposure during pregnancy, and its influence on the chromosome constitution of the pre-ovulatory egg. *Alcohol & Alcoholism, 32*, 113–128.

Kawachi, I., & Kennedy, B.P. (2002). *The health of nations: Why inequality is harmful to your health.* New York, NY: The New Press.

Kazdin, A.E., & Benjet, C. (2003). Spanking children: Evidence and issues. *Current Directions in Psychological Science, 12*(3), 99–103.

Keen, R. (2003). Representation of objects and events: Why do infants look so smart and toddlers look so dumb? *Current Directions in Psychological Science, 12*, 79–83.

Keen, R. & Shutts, K. (2007). Object and event representation in toddlers. *Progress in Brain Research, 164,* 227–235.

Keene, J., Hope, T., Rogers, P., & Elliman, N. (1998). An investigation of satiety in ageing, dementia, and hyperphagia. *International Journal of Eating Disorders, 23,* 409–418.

Keep Kids Healthy (2003). Choosing toys for your kids. Retrieved from www.keepkidshealthy.com/development/choosing_toys.html

Keith, P.M. (1981/1982). Perception of time remaining and distance from death. *Omega, 12,* 307–318.

Kelley, M.L., Sanches-Hucles, J., & Walker, R.R. (1993). Correlates of disciplinary practices in working- to middle-class African-American mothers. *Merrill-Palmer Quarterly, 39,* 252–264.

Kendler, K., Kessler, R., Walters, E., MacLean, C., Neale, M., Heath, A., & Eaves, L. (1995). Stressful life events, genetic liability, and onset of an episode of major depression in women. *American Journal of Psychiatry, 152,* 833–842.

Kendler, K., Thornton, L., Gilman, S., & Kessler, R. (2000). Sexual orientation in a U.S. national sample of twin and nontwin sibling pairs. *American Journal of Psychiatry, 157,* 1843–1846.

Kensinger, E., Clarke, R., & Corkin, S. (2003). What neural correlates underlie successful encoding and retrieval? A functional magnetic resonance imaging study using a divided attention paradigm. *Journal of Neuroscience, 23,* 2407–2415.

Kent, H. (2001). Eighteen months, 12 suicides. *Canadian Medical Association Journal, 164*(13), 1940.

Kercsmar, C. (1998). The respiratory system. In R. Behrman & R. Kliegman (Eds.), *Nelson essentials of pediatrics* (3rd ed.). Philadelphia, PA: W.B. Saunders.

Kerr, D.A., Llado, J., Shamblott, M., Maragakis, N., Irani, D.N., Dike, S., . . . Rothstein, J.D. (2001). Human embryonic germ cell derivatives facilitate motor recovery of rats with diffuse motor neuron injury. *The Journal of Neuroscience, 23*(12), 5131–5140.

Kerr, M. (2006, March 13). *Menstrual blood shows good potential as stem cell source.* Reuter's Health Information. Retrieved from www.medscape.com/viewarticle/527401

Keskinen, E., Ota, H., & Katila, A. (1998). Older drivers fail in intersections: Speed discrepancies between older and younger male drivers. *Accident Analysis & Prevention, 30,* 323–330.

Kessler, R., Berglund, P., Demler, O., Jin, R., Merikangas, K., & Walters, E. (2005). Lifetime prevalence and age-of-onset distributions of DSM-IV disorders in the national comorbidity survey replication.
Archives of General Psychiatry, 62, 593–602.

Khanna, G., & Kapoor, S. (2004). Secular trend in stature and age at menarche among Punjabi Aroras residing in New Delhi, India. *Collegium Antropologicum, 28,* 571–575.

Khlat, M., Sermet, C., & Le Pape, A. (2000). Women's health in relation with their family and work roles: France in the early 1990s. *Social Science & Medicine, 50,* 1807–1825.

Khoury, M.J. (2003). Genetics and genomics in practice: The continuum from genetic disease to genetic information in health and disease. *Genetics in Medicine, 5*(4), 261–268.

Kiecolt-Glaser, J.K., & Glaser, R. (1995). Measurement of immune response. In S. Cohen, R.C. Kessler, & L.U. Gordon (Eds.), *Measuring stress: A guide for health and social scientists* (pp. 213–229). New York, NY: Oxford University Press.

Kiecolt-Glaser, J.K., Glaser, R., Suttleworth, E.E., Dyer, C.S., Ogrocki, P., & Speicher, C.E. (1987). Chronic stress and immunity in family caregivers of Alzheimer's disease patients. *Psychosomatic Medicine, 49,* 523–535.

Kikhavani, S., & Kumar, S. (2005). Life events, coping resources, and depression. *Psychological Studies, 50,* 298–302.

Kilbride, H., Castor, C., Hoffman, E., & Fuger, K. (2000). Thirty-six month outcome of prenatal cocaine exposure for term or near-term infants: Impact of early case management. *Journal of Developmental Pediatrics, 21,* 19–26.

Kilbride, H.W., Castor, C.A., & Fuger, K.L. (2006). School-age outcome of children with prenatal cocaine exposure following early case management. *Journal of Developmental & Behavioral Pediatrics, 27*(3), 181–187.

Kilic, C., & Ulusoy, M. (2003). Psychological effects of the November 1999 earthquake in Turkey: An epidemiological study. *Psychiatrica Scandinavica, 108,* 232–238.

Kilpatrick, S.J., & Laros, R.K. (1989). Characteristics of normal labor. *Obstetrics and Gynecology, 74,* 85–87.

Kim T.J., Laufer, L.R., & Wook Hong, S. (2010). Vitrification of oocytes produces high pregnancy rates when carried out in fertile women. *Fertility and Sterility, 93*(2), 467–474.

Kimmins, S., & Sassone-Corsi, P. (2005). Chromatin remodeling and epigenetic features of germ cells. *Nature, 434*(7033), 583–589.

King, P.M., & Kitchener, K.S. (2004). Reflective judgment: Theory and research on the development of epistemic assumption through adulthood. *Educational Psychologist, 39*(1), 5–18.

Kinney, D.A. (1993). From "nerds" to "normals": Adolescent identity recovery within a changing social system. *Sociology of Education, 66,* 21–40.

Kinzl, J., Mangweth, B., Traweger, C., & Biebl, W. (1996). Sexual dysfunction in males: Significance of adverse childhood experiences. *Child Abuse & Neglect, 20,* 759–766.

Kirby, D. (2000). School-based interventions to prevent unprotected sex and HIV among adolescents. In J. Peterson & D. Diclemente (Eds.), *Handbook of HIV prevention* (pp. 83–97). New York, NY: Plenum Publishers.

Kirkcaldy, B.D., Siefen, G., Surall, D., & Bischoff, R.J. (2004) Predictors of drug and alcohol abuse among children and adolescents. *Personality and Individual Differences, 36,* 247–265.

Kirkness, V.J. (1999). The critical state of aboriginal languages in Canada. *Canadian Journal of Native Education, 22,* 1–15.

Kisilevsky, B.S., Hains, S.M.J., Lee, K., Xie, X., Huang, H., Ye, H.H., . . . Wang, Z. (2003). Effects of experience on fetal voice recognition. *Psychological Science, 14*(3), 220–224.

Kitzan, L., Ferraro, F., Petros, T., & Ludorf, M. (1999). The role of vocabulary ability during visual word recognition in younger and older adults. *Journal of General Psychology, 126,* 6–16.

Klaczynski, P.A., Fauth, J.M., & Swanger, A. (1998). Adolescent identity: Rational vs. experiential processing, formal operations and critical thinking beliefs. *Journal of Youth and Adolescence, 27*(2), 185–207.

Klahr, D. (1992). Information-processing approaches to cognitive development. In M.H. Bernstein & M.E. Lamb (Eds.), *Developmental psychology: An advanced textbook* (3rd ed., pp. 273–335). Hillsdale, NJ: Erlbaum.

Klaiber, E., Broverman, D., Vogel, W., Peterson, L., & Snyder, M. (1997). Relationships of serum estradiol levels, menopausal duration, and mood during hormonal replacement therapy. *Psychoneuroendocrinology, 22,* 549–558.

Klebanov, P.K., Brooks-Gunn, J., Hofferth, S., & Duncan, G.J. (1995, March). *Neighborhood resources, social support and maternal competence.* Paper presented at the biennial meetings of the Society for Research in Child Development, Indianapolis, IN.

Kleemeier, R.W. (1962). Intellectual changes in the senium. *Proceedings of the Social Statistics Section of the American Statistics Association, 1,* 290–295.

Klein, A., & Swartz, S. (1996). *Reading Recovery in California: Program overview.* San Francisco, CA: San Francisco Unified School District.

Klein, J.S., & Bisanz, J. (2000). Preschoolers doing arithmetic: The concepts are willing but the working memory is weak. *Canadian Journal of Experimental Psychology, 54*(2), 105–115.

Klerman, L.V. (1991). The health of poor children: Problems and programs. In A.C. Huston (Ed.), *Children in poverty: Child development and public policy* (pp. 136–157). Cambridge, England: Cambridge University Press.

Kletzky, O.A., & Borenstein, R. (1987). Vasomotor instability of the menopause. In D.R. Mishell, Jr. (Ed.), *Menopause: Physiology and pharmacology.* (pp. 53–66). Chicago, IL: Year Book Medical Publishers.

Kliegl, R., Smith, J., & Baltes, P.B. (1989). Testing-the-limits and the study of adult age differences in cognitive plasticity of a mnemonic skill. *Developmental Psychology, 25,* 247–256.

Kliegl, R., Smith, J., & Baltes, P.B. (1990). On the locus and process of magnification of age differences during mnemonic training. *Developmental Psychology, 26,* 894–904.

Kliegman, R. (1998). Fetal and neonatal medicine. In R. Behrman & R. Kliegman (Eds.), *Nelson essentials of pediatrics* (3rd ed., pp. 167–225). Philadelphia, PA: W.B. Saunders.

Kline, D.W., & Scialfa, C.T. (1996). Visual and auditory aging. In J.E. Birren & K.W. Schaie (Eds.), *Handbook of the psychology of aging* (4th ed., pp. 181–203). San Diego, CA: Academic Press.

Kline, D.W., Kline, T.J.B., Fozard, J.L., Kosnik, W., Schieber, F., & Sekuler, R. (1992). Vision, aging, and driving: The problem of older drivers. *Journals of Gerontology: Psychological Sciences, 47,* P27–34.

Kline, G., Stanley, S., Markman, H., & Olmos-Gallo, P. (2004). Timing is everything: Pre-engagement cohabitation and increased risk for poor marital outcomes. *Journal of Family Psychology, 18*(2), 311–318.

Kline, S. (1998). *Video game culture: Leisure and play preferences of BC teens.* Vancouver, BC: Simon Fraser University Media Analysis Laboratory.

Kline, S. (2002). *Moral panics and video games.* Vancouver, BC: Simon Fraser University Media Analysis Laboratory. Retrieved from www2.sfu.ca/media-lab/

Kline, S. (2003). *Media consumption as a health and safety risk factor.* Vancouver, BC: Simon Fraser University Media Analysis Laboratory. Retrieved from www2.sfu.ca/media-lab/risk/docs/kline_media_risk_reduction5.doc

Klingbeil, D.A. (2009). Test review: A review of the Five Factor Personality Inventory—Children. *Assessment for Effective Intervention, 35*(1), 61–64. doi: 10.1177/1534508408326248

Klomsten, A., Skaalvik, E., & Espnes, G. (2004). Physical self-concept and sports: Do gender differences still exist? *Sex Roles: A Journal of Research, 50,* 119–127.

Ko, H., Mehta, K.K., & Meng, K.S. (2006). *Understanding and counselling older persons: A handbook.* Singapore: Sage Counselling Centre.

Kochanska, G. (1997a). Multiple pathways to conscience for children with different temperaments: From toddlerhood to age 5. *Developmental Psychology, 33,* 228–240.

Kochanska, G. (1997b). Mutually responsive orientation between mothers and their young: Implications for early socialization. *Child Development, 68,* 94–112.

Kochanska, G., Murray, K., & Coy, K. (1997). Inhibitory control as a contributor to conscience in childhood: From toddler to early school age. *Child Development, 68,* 263–277.

Kochanska, G., Murray, K., Jacques, T., Koenig, A., & Vandegeest, K. (1996). Inhibitory control in young children and its role in emerging internalization. *Child Development, 67,* 490–507.

Kochenderfer, B.J., & Ladd, G.W. (1996). Peer victimization: Cause or consequence of school maladjustment. *Child Development, 67*(4), 1305–1317.

Kocsis, J. (1998). Geriatric dysthymia. *Journal of Clinical Psychiatry, 59,* 13–15.

Koenig, A.L., Cicchetti, D., & Rogosch, F.A. (2004). Moral development: The association between maltreatment and young children's prosocial behaviors and moral transgressions. *Social Development, 13*(1), 87–106.

Koerner, S., & Kenyon, D. (2007). Understanding "good days" and "bad days": Emotional and physical reactivity among caregivers for elder relatives. *Family Relations, 56,* 1–11.

Kohlberg, L. (1964). Development of moral character and moral ideology. In M.L. Hoffman & L.W. Hoffman (Eds.), *Review of child development research: Vol. 1* (pp. 283–332). New York, NY: Russell Sage Foundation.

Kohlberg, L. (1966). A cognitive-developmental analysis of children's sex-role concepts and attitudes. In E.E. Maccoby (Ed.), *The development of sex differences* (pp. 82–172). Stanford, CA: Stanford University Press.

Kohlberg, L. (1969). Stage and sequence: The cognitive-develpmental approach to socialization. In D. Goslin (Ed.), *Handbook of socialization theory and research* (pp. 347–480). Chicago, IL: Rand McNally.

Kohlberg, L. (1976). Moral stages and moralization: The cognitive developmental approach. In T. Lickona (Ed.), *Moral development and behavior: Theory, research, and social issues* (pp. 31–53). New York, NY: Holt.

Kohlberg, L. (1981). *Essays on moral development: Vol. 1. The philosophy of moral development.* New York, NY: Harper & Row.

Kohlberg, L., & Elfenbein, D. (1975). The development of moral judgments concerning capital punishment. *American Journal of Orthopsychiatry, 54,* 614–640.

Kohlberg, L., & Ullian, D.Z. (1974). Stages in the development of psychosexual concepts and attitudes. In R.C. Friedman, R.M. Richart, & R.L. Vande Wiele (Eds.), *Sex differences in behavior* (pp. 209–222). New York, NY: Wiley.

Kohlberg, L., Levine, C., & Hewer, A. (1983). *Moral stages: A current formulation and a response to critics.* Basel, Switzerland: S. Karger.

Kohli, M. (1994). Work and retirement: A comparative perspective. In M.W. Riley, R.L. Kahn, & A. Foner (Eds.), *Age and structural lag* (pp. 80–106). New York, NY: Wiley-Interscience.

Kondro, W. (2004). UK bans, Health Canada warns about anti-depressants. *Canadian Medical Association Journal, 170*(4), 23.

Kong, R., Johnson, H., Beattie, S., & Cardillo, A. (2003). Sexual offences in Canada (Cat. No. 85-002-XPE). Ottawa, ON: Statistics Canada.

Koppenhaver, D., Hendrix, M., & Williams, A. (2007). Toward evidence-based literacy interventions for children with severe and multiple disabilities. *Seminars in Speech & Language, 28,* 79–90.

Koren, G., Nulman, I., Chudley, A.E., & Loocke, C. (2003). Fetal alcohol spectrum disorder. *Canadian Medical Association Journal, 169*(11), 1181–1185.

Korobv, N., & Thorne, A. (2006). Intimacy and distancing: Young men's conversations about romantic relationships. *Journal of Adolescent Research, 21,* 27–55.

Koskinen, P., Blum, I., Bisson, S., Phillips, S., Creamer, T., & Baker, T.K. (2000). Book access, shared reading, and audio models: The effects of supporting the literacy learning of linguistically diverse students in school and at home. *Journal of Educational Psychology, 92,* 23–36.

Kost, K. (1997). The effects of support on the economic well-being of young fathers. *Families in Society, 78,* 370–382.

Kostanski, M., & Gullone, E. (1999). Dieting and body image in the child's world: Conceptualization and behavior. *Journal of Genetic Psychology, 160,* 488–499.

Kozey, M., & Siegel, L.S. (2008). Definitions of learning disabilities in Canadian provinces and territories. *Canadian Psychology, 49*(2), 162–172.

Kozma, A., Stones, M.J., & Hannah, T.E. (1991). Age, activity, and physical performance: An evaluation of performance models. *Psychology and Aging, 6,* 43–49.

Kozu, J. (1999). Domestic violence in Japan. *American Psychologist, 54,* 50–54.

Kramer, J.H., Mungas, D., Reed, B.R., Wetzel, M.E., Burnett, M.M., Miller, B.L., . . . Chui, HC. (2007). Longitudinal MRI and cognitive change in healthy elderly. *Neuropsychology, 21*(4), 412–418.

Kramer, M.S., & Kakuma, R. (2009). Optimal duration of exclusive breastfeeding (review). Retrieved from Cochrane Library—Cochrane Database of Systematic Reviews website: http://mrw.interscience.wiley.com/cochrane/clsysrev/articles/CD003517/frame.html

Krause, N., Ingersoll-Dayton, B., Liang, J., & Sugisawa, H. (1999). Religion, social support, and health among the Japanese elderly. *Journal of Health Behavior & Health Education, 40,* 405–421.

Kraut, R., Patterson, M., Lundmark, V., Kiesler, S., Mukophadhyay, T., & Schertis, W. (1998). Internet paradox: A social technology that reduces social involvement and psychological well-being? *American Psychologist, 53,* 1017–1031.

Krebs, D., & Denton, K. (2006). Explanatory limitations of cognitive-developmental approaches to morality. *Psychological Review, 113,* 672–675.

Kristenson, H., Österling, A., Nilsson, J., & Lindgärde, F. (2002). Alcoholism: Clinical and experimental research. *Alcoholism: Clinical and Experimental Research, 26,* 478–484.

Kristjanson, L.J., & Aoun, S. (2004). Palliative care for families: Remembering the hidden patients. *Canadian Journal of Psychiatry, 49*(6), 359–365.

Kronenberg, F. (1994). Hot flashes: Phenomenology, quality of life, and search for treatment options. *Experimental Gerontology, 29,* 319–336.

Krueger-Lebus, S., & Rauchfleisch, U. (1999). Level of contentment in lesbian partnerships with and without children. *System Familie, 12,* 74–79.

Kruk, E. (1995). Grandparent-grandchild contact loss: Findings from a study of "grandparent rights" members. *Canadian Journal on Aging, 14*(4), 737–754.

Ku, S., Kang, J., Kim, H., Kim, Y., Jee, B., Suh, C., . . . Kim, S. (2006). Age at menarche and its influencing factors in North Korean female refugees. *Human Reproduction, 21,* 833–836.

Kubzansky, L., Cole, S., Kawachi, I., Vokonas, P., & Sparrow, D. (2006). Shared and unique contributions of anger, anxiety, and depression to coronary heart disease: A prospective study in the normative aging study. *Annals of Behavioral Medicine, 31,* 21–29.

Kübler-Ross, E. (1969). *On death and dying.* New York, NY: Macmillan.

Kübler-Ross, E. (1974). *Questions and answers on death and dying.* New York, NY: Macmillan.

Kuhn, D., Kohlberg, L., Languer, J., & Haan, N. (1977). The development of formal operations in logical and moral judgment. *Genetic Psychology Monographs, 95,* 97–188.

Kumabe, C. (2006). Factors influencing contemporary Japanese attitudes regarding life and death. Japanese Journal of *Health Psychology, 19,* 20–24.

Kunkel, S.R., & Applebaum, R.A. (1992). Estimating the prevalence of long-term disability for an aging society. *Journals of Gerontology: Social Sciences, 47,* S253–260.

Kupersmidt, J.B., Griesler, P.C., DeRosier, M.E., Patterson, C.J., & Davis, P.W. (1995). Childhood aggression and peer relations in the context of family and neighborhood factors. *Child Development, 66,* 360–375.

Kurdek, L. (1997). Relation between neuroticism and dimensions of relationship commitment: evidence from gay, lesbian, and heterosexual couples. *Journal of Family Psychology, 11,* 109–124.

Kurdek, L. (2000). The link between sociotropy/autonomy and dimensions of relationship commitment: Evidence from gay and lesbian couples. *Personal Relationships, 7,* 153–164.

Kurdek, L. A. (2003). Differences between gay and lesbian cohabiting couples. *Journal of Social & Personal Relationships, 20,* 411–436.

Kurdek, L.A. (1995). Developmental changes in relationship quality in gay and lesbian cohabiting couples. *Developmental Psychology, 31,* 86–94.

Kurz, A., Erkinjuntti, T., Small, G., Lilienfeld, S., & Damaraju, C. (2003). Long-term safety and cognitive effects of galantamine in the treatment of probable vascular dementia or Alzheimer's disease with cerebrovascular disease. *European Journal of Neurology, 10,* 633–640.

Kushi, L., & Giovannucci, E. (2002). Dietary fat and cancer. *The American Journal of Medicine, 113*(9), 63–70.

Kuttler, A., LaGreca, A., & Prinstein, M. (1999). Friendship qualities and social-emotional functioning of adolescents with close, cross-sex friendships. *Journal of Research on Adolescence, 9,* 339–366.

Kyriacou, D., Anglin, D., Taliaferro, E., Stone, S., Tubb, T., Linden, J., . . . Kraus, J. (1999). Risk factors for injury to women from domestic violence. *New England Journal of Medicine, 341,* 1892–1898.

la Cour, P., Avlund, K., & Schultz-Larsen, K. (2006). Religion and survival in a secular region. A twenty year follow-up of 734 Danish adults born in 1914. *Social Science & Medicine, 62,* 157–164.

La Freniere, P., Strayer, F.F., & Gauthier, R. (1984). The emergence of same-sex affiliative preferences among preschool peers. A developmental/ethological perspective. *Child Development, 55,* 1958–1965.

Labouvie-Vief, G. (1980). Beyond formal operations: Uses and limits of pure logic in life-span development. *Human Development, 23,* 141–161.

Labouvie-Vief, G. (1990). Modes of knowledge and the organization of development. In M.L. Commons, C. Armon, L. Kohlberg, F.A. Richards, T.A. Grotzer, & J.D. Sinnott (Eds.), *Adult development: Vol. 2. Models and methods in the study of adolescent and adult thought* (pp. 43–62). New York, NY: Praeger.

Labouvie-Vief, G. (2006). Emerging structures of adult thought. In J. Arnett & J. Tanner (Eds.), *Emerging adults in America: Coming of age in the 21st century* (pp. 59–84). Washington, DC: American Psychological Association.

Lachman, M. (2004). Development in midlife. *Annual Review of Psychology, 55,* 305–331.

Lachman, M. (2004). Development in midlife. *Annual Review of Psychology, 55,* 305–331.

Lachman, M., & Weaver, S. (1998). Sociodemographic variations in the sense of control by domain: Findings from the MacArthur studies of midlife. *Psychology & Aging, 13,* 553–562.

Ladouceur, R., Boudreault, N., Jacques, C., and Vitaro, F. (1999). Pathological gambling and related problems among adolescents. *Journal of Child and Adolescent Substance Abuse, 8,* 55–68.

Ladouceur, R., Dubé, D., & Bujold, A. (1995). Gambling among primary school students. In E. Eadington (Ed.), *Gambling behavior and gambling problem.* Reno, NV: University of Nevada Press.

Laird, P.W. (2005). Cancer epigenetics. *Human Molecular Genetics, 14*(Review Issue 1), R65–R76.

Laird, R., Pettit, G., Dodge, K., & Bates, J. (1999). Best friendships, group relationships, and antisocial behavior in early adolescence. *Journal of Early Adolescence, 19,* 413–437.

Lakatos, K., Nemoda, Z., Birkas, E., Ronai, Z., Kovacs, E., Ney, K., . . . Gervai, J. (2003). Association of D4 dopamine receptor gene and serotonin transporter promoter polymorphisms with infants' response to novelty. *Molecular Psychiatry, 8,* 90–97.

Lakatta, E.G. (1990). Heart and circulation. In E.L. Schneider & J.W. Rowe (Eds.), *Handbook of the biology of aging* (3rd ed., pp. 181–217). San Diego, CA: Academic Press.

Lam, R., Pacala, J., & Smith, S. (1997). Factors related to depressive symptoms in an elderly Chinese American sample. *Gerontologist, 17,* 57–70.

Lamb, M.E. (1981). The development of father-infant relationships. In M.E. Lamb (Ed.), *The role of the father in child development* (2nd ed., pp. 459–488). New York, NY: Wiley.

Lambert, W., & Tucker, G.R. (1972). *Bilingual education of children: The St. Lambert experiment.* Rowley, MA: Newbury House.

Lampard, R., & Peggs, K. (1999). Repartnering: The relevance of parenthood and gender to cohabitation and remarriage among the formerly married. *British Journal of Sociology, 50,* 443–465.

Landolt, M., & Dutton, D. (1997). Power and personality: An analysis of gay male intimate abuse. *Sex Roles, 37,* 335–359.

Landry, S.H., Garner, P.W., Swank, P.R., & Baldwin, C.D. (1996). Effects of maternal scaffolding during joint toy play with preterm and full-term infants. *Merrill-Palmer Quarterly, 42,* 177–199.

Landy, S., & Tam, K.K. (1996). "Yes, parenting does make a difference to the development of children in Canada." In *Growing up in Canada: National longitudinal survey of children and youth.* Ottawa, ON: Human Resources Development Canada and Statistics Canada.

Landy, S., & Tam, K.K. (1998). Understanding the contribution of multiple risk factors on child development at various ages (Cat. No. W-98-22E). Ottawa, ON: Human Resources Development Canada.

Langer, G., Arnedt, C., & Sussman, D. (2004). Primetime Live poll: American sex survey analysis. Retrieved from http://abcnews.go.com/Primetime/PollVault/story?id=156921&page=1

Langille, D.B. (2007). Teenage pregnancy: Trends, contributing factors and the physician's role. *Canadian Medical Association Journal, 176*(11), 1601–1602.

Langlois, A. (2004, May). Retiring on the instalment plan. *CAmagazine.com.* Retrieved from www.camagazine.com/index.cfm/ci_id/20901/la_id/1/camagazine/1/print/true.htm

Langlois, J.H., Kalakanis, L.E., Rubenstein, A.J., Larson, A.D., Hallam, M.J., & Smoot, M.T. (2000). Maxims and myths of beauty: A meta-analytic and theoretical review. *Psychological Bulletin, 126,* 390–423.

Langlois, J.H., Ritter, J.M., Roggman, L.A., & Vaughn, L.S. (1991). Facial diversity and infant preferences for attractive faces. *Developmental Psychology, 27,* 79–84.

Langlois, J.H., Roggman, L.A., & Rieser-Danner, L.A. (1990). Infants' differential social responses to attractive and unattractive faces. *Developmental Psychology, 26,* 153–159.

Langlois, J.H., Roggman, L.A., Casey, R.J., Ritter, J.M., Rieser-Danner, L.A., & Jenkins, V.Y. (1987). Infant preferences for attractive faces: Rudiments of a stereotype? *Developmental Psychology, 23,* 363–369.

Langlois, S. & Morrison, P. (2002). Suicide deaths and suicide attempts (Cat. No. 82-003). *Health Reports, 13*(2), 9–22.

Lanius, R.A., Williamson, P.C., Densmore, M., Boksman, K., Neufeld, R.W., Gati, J.S., & Menon, R.S. (2004). The nature of traumatic memories: A 4-T fMRI functional connectivity analysis. *American Journal of Psychiatry, 161*(1), 36–44.

Lanius, R.A., Williamson, P.C., Hopper, J., Densmore, M., Boksman, K., Gupta, M.A., . . . Menon, R.S. (2003). Recall of emotional states in posttraumatic stress disorder: An fMRI investigation. *Biological Psychiatry, 53*(3), 204–210.

Lansdown, R., & Benjamin, G. (1985). The development of the concept of death in children aged 5–9 years. *Child Care, Health and Development, 11,* 13–30.

Larson, R. (2000). Toward a psychology of positive youth development. *American Psychologist, 55,* 170–183.

Larson, R., Mannell, R., & Zuzanek, J. (1986). Daily well-being of older adults with friends and family. *Psychology and Aging, 1,* 117–126.

Larzelere, R.E. (2000). Child outcomes of non-abusive and customary physical punishment by parents: An updated literature review. *Clinical Child and Family Psychology Review, 3*(4), 199–221.

Larzelere, R.E. (2003, April). *A meta-analysis comparing the effect sizes and correlates of corporal punishment with alternative disciplinary tactics.* Paper presented at the Society for Research in Child Development, Tampa, FL.

Larzelere, R.E., Kuhn, B.R., & Johnson, B. (2004). The intervention selection bias: An underrecognized confound in intervention research. *Psychological Bulletin, 130*(2), 289–303.

LaSala, M. (2001). Monogamous or not: Understanding and counseling gay male couples. *Families in Society, 82,* 605–611.

Laso, F., Iglesias-Osma, C., Ciudad, J., Lopez, A., Pastor, I., & Orfao, A. (1999). Chronic alcoholism is associated with an imbalanced production of the Th-a/Th-2 cytokines by peripheral blood T cells. *Alcoholism: Clinical & Experimental Research, 23,* 1306–1311.

Laumann, E.O., Gagnon, J.H., Michael, R.T., & Michaels, S. (1994). *The social organization of sexuality: Sexual practices in the United States.* Chicago, IL: University of Chicago Press.

Lauriello, J., McEvoy, J., Rodriguez, S., Bossie, C., & Lasser, R. (2005). Long-acting risperidone vs. placebo in the treatment of hospital inpatients with schizophrenia. *Schizophrenia Research, 72,* 249–258.

Laursen, B. (1995). Conflict and social interaction in adolescent relationships. *Journal of Research on Adolescence, 5,* 55–70.

Lavoie, M., & Ladouceur, R. (2004, February). Prevention of gambling among youth: Increasing knowledge and modifying attitudes towards gambling. *eGambling: The Electronic Journal of Gambling Issues, 10,* 1–10. Retrieved from www.camh.net/egambling/issue10/ejgi_10_lavoie_ladouceur.html

Lawrence, K., Yardley, J., Root, L., Canham, B., & McPhee, J. (2002). *Report on adolescent gambling: Attitudes and behaviours of Niagara Region youth.* St. Catharines, ON: Brock University. Retrieved from Ontario Problem Gambling website: www.gamblingresearch.org/download.sz/037%20Report%20web%20version.pdf?docid=5372

Lawrence, R.H., Bennett, J.M., & Markides, K.S. (1992). Perceived intergenerational solidarity and psychological distress among older Mexican Americans. *Journals of Gerontology: Social Sciences, 47,* S55–65.

Lawton, M.P. (1985). Housing and living environments of older people. In R.H. Binstock & E. Shanas (Eds.), *Aging and the social sciences* (2nd ed., pp. 450–478). New York, NY: Van Nostrand Reinhold.

Lawton, M.P. (1990). Residential environment and self-directedness among older people. *American Psychologist, 45,* 638–640.

Layton, L., Deeny, K., Tall, G., & Upton, G. (1996). Researching and promoting phonological awareness in the nursery class. *Journal of Research in Reading, 19,* 1–13.

Le Grand, R., Mondloch, C.J., Maurer, D., & Brent, H.P. (2001). Early visual experiences and face processing. *Nature, 410,* 890.

Le Grand, R., Mondloch, C.J., Maurer, D., & Brent, H.P. (2003). Expert face processing requires visual input to the right hemisphere during infancy. *Nature Neuroscience, 6*(10), 1108–1112.

Le Grand, R., Mondloch, C.J., Maurer, D., & Brent, H.P. (2004). Impairment in holistic face processing following early visual deprivation. *Psychological Science, 15*(11), 762–768.

Le Mare, L., Fernyhough, L., & Warford, L. (2001, April 19–22). *Intellectual and academic performance of Romanian orphans 10 years after being adopted to Canada.* Poster presented at the Biennial Meeting of the Society for Research in Child Development, Minneapolis, MN.

Le Mare, L., Warford, L., & Fernyhough, L. (2001, April 19–22). *Peer relationships of Romanian orphans 10 years after being adopted to Canada.* Poster presented at the Biennial Meeting of the Society for Research in Child Development, Minneapolis, MN.

Leaper, C. (1991). Influence and involvement in children's discourse: Age, gender, and partner effects. *Child Development, 62,* 797–811.

Leaper, C., & Friedman, C.K. (2007) The socialization of gender. In J.E. Grusec & P.D. Hastings (Eds.), *Handbook of socialization: Theory and research* (pp. 561–587). New York, NY: Guilford.

Learning Disabilities Association of Canada (2000). *Children with learning disabilities and dyslexia.* Ottawa, ON: Author. Retrieved from: www.ldac-taac.ca/LDindepth/childrenwithld.htm

Learning Disabilities Association of Canada (2002). *Official definition of learning disabilities.* Ottawa, ON: Author. Retrieved from www.ldac-taac.ca/english/defined/jan02eng.pdf

Learning without learning; Epigenetics. (Sept 23, 2006). *The Economist (London), 380*(8496), 93.

LeBlanc, J.C., Pless, I.B., King, W.J., Bawden, H., Bernard-Bonnin, A., Klassen, T., . . . Tenenbein, M. (2006). Home safety measure and the risk of unintentional injury among young children: a multicentre case-control study. *Canadian Medical Association Journal, 175*(8), 883–887.

Lee, C. (2004). Physical punishment of children: A psychological perspective. *Canadian Clinical Psychologist, 14*(2), 4–5.

Lee, D.S., Chiu, M., Manuel, D.G., Tu, K., Wang, X., Austin, P.C., . . . Tu, J. (2009). Trends in risk factors for cardiovascular disease in Canada: Temporal, socio-demographic and geographic factors. *Canadian Medical Association Journal, 181*(3–4), E55–E65.

Lee, G., & DeMaris, A. (2007). Widowhood, gender, and depression: A longitudinal analysis. *Research on Aging, 29*(1), 56–72.

Lee, I., Manson, J.E., Hennekens, C.H., & Paffenbarger, R.S., Jr. (1993). Body weight and mortality: A 27-year follow-up of middle-aged men. *Journal of the American Medical Association, 270,* 2823–2828.

Lee, I.-M., Hsieh, C., & Paffenbarger, R.S. (1995). Exercise intensity and longevity in men. *Journal of the American Medical Association, 273,* 1179–1184.

Lee, J. (1996). *What your doctor may not tell you about menopause.* New York, NY: Warner Books.

Lee, M., Law, C., & Tam, K. (1999). Parenthood and life satisfaction: A comparison of single and dual-parent families in Hong Kong. *International Social Work, 42,* 139–162.

LeFevre, J., Skwarchuk, S., Smith-Chant, B. L., Fast, L., Kamawar, D., & Bisanz, J. (2009). Home numeracy experiences and children's math performance in the early school years. *Canadian Journal of Behavioural Science, 41*(2), 55–66.

Legendre, G. (2006). Early child grammars: Qualitative and quantitative analysis of morphosyntactic production. *Cognitive Science, 30,* 803–835.

Legerstee, M., & Markovaa, G. (2008). Variations in 10-month-old infant imitation of people and things. *Infant Behavior and Development, 31*(1), 81–91.

Legerstee, M., & Markovaa, G. (2008). Variations in 10-month-old infant imitation of people and things. *Infant Behavior and Development, 31*(1), 81–91.

Legerstee, M., Anderson, D., & Schaffer, A. (1998). Five- and eight-month-old infants recognize their faces and voices as familiar and social stimuli. *Child Development, 69,* 37–50.

Legerstee, M., Pomerleau, A., Malcuit, G., & Feider, H. (1987). The development of infants' response to people and a doll: Implications for research communication. *Infant Behavior and Development, 10,* 82–95.

Lehman, D., & Nisbett, R. (1990). A longitudinal study of the effects of undergraduate training on reasoning. *Developmental Psychology, 26,* 952–960.

Lemaire, P., & Lecacheur, M. (2004). Five-rule effects in young and older adults' arithmetic: Further evidence for age-related differences in strategy selection. *Current Psychology Letters: Behavior, Brain, & Cognition, 12.* Retrieved from Current Psychology Letters website: http://cpl.revues.org/ document412.html.

Lenhardt, A., & McCourt, B. (2000). Adolescent unresolved grief in response to the death of a mother. *Professional School Counseling, 3,* 189–196.

Lenroot, R. K., Gogtay, N., Greenstein, D.K., Wells, E.M., Wallace, G.L., Clasen, L.S., . . . Giedd, J.N. (2007). Sexual dimorphism of brain developmental trajectories during childhood and adolescence. *Neuroimage, 36*(4), 1065–1073.

Lenroot, R.K., & Giedd, J.N. (2006). Brain development in children and adolescents: Insights from anatomical magnetic resonance imaging. *Neuroscience and Biobehavioral Reviews, 30*(6), 718–729.

Lenroot, R.K., Gogtay, N., Greenstein, D.K., Wells, E.M., Wallace, G.L., Clasen, L.S., . . . Giedd, J. (2007). Sexual dimorphism of brain developmental trajectories during childhood and adolescence. *Neuroimage, 36*(4), 1065–1073.

Lester, D. (1990). The Collett-Lester fear of death scale: The original version and a revision. *Death Studies, 14,* 451–468.

Leve, L.D., & Fagot, B.I. (1995, April). *The influence of attachment style and parenting behavior on children's prosocial behavior with peers.* Paper presented at the biennial meetings of the Society for Research in Child Development, Indianapolis, IN.

Levenson, R.W., Carstensen, L.L., & Gottman, J.M. (1993). Long-term marriage: Age, gender, and satisfaction. *Psychology and Aging, 8,* 301–313.

Levine, L., & Bluck, S. (1997). Experienced and remembered emotional intensity in older adults. *Psychology of Aging, 12,* 514–523.

Levinson, D.J. (1978). *The seasons of a man's life.* New York, NY: Knopf.

Levinson, D.J. (1986). A conception of adult development. *American Psychologist, 41,* 3–13.

Levinson, D.J. (1990). A theory of life structure development in adulthood. In C.N. Alexander & E.J. Langer (Eds.), *Higher stages of human development* (pp. 35–54). New York, NY: Oxford University Press.

Levitt, M.J., Weber, R.A., & Guacci, N. (1993). Convoys of social support: An intergenerational analysis. *Psychology and Aging, 8,* 323–326.

Levy, G.D., & Fivush, R. (1993). Scripts and gender: A new approach for examining gender-role development. *Developmental Review, 13,* 126–146.

Levy-Shiff, R., Vakil, E., Dimitrovsky, L., Abramovitz, M., Shahar, N., Har-Even, D., . . . Fish, B. (1998). Medical, cognitive, emotional, and behavioral outcomes in school-age children conceived by in-vitro fertilization. *Journal of Clinical Child Psychology, 27,* 320–329.

Lewis, C., & Lamb, M.E. (2003). Fathers' influences on children's development: The evidence from two-parent families. *European Journal of Psychology of Education, 18,* 211–228.

Lewis, J., Malow, R., & Ireland, S. (1997). HIV/AIDS in hetero-sexual college students: A review of a decade of literature. *Journal of American College Health, 45,* 147–158.

Lewis, M. (1990). Social knowledge and social development. *Merrill-Palmer Quarterly, 36,* 93–116.

Lewis, M. (1991). Ways of knowing: Objective self-awareness of consciousness. *Developmental Review, 11,* 231–243.

Lewis, M., & Brooks, J. (1978). Self-knowledge and emotional development. In M. Lewis & L.A. Rosenblum (Eds.), *The development of affect* (pp. 205–226). New York, NY: Plenum.

Lewis, M., Allesandri, S.M., & Sullivan, M.W. (1992). Differences in shame and pride as a function of children's gender and task difficulty. *Child Development, 63,* 630–638.

Lewis, M., Sullivan, M.W., Stanger, C., & Weiss, M. (1989). Self development and self-conscious emotions. *Child Development, 60,* 146–156.

Lewis, M.D. (1993). Early socioemotional predictors of cognitive competence at 4 years. *Developmental Psychology, 29,* 1036–1045.

Lewis, T.L., & Maurer, D. (2005). Multiple sensitive periods in human visual development: Evidence from visually deprived children. *Developmental Psychobiology, 46*(3), 163–183.

Ley, D.C.H., & van Bommel, H. (1994). *The heart of hospice.* Toronto, ON: NC Press Limited.

Li, L., & Seltzer, M. (2003). Parent care, intergenerational relationship quality, and mental health of adult daughters. *Research on Aging, 25,* 484–504.

Li, S., Lindenberger, B., Aschersleben, G., Prinz, W., & Baltes, P. (2004). Transformations in the couplings among intellectual abilities and constituent cognitive processes across the life span. *Psychological Science, 15,* 155–163.

Li, S., Lindenberger, U., Hommel, B., Aschersleben, G., Prinz, W., & Baltes, P.B. (2004). Transformations in the coupling among intellectual abilities and constituent cognitive processes across the life span. *Psychological Science, 15*(3), 155–163.

Lickona, T. (1978). Moral development and moral education. In J.M. Gallagher & J.J.A. Easley (Eds.), *Knowledge and development: Vol. 2* (pp. 21–74). New York, NY: Plenum.

Lickona, T. (1983). *Raising good children.* New York, NY: Bantam Books.

Lieberman, D.A. (1997). Interactive video games for health promotion: Effects on knowledge, self-efficacy, social support, and health. In R.L. Street, W.R. Gold, & T. Manning (Eds.), *Health promotion and interactive technology: Theoretical applications and future directions* (pp. 103–120). Mahwah, NJ: Erlbaum.

Lieberman, M., Doyle, A., & Markiewicz, D. (1995, March). *Attachment to mother and father: Links to peer relations in children.* Paper presented at the biennial meetings of the Society for Research in Child Development, Indianapolis, IN.

Lieberman, M.A. (1965). Psychological correlates of impending death: Some preliminary observations. *Journal of Gerontology, 20,* 182–190.

Lieberman, M.A., & Coplan, A.S. (1970). Distance from death as a variable in the study of aging. *Developmental Psychology, 2,* 71–84.

Liebermann, J., & Tucker, M.J. (2002). Effect of carrier system on the yield of human oocytes and embryos as assessed by survival and developmental potential after vitrification. *Reproduction, 124,* 483–489.

Liebermann, J., & Tucker, M.J. (2006). Comparison of vitrification and conventional cryopreservation of day 5 and day 6 blastocysts during clinical application. *Fertility and Sterility, 86*(1), 20–25.

Li, S-C., Lindenberger, U., Hommel, B., Aschersleben, G., Prinz, W., & Baltes, P.B. (2004). Transformations in the couplings among intellectual abilities and constituent cognitive processes across the life span. *Psychological Science, 15*(3), 155–163.

Li-Grining, C. (2007). Effortful control among low-income preschoolers in three cities: Stability, change, and individual differences. *Developmental Psychology, 43,* 208–221.

Lim, K.O., Zipursky, R.B., Watts, M.C., & Pfefferbaum, A. (1992). Decreased gray matter in normal aging: An in vivo magnetic resonance study. Journals of Gerontology: *Biological Sciences, 47*(1), B26–30.

Lin, C., Hsiao, C., & Chen, W. (1999). Development of sustained attention assessed using the Continuous Performance Test among children 6–15 years of age. *Journal of Abnormal Child Psychology, 27,* 403–412.

Lincourt, A., Rybash, J., & Hoyer, W. (1998). Aging, working memory, and the development of instance-based retrieval. *Brain & Cognition, 37,* 100–102.

Lindahl, K., Clements, M., & Markman, H. (1997). Predicting marital and parent functioning in dyads and triads: A longitudinal investigation of marital processes. *Journal of Family Psychology, 11,* 139–151.

Lindgren, C., Connelly, C., & Gaspar, H. (1999). Grief in spouse and children caregivers of dementia patients. *Western Journal of Nursing Research, 21,* 521–537.

Lindo, G., & Nordholm, L. (1999). Adaptation strategies, well-being, and activities of daily living among people with low vision. *Journal of Visual Impairment & Blindness, 93,* 434–446.

Lindsay, C. (2008). *Canadians attend weekly religious services less than 20 years ago (89-630-X).* Ottawa, ON: Statistics Canada. Retrieved from www.statcan.gc.ca/pub/89-630-x/2008001/article/10705-eng.pdf

Lindsay, J. (2000). An ambiguous commitment: Moving in to a cohabiting relationship. *Journal of Family Studies, 6,* 120–134.

Lindsay, J., Sykes, E., McDowell, I., Verreault, R., & Laurin, D. (2004). More than the epidemiology of Alzheimer's disease: Contributions of the Canadian study of health and aging. *Canadian Journal of Psychiatry, 49*(2), 83–91.

Lindsay, R. (1985). The aging skeleton. In M.R. Haug, A.B. Ford, & M. Sheafor (Eds.), *The physical and mental health of aged women* (pp. 65–82). New York, NY: Springer.

Lindstrom, T. (1997). Immunity and somatic health in bereavement. A prospective study of 39 Norwegian widows. *Omega: Journal of Death & Dying, 35,* 231–241.

Lindvall, O. (2003). Stem cells for cell therapy in Parkinson's disease. *Pharmacological Research, 47*(4), 279–287.

Linebarger, D.L. & Walker, D. (2005). Infants' and toddlers' television viewing and language outcomes. *American Behavioral Scientist, 48*(5), 624–645.

Linebarger, D.L., & Wainwright, D.K. (2006). *Television can teach: Elements of effective educational television.* Philadelphia, PA: Annenberg School for Communication, University of Pennsylvania.

Lines, E. (2007). *Cyber-bullying: Our kids' new reality.* Toronto, ON: Kids Help Phone. Retrieved from www.kidshelpphone.ca/beingthereforkids/newsroom/images/Cyber-Bullying_Report_2007_full.pdf

Lineweaver, T., & Hertzog, C. (1998). Adults' efficacy and control beliefs regarding memory and aging: Separating general from personal beliefs. *Aging, Neuropsychology, & Cognition, 5,* 264–296.

Lineweaver, T.T., Berger, A.K., & Hertzog, C. (2009). Expectations about memory change across the life span are impacted by aging stereotypes. *Psychology and Aging, 24*(1), 169–176.

Links, P.S., Gould, B., & Ratnayake, R. (2003). Assessing suicidal youth with antisocial, borderline, or narcissistic personality disorder. *Canadian Journal of Psychiatry, 48*(5), 301–310.

Lippa, R. (2005). *Gender, nature, and nurture.* Hillsdale, NJ: Lawrence Erlbaum Associates.

Lissner, L., Bengtsson, C., Björkelund, C., & Wedel, H. (1996). Physical activity levels and changes in relation to longevity: A prospective study of Swedish women. *American Journal of Epidemiology, 143,* 54–62.

Litwak, E., & Longino, C.F., Jr. (1987). Migration patterns among the elderly: A developmental perspective. *The Gerontologist, 27,* 266–272.

Liu, W., & Aaker, J. (2007). Do you look to the future or focus on today? The impact of life experience on intertemporal decisions. *Organizational Behavior and Human Decision Processes, 102,* 212–225.

Livesley, W.J., & Bromley, D.B. (1973). *Person perception in childhood and adolescence.* London, England: Wiley.

Lobel, T., Slone, M., & Winch, G. (1997). Masculinity, popularity, and self-esteem among Israeli preadolescent girls. *Sex Roles, 36,* 395–408.

Loeb, S., Fuller, B., Kagan, S., & Carrol, B. (2004). Child care in poor communities: Early learning effects of type, quality, and stability. *Child Development, 75,* 47–65.

Loehlin, J.C., Horn, J.M., & Willerman, L. (1994). Differential inheritance of mental abilities in the Texas Adoption Project. *Intelligence, 19,* 325–336.

Lofti, M. (2001). *Experiences and issues in controlling micronutrient malnutrition.* Ottawa, ON: International Development Research Centre.

Lohan, J., & Murphy, S. (2001/2002). Parents' perceptions of adolescent sibling grief responses after an adolescent or young adult child's sudden, violent death. *Omega, 44,* 195–213.

Longino, C.F., Jr. (1990). Geographical distribution and migration. In R.H. Binstock & L.K. George (Eds.), *Handbook of aging and the social sciences* (3rd ed., pp. 45–63). San Diego, CA: Academic Press.

Longino, C.F., Jr., Jackson, D.J., Zimmerman, R.S., & Bradsher, J.E. (1991). The second move: Health and geographic mobility. *Journals of Gerontology: Social Sciences, 46,* S218–224.

López-Alarcón, M., Villapando, S., & Fajardo, A. (1997). Breastfeeding lowers the frequency and duration of acute respiratory infection and diarrhea in infants under six months of age. *Journal of Nutrition, 127,* 436–443.

Lorant, V., Kunst, A., Huisman, M., Bopp, M., & Mackenbach, J. (2005). *Social Science & Medicine, 60,* 2431–2441.

Loutfy, M R., Hart, T.A., Mohammed, S.S., Su, D., Ralph, E.D., Walmsley, S.L., . . . Yudin, M.H. (2009). Fertility desires and intentions of HIV-positive women of reproductive age in Ontario, Canada: a cross-sectional study. *PLoS One, 4*(12), 1–7.

Loutradi, K.E., Kolibianakis, E.M., Venetis, C.A., Papanikolaou, E.G., Pados, G., Bontis, I., & Tarlatzis, B.C. (2008). Cryopreservation of human embryos by vitrification of slow freezing: A systematic review and meta-analysis. *Fertility and Sterility, 90*(1), 186–193.

Love, J., Harrison, L., Sagi-Schwartz, A., van IJzendoorn, M., Ross, C., Ungerer, J., . . . Chazan-Cohen, R. (2003). Child care quality matters: How conclusions may vary with context. *Child Development, 74,* 1021–1033.

Low, C., Stanton, A., Thompson, N., Kwan, L., & Ganz, P. (2006). Contextual life stress and coping strategies as predictors of adjustment to breast cancer survivorship. *Annals of Behavioral Medicine, 32,* 235–244.

Lowenstein, D., Acevedo, A., Czaja, S., & Duara, R. (2004). Cognitive rehabilitation of mildly impaired Alzheimer disease patients on cholinesterase inhibitors. *American Journal of Geriatric Psychiatry, 12,* 395–402.

Luch, A. (2005). Nature and nurture—lessons from chemical carcinogenesis. *Nature Reviews Cancer, 5*(2), 113–125.

Lugo-Gil, J., & Tamis-LeMonda, C.S. (2008). Family resources and parenting quality: Links to children's cognitive development across the first three years. *Child Development, 79*(4), 1065–1085.

Lundh, W., & Gyllang, C. (1993). Use of the Edinburgh Postnatal Depression Scale in some Swedish child health care centres. *Scandinavian Journal of Caring Sciences, 7,* 149–154.

Luo, Z.C., Wilkins, R., Heaman, M., Martens, P., Smylie, J., Hart, L., . . . Fraser, W.D. (2010). Birth outcomes and infant mortality by the degree of rural isolation among First Nations and non-First Nations in Manitoba, Canada. *The Journal of Rural Health, 26*(2), 175–181. doi: 10.1111/j.1748-0361.2010.00279.x

Luong, M. (2008). Life after teenage motherhood (75-001-X). *Perspectives on Labour and Income, 9*(5), 5–13. Retrieved from Statistics Canada website: www.statcan.gc.ca/pub/75-001-x/2008105/pdf/10577-eng.pdf

Lyons, N.P. (1983). Two perspectives: On self, relationships, and morality. *Harvard Educational Review, 53,* 125–145.

Ma, H. (2003). The relation of moral orientation and moral judgement to prosocial and antisocial behaviour of Chinese adolescents. *International Journal of Psychology, 38*(2), 101–111.

Ma, H., Shek, D., Cheung, P., & Oi Bun Lam, C. (2000). Parental, peer and teacher influences on the social behavior of Hong Kong Chinese adolescents. *Journal of Genetic Psychology, 161,* 65–78.

Maas, H.S., & Kuypers, J.A. (1974). *From thirty to seventy*. San Francisco, CA: Jossey-Bass.

Maccoby, E., & Lewis, C. (2003). Less day care or different day care? *Child Development, 74*, 1069–1075.

Maccoby, E.E. (1980). *Social development: Psychological growth and the parent-child relationship*. New York, NY: Harcourt Brace Jovanovich.

Maccoby, E.E. (1990). Gender and relationships: A developmental account. *American Psychologist, 45*, 513–520.

Maccoby, E.E. (1995). The two sexes and their social systems. In P. Moen, G.H. Elder, Jr., & K. Lüscher (Eds.), *Examining lives in context: Perspectives on the ecology of human development* (pp. 347–364). Washington, DC: American Psychological Association.

Maccoby, E.E., & Martin, J.A. (1983). Socialization in the context of the family: Parent-child interaction. In E.M. Hetherington (Ed.), *Handbook of child psychology: Socialization, personality, and social development: Vol. 4* (pp. 1–102). New York, NY: Wiley.

MacDonald, S.W.S., Hultsch, D.F., & Dixon, R.A. (2008). Predicting impending death: Inconsistency in speed is a selective and early marker. *Psychology and Aging, 23*(3), 595–607. doi: 10.1037/0882-7974.23.3.595

MacDorman, M., & Atkinson, J. (1999, July 30). Infant mortality statistics from the 1997 period. Linked birth/infant death data set. *National Vital Statistics Reports, 47*(23), 1–24.

Mackey, E., & La Greca, A. (2007). Adolescents' eating, exercise, and weight control behaviors: Does peer crowd affiliation play a role? *Journal of Pediatric Psychology, 32*, 13–23.

MacMaster, F.P., & Kusumakar, V. (2004). Hippocampal volume in early onset depression. *BMC Medicine, 2*(2).

MacMillan, H.L., Boyle, M.H., Wong, M.Y.Y., Duku, E.K., Fleming, J.E., & Walsh, C.A. (1999). Slapping and spanking in childhood and its association with lifetime prevalence of psychiatric disorders in a general population sample. *Canadian Medical Association Journal, 161*(7), 805–809.

Macrae, C., & Bodenhausen, G. (2000). Social cognition: Thinking categorically about others. *Annual Review of Psychology, 51*, 93–120.

Mael, F., Morath, R., & McLellan, J. (1997). Dimensions of adolescent employment. *Career Development Quarterly, 45*, 351–368.

Maguire, M., & Dunn, J. (1997). Friendships in early childhood and social understanding. *International Journal of Behavioral Development, 21*, 669–686.

Main, M., & Hesse, E. (1990). Parents' unresolved traumatic experiences are related to infant disorganized attachment status: Is frightened and/or frightening parental behavior the linking mechanism? In M.T. Greenberg, D. Cicchetti, & E.M. Cummings (Eds.), *Attachment in the preschool years: Theory, research, and intervention* (pp. 161–182). Chicago, IL: University of Chicago Press.

Main, M., & Solomon, J. (1990). Procedures for identifying infants as disorganized/disoriented during the Ainsworth Strange Situation. In M.T. Greenberg, D. Cicchetti, & E.M. Cummings (Eds.), *Attachment in the preschool years: Theory, research, and intervention* (pp. 121–160). Chicago, IL: University of Chicago Press.

Maitel, S., Dromi, E., Sagi, A., & Bornstein, M. (2000). The Hebrew Communicative Development Inventory: Language-specific properties and cross-linguistic generalizations. *Journal of Child Language, 27*, 43–67.

Maitra, A., Arking, D.E., Shivapurkar, N., Ikeda, M., Stastny, V., Kassauei, K., . . . Chakravarti, A. (2005). Genomic alterations in cultured human embryonic stem cells. *Nature Genetics 37*(10), 1099–1103.

Maki, P., Veijola, J., Rantakallio, P., Jokelainen, J., Jones, P., & Isohanni, M. (2004). Schizophrenia in the offspring of antenatally depressed mothers: A 31-year follow-up of the Northern Finland 1966 Birth Cohort. *Schizophrenia Research, 66*, 79–81.

Malabonga, V., & Pasnak, R. (2002). Hierarchical categorization by bilingual Latino children: Does a basic-level bias exist? *Genetic, Social, & General Psychology Monographs, 128*, 409–441.

Malina, R.M. (1982). Motor development in the early years. In S.G. Moore & C.R. Cooper (Eds.), *The young child: Reviews of research: Vol. 3* (pp. 211–232). Washington, DC: National Association for the Education of Young Children.

Malina, R.M. (1990). Physical growth and performance during the transition years. In R. Montemayor, G.R. Adams, & T.P. Gullotta (Eds.), *From childhood to adolescence: A transitional period?* (pp. 41–62). Newbury Park, CA: Sage.

Malinosky-Rummell, R., & Hansen, D. (1993). Long-term consequences of childhood physical abuse. *Psychological Bulletin, 114*, 68–79.

Malkinson, R., & Bar-Tur, L., (1999). The aging of grief in Israel: A perspective of bereaved parents. *Death Studies, 23*, 413–431.

Mallet, P., Apostolidis, T., & Paty, B. (1997). The development of gender schemata about heterosexual and homosexual others during adolescence. *Journal of General Psychology, 124*, 91–104.

Mamayson, S. (2009). *What is down syndrome?* Retrieved from Canadian Down Syndrome Society website: www.cdss.ca/information/general-information/what-is-down-syndrome.html

Mandrioli, M. (2004). Epigenetic tinkering and evolution: Is there any continuity in the role of cytosine methylation from invertebrates to vertebrates? *Cellular and Molecular Life Sciences, 61*(19–20), 2425–2427.

Manson, J.E., Willett, W.C., Stampfer, M.J., Colditz, G.A., Hunter, D.J., Hankinson, S.E., . . . Speizer, F.E. (1995). Body weight and mortality among women. *New England Journal of Medicine, 333*, 677–685.

Manzoli, L., Villari, P., Pironec, G., & Boccia, A. (2007). Marital status and mortality in the elderly: A systematic review and meta-analysis. *Social Science & Medicine, 64*, 77–94.

Mao, H. (2003). The relationship between voluntary employer changes and perceived job stress in Taiwan. International Journal of Stress Management, *10*, 75–85.

Maratsos, M. (1983). Some current issues in the study of the acquisition of grammar. In J. H. Flavell & E. M. Markman (Eds.), *Handbook of child psychology: Cognitive development* (pp. 707–786). New York, NY: Wiley.

Maratsos, M. (1998). The acquisition of grammar. In W. Damon (Ed.), *Handbook of child psychology: Vol. 2, Cognition, perception, and language* (5th ed., pp. 421–466). New York, NY: Wiley.

Maratsos, M. (2000). More overregularizations after all: New data and discussion on Marcus, Pinker, Ullman, Hollander, Rosen & Xu. *Journal of Child Language, 27*, 183–212.

Marcia, J.E. (1966). Development and validation of ego identity status. *Journal of Personality and Social Psychology, 3*, 551–558.

Marcia, J.E. (1980). Identity in adolescence. In J. Adelson (Ed.), *Handbook of adolescent psychology* (pp. 159–187). New York, NY: Wiley.

Marcia, J.E. (1993). The ego identity status approach to ego identity. In J.E. Marcia, A.S. Waterman, D.R. Matheson, S.L. Archer, & J.L. Orlofsky (Eds.), *Ego identity: A handbook for psychsocial research* (pp. 1–21). New York, N.Y.: Springer-Verlag.

Marcia, J.E. (2001). A commentary on Seth Schwartz's review of identity theory and research. *Identity: An International Journal of Theory and Research, 1*(1), 59–65.

Marcia, J.E. (2002). Adolescence, identity, and the Bernardone family. *Identity: An International Journal of Theory and Research, 2*(3), 199–209.

Marcus, D.E., & Overton, W.F. (1978). The development of cognitive gender constancy and sex role preferences. *Child Development, 49*, 434–444.

Marcus, R.F. (1986). Naturalistic observation of cooperation, helping, and sharing and their association with empathy and affect. In C. Zahn-Waxler, E.M. Cummings, & R. Iannotti (Eds.), *Altruism and aggression: Biological and social origins* (pp. 256–279). Cambridge, England: Cambridge University Press.

Marean, G.C., Werner, L.A., & Kuhl, P.K. (1992). Vowel categorization by very young infants. *Developmental Psychology, 28*, 396–405.

Mares, M.L., & Woodard, E. (2005). Positive Effects of Television on Children's Social Interactions: A Meta-Analysis. *Media Psychology, 7*(3), 301–322.

Mares, M.L., & Woodard, E.H. (2001). Prosocial effects on children's social interactions. In: D.G. Singer & J.D. Singer (Eds.), *Handbook of Children and the Media* (pp. 183–205). Thousand Oaks, CA: Sage Publications.

Margolin, G., & Gordis, E. (2000). The effects of family and community violence on children. *Annual Review of Psychology, 51*, 445–479.

Mark, A.E., Boyce, W.F., & Janssen, I. (2006). Television viewing, computer use, and total screen time in Canadian youth. *Paediatrics & Child Health, 11*(9), 595–599.

Market Wire. (2003). *Research from Quality Planning Corporation shows elderly drivers involved in more accidents, fewer violations than younger drivers.* Retrieved from http://findarticles.com/p/articles

Markey, P., Markey, C., & Tinsley, B. (2004). Children's behavioral manifestations of the five-factor model of personality. *Personality & Social Psychology Bulletin, 30*(4), 423–432.

Markman, E.M. (1992). Constraints on word learning: Speculations about their nature, origins, and domain specificity. In M.R. Gunnar & M. Maratsos (Eds.), *Minnesota Symposia on Child Psychology: Vol. 25* (pp. 59–101). Hillsdale, NJ: Erlbaum.

Markova, M., & Legerstee, M. (2008). How infants come to learn about the minds of others. *Zero to Three Journal, 28*(3), 26–31.

Marks, N., & Lamberg, J. (1998). Marital status continuity and change among young and midlife adults. *Journal of Family Issues, 19*, 652–686.

Marquardt, R. (1998). Quality of youth employment. In Human Resources Development Canada, *High school may not be enough: An analysis of results from the school leavers follow-up survey, 1995* (Cat. No. MP43-380/1998E). Ottawa, ON: Author. Retrieved from www.hrdc-drhc.gc.ca/arb/publications/books/notenough/c5_e.shtml#anchor1533972

Marsh, H., Craven, R., & Debus, R. (1999). Separation of competency and affect components of multiple dimensions of academic self-concept: A developmental perspective. *Merrill-Palmer Quarterly, 45*, 567–601.

Marshall, K. (2003). Parental leave: More time off for baby. (11–008–XPE) in *Canadian Social Trends, Winter* (71), 13–18.

Marshall, K. (2006). Converging gender roles (75-001-XPE). *Perspectives on Labour and Income, 18*(2), 14–22.

Marshall, K. (2007). The busy lives of teens. *Perspectives on Labour and Income, 8*(5), 5–25.

Marshall, K. (2008). Fathers' use of paid parental leave. In *Perspectives* (75-001-X). Ottawa, ON: Statistics Canada. Retrieved from www.statcan.gc.ca/pub/75-001-x/2008106/pdf/10639-eng.pdf

Marshall, N., Coll, C., Marx, F., McCartney, K., Keefe, N., & Ruh, J. (1997). After-school time and children's behavioral adjustment. *Merrill-Palmer Quarterly, 43*, 497–514.

Marshall, V.W. (1975). Age and awareness of finitude in developmental gerontology. *Omega, 6*, 113–129.

Marshall, V.W., & Levy, J.A. (1990). Aging and dying. In R.H. Binstock & L.K. George (Eds.), *Handbook of aging and the social sciences* (3rd ed., pp. 245–260). San Diego, CA: Academic Press.

Marsiglio, W., & Donnelly, D. (1991). Sexual relations in later life: A national study of married persons. *Journals of Gerontology: Social Sciences, 46*, S338–344.

Martin, C.L. (1991). The role of cognition in understanding gender effects. In H.W. Reese (Ed.), *Advances in child development and behavior, Vol. 23* (pp. 113–150). San Diego, CA: Academic Press.

Martin, C.L. (1993). New directions for investigating children's gender knowledge. *Developmental Review, 13*, 184–204.

Martin, C.L., & Halverson, C.F., Jr. (1981). A schematic processing model of sex typing and stereotyping in children. *Child Development, 52*, 1119–1134.

Martin, C.L., & Little, J.K. (1990). The relation of gender understanding to children's sex-typed preferences and gender stereotypes. *Child Development, 61*, 1427–1439.

Martin, C.L., & Ruble, D.N. (2004). Children's search for gender cues: cognitive perspectives on gender development. *Current Directions in Psychological Science, 13*, 67–70.

Martin, C.L., & Ruble, D.N. (2010). Patterns of Gender Development. *Annual Review of Psychology, 61*, 353–381.

Martin, C.L., Ruble, D.N., & Szkrybalo. J. (2002). Cognitive theories of early gender development. *Psychological Bulletin, 128*(6), 903–33.

Martin, C.L., Wood, C.H., & Little, J.K. (1990). The development of gender stereotype components. *Child Development, 61*, 1891–1904.

Martin, D.I., Ward, R., & Suter, C.M. (2005). Germline epimutation: A basis for epigenetic disease in humans. *Annals of the New York Academy of Sciences, 1054*(1), 68–77.

Martin, G.M. (2005). Epigenetic drift in aging identical twins. *Proceedings of the National Academy of Sciences of the United States of America, 102*(30), 10413–10414.

Martin, J.A., Hamilton, B.E., Sutton, P.D., Ventura, S.J., Menacker, F., Kimeyer, S., & Matthews, T.J. (2009). Births: Final data for 2006. *National Vital Statistics Reports, 57*(7).

Martin, R., Annis, S., Darling, L., Wadley, V., Harrell, L., & Marson, D. (2003). Loss of calculation abilities in patients with mild and moderate Alzheimer disease. *Archives of Neurology, 60*, 1585–1589.

Martin, R.P., Wisenbaker, J., & Huttunen, M. (1994). Review of factor analytic studies of temperament measures based on the Thomas-Chess structural model: Implications for the Big Five. In C.F. Halverson, Jr., G.A. Kohnstamm, & R.P. Martin (Eds.), *The developing structure of temperament and personality from infancy to adulthood* (pp. 157–172). Hillsdale, NJ: Erlbaum.

Martin-Matthews, A.E. (2001). *The ties that bind aging families: Caregiving roles and relationships.* Ottawa, ON: Vanier Institute of the Family. Retrieved December 23, 2001 from www.vifamily.ca/cft/aging/caregiving.htm

Martinez, L. (2002). Teratogen hot topic: Anticoagulants. *The Genetic Drift 20*(4), Retrieved from Mountain States Genetics Foundation website: www.mostgene.org/gd/gdvol20e.htm

Martini, T.S., Root, C.A., & Jenkins, J.M. (2004). Low and middle income mothers' regulation of negative emotion: Effects of children's temperament and situational emotional responses. *Social Development. 13*(4), 515–530.

Martorano, S.C. (1977). A developmental analysis of performance on Piaget's formal operations tasks. *Developmental Psychology, 13*, 666–672.

Maruyama, M., Arai, H., Ootsuki, M., Okamura, N., Matsui, T., Sasaki, H., . . . Kaneta, T. (2003). Biomarkers in subjects with amnestic mild cognitive impairment. *Journal of the American Geriatrics Society, 51*, 1671–1672.

Mascolo, M.F., & Fischer, K.W. (1995). Developmental transformations in appraisals for pride, shame, and guilt. In J.P. Tangney & K.W. Fischer (Eds.), *Self-conscious emotions: The psychology of shame, guilt, embarrassment, and pride* (pp. 64–113). New York, NY: Guilford Press.

Masi, R. (1988). Multiculturalism, medicine and health, Part I: Multicultural healthcare. *Médecin de Famille Canadien, 34*.

Maslow, A.H. (1968). *Toward a psychology of being* (2nd ed.). New York, NY: Van Nostrand Reinhold.

Maslow, A.H. (1970). *Motivation and personality* (2nd ed.). New York, NY: Harper & Row.

Mason, B., Goodman, A., Chabac, S., & Lehert, P. (2006). Effect of oral acamprosate on abstinence in patients with alcohol dependence in a double-blind, placebo-controlled trial: The role of patient motivation. *Journal of Psychiatric Research, 40*, 383–393.

Mason, J., & Chuang, S. (2001). Culturally-based after-school arts programming for low-income urban children: Adaptive and preventive effects. *Journal of Primary Prevention, 22*(1), 45–54.

Mast, B., Azar, A., MacNeill, S., & Lichtenberg, P. (2004). Depression and activities of daily living predict rehospitalization within 6 months of discharge from geriatric rehabilitation. *Rehabilitation Psychology, 49*, 219–223.

Maszk, P., Eisenberg, N., & Guthrie, I. (1999). Relations of children's social status to their emotionality and regulation: A short-term longitudinal study. *Merrill-Palmer Quarterly, 454*, 468–492.

Mathers, J.C., & Hesketh, J.E. (2007). The biological revolution: Understanding the impact of SNPs on diet-cancer interrelationships. *The Journal of Nutrition, 137*(1), 253S–258S.

Mathew, A., & Cook, M. (1990). The control of reaching movements by young infants. *Child Development, 61*, 1238–1257.

Mattson, S., & Riley, E. (1999). Implicit and explicit memory functioning in children with heavy prenatal alcohol exposure. *Journal of the International Neuropsychological Society, 5*, 462–471.

Maughan, B., Pickles, A., & Quinton, D. (1995). Parental hostility, childhood behavior, and adult social functioning. In J. McCord (Ed.), *Coercion and punishment in long-term perspectives* (pp. 34–58). Cambridge, England: Cambridge University Press.

Mauldin, J. (2005). The new retirement model. Retrieved from AgeWave website: www.agewave.com/media_files/ota.htm.

Maurer, D., & Maurer, C. (1988). *The world of the newborn.* New York, NY: Basic Books.

Maurer, D., Ellemberg, D., & Lewis, T.L. (2006). Repeated measurements of contrast sensitivity reveal limits to visual plasticity after early binocular deprivation in humans. *Neuropsychologia, 44*, 2104–2112.

Maurer, D., Mondloch, C.J., & Lewis, T.L. (2007). Sleeper effects. *Developmental Science, 10*(1), 40–47.

Mayeux, L., & Cillissen, A. (2003). Development of social problem solving in early childhood: Stability, change, and associations with social competence. *Journal of Genetic Psychology, 164*, 153–173.

Maylor, D., Vousden, J., & Brown, D. (1999). Adult age differences in short-term memory for serial order: Data and a model. *Psychology & Aging, 14*, 572–594.

Maylor, E. (1998). Changes in event-based prospective memory across adulthood. *Aging, Neuropsychology, & Cognition, 5*, 107–128.

Mayringer, H., & Wimmer, H. (2000). Pseudoname learning by German-speaking children with dyslexia: Evidence for a phonological learning deficit. *Journal of Experimental Child Psychology, 75*, 116–133.

Mayseless, O., & Scharf, M. (2007). Adolescents' attachment representations and their capacity for intimacy in close relationships. *Journal of Research on Adolescence, 17*, 23–50.

McAdams, D., & Pals, J. (2006). A new Big Five: Fundamental principles for an integrative science of personality. *American Psychologist, 61*, 204–217.

McAllister, D., Kaplan, B., Edworthy, S., Martin, L., Crawford, S., Ramsay-Goldman, R. . . . Sibley, J. (1997). The influence of systemic lupus erythematosus on fetal development: Cognitive, behavioral, and health trends. *Journal of the International Neurological Society, 3*, 370–376.

McBride-Chang, C. (1998). The development of invented spelling. *Early Education & Development, 9*, 147–160.

McBride-Chang, C., & Ho, C. (2000). Developmental issues in Chinese children's character acquisition. *Journal of Educational Psychology, 92*, 50–55.

McBride-Chang, C., Shu, H., Zhou, C., & Wagner, R. (2004). Morphological awareness uniquely predicts young children's Chinese character recognition. *Journal of Educational Psychology, 96*, 743–751.

McBurney, K. (Spring, 2008). *Leading the Integration of Compassion: Winnipeg's palliative care program.* Winnipeg, MB: Aspire. Retrieved from Winnipeg Regional Health Authority website: www.wrha.mb.ca/media/files/Aspire_Spring08_E.pdf

McCain, M., & Mustard, F. (1999). *Early years study: Reversing the real brain drain.* Toronto, ON: Ontario Children's Secretariat.

McCain, M.N., & Mustard, J.F. (2002). *The early years study three years later.* Toronto, ON: The Founders' Network.

McCall, B., Cavanaugh, M., Arvey, R., & Taubman, P. (1997). Genetic influences on job and occupational switching. *Journal of Vocational Behavior, 50*, 60–77.

McCall, R.B. (1993). Developmental functions for general mental performance. In D.K. Detterman (Ed.), *Current topics in human intelligence: Vol. 3. Individual differences and cognition* (pp. 3–30). Norwood, NJ: Ablex.

McCartney, K., Burchinal, M., Clarke-Stewart, A., Bub, K.L., Owen, M.T., & Belsky, J. (2010). Testing a series of causal propositions relating time in child care to children's externalizing behavior. *Developmental Psychology, 46*(1), 1–17a.

McClun, L., & Merrell, K. (1998). Relationship of perceived parenting styles, locus of control orientation, and self-concept among junior high age students. *Psychology in the Schools, 35*, 381–390.

McCoy, N. (1998). Methodological problems in the study of sexuality and the menopause. *Maturitas, 29*, 51–60.

McCrae, R., & Costa, P. (1990). *Personality in adulthood.* New York, NY: Guilford.

McCrae, R., Costa, P., Ostendord, F., & Angleitner, A. (2000). Nature over nurture: Temperament, personality, and life span development. *Journal of Personality & Social Psychology, 78*, 173–186.

McCrae, R.R., & Costa, P.T., Jr. (1984). *Emerging lives, enduring dispositions: Personality in adulthood.* Boston, MA: Little, Brown.

McCrae, R.R., & John, O.P. (1992). An introduction to the Five-Factor Model and its applications. *Journal of Personality, 60*, 175–215.

McDaniel, S. (1994). *Family and friends: General Social Survey analysis series* (Cat. No. 11-612E—No. 9). Ottawa, ON: Statistics Canada.

McDevitt, N. (2006). The nurture of things. *Headway, 2*(1), 16–19.

McDonald, P.L., & Wanner, R.A. (1990). *Retirement in Canada.* Toronto, ON: Butterworths.

McFadden, D. (1998). Sex differences in the auditory system. *Developmental Neuropsychology, 14*, 261–298.

McFalls, J.A., Jr. (1990). The risks of reproductive impairment in the later years of childbearing. *Annual Review of Sociology, 16*, 491–519.

McGregor, K., Sheng., L., & Smith, B. (2005). The precocious two-year-old: Status of the lexicon and links to the grammar. *Journal of Child Language, 32*, 563–585.

McHale, S., Crouter, A., & Tucker, C. (1999). Family context and gender role socialization in middle childhood: Comparing girls to boys and sisters to brothers. *Child Development, 70*, 990–1004.

McHugh, M. (2005). Understanding gender and intimate partner abuse. *Sex Roles: A Journal of Research, 52*, 717–724.

McIntosh, B.R., & Danigelis, N.L. (1995). Race, gender, and the relevance of productive activity for elders' affect. *Journals of Gerontology: Social Sciences, 50B*, S229–239.

McIntosh, C.G., Tonkin, S.L., & Gunn, A.J. (2009). What is the mechanism of sudden infant deaths associated with co-sleeping? *New Zealand Medical Journal, 122*, 69–75.

McIntosh, C.N., Finès, P., Wilkins, R., & Wolfson, M.C. (2009). Income disparities in health adjusted life expectancy for Canadian adults, 1991 to 2001. *Health Reports, 20*(4), 1–10.

McIntyre, L., Walsh, G., & Conner, S.K. (2001). A follow-up study on child hunger in Canada (Cat. No. W-01-1-2E). Ottawa, ON: Human Resources Development Canada. Retrieved from www.hrdc-drhc.gc.ca/stratpol/arb/publications/research/2001docs/abw-01-1-2e.shtml

McKay, A. (2005). *Sexual health education in the schools: Questions & answers.* Toronto, ON: Sex Information and Education Council of Canada (SIECCAN). Retrieved from www.sieccan.org/pdf/SHES_QA.pdf

McKim, M.K., Cramer, K.M., Stuart, B., & O'Connor, D.L. (1999). Infant care decisions and attachment security: The Canadian transition to child care study. *Canadian Journal of Behavioural Science, 31*(2), 92–106.

McLanahan, S., & Sandefur, G. (1994). *Growing up with a single parent: What hurts, what helps.* Cambridge, MA: Harvard University Press.

McLoyd, V. (1998). Socioeconomic disadvantage and child development. *American Psychologist, 53*, 185–204.

McMillan, R. (2010). Voices from the field—Early learning care and education: Applying an integrated approach. In R.E. Tremblay, R.G. Barr, R.D. Peters, & M. Boivin (Eds.), *Encyclopedia on Early Childhood Development.* Montreal, QC: Centre of Excellence for Early Childhood Development. Retrieved from www.child-encyclopedia.com/documents/McMillanANGps.pdf.

McMullen, K., Gilmore, J., & Le Petit, C. (2010). *Women in non-traditional occupations and fields of study.* (81-004-X). Ottawa, ON: Statistics Canada. Retrieved from www.statcan.gc.ca/pub/81-004-x/2010001/article/11151-eng.htm

McNally, E., Hendricks, S., & Horowitz, I. (1985). A look at breast-feeding trends in Canada (1963–1982). *Canadian Journal of Public Health, 76*, 101–107.

McNeal, C., & Amato, P. (1998). Parents' marital violence: Long-term consequences for children. *Journal of Family Issues, 19,* 123–139.

McNeal, R. (1997). Are students being pulled out of high school? The effect of adolescent employment on dropping out. *Sociology of Education, 70,* 206–220.

McShane, K., Smylie, J., & Adomako, P. (2009). Health of First Nations, Inuit, and Métis children in Canada. In J. Smylie & P. Adomako (Eds.), *Indigenous Children's Health Report: Health Assessment in Action.* Ottawa, ON: Health Canada.

Mead, S., & Fisk, A. (1998). Measuring skill acquisition and retention with an ATM simulator: The need for age-specific training. *Human Factors, 40,* 516–523.

Meaney, M. (2010). Epigenetics and the biological definition of Gene x Environment interactions. *Child Development, 81,* 41–79.

Meaney, M.J., & Szyf, M. (2005). Maternal care as a model for experience-dependent chromatin plasticity? *Trends in Neuroscience, 28*(9), 456–463.

Media Awareness Network. (2001a). Young Canadians in a wired world: The students' view. Media Awareness Network. Retrieved from www.media-awareness.ca/eng/webaware/netsurvey/pdf/reportoct.pdf

Media Awareness Network. (2001b). Young Canadians in a wired world: The students' view—key findings. Media Awareness Network. Retrieved from www.media-awareness.ca/eng/webaware/netsurvey/students/keyfindingsoct.htm

Media Awareness Network. (2004a). *Video games.* Retrieved from www.media-awareness.ca/english/parents/video_games/index.cfm

Media Awareness Network. (2004b). Young Canadians in a wired world—Phase II: A qualitative research report. Media Awareness Network. Ottawa, ON: Author. Retrieved from www.media-awareness.ca/english/special_initiatives/surveys/phase_two/index.cfm

Media Awareness Network. (2005). *Young Canadians in a Wired World—Phase II.* Retrieved from www.media-awareness.ca/english/research/YCWW/phaseII/upload/YCWWII_Student_Survey.pdf

Mediascope, Inc. (1999). *The social effects of electronic interactive games: An annotated bibliography.* Studio City, CA: Mediascope Press.

Mediascope Press. (1999). *Substance use in popular movies and music* (Issue Brief Series). Studio City, CA: Author.

Mediascope Press. (2000). Teens, sex and the media (Issue Brief Series). Studio City, CA: Mediascope Inc.

Medvedova, L. (1998). Personality dimensions—"little five"—and their relationships with coping strategies in early adolescence. *Studia Psychologica, 40,* 261–265.

Meek, C. (2004). UK psychiatrists question SSRI warnings for under-18s. *Canadian Medical Association Journal, 170*(4), 455.

Meeks, S. (1997). Illnesses in late life: Short-term course of mental illness in middle age and late life. *International Psychogeriatrics, 9,* 343–358.

Meeus, W., Dekovic, M., & Iedema, J. (1997). Unemployment and identity in adolescence: A social comparison perspective. *Career Development Quarterly, 45,* 369–380.

Mehta, K. (1997). The impact of religious beliefs and practices on aging: A cross-cultural comparison. *Journal of Aging Studies, 11,* 101–114.

Meisenhelder, J., & Chandler, E. (2000). Faith, prayer, and health outcomes in elderly Native Americans. *Clinical Nursing Research, 9,* 191–203.

Melot, A., & Houde, O. (1998). Categorization and theories of mind: The case of the appearance/reality distinction. *Cahiers de Psychologie Cognitive/Current Psychology of Cognition, 17,* 71–93.

Meltzoff, A.N., & Moore, M.K. (1977). Imitation of facial and manual gestures by human neonates. *Science, 198,* 75–78.

Menesini, E., Sanchez, V., Fonzi, A., Ortega, R., Costabile, A., & Lo Feudo, G. (2003). Moral emotions and bullying: A cross-national comparison of differences between bullies, victims and outsiders. *Aggressive Behavior, 29,* 515–530.

Mental Health Foundation of New Zealand. (2002). *Bulimia Nervosa.* Auckland, NZ: Author. Retrieved from www.mentalhealth.org.nz/conditions/docs/pdf8.pdf

Meredith, K., & Rassa, G. (1999). Aligning the levels of awareness with the stages of grieving. *Journal of Cognitive Rehabilitation, 17,* 10–12.

Merikangas, K.R., & Angst, J. (1995). The challenge of depressive disorders in adolescence. In M. Rutter (Ed.), *Psychosocial disturbances in young people: Challenges for prevention* (pp. 131–165). Cambridge, England: Cambridge University Press.

Meritesacker, B., Bade, U., Haverkock, A., & Pauli-Pott, U. (2004). Predicting maternal reactivity/sensitivity: The role of infant emotionality, maternal depressiveness/anxiety, and social support. *Infant Mental Health Journal, 25,* 47–61.

Meyer-Bahlburg, H.F.L., Ehrhardt, A.A., Rosen, L.R., Gruen, R.S., Veridiano, N.P., Vann, F.H., & Neuwalder, H.F. (1995). Prenatal estrogens and the development of homosexual orientation. *Developmental Psychology, 31,* 12–21.

Michael, R.T., Gagnon, J.H., Laumann, E.O., & Kolata, G. (1994). *Sex in America.* Boston, MA: Little, Brown.

Miech, R., & Shanahan, M. (2000). Socioeconomic status and depression over the life course. *Journal of Health & Social Behavior, 41,* 162–176.

Milan, A. (2003). Would you live common-law? (Cat. No. 11-008). *Canadian Social Trends, Autumn*(70), 2–6.

Milan, A., & Hamm, B. (2003). Across the generations: Grandparents and grandchildren (Cat. No. 11-008). *Canadian Social Trends, Winter*(71), 2–7.

Milan, A., Maheux, H., & Chui, T. (2010). A portrait of couples in mixed unions. *Canadian Social Trends, 89.*

Millar, W.J., & Hill, G. (2004). Pregnancy and smoking (Cat. No. 82–003). *Health Reports, 15*(4), 53–56.

Miller, B., Norton, M., Curtis, T., Hill, E., Schvaneveldt, P., & Young, M. (1998). The timing of sexual intercourse among adolescents: Family, peer, and other antecedents: Erratum. *Youth & Society, 29,* 390.

Miller, B.C., & Moore, K.A. (1990). Adolescent sexual behavior, pregnancy, and parenting: Research through the 1980s. *Journal of Marriage and the Family, 52,* 1025–1044.

Miller, F., Jenkins, J., & Keating, D. (2002). Parenting and children's behaviour problems. In J.D. Willms (Ed.), *Vulnerable children* (pp. 71–102). Edmonton, AB: The University of Alberta Press.

Miller, P., Eisenberg, N., Fabes, R., & Shell, R. (1996). Relations of moral reasoning and vicarious emotion to young children's prosocial behavior toward peers and adults. *Developmental Psychology, 29,* 3–18.

Miller, P., Wang, S., Sandel, T., & Cho, G. (2002). Self-esteem as folk theory: A comparison of European American and Taiwanese mothers' beliefs. *Science & Practice, 2*(3), 209–239.

Miller, R.A. (1996). Aging and the immune response. In E.L. Schneider & J.W. Rowe (Eds.), *Handbook of the biology of aging* (4th ed., pp. 355–392). San Diego, CA: Academic Press.

Miller, T.Q., Turner, C.W., Tindale, R.S., Posavac, E.J., & Dugoni, B.L. (1991). Reasons for the trend toward null findings in research on Type A behavior. *Psychological Bulletin, 110,* 469–495.

Mills, D., Coffey-Corina, S., & Neville, H. (1994). Variability in cerebral organization during primary language acquisition. In G. Dawson & K. Fischer (Eds.), *Human behavior and the developing brain.* New York, NY: Guilford Press.

Mills, R.S.L., & Rubin, K.H. (1998). Are behavioural and psychological control both differentially associated with childhood aggression and social withdrawal? *Canadian Journal of Behavioural Science, 30*(2), 132–136.

Min, J., Breheny, S., MacLachlan, V., & Healy, D. (2004). What is the most relevant standard of success in assisted reproduction? The singleton, term gestation, live birth rate per cycle initiated: the BESST endpoint for assisted reproduction. *Human reproduction, 19*(1), 3–7.

Min, J., Claman, P., & Hughes, E. (2006). Guidelines for the number of embryos to transfer following in vitro fertilization. *Journal of Obstetrics Gynaecology Canada, 28*(9), 799–813.

Minkler, M., & Fadem, P. (2002). "Successful aging": A disability perspective. *Journal of Disability Policy Studies, 12*, 229–235.

Mischel, W. (1966). A social learning view of sex differences in behavior. In E.E. Maccoby (Ed.), *The development of sex differences* (pp. 56–81). Stanford, CA: Stanford University Press.

Mischel, W. (1970). Sex typing and socialization. In P.H. Mussen (Ed.), *Carmichael's manual of child psychology: Vol. 2* (pp. 3–72). New York, NY: Wiley.

Mishra, R.C. (1997). Cognition and cognitive development. In J. Berry, P. Dasen, & T. Sarswathi (Eds.), *Handbook of cross-cultural psychology: Vol. 2*. Boston, MA: Allyn & Bacon.

Mitchell, B.A. (2000). The refilled "nest": Debunking the myth of families-in-crisis. In E.M. Gee & G. Gutman (Eds.), *The overselling of population aging: Apocalyptic demography and intergenerational challenges* (pp. 80–99). Toronto, ON: Oxford University Press.

Mitchell, P.R., & Kent, R.D. (1990). Phonetic variation in multisyllable babbling. *Journal of Child Language, 17*, 247–265.

Moen, P. (1996). Gender, age, and the life course. In R.H. Binstock & L.K. George (Eds.), *Handbook of aging and the social sciences* (4th ed., pp. 171–187). San Diego, CA: Academic Press.

Moen, P. (2005). Beyond the career mystique: "Time in," "time out," and "second acts." *Sociological Forum, 20*, 187–208.

Mohan, J. (2006). Cardiac psychology. *Journal of the Indian Academy of Applied Psychology, 32*, 214–220.

Mohanty, A. & Perregaux, C. (1997). Language acquisition and bilingualism. In J. Berry, P. Dasen, & T. Saraswath (Eds.), *Handbook of cross-cultural psychology: Vol. 2*. Boston, MA: Allyn & Bacon.

Monarch, E., Saykin, A., & Flashman, L. (2004). Neuropsychological impairment in borderline personality disorder. *Psychiatric Clinics of North America, 27*, 67–82.

Mondloch, C.J., Dobson, K.S., Parsons, J., & Maurer, D. (2004). Why 8-year-olds cannot tell the difference between Steve Martin and Paul Newman: Factors contributing to the slow development of sensitivity to the spacing of facial features. *Journal of Experimental Child Psychology, 89*, 159–181.

Mondloch, C.J., Geldart, S., Maurer, D., & Le Grand, R. (2003). Developmental changes in face processing skills. *Journal of Experimental Child Psychology, 86*, 67–84.

Mondloch, C.J., Le Grand, R., & Maurer, D. (2002). Configural face processing develops more slowly than featural face processing. *Perception, 31*, 553–566.

Mondloch, C.J., Leis, A., & Maurer, D. (2006). Recognizing the face of Johnny, Suzy, and me: Insensitivity to the spacing among features at 4 years of age. *Child Development, 77*(1), 234–243.

Mondloch, C.J., Maurer, D., & Ahola, S. (2006). Becoming a face expert. *Psychological Science, 17*(11), 930–934.

Monk, C., Webb, S., & Nelson, C. (2001). Prenatal neurobiological development: Molecular mechanisms and anatomical change. *Developmental Neuropsychology, 19*, 211–236.

Monroy, T. (2000, March 15). Boomers alter economics. *Interactive Week*. Retrieved from ZDNet website: www.ZDNet.com

Montemayor, R., & Eisen, M. (1977). The development of self-conceptions from childhood to adolescence. *Developmental Psychology, 13*, 314–319.

Montero, I., & De Dios, M. (2006). Vygotsky was right: An experimental approach to the relationship between private speech and task performance. *Estudios de Psicología, 27*, 175–189.

Montgomery, M., & Sorel, G. (1998). Love and dating experience in early and middle adolescence: Grade and gender comparisons. *Journal of Adolescence, 21*, 677–689.

Moody, E. (1997). Lessons from pair counseling with incarcerated juvenile delinquents. *Journal of Addictions & Offender Counseling, 18*, 10–25.

Moon, C., & Fifer, W.P. (1990). Syllables as signals for 2-day-old infants. *Infant Behavior and Development, 13*, 377–390.

Mooney, L., Knox, D., & Schacht, C. (2010). *Understanding social problems* (7th ed.). Thousand Oaks, CA: Wadsworth.

Moore, C. (2007). Maternal behavior, infant development, and the question of developmental resources. *Developmental Psychobiology, 49*, 45–53.

Moore, C., Barresi, J., & Thompson, C. (1998). The cognitive basis of future-oriented prosocial behavior. *Social Development, 7*, 198–218.

Moore, C. & D'Entremont, B. (2001). Developmental changes in pointing as a function of attentional focus. Journal of Cognition and Development, 2, 109–129.

Moore, E.R., Anderson G.C., & Bergman, N. (2007). Early skin-to-skin contact for mother and their healthy newborn infants. *Cochrane Database of Systematic Reviews, 3*.

Moore, K.L., & Persaud, T.V.N. (1993). *The developing human: Clinically oriented embryology* (5th ed.). Philadelphia, PA: Saunders.

Morfei, M., Hooker, K., Carpenter, J., Mix, C., & Blakeley, E. (2004). Agentic and communal generative behavior in four areas of adult life: Implications for psychological well-being. *Adult Development, 11*, 55–58.

Morgan, C., Covington, J., Geisler, M., Polich, J., & Murphy, C. (1997). Olfactory event-related potentials: Older males demonstrate the greatest deficits. *Electroencephalography & Clinical Neurophysiology, 104*, 351–358.

Morgan, D.G. (1992). Neurochemical changes with aging: Predisposition towards age-related mental disorders. In J.E. Birren, R.B. Sloane, & G.D. Cohen (Eds.), *Handbook of mental health and aging* (2nd ed., pp. 175–200). San Diego, CA: Academic Press.

Mork, J., Lie, K., Glattre, E., Clark, S., Hallmans, G., Jellum, E., . . . Dillner, J. (2001). Human papillomavirus infection as a risk factor for squamous-cell carcumoma of the head and neck. *New England Journal of Medicine, 344*, 1125–1131.

Morris, D.L., Kritchevsky, S.B., & Davis, C.E. (1994). Serum carotenoids and coronary heart disease. The Lipid Research Clinics Coronary Primary Prevention Trial and Follow-up Study. *Journal of the American Medical Association, 272*, 1439–1441.

Morrison, N.A., Qi, J.C., Tokita, A., Kelly, P.J., Crofts, L., Nguyen, T.V., . . . Eisman, J.A. (1994). Prediction of bone density from vitamin D receptor alleles. *Nature, 367*, 284–287.

Morrissette, P. (1999). Post-traumatic stress disorder in child sexual abuse: Diagnostic and treatment considerations. *Child & Youth Care Forum, 28*, 205–219.

Morrongiello, B.A. (1988). Infants' localization of sounds along the horizontal axis: Estimates of minimum audible angle. *Developmental Psychology, 24*(1), 8–13.

Morrongiello, B.A., Walpole, B., & McArthur, B.A. (2009). Young children's risk of unintentional injury: A comparison of mothers' and fathers' supervision beliefs and reported practices. *Journal of Pediatric Psychology, 34*(10), 1063–1068. doi:10.1093/jpepsy/jsp011

Morrongiello, B., Corbett, M., & Bellissimo, A. (2008). "Do as I say, not as I do': Family influences on children's safety and risk behaviors. *Health Psychology, 27*(4), 498–503.

Morrongiello, B.A., & Dawber, T. (1999). Parental influences on toddlers' injury-risk behaviors: Are sons and daughters socialized differently? *Journal of Applied Developmental Psychology, 20*, 227–251.

Morrongiello, B.A., Fenwick, K.D., & Chance, G. (1990). Sound localization acuity in very young infants: An observer-based testing procedure. Developmental Psychology, 24, 75–84.

Morrongiello, B.A., & House, K. (2004). Measuring parent attributes and supervision behaviors relevant to child injury risk: Examining the usefulness of questionnaire measures. *Injury Prevention, 10*(2), 114–119.

Morrongiello, B.A., & Kiriakou, S. (2004). Mothers' home-safety practices for preventing six types of childhood injuries: What do they do, and why? *Journal of Pediatric Psychology, 29*(4), 285–297.

Morrongiello, B.A., Midgett, C., & Shields, R. (2001). Don't run with scissors: Young children's knowledge of home safety rules. Journal of Pediatric Psychology, 26, 105–115.

Morrongiello, B.A., & Rennie, H. (1998). Why do boys engage in more risk taking than girls? The role of attributions, beliefs, and risk appraisal. *Journal of Pediatric Psychology, 23*, 33–44.

Morrow, D., Menard, W., Ridolfo, H., Stine-Morrow, E., Teller, T., & Bryant, D. (2003). Expertise, cognitive ability, and age effects on pilot communication. *International Journal of Aviation Psychology, 13,* 345–371.

Morse, P.A., & Cowan, N. (1982). Infant auditory and speech perception. In T.M. Field, A. Houston, H.C. Quay, L. Troll, & G.E. Finley (Eds.), *Review of human development* (pp. 32–61). New York, NY: Wiley.

Mosher, W.D. (1987, June). Infertility: Why business is booming. *American Demography,* 42–43.

Mosher, W.D., & Pratt, W.F. (1987). *Fecundity, infertility, and reproductive health in the United States, 1982: Vital Health Statistics, Series 23, No. 14. National Center for Health Statistics, U.S. Public Health Service.* Washington, DC: USGPO.

Moss, E., St-Laurent, D., Rousseau, D., Parent, S., Gosselin, C., & Saintange, J., (1999). L'attachement à l'âge scolaire et le développement des troubles de comportement. *Canadian Journal of Behavioural Science, 31*(2), 107–118.

Mott, J., Crowe, P., Richardson, J., & Flay, B. (1999). After-school supervision and adolescent cigarette smoking: Contributions of the setting and intensity of after-school self-care. *Journal of Behavioral Medicine, 22,* 35–58.

Mounts, N.S., & Steinberg, L. (1995). An ecological analysis of peer influence on adolescent grade point average and drug use. *Developmental Psychology, 31,* 915–922.

Müller, U., Carpendale, J.I.M., Bibok, M., & Racine, T.P. (2006). Subjectivity, identification and differentiation: key issues in early social development. *Monographs of the Society for Research in Child Development, 71*(2), 167–179.

Mueller, U., Overton, W., & Reene, K. (2001). Development of conditional reasoning: A longitudinal study. *Journal of Cognition & Development, 2,* 27–49.

Muhajarine, N., & D'Arcy, C. (1999). Physical abuse during pregnancy: prevalence and risk factors. *Canadian Medical Association Journal, 160*(4), 1007–1011.

Mullins, L.C., & Mushel, M. (1992). The existence and emotional closeness of relationships with children, friends, and spouses. The effect on loneliness among older persons. *Research on Aging, 14,* 448–470.

Munroe, R.H., Shimmin, H.S., & Munroe, R.L. (1984). Gender understanding and sex role preference in four cultures. *Developmental Psychology, 20,* 673–682.

Munroe, R.L. & Romney, A.K. (2006). Gender and age differences in same-sex aggregation and social behavior: A four-culture study. *Journal of Cross-Cultural Psychology, 37,* 3–19. doi: 10.1177/0022022105282292

Murnen, S., Smolak, L., Mills, J., & Good, L. (2003). Thin, sexy women and strong, muscular men: Grade-school children's responses to objectified images of women and men. *Sex Roles, 49,* 427–437.

Murphy, C.C., Schei, B., Myhr, T.L., & Du Mont, J. (2001). Abuse: a risk factor for low birth weight? A systematic review and meta-analysis. *Canadian Medical Association Journal, 164*(11), 1567–1572.

Murphy, S., Johnson, L., & Lohan, J. (2003). Finding meaning in a child's violent death: A five-year propective analysis of parents' personal narratives and empirical data. *Death Studies, 27,* 381–404.

Murray, J., Liotti, M., Ingmundson, P., Mayberg, H., Pu U., Zamarripa, F., . . . Fox, T. (2006). Children's brain activations while viewing televised violence revealed by MRO. *Media Psychology, 8*(1), 25–37.

Murray, L., Sinclair, D., Cooper, P., Ducournau, P., Turner, P. & Stein, A. (1999). The socioemotional development of 5-year-old children of postnatally depressed mothers. *Journal of Child Psychology & Psychiatry & Allied Disciplines, 40,* 1259–1271.

Mutagens. (1995, Spring). *Genetic Drift, 12.* Retrieved from Mountain States Genetics Foundation website: www.mostgene.org/gd/gdvol12f.htm

Mutch, L., Leyland, A., & McGee, A. (1993). Patterns of neuropsychological function in a low-birth-weight population. *Developmental Medicine & Child Neurology, 35,* 943–956.

Muzi, M. (2000). *The experience of parenting.* Upper Saddle River, NJ: Prentice Hall.

Mwamwenda, T. (1999). Undergraduate and graduate students' combinatorial reasoning and formal operations. *Journal of Genetic Psychology, 160,* 503–506.

Myerowitz, R., & Hogikyan, N.D. (1987). A deletion involving Alu sequences in the beta-hexosaminidase alpha-chain gene of French Canadians with Tay-Sachs disease. *Journal of Biological Chemistry, 15*:262(32), 15396–15399.

Nagamine, S. (1999). Interpersonal conflict situations: Adolescents' negotiation processes using an interpersonal negotiation strategy model: Adolescents' relations with their parents and friends. *Japanese Journal of Educational Psychology, 47,* 218–228.

Nagy, W., Berninger, V., Abbott, R., Vaughan, K., & Vermeulen, K. (2004). Relationship of morphology and other language skills to literacy skills in at-risk second-grade readers and at-risk fourth-grade writers. *Journal of Educational Psychology, 96,* 730–742.

Narvaez, D. (1998). The influence of moral schemas on the reconstruction of moral narratives in eighth graders and college students. *Journal of Educational Psychology, 90,* 13–24.

Nathanson, C.A., & Lorenz, G. (1982). Women and health: The social dimensions of biomedical data. In J.Z. Giele (Ed.), *Women in the middle years* (pp. 37–88). New York, NY: Wiley.

National Advisory Committee on Immunization. (2007). *Statement on human papillomavirus vaccine. Canadian Communicable Disease Report 2007; 33(ACS–2):1–32.* Ottawa, ON: Author. Retrieved from Public Health Agency of Canada website: www.phac-aspc.gc.ca/publicat/ccdr-rmtc/07pdf/acs33-02.pdf

National Cancer Institute of Canada. (2000). *Canadian cancer statistics 2000.* Toronto, ON: Author. Retrieved from www.ncic.cancer.ca

National Cancer Institute. (2006). *Breast cancer and the environment research centers chart new territory.* Retrieved from www.nci.nih.gov/ncicancerbulletin/NCI_Cancer_Bulletin_081506/page9

National Center for Chronic Disease Prevention and Health Promotion. (2000). *Obesity epidemic increases dramatically in the United States* [Online press release]. Retrieved from www.cdc.gov

National Center for Educational Statistics. (1997). *National Assessment of Educational Progress: 1996 Long-Term Trend Assessment.* Washington, DC: U.S. Department of Education.

National Center for Health Statistics (NCHS). (1996). Guidelines for school health programs to promote lifelong healthy eating. *Morbidity and Mortality Weekly Report, 45,* 1–33.

National Centre for Injury Prevention and Control (NCIPC). (2000). Fact book for the year 2000. Washington, DC: Author

National Center for Injury Prevention and Control (NCIPC). (2006). *Intimate partner violence.* Retrieved from www.cdc.gov/ncipc/factsheets/ipvfacts.htm

National Institute of Child Health & Human Development Early Child Care Research Network. (1999). Chronicity of maternal depressive symptoms, maternal sensitivity, and child functioning at 36 months. *Developmental Psychology, 35,* 1297–1310.

National Institute of Child Health and Human Development Early Child Care Research Network. (2004a). Affect dysregulation in the mother-child relationship in the toddler years: Antecedents and consequences. *Development & Psychopathology, 16,* 43–68.

National Institute of Child Health and Human Development Early Child Care Research Network. (2004b). Are child developmental outcomes related to before- and after-school care arrangements? Results from the NICHD Study of Early Child Care. *Child Development, 75*(1), 280–295.

National Institute of Child Health and Human Development Early Child Care Research Network. (Eds.). (2005). *Child care and child development: Results of the NICHD Study of early child care and youth development.* New York, NY: Guilford Press.

National Institute of Child Health and Human Development Early Child Care Research Network. (2006). Child-care effect sizes for the NICHD study of early child care and youth development. *American Psychologist, 61*(2), 99–116.

National Institute of Health (2005). Menopausal hormone therapy (NIH Publication No. 05-5200). Bethesda, MD: Author. Retrieved from www.nhlbi.nih.gov/health/women/pht_facts.pdf

National Institute on Aging. (2000a) *Depression: A serious but treatable illness* [Online "Age Page"]. Retrieved from www.nih.gov/nia

National Institute on Aging. (2000b). *Sexuality in later life* [Online "Age Page"]. Retrieved from www.nih.gov/nia

National Institutes of Health. (2004). *Stem cell basics*. Author. Retrieved from http://stemcells.nih.gov/info/basics/basics4.asp.

Natural Resources Canada (2010). *2007 survey of household energy use-summary report*. Ottawa, ON: Author. Retrieved from http://oee.nrcan.gc.ca/publications/statistics/sheu-summary07/home-electronics.cfm?attr=0

Neild, R., & Balfanz, R. (2006). An extreme degree of difficulty: The educational demographics of urban neighborhood high schools. *Journal of Education for Students Placed at Risk, 11*, 123–141.

Neill, M. (1998). *High stakes tests do not improve student learning*. Retrieved from National Center for Fair & Open Testing website: www.fairtest.org

Neimeyer, R., Prigerson, H., & Davies, B. (2002). Mourning and meaning. *American Behavioral Scientist, 46*(2), 235–251.

Neimeyer, R.A., Wittkowski, J., & Moser, R.P. (2004). Psychological research on death attitudes: An overview and evaluation. *Death Studies, 28*(4), 309–340.

Neisser, U., Boodoo, G., Bouchard, T.J., Jr., Boykin, A.W., Brody, N., Ceci, S.J., . . . Urbina, S. (1996). Intelligence: Knowns and unknowns. *American Psychologist, 51*, 77–101.

Neitzel, C., & Stright, A. (2003). Mothers' scaffolding of children's problem solving: Establishing a foundation of academic self-regulatory competence. *Journal of Family Psychology, 17*, 147–159.

Nelson, E.A., & Dannefer, D. (1992). Aged heterogeneity: Fact or fiction? The fate of diversity in gerontological research. *The Gerontologist, 32*, 17–23.

Nelson, K. (1973). Structure and strategy in learning to talk. *Monographs of the Society for Research in Child Development, 38* (Serial No. 149).

Nelson, K. (1977). Facilitating children's syntax acquisition. *Developmental Psychology, 13*, 101–107.

Nelson, M.E., Fiatarone, M.A., Morganti, C.M., Trice, I., Greenberg, R.A., & Evans, W.J. (1994). Effects of high-intensity strength training on multiple risk factors for osteoporotic fractures. *Journal of the American Medical Association, 272*, 1909–1914.

Nelson, S. (1980). Factors influencing young children's use of motives and outcomes as moral criteria. *Child Development, 51*, 823–829.

Neshat-Doost, H., Taghavi, M., Moradi, A., Yule, W., & Dalgleish, T. (1998). Memory for emotional trait adjectives in clinically depressed youth. *Journal of Abnormal Psychology, 107*, 642–650.

Neugarten, B.L. (1970). Dynamics of transition of middle age to old age. *Journal of Geriatric Psychiatry, 4*, 71–87.

Neugarten, B.L. (1979). Time, age, and the life cycle. *American Journal of Psychiatry, 136*, 887–894.

Neugebauer, R., Hoek, H., & Susser, E. (1999). Prenatal exposure to wartime famine and development of antisocial personal disorder in early adulthood. *Journal of the American Medical Association, 282*, 455–462.

Nevid, J.S., Greene, B., Johnson, P.A, & Taylor, S. (2009), *Essentials of Abnormal Psychology*, 2nd Canadian Edition. Toronto, ON: Pearson Education Canada.

Newcomb, A.F., & Bagwell, C.L. (1995). Children's friendship relations: A meta-analytic review. *Psychological Bulletin, 117*, 306–347.

Newcomb, A.F., Bukowski, W.M., & Pattee, L. (1993). Children's peer relations: A meta-analytic review of popular, rejected, neglected, controversial, and average sociometric status. *Psychological Bulletin, 113*, 99–128.

Newman, J., & Pittman, T. (2003). *Dr. Jack Newman's guide to breastfeeding* (rev. ed.). Toronto, ON: Harper Collins Canada.

Ni, Y. (1998). Cognitive structure, content knowledge, and classificatory reasoning. *Journal of Genetic Psychology, 159*, 280–296.

Nichols, D., & Melov, S. (2004). The aging cell. *Aging, 3*, 1474–1497.

Nicholson, J. (1998). Inborn errors of metabolism. In R. Behrman & R. Kliegman (Eds.), *Nelson essentials of pediatrics* (3rd ed., pp. 147–166). Philadelphia, PA: W.B. Saunders.

Nicholson, R., Houle, T., Rhudy, J., & Norton, P. (2007). Psychological risk factors in headache. *Headache: The Journal of Head and Face Pain, 47*, 413–426.

Nicoladis, E., & Genesee, F. (1996). A longitudinal study of pragmatic differentiation in young bilingual children. *Language Learning, 46*, 439–464.

Nicoladis, E., & Genesee, F. (1997). Language development in preschool bilingual children. *Journal of Speech-Language Pathology and Audiology, 21*(4), 258–270.

Nilsson, E., Gillberg, C., Gillberg, I., & Rastam, M. (1999). Ten-year follow-up of adolescent-onset anorexia nervosa: Personality disorders. *Journal of the American Academy of Child & Adolescent Psychiatry, 38*, 1389–1395.

Nilsson, L., Baeckman, L., Erngrund, K., & Nyberg, L. (1997). The Betula prospective cohort study: Memory, health, and aging. *Aging, Neuropsychology, & Cognition, 4*, 1–32.

Nisan, M., & Kohlberg, L. (1982). Universality and variation in moral judgment: A longitudinal and cross-sectional study in Turkey. *Child Development, 53*, 865–876.

Niska, K., Snyder, M., & Lia-Hoagberg, B. (1998). Family ritual facilitates adaptation to parenthood. *Public Health Nursing, 15*, 329–337.

Noh, S.R., Shake, M.C., Parisi, J.M., Joncich, A.D., Morrow, D.G., & Stine-Morrow, E.A.L. (2007). Age differences in learning from text: The effects of content preexposure on reading. *International Journal of Behavioral Development, 31*, 133–148.

Nolen-Hoeksema, S., & Girgus, J.S. (1994). The emergence of gender differences in depression during adolescence. *Psychological Bulletin, 115*, 424–443.

Noonan, G., Turner, N.E., & Macdonald, J. (1999). *Gambling and problem gambling amongst students in grades 5 to 11*. Centre for Addiction and Mental Health, May, 1–22. Retrieved from www.cfcg.org/search/documents/Gambling _and_problem_gambling_amongst_students_in_grades_5_to_11-14_02_2000-15_11_09.pdf

Norboru, T. (1997). A developmental study of wordplay in preschool children: The Japanese game of "Shiritori." *Japanese Journal of Developmental Psychology, 8*, 42–52.

Norris, F.H., & Murrell, S.A. (1990). Social support, life events, and stress as modifiers of adjustment to bereavement by older adults. *Psychology and Aging, 5*, 429–436.

Norris, J.E. (1994). Widowhood in later life. In *Writings in gerontology, (14) Late-life marital disruptions* (pp. 34–45). Ottawa, ON: National Advisory Council on Aging.

Norris, J.E., & Tindale, J.A. (1994). *Among generations: The cycle of adult relationships*. New York, NY: W.H. Freeman.

Norton, A.J. (1983). Family life cycle: 1980. *Journal of Marriage and the Family, 45*, 267–275.

Norwood, T.H., Smith, J.R., & Stein, G.H. (1990). Aging at the cellular level: The human fibroblastlike cell model. In E.R. Schneider & J.W. Rowe (Eds.), *Handbook of the biology of aging* (3rd ed., pp. 131–154). San Diego, CA: Academic Press.

Nucci, L., & Smetana, J. (1996). Mothers' concepts of young children's areas of personal freedom. *Child Development, 67*, 1870–1886.

Nutter, J. (1997). Middle school students' attitudes and use of anabolic steroids. *Journal of Strength Conditioning Research, 11*, 35–39.

Nygren, K.G. (2007). Single embryo transfer: The role of natural cycle/minimal stimulation IVF in the future. *Reproductive Biomedicine Online, 14*(5), 626–627.

O'Beirne, H., & Moore, C. (1995, March). *Attachment and sexual behavior in adolescence*. Paper presented at the biennial meetings of the Society for Research in Child Development, Indianapolis, IN.

O'Connor, N.J., Manson, J.E., O'Connor, G.T., & Buring, J.E. (1995). Psychosocial risk factors and nonfatal myocardial infarction. *Circulation, 92*, 1458–1464.

O'Hara, M.W., Schlechte, J.A., Lewis, D.A., & Varner, M.W. (1992). Controlled prospective study of postpartum mood disorders: Psychological, environmental, and hormonal variables. *Journal of Abnormal Psychology, 100*, 63–73.

O'Leary, K.D., & Smith, D.A. (1991). Marital interactions. *Annual Review of Psychology, 42*, 191–212.

O'Leary, S., Slep, A.S., & Reid, M. (1999). A longitudinal study of mothers' overreactive discipline and toddlers' externalizing behavior. *Journal of Abnormal Child Psychology, 27,* 331–341.

O'Neill, D.K., Astington, J.W., & Flavell, J.H. (1992). Young children's understanding of the role that sensory experiences play in knowledge acquisition. *Child Development, 63,* 474–490.

Oates, J. (1998). Risk factors for infant attrition and low engagement in experiments and free-play. *Infant Behavior & Development, 21,* 555–569.

Oates, M., Cox, J., Neema, S., Asten, P., Glangeaud-Freudenthal, N., Figueiredo, B., . . . Yoshida, K. (2004). Postnatal depression across countries and cultures: A qualitative study. *British Journal of Psychiatry, 184* (Supp. 146), s10–s16.

Oatley, K., & Jenkins, J. (1996). *Understanding emotions.* Cambridge, MA: Blackwell Publishers.

Offord, D.R., Boyle, M.H., & Racine, Y.A. (1991). The epidemiology of antisocial behavior in childhood and adolescence. In D.J. Pepler & K.H. Rubin (Eds.), *The development and treatment of childhood aggression* (pp. 31–54). Hillsdale, NJ: Erlbaum.

Ofstedal, M., Zimmer, Z., & Lin, H. (1999). A comparison of correlates of cognitive functioning in older persons in Taiwan and the United States. *Journals of Gerontology: Series B: Psychological Sciences & Social Sciences. 54B,* S291–S301.

Oggins, J. (2003). Topics of marital disagreement among African-American and Euro-American newlyweds. *Psychological Reports, 92,* 419–425.

Okamoto, K., & Uechi, Y. (1999). Adolescents' relations with parents and friends in the second individuation process. *Japanese Journal of Educational Psychology, 47,* 248–258.

Okuma, K., & Tanimura, M. (2009). A preliminary study on the relationship between characteristics of TV content and delayed speech development in young children. *Infant Behavior and Development, 32*(3), 312–321.

Okwumabua, J., Baker, F., Wong, S., & Pilgram, B. (1997). Characteristics of depressive symptoms in elderly urban and rural African Americans. *Journal of Gerontology, 52A,* M241–M246.

Oldershaw, L. (2002). *A national survey of parents of young children.* Toronto, ON: Invest in Kids. Retrieved from www.investinkids.ca/content/documents/parent_poll_10_29_02.pdf

Olds, D.L., Sadler, L., & Kitzman, H. (2007). Programs for parents of infants and toddlers: Recent evidence from randomized trials. *Journal of Child Psychology and Psychiatry, 48*(3–4), 355–391.

Olin, J., & Zelinski, E. (1997). Age differences in calibration of comprehension. *Educational Gerontology, 23,* 67–77.

Oliver, L.N., & Hayes, M.W. (2005). Neighbourhood socio-economic status and the prevalence of overweight Canadians. *Canadian Journal of Public Health, 96*(6), 415–420.

Oller, D., Cobo-Lewis, A., & Eilers, R. (1998). Phonological translation in bilingual and monolingual children. *Applied Psycholinguistics, 19,* 259–278.

Oller, D.K. (1981). Infant vocalizations: Exploration and reflectivity. In R.E. Stark (Ed.), *Language behavior in infancy and early childhood* (pp. 85–104). New York, NY: Elsevier North-Holland.

Olshansky, S.J., Passaro, D.J., Hershow, R.C., Layden, J., Carnes, B.A., Brody, J., . . . Ludwig, D. (2005). A potential decline in life expectancy in the United States in the 21st century. *New England Journal of Medicine, 352,* 1138–1145.

Olson, J.M., Vernon, P.A., Aitken Harris, J., & Jang, K.L. (2001). The heritability of attitudes: A study of twins. *Journal of Personality and Social Psychology, 80*(6), 845–860.

Olson, M., Krantz, D., Kelsey, S., Pepine, C., Sopko, G., Handberg, E., . . . Merz, N. (2005). Hostility scores are associated with increased risk of cardiovascular events in women undergoing coronary angiography: A report from the NHLBI-sponsored WISE study. *Psychosomatic Medicine, 67,* 546–552.

Olson, S.L., Bates, J.E., & Kaskie, B. (1992). Caregiver-infant interaction antecedents of children's school-age cognitive ability. *Merrill-Palmer Quarterly, 38,* 309–330.

Olweus, D. (1995). Bullying or peer abuse at school: Facts and intervention. *Current Directions in Psychological Science, 4*(6), 196–200.

Oman, D., & Reed, D. (1998). Religion and mortality among the community-dwelling elderly. *American Journal of Public Health, 88,* 1469–1475.

Omiya, A., & Uchida, N. (2002). The development of children's thinking strategies: The retrieval of alternatives based on the categorization with conditional reasoning tasks. *Japanese Journal of Psychology, 73,* 10–17.

Onen, S., Onen, F., Mangeon, J., Abidi, H., Courpron, P., & Schmidt, J. (2005). Alcohol abuse and dependence in elderly emergency department patients. *Archives of Gerontology and Geriatrics, 41,* 191–200.

Onrust, S., & Cuijpers, P. (2006). Mood and anxiety disorders in widowhood: A systematic review. *Aging & Mental Health, 10*(4), 327–334.

Onrust, S., Cuijpers, P., Smit, F., & Bohlmeijer, E. (2007). Predictors of psychological adjustment after bereavement. *International Psychogeriatrics, 19*(5), 921–934.

Ontario Hospital Association. (2009). *Cytomegalovirus surveillance protocol for Ontario hospitals* (#295). Toronto, ON: Author.

Onyskiw, J.E., Harrison, M.J., & Magill-Evans, J.E. (1997). Past childhood experiences and current parent-infant interactions. *Western Journal of Nursing Research, 19,* 501–518.

Organization of Teratology Information Specialists. (2005). *Acetaminophen and pregnancy.* Retrieved from www.otispregnancy.org/pdf/acetaminophen.pdf

Organization of Teratology Information Specialists. (2010). *Parental exposures and pregnancy.* Retrieved from www.otispregnancy.org/files/paternal.pdf

Ornish, D. (1993). *Eat more, weigh less.* New York, NY: HarperCollins.

Ornoy, A. (2002). The effects of alcohol and illicit drugs on the human embryo and fetus. *Israel Journal of Psychiatry & Related Sciences, 39,* 120–132.

Orth-Gomér, K., Rosengren, A., & Wilhelmsen, L. (1993). Lack of social support and incidence of coronary heart disease in middle-aged Swedish men. *Psychosomatic Medicine, 55,* 37–43.

Orwoll, L., & Perlmutter, M. (1990). The study of wise persons: Integrating a personality perspective. In R.J. Sternberg (Ed.), *Wisdom: Its nature, origins, and development* (pp. 160–180). Cambridge, England: Cambridge University Press.

Osadchy, A., Kazmin. A., & Koren, G. (2009). Nicotine replacement therapy during pregnancy: recommended or not recommended? *Journal of Obstetrics and Gynaecology Canada, 31*(8), 744–777.

Osana, H. P., & Rayner, V. (2010). Developing numeracy: Promoting a rich learning environment for young children. In *Encyclopedia of Language and Literacy Development* (pp. 1–12). London, ON: Canadian Language and Literacy Research Network. Retrieved from www.literacyencyclopedia.ca/pdfs/topic.php?topId=286

Osofsky, J.D., Hann, D.M., & Peebles, C. (1993). Adolescent parenthood: Risks and opportunities for mothers and infants. In C.H. Zeanah, Jr. (Ed.), *Handbook of infant mental health* (pp. 106–19). New York, NY: Guilford Press.

Ostoja, E., McCrone, E., Lehn, L., Reed, T., & Sroufe, L.A. (1995, March). *Representations of close relationships in adolescence: Longitudinal antecedents from infancy through childhood.* Paper presented at the biennial meetings of the Society for Research in Child Development, Indianapolis, IN.

Ostrov, J.M., Gentile, D.A., & Crick, N.R. (2006). Media exposure, aggression and prosocial behavior during early childhood: A longitudinal study. *Social Development, 15*(4), 612–627.

Ostrove, J.M., & Stewart, A.J. (1998). Representing Radcliffe: Perceptions and consequences of social class. *Journal of Adult Development, 5*(3), 183–193.

Ottawa Citizen (April 25, 2005). *A moral force: The story of Dr. Balfour Mount.* Winnipeg, MB: Canwest Global Communications Corp. Retrieved from www.canada.com/ottawacitizen/story.html?id=896d005a-fedd-4f50-a2d9-83a95fc56464

Owens, G., Crowell, J.A., Pan, H., Treboux, D., O'Connor, E., & Waters, E. (1995). The prototype hypothesis and the origins of attachment working models: Adult relationships with parents and romantic partners. *Monographs of the Society for Research in Child Development, 60*(244, No. 2–3), 216–233.

Ozman, H.A., & Craver, S.M. (1986). *Philosophical foundations of education.* Columbus, OH: Merrill.

Paden, S.L., & Buehler, C. (1995). Coping with the dual-income lifestyle. *Journal of Marriage and the Family, 57,* 101–110.

Paffenbarger, R.S., Hyde, R.T., Wing, A.L., & Hsieh, C. (1987). Physical activity, all-cause mortality, and longevity of college alumni. *New England Journal of Medicine, 314,* 605–613.

Pagani, L., Boulerice, B., Tremblay, R., & Vitaro, F. (1997). Behavioural development in children of divorce and remarriage. *Journal of Child Psychology & Psychiatry & Allied Disciplines, 38,* 769–781.

Pagani, L.S., Derevesnky, J.L., & Japel, C. (2009). Predicting gambling behavior in sixth grade from kindergarten impulsivity. *Archives of Pediatric Adolescent Medicine, 163*(3), 238–240.

Painter, M., & Bergman, I. (1998). Neurology. In R. Behrman & R. Kliegman (Eds.), *Nelson essentials of pediatrics* (3rd ed., pp. 694–745). Philadelphia, PA: W.B. Saunders.

Pajares, F. (2004). *Albert Bandura: Biographical sketch.* Retrieved from Dision of Educational Studies website: www.des.emory.edu/mfp/banconversion.html

Pajares, F., & Graham, L. (1999). Self-efficacy, motivation constructs, and mathematics performance of entering middle school students. *Contemporary Educational Psychology, 24,* 124–139.

Pajares, F., & Valiante, G. (1999). Grade level and gender differences in the writing self-beliefs of middle school students. *Contemporary Educational Psychology, 24,* 390–405.

Paley, V. (1986). *Mollie is three: Growing up in school.* Chicago, IL: University of Chicago Press.

Palla, B., & Litt, I.R. (1988). Medical complications of eating disorders in adolescents. *Pediatrics, 81,* 613–623.

Palmore, E. (1981). *Social patterns in normal aging: Findings from the Duke Longitudinal Study.* Durham, NC: Duke University Press.

Pang, T., & Lam, C. (2002). The widowers' bereavement process and death rituals: Hong Kong experiences. *Illness, Crisis, & Loss, 10,* 294–303.

Papadimitropoulos, E.A., Coyte, P.C., Josse, R.G., & Greenwood, C.E. (1997). Current and projected rates of hip fracture in Canada. *Canadian Medical Association Journal, 157*(10), 1357–1363.

Parault, S., & Schwanenflugel, P. (2000). The development of conceptual categories of attention during the elementary school years. *Journal of Experimental Child Psychology, 75,* 245–262.

Parent, S., Tillman, G., Jule, A., Skakkebaek, N., Toppari, J., & Bourguignon, J. (2003). The timing of normal puberty and the age limits of sexual precocity: Variations around the world, secular trends, and changes after migration. *Endocrine Review, 24,* 668–693.

Parham, T. (1989). Cycles of psychological Nigrescence. *The Counseling Psychologist, 17*(2), 187–226.

Park, J. (2003). Adolescent self-concept and health into adulthood (Cat. No. 82-003). *Health Reports, 14*(Supplement), 41–52.

Parke, R.D., & Tinsley, B.R. (1981). The father's role in infancy: Determinants of involvement in caregiving and play. In M.E. Lamb (Ed.), *The role of the father in child development* (2nd ed., pp. 429–458). New York, NY: Wiley.

Parke, R. (2004). The Society for Research in Child Development at 70: Progress and promise. Child Development, 75(1), 1–24.

Parker, R. (1999). Reminiscence as continuity: Comparison of young and older adults. *Journal of Clinical Geropsychology, 5,* 147–157.

Parks, M., & Roberts, L. (1998). "Making MOOsic": The development of personal relationships on line and a comparison to their off-line counterparts. *Journal of Social & Personal Relationships, 15,* 517–537.

Parmelee, A.H., Jr., Wenner, W.H., & Schulz, H.R. (1964). Infant sleep patterns from birth to 16 weeks of age. *Journal of Pediatrics, 65,* 576–582.

Parnes, H.S., & Sommers, D.G. (1994). Shunning retirement: Work experience of men in their seventies and early eighties. *Journals of Gerontology: Social Sciences, 49,* S117–124.

Parrila, R., Kirby, J., & McQuarrie, L. (2004). Articulation rate, naming speed, verbal short-term memory, and phonological awareness: Longitudinal predictors of early reading development? *Scientific Studies of Reading, 8,* 3–26.

Parsons, G. & McMullen, K. (2009). *Trends in university graduation, 1992 to 2007* (81-004-X). Ottawa, ON: Statistics Canada. Retrieved from www.statcan.gc.ca/pub/81-004-x/2009005/article/11050-eng.htm

Parten, M. (1932). Social participation among preschool children. *Journal of Abnormal and Social Psychology, 27*(3), 243–269.

Pascalis, O., de Schonen, S., Morton, J., Derulle, C., & Fabre-Grenet, M. (1995). Mother's face recognition by neonates: A replication and extension. *Infant Behavior and Development, 18,* 79–85.

Pascarella, E. (1999). The development of critical thinking: Does college make a difference? *Journal of College Student Development, 40,* 562–569.

Pascarella, E., & Terenzi, P. (1991). *How college affects students: Findings and insights from twenty years of research.* San Francisco, CA: Jossey-Bass.

Pascual-Leone, J. (1987). Organismic processes for Neo-Piagetian theories: A dialectical causal account of cognitive development. *International Journal of Psychology, 22,* 531–570.

Patten, S.B. (2000). Incidence of major depression in Canada. *Canadian Medical Association Journal, 163*(6), 714–715.

Patterson, C. (1994). Screening for cognitive impairment in the elderly. In Health Canada, *The Canadian guide to clinical preventive health care* (Section 11, Chapter 75). Ottawa, ON: Health Canada. Retrieved from www.hc-sc.gc.ca/hppb/healthcare/pubs/clinical_preventive/pdf/s11c75e.pdf

Patterson, C.J. (2006). Children of lesbian and gay parents. *Current Directions in Psychological Science, 15*(5), 241–243.

Patterson, C.J. (2009). Children of lesbian and gay parents: Psychology, law and policy. *American Psychologist, 64*(8), 727–36.

Pauen, S. (2000). Early differentiation within the animate domain: Are humans something special? *Journal of Experimental Child Psychology, 75,* 134–151.

Pauen, S. (2002). The global-to-basic level shift in infants' categorical thinking: First evidence from a longitudinal study. *International Journal of Behavioral Development, 26*(6), 492–499.

Pearce, P. (1997). Postpartum depression more than "the blues." *Canadian Journal of Continuing Medical Education, 9*(2), 31–5.

Pease-Alvarez, L. (1993). *Moving in and out of bilingualism: Investigating native language maintenance and shift in Mexican-descent children.* (Research Report). Washington, DC: National Council on Bilingual Education.

Peaston, A.E., & Whitelaw, E. (2006). Epigenetics and phenotypic variation in mammals. *Mammalian Genome, 17*(5), 365–374.

Pedersen, N.L., & Harris, J.R. (1990). Developmental behavioral genetics and successful aging. In P.B. Baltes & M.M. Baltes (Eds.), *Successful aging* (pp. 359–380). Cambridge, England: Cambridge University Press.

Pederson, D., & Moran, G. (1996). Expressions of the attachment relationship outside of the Strange Situation. *Child Development, 67,* 915–927.

Pederson, D.R., & Moran, G. (1995). A categorical description of infant-mother relationships in the home and its relation to Q-sort measures of infant-mother interaction. *Monographs of the Society for Research in Child Development, 60*(244, Nos. 2–3), 111–132.

Pederson, D.R., Gleason, K.E., Moran, G., & Bento, S. (1998). Maternal attachment representations, maternal sensitivity, and the infant-mother attachment relationship. *Developmental Psychology, 34,* 925–933.

Pederson, D.R., Moran, G., Sitko, C., Campbell, K., Ghesquire, K., & Acton, H. (1990). Maternal sensitivity and the security of infant-mother attachment: A Q-sort study. *Child Development, 61,* 1974–1983.

Pedlow, R., Sanson, A., Prior, M., & Oberklaid, F. (1993). Stability of maternally reported temperament from infancy to 8 years. *Developmental Psychology, 29,* 998–1007.

Pegg, J.E., Werker, J.F., & McLeod, P.J. (1992). Preference for infant-directed over adult-directed speech: Evidence from 7-week-old infants. *Infant Behavior & Development, 15*, 325–345.

Peigneux, P., & van der Linden, M. (1999). Influence of ageing and educational level on the prevalence of body-part-as-objects in normal subjects. *Journal of Clinical & Experimental Neuropsychology, 21*, 547–552.

Pelletier, L., Dion, S., & Levesque, C. (2004). Can self-determination help protect women against sociocultural influences about body image and reduce their risk of experiencing bulimic symptoms? *Journal of Social & Clinical Psychology, 23*, 61–88.

Pelligrini, A., & Smith, P. (1998). Physical activity play: The nature and function of a neglected aspect of play. *Child Development, 69*, 577–598.

Peplau, L. A. (1991). Lesbian and gay relationships. In J. C. Gonsiorek & J. D. Weinrich (Eds.), *Homosexuality: Research implications for public policy* (pp. 177–196). Newbury Park, CA: Sage.

Pepler, D.J., Craig, W.M., Connolly, J.A., Yuill, A., McMaster, L., & Jiang, D (2006). A developmental perspective on bullying. *Aggressive Behavior, 32*(4), 376–384.

Pereverzeva, M., Hui-Lin Chien, S., Palmer, J., & Teller, D. (2002). Infant photometry: Are mean adult isoluminance values a sufficient approximation to individual infant values? *Vision Research, 42*, 1639–1649.

Pérez, C.E. (2003). Children who become active. Supplement to Health Reports, 2003 (Cat. No. 82-003). Ottawa, ON: Statistics Canada.

Perho, H., & Korhonen, M. (1999). Coping in work and marriage at the onset of middle age. *Psykologia, 34*, 115–127.

Perry, B.D. (2001). The neuroarcheology of childhood maltreatment: The neurodevelopmental costs of adverse childhood events. In K. Franey, R. Geffner, & R. Falconer (Eds), *The cost of maltreatment: Who pays? We all do* (pp. 15–37). San Diego, CA: Family Violence and Sexual Assault Institute.

Perry, B.D. (2002). Stress, trauma and post-traumatic stress disorders in children: An introduction. Houston, TX: ChildTrauma Academy. Retrieved from Child Trauma Academy website: www.childtrauma.org/CTAMATERIALS/PTSDfn_03_v2.pdf

Perry, B.D., Pollard, R., Blakely, T., Baker, W., & Vigilante, D. (1995). Childhood trauma, the neurobiology of adaptation and 'use-dependent' development of the brain: How "states" become "traits." *Infant Mental Health Journal, 16*(4), 271–291.

Perry, W. (1968). *Forms of intellectual and ethical development in the college years.* New York, NY: Holt, Rinehart & Winston.

Peskin, J. (1992). Ruse and representations: On children's ability to conceal information. *Developmental Psychology, 28*(1), 84–89.

Pesonen, A., Raikkonen, K., Strandberg, T., Kelitikangas-Jarvinen, & L., Jarvenpaa, A. (2004). Insecure adult attachment style and depressive symptoms: Implications for parental perceptions of infant temperament. *Infant Mental Health Journal, 25*, 99–116.

Petersen, A.C., Compas, B.E., Brooks-Gunn, J., Stemmler, M., Ey, S., & Grant, K.E. (1993). Depression in adolescence. *American Psychologist, 48*, 155–168.

Peterson, A.C., & Taylor, B. (1980). The biological approach to adolescence. In J. Adelson (Ed.), *Handbook of adolescent psychology* (pp. 117–158). New York, NY: Wiley.

Peterson, B. (2002). Longitudinal analysis of midlife generativity, intergenerational roles, and caregiving. *Psychology & Aging, 17*, 161–168.

Peterson, C. (2002). Children's long-term memory for autobiographical events. *Developmental Review, 22*(3), 370–402.

Peterson, C., Seligman, M.E.P., & Vaillant, G.E. (1988). Pessimistic explanatory style is a risk factor for physical illness: A thirty-five-year longitudinal study. *Journal of Personality and Social Psychology, 55*, 23–27.

Peterson, L., Ewigman, B., & Kivlahan, C. (1993). Judgments regarding appropriate child supervision to prevent injury: The role of environmental risk and child age. *Child Development, 64*, 934–950.

Petitto, L.A., & Holowka, S. (2002). Evaluating attributions of delay and confusion in young bilinguals: Special insights from infants acquiring a signed and spoken language. *Sign Language Studies, 3*(1), 4–34.

Petronis, A. (2003). Epigenetics and bipolar disorder: New opportunities and challenges. *American Journal of Medical Genetics, 123*(1), 65–75.

Petronis, A. (2004). The origin of schizophrenia: Genetic thesis, epigenetic antithesis, and resolving synthesis. *Biological Psychiatry, 55*(10), 965–970.

Petronis, A. (2006). Epigenetics and twins: Three variations on the theme. *Trends in Genetics, 22*(7), 347–350.

Petronis, A., Gottesman, I.I., Crow, T.J., DeLisi, L.E., Klar, A.J., Macciardi, F., . . . Sutherland, G.R.. (2000). Psychiatric epigenetics: A new focus for the new century. *Molecular Psychiatry, 5*(4), 342–346.

Pettingale, K.W., Morris, T., Greer, S., & Haybittle, J.L. (1985). Mental attitudes to cancer: An additional prognostic factor. *Lancet, 85.*

Pettit, G., Laird, R., Bates, J., & Dodge, K. (1997). Patterns of after-school care in middle childhood: Risk factors and developmental outcomes. *Merrill-Palmer Quarterly, 43*, 515–538.

Pettit, G.S., Clawson, M.A., Dodge, K.A., & Bates, J.E. (1996). Stability and change in peer-rejected status: The role of child behavior, parenting, and family ecology. *Merrill-Palmer Quarterly, 42*, 295–318.

Pezdek, K., Blandon-Gitlin, I., & Moore, C. (2003). Children's face recognition memory: More evidence for the cross-race effect. *Journal of Applied Psychology, 88*, 760–763.

Phillips, A., Wellman, H., & Spelke, E. (2002). Infants' ability to connect gaze and emotional expression to intentional action. *Cognition, 85*, 53–78.

Phillips, D., Schwean, V., & Saklofske, D. (1997). Treatment effect of a school-based cognitive-behavioral program for aggressive children. *Canadian Journal of School Psychology, 13*, 60–67.

Phillips, S. (2010, March 8). Women's equity a long way off in Alberta: Alberta most unequal province in Canada. Edmonton, AB: Parkland Institute. Retrieved from http://parklandinstitute.ca/research/summary/womens_equality_a_long_way_off_in_alberta/

Phillips, S.K., Bruce, S.A., Newton, D., & Woledge, R.C. (1992). The weakness of old age is not due to failure of muscle activation. *Journals of Gerontology: Medical Sciences, 47*, M45–49.

Phillipsen, L. (1999). Associations between age, gender, and group acceptance and three components of friendship quality. *Journal of Early Adolescence, 19*, 438–464.

Phinney, J.S. (1990). Ethnic identity in adolescents and adults: Review of research. *Psychological Bulletin, 108*, 499–514.

Phinney, J. (1993). A three stage model of ethnic identity development in adolescents. In M.E. Bernal & G.P. Knight (Eds.), *Ethnic identity: Formation and transmission among Hispanic and other minorities* (pp. 61–80). Albany, NY: State University of New York Press.

Phinney, J., Baumann, K., & Blanton, S. (2001). Life goals and attributions for expected outcomes among adolescents from five ethnic groups. *Hispanic Journal of Behavioral Sciences, 23*, 363–377.

Phinney, J.S., & Alipuria, L.L. (1996). At the interface of cultures: Multi-ethnic/multiracial high school and college students. *Journal of Social Psychology, 136*(2), 139–158.

Phinney, J.S., & Kohatsu, E.L. (1997). Ethnic and racial identity development and mental health. In J. Schulenberg, J.L. Maggs, & K. Hurrelmann (Eds.), *Health risks and developmental transitions during adolescence* (pp. 420–443). Cambridge, England: Cambridge University Press.

Phinney, J.S., Ferguson, D.L., & Tate, J.D. (1997). Intergroup attitudes among ethnic minority adolescents: A causal model. *Child Development, 68*(5), 955–969.

Phinney, J.S., Ong, A., & Madden, T. (2000). Cultural values and intergenerational value discrepancies in immigrant and non-immigrant families. *Child Development, 71*(2), 528–539.

Phipps, S., & Lethbridge, L. (2006). Incomes and the outcomes of children (11F0019MIE—No. 281). Ottawa, ON: Ministry of Industry.

Piaget, J. (1932). *The moral judgment of the child*. New York, NY: Macmillan.

Piaget, J. (1952). *The origins of intelligence in children*. New York, NY: International Universities Press.

Piaget, J. (1954). *The construction of reality in the child*. New York, NY: Basic Books. (Originally published 1937.)

Piaget, J. (1965). *The moral judgment of the child*. New York, NY: Free Press.

Piaget, J. (1970). Piaget's theory. In P.H. Mussen (Ed.), *Carmichael's manual of child psychology: Vol. 1* (3rd ed., pp. 703–732). New York, NY: Wiley.

Piaget, J. (1977). *The development of thought: Equilibration of cognitive structures*. New York, NY: Viking.

Piaget, J., & Inhelder, B. (1959). *La gènese des structures logiques élémentaires: Classifications et sériations [The origin of elementary logical structures: Classification and seriation]*. Neuchâtel, Switzerland: Delachaux et Niestlé.

Piaget, J., & Inhelder, B. (1969). *The psychology of the child*. New York, NY: Basic Books.

Pianta, R.C., & Egeland, B. (1994). Predictors of instability in children's mental test performance at 24, 48, and 96 months. *Intelligence, 18*, 145–163.

Picard, A. (2010, March 4). The budget's fine print matters to health. *The Globe and Mail*. Retrieved from www.theglobeandmail.com/life/health/the-budgets-fine-print-matters-to-health/article1489327/

Picard, C. (1999). The level of competition as a factor for the development of eating disorders in female collegiate athletes. *Journal of Youth and Adolescence, 28*, 583–594.

Pickering, L., Granoff, D., Erickson, J., Masor, M., Cordle, C., Schaller, J., . . . Hilty, M. (1998). Modulation of the immune system by human milk and infant formula containing nucleotides. *Pediatrics, 101*, 242–249.

Pierce, M., & Leon, D. (2005). Age at menarche and adult BMI in the Aberdeen children of the 1950s cohort study. *American Journal of Clinical Nutrition, 82*, 733–739.

Pies, R. (2003). *Body image*. Irvine, CA: Continuing Medical Education. Inc. Retrieved from www.mhsource.com/expert/exp1090803c.html

Pilgrim, C., Luo, Q., Urberg, K., & Fang, X. (1999). Influence of peers, parents, and individual characteristics on adolescent drug use in two cultures. *Merrill-Palmer Quarterly, 45*, 85–107.

Pillemer, K., & Suitor, J.J. (1990). Prevention of elder abuse. In R. Ammerman & M. Hersen (Eds.), *Treatment of family violence: A sourcebook* (pp. 406–422). New York, NY: Wiley.

Pillemer, K., & Suitor, J.J. (1992). Violence and violent feelings: What causes them among family caregivers? *Journals of Gerontology: Social Sciences, 47*, S165–172.

Pillow, B. (1999). Children's understanding of inferential knowledge. *Journal of Genetic Psychology, 160*, 419–428.

Pine, J.M., Lieven, E.V.M., & Rowland, C.F. (1997). Stylistic variation at the "single-word" stage: Relations between maternal speech characteristics and children's vocabulary composition and usage. *Child Development, 68*, 807–819.

Pinker, S. (1994). *The language instinct: How the mind creates language*. New York, NY: Morrow.

Pinker, S. (1997). *How the mind works*. New York, NY: Norton.

Pinker, S. (2002). *The blank slate: The modern denial of human nature*. New York, NY: Viking.

Pinquart, M., & Soerensen, S. (2000). Influences of socioeconomic status, social network, and competence on subjective well-being in later life: A meta-analysis. *Psychology & Aging, 15*, 187–224.

Pinquart, M., & Sorensen, S. (2006a). Gender differences in caregiver stressors, social resources, and health: An updated meta-analysis. *Journals of Gerontology: Series B: Psychological Sciences and Social Sciences, 61B*, P33–P45.

Pinquart, M., & Sorensen, S. (2006b). Helping caregivers of persons with dementia: Which interventions work and how large are their effects? *International Geriatrics, 18*, 577–595.

Pisani, J. (2006, November 29). The making of . . . a LEGO. *Bloomberg Business Week*. Retrieved from www.businessweek.com/bwdaily/dnflash/content/nov2006/db20061127_153826.htm

Plaud, J., Plaud, D., & von Duvillard, S. (1999). Human behavioral momentum in a sample of older adults. *Journal of General Psychology, 126*, 165–175.

Plomin, R., & McClearn, G.E. (1990). Human behavioral genetics of aging. In J.E. Birren & K.W. Schaie (Eds.), *Handbook of the psychology of aging* (3rd ed., pp. 67–79). San Diego, CA: Academic Press.

Plomin, R., & Rende, R. (1991). Human behavioral genetics. *Annual Review of Psychology, 42*, 161–190.

Plomin, R., Emde, R.N., Braungart, J.M., Campos, J., Corley, R., Fulker, D.W., . . . DeFries, J.C. (1993). Genetic change and continuity from fourteen to twenty months: The MacArthur longitudinal twin study. *Child Development, 64*, 1354–1376.

Pluess, M., & Belsky, J. (2010). Differential susceptibility to parenting and quality child care. *Developmental Psychology, 46*(2), 379–90.

Polivy, J., & Herman, P. (2002). Causes of eating disorders. *Annual Review of Psychology, 53*, 187–213.

Polka, L., & Werker, J.F. (1994). Developmental changes in perception of nonnative vowel contrasts. *Journal of Experimental Psychology: Human Perception and Performance, 20*, 421–435.

Pollack, J.M. (1979/1980). Correlates of death anxiety: A review of empirical studies. *Omega, 10*, 97–121.

Pollitt, E., & Gorman, K.S. (1994). Nutritional deficiencies as developmental risk factors. In C.A. Nelson (Ed.), *The Minnesota Symposia on Child Development: Vol. 27* (pp. 121–144). Hillsdale, NJ: Erlbaum.

Polo, M., Escera, D., Gual, A., & Grau, C. (1999). Mismatch negativity and auditory sensory memory in chronic alcoholics. *Clinical & Experimental Research, 23*, 1744–1750.

Pomerantz, E., & Ruble, D. (1998). The role of maternal control in the development of sex differences in child self-evaluative factors. *Child Development, 69*, 458–478.

Ponds, R., Commissaris, K., & Jolles, J. (1997). Prevalence and covariates of subjective forgetfulness in a normal population in the Netherlands. *International Journal of Aging and Human Development, 45*, 207–221.

Porter, R., Making, J., Davis, L., & Christensen, K. (1992). Breast-fed infants respond to olfactory clues from their own mother and unfamiliar lactating females. *Infant Behavior and Development, 15*(1), 85–93.

Portnoy, V. (1999). Progressing from disease prevention to health promotion. *Journal of the American Medical Association, 282*, 1813.

Posner, J., & Vandell, D. (1994). Low-income children's after-school care: Are there beneficial effects of after-school programs? *Child Development, 65*, 440–456.

Posthuma, W.F.M., Westendorp, R.G.J., & Vandenbroucke, J.P. (1994). Cardioprotective effect of hormone replacement therapy in postmenopausal women: Is the evidence biased? *British Medical Journal, 308*, 1268–1269.

Poulin, F., & Boivin, M. (1999). Proactive and reactive aggression and boys' friendship quality in mainstream classrooms. *Journal of Emotional & Behavioral Disorders, 7*, 168–177.

Poulson, C.L., Nunes, L.R.D., & Warren, S.F. (1989). Imitation in infancy: A critical review. In H.W. Reese (Ed.), *Advances in child development and behavior: Vol. 22* (pp. 272–298). San Diego, CA: Academic Press.

Powell, R. (May 31, 2006). The $400 billion income shortfall: Baby-boomer women have tougher road to retirement. *Market Watch*. Retrieved from www.marketwatch.com/News/Story/Story.aspx?guid=%7B107BAF88-C68D-473E-B022-6C3533D216AD%7D.

Powlishta, K.K. (1995). Intergroup processes in childhood: Social categorization and sex role development. *Developmental Psychology, 31*, 781–788.

Powlishta, K.K., Serbin, L.A., Doyle, A., & White, D.R. (1994). Gender, ethnic, and body type biases: The generality of prejudice in childhood. *Developmental Psychologym, 30*, 526–536.

Prager, E. (1998). Men and meaning in later life. *Journal of Clinical Geropsychology, 4*, 191–203.

Prasad, K.N., Cole, W.C., & Hasse, G.M. (2004). Health risks of low dose ionizing radiation in humans: A review. *Experimental Biology and Medicine, 229*(5), 378–382.

Prat-Sala, M., Shillcock, R., & Sorace, A. (2000). Animacy effects on the production of object-dislocated descriptions by Catalan-speaking children. *Journal of Child Language, 27*, 97–117.

Pratt, M., Arnold, M., & Pratt, A. (1999). Predicting adolescent moral reasoning from family climate: A longitudinal study. *Journal of Early Adolescence, 19*, 148–175.

Prechtl, H.F.R., & Beintema, D.J. (1964). *The neurological examination of the full-term newborn infant: Clinics in Developmental Medicine, 12*. London, England: Heinemann.

Prentice, A. (1994). Extended breast-feeding and growth in rural China. *Nutrition Reviews, 52*, 144–146.

Pressley, M., & Dennis-Rounds, J. (1980). Transfer of a mnemonic keyword strategy at two age levels. *Journal of Educational Psychology, 72*, 575–582.

Pressman, E., DiPietro, J., Costigan, K., Shupe, A., & Johnson, T. (1998). Fetal neurobehavioral development: Associations with socioeconomic class and fetal sex. *Developmental Psychobiology, 33*, 79–91.

Price, C., & Kunz, J. (2003). Rethinking the paradigm of juvenile delinquency as related to divorce. *Journal of Divorce & Remarriage, 39*, 109–133.

Prigerson, H., Bierhals, A., Kasl, S., Reynolds, C., Shear, M.K., Day, N. . . . Jacobs, S. (1997). Traumatic grief as a risk factor for mental and physical morbidity. *American Journal of Psychiatry, 154*, 616–623.

Prigerson, H., Bridge, J., Maciejewski, P., Beery, L., Rosenheck, R., Jacobs, S., . . . Brent, D. (1999). Influence of traumatic grief on suicidal ideation among young adults. *American Journal of Psychiatry, 156*, 1994–1995.

Prince, A. (1998). Infectious diseases. In R. Behrman & R. Kliegman (Eds.), *Nelson essentials of pediatrics* (3rd ed., pp. 315–418). Philadelphia, PA: W.B. Saunders.

Prinstein, M., & La Greca, A. (1999). Links between mothers' and children's social competence and associations with maternal adjustment. *Journal of Clinical Child Psychology, 28*, 197–210.

Provasi, J., Dubon, C., & Bloch, H. (2001). Do 9- and 12-month-olds learn means-ends relation by observing? *Infant Behavior & Development, 24*, 195–213.

Public Health Agency of Canada. (2006a). *HIV and AIDS in Canada.* Surveillance Report to June 30, 2006. Surveillance and Risk Assessment Division, Centre for Infectious Disease Prevention and Control. Ottawa, ON: Author.

Public Health Agency of Canada. (2006b). Canada. *Canadian immunization guide* (7th ed.) (Cat. No. HP40-4/2006E). Ottawa, ON: Author. Retrieved from www.phac-aspc.gc.ca/publicat/cig-gci/pdf/cig-gci-2006_e.pdf

Public Health Agency of Canada. (2006c). 2004 Canadian Sexually Transmitted Infections Surveillance Report: Pre-Release. In *Sexual Health and Sexually Transmitted Infections.* Retrieved from www.phac-aspc.gc.ca/std-mts/stddata_pre06_04/tab1-1_ e.html

Public Health Agency of Canada (2007). Canada's physical activity guide to healthy living for older adults (Cat. No. H39-429/1999-1E). Ottawa, ON: Health Canada. Retrieved from www.phac-aspc.gc.ca/hp-ps/hl-mvs/pag-gap/pdf/guide-older-eng.pdf

Public Health Agency of Canada. (2008a). *Canadian perinatal health report* (2008 ed.) (HP10-12/2008E-PDF). Ottawa, ON: Ministry of Health. Retrieved from www.phac-aspc.gc.ca/publicat/2008/cphr-rspc/pdf/cphr-rspc08-eng.pdf

Public Health Agency of Canada (2008b). *Leading causes of hospitalizations, Canada, 2005/06, Males and females cmbined.* Ottawa, ON: Author. Retrieved on from www.phac-aspc.gc.ca/publicat/lcd-pcd97/pdf/lcd-pcd-t2-eng.pdf

Public Health Agency of Canada (2008c). *Canadian guidelines for sexual health education* (HP40-25/2008E). Ottawa, ON: Author. Retrieved from www.phac-aspc.gc.ca/publicat/cgshe-ldnemss/pdf/guidelines-eng.pdf

Public Health Agency of Canada (2008d). *Leading causes of death and hospitalization in Canada.* Ottawa, ON: Author. Retrieved from www.phac-aspc.gc.ca/publicat/lcd-pcd97/index-eng.php

Public Health Agency of Canada (2009a). *Breastfeeding and infant nutrition.* Ottawa, ON: Ministry of Health. Retrieved from www.phac-aspc.gc.ca/dca-dea/prenatal/nutrition-eng.php

Public Health Agency of Canada (2009b). *Child and youth injury in review, 2009 edition* (HP15-5/2009). Ottawa, ON: Author. Retrieved from www.publichealth.gc.ca/InjuryReview2009

Public Health Agency of Canada. (2009c). *Tracking heart disease and stroke in Canada 2009* (HP32-3/2009E). Ottawa, ON: Ministry of Health. Retrieved from www.phac-aspc.gc.ca/publicat/2009/cvd-avc/pdf/cvd-avs-2009-eng.pdf

Public Health Agency of Canada (2010). *Childhood obesity and the role of the Government of Canada.* Ottawa, ON: Author. Retrieved from www.phac-aspc.gc.ca/ch-se/obesity/obesity-eng.php

Purnine, D., & Carey, M. (1998). Age and gender differences in sexual behavior preferences: A follow-up report. *Journal of Sex & Marital Therapy, 24*, 93–102.

Putnins, A. (1997). Victim awareness programs for delinquent youths: Effects on moral reasoning maturity. *Adolescence, 32*, 709–714.

Pyne, D. (2008). *A Model of Religion and Death.* Papers on Economics of Religion 08/06, Department of Economic Theory and Economic History of the University of Granada. Retrieved from www.ugr.es/~teoriahe/RePEc/gra/paoner/per08_06.pdf

Pynoos, J., & Golant, S. (1996). Housing and living arrangements for the elderly. In R.H. Binstock & L.K. George (Eds.), *Handbook of aging and the social sciences* (4th ed., pp. 303–324). San Diego, CA: Academic Press.

Quadagno, J., & Hardy, M.A. (1996). Work and retirement. In R.H. Binstock & L.K. George (Eds.), *Handbook of aging and the social sciences* (4th ed., pp. 325–345). San Diego, CA: Academic Press.

Quick, H., & Moen, P. (1998). Gender, employment and retirement quality: A life course approach to the differential experiences of men and women. *Journal of Occupational Health Psychology, 3*, 44–64.

Raaijmakers, Q., Verbogt, T., & Vollebergh, W. (1998). Moral reasoning and political beliefs of Dutch adolescents and young adults. *Journal of Social Issues, 54*, 531–546.

Rabasca, L. (1999, October). *Ultra-thin magazine models found to have little negative effect on adolescent girls.* APA Monitor Online, 30. Retrieved from www.apa.org/monitor/oct99

Racine, T.P., & Carpendale, J.I.M. (2007). The role of shared practice in joint attention. *British Journal of Developmental Psychology, 25*(1), 3–25.

Radmacher, K., & Azmitia, M. (2006). Are there gendered pathways to intimacy in early adolescents' and emerging adults' friendships? *Journal of Adolescent Research, 21*, 415–448.

Raffaelli, M., & Ontai, L. (2004). Gender socialization in Latino/a families: Results from two retrospective studies. *Sex Roles, 50*, 287–299.

Ragnarsdottir, H., Simonsen, H., & Plunkett, K. (1999). The acquisition of past tense morphology in Icelandic and Norwegian children: An experimental study. *Journal of Child Language, 26*, 577–618.

Rahman, A., Lovel, H., Bunn, J., Igbal, A., & Harrington, R. (2004). Mothers' mental health and infant growth: A case-control study from Rawalpindi, Pakistan. *Child: Care, Health, & Development, 30*, 21–27.

Rahman, O., Strauss, J., Gertler, P., Ashley, D., & Fox, K. (1994). Gender differences in adult health: An international comparison. *The Gerontologist, 34*, 463–469.

Rahman, Q., & Wilson, G. (2003). Born gay? The psychobiology of human sexual orientation. *Personality and Individual Differences, 34*, 1337–1382.

Raja, S.N., McGee, R., & Stanton, W.R. (1992). Perceived attachments to parents and peers and psychological well-being in adolescence. *Journal of Youth and Adolescence, 21*, 471–485.

Ramey, C., & Ramey, S. (1998). Early intervention and early experience. *American Psychologist, 53*, 109–120.

Ramey, C.T. (1992). High-risk children and IQ: Altering intergenerational patterns. *Intelligence, 16*, 239–256.

Ramey, C.T. (1993). A rejoinder to Spitz's critique of the Abecedarian experiment. *Intelligence, 17,* 25–30.

Ramey, C.T., & Campbell, F.A. (1987). The Carolina Abecedarian Project: An educational experiment concerning human malleability. In J.J. Gallagher & C.T. Ramey (Eds.), *The malleability of children* (pp. 127–140). Baltimore, MD: Paul H. Brookes.

Randall, K. (2007). Examining the relationship between burnout and age among Anglican clergy in England and Wales. *Mental Health, Religion, & Culture, 10,* 39–46.

Rao G., & Rao, S. (1997). Sector and age differences in productivity. *Social Science International, 13,* 51–56.

Raskind, M.A., & Peskind, E.R. (1992). Alzheimer's disease and other dementing disorders. In J.E. Birren, R.B. Sloane, & G.D. Cohen (Eds.), *Handbook of mental health and aging* (2nd ed., pp. 478–515). San Diego, CA: Academic Press.

Ravanera, Z.R., & Rajulton, F. (1998, April 2–4). *Variations in the length of male parenting: Evidence from the 1995 GSS Canada* (Discussion Paper No. 98-6). Paper presented at the Annual Meeting of the Population Association of America, Chicago, IL. Retrieved from The University of Western Ontario, Faculty of Social Science website: www.ssc.uwo.ca/sociology/popstudies/dp/dp98-6.pdf

Ray, J.G., Vermeulen, M.J., Schull, M.J., Singh, G., Shah, R., & Redelmeier, D.A. (2007). Results of the recent immigrant pregnancy and perinatal long-term evaluation study (RIPPLES). *Canadian Medical Association Journal, 176*(10), 1419–1426.

Raz, N., & Rodrigue, K. (2006). Differential aging of the brain: Patterns, cognitive correlates and modifiers. *Neuroscience and Biobehavioral Reviews, 30,* 730–748.

Raz, N., Rodrigue, K., Kennedy, K., & Acker, J. (2007). Vascular health and longitudinal changes in brain and cognition in middle-aged and older adults. *Neuropsychology, 21,* 149–157.

Recker, R., Lappe, J., Davies, M., & Heaney, R. (2000). Characterization of perimenopausal bone loss: A prospective study. *Journal of Bone and Mineral Research, 15,* 1965–1973.

Reefhuis, J., & Honein, MA. (2004). Maternal age and non-chromosomal birth defects, Atlanta—1968–2000. Teenager or thirty-something, who is at risk? *Birth defects research. Part A, Clinical and molecular teratology, 70*(9), 572–579.

Regidor, E., Ronda, E., Garcia, A.M., & Dominguez, V. (2004). Paternal exposure to agricultural pesticides and cause specific fetal death. Occupational and Environmental Medicine, 61, 334–339.

Reichle, B., & Gefke, M. (1998). Justice of conjugal divisions of labor—you can't always get what you want. *Social Justice Research, 11,* 271–287.

Reiman, E. E., Webster, J., Myers, A., Hardy, J., Dunckley, T., Zismann, V., . . . Stephan, D. (2007). GAB2 alleles modify Alzheimer's risk in ApoE 4 carriers. *Neuron, 54,* 713–720.

Reiner, W., & Gearheart, J. (2004). Discordant sexual identity in some genetic males with cloacal extrophy assigned to female sex at birth. *The New England Journal of Medicine, 350,* 333–341.

Reisman, J.E. (1987). Touch, motion, and proprioception. In P. Salapatek & L. Cohen (Eds.), *Handbook of infant perception: Vol. 1. From sensation to perception* (pp. 265–304). Orlando, FL: Academic Press.

Remafedi, G., Resnick, M., Blum, R., & Harris, L. (1998). Demography of sexual orientation in adolescents. *Pediatrics, 89,* 714–721.

Remsberg, K., Demerath, E., Schubert, C., Chumlea, W., Sun, S., & Siervoge, R. (2004). Early menarche and the development of cardiovascular disease risk factors in adolescent girls: The Fels Longitudinal Study. *Journal of Clinical Endocrinology & Metabolism, 90,* 2718–2724.

Rendell, P., & Thomson, D. (1999). Aging and prospective memory: Differences between naturalistic and laboratory tasks. *Journals of Gerontology, 54B,* P256–P269.

Repetto, P., Caldwell, C., & Zimmerman, M. (2004). Trajectories of depressive symptoms among high risk African-American adolescents. *Journal of Adolescent Health, 35,* 468–477.

Rhodes, G. (2006). The evolutionary psychology of facial beauty. *Annual Review of Psychology, 57,* 199–226.

Rhodes, G., Lee, K., Palermo, R., Weiss, M., Yoshikawa, S., Clissa, P., . . . Jeffery, L. (2005). Attractiveness of own-race, other-race and mixed-race faces. *Perception, 34,* 319–340.

Rhodes, G., Yoshikawa, S., Palermo, R., Simmons, L.W., Peters, M., Les, K., . . . Crawford, J.R. (2007). Perceived health contributions to the attractiveness of facial symmetry, averageness and sexual dimorphism. *Perception, 36,* 1244–1252.

Rhodes, J., van Praag, H., Jeffrey, S., Girard, I., Mitchell, G., Garland, T., & Gage, F. (2003). Exercise increases hippocampal neurogenesis to high levels but does not improve spatial learning in mice bred for increased voluntary wheel running. *Behavioral Neuroscience, 117,* 1006–1016.

Rholes, W., Simpson, J., Blakely, B., Lanigan, L., & Allen, D. (1997). Adult attachment styles, the desire to have children, and working models of parenthood. *Journal of Personality, 65,* 357–385.

Rholes, W.S., & Ruble, D.N. (1984). Children's understanding of dispositional characteristics of others. *Child Development, 55,* 550–560.

Ricciardelli, L.A., & McCabe, M.P. (2004). A biopsychosocial model of disordered eating and the pursuit of muscularity in adolescent boys. *Psychological Bulletin, 130*(2), 179–205.

Richards, E.J. (2006). Inherited epigenetic variation—revisiting soft inheritance. *Nature Reviews. Genetics, 7*(5), 395–401.

Richardson, B. (2003). Impact of aging on DNA methylation. *Ageing Research Reviews, 2*(3), 245–61.

Rich-Edwards, J.W., Manson, J.E., Hennekens, C.H., & Buring, J.E. (1995). The primary prevention of coronary heart disease in women. *New England Journal of Medicine, 332,* 1758–1766.

Riediger, M., Freund, A.M., & Baltes, P.B. (2005). Managing life through personal goals: Intergoal facilitation and intensity of goal pursuit in younger and older adulthood. *The Journals of Gerontology. Series B, Psychological sciences and social sciences, 60*(2), 84–91.

Riggs, A. (1997). Men, friends, and widowhood: Towards successful aging. *Australian Journal on Ageing, 16,* 182–185.

Righetti, P. (1996). The emotional experience of the fetus: A preliminary report. *Pre- & Peri-Natal Psychology Journal, 11,* 55–65.

Rinaldi, P., Polidori, M., Metastasio, A., Mariani, E., Mattioli, P., Cherubini, A., . . . Mecocci, P. (2003). Plasma antioxidants are similarly depleted in mild cognitive impairment and in Alzheimer's disease. *Neurobiology of Aging, 24,* 915–919.

Rique, J., & Camino, C. (1997). Consistency and inconsistency in adolescents' moral reasoning. *International Journal of Behavioral Development, 21,* 813–836.

Risch, H.A., Jain, M., Marrett, L.D., & Howe, G.R. (1994). Dietary fat intake and risk of epithelial ovarian cancer. *Journal of the National Cancer Institute, 86,* 1409–1415.

Roberts, M. (May 22, 2007). Canadian women offered chance to delay motherhood. *BioNews.* Retrieved from www.bionews.org.uk/new.lasso?storyid=3447

Roberts, R.E., & Sobhan, M. (1992). Symptoms of depression in adolescence: A comparison of Anglo, African, and Hispanic Americans. *Journal of Youth and Adolescence, 21,* 639–651.

Roberts, W., & Strayer, J. (1996). Empathy, emotional expressiveness, and prosocial behavior. *Child Development, 67,* 449–470.

Robins, L.N., & McEvoy, L. (1990). Conduct problems as predictors of substance abuse. In L.N. Robins & M. Rutter (Eds.), *Straight and devious pathways from childhood to adulthood* (pp. 182–204). Cambridge, England: Cambridge University Press.

Robins, R., Caspi, A., & Moffitt, T. (2000). Two personalities, one relationship: Both partners' personality traits shape the quality of their relationship. *Journal of Personality & Social Psychology, 79,* 251–259.

Robinson, J.L., & Lee, B.E. (2000). Prevention of perinatal transmission of HIV infection. *Canadian Medical Association Journal, 163*(7), 831–832.

Robinson, N., Lanzi, R., Weinberg, R., Ramey, S., & Ramey, C. (2002). Family factors associated with high academic competence in former Head Start children at third grade. *Gifted Child Quarterly, 46,* 278–290.

Robinson, P. (2004). Youth court statistics, 2002/03 (Cat. No. 85-002-XPE). *Juristat, 24*(2), 1–20.

Robinson-Whelen, S., & Kiecolt-Glaser, N. (1997). The importance of social versus temporal comparison appraisals among older adults. *Journal of Applied Social Psychology, 27,* 959–966.

Roche, A.F. (1979). Secular trends in human growth, maturation, and development. *Monographs of the Society for Research in Child Development, 44*(3–4, Serial No. 179).

Rockwood, K., & Stadnyk, K. (1994). The prevalence of dementia in the elderly: A review. *Canadian Journal of Psychiatry, 29,* 253–257.

Roderick, M., & Camburn, E. (1999). Risk and recovery from course failure in the early years of high school. *American Educational Research Journal, 36,* 303–343.

Rodkin, P., Farmer, T., Pearl, R., & Van Acker, R. (2000). Heterogeneity of popular boys: Antisocial and prosocial configurations. *Developmental Psychology, 36,* 14–24.

Rodrigo, M., Janssens, J., & Ceballos, E. (1999). Do children's perceptions and attributions mediate the effects of mothers' child rearing actions? *Journal of Family Psychology, 13,* 508–522.

Rodriguez, C., Calle, E.E., Coates, R.J., Miracle-McMahil, H.L., Thun, M.J., & Heath, C.W., Jr. (1995). Estrogen replacement therapy and fatal ovarian cancer. *American Journal of Epidemiology, 141,* 828–835.

Roemer, I., Reik, W., Dean, W., & Klose, J. (1997). Epigenetic inheritance in the mouse. *Current Biology, 7*(4), 277–280.

Roeser, R., & Eccles J. (1998). Adolescents' perceptions of middle school: Relation to longitudinal changes in academic and psychological adjustment. *Journal of Research on Adolescence, 8,* 123–158.

Rogers, C.R. (1961). *On becoming a person.* Boston, MA: Houghton Mifflin.

Rogers, J.L., Rowe, D.C., & May, K. (1994). DF analysis of NLSY IQ/Achievement data: Nonshared environmental influences. *Intelligence, 19,* 157–177.

Rogers, R.L., Meyer, J.S., & Mortel, K.F. (1990). After reaching retirement age physical activity sustains cerebral perfusion and cognition. *Journal of the American Geriatric Society, 38,* 123–128.

Rogoff, B. (1990). *Apprenticeship in thinking: Cognitive development in social contexts.* New York, NY: Oxford University Press.

Rogosch, F., Cicchetti, D., & Aber, J. (1995). The role of child maltreatment in early deviations in cognitive and affective processing abilities and later peer relationship problems. *Development and Psychopathology, 7,* 591–609.

Roisman, G., Masten, A., Coatsworth, J., & Tellegen, A. (2004). Salient and emerging developmental task in the transition to adulthood. *Child Development, 75,* 123–133.

Rollins, B.C., & Feldman, H. (1970). Marital satisfaction over the family life cycle. *Journal of Marriage and the Family, 32,* 20–27.

Rolls, E. (2000). Memory systems in the brain. *Annual Review of Psychology, 51,* 599–630.

Romano, E., Baillargeon, R.H., Fortier, I., Wu, H.X., Robaey, P., Zoccolillo, M., Tremblay, R.E. (2005). Individual change in methylphenidate use in a national sample of children aged 2 to 11 years. *Canadian Journal of Psychiatry, 50*(3), 144–152.

Romano, E., Baillargeon, R.H., & Tremblay, R.E. (2002). *Prevalence of hyperactivity-impulsivity and inattention among Canadian children: Findings from the first data collection cycle (1994–1995) of the National Longitudinal Survey of Children and Youth* (Cat. No. RH63-1/561-01-03E). Ottawa, ON: Human Resources Development Canada.

Rosander, K., & von Hofsten, C. (2004). Infants' emerging ability to represent occluded object motion. *Cognition, 91,* 1–22.

Rosario, M., Schrimshaw, E., & Hunter, J. (2004). Ethnic/racial differences in the coming-out process of lesbian, gay, and bisexual youths: A comparison of sexual identity development over time. *Cultural Diversity and Ethnic Minority Psychology, 10,* 215–228.

Rosario, M., Schrimshaw, E., Hunter, J., & Braun, L. (2006). Sexual identity development among lesbian, gay, and bisexual youths: Consistency and change over time. *Journal of Sex Research, 43,* 46–58.

Rose, A.J., & Asher, S.R. (2004). Children's strategies and goals in response to help-giving and help-seeking tasks within a friendship. *Child Development, 75*(3), 749–763.

Rose, A.J., & Montemayor, R. (1994). The relationship between gender role orientation and perceived self-competence in male and female adolescents. *Sex Roles, 31,* 579–595.

Rose, D.P. (1993). Diet, hormones, and cancer. *Annual Review of Public Health, 14,* 1–17.

Rose, R.J. (1995). Genes and human behavior. *Annual Review of Psychology, 56,* 625–654.

Rose, S.A., & Feldman, J.F. (1995). Prediction of IQ and specific cognitive abilities at 11 years from infancy measures. *Developmental Psychology, 31,* 685–696.

Rose, S.A., & Ruff, H.A. (1987). Cross-modal abilities in human infants. In J.D. Osofsky (Ed.), *Handbook of infant development* (2nd ed., pp. 318–362). New York, NY: Wiley-Interscience.

Rose, S.A., Feldman, J.F., & Janowski, J.J. (2001). Attention and recognition memory in the 1st year of life: A longitudinal study of preterm and full-term infants. *Developmental Psychology, 37*(1), 135–151.

Rosenberg, M. (1986). Self-concept from middle childhood through adolescence. In J. Suls & A.G. Greenwald (Eds.), *Psychological perspectives on the self: Vol. 3* (pp. 107–136). Hillsdale, NJ: Erlbaum.

Rosenberg, M. (2003). Recognizing gay, lesbian, and transgender teens in a child and adolescent psychiatry practice. *Journal of the American Academy of Child and Adolescent Psychiatry, 42,* 1517–1521.

Rosenblith, J.F. (1992). *In the beginning* (2nd ed.). Thousand Oaks, CA: Sage.

Rosenkrantz, S., Aronson, S., & Huston, A. (2004). Mother-infant relationship in single, cohabiting, and married families: A case for marriage? *Journal of Family Psychology, 18,* 5–18.

Rosenman, R.H., & Friedman, M. (1983). Relationship of type A behavior pattern to coronary heart disease. In H. Selye (Ed.), *Selye's guide to stress research: Vol. 2* (pp. 47–106). New York, NY: Scientific and Academic Editions.

Rosenthal, C.J. (1987). Aging and intergenerational relations in Canada. In V.W. Marshall (Ed.). *Aging in Canada: Social perspectives* (2nd ed., Chapter 17, pp. 311–342). Markam, ON: Fitzhenry and Whiteside.

Rosenthal, C.J., & Gladstone, J. (2000). *Grandparenthood in Canada.* Ottawa, ON: The Vanier Institute of the Family. Retrieved from www.vifamily.ca/cft/grandpt/CONTEXT.HTM

Rosenthal, S., & Gitelman, S. (2002). Endocrinology. In A. Rudolph, R. Kamei, & K. Overby (Eds.), *Rudolph's fundamentals of pediatrics* (3rd ed.) (pp. 747–795). New York, NY: McGraw-Hill.

Ross, D. (1998a). *Child poverty in Canada: Recasting the issue.* Ottawa, ON: Canadian Council on Social Development. Retrieved from www.ccsd.ca/pubs/recastin.htm

Ross, D.P. (1998b). *Rethinking child poverty. Perception, 22*(1), Insight #8. Retrieved from www.ccsd.ca/perception/insite8.htm

Ross, D.P., Roberts, P.A., & Scott, K. (1998). *Mediating factors in child development outcomes: Children in lone-parent families* (Cat. No. W-98-8E). Ottawa, ON: Human Resources Development Canada.

Ross, N.A., Wolfson, M.C., Dunn, J.R., Berthelot, J-M., Kaplan, G.A., & Lynch, J.W. (2000). Relation between income inequality and mortality in Canada and in the United States. *British Medical Journal, 320*(7239), 898–902.

Ross, R.K., Paganini-Hill, A., Mack, T.M., & Henderson, B.E. (1987). Estrogen use and cardiovascular disease. In D.R. Mishell, Jr. (Ed.), *Menopause: Physiology and pharmacology* (pp. 209–224). Chicago, IL: Year Book Medical Publishers.

Rossman, T.G. (2003). Mechanism of arsenic carcinogenesis: An integrated approach. *Mutation Research/Fundamental and Molecular Mechanisms of Mutagenesis, 533*(1–2), 37–65.

Rossouw, J., Anderson, G., Prentice, R., LaCroix, A., Kooperberg, C., Stefanick, M., . . . Ockene, J. (2002). Risks and benefits of estrogen plus progestin in healthy postmenopausal women: Principal results from the Women's Health Initiative randomized controlled trial. *Journal of the American Medical Association, 288,* 321–333.

Rossow, I., & Amundsen, A. (1997). Alcohol abuse and mortality: A 40-year prospective study of Norwegian conscripts. *Social Science & Medicine, 44,* 261–267.

Rotermann, M. (2007). Marital breakdown and subsequent depression (82–033). *Health Reports, 18*(2), 33–44.

Rotermann, M. (2008). Trends in teen sexual behaviour and condom use. *Health Reports, 19*(3), 1–5.

Roth, M. (2003). Validation of the Arnett Inventory of Sensation Seeking (AISS): Efficiency to predict the willingness towards occupational change, and affection by social desirability. *Personality & Individual Differences, 35,* 1307–1314.

Rothbard, J.C., & Shaver, P.R. (1994). Continuity of attachment across the life span. In M.B. Sperling & W.H. Berman (Eds.), *Attachment in adults. Clinical and developmental perspectives* (pp. 31–71). New York, NY: Guilford Press.

Rothbart, M., Ahadi, S., & Evans, D. (2000). Temperament and personality: Origins and outcomes. *Journal of Personality & Social Psychology, 78,* 122–135.

Rothbart, M.K., Derryberry, D., & Posner, M.I. (1994). A psychobiological approach to the development of temperament. In J.E. Bates & T.D. Wachs (Eds.), *Temperament: Individual differences at the interface of biology and behavior* (pp. 83–116). Washington, DC: American Psychological Association.

Rotter, J. (1990). Internal versus external control of reinforcement: A case history of a variable. *American Psychologist, 45*(4), 489–493.

Roumeliotis, P. (2010a). *Colic and babies.* Canadian Parents, Retrieved from www.canadianparents.com/article/colic-and-babies

Roumeliotis, P. (2010b). *Newborn issues: Colic and the newborn.* Retrieved from www.drpaul.com/newborn/colic.html

Rovee-Collier, C. (1993). The capacity for long-term memory in infancy. *Current Directions in Psychological Science, 2,* 130–135.

Rowe, J., & Kahn, R. (1997). Successful aging. *Gerontologist, 37,* 433–440.

Rowe, J., & Kahn, R. (1998). *Successful aging.* New York, NY: Pantheon.

Rowland, D., & Tai, W. (2003). A review of plant-derived and herbal approaches to the treatment of sexual dysfunctions. *Journal of Sex & Marital Therapy, 29,* 185–205.

Roy, E., Bryden, P., & Cavill, S. (2003). Hand differences in pegboard performance through development. *Brain & Cognition, 53,* 315–317.

Roy, F. (2006). From she to she: Changing patterns of women in the Canadian labour force. (11-010-XPB) in *Canadian Economic Observer, 19*(6), 1–10. Ottawa, ON: Statistics Canada.

Rubin, K., Burgess, K., & Hastings, P. (2002). Stability and social-behavioral consequences of toddlers' inhibited temperament and parenting behaviors. *Child Development, 73,* 483–495.

Rubin, K., Burgess, K., Dwyer, K., & Hastings, P. (2003). Predicting preschoolers' externalizing behaviors from toddler temperament, conflict, and maternal negativity. *Developmental Psychology, 39,* 164–176.

Rubin, K.H., Hymel, S., Mills, R.S.L., & Rose-Krasnor, L. (1991). Conceptualizing different developmental pathways to and from social isolation in childhood. In D. Cicchetti & S.L. Toth (Eds.), *Internalizing and externalizing expressions of dysfunction: Rochester Symposium on Developmental Psychopathology: Vol. 2* (pp. 91–122). Hillsdale, NJ: Erlbaum.

Rubin, S., & Schechter, N. (1997). Exploring the social construction of bereavement: Perceptions of adjustment and recovery in bereaved men. *American Journal of Orthopsychiatry, 67,* 279–289.

Rubinstein, R.L. (1986). *Singular paths: Old men living alone.* New York, NY: Columbia University Press.

Ruble, D., & Dweck, C. (1995). Self-conceptions, person conceptions, and their development. In N. Eisenberg (Ed.), *Social development.* Thousand Oaks, CA: Sage.

Ruble, D.N. (1987). The acquisition of self-knowledge: A self-socialization perspective. In N. Eisenberg (Ed.), Contemporary topics in developmental psychology (pp. 243–270). New York, NY: Wiley-Interscience.

Rudd, M., Viney, L., & Preston, C. (1999). The grief experienced by spousal caregivers of dementia patients: The role of place of care of patient and gender of caregiver. *International Journal of Aging & Human Development, 48,* 217–240.

Rummens, J. (2001). *Canadian identities: An interdisciplinary overview of Canadian research on identity. Commissioned by the Department of Canadian Heritage for the Ethnocultural, Racial, Religious, and Linguistic Diversity and Identity Seminar Halifax, Nova Scotia November 1–2, 2001.* Retrieved from Metropolis Canada website: http://canada.metropolis.net/events/ethnocultural/publications/identity_e.pdf

Rutten, B. P. F., & Mill. J. (2009). Epigenetic mediation of environmental influences in major psychotic disorders. *Schizophrenia Bulletin, 35,* 10450–1056.

Rutter, M. (2007). Gene-environment interdependence. *Developmental Science, 10*(1), 12–18.

Rys, G., & Bear, G. (1997). Relational aggression and peer relations: Gender and developmental issues. *Merrill-Palmer Quarterly, 43,* 87–106.

Saavedra, M., Ramirez, A., & Contreras, C. (1997). Interactive interviews between elders and children: A possible procedure for improving affective state in the elderly. *Acta Psiquiatrica y Psicologica de America Latina, 43,* 63–66.

Safety Canada Online (2000). Youth and road crashes. Ottawa, ON: Canada Safety Council, (Vol. XLIV, No. 2). Retrieved from: www.safety-council.org/index.html

Safty, A. (1995). French immersion and the making of a bilingual society: A critical review and discussion. In L.W. Roberts & R.A. Clifton (Eds.), *Contemporary Canadian educational issues.* Toronto, ON: Nelson.

Sagi, A., Koren-Karie, N., Gini, M., Ziv, Y., & Joels, T. (2002). Shedding further light on the effects of various types and quality of early child care on infant-mother attachment relationship: The Haifa Study of early child care. *Child Development, 73*(4), 1166.

Sagiv, M., Vogelaere, P., Soudry, M., & Shrsam, R. (2000). Role of physical activity training in attenuation of height loss. *Gerontology, 46,* 266–270.

Sak, U., & Maker, C. (2006). Developmental variation in children's creative mathematical thinking as a function of schooling, age, and knowledge. *Creativity Research, 18,* 279–291.

Salari, S., & Zhang, W. (2006). Kin keepers and good providers: Influence of gender socialization on well-being among USA birth cohorts. *Aging and Mental Health, 10*(5), 485–496.

Salari, S.M., & Baldwin, B.M. (2002). Verbal, physical and injurious aggression among intimate couples over time. *Journal of Family Issues, 23*(4), 523–550.

Saltaris, C., Serbin, L.A., Stack, D.M., Karp, J.A., Schwartzman, A.E., & Ledingham, J.E. (2004). Nurturing cognitive competence in preschoolers: A longitudinal study of intergenerational continuity and risk. *International Journal of Behavioral Development, 28*(20), 105–115.

Salthouse, T. A. (1991). *Theoretical perspectives on cognitive aging.* Hillsdale, NJ: Erlbaum.

Salthouse, T. (2004). What and when of cognitive aging. *Current Directions in Psychological Science, 13,* 140–144.

Salthouse, T. (2004). What and when of cognitive aging. *Current Directions in Psychological Science, 13,* 140–144.

Salthouse, T.A. (1991). *Theoretical perspectives on cognitive aging.* Hillsdale, NJ: Erlbaum.

Saltz, R. (1979). Children's interpretation of proverbs. *Language Arts, 56,* 508–514.

Saluja, G., Brenner, R., Morrongiello, B.A., Haynie, D., Rivera, M., Cheng, T.L. (2004). The role of supervision in child injury risk: Definition, conceptual and measurement issues. *Injury Control & Safety Promotion, 11*(1), 17–23.

Sammartino, F.J. (1987). The effect of health on retirement. *Social Security Bulletin, 50*(2), 31–47.

Sampson, R.J., & Laub, J.H. (1994). Urban poverty and the family context of delinquency: A new look at structure and process in a classic study. *Child Development, 65,* 523–540.

Samuels, S., & Flor, R. (1997). The importance of automaticity for developing expertise in reading. *Reading & Writing Quarterly: Overcoming Learning Difficulties, 13,* 107–121.

Sandman, C., Wadhwa, P., Chicz-DeMet, A., Porto, M., & Garite, T. (1999). Maternal corticotropin-releasing hormone and habituation in the human fetus. *Developmental Psychobiology, 34,* 163–173.

Sandman, C., Wadhwa, P., Hetrick, W., Porto, M., & Peeke, H. (1997). Human fetal heart rate dishabituation between thirty and thirty-two weeks. *Child Development, 68,* 1031–1040.

Sandnabba, N., & Ahlberg, C. (1999). Parents' attitudes and expectations about children's cross-gender behavior. *Sex Roles, 40,* 249–263.

Sands, L.P., & Meredith, W. (1992). Blood pressure and intellectual functioning in late midlife. *Journals of Gerontology: Psychological Sciences, 47,* P81–84.

Sands, L.P., Terry, H., & Meredith, W. (1989). Change and stability in adult intellectual functioning assessed by Wechsler item responses. *Psychology and Aging, 4,* 79–87.

Sandson, T., Bachna, K., & Morin, M. (2000). Right hemisphere dysfunction in ADHD: Visual hemispatial inattention and clinical subtype. *Journal of Learning Disabilities, 33,* 83–90.

Sanford, K., & Madill, L. (2006). Resistance through video game play: It's a boy thing. *Canadian Journal of Education, 29,* 287–306.

Sanmartin, C., & Ng, E. (2004). Joint Canada/United States survey of health, 2002–3 (Cat. No. 82M0022XIE). Ottawa, ON: Statistics Canada. Retrieved from www.statcan.ca/english/freepub/82M0022XIE/2003001/pdf/82M0022XIE2003001.pdf

Sano, M., Ernesto, C., Thomas, R., Kauber, M., Schafer, K., Grundman, M., . . . Thal, L. (1997). A controlled trial of selegiline, alpha-tocopherol, or both as treatment for Alzheimer's disease. *New England Journal of Medicine, 336,* 1216–1222.

Sanson, A., Hemphill, S., & Smart, D. (2004). Connections between temperament and social development: A review. *Social Development, 13,* 142–170.

Sanz, A., Pamplona, R., & Barja, G. (2006). Is the mitochondrial free radial theory of aging intact? *Antioxidants and Redox Signaling, 8,* 582–599.

Sarkar, N.N. (2008). The impact of intimate partner violence on women's reproductive health and pregnancy outcome. *Journal of Obstetricians and Gynaecology, 28*(3), 266–271.

Sarma. S., Hawley. G., & Basu, K. (2009). Transitions in living arrangements of Canadian seniors: findings from the NPHS longitudinal data. *Social Science and Medicine. 68*(6), 1106–1113.

Sartorius, G.A., & Nieschlag, E. (2010). Paternal age and reproduction. *Human Reproduction Update, 16*(1), 65–79.

Sarwal, S., Wong, T., Sevigny, C., & Ng, L.K. (2003). Increasing incidence of ciprofloxacin-resistant Neisseria gonorrhoeae infection in Canada. *Canadian Medical Association Journal, 168*(7), 872–873.

Sato, S., Shimonaka, Y., Nakazato, K., & Kawaai, C. (1997). A life-span developmental study of age identity: Cohort and gender differences. *Japanese Journal of Developmental Psychology, 8,* 88–97.

Savage, M., & Holcomb, D. (1999). Adolescent female athletes' sexual risk-taking behaviors. *Journal of Youth and Adolescence, 28,* 583–594.

Sax, L., & Bryant, A. (2006). The impact of college on sex-atypical career choices of men and women. *Journal of Vocational Behavior, 68,* 52–63.

Scarr, S., & McCartney, K. (1983). How people make their own environments: A theory of genotype/environment effects. *Child Development, 54,* 424–435.

Scarr, S., Weinberg, R.A., & Waldman, I.D. (1993). IQ correlations in transracial adoptive families. *Intelligence, 17,* 541–555.

Schaal, B., Marlier, L., & Soussignan, R. (1998). Olfactory function in the human fetus: Evidence from selective neonatal responsiveness to the odor of amniotic fluid. *Behavioral Neuroscience, 112,* 1438–1449.

Schachter, H.M., Pham, B., King, J., Langford, S., & Moher, D. (2001). How efficacious and safe is short-acting methylphenidate for the treatment of attention-deficit disorder in children and adolescents? A meta-analysis. *Canadian Medical Association Journal, 165*(11), 1475–1488.

Schadt, D. (1997). The relationship of type to developmental issues of midlife women: Implications for counseling. *Journal of Psychological Type, 43,* 12–21.

Schaffer, H., & Emerson, P. (1964). The development of social attachments in infancy. *Monographs of the Society for Research in Child Development, 29*(3, Serial No. 94).

Schaie, K.W. (1983). The Seattle longitudinal study: A 21-year exploration of psychometric intelligence in adulthood. In K.W. Schaie (Ed.), *Longitudinal studies of adult psychological development* (pp. 64–135). New York, NY: Guilford Press.

Schaie, K.W., & Hertzog, C. (1983). Fourteen-year cohort-sequential analyses of adult intellectual development. *Developmental Psychology, 19,* 531–543.

Schaie, K.W., Nguyen, H., Willis, S., Dutta, R., & Yue, G. (2001). Environmental factors as a conceptual framework for examining cognitive performance in Chinese adults. *International Journal of Behavioral Development, 25,* 193–202.

Schaie, W., & Willis, S. (2005). *Mind alert: Intellectual functioning in adulthood: Growth, maintenance, decline, and modifiability.* Lecture presented at the Joint Conference of the American Society on Aging and the National Council on Aging as part of the Mind-Alert Program. Retrieved from http://geron.psu.edu/sls/publications/MindAlert.pdf

Schatschneider, C., Fletcher, J., Francis, D., Carlson, C., & Foorman, B. (2004). Kindergarten prediction of reading skills: A longitudinal comparative analysis. *Journal of Educational Psychology, 96,* 265–282.

Schatschneider, C., Francis, D., Foorman, B., Fletcher, J., & Mehta, P. (1999). The dimensionality of phonological awareness: An application of item response theory. *Journal of Educational Psychology, 91,* 439–449.

Scheibel, A.B. (1992). Structural changes in the aging brain. In J.E. Birren, R.B. Sloane, & G.D. Cohen (Eds.), *Handbook of mental health and aging* (2nd ed., pp. 147–174). San Diego, CA: Academic Press.

Scheibel, A.B. (1996). Structural and functional changes in the aging brain. In J.E. Birren & K.W. Schaie (Eds.), *Handbook of the psychology of aging* (4th ed., pp. 105–128). San Diego, CA: Academic Press.

Scheidt, R., Humpherys, D., & Yorgason, J. (1999). Successful aging: What's not to like? *Journal of Applied Gerontology, 18,* 277–282.

Schellenberg, G. & Ostrovsky, Y. (2008). The retirement plans and expectations of older workers. In *2007 General Social Survey Report* (11-008-X). Ottawa, ON: Statistics Canada. Retrieved from www.statcan.gc.ca/pub/11-008-x/2008002/article/10666-eng.pdf

Schieber, F. (1992). Aging and the senses. In J.E. Birren, R.B. Sloane, & G.D. Cohen (Eds.), *Handbook of mental health and aging* (2nd ed., pp. 252–306). San Diego, CA: Academic Press.

Schliemann, A., Carraher, D., & Ceci, S. (1997). Everyday cognition. In J. Berry, P. Dasen, & T. Saraswathi (Eds.), *Handbook of cross-cultural psychology: Vol. 2. Basic processes and human development.* Needham Heights, MA: Allyn & Bacon.

Schmid, T.E., Eskenazi, B., Baumgartner, A., Marchetti, F., Young, S., Weldon, R., . . . Wyrobek, A. J. (2007). The effects of male age on sperm DNA damage in healthy non-smokers. *Human Reproduction, 22,* 180–187.

Schmidt, M., DeMulder, E., & Denham, S. (2002). Kindergarten social-emotional competence: Developmental predictors and psychosocial implications. *Early Child Development & Care, 172,* 451–461.

Schmitt, D., Shackelford, T., & Buss, D. (2001). Are men really more "oriented" toward short-term mating than women? A critical review of theory and research. *Psychology, Evolution, & Gender, 3,* 211–239.

Schmitz, S., Fulker, D., Plomin, R., Zahn-Waxler, C., Emde, R., & DeFries, J. (1999). Temperament and problem behavior during early childhood. *International Journal of Behavioral Development, 23*, 333–355.

Schnarch, D. (1997). Sex, intimacy, and the Internet. *Journal of Sex Education & Therapy, 22*, 15–20.

Schoenhals, M., Tienda, M., & Schneider, B. (1998). The educational and personal consequences of adolescent employment. *Social Forces, 77*, 723–762.

Scholle, S., Buranosky, R., Hanusa, B., Ranieri, L., Dowd, K., & Valappil, B. (2003). Routine screening for intimate partner violence in an obstetrics and gynecology clinic. *American Journal of Public Health, 93*, 1070–1072.

Schöner, G., & Thelen, E. (2006). Using dynamic field theory to rethink infant habituation. *Psychological Review, 113*(2), 273–299.

Schonert-Reichl, K. (1999). Relations of peer acceptance, friendship adjustment, and social behavior to moral reasoning during early adolescence. *Journal of Early Adolescence, 19*, 249–279.

Schothorst, P., & van Engeland, H. (1996). Long-term behavioral sequelae of prematurity. *Journal of the American Academy of Child & Adolescent Psychiatry, 35*, 175–183.

Schraf, M., & Hertz-Lazarowitz, R. (2003). Social networks in the school context: Effects of culture and gender. *Journal of Social & Personal Relationships, 20*, 843–858.

Schroeder, D., & Salthouse, T. (2004). Age-related effects on cognition between 20 and 50 years of age. *Personality & Individual Differences, 36*, 393–404.

Schultz, N.R., Jr., Elias, M.F., Robbins, M.A., Streeten, D.H.P., & Blakeman, N. (1986). A longitudinal comparison of hypertensives and normotensives on the Wechsler Adult Intelligence Scale: Initial findings. *Journal of Gerontology, 41*, 169–175.

Schulz, J.H. (1995). *The economics of aging* (6th ed.). Westport, CT: Auburn House.

Schulz, R., Visintainer, P., & Williamson, G.M. (1990). Psychiatric and physical morbidity effects of caregiving. *Journals of Gerontology: Psychological Sciences, 45*, 181–191.

Schumacher, A., & Petronis, A. (2006). Epigenetics of complex diseases: From general theory to laboratory experiments. *Current Topics in Microbiology and Immunology, 310*, 81–115.

Schunk, D.H. (1983). Reward contingencies and the development of children's skills and self-efficacy. *Educational Psychologist, 75*, 511–518.

Schuster, C. (1997). Condom use behavior: An assessment of United States college students' health education needs. *International Quarterly of Community Health Education, 17*, 237–254.

Schuster, M., Bell, R., Berry, S., & Kanouse, D. (1998). Impact of a high school condom availability program on sexual attitudes and behaviors. *Family Planning Perspectives, 30*, 67–72.

Schvaneveldt, P., Miller, B., Berry, E., & Lee, T. (2001). Academic goals, achievement, and age at first sexual intercourse: Longitudinal, bidirectional influences. *Adolescence, 36*, 767–787.

Schwartz, D., Dodge, K.A., & Coie, J.D. (1993). The emergence of chronic peer victimization in boys' play groups. *Child Development, 64*(6), 1755–1772.

Schwartz, R.M., Anastasia, M.L., Scanlon, J.W., & Kellogg, R.J. (1994). Effect of surfactant on morbidity, mortality, and resource use in newborn infants weighing 500 to 1500 g. *New England Journal of Medicine, 330*, 1476–1480.

Schwartz, S.J. (2001). The evolution of Eriksonian and Neo-Eriksonian identity theory and research: A review and integration. *Identity: An International Journal of Theory and Research, 1*(1), 7–58.

Schwebel, D., Rosen, C., & Singer, J. (1999). Preschoolers' pretend play and theory of mind: The role of jointly constructed pretence. *British Journal of Developmental Psychology, 17*, 333–348.

Schweinhart, L.J. (2003, April). *Benefits, costs, and explanation of the High/Scope Perry Preschool Program.* Paper presented at the Meeting of the Society for Research in Child Development, Tampa, FL. Retrieved from www.highscope.org/Research/PerryProject/Perry-SRCD-2003.pdf

Scott, J. (1998). Hematology. In R. Behrman & R. Kliegman (Eds.), *Nelson essentials of pediatrics* (3rd ed., pp. 545–582). Philadelphia, PA: W.B. Saunders.

Sebanc, A. (2003). The friendship features of preschool children: Links with prosocial behavior and aggression. *Social Development, 12*, 249–268.

Segatto, B., & Di Filippo, L. (2003). Vita relazionale ed emozioni nelle coppie in fase di pensionamento e/o nido vuoto. *Eta Evolutiva, 74*, 5–20.

Segerstrom, S.C., Taylor, S.E., Kemeny, M.E., & Fahey, J.L. (1998). Optimism is associated with mood, coping and immune change in response to stress. *Journal of Personality and Social Psychology, 74*(6), 1646–1655.

Séguin, L., Xu, Q., Potvin, L., Zunzunegui, M.V., & Frohlich, K.L. (2003). Effects of low income on infant health. *Canadian Medical Association Journal, 168*(12), 1533–1538.

Seifer, R., Schiller, M., Sameroff, A.J., Resnick, S., & Riordan, K. (1996). Attachment, maternal sensitivity, and infant temperament during the first year of life. *Developmental Psychology, 32*, 12–25.

Seligman, M.E.P. (1991). *Learned optimism.* New York, NY: Knopf.

Selman, R.L. (1980). *The growth of interpersonal understanding.* New York, NY: Academic Press.

Semrud-Clikeman, M., Nielsen, K., Clinton, A., Sylvester, L., Parle, N., & Connor, R.T. (1999). An intervention approach for children with teacher- and parent-identified attentional difficulties. *Journal of Learning Disabilities, 32*, 581–590.

Sénéchal, M. (1997). The differential effect of storybook reading on preschooler's expressive and receptive vocabulary acquisition. *Journal of Child Language, 24*, 123–138.

Sénéchal, M., & Cornell, E.H. (1993). Vocabulary acquisition through shared reading experiences. *Reading Research Quarterly, 28*, 360–374.

Sénéchal, M., & LeFevre, J. (1998). *Long-term consequences of early home literacy experiences.* Paper presented at the annual meeting of the Canadian Psychological Conference, Edmonton, AB.

Sénéchal, M., & LeFevre, J. (2002). Parental involvement in the development of children's reading skill: A 5-year longitudinal study. *Child Development, 73*(2), 445–460.

Sénéchal, M., & Young, L. (2008). The effect of family literacy interventions on children's acquisition of reading from kindergarten to grade 3: A meta-analytic review. *Review of Educational Research, 78*, 880–890.

Sénéchal, M., Cornell, E.H., & Broda, L.S. (1995). Age-related differences in the organization of parent-infant interactions during picture-book reading. *Early Childhood Research Quarterly, 10*, 317–337.

Sénéchal, M., LeFevre, J., Thomas, E., & Daley, K. (1998). Differential effects of home literacy experiences on the development of oral and written language. *Reading Research Quarterly, 32*, 96–116.

Sénéchal, M., Thomas, E., & Monker, J. (1995). Individual differences in 4-year-old children's acquisition of vocabulary during storybook reading. *Journal of Educational Psychology, 87*, 218–229.

Serbin, L., Poulin-Dubois, D., Colbourne, K., Sen, M., & Eichstedt, J. (2001). Gender stereotyping in infancy: Visual preferences for and knowledge of gender-stereotyped toys in the second year. *International Journal of Behavioral Development, 25*, 7–15.

Serbin, L.A., Cooperman, J.M., Peters, P.L., Lehoux, P.M, Stack, D.M., & Schwartzman A.E. (1998). Intergenerational transfer of psychosocial risk in women with childhood histories of aggression, withdrawal. *Developmental Psychology, 34*, 1246–1262.

Serbin, L.A., Poulin-Dubois, D., & Eichstedt, J.A. (2002). Infants' responses to gender-inconsistent events. *Infancy, 3*(4), 531–542.

Serbin, L.A., Powlishta, K.K., & Gulko, J. (1993). The development of sex typing in middle childhood. *Monographs of the Society for Research in Child Development, 58*(2, Serial No. 232).

Serdula, M.K., Ivery, D., Coates, R.J., Freedman, D.S., Williamson, D.F., & Byers, T. (1993). Do obese children become obese adults? A review of the literature. Preventive Medicine, 22, 167–177.

Serpell, R., & Hatano, G. (1997). Education, schooling, and literacy. In J. Berry, P. Dasen, & T. Saraswathi (Eds.), *Handbook of cross-cultural psychology: Vol. 2. Basic processes and human development*. Needham Heights, MA: Allyn & Bacon.

Service Canada (2010). *Canadian retirement income calculator*. Ottawa, ON: Author. Retrieved from www.servicecanada.gc.ca/eng/isp/common/cricinfo.shtml

Settlement.org (2001). First-language literacy and heritage: Heritage language programs. Retrieved from www.settlement.org/site/LL/firstlanguage_heritage.asp

Sewell, A. (2009). Evoking children's spirituality in the reciprocal relationships of a learning community. *International Journal of Children's Spirituality, 14*(1), 5–16.

Sexualityandu.ca (2009). *Talking contraception and sexuality with your child same-sex parenting: Creating a strong family life as a gay couple. Ottawa, ON: Society of Obstetricians and Gynaecologists of Canada*. Retrieved from www.sexualityandu.ca/parents/talk-7.aspx

Shackelford, T.K. (2001). Cohabitation, marriage and murder. *Aggressive Behavior, 27*(4), 284–291.

Shaffer, D., Garland, A., Gould, M., Fisher, P., & Trautman, P. (1988). Preventing teenage suicide: A critical review. *Journal of the American Academy of Child and Adolescent Psychiatry, 27*, 675–687.

Shaffer, H.J. & Hall, M.N. (1996). Estimating prevalence of adolescent gambling disorders: A quantitative synthesis and guide toward standard gambling nomenclature. *Journal of Gambling Studies, 142*, 193–214.

Shah, S.P., Morin, R.D., Khattra, J., Prentice, L., Pugh, T., Burleigh, A., . . . Aparicio, S. (2009). Mutational evolution in a lobular breast tumour profiled at single nucleotide resolution. *Nature, 461*, 809–813.

Shannon, T. (2004). *Stem cell research: How Catholic ethics guides us*. Catholic Update. Retrieved from www.usccb.org/prolife/issues/bioethic/stemcelltest71801.htm.

Shapiro, E. (2002). Family bereavement after collective trauma: Private suffering, public meanings, and cultural contexts. *Journal of Systemic Therapies, 21*, 81–92.

Sharma, S., Monsen, R., & Gary, B. (1997). Comparison of attitudes toward death and dying among nursing majors and other college students. *Omega: Journal of Death & Dying, 34*, 219–232.

Shaw, D.S., Kennan, K., & Vondra, J.I. (1994). Developmental precursors of externalizing behavior: Ages 1 to 3. *Developmental Psychology, 30*, 355–364.

Shaw, P., Kabani, N.J., Lerch, J.P., Eckstrand, K., Lenroot, R., Gogtay, N., . . . Wise, S.P. (2008). Neurodevelopmental trajectories of the human cerebral cortex. *Journal of Neuroscience, 28*(14), 3586–3594.

Shaw, R., Ryst, E., & Steiner, H. (1996). Temperament as a correlate of adolescent defense mechanisms. *Child Psychiatry & Human Development, 27*, 105–114.

Shea, S.E., Gordon, K., Hawkins, A., Kawchuk, J., & Smith, D. (2000). Pathology in the Hundred Acre Wood: A neurodevelopmental perspective on A.A. Milne. *Canadian Medical Association Journal, 163*(12), 1557–1559.

Sher, L. (2004). Type D personality, cortisol and cardiac disease. *Australian and New Zealand Journal of Psychiatry, 38*, 652–653.

Sherman, A., Lansford, J., & Volling, B. (2006). Sibling relationships and best friendships in young adulthood: Warmth, conflict, and well-being. *Personal Relationships, 13*, 151–165.

Shi, R., & Werker, J.F. (2001). Six-month-old infants' preference for lexical over grammatical words. *Psychological Science, 12*(1), 70–75.

Shi, R., Werker, J.F., & Morgan, J.L. (1999). Newborn infants' sensitivity to perceptual cues to lexical and grammatical words. *Cognition, 72*, B11–B12.

Shields, M. (2008). *Measured obesity: Overweight Canadian children and adolescents*. (Cat. No. 82-620-MWE2005001). Ottawa, ON: Statistics Canada. Retrieved from www.statcan.ca/english/research/82-620-MIE/2005001/pdf/cobesity.pdf.

Shiner, R. (2000). Linking childhood personality with adaptation: Evidence for continuity and change across time into late adolescence. *Journal of Personality & Social Psychology, 78*, 310–325.

Shneidman, E.S. (1980). *Voices of death*. New York, NY: Harper & Row.

Shneidman, E.S. (1983). *Deaths of man*. New York, NY: Jason Aronson.

Shock, N.W., Greulich, R.C., Andres, R., Arenberg, D., Costa, P.T., Jr., Lakatta, E.G., & Tobin, J.D. (1984). *Normal human aging: The Baltimore Longitudinal Study of Aging*. NIH Publication No. 84–2450, U.S. Department of Health and Human Services, National Institute on Aging. Washington, DC: U.S. Government Printing Office.

Shonkoff, J.P. (1984). The biological substrate and physical health in middle childhood. In W.A. Collins (Ed.), *Development during middle childhood: The years from six to twelve* (pp. 24–69). Washington, DC: National Academy Press.

Shonkoff, J.P. (2010). Building a new biodevelopmental framework to guide the future of early childhood policy. *Child Development, 81*(1), 357–367.

Shore, C.M. (1995). *Individual differences in language development*. Thousand Oaks, CA: Sage.

Shu, H., Anderson, R., & Wu, N. (2000). Phonetic awareness: Knowledge of orthography-phonology relationships in the character acquisition of Chinese children. *Journal of Educational Psychology, 92*, 56–62.

Shumaker, S., Legault, C., Rapp, S., Thal, L., Wallace, R., Ockene, J., et al. (2003). Estrogen plus progestin and the incidence of dementia and mild cognitive impairment in postmenopausal women: The Women's Health Initiative memory study: A randomized controlled trial. *Journal of the American Medical Association, 289*, 2651–2662.

Sibbald, B. (2004). Legal action against GSK over SSRI data. *Canadian Medical Association Journal, 170*(4), 23.

Siegel, L.S. (2008). Morphological awareness skills of English language learners and children with dyslexia. *Topics in Language Disorders, 28*(1), 15–27. doi: 10.1097/01.adt.0000311413.75804.60

Siegler, I.C. (1983). Psychological aspects of the Duke Longitudinal Studies. In K.W. Schaie (Ed.), *Longitudinal studies of adult psychological development* (pp. 136–190). New York, NY: Guilford Press.

Siegler, R., & Chen, Z. (2002). Development of rules and strategies: Balancing the old and the new. *Journal of Experimental Child Psychology, 81*, 446–457.

Siegler, R.S. (1994). Cognitive variability: A key to understanding cognitive development. *Current Directions in Psychological Science, 3*, 1–5.

Sigman, M., Neumann, C., Carter, E., Cattle, D.J., D'Souza, S., & Bwibo, N. (1988). Home interactions and the development of Embu toddlers in Kenya. *Child Development, 59*, 1251–1261.

Silver, M., Newell, K., Brady, C., Hedley-White, E., & Perls, T. (2002). Distinguishing between neurodegenerative disease and disease-free aging: Correlating neuropsychological evaluations and neuropathological studies in centenarians. *Psychosomatic Medicine, 64*, 493–501.

Silverman, J., Ciresi, G., Smith, C., Marin, D., & Schnaider-Beeri, M. (2005). Variability of familial risk of Alzheimer's disease across the late life span. *Archives of General Psychiatry, 62*, 565–573.

Silverstein, J., & Lasky, M. (2003). *Online Dating For Dummies*. Mississauga, ON: Wiley Canada.

Silverstein, M., & Long, J. (1998). Trajectories of grandparents' perceived solidarity with adult grandchildren: A growth curve analysis over 23 years. *Journal of Marriage & the Family, 60*, 912–923.

Simoneau, G.G., & Liebowitz, H.W. (1996). Posture, gait, and falls. In J.E. Birren & K.W. Schaie (Eds.), *Handbook of the psychology of aging* (4th ed., pp. 204–217). San Diego, CA: Academic Press.

Simons, R.L., Robertson, J.F., & Downs, W.R. (1989). The nature of the association between parental rejection and delinquent behavior. *Journal of Youth and Adolescence, 18*, 297–309.

Simonton, D. (2000). Creativity: Cognitive, personal, developmental, and social aspects. *American Psychologist, 55*, 151–158.

Simonton, D.K. (1988). Age and outstanding achievement: What do we know after a century of research? *Psychological Bulletin, 104,* 251–267.

Simonton, D.K. (1991). Career landmarks in science: Individual differences and interdisciplinary contrasts. *Developmental Psychology, 27,* 119–130.

Sims, M., Hutchins, T., & Taylor, M. (1997). Conflict as social interaction: Building relationship skills in child care settings. *Child & Youth Care Forum, 26,* 247–260.

Singh, L., Nestor, S., Parikh, C., & Yull, A. (2009). *Influences of infant-directed speech on early word recognition. Infancy, 14*(6), 654–666.

Skaalvik, E., & Valas, H. (1999). Relations among achievement, self-concept and motivation in mathematics and language arts: A longitudinal study. *Journal of Experimental Education, 67,* 135–149.

Skinner, B.F. (1953). *Science and human behavior.* New York, NY: Macmillan.

Skinner, B.F. (1957). *Verbal behavior.* New York: Prentice Hall.

Skinner, B.F. (1980). The experimental analysis of operant behavior: A history. In R.W. Riebes & K. Salzinger (Eds.), *Psychology: Theoretical-historical perspectives.* New York, NY: Academic Press.

Skoe, E., Hansen, K., Morch, W., Bakke, I., Hoffman, T., Larsen, B., & Aasheim, M. (1999). Care-based moral reasoning in Norwegian and Canadian early adolescents: A cross-national comparison. *Journal of Early Adolescence, 19,* 280–291.

Skoumal, R., Chen, J., Kula, K., Breza, J., Calomfirescu, N., Basson, B., & Kopernicky, V. (2004). Efficacy and treatment satisfaction with on-demand tadalafil (Cialis) in men with erectile dysfunction. *European Urology, 46,* 362–369.

Slaby, R.G., & Frey, K.S. (1975). Development of gender constancy and selective attention to same-sex models. *Child Development, 46,* 849–856.

Slater, A. (1995). Individual differences in infancy and later IQ. *Journal of Child Psychology and Psychiatry, 36,* 69–112.

Slaughter, V. (2005). Young children's understanding of death. *Australian Psychologist, 40*(3), 179–186.

Slaughter, V., & Lyons, M. (2003). Learning about life and death in early childhood. *Cognitive Psychology, 46,* 1–30.

Slobounov, S., Moss, S., Slobounova, E., & Newell, K. (1998). Aging and time to instability in posture. *Journals of Gerontology: Series A: Biological Sciences & Medical Sciences, 53A,* B71–B78.

Smeeding, T.M. (1990). Economic status of the elderly. In R.H. Binstock & L.K. George (Eds.), *Handbook of aging and the social sciences* (3rd ed., pp. 362–381). San Diego, CA: Academic Press.

Smetana, J., Schlagman, N., & Adams, P. (1993). Preschool children's judgments about hypothetical and actual transgressions. *Child Development, 64,* 202–214.

Smetana, J.G., Killen, M., & Turiel, E. (1991). Children's reasoning about interpersonal and moral conflicts. *Child Development, 62,* 629–644.

Smith, A., Lalonde, R., & Johnson, S. (2004). Serial migration and its implications for the parent–child relationship: A retrospective analysis of the experiences of the children of Caribbean immigrants. *Cultural Diversity & Ethnic Minority Psychology, 10,* 107–122.

Smith, C., Umberger, G., Manning, E., Sleven, J., Wekstein, D., Schmitt, F., . . . Zhang, Z. (1999). Critical decline in fine motor hand movements in human aging. *Neurology, 53,* 1458–1461.

Smith, D., & Moen, P. (2004). Retirement satisfaction for retirees and their spouses: Do gender and the retirement decision-making process matter? *Journal of Family Issues, 25,* 262–285.

Smith, E.L. (1982). Exercise for prevention of osteoporosis: A review. *Physician and Sportsmedicine, 10,* 72–83.

Smith, G., & Palmieri, P. (2007). Risk of psychological difficulties among children raised by custodial grandparents. *Psychiatric Services, 58,* 1303–1310.

Smith, L., Fagan, J., & Ulvund, S. (2002). The relation of recognition memory in infancy and parental socioeconomic status to later intellectual competence. *Intelligence, 30,* 247–259.

Smith, M., Sharit, J., & Czaja, S. (1999). Aging, motor control, and the performance of computer mouse tasks. *Human Factors, 41,* 389–396.

Smith, P., White, J., & Holland, L. (2003). A longitudinal perspective on dating violence among adolescent and college-age women. *American Journal of Public Health, 93,* 1104–1109.

Smith, W. (2004, January 19). Disabling assisted suicide: Why a deadly movement hasn't been contagious. *National Review Online.* Retrieved from www.nationalreview.com/script/printpage.asp?ref_/comment/smith200401190806.asp.

Smith, Y., van Goozen, S., Kuiper, A., & Cohen-Kettenis, P. (2005). Sex reassignment: Outcomes and predictors of treatment for adolescent and adult transsexuals. *Psychological Medicine, 35,* 89–99.

Smoll, F.L., & Schutz, R.W. (1990). Quantifying gender differences in physical performance: A developmental perspective. *Developmental Psychology, 26,* 360–369.

Snarey, J., Son, L., Kuehne, V.S., Hauser, S., & Vaillant, G. (1987). The role of parenting in men's psychosocial development: A longitudinal study of early adulthood infertility and midlife generativity. *Developmental Psychology, 23,* 593–603.

Snarey, J.R. (1985). Cross-cultural universality of social-moral development: A critical review of Kohlbergian research. *Psychological Bulletin, 97,* 202–232.

Snarey, J. (1995). In communitarian voice: The sociological expansion of Kohlbergian theory, research, and practice. In W.M. Kurtines & J.L. Gerwitz (Eds.), *Moral development: An introduction* (pp. 109–134). Boston, MA: Allyn & Bacon.

Snarey, J.R., Reimer, J., & Kohlberg, L. (1985). Development of social-moral reasoning among kibbutz adolescents: A longitudinal cross-sectional study. *Developmental Psychology, 21,* 3–17.

Snow, C.E. (1997, April). *Cross-domain connections and social class differences: Two challenges to nonenvironmentalist views of language development.* Paper presented at the biennial meetings of the Society for Research in Child Development, Washington, DC.

Snyder, C. (1997). Unique invulnerability: A classroom demonstration in estimating personal mortality. *Teaching of Psychology, 24,* 197–199.

Society of Obstetricians and Gynaecologists of Canada. (2001). *The Society of Obstetricians and Gynaecologists of Canada dispels myths and misconceptions about change of life.* Ottawa, ON: Author. Retrieved from www.sogc.org/SOGCnet/sogc_docs/press/releases2001/oct12_01_e.htm

Society of Obstetricians and Gynaecologists of Canada. (2002). *The SOGC statement on the WHI report on estrogen and progestin use in postmenopausal women: Appendix: Revisions to recommendations: Canadian consensus conference on menopause and osteoporosis.* Ottawa, ON: Author. Retrieved from http://sogc.medical.org/sogcnet/pdfs/rev_recommend.pdf

Society of Obstetricians and Gynaecologists of Canada. (2004). C-sections on demand—SOGC's position. *SOGC Advisory* (March 10, 2004). Retrieved from www.sogc/org/sogcnet/sogc%5Fdocs/press/releases2004/pdfs/electivecaesareanspart%20ii.pdf

Society of Obstetricians and Gynaecologists of Canada. (2007). *SOGC Statement on CMAJ Commentary, "Human papillomavirus, vaccines and women's health: questions and cautions."* Ottawa, ON: Author. Retrieved from sogc.medical.org/media/guidelines-hpv-commentary_e.asp

Society of Obstetricians and Gynecologists of Canada. (2007b). Women's Health Information: Pregnancy—multiple births. Retrieved from www.sogc.org/health/pregnancy-multiple_e.asp

Sodhi Kalsi, P. (2003). *"The best of both worlds": Bicultural identity formation of Punjabi women living in Canada.* Canadian Association for the Study of Adult Education—Online Proceedings 2003. University of Toronto. Retrieved from www.oise.utoronto.ca/CASAE/cnf2003/2003_papers/psodhiCAS03.pdf

Soken, N., & Pick, A. (1999). Infants' perception of dynamic affective expressions: Do infants distinguish specific expressions? *Child Development, 70,* 1275–1282.

Sokol, R.J., Delaney-Black, V., & Nordstrom, B. (2003). Fetal alcohol spectrum disorder. *Journal of the American Medical Association, 290*(22), 2996–2999.

Sola, A., Rogido, M., & Partridge, J. (2002). The perinatal period. In A. Rudolph, R. Kamei, & K. Overby (Eds.), *Rudolph's fundamental of pediatrics* (3rd ed., pp. 125–183). New York, NY: McGraw-Hill.

Soldo, B.J., Wolf, D.A., & Agree, E.M. (1990). Family, households, and care arrangements of frail older women: A structural analysis. *Journals of Gerontology: Social Sciences, 45,* S238–249.

Solomon, S., Rothblum, E., & Balsam, K. (2004). Pioneers in partnership: Lesbian and gay male couples in civil unions compared with those not in civil unions and married heterosexual siblings. *Journal of Family Psychology, 18,* 275–286.

Somani, S., Hoskin-Mott, A., Mishra, A., Bois, A., Book, B.H., Chute, M., et al. (2009). Managing patients at risk for age-related macular degeneration: A Canadian strategy. *Canadian Journal of Optometry, 71*(2), 14–20.

Somers, M.D. (1993). A comparison of voluntarily childfree adults and parents. *Journal of Marriage and the Family, 55,* 643–650.

Sommer, B., Avis, N., Meyer, P., Ory, M., Madden, T., Kagawa-Singer, M., . . . Adler, S. (1999). Attitudes toward menopause and aging across ethnic/racial groups. *American Psychosomatic Society, 61,* 868–875.

Song, H.J., & Baillargeon, R. (2008). Infants' reasoning about others' false perceptions. *Developmental Psychology, 44*(6), 1789–1795.

Soori, H., & Bhopal, R. (2002). Parental permission for children's independent outdoor activities: Implications for injury prevention. *European Journal of Public Health, 12,* 104–109.

Sophian, C. (1995). Representation and reasoning in early numerical development: Counting, conservation, and comparisons between sets. *Child Development, 66,* 559–577.

Sotelo, M., & Sangrador, J. (1999). Correlations of self-ratings of attitude towards violent groups with measures of personality, self-esteem, and moral reasoning. *Psychological Reports, 84,* 558–560.

Sowell, E.R., Peterson, B.S., Thompson, P.M., Welcome, S.E., Henkenius, A.L., & Toga, A.W. (2003). Mapping cortical change across the human life span. *Nature Neuroscience, 6*(3), 309–315.

Sowell, E.R., Thompson, P.M., & Toga, A.W. (2004). Mapping changes in the human cortex throughout the span of life. *Neuroscientist, 10*(4), 372–392.

Sowell, E.R., Thompson, P.M., Holmes, C.J., Jernigan, T.L., & Toga, A.W. (1999). *In vivo* evidence for post-adolescent brain maturation in frontal and striatal regions. *Nature Neuroscience, 2*(10), 859–861.

Sowell, E.R., Thompson, P.M., Tessner, K.D., & Toga, A.W. (2001). Mapping continued brain growth and gray matter density reduction in dorsal frontal cortex: Inverse relationships during post-adolescent brain maturation. *The Journal of Neuroscience, 21*(22), 8819–8829.

Sparrow, P.R., & Davies, D.R. (1988). Effects of age, tenure, training, and job complexity on technical performance. *Psychology and Aging, 3,* 307–314.

Spelke, E.S. (1979). Exploring audible and visible events in infancy. In A.D. Pick (Ed.), *Perception and its development: A tribute to Eleanor J. Gibson* (pp. 221–236). Hillsdale, NJ: Erlbaum.

Spelke, E.S. (1982). Perceptual knowledge of objects in infancy. In J. Mehler, E.C.T. Walker, & M. Garrett (Eds.), *Perspectives on mental representation* (pp. 409–430). Hillsdale, NJ: Erlbaum.

Spelke, E.S. (1985). Perception of unity, persistence, and identity: Thoughts on infants' conceptions of objects. In J. Mehler & R. Fox (Eds.), *Neonate cognition* (pp. 89–113). Hillsdale, NJ: Erlbaum.

Spelke, E.S. (1991). Physical knowledge in infancy: Reflections on Piaget's theory. In S. Carey & R. Gelman (Eds.), *The epigenesis of mind. Essays on biology and cognition* (pp. 133–169). Hillsdale, NJ: Erlbaum.

Spelke, E.S., von Hofsten, C., & Kestenbaum, R. (1989). Object perception in infancy: Interaction of spatial and kinetic information for object boundaries. *Developmental Psychology, 25,* 185–196.

Spence, J.T., & Helmreich, R.L. (1978). *Masculinity and femininity.* Austin, TX: University of Texas Press.

Spencer, C. (2008). *Grandparent rights.* Retrieved from www.canadianelderlaw.ca/GrandparentsRights.htm

Spieler, D., & Griffin, Z. (2006). The influence of age on the time course of word preparation in multiword utterances. *Language and Cognitive Processes, 21,* 291–321.

Spitze, G. (1988). Women's employment and family relations: A review. *Journal of Marriage and the Family, 50,* 595–618.

Spokane, A., & Cruza-Guet, M. (2005). Holland's theory of vocational personalities in work environments. In S. Brown & R. Lent (Eds.), *Career development and counseling: putting theory and research to work* (pp. 24–41). Hoboken, NJ: John Wiley & Sons.

Spreen, O., Risser, A., & Edgell, D. (1995). *Developmental neuropsychology.* New York, NY: Oxford University Press.

Srivastava, S., John, O.P., Gosling, S.D., & Potter, J. (2003). Development of personality in early and middle adulthood: Set like plaster or persistent change? *Journal of Personality and Social Psychology, 84*(5), 1041–1053.

Sroufe, L.A., Carlson, E., & Schulman, S. (1993). Individuals in relationships: Development from infancy through adolescence. In D.C. Funder, R.D. Parke, C. Tomlinson-Keasey, & K. Widaman (Eds.), *Studying lives through time: Personality and development* (pp. 315–342). Washington, DC: American Psychological Association.

St. James-Roberts, I., Bowyer, J., Varghese, S., & Sawdon, J. (1994). Infant crying patterns in Manila and London. *Child: Care, Health and Development, 20,* 323–337.

Stager, C.L., & Werker, J.F. (1997). Infants listen for more phonetic detail in speech perception than in word learning tasks. *Nature, 388,* 381–382.

Stallworth, J., & Lennon, J. (2003). An interview with Dr. Lester Breslow: A pioneer in chronic disease prevention and health behavior intervention shares insights from his professional and personal experiences. *American Journal of Public Health, 93,* 1803–1805.

Stambrook, M., & Parker, K.C.H. (1987). The development of the concept of death in childhood: A review of the literature. *Merrill-Palmer Quarterly, 33,* 133–158.

Stampfer, M.J., Colditz, G.A., Willett, W.C., Manson, J.E. Rosner, B., Speizer, F.E., & Hennekens, C.H. (1991). Postmenopausal estrogen therapy and cardiovascular disease: Ten-year follow-up from the Nurses' Health Study. *New England Journal of Medicine, 325,* 756–762.

Stampfer, M.J., Hennekins, C.H., Manson, J.E., Colditz, G.A., Rosner, B., & Willett, W.C. (1993). Vitamin E consumption and the risk of coronary disease in women. *New England Journal of Medicine, 328,* 1444–1449.

Stanford, E.P., Happersett, C.J., Morton, D.J., Molgaard, C.A., & Peddecord, K.M. (1991). Early retirement and functional impairment from a multiethnic perspective. *Research on Aging, 13,* 5–38.

Statistics Canada. (1998). *The Daily* (October 28). National Longitudinal Survey of Children and Youth, Cycle 2, 1996. Ottawa, ON: Author. Retrieved from www.statcan.ca:80/Daily/English/981028/d981028.htm

Statistics Canada. (2000a). *Canada at a Glance* (2nd ed.). (Cat. No. 12-581-XPE.) Ottawa, ON: Communications Division. Retrieved from www.statcan.ca/english/freepub/12-581-XIE/12-581-XIE.pdf

Statistics Canada. (2000b). *The Daily* (October 20). Teenage pregnancy. Ottawa, ON: Author. Retrieved from www.statcan.ca/Daily/English/001020/d001020b.htm

Statistics Canada. (2000c). *The Daily* (July 25, 2000). Family violence. Ottawa, ON: Author. Retrieved from www.statcan.ca/Daily/English/000725/d000725b.htm

Statistics Canada. (2000d). *The Daily* (March 31, 2000). Health Reports: How healthy are Canadians? Ottawa, ON: Author. Retrieved from www.statcan.ca/Daily/English/000331/d000331a.htm

Statistics Canada. (2000e). *Exercise frequency.* Ottawa, ON: Author. Retrieved from www.statcan.ca/english/Pgdb/People/Health/health19b.htm

Statistics Canada. (2001a). *The Daily* (June 22). Impact of smoking on life expectancy and disability. Ottawa, ON: Author. Retrieved from www.statcan.ca/Daily/English/010622/d010622a.htm

Statistics Canada. (2001b). *The Daily* (June 28). Family violence: Focus on child abuse and children at risk. Ottawa, ON: Author. Retrieved from www.statcan.ca/Daily/English/010628/d010628b.htm

Statistics Canada. (2001c). *The Daily* (May 30). National Longitudinal Survey of children and Youth: Participation in activities 1998/99. Ottawa, ON: Author. Retrieved from www.statcan.ca/Daily/English/010530/ d010530a.htm

Statistics Canada. (2001d). *The Daily* (January 25). Television viewing. Ottawa, ON: Author. Retrieved from www.statcan.ca/Daily/English/010125/d010125a.htm

Statistics Canada. (2001e, June). Frequency of heavy drinking. In *Health Indicators* (Cat. No. 82-221-XIE). Ottawa, ON: Author. Retrieved from www.statcan.ca/english/freepub/82-221-XIE/00601/high/drink/htm

Statistics Canada. (2001f). *Children and Youth in Canada* (Cat. No. 85F0033MIE-01005). Ottawa, ON: Author. Retrieved from www.statcan.ca/english/freepub/85F0033MIE/85F0033MIE01005.pdf

Statistics Canada. (2001g). *The Daily* (October 31). Homicide statistics, 2000. Ottawa, ON: Author. Retrieved from www.statcan.ca/Daily/English/011031/d011031b.htm

Statistics Canada. (2001h). *Family violence in Canada: A statistical profile* (Cat. No. 85-224-XIE). Ottawa, ON: Author. Retrieved from www.statcan.ca/english/freepub/85-224-XIE/0100085-224-XIE.pdf

Statistics Canada. (2001i). Participation rates and unemployment rates by age and sex, Canada and selected countries (Canadian Statistics: Labour, employment and unemployment—Participation, employment and unemployment). Ottawa, ON: Author. Retrieved from www.statcan.ca/english/Pgdb/People/Labour/labor23a.htm

Statistics Canada. (2001j). *The Daily* (May 23). Deaths, 1998. Ottawa, ON: Author. Retrieved from www.statcan.ca/Daily/English/010523/d010523e.htm

Statistics Canada. (2001k). Retirement by sex, class of worker, Canada, annual average (File No. CDIT28AN). *Labour Force Survey, 2000–2001* (CD-ROM, Cat. No. 71F0004XCB). Ottawa, ON: Author.

Statistics Canada. (2002a). *2001 Census: Analysis series.* Profile of languages in Canada: English, French and many others (96F0030XIE2001005). Ottawa, ON: Ministry of Industry. Retrieved from www12.statcan.ca/english/census01/products/analytic/companion/lang/pdf/96F0030XIE2001005.pdf

Statistics Canada. (2002b). *Statistics Canada, 2001 Census.* More children living with common-law parents (Table—Distribution of children aged 0 to 14 by family structure, Canada, provinces and territories, 2001). Retrieved from www12.statcan.ca/english/census01/products/analytic/companion/fam/children

Statistics Canada. (2002c). *General Social Survey—Cycle 15: Changing conjugal life in Canada* (Cat. No. 89-576-XIE). Ottawa, ON: Author. Retrieved from www.statcan.ca/english/freepub/89-576-XIE/89-576-XIE2001001.pdf

Statistics Canada. (2002d). *Profile of the Canadian population by age and sex: Canada ages* (Cat. No. 96F0030XIE2001002). Ottawa, ON: Author. Retrieved from www12.statcan.ca/english/census01/Products/Analytic/companion/age/images/96F0030XIE2001002.pdf

Statistics Canada. (2002e). *Risk of depression, by age group and sex, household population aged 12 and over, Canada, 2000/01*(Health indicators Cat. No. 82-221). Ottawa, ON: Author. Retrieved from www.statcan.ca/english/freepub/82-221-XIE/00604/tables/pdf/1295.pdf

Statistics Canada. (2003). *The Daily,* (July 25). Sexual offences. (Cat. No. 11-001.) Ottawa, ON: Author. Retrieved from www.statcan.ca/Daily/English/030725/d030725.pdf

Statistics Canada. (2004a). *The Daily,* May 4, 2004: Divorces. Ottawa, ON: Author. Retrieved from www.statcan.ca/Daily/English/040504/d040504.pdf

Statistics Canada. (2004b). *Women in Canada: Work chapters updates, 2003* (Cat. No. 89F0133XIE), March 25. Ottawa, ON: Author. Retrieved from www.statcan.ca/english/freepub/89F0133XIE/89F0133XIE2003000.pdf

Statistics Canada. (2004c). Table 102-0511—Life expectancy—abridged life table, at birth and at age 65, by sex, Canada, provinces and territories, annual (years). Ottawa, ON: Author. Retrieved from http://cansim2.statcan.ca/cgi-win/CNSMCGI.EXE?Lang=E&ArrayId=01020511&Array_Pick=1&Detail=1&ResultTemplate=CII/CII___&RootDir=CII/&TblDetail=1&C2SUB=HEALTH

Statistics Canada. (2004d). *Self-rated health, by age group and sex, household population aged 12 and over, Canada, 2003* (Health Indicators Cat. No. 82-221). Ottawa, ON: Author. Retrieved from www.statcan.ca/english/freepub/82-221-XIE/00604/tables/pdf/1117_03.pdf

Statistics Canada. (2004e). Fact-sheet on retirement (Cat. No. 75-001). *Perspectives on Labour and Income, 5*(2), 1–7. Retrieved from www.statcan.ca/english/studies/75-001/10204/200402_04.pdf

Statistics Canada. (2004f, June 15). *The Daily* Canadian Community Health Survey (Cat. No. 82-221). Ottawa, ON: Author. Retrieved from www.statcan.ca/Daily/English/040615/d040615b.htm

Statistics Canada. (2005). *National Longitudinal Survey of Children and Youth: Home environment, income and child behaviour.* Ottawa, ON: *The Daily* (February 21). Retrieved from www.statcan.ca/Daily/English/050221/d050221b.htm

Statistics Canada. (2006). Television viewing. In *The Daily* March 31, 2006. Retrieved from www.statcan.ca/Daily/English/060331/d060331b.htm

Statistics Canada. (2007, January 17). *The Daily.* Ottawa, ON: Author. Retrieved from www.statcan.gc.ca/daily-quotidien/070117/dq070117a-eng.htm

Statistics Canada. (2008a). *Window on the National Longitudinal Survey of Children and Youth.* Ottawa, ON: Author. Retrieved from www.statcan.gc.ca/imdb-bmdi/document/4450_D3_T9_V2-eng.pdf

Statistics Canada. (2008b). *Numeracy.* Ottawa, ON: Minister of Industry. Retrieved from www.statcan.gc.ca/pub/81-004-x/def/4068737-eng.htm

Statistics Canada. (2008c). *Pregnancy outcomes 2005* (82-224-X). Ottawa, ON: Minister of Industry. Retrieved from http://dsp-psd.pwgsc.gc.ca/collection_2008/statcan/82-224-X/82-224-XIE2005000.pdf

Statistics Canada. (2008d). Early indicators of students at risk of dropping out of high school (81-004-XIE). In *Education Matters*, Ottawa, ON: Author. Retrieved from www.statcan.gc.ca/pub/81-004-x/2004006/7781-eng.htm

Statistics Canada. (2008e). *2006 census information on same-sex common-law and married couples.* Ottawa, ON: Minister of Industry. Retrieved from Statistics Canada website: www12.statcan.ca/census-recensement/2006/ref/info/same_sex-meme_sexe-eng.cfm

Statistics Canada. (2009a). *Deaths 2006* (84F0211XIE). Ottawa, ON: Minister of Industry. Retrieved from www.statcan.gc.ca/pub/84f0211x/84f0211x2006000-eng.pdf

Statistics Canada. (2009b). *Canada at a Glance 2009* (12-581-XIE). Ottawa, ON: Author. Retrieved from www.statcan.gc.ca/pub/12-581-x/12-581-x2008001-eng.pdf

Statistics Canada. (2009c). *Births 2007* (84F0210X). Ottawa, ON: Minister of Industry. Retrieved from www.statcan.gc.ca/pub/84f0210x/84f0210x2007000-eng.pdf

Statistics Canada. (2009d). *Mean age of mothers a time of delivery (live births), Canada, provinces and territories, annual (years).* CANSIM. Retrieved from http://cansim2.statcan.gc.ca/cgi-win/cnsmcgi.exe?Lang=E&RootDir=CII/&ResultTemplate=CII/CII___&Array_Pick=1&ArrayId=1024504

Statistics Canada. (2009e). *The Canadian labour market at a glance 2007* (71-222-X). Ottawa, ON: Minister of Industry. Retrieved from www.statcan.gc.ca/pub/71-222-x/71-222-x2008001-eng.pdf

Statistics Canada. (2009f). *School-age population living in low-income circumstances* (81-599-X). Ottawa, ON: Minister of

Industry. Retrieved from www.statcan.gc.ca/bsolc/olc-cel/olc-cel?catno=81-599-X2009004&lang=eng

Statistics Canada. (2009g). *2006 census: Family portrait: continuity and change in Canadian families and households in 2006: National portrait: Census families.* Ottawa, ON, Minister of Industry. Retrieved from www12.statcan.ca/census-recensement/2006/as-sa/97-553/index-eng.cfm

Statistics Canada. (2009h). *Leading causes of death, by selected age groups, by sex, Canada, 2001 to 2005* (Cat. No. 84-215-X). Ottawa, ON: Author. Retrieved from www.statcan.gc.ca/pub/84-215-x/2009000/tbl-eng.htm

Statistics Canada. (2009i). *Education indicators in Canada: An international perspective.* Ottawa, ON: Author. Retrieved from www.statcan.gc.ca/daily-quotidien/090908/dq090908b-eng.htm

Statistics Canada. (2009j). *University degrees, diplomas and certificates awarded.* Ottawa, ON: Author. Retrieved from www.statcan.gc.ca/daily-quotidien/090713/t090713b1-eng.htm

Statistics Canada. (2009k). *Employment rates of 25- to 64-year-olds, by highest level of education attained, 2007.* Ottawa, ON: Author. Retrieved from www.statcan.gc.ca/daily-quotidien/090908/t090908b2-eng.htm

Statistics Canada. (2009k). *Leading causes of death in Canada* (84-215-XWE). Ottawa, ON: Minister of Industry. Retrieved from www.statcan.gc.ca/pub/84-215-x/2008000/hl-fs-eng.htm

Statistics Canada. (2009l, November 27). *The Daily: Canada's population estimates: Age and sex.* Ottawa, ON: Author. Retrieved from www.statcan.gc.ca/daily-quotidien/091127/dq091127b-eng.htm

Statistics Canada. (2010a). *Father's Day . . . by the numbers.* Ottawa, ON, Minister of Industry, Retrieved from www42.statcan.ca/smr08/2006/smr08_051_2006-eng.htm

Statistics Canada. (2010b). *Healthy people, healthy places: Perceived life stress* (82-229-XWE). Ottawa, ON: Minister of Industry. Retrieved from www.statcan.gc.ca/pub/82-229-x/2009001/status/pls-eng.htm

Statistics Canada. (2010c, February 23). *The Daily: Deaths.* Ottawa, ON: Author. Retrieved from www.statcan.gc.ca/daily-quotidien/100223/dq100223a-eng.htm

Statistics Canada. (2010d). *Religious attendance rates, by sex, 1985 to 2008* (11-008-X). Ottawa, ON: Author. Retrieved from www.statcan.gc.ca/pub/11-008-x/2010001/c-g/11132/desc/desc001-eng.htm

Steele, J., & Mayes, S. (1995). Handedness and directional asymmetry in the long bones of the human upper limb. *International Journal of Osteoarchaeology, 5,* 39–49.

Steele, M., Hodges, J., Kaniuk, J., Hillman, S., & Henderson, K. (2003). Attachment representations and adoption: Associations between maternal states of mind and emotion narratives in previously maltreated children. *Journal of Child Psychotherapy, 29,* 187–205.

Stein, C., Wemmerus, V., Ward, M., Gaines, M., Freeberg, A., & Jewell, T. (1998). "Because they're my parents": An intergenerational study of felt obligation and parental caregiving. *Journal of Marriage & the Family, 60,* 611–622.

Stein, K., Roeser, R., & Markus, H. (1998). Self-schemas and possible selves as predictors and outcomes of risky behaviors in adolescents. *Nursing Research, 47,* 96–106.

Steinberg, L. (1988). Reciprocal relation between parent-child distance and pubertal maturation. *Developmental Psychology, 24,* 122–128.

Steinberg, L., Fletcher, A., & Darling, N. (1994). Parental monitoring and peer influences on adolescent substance use. *Pediatrics, 93,* 1060–1064.

Steiner, J.E. (1979). Human facial expressions in response to taste and smell stimulation. In H. W. Reese & L. P. Lipsitt (Eds.), *Advances in child development and behavior: Vol. 13* (pp. 257–296). New York, NY: Academic Press.

Steinhauser, K., Christakis, N., Clipp, E., McNeilly, M., Grambow, S., Parker, J., & Tulsky, J.A. (2001). Preparing for the end of life: Preferences of patients, families, physicians, and other care providers. *Journal of Pain & Symptom Management, 22,* 727–737.

Stephen, J.E., Rahn, M., Verhoef, M., & Leis, A. (2007). What is the state of the evidence on the mind–cancer survival question, and where do we go from here? A point of view. *Supportive Care in Cancer, 15*(8), 903–1010.

Stephens, T., Dulberg, C., & Joubert, N. (2000). Mental health of the Canadian population: A comprehensive analysis. *Chronic Diseases in Canada, 20*(3), 118–126. Retrieved from Public Health Agency of Canada website: www.phac-aspc.gc.ca/publicat/cdic-mcc/20-3/index.html

Sternberg, R. (1988). *The triarchic mind: A new theory of intelligence.* New York, NY: Viking Press.

Sternberg, R., & Grigorenko, E. (2006). Cultural intelligence and successful intelligence. *Group & Organization Management, 31,* 37–39.

Sternberg, R., Wagner, R., Williams, W., & Horvath, J. (1995). Testing common sense. *American Psychologist, 50,* 912–927.

Sternberg, R.J. (1987). Liking versus loving: A comparative evaluation of theories. *Psychological Bulletin, 102,* 331–345.

Sternberg, R.J., & Wagner, R.K. (1993). The g-ocentric view of intelligence and job performance is wrong. *Current Directions in Psychological Science, 2,* 1–5.

Stetson, B. (2002). *Living victims, stolen lives: Parents of murdered children speak to American about death value, and meaning.* New York, NY: Baywood Publishing Company.

Stevens, J., & Choo, K. (1998). Temperature sensitivity of the body surface over the life span. *Somatosensory & Motor Research, 15,* 13–28.

Stewart, A., & Ostrove, J. (1998). Women's personality in middle age: Gender, history, and midcourse corrections. *American Psychologist, 53,* 1185–1194.

Stewart, C. (2004). The physiology of stem cells: Potential for the elderly patient. *Journal of Musculoskeletal Neuron Interaction, 4,* 179–183.

Stipek, D., Gralinski, J., & Kopp, C. (1990). Self-concept development in the toddler years. *Developmental Psychology, 26,* 972–977.

Stobert, S. & Kemeny, A. (2003). Childfree by choice (Cat. No. 11-008). *Canadian Social Trends, Summer*(69), 7–10.

Stormshak, E., Bierman, K., McMahon, R., & Lengua, L. (2000). Parenting practices and child disruptive behavior problems in early elementary school. *Journal of Clinical Child Psychology, 29,* 17–29.

Stoutjesdyk, D., & Jevne, R. (1993). Eating disorders among high performance athletes. *Journal of Youth and Adolescence, 22,* 271–282.

Strawbridge, W.J., Camacho, T.C., Cohen, R.D., & Kaplan, G.A. (1993). Gender differences in factors associated with change in physical functioning in old age: A 6-year longitudinal study. *The Gerontologist, 33,* 603–609.

Strayer, J., & Roberts, W. (1997). Children's personal distance and their empathy: Indices of interpersonal closeness. *International Journal of Behavioral Development, 20*(3), 385–403.

Strayer, J., & Roberts, W. (2004). Children's anger, emotional expressiveness, and empathy: Relations with parents' empathy, emotional expressiveness, and parenting practices. *Social Development, 13*(2), 229–254.

Strayer, J., & Roberts, W. (2004b). Empathy and observed anger and aggression in five-year-olds. *Social Development, 13,* 1–13.

Streiner, D.L., Cairney, J., & Veldhuizen, S. (2006). The epidemiology of psychological problems in the elderly. *Canadian Journal of Psychiatry, 51*(3), 185–191.

Striano, T., & Rochat, P. (1999). Developmental link between dyadic and triadic social competence in infancy. *British Journal of Developmental Psychology, 17,* 551–562.

Stroebe, M., van Son, M., Stroebe, W., Kleber, R., Schut, H., & van den Bout, J. (2000). On the classification and diagnosis of pathological grief. *Clinical Psychology Review, 20,* 57–75.

Stroebe, M.S., & Stroebe, W. (1993). The mortality of bereavement: A review. In M.S. Stroebe, W. Stroebe, & R.O. Hansson (Eds.), *Handbook of bereavement: Theory, research, and intervention* (pp. 175–195). Cambridge, England: Cambridge University Press.

Stroebe, W., & Stroebe, M.S. (1993). Determinants of adjustment to bereavement in younger widows and widowers. In M.S. Stroebe, W. Stroebe, & R.O. Hansson (Eds.), *Handbook of bereavement. Theory, research, and intervention* (pp. 208–226). Cambridge, England: Cambridge University Press.

Stroganova, T., Posikera, I., Pushina, N., & Orekhova, E. (2003). Lateralization of motor functions in early human ontogeny. *Human Physiology, 29,* 48–58.

Students Commission. (1992). Being Canadian: Culture, heritage, and identity. Students Commission. Retrieved from http://collections.ic.gc.ca/sharing/B_C_e.html

Students Commission. (1995). History. Students commission. Retrieved from http://collections.ic.gc.ca/sharing/history_e.html

Students Commission. (2004). *The Students Commission.* Toronto, ON: Author. Retrieved from Tiny Giant Magazine website: www.tgmag.ca/index_e.htm

Stull, D.E., & Hatch, L.R. (1984). Unravelling the effects of multiple life changes. *Research on Aging, 6,* 560–571.

Sturm, J., & Seery, C. (2007). Speech and articulatory rate of school-aged children in conversation and narrative contexts. *Language, Speech, and Hearing Services in Schools, 38,* 47–59.

Sudworth, M. & deSouza, P. (2000). *Youth court statistics, 1999/00* (Vol. 21, No. 3). (Cat. No. 85-002-XPE). Ottawa, ON: Statistics Canada. Retrieved from http://www.statcan.ca/english/previews/85-002-XIE/P0030185-002-XIE.pdf

Sugisawa, H., Liang, J., & Liu, X. (1994). Social networks, social support, and mortality among older people in Japan. *Journals of Gerontology: Social Sciences, 49,* S3–13.

Suicide Information & Education Centre. (1998). *SIEC Alert: Trends in Canadian suicide.* Calgary: Author. Retrieved from www.suicideinfo.ca/library/alert/alert30.pdf

Sulkes, S. (1998). Developmental and behavioral pediatrics. In R. Behrman & R. Kliegman (Eds.), *Nelson essentials of pediatrics* (3rd ed., pp. 1–55). Philadelphia, PA: W.B. Saunders.

Sullivan, K., Zaitchik, D., & Tager-Flusberg, H. (1994). Preschoolers can attribute second-order beliefs. *Developmental Psychology, 30,* 395–402.

Sullivan, M., Ormel, J., Kempen, G., & Tymstra, T. (1998). Beliefs concerning death, dying, and hastening death among older, functionally impaired Dutch adults: A one-year longitudinal study. *Journal of the American Geriatrics Society, 46,* 1251–1257.

Suman, R. P.N., Udani, R., & Nanavati, R. (2007). Kangaroo mother care for low birth weight infants: A randomized controlled trial. *Indian Pediatrics, 45,* 17–23.

Super, D. (1990). A life-span, life-space approach to career development. In D. Brown & L. Brooks (Eds.), *Applying contemporary theories to practice.* (2nd ed.) (pp. 197–261). The Jossey-Bass management series and the Jossey-Bass social and behavioral science series. San Francisco, CA: Jossey-Bass.

Suryadevara, V., Storey, S., Aronow, W., & Ahn, C. (2003). Association of abnormal serum lipids in elderly persons with atherosclerotic vascular disease and dementia, atherosclerotic vascular disease without dementia, dementia without atherosclerotic vascular disease, and no dementia or atherosclerotic vascular disease. *Journals of Gerontology, Series A: Biological Sciences & Medical Sciences, 58A,* 859–861.

Susser, E., & Lin, S. (1992). Schizophrenia after prenatal exposure to the Dutch hunger winter of 1944–45. *Archives of General Psychiatry, 49,* 983–988.

Svrakic, N., Svrakic, D., & Cloninger, C. (1996). A general quantitative theory of personality development: Fundamentals of a self-organizing psychobiological complex. *Development & Psychopathology, 8,* 247–272.

Swaim, K., & Bracken, B. (1997). Global and domain-specific self-concepts of a matched sample of adolescent runaways and non-runaways. *Journal of Clinical Child Psychology, 26,* 37–403.

Swanson, L., & Kim, K. (2007). Working memory, short-term memory, and naming speed as predictors of children's mathematical performance. *Intelligence, 35,* 151–168.

Swanson, S.M. (1999). *Abuse and neglect of older adults.* Ottawa, ON: Health Canada, The National Clearinghouse on Family

Violence. Retrieved from www.hc-sc.gc.ca/hppb/familyviolence/pdfs/abuseneg98en.pdf

Swedo, S.E., Rettew, D.C., Kuppenheimer, M., Lum, D., Dolan, S., & Goldberger, E. (1991). Can adolescent suicide attempters be distinguished from at-risk adolescents? *Pediatrics, 88,* 620–629.

Sweeting, H., & West, P. (2002). Gender differences in weight related concerns in early to late adolescence. *Journal of Family Issues, 23,* 728–747.

Swendsen, J., & Mazure, C. (2000). Life stress as a risk factor for postpartum depression: Current research and methodological issues. *Clinical Psychology, 7,* 17–31.

Swensen, C.H., Eskew, R.W., & Kohlhepp, K.A. (1981). Stage of family life cycle, ego development, and the marriage relationship. *Journal of Marriage and the Family, 43,* 841–853.

Symister, P., & Friend, R. (2003). The influence of social support and problematic support on optimism and depression in chronic illness: A prospective study evaluating self-esteem as a mediator. *Health Psychology, 22,* 123–129.

Szyf, M. (2006). Letter from the editor. *Epigenetics, 1*(1), i–i.

Szyf, M. (2009). The early life environment and the epigenome. *Biochimica et Biophysica Acta (BBA)—General Subjects, 1790*(9), 878–885.

Taga, K., Markey, C., & Friedman, H. (2006). A longitudinal investigation of associations between boys' pubertal timing and adult behavioral health and well-being. *Journal of Youth and Adolescence, 35,* 401–411.

Tai, M.H., Chang, C.C., Kiupel, M., Webster, J.D., Olson, L.K., & Trosko, J.E. (2005). Oct4 expression in adult human stem cells: Evidence in support of the stem cell theory of carcinogenesis. *Carcinogenesis 26*(2), 495–502.

Tait, M., Padgett, M.Y., & Baldwin, T.T. (1989). Job and life satisfaction: A reevaluation of the strength of the relationship and gender effects as a function of the date of the study. *Journal of Applied Psychology, 74,* 502–507.

Takahashi, K., Tamura, J., & Tokoro, M. (1997). Patterns of social relationships and psychological well-being among the elderly. *International Journal of Behavioral Development, 21,* 417–430.

Takata, T. (1999). Development process of independent and interdependent self-construal in Japanese culture: Cross-cultural and cross-sectional analyses. *Japanese Journal of Educational Psychology, 47,* 480–489.

Talan, J. (1998, October 28). Possible genetic link found for right-handedness, not for left. *Seattle Times.*

Talbott, M. (1998). Older widows' attitudes towards men and remarriage. *Journal of Aging Studies, 12,* 429–449.

Talge, N.M., Neal, C., & Glover, V. (2007). Antenatal maternal stress and long-term effects on child neurodevelopment: how and why? *Journal of Child Psychology and Psychiatry and Allied Disciplines, 48*(3–4), 245–261.

Tani, F., Greenman, P. S., Schneider, B. H., & Fregoso, M. (2003). Bullying and the Big Five: A study of childhood personality and participant roles in bullying incidents. *School Psychology International,24*(2), 131–146.

Tanimura, M., Okuma, K., & Kyoshima, K. (2007). Television viewing, reduced parental utterance, and delayed speech development in infants and young children. *Archives of Pediatric & Adolescent Medicine, 161*(6), 618–619.

Tanner, J.M. (1990). *Foetus into man: Physical growth from conception to maturity* (2nd ed.). Cambridge, MA: Harvard University Press.

Tan-Niam, C., Wood, D., & O'Malley, C. (1998). A cross-cultural perspective on children's theories of mind and social interaction. *Early Child Development & Care, 144,* 55–67.

Tanofsky-Kraff, M., Yanovski, S., Wilfley, D., Marmarosh, C., Morgan, C., & Yanovski, J. (2004). Eating-disordered behaviors, body fat, and psychopathology in overweight and normal-weight children. *Journal of Consulting and Clinical Psychology, 72,* 53–61.

Tapanya, S., Nicki, R., & Jarusawad, O. (1997). Worry and intrinsic/extrinsic religious orientation among Buddhist (Thai) and Christian (Canadian) elderly persons. *International Journal of Aging and Human Development, 44,* 73–83.

Tarter, R., Panzak, G., Switala, J., Lu, S., Simkevitz, H. & Van Thiel, D. (1997). Isokinetic muscle strength and its association with neuropsychological capacity in cirrhotic alcoholics. *Alcoholism: Clinical & Experimental Research, 21*, 191–196.

Taylor, M., Cartwright, B.S., & Carlson, S.M. (1993). A developmental investigation of children's imaginary companions. *Developmental Psychology, 29*, 276–285.

Taylor, P., Funk, C., & Clark, A. (2007). *Generation gap in values, behaviors: As marriage and parenthood drift apart, public is concerned about social impact.* Pew Research Center. Retrieved from http://pewresearch.org/assets/social/pdf/Marriage.pdf.

Taylor, P., Funk, C., Craighill, P., & Kennedy, C. (2006). *Families drawn together by communication revolution.* Retrieved from http://pewsocialtrends.org/assets/pdf/FamilyBonds.pdf

Taylor, R.D., & Roberts, D. (1995). Kinship support and maternal and adolescent well-being in economically disadvantaged African-American families. *Child Development, 66*, 1585–1597.

Taylor, R.J., Chatters, L.M., Tucker, M.B., & Lewis, E. (1990). Developments in research on black families: A decade review. *Journal of Marriage and the Family, 52*, 993–1014.

Teachman, J. (2003). Premarital sex, premarital cohabitation and the risk of subsequent marital dissolution among women. *Journal of Marriage & the Family, 65*(2), 444–455.

Teicher, M.H. (2002). Scars that won't heal: The neurobiology of child abuse. *Scientific American, 286*(3), 68–75.

Terashima, K., Mikami, A., Tachibana, N., Kumano-Go, T., Teshima, Y., Sugita, & Takeda, M. (2004). Sleep characteristics of menopausal insomnia: A polysomnographic study. *Psychiatry & Clinical Neurosciences, 58*, 179–185.

Terman, L. (1916). *The measurement of intelligence.* Boston, MA: Houghton Mifflin.

Terman, L., & Merrill, M.A. (1937). *Measuring intelligence: A guide to the administration of the new revised Stanford-Binet tests.* Boston, MA: Houghton Mifflin.

Terracciano, A., Abdel-Khalek, A.M., Adam, N., Adamovova, L., Ahn, C.K., Ahn, H.N., . . . McCrae, R. (2005). National character does not reflect mean personality trait levels in 49 cultures. *Science, 310*, 96.

Tershakovec, A., & Stallings, V. (1998). Pediatric nutrition and nutritional disorders. In R. Behrman & R. Kliegman (Eds.), *Nelson essentials of pediatrics* (3rd ed.). Philadelphia, PA: W.B. Saunders.

Tervo, S., Kivipelto, M., Hänninen, T., Vanhanen, M., Hallikainen, M., Mannermaa, A., & Soininena, H. (2004). Incidence and risk factors for mild cognitive impairment: A population-based three-year follow-up study of cognitively healthy elderly subjects. *Dementia & Geriatric Cognitive Disorders, 17*, 196–203.

Tessier, R., Charpak, N., Giron, M., Cristo, M., de Calume, Z.F., & Ruiz-Palaez, J.G. (2009). Kangaroo mother care, home environment and father involvement in the first year of life: a randomized controlled study. *Acta Paediatrica, 98*, 1444–1450.

Teti, D.M., Gelfand, D.M., Messinger, D.S., & Isabella, R. (1995). Maternal depression and the quality of early attachment: An examination of infants, preschoolers, and their mothers. *Developmental Psychology, 31*, 364–376.

Thagard, P. (1996). *Mind: Introduction to cognitive science.* Cambridge, MA: MIT Press/Bradford Books.

Thagard, P. (2002). Cognitive science. In *The Stanford Encyclopedia of Philosophy* (Winter 2002 Edition), Edward N. Zalta (Ed.). Retrieved from http://plato.stanford.edu/archives/win2002/entries/cognitive-science/

Thal, D., & Bates, E. (1990). Continuity and variation in early language development. In J. Colombo & J. Fagen (Eds.), *Individual differences in infancy: Reliability, stability, prediction* (pp. 359–385). Hillsdale, NJ: Erlbaum.

Thal, D., Tobias, S., & Morrison, D. (1991). Language and gesture in late talkers: A 1-year follow-up. *Journal of Speech & Hearing Research, 34*, 604–612.

Tharenou, P. (1999). Is there a link between family structures and women's and men's managerial career advancement? *Journal of Organizational Behavior, 20*, 837–863.

Tharp, R.G., & Gallimore, R. (1988). *Rousing minds to life.* New York, NY: Cambridge University Press.

Thelen, E. (1995). Motor development: A new synthesis. *American Psychologist, 50*, 79–95.

Thelen, E., & Adolph, K.E. (1992). Arnold L. Gesell: The paradox of nature and nurture. *Developmental Psychology, 28*, 368–380.

Theriault, J. (1998). Assessing intimacy with the best friend and the sexual partner during adolescence: The PAIR-M inventory. *Journal of Psychology, 132*, 493–506.

Thiessen, V., & Nickerson, C. (2001). *Canadian gender trends in education and work* (Cat. No. MP32-30/00-4E). Ottawa, ON: Human Resources Development Canada. Retrieved from www.hrdc-drhc.gc.ca/arb/publications/research/2000docs/t-00-4e.pdf

Thorn, A., & Gathercole, S. (1999). Language-specific knowledge and short-term memory in bilingual and non-bilingual children. *Quarterly Journal of Experimental Psychology: Human Experimental Psychology, 52A*, 303–324.

Thomas, A., & Chess, S. (1977). *Temperament and development.* New York, NY: Brunner/Mazel.

Thomas, E.M. (2004). *Aggressive behaviour outcomes for young children: Change in parenting environment predicts change in behaviour* (Cat. No. 89-599-MIE2004001). Ottawa, ON: Statistics Canada.

Thomas, E.M. (2006). *Readiness to learn at school among five-year-old children in Canada.* (89-599-MIE-no. 004). Ottawa, ON: Special Surveys Division, Statistics Canada.

Thomas, M. (1996). *Comparing theories of child development* (4th ed.). New York, NY: Norton.

Thomas, M.H. (2000). Abstinence-based programs for prevention of adolescent pregnancies: A review. *Journal of Adolescent Health, 26*, 5–17.

Thomas, R.M. (Ed.). (1990). *The encyclopedia of human development and education: Theory, research, and studies.* Oxford, England: Pergamon Press.

Thorne, B. (1986). Girls and boys together . . . but mostly apart: Gender arrangements in elementary schools. In W.W. Hartup & Z. Rubin (Eds.), Relationships and development (pp. 167–184). Hillsdale, NJ: Erlbaum.

Thompson, G.N., & Chochinov, H.M. (2008). Dignity-based approaches in the care of terminally ill patients. *Current Opinion in Supportive and Palliative Care, 2*(1), 49–53.

Thompson, G.N., Chochinov, H.M., Wilson, K.G., McPherson, C.J., Chary, S., O'Shea, F.M. . . . Macmillan, K. (2009). Prognostic Acceptance and the Well-Being of Patients Receiving Palliative Care for Cancer. *Journal of Clinical Oncology, 27*(34), 5757–5762.

Thompson, R., & Goodvin, R. (2005). The individual child: Temperament, emotion, self, and personality. In M. Bornstein & M. Lamb (Eds.), *Developmental science: An advanced textbook* (5th ed.). Hillsdale, NJ: Lawrence Erlbaum.

Thompson, W., & Lande, R. (2007). *Alcoholism.* Retrieved from eMedicine website: www.emedicine.com/med/topic98.htm

Thorson, J.A., & Powell, F.C. (1992). A revised death anxiety scale. *Death Studies, 16*, 507–521.

Tice, R.R., & Setlow, R.B. (1985). DNA repair and replication in aging organisms and cells. In C.E. Finch & E.L. Schneider (Eds.), *Handbook of the biology of aging* (2nd ed., pp. 173–224). New York, NY: Van Nostrand Reinhold.

Tinnitus Association of Canada. (2001). *Questions & Answers.* Toronto, ON: Author. Retrieved from http://www.kadis.com/ta/faq.htm

Todd, R.D., Swarzenski, B., Rossi, P.G., & Visconti, P. (1995). Structural and functional development of the human brain. In D. Cicchetti & D.J. Cohen (Eds.), *Developmental psychopathology: Vol. 1. Theory and methods* (pp. 161–194). New York, NY: Wiley.

Toh, S., Hernández-Díaz, S., Logan, R., Rossouw, J.E., & Hernán, M.A. (2010). Coronary heart disease in postmenopausal recipients of estrogen plus progestin therapy: Does the increased risk ever disappear? *Annals of Internal Medicine, 152*(4), 211–217.

Tomasello, M. (1999). *The cultural origins of human cognition.* Cambridge, MA: Harvard University Press.

Tomasello, M. (2008). *Origins of human communication.* Cambridge, MA: MIT Press.

Tomassini, C., Kalogirou, S., Grundy, E., Fokkema, T., Martikainen, P., van Groenou, M., . . . Karisto, A. (2004). Contacts between elderly parents and their children in four European countries: Current patterns and future prospects. *European Journal of Ageing, 1,* 54–63.

Tomlinson-Keasey, C., Eisert, D.C., Kahle, L.R., Hardy-Brown, K., & Keasey, B. (1979). The structure of concrete operational thought. *Child Development, 50,* 1153–1163.

Tooby, J., Cosmides, L. & Barrett, H. C. (2005). Resolving the debate on innate ideas: Learnability constraints and the evolved interpenetration of motivational and conceptual functions. In Carruthers, P., Laurence, S. & Stich, S. (Eds.), *The Innate Mind: Structure and Content.* New York, NY: Oxford University Press.

Toomela, A. (1999). Drawing development: Stages in the representation of a cube and a cylinder. *Child Development, 70,* 1141–1150.

Torgerson, D., Thomas, R., Campbell, M., & Reid, D. (1997). Alcohol consumption and age of maternal menopause are associated with menopause onset. *Maturitas, 26,* 21–25.

Torgesen, J., Wagner, R., Rashotte, C., Rose, E., Lindamood, P., Conway, T. & Garvan, C. (1999). Preventing reading failure in young children with phonological processing disabilities: Group and individual responses to instruction. *Journal of Educational Psychology, 91,* 594–603.

Toronto District School Board (2001). *Facts and figures about the TDSB.* Toronto, ON: Author. Retrieved from www.tdsb.on.ca/communications/TDSBFacts.html

Tortora, G., & Grabowski, S. (1993). *Principles of anatomy and physiology.* New York, NY: HarperCollins.

Toy Retailers Association (n.d.) *Toy of the Century.* Retrieved from www.toyretailersassociation.co.uk/toty/totc20.htm

Traffic Injury Research Foundation (2001). *Graduated licensing: A blueprint for North America.* Ottawa, ON: Author.

Trasler, J.M. (2009). Epigenetics in spermatogenesis. *Molecular and Cellular Endocrinology, 306,* 33–36.

Trasler, J.M., & Doerksen, T. (1999). Teratogen update: Paternal exposures-reproductive risks. *Teratology, 60*(3), 161–172.

Trautner, H., Gervai, J., & Nemeth, R. (2003). Appearance-reality distinction and development of gender constancy understanding in children. *International Journal of Behavioral Development, 27,* 275–283.

Treas, J. & Giesen, D. (2000). Sexual infidelity among married and cohabiting Americans. *Journal of Marriage & the Family, 62*(1), 48–60.

Trebay, G. (2008, February 7). The Vanishing Point. *The New York Times.* Retrieved from www.nytimes.com/2008/02/07/fashion/shows/07DIARY.html?pagewanted=1

Trehub, S.E., & Rabinovitch, M.S. (1972). Auditory-linguistic sensitivity in early infancy. *Developmental Psychology, 6,* 74–77.

Trehub, S.E., Bull, D., & Thorpe, L.A. (1984). Infants' perception of melodies: The role of melodic contour. *Child Development, 55,* 821–830.

Trehub, S.E., Plantinga, J., & Brcic, J. (2009). Infants detect cross-modal cues to identity in speech and singing. *Annals of the New York Academy of Sciences, 1169,* 508–511.

Trehub, S.E., Thorpe, L.A., & Morrongiello, B.A. (1985). Infants' perception of melodies: Changes in a single tone. *Infant Behavior & Development, 8,* 213–223.

Tremblay, D.G. (2010). Paid parental leave: An employee right or still an ideal? An analysis of the situation in Quebec in comparison with North America. *Employee Responsibilities and Rights Journal, 22*(2), 83–100.

Tremblay, R.E., Nagin, D.S., Séguin, J.R., Zoccolillo, M., Zelazo, P.D., Boivin, M., . . . Japel, C. (2004). Physical aggression during early childhood: trajectories and predictors. *Canadian Child and Adolescent Psychiatry Review, 14*(1), 3–9.

Tremblay, M.S., Shields, M., Laviolette, M., Craig, C.L., Janssen, I., & Connor Gorber, S. (2010). Fitness of Canadian children and youth: Results from the 2007–2009 Canadian Health Measures Survey. *Health Reports, 21*(1), 7–20.

Tremblay, R.E. (2000). The origins of youth violence. *Isuma, 1*(2), 19–24.

Tremblay, R.E. (2008a). Development of physical aggression from early childhood to adulthood. In Centres of Excellence for Children's Well-Being (Eds.), *Encyclopedia on Early Childhood Development.* Retrieved from www.enfant-encyclopedie.com/pages/PDF/TremblayANGxp_rev.pdf

Tremblay, R.E. (2008b). Understanding development and prevention of chronic physical aggression: Towards experimental epigenetic studies. *Philosophical Transaction of the Royal Society B, 363,* 2613–2622.

Tremblay, R.E. (2010). Developmental origins of disruptive behaviour problems: the "original sin" hypothesis, epigenetics and their consequences for prevention. *Journal of Child Psychology and Psychiatry, 51*(4), 341–367.

Tremblay, R.E., Boulerice, B., Harden, P.W., McDuff, P., Perusse, D., Pihl, R.O., & Zoccolillo, M. (1996). Do children in Canada become more aggressive as they approach adolescence? In Human Resources Development Canada & Statistics Canada, *Growing up in Canada: National longitudinal survey of children and youth.* Ottawa, ON: Author.

Tremblay, R.E., Masse, L.C., Vitaro, F., & Dobkin, P.L. (1995). The impact of friends' deviant behavior on early onset of delinquency: Longitudinal data from 6 to 13 years of age. *Development and Psychology, 7,* 649–667.

Trifunov, W. (2009). *The practice of bed sharing: A systematic literature and policy review.* Ottawa, ON: Public Health Agency of Canada. Retrieved from www.phac-aspc.gc.ca/dca-dea/prenatal/pbs-ppl-eng.php

Triggs-Raine, B., Richard, M., Wasel, N., Prence, E.M., & Natowicz, M.R. (1995) Mutational analyses of Tay-Sachs disease: Studies on Tay-Sachs carriers of French Canadian background living in New England. *American Journal of Human Genetics, 56*(4), 870–879.

Trivers, R. (1972). Parental investment and sexual selection. In B. Campbell (Ed.), *Sexual selection and the descent of man: 1871–1971* (pp. 136–179). Chicago, IL: Aldine.

Trocmé, N., Durrant, J., Ensom, R., & Marwah, I. (2004). *Physical abuse of children in the context of punishment.* CECW Information Sheet #8E. Toronto, Canada: Faculty of Social Work, University of Toronto.

Trocmé, N., Fallon, B., MacLaurin, B., Daciuk, J., Felstiner, T.B., Tommyr, L., . . . Black, T. (2005). *Canadian Incidence Study of Reported Child Abuse and Neglect—2003: Major Findings* (HP5-1/2005E). Ottawa, ON: Minister of Public Works and Government Services Canada. Retrieved from www.phac-aspc.gc.ca/cm-vee/csca-ecve/pdf/childabuse_final_e.pdf

Trovato, F. (1991). Early childhood mortality 1926–1986. *Canadian Social Trends (Summer),* 6–10. Ottawa, ON: Statistics Canada.

Truluck, J., & Courtenay, B. (1999). Learning style preferences among older adults. *Educational Gerontology, 25,* 221–236.

Trusty, J. (1999). Effects of eighth-grade parental involvement on late adolescents' educational expectations. *Journal of Research & Development in Education, 32,* 224–233.

Tsang, P. (1998). Age, attention, expertise, and time-sharing performance. *Psychology & Aging, 13,* 323–347.

Tsang, W., & Hui-Chan, C. (2003). Effects of Tai Chi on joint proprioception and stability limits in elderly subjects. *Medicine & Science in Sports & Exercise, 35,* 1962–1971.

Tsang, W., & Hui-Chan, C. (2004). Effects of exercise on joint sense. *Medicine and Science in Sports and Exercise, 36*(4), 658–667.

Tu, J.V., Nardi, L., Fang, J., Liu, J., Khalid, L., & Johansen, H. (2009). National trends in rates of death and hospital admissions related to acute myocardial infarction, heart failure and stroke, 1994–2004. *Canadian Medical Association Journal, 180*(13), 188–125. doi:10.1503/cmaj.081197.

Tulving, E. (1972). Episodic and semantic memory. In E. Tulving & W. Donaldson (Eds.), *Organization of memory* (pp. 381–403). New York, NY: Academic Press.

Tulving, E. (1999). *What is episodic memory and why is it unique?* Bauer Colloquium Series. Toronto, ON: University of Toronto. Retrieved from www.bio.brandeis.edu/news/bauer/1999/tulving.html

Tulving, E. (2004). Episodic memory: from mind to brain. *Revue Neurologique (Paris), 160*(4), 9–23.

Turcotte, M. & Schellenberg, G. (2007). *A portrait of seniors in Canada 2006* (89-519-XIE). Ottawa, ON: Statistics Canada. Retrieved from www.statcan.gc.ca/pub/89-519-x/89-519-x2006001-eng.pdf

Turcotte, M. (2006). Parents with adult children living at home (11–008). *Canadian Social Trends, 80*, 2–9.

Turcotte, M. (2007). Time spent with family during a typical work-day, 1986 to 2005 (11–008). *Canadian Social Trends, 83*, 2–11.

Turcotte, N., & Schellenberg, G. (2007). *A Portrait of Seniors in Canada 2006* (89–519 XPE). Ottawa, ON: Statistics Canada.

Turcotte, P. (2003). Update on families (Cat. No. 11-008-XPE). *Canadian Social Trends, Summer*(69), 11–13.

Turcotte, P. (2003). *Update on families.* Ottawa, ON: Statistics Canada. Retrieved from www.statcan.gc.ca/pub/11-008-x/2003001/article/6529-eng.pdf

Turnage, B.F. (2004). African American mother-daughter relationships mediating daughter's self-esteem. *Child and Adolescent Social Work Journal, 21*(2), 155–173.

Turner, N.E., Toneatto, T., & Stanovich, K. (1999, February). Cognitive Biases in Problem Gamblers. *New Directions in Gambling Research Conference of the National Centre for Responsible Gaming.*

Twenge, J., Campbell, W., & Foster, C. (2003). Parenthood and marital satisfaction: A meta-analytic review. *Journal of Marriage & the Family, 65*, 574–583.

Twycross, R.G. (1996). Euthanasia: Going Dutch? *Journal of the Royal Society of Medicine, 89*, 61–63.

Tzschentke, B., & Plagemann, A. (2006). Imprinting and critical periods in early development. *World's Poultry Science Journal, 62*(4), 626–637.

Uemura, N., Okamoto, S., Yamamoto, S., Matsumura, N., Yamaguchi, S., Yamakido, M., . . . Schlemper, R. (2001). *Helicobacter pylori* infection and the development of gastric cancer. *New England Journal of Medicine, 345*, 784–789.

Uhlenberg, P., Cooney, T., & Boyd, R. (1990). Divorce for women after midlife. *Journals of Gerontology: Social Sciences, 45*, S3–11.

Umberson, D. (1992). Relationships between adult children and their parents: Psychological consequences for both generations. *Journal of Marriage and the Family, 54*, 664–674.

Underwood, M. (1997). Peer social status and children's understanding of the expression and control of positive and negative emotions. *Merrill-Palmer Quarterly, 43*, 610–634.

Underwood, M.K., Kupersmidt, J.B., & Coie, J.D. (1996). Childhood peer sociometric status and aggression as predictors of adolescent childbearing. *Journal of Research on Adolescence, 6*, 201–224.

United Nations Development Programme (2009). *Human development report 2009.* New York, NY: Author. Retrieved from http://hdr.undp.org/en/statistics/indices/hdi/

Uno, D., Florsheim, P., & Uchino, B. (1998). Psychosocial mechanisms underlying quality of parenting among Mexican-American and White adolescent mothers. *Journal of Youth & Adolescence, 27*, 585–605.

Updegraff, K., & Obeidallah, D. (1999). Young adolescents' patterns of involvement with siblings and friends. *Social Development, 8*, 52–69.

Urban, J., Carlson, E., Egeland, B., & Sroufe, L A. (1991). Patterns of individual adaptation across childhood. *Development and Psychopathology, 3*, 445–460.

Urberg, K., Degirmencioglu, S., & Pilgrim, C. (1997). Close friend and group influence on adolescent cigarette smoking and alcohol use. *Developmental Psychology, 33*, 834–844.

Urberg, K., Degirmencioglu, S., & Tolson, J. (1998). Adolescent friendship selection and termination: The role of similarity. *Journal of Social & Personal Relationships, 15*, 703–710.

Urberg, K.A., Degirmencioglu, S.M., Tolson, J.M., & Halliday-Scher, K. (1995). The structure of adolescent peer networks. *Developmental Psychology, 31*, 540–547.

Urdan, T. (1997). Examining the relations among early adolescent students' goals and friends' orientation toward effort and achievement in school. *Contemporary Educational Psychology, 22*, 165–191.

Uriarte-Landa, J., & Hebert, B. (2009). Work-life balance of older workers. In *Perspectives* (75-001-X). Ottawa, ON: Statistics Canada. Retrieved from www.statcan.gc.ca/pub/75-001-x/2009110/pdf/10944-eng.pdf

Ushikubo, M. (1998). A study of factors facilitating and inhibiting the willingness of the institutionalized disabled elderly for rehabilitation: A United States–Japanese comparison. Journal of Cross-Cultural Gerontology, 13, 127–157.

Uylings, H. (2006). Development of the human cortex and the concept of "critical" or "sensitive" periods. *Language Learning, 56*, 59–90.

Vaeisaenen, L. (1998). Family grief and recovery process when a baby dies. *Psychiatria Fennica, 29*, 163–174.

Vaillant, G. (2002). *Aging well: Surprising guideposts to a happier life from the landmark Harvard Study of Adult Development.* New York, NY: Little, Brown & Company.

Vaillant, G.E. (1991). The association of ancestral longevity with successful aging. *Journals of Gerontology: Psychological Sciences, 46*, P292–298.

Valenza, E., Leo, I., Gava, L., & Simion, F. (2006). Perceptual completion in newborn human infants. *Child Development, 8*, 1–12.

Van Allen, M.I., McCourt, C., & Lee, N.S. (2002). *Preconception health: folic acid for the primary prevention of neural tube defects. A resource document for health professionals, 2002* (Cat. Number H39-607/2002E). Ottawa, ON: Minister of Public Works and Government Services Canada.

van Balen, F. (1998). Development of IVF children. *Developmental Review, 18*, 30–46.

van Bommel, H. (1992). *Dying for care: Hospice care or euthanasia.* Toronto, ON: NC Press Limited.

van Bommel, H. (2002). *Family hospice care: Pre-planning and care guide* (16th Anniversary Edition). Scarborough, ON: Resources Supporting Family and Community Legacies Inc. Retrieved from www.legacies.ca/Family_Hospice_ Care%20Index.htm

Van Boxtel, M., Paas, F., Houx, P., Adam, J., Teeken, J., & Jolles, J. (1997). Aerobic capacity and cognitive performance in a cross-sectional aging study. *Medicine & Science in Sports & Exercise, 29*, 1357–1365.

van den Boom, D. (1995). Do first-year intervention effects endure? Follow-up during toddlerhood of a sample of Dutch irritable infants. *Child Development, 66*, 1798–1816.

van den Boom, D.C. (1994). The influence of temperament and mothering on attachment and exploration: An experimental manipulation of sensitive responsiveness among lower-class mothers with irritable infants. *Child Development, 65*, 1457–1477.

Van den Broek, P., Lynch, J., Naslund, J., Ievers-Landis, C., & Verduin, K. (2004). The development of comprehension of main ideas in narratives: Evidence from the selection of titles. *Journal of Educational Psychology, 96*, 707–718.

van der Molen, M., & Molenaar, P. (1994). Cognitive psychophysiology: A window to cognitive development and brain maturation. In G. Dawson & K. Fischer (Eds.), *Human behavior and the developing brain* (pp. 456–492). New York, NY: Guilford Press.

van Doornen, L., Snieder, H., & Boomsma, D. (1998). Serum lipids and cardiovascular reactivity to stress. *Biological Psychology, 47*, 279–297.

Van Duuren, M., Kendell-Scott, L., & Stark, N. (2003). Early aesthetic choices: Infant preferences for attractive premature infant faces. *International Journal of Behavioral Development, 27*, 212–219.

van Grootheest, D., Beekman, A., van Groenou, M., & Deeg, D. (1999). Sex differences in depression after widowhood: Do men suffer more? *Social Psychiatry & Psychiatric Epidemiology, 34*, 391–398.

van Heeringen, K. (2003). The neurobiology of suicide and suicidality. *Canadian Journal of Psychiatry, 48*(5), 292–300.

van IJzendoorn, M. (2005). Attachment at an early age (0–5) and its impact on children's development. In Centres of Excellence for Children's Well-Being (Ed.), *Encyclopedia on Early Childhood Development*. Retrieved from www.excellence-earlychildhood.ca/documents/van_IJzendoornANGxp.pdf

van IJzendoorn, M.H. (1995). Adult attachment representations, parental responsiveness, and infant attachment: A meta-analysis on the predictive validity of the Adult Attachment Interview. *Psychological Bulletin, 117*, 387–403.

Van Lange, P., DeBruin, E., Otten, W., & Joireman, J. (1997). Development of prosocial, individualistic, and competitive orientations: Theory and preliminary evidence. *Journal of Personality & Social Psychology, 73*, 733–746.

Van Mierlo, J., & Van den Bulck, J. (2004). Benchmarking the cultivation approach to video game effects: a comparison of the correlates of TV viewing and game play. *Journal of Adolescence, 27*(1), 97–111.

van Solinge, H. (2007). Health change in retirement: A longitudinal study among older workers in the Netherlands. *Research on Aging, 29*, 225–256.

van Wel, F. (1994). "I count my parents among my best friends": Youths' bonds with parents and friends in the Netherlands. *Journal of Marriage and the Family, 56*, 835–843.

Vanier Institute of the Family (2001). Did you know? How much time do Canadians spend watching television? Ottawa, ON: Author. Retrieved from www.vifamily.ca/faqs/didyouknow.htm

Vartanian, L. (2000). Revisiting the imaginary audience and personal fable constructs of adolescent egocentrism: A conceptual review. *Adolescence, 35*, 639–661.

Vartanian, L. (2001). Adolescents' reactions to hypothetical peer group conversations: Evidence for an imaginary audience? *Adolescence, 36*, 347–380.

Vaudry, W., Lee. B., Rosychuk, R., & Pelletier, L. (2009). Congenital cytomegalovirus infection. *Canadian Paediatric Surveillance Program (CPSP) 2008 Results*, 17–20.

Veenhof, B., & Timusk, P. (2009). Online activities of Canadian boomers and seniors (Chart 1) (Cat. no. 11-008-X). *Canadian Social Trends, Winter*, (88), 25–32.

Venkatraman, M.M. (1995). A cross-cultural study of the subjective well-being of married elderly persons in the United States and India. *Journals of Gerontology: Social Sciences, 50B*, S35–44.

Verbrugge, L.M. (1989). Gender, aging, and health. In K.S. Markides (Ed.), *Aging and health* (pp. 23–78). Newbury Park, CA: Sage.

Verbrugge, L.M., & Wingard, D.L. (1987). Sex differentials in health and mortality. *Women and Health, 12*, 103–145.

Verhaeghen, P., Marcoen, A., & Goossens, L. (1992). Improving memory performance in the aged through mnemonic training: A meta-analytic study. Psychology and Aging, 7, 242–251.

Verhaeghen, P., & Marcoen, A. (1993). Memory aging as a general phenomenon: Episodic recall of older adults is a function of episodic recall of young adults. *Psychology and Aging, 8*, 380–388.

Verhaeghen, P., Marcoen, A., & Goossens, L. (1992). Improving memory performance in the aged through mnemonic training: A meta-analytic study. *Psychology and Aging, 7*, 242–251.

Verkooijen, K., de Vries, N., & Nielsen, G. (2007). Youth crowds and substance use: The impact of perceived group norm and multiple group identification. *Psychology of Addictive Behaviors, 21*, 55–61.

Vermeer, H., & van IJzendoorn, M. (2006). Children's elevated cortisol levels at daycare. *Early Childhood Research Quarterly, 21*, 390–401.

Veroff, J., Douvan, E., & Kulka, R.A. (1981). *The inner American: A self-portrait from 1957 to 1976*. New York, NY: Basic Books.

Vézina, M., & Turcotte, M. (2009). *Forty-year-old mothers of preschool children: A profile*. (11-008-XWE). Ottawa, ON: Statistics Canada. Retrieved from www.statcan.gc.ca/pub/11-008-x/2009002/article/10918-eng.htm

Vig, E.K., & Pearlman, R.A.. (2003). Quality of life while dying: a qualitative study of terminally ill older men. *Journal of the American Geriatrics Society, 51*(11), 1595–601.

Ville, I., & Khlat, M. (2007). Meaning and coherence of self and health: An approach based on narratives of life events. *Social Science & Medicine, 64*, 1001–1014.

Vinokur, A.D., & van Ryn, M. (1993). Social support and undermining in close relationships: Their independent effects on the mental health of unemployed persons. *Journal of Personality and Social Psychology, 65*, 350–359.

Vitaro, F., Tremblay, R., Kerr, M., Pagani, L., & Bukowski, W. (1997). Disruptiveness, friends' characteristics, and delinquency in early adolescence: A test of two competing models of development. *Child Development, 68*, 676–689.

Vogin, J. (2005). Taking medication while pregnant. Retrieved from www.medicinenet.com/script/main/art.asp?articlekey=51639

Volz, J. (2000). Successful aging: The second 50. *Monitor, 31*, 24–28.

Vouloumanos, A., & Werker, J.F. (2004). Tuned to the signal: the privileged status of speech for young infants. *Developmental Science, 7*(3), 270–276.

Vouloumanos, A., & Werker, J.F. (2007a). Listening to language at birth: Evidence for a bias for speech in neonates. *Developmental Science, 10*(2), 159–164.

Vouloumanos, A., & Werker, J.F. (2007b). Why voice melody alone cannot explain neonates' preference for speech. *Developmental Science, 10*(2), 170–172.

Voyer, D., Voyer, S., & Bryden, M.P. (1995). Magnitude of sex differences in spatial abilities: A meta-analysis and consideration of critical variables. *Psychological Bulletin, 117*, 250–270.

Vuorenkoski, L., Kuure, O., Moilanen, I., & Peninkilampi, V. (2000). Bilingualism, school achievement, and mental wellbeing: A follow-up study of return migrant children. *Journal of Child Psychology & Psychiatry & Allied Disciplines, 41*, 261–266.

Vygotsky, L.S. (1962). Thought and language. Cambridge, MA: MIT Press. (Original work published 1934)

Vygotsky, L.S. (1978). *Mind and society: The development of higher mental processes*. Cambridge, MA: Harvard University Press. (Original works published 1930, 1933, and 1935.)

Wade, T.J., & Cairney, J. (1997). Age and depression in a nationally representative sample of Canadians: A preliminary look at the National Population Health Survey. *Canadian Journal of Public Health, 88*(5), 297–302.

Waggoner, G. (2000). The new grandparents: What they buy, what they think. *Modern Maturity, 43*, 85, 91.

Walden, T.A. (1991). Infant social referencing. In J. Garber & K.A. Dodge (Eds.), *The development of emotion regulation and dysregulation* (pp. 69–88). Cambridge, England: Cambridge University Press.

Walker, H., Messinger, D., Fogel, A., & Karns, J. (1992). Social and communicative development in infancy. In V.B.V. Hasselt & M. Hersen (Eds.), *Handbook of social development: A lifespan perspective* (pp. 157–181). New York, NY: Plenum.

Walker, L. (1980). Cognitive and perspective-taking prerequisites for moral development. *Child Development, 51*, 131–139.

Walker, L.J. (1989). A longitudinal study of moral reasoning. *Child Development, 60*, 157–160.

Walker, L.J., de Vries, B., & Trevethan, S.D. (1987). Moral stages and moral orientations in real-life and hypothetical dilemmas. *Child Development, 58*, 842–858.

Walker-Andrews, A., & Kahana-Kalman, R. (1999). The understanding of pretence across the second year of life. *British Journal of Developmental Psychology, 17*, 523–536.

Walker-Andrews, A. S. (1997). Infants' perception of expressive behaviors: Differentiation of multimodal information. *Psychological Bulletin, 121*(3), 437–456.

Walker-Andrews, A.S., & Lennon, E. (1991). Infants' discrimination of vocal expressions: Contributions of auditory and visual information. *Infant Behavior and Development, 14*, 131–142.

Wallace, G.L., Schmitt, E.J., Lenroot, R., Viding, E., Ordaz, S., Rosenthal, M.A., et al. (2006). A pediatric twin study of brain morphometry. *Journal of child psychology and psychiatry, and allied disciplines, 47*(10), 987–993.

Wallace, M. (2003). Crime statistics in Canada, 2002. (Cat. No. 85-002-XPE). *Juristat, 23*(5), n.p.

Wallace, M. (2004). Crime statistics in Canada, 2003. (Cat. No. 85-002-XPE). *Juristat, 24*(6), n.p.

Wallerstein, J., & Lewis, J. (1998). The long-term impact of divorce on children: A first report from a 25-year study. Family & Conciliation Courts Review, 36, 368–383.

Walmsley, S. (2003). Opt in or opt out: What is optimal for prenatal screening for HIV infection? *Canadian Medical Association Journal, 168*(6), 707–708.

Walton, G.E., Bower, N.J.A., & Bower, T.G.R. (1992). Recognition of familiar faces by newborns. *Infant Behavior and Development, 15,* 265–269.

Walusinski, O., Kurjak, A., Andonotopo, W., & Azumendi, G. (2005). Fetal yawning: A behavior's birth with 4D US revealed. *The Ultrasound Review of Obstetrics & Gynecology, 5,* 210–217.

Wang, C., & Phinney, J. (1998). Differences in child rearing attitudes between immigrant Chinese mothers and Anglo-American mothers. *Early Development & Parenting, 7,* 181–189.

Wang, Y. (2002). Is obesity associated with early sexual maturation? A comparison of the association in American boys versus girls. *Pediatrics, 110,* 903–910.

Wang, Y., & Ollendick, T. (2001). A cross-cultural and developmental analysis of self-esteem in Chinese and Western children. *Clinical Child and Family Psychology Review, 4*(3), 253–271.

Wang, X., Dow-Edwards, D., Anderson, V., Minkoof, H., & Hurd, Y.L. (2004). In utero marijuana exposure associated with abnormal amygdala dopamine *D2* gene expression in the human fetus. *Biological Psychiatry, 56*(12), 909–915.

Warburton, J., Le Brocque, R., & Rosenman, L. (1998). Older people: the reserve army of volunteers? An analysis of volunteerism among older Australians. *International Journal of Aging & Human Development, 46,* 229–245.

Ward, S.L., & Overton, W.F. (1990). Semantic familiarity, relevance, and the development of deductive reasoning. *Developmental Psychology, 26,* 488–493.

Wark, G.R., & Krebs, D.L. (1996). Gender and dilemma differences in real-life moral judgment. *Developmental Psychology, 32,* 220–230.

Warr, P., Jackson, P., & Banks, M. (1988). Unemployment and mental health: Some British studies. *Journal of Social Issues, 44,* 47–68.

Warren, S., Gunnar, M., Kagan, J., Anders, T., Simmens, S., Rones, M., . . . Sroufe, A. (2003). Maternal panic disorder: Infant temperament, neurophysiology, and parenting behaviors. *Journal of the American Academy of Child & Adolescent Psychiatry, 42,* 814–825.

Watamura, S., Donzella, B., Alwin, J., & Gunnar, M. (2003). Morning-to-afternoon increases in cortisol concentrations for infants and toddlers at child care: Age differences and behavioral correlates. *Child Development, 74,* 1006–1020.

Waterman, R.A. Critical experiments to determine if early nutritional influences on epigenetics mechanisms cause metabolic imprinting in humans. In M.E. Wintour & J.A. Owens (Eds.), *Early life origins of health and disease. Advances in Experimental medicine and biology: Vol. 573* (pp. 79–86). New York, NY: Springer Science & Business Media.

Waters, E., Treboux, D., Crowell, J., Merrick, S., & Albersheim, L. (1995, March). *From the Strange Situation to the Adult Attachment Interview: A 20-year longitudinal study of attachment security in infancy and early adulthood.* Paper presented at the biennial meetings of the Society for Research in Child Development, Indianapolis, IN.

Watkins, S.C., Menken, J.A., & Bongaarts, J. (1987). Demographic foundations of family change. *American Sociological Review, 52,* 346–358.

Watson, A., Nixon, C., Wilson, A., & Capage, L. (1999). Social interaction skills and theory of mind in young children. *Developmental Psychology, 35,* 386–391.

Watson, J. (1997). Grandmothering across the lifespan. *Journal of Gerontological Social Work, 28,* 45–62.

Waxman, S.R., & Kosowski, T.D. (1990). Nouns mark category relations: Toddlers' and preschoolers' word-learning biases. *Child Development, 61,* 1461–1473.

Weaver, I.C., Meaney, M.J., & Szyf, M. (2006). Maternal care effects on the hippocampal transcriptome and anxiety-mediated behaviors in the offspring that are reversible in adulthood. *Proceedings of the National Academy of Sciences of the United States of America, 103*(9), 3480–3485.

Weaver, I.C.G., Cervoni, N., Champagne, F.A., D'Alessio, A.C., Sharma1, S., Seck, J.R., . . . Meaney, M.J. (2004). Epigenetic programming by maternal behavior. *Nature Neuroscience, 7*(8), 847–854.

Weaver, I.C.G., Champagne, F.A., Brown, S.E., Dymov, S., Sharma, S., Meaney, M.J., & Szyf, M. (2005). Reversal of maternal programming of stress responses in adult offspring through methyl supplementation: Altering epigenetic marking later in life. *The Journal of Neuroscience, 25*(47), 11045–11054.

Weaver, I.C.G., D'Alessio, A.C., Brown, S.E., Hellstrom, I.C., Dymov, S., Sharma, S., . . . Meaney, M.J. (2007). The transcription factor nerve growth factor-inducible protein a mediates epigenetic programming: Altering epigenetic marks by immediate–early genes. *The Journal of Neuroscience, 27*(7), 1756–1768.

Weaver, J. (1999). Gerontology education: A new paradigm for the 21st century. *Educational Gerontology, 25,* 479–490.

Weaver, S., Clifford, E., Hay, D., & Robinson, J. (1997). Psychosocial adjustment to unsuccessful IVF and GIFT treatment. *Patient Education & Counseling, 31,* 7–18.

Weber, K. (1993). *Special Education in Ontario Schools.* Thornhill, ON: Highland Press.

Webster, J., & McCall, M. (1999). Reminiscence functions across adulthood: A replication and extension. *Journal of Adult Development, 6,* 73–85.

Webster, M.L., Thompson, J.M., Mitchell, E.A., & Werry, J.S. (1994). Postnatal depression in a community cohort. *Australian & New Zealand Journal of Psychiatry, 28,* 42–49.

Wechsler, D. (2003). *Wechsler Intelligence Scale for Children—Fourth Edition.* San Antonio, TX: Harcourt Assessment, Inc.

Wechsler, H., Davenport, A., Dowdall, G., Moeykens, B., & Castillo, S. (1994). Health and behavioral consequences of binge drinking in college. *Journal of the American Medical Association, 272,* 1672–1677.

Wechsler, H., Dowdall, G., Maenner, G., Gledhill-Hoyt, J., & Lee, H. (1998). Changes in binge drinking and related problems among American college students between 1993 and 1997. *Journal of American College Health, 47,* 57–68.

Wedding, D., Kohout, J., Mengel, M.B., Ohlemiller, M., Ulione, M., Cook, K., . . . Braddock, S. (2007). Psychologists' knowledge and attitudes about fetal alcohol syndrome, fetal alcohol spectrum disorder, and alcohol use during pregnancy. *Professional Psychology: Research and Practice, 38*(2), 208–213.

Weeks, J. (2004). Same-sex partnerships. *Feminism & Psychology, 14,* 158–164.

Weikum, W., Vouloumanos, A., Navarro, J., Soto-Faraco, S., Sebastian-Galles, N., & Werker, J.F. (2007). Visual language discrimination in infancy. *Science, 316*(5828), 1159.

Weimer, B.L., Kerns, K.A., & Oldenburg, C.M. (2004). Adolescent's interaction with a best friend: Association with attachment style. *Journal of Experimental Child Psychology, 88*(1), 102–122.

Weinberg, R.A. (1989). Intelligence and IQ: Landmark issues and great debates. *American Psychologist, 44,* 98–104.

Weindrich, D., Jennen-Steinmetz, C., Laucht, M., & Schmidt, M.H. (2003). Late sequelae of low birthweight: mediators of poor school performance at 11 years. *Developmental Medicine and Child Neurology, 45*(7), 463–469.

Weinfield, N., & Egeland, B. (2004). Continuity, discontinuity, and coherence in attachment from infancy to late adolescence: Sequelae of organization and disorganization. *Attachment & Human Development, 6,* 73–97.

Weinhold, B. (2006). Epigenetics: The science of change. *Environmental Health Perspectives, 114*(3), A160–A167.

Weinstock, L. (1999). Gender differences in the presentation and management of social anxiety disorder. *Journal of Clinical Psychiatry, 60,* 9–13.

Weisner, T., & Wilson-Mitchell, J. (1990). Nonconventional family lifestyles and sex typing in six-year olds. *Child Development, 62,* 1915–1933.

Weisse, C.S. (1992). Depression and immunocompetence: A review of the literature. *Psychological Bulletin, 111,* 475–489.

Welch-Ross, M. (1997). Mother-child participation in conversation about the past: Relationships to preschoolers' theory of mind. *Developmental Psychology, 33,* 618–629.

Welford, A.T. (1993). The gerontological balance sheet. In J. Cerella, J. Rybash, W. Hoyer, & M.L. Commons (Eds.), *Adult information processing: Limits on loss* (pp. 3–10). San Diego, CA: Academic Press.

Wellman, H.M. (1982). The foundations of knowledge: Concept development in the young child. In S.G. Moore & C.C. Cooper (Eds.), *The young child: Reviews of research: Vol. 3* (pp. 115–134). Washington, DC: National Association for the Education of Young Children.

Wentzel, K.R., & Asher, S.R. (1995). The academic lives of neglected, rejected, popular, and controversial children. *Child Development, 66,* 754–763.

Werker, J., Pons, F., Dietrich, C., Kajikawa, S., Fais, L., & Amano, S. (2007). Infant directed speech supports phonetic category learning in English and Japanese. *Cognition, 103,* 147–162.

Werker, J.F. (1989). Becoming a native listener: A developmental perspective on human speech perception. *American Scientist, 77*(1), 54–59.

Werker, J.F. (1995). Exploring developmental changes in cross-language speech perception. In D.N. Osherson (Ed.), *An invitation to cognitive science: Language: Vol. 1.* Cambridge, MA: MIT Press.

Werker, J.F., & Tees, R.C. (1984). Phonemic and phonetic factors in adult cross-language speech perception. *Journal of the Acoustical Society of America, 75*(6), 1866–1878.

Werker, J.F., Byers-Heinlein, K., & Fennell. C.T. (2009). Bilingual beginnings to learning words. *Philosophical Transactions of the Royal Society of London. Series B, Biological sciences, 364*(1536), 3649–3663.

Werker, J.F., Cohen, L.B., Lloyd, V., Casosola, M., & Stager, C. (1998). Acquisition of word-object associations by 14-month-old infants. *Developmental Psychology, 34*(6), 1289–1309.

Werker, J.F., Pegg, J.E., & McLeod, P.J. (1994). A cross-language investigation of infant preference for infant-directed communication. *Infant Behavior & Development, 17,* 323–333.

Werker. J.F., & Byers-Heinlein, K. (2008). Bilingualism in infancy: First steps in perception and comprehension. *Trends in Cognitive Sciences 12*(4), 144–51. doi:10.1016/j.tics.2008.01.008

Werner, L.A., & Gillenwater, J.M. (1990). Pure-tone sensitivity of 2- to 5-week-old infants. *Infant Behavior & Development, 13,* 355–375.

West, P., Sweeting, H., & Ecob, R. (1999). Family and friends' influences on the uptake of regular smoking from mid-adolescence to early adulthood. *Addiction, 97,* 1397–1411.

West, R.L., & Crook, T.H. (1990). Age differences in everyday memory: Laboratory analogues of telephone number recall. *Psychology and Aging, 5,* 520–529.

White, M., Wilson, M., Elander, G., & Persson, B. (1999). The Swedish family: Transition to parenthood. *Scandinavian Journal of Caring Sciences, 13,* 171–176.

White, W.H. (1992). G. Stanley Hall: From philosophy to developmental psychology. *Developmental Psychology, 28,* 25–34.

Whitelaw, N.C., & Whitelaw, E. (2006). How lifetimes shape epigenotype within and across generations. *Human Molecular Genetics, 15*(Review Issue No. 2), 131–137.

White-Traut, R., Nelson, M., Silvestri, J., Vasan, U., Littau, S., Meleedy-Rey, P., . . . Patel, M. (2002). Effect of auditory, tactile, visual, and vestibular intervention on length of stay, alertness, and feeding progression in preterm infants. *Developmental Medicine & Child Neurology, 44,* 91–97.

Whittaker, R. (1998). Re-framing the representation of women in advertisements for hormone replacement therapy. *Nursing Inquiry, 5,* 77–86.

Whitty, M. (2003). Pushing the wrong buttons: Men's and women's attitudes toward online and offline infidelity. *CyberPsychology & Behavior, 6,* 569–579.

Wich, B.K., & Carnes, M. (1995). Menopause and the aging female reproductive system. *Endocrinology and Metabolism Clinics of North America, 24,* 273–295.

Wiederman, M., & Allgeier, E. (1992). Gender differences in mate selection criteria: Sociobiological or socioeconomic explanation? *Ethology and Sociobiology, 13,* 115–124.

Wiencek, H. (1987). *The world of LEGO toys.* New York, NY: Harry N. Abrams, Inc.

Wigfield, A., Eccles, J.S., MacIver, D., Reuman, D.A., & Midgley, C. (1991). Transitions during early adolescence: Changes in children's domain-specific self-perceptions and general self-esteem across the transition to junior high school. *Developmental Psychology, 27,* 552–565.

Wilkins, K., & Park, E. (1996). Chronic conditions, physical limitations and dependency among seniors living in the community (Cat. No. 82-003-XPB). *Health Reports, 8*(3), 7–15.

Wilkins, R., Houle, C., Berthelot, J., & Ross, N. (2000). The changing health status of Canada's children. *Isuma, 1*(2), 57–63.

Williams, C. (2001). Family disruptions and childhood happiness (Cat. No. 11-008-XPE). *Canadian Social Trends, Autumn,* 2–4.

Williams, C. (2005). The sandwich generation (11–008). *Canadian Social Trends, 77,* 16–21.

Willis, S.L. (1996). Everyday problem solving. In J.E. Birren & K.W. Schaie (Eds.), *Handbook of the psychology of aging* (4th ed., pp. 287–307). San Diego, CA: Academic Press.

Willis, S.L., Jay, G.M., Diehl, M., & Marsiske, M. (1992). Longitudinal change and prediction of everyday task competence in the elderly. *Research on Aging, 14,* 68–91.

Willms, J.D. (2002a). Research findings bearing on Canadian social policy. In J.D. Willms (Ed.), *Vulnerable children* (pp. 331–358). Edmonton, AB: The University of Alberta Press.

Willms, J.D. (2002b). Socioeconomic gradients for childhood vulnerability. In J.D. Willms (Ed.), *Vulnerable children* (pp. 71–102). Edmonton, AB: The University of Alberta Press.

Wilmore, J., Stanforth, P., Gagnon, J., Rice, T., Mandel, S., Leon, A., . . . Bouchard, C. (2001). Cardiac output and stroke volume changes with endurance training: The HERITAGE Family Study. *Medical Science & Sports Exercise, 33,* 99–106.

Wilson, S.L. (2009). Understanding and promoting attachment. *Journal of Psychosocial Nursing and Mental Health Services, 47*(8), 23–7. doi: 10.3928/02793695-20090706-04

Wilson, W.J. (1995). Jobless ghettos and the social outcome of youngsters. In P. Moen, G.H. Elder, Jr., & K. Lüscher (Eds.), *Examining lives in context: Perspectives on the ecology of human development* (pp. 527–543). Washington, DC: American Psychological Association.

Wimmer, H., Mayringer, H., & Landerl, K. (1998). Poor reading: A deficit in skill-automatization or a phonological deficit? *Scientific Studies of Reading, 2,* 321–340.

Winter, L., Lawton, M., Casten, R., & Sando, R. (2000). The relationship between external events and affect states in older people. *International Journal of Aging & Human Development, 50,* 85–96.

Winter, R. (1999). A Biblical and theological view of grief and bereavement. *Journal of Psychology & Christianity, 18,* 367–379.

Wintre, M., & Yaffe, M. (2000). First-year students' adjustment to university life as a function of relationships with parents. *Journal of Adolescent Research, 15,* 9–37.

Winzer, M. (1993). *Children with exceptionalities* (3rd ed.). Scarborough, ON: Prentice-Hall Canada.

Wolak, J., Mitchell, K., & Finkelhor, D. (2002). Close online relationships in a national sample of adolescents. *Adolescence, 37,* 441–455.

Women's Health Initiative Steering Committee (2004). Effects of conjugated equine estrogen in postmenopausal women with hysterectomy. The Women's Health Initiative randomized controlled trial. *Journal of the American Medical Association, 291*(14), 1701–1712.

Wong, A.H.C., Gottesman, I.I., & Petronis, A. (2005). Phenotypic differences in genetically identical organisms: The epigenetic perspective. *Human Molecular Genetics, 14* (Review Issue 1), R11–R18.

Wong, C., & Tang, C. (2004). Coming out experiences and psychological distress of Chinese homosexual men in Hong Kong. *Archives of Sexual Behavior, 33,* 149–157.

Wong, D. (1993). *Whaley & Wong's essentials of pediatric nursing.* St. Louis, MO: Mosby-Yearbook, Inc.

Wong, P.T.P. (2000). Meaning in life and meaning in death in successful aging. In A. Tomer (Ed.), *Death Attitudes and the Older Adult: Theories, Concepts, and Applications* (pp. 23–36). Philadelphia, PA: Brunner/Mazel.

Wong, P.T.P. (2003). *From death anxiety to death acceptance: A meaning management model.* Langley, BC: International Network on Personal Meaning. Retrieved from www.meaning.ca/articles/death_acceptance.htm

Woo, M., & Oei, T. (2006). The *MMPI-2* gender-masculine and gender-feminine scales: Gender roles as predictors of psychological health in clinical patients. *International Journal of Psychology, 41,* 413–422.

Wood, C., & Terrell, C. (1998). Pre-school phonological awareness and subsequent literacy development. *Educational Psychology, 18,* 253–274.

Woodward, M., & Tunstall-Pedoe, H. (1995). Alcohol consumption, diet, coronary risk factors, and prevalent coronary heart disease in men and women in the Scottish heart health study. *Journal of Epidemiology and Community Health, 49,* 354–362.

Woolfolk, A. E., Winne, P. H., & Perry, N. E. (2009). *Educational Psychology* (3rd CDN ed.). Toronto, ON: Pearson Education Canada.

Working Group for the PEPI Trial, The (1995). Effects of estrogen or estrogen/progestin regimens on heart disease risk factors in postmenopausal women: The Postmenopausal Estrogen/Progestin Interventions (PEPI) Trial. Journal of the American Medical Association, *273,* 199–208.

World Health Organization. (2000). *Violence against women* [Online report]. Retrieved from www.who.int

World Health Organization. (2002). Abuse of the elderly (Chapter 5). In E.G. Krug, L.L. Dahlberg, J.A. Mercy, A.B. Zwi, & R. Lozano (Eds.), *World report on violence and health* (pp. 123–145). Retrieved from www.who.int/violence_injury_prevention/violence/world_report/en/full_en.pdf

World Health Organization. (2010). *The WHO child growth standards.* Retrieved from www.who.int/childgrowth/en/

Worrell, F. (1997). Predicting successful or non-successful at-risk status using demographic risk factors. *High School Journal, 81,* 46–53.

Wright, C., & Birks, E. (2000). Risk factors for failure to thrive: A population-based survey. *Child: Care, Health & Development, 26,* 5–16.

Wright, M.J, & Myers, C. (1982). *History of academic psychology in Canada.* Toronto, ON: C.J. Hogrefe, Inc.

Wright, M.J. (1993). Women groundbreakers in Canadian psychology: World War II and its aftermath. *Canadian Psychology, 33*(2), Abstract.

Wright, S., Taylor, D., & Macarthur, J. (2000). Subtractive bilingualism and the survival of the Inuit language: Heritage versus second-language education. *Journal of Educational Psychology, 92,* 63–84.

Wright, T., & Bonett, D. (2007). Job satisfaction and psychological well-being as nonadditive predictors of workplace turnover. *Journal of Management, 33,* 141–160.

Wu, Z., & Penning, M. (1997). Marital instability after midlife. *Journal of Family Issues, 18,* 459–478.

Wyatt, J.M., & Carlo, G. (2002). What will my parents think? Relations among adolescents' expected parental reactions, prosocial moral reasoning, and prosocial and antisocial behaviours. *Journal of Adolescent Research, 17*(6), 646–66.

Wyatt, N. (2004, August 8). Survey: Online dating dangerous. *CNEWS.* Retrieved from http://cnews.canoe.ca/CNEWS/Canada/2004/08/08/pf-575064.html

Xie, H., Cairns, R., & Cairns, B. (1999). Social networks and configurations in inner-city schools: Aggression, popularity, and implications for students with EBD. *Journal of Emotional & Behavioral Disorders, 7,* 147–155.

Xu, F. (2003). The development of object individuation in infancy. In H. Hayne & J. Fagen (Eds.), *Progress in Infancy Research: Vol. 3* (pp. 159–192). Mahwah, NJ: Lawrence Erlbaum.

Xu, F. (2005). Categories, kinds, and object individuation in infancy. In L. Gershkoff-Stowe and D. Rakison (Eds.), *Building object categories in developmental time* (pp. 63–89). Papers from the 32nd Carnegie Symposium on Cognition. New Jersey: Lawrence Erlbaum.

Xu, F., & Baker, A. (2005). Object individuation in 10-month-old infants using a simplified manual search method. *Journal of Cognition and Development, 6*(3), 307–323.

Xu, F., & Carey, S. (1996). Infants' metaphysics: the case of numerical identity. *Cognitive Psychology, 30*(2), 111–153.

Yang, H., Lu, S., Liaw, Y., You, S., Sun, C., Wang, L., . . . Chen, C. (2002). Hepatitis B/e antigen and the risk of hepatocellular carcinoma. *New England Journal of Medicine, 347,* 168–174.

Yang, Q., Wen, S.W., Leader, A., Chen X.K., Lipson, J., & Walker, M. (2007). Paternal age and birth defects: how strong is the association? *Human Reproduction, 22*(3), 696–701.

Yeung, A., Chui, H., & Lau, I. (1999). Hierarchical and multidimensional academic self-concept of commercial students. *Contemporary Educational Psychology, 24,* 376–389.

Yirmiya, N., & Shulman, C. (1996). Seriation, conservation, and theory of mind abilities in individuals with autism, individuals with mental retardation, and normally developing children. *Child Development, 67,* 2045–2059.

Yonas, A., & Owsley, C. (1987). Development of visual space perception. In P. Salpatek & L. Cohen (Eds.), *Handbook of infant perception: Vol. 2. From perception to cognition* (pp. 80–122). Orlando, FL: Academic Press.

Yonas, A., Elieff, C., & Atterberry, M. (2002). Emergence of sensitivity to pictorial depth cues: Charting development in individual infants. *Infant Behavior & Development, 25,* 495–514.

Yordanova, J., Kolev, V., & Basar, E. (1998). EEG theta and frontal alpha oscillations during auditory processing change with aging. *Electroencephalography & Clinical Neurophysiology: Evoked Potentials, 108,* 497–505.

Young, A. (1997). I think, therefore I'm motivated: The relations among cognitive strategy use, motivational orientation and classroom perceptions over time. *Learning & Individual Differences, 9,* 249–283.

Young, J., & Rodgers, R. (1997). A model of radical career change in the context of psychosocial development. *Journal of Career Assessment, 5,* 167–182.

Young, S., Fox, N., & Zahn-Waxler, C. (1999). The relations between temperament and empathy in 2-year-olds. *Developmental Psychology, 35,* 1189–1197.

Young, T.K, Reading, J., Elias, B. & O'Neil, J.D. (2000). Type 2 diabetes mellitus in Canada's First Nations: Status of an epidemic in progress. *Canadian Medical Association Journal, 163*(5), 561–566.

Yuill, N. (1997). English children as personality theorists: Accounts of the modifiability, development, and origin of traits. *Genetic, Social & General Psychology Monographs, 123,* 5–26.

Zahn-Waxler, C., & Radke-Yarrow, M. (1982). The development of altruism: Alternative research strategies. In N. Eisenberg (Ed.), *The development of prosocial behavior* (pp. 109–138). New York, NY: Academic Press.

Zahn-Waxler, C., Radke-Yarrow, M., Wagner, E., & Chapman, M. (1992). Development of concern for others. *Developmental Psychology, 28,* 126–136.

Zakriski, A., & Coie, J. (1996). A comparison of aggressive-rejected and nonaggressive-rejected children's interpretation of self-directed and other-directed rejection. *Child Development, 67,* 1048–1070.

Zamboni, B. (2006). Therapeutic considerations in working with the family, friends, and partners of transgendered individuals. *The Family Journal, 14,* 174–179.

Zelazo, N.A., Zelazo, P.R., Cohen, K.M., & Zelazo, P.D. (1993). Specificity of practice effects on elementary neuromotor patterns. *Developmental Psychology, 29,* 686–691.

Zelazo, P., Helwig, C., & Lau, A. (1996). Intention, act, and outcome in behavioral prediction and moral judgment. *Child Development, 67,* 2478–2492.

Zelazo, P.D., & Boseovski, J.J. (2001). Video reminders in a representational change task: Memory for cues but not beliefs or statements. *Journal of Experimental Child Psychology, 78,* 107–129.

Zelazo, P.R., Zelazo, N.A., & Kolb, S. (1972). "Walking" in the newborn. *Science, 176,* 314–315.

Zelinski, E., & Burnight, K. (1997). Sixteen-year longitudinal and time lag changes in memory and cognition in older adults. *Psychology & Aging, 12,* 503–513.

Zelinski, E.M., Gilewski, M.J., & Schaie, K.W. (1993). Individual differences in cross-sectional and 3-year longitudinal memory performance across the adult life span. *Psychology and Aging, 8,* 176–186.

Zhang, R., & Yu, Y. (2002). A study of children's coordinational ability for outcome and intention information. *Psychological Science* (China), *25,* 527–530.

Zhang, X. (2009). Earnings of women with and without children. In *Perspectives.* Ottawa, ON: Statistics Canada. Retrieved from www.statcan.gc.ca/cgi-bin/af-fdr.cgi?l=eng&loc=../pdf/10823-eng.pdf

Zhou, M., Yao, L., & Xu, J. (2002). Studied the influence of Taoist education on the subjective well-being of the elderly. *Chinese Mental Health Journal, 16,* 175–176.

Zick, C., & Holden, K. (2000). An assessment of the wealth holdings of recent widows. *Journal of Gerontology, 55B,* S90–S97.

Zigler, E., & Finn-Stevenson, M. (1993). *Children in a changing world: Developmental and social issues.* Pacific Grove, CA: Brooks/Cole.

Zigler, E., & Hodapp, R.M. (1991). Behavioral functioning in individuals with mental retardation. *Annual Review of Psychology, 42,* 29–50.

Zigler, E., & Styfco, S.J. (1993). Using research and theory to justify and inform Head Start expansion. *Social Policy Report, Society for Research in Child Development, VII*(2), 1–21.

Zimmer, Z., Hickey, T., & Searle, M.S. (1995). Activity participation and well-being among older people with arthritis. *The Gerontologist, 35,* 463–471.

Zimmer-Gembeck, M. (1999). Stability, change and individual differences in involvement with friends and romantic partners among adolescent females. *Journal of Youth & Adolescence, 28,* 419–438.

Zimmerman, B.J., & Schunk, D.H. (2002). Albert Bandura: The man and his contributions to educational psychology. In B.J. Zimmerman, & H. Schunk (Eds.), *Educational psychology: A century of contributions* (pp. 431–459). Mahwah, NJ: L. Erlbaum Associates.

Zimmerman, C. (2000). The development of scientific reasoning skills. *Developmental Review, 20,* 99–149.

Zimmerman, F.J., & Christakis, D.A. (2005). Children's television viewing and cognitive outcomes: A longitudinal analysis of national data. *Archives of Pediatric & Adolescent Medicine, 159*(7), 619–625.

Zimmerman, F.J., Christakis, D.A., & Meltzoff, A.N. (2007). Television and DVD/video viewing in children younger than 2 years. *Archives of Pediatrics and Adolescent Medicine, 161*(5), 473–479.

Zimmerman, M., Copeland, L., Shope, J., & Dielman, T. (1997). A longitudinal study of self-esteem: Implications for adolescent development. *Journal of Youth & Adolescence, 26,* 117–141.

Zimmermann, P. (2004). Attachment representations and characteristics of friendship relations during adolescence. *Journal of Experimental Child Psychology, 88*(1), 83–101.

Zisook, S., Chentsova-Dutton, Y., & Shuchter, S. (1998). PTSD following bereavement. *Annals of Clinical Psychiatry, 10,* 157–163.

Zisook, S., Paulus, M., Shuchter, S., & Judd, L. (1997). The many faces of depression following spousal bereavement. *Journal of Affective Disorders, 45,* 85–94.

Zola, S., & Squire, L. (2003). Genetics of childhood disorders: Learning and memory: Multiple memory systems. *Journal of the American Academy of Child and Adolescent Psychiatry, 42,* 504–506.

Zosuls, K.M., Ruble, D.N., Tamis-LeMonda, C.S., Shrout, P.E., Bornstein, M.H., & Greulich, F.K. (2009). The acquisition of gender labels in infancy: implications for sex-typed play. *Developmental Psychology, 45,* 688–701.

Zucker, A., Ostrove, J., & Stewart A. (2002). College-educated women's personality development in adulthood: Perceptions and age differences. *Psychology & Aging, 17,* 236–244.

Zunker, V. (1994). *Career counseling.* Pacific Grove, CA: Brooks/Cole.

Zunzunegui, M., Alvarado, B., Del Ser, T., & Otero, A. (2003). Social networks, social integration, and social engagement determine cognitive decline in community-dwelling Spanish older adults. *Journals of Gerontology, Series B: Psychological Sciences & Social Sciences, 58B,* S93–S100.

Zuzanek, J. (2000). *The effects of time use and time pressure on child-parent relationships.* Waterloo, ON: Otium Publications. Retrieved from Health Canada website: www.hc-sc.gc.ca/dca-dea/publications/pdf/timepcr-tempsrpe_e.pdf

Zysset, S., Schroeter, M., Neumann, J., & von Cramon, D. (2007). Stroop interference, hemodynamic response and aging: An event-related fMRI study. *Neurobiology of Aging, 28,* 937–946.

NAME INDEX

Maslow, A.H., 37, 38n
Mason, B., 439
Mason, J., 298
Masse, L.C., 355
Masson, M.E.J., 497
Mast, B., 493
Masten, A., 399
Maszk, P., 296
Matheny, L.S., 95
Mathers, J.C., 31
Matheson, C.C., 224
Mathew, A., 175n
Mattia, F., 117
Mattson, S., 76
Maughan, B., 212
Mauldin, J., 468
Maurer, C., 83
Maurer, D., 83, 107, 108, 112, 115–116
Maviolette, M., 311n
May, K., 203
Mayes, S., 178
Mayeux, L., 230
Maylor, D., 498
Maylor, E., 443
Mayringer, H., 263, 269
Mayseless, O., 358
Mazure, C., 409
McAdams, D., 453
McAllister, D., 78
McArthur, B.A., 180
McBride-Chang, C., 195, 262
McBurney, K., 533
McCabe, M.P., 321
McCain, M., 214, 224, 246
McCall, B., 467
McCall, M., 505
McCall, R.B., 200
McCartney, K., 158, 161, 169
McClearn, G.E., 478
McClelland, A., 272
McClun, L., 358
McCourt, B., 548
McCourt, C., 77
McCoy, N., 428
McCrae, R., 159, 232, 279n, 452, 463
McCrae, R.R., 279
McCrone, E., 158
McDaniel, S., 517
McDermott, K., 429
McDevitt, N., 27
McDonald, P.L., 521
McDonald-Miszak, L., 498
McDowell, I., 492
McDuff, P., 308
McEvoy, J., 387
McEvoy, L., 317
McFadden, D., 67
McFadden, M., 426
McFalls, J.A.Jr., 375n, 376
McGee, A., 77
McGee, R., 357
McGowan, J., 489
McGregor, K., 193
McHale, S., 291
McHugh, M., 381, 382
McIntosh, B.R., 506
McIntosh, C.G., 106
McIntosh, C.N., 370–371, 371n
McIntyre, L., 245
McKay, A., 313
McKeen, N.A., 175
McKim, M.K., 167
McKinlay, 375n
McKusick, V.A., 31
McLanahan, S., 223, 516
McLaughlin, J., 408
McLellan, J., 334
McLeod, P.J., 135
McLoyd, V., 246
McMillan, R., 170
McMullen, K., 414
McMullin, J.A., 518

McNally, E., 101
McNeal, C., 383
McPhee, J., 366
McQuarrie, L., 262
McQueen, M., 492
McRae, C., 222, 232
McShane, K., 105
Mead, S., 527
Meaney, M., 229
Meaney, M.J., 27–28, 31
Meek, C., 324
Meeks, S., 438
Meeus, W., 358, 413
Mehta, K.K., 511, 512
Mehta, P., 195
Meisenhelder, J., 511
Melot, A., 188
Melov, S., 485
Meltzoff, A.N., 125, 126n, 127
Mendez, J., 224
Menesini, E., 295
Meng, K.S., 511
Menken, J.A., 455
Mercke, A., 151
Meredith, K., 534
Meredith, W., 390, 440
Merikangas, K.R., 323
Meritesacker, B., 157
Merrell, K., 358
Merrick, S., 155
Merrill, M.A., 198
Mervis, C.V., 139
Messinger, D., 152
Messinger, D.S., 157
Metallidou, P., 295
Metter, E.J., 375n
Meyer, J.S., 442
Meyer-Bahlberg, H.F.L., 315
Michael, R.T., 430
Michaels, S., 430
Midgett, C., 180
Midgley, C., 330, 343
Miech, R., 494
Miedema, S., 150
Milan, A., 399, 400n, 405, 458–459, 459n
Mill, J., 59
Millar, W.J., 76
Miller, B., 312
Miller, B.C., 363
Miller, F., 156, 218
Miller, P., 283
Miller, R., 377
Miller, R.A., 375n
Miller, T., 493
Miller, T.Q., 437
Miller-Johnson, S., 202
Milligan, K., 166, 168
Mills, D., 177
Mills, J., 322
Mills, R.S.L., 289, 296
Milne, B.J., 299
Min, J., 60
Minkler, M., 510
Minkoof, H., 68
Minsky, D., 383
Minton, B., 428
Mintzer, A., 407
Mintzes, B., 324
Mischel, W., 236
Mishra, R.C., 6, 263
Mitchell, B.A., 458
Mitchell, E.A., 409
Mitchell, J., 211
Mitchell, K., 401
Mitchell, P.R., 136
Mitchell, R., 370
Mitchell, V., 10
Mix, C., 451
Moane, G., 10
Modvig, J., 463
Moen, P., 412, 417, 522, 524
Moeykens, B., 386
Moffitt, T., 402, 411

Moffitt, T.E., 279n
Mohan, J., 437
Mohanty, A., 272
Moher, D., 271
Moilanen, I., 142
Moise-Titus, J., 300
Moldofsky, H., 270
Molenaar, P., 250
Molgaard, D.J., 521
Molinari, L., 240
Molloy, A., 77
Monarch, E., 385
Mondloch, C.J., 107, 112, 115–116
Monk, C., 95
Monker, J., 196
Monroy, T., 468
Monsen, R., 537
Monsour, A., 340
Montemayor, R., 281, 340, 340n, 342, 357
Montero, I., 192
Montgomery, M., 363
Moody, C., 355
Moon, C., 131
Mooney, 494
Mooney, L., 181
Moore, C., 151, 164, 188, 209, 233
Moore, C.F., 353
Moore, E.R., 104
Moore, K.A., 363
Moore, K.L., 66, 72, 73n
Moore, M.K., 126n
Morabia, A., 433
Moradi, A., 323
Moran, G., 155, 156
Moran, V., 142
Morath, R., 334
Morfei, M., 451
Morgan, C., 483
Morgan, D.G., 481
Morgan, J.L., 138
Morgan, J.N., 467
Morin, M., 270
Mork, J., 435
Morley, K.I., 31
Morrell, R., 508
Morris, D.L., 435n
Morris, E., 266
Morris, T., 544
Morrison, D., 141
Morrison, N.A., 431n
Morrison, P., 494, 494n
Morrissette, P., 181
Morrongiello, B.A., 108, 180
Morrow, D., 444
Morse, P.A., 117
Mortel, K.F., 442
Morton, D.J., 521
Morton, J., 114
Morton, J.B., 240
Mory, M.S., 362
Moser, R.P., 539
Mosher, M., 293
Mosher, W.D., 376
Moskowitz, D.S., 451
Moss, E., 211
Moss, S., 487
Mott, J., 320
Mounts, N.S., 356
Mousmanis, P., 246
Mueller, R., 413
Mueller, U., 327
Muhajarine, N., 81
Muir, D.W., 164
Mulder, G., 425–426
Mulder, R., 346
Muller, D., 375n
Müller, U., 164
Mullet, E., 527
Mullin, K., 492
Multon, K., 467
Mundy, 375n
Mung'ala-Odera, V., 263
Munroe, R.H., 238

Munroe, R.L., 238
Murell, S.A., 549
Murnen, S., 322
Murphy, C., 483
Murphy, C.C., 80–81
Murphy, M., 80
Murphy, S., 548
Murray, J., 300
Murray, K., 216, 234
Murray, L., 157
Murstein, 402
Must, A., 307
Mustard, F., 214, 224, 246
Mutch, L., 77
Muzi, M., 408, 458
Mwamwenda, T., 327
Myerowitz, R., 71
Myers, B., 253
Myers, C., 6, 7
Myerson, J., 496
Myhr, T.L., 80

N

Nagamine, S., 359
Nagin, D., 383
Nagin, D.S., 226
Nagy, W., 262
Najam, N., 410
Nakazato, K., 339
Nanavati, R., 105
Nanin, J., 364
Nansen, M.A., 30n
Narvaez, D., 352
Naslund, J., 262
Nathanson, C.A., 429
Natowicz, M.R., 71
Navarro, E., 508
Neal, C., 79
Nederend, S., 241
Neeper, S., 498
Neild, R., 331
Neill, M., 264–265
Neimeyer, R., 548, 552
Neimeyer, R.A., 539, 540
Neisser, U., 200, 203
Neitzel, C., 49, 192
Nelson, C., 95, 117
Nelson, E.A., 463
Nelson, K., 136, 142, 144
Nelson, M.E., 431
Nelson, N.M., 236
Nelson, S., 211
Nemeth, R., 238
Neshat-Doost, H., 323
Nesselroade, J.R., 432
Nestor, S., 136
Neugarten, B.L., 11, 538
Neugebauer, R., 77
Neumann, J., 425
Nevid, J.S., 24n
Neville, H., 177
Newberger, E., 181
Newcomb, A.F., 291, 296
Newell, K., 487, 490
Newman, J., 102
Newsome, M., 139
Newton, C.R.J.C., 263
Newton, D., 376
Ng, E., 372
Ng, L.K., 378
Nguyen, H., 444
Ni, Y., 260
Nichols, D., 485
Nichols, R., 551
Nicholson, J., 70
Nicholson, R., 380
Nickerson, C., 413
Nicoladis, E., 136
Nielsen, G., 361
Nieschlag, E., 80
Nilsson, E., 322
Nilsson, J., 439
Nilsson, L., 443
Nisan, M., 351

SUBJECT INDEX